Lecture Notes in Computer Science 11269

Commenced Publication in 1973
Founding and Former Series Editors:
Gerhard Goos, Juris Hartmanis, and Jan van Leeuwen

More information about this series at http://www.springer.com/series/7412

Thomas Brox · Andrés Bruhn
Mario Fritz (Eds.)

Pattern Recognition

40th German Conference, GCPR 2018
Stuttgart, Germany, October 9–12, 2018
Proceedings

Springer

Editors
Thomas Brox
University of Freiburg
Freiburg, Germany

Andrés Bruhn
University of Stuttgart
Stuttgart, Germany

Mario Fritz
CISPA Helmholtz Center
for Information Security
Saarbrücken, Germany

ISSN 0302-9743   ISSN 1611-3349   (electronic)
Lecture Notes in Computer Science
ISBN 978-3-030-12938-5   ISBN 978-3-030-12939-2   (eBook)
https://doi.org/10.1007/978-3-030-12939-2

Library of Congress Control Number: 2019930850

LNCS Sublibrary: SL6 – Image Processing, Computer Vision, Pattern Recognition, and Graphics

This Springer imprint is published by the registered company Springer Nature Switzerland AG
The registered company address is: Gewerbestrasse 11, 6330 Cham, Switzerland

Preface

It was an honor and pleasure to organize the 40th German Conference on Pattern Recognition (GCPR 2018) in Stuttgart during October 9–12, 2018. With the first GCPR conference dating back to Oberpfaffenhofen in 1978 and no conference being held in 1982, this year's event in Stuttgart was the 40th annual meeting in the long tradition of the DAGM conference series. Moreover, this year, it was the second time that the GCPR took place in Stuttgart (following DAGM 1998) and it was the second time (after GCPR 2015) that it was co-located with the International Symposium on Vision, Modeling, and Visualization (VMV). This volume comprises its refereed proceedings.

To increase the emphasis on applied research, GCPR 2018 offered additional tracks with dedicated track chairs for computer vision systems and applications, for pattern recognition in life and natural sciences, as well as for photogrammetry and remote sensing. Moreover, the page limit was extended from ten pages to 14 pages plus two pages of references to match the standard paper length of other top conferences in the field. As a consequence, the call for papers resulted in 123 submissions from institutions from 23 countries. Thereby, each paper underwent a strict double-blind reviewing process, in almost all cases based on reviews from three Program Committee (PC) members, sometimes with support from additional experts. In total, 48 papers were accepted for publication, resulting in an acceptance rate of 39%, which is one of the lowest acceptance rates in the history of GCPR. From those submission, 22 papers were accepted for oral presentation, whereas 26 contributions were accepted as posters. The resulting high-quality single-track program covered the entire spectrum of pattern recognition, machine learning, image processing, and computer vision. This would not have been possible without the Program Committee members, the track chairs, and the auxiliary reviewers, whose valuable service to our scientific community we highly appreciate, as well as without the authors., whom we would like to thank for submitting many innovative papers to GCPR this year.

Moreover, we are glad that four world-leading experts in the field of computer graphics, autonomous driving small-scale soft robotics, and visual effects accepted our invitation to give keynote talks, namely:

- Michael Cohen (Facebook, University of Washington, USA)
- Raquel Urtasun (Uber ATG Toronto, University of Toronto, Canada)
- Metin Sitti (MPI for Intelligent Systems, CMU, Germany/USA)
- Juri Stanossek (Mackevision, Film Academy of Ludwigsburg, Germany)

Their talks were truly inspiring showing visionary ideas as well as recent progress in the respective fields. These keynotes were complemented by additional talks related to the 40th anniversary of the GCPR. While the current and former presidents of the German Pattern Recognition Society (DAGM) took us on a fascinating journey from the past to the future of the DAGM, experts from medical image analysis

(Joachim Hornegger, University of Erlangen-Nuremberg, Germany) and human motion estimation (Michael Black, MPI for Intelligent Systems, Germany) gave overview talks outlining the development in these two areas.

In the tradition of the GCPR, the conference program was further accompanied by a number of workshops and tutorials that took place on the day before the actual conference. These events included a workshop on "Computer Vision Challenges in Industry" organized by Alexander Freytag (Zeiss Cooperate Research), Carsten Steger (MVTec Software GmbH) and Bodo Rosenhahn (University of Hannover), as well as two half-day tutorials on Light Fields and Visual Tracking organized by Bastian Goldlücke/Ole Johannsen (University of Konstanz, Germany) and Martin Danelljan (Linköping University, Sweden), respectively.

Finally, it is our pleasure to thank our generous sponsors as well as all the people involved in the organization of the confernece. In this context, we would like to thank Daimler, MVTec, and Zeiss (all as Gold Sponsors) as well as Bosch, Sony, and TeamViewer (all as Silver Sponsors). Moreover, we thank INFOS e.V. and in particular Michael Matthiesen for the great organizational support regarding logistics and finances. A final thank you goes to Tina Barthelmes, Petra Enderle, Anton Malina, Petra van Schayck, Maria Schulz, Nils Rodrigues, Margot Roubicek, and Karin Vrana from VIS and VISUS at the University of Stuttgart and to Yang He from the Max Planck Institute for Informatics for all their efforts to make this conference a huge success.

We are happy that we hosted the 40th German Conference on Pattern Recognition in 2018 in Stuttgart, and we look forward to having a great GCPR next year in Dortmund.

October 2018

Thomas Brox
Andrés Bruhn
Mario Fritz

Organization

General Chair

Andrés Bruhn   University of Stuttgart, Germany

Program Chairs

Thomas Brox   University of Freiburg, Germany
Mario Fritz   CISPA Helmholtz Center i.G., Germany

Programme Committee

Christian Bauckhage	Fraunhofer IAIS, Germany
Horst Bischof	TU Graz, Austria
Joachim Buhmann	ETH Zurich, Switzerland
Daniel Cremers	TU Munich, Germany
Dietrich Paulus	University of Koblenz, Germany
Gernot Fink	University of Dortmund, Germany
Wolfgang Förstner	University of Bonn, Germany
Uwe Franke	Daimler AG, Germany
Jürgen Gall	University of Bonn, Germany
Peter Gehler	University of Tübingen, Germany
Michael Goesele	TU Darmstadt, Germany
Bastian Goldlücke	University of Konstanz, Germany
Fred Hamprecht	Heidelberg University, Germany
Matthias Hein	University of Tübingen, Germany
Stefan Hinz	KIT, Germany
Margret Keuper	University of Mannheim, Germany
Walter Kropatsch	TU Wien, Austria
Reinhard Koch	University of Kiel, Germany
Ullrich Köthe	Heidelberg University, Germany
Arjan Kuijper	TU Darmstadt, Fraunhofer IGD, Germany
Christoph Lampert	IST Austria, Austria
Laura Leal-Taixe	TU Munich, Germany
Bastian Leibe	RWTH Aachen University, Germany
Andreas Maier	University of Erlangen, Germany
Peter Ochs	University of Freiburg, Germany
Björn Ommer	Heidelberg University, Germany
Josef Pauli	University of Duisburg-Essen, Germany
Thomas Pock	TU Graz, Austria

Volker Roth   University of Basel, Switzerland
Stefan Roth   TU Darmstadt, Germany
Carsten Rother   Heidelberg University, Germany
Torsten Sattler   ETH Zurich, Switzerland
Hanno Scharr   FZ Jülich, Germany
Bernt Schiele   MPI for Informatics, Germany
Christoph Schnörr   Heidelberg University, Germany
Cyrill Stachniss   University of Bonn, Germany
Rainer Stiefelhagen   KIT, Germany
Christian Theobalt   MPI for Informatics, Germany
Thomas Vetter   University of Basel, Switzerland
Angela Yao   University of Bonn, Germany

Track Chairs

Joachim Denzler   University of Jena, Germany
Xiaoyi Jiang   University of Münster, Germany
Helmut Mayer   Bundeswehr University of Munich, Germany
Bodo Rosenhahn   University of Hannover, Germany
Uwe Sörgel   University of Stuttgart, Germany
Carsten Steger   TU Munich, MVTec Software GmbH, Germany

Additional Reviewers

Pasquale Foggia   University of Salerno, Italy
Olaf Hellwich   TU Berlin, Germany
Kun Liu   Hella Aglaia Mobile Vision GmbH, Germany
Eckart Michaelsen   Fraunhofer IOSB, Germany
Tuan Pham   Linköping University, Sweden
Nicola Strisiciuglio   University of Groningen, The Netherlands
Klaus Toennies   University of Magdeburg, Germany
Jan Dirk Wegner   ETH Zurich, Switzerland
Jane You   Hong Kong Polytechnic University, SAR China

Awards

GPCR Paper Awards

From all papers accepted at GCPR 2018, the following three papers were selected by the PC as award winners:

GCPR 2018 Best Paper Award

"End-to-End Learning of Deterministic Decision Trees"
Thomas M. Hehn, Fred Hamprecht

GCPR 2018 Honorable Mentions

"3D Fluid Flow Estimation with Integrated Particle Reconstruction"
Katrin Lasinger, Christoph Vogel, Thomas Pock, Konrad Schindler

"A Randomized Gradient-Free Attack to ReLU Networks"
Francesco Croce, Matthias Hein

DAGM Awards

The following DAGM Prizes were awarded at GCPR 2018:

DAGM German Pattern Recognition Award 2018

Prof. Dr. Angela Yao
University of Singapore, Singapore (previously University of Bonn, Germany)

The award was given to Prof. Angela Yao for her outstanding contributions to the area of hand pose estimation and action recognition.

DAGM MVTec Dissertation Awards 2018

Dr. Mateusz Malinowski
Max Planck Institute for Informatics, Saarbrücken, Germany
"Towards Holistic Machines:
From Visual Recognition to Question Answering About Real-world Images"
PhD Thesis, Saarland University, 2017

Dr. Siyu Tang
Max Planck Institute for Informatics, Saarbrücken, Germany
"People Detection and Tracking in Crowded Scenes"
PhD Thesis, Saarland University, 2017

DAGM Best Master Thesis Award 2018

"Sublabel-Accurate Convex Relaxation with Total Generalized Variation Regularization"
Michael Strecke (Master Student), Bastian Goldlücke (Supervisor)

Contents

Oral Session 4: Learning II

Oral Session 5: Optimization and Clustering

Oral Session 5: Optimization and Clustering

Poster Session 1

Poster Session I

Topology-Based 3D Reconstruction of Mid-Level Primitives in Man-Made Environments

Dominik Wolters[✉][iD] and Reinhard Koch

Department of Computer Science, Kiel University, Kiel, Germany
dwol@informatik.uni-kiel.de

Abstract. In this paper a novel reconstruction method is presented that uses the topological relationship of detected image features to create a highly abstract but semantically rich 3D model of the reconstructed scenes. In the first step, a combined image-based reconstruction of points and lines is performed based on the current state of art structure from motion methods. Subsequently, connected planar three-dimensional structures are reconstructed by a novel method that uses the topological relationships between the detected image features. The reconstructed 3D models enable a simple extraction of geometric shapes, such as rectangles, in the scene.

1 Introduction

One of the key tasks of computer vision is the image-based 3D scene reconstruction, which aims to calculate a 3D model of the scene from an image sequence with different viewpoints. In the simplest case, the model can be a set of 3D points. More sophisticated methods create a complete 3D surface model.

Traditionally, these reconstruction methods, such as structure from motion (SfM), make use of interest points. This is a challenge especially in urban and man-made environments, as only a few textured surfaces are available. This results in very sparse point clouds that have limited meaning and make it difficult to analyze and understand the scene. Subsequent multi-view stereo reconstruction can often generate dense point clouds, but these methods have a high computational complexity and generate large amounts of data.

We propose a method that enables the reconstruction of highly abstract but semantically rich 3D models in man-made environments. In the first step, we perform a combined image-based reconstruction of points and lines based on the current state of art SfM methods. Subsequently, connected three-dimensional structures are reconstructed by a novel method that uses the topological relationships between the detected image features. The reconstructed models enable a simple extraction of geometric shapes, such as rectangles, in the scene.

Related Work. For the three-dimensional reconstruction of objects from an image sequence with different viewpoints, correspondences between images must

© Springer Nature Switzerland AG 2019
T. Brox et al. (Eds.): GCPR 2018, LNCS 11269, pp. 3–17, 2019.
https://doi.org/10.1007/978-3-030-12939-2_1

be found. For this purpose, image features, such as corners and lines, are tracked from one image to the next. The result of a SfM procedure usually consists of the camera poses at which the images were taken and a sparse three-dimensional point cloud of the scene.

First methods that enabled the reconstruction of sights from large unsorted Internet photo collections [15] have contributed to the popularity of SfM applications. In the following years, the efficiency of the processes was further increased so that complete cities could be reconstructed from huge data sets [2,6]. The state of the art SfM methods generally use point features. There are only a small number of line-based reconstruction methods that can handle realistic datasets. A complete line-based SfM pipeline is presented in [21]. They use their proposed Line Band Descriptor (LBD) [20] for line matching and their Robust Perspective-n-Line (RPnL) [19] algorithm to estimate the camera pose. Because point-based SfM methods are widely used and enable reliable pose estimation, many approaches use a point-based reconstruction as a prerequisite. If the camera positions are known, line-based reconstruction is substantially simplified and is used as a post-processing step to improve the SfM results with 3D lines [8].

A number of methods that are concerned with line-based reconstruction use the lines as starting point to build a piecewise planar 3D model of the scene. These methods usually focus on the reconstruction of buildings. Using 3D lines to create planes has advantages compared to 3D points, since two 3D lines are sufficient to create a plane hypothesis and the reconstructed lines normally represent the intersection of two 3D planes. The method presented in [16] uses the reconstructed lines to determine the main directions of the scene, which are used to detect the dominant planes. A similar procedure is proposed by [14]. Starting from a sparse 3D reconstruction of points and lines, planes are extracted and then piecewise planar depth maps are generated by graph-cut based minimization. The interpretation of buildings and especially of their facades has been researched for a long time. Early approaches have focused on facade segmentation and window detection using image sequences [10,16]. Most recent works on facade segmentation are based on single images [9,12,13]. For the facade segmentation, the images usually have to be rectified. Furthermore, architectural assumptions are often used, for example that the windows are arranged in rows or columns.

Contribution. With the common SfM methods, each image feature is reconstructed independently, even if it belongs to structures that are connected in the scene. In particular, line segments that describe a contiguous planar object in the scene are generally not in the same plane in the reconstructed model, which makes it impossible to directly determine contiguous 3D structures.

The main contribution of this paper is that we introduce a new method that reconstructs planar three-dimensional structures based on a SfM reconstruction. The structures are composed of points and lines whose connections are stored in a graph describing the topological relationships. In this way, a highly abstract but semantically rich 3D model of the scene is obtained. The topology graph allows searching for more complex geometric shapes. To show this, we present a method that automatically extracts rectangles in the reconstructed 3D models.

Overview. The reconstruction method we propose consists of several steps (Fig. 1). In the first step, a feature-based reconstruction is performed which reconstructs points and lines and determines the camera poses. Then the main planes of the scene are determined. These are the basis for our novel topology-based reconstruction method, which makes it possible to reconstruct contiguous planar structures. Finally, geometric shapes can be easily extracted in the reconstructed 3D model.

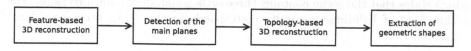

Fig. 1. Flowchart of the reconstruction process.

2   Feature-Based 3D Reconstruction

In this section, we show the structure of our feature-based reconstruction pipeline, which is the first step in our reconstruction process. We use a combination of state of the art methods that allow a reliable reconstruction of point and line primitives.

The first step of the reconstruction is *feature extraction*. We use the method proposed by [18] to detect the image features. The method enables an accurate and robust detection of points, lines and arcs. In addition to the image features, the method returns a graph that describes the topological relationships of the features. In addition, we extract a FREAK [3] descriptor for each point. The next step is *point matching*. Here visually similar pairs of features are determined in two different images. In the third step, the *geometric verification* is performed. In the verification step the relative poses between the matched camera pairs are determined. The fourth step is the *reconstruction* of the points. Starting from an initial camera pair, a 3D model is incrementally built up. All matched image features are triangulated so that a sparse three-dimensional point cloud is generated. The last step is *bundle adjustment*. The aim of bundle adjustment is to determine 3D point positions and camera parameters that minimize the reprojection error. For the final bundle adjustment, we use Ceres [1].

In order to enable the reconstruction of line primitives, the described reconstruction process is extended. We take advantage of the fact that the camera poses are already known through point-based reconstruction. The combined detection method detects the lines at the same time as the points, so that the 2D line features are already available. To characterize the local appearance of line segments we use the Line Band Descriptor (LBD) [20]. The next step is *line matching*. For line matching, we use the method presented by Zhang et al. [20] accordingly. The final step is the *reconstruction* of the lines. Starting with an initial camera pair, the matched line segments are triangulated. Iteratively, observations from further cameras are added. The triangulated 3D lines are then verified by their reprojection error.

3   Topology-Based Reconstruction

3.1   Detection of the Main Planes

The first step of the topology-based reconstruction method developed by us is the detection of the main planes of the scene. We are using an approach based on a method for the automatic indoor reconstruction using dense point clouds proposed by [4]. The approach uses the Manhattan world assumption [5], which states that the scene contains three orthogonal, dominant directions. The architecture of buildings generally corresponds to this assumption to a large extent.

Determining the Manhattan World Directions. First the vertical or the gravity direction is determined. This can either be given by an inertial navigation system (INS) or estimated from the vanishing points. In our case, the corresponding gravity vector is given by an INS for each image.

To determine the normals of the facade planes, we use the assumption that they are perpendicular to the gravity direction. In addition, we use the assumption that the facade planes are orthogonal to each other. Both facade normals can therefore be determined by only one rotation around the gravity direction.

We use an entropy-based method to determine the rotation. The analysis of the entropy of distribution of point coordinates is a common approach in literature to determine the main directions of a point cloud [7,11,17].

Plane-Sweep. In point clouds, planes can be detected by a plane sweep [4]. This is achieved by moving a plane through the three-dimensional space at discrete intervals along a given direction. For each step, the number of points is determined that lie within a predefined range around the plane. This creates a histogram of the sweep area. For each sweep step, a bin is created in the histogram with the number of points as value. The peaks in the histogram correspond to areas with a high point density and represent areas of potential planes. The peaks are determined using non-maxima suppression. In addition, a threshold value is used to suppress local maxima in areas with few points. We use a fixed minimum threshold of 100 for the frequency.

Finally, the minimum bounding rectangle (MBR) is determined on the plane. This is the smallest possible rectangle parallel to the axis that encloses all points of the point cloud that lie on the plane or have a distance of less than 2.5 cm to the plane.

To illustrate the computation, we consider the determination of the main planes using the example of a real scene. Figure 2 (a) shows one of the input images and Fig. 2 (b) shows the point cloud generated from the reconstructed points and lines and the detected main planes. The planes represent a suitable approximation of the scene and represent the main surfaces of the building.

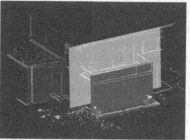

(a) Input image   (b) Point cloud with planes

Fig. 2. (a) One of the input images used for the feature-based reconstruction and (b) generated point cloud with the detected main planes.

3.2 Topology-Based 3D Reconstruction

The main planes are the basis for the topology-based reconstruction method we propose. The reconstruction process (Listing 1) is performed successively for all detected main planes and consists of three steps, which are explained in detail below.

Listing 1. Pseudocode for topology-based 3D reconstruction

```
Input:   P_1,..,P_m - detected planes
         F_1,..,F_n - detected features of images 1,..,n
         C_1,..,C_n - camera poses of images 1,..,n

Output:  M - reconstructed 3D model
         G - 3D topology graph

for each P in {P_1,..,P_m}
  // pairwise matching
  for i = 1 to n-1
    backproject features F_i and F_(i+1) to plane P
    for each feature in F_i find most similar in F_(i+1)
    for each feature in F_(i+1) find most similar in F_i
    cross check
  end

  // generate feature hypotheses
  build feature trails based on the pairwise matches
  for each trail
    if trail has at least 4 observations
      create 3D feature hypothesis
    end
  end

  // establishment and verification topology
  for each 3D feature pair
    if at least 3 associated 2D observations are connected
      connect 3D features in the topology graph
    end
  end
  remove unconnected 3D feature hypotheses
end

return 3D model M and topology graph G
```

Pairwise Matching. In the matching step, corresponding image features are determined between successive images of the image sequence. The matching process proceeds as follows. First, all image features that have been detected are backprojected to the current 3D plane. For a camera pair, for each image feature from the first image, the feature from the second image that is most similar to it is determined. Additionally we use a cross check of the matches. To determine the similarity of point features, we consider the Euclidean distance between the features backprojected to the planes. For the lines, the sum of the perpendicular distances from the start and end point of the line feature from the first image to the line feature from the second image is used to determine the similarity.

Generation of Feature Hypotheses. The aim of the next step is to determine hypotheses for 3D features that are supported by multiple image observations. Starting from a pair of images, supporting observations from other images are searched on the basis of the matching results. In this way, trails of corresponding image features are created across multiple images. For all features supported by at least four image observations, a 3D feature hypothesis is determined. The position of the feature on the 3D plane is determined by fitting it to the image features backprojected onto the plane.

Establishment and Verification of the Topology. In the third step, the topological relationships between the 3D features are established. At the same time, this step is used to verify the feature hypotheses. To establish the topological relationships between the 3D feature hypotheses, it is examined for each feature pair whether a topological relationship exists between at least three of the associated 2D observations. If this is the case, the nodes associated with the 3D feature hypotheses are connected in the corresponding topology graph. All feature hypotheses that are not part of a connected component of the graph with at least three nodes are removed after this process. These are usually caused by mismatches. Furthermore, the aim of the method is to identify more complex planar structures.

3.3   Extraction of Geometric Shapes

Based on the 3D model of topology-based reconstruction, we have developed a method that enables the extraction of specific geometric shapes. We use the topological information to automatically extract rectangles. In man-made environments, this method is a simple way to detect candidates for windows in facades, as these can usually be assumed to be rectangular.

To extract the rectangles we use the topology graph, which describes the relationships between the reconstructed image features. We use the assumption that a rectangle in the reconstructed 3D model consists of four line segments and four corner points that are part of a common connected component of the topology graph. First, simple cycles are searched in the graph. In graph theory, a simple cycle of a graph $G = (V, E)$ is a path $(v_1, \ldots, v_n)$ with $v_i \in V$ for $i = 1, \ldots, n$ to which applies:

$$v_1 = v_n \tag{1}$$

$$v_i \neq v_j \text{ for } i, j \in 1, \ldots, n - 1 \text{ and } i \neq j \tag{2}$$

The length of a simple cycle $(v_1, \ldots, v_n)$ is defined as $n - 1$. For each simple cycle of length eight of the topology graph, it is checked whether it consists of an alternating sequence of point nodes and line nodes. If this is the case, it is validated whether the associated reconstructed features fulfill the properties of a rectangle, i. e. that all line segments connected by a point node have an angle of $90°$ to each other and that the point node corresponds to the intersection of the two line segments. In this way, planar rectangular structures can be identified in the scene.

4 Evaluation

4.1 Synthetic Scenes

In a first evaluation, we analyze the detection accuracy and the localization error of our topology-based reconstruction and compare it with the common SfM reconstruction. We use computer-generated images of a synthetic building with known ground truth as input for the reconstruction. Figure 3 (a) shows one of the computer-generated input images. The building has a width of 15 m. In total, we use eight sequences with ten images each with a resolution of 3 MP. In the evaluation, we determine the detection rate. It indicates how many of the geometric structures of the building, i. e. window corners and frames, have been reconstructed. In total, the building has 138 features that must be detected. To evaluate the accuracy of the reconstruction, we measure the localization error. The localization error is calculated as the error distance in 3D space.

The results are given in Table 1. For topology-based reconstruction, the detection rate of automatic rectangle detection is also specified. Although the detection rate of the SfM reconstruction on the synthetic data is already high at 94.2%, the value can be further increased by the topology-based reconstruction. The average localization error for both methods is on a similar level. Furthermore, all rectangles are detected correctly on the synthetic scenes by our method. Examples of the results of the SfM reconstruction, the topology-based reconstruction and the rectangle detection are shown in Fig. 3.

4.2 Real-World Scenes

Test Dataset. For the evaluation of our method in real-world applications, we use a dataset consisting of six scenes with real-world images showing buildings. Each scene contains between 11 and 32 images, which have a resolution of 3 MP. In addition, the scenes contain reference objects of known size. These are special customized boards with dot patterns that can be detected in the images. The

Table 1. Evaluation of detection accuracy of the SfM reconstruction and the topology-based reconstruction using eight synthetic scenes.

Method	Detection rate	Localization error	Rectangle detection rate
SfM reconstruction	94.2%	0.017 m	–
Topol.-based reconstruction	100%	0.016 m	100%

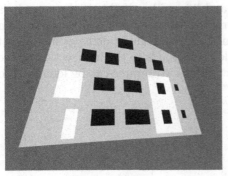

(a) Input image

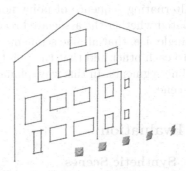

(b) SfM reconstruction

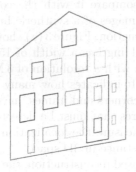

(c) Topology-based reconstruction

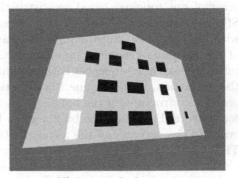

(d) Rectangle detection

Fig. 3. The individual steps of the reconstruction process using the example of a computer-generated scene of a synthetic building: (a) One of the input images, (b) SfM reconstruction and camera positions, (c) topology-based reconstruction and (d) automatic rectangle detection (highlighted yellow). (Color figure online)

diagonal size of the boards is 60 cm. They are used to determine the correct scaling of the scene to metric coordinates.

In order to provide more than just a qualitative evaluation, the essential geometric structures, e.g. the corners and edges of the buildings and windows in the facade, were labeled by humans for two of the scenes. In addition, the corresponding features in successive images of the scenes were labeled.

Consistency of the Topology Between Images. The idea of the first experiment is to determine the consistency of the extracted topology on real-world images. We determine the detected features and the topological relationships between them for all images of a scene. For all detected features for which a human labeled ground truth feature exist, we determine whether a path exists between them in the topology graph, that is, whether they belong to the same connected component of the graph. Then we look at all successive image pairs of the scene and determine how many of the feature pairs that are connected in the first image of the image pair are also connected in the second image.

The results of the experiment are given in Table 2. The evaluation is made separately for corners and line segments. Although the real-world images contain partial occlusions and strong changes of the viewpoint, the proportion of topologically consistent feature pairs in successive images is between 66% and 88%. The extracted topological relationships are therefore largely consistent across several images of the scenes. The topology graph can thus provide valuable information to support matching and correspondence search between images.

Table 2. Consistency of the extracted topology between successive images of real-world scenes for corners and line segments.

Scene	Corners			Line segments		
	# Pairs	# Matched	Prop.	# Pairs	# Matched	Prop.
No. 1	129	106	82%	187	165	88%
No. 2	1821	1198	66%	956	724	76%

Reconstruction Results. In the second experiment, we perform a qualitative evaluation of the reconstructed 3D models. We have tested it on the dataset with six real-world scenes showing buildings. Figures 4, 5 and 6 show the results of the SfM reconstruction in the first row and the results of the topology-based reconstruction in the second row for all six test scenes. The topology-based reconstruction was performed for all vertical main planes detected in the scene. Then the partial reconstructions are combined to one three-dimensional model. All image features associated to a connected component of the topology graph are drawn in the same color.

It is clearly visible that the related structures, such as the windows, are also present in the topology-based reconstructed 3D model as a connected structure. The topological relationships of the features can therefore also be preserved by the method during the reconstruction. The contiguous planar objects of a scene are thus also connected in the reconstructed model and on a common plane.

The advantages of the topology-based reconstruction approach become particularly clear in the second scene from Fig. 4. The facades of the neighboring half-timbered houses are reliably reconstructed. The panels between the timbers are each identified and reconstructed as a connected planar structure. In the

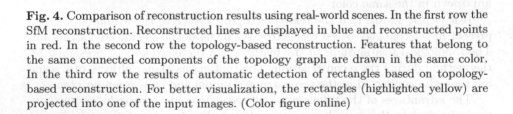

Fig. 4. Comparison of reconstruction results using real-world scenes. In the first row the SfM reconstruction. Reconstructed lines are displayed in blue and reconstructed points in red. In the second row the topology-based reconstruction. Features that belong to the same connected components of the topology graph are drawn in the same color. In the third row the results of automatic detection of rectangles based on topology-based reconstruction. For better visualization, the rectangles (highlighted yellow) are projected into one of the input images. (Color figure online)

Fig. 5. Comparison of reconstruction results using real-world scenes. In the first row the SfM reconstruction. Reconstructed lines are displayed in blue and reconstructed points in red. In the second row the topology-based reconstruction. Features that belong to the same connected components of the topology graph are drawn in the same color. In the third row the results of automatic detection of rectangles based on topology-based reconstruction. For better visualization, the rectangles (highlighted yellow) are projected into one of the input images. (Color figure online)

Fig. 6. Comparison of reconstruction results using real-world scenes. In the first row the SfM reconstruction. Reconstructed lines are displayed in blue and reconstructed points in red. In the second row the topology-based reconstruction. Features that belong to the same connected components of the topology graph are drawn in the same color. In the third row the results of automatic detection of rectangles based on topology-based reconstruction. For better visualization, the rectangles (highlighted yellow) are projected into one of the input images. (Color figure online)

result of the SfM reconstruction, only a small part of the area is reconstructed and there is no information about the connection to each other.

The third row of the figures shows the rectangles detected by our methods. For better visualization, the reconstructed rectangles are projected into one of the input images. This enables an easier assessment of the quality of the detection. Only the rectangle with the longest perimeter is displayed for each connected component of the topology graph. It is clearly visible that most rectangular structures in the scenes are already extracted by this relatively simple approach. In addition, the assumption that the rectangular structures in man-made environments often correspond to the windows is confirmed by the results.

Computational Performance. The runtimes for the SfM reconstruction and the topology-based reconstruction on a laptop with a Core i5 are given in Table 3. The algorithms are implemented as unoptimized C++ code. The runtime of the SfM reconstruction depends mainly on the number of images in the scene and the number of features that are detected in the images. The runtime per image is between 7.5 s and 17.9 s. The reconstruction of a complete scene is thus completed after a few minutes.

The detection of the main planes in the point cloud of the SfM reconstruction takes only a few seconds. The proposed method thus enables an efficient detection of the main structures of a scene based on a sparse SfM reconstruction. The runtime depends only on the size of the point cloud and the bin width of the histograms. The subsequent topology-based reconstruction method has a runtime similar to the SfM reconstruction. The average runtime per image is between 4.1 s and 14.1 s.

The runtime depends mainly on the number of planes and the number of image features found on them. Scenes with few planes and a simple structure can be reconstructed faster than scenes with many planes and a lot of image features. Therefore, scene no. 3 (Fig. 5, left column) has the shortest runtime, since it is composed of only one plane and has a simple structure with few image features. For scenes with several planes, e.g. no. 1 (Fig. 4, left column), or a lot of image features, e.g. no. 6 (Fig. 6, right column), the runtime is longer. The overall runtime of the proposed topology-based reconstruction method is thus at a level that allows practical application in reconstruction frameworks.

The detection of rectangles in topology-based reconstruction is very efficient because the information about the connections between the characteristics is available in the topology graph, so that the desired structures can be determined with a simple search algorithm. The runtime for the detection of the rectangles in the six real-world scenes is between 1.5 s and 3.4 s.

Table 3. Evaluation of the runtime of the SfM reconstruction, plane detection, topology-based reconstruction and rectangle detection using six real-world scenes. Indicated is the total time as well as the average per image.

Scene	Num. of images	SfM reconstr.	Plane detection	Topol.-based reconstr.	Rectangle detection
No. 1	17	239.6 s (∅ 14.1 s)	7.3 s	239.7 s (∅ 14.1 s)	1.1 s
No. 2	11	82.1 s (∅ 7.5 s)	4.4 s	141.0 s (∅ 12.8 s)	2.0 s
No. 3	21	259.5 s (∅ 12.4 s)	2.0 s	86.1 s (∅ 4.1 s)	1.8 s
No. 4	14	215.6 s (∅ 15.4 s)	3.1 s	155.8 s (∅ 11.1 s)	1.5 s
No. 5	24	430.2 s (∅ 17.9 s)	3.5 s	249.6 s (∅ 10.4 s)	3.4 s
No. 6	32	522.7 s (∅ 16.3 s)	4.1 s	400.2 s (∅ 12.5 s)	3.2 s

5   Conclusion

In this paper, we have presented a novel reconstruction method that uses the topological relationship of the features to create a highly abstract but semantically rich 3D model of the reconstructed scenes, in which certain geometric structures can easily be detected. The presented method can make a meaningful contribution to the understanding and analysis of scenes, without the need to perform a computationally complex multi-view stereo reconstruction.

References

1. Agarwal, S., Mierle, K., et al.: Ceres Solver
2. Agarwal, S., Snavely, N., Simon, I., Sietz, S.M., Szeliski, R.: Building Rome in a day. In: Twelfth IEEE International Conference on Computer Vision (ICCV 2009). IEEE, Kyoto, September 2009
3. Alahi, A., Ortiz, R., Vandergheynst, P.: FREAK: fast retina keypoint. In: 2012 IEEE Conference on Computer Vision and Pattern Recognition (CVPR), pp. 510–517. IEEE, June 2012
4. Budroni, A., Böhm, J.: Automatic 3D modelling of indoor manhattan-world scenes from laser data. In: Proceedings of the International Archives of Photogrammetry, Remote Sensing and Spatial Information Sciences, pp. 115–120 (2010)
5. Coughlan, J., Yuille, A.: Manhattan world: compass direction from a single image by Bayesian inference. In: Proceedings of the Seventh IEEE International Conference on Computer Vision, vol. 2, pp. 941–947. IEEE (1999)
6. Frahm, J.-M., et al.: Building Rome on a cloudless day. In: Daniilidis, K., Maragos, P., Paragios, N. (eds.) ECCV 2010. LNCS, vol. 6314, pp. 368–381. Springer, Heidelberg (2010). https://doi.org/10.1007/978-3-642-15561-1_27
7. Gallup, D., Frahm, J.M., Mordohai, P., Yang, Q., Pollefeys, M.: Real-time plane-sweeping stereo with multiple sweeping directions. In: 2007 IEEE Conference on Computer Vision and Pattern Recognition, pp. 1–8. IEEE, June 2007
8. Hofer, M., Maurer, M., Bischof, H.: Improving sparse 3D models for man-made environments using line-based 3D reconstruction. In: 2014 2nd International Conference on 3D Vision, vol. 1, pp. 535–542, December 2014
9. Mathias, M., Martinović, A., Van Gool, L.: ATLAS: a three-layered approach to facade parsing. Int. J. Comput. Vis. **118**(1), 22–48 (2016)

10. Mayer, H., Reznik, S.: Building Façade interpretation from image sequences. In: Proceedings of the ISPRS Workshop CMRT, pp. 55–60 (2005)
11. Olufs, S., Vincze, M.: Room-structure estimation in Manhattan-like environments from dense 2 1/2D range data using minumum entropy and histograms. In: 2011 IEEE Workshop on Applications of Computer Vision (WACV), pp. 118–124. IEEE, January 2011
12. Rahmani, K., Mayer, H.: High quality facade segmentation based on structured random forest, region proposal network and rectangular fitting. ISPRS Ann. Photogram. Remote Sens. Spat. Inf. Sci. **IV–2**, 223–230 (2018)
13. Schmitz, M., Mayer, H.: A convolutional network for semantic facade segmentation and interpretation. ISPRS - Int. Arch. Photogr. Remote Sens. Spat. Inf. Sci. **XLI–B3**, 709–715 (2016). https://doi.org/10.5194/isprsarchives-XLI-B3-709-2016
14. Sinha, S.N., Steedly, D., Szeliski, R.: Piecewise planar stereo for image-based rendering. In: ICCV, pp. 1881–1888. Citeseer (2009)
15. Snavely, N., Seitz, S.M., Szeliski, R.: Photo tourism: exploring photo collections in 3D. In: ACM Transactions on Graphics (TOG), vol. 25, pp. 835–846. ACM (2006)
16. Werner, T., Zisserman, A.: New techniques for automated architectural reconstruction from photographs. In: Heyden, A., Sparr, G., Nielsen, M., Johansen, P. (eds.) ECCV 2002. LNCS, vol. 2351, pp. 541–555. Springer, Heidelberg (2002). https://doi.org/10.1007/3-540-47967-8_36
17. Wolters, D.: Automatic 3D reconstruction of indoor manhattan world scenes using kinect depth data. In: Jiang, X., Hornegger, J., Koch, R. (eds.) GCPR 2014. LNCS, vol. 8753, pp. 715–721. Springer, Cham (2014). https://doi.org/10.1007/978-3-319-11752-2_59
18. Wolters, D., Koch, R.: Combined precise extraction and topology of points, lines and curves in man-made environments. In: Roth, V., Vetter, T. (eds.) GCPR 2017. LNCS, vol. 10496, pp. 115–125. Springer, Cham (2017). https://doi.org/10.1007/978-3-319-66709-6_10
19. Xu, C., Zhang, L., Cheng, L., Koch, R.: Pose estimation from line correspondences: a complete analysis and a series of solutions. IEEE Trans. Pattern Ana. Mach. Intell. **39**(6), 1209–1222 (2017). https://doi.org/10.1109/TPAMI.2016.2582162
20. Zhang, L., Koch, R.: An efficient and robust line segment matching approach based on LBD descriptor and pairwise geometric consistency. J. Vis. Commun. Image Represent. **24**(7), 794–805 (2013)
21. Zhang, L., Koch, R.: Structure and motion from line correspondences: representation, projection, initialization and sparse bundle adjustment. J. Vis. Commun. Image Represent. **25**(5), 904–915 (2014)

Associative Deep Clustering:
Training a Classification Network
with No Labels

Philip Haeusser[(✉)], Johannes Plapp, Vladimir Golkov, Elie Aljalbout,
and Daniel Cremers

Department of Informatics, TU Munich, Munich, Germany
haeusser@cs.tum.edu
http://vision.in.tum.de

Abstract. We propose a novel end-to-end clustering training schedule
for neural networks that is direct, i.e. the output is a probability distribution over cluster memberships. A neural network maps images to
embeddings. We introduce centroid variables that have the same shape
as image embeddings. These variables are jointly optimized with the
network's parameters. This is achieved by a cost function that associates
the centroid variables with embeddings of input images. Finally, an additional layer maps embeddings to logits, allowing for the direct estimation
of the respective cluster membership. Unlike other methods, this does
not require any additional classifier to be trained on the embeddings in a
separate step. The proposed approach achieves state-of-the-art results in
unsupervised classification and we provide an extensive ablation study
to demonstrate its capabilities.

1 Introduction

1.1 Towards Direct Deep Clustering

Deep neural networks have shown impressive potential on a multitude of computer vision challenges [5,8,27,35–37]. A fundamental limitation in many applications is that they traditionally require huge amounts of labeled training data.
To circumvent this problem, a plethora of semi-supervised and unsupervised
training schemes have been proposed [4,7,17,24]. They all aim at reducing the
number of labeled data while leveraging large quantities of unlabeled data.

It is an intriguing idea to train a neural network without any labeled data at
all by automatically discovering structure in data, given the number of classes
as minimal prior knowledge. In many real-world applications beyond the scope
of academic research, it is desired to discover structures in large unlabeled data
sets. When the goal is to separate date into groups, this maneuver is called
clustering. Deep neural networks are the model of choice when it comes to image
understanding. In the past, however, deep neural networks have rarely been
trained for clustering directly. A more common approach is *feature learning*.

© Springer Nature Switzerland AG 2019
T. Brox et al. (Eds.): GCPR 2018, LNCS 11269, pp. 18–32, 2019.
https://doi.org/10.1007/978-3-030-12939-2_2

Here, a proxy task is designed to generate a loss signal that can be used to update the model parameters in an entirely unsupervised manner. Such a task can be the reconstruction of the input image from the internal representation. This setup is called "auto-encoder" [14]. Other tasks enforce similarities in representation space under transformations in pixel space [7]. There are generative adversarial approaches [9] or context prediction proxy tasks [4].

An exhaustive comparison of previous works is collected in Sect. 1.2. All these approaches aim at transforming an input image x_i to a representation or embedding z_i that allows for clustering the data. In order to perform this last step, a mapping from embedding space to clusters is necessary, e.g. by training an additional classifier on the features, such as k-means [26] or an SVM [34] in a separate step.

A common problem in unsupervised learning is that there is no signal that tells the network to cluster different examples from the same class together although they look very different in pixel space. We call this the *blue sky problem* with the pictures of a flying bird and a flying airplane in mind, both of which will contain many blue pixels but just a few others that make the actual distinction. In particular, auto-encoder approaches suffer from the blue sky problem as their cost function usually penalizes reconstruction in pixel space and hence favors the encoding of potentially unnecessary but space consuming information such as the sky (Fig. 1).

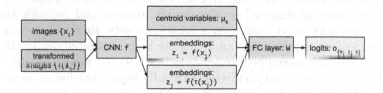

Fig. 1. Associative deep clustering. Images (x_i) and transformations of them $(\tau(x_j))$ are sent through a CNN in order to obtain embeddings z. We introduce k centroid variables μ_k that have the same dimensionality as the embeddings. Our proposed loss function simultaneously trains these centroids and the network's parameters along with a mapping from embedding space to a cluster membership distribution.

1.2 Related Work

Most classical clustering approaches are limited to the original data space and are thus not very effective in high-dimensional spaces with complicated data distributions such as images. Early deep-learning-based clustering methods first train a feature extractor, and in a separate step apply a clustering algorithm to the features [9, 29, 31].

Well-clusterable deep representations are characterized by high within-cluster similarities of points compared to low across-cluster similarities. Some loss functions optimize only one of these two aspects. Particularly, methods that do not encourage across-cluster dissimilarities are at risk of producing worse (or theoretically even trivial) representations/results [39], but some of them nonetheless work well in practice. Other methods avoid trivial representations by using additional techniques unrelated to clustering, such as an auto-encoder reconstruction loss [18,25,38,39].

The Deep Embedded Clustering (DEC) [38] model simultaneously learns feature representations and cluster assignments using a deep network. The goal is to optimize the KL divergence between the cluster assignment probability distribution of embedded data points and a target distribution, hence enforcing stricter and more confident assignments (close to 0 or 1). To get a good initialization, DEC needs an auto-encoder pre-training. Moreover, the approach has some difficulties scaling to larger data sets such as STL-10.

In addition to DEC, several other works used similar approaches combining initialization with auto-encoders and fine-tuning with some clustering objectives (sometimes in combination with an auto-encoder reconstruction during fine-tuning as well) [18,25,39].

Variational Deep Embedding (VaDE) [41] is a generative clustering approach based on variational auto-encoders. This method achieves significantly more accurate results on small data sets, but does not scale to larger, higher-resolution ones. For STL-10, it uses a network pre-trained on the dramatically larger Imagenet data set [30].

Joint Unsupervised Learning (JULE) of representations and clusters [40] is based on agglomerative clustering. In contrast to our method, JULE's network training procedure alternates between cluster updates and network training. JULE achieves very good results on several data sets. However, its computational and memory requirements are relatively high as pointed out in [15].

Clustering convolutional neural networks (CCNN) [15] predict cluster assignments at the last layer, and a clustering-friendly representation at an intermediate layer. The training loss is the difference between the clustering predictions and the results of k-means applied to the learned representation. Interestingly, CCNN yields good results in practice, despite both the clustering features and the cluster predictions being initialized in random and contradictory ways. An important distinction to our work is that CCNN requires running k-means in each iteration.

Deep Embedded Regularized Clustering (DEPICT) [3] is similar to DEC in that feature representations and cluster assignments are simultaneously learned using a deep network. An additional regularization term is used to balance the cluster assignment probabilities allowing to get rid of the pre-training step. This method achieved a performance comparable to ours on MNIST and FGRC. However, it requires pre-training using the autoencoder reconstruction loss.

In Categorical Generative Adversarial Networks (CatGANs) [33], unlike standard GANs, the discriminator learns to separate the data into k categories instead of learning a binary discriminative function. The authors achieve this by introducing an objective function assuring confident class assignments for samples drawn from the unlabeled data set and uncertain ones for outputs of the generator, in addition to a balanced class usage. In consequence, the network was able to generate images with high visual fidelity and cluster its data with high accuracy. However, it was only tested on the MNIST data set and the "circles" data set. Results on large data sets are not reported.

Information-Maximizing Self-Augmented Training (IMSAT) [16] is based on Regularized Information Maximization (RIM) [20], which learns a probabilistic classifier that maximizes the mutual information between the input and the class assignment. In IMSAT this mutual information is represented by the difference between the marginal and conditional distribution of those values. IMSAT also introduces regularization via self-augmentation. For large data sets, IMSAT uses fixed pre-trained network layers.

In summary, previous methods either do not scale well to large data sets [33, 38,41], have high computational and/or memory cost [40], require a clustering algorithm to be run during or after the training (most methods, e.g. [15,40]), are at risk of producing trivial representations, and/or require some labeled data [16] or clustering-unrelated losses (for example additional autoencoder loss [1,3,18, 25,38,39,41]) to (pre-)train (parts of) the network. In particular, reconstruction losses tend to overestimate the importance of low level features such as colors. In order to solve these problems, it is desirable to develop new training schemes that tackle the clustering problem as a *direct* end-to-end training of a neural network.

1.3   Contribution

In this paper, we propose *Associative Deep Clustering* as an end-to-end framework that allows to train a neural network directly for clustering. In particular, we introduce *centroid embeddings*: variables that look like embeddings of images but are actually part of the model. They can be optimized and they are used to learn a projection from embedding space to the desired output space, e.g. logits $\in \mathbb{R}^k$ where k is the number of classes. The intuition is that the centroid variables carry over high-level information about the data structure (i.e. cluster centroid embeddings) from iteration to iteration. It makes sense to train a neural network directly for a clustering task, rather than a proxy task (such as reconstruction from embeddings) since the ultimate goal is actually clustering.

To facilitate this, we introduce a cost function which encourages clusters to separate well and to associate similar images. *Associations* [12] are made between centroids and image embeddings, and between embeddings of images and their transformations. Unlike previous methods, we use clustering-specific loss terms that allow to directly learn the assignment of an image to a cluster. There is no need for a subsequent training procedure on the embeddings. The output of the network is a cluster membership distribution for a given input image. We demonstrate that this approach is useful for clustering images without any prior knowledge other than the number of classes.

The resulting learned cluster assignments are so good that subsequently re-running a clustering algorithm on the learned embeddings does not further improve the results (unlike e.g. [40]).

To the best of our knowledge, we are the first to introduce a joint training scheme that directly optimizes network parameters and the resulting cluster representations. This is opposed to feature learning approaches where the obtained features require an additional clustering algorithm such as k-means to be run on top of them in order to produce actual clusters, or to methods where the clustering is directly learned but parts of the network are pre-trained and then fixed [16].

Moreover, unlike most previous methods, we use *only* clustering-specific and invariance-imposing losses and no clustering-unrelated losses such as auto-encoder reconstruction or classification-based pre-training.

In summary, our contributions are:

- We introduce centroid variables that are jointly optimized with the network's weights.
- This is facilitated by our clustering cost function that makes *associations* between cluster centroids and image embeddings. No labels are needed at any time. In particular, there is no subsequent clustering step necessary.
- We conducted an extensive ablation study demonstrating the effects of our proposed training schedule.
- Our method outperforms the current state of the art on a number of data sets.
- All code is available as an open-source implementation in TensorFlow[1].

2   Associative Deep Clustering

In this section, we describe our setup and the cost function. Figure 2 depicts an overall schematic which will be referenced in the following.

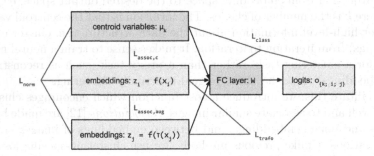

Fig. 2. Schematic of the framework and the losses. Green boxes are trainable variables. Yellow boxes are representations of the input. Red lines connect the losses with their inputs. Please find the definitions in Sect. 2.2 (Color figure online)

---

[1] github.com/haeusser.

2.1 Associative Learning

Recent works have shown that *associations* in embedding space can be used for semi-supervised training and domain adaptation [11,12]. Both applications require an amount of labeled training data which is fed through a neural network along with unlabeled data. Then, an imaginary walker is sent from embeddings of labeled examples to embeddings of unlabeled examples and back. From this idea, a cost function is constructed that encourages consistent association cycles, meaning that two labeled examples are associated via an unlabeled example with a high probability if the labels match and with a low probability otherwise. It is important to note that only probability distributions for these "walks" are computed. The concept of a "walker" is just used to illustrate the rationale. Let us introduce this more formally with the case where labeled data is available: Let A_i and B_j be embeddings of labeled and unlabeled data, respectively. Then a similarity matrix $M_{ij} := A_i \cdot B_j$ can be defined. These similarities can now be transformed into a transition probability matrix by softmaxing M over columns:

$$P_{ij}^{ab} = P(B_j|A_i) := (\text{softmax}_{\text{cols}}(M))_{ij} = \exp(M_{ij}) / \sum_{j'} \exp(M_{ij'}) \qquad (1)$$

Analogously, the transition probabilities in the other direction (P^{ba}) are obtained by replacing M with M^T. Finally, the metric of interest is the probability of an association cycle from A to B to A:

$$P_{ij}^{aba} := (P^{ab}P^{ba})_{ij} = \sum_k P_{ik}^{ab} P_{kj}^{ba} \qquad (2)$$

Since the labels of A are known, it is possible to define a target distribution where inconsistent association cycles (where labels mismatch) have zero probability:

$$T_{ij} := \begin{cases} 1/\#\text{class}(A_i) & \text{class}(A_i) = \text{class}(A_j) \\ 0 & \text{else} \end{cases} \qquad (3)$$

Now, the associative loss function becomes

$$\mathcal{L}_{\text{assoc}}(A, B) := \text{crossentropy}(T_{ij}; P_{ij}^{ab}) \qquad (4)$$

In other words, $\mathcal{L}_{\text{assoc}}(A, B)$ encourages the network to find weights that transform an input image to an embedding such that the transition probability from labeled examples to unlabeled ones and back is zero if the labels mismatch and uniform otherwise. The uniform probability causes the network to make no difference between multiple embeddings that belong to the same class.

For the complete derivation, the reader is kindly referred to [12].

2.2 Clustering Loss Function

In this work, we further develop this setup since there is no labeled batch A. In its stead, we introduce centroid variables μ_k with the same dimensionality as the image embeddings. The centroid variables have surrogate labels $0, 1, \ldots, k - 1$. With them and embeddings of (augmented) images, we can define clustering associations. In the following, we use the following variables:

- $x_i \in \mathbb{R}^{H \times W \times C}$: the i-th input image with height H, width W and number of channels C
- $\tau : \mathbb{R}^{H \times W \times C} \to \mathbb{R}^{H \times W \times C}$: an image transformation function
- $f : \mathbb{R}^{H \times W \times C} \to \mathbb{R}^{128}$: the mapping from input space to embedding space represented by the neural network
- $\mathbb{R}^{128} \ni z_i := f(x_i)$: the embedding of an image x_i
- $\mu_k \in \mathbb{R}^{128}$: the k-th centroid variable
- $W \in \mathbb{R}^{128 \times K}$: the weights of a fully-connected layer mapping embeddings z_i to logits o_i representing K classes
- $o_i \in \mathbb{R}^K$: the logit for image x_i

We define two associative loss terms:

- $\mathcal{L}_{\text{assoc,c}} := \mathcal{L}_{\text{assoc}}(\mu_k; z_i)$ where associations are made between ("labeled") centroid variables μ_k (instead of A) and (unlabeled) image embeddings z_i.
- $\mathcal{L}_{\text{assoc,aug}} := \mathcal{L}_{\text{assoc}}(z_i; f(\tau(x_j)))$ where we apply 4 random transformations τ to each image x_j resulting in 4 "augmented" embeddings z_j that share the same surrogate label. The "labeled" batch A then consists of all augmented images, the "unlabeled" batch B of embeddings of the unaugmented images x_i.

For simplicity, we imply a sum over all examples x_i and x_j in the batch. The loss is then divided by the number of summands.

The transformation τ randomly applies cropping and flipping, Gaussian noise, small rotations and changes in brightness, saturation and hue.

All embeddings and centroids are normalized to 1 with an L2 loss $\mathcal{L}_{\text{norm}}$.

A fully-connected layer W projects embeddings (μ_k, z_i and z_j) to logits $o_{k,i,j} \in \mathbb{R}^k$. After a softmax operation, each logit vector entry can be interpreted as the probability of membership in the respective cluster just as in a conventional classification output layer [22]. W is optimized through a standard cross-entropy classification loss $\mathcal{L}_{\text{classification}}$ where the inputs are μ_k and the desired outputs are the surrogate labels of the centroids.

Finally, we define a transformation loss

$$\mathcal{L}_{\text{trafo}} := |1 - f(x_i)^T f(\tau(x_j)) - \text{crossentropy}(o_i, o_j)| \tag{5}$$

We have two settings for τ: In the first one, we set τ to a random image transformation as described above. In this case, $\mathcal{L}_{\text{trafo}}$ causes the embedding of an image $f(x_i)$ to be similar to the embedding of another transformed image $f(\tau(x_j))$ if their estimated cluster membership distribution o_i, o_j, respectively, is similar. A similar trick has been used before [6], however, only with the requirement that an image and its transformed version should have the same embedding. Since we introduce crossentropy(o_i, o_j) as a weak label loss, we can generalize this to different images x_i, x_j where $i \neq j$.

Table 1. Clustering. Accuracy (%) on the test sets (higher is better). Standard deviation in parentheses where available. We report the mean and best of 20 runs for two architectures. For ResNet, we also report the accuracy when k-means is run on top of the obtained embeddings after convergence. [†]: Using features after pre-training on Imagenet. [‡]: Using GIST features. [††]: Using histogram-of-oriented-gradients (HOG) features. [‡‡]: Using 5k labels to train a classifier on top of the features from clustering. [*]: For DEPICT and IMSAT, we carried out additional experiments without pre-training, i.e. unsupervisedly and from scratch. We report mean and standard deviation from 10 runs.

	MNIST	FRGC	SVHN	CIFAR-10	STL-10
k-means on pixels	53.49	24.3	12.5	20.8	22.0
DEC [38]	84.30	37.8	-	-	35.9[‡†]
pre-train+DEC [16]	-	-	11.9 (0.4)[†]	46.9 (0.9)[†]	78.1 (0.1)[†]
VaDE [41]	94.46	-	-	-	84.5[†]
CatGAN [33]	95.73	-	-	-	-
JULE [40]	96.4	46.1	-	63.5[‡‡]	-
DEPICT [3]	96.5	**47.0**	-	-	-
DEPICT unsupervised[*]	-	-	18.6 (1.1)	12.4 (0.5)	22.8 (1.5)
IMSAT [16]	**98.4 (0.4)**	-	57.3 (3.9) [‡]	45.6 (2.9)[†]	94.1[†]
IMSAT unsupervised[*]	-	-	23.2 (0.4)	19.9 (0.2)	24.3 (0.9)
CCNN [15]	91.6	-	-	-	-
Ours (VCNN): mean	**98.7 (0.6)**	43.7 (1.9)	37.2 (4.6)	26.7 (2.0)	38.9 (5.9)
Ours (VCNN): best	99.2	46.0	43.4	28.7	41.5
Ours (ResNet): mean	95.4 (2.9)	21.9 (4.9)	**38.6 (4.1)**	**29.3 (1.5)**	**47.8 (2.7)**
Ours (ResNet): best	97.3	29.0	**45.3**	**32.5**	**53.0**
Ours (ResNet): K-means	93.8 (4.5)	24.0 (3.0)	35.4 (3.8)	30.0 (1.8)	47.1 (3.2)

In the second setting, we set τ to the identity function. This basically reduces $\mathcal{L}_{trafo}$ to a generalized weak "triplet loss" [32] where again the crossentropy term acts as a weak label loss. $\mathcal{L}_{trafo}$ should be small if the embeddings $f(x_i)$ and $f(x_j)$ are similar *and* their cluster membership distribution o_i and o_j, respectively.

In summary, particularly, $\mathcal{L}_{trafo}$ serves the following purposes:

- The logit o_i of an image x_i and the logit o_j of the transformed version $\tau(x_j)$ should be similar for $i = j$.
- Images that the network thinks belong to the same cluster (i.e. their centroid distribution o is similar) should also have similar embeddings, regardless of whether τ was applied.
- Embeddings of one image and a different image are allowed to be similar if the centroid membership is similar.
- Embeddings are forced to be dissimilar if they do not belong to the same cluster.

The final cost function now becomes

$$\mathcal{L} = \alpha\mathcal{L}_{assoc,c} + \beta\mathcal{L}_{assoc,aug} + \gamma\mathcal{L}_{norm} + \delta\mathcal{L}_{trafo} + \mathcal{L}_{classification}$$

with the loss weights $\alpha, \beta, \gamma, \delta$.

By using image augmentations as transformations, $\mathcal{L}_{\mathrm{assoc,aug}}$ and $\mathcal{L}_{\mathrm{trafo}}$ are used to make the clustering invariant to such transformations, allowing the network to learn higher-level abstractions. This can be seen as a form of user input, however only common augmentations are used here.

In the remainder of this paper, we present an ablation study to demonstrate that the loss terms do in fact support the clustering performance. From this study, we conclude on a set of hyper parameters to be held fixed for all data sets. With these fixed parameters, we finally report clustering scores on various data sets along with a qualitative analysis of the clustering results.

3 Experiments

3.1 Training Procedure

For all experiments, we start with a warm-up phase where we set all loss weights to zero except $\beta = 0.9$ and $\gamma = 10^{-5}$. $\mathcal{L}_{\mathrm{assoc,aug}}$ is used to initialize the weights of the network. After $5,000$ steps, we find an initialization for μ_k by running k-means on the training embeddings. Then, we activate the other loss weights.

We use the Adam optimizer [19] with ($\beta_1 = 0.8$, $\beta_2 = 0.9$) and a learning rate of 0.0008. This learning rate is divided by 3 every $10,000$ iterations. Following [10], we also adopt a warmup-phase of $2,000$ steps for the learning rate.

We report results on two architectures: a vanilla convolutional neural net from [12] (in the following referred to as VCNN) and the commonly used ResNet architecture [13]. For VCNN, we adopt the hyper-parameters used in the original work, specifically the mini-batch size of 100 and the embedding size 128.

For ResNet, we use the architecture specified for CIFAR-10 by [13] for all data sets except STL-10. Due to the larger resolution of this data set, we adopt the ImageNet variant, and modify it in the following way:

- The kernel size for the first convolutional layer becomes 3, with a stride of 1.
- The subsequent max-pooling layer is set to 2×2
- We reduce the number of filters by a factor of 2.

We use a mini-batch size of 128 images. For ResNet, we use 64-dimensional embedding vectors, as the CIFAR10-variant only has 64 filters in the last layer. We use a block size of 5 for SVHN and CIFAR-10 and 3 for all other sets.

The visit weight for both association losses is set to 0.3.

In order to find reasonable loss weights and investigate the importance, we conducted an ablation study which is described in the following section.

3.2 Ablation Study

We randomly sampled the loss weights for all previously introduced losses in the range $[0; 1]$ except for the normalization loss weight γ and ran $1,061$ experiments on MNIST. Then, we used this clustering model to assign classes to the MNIST test set. Following [38], we picked the permutation of class labels that reflects the true class labels best and summarized the respective accuracies in Fig. 3. For each point in a plot, we held only the one parameter fixed and averaged all according runs. This explains the error bars which arise from variance of all other parameters. It can still be seen very clearly that each loss has an important contribution to the test accuracy indicating the importance of the respective terms in our cost function.

We carried out similar experiments for other data sets which allowed to choose one set of hyper parameters for all subsequent experiments, which is described in the next section.

In Table 2, we report the results of an ablation study of the different loss terms. It becomes evident that the contribution of each individual loss term is crucial.

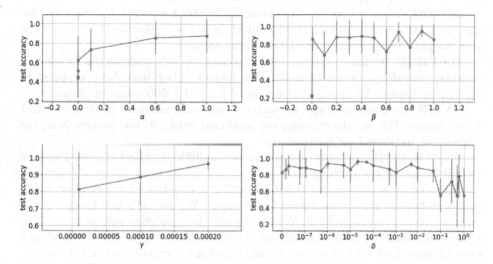

Fig. 3. Ablation study for different hyper-parameters on MNIST.

Table 2. Ablation study for different loss terms. We report the mean classification test error mean and standard deviation of 10 runs. In the first column, as no centroids are trained, we report scores using direct classification (left), and using k-means on embeddings after the warm-up phase (right). In general, all loss terms contribute to the final results. Also, especially on more complex data sets such as STL-10, associations with augmented samples are important.

Active loss terms:	$\mathcal{L}_{assoc,aug}$	$\mathcal{L}_{assoc,c} + \mathcal{L}_{norm}$	$\mathcal{L}_{assoc,c} + \mathcal{L}_{norm} + \mathcal{L}_{assoc,aug}$	All (cf. Table 1)
MNIST VCNN	27.6 (3.8)/85.3 (6.4)	66.7 (8.7)	97.0 (3.8)	98.7 (0.6)
CIFAR-10 ResNet	19.4 (0.5)/30.2 (1.2)	17.8 (0.8)	27.1 (0.9)	29.3 (1.5)
STL-10 ResNet	19.5 (2.7)/42.0 (1.3)	16.2 (1.1)	45.6 (3.1)	47.8 (2.7)

3.3 Evaluation Protocol

From the previous section, we chose the following hyper parameters to hold fixed for all data sets: $\alpha = 1; \beta = 0.9; \gamma = 10^{-5}; \delta = 2 \times 10^{-5}$

Following [38], we set k to be the number of ground-truth classes in each data set, and evaluate the clustering performance using the unsupervised clustering accuracy (ACC) metric. For every data set, we run our proposed algorithm 10 times, and report the mean, standard deviation and maximum accuracy of all clustering runs.

3.4 Data Sets

We evaluate our algorithm on the following, widely-used image data sets:

MNIST [23] is a benchmark containing 70,000 handwritten digits. We use all images from the training set without their labels. Following [12], we set the visit weight to 0.8. We also use 1,000 warm-up steps.

For **FRGC**, we follow the protocol introduced in [40], and use the 20 selected subsets, providing a total of 2,462 face images. They have been cropped to 32×32 px images. We use a visit weight of 0.1 and 1,000 warm-up steps.

SVHN [28] contains digits extracted from house numbers in Google Street View images. We use the training set combined with 150,000 images from the additional, unlabeled set for training.

CIFAR-10 [21] contains tiny images of ten different object classes. Here, we use all images of the training set.

STL-10 [2] is similar to CIFAR-10 in that it also has 10 object classes, but at a significantly higher resolution (96×96 px). We use all 5,000 images of the training set for our algorithm. We do not use the unlabeled set, as it contains images of objects of other classes that are not in the training set. We randomly crop images to 64×64 px during training, and use a center crop of this size for evaluation.

Table 1 summarizes the results. We achieve state-of-the-art results on MNIST, SVHN, CIFAR-10 and STL-10.

3.5 Qualitative Analysis

Figure 4 shows images from the MNIST and STL-10 test set, respectively. The examples shown have the highest probability to belong to the respective clusters (logit argmax). The MNIST examples reveal that the network has learned to cluster hand-written digits well while generalizing to different ways how digits can be written. For example, *2* can be written with a little loop. Some examples of *8* have a closed loop, some don't. The network does not make a difference here which shows that the proposed training scheme does learn a high-level abstraction.

Analogously, for STL-10, nearly all images are clustered correctly, despite a broad variance in colors and shapes. It is interesting to see that there is no bird among the top-scoring samples of the *airplane*-cluster, and all birds are correctly

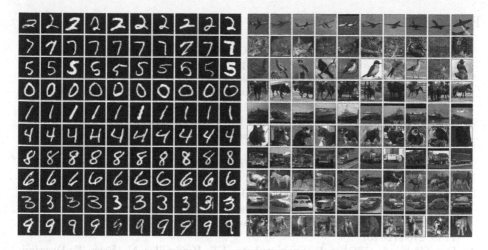

Fig. 4. Left: clustering examples from MNIST. Right: clustering examples from STL-10. Each row contains the examples with the highest probability to belong to the respective cluster.

clustered even if they are in front of a blue background. This demonstrates that our proposed algorithm does not solely rely on low-level features such as color (cf. the *blue sky problem*) but actually finds common patterns based on more complex similarities.

4 Conclusion

We have introduced *Associative Deep Clustering* as a novel, direct clustering algorithm for deep neural networks. The central idea is to jointly train centroid variables with the network's weights by using a clustering cost function. No labels are needed at any time and our approach does not require subsequent clustering such as many feature learning schemes. The importance of the loss terms were demonstrated in an ablation study and the effectiveness of the training schedule is reflected in state-of-the-art results in classification. A qualitative investigation suggests that our method is able to successfully discover structure in image data even when there is high intra-class variation. In clustering, there is no absolute right or wrong - multiple solutions can be valid, depending on the categories that a human introduces. We believe, however, that our formulation is applicable to many real world problems and that the simple implementation will hopefully inspire many future works.

References

1. Aljalbout, E., Golkov, V., Siddiqui, Y., Cremers, D.: Clustering with deep learning: taxonomy and new methods. arXiv preprint arXiv:1801.07648 (2018)
2. Coates, A., Ng, A., Lee, H.: An analysis of single-layer networks in unsupervised feature learning. In: Proceedings of the Fourteenth International Conference on Artificial Intelligence and Statistics, pp. 215–223 (2011)
3. Dizaji, K.G., Herandi, A., Huang, H.: Deep clustering via joint convolutional autoencoder embedding and relative entropy minimization. arXiv preprint arXiv:1704.06327 (2017)
4. Doersch, C., Gupta, A., Efros, A.A.: Unsupervised visual representation learning by context prediction. In: Proceedings of the IEEE International Conference on Computer Vision, pp. 1422–1430 (2015)
5. Dosovitskiy, A., et al.: FlowNet: learning optical flow with convolutional networks. In: Proceedings of the IEEE International Conference on Computer Vision, pp. 2758–2766 (2015)
6. Dosovitskiy, A., Fischer, P., Springenberg, J.T., Riedmiller, M., Brox, T.: Discriminative unsupervised feature learning with exemplar convolutional neural networks. IEEE Trans. Pattern Anal. Mach. Intell. **38**(9), 1734–1747 (2016)
7. Dosovitskiy, A., Springenberg, J.T., Riedmiller, M., Brox, T.: Discriminative unsupervised feature learning with convolutional neural networks. In: Advances in Neural Information Processing Systems, pp. 766–774 (2014)
8. Eigen, D., Puhrsch, C., Fergus, R.: Depth map prediction from a single image using a multi-scale deep network. In: Advances in Neural Information Processing Systems, pp. 2366–2374 (2014)
9. Goodfellow, I., et al.: Generative adversarial nets. In: Advances in Neural Information Processing Systems, pp. 2672–2680 (2014)
10. Goyal, P., et al.: Accurate, large minibatch SGD: training imagenet in 1 hour. arXiv preprint arXiv:1706.02677 (2017)
11. Haeusser, P., Frerix, T., Mordvintsev, A., Cremers, D.: Associative domain adaptation. In: IEEE International Conference on Computer Vision (ICCV) (2017)
12. Haeusser, P., Mordvintsev, A., Cremers, D.: Learning by association - a versatile semi-supervised training method for neural networks. In: IEEE Conference on Computer Vision and Pattern Recognition (CVPR) (2017)
13. He, K., Zhang, X., Ren, S., Sun, J.: Deep residual learning for image recognition. In: Proceedings of the IEEE Conference on Computer Vision and Pattern Recognition, pp. 770–778 (2016)
14. Hinton, G.E., Salakhutdinov, R.R.: Reducing the dimensionality of data with neural networks. Science **313**(5786), 504–507 (2006)
15. Hsu, C.C., Lin, C.W.: CNN-based joint clustering and representation learning with feature drift compensation for large-scale image data. arXiv preprint arXiv:1705.07091 (2017)
16. Hu, W., Miyato, T., Tokui, S., Matsumoto, E., Sugiyama, M.: Learning discrete representations via information maximizing self augmented training. arXiv preprint arXiv:1702.08720 (2017)
17. Huang, C., Change Loy, C., Tang, X.: Unsupervised learning of discriminative attributes and visual representations. In: Proceedings of the IEEE Conference on Computer Vision and Pattern Recognition, pp. 5175–5184 (2016)
18. Huang, P., Huang, Y., Wang, W., Wang, L.: Deep embedding network for clustering. In: 2014 22nd International Conference on Pattern Recognition (ICPR), pp. 1532–1537. IEEE (2014)

19. Kingma, D., Ba, J.: Adam: a method for stochastic optimization. arXiv preprint arXiv:1412.6980 (2014)
20. Krause, A., Perona, P., Gomes, R.G.: Discriminative clustering by regularized information maximization. In: Advances in Neural Information Processing Systems, pp. 775–783 (2010)
21. Krizhevsky, A., Hinton, G.: Learning multiple layers of features from tiny images (2009)
22. Krizhevsky, A., Sutskever, I., Hinton, G.E.: ImageNet classification with deep convolutional neural networks. In: Proceedings of the 25th International Conference of Neural Information Processing Systems (2012)
23. LeCun, Y.: The MNIST database of handwritten digits (1998). http://yann.lecun.com/exdb/mnist/
24. Lee, D.H.: Pseudo-label: the simple and efficient semi-supervised learning method for deep neural networks. In: Workshop on Challenges in Representation Learning, ICML, vol. 3, p. 2 (2013)
25. Li, F., Qiao, H., Zhang, B., Xi, X.: Discriminatively boosted image clustering with fully convolutional auto-encoders. arXiv preprint arXiv:1703.07980 (2017)
26. MacQueen, J., et al.: Some methods for classification and analysis of multivariate observations. In: Proceedings of the Fifth Berkeley Symposium on Mathematical Statistics and Probability, Oakland, CA, USA, vol. 1, pp. 281–297 (1967)
27. Mayer, N., et al.: A large dataset to train convolutional networks for disparity, optical flow, and scene flow estimation. In: Proceedings of the IEEE Conference on Computer Vision and Pattern Recognition, pp. 4040–4048 (2016)
28. Netzer, Y., Wang, T., Coates, A., Bissacco, A., Wu, B., Ng, A.Y.: Reading digits in natural images with unsupervised feature learning. In: NIPS workshop on deep learning and unsupervised feature learning, vol. 2011, p. 5 (2011)
29. Radford, A., Metz, L., Chintala, S.: Unsupervised representation learning with deep convolutional generative adversarial networks. arXiv preprint arXiv:1511.06434 (2015)
30. Russakovsky, O., et al.: ImageNet large scale visual recognition challenge. Int. J. Comput. Vis. (IJCV) 115(3), 211–252 (2015). https://doi.org/10.1007/s11263-015-0816-y
31. Salimans, T., Goodfellow, I., Zaremba, W., Cheung, V., Radford, A., Chen, X.: Improved techniques for training GANs. arXiv preprint arXiv:1606.03498 (2016)
32. Schroff, F., Kalenichenko, D., Philbin, J.: FaceNet: a unified embedding for face recognition and clustering. In: Proceedings of the IEEE Conference on Computer Vision and Pattern Recognition, pp. 815–823 (2015)
33. Springenberg, J.T.: Unsupervised and semi-supervised learning with categorical generative adversarial networks. arXiv preprint arXiv:1511.06390 (2015)
34. Suykens, J.A., Vandewalle, J.: Least squares support vector machine classifiers. Neural Process. Lett. 9(3), 293–300 (1999)
35. Szegedy, C., et al.: Going deeper with convolutions. In: Proceedings of the IEEE Conference on Computer Vision and Pattern Recognition, pp. 1–9 (2015)
36. Szegedy, C., Toshev, A., Erhan, D.: Deep neural networks for object detection. In: Advances in Neural Information Processing Systems, pp. 2553–2561 (2013)
37. Toshev, A., Szegedy, C.: DeepPose: human pose estimation via deep neural networks. In: Proceedings of the IEEE Conference on Computer Vision and Pattern Recognition, pp. 1653–1660 (2014)
38. Xie, J., Girshick, R., Farhadi, A.: Unsupervised deep embedding for clustering analysis. In: International Conference on Machine Learning, pp. 478–487 (2016)

39. Yang, B., Fu, X., Sidiropoulos, N.D., Hong, M.: Towards k-means-friendly spaces: simultaneous deep learning and clustering. arXiv preprint arXiv:1610.04794 (2016)
40. Yang, J., Parikh, D., Batra, D.: Joint unsupervised learning of deep representations and image clusters. In: Proceedings of the IEEE Conference on Computer Vision and Pattern Recognition, pp. 5147–5156 (2016)
41. Zheng, Y., Tan, H., Tang, B., Zhou, H., et al.: Variational deep embedding: a generative approach to clustering. arXiv preprint arXiv:1611.05148 (2016)

A Table Tennis Robot System Using an Industrial KUKA Robot Arm

Jonas Tebbe[✉], Yapeng Gao[✉], Marc Sastre-Rienietz[✉], and Andreas Zell[✉]

Cognitive Systems, Eberhard Karls University, Tübingen, Germany
{jonas.tebbe,yapeng.gao,andreas.zell}@uni-tuebingen.de,
marc.sastre-rienitz@student.uni-tuebingen.de
http://www.cogsys.cs.uni-tuebingen.de/

Abstract. In recent years robotic table tennis has become a popular research challenge for image processing and robot control. Here we present a novel table tennis robot system with high accuracy vision detection and fast robot reaction. Our system is based on an industrial KUKA Agilus R900 sixx robot with 6 DOF. Four cameras are used for ball position detection at 150 fps. We employ a multiple-camera calibration method, and use iterative triangulation to reconstruct the 3D ball position with an accuracy of 2.0 mm. In order to detect the flying ball with higher velocities in real-time, we combine color and background thresholding. For predicting the ball's trajectory we test both a curve fitting approach and an extended Kalman filter. Our robot is able to play rallies with a human counting up to 50 consequential strokes and has a general hitting rate of 87%.

Keywords: Table tennis robot · Ball detection · Trajectory prediction

1 Introduction

In March 2014 KUKA was very successful with a commercial video of the best german table tennis player Timo Boll facing a KUKA Agilus R900 sixx robot [8]. As the robot could not really play table tennis, the producers used modern video editing to give "a realistic vision of what robots can be capable of in the future". Shortly afterward another video [11] went viral, showing a self-built robot arm playing table tennis in a garage. Several inconsistencies pointed to manipulation of the video. With the same KUKA robot as in the first video we want to test the current limits of real robotic table tennis.

1.1 Related Work

Robotic table tennis has been attracting many researchers in the domain of image processing and robot control since Billingsley [5] in 1983 announced a robot table tennis competition with 20 rules for improving the successful hitting rate. Following these rules, Anderson [3] developed the first robot able to play

© Springer Nature Switzerland AG 2019
T. Brox et al. (Eds.): GCPR 2018, LNCS 11269, pp. 33–45, 2019.
https://doi.org/10.1007/978-3-030-12939-2_3

with human ping-pong players. He employed four cameras to detect the incoming ball and a 6-DOF PUMA 260 arm to return the ball. Other early robot systems were designed to continue this work with some limitations like using low frame rate camera or playing just in a well defined environment [1, 7, 16].

In recent years, there have been multiple robots of different accuracy defining the current state of the art. Xiong et al. [28] developed two humanoid robots named Wu & Kong, which can rally with each other more than 100 rounds. Each humanoid robot has 30 DOF in total, which are composed of two 7-DOF arms, two 6-DOF legs, and 4-DOF for head and waist. Every robot was equipped with four cameras to detect the ball. Muelling et al. [17–19] learned a generalized stroke motion from different elementary hitting movements taught by a human tutor. They used an anthropomorphic 7-DOF robot arm, which could generate smooth hitting movements capable of adapting to the changes in ball speed and position. Nakashima et al. [20–22] designed the joint trajectory of a 7-DOF robot arm which hits a back-spin ball to target points at the speed of 2–3 m/s. The success hitting rate was 70% in 20 trials. Li et al. presented a robot system in [14] consisting of two high-speed cameras and a universal 7-DOF robot arm. He applied a novel two-phase trajectory prediction to determine the hitting position, and finally achieved a success rate of 88%. Silva et al. [25] attached a light card-board racket and an onboard camera to a quadrotor drone and utilized imitation learning adopted from [19] to reach hitting rates of 30% in simulation and 20% with a real quadrotor. There are also some industrial companies following the same work. Omron [12] has shown an impressive demonstration at various robotics fairs. The Forpheus robot repurposed from an Omron 5-axis parallel robot, seems to have the best hitting accuracy at the moment and as a robotic tutor it can evaluate the ability level of its opponent with deep learning. SIASUN [24] exhibited its table tennis robot named Pongbot. It can predict the hitting position within 4 ms with 20 mm error using a high-speed stereo camera, and they developed a 6-DOF flexible robot arm to hit the ball back with an intelligent strategy.

1.2 Our System

In this paper, we present a novel table tennis robot system (Fig. 1) with high accuracy vision detection and fast robot reaction. Four PointGrey Chameleon3 cameras which are mounted in the corners of the ceiling are used for ball position detection. A table tennis paddle is rigidly fixed at the end-effector of a 6-DOF KUKA Agilus robot, and two Sick S300 laser scanners mounted on the floor are used in a safety system for area protection and access prevention. The whole system is controlled by one host computer with a 4×3.3 GHz Intel i5-4590 CPU and 16GB RAM. We implement the proposed approaches using the Robot Operating System (ROS) [23] nodes with message communication between each other and OpenCV [6] for image processing.

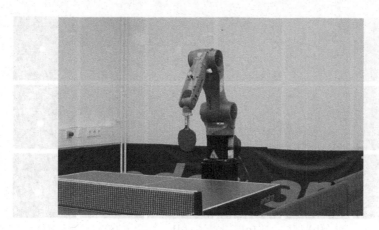

Fig. 1. Table tennis robot system with KUKA Agilus robot. The cameras, which are mounted on the ceiling, are not visible.

2   Methods

2.1   Ball Detection

There is a ROS ball detection node which outputs the 3D ball positions. The method adopted in this paper is fusing multiple features including motion, color, area and shape, which are used in [14,29]. To improve the robustness of image segmentation, we transfer the raw images read from the cameras into HSV color space. Multiple CPU threads are generated for each camera to accelerate the processing. Figure 2 shows the ball detection process using motion and color features for three examples cropped to the regions of interest. The top row depicts a position close to racket and player's hand. The middle row details a state on the table and in the last row the ball is crossing the net.

We want to avoid the crescent shaped ball shown in [34] when using adjacent frame difference because of a slow ball and high frame rate. Therefore we store the images in a queue and compare the current (n-th) to the $n - 7$th image, which is shown in Fig. 2(a)–(c). The binary shown in Fig. 2(d) uses thresholding according to the following equation:

$$Binary_n(u,v) = \begin{cases} 255 & \text{if } L \leqslant HSV_n(u,v) - HSV_{n\text{-}7}(u,v) \leqslant U \\ 0 & otherwise \end{cases} \tag{1}$$

$HSV_n(u,v)$ is the vector of HSV values of the pixel (u,v) in the nth image and comparison is done component-wise. L and U are the lower and upper HSV boundary values which are selected manually.

Restricting the setup to orange table tennis balls we are able to get the benefit of color thresholding the nth frame, which results in Fig. 2(e). By means of computing the bitwise conjunction of (d) and (e) in Fig. 2(f), we can extract the orange moving objects including balls and possibly skin regions, the moving

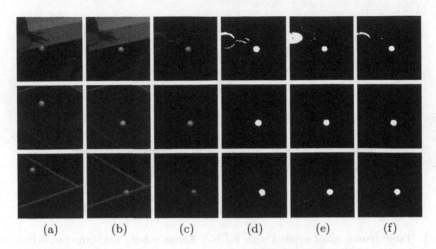

(a)   (b)   (c)   (d)   (e)   (f)

Fig. 2. Ball detection process using motion and color features: (a): the $(n-7)^{th}$ frame. (b): the nth frame. (c): subtracting frame (a) from (b). (d): color thresholding of (c). (e): color thresholding of (b). (f): bitwise AND operation between (d) and (e).

bat and the robot. To extract the correct blob belonging to the ball, we exploit size and shape features to filter out non-ball objects described as follows:

$$\begin{cases} 10px \leqslant & Area & \leqslant 800px \\ 0.5 \leqslant & AreaExtent \leqslant 1 \\ 1/1.4 \leqslant & AspectRatio \leqslant 1.4 \end{cases} \quad (2)$$

where $Area$ is the contour area extracted from the Fig. 2(f) in pixels. $AreaExtent$ is the ratio of $Area$ to the area of the minimal containing up-right bounding box. $AspectRatio$ is the aspect ratio of the bounding box. In rare cases this process results in multiple candidates because of other moving objects with similar properties existing. Therefore we select the one with the largest area as the detected ball.

Once a ball is recognized in the current frame, a region of interest (ROI) will be computed around the ball's center. Then we can track the next ball in this ROI within 5 ms/image. Processing in parallel gives real-time performance for a frame rate of 150fps.

The balls central pixel positions in multiple images are undistorted and triangulated to a 3d position according to calibration and triangulation described in Sect. 3.1.

2.2   Ball Trajectory Prediction

Given the observation of the positions of the ball until the current time, we need to predict the future trajectory of the ball to plan the hitting stroke of our robot. The flying ball is exposed to three forces: Gravity, air resistance, and the Magnus force (caused by spin) as depicted in Fig. 3. Even for humans this prediction is difficult and requires years to get a good estimation of balls with heavy spin. This is in particular due to the difficulty of measuring spin. Various research has been done on this topic. In [18] a physical model was used. The model in [32] could learn its parameters using a neural network. Many systems use an extended or unscented Kalman filter [18, 27, 30, 31] or curve fitting [14, 34]. For our system we employed both an extended Kalman filter and a curve fitting approach.

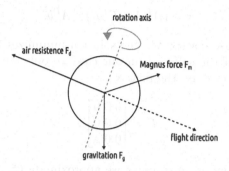

Fig. 3. Acting forces on a ball: gravitation pointing downwards, air resistance in the opposite direction of flight and Magnus force perpendicular to the spin axis and flight direction.

Curve Fitting. For the curve fitting approach the 3d trajectory points are separated for every axis. In our case the x-axis is along the large side of table, the y-axis is parallel to the net and the z-axis gives the height of a point. A quadratic polynomial $P(t) = at^2 + bt + c$ is fitted to the data for each axis, where the input is the time and the output is the ball's position on the specific axis. Its coefficients can be easily solved as this is a linear least squares problem. These polynomials describe the flight before bouncing on the table. With the roots of the z-axis polynomial we have the bounce time t_{bounce}. For the post-bounce trajectory we derive another set of polynomials Q. For the x-axis we define factors s_x and a_x for the change of velocity and acceleration in x-direction after the bounce. Without considering spin on the bounce we assume the post-bounce polynomial Q_x satisfies

$$Q_x(t_{\text{bounce}}) = P_x(t_{\text{bounce}}) \tag{3}$$

$$Q'_x(t_{\text{bounce}}) = s_x * P'_x(t_{\text{bounce}}) \tag{4}$$

$$Q''_x(t_{\text{bounce}}) = a_x * P''_x(t_{\text{bounce}}). \tag{5}$$

Analogously we have conditions for the other polynomials. With these conditions we can find unique solutions. The hitting point defined by the intersection with the plane $x = 0.1$ (in meters) can be solved from the post-bounce polynomials. The values used in our experiments are $s_x = s_y = 0.73$, $s_z = -0.85$, $a_x = a_y = 0.3$ and $a_z = -0.92$. Note that s_z and a_z are negative to affect for bouncing of the table in the opposite direction.

A disadvantage of the curve fitting approach is the large error for the first estimations, where only 5–10 ball positions have been recorded. To overcome this we suggest to use Tikhonov regularization for least-square solving the polynomial while regularizing the curvature. For a linear least squares problem $Ax = b$ we have an optimal solution

$$\hat{x} = (A^T A)^{-1} A^T b. \tag{6}$$

In Tikhonov regularization one defines a Tikhonov matrix Γ and

$$\hat{x} = (A^T A + \Gamma^T \Gamma)^{-1} A^T b. \tag{7}$$

For a typical Tikhonov matrix λI_n the solution minimizes the error while regularizing the norm of the solution. In our case we only want to regularize the acceleration $P''(t)$, so we use the matrix

$$\Gamma = \begin{bmatrix} 0 & 0 & 0 \\ 0 & 0 & 0 \\ 0 & 0 & \lambda \end{bmatrix}. \tag{8}$$

Using the z-polynomial as an example we approximate $(z_i - a_{\mathrm{prior}} t_i^2)_i$ with the Tikhonov matrix Γ. In this case the curvature a of the polynomial has a penalty to differ from 0. Therefore replacing the curvature a by $a' = a + a_{\mathrm{prior}}$ results in a polynomial with a curvature near a_{prior} approximating the values $(z_i)_i$. We use the curvature from prior experiments which includes an approximation for gravity and air drag. This can significantly improve the first predictions. With a smaller λ for more ball position measurement the curve fitting is drawn less to the prior curvatures and more to the real one. Using Tikhonov regularization we could lower the average bounce point error after 5 balls from unreasonable values to 70 mm, which is acceptable for initially moving the robot arm in the right direction.

EKF Approach. Relative to the balls speed v and angular velocity ω the gravitation force F_g, drag force F_d and Magnus force F_m in Fig. 3 are defined by the formulas

$$F_g = (0, 0, -mg)^T. \tag{9}$$

$$F_d = -\frac{1}{2} C_D \rho_a A \|v\| v \tag{10}$$

$$F_m = \frac{1}{2} C_M \rho_a A r (\omega \times v). \tag{11}$$

The constants appearing are the mass of the ball $m = 2.7$ g, the gravitational constant $g = 9.81$ m/s^2, the drag coefficient $C_D = 0.4$, the density of the air $\rho_a = 1.29$ kg/m^3, the lift coefficient $C_M = 0.6$, the ball radius $r = 0.02$ m, and the ball's cross-section $A = r^2 \pi$. A discrete motion model is defined by

$$p_{t+1} = f(p_t) = \begin{pmatrix} x + v_x \Delta t \\ y + v_y \Delta t \\ z + v_z \Delta t \\ v_x - k_D \Delta t \, \|v\| \, v_x + k_M \Delta t (\omega_y v_z - \omega_z v_y) \\ v_y - k_D \Delta t \, \|v\| \, v_y + k_M \Delta t (\omega_z v_x - \omega_x v_z) \\ v_z - k_D \Delta t \, \|v\| \, v_z + k_M \Delta t (\omega_x v_y - \omega_y v_x) - g \Delta t \end{pmatrix}. \tag{12}$$

Here we shorten the coefficients to $k_D = \frac{1}{2} C_D \rho_a A$ and $k_M = \frac{1}{2} C_M \rho_a A r$. The state is defined as $p_t = (x, y, z, v_x, v_y, v_z)$ and can be estimated by an extended Kalman filter [31]. Using the estimated state we can predict the future trajectory using the discrete model. At the bounce point the speed and angular velocity from directly before the bounce denoted by $*^-$ are transformed to $*^+$ as follows

$$v_x^+ = \alpha_x v_x^- + \beta_x \omega_y^- \tag{13}$$

$$v_y^+ = \alpha_y v_y^- + \beta_y \omega_x^- \tag{14}$$

$$v_z^+ = -\alpha_z v_z^- \tag{15}$$

$$\omega_x^+ = \gamma_x \omega_x^- + \delta_x v_y^- \tag{16}$$

$$\omega_y^+ = \gamma_y \omega_y^- + \delta_y v_x^- \tag{17}$$

$$\omega_z^+ = \gamma_z \omega_z^-. \tag{18}$$

The values used in our experiments are $\alpha_x = \alpha_y = 0.75$, $\alpha_z = -0.97$, $\beta_x = \beta_y = 0.0015$, $\gamma_x = 0.53$, $\gamma_y = 0.6$, $\gamma_z = 0.9$, $\delta_x = -26$ and $\delta_y = 25$ according to [31].

A dataset is recorded with 50 balls played in by a human player with low spin, similar to the ones shown in the video. Our results on the data are shown in Tables 1 and 2. For the accuracy after the first quarter (first half) 14.5 balls (32.2 balls) are used on average. For this data we are not considering spin, which is difficult to measure and is part of further research, such that the angular velocity ω used in the EKF is zero. In the future a constant spin value measured by another system can be integrated.

In evaluation the EKF and curve fitting are on par with each other. If only ball position from the first quarter are given the EKF gives better results and with positions from the first half the curve fitting is more accurate. The EKF may have the advantage to use a physical model, but ball positions early in time are getting out of the scope. In contrast, the curve fitting uses all available data to fit the curve. Therefore, it gets more accurate with more ball positions. It can also cope with small amounts of spin as such a trajectory can also be approximated by a parabola.

2.3 Robot Control

The robotic arm in the system (KUKA AGILUS KR6 R900 sixx) is a high speed industrial robot with six DOF, mounted on the floor and capable of achieving linear velocities of over $4\,\text{m/s}$.

The robot is controlled by its own computer, integrated in the KR-C4 controller, which provides an interface to the user. The user of the robot can then

Table 1. Bounce and hitting point errors on balls measured until the first quarter of the table and until the first half of the table

/mm	After first quarter		After first half	
	Error	Stddev	Error	Stddev
Bounce point curve fitting	72.7	32.3	19.9	13.7
Bounce point EKF	46.6	29.4	27.8	15.2
Hitting point curve fitting	69.9	25.6	18.3	11.1
Hitting point EKF	55.3	22.8	34.7	13.2

Table 2. Bounce and hitting time errors on balls measured until the first quarter of the table and until the first half of the table

/ms	After first quarter		After first half	
	Error	Stddev	Error	Stddev
Bounce time curve fitting	21.8	5.5	6.5	2.7
Bounce time EKF	26.8	5.0	15.3	3.9
Hitting time curve fitting	64.9	9.2	8.4	7.3
Hitting time EKF	45.4	24.3	27.1	9.6

move it manually at low velocities or move it via a program written in the KRL programming language. While we could not use the industrial controller for frequent dynamic trajectory changes, we used approximate movements described below for a similar effect for up to 3 end-effector target point changes.

We can establish a connection to the controller PC via the network using the KUKA ETHERNETKRL package, which allows to read or write KRL variables from an external PC via an Ethernet connection. Figure 4 shows a diagram of the communication system. The delay in sending or receiving data via the ETHERNETKRL connection depends on the amount of read/write function calls on the robot side (about 4 to 12 ms per call). In order to minimize the delay, we put all the data of a message in a single array so that we only need one function call on the robot computer.

We use two kinds of motions: exact and approximate. Exact motions move the robot exactly to a specified point, whilst approximate motions move the robot in the direction of the specified point, as if it were an exact motion, but changing direction to the next point in the trajectory when a certain limit distance to the initial point is achieved (see Fig. 5). Approximated motions allow for the trajectory of the robot to change before it arrives to the initial target. Thus we are able to send an initial guess of the hitting point ahead of time and then send corrections with more precise information of the hitting point as we get to see more of the actual trajectory of the ball.

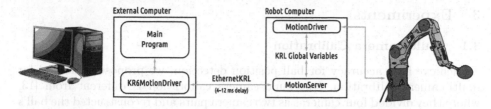

Fig. 4. To control the robot, two programs run on the robot controller: the `MotionServer`, which runs on the Submit Interpreter, handles the connection and is responsible for reading or writing the data that the connected PC requests, while the other program called `MotionDriver`, running with higher priority, is the one that executes all movement commands. On the external PC side, the C++ class called `KR6MotionDriver` communicates with the `MotionServer` on the robot side.

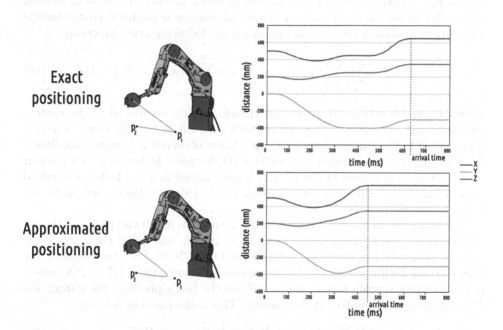

Fig. 5. On the left side we can see the difference between the spatial trajectories of the robotic motion when the point p_1 is reached exactly vs. approximately. On the right side, we plot two real trajectories between the points $p_0 = (500, 0, 200)$, $p_1 = (450, -400, 250)$ and $p_2 = (650, -300, 350)$. When p_1 is reached using exact positioning, the robot lowers the velocity extremely near p_1 giving the impression that it stays still for a little moment and reaching the point p_2 about 175 ms later than with approximate positioning.

3   Experiments

3.1   Multi-camera Calibration

To achieve high accuracy for ball position detection, we propose a method for multi-camera calibration. Our multi-camera calibration is different from [13] where they divided four cameras as two camera pairs and reconstructed the ball's 3D position from one pair. Our system can estimate the 3D position from more than two cameras which has the same idea as [15]. We first estimate the camera intrinsics, distortion coefficients based on [33] with a 4×11 asymmetric circle grid pattern. We use the stereo calibration method in [9] to initialize the extrinsic camera parameters, which denote the coordinate system transformations from three slave cameras to the master camera. To optimize these extrinsic matrices simultaneously, we place the pattern at different locations and orientations in overlapping fields of view of all cameras in order to extract the same centers of circular blobs for every camera. Then, we employ a modified sparse bundle adjustment approach [26], which minimizes the following error function:

$$E(P, X) = \sum_{i=1}^{m} \sum_{j=1}^{n} \|P_j X_i - x_{ij}\|^2 + \lambda \sum_{i=1}^{m} |\|X_{i+1} - X_i\| - D|^2 \tag{19}$$

where P_j is the estimated projection transformation composed of the camera intrinsics and extrinsics. X_i is the center's position in the 3D scene, which is reprojected to the image plane by P_j. x_{ij} is the observed 2D image coordinate. The second error term accounts for the 3D distance D between two circular blobs, which is not used in the normal bundle adjustment. A factor λ is added to account for the different units (pixels, mm). This equation is solved by the Ceres Solver library [2].

If a ball is found in every camera image, we need to find its 3d position. We use an iterative N-view triangulation method, as in [10], instead of the linear least-squares triangulation, which is performed in OpenCV [6]. For every camera, the linear triangulation solves the homogeneous equation $\alpha(u, v, 1)^\mathsf{T} = PX$, where α is an unknown scale factor and $(u, v)^\mathsf{T}$ are the ball's pixels in the image, and P is the projection matrix of the camera. This is the same as solving:

$$uP_3X = P_1X, \quad vP_3X = P_2X, \quad \alpha = P_3X \tag{20}$$

where P_i denotes the i-th row of P. So in linear least square triangulation the u-error $e_u = uP_3X = P_1X$ is minimized and similar the v-error. Ideally we would like to minimize the error $e'_u = u - P_1X/P_3X$ where P_1X/P_3X is the reprojection of X to the image plane. To come nearer to the ideal solution [10] iteratively solves $X = X_i$ from the error function $e'_u = e_v/w_i$ where $w_0 = 1$ and $w_i = P_3X_i$. Likewise, it is done for v and all other cameras.

The system's accuracy is evaluated by mounting a table tennis ball on the end-effector and comparing against the robot's end-effector localization including the difference vector from end-effector to fixed ball. In this fashion we capture 40 static locations of the ball with both systems resulting in two 3D points sets. The two systems operate in different coordinate systems and a coordinate transformation is estimated using the two 3D points sets according to [4]. The camera calibration errors are shown in Table 3, which includes two tests using both two and four cameras. Adopting our multi-camera calibration and linear least-squares triangulation we achieve an error of 2.5 mm for four cameras. Iterative triangulation improves the error to 2.0 mm.

Table 3. Calibration errors comparison in mm

	Stereo calibration	Multi-view calibration	Iterative triangulation
Two cameras	11.0	3.2	3.2
Four cameras	15.0	2.5	2.0

3.2 Cooperative Play Against a Human

Even without considering spin we were able to play consistent rallies against a human player. In the experiment the player plays a simple stroke using the counter-hitting technique. For predicting the table tennis ball trajectory we use the extended Kalman Filter. An initial position near the base line is sent to the robot at 400 ms before the predicted hitting time. The actual stroke is sent 300 ms before hitting. It consists of a two movements, first to a preparation position and then to the hitting point. In that way we can cope with the lack of velocity control and hit the ball at the predicted hitting point with an approximated velocity between 2 and 4 m/s. On a total of 315 strokes our robots was able to return 87% of the balls back to the table. A video of several such rallies can be found on our YouTube channel (https://youtu.be/AxSyXMbV3Yg).

4   Conclusion and Future Work

In this paper we present a new table tennis robot system. Against balls played from a human with little topspin or no spin, the robot is very successful. In a next step we need to adapt to different spin types. Using a fifth high-speed camera we already started to detect the rotation of the table tennis ball using its logo brand. In the future we will use the system to make the robot play different types of strokes depending on the ball's spin.

Acknowledgement. This work was supported in part by the Vector Stiftung and KUKA.

References

1. Acosta, L., Rodrigo, J.J., Mendez, J.A., Marichal, G.N., Sigut, M.: Ping-pong player prototype. IEEE Robot. Autom. Mag. **10**(4), 44–52 (2003). https://doi.org/10.1109/MRA.2003.1256297
2. Agarwal, S., Mierle, K., et al.: Ceres solver. http://ceres-solver.org

3. Anderson, R.L.: A Robot Ping-Pong Player: Experiment in Real-time Intelligent Control. MIT Press, Cambridge (1988)
4. Arun, K.S., Huang, T.S., Blostein, S.D.: Least-squares fitting of two 3-D point sets. IEEE Trans. Pattern Anal. Mach. Intell. PAMI **9**(5), 698–700 (1987). https://doi.org/10.1109/TPAMI.1987.4767965
5. Billingsley, J.: Robot ping pong, May 1983
6. Bradski, G.: The OpenCV Library. Dr. Dobb's J. Softw. Tools (2000)
7. Fässler, H., Beyer, H.A., Wen, J.T.: Robot ping pong player: optimized mechanics, high performance 3D vision, and intelligent sensor control. Robotersysteme **6**, 161–170 (1990)
8. Group, K.R.: The duel: timo boll vs. kuka robot, March 2014. https://www.youtube.com/watch?v=tIIJME8-au8
9. Hartley, R.I., Zisserman, A.: Multiple View Geometry in Computer Vision, 2nd edn. Cambridge University Press, Cambridge (2004). ISBN 0521540518
10. Hartley, R.I., Sturm, P.: Triangulation. Comput. Vis. Image Underst. **68**(2), 146–157 (1997). https://doi.org/10.1006/cviu.1997.0547
11. Hoffmann, U.: Mann gegen maschine - ulf hoffmann tischtennis roboter (uhttr-1), March 2014. https://www.youtube.com/watch?v=imVNg9j7rvU
12. Kawakami, S., Ikumo, M., Oya, T.: Omron table tennis robot forpheus. https://www.omron.com/innovation/forpheus.html
13. Lampert, C.H., Peters, J.: Real-time detection of colored objects in multiple camera streams with off-the-shelf hardware components. J. Real-Time Image Process. **7**(1), 31–41 (2012). https://doi.org/10.1007/s11554-010-0168-3
14. Li, H., Wu, H., Lou, L., Kühnlenz, K., Ravn, O.: Ping-pong robotics with high-speed vision system. In: 2012 12th International Conference on Control Automation Robotics Vision (ICARCV), pp. 106–111 (2012). https://doi.org/10.1109/ICARCV.2012.6485142
15. Lourakis, M., Argyros, A.: SBA: a generic sparse bundle adjustment C/C++ package based on the Levenberg-Marquardt algorithm, January 2008
16. Miyazaki, F., Matsushima, M., Takeuchi, M.: Learning to dynamically manipulate: a table tennis robot controls a ball and rallies with a human being. In: Kawamura, S., Svinin, M. (eds.) Advances in Robot Control, pp. 317–341. Springer, Heidelberg (2006). https://doi.org/10.1007/978-3-540-37347-6_15
17. Müling, K., Kober, J., Peters, J.: A biomimetic approach to robot table tennis. Adapt. Behav. **19**(5), 359–376 (2011). https://doi.org/10.1177/1059712311419378
18. Mülling, K., Kober, J., Peters, J.: Simulating human table tennis with a biomimetic robot setup. In: Doncieux, S., Girard, B., Guillot, A., Hallam, J., Meyer, J.-A., Mouret, J.-B. (eds.) SAB 2010. LNCS (LNAI), vol. 6226, pp. 273–282. Springer, Heidelberg (2010). https://doi.org/10.1007/978-3-642-15193-4_26
19. Mülling, K., Kober, J., Kroemer, O., Peters, J.: Learning to select and generalize striking movements in robot table tennis. Int. J. Robot. Res. **32**(3), 263–279 (2013). https://doi.org/10.1177/0278364912472380
20. Nakashima, A., Ito, D., Hayakawa, Y.: An online trajectory planning of struck ball with spin by table tennis robot. In: 2014 IEEE/ASME International Conference on Advanced Intelligent Mechatronics, pp. 865–870, July 2014. https://doi.org/10.1109/AIM.2014.6878188
21. Nakashima, A., Ogawa, Y., Kobayashi, Y., Hayakawa, Y.: Modeling of rebound phenomenon of a rigid ball with friction and elastic effects. In: Proceedings of the 2010 American Control Conference, pp. 1410–1415, June 2010. https://doi.org/10.1109/ACC.2010.5530520

22. Nakashima, A., Nonomura, J., Liu, C., Hayakawa, Y.: Hitting back-spin balls by robotic table tennis system based on physical models of ball motion. IFAC Proc. Vol. **45**(22), 834–841 (2012). https://doi.org/10.3182/20120905-3-HR-2030.00107. 10th IFAC Symposium on Robot Control. http://www.sciencedirect.com/science/article/pii/S1474667016337132

23. Quigley, M., et al.: ROS: an open-source robot operating system. In: Proceedings of the IEEE International Conference on Robotics and Automation (ICRA) Workshop on Open Source Robotics, Kobe, Japan, May 2009

24. SIASUN: Siasun table tennis robot pongbot. https://youtu.be/Ov8jwAKucmk

25. Silva, R., Melo, F.S., Veloso, M.: Towards table tennis with a quadrotor autonomous learning robot and onboard vision. In: 2015 IEEE/RSJ International Conference on Intelligent Robots and Systems (IROS), pp. 649–655, September 2015. https://doi.org/10.1109/IROS.2015.7353441

26. Triggs, B., McLauchlan, P.F., Hartley, R.I., Fitzgibbon, A.W.: Bundle adjustment—a modern synthesis. In: Triggs, B., Zisserman, A., Szeliski, R. (eds.) IWVA 1999. LNCS, vol. 1883, pp. 298–372. Springer, Heidelberg (2000). https://doi.org/10.1007/3-540-44480-7_21

27. Wang, Q., Zhang, K., Wang, D.: The trajectory prediction and analysis of spinning ball for a table tennis robot application. In: The 4th Annual IEEE International Conference on Cyber Technology in Automation, Control and Intelligent, pp. 496–501, June 2014. https://doi.org/10.1109/CYBER.2014.6917514

28. Xiong, R., Sun, Y., Zhu, Q., Wu, J., Chu, J.: Impedance control and its effects on a humanoid robot playing table tennis. Int. J. Adv. Robot. Syst. **9**(5), 178 (2012). https://doi.org/10.5772/51924

29. Zhang, H., Wu, Y., Yang, F.: Ball detection based on color information and hough transform. In: 2009 International Conference on Artificial Intelligence and Computational Intelligence, vol. 2, pp. 393–397 (2009). https://doi.org/10.1109/AICI.2009.21

30. Zhang, Y., Xiong, R., Zhao, Y., Wang, J.: Real-time spin estimation of ping-pong ball using its natural brand. IEEE Trans. Instrum. Measure. **64**(8), 2280–2290 (2015). https://doi.org/10.1109/TIM.2014.2385173

31. Zhang, Y., Zhao, Y., Xiong, R., Wang, Y., Wang, J., Chu, J.: Spin observation and trajectory prediction of a ping-pong ball. In: 2014 IEEE International Conference on Robotics and Automation (ICRA), pp. 4108–4114, May 2014. https://doi.org/10.1109/ICRA.2014.6907456

32. Zhang, Y., Xiong, R., Zhao, Y., Chu, J.: An adaptive trajectory prediction method for ping-pong robots. In: Su, C.-Y., Rakheja, S., Liu, H. (eds.) ICIRA 2012. LNCS (LNAI), vol. 7508, pp. 448–459. Springer, Heidelberg (2012). https://doi.org/10.1007/978-3-642-33503-7_44

33. Zhang, Z.: A flexible new technique for camera calibration. IEEE Trans. Pattern Anal. Mach. Intell. **22**(11), 1330–1334 (2000). https://doi.org/10.1109/34.888718

34. Zhang, Z., Xu, D., Tan, M.: Visual measurement and prediction of ball trajectory for table tennis robot. IEEE Trans. Instrum. Measure. **59**(12), 3195–3205 (2010). https://doi.org/10.1109/TIM.2010.2047128

View-Aware Person Re-identification

Gregor Blott[1,2]([✉]) [iD], Jie Yu[1] [iD], and Christian Heipke[2] [iD]

[1] Computer Vision Research Lab, Robert Bosch GmbH, Hildesheim, Germany
{gregor.blott,jie.yu}@de.bosch.com
[2] Institute of Photogrammetry and GeoInformation, Leibniz Universität Hannover,
Hannover, Germany
heipke@ipi.uni-hannover.de

Abstract. Appearance-based person re-identification (PRID) is currently an active and challenging research topic. Recently proposed approaches have mostly dealt with low- and middle-level processing of images. Furthermore, there is very limited research that has focused on view information. View variation limits the performance of most approaches because a person's appearance from one view can be completely different from that of another view, which makes the re-identification challenging. In this work, we study the influence of the view on PRID and propose several fusion strategies that utilize multi-view information to handle the PRID problem. We perform experiments on a re-mapped version of Market-1501 dataset and an internal dataset. Our proposed multi-view strategy increases the recognition rate at rank-one by a large margin in comparison with that obtained via random view matching or multi-shot.

Keywords: Person Re-identification · PRID · Re-ID

1 Introduction

Appearance-based person re-identification (PRID) is one of the core technologies in multi-camera systems, which enables large-scale video surveillance, such as in airports. The fundamental re-identification problem involves matching a person of interest observed in a "probe" camera view to a sample of the same person from a "gallery" of candidates captured at a different time by another camera, which does not necessarily have a field of view overlapping with that of the probe camera. Recently, considerable progress has been achieved in this domain, resulting from the development of relevant computer vision and machine learning algorithms. However, this problem has not yet been completely solved. An essential problem is the conflict between high intra-variations and low inter-variations among different person identities. For example, different persons seen from an identical perspective may appear more similar than one and the same person as viewed from different perspectives. Figure 1 shows a difficult example of practical relevance. The top four matches per approach show a subset of most similar persons wearing the same type of clothes as the queried person.

T. Brox et al. (Eds.): GCPR 2018, LNCS 11269, pp. 46–59, 2019.
https://doi.org/10.1007/978-3-030-12939-2_4

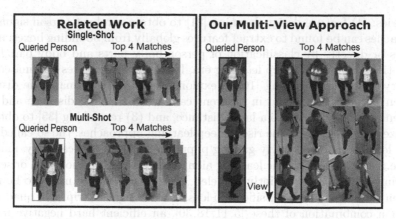

Fig. 1. Difference between related work (left) and our approach (right). We exploit a triplet of three views per person per camera for finding the match.

In this study, we address high intra-variations and low inter-variations of a person by utilizing high-level pose information, which is orthogonal to low- and mid-level feature extraction. Therefore, our approach can be combined with most recent PRID approaches with the hope to achieve improved results, as multiple views are available. The contributions of this study include the following:

- We propose the first two multi-view datasets for PRID in which each person can be analyzed in three orthogonal views per camera: A front view, a side view and a back view. We call this a view-triplet.
- Six strategies are proposed for merging non-synchronized view-triplets to decrease intra-person variations. Not surprisingly, the best of these strategies increases the recognition rate by a large margin.
- Experiments were performed to determine the influence of different views and demonstrate the high impact of view-specific matching. In contrast to [23] in which only random persons are used, we used fixed unique person IDs for all experiments and only changed the view for a specific person for different view-aware experiments.

The remainder of this paper is structured as follows. Related work is discussed in Sect. 2. Section 3 presents our methods, and Sect. 4 presents the results of the experiments performed herein, including a discussion. Finally, Sect. 5 concludes the study.

2 Related Work

Apperance based PRID is a considerably active research topic, more than 400 research papers have been published in the past four years.[1] Detailed reviews are given in e.g. [2,25,34]. The main contributions can be clustered into three

---

[1] Including conference papers, journals, arxiv and technical reports.

categories: (1) feature design/learning [21] to obtain a robust person signature. Approaches can be found to extract features globally from bounding boxes, image patches or directly by classification of person body parts and body part based descriptions. Before the deep learning era, hand crafted features dominated this category. (2) metric learning [16] to exploit a function that maps the distance between an identical person in different cameras to a small distance and that between different persons to a large distance, and (3) re-ranking [35] to obtain a optimized solution. With the rise of deep learning approaches, the so-called end-to-end learning is increasingly gaining popularity [11]. In this category, multiple tasks, e.g. feature and metric learning along with pose estimation [31], or semantic segmentation [19] are jointly modeled. Moreover, a choice needs to be made between verification loss, classification loss, embedding loss, triplet or quadruplet loss, or a combination of these [5,11,18,30], an efficient hard negative mining strategy [11] and a promising network architecture, e.g. Siamese architecture [24], recurrent architecture [22,28,36], or the underlying base feature extraction network, for achieving state-of-the-art performance.

At present, algorithms designed for supervised learning mostly outperform unsupervised learning approaches [29] and additional information from active sensors such as the Kinect [9,12,27] or passive sensors such as stereo cameras [3] could be helpful for preprocessing or used to extract additional features.

In this work, we focus on fusion of the view-triplet content per person per camera to reduce intra-person variation, which has not been studied in previous research. Consequently, all feature extracting methods are also relevant in our context, as we need a base feature extraction strategy before our fusion can be performed.

3   Methods

Commonly employed approaches use a one-person image (single-shot) or multiple person images (multi-shot, multi-query) mostly from the same view in the probe to find a queried person in an arbitrary view from a person gallery. Even for a human, image based PRID with classical security cameras in arbitrary poses may be a difficult problem. If the person of interest is only recorded from one view (e.g. back view with huge black bag pack) and in the gallery only one image of opposite view exists (e.g. front view with open green jacket and orange t-shirt), with increasing dataset size and decreasing dataset diversity the correct association can not always be guaranteed. To overcome this issue more views per person are desired. Figure 1 (left) demonstrates a typical situation. The top four matches show a subset of most similar persons wearing the same clothes as the queried person. However, the correct match is not included. For a human, it is only possible to find outliers by analyzing attributes such as the hair style, the colour of the shoes, and bag on the right side. These details are typically not visible from an arbitrary viewing direction.

We address security fisheye cameras in nadir pose for PRID (cf. Fig. 2(b)). This special configuration allows for the extraction of several views per person, especially the view-triplets, after the relevant person image-region was detected in the fisheye image (e.g. [4]), de-warped, and furthermore the view classification was done. To perform view classification, intra-camera tracking incl. the angle of the movement relative to the camera orientation, or appearance based classification can be used. For the purpose of multi-view images obtained from fisheye camera, we primarily conducted this study to find an efficient view-triplet content fusion for PRID. The goal is to measure the improvements by using the view-triplets compared to baseline strategies such as single-shot and multi-shot. As a side effect we evaluate the influence of different views. Note that the tasks of obtaining multi-view images from fisheye images and of view classification are beyond the scope of this study since we want to show which performance can be expected in the best case. Therefore, we use images taken by central projection and known views to determine an upper border of performance. In comparison to actual fisheye images we expect a better performance by using images taken by central projection, since we do not have to de-warp and align the persons in the images.

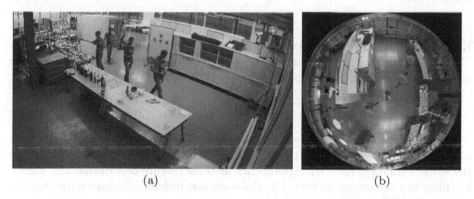

(a)   (b)

Fig. 2. Comparison of two camera models for obtaining more person views. (a) Input image from a wall-mounted camera (central projection) with person (multiple exposures). The person can only be seen from the front. (b) Fisheye camera image with the same person (again multiple exposures). The person can be analyzed from various views.

3.1 Fusion Approaches

Six fusion strategies for multi-view PRID are investigated and evaluated: two early fusion strategies, three late fusion strategies and one deep fusion strategy. For early fusion, images or features extracted from images are first concatenated, after which the resulting feature vector is used for matching; for late fusion, matching of descriptors is performed separately for each image (person view), after which fusion is applied to the results. The latter enables view-dependent learning before fusion. In contrast to the rule-based early and late fusion, deep fusion allows for a dataset depending learning. The principle data flow is illustrated in Fig. 3. In the following the different strategies are explained in detail:

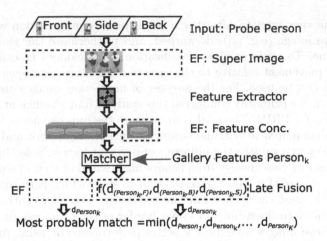

Fig. 3. Visualization for different fusion strategies. Different strategies are illustrated by dashed lines (EF: Early Fusion). Note, deep fusion is not depicted, details can be found in [22].

Early Fusion: Super Images. The first approach involves super image fusion. The view-triplet is projected onto a canvas of triple single image width. A feature vector for one person in one camera is described as $\vec{F} = f(I_{Super})$; where,

$$I_{Super}^{(m \times 3 \cdot n)} = [I_{Front}^{(m \times n)}, I_{Side}^{(m \times n)}, I_{Back}^{(m \times n)}],$$

is a super image and comprises three view images (I_{Front}, I_{Side}, and I_{Back}) with m pixels image height and n pixels width. The images are sub-sampled here to the same resolution ($m \times n$). Approaches used for feature description and metric learning are presented in Sect. 3.2, since we use different feature extractors to analyse the different fusion strategies.

Early Fusion: Feature Concatenation. In contrast to the first strategy, descriptors are first extracted from each image view separately, after which the resulting three feature vectors are concatenated. The feature vector for one person in one camera can be written as

$$\vec{F}^{(1 \times (a+b+c))} = [\vec{F}_{Front}^{(1 \times a)}, \vec{F}_{Side}^{(1 \times b)}, \vec{F}_{Back}^{(1 \times c)}],$$

where $\vec{F}_{Front} = f(I_{Front})$, $\vec{F}_{Back} = f(I_{Back})$, and $\vec{F}_{Side} = f(I_{Side})$ and a, b, c are the dimensions of the view-depending feature vectors.

Late Fusion: Inverse Rank Position Algorithm (IRPA) is an algorithm for merging multiple feature similarity lists into a single overall similarity ranking list, which is proposed for database retrieval [13]. After an initial view specific matching, the fusion is performed. The ranking results of front–front, back–back, and side–side matching for all person IDs are transformed into a new ranking result as follows:

$$r(P, id_n) = \frac{1}{\frac{1}{r_{Front}(P_{Front}, id_{n_{Front}})} + \frac{1}{r_{Back}(P_{Back}, id_{n_{Back}})} + \frac{1}{r_{Side}(P_{Side}, id_{n_{Side}})}},$$

where P is the queried probe person, id_n a currently compared person from the gallery and r the corresponding rank. The final ranks are estimated according to the fused and re-ranked ranking list.

Late Fusion: Inverse Score Position Algorithm (ISPA) is motivated by IRPA in that the rank is replaced by a distance. In our case, the Euclidean distance between the queried probe person and one person in the gallery after comparing the distance between the two feature vectors. By taking a distance instead of a rank, detailed information on person similarity is utilized. The distance between persons is shorter or longer depending on the similarity, whereas by considering absolute ranks, the distance is disregarded. Mathematics behind IRPA and ISPA is the *harmonic mean*.

Late Fusion: Product Rule (PR). Furthermore, we employ the product rule (PR). Previous works on biometric multi-modality fusion [1,15] have demonstrated that the PR adapts well to input data of various scales and does not require extensive normalization of the data [33]. The resulting distance between a probe and one gallery sample after fusion can be calculated as follows:

$$d(P, id_n) = d_{Front}(P_{Front}, id_{n_{Front}}) \cdot d_{Back}(P_{Back}, id_{n_{Back}}) \cdot d_{Side}(P_{Side}, id_{n_{Side}}),$$

where P is the queried probe person, id_n a currently compared person from the gallery and d the corresponding distance.

Deep Fusion: Recurrent Neural Network (RNN). In addition to rule based fusion, we exploit learning based fusion via a recurrent neural network, where the fusion scheme is learned from training data. Instead of multiple consecutive samples used in the original approach [22], multi-view samples are applied. Thus, view information is encoded as prior knowledge in the network and a higher learning efficiency is expected. Note, that in our setup, optical flow, which contributes to multi-shot PRID [22], is no longer beneficial due to the lack of matching flows. Details are given in the next paragraph.

3.2 Feature Extraction and Metric Learning

For feature extraction and metric learning we use three strategies as baselines:

- Best performing handcrafted approach: *GOG* for feature description [21] and *XQDA* [20] for metric learning. We exploit this approach since later we use also a dataset of small training size which is not sufficient for deep learning approaches.

- State-of-the-Art deep learning based approach: Triplet-Loss (*TriNet*) [11] with batch hard loss, enabling an efficient way to teach and learn. The batch hard loss allows for the mining of hard negatives (a different person with very similar appearance), and hard positives (the same person with slightly different appearance).
- Deep learning based approach with recurrent architecture: Siamese+RNN [22]. In contrast to both other approaches the Siamese+RNN architecture proved to be an efficient multi-shot fusion approach by aggregating features of images acquired one after another. We use this approach to evaluate quantitative if the exactly same approach without optical flow information outperforms by using multiple views.

4   Experiments and Results

In this section we evaluate the proposed multi-view fusion strategies and demonstrate the advantages of multi-view fusion compared to the classical single- and multi-shot approaches for person re-identification. For a general comparison, we use standard feature extraction approaches introduced in Sect. 3.2, which cover both handcrafted and deep features. The feature descriptor and metric learning approach model are then fixed to compare single-shot, multi-shot and multi-view approaches. Note, that rather than comparing the baseline approaches [11, 20–22] we focus on the potential of using additional views employing the different fusion schemes.

4.1   Datasets

Most of available PRID datasets like CUHK03 [17], Market-1501 [32] and Airport [14] do not provide labels for views of persons. For our experiments we annotate the Market-1501 dataset with additional view information. Each image is assigned with a label of "front", "back", "side", and "neither". The original Market-1501 dataset comprises 1501 unique persons with over 36,000 samples. After annotation the dataset is re-mapped (cf. Fig. 4) to a multi-view dataset (MuVi-Market), four single-shot datasets [SiSo-Market (front, back, side and random)], and a multi-shot dataset (MuSo-Market; random views and continuous time frames). The re-mapped dataset is divided into two virtual cameras for probe and gallery set, respectively.[2] By following this procedure, we obtain 800 unique person IDs that occur in each of the shot- and view-dependent datasets. We call the dataset Market-800. Additionally, we recorded a new dataset with 85 unique person IDs from three ceiling mounted cameras of eight-meter elevations. Three views (front, back and side) per person per camera are annotated with bounding boxes. Compared to the Market datasets, camera positions are much higher and changes in appearance due to high viewpoint of person in images is

---

[2] Cameras 1–3 from the original dataset were used for virtual camera 1, and cameras 4–6 were used for virtual camera 2.

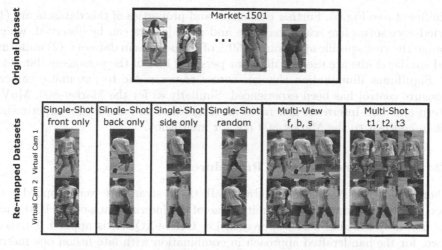

Fig. 4. Illustration for our market dataset re-mapping.

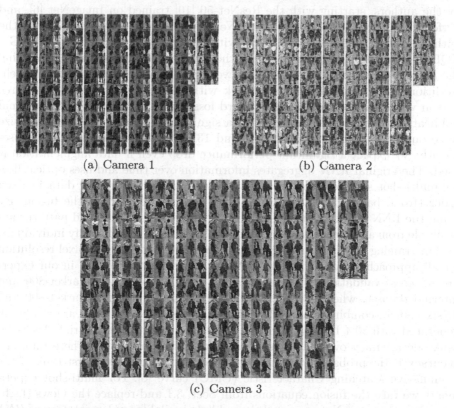

(a) Camera 1   (b) Camera 2

(c) Camera 3

Fig. 5. Our multi-view dataset: persons in three views (side, front, and back). For visualization, all person images are downscaled to an equal image resolution.

significant (see Fig. 5). Further challenges and properties of this datasets are (1) varied accessories like scarfs, baggage and open jackets can be observed, which change the view specific appearance (50% of the persons in dataset). (2) uniforms and similar cloths are used by different persons (10% of the persons in dataset). (3) Significant illumination changes across cameras due to automatic camera exposure control has been experienced. Similarly as for the Market-800, MuVi-Intern and SiSo-Intern are generated for single-shot and multi-view experiments but in contrast to the Market-800 not for multi-shot.

4.2 Training and Inference Procedure

Whereas for the Market-800 dataset all three strategies were applied (see Sect. 3.2), considering the very limited size of the internal dataset (85 IDs), only the non-deep-learning based approach, i.e. GOG+XQDA, is applied. Furthermore, for the handcrafted approach in combination with late fusion one metric is learnt per view. For *TriNet*, we re-train our model with source codes provided by the authors, starting with the ResNet-50 [10] trained on ImageNet [6], and perform test-time data augmentation. We did not use the model provided by the authors since it potentially was learnt with our test data. In contrast to GOG+XQDA+ late fusion, training is done without view dedicated learning since using the hard negative and positive mining we expect the network is learning itself. Additionally, we can teach the network with much more samples since three person views are used for the batch hard loss. Note, in contrast to the original publication we train the network with a significantly smaller training data size since our dataset consists of only around 13% of the original samples. Consequently, we expect a significant performance drop even if data augmentation is used. The original *RNN* aggregates information over time and uses optical flow for multi-shot samples. For our multi-view experiments we feed data in fixed order (front, back and side view) into the network to perform the fusion. By using the RNN we expect that the model learns which colours and patterns are available from all three views and which are important to re-identify individuals.

For training and inference all images are sampled to 128×64 pixel resolution for all approaches. Following the VIPeR [8] benchmark protocol, in our experiments cross validation [26] is applied on both datasets, the Market-800 and internal dataset, where 10 different dataset splits (trials) for Market-800 and 6 (six camera combinations) x 10 different dataset splits (trials) are randomly generated with 50% IDs for training and 50% for testing at each trial. Averaged rank-one accuracy over all trials of each dataset are reported, where rank-one accuracy is the probability of finding the correct match in the first rank of the Cumulative Matching Characteristic (CMC) curve [8]. For multi-shot experiments we take the fusion equations from Sect. 3.1 and replace the views (f,s,b) with time (t_1, t_2, t_3). Note, we used the publicly available implementation of *RNN* [22], change the dataset, and fixed the train and test splits to the one used for the other experiments. Furthermore, optical flow was disabled for multi-view experiments.

4.3   Fusion Evaluation and Discussion

Comparison of Single-Shot, Multi-shot and Multi-view: In this subsection we compare our proposed view-triplet fusion strategies to the conventional single-shot and multi-shot matching approaches. The three feature baselines are combined with the corresponding strategies of the three categories. The result is not surprising (cf. Table 1 and Fig. 6), since multi-shot uses more person information than single-shot, for multi-shot a much higher performance is obtained. Compared to the other two categories our multi-view approaches improve the performance further, independent of feature baselines. For example, with GOG+XQDA, multi-view approaches increase the maximum recognition rate by +47% and +25% compared to single- and multi-shot with random views. Similar trends can be observed by using TriNet (+21% and 18%, respectively) and RNN (+48% and +23%, respectively). These improvements show the impact of additional person and view information for the re-identification task. With deep features, the improvement is less significant, probably because they extract rich information at mid-level already, as shown in [7]. View knowledge seems to be also very useful for single-shot matching since rank-one could be improved from 40% random view matching to 65% for front view only matching. The results for the internal dataset show that the performance slightly decreases compared to the same strategies on the huge Market-800 dataset which probably is caused by the small training dataset, combined with the much higher camera view, where the latter results in the different perspectives becoming more and more similar. Even though, 82% rank-one recognition rate is obtained by using the multi-view strategy, it is interesting to note, that the remaining miss-matches, even if the view-triplet is used, and a person can be analysed by

Table 1. Rank-one recognition rate (%) of conducted experiments, results are averaged over 10 trials. No multi-shot is performed for the internal dataset due to lack of data.

Fusion	Feat. Ext.		
	GOG+XQDA	TriNet	GOG+XQDA
Single-shot	SiSo-Market		SiSo-Intern
Random views	40	74	43
Front views only	65	78	59
Back views only	64	78	64
Side views only	51	73	58
Multi-shot	MuSo-Market		-
Super Images	58	70	-
CFV	55	73	-
IRPA	58	74	-
ISPA	62	77	-
PR	61	76	-
Multi-view	MuVi-Market		MuVi-Intern
Super images	85	84	68
CFV	83	87	73
IRPA	83	91	80
ISPA	**87**	95	**82**
PR	86	94	81

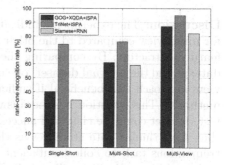

Fig. 6. Comparison of different rank-one recognition rates (%) for the Market-800 dataset. Best performing rule-based fusion and Siamese-RNN fusion are illustrated for single-shot, multi-shot and multi-view.

almost 270°, the re-identification challenge is not solved and on average 5% are incorrectly associated.

Deep Features vs. Handcrafted Features for Multi-view Fusion: In this subsection we examine the impacts of multi-shot and multi-view fusion on both, deep learning and the handcrafted feature baselines. For GOG+XQDA, multi-shot and multi-view increase the performance significantly compared to single-shot random views. However, for TriNet there is no significant difference between single and multi-shot matching. The RNN seems to be an effective fusion for the Siamese features since rank-one was improved by +25% (34% to 59%). Multi-view fusion increases all feature baselines significantly for all three feature baselines. The performance variations between feature baselines were reduced from 38% (max. performance minus min. performance for single-shot) to 12% (max. performance minus min. performance) after multi-view fusion. These results show that view information is orthogonal to the PRID features learned from images, therefore, both strategies can be very effectively combined.

Comparison of Fusion Strategies: The proposed fusion schemes have been applied on both multi-shot and multi-view experiments. As shown in Table 1 and Fig. 6, ISPA and PR are the most effective approaches. RNN improves results of Siamese features from 34% for single-shot to 59% for multi-shot to 82% for multi-view (note that we cannot compare it to other publications directly since we use the re-mapped dataset). By considering the complexity and generalization, ISPA and PR are recommended to be used, as they are simple to perform and no data specific training is necessary. It is worth mentioning that the best performance of our fusion on Market-800 is on average 95%, which is at a very high level.

Discussion: The experiments indicate a much higher rank-one recognition rate for multi-view compared to the other approaches independently of datasets and feature extractors. By comparing the improvements on the re-mapped Market dataset and the internal dataset, one question could arise: is the proposed multi-view approach still beneficial if sufficient training data is available for baseline methods? This question can be answered from two aspects: Firstly, a certain test dataset could be classified successfully, if enough training data is collected that have similar data statistics as the test dataset. However, it can become a tremendous task to collect sufficient training data to cover all variations in a real world scenario. Secondly, multi-view information is orthogonal to most of the baseline approaches, which assume a view-invariant appearance model to perform re-identification, which in many applications is not valid.

5   Conclusion

In this paper we investigated several multi-view fusion strategies for person re-identification and demonstrate that the proposed fusion approaches outperform the baseline single-shot and multi-shot strategies by a large margin. The rank-one recognition rates after applying ISPA are between 82% and 95% on both test datasets with any of three feature extractors. Our experiments indicated that view-aware fusion is a new but promising research direction to handle the very challenging person re-identification problem. It is complementary to varied feature extraction approaches. Our future work is to complete the whole pipeline for real-world applications by extracting views of persons using motion estimation or additional classifiers.

References

1. Alkoot, F.M., Kittler, J.: Experimental evaluation of expert fusion strategies. Pattern Recogn. Lett. **20**(11–13), 1361–1369 (1999). https://doi.org/10.1016/S0167-8655(99)00107-5
2. Bedagkar-Gala, A., Shah, S.K.: A survey of approaches and trends in person re-identification. Image Vis. Comput. **32**(4), 270–286 (2014). https://doi.org/10.1016/j.imavis.2014.02.001
3. Blott, G., Heipke, C.: Bifocal stereo for multipath person re-identification. In: ISPRS - International Archives of the Photogrammetry, Remote Sensing and Spatial Information Sciences, vol. XLII-2/W8, pp. 37–44 (2017). https://doi.org/10.5194/isprs-archives-XLII-2-W8-37-2017
4. Blott, G., Takami, M., Heipke, C.: Semantic segmentation of fisheye images. In: Leal-Taixé, L., Roth, S. (eds.) ECCV 2018 Workshops. LNCS, vol. 11129, pp. 181–196. Springer, Cham (2019). https://doi.org/10.1007/978-3-030-11009-3_10
5. Chen, W., Chen, X., Zhang, J., Huang, K.: Beyond triplet loss: a deep quadruplet network for person re-identification. In: CVPR, pp. 1320–1329. IEEE (2017). https://doi.org/10.1109/CVPR.2017.145
6. Deng, J., Dong, W., Socher, R., Li, L., Li, K., Li, F.: ImageNet: a large-scale hierarchical image database. In: CVPR, pp. 248–255. IEEE (2009). https://doi.org/10.1109/CVPR.2009.5206848
7. Geng, M., Wang, Y., Xiang, T., Tian, Y.: Deep transfer learning for person re-identification. CoRR abs/1611.05244 (2016)
8. Gray, D., Brennan, S., Tao, H.: Evaluating appearance models for recognition, reacquisition, and tracking. In: International Workshop on Performance Evaluation for Tracking and Surveillance, Rio de Janeiro. IEEE (2007)
9. Haque, A., Alahi, A., Fei-Fei, L.: Recurrent attention models for depth-based person identification. In: CVPR, pp. 1229–1238. IEEE (2016). https://doi.org/10.1109/CVPR.2016.138
10. He, K., Zhang, X., Ren, S., Sun, J.: Deep residual learning for image recognition. In: CVPR, pp. 770–778. IEEE (2016). https://doi.org/10.1109/CVPR.2016.90
11. Hermans, A., Beyer, L., Leibe, B.: In defense of the triplet loss for person re-identification. CoRR abs/1703.07737 (2017)
12. Imani, Z., Soltanizadeh, H.: Person reidentification using local pattern descriptors and anthropometric measures from videos of kinect sensor. IEEE Sens. J. **16**(16), 6227–6238 (2016). https://doi.org/10.1109/JSEN.2016.2579645
13. Jović, M., Hatakeyama, Y., Dong, F., Hirota, K.: Image retrieval based on similarity score fusion from feature similarity ranking lists. In: Wang, L., Jiao, L., Shi, G., Li, X., Liu, J. (eds.) FSKD 2006. LNCS (LNAI), vol. 4223, pp. 461–470. Springer, Heidelberg (2006). https://doi.org/10.1007/11881599_54

14. Karanam, S., Gou, M., Wu, Z., Rates-Borras, A., Camps, O.I., Radke, R.J.: A comprehensive evaluation and benchmark for person re-identification: features, metrics, and datasets. CoRR abs/1605.09653 (2016)
15. Kittler, J., Hatef, M., Duin, R.P.W., Matas, J.: On combining classifiers. IEEE Trans. Pattern Anal. Mach. Intell. **20**(3), 226–239 (1998). https://doi.org/10.1109/34.667881
16. Köstinger, M., Hirzer, M., Wohlhart, P., Roth, P.M., Bischof, H.: Large scale metric learning from equivalence constraints. In: CVPR, pp. 2288–2295. IEEE (2012). https://doi.org/10.1109/CVPR.2012.6247939
17. Li, W., Zhao, R., Xiao, T., Wang, X.: DeepReID: deep filter pairing neural network for person re-identification. In: CVPR, pp. 152–159. IEEE (2014). https://doi.org/10.1109/CVPR.2014.27
18. Li, W., Zhu, X., Gong, S.: Person re-identification by deep joint learning of multi-loss classification. In: Sierra, C. (ed.) IJCAI, pp. 2194–2200 (2017). https://doi.org/10.24963/ijcai.2017/305
19. Li, X., et al.: Video object segmentation with re-identification. CoRR abs/1708.00197 (2017)
20. Liao, S., Hu, Y., Zhu, X., Li, S.Z.: Person re-identification by local maximal occurrence representation and metric learning. In: CVPR, pp. 2197–2206. IEEE (2015). https://doi.org/10.1109/CVPR.2015.7298832
21. Matsukawa, T., Okabe, T., Suzuki, E., Sato, Y.: Hierarchical Gaussian descriptor for person re-identification. In: CVPR, pp. 1363–1372. IEEE (2016). https://doi.org/10.1109/CVPR.2016.152
22. McLaughlin, N., del Rincón, J.M., Miller, P.C.: Recurrent convolutional network for video-based person re-identification. In: CVPR, pp. 1325–1334. IEEE (2016). https://doi.org/10.1109/CVPR.2016.148
23. Riachy, C., Bouridane, A.: Person re-identification: attribute-based feature evaluation. In: 16th World Symposium on Applied Machine Intelligence and Informatics (SAMI), pp. 85–90. IEEE (2018)
24. Varior, R.R., Shuai, B., Lu, J., Xu, D., Wang, G.: A siamese long short-term memory architecture for human re-identification. In: Leibe, B., Matas, J., Sebe, N., Welling, M. (eds.) ECCV 2016. LNCS, vol. 9911, pp. 135–153. Springer, Cham (2016). https://doi.org/10.1007/978-3-319-46478-7_9
25. Vezzani, R., Baltieri, D., Cucchiara, R.: People reidentification in surveillance and forensics: a survey. ACM Comput. Surv. **46**(2), 29–37 (2013). https://doi.org/10.1145/2543581.2543596
26. Witten, I.H., Eibe, F., Hall, M.A.: Data Mining: Practical Machine Learning Tools and Techniques, 3rd edn. Morgan Kaufmann, Elsevier (2011)
27. Wu, A., Zheng, W., Lai, J.: Robust depth-based person re-identification. IEEE Trans. Image Process. **26**(6), 2588–2603 (2017). https://doi.org/10.1109/TIP.2017.2675201
28. Yan, Y., Ni, B., Song, Z., Ma, C., Yan, Y., Yang, X.: Person re-identification via recurrent feature aggregation. In: Leibe, B., Matas, J., Sebe, N., Welling, M. (eds.) ECCV 2016. LNCS, vol. 9910, pp. 701–716. Springer, Cham (2016). https://doi.org/10.1007/978-3-319-46466-4_42
29. Yu, H., Wu, A., Zheng, W.: Cross-view asymmetric metric learning for unsupervised person re-identification. In: ICCV, pp. 994–1002. IEEE (2017). https://doi.org/10.1109/ICCV.2017.113
30. Zhang, Y., Xiang, T., Hospedales, T.M., Lu, H.: Deep mutual learning. CoRR abs/1706.00384 (2017)

31. Zhao, H., et al.: Spindle net: person re-identification with human body region guided feature decomposition and fusion. In: CVPR, pp. 907–915. IEEE (2017). https://doi.org/10.1109/CVPR.2017.103
32. Zheng, L., Shen, L., Tian, L., Wang, S., Wang, J., Tian, Q.: Scalable person re-identification: a benchmark. In: ICCV, pp. 1116–1124. IEEE (2015). https://doi.org/10.1109/ICCV.2015.133
33. Zheng, L., Wang, S., Tian, L., He, F., Liu, Z., Tian, Q.: Query-adaptive late fusion for image search and person re-identification. In: CVPR, pp. 1741–1750. IEEE (2015). https://doi.org/10.1109/CVPR.2015.7298783
34. Zheng, L., Yang, Y., Hauptmann, A.G.: Person re-identification: past, present and future. CoRR abs/1610.02984 (2016)
35. Zhong, Z., Zheng, L., Cao, D., Li, S.: Re-ranking person re-identification with k-reciprocal encoding. In: CVPR, pp. 3652–3661. IEEE (2017). https://doi.org/10.1109/CVPR.2017.389
36. Zhou, Z., Huang, Y., Wang, W., Wang, L., Tan, T.: See the forest for the trees: joint spatial and temporal recurrent neural networks for video-based person re-identification. In: CVPR, pp. 6776–6785. IEEE (2017). https://doi.org/10.1109/CVPR.2017.717

MC2SLAM: Real-Time Inertial Lidar Odometry Using Two-Scan Motion Compensation

Frank Neuhaus[(⊠)], Tilman Koß, Robert Kohnen, and Dietrich Paulus

University of Koblenz-Landau, Universitätsstr. 1, 56070 Koblenz, Germany
{fneuhaus,tkoss,rkohnen,paulus}@uni-koblenz.de

Abstract. We propose a real-time, low-drift laser odometry approach that tightly integrates sequentially measured 3D multi-beam LIDAR data with inertial measurements. The laser measurements are motion-compensated using a novel algorithm based on non-rigid registration of two consecutive laser sweeps and a local map. IMU data is being tightly integrated by means of factor-graph optimization on a pose graph. We evaluate our method on a public dataset and also obtain results on our own datasets that contain information not commonly found in existing datasets. At the time of writing, our method was ranked within the top five laser-only algorithms of the KITTI odometry benchmark.

1   Introduction

Building three-dimensional maps of the world is commonly considered an essential prerequisite for autonomous robots and cars. However, there are other applications where the motion patterns are less constrained and that thus call for very general and robust methods. Examples come from the field of surveying where the goal is to quickly map difficult-to-reach areas using hand-held devices, or applications in disaster response where the goal is to quickly perform damage- or situation assessment. We propose a generic approach to LIDAR odometry[1]—a crucial requirement for full SLAM—that supports all of these use-cases, including automotive and hand-held use. For all of our tests, we use different types of Velodyne LIDAR sensors, which we generically call multi-beam LIDARs (MBL); revolutions of the sensor are generically referred to as *sweeps*.

We use *two* consecutive laser sweeps to estimate the motion during the first sweep. In a single step, our algorithm registers the sweeps against a local map and performs motion compensation, which means that the sweeps are undistorted so

---

[1] Our implementation is also able to close loops, but to maintain focus of this work, we decided to focus on the odometry part of the SLAM problem, whose accuracy is essential to obtain accurate maps—even when loops are being closed.

Electronic supplementary material The online version of this chapter (https://doi.org/10.1007/978-3-030-12939-2_5) contains supplementary material, which is available to authorized users.

© Springer Nature Switzerland AG 2019
T. Brox et al. (Eds.): GCPR 2018, LNCS 11269, pp. 60–72, 2019.
https://doi.org/10.1007/978-3-030-12939-2_5

that the ego-motion of the device is taken into account. Combination of these steps ensures that motion compensation quality is on par with the quality of the odometric computations.

To cope with erratic, high-frequency motion—particularly in cases where the system is carried by a human—we bootstrap the motion compensation with predictions based on IMU data. Conversely, motion compensation results are fused with raw inertial measurements by means of factor-graph-based optimization which refines poses and estimates IMU biases. An additional benefit of this fusion is the correct alignment of the map's gravitational vector with that of the real world. The trajectory is automatically leveled, virtually eliminating two dimensions in which the trajectory could otherwise have drifted, namely roll and pitch. Our IMU integration is tight because estimated biases and velocities are used for motion prediction. Results of our algorithm are shown in Fig. 1.

Fig. 1. Results on our own dataset (left), recorded with a head-mounted Velodyne LIDAR (middle). Right: Result on a dataset recorded on a car.

Our contributions in this paper are:

- We describe a novel way to motion-compensate sweeps and show how to tightly integrate an IMU into the system.
- We describe a local map data structure that approximates a Poisson disk downsampling. Despite its simplicity, we show that it yields results equivalent to previous work (see Sect. 5) while being computationally more efficient.
- We show that our method is fast and performs well both on the highly competitive KITTI odometry dataset and on our own challenging datasets recorded with a head-mounted MBL.

2   Related Work

The LOAM-method [21,22,24] proposed by Zhang and Singh is related to our approach. It performs LIDAR odometry only, separating the problem into *odometry* and *mapping*. Within the former, the current sensor sweep is matched against the previous—already motion-compensated—laser sweep only. Motion compensation is performed using a variant of the ICP algorithm that assumes linear motion during the sweep. Instead of exclusively using point-to-plane features that are relatively common within the scan-matching community [15], Zhang and

Singh additionally define so-called *sharp* features. Points are classified as either sharp or planar using a 'smoothness'-metric. Sharp features are then incorporated as point-to-line errors into an ICP error function. The mapping part of their algorithm matches the now-undistorted point cloud against a local map, i. e. is a temporally windowed accumulation of a number of recent point clouds.

Zhang and Singh also propose extensions of their approach to the visual domain [20,23]. This combination is beyond the scope of our work though, since we are currently focusing on the laser domain only.

Bosse et al. [4] present a hand-held 3D laser mapping system based on a spring-mounted 2D LRF whose motion is characterized by a motion model, and an IMU. Their trajectory is sampled at discrete intervals but interpolated in between, making it continuous. Instead of pre-integrating inertial measurements—which is what we propose—they directly integrate individual IMU measurements into least-squares optimization. The underlying assumption is that the trajectory is smooth, which is an assumption we do not have to make.

Moosmann and Stiller [16] as well as Deschaud [6] motion-compensate Velodyne scans based on the previous registration step without any IMU, limiting applications to relatively low-frequency, smooth motion that does not change much between two consecutive laser scans. Both approaches also propose matching the undistorted scan against a local map. Deschaud's approach represents the local map as an implicit moving least squares surface and uses only point-to-plane features selected by a criterion that aims to constrain all six degrees of freedom. At the time of writing, the IMLS method was the best-ranked, fully published method on the KITTI odometry dataset[2].

The approach of Nüchter et al. [18] slices the raw sweep into multiple segments that are assumed rigid. Their algorithm relies on a strong planarity constraint of the ground. They extended their algorithm in [17] to bootstrap it with data from the Google Cartographer library, no longer requiring geometric constraints. The authors mention processing times in the order of days, making the algorithm offline.

There are also commercially available solutions for backpack mapping such as the Leica Pegasus system which is based on two Veloyne LIDARs, cameras, GPS and IMU sensors. However, little is known about the used algorithms. An attempt to quantify the quality of a similar backpack mapping system was conducted by Rönnholm et al. [19] who compared the results with data acquired by a UAV. Kukko et al. [13] used surveyed fiducials for comparison. Revealing absolute accuracies of their backpack mapping system of about two centimeters. However, the analyzed mapping systems make strong use of GPS, making their results not directly comparable to our solution, which does not rely on GPS and instead fuses IMU measurements directly with the laser data.

---

[2] At the time of writing, the best method using only laser data was the LOAM method by Zhang and Singh. However, the results reported on the KITTI benchmark webpage are no longer equivalent to those reported in their paper [22], indicating that their solution has been updated. The updated algorithm is no longer publicly available.

3 Laser Odometry

Since our MBL sensors are being moved while the devices are measuring, assembling the data of a sweep into a correct 3D scan requires motion compensation. This refers the process of transforming all points within a sweep into a common coordinate frame. The k-th sweep is expected to start at the coordinate frame F_{t_k} with timestamp t_k.

A scan is an aggregate of all measurements acquired during one sweep and is assumed to be a set $S_k = \{\langle \mathbf{p}_i, t_i \rangle \mid i \in \{1, \ldots, n\}\}$ of tuples, each consisting of a point $\mathbf{p}_i$ and a corresponding timestamp t_i. Points are represented in the sensor's local coordinate system at the time they were measured, i.e. F_{t_i}.

3.1 Selection of Query Points

Due to the measuring principle of laser scanners there are significantly more points in the immediate vicinity of the laser than at greater distances. As Deschaud [6] observed in his work, points in close distance are not very effective at constraining the rotation of a scan registration problem. This is because even small rotational errors lead to large, measurable deviations at large distances, while at small distances the deviations are much smaller and therefore disappear in measurement noise. Deschaud proposes a clever sampling strategy that however requires normals which are expensive to compute.

We propose a much simpler approach, where we extract a set of *query points* $Q_k \subseteq S_k$ from the point cloud. Points are selected from S_k so that a minimum distance of $\delta_Q \approx 20\,\mathrm{cm}$ between the points is maintained within Q_k. Technically, this is achieved by storing points in a uniform grid and performing radius queries against it for every considered point. The minimum distance between the points mitigates the non-uniform point density of laser scans and results in a Poisson disk sampling of the scan. The obtained set of points is further subsampled by randomly selecting N_Q points.

3.2 Motion Compensation

For motion compensation, we consider the query points from two consecutive sweeps of the Velodyne sensor at once: $Q_{k,k+1} = Q_k \bigcup Q_{k+1}$. This is one of the key differences to prior work, such as [22], where only the current sweep is considered. The use of two sweeps better constrains the optimization problem for the first sweep, because optimization has to ensure, the trajectory is appropriate beyond the first sweep. In our experiments, we observed significantly reduced noise on the estimation results using this method.

The goal of our motion compensation is to approximate a function $\zeta_k : [t_k, t_{k+2}] \to \mathbb{R}^3 \times S^3$ that for a given timestamp returns the relative pose (translation and unit quaternion) from F_{t_i} with $t_k \leq t_i \leq t_{k+2}$ to the coordinate frame F_{t_k} at the start of the first sweep. The trajectory models the motion between the start of the first and the end of the second sweep and can be used to motion-compensate the two sweeps. See Fig. 2 for an overview of the coordinate systems.

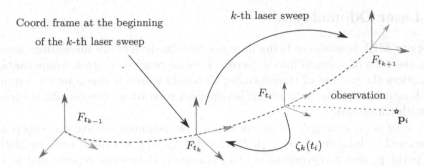

Fig. 2. Overview of the coordinate frames. F_{t_k} refers to the coordinate frame of the laser sensor at the start of the k-th sweep. A point $\mathbf{p}_i$ that is observed from the sensor at time t_i is represented in the coordinate system F_{t_i}. The function $\zeta_k(t)$ introduced in Sect. 3.2 models the relative pose of F_t w.r.t. F_{t_k}.

Trajectory Model. We assume having an initial guess $\bar{\zeta}_k$ for the trajectory. Being a constant during subsequent optimization, it can be arbitrarily complex. In practice, we obtain this trajectory by integrating IMU measurements for the duration of $[t_k, t_{k+2}]$ using the same method shown in Sect. 4. Required biases are taken from the most recent available result from graph optimization. If no IMU is used, $\bar{\zeta}_k$ can be chosen such that it predicts the motion of the LIDAR for the considered duration by linear extrapolation of the previously computed sensor motion. We choose this approach when IMU data is unavailable or when we compare against a non-inertial variant of our algorithm.

For optimization, we model the actual deviation from the predicted trajectory $\bar{\zeta}_k$ with a bias $\mathbf{b} \in \mathbb{R}^6$. We use an exponential map representation for the bias, allowing it to be 'added' on top of the pose from the prediction using a specialized $\boxplus$-operator (see [9]). Hence, our function is linear in the log map of the trajectory. Our complete model for the trajectory can be written as follows:

$$\hat{\zeta}_k(t, \mathbf{b}) = \bar{\zeta}_k(t) \boxplus \left(\mathbf{b} \frac{t - t_k}{t_{k+2} - t_k} \right) \tag{1}$$

Using this model, we are able to transform a point measured at time t to the start of the current (k-th) sweep. We now proceed to define a set of error functions that can be used to determine the unknown bias.

Residuals. We assume already having a local map (see next section) containing reference points $\mathcal{R}_{k-1}$ that are represented in frame $F_{t_{k-1}}$. We transform it to F_{t_k} and obtain $\hat{\mathcal{R}}_k$. In analogy to the point-to-plane ICP algorithm [2,15], every query point $\langle \mathbf{p}_i, t_i \rangle \in \mathcal{Q}_{k,k+1}$ is also transformed into the coordinate frame F_{t_k} using $\hat{\zeta}_k$ in order to determine a set of neighbors in $\hat{\mathcal{R}}_k$ within some radius ϵ. If not enough points are found within the given radius, no residual is generated for the given query point. Otherwise, we extract the normal $\mathbf{n}$ of the reference 'surface' using eigen analysis[3]. The support vector $\mathbf{q}$ of the plane is the mean of the neighbor points. Therefore, our residual functions are defined as

$$r_i(\mathbf{b}) = \mathbf{n}^T(\hat{\zeta}_k(t_i, \mathbf{b}) * \mathbf{p}_i - \mathbf{q}). \tag{2}$$

We use the $*$ operator to indicate rigid transformation of a point with a pose.

Local Reference Map. Since data from one sweep of a MBL is typically very sparse, determining neighbors for a query point $\mathbf{p}_i$ only from *the* most recent compensated point cloud is not sufficient and leads to universally bad performance on all datasets we tested on (see Sect. 5). Instead, we choose a denser approximation of the local vicinity current position: All compensated points within the last $N_{LM} \approx 100$ sweeps (excluding the k-th sweep) are stored in a local map $\mathcal{R}_k$ at coordinate frame F_{t_k}. By only storing new points whose distance to points already stored exceeds a threshold $\delta_{LM} \approx 5\,\mathrm{cm}$, we effectively approximate a Poisson disk sampling of the scans. As a result, the covariance estimation in a radius ϵ around a query point $\mathbf{p}_i$ is more robust and not as prone to inhomogeneous point densities of the individual sweeps. Note that we insert *all* points from the laser scan in this set, not only the selected query points.

To accelerate neighbor search, the local map is stored in a uniform grid data structure. All tuples $\langle \mathbf{p}_i, t_i \rangle$ of the laser points are stored in ascending order of timestamps, making it efficient to remove points from old laser scans that are no longer needed in the local map.

Optimization. The goal of motion compensation is to solve the problem

$$\arg\min_{\mathbf{b}} \sum_i \rho(||r_i(\mathbf{b})||_{\Sigma_i}^2), \tag{3}$$

where $||.||_{\Sigma_i}^2$ corresponds to the squared Mahalanobis distance, Σ_i is the variance of the i-th measurement, and where $\rho(.)$ is the Tukey loss function that reduces the influence of outliers. Instead of selecting hard-coded uncertainties Σ_i for the individual residuals, we robustly estimate them from the data. To this end, we compute the median absolute deviation (MAD) of the residuals, which is known to be able to be robust for up to 50% of outliers. It can be used as a consistent estimator of the standard deviation by multiplying it with a scaling factor $c = 1.4826$, which is correct for normally distributed values. Thus, the standard deviation can be estimated using

$$\hat{\sigma}(\{r_i\}) = c \cdot \mathrm{median}(\{|r_i - \mathrm{median}(\{r_i\})|\}). \tag{4}$$

Therefore, we set $\Sigma_i = \hat{\sigma}(\{r_i\})^2$ and solve the problem using the Ceres solver [1]. Having estimated $\mathbf{b}$, we motion-compensate $\mathcal{S}_k$ (not $\mathcal{S}_{k+1}$) and insert its points into the local map $\mathcal{R}_k$. Note, how our motion estimation algorithm uses the sweeps in an overlapping fashion: Two consecutive sweeps are used to motion-compensate only one sweep.

---

[3] This is relatively efficient, because it is done for the set of query points and not for the whole point cloud.

4 IMU Integration

For mapping and IMU integration, we build an online factor graph for a global optimization problem. Nodes correspond to random variables that represent system's state at the beginning of a sweep. We define random variables

$$\mathbf{x}_t = (\mathbf{p}, \mathbf{q}) \in \mathbb{R}^3 \times S^3 \tag{5}$$

for the pose of the system at time step t, comprising both the position $\mathbf{p} \in \mathbb{R}^3$ and a normalized orientation quaternion $\mathbf{q} \in S^3$. The random variables

$$\mathbf{u}_t = (\mathbf{v}, \mathbf{b}^a, \mathbf{b}^g) \in \mathbb{R}^3 \times \mathbb{R}^3 \times \mathbb{R}^3 \tag{6}$$

are used for the dynamic state of the system and contain linear velocity $\mathbf{v}$ (represented in inertial space) and biases $\mathbf{b}^a$ and $\mathbf{b}^g$ for the accelerometer and gyro. The amount of dynamic state random variables added to the system is configurable. We currently create one for every five system state nodes.

4.1 Cost Functions

We use three types of factors that are defined by their residual function within a least-squares problem.

Pose Prior Factor. We put a prior

$$\mathbf{r}_{\text{Prior}} : \mathbb{R}^3 \times S^3 \to \mathbb{R}^6 \tag{7}$$

$$\mathbf{r}_{\text{Prior}}(\mathbf{x}_t) = \mathbf{x}_t \boxminus (0, 0, 0, 1, 0, 0, 0)^T \tag{8}$$

on the first node so that the optimization problem is constrained. The given seven-dimensional vector represents the world origin with three translational components, which are zero, and four rotational components, which represent a unit quaternion in the order w, x, y, z. The used $\boxminus$ operator computes a 6D pose error on the SE3 manifold (see [9]). The covariance associated with the residual function is chosen such that the rotational part is only constrained along the yaw axis, ensuring that the initialization is still appropriate in cases where the device does not start up in alignment with gravity. The positional part of the first pose is held constant at the world origin during optimization. Hence, the associated covariances are not relevant and we simply set them to 1.

Laser Odometry Factor. The $\hat{\zeta}_k$ function from Sect. 3 allows motion-compensation of the k-th laser sweep. Assuming this sweep begins at time t_1 and ends at t_2, we can obtain an estimate $\hat{\mathbf{z}}_{t_1, t_2}$ for the relative pose between the end- and the beginning of this sweep as $\hat{\mathbf{z}}_{t_1, t_2} = \hat{\zeta}_k(t_2)$. We use this pose in a factor

$$\mathbf{r}_{\text{Odo}} : (\mathbb{R}^3 \times S^3) \times (\mathbb{R}^3 \times S^3) \to \mathbb{R}^6 \tag{9}$$

$$\mathbf{r}_{\text{Odo}}(\mathbf{x}_{t_1}, \mathbf{x}_{t_2}) = (\mathbf{x}_{t_1} \ominus \mathbf{x}_{t_2}) \boxminus \hat{\mathbf{z}}_{t_1, t_2} \tag{10}$$

to softly constrain the relative pose between two consecutive sweep poses in the factor graph. The $\ominus$ operator computes the current relative pose between the two pose nodes. A covariance matrix needed to weigh the residual is obtained as a part of the optimization during motion compensation.

IMU-based Relative Pose Factor. We use a pre-integrated factor

$$r_{\text{IMU}} : (\mathbb{R}^3 \times S^3) \times (\mathbb{R}^3 \times S^3) \times \mathbb{R}^9 \times \mathbb{R}^9 \to \mathbb{R}^{15} \tag{11}$$

$$r_{\text{IMU}}(\mathbf{x}_{t_1}, \mathbf{x}_{t_2}, \mathbf{u}_{t_1}, \mathbf{u}_{t_2}) = \begin{pmatrix} \hat{\mathbf{p}}_n - \mathbf{p}_{t_2} \\ \log(\hat{\mathbf{q}}_n^{-1} \mathbf{q}_{t_2}) \\ \hat{\mathbf{v}}_n - \mathbf{v}_{t_2} \\ \hat{\mathbf{b}}_n^g - \mathbf{b}_{t_2}^g \\ \hat{\mathbf{b}}_n^a - \mathbf{b}_{t_2}^a \end{pmatrix} \tag{12}$$

that computes the residual[4] between the 'new' state—as predicted by integrating n IMU measurements on top of the 'old' state—and the actual 'new' state. To obtain predictions for the 'new' state, we follow established methods from the vision area [10,14]. Given n IMU measurements between t_1 and t_2, we denote accelerometer and gyro measurements a_j and ω_j and time τ_j, $j = 1, \ldots, n$.

We iteratively integrate over these measurements using simple motion equations to obtain an updated state estimate as well as an associated covariance matrix. This iteration is essentially multiple repetitions of an Extended Kalman Filter prediction. For notational brevity, we define

$$\bar{\omega}_j = \tfrac{1}{2}(\omega_j + \omega_{j+1}) - \mathbf{b}_{t_1}^g \quad \bar{\mathbf{a}}_j' = \tfrac{1}{2}(\mathbf{a}_j + \mathbf{a}_{j+1}) - \mathbf{b}_{t_1}^a - \hat{\mathbf{q}}_j^{-1} * \mathbf{g} \quad \Delta_{\tau_j} = \tau_{j+1} - \tau_j \tag{13}$$

where $\mathbf{g}$ is the gravity vector. In both $\bar{\omega}_j$ as well as $\bar{\mathbf{a}}_j'$, the respective biases are subtracted from the average of successive measurements. In $\bar{\mathbf{a}}_j'$, we also remove the gravity vector from the measurements after transforming into inertial space.

Starting with $\hat{\mathbf{p}}_0 = \mathbf{p}_{t_1}, \hat{\mathbf{q}}_0 = \mathbf{q}_{t_1}, \hat{\mathbf{v}}_0 = \mathbf{v}_{t_1}, \hat{\mathbf{b}}_0^g = \mathbf{b}_{t_1}^g, \hat{\mathbf{b}}_0^a = \mathbf{b}_{t_1}^a$ and an initial covariance matrix $\Sigma_0 = \mathbf{0}_{15 \times 15}$, we apply the following iteration for $j = 0, \ldots, n - 1$:

$$\hat{\mathbf{p}}_{j+1} = \hat{\mathbf{p}}_j + \Delta_{\tau_j}(\hat{\mathbf{q}}_j * (\hat{\mathbf{v}}_j + \frac{\Delta_{\tau_j}}{2}\bar{\mathbf{a}}_j')) \qquad \hat{\mathbf{b}}_{j+1}^g = \hat{\mathbf{b}}_j^g \tag{14}$$

$$\hat{\mathbf{q}}_{j+1} = \hat{\mathbf{q}}_j \cdot \exp(\Delta_{\tau_j} \cdot \bar{\omega}_j) \qquad \hat{\mathbf{b}}_{j+1}^a = \hat{\mathbf{b}}_j^a \tag{15}$$

$$\hat{\mathbf{v}}_{j+1} = \hat{\mathbf{v}}_j + \Delta_{\tau_j}(\bar{\mathbf{a}}_j' - [\bar{\omega}_j]^\times \hat{\mathbf{v}}_j) \qquad \Sigma_{j+1} = \mathbf{J}\Sigma_j\mathbf{J}^T + \mathbf{G}\Delta_{\tau_j}^2\mathbf{N}\mathbf{G}^T \tag{16}$$

Here, $\mathbf{J} \in \mathbb{R}^{15 \times 15}$ is the Jacobian of the full state propagation function. $\mathbf{G} \in \mathbb{R}^{15 \times 12}$ is the derivative of the same propagation function by the inertial noise variables which are assumed to additively corrupt the inertial measurements. We omit the actual values here for brevity. $\mathbf{N}$ is a block-diagonal matrix with

$$\mathbf{I}_{3 \times 3}\sigma_g^2, \mathbf{I}_{3 \times 3}\sigma_{bg}^2, \mathbf{I}_{3 \times 3}\sigma_a^2, \mathbf{I}_{3 \times 3}\sigma_{ba}^2 \tag{17}$$

---

[4] Note that we use a log map of S^3 to $\mathbb{R}^3$ for measuring the 'difference' between the orientations [11].

on the diagonal corresponding to the noise strength of gyroscope, gyroscope bias, accelerometer and accelerometer bias. They can be determined for a given IMU using the Allan variance method [3]. The variable Σ corresponds to the uncertainty of the integration that is used to weigh the residual during optimization.

IMU factors are re-integrated every time the base state $\mathbf{x}_{t_1}$ changes. This could potentially be an issue for very long trajectories that we plan to solve using [7] combined with an incremental least-squares solver [12] in future work.

4.2 Optimization

Optimization of the covariance-weighted squared sum of all residual functions is carried out using the Ceres solver [1]. All occurring quaternions are optimized using a local parametrization included in Ceres that allows for an efficient and mathematically sound optimization on the underlying S^3 manifold.

5 Experiments

KITTI Dataset. The KITTI odometry benchmark [8] is widely accepted for evaluating large-scale, outdoor odometry algorithms. The associated dataset contains 22 sequences featuring laser scans from a Velodyne HDL 64 MBL. Ground truth derived from a high-quality commercial GPS/INS is provided for half of the sequences, serving as a training set, while the rest forms the test set. Scans in the KITTI odometry dataset are already motion-compensated using an unknown trajectory which—as we suppose—is the ground truth trajectory of the vehicle. Scan points are represented at the time where the laser faced exactly forward which complicates processing for our algorithm that requires raw, *uncompensated* Velodyne point clouds. Therefore, for each sweep, we take the relative pose from the previous sweep and use this to undo this motion compensation of the current one, making the data raw as possible. This allows us to run the benchmark without major changes in our method but introduces potential errors into the results.

As Deschaud [6] and others have observed, the point clouds in the dataset suffer from bad intrinsic calibration. Deschaud came up with a simple approximate calibration for the data which we also use for our experiments (see [6]).

The IMU part of our algorithm is not applicable to the KITTI dataset since IMU data is not provided as a part of the odometry benchmark.

Our results on the training set are given in Table 1. It can be seen that we outperform IMLS on 6 from 10 datasets, yet both methods appear to be relatively similar in performance. We believe that the map representation and feature selection advocated by IMLS may result in similar quantitative benefits over LOAM as our proposed method. The main advantage of our algorithm is the runtime, which makes it suitable for real-time operation. It is possible that the two algorithms have other strengths and weaknesses that are not visible in this purely quantitative analysis on a car-mounted dataset, however, no direct in-depth comparison was made in the context of this work.

Table 1. Comparison of the translation drift per meter (in %) of LOAM [24], IMLS [6] and our algorithm on the KITTI training dataset.

Seq.	Environment	LOAM	IMLS	Ours	Seq.	Environment	LOAM	IMLS	Ours
00	Urban	0.78	**0.50**	0.51	06	Urban	0.65	0.33	**0.31**
01	Highway	1.43	0.82	**0.79**	07	Urban	0.63	**0.33**	0.34
02	Urban+Country	0.92	**0.53**	0.54	08	Urban+Country	1.12	**0.80**	0.84
03	Country	0.86	0.68	**0.65**	09	Urban+Country	0.77	0.55	**0.46**
04	Country	0.71	**0.33**	0.44	10	Urban+Country	0.79	0.53	**0.52**
05	Urban	0.57	0.32	**0.27**					

Results on the KITTI test set are provided on the KITTI website[5], where our approach is called MC2SLAM. We hold the shared 4th/5th place of all laser-based algorithms with a translational error of 0.69%. We do however feature a better rotational error and lower run time than the equally ranked IMLS method (see 'Runtime' paragraph below).

Own Datasets. Our own datasets[6] were all recorded on a Velodyne HDL 32 sensor which handily features a built-in IMU. We associate individual timestamps with each point based on the specifications in the manufacturer's datasheet. This is in contrast to the KITTI dataset, where we can only roughly estimate a point's timestamp using its azimuth angle, lowering accuracy of our computations.

For the datasets CAMPUS_DRIVE and FIELD we mounted the sensor on a car, comparable to the KITTI dataset. For CAMPUS_RUN the sensor was mounted on a helmet so that a person could walk around to record data (see Fig. 1). Due to erratic motion from head movements, we expect the IMU to have much more impact in comparison to the very smooth motion patterns of a vehicle.

For large datasets, it is very difficult to determine an accurate, 6-DoF ground truth. Even on the KITTI dataset, the accuracy of the ground truth—especially at small scales—is limited, as has been noticed by other authors [5]. To some extent, specialized evaluation metrics accommodate for these issues and allow to obtain reasonable quantitative results. However, since the wheel-odometry, GPS/INS based solution can not be applied to our head-mounted datasets containing both indoor and outdoor data, we introduce the concept of *checkpoints*. A checkpoint is a point at which a loop in the data could be closed, making it possible to determine the relative pose between the two scans involved. No actual loop closing has to be performed, only the relative pose error at this trajectory position is computed. It represents the amount of drift that has accumulated over the course of the loop. We compute the translational- and rotational drift per meter, comparable to the KITTI evaluation by averaging over the errors

---

[5] http://www.cvlibs.net/datasets/kitti/eval_odometry.php see entry 'MC2SLAM'.
[6] See URL: https://agas.uni-koblenz.de/data/datasets/mc2slam/.

Table 2. Comparison of the translation drift per meter (in %) using different settings of our algorithm.

Local Map	✓	✗	✓
IMU	✓	✓	✗
CAMPUS_RUN_1	**0.41**	1.90	8.96
CAMPUS_RUN_2	**0.54**	2.13	15.65
CAMPUS_DRIVE	**0.10**	0.64	0.30
FIELD	**0.42**	7.50	0.43

Fig. 3. Trajectory of the FIELD dataset drawn on top of a screenshot from Google Maps with and without using a local map for reference point matching in magenta resp. cyan. (Color figure online)

divided by the loop lengths. We specifically choose this metric to make our results comparable to the KITTI results.

For our datasets, checkpoints have been obtained manually using a specialized tool to perform and verify the registration. All our datasets contain at least one loop between the beginning and the end. Some contain several loops, improving the reliability of the chosen evaluation approach.

Our algorithm randomly selects feature points during motion compensation. For this reason, we ran our algorithm 10 times[7] with different random seeds, in order to obtain a precise measure of accuracy. Our averaged results are shown in Table 2. The results emphasize the importance of a local map, and highlight the versatility of our method: The datasets contain head-mounted in- and outdoor scenarios as well as car-mounted ones. Yet we are seeing low very low drift in all of them. As seen in the plot of the trajectory in Fig. 3, the local map is particularly important to keep the drift low in the long term.

Integration of an IMU is particularly important for head-mounted datasets. For example, we observe that the drift on the CAMPUS_RUN dataset is unacceptable without the integration of an IMU. Motion compensation for those kinds of datasets appears to heavily rely on inertial sensing. For the datasets CAMPUS_DRIVE as well as FIELD, we are seeing smaller benefits from the IMU, which we attribute to the much smoother motion patterns within a car-mounted setting that make linear motion predictions during motion-compensation relatively accurate. However, there are also car-mounted applications in off-road environments, which we did not include in our evaluation. These applications would probably benefit from the IMU integration in a similar way than the head-mounted datasets we evaluated.

For more information about the datasets evaluated in Table 2, please refer to the supplemental material and the given web page.

---

[7] This number was manually determined to be sufficient to reduce the deviation of the results to negligible values.

Runtime. For our own recorded datasets, the SLAM problem is generally solved in real time on an Intel i7-3700K processor. Precise runtimes were determined by running our algorithm and averaging over 1000 frames of the CAMPUS_RUN_1 dataset: The actual motion compensation algorithm takes about 32 ms per sweep in total. The selection of reference points takes 7.7 ms, estimation of the bias variable b for the motion compensation trajectory takes 17.6 ms and applying the resulting trajectory to the full sweep S_k takes 3.7 ms. Insertion of the compensated sweep into the local map is done in a background thread and does not block the main thread. Pose graph optimization is also executed in a separate thread and only needs to be performed every five sweeps (see Sect. 4.2). For this dataset, this step took around 108.6 ms per run.

The runtime of bias estimation depends on the number of query points N_Q matched with the local map. In this example 500 reference points were used for the optimization. While using 1500 points slightly increases accuracy, runtime is more than doubled, increasing the duration of this step from 17.6 ms to 37.8 ms.

6   Conclusion

We have presented an algorithm for laser-based odometry that is applicable to a broad range of domains. The two-scan motion compensation against a local Poisson map yields fast and reliable pose-estimates with low long-term drift, which we were able to show using the KITTI benchmark, as well as on our own datasets. Tight integration of an IMU allows for erratic motion, allowing the use of hand-held or even head-mounted sensors for mapping hard-to-reach areas. In contrast to many existing backpack mapping solutions, our approach does not require GPS, making it suitable for a wide variety of use cases.

Acknowledgement. The authors would like to thank three anonymous reviewers for their helpful comments.

References

1. Agarwal, S., Mierle, K., et al.: Ceres solver. http://ceres-solver.org
2. Besl, P.J., McKay, N.D.: Method for registration of 3-D shapes. In: Sensor Fusion IV: Control Paradigms and Data Structures, vol. 1611, pp. 586–607. International Society for Optics and Photonics (1992)
3. Board, I.: IEEE standard specification format guide and test procedure for single-axis interferometric fiber optic gyros. IEEE Std., pp. 952–1997 (1998)
4. Bosse, M., Zlot, R., Flick, P.: Zebedee: design of a spring-mounted 3-D range sensor with application to mobile mapping. IEEE Trans. Robot. **28**(5), 1104–1119 (2012)
5. Cvišić, I., Petrović, I.: Stereo odometry based on careful feature selection and tracking. In: 2015 European Conference on Mobile Robots, ECMR, pp. 1–6. IEEE (2015)
6. Deschaud, J.: IMLS-SLAM: scan-to-model matching based on 3D data. CoRR abs/1802.08633 (2018). http://arxiv.org/abs/1802.08633

7. Forster, C., Carlone, L., Dellaert, F., Scaramuzza, D.: IMU preintegration on manifold for efficient visual-inertial maximum-a-posteriori estimation. In: Proceedings of Robotics: Science and Systems, Rome, Italy, July 2015. https://doi.org/10.15607/RSS.2015.XI.006

8. Geiger, A., Lenz, P., Urtasun, R.: Are we ready for autonomous driving? The KITTI vision benchmark suite. In: Conference on Computer Vision and Pattern Recognition, CVPR (2012)

9. Hertzberg, C., Wagner, R., Frese, U., Schröder, L.: Integrating generic sensor fusion algorithms with sound state representations through encapsulation of manifolds. Inf. Fusion 14(1), 57–77 (2013)

10. Hesch, J.A., Kottas, D.G., Bowman, S.L., Roumeliotis, S.I.: Consistency analysis and improvement of vision-aided inertial navigation. IEEE Trans. Robot. 30(1), 158–176 (2014)

11. Kaess, M.: Simultaneous localization and mapping with infinite planes. In: ICRA, vol. 1, p. 2 (2015)

12. Kaess, M., Johannsson, H., Roberts, R., Ila, V., Leonard, J.J., Dellaert, F.: iSAM2: Incremental smoothing and mapping using the Bayes tree. Int. J. Robot. Res. 31(2), 216–235 (2012)

13. Kukko, A., Kaartinen, H., Hyyppä, J., Chen, Y.: Multiplatform mobile laser scanning: usability and performance. Sensors 12(9), 11712–11733 (2012)

14. Leutenegger, S., Lynen, S., Bosse, M., Siegwart, R., Furgale, P.: Keyframe-based visual–inertial odometry using nonlinear optimization. Int. J. Robot. Res. 34(3), 314–334 (2015)

15. Low, K.L.: Linear least-squares optimization for point-to-plane ICP surface registration, no. 4. Chapel Hill, University of North Carolina (2004)

16. Moosmann, F., Stiller, C.: Velodyne SLAM. In: Proceedings of the IEEE Intelligent Vehicles Symposium, pp. 393–398, Baden-Baden, Germany, June 2011

17. Nüchter, A., Bleier, M., Schauer, J., Janotta, P.: Improving Google's cartographer 3D mapping by continuous-time SLAM. Int. Arch. Photogram. Remote Sens. Spat. Inf. Sci. 42, 543 (2017)

18. Nüchter, A., Borrmann, D., Koch, P., Kühn, M., May, S.: A man-portable, IMU-free mobile mapping system. ISPRS Ann. Photogram. Remote Sens. Spat. Inf. Sci. 2, 17–23 (2015). https://www.isprs-ann-photogramm-remote-sens-spatial-inf-sci.net/II-3-W5/17/2015/

19. Rönnholm, P., Liang, X., Kukko, A., Jaakkola, A., Hyyppä, J.: Quality analysis and correction of mobile backpack laser scanning data. ISPRS Ann. Photogram. Remote Sens. Spat. Inf. Sci. 3, 41 (2016)

20. Zhang, J., Kaess, M., Singh, S.: Real-time depth enhanced monocular odometry. In: 2014 IEEE/RSJ International Conference on Intelligent Robots and Systems, IROS 2014, pp. 4973–4980. IEEE (2014)

21. Zhang, J., Kaess, M., Singh, S.: A real-time method for depth enhanced visual odometry. Auton. Robots 41(1), 31–43 (2017)

22. Zhang, J., Singh, S.: LOAM: lidar odometry and mapping in real-time. In: Robotics: Science and Systems, vol. 2 (2014)

23. Zhang, J., Singh, S.: Visual-lidar odometry and mapping: low-drift, robust, and fast. In: 2015 IEEE International Conference on Robotics and Automation, ICRA, pp. 2174–2181. IEEE (2015)

24. Zhang, J., Singh, S.: Low-drift and real-time lidar odometry and mapping. Auton. Robots 41(2), 401–416 (2017)

An Analysis by Synthesis Approach for Automatic Vertebral Shape Identification in Clinical QCT

Stefan Reinhold[1]([⊠]) [ID], Timo Damm[2] [ID], Lukas Huber[2] [ID], Reimer Andresen[3] [ID], Reinhard Barkmann[2], Claus-C. Glüer[2] [ID], and Reinhard Koch[1] [ID]

[1] Department of Computer Science, Kiel University, Kiel, Germany
sre@informatik.uni-kiel.de
[2] Section Biomedical Imaging,
Molecular Imaging North Competence Center (MOIN CC),
Department of Radiology and Neuroradiology,
University Medical Center Schleswig-Holstein (UKSH), Kiel University,
Kiel, Germany
[3] Institute of Diagnostic and Interventional Radiology/Neuroradiology,
Westküstenklinikum Heide, Academic Teaching Hospital of the Universities of Kiel,
Lübeck and Hamburg, Heide, Germany

Abstract. Quantitative computed tomography (QCT) is a widely used tool for osteoporosis diagnosis and monitoring. The assessment of cortical markers like cortical bone mineral density (BMD) and thickness is a demanding task, mainly because of the limited spatial resolution of QCT. We propose a direct model based method to automatically identify the surface through the center of the cortex of human vertebra. We develop a statistical bone model and analyze its probability distribution after the imaging process. Using an as-rigid-as-possible deformation we find the cortical surface that maximizes the likelihood of our model given the input volume. Using the European Spine Phantom (ESP) and a high resolution μCT scan of a cadaveric vertebra, we show that the proposed method is able to accurately identify the real center of cortex ex-vivo. To demonstrate the in-vivo applicability of our method we use manually obtained surfaces for comparison.

Keywords: Biomedical image analysis ·
Quantitative computed tomography · Cortex identification ·
Bone densitometry · Analysis by synthesis

1 Introduction

Osteoporosis is a systematic skeletal disease that is characterized by low bone mass and deterioration of bone microstructure resulting in high fracture risk [6]. Its high prevalence of 24% in women beyond age of 65 makes osteoporosis a wide spread disease and a highly relevant research topic [7]. Quantitative computed tomography (QCT) has become a reliable tool for osteoporotic fracture

T. Brox et al. (Eds.): GCPR 2018, LNCS 11269, pp. 73–88, 2019.
https://doi.org/10.1007/978-3-030-12939-2_6

risk prediction [1,11] and monitoring [8,10]. Volumetric trabecular *bone mineral density* (BMD) was identified as a good marker for bone strength. Still, the high under-diagnosis rate of 84% [28] indices that trabecular BMD alone is not sufficient as a bone strength marker. In osteoporotic patients the cortex takes the main load [25]. Therefore, the vertebral cortical bone is a worthwhile subject of study [12,13]. However, the assessment of cortical markers like cortical thickness or cortical BMD is a challenging task [22]: the spatial resolution of clinical QCT ranges from 0.3–0.5 mm in-plane and from 1–3 mm out-of-plane. The thickness of the cortex of a vertebral body is reported [24,27] to range from 0.25 mm to 0.4 mm and is therefore clearly below the Nyquist-Frequency, resulting in tremendous overestimation of cortical thickness in clinical QCT. Using high resolution QCT (HR-QCT) an in-plane resolution of up to 0.15 mm and an out-of-plane resolution of about 0.3 mm can be achieved at the expense of higher radiation dose, but cortical thickness is still clearly overestimated [10].

In this paper we address the problem of identifying the center of the cortex of a vertebral body from clinical QCT scans without any user interaction. As can be seen in Fig. 1 the apparent ridge of the cortical bone, i.e. the surface of maximum intensity, moves when the ratio of cortical to trabecular BMD changes. The same is true for different scanner resolutions [22] and cortical thicknesses. The strength of this effect does also vary with scanner, resolution and reconstruction kernel, making results from different scanners hard to compare [9]. A direct deconvolution of the resulting image is not applicable due to low signal to noise ratio.

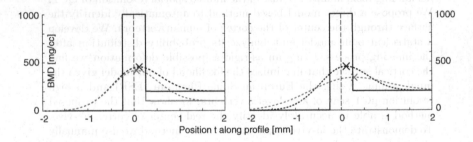

Fig. 1. Cortex center shift by different trabecular BMD and resolution. Left: a simulated BMD profile trough an idealized cortex (center at $t = 0$, width 0.5 mm, mineralization 1000 mg/cc). The trabecular BMD is 100 mg/cc (red, left) and 200 mg/cc (black). The dashed lines show the corresponding signals after convolution with a gaussian with $\sigma = 0.5$ (black) and $\sigma = 0.8$ (red, right) simulating a clinical QCT. The crosses mark the cortical ridges (maximum intensities). (Color figure online)

Related Work. Shape identification and segmentation of vertebral bodies has been a research topic for a long time. Kang et al. [17] use a region growing approach followed by a refinement step based on relative thresholding to distinguish soft tissue from bone. While the method yields accurate results for thick cortices (5 times the voxel size and above), it shows the typical overestimation for thin cortices as present in human vertebrae. Mastmayer et al. [18,19] proposed a multi step semi-automatic segmentation method based on the Euler-Lagrange equation and local adaptive volume growing that yields promising results, but again suffers from partial volume effects for thin cortices. The graph cut method proposed by Aslan et al. [2,3] shows superior performance over previous work, but since the segmentation is voxel based, voxel size, especially out-of-plane, remains the limiting factor.

All of the methods mentioned yield voxel masks as the segmentation result. Therefore, the voxel size constraints the accuracy of cortex identification. Treece et al. [30] developed a mathematical model of the bone anatomy and applied a simplified model of the imaging system. The resulting measurement model is then fitted to the data given an initial segmentation of the target bone. This way they were able to provide an unbiased cortical thickness estimate down to 0.3 mm on proximal femur.

Our Approach. We propose an analysis by synthesis (AbS) based approach (also called direct method) to accurately fit a template surface to the center of the cortical bone underlying a clinical QCT scan. The idea behind AbS based image analysis is not to analyze image features directly but instead synthesize an artificial image of a parametrizable model and find the parameters for which the synthetic and the input image match best. This way no image derivatives are required, making the process robust to noise. This model based approach can, to a certain degree, compensate for loss of information in the imaging process by incorporating prior knowledge into the model. However, for CT a full synthesis would require a radon transform of the full model followed by a CT reconstruction. Since this full synthesis is very expensive computationally, we simplify the scanning process to a blur, implemented by a convolution with the point spread functions (PSF) of the system. To simplify the synthesis further, we make use of *sparse synthesis* [14,23] where not the whole image is synthesized, but only a sparse subset of it. Here, the result of the sparse synthesis is a set of one dimensional profiles orthogonal to the cortical surface, equivalent to a sparse sampling of a full synthesis[1]. Our model consists of a closed genus 0 surface representing the center of the cortex. As in medial representations [26], we assign a thickness and a BMD value to every point on the surface. The trabecular region inside the bone and the soft tissue region outside are represented by BMD distributions. Using a maximum a posteriori (MAP) estimation, we find the surface that maximizes the likelihood of the model parameters given measurements of the input volume.

In Sect. 2 we give a detailed insight into the proposed method. We develop a statistical model of bone by extending the deterministic model of Treece et al. [30] in Sect. 2.1. The sparse synthesis yields a statistical measurement model which we derive in Sect. 2.2. In Sect. 2.3 we show how the MAP estimation can

---

[1] The equivalence is actually not given for the full volume. In areas where two cortices are close together, the sparse synthesis differs from the full synthesis. However, these regions are not critical for clinical routine.

be carried out in a data parallel process by employing the as-rigid-as-possible (ARAP [29]) deformation scheme. In Sect. 3, we evaluate the accuracy of our method by using the European Spine Phantom (ESP, [16]). In addition, we further evaluate the accuracy using a μCT scan of a cadaveric human vertebra. To show the applicability of our method to clinical data we compare our results on 100 in-vivo QCT scans with manually obtained annotations. Finally, in Sect. 4 we conclude this article and discuss future work.

2   Method

The input to our method is a calibrated[2] QCT scan of a vertebra, a pre-estimated statistical measurement model and a labeled three-dimensional sketch of the target bone as depicted in Fig. 2(a). Each label of the template corresponds to a differently parameterized statistical bone model. The output is a triangle mesh representing the unbiased surface of the cortex center.

2.1   Statistical Bone Model

We model the surface of the cortex center as a closed genus 0 triangle mesh S with N vertices. Its piecewise linear embedding is given by the vertex positions $V \subseteq \mathbb{R}^3$. When we look at a one dimensional profile orthogonal to the surface at any point on S (Fig. 2(b)), then the BMD graph is a piecewise constant function of the signed distance t to the cortex center. By modeling the three density levels (soft tissue density, cortical BMD, trabecular BMD) as gaussian random variables $Y_i \sim \mathcal{N}(\mu_{Y_i}, \sigma_{Y_i}^2), i = 0, 1, 2$ and by modeling the cortical thickness[3] as a random variable W with[4] $\log W \sim \mathcal{N}(\mu_W, \sigma_W^2)$, we obtain a stochastic process $Y(t)$ of the profile:

$$Y(t) = Y_0 + (Y_1 - Y_0) \cdot H(t + W) + (Y_2 - Y_1) \cdot H(t - W), \tag{1}$$

where H denotes the Heaviside step function. Note that (1) takes a similar form as [30, Eq. 1] with all unknowns replaced by random variables.

Since the density distribution of the soft tissue is not equal everywhere, for example the intervertebral discs have higher density than muscles, we use differently parameterized random processes for different sections of the bone. Figure 2(a) depicts the three different regions used in our model: vertical cortex (green), endplates (red), foramen (yellow). The "cut pedicles" region (blue in Fig. 2(a)) is not used in the model.

---

[2] Houndsfield units are converted to bone mineral equivalents using known densities of a calibration phantom which is simultaneously scanned with the patient.

[3] The cortical thickness is $2 \cdot W$.

[4] W is a non-negative size quantity which is commonly modeled as a log-normal distribution.

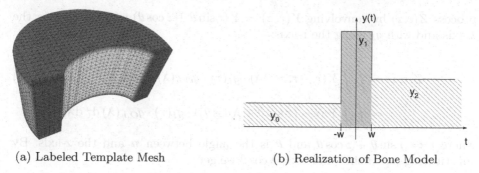

(a) Labeled Template Mesh   (b) Realization of Bone Model

Fig. 2. (a) Labeled vertebra template used in the proposed method. Different colors correspond to different regions with distinct bone models: vertical cortex (green), endplates (red), foramen (yellow), cut pedicles (blue). (b) Realization $y(t)$ of random process $Y(t)$, see Eq. 1. The cortex is depicted in green. (Color figure online)

2.2   Measurement Model

The next step in the AbS framework is the synthesis step where the imaging system is simulated by applying the in-plane and out-of-plane PSF to the bone model. By sampling the resulting image one can then acquire observable profiles. However, with sparse synthesis we are able to simplify the process by not performing the convolutions in the global coordinate system, but in the local system of the profile.

Combined PSF. The slice sensitivity profile (SSP) of a spiral CT can be approximated by the convolution of the rectangular profile of helical CT by the triangular table movement function [15]. The width of the rectangular profile is determined by the collimation, while the width of the movement function is determined by the table feed. We therefore approximate the out-of-plane PSF (perpendicular to a CT slice) for pitch factor of 1 with

$$g_{O,h}(z) := \tilde{g}_O\left(\frac{z}{h}\right), \tag{2}$$

where $\tilde{g}_O(z) := \Pi(z) * \Lambda(2z)$ and h is the slice width. Like [30] we approximate the in-plane PSF with a rotational invariant gaussian of width σ:

$$g_I(x,y) := \frac{1}{\sqrt{2\pi}\sigma} \exp\left(-\frac{x^2 + y^2}{2\sigma^2}\right). \tag{3}$$

If we slice through the cortex at $x \in \mathcal{S}$ with a plane defined by the z-axis and the surface normal n at x, we can define a local coordinate system centered on x with the z-axis as the ordinate and the projection of n onto the x-y-plane as the abscissa (r-axis) as depicted in Fig. 3. Since the profile now lies inside r-z-plane and because g_I is rotational invariant, we can obtain the measurement process $\tilde{Z}(r,z)$ by convolving $\tilde{Y}(r,z) := Y(r\sin\theta + z\cos\theta)$ with $g_{O,h}$ along the z-axis and with g_I along the r-axis:

$$\tilde{Z}(r,z) = \int\int \tilde{Y}(r-\tau, z-\lambda)\cdot g_I(\tau)\cdot g_{O,h}(\lambda)\,\mathrm{d}\tau\,\mathrm{d}\lambda \tag{4}$$

$$= \int\int Y\left(t-(\tau\sin\theta+\lambda\cos\theta)\right)\cdot g_I(\tau)\cdot g_{O,h}(\lambda)\,\mathrm{d}\tau\,\mathrm{d}\lambda,$$

where $t := r\sin\theta + z\cos\theta$ and θ is the angle between $\boldsymbol{n}$ and the z-axis. By substituting $\phi := \tau\sin\theta$ and $\psi := \lambda\cos\theta$ we get

$$\tilde{Z}(r,z) = \int\int Y(t-\phi-\psi)\cdot g_I\left(\frac{\phi}{\sin\theta}\right)\cdot g_{O,h}\left(\frac{\psi}{\cos\theta}\right)\cdot\frac{1}{\sin\theta\cos\theta}\,\mathrm{d}\phi\,\mathrm{d}\psi$$

$$= Y(t) * \left\{\frac{1}{\sin\theta}\cdot g_I\left(\frac{t}{\sin\theta}\right) * \frac{1}{\cos\theta}\cdot g_{O,h}\left(\frac{t}{\cos\theta}\right)\right\} \tag{5}$$

$$= Y(t) * g_\theta(t).$$

Hence, we can simplify the two dimensional convolution by a single convolution of the one-dimensional process from (1) with an angle dependent PSF g_θ.

Although, we used a gaussian for the in-plane PSF in the derivation of the combined PSF, we note that any symmetric square integrable PSF can be used here. Ohkubo et al. [21] determined the PSFs for several reconstruction kernels. Based on their measurements one can observe that a gaussian is a good approximation for smooth kernels like the Siemens B40, but for sharper kernels like the Siemens B80 it is not: the B80 amplifies some higher frequencies in a narrow band to enhance edges while the gaussian damps all high frequencies.

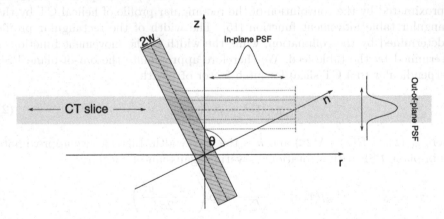

Fig. 3. Schematic view of an orthogonal cut through a cortex segment of width $2w$ (shaded green). The resulting spatial density is sampled along the surface normal $\boldsymbol{n}$ at an angle θ with the z-axis after convolution with the in-plane PSF along r and with the out-of-plane PSF along z. (Color figure online)

Stochastic Measurement Process. Let $G_\theta := \int g_\theta(t)\,dt$ be the primitive function of the angle dependent PSF g_θ from (5). Since g_θ has finite energy, we know that $\lim\limits_{t\to-\infty} G_\theta(t) = 0$ and $\lim\limits_{t\to+\infty} G_\theta(t) = 1$. With this we can define the optimal (i.e. noise free) stochastic measurement process $Z(t)$ as

$$Z(t) := Y(t) * g_\theta(t) \tag{6}$$
$$= Y_0 + (Y_1 - Y_0) \cdot G_\theta(t + W) + (Y_2 - Y_1) \cdot G_\theta(t - W).$$

Since Y_0, Y_1, Y_2 are stochastically independent normally distributed random variables the conditional stochastic process $\zeta(t) := Z(t)|W$ is gaussian with mean and variance function given as:

$$\mu_\zeta(t|w) = \mu_0 + (\mu_{Y_1} - \mu_{Y_0}) \cdot G_\theta(t + w) + (\mu_{Y_2} - \mu_{Y_1}) \cdot G_\theta(t - w), \tag{7}$$
$$\sigma_\zeta^2(t|w) = \sigma_{Y_0}^2(1 - G_\theta(t + w))^2 + \sigma_{Y_1}^2(G_\theta(t + w) - G_\theta(t - w))^2 +$$
$$\sigma_{Y_2}^2 G_\theta^2(t - w).$$

Thus the probability density function (PDF) f_ζ of $\zeta(t)$ is given by

$$f_\zeta(z, t|w) = N\left(z \mid \mu_\zeta(t|w), \sigma_\zeta^2(t|w)\right). \tag{8}$$

With the joint probability density function of $Z(t)$ and W

$$f_{Z,W}(z, w, t) = f_\zeta(z, t|w) f_W(w), \text{ with} \tag{9}$$
$$f_W(w) = \frac{1}{w} \cdot \frac{1}{\sqrt{2\pi}\sigma_W} \exp\left(-\frac{(\ln w - \mu_W)^2}{2\sigma_W^2}\right),$$

the probability density function f_Z of $Z(t)$ is obtained by marginalizing out W:

$$f_Z(z, t) = \int f_\zeta(z, t|w) f_W(w)\,dw. \tag{10}$$

2.3 Deformation Model and Optimization

Given a profile through a point $x \in S$ of an input volume I, we can express the degree of conformity of the profile with a synthetic profile by means of the likelihood of the measurement model. The optimal surface S' is then defined by the linear embedding $V' \subset \mathbb{R}^3$ for which the likelihood of all profiles through S' are maximal. However, this is an ill posed problem, because it is not guaranteed that the maximizer yields a realistic shape. By constraining the deformation between an initial surface S and S' to be as rigid as possible, shape degeneration can be avoided and the problem becomes well formed.

We modify the as-rigid-as-possible (ARAP) energy term from [29] to act as a shape prior in the MAP framework as follows:

$$E(\hat{S}) = \min_{R_i \in SO(3)} \left\{ \sigma_E^{-2} \sum_{i=1}^N \gamma_i \sum_{j \in \mathcal{N}(i)} \omega_{ij} \|(\hat{x}_i - \hat{x}_j) - R_i(x_i - x_j)\|_2^2 \right\}, \tag{11}$$

where ω_{ij} are the cotangent weights of edge (i,j) [20], γ_i are per-vertex weights and $\mathcal{N}(i)$ contains all vertices of the 1-ring of vertex i. $\boldsymbol{R}_i \in SO(3)$ are per-vertex rotation matrices adding additional $3N$ degrees of freedom to the deformation. $E(\hat{S})$ can be seen as a measure of how far the deformation is from an isometry [4]. With the scale σ_E^{-2} Eq. (11) is equivalent (up to constants) to the negative log likelihood function of a gaussian random variable E modeling the ARAP energy of $\mathcal{S}'$.

Now, let $\boldsymbol{t} = (t_i)_{1,\ldots,2K+1}$ be a vector of $2K+1$ samples from $[-t_0, t_0] \subset \mathbb{R}$ with a sampling interval δ_t. For all $i = 1, \ldots, N$ let $\hat{\boldsymbol{l}}_i := \{\hat{\boldsymbol{x}}_i + t_j \cdot \hat{\boldsymbol{n}}_i \,|\, j = 1, \ldots, 2K+1\}$ be a vector of discrete samples of a profile through position $\hat{\boldsymbol{x}}_i \in \hat{V}$ and let $\hat{\boldsymbol{\rho}}_i := I(\hat{\boldsymbol{l}}_i)$ be the densities obtained by sampling the interpolated[5] input volume I at positions $\hat{\boldsymbol{l}}_i$. The log likelihood $\mathcal{L}(\hat{\boldsymbol{x}}_i|\hat{\boldsymbol{\rho}}_i)$ of $\hat{\boldsymbol{x}}_i$ given measurements $\hat{\boldsymbol{\rho}}_i$ is given with (10) by[6]

$$\mathcal{L}_Z(\hat{\boldsymbol{x}}_i|\hat{\boldsymbol{\rho}}_i) = \sum_{j=1}^{2K+1} \log f_Z(\hat{\rho}_{ij}, t_j). \tag{12}$$

The posterior log likelihood is then proportional to

$$\mathcal{L}_{E|Z}(\hat{S}_i|\hat{\boldsymbol{\rho}}_i) \propto \mathcal{L}_Z(\hat{\boldsymbol{x}}_i|\hat{\boldsymbol{\rho}}_i) - E(\hat{S}) - \log \int f_{Z|E}(\hat{\boldsymbol{\rho}}_i|\hat{S}) \, d\hat{S}. \tag{13}$$

The direct optimization of (13) is analytically intractable and numerical optimization would either require the computation of image gradients, which we are tying to avoid, or gradient less optimization methods which do not perform very well on high dimensional optimization problems. We therefore split the optimization into two sub problems that can be efficiently solved: first the optimal displacement along the surface normal for each profile is estimated. Afterwards, the surface is optimized to match the displaced positions under ARAP constraints. This two step optimization scheme is iterated until convergence.

Optimal Displacements. We first modify Eq. (12) by adding a latent variable $s_i \sim \mathcal{N}(0, \sigma_{s_i}^2)$ as follows:

$$\mathcal{L}_{Z|s_i}(\boldsymbol{x}_i|\boldsymbol{\rho}_i, s_i) = \mathcal{L}_Z(\boldsymbol{x}_i + s_i\boldsymbol{n}_i|\boldsymbol{\rho}_i). \tag{14}$$

Using MAP estimation we can find the optimal displacement $\hat{s}_i$ by maximizing the posterior likelihood

$$\mathcal{L}_{s_i|Z}(s_i|\boldsymbol{x}_i, \boldsymbol{\rho}_i) = \tag{15}$$

$$\mathcal{L}_{Z|s_i}(\boldsymbol{x}_i|\boldsymbol{\rho}_i, s_i) + \mathcal{L}_{s_i}(s_i) - \log \int f_{Z|s_i}(\boldsymbol{\rho}_i|\boldsymbol{t}_i + \tau)f_{s_i}(\tau) \, d\tau.$$

---

[5] In our implementation we use trilinear interpolation for performance reasons.

[6] To keep the derivation simple, we assume independence here. In general the samples are correlated by the interpolation method.

In our implementation we pre-evaluate f_Z for discrete samples of t, θ and z to a three dimensional histogram and approximate f_Z by histogram lookup with trilinear interpolation. This way, Eq. (15) can be maximized very efficiently using data parallel exhaustive search along s_i at discrete steps.

Surface Fitting. Now that the optimal displacements are known, the surface needs to be fitted to the displaced positions $y_i := x_i + \hat{s}_i n_i$ under ARAP constraints. We therefore minimize the following energy term:

$$E_{\text{shape}}(\hat{S}) = \sum_{i=1}^{N} \gamma_i \left((\hat{x}_i - y_i)^T n_i\right)^2 + E(\hat{S}), \qquad (16)$$

where the first term addresses the point to plane distances and the second term the ARAP constraints. There might be profiles ρ_i where no cortex can be observed. Since the estimated displacements from those profiles are meaningless, we use the per-vertex weights γ_i to down-weight those estimates by using the posterior PDF: $\gamma_i := f_{s_i|Z}(\hat{s}_i|x_i, \rho_i)$.

Like in [29] we use an alternating iterative optimization scheme to optimize (16): we first keep the rotations R_i fixed and optimize for the positions $\hat{x}_i$ and then optimize for the rotations while keeping the positions fixed. For fixed positions, the optimal rotations can be found by SVD (refer to [29, Eqs. 5 and 6] for details). The optimal positions $\hat{x}_i$ can be found by setting the partial derivatives of E_{shape} to zero, which results in the following sparse linear system of equations:

$$\left(2\sigma_E^{-2} L \otimes I_3 + B\right) x = 2\sigma_E^{-2} c + d, \qquad (17)$$

where $x = \left(x_1^T, \ldots, x_N^T\right)^T$, L is the Laplacian matrix of S, B is a block diagonal matrix with entries $(\gamma_i n_i n^T)_{ii}$ and $\otimes$ denotes the Kronecker product. The vector c contains the ARAP constraints as a concatenations of vectors $c_i = \sum_j L_{ij} \frac{(R_i + R_j)}{2}(x_i - x_j)$ and d consist of concatenations of vectors $d_i = \gamma_i n_i n_i^T(x_i + \hat{s}_i n_i)$. Equation (17) can be efficiently solved using a preconditioned conjugate gradient solver (PCG). The alternating optimization scheme is iterated until convergence.

3   Experiments and Results

We implemented the proposed method using MATLAB and C++. The measurement model requires the slice spacing h and the width σ of the in-plane PSF as input parameters. The value of σ can be easily estimated from phantom scans[7]. The parameters of the BMD priors Y_i, can be estimated from single measurements or prior knowledge. The parameters of the width prior W are set to reflect the range of reported cortical thicknesses. For each scanner

---

[7] Since the calibration phantom is present in all QCT scans, no separate scanning process is required.

configuration (h, σ) we pre-computed f_Z for discrete samples from $(t, \theta, z) \in$ $[-2, 2] \times [0°, 90°] \times [-1000, 2000]$ (41, 91 and 3001 samples, respectively) data parallel on a GPGPU and saved the result as a 3D histogram as described in Sect. 2.3. We set $\sigma_{s_i} = 2$ and $\sigma_E = 2$ for all experiments. The optimization usually provides good results after a few iterations and takes about 1 to 5 min to complete on our system (Intel® Core™ i7-4790 CPU @ 3.60 GHz, 4 Cores), depending on the image size and number of iterations[8].

Table 1. Results of the phantom experiment. Given are for each of the three ESP vertebrae the radii and heights of the estimated surface. For both variables the mean, the standard deviation (SD) and the difference to the ground truth values (Diff) are shown. All measures are in mm. N denotes the number of samples on each surface (vertical cortex for radius, endplates for height).

Vertebra	Radius				Height			
	N	Mean	Diff	SD	N	Mean	Diff	SD
Low	10072	17.73	−0.02	0.14	6101	23.95	−0.05	0.28
Medium	9897	17.52	0.02	0.16	6239	23.64	−0.36	0.42
High	9602	17.23	−0.02	0.16	23306	23.00	0.00	0.30

3.1   Ex-Vivo

To evaluate the accuracy of the proposed method, we scanned the ESP with a clinical CT scanner using a low dose protocol (Siemens Somatom 64, 120 kV, 80 mAs, kernel B40s) at an in-plane resolution of 0.4 mm and a slice spacing of 1 mm. The ESP consists of three geometrical phantom vertebra (low, medium and high), each with different wall thicknesses and densities. The proposed method was used to acquire the cortical surfaces $\mathcal{S}_i$ of the three phantom vertebrae. To gain a dense surface, we used random mesh sampling of $\mathcal{S}_i$ using the method described in [5]. For the accuracy evaluation of the vertical cortex, we first fit a cylinder to the point cloud belonging to the vertical cortex and then computed the radius for each point separately. Since the vertebral bodies of the ESP have a diameter of 36 mm, the optimal radii of the cylindrical surfaces through the cortex centers are 17.75 mm (0.5 mm wall), 17.5 mm (1 mm wall) or 17.25 mm (1.5 mm wall), for the low, medium and high vertebra, respectively. To evaluate the accuracy of the endplate surface we fit two planes to our point cloud: one for the upper endplate and one for the lower endplate. Hereafter, the point to plane distance of each sample to its opposite plane was computed. All bodies of the phantom have a height of 25 mm, so the optimal distances are 24 mm for the low and medium vertebra (1 mm wall) and 23 mm (2 mm wall) for the high vertebra.

---

[8] In our prototype implementation, the optimization does not utilize the GPU, yet, but we note that all operations can be easily ported to the GPU.

Table 1 summarizes the results of the ESP experiment. For all vertebra levels, the difference between the mean radius of the estimated surface and the ground truth radius is near zero. The standard deviation is below one half of the in-plane resolution. The same applies for the estimated heights, noting that the out-of-plane resolution is 2.5-times lower than the in-plane resolution.

Since the shape of the ESP is very simple, we used a cadaveric vertebra embedded in resin for a more realistic reference. The embedded vertebra was scanned with a µCT system (SCANCO Medical, 70 kV, 360 mAs) with an isotropic resolution of 31 µm and with a clinical QCT system (Siemens Somatom 64, 120 kV, 100 mAs, kernel B40s) with an in-plane resolution of 0.2 mm and a slice spacing of 1 mm. Both scans where calibrated and the QCT scan was resampled and rigidly registered to the µCT scan. The resulting rigid transformation matrix was saved for later use. We applied our method to the unregistered QCT scan of the embedded vertebra and sampled the resulting surface as above. Using the inverse transformation matrix the point cloud was transformed into the coordinate system of the µCT scan. To evaluate the accuracy of the cortical surface we first need to identify the ground-truth cortex in the µCT scan. We sampled the µCT scan along lines orthogonal to the acquired surface at every sample point, from 5 mm outside to 5 mm inside the volume defined by the surface using 2001 samples per line (5 µm spacing). We binarized the profile using a threshold of 500 mg/cc. To fill small cavities in the cortex (see Fig. 5), we applied a morphological closing operation to the binarized signals. We defined the periosteal (outer) surface as the first rising edge and the endosteal (inner) surface as the first falling edge. The center of the cortex is then the midpoint between the periosteal and the endosteal surface. Since the surface estimated by the proposed method is located at the center of the sampled line ($t = 0$), the signed distance to the real cortex center is simply the location of the midpoint.

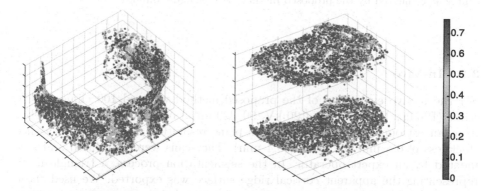

Fig. 4. Spatial distribution of absolute distances [mm] to cortex centers of the µCT experiment. Left: vertical cortex, right: endplates. The distances are encoded as colors.

We were able to identify the cortex center for 8506 samples for the vertical cortex and for 8273 samples for the endplates using this method. The average distance to the center of the vertical cortex was 0.0662 ± 0.2327 mm (mean ± standard deviation) and 0.0607 ± 0.2347 mm for the endplates. The absolute error was below 0.075 mm for 25%, below 0.16 mm for 50% and below 0.28 mm for 75% of the samples. Figure 4 depicts the spatial distribution of the absolute errors on the surface. The highest errors are scattered around the surface, but do not form larger clusters. We manually inspected the profiles with the highest errors and found that most of them are located at positions where the real cortex is hard to identify by the thresholding method. Figure 5 shows an example of such a location. While the cortex centers identified by the thresholding method vary quite widely, the estimated surface stays smooth between the periosteal and the endosteal surfaces.

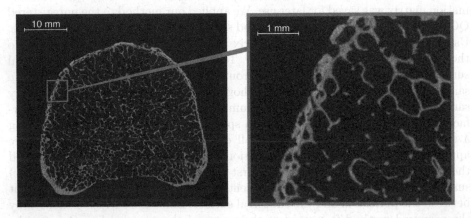

Fig. 5. Left: central slice of the embedded vertebra acquired with μCT. Right: zoom to a region where cortex definition is problematic. The green contour shows the cortex center as estimated by the proposed method. (Color figure online)

3.2   In-Vivo

For the in-vivo evaluation of the proposed method we used 100 clinical QCT scans (Phillips Brilliance 16, 120 kV, 90–420 mAs) of the first lumbar vertebra from an osteoporosis study with an in-plane resolution of 0.7 mm and a slice thickness of 0.8 mm (increment 0.4 mm). The scans were calibrated and segmented by an expert operator. In the segmentation process, a triangle mesh representing the apparent cortical ridge surface was exported. We used those meshes as a reference to evaluate the applicability of the proposed method to in-vivo data. However, since the manually obtained meshes do not identify the center of the cortex but the apparent cortical ridge, a bias is unavoidable. After applying the proposed method to the in-vivio scans, we did the same random sampling as in the ex-vivo case and afterwards computed for each sample the distance to the reference mesh using [5].

For the vertical cortex we acquired 98000 samples (980 samples per patient) with an average distance of 0.25 ± 0.52 mm (mean $\pm$ standard deviation). For the endplates we acquired 101600 samples (1016 samples per patient) with an average distance of 0.19 ± 0.56 mm. By visual inspection of the spatial distribution of absolute errors, we found that the majority of high errors are located in the transition area between the vertical cortex and the endplates.

To check if the bias could be explained by the displacement between ridge and cortex center (cf. Fig. 1), we evaluated the 99% confidence intervals of ζ (8) for a cortical thickness of 0.3 mm and for priors Z_0 and Z_2 estimated from the 100 in-vivo scans. For an angle of $\theta = 90°$, the displacement between the cortical ridge and the cortex center lies between 0.1 mm and 0.3 mm and for an angle of $\theta = 0°$ between 0.09 mm and 2.3 mm. This could explain the observed bias, but for the in-vivo case it cannot be directly verified. To substantiate our hypothesis, we did a statistical analysis based on measurements obtained using the original manual segmentation of the 100 in-vivo scans. There were no significant correlations between the bias and the integral BMD, cortical thickness, the total volume or the ratio of cortical to trabecular BMD. However, the cortical thickness measure that was used is based on voxel distances and therefore it is not very expressive. Therefore, we also investigated the density weighted cortical thickness (cortical thickness multiplied by cortical BMD divided by 1200 mg/cc). We found a significant negative linear relationship between the bias and density weighted cortical thickness (wCt.Th). Figure 6 shows a scatter plot with the regression line. There is a significant negative slope of -0.94 ($p = 0.019$). Therefore, if the cortex gets thicker, the bias gets lower. This is consistent with the cortex center shift as depicted in Fig. 1: a thicker cortex is equivalent to a higher resolution resulting in a better agreement between the cortical ridge and the cortex center.

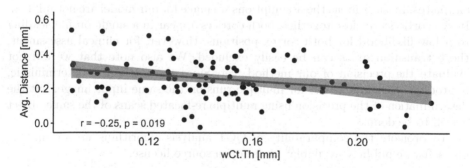

Fig. 6. Scatterplot of the average distance of the estimated to the manual obtained mesh by weighted cortical thickness (wCt.Th). The regression line has a significant negative slope of -0.94 ($p = 0.019$) indicating a negative linear relationship. The confidence interval is depicted as the shaded blue region. (Color figure online)

4   Conclusion

We presented an analysis by synthesis approach for automatic vertebral shape identification in clinical QCT. The foundation of our method is a statistical model of bone which is convolved with the in-plane and out-of-plane PSF of spiral CT resulting in a statistical measurement model. We use an as-rigid-as-possible deformation scheme to find the surface of the center of cortical bone that maximizes the posterior likelihood of the model given the image. Since the posterior likelihood is analytically intractable, we propose an alternating optimization scheme to find an approximate solution using an efficient data parallel process.

The evaluation of the proposed method using a clinical QCT scan of the ESP and a µCT scan of an embedded vertebra demonstrates its high sub-voxel accuracy. The applicability to in-vivo data was shown by comparing the estimated surfaces to manual annotations of 100 in-vivo QCT scans from an osteoporosis study. The remaining bias to the manually obtained meshes might be explained by the displacement of the apparent cortical ridge to the cortex center due to low spatial resolution. We substantiated this hypothesis by a statistical correlation analysis.

We think the proposed method is a good starting point for further assessment of cortical bone markers. The estimation of the (local) cortical thickness and the cortical BMD should be possible by maximizing the posterior probability of the respective parameters, like we did for the displacements. We may also note that, although we presented our method here for vertebral shape identification, it is not limited to vertebrac. Using a different template mesh the method can also be applied to other bones or bone parts, e.g. proximal femur.

There are of course limitations of our method: it fails to accurately estimate the cortex center at the transition area between the vertical cortex and the endplates. In these areas the assumptions we make for our model are not fulfilled. If two cortices are close together, both cortices appear in a single profile, leading to a low likelihood for both cortex positions. However, for clinical assessment, those transition areas can be easily excluded. We also note that we did not evaluate the precision of our method, yet. Since the method is deterministic, it produces the same result for multiple runs on the same input image, but the determination of the precision using multiple re-located scans of the same object is still to be done.

To promote the comparability of QCT analysis algorithms we are making our software publicly available[9] under open source license.

Acknowledgments. This work was part of the Diagnostik Bilanz Study which is part of the BioAsset project. BioAsset is funded by a grant of the Bundesministerium für Bildung und Forschung (BMBF), Germany, Föderkennzeichen 01EC1005. This work was also supported by the German Research Foundation, DFG, No. KO2044/9-1.

---

[9] https://github.com/ithron/CortidQCT.

References

1. Andresen, R., Haidekker, M., Radmer, S., Banzer, D.: CT determination of bone mineral density and structural investigations on the axial skeleton for estimating the osteoporosis-related fracture risk by means of a risk score. Br. J. Radiol. **72**(858), 569–578 (1999)
2. Aslan, M.S., Ali, A., Chen, D., Arnold, B., Farag, A.A., Xiang, P.: 3D vertebrae segmentation using graph cuts with shape prior constraints. In: 2010 17th IEEE International Conference on Image Processing (ICIP), pp. 2193–2196. IEEE (2010)
3. Aslan, M.S., et al.: A novel 3D segmentation of vertebral bones from volumetric CT images using graph cuts. In: Bebis, G., et al. (eds.) ISVC 2009. LNCS, vol. 5876, pp. 519–528. Springer, Heidelberg (2009). https://doi.org/10.1007/978-3-642-10520-3_49
4. Chao, I., Pinkall, U., Sanan, P., Schröder, P.: A simple geometric model for elastic deformations. ACM Trans. Graph. (TOG) **29**, 38 (2010)
5. Cignoni, P., Rocchini, C., Scopigno, R.: Metro: measuring error on simplified surfaces. In: Computer Graphics Forum, vol. 17, pp. 167–174. Wiley Online Library (1998)
6. Consensus, A.: Consensus development conference: diagnosis, prophylaxis, and treatment of osteoporosis. Am. J. Med. **94**(6), 646–650 (1993)
7. Fuchs, J., Scheidt-Nave, C., Kuhnert, R.: 12-month prevalence of osteoporosis in Germany. Robert Koch-Institut, Epidemiologie und Gesundheitsberichterstattung (2017)
8. Genant, H.K., et al.: Effects of romosozumab compared with teriparatide on bone density and mass at the spine and hip in postmenopausal women with low bone mass. J. Bone Mineral Res. **32**(1), 181–187 (2017)
9. Giambini, H., Dragomir-Daescu, D., Huddleston, P.M., Camp, J.J., An, K.N., Nassr, A.: The effect of quantitative computed tomography acquisition protocols on bone mineral density estimation. J. Biomech. Eng. **137**(11), 114502 (2015)
10. Glüer, C.C., et al.: Comparative effects of teriparatide and risedronate in glucocorticoid-induced osteoporosis in men: 18-month results of the eurogiops trial. J. Bone Mineral Res. **28**(6), 1355–1368 (2013)
11. Guglielmi, G., Grimston, S.K., Fischer, K.C., Pacifici, R.: Osteoporosis: diagnosis with lateral and posteroanterior dual X-ray absorptiometry compared with quantitative CT. Radiology **192**(3), 845–850 (1994)
12. Haidekker, M., Andresen, R., Evertsz, C., Banzer, D., Peitgen, H.: Evaluation of the cortical structure in high resolution CT images of lumbar vertebrae by analysing low bone mineral density clusters and cortical profiles. Br. J. Radiol. **70**(840), 1222–1228 (1997)
13. Haidekker, M., Andresen, R., Werner, H.: Relationship between structural parameters, bone mineral density and fracture load in lumbar vertebrae, based on high-resolution computed tomography, quantitative computed tomography and compression tests. Osteoporos. Int. **9**(5), 433–440 (1999)
14. Jordt, A., Koch, R.: Fast tracking of deformable objects in depth and colour video. In: BMVC, pp. 1–11 (2011)
15. Kalender, W.: Technical foundations of spiral CT. J. belge de radiologie **78**(2), 68–74 (1995)
16. Kalender, W.A., Felsenberg, D., Genant, H.K., Fischer, M., Dequeker, J., Reeve, J.: The European spine phantom–a tool for standardization and quality control in spinal bone mineral measurements by DXA and QCT. Eur. J. Radiol. **20**(2), 83–92 (1995)

17. Kang, Y., Engelke, K., Kalender, W.A.: A new accurate and precise 3-D segmentation method for skeletal structures in volumetric CT data. IEEE Trans. Med. Imaging **22**(5), 586–598 (2003)
18. Mastmeyer, A., Engelke, K., Fuchs, C., Kalender, W.A.: A hierarchical 3D segmentation method and the definition of vertebral body coordinate systems for QCT of the lumbar spine. Med. Image Anal. **10**(4), 560–577 (2006)
19. Mastmeyer, A., Engelke, K., Meller, S., Kalender, W.: A new 3D method to segment the lumbar vertebral bodies and to determine bone mineral density and geometry. In: Proceedings of Medical Image Understanding and Analysis. University of Bristol, UK (2005)
20. Meyer, M., Desbrun, M., Schröder, P., Barr, A.H.: Discrete differential-geometry operators for triangulated 2-manifolds. In: Hege, H.C., Polthier, K. (eds.) Visualization and Mathematics III. Mathematics and Visualization, pp. 35–57. Springer, Heidelberg (2003). https://doi.org/10.1007/978-3-662-05105-4_2
21. Ohkubo, M., et al.: Determination of point spread function in computed tomography accompanied with verification. Med. Phys. **36**(6Part1), 2089–2097 (2009)
22. Prevrhal, S., Engelke, K., Kalender, W.A.: Accuracy limits for the determination of cortical width and density: the influence of object size and CT imaging parameters. Phys. Med. Biol. **44**(3), 751 (1999)
23. Reinhold, S., Jordt, A., Koch, R.: Randomly sparsified synthesis for model-based deformation analysis. In: Rosenhahn, B., Andres, B. (eds.) GCPR 2016. LNCS, vol. 9796, pp. 143–154. Springer, Cham (2016). https://doi.org/10.1007/978-3-319-45886-1_12
24. Ritzel, H., Amling, M., Pösl, M., Hahn, M., Delling, G.: The thickness of human vertebral cortical bone and its changes in aging and osteoporosis: a histomorphometric analysis of the complete spinal column from thirty-seven autopsy specimens. J. Bone Mineral Res. **12**(1), 89–95 (1997)
25. Rockoff, S.D., Sweet, E., Bleustein, J.: The relative contribution of trabecular and cortical bone to the strength of human lumbar vertebrae. Calcif. Tissue Res. **3**(1), 163–175 (1969)
26. Siddiqi, K., Pizer, S.: Medial Representations: Mathematics, Algorithms and Applications, vol. 37. Springer, Heidelberg (2008)
27. Silva, M., Wang, C., Keaveny, T., Hayes, W.: Direct and computed tomography thickness measurements of the human, lumbar vertebral shell and endplate. Bone **15**(4), 409–414 (1994)
28. Smith, M., Dunkow, P., Lang, D.: Treatment of osteoporosis: missed opportunities in the hospital fracture clinic. Ann. Roy. Coll. Surg. Engl. **86**(5), 344 (2004)
29. Sorkine, O., Alexa, M.: As-rigid-as-possible surface modeling. In: Symposium on Geometry Processing, vol. 4, pp. 109–116 (2007)
30. Treece, G.M., Gee, A.H., Mayhew, P., Poole, K.E.: High resolution cortical bone thickness measurement from clinical CT data. Med. Image Anal. **14**(3), 276–290 (2010)

Parcel Tracking by Detection in Large Camera Networks

Sascha Clausen(✉), Claudius Zelenka, Tobias Schwede,
and Reinhard Koch

Department of Computer Science, Kiel University, Kiel, Germany
{sac,cze,tosc,rk}@informatik.uni-kiel.de

Abstract. Inside parcel distribution hubs, several tenth of up 100 000 parcels processed each day get lost. Human operators have to tediously recover these parcels by searching through large amounts of video footage from the installed large-scale camera network. We want to assist these operators and work towards an automatic solution. The challenge lies both in the size of the hub with a high number of cameras and in the adverse conditions. We describe and evaluate an industry scale tracking framework based on state-of-the-art methods such as Mask R-CNN. Moreover, we adapt a siamese network inspired feature vector matching with a novel feature improver network, which increases tracking performance. Our calibration method exploits a calibration parcel and is suitable for both overlapping and non-overlapping camera views. It requires little manual effort and needs only a single drive-by of the calibration parcel for each conveyor belt. With these methods, most parcels can be tracked start-to-end.

Keywords: Multi-object tracking · Tracking by Detection ·
Instance segmentation · Camera network calibration

1 Introduction

Parcel delivery is a vital part of today's society. Parcel delivery companies process their parcels in parcel hubs, so that every parcel reaches the right recipient. Some parcels are directed to the wrong destination or simply get lost by falling off the conveyor belts. This can pertain several tenth per 100 000 parcels sent. To recover them, parcel hubs are equipped with large-scale camera networks to surveil the parcels. A camera network may consist of up to 200 cameras inside a single distribution hub. When a parcel gets lost, a human operator views videos starting from the entry scan to see where it got lost. This is a tedious, time consuming and tiring task. We propose a tracking framework to assist the operators in their work. It is important to note that our framework operates on

Electronic supplementary material The online version of this chapter (https://doi.org/10.1007/978-3-030-12939-2_7) contains supplementary material, which is available to authorized users.

© Springer Nature Switzerland AG 2019
T. Brox et al. (Eds.): GCPR 2018, LNCS 11269, pp. 89–104, 2019.
https://doi.org/10.1007/978-3-030-12939-2_7

an existing camera network and that no extra hardware such as RFID scanners are required.

Parcel hubs are highly heterogeneous: Different conveyor belt types and colors, different conveyor belt and camera topology, manual or (semi-)automatic sorting, varying illumination and strongly varying viewpoints (Fig. 1). Also the parcels can be very diverse and occur in all materials, colors and dimensions. It is possible to see car tires next to very small brown paper board parcels. However, depending on operating conditions, there may also be a large number of the same kind of parcels. Traditional approaches and trackers such as background subtraction have problems with changing illumination, occlusions and especially with separating touching parcels, which occur in case of parcel jams. These conditions in combination with a low frame rate of approx. 5 fps and a high maximum object velocity of approx. $2\,\mathrm{ms^{-1}}$ define the setting for this application oriented research in tracking algorithms.

Fig. 1. Example images from four parcel hubs (Color figure online)

1.1 Related Work

There are only few related works in the domain of camera based tracking of parcels in multi-camera systems. [15] proposes a multi-camera system to track parcels on a short conveyor belt with 7 m length, which is a much smaller problem setting than a large-scale parcel hub. Their solution is based on applying the KLT-tracker [31] on feature corner points, which is not practical for our problem with much lower frame rates, larger intra-frame motion, variation, and background variability. Other systems are optimized for robot vision on conveyor belts [29] and focus more on how to grab an object with a robotic arm, than fast tracking with low frame-rate. In [32] for a related task, tracking persons across non overlapping camera, albeit with a higher frame rate, the Hungarian algorithm [17] for label assignment and Kalman filter for prediction is used.

One aspect of tracking parcels is that the process of detecting parcels can be seen as separating them from background. However, background subtraction techniques [26,30] are very fast, but cannot handle very dirty or irregular backgrounds and touching objects cannot be separated. Large progress has been made in recent years in deep learning based general object detection algorithms, examples are Faster R-CNN [28] and SSD [21]. Even more useful for our task are algorithms, which also provide instance segmentation, i.e. FCIS [19] and Mask R-CNN [9] and thus allow more accurate localization.

The second aspect is the tracking itself, but we must consider that detection quality is key for tracking performance, as shown in [2], where an increase of 18.9% in performance is made by changing the detector. In our task, we have a lower frame rate compared to benchmarks (e.g. [24]), which means that objects can change their appearance significantly between frames and their motion is not constant, but depends on the interaction of the parcels. Hence, some approaches that provide very high benchmark results, such as Tubelets [14], are clearly not suitable for our task. Also, we are strongly limited in the amounts of training data for the tracking task, especially for longer sequences. This problem of insufficient training data is even more severe for recurrent neural networks, which have recently shown good results [25].

Also highly successful in benchmarks, but easier to train and not as dependent on high frame rates is the approach of [18], where siamese networks are used to solve the problem of re-identifying the tracked objects and [5], where the feature vectors of the CNN backbone of the detector are used as identifying features.

1.2   Contribution

The difficult conditions are what separates our application oriented research from many of the related works optimized for benchmark data introduced above. The contribution of this article lies in the industrial large scale application and adaptation of these previously benchmark optimized algorithms.

Inspired by this recent success of deep architectures on benchmark data we propose a two-stage Tracking-by-Detection approach via [9] by detecting the parcels with a CNN and assigning the detections between frames similar to [5,18,32], with an additional novel feature improver network. We show that even though benchmark optimized, their approach and ideas are transferable and adaptable to tracking parcels across multiple camera in parcel distribution hubs.

2 Detection

The parcels are detected via state-of-the-art instance segmentation with Mask R-CNN [9], because the precise contour of the parcels gives additional informations to tell them apart. We use the implementation of Matterport [23] with pre-trained weights on the COCO data set [20]. The model is fine-tuned on 3306 hand-labeled images from 37 different cameras containing 14 284 parcels. The training data is augmented by horizontal flipping, darkening the images by adjusting the gamma value and using random crops of the image.

We train the network with stochastic gradient descent and a learning rate of 0.002. The training is split in two stages: First, the RPN, the classifier and the mask heads are trained for 70 000 iterations. Then the stages 4 and 5 of the ResNet backbone are additionally trained for another 200 000 iterations. We use a weight decay of 0.0001, a momentum of 0.9 and a batch size of 2. The learning rate is smaller by a factor of 10 compared to [9] because larger learning rates lead to worse results and exploding gradients [23].

2.1 Feature Improver Network

Mask R-CNN uses the output of the ROIAlign layer for the classification and segmentation of each region proposal. This output can be seen as a feature vector for each region proposal. We define the similarity of two parcel feature vectors as the normalized scalar product between them to get a similarity value between 0 and 1. We observed that feature vectors of visually similar parcel images (e.g. images of the same parcel in adjacent frames) have a higher similarity than parcel images of different parcels. The similarity can thus be used to assign the detections in adjacent frames to the correct parcels (for details see Sect. 4). Inspired by siamese networks [4,5,18], we propose a *feature improver network* as an additional head for Mask R-CNN (Fig. 2). This head is supposed to make the feature vectors more distinguishable via the scalar product.

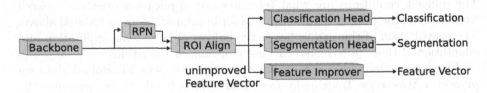

Fig. 2. Structure of our neural network

The feature improver network is a simple fully connected network with one layer consisting of 1024 neurons. As a proof of concept, we first train Mask R-CNN and extract the outputs of the ROIAlign layer afterwards. The feature improver network is then trained with these unimproved feature vectors in a siamese network fashion, i.e. we normalize the unimproved feature vectors and calculate the dot product of the two siamese network branches. As a result, the output lies in the interval [0, 1] and we can use binary cross entropy as loss function. The training target is to maximize the scalar product of feature vectors from the same parcel in adjacent images and to minimize the scalar product of feature vectors from different parcels. We train the feature improver network on the same data set as Mask R-CNN with the Adadelta [34] optimizer for 1000 iterations using a batch size of 200 and a learning rate of 0.01.

3 Calibration

For the tracking across different cameras, we require the exact topology of the conveyor belts, the cameras and their viewpoints. Therefore, before discussing the tracking component of our system, we will briefly introduce our calibration method.

Our system is designed to be in large parts automatic without requiring additional external knowledge of the network. Our approach consists of a calibration parcel, which is filmed as it moves across every conveyor belt, as in Fig. 3a. The calibration parcel has an ArUco [7] marker on each side to provide at least one calibration target from each viewing direction.

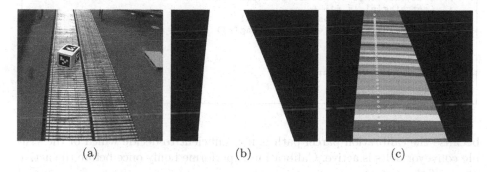

(a)   (b)   (c)

Fig. 3. (a) shows one recording of the calibration parcel on the conveyor belt. The manually annotated mask for the same camera view as in (a) can be seen in (b). In (c) the reconstructed surface of the conveyor belt is displayed. The different colored pieces are the planar elements, the surface is constructed of. The yellow circles are the projected positions of the calibration parcel and describe its trajectory during the calibration. (Color figure online)

The marker can be easily detected and used as a reference to intrinsically calibrate each camera. A further result of the calibration are relative 3D positions of the calibration parcel to each camera. We can approximate the conveyor belt's surface with piecewise planar segments, see Fig. 3c. Furthermore, we capture the calibration images with their timestamps. The 3D positions combined with their respective timestamps results in the calibration parcel path. With the help of this path we can predict the position of other parcels.

Knowledge about the conveyor belt region is needed to identify and ignore parcels besides it. The external contour of the conveyor belt is manually annotated, resulting in a mask as in Fig. 3b. This cannot be done automatically,

Listing 1. Pseudocode for the intra-camera tracking

```
Input: parcels  - the parcels from the last frame
       contours - the detected contours from the current frame

costMatrix = array[size(parcels)][size(contours)]
unassignedContours = set()

for p ∈ parcels {
  prediction = predictionForCurrentFrame(p)
  vp = getFeatureVector(p)
  for c ∈ contours {
    unassignedContours.add(c)
    vc = getFeatureVector(c)
    distance = computeDistance(prediction, c)
    //The value 0.0027 was chosen empirically
    s = max(0, 1 - (distance * 0.0027))
    similarity = scalarProduct(vp, vc)
    costs = 1 - (s * similarity)
    costMatrix[p][c] = costs
  }
}

//Matching is a p × 1 vector that contains the assigned
//contour for every parcel.
matching = hungarianMatching(costMatrix)

for p ∈ parcels {
  //-1 defines that no matching is possible
  if (matching[p] != -1) {
    addContourToParcel(matching[p], p)
    unassignedContours.remove(matching[p])
  }
}

for c ∈ unassignedContours {
  createNewParcel(c)
}
```

because the calibration parcel path is not sufficient to decide which of the visible conveyor belts is active. Calibration is performed only once before the active phase of the system.

4   Tracking

An investigation process is started when a parcel gets lost. This process tracks the lost parcel from the last known position, which is marked by a human operator. The tracking consists of the tracking inside camera views (intra-camera tracking) and the tracking between overlapping and non-overlapping camera views (inter-camera tracking). The intersection points of different camera views are determined by the calibration.

In the following, we explain the steps of our intra-camera tracking as specified with pseudo code in Listing 1. The intra-camera assignment can be seen as a weighted bipartite matching problem where every parcel in frame f has a corresponding one in frame $f+1$. Therefore, we compute a cost matrix for all possible matchings of the detections in both frames. The matching cost of two detections is defined as the scalar product of their feature vectors. The feature vectors are computed by the neural network proposed in Sect. 2.1. To improve the matching, we predict the positions of the detections in frame f for the frame $f + 1$ with the optical flow algorithm proposed in [16]. The similarity is then scaled with the distance between the predicted and detected positions. From a cost matrix, the matching with the lowest costs is computed using the Hungarian algorithm [17]. Besides matching the contours of the current and the next frame as outlined in pseudo code, we implement an occlusion handling technique, which also handles spurious missed detection. We include the unassigned contours in the current frame, shifted by the optical flow, as additional matching candidates in the next frame.

A parcel can only be tracked in this way a limited amount of times, without getting assigned to a detected contour. After that it is marked as lost and not further handled in this camera. This allows us to continue tracking a parcel even if it has not been tracked in some frames in between for various reasons.

(a) Camera view with the overlapping area in the right upper corner (b) Enlarged view of the overlapping area

(c) Image from the next camera at the same time

Fig. 4. Parcels may look very different from neighboring cameras.

In contrast, the inter-camera assignment can not be done by the visual appearance of the parcels because neighboring cameras can have very different poses, as can be seen in Fig. 4. The reasons for the differences between two view include destination labels, which are only on one side of the parcel, and asymmetric applied tape. Therefore, the inter-camera assignment is performed by projecting the parcels from one camera to the next by using their extrinsic calibration. Although the contour of a parcel is known from the detection, we do not have the 3D shape or height. Therefore, we use the conveyor belt surface as an intermediate step for the projection.

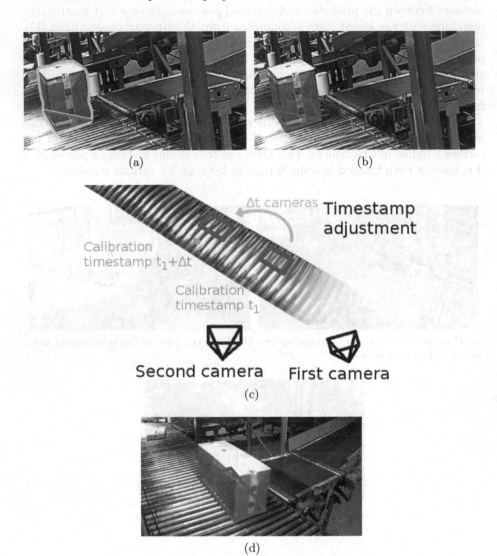

Fig. 5. Illustration of the different steps for the inter-camera tracking. (a) shows the approximation of a triangle (red) for the visible bottom part of a contour (yellow). In (b) the estimated parallelogram for the parcel base (blue) based on the previous approximated triangle can be seen. The schematic projection onto the conveyor plane surface and the time adjustment can be viewed in (c). In this drawing the time difference between both cameras images is defined by Δt. The calibration parcel movement in the time Δt is depicted in orange. Furthermore, the positions of the quadrangle before and after the time adjustment are shown. (d) shows the projection from the conveyor plane surface to the image plane of the second camera. (Color figure online)

The different steps of the inter-camera tracking are shown in Fig. 5. In the first step, we regard the upward surface normal direction and select those parcel contour points, which are located in the opposite direction. This results in the bottom part of the parcel contour, which is in-plane with the conveyor belt. Then we approximate it with a triangle, shown in Fig. 5a. The second step is to estimate the parcel base by extending the triangle to a parallelogram, as shown in Fig. 5b. In the third step, we project the parallelogram onto the conveyor belt surface. The projected position is adjusted using the time difference between both cameras and the calibration parcels velocity and direction, for this point. Lastly, the quadrangle is projected from the conveyor belt surface into the image plane of the second camera, as shown in Fig. 5d. All relevant contours in a frame are projected in this way into the next camera. Then these projected contours have to be matched with the detected ones. This is done by defining the costs c as $c = 1 - IoU$ and solving the problem with the Hungarian algorithm. Examples of the tracking can be seen in Figs. 6 and 7.

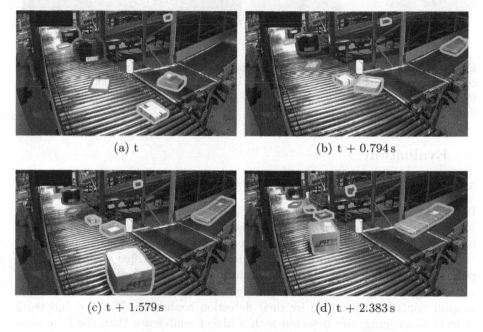

(a) t

(b) t + 0.794 s

(c) t + 1.579 s

(d) t + 2.383 s

Fig. 6. These images show the tracking of multiple parcels in one camera view. The color of the contours depends on the parcel they are assigned to, whereas every parcel has its own unique color. The images (a) to (d) show subsequent moments of the tracking. (Color figure online)

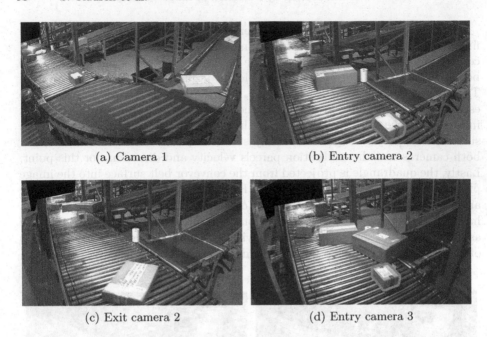

(a) Camera 1   (b) Entry camera 2

(c) Exit camera 2   (d) Entry camera 3

Fig. 7. These images show the tracking of one parcel over multiple cameras. The orange contour highlights the tracked parcel. The images (a) to (d) show the tracked parcel from different camera views over time, as it progresses along the conveyor belt. (Color figure online)

5   Evaluation

5.1   Detection

If not stated otherwise, the training is conducted with a training set of 3306 images with a ResNet-101 backbone. For evaluation purposes a sequence of 857 images is used. The threshold confidence for the detections is set to 0.8.

Usually, the performance of object detectors is quantified with the average precision (AP) [9,21,28]. The AP emphasizes accurate bounding boxes while neglecting classification accuracy [27] by ordering all detections above a given ground truth IoU threshold by their detection confidence. If all ground truth objects of an image are detected with a higher confidence than the false positive detections, the AP gets misleading: It reaches 1 and is not affected by any low-confidence false-positive detections. Because false positive detections could confuse our tracking algorithm, we propose a different metric to compare our results. Instead of calculating the scores for each image independently and averaging the values over the whole validation set, we count the true positives, the false positives and the ground truth annotations for all validation image and calculate one global precision, recall and F1 score. These global scores allow us to select the best training result for the requirements of our tracking algorithm.

Different training and network configurations have been tested (Table 1):

- **Backbone network:** A deeper architecture improves the accuracy, but results in a slightly longer inference time of ~170 ms instead of ~150 ms per image on a Nvidia Titan Xp.
- **Data augmentation by darkening the training images:** Because some parcel hubs have darker areas, we darken some training images to simulate bad lighting conditions. This augmentation does not change the F1 score significantly, but increases the precision at the cost of lower recall.
- **Data augmentation by using random crops of the training images:** Random crops of the training images are used to simulate only partly visible parcels at the image borders.

Table 1. Comparison of different training results with IoU = 0.5

	Precision	Recall	F1
Reference ResNet-101	0.92	0.812	0.863
ResNet-50	0.927	0.78	0.847
Without darkening	0.952	0.794	0.866

5.2   Tracking

Because tracking is conducted in two phases (inter-camera tracking and intra-camera tracking), we also have two different tests to evaluate the tracking performance. The first test aims at evaluating the intra-camera tracking performance, while the second test evaluates the combined performance of inter- and intra-camera tracking.

The test set for the first test contains data of three different cameras. The first two cameras have a frame rate of 8 and the third of 5 fps. The data set contains 236, 233 and 161 images for the cameras respectively. For each tracking test we compare different configurations of the intra-camera tracking. We test the tracking as described in Sect. 4 with the improved feature vector, unimproved feature vector and IoU of the prediction for the similarity computation of parcels. Furthermore, we test the tracking with the improved and unimproved feature vector without the optical flow prediction and the distance based scaling. All configurations are compared by computing the MOTA-score [1]. For the computation of this score, detected contours are matched with ground truth contours, if their IoU ratio is not less than 0.5.

In the second test, the parcels are tracked across four cameras up to a specific point. We evaluate the tracking performance end-to-end. If for a track the initial parcel is the same as the tracked object at the specified point, the track is labeled successful. This also applies if the tracked parcel was mismatched in the tracking process, but was recovered to the correct parcel. The data set for the test contains the start positions of 38 parcels. The cameras have an average frame rate of 5 fps.

Table 2. Results of the intra-camera tracking and combined tracking test. The segmentation model for intra-camera tracking achieves 111 false positives and 455 false negatives for the 2742 annotated parcels. For the combined test, single parcels are tracked across multiple cameras up to a specific point.

	Intra-camera		Combined
	Mismatches	MOTA-score	Correctly tracked parcels
Without optical flow prediction:			
Feature vector	78	0.7651	26.32%
Improved feature vector	54	0.7739	31.58%
With optical flow prediction:			
IoU	59	0.7721	65.79%
Feature vector	30	0.7826	78.95%
Improved feature vector	22	0.7856	81.58%

As seen in Table 2, using the improved feature vectors without optical flow decreases the mismatches from 78 to 54. Using optical flow prediction further decreases to 30 and 22 respectively. Causes for remaining errors are sudden changes in the velocity or direction or occlusion by body parts or held parcels and other objects. If the matching is done with the IoU ratio, 59 mismatches are encountered, caused by relatively large parcel movements between following frames induced by the low rate of the cameras. Furthermore, the usage of feature vectors allows rediscovering similar parcels, even if the prediction does not overlap with the contour in the next frame.

The results of the second test in Table 2 are similar. The optical flow prediction results in tracking more than twice as many parcels correctly. The usage of the improved feature vector raises performance slightly compared to the unimproved one. Surprisingly, there are cases in which the tracking is successful with the unimproved feature vector, but fails with the improved one. In these cases both trackers switch targets to a wrong parcel. However, the tracker with the unimproved feature vector switches back one or two frames later. We reason that this is caused by the high similarity of the unimproved feature vectors to each other. This allows mismatches between similar parcels to occur more often and also makes it easier to switch back to the correct parcel after mismatching. Another interesting aspect is the comparison between the IoU tracking and the improved feature vector tracking without the optical flow prediction. Although the numbers of mismatches are similar, the IoU tracking tracks twice as many parcels correctly. We conclude that the differences in performance are caused by the sensitivity of the feature vector matching to lighting changes and similar parcels.

Tracking Baseline Comparison. For baseline comparison we conduct the tracking evaluation on the test data with the OpenCV implementations of the following tracking algorithms: Boosting [8], KCF [6,11], MedianFlow [12], TLD [13], GOTURN [10], MOSSE [3] and CSRT [22]. The tracker's parameters were optimized for the best results on the test set.

(a) Initialization bounding box   (b) All OpenCV trackers except for CSRT lost the package

(c) CSRT lost the parcel   (d) Only our algorithm tracks the parcel until the end

Fig. 8. These images show a comparison between our tracking algorithm and the tracking algorithms of OpenCV. The change of direction and the shadow lead to failure of the other tracking algorithms.

A challenging part of the test set can be seen in Fig. 8. All tracking algorithms get initialized with the same bounding box (Fig. 8a). Most trackers work well as long as the target parcel does not change direction. When the parcel changes direction and reaches the shadow, only CSRT manages to stay on target (Fig. 8b), but loses the parcel five frames later (Fig. 8c). A similar tracking behavior can be seen for all other test parcels, which results in no correctly tracked parcel in the test set.

6 Conclusion

We presented a multi-object, multi-camera tracking system for parcels, designed for large parcel hubs. The system is designed to work in large scale industrial environments. It profits from the automatic calibration process, which reduces the calibration effort significantly. With this system and our novel feature vector improver network, we are currently able to track about 81% of the parcels correctly. While in most cases the tracking works smoothly, especially cases of human interaction with parcels cause the tracking to fail. In these cases human operators are still needed. Furthermore, a human operator is additionally needed to initialize the tracking process by selecting the parcel in the image.

In the future we plan to automate the tracking initialization by using timestamps and compulsory barcode scans at the entrance of the parcel hub. A possibility to improve the runtime performance is to use SSD [21] or YOLO [27] for the detection and only compute segmentations when they are needed. Another direction could be the exploration of more dedicated architectures or specialized loss functions like triplet loss [33] for the feature improver head, to minimize the number of mismatches. Considering the current need to capture all possible paths to neighboring cameras, the calibration effort can be reduced by changing the routine for the inter-camera tracking, so that it does not rely on the path of the calibration parcel. Another possible avenue of improvement is of course increasing our set of training data for both tracking and detection.

Our evaluation data set was assembled to provide a realistic impression of overall tracking performance. We are planning to assemble different evaluation data sets with only common or only particular difficult situations, to be able to analyze tracking behavior in more detail.

Even if our system is not able to track all parcels fully automatic yet, we have done a major step in this direction. We are confident that this research helps reducing the occasions human operators are needed to manually track parcels in video data.

Acknowledgments. This work was supported by the Central Innovation Programme for SMEs of the Federal Ministry for Economic Affairs and Energy of Germany under grant agreement number 16KN044302.

References

1. Bernardin, K., Stiefelhagen, R.: Evaluating multiple object tracking performance: the CLEAR MOT metrics. EURASIP J. Image Video Process. **2008** (2008). https://doi.org/10.1155/2008/246309
2. Bewley, A., Ge, Z., Ott, L., Ramos, F.T., Upcroft, B.: Simple online and realtime tracking. In: 2016 IEEE International Conference on Image Processing, pp. 3464–3468 (2016). https://doi.org/10.1109/ICIP.2016.7533003
3. Bolme, D.S., Beveridge, J.R., Draper, B.A., Lui, Y.M.: Visual object tracking using adaptive correlation filters. In: The Twenty-Third IEEE Conference on Computer Vision and Pattern Recognition, pp. 2544–2550 (2010). https://doi.org/10.1109/CVPR.2010.5539960
4. Bromley, J., Guyon, I., LeCun, Y., Säckinger, E., Shah, R.: Signature verification using a Siamese time delay neural network. In: Advances in Neural Information Processing Systems, vol. 6, pp. 737–744 (1993)
5. Chahyati, D., Fanany, M.I., Arymurthy, A.M.: Tracking people by detection using CNN features. Proc. Comput. Sci. **124**, 167–172 (2017). https://doi.org/10.1016/j.procs.2017.12.143

6. Danelljan, M., Khan, F.S., Felsberg, M., van de Weijer, J.: Adaptive color attributes for real-time visual tracking. In: 2014 IEEE Conference on Computer Vision and Pattern Recognition, pp. 1090–1097 (2014). https://doi.org/10.1109/CVPR.2014.143

7. Garrido-Jurado, S., Muñoz-Salinas, R., Madrid-Cuevas, F.J., Marín-Jiménez, M.J.: Automatic generation and detection of highly reliable fiducial markers under occlusion. Pattern Recogn. **47**(6), 2280–2292 (2014). https://doi.org/10.1016/j.patcog.2014.01.005

8. Grabner, H., Grabner, M., Bischof, H.: Real-time tracking via on-line boosting. In: Proceedings of the British Machine Vision Conference 2006, pp. 47–56 (2006). https://doi.org/10.5244/C.20.6

9. He, K., Gkioxari, G., Dollár, P., Girshick, R.B.: Mask R-CNN. In: IEEE International Conference on Computer Vision, pp. 2980–2988 (2017). https://doi.org/10.1109/ICCV.2017.322

10. Held, D., Thrun, S., Savarese, S.: Learning to track at 100 FPS with deep regression networks. In: Leibe, B., Matas, J., Sebe, N., Welling, M. (eds.) ECCV 2016. LNCS, vol. 9905, pp. 749–765. Springer, Cham (2016). https://doi.org/10.1007/978-3-319-46448-0_45

11. Henriques, J.F., Caseiro, R., Martins, P., Batista, J.: Exploiting the circulant structure of tracking-by-detection with kernels. In: Fitzgibbon, A., Lazebnik, S., Perona, P., Sato, Y., Schmid, C. (eds.) ECCV 2012. LNCS, vol. 7575, pp. 702–715. Springer, Heidelberg (2012). https://doi.org/10.1007/978-3-642-33765-9_50

12. Kalal, Z., Mikolajczyk, K., Matas, J.: Forward-backward error: automatic detection of tracking failures. In: 20th International Conference on Pattern Recognition, pp. 2756–2759 (2010). https://doi.org/10.1109/ICPR.2010.675

13. Kalal, Z., Mikolajczyk, K., Matas, J.: Tracking-learning-detection. IEEE Trans. Pattern Anal. Mach. Intell. **34**(7), 1409–1422 (2012). https://doi.org/10.1109/TPAMI.2011.239

14. Kang, K., Ouyang, W., Li, H., Wang, X.: Object detection from video tubelets with convolutional neural networks. In: 2016 IEEE Conference on Computer Vision and Pattern Recognition, pp. 817–825 (2016). https://doi.org/10.1109/CVPR.2016.95

15. Karaca, H.N., Akınlar, C.: A multi-camera vision system for real-time tracking of parcels moving on a conveyor belt. In: Yolum, I., Güngör, T., Gürgen, F., Özturan, C. (eds.) ISCIS 2005. LNCS, vol. 3733, pp. 708–717. Springer, Heidelberg (2005). https://doi.org/10.1007/11569596_73

16. Kroeger, T., Timofte, R., Dai, D., Van Gool, L.: Fast optical flow using dense inverse search. In: Leibe, B., Matas, J., Sebe, N., Welling, M. (eds.) ECCV 2016. LNCS, vol. 9908, pp. 471–488. Springer, Cham (2016). https://doi.org/10.1007/978-3-319-46493-0_29

17. Kuhn, H.W., Yaw, B.: The Hungarian method for the assignment problem. Naval Res. Logist. Q. **2**, 83–97 (1955)

18. Leal-Taixé, L., Canton-Ferrer, C., Schindler, K.: Learning by tracking: Siamese CNN for robust target association. In: 2016 IEEE Conference on Computer Vision and Pattern Recognition Workshops, pp. 418–425 (2016). https://doi.org/10.1109/CVPRW.2016.59

19. Li, Y., Qi, H., Dai, J., Ji, X., Wei, Y.: Fully convolutional instance-aware semantic segmentation. In: 2017 IEEE Conference on Computer Vision and Pattern Recognition, pp. 4438–4446 (2017). https://doi.org/10.1109/CVPR.2017.472

20. Lin, T.-Y., et al.: Microsoft COCO: common objects in context. In: Fleet, D., Pajdla, T., Schiele, B., Tuytelaars, T. (eds.) ECCV 2014. LNCS, vol. 8693, pp. 740–755. Springer, Cham (2014). https://doi.org/10.1007/978-3-319-10602-1_48

21. Liu, W., et al.: SSD: single shot multibox detector. In: Leibe, B., Matas, J., Sebe, N., Welling, M. (eds.) ECCV 2016. LNCS, vol. 9905, pp. 21–37. Springer, Cham (2016). https://doi.org/10.1007/978-3-319-46448-0_2
22. Lukezic, A., Vojír, T., Zajc, L.C., Matas, J., Kristan, M.: Discriminative correlation filter tracker with channel and spatial reliability. Int. J. Comput. Vis. 126(7), 671–688 (2018). https://doi.org/10.1007/s11263-017-1061-3
23. Matterport: Mask R-CNN for object detection and segmentation. https://github.com/matterport/Mask_RCNN
24. Milan, A., Leal-Taixé, L., Reid, I.D., Roth, S., Schindler, K.: MOT16: a benchmark for multi-object tracking (2016). https://arxiv.org/abs/1603.00831
25. Milan, A., Rezatofighi, S.H., Dick, A.R., Reid, I.D., Schindler, K.: Online multi-target tracking using recurrent neural networks. In: Proceedings of the Thirty-First AAAI Conference on Artificial Intelligence, pp. 4225–4232 (2017)
26. Radke, R.J., Andra, S., Al-Kofahi, O., Roysam, B.: Image change detection algorithms: a systematic survey. IEEE Trans. Image Process. 14(3), 294–307 (2005). https://doi.org/10.1109/TIP.2004.838698
27. Redmon, J., Farhadi, A.: YOLOv3: an incremental improvement (2018). https://arxiv.org/abs/1804.02767
28. Ren, S., He, K., Girshick, R.B., Sun, J.: Faster R-CNN: towards real-time object detection with region proposal networks. IEEE Trans. Pattern Anal. Mach. Intell. 39(6), 1137–1149 (2017). https://doi.org/10.1109/TPAMI.2016.2577031
29. Shin, I.S., Nam, S.H., Yu, H.G., Roberts, R.G., Moon, S.B.: Conveyor visual tracking using robot vision. In: Proceedings of 2006 Florida Conference on Recent Advances in Robotics, pp. 1–5. Citeseer (2006)
30. Tang, Z., Miao, Z., Wan, Y.: Background subtraction using running Gaussian average and frame difference. In: Ma, L., Rauterberg, M., Nakatsu, R. (eds.) ICEC 2007. LNCS, vol. 4740, pp. 411–414. Springer, Heidelberg (2007). https://doi.org/10.1007/978-3-540-74873-1_50
31. Tomasi, C., Kanade, T.: Detection and tracking of feature points. Technical report. Carnegie Mellon University, Technical Report CMU-CS-91-132 (1991)
32. Wang, X., Türetken, E., Fleuret, F., Fua, P.: Tracking interacting objects optimally using integer programming. In: Fleet, D., Pajdla, T., Schiele, B., Tuytelaars, T. (eds.) ECCV 2014. LNCS, vol. 8689, pp. 17–32. Springer, Cham (2014). https://doi.org/10.1007/978-3-319-10590-1_2
33. Weinberger, K.Q., Blitzer, J., Saul, L.K.: Distance metric learning for large margin nearest neighbor classification. In: Advances in Neural Information Processing Systems, vol. 18, pp. 1473–1480 (2005)
34. Zeiler, M.D.: ADADELTA: an adaptive learning rate method (2012). https://arxiv.org/abs/1212.5701

Segmentation of Head and Neck Organs at Risk Using CNN with Batch Dice Loss

Oldřich Kodym[1(✉)], Michal Španěl[1,2], and Adam Herout[1]

[1] Graph@FIT, Brno University of Technology, Brno, Czech Republic
ikodym@fit.vutbr.cz
[2] TESCAN 3DIM, Brno, Czech Republic
spanel@3dim-laboratory.cz

Abstract. This paper deals with segmentation of organs at risk (OAR) in head and neck area in CT images which is a crucial step for reliable intensity modulated radiotherapy treatment. We introduce a convolution neural network with encoder-decoder architecture and a new loss function, the batch soft Dice loss function, used to train the network. The resulting model produces segmentations of every OAR in the public MICCAI 2015 Head And Neck Auto-Segmentation Challenge dataset. Despite the heavy class imbalance in the data, we improve accuracy of current state-of-the-art methods by 0.33 mm in terms of average surface distance and by 0.11 in terms of Dice overlap coefficient on average.

Keywords: Convolutional neural networks ·
Computed Tomography · Multi-label segmentation ·
Head and neck radiotherapy

1 Introduction

Organs at risk (OAR) in head and neck area is a group of organs at potential risk of damage during radiotherapy application. Their three-dimensional segmentation in medical Computed Tomography (CT) images is a first step required for reliable planning in image-guided radiotherapy during head and neck cancer treatment [1]. Producing 3D segmentation in clinical data manually is a tedious task and therefore effort is being put into developing automatic methods that would be able to produce accurate segmentation masks for the objects of interest. In area of head and neck OAR, however, this is a very challenging task as the soft tissue structures have very little contrast.

The MICCAI 2015 Head and Neck Auto Segmentation Challenge [2] provides a dataset for evaluation of head and neck OAR segmentation methods. Furthermore, the challenge also defined baseline methods for head and neck segmentation for each structure. Most of the approaches relied on statistical shape model [3] or active appearance model [4] registration with atlas-based initialization during the challenge. Although several methods where able to produce

© Springer Nature Switzerland AG 2019
T. Brox et al. (Eds.): GCPR 2018, LNCS 11269, pp. 105–114, 2019.
https://doi.org/10.1007/978-3-030-12939-2_8

segmentations of every structure, especially smaller objects such as submandibular glands, optic nerves and optic chiasm didn't reach a satisfactory accuracy required for clinical application. More recent methods made use of more modern machine learning methods such as convolutional neural networks (CNN) that have been gaining a lot of popularity since the introduction of AlexNet in 2012 [5] in most of computer vision fields including medical image data analysis.

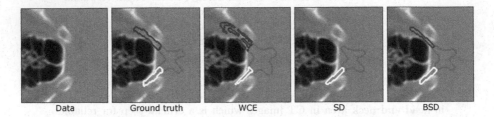

Fig. 1. Examples of optic nerves (blue, yellow) and chiasm (red) segmentation using various standard loss function such as weighted cross-entropy (WCE) and soft Dice (SD) and our Batch soft Dice (BSD) loss. (Color figure online)

Fritscher et al. [6] first used a patch-based CNN with 3 orthogonal input patches to obtain a pixel-wise prediction map for each structure, using atlas-based probability map for each structure as an additional input, slightly increasing accuracy of parotid and submandibular gland segmentation. Coincidentally, Ibragimov et al. [7] used a very similar model with a Markov random field post processing step. They obtained segmentation of all OARs but reaching accuracy of only 37% for optic chiasm and under 65% for optic nerves. Most recently, Wang et al. [8] applied a hierarchical random forest vertex regression method for some of the OAR, showing further improvement of accuracy of brain stem, mandible, and parotid gland segmentation.

In this paper we design a CNN with encoder-decoder architecture, first used in biomedical segmentation by Ronneberger et al. [9], and evaluate its performance on head and neck OAR segmentation task. Since the model fails to learn some of the structures when trained using the standard cross-entropy loss, we make use of Dice loss function introduced first by Pastor-Pellicer et al. [11] and later used for medical segmentation by Milletari et al. [10]. This form of *soft Dice loss* has been employed quite extensively in recent literature [12,13]. Despite obtaining acceptable results on most of the structures, we also observed rather low performance on smaller low-contrast structures when using standard Dice loss. We propose a modification to the standard soft Dice loss function – the *Batch soft Dice Loss* – to overcome this problem and show that it enables the model to outperform models trained using other loss functions. In case of optic chiasm and nerves segmentation we reach as much as 59% improvement over current state-of-the-art methods in terms of Dice overlap measure.

2   Proposed Method for Organ Segmentation

In this section, we describe the architecture of our CNN model and different loss functions that have been evaluated. We also give details on the training phase and data preprocessing.

2.1   Head and Neck Segmentation Challenge

The dataset includes CT scans of patients with manual segmentations of 6 anatomical structures which include brain stem (BS), mandible (MA), optic chiasm (OC), bilateral optic nerves (ON), parotid glands (PG), and submandibular glands (SG). Total of 48 patient scans of head and neck area are available in the challenge dataset. However, 18 of these scans contain incomplete ground truth annotation for some structures. Since our model is trained using image patches that span across almost complete head area, these scans had to be excluded from our experiments to prevent introducing false background voxels into the ground truth.

2.2   Model Architecture

Our segmentation model architecture is of encoder-decoder type [9]. Convolutional layers are coupled with max-pooling layers to increase the field of view of deeper features while decreasing their resolution in the first, encoder part. In the second, decoder part, the features are upscaled again using bilinear interpolation. Each upscaling step is accompanied by concatenating the feature maps from the encoder part of the model with matching resolution to improve the gradient flow through the model.

We limit our model to only operate on two-dimensional axial slices for the following two reasons. First, because we use 140×140 image patches to include enough context, there is an intra-image class imbalance issue. Although we compensate for this during the training as mentioned in the following sections, using three-dimensional image patches results in amplification of this issue because some structures, such as optic chiasm, are highly planar in the axial plane. Second, memory requirements are an issue here as well. The nature of multi-class segmentation requires mini-batches of data used in the training phase to contain a balanced number of image patches containing each of the structures in order to correctly compute the gradient step. This is easier to accomplish when using 2D image patches. Our results show that the two-dimensional approach has only small impact on the z-dimension discontinuities and the overall performance.

The architecture scheme is shown in Fig. 2. We only use standard 3×3 convolution kernel size. Each convolutional block encompasses convolution kernel filtering, batch normalization, and ReLU activation, except for the last convolutional block which uses softmax activation to produce the final label probabilities. Unlike U-net, we do not use any further regularization beyond batch normalization since the model does not tend to overfit. *Concatenation skip connections* that we employ have been shown to perform better than the popular

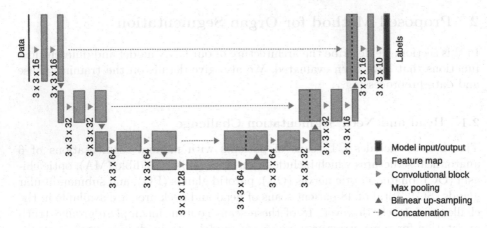

Fig. 2. Proposed segmentation model architecture. Series of two convolutions, batch normalizations and ReLU activations are used in each block. Down- and up-sampling is done using max-pooling and bilinear interpolation, respectively, with concatenation skip connections providing additional spatial information during up-sampling.

residual skip connections in segmentation of medical volumetric data [14]. U-net uses deconvolution layer to perform feature map upscaling but our experiments showed that bilinear interpolation performs at least as well. This is likely caused by the fact that the concatenation skip connections that were not being used when deconvolutional CNNs were first introduced provide sufficient information about fine structure to the model during upscaling.

2.3   Loss Functions and Optimization

Several different multi-class loss functions used for segmentation in current literature were evaluated in this paper along with our proposed batch Dice loss. We will use the following notation to introduce different loss functions used in our experiments. Let the number of image patches x_i in our training mini-batches be I and let each image patch consist of C pixels. The segmentation model then maps each of $I \times C = N$ pixels in the mini-batch to probability p_l for each of L labels. The training procedure ensures that the resulting output label probability vectors p_l^c correspond to one-hot encoded ground truth label vectors r_l^c as best as possible on the training data. During inference, we choose the output label l of each pixel c as

$$l^c = \arg \max_l \{p_l^c\}. \tag{1}$$

Cross-Entropy. Also known as log-loss, cross-entropy is the most widely used loss function for classification CNN. When applied to a segmentation task, cross-entropy measures the divergence of the predicted probability from the ground truth label for each pixel separately and then averages the value over all pixels in the mini-batch:

$$\mathcal{L}_{CE} = -\frac{1}{N} \sum_{c=1}^{N} \sum_{l=1}^{L} r_l^c \log(p_l^c) \tag{2}$$

This loss function tends to under-estimate the prediction probabilities for classes that are under-represented in the mini-batch which is inevitable in our training data, as can also be seen on Fig. 3.

Weighted Cross-Entropy. The tendency to under-estimate can be mitigated by assigning higher weights to loss contributions from pixels with under-represented class labels:

$$\mathcal{L}_{WCE} = -\frac{1}{N} \sum_{c=1}^{N} \frac{1}{w_c} \sum_{l=1}^{L} r_l^c \log(p_l^c), \tag{3}$$

where w_c is a weight assigned to pixel c computed as a prior probability of ground truth label r_l^c in the given mini-batch.

Soft Dice. Inspired by the Dice coefficient [15] often used to evaluate binary segmentation accuracy, the differentiable soft Dice loss was introduced by Milletari et al. [10] to tackle the class imbalance issue without the need for explicit weighting. One possible formulation is

$$\mathcal{L}_{SD} = \frac{1}{I} \sum_{i=1}^{I} 1 - \frac{2 \sum_{l=1}^{L} \sum_{c=1}^{C} p_l^c r_l^c}{\sum_{l=1}^{L} \sum_{c=1}^{C} p_l^c + r_l^c}. \tag{4}$$

This allows easy generalization to multi-class segmentation where $L > 2$ by treating each image as a 3D volume where the third dimension is the position in the one-hot encoded label vector.

Batch Soft Dice. We hypothesize that one of the advantages of the soft Dice loss is that it is a global operator as opposed to point-wise cross-entropy and therefore it is able to better estimate the correct overall gradient direction. Our modification lies in extending the computation by treating the whole data mini-batch as a single 4-dimensional tensor during the loss computation. In other words, instead of computing the Dice loss over C voxels I times and then averaging, we compute a single Dice loss over all N voxels without averaging.

$$\mathcal{L}_{BSD} = 1 - \frac{2 \sum_{l=1}^{L} \sum_{c=1}^{N} p_l^c r_l^c}{\sum_{l=1}^{L} \sum_{c=1}^{N} p_l^c + r_l^c} \tag{5}$$

Our intuition behind this choice is that during the training phase, the standard Dice loss gradient estimation on a single image/slice does not take into account the fact that the same set of filters should also be capable of segmenting structures not present in the current training slice. This is tackled by averaging the gradient over multiple slices in the batch. This can, however, cause individual gradients to more or less cancel out if their directions are very different. By contrast, computing the Dice loss gradient over the whole batch of slices as a single global operator should enforce the gradient to steadily push the filter weights towards the correct segmentation of each structure in the batch.

It should be noted that in all of the above equations we omitted regularizing term used to avoid zero division for clarity.

In the training phase, the model weights are updated through Adam optimizer with step 10^{-4} computed over mini-batches of 30 image patches. As some structures are under-represented in the dataset, we use standard data augmentation techniques such as random flips, translations and elastic transformations to prevent overfitting.

3   Experimental Results

We optimized our model until convergence using each of the loss functions with 25 training patient scans to keep the challenge format [2]. We cross-validated the models on different test and training scan subsets so that total of 10 scans were used for testing.

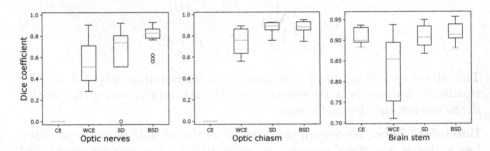

Fig. 3. Optic nerves, chiasm and brain stem segmentation results for models trained with cross-entropy (CE), weighted cross-entropy (WCE), soft Dice (SD) and batch soft Dice (BSD) loss functions. In all cases, BSD loss performs best.

We first demonstrate the performance of the models on the case of optic nerves, optic chiasm, and brain stem segmentation. On other structures, the difference between performance of models trained with different loss functions is less significant. The results in terms of Dice coefficient (measure of segmentation quality on which the loss function is based) are shown in Fig. 3. Superiority of soft Dice-trained models can be observed. However, standard soft Dice-trained model reaches a significantly smaller precision in case of optic nerves and sometimes misses the structure altogether as also illustrated by Fig. 1. The model trained using the proposed batch soft Dice loss does not seem to suffer from this

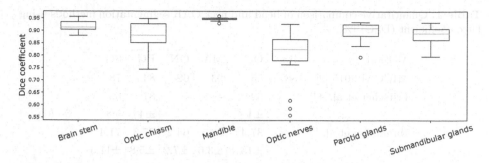

Fig. 4. Performance of segmentation model trained using $\mathcal{L}_{\text{BSD}}$ loss function (5) on individual OARs.

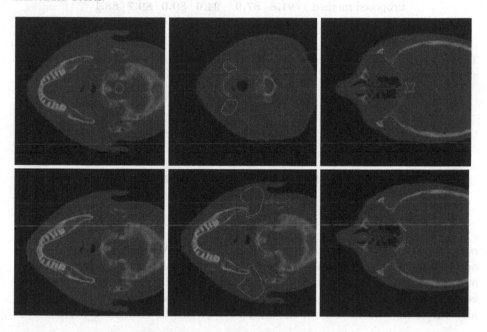

Fig. 5. Examples of successful segmentation outputs (green) with corresponding ground truth annotations (red). Upper row from left to right: brain stem, submandibular glands, optic chiasm, lower row from left to right: mandible, parotid glands, optic nerves. (Color figure online)

issue and we therefore conclude that it is more suitable for training models for segmentation of small anatomical structures with low contrast such as head and neck OAR.

The overall performance of our model for each individual OAR is shown in Fig. 4. Specific examples of successful segmentation for each tissue is shown in Fig. 5. Except for several outlier cases where optic nerve segmentation reached a lower precision with the Dice coefficient around 0.6, we obtained acceptable

Table 1. Quantitative comparison of head and neck OAR segmentation methods using Dice coefficient (DSC) [%].

Method	BS	OC	MA	ON	PG	SG
MICCAI 2015 [2]	88	55	93	62	84	78
Fritscher et al. [6]	-	52	-	-	81	65
		±1			±4	±8
Ibragimov et al. [7]	-	37.4	89.5	64.2	77.3	71.4
		±13.4	±3.6	±7.2	±5.8	±11.3
Wang et al. [8]	90.3	-	94.4	-	82.6	-
	±3.8		±1.3		±5.7	
Proposed method	**91.8**	**87.9**	**94.6**	**80.0**	**89.7**	**88.1**
	±2.2	±5.9	±0.7	±9.9	±3.7	±3.6

Table 2. Quantitative comparison of head and neck OAR segmentation methods using average surface distance (ASD) [mm].

Method	BS	OC	MA	ON	PG	SG
MICCAI 2015 [2]	1.1	1.0	0.5	0.8	1.6	1.4
Wang et al. [8]	0.91	-	0.43	-	1.83	-
	±0.32		±0.12		±0.78	
Proposed method	**0.63**	**0.16**	**0.29**	**0.35**	**0.82**	**1.08**
	±0.24	±0.05	±0.03	±0.9	±0.66	±1.47

results with Dice coefficient over 0.8 for all structures. We quantitatively compare our method with other published methods in terms of Dice coefficient (Table 1) and in terms of average surface distance [16] (Table 2). Although the difference is most accentuated in cases of optic nerves and chiasm segmentation, our model also surpasses current state-of-the-art results on all the remaining OARs.

4   Conclusions

We designed an encoder-decoder CNN model for head and neck OAR segmentation and proposed the Batch Dice Loss for multi-class segmentation of structures with small sizes. We compared the loss function to other standard loss functions in terms of their ability to optimize a model for OAR segmentation. The model trained using the batch Dice loss reached the best performance when compared to other loss functions and also to current state-of-the-art methods on this dataset.

In the future work we are going to evaluate the performance of batch Dice loss when applied to optimization of different models. These could include models trained on different datasets where three-dimensional models would be feasible. We are also going to assess whether it is also beneficial in the case of binary segmentation. Another potential area to explore is explicitly weighting the loss function according to current classification performance rather than prior occurrence probabilities.

Acknowledgements. This work was supported in part by the company TESCAN 3DIM (fka 3Dim Laboratory) and by the Technology Agency of the Czech Republic project TE01020415 (V3C – Visual Computing Competence Center).

References

1. Dawson, L.A., Sharpe, M.B.: Image-guided radiotherapy: rationale, benefits, and limitations. Lancet Oncol. **7**(10), 848–858 (2006)
2. Raudaschl, P.F., et al.: Evaluation of segmentation methods on head and neck CT: auto-segmentation challenge 2015. Med. Phys. **44**(5), 2020–2036 (2017)
3. Heimann, T., Meinzer, H.P.: Statistical shape models for 3D medical image segmentation: a review. Med. Image Anal. **13**, 543–563 (2009)
4. Jung, F., Steger, S., Knapp, O., Noll, M., Wesarg, S.: COSMO - coupled shape model for radiation therapy planning of head and neck cancer. In: Linguraru, M.G., et al. (eds.) CLIP 2014. LNCS, vol. 8680, pp. 25–32. Springer, Cham (2014). https://doi.org/10.1007/978-3-319-13909-8_4
5. Krizhevsky, A., Sutskever, I., Hinton, G.E.: ImageNet classification with deep convolutional neural networks. In: Advance in Neural Information Processing Systems, pp. 1097–1105 (2012)
6. Fritscher, K., Raudaschl, P., Zaffino, P., Spadea, M.F., Sharp, G.C., Schubert, R.: Deep neural networks for fast segmentation of 3D medical images. In: Ourselin, S., Joskowicz, L., Sabuncu, M.R., Unal, G., Wells, W. (eds.) MICCAI 2016. LNCS, vol. 9901, pp. 158–165. Springer, Cham (2016). https://doi.org/10.1007/978-3-319-46723-8_19
7. Ibragimov, B., Xing, L.: Segmentation of organs-at-risks in head and neck CT images using convolutional neural networks. Med. Phys. **44**(2), 547–557 (2017)
8. Wang, Z., Wei, L., Wang, L., Gao, Y., Chen, W., Shen, D.: Hierarchical vertex regression-based segmentation of head and neck CT images for radiotherapy planning. IEEE Trans. Image Process. **27**(2), 923–937 (2018)
9. Ronneberger, O., Fischer, P., Brox, T.: U-Net: convolutional networks for biomedical image segmentation. In: Navab, N., Hornegger, J., Wells, W.M., Frangi, A.F. (eds.) MICCAI 2015. LNCS, vol. 9351, pp. 234–241. Springer, Cham (2015). https://doi.org/10.1007/978-3-319-24574-4_28
10. Milletari, F., Navab, N., Ahmadi, S.: V-Net: fully convolutional neural networks for volumetric medical image segmentation. In: Fourth International Conference on 3D Vision, 3DV, Stanford, CA, pp. 565–571 (2016)
11. Pastor-Pellicer, J., Zamora-Martínez, F., España-Boquera, S., Castro-Bleda, M.J.: International Work-Conference on Artificial Neural Networks, pp. 376–384 (2013)
12. Sudre, C.H., Li, W., Vercauteren, T., Ourselin, S., Jorge Cardoso, M.: Generalised dice overlap as a deep learning loss function for highly unbalanced segmentations. In: Cardoso, M.J., et al. (eds.) DLMIA/ML-CDS -2017. LNCS, vol. 10553, pp. 240–248. Springer, Cham (2017). https://doi.org/10.1007/978-3-319-67558-9_28
13. Fidon, L., et al.: Generalised Wasserstein dice score for imbalanced multi-class segmentation using holistic convolutional networks. In: Crimi, A., Bakas, S., Kuijf, H., Menze, B., Reyes, M. (eds.) BrainLes 2017. LNCS, vol. 10670, pp. 64–76. Springer, Cham (2018). https://doi.org/10.1007/978-3-319-75238-9_6

14. Kayalibay, B., Jensen, G., Smagt, P.: CNN-based segmentation of medical imaging data (2017). https://arxiv.org/pdf/1701.03056.pdf
15. Dice, L.R.: Measures of the amount of ecologic association between species. Ecology **26**(3), 297–302 (1945)
16. Van Ginneken, B., Heimann, T., Styner, M.: 3D segmentation in the clinic: a grand challenge. In: MICCAI Workshop on 3D Segmentation in the Clinic: A Grand Challenge (2007)

Detection of Mechanical Damages in Sawn Timber Using Convolutional Neural Networks

Nikolay Rudakov[1,3], Tuomas Eerola[1(✉)] ⓘ, Lasse Lensu[1] ⓘ,
Heikki Kälviäinen[1] ⓘ, and Heikki Haario[2] ⓘ

[1] School of Engineering Science, Machine Vision and Pattern Recognition
Laboratory, Lappeenranta University of Technology,
P.O. Box 20, 53851 Lappeenranta, Finland
{nikolay.rudakov,tuomas.eerola,lasse.lensu,heikki.kalviainen}@lut.fi
[2] School of Engineering Science, Inverse Problems Research Group,
Lappeenranta University of Technology,
P.O. Box 20, 53851 Lappeenranta, Finland
heikki.haario@lut.fi
[3] FinScan Oy, Lukupurontie 2, 02200 Espoo, Finland
nikolay.rudakov@finscan.fi

Abstract. The quality control of timber products is vital for the sawmill industry pursuing more efficient production processes. This paper considers the automatic detection of mechanical damages in wooden board surfaces occurred during the sawing process. Due to the high variation in the appearance of the mechanical damages and the presence of several other surface defects on the boards, the detection task is challenging. In this paper, an efficient convolutional neural network based framework that can be trained with a limited amount of annotated training data is proposed. The framework includes a patch extraction step to produce multiple training samples from each damaged region in the board images, followed by the patch classification and damage localization steps. In the experiments, multiple network architectures were compared: the VGG-16 architecture achieved the best results with over 92% patch classification accuracy and it enabled accurate localization of the mechanical damages.

1 Introduction

Automated quality control plays an important role in the sawmill process where end products, i.e., boards and planks need to be efficiently sorted into different grades. Higher board grades can be sold at a higher price, resulting in more profit for the sawmill. At the same time, selling low quality boards as high grade products causes reclamations from the customers. Therefore, it is vital to be able to define the grade as accurately as possible. For automating the quality control, computer vision techniques provide an attractive tool for grading of the boards and planks.

© Springer Nature Switzerland AG 2019
T. Brox et al. (Eds.): GCPR 2018, LNCS 11269, pp. 115–126, 2019.
https://doi.org/10.1007/978-3-030-12939-2_9

Timber can be mechanically damaged in the sawing process. The most common cause for the mechanical damages is that the feed rollers excessively press the board with spikes while moving it through the sawing machine [11]. Such defects appear as series of marks or traces along the board. However, several other mechanical damages may occur during the process, resulting in large variations in the appearance of the damages. Examples of mechanical damages on sawn timber are shown in Fig. 1. It should be emphasized that the defect type affects the grading of the boards and the end use of the product. Therefore, it is essential to distinguish mechanical damages from the other defects.

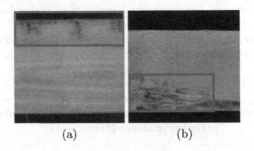

(a)   (b)

Fig. 1. Examples of the mechanical damages: (a) Periodic mechanical damage caused by a feed roller; (b) Another type of non-periodic mechanical damage.

Convolutional neural networks (CNNs) are the leading technique for image classification and object detection [17]. Being a universal function approximator, CNN can be potentially trained to extract almost any high-level features from the input image including features of mechanical damages of sawn timber. However, applying an existing state-of-the-art CNN-based general object detection method such as YOLO [14] or Faster R-CNN [16] for the detection of defects, especially mechanical damages, is challenging due to the following characteristics of the data: (1) the board images have a very high width to height ratio, (2) annotated data are difficult to obtain resulting in a small amount of training data, and (3) defect (bounding box) sizes and aspect ratios vary considerably.

In this paper, the above problems are tackled by proposing an efficient CNN-based method for detecting mechanical damages from board images by utilizing a one-dimensional sliding window approach. The proposed method is based on the fact that the damage localization is relevant only along the longitudinal direction of the board since the defected parts of the board are sawn off. This makes it possible implement the sliding window based detection method with only one scale and with a relatively small amount of image patches per image to be classified with CNN. Since most of the individual mechanical damages are large, each of them is represented by numerous image patches resulting in a large amount of positive examples for the training. We further utilize data augmentation and transfer learning to make it possible to train CNNs with a relatively small amount of data. Finally, we evaluate multiple CNN architectures for the classification task, and demonstrate the efficiency of the approach.

2   Related Work

Numerous computer vision based methods for surface inspection of sawn timber including defect detection can be found in the literature. However, most of the existing studies consider the detection of natural timber defects such as different kinds of knots, bark pockets, wane, fungus, worm holes, cracks, and resin leaving out mechanical damages [6].

The existing approaches vary between the different defect types, but three common stages can be highlighted [6]: (1) The defects are localized, (2) features are extracted from each defect, and (3) feature-based classification of the defects is performed. Several reviews on the existing solutions for the timber surface inspection exist [6,15,23]. They categorize the approaches based on the methods used for defect localization, feature extraction, and classification, and compare the method performances.

The feature localization stage can be implemented with the combination of various image filtering, segmentation, thresholding, connected components labeling, region merging, and many other image processing techniques. Most of the previous studies have used texture features for the timber defect classification [23]. The most common feature extraction methods are local binary patterns (LBP) [12], gray-level co-occurrence matrix (GLCM) [5], scale-invariant feature transform (SIFT) [10], speeded up robust features (SURF) [1] and Tamura texture features [22].

With the increase of computing performance, deep learning approaches have become more popular in image processing [21]. The most recent articles considering defect detection rely on CNNs. In [15], a generic deep-learning-based approach for automated surface inspection was introduced. The method utilizes a pretrained Decaf CNN [3] to generate a heatmap of defects on the surface. The heatmap is further binarized and segmented using the graph-based Felzenszwalb's segmentation method [4]. In [2], a method for crack detection on concrete surface using a single CNN was introduced. The image is processed using a sliding window, and the corresponding part of the image is fed to CNN for each position of the window.

3   Proposed Method

The scheme of the proposed method is illustrated in Fig. 2. The method starts with the patch extraction procedure where the board image is divided into overlapping image patches. The patches are classified using CNN according to the defect type located within the patch. Finally, the mechanical damages are localized based on the coordinates of the patches.

The sawn timber boards are long and narrow, and that is why their surface images have the high width-to-height ratio. At the same time, the existing trained CNN architectures require input images to be typically scaled to a fixed size with the aspect ratio of 1. Since the mechanical damages caused by feed rollers consist of quite narrow notches scaling a board image to the required

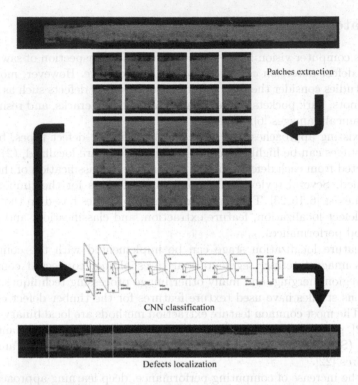

Patches extraction

CNN classification

Defects localization

Fig. 2. The scheme of the proposed method for mechanical damage detection from sawn timber images: the board image is split into overlapping patches, the patches are fed to CNN, and then the classified patches and their original locations determine the beginning (green line) and the end (red line) positions of mechanical damages in the longitudinal direction. (Color figure online)

dimensions (approximately 8 times in the horizontal dimension) leads to losing the significant information about defect appearance and causes difficulties in the learning process as a consequence.

To resolve this problem, the patch extraction method is used. The general idea is to segment the board from the image and to split the segmented region into a series of small overlapping patches with the required size. The proposed patch extraction technique turns the problem of the mechanical damage detection into a patch classification task.

3.1 Patch Extraction

Before the image patch extraction, the board needs to be detected from the image. Typical board images captured in the sawmill process consist of a bright board with a dark background. For the board segmentation, the image is converted from RGB to grayscale, and the Otsu's thresholding method [13] is applied. After this, the largest connected component is searched.

The coordinates of the bounding box for the board are computed using the coordinates of the top-, bottom-, left- and right-most pixels of the connected component. The board in the image could be located imprecisely in the horizontal direction and its orientation could be different from the one of the image. The non-ideal orientation and possible presence of slivers makes the direct use of connected component extreme points unreliable for accurate extraction of the patches. Nevertheless, the left and right sides of the bounding box can be used as reference points.

To locate the board more accurately, the following steps are performed. First, the board centroid is calculated as the mean value of the connected component pixels coordinates. Then, the angle to the horizontal direction θ and the minor axis length of the ellipse with the same normalized central moment as the connected component are computed. To find the ellipse, the origin of the pixels' coordinates is shifted to the position of the centroid. If the height of the bounding box is smaller than the minor ellipse axis multiplied by $\cos\theta$ then the bounding box is assumed to be correct and the upper board edge is approximated using the coordinates of one of the top bounding box corners as a reference. The lower board edge is a parallel line that goes under the upper edge at the approximated board height distance. If the height of the bounding box is larger than the minor ellipse axis multiplied by $\cos\theta$ then the reference is the central line passing through the centroid with the angle to the horizontal direction θ. The upper and lower edges are at the distance of half board height from the central line.

The patch positions are computed using the top and bottom board edges, and the left and right bounding box sides. Moreover, the top and bottom parts of all the patches include the background margins with the size of 10% of the board height. This is done because the mechanical damages are often located close to or at the edges of the board. Also, the background margin of 10 pixels is added to the left and right ends of the board. The patches have a square shape and adjacent patches have 50% overlap with each other. Finally, the patches are scaled to the input size of the CNN architecture. An example of localized patches is shown in Fig. 3.

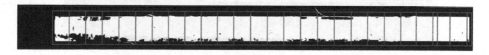

Fig. 3. Extraction the overlapping image patches from the segmented board image. The rightmost patch is aligned with the end of the board and has, therefore, a larger overlap with the neighboring patch.

3.2 Patch Classification and Damage Localization

After the patches have been extracted they are fed to the CNN network in which binary classification between the defected and non-defected patches is made. During the extraction step, the patch coordinates of the entire image are preserved. The patch is considered to contain the mechanical damage if the damage covers more than the half of the patch in the longitudinal direction of the board. Also, the patch overlap is half of their width. To deduce the localization, the left border of the defect is considered to be at $x + 0.25w$ of the first patch in a sequence of defective patches while the right border is considered be at $x + 0.75w$ of the last patch in a sequence of defective patches where x is the longitudinal coordinate of the top left corner of the patch and w is the width of the patch. The damage localization is visualized in Fig. 4.

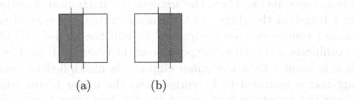

(a)   (b)

Fig. 4. Damage localization: (a) The first defective patch in a sequence; (b) The last defective patch in a sequence.

4   Experiments

4.1   Data

The data consists of images of 127 sawn timber boards (see Fig. 5). Six overlapping images (three from the top and three from the bottom sides) were taken from every board to cover the whole length of the board. The images were manually annotated for the following defect types: periodic mechanical damages caused by feed rollers and non-periodic mechanical damages. The defect examples are shown in Fig. 1.

Fig. 5. An example of feed roller traces as mechanical damage (green bounding box) and wane not considered as mechanical damage (red bounding box). (Color figure online)

The patch extraction algorithm was applied to the labeled data. As a result, 10808 image patches were extracted from the board images. All patches overlapping with a bounding box of a mechanical damage at least 50% of its width were labeled as containing a defect. Most of the patches represent defectless parts of the board, and therefore, there is a large class imbalance in the dataset. For example, in the case of periodic mechanical damages, there are 8683 clear patches and only 2125 defective. The number of defective patches was increased by generating augmented image patches with horizontal and vertical mirroring and 180° rotation. As a result, the number of defective patches was 8500. The patches were board-wise randomly split into the training (70%) and test sets (30%). This means that all the patches from one board were used either in the training phase or in the test phase. The augmented image patches were used only in the training phase. The vast majority of mechanical damages belong to the group of periodic mechanical damages. Therefore, for the further experiments, two datasets were constructed. In the first dataset, all mechanical damages were combined into one defect class and, in the second dataset, non-periodic mechanical damages were eliminated causing the defect class to contain only periodic mechanical damages. Table 1 shows the numbers of images and patches in the datasets.

Table 1. The number of images in the datasets.

Defects	Training					Test				
	Boards	Images	Patches			Boards	Images	Patches		
			Clear	Defect	Total			Clear	Defect	Total
Combined	89	597	5490	7840	13330	38	229	2667	691	3358
Periodic	89	534	6045	6164	12209	38	228	2638	584	3222

4.2 Evaluation Criteria

The accuracy (ACC) of image patch classification was measured as the percentage of correctly classified patches over all test images. Additionally, the damage localization accuracy was measured using the Jaccard metric. The Jaccard metric is typically defined as follows:

$$S_{\text{Jaccard}} = \frac{|A_P \cap A_{GT}|}{|A_P \cup A_{GT}|} \tag{1}$$

where A_P is the area of the predicted object bounding box and A_{GT} is the area of the ground truth bounding box. In our experiments, comparing detections and ground truth this way is problematic since a portion of the test images does not contain any mechanical damages causing the intersection $|A_P \cap A_{GT}|$ to be zero even if the method works correctly, i.e. it does not detect any false positives. This further results in the Jaccard metric values to be unreliable. To avoid this, the Jaccard metric was used to measure the accuracy of detecting the non-damaged parts of the boards, i.e., how well the method predicts the regions that do not contain mechanical damages. This means that A_{GT} in (1) defines the ground truth for non-damaged areas and A_P defines the areas where no mechanical damages were detected. It should be noted that the dataset does not contain any image that is fully covered with mechanical damages, and therefore, the intersection is zero only if the method fails, i.e. does not detect any non-damaged regions. An example of the intersection and the union of the ground truth, and the predicted mechanically damaged one-dimensional regions of the board is shown in Fig. 6. The average Jaccard metric over all the test images was used as the performance measure.

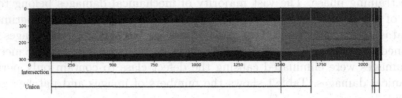

Fig. 6. Jaccard metric in case of one-dimensional mechanical damage localization from a board image. The ground truth defect borders are red and the predicted defect borders are green. (Color figure online)

4.3   Results

Two experiments were carried out. In the first experiment, the method was trained to detect any mechanical damages, i.e., the both periodic and non-periodic mechanical damages were considered to belong to the same class (combined). In the second experiment, the method was trained to detect the periodic mechanical damages only. The purpose of the first experiment was to evaluate the ability of the selected CNN architecture to distinguish the mechanically damaged parts of the board regardless of the damage type. The non-periodic mechanical damages may significantly affect the accuracy because they are more variable in their appearance and less common in the existing dataset. That is why the second experiment was carried out to evaluate the performance of the CNN to classify periodic mechanical damages. Since the non-periodic mechanical damages are considerably less common, it was not possible to train a CNN to detect them alone.

Four CNN architectures were selected for the comparison concerning their ability to recognize mechanical damages in sawn timber patches. These architectures were AlexNet [9], GoogLeNet [20], ResNet-50 [7] and VGG-16 [19]. The architectures were trained with the Caffe deep learning framework [8]. To reduce the training time and to increase the classification accuracy, the transfer learning approach was applied. The selected CNNs were initialized with pretrained models trained for wood species identification using a similar but more extensive dataset [18].

The performance for localization and binary classification of the combined periodic and non-periodic mechanical damages to a single class is provided in Table 2. The performance for localization and binary classification of the periodic mechanical damages is provided in Table 3. The percentages of images that were analyzed correctly, i.e., all the mechanical damages were correctly detected with respect to the Jaccard metric threshold, are shown in Fig. 7. Examples of periodic damage detection results with the GoogLeNet CNN architecture are given in Fig. 8.

Table 2. Performance comparison of different CNN architectures in case of the combined binary classification. Accuracy refers to the classification accuracy for individual patches and $S_{Jaccard}$ measures the defect location accuracy for the full images.

Architecture	Accuracy	$S_{Jaccard}$	Confusion matrix		
AlexNet	0.800	0.692		Predicted 0	Predicted 1
			True 0	0.86	0.14
			True 1	0.42	0.58
GoogLeNet	0.860	0.700		Predicted 0	Predicted 1
			True 0	0.87	0.13
			True 1	0.16	0.84
ResNet-50	0.799	0.624		Predicted 0	Predicted 1
			True 0	0.79	0.21
			True 1	0.17	0.83
VGG-16	0.861	0.696		Predicted 0	Predicted 1
			True 0	0.85	0.15
			True 1	0.11	0.89

The most time consuming stage of the proposed method is the sequential patch classification with CNN. The lower the inference time consumed by a single patch classification is, the more effective is the given CNN architecture. The inference times for all the CNNs were measured on a MSI GE70 laptop with Intel Core i7-4700MQ @ 2.4 GHz processor, NVIDIA GeForce GTX 760M single GPU, and Ubuntu 17.10 operating system. Table 4 contains the average time required to classify one patch of a board image.

As it can be seen, the VGG-16 architecture achieves the best patch classification accuracy of more than 92% for the periodic mechanical damages and 86% for all the mechanical damages. At the same time, the GoogLeNet architecture achieves the lowest false negative and false positive rates and it is four times faster in the single patch processing than the VGG-16. The worst classification and detection accuracy was shown by the AlexNet architecture, and it showed the worst false positive rate of 41%.

Table 3. Performance comparison of different CNN architectures in case of the periodic mechanical damages binary classification.

Architecture	Accuracy	S_{Jaccard}	Confusion matrix		
AlexNet	0.857	0.779		Predicted 0	Predicted 1
			True 0	0.92	0.08
			True 1	0.41	0.59
GoogLeNet	0.907	0.795		Predicted 0	Predicted 1
			True 0	0.91	0.09
			True 1	0.09	0.91
ResNet-50	0.913	0.829		Predicted 0	Predicted 1
			True 0	0.94	0.06
			True 1	0.20	0.80
VGG-16	0.927	0.840		Predicted 0	Predicted 1
			True 0	0.95	0.05
			True 1	0.16	0.84

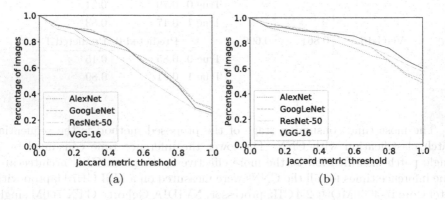

Fig. 7. Percentage of images with correctly detected damages with respect to the Jaccard metric threshold: (a) Combined mechanical damages; (b) Periodic mechanical damages only.

Table 4. Single patch average inference time for each of the trained CNN architectures.

Architecture	Inference time, seconds
AlexNet	0.022
GoogLeNet	0.023
ResNet-50	0.051
VGG-16	0.101

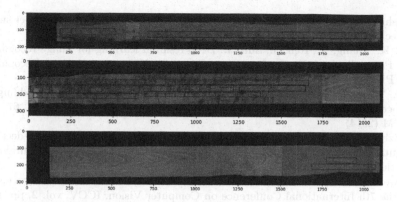

Fig. 8. Examples of the periodic mechanical damage detection with the GoogLeNet CNN architecture: the ground truth damage areas (red bounding boxes) and the predicted defective parts (green overlay). (Color figure online)

5   Conclusion

In this paper, a method for mechanical damage detection on sawn timber images was proposed. The proposed method segments the board on the image, splits the part of the image containing the board into overlapping patches, classifies the patches with the CNN, and, finally, determines the defect location based on classification results and the coordinates of the patches. The experiments compared the performance of the following four CNN architectures: AlexNet, GoogLeNet, VGG-16, and ResNet-50. The VGG-16 architecture produced the best results with a promising classification accuracy of more than 92% for individual patches.

Acknowledgements. The research was carried out in the DigiSaw project (No. 2894/31/2017) funded by Business Finland. The authors would to thank FinScan Oy for providing the data for the experiments.

References

1. Bay, H., Ess, A., Tuytelaars, T., Van Gool, L.: Speeded-up robust features SURF. Comput. Vis. Image Underst. **110**(3), 346–359 (2008)
2. Cha, Y.J., Choi, W., Büyüköztürk, O.: Deep learning-based crack damage detection using convolutional neural networks. Comput.-Aided Civ. Infrastruct. Eng. **32**(5), 361–378 (2017)
3. Donahue, J., et al.: DeCAF: a deep convolutional activation feature for generic visual recognition. In: Proceedings of the 31st International Conference on Machine Learning, ICML, vol. 32, pp. 647–655. PMLR (2014)
4. Felzenszwalb, P.F., Huttenlocher, D.P.: Efficient graph-based image segmentation. Int. J. Comput. Vis. **59**(2), 167–181 (2004)
5. Haralick, R.M., Shanmugam, K., Dinstein, I.: Textural features for image classification. IEEE Trans. Syst. Man Cybern. SMC **3**(6), 610–621 (1973)

6. Hashim, U., Hashim, S., Muda, A.: Automated vision inspection of timber surface defect: a review. Jurnal Teknologi **77**(20), 127–135 (2015)
7. He, K., Zhang, X., Ren, S., Sun, J.: Deep residual learning for image recognition. In: Proceedings of the Conference on Computer Vision and Pattern Recognition, CVPR, pp. 770–778. IEEE (2016)
8. Jia, Y., et al.: Caffe: convolutional architecture for fast feature embedding. In: Proceedings of the 22nd International Conference on Multimedia, pp. 675–678. ACM (2014)
9. Krizhevsky, A., Sutskever, I., Hinton, G.E.: ImageNet classification with deep convolutional neural networks. In: Proceedings of the 25th Conference on Neural Information Processing Systems, NIPS, pp. 1097–1105 (2012)
10. Lowe, D.G.: Object recognition from local scale-invariant features. In: Proceedings of the 7th International Conference on Computer Vision, ICCV, vol. 2, pp. 1150–1157. IEEE (1999)
11. Nuutinen, Y., Väätäinen, K., Asikainen, A., Prinz, R., Heinonen, J.: Operational efficiency and damage to sawlogs by feed rollers of the harvester head. Silva Fennica **44**(1), 121–139 (2010)
12. Ojala, T., Pietikäinen, M., Harwood, D.: A comparative study of texture measures with classification based on featured distributions. Pattern Recognit. **29**(1), 51–59 (1996)
13. Otsu, N.: A threshold selection method from gray-level histograms. IEEE Trans. Syst. Man Cybern. **9**(1), 62–66 (1979)
14. Redmon, J., Divvala, S., Girshick, R., Farhadi, A.: You only look once: unified, real-time object detection. In: Proceedings of the Conference on Computer Vision and Pattern Recognition, CVPR, pp. 779–788. IEEE (2016)
15. Ren, R., Hung, T., Tan, K.C.: A generic deep-learning-based approach for automated surface inspection. IEEE Trans. Cybern. **48**(3), 929–940 (2018)
16. Ren, S., He, K., Girshick, R., Sun, J.: Faster R-CNN: towards real-time object detection with region proposal networks. In: Proceedings of the 28th Conference on Neural Information Processing Systems, NIPS, pp. 91–99 (2015)
17. Russakovsky, O., et al.: ImageNet large scale visual recognition challenge. Int. J. Comput. Vis. (IJCV) **115**(3), 211–252 (2015). https://doi.org/10.1007/s11263-015-0816-y
18. Shustrov, D.: Species identification of wooden material using convolutional neural networks. Master's thesis. Lappeenranta University of Technology, Finland (2018)
19. Simonyan, K., Zisserman, A.: Very deep convolutional networks for large-scale image recognition. In: Proceedings of the International Conference on Learning Representations, ICLR (2014)
20. Szegedy, C., et al.: Going deeper with convolutions. In: Proceedings of the Conference on Computer Vision and Pattern Recognition, CVPR, pp. 1–9. IEEE (2015)
21. Szegedy, C., Vanhoucke, V., Ioffe, S., Shlens, J., Wojna, Z.: Rethinking the inception architecture for computer vision. In: Proceedings of the Conference on Computer Vision and Pattern Recognition, CVPR, pp. 2818–2826. IEEE (2016)
22. Tamura, H., Mori, S., Yamawaki, T.: Textural features corresponding to visual perception. IEEE Trans. Syst. Man Cybern. **8**(6), 460–473 (1978)
23. Tong, H.L., Ng, H., Yap, T.V.T., Ahmad, W.S.H.M.W., Fauzi, M.F.A.: Evaluation of feature extraction and selection techniques for the classification of wood defect images. J. Eng. Appl. Sci. **12**(3), 602–608 (2017)

Compressed-Domain Video Object Tracking Using Markov Random Fields with Graph Cuts Optimization

Fernando Bombardelli[✉], Serhan Gül, and Cornelius Hellge

Department of Video Coding and Analytics, Fraunhofer Heinrich Hertz Institute,
Berlin, Germany
{fernando.bombardelli,serhan.guel,cornelius.hellge}@hhi.fraunhofer.de

Abstract. We propose a method for tracking objects in H.264/AVC compressed videos using a Markov Random Field model. Given an initial segmentation of the target object in the first frame, our algorithm applies a graph-cuts-based optimization to output a binary segmentation map for the next frame. Our model uses only the motion vectors and block coding modes from the compressed bitstream. Thus, complexity and storage requirements are significantly reduced compared to pixel-domain algorithms. We evaluate our method over two datasets and compare its performance to a state-of-the-art compressed-domain algorithm. Results show that we achieve better results in more challenging sequences.

1 Introduction

Visual object tracking is an important task in many applications of computer vision such as human-computer interaction, motion-based recognition, video surveillance, traffic control, and vehicle navigation [25]. Although some efficient algorithms have been proposed recently [7,11], many high-accuracy visual tracking algorithms consist of multistage, complex solutions that require large amounts of processing. Such high computational complexity can be a limiting factor in environments with limited processing resources, such as embedded systems, and in scenarios that require efficient processing of several video streams in parallel. A typical example of such an application is the large-scale analysis of videos from surveillance cameras deployed in a smart city [4].

An alternative to tracking algorithms that operate on decoded and reconstructed pixels are the so-called *compressed-domain* algorithms that directly operate on compressed video data. These algorithms operate on features extracted from the video bitstream such as prediction block types, motion vectors (MVs) and transform coefficients. They do not require a full decoding of the video bitstream and have a reduced amount of storage and processing requirements (due to compression) with significantly lower computational complexity.

In this paper, we present a compressed-domain object tracking method that uses only the extracted MVs and block coding modes from a H.264/AVC video

© Springer Nature Switzerland AG 2019
T. Brox et al. (Eds.): GCPR 2018, LNCS 11269, pp. 127–139, 2019.
https://doi.org/10.1007/978-3-030-12939-2_10

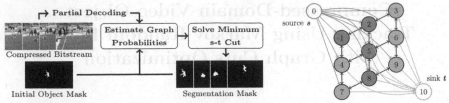

(a) Processing pipeline of the proposed approach. Given an H.264/AVC compressed video bitstream and an initial object mask, for each frame we (i) extract its motion vectors, (ii) estimate the probabilities in our Markov Random Field model, (iii) generate its corresponding graph, and (iv) infer the new object's mask by finding an exact solution of a minimum s-t cut optimization problem.

(b) Example of a constructed graph. Supposing a minimum s-t cut that yields the partition depicted by the blue and red-colored nodes, then setting $\omega_1^t, \omega_2^t, \omega_5^t, \omega_8^t = 1$ and $\omega_3^t, \omega_4^t, \omega_6^t, \omega_7^t, \omega_9^t = 0$ determines an optimal solution to the problem.

Fig. 1. Overview of our method

bitstream. Our approach is also applicable to the newer H.265/HEVC standard and other block-based video compression schemes. However, we chose H.264/AVC since it is still the most widely used standard, especially for surveillance cameras and embedded systems. We define the problem as tracking-by-segmentation as follows: H and W denote the height and the width of the pictures, then, given a sequence of frames $\{F_t\}_{t \in \mathbb{N}}$ and a binary matrix $M_1 \in \{0,1\}^{H \times W}$ labeling the object in the frame F_1, the objective is to infer for every $t > 1$ the matrix $M_t \in \{0,1\}^{H \times W}$, which segments the pixels of the frame F_t into the classes *object* and *non-object*. An overview of our approach is shown in Fig. 1(a).

Our main contributions are: (i) formulation of the compressed-domain tracking task as an optimization problem over a Markov Random Field (MRF) by defining the appropriate energy (potential) functions; (ii) application of a graph-cuts-based solution to perform binary segmentation relying only on MVs from the compressed bitstream.

2 Related Work

Various compressed-domain tracking and moving object detection methods were proposed in literature with recent work focusing on tracking rigid objects in H.264/AVC and H.265/HEVC video bitstreams [3]. Some works on moving object detection solely rely on macroblock (MB) types [16–18]. Poppe *et al.* [18] analyze the bitstreams on a MB level and introduced a syntax level algorithm based on MB sizes in bits. Their algorithm learns a background model in an initial training phase and uses this model as a benchmark in the following steps to determine MBs corresponding to moving objects. Laumer *et al.* [16] define weights for all possible MB types considering the decision process of the encoder while selecting the MB types. Assigned weights indicate the probability that a MB belongs to a moving object.

Other approaches rely either solely on the extracted MVs or a combination of MB types and MVs [13,24,26]. Käs and Nicolas [13] use global motion estimation to filter out outlier MVs and use the filtered MVs to estimate the trajectory of moving objects in the scene. Wojaczek et al. [24] utilize MB types at a preprocessing step for fast evaluation of video streams. If an object is detected, a more precise pixel-domain object detector is employed to obtain a finer segmentation.

Most successful tracking results in compressed domain were obtained by using statistical inference models, specifically MRFs. Zeng et al. [27] published one of the earliest works that employed an MRF model for MV-based tracking. Their approach merges similar MVs into moving objects by minimizing the MRF energy and defining different MV types. Their model considers the spatial continuity and temporal consistency of MVs to identify groups of MVs belonging to the tracking object. However, it is only suitable for static scenes since the method does not take into account the camera motion. Khatoonabadi and Bajić [14] treat the tracking problem in a Bayesian framework and use MVs to compute a motion coherence metric. Furthermore, they employ global motion compensation to deal with dynamic scenes and propose an interpolation technique to assign motion information to intra-coded blocks based on the MVs of their neighboring blocks. Enhancing the objective function of [14], Gül et al. [10] use the color information from the first intra-coded frame (I frame) to create a Gaussian Mixture Model (GMM) based on the color distributions of the object and the background, provided by initial labeling, and update the solution at every I frame. Their approach increases the tracking accuracy with a negligible loss in terms of computational speed caused by the sparse sampling of color information from I frames.

3 Proposed Method

The video object tracking problem can be considered as finding an optimal segmentation of the current video frame into *object* and *non-object* classes based on the binary segmentation from the previous one. We assume that pixelwise ground truth annotation of the tracking object is given for the first frame as initial input. We then treat the tracking problem as an inference problem on an MRF model (Sect. 3.1) and use minimum s-t cut (*i.e.* graph cuts) method [19] to solve the optimization problem (Sect. 3.2). Our method operates on a uniformly sampled motion vector field. Since H.264/AVC has variable prediction block sizes and intra-coded blocks without MVs [23], we apply some preprocessing steps to obtain such a uniform MV field (Sect. 3.4).

3.1 Probabilistic Framework

Our approach is based on the work of Khatoonabadi and Bajić [14] who model the object tracking task as an inference problem using an MRF. Their idea is to have for each frame t one random variable ω^t representing the binary segmentation of the respective frame. So, the problem is to find the most likely labeling ω^t given the previous one ω^{t-1} and the motion information.

In contrast to them, we assign every block a random variable which may assume the values 1, for *object*, or 0, for *non-object*. In order to model the relations between adjacent blocks in a uniform manner, we construct a uniformly sampled MV field by preprocessing, and obtain a grid with N blocks. In our probabilistic framework, for each block $n = 1, \ldots, N$, the corresponding observed MV $\mathbf{x}_n$ is conditionally dependent on the respective block state $\omega_n^t \in \{0, 1\}$, and each block state is conditionally dependent on its four-connected neighbors and its state ω_n^{t-1} in the previous frame.

The inference problem can then be stated as a maximum-a-posteriori optimization problem, that is,

$$\max_{\omega_1^t, \ldots, \omega_N^t} P(\omega_1^t, \ldots, \omega_N^t \mid \mathbf{x}_1, \ldots, \mathbf{x}_N, \omega_1^{t-1}, \ldots, \omega_N^{t-1}). \tag{1}$$

For convenience we denote $\omega_1^t, \ldots, \omega_N^t$ as $\boldsymbol{\omega}^t$; $\omega_1^{t-1}, \ldots, \omega_N^{t-1}$ as $\boldsymbol{\omega}^{t-1}$; and the objective function of (1) as f. From Bayes' theorem and the conditional independences implied by the MRF it follows that

$$f(\boldsymbol{\omega}^t) = \frac{P(\mathbf{x}_1, \ldots, \mathbf{x}_N | \boldsymbol{\omega}^t, \boldsymbol{\omega}^{t-1}) P(\boldsymbol{\omega}^t, \boldsymbol{\omega}^{t-1})}{P(\mathbf{x}_1, \ldots, \mathbf{x}_N, \boldsymbol{\omega}^{t-1})} = \left[\prod_{n=1}^{N} P(\mathbf{x}_n | \omega_n^t) \right] \frac{P(\boldsymbol{\omega}^t, \boldsymbol{\omega}^{t-1})}{P(\mathbf{x}_1, \ldots, \mathbf{x}_N, \boldsymbol{\omega}^{t-1})}. \tag{2}$$

Consider the undirected graph relating the random variables $\boldsymbol{\omega}^t$ and $\boldsymbol{\omega}^{t-1}$, and note that every maximal clique in it contains exactly two vertices. Moreover, the set of its maximal cliques $\mathcal{C}$ can be partitioned into three subsets: the set $\mathcal{C}_1 = \{\{\omega_n^t, \omega_n^{t-1}\} \mid n = 1, \ldots, N\}$ of pair of vertices corresponding to the same blocks in different frames; the set $\mathcal{C}_2 = \{\{\omega_i^t, \omega_j^t\} \mid \{i, j\} \in \mathcal{L}\}$ of neighboring blocks in the frame t; and the set $\mathcal{C}_3 = \{\{\omega_i^{t-1}, \omega_j^{t-1}\} \mid \{i, j\} \in \mathcal{L}\}$ of neighboring blocks in the frame $t - 1$. ($\mathcal{L}$ denotes the set of indices of the adjacent blocks in a same frame.) Then, its joint probability can be factorized by the Hammersley-Clifford theorem [5] as

$$P(\boldsymbol{\omega}^t, \boldsymbol{\omega}^{t-1}) = \frac{1}{Z} \exp\left(-\sum_{W_n \in \mathcal{C}_1} \Psi_n^1(W_n) - \sum_{W_{\{ij\}} \in \mathcal{C}_2} \Psi_{\{ij\}}^2(W_{\{ij\}}) - \sum_{W_{\{ij\}} \in \mathcal{C}_3} \Psi_{\{ij\}}^3(W_{\{ij\}}) \right), \tag{3}$$

where Z is a normalization constant, and Ψ^k, $k = 1, 2, 3$, are the potential functions. Eliminating the terms that do not depend on the $\boldsymbol{\omega}^t$ (since they do not affect the result of the optimization), we obtain the following from (2) and (3)

$$f(\boldsymbol{\omega}^t) \propto \left[\prod_{n=1}^{N} P(\mathbf{x}_n | \omega_n^t) \right] \exp\left(-\sum_{n=1}^{N} \Psi_n^1(\omega_n^t, \omega_n^{t-1}) - \sum_{\{i,j\} \in \mathcal{L}} \Psi_{\{ij\}}^2(\{\omega_i^t, \omega_j^t\}) \right). \tag{4}$$

Finally, the optimization problem can be solved by minimizing the negative logarithm of f, that is,

$$\min_{\omega_1^t, \ldots, \omega_N^t} E(\boldsymbol{\omega}^t) := \sum_{n=1}^{N} \Psi_n^1(\omega_n^t, \omega_n^{t-1}) - \ln P(\mathbf{x}_n | \omega_n^t) + \sum_{\{i,j\} \in \mathcal{L}} \Psi_{\{ij\}}^2(\{\omega_i^t, \omega_j^t\}). \quad (5)$$

3.2 Solving Through Minimum s-t Cut

In order to solve (5) through minimum s-t cut, we construct a graph $G = (V, A)$ from the current frame. For that, let N be the number of blocks in the frame, and define the set V of vertices of G as $V = \{0, 1, \ldots, N, N+1\}$. In this set, 0 corresponds to the *source* vertex, $N+1$ to the *sink* vertex, and for all $n = 1, \ldots, N$ the vertex n corresponds to the random variable ω_n^t. Furthermore, define the set A of arcs of G as the union of three subsets A_1, A_2, A_3, where $A_1 := \{(0, n) | n = 1, ..., N\}$ is the set of arcs going from the source to every other vertex (except the sink); $A_2 := \{(n, N+1) | n = 1, \ldots, N\}$ is the set of arcs going from every vertex (except the source) to the sink; and A_3 is the set of arcs linking adjacent blocks in the frame in both directions. Figure 1(b) shows an example of the constructed graph.

To determine the arc capacities, we first split the terms of the objective function (5) and define $U_n(\omega_n^t) := \Psi_n^1(\omega_n^t, \omega_n^{t-1}) - \ln P(\mathbf{x}_n | \omega_n^t)$ for all $n = 1, \ldots, N$, and $B_{ij}(\omega_i^t, \omega_j^t) := \Psi_{\{ij\}}^2(\{\omega_i^t, \omega_j^t\})$ for all arcs $(i, j) \in A_3$. Then, we set for all $n = 1, \ldots, N$, the arc capacities $u_{0,n} = U_n(0)$, and $u_{n,N+1} = U_n(1)$. And for all arcs $(i, j) \in A_3$ we set $u_{i,j} = B_{ij}(0, 1)$. Note that $B_{ij}(0, 1) = B_{ij}(1, 0)$ and $B_{ij} \equiv B_{ji}$.

Once we have found a minimum s-t cut in G which partitions the set V into S and T with the *source* $0 \in S$ and the *sink* $N + 1 \in T$, we determine the optimal solution $\boldsymbol{\omega}^t$ to (5) by setting, for all $n \in \{1, \ldots, N\}$, $\omega_n^t = 1$ if $n \in S$, and $\omega_n^t = 0$ otherwise.

Among the several algorithms for solving the minimum s-t cut problem [6], we have chosen Excesses Incremental Breadth-First Search (EIBFS) [8,9], which finds global minima in polynomial time. Moreover, this algorithm allows the optimal solution of a given frame to be used as an initial, near-optimal solution in the next one, substantially reducing the computational effort.

3.3 Probability Models

In our approach, the probabilities $P(\mathbf{x}_n | \omega_n^t = 0)$ and $P(\mathbf{x}_n | \omega_n^t = 1)$ are estimated by computing the two-dimensional histogram of vectors from the background and from the object, respectively. Although the exact regions of the MVs belonging to *object* and *non-object* classes are unknown at the current frame, the previously computed object's mask M_{t-1} gives the best estimate of these regions at the previous frame. Therefore, assuming that the tracking object moves smoothly, we can use the vectors of the current frame in the area occupied by M_{t-1} as object samples, and the vectors outside this area as non-object samples. In order to obtain a more robust sample of MVs for the *object* class, we apply an erosion morphological transformation with a predefined kernel size C_1 on M_{t-1}, which removes its borders.

Moreover, we compute these probabilities using additive smoothing with parameter $\alpha > 0$. In other words, given the histogram of a class ω_n^t with a total of B bins and for which K vectors were used to create it, if k is the number of samples inside the bin corresponding to a given MV $\mathbf{x}_n$, then its conditional probability is given by

$$P(\mathbf{x}_n|\omega_n^t) = \frac{k + \alpha}{K + \alpha B}. \tag{6}$$

This procedure not only smooths the histogram, but also guarantees non-zero probabilities, which is necessary to calculate their logarithms in Eq. (5).

For modeling the potential functions Ψ_n^1, note that they should indicate a temporal relation between the current frame and the previous one. We, therefore, follow the proposal of Khatoonabadi and Bajić [14] of using a measure of temporal continuity of the blocks. In summary, to determine the temporal continuity $D_n \in [0,1]$ of a block $n \in \{1, \ldots, N\}$, one firstly projects it backwards onto the previous frame according to its MV, and then determines how much of its area lies on a block labeled as *object*. On the matrix yielded by calculating this measure on the whole frame we apply a Gaussian filter with predefined standard deviation σ in order to make it more robust to noisy MVs. Then, for all $n = 1, \ldots, N$, we define Ψ_n^1 parametrized by $C_2 > 0$ as follows:

$$\Psi_n^1(\omega_n^t, \omega_n^{t-1}) = \begin{cases} C_2 \, D_n & \text{if } \omega_n^t = 0, \\ C_2 \, (1 - D_n) & \text{if } \omega_n^t = 1. \end{cases} \tag{7}$$

The potential function $\Psi_{\{ij\}}^2$ models the relation between adjacent blocks i and j in the current frame t as a cost, which is positive if the labels are different and zero otherwise. We empirically define it as being inversely proportional to the distance between the respective MVs $\mathbf{x}_i$ and $\mathbf{x}_j$, as follows:

$$\Psi_{\{ij\}}^2(\{\omega_i^t, \omega_j^t\}) = \begin{cases} \gamma \left(\|\mathbf{x}_i - \mathbf{x}_j\|^2 + \gamma^2 \right)^{-1.5} & \text{if } \omega_i^t \neq \omega_j^t, \\ 0 & \text{if } \omega_i^t = \omega_j^t, \end{cases} \tag{8}$$

where $\gamma > 0$ is a parameter of the function.

3.4 Preprocessing

Our proposed tracking algorithm uses two types of information from the encoded video stream: MVs and block coding modes (macroblock partitioning). H.264/AVC allows for four block partitioning modes: 16×16, 8×16, 16×8, and 8×8 where the 8×8 blocks can further be partitioned into 8×4, 4×8, and 4×4 sub-blocks. In order to fulfill the input assumptions of the proposed model, a uniformly sampled MV field needs to be constructed. Since the smallest partition in H.264/AVC is 4×4, we map all MVs to 4×4 blocks. Specifically, we apply the following preprocessing steps: (i) partially decode the video stream (as in [12]), yielding a list of prediction blocks and respective MVs. (ii) Arrange these MVs into a two-channel matrix in order to produce a uniform grid of vectors, where every entry corresponds to a 4×4 block. (iii) For intra-predicted blocks, which have no associated MVs, we compute the Polar Vector Median as defined in [14] by employing the MVs of the not intra-coded neighboring blocks.

Although these preprocessing steps may be sufficient for the case of static camera, the method could fail in the presence of camera motion. Therefore, we estimate global motion with the method introduced by Smolić et al. in [21] and improved by Arvanitidou et al. in [2]. In this model, six parameters $a_1, \ldots, a_6$ are used to obtain an approximation $\tilde{\mathbf{v}}_{x,y}(\mathbf{a})$ of the MV at the position (x, y) by

$$\tilde{\mathbf{v}}_{x,y}(\mathbf{a}) = \begin{bmatrix} a_1 x + a_2 y + a_3 - x \\ a_4 x + a_5 y + a_6 - y \end{bmatrix}. \tag{9}$$

Then, given M MVs $\mathbf{v}_{x^1,y^1}, \ldots, \mathbf{v}_{x^M,y^M}$, the goal is to find the global motion parameter $\mathbf{a} \in \mathbb{R}^6$ which minimizes the error $\sum_{k=1}^{M} \|\tilde{\mathbf{v}}_{x^k,y^k}(\mathbf{a}) - \mathbf{v}_{x^k,y^k}\|^2$. The optimal solution $\mathbf{a}^*$ is determined by solving this least squares problem using an M-estimator. As in [2], we only use MVs of prediction blocks larger than or equal to 8×8 pixels since they are less likely to belong to moving foreground. Finally, in order to compensate the camera motion, we subtract from the MV field the estimates $\tilde{\mathbf{v}}_{x,y}(\mathbf{a}^*)$ since they indicate the effect of global motion at the respective coordinates.

4 Experiments

We evaluated our method on two different datasets and compared its tracking performance with the ST-MRF method in [14]. For evaluation, we use the commonly employed metrics in tracking literature: Precision, Recall and F-Measure [25]. These three measures are computer at each video frame and their values are averaged for each sequence.

4.1 Experimental Setup

The first dataset (referred to as *derf*), also used in [14], comprises nine standard test sequences with formats CIF (352×288 pixels) and SIF (352×240 pixels) encoded by the H.264/AVC JM 18.0 Reference Software [22]. Their group-of-pictures (GOP) structure is IPPP..., *i.e.*, the first frame is an intra-predicted picture (predicted from previously decoded data from the same picture), and each frame after the first one is a forward-predicted picture (predicted from a picture that has been previously coded and transmitted) containing MVs pointing to the previous reference pictures [20].

Since the ground truth segmentations of the *derf* dataset are not available over the entire duration of the sequences (but only on a relatively small portion), performance of the tracking algorithms can only be evaluated over a limited portion of each sequence. Moreover, *derf* contains test sequences that were originally

Table 1. Evaluation results in percentages for both datasets. Columns *Prec.*, *Rec.* and *F-Me.* show averaged precision, recall and F-measure, respectively. Numbers in bold face correspond to the method which obtained the highest F-measure for the respective video sequence.

Derf	ST-MRF [14]			Proposed		
Sequence	Prec.	Rec.	F-Me.	Prec.	Rec.	F-Me.
Mobile Calendar	**75.9**	**88.4**	**81.2**	70.8	95.9	80.8
Coastguard	**64.3**	**89.4**	**74.4**	43.0	98.7	57.8
Stefan (CIF)	**84.2**	**68.3**	**74.1**	75.8	72.2	73.6
Stefan (SIF)	**84.7**	**67.8**	**74.3**	69.5	79.0	73.2
Hall Monitor	72.8	84.4	78.1	**71.7**	**87.4**	**78.6**
Flower Garden	**82.9**	**95.8**	**88.8**	70.6	98.4	81.5
Table Tennis	**94.1**	**88.0**	**90.8**	89.0	92.1	90.5
City	**92.9**	**96.5**	**94.6**	91.3	97.4	94.2
Foreman	**92.3**	**90.4**	**91.2**	98.0	76.1	85.2
Average	**82.7**	**85.4**	**83.1**	75.5	88.6	79.5

VOT2016	ST-MRF [14]			Proposed		
Sequence	Prec.	Rec.	F-Me.	Prec.	Rec.	F-Me.
fish1	19.7	21.0	19.2	**17.2**	**34.5**	**22.6**
fish2	**36.0**	**37.1**	**34.2**	25.9	45.8	31.5
fish3	24.9	25.7	21.2	**64.5**	**56.7**	**50.5**
fish4	8.0	8.0	7.5	**54.7**	**79.1**	**63.1**
graduate	5.1	1.7	2.3	**45.3**	**48.4**	**45.7**
gymnastics1	2.3	1.1	1.3	**20.3**	**29.2**	**21.2**
gymnastics2	42.1	25.7	27.4	**30.7**	**45.5**	**36.1**
gymnastics4	4.8	1.7	2.2	**63.0**	**66.5**	**63.3**
hand	10.3	20.7	11.6	**31.8**	**69.4**	**41.1**
handball2	**17.7**	**91.4**	**25.0**	9.5	61.4	15.9
helicopter	27.2	89.9	26.5	**21.5**	**52.1**	**28.7**
marching	**23.9**	**39.6**	**22.8**	3.3	5.3	3.9
matrix	9.4	5.6	6.3	**18.6**	**29.0**	**22.2**
nature	23.1	12.4	14.8	**26.9**	**21.1**	**22.0**
octopus	54.9	98.3	67.8	**56.5**	**88.0**	**68.2**
racing	31.7	84.7	40.5	**33.1**	**92.1**	**46.2**
shaking	17.0	89.0	24.0	**28.8**	**90.1**	**42.7**
sheep	2.8	1.5	1.8	**25.9**	**92.8**	**38.0**
singer1	**47.3**	**33.8**	**35.4**	23.4	82.2	34.4
singer2	13.7	89.0	22.4	**23.9**	**63.9**	**32.8**
singer3	**37.1**	**92.9**	**48.5**	17.9	33.0	19.5
soldier	**40.5**	**83.8**	**51.9**	32.8	74.5	42.7
sphere	26.1	84.7	37.7	**40.3**	**43.2**	**40.3**
tiger	10.3	27.6	13.7	**30.2**	**53.9**	**34.5**
traffic	**14.9**	**72.1**	**21.5**	1.7	12.4	2.8
Average	24.4	50.2	27.0	**32.4**	**57.9**	**37.6**

VOT2016	ST-MRF [14]			Proposed		
Sequence	Prec.	Rec.	F-Me.	Prec.	Rec.	F-Me.
bag	17.9	90.7	28.3	**34.8**	**79.0**	**47.1**
birds2	8.7	5.9	6.7	**31.5**	**47.1**	**37.5**
blanket	20.8	30.9	22.3	**40.3**	**69.1**	**49.6**
bmx	**55.4**	**77.1**	**62.8**	60.4	41.3	48.1
crossing	36.1	92.9	**49.4**	22.2	85.7	33.9
dinosaur	39.7	88.0	52.7	**45.9**	**87.3**	**58.6**
fernando	51.5	81.5	53.2	**55.4**	**74.1**	**59.8**

collected for evaluation of video codecs. As a result, the sequences do not thoroughly address the challenging situations (*e.g.* complex camera motion, multiple similar objects) that a tracking algorithm may encounter. To address these issues, we performed further experiments on a second, larger dataset created for Visual Object Tracking (VOT) Challenge 2016 [15]. The dataset has 60 sequences with resolutions varying from 320×240 to 1280×720 pixels. VOT 2016 challenge aims at comparing single-object visual trackers most of which were published at major computer vision conferences and journals in recent years. Therefore, the dataset contains challenging sequences with strong camera motion and cluttered scenes with distracting objects. Since the sequences are originally available as JPEG images, we re-encoded them as H.264/AVC sequences with a GOP structure IPPP...IPPP... using the x264 encoder [1].

We implemented our tracker in Python[1] and integrated the minimum s-t cut solver (developed in C++ [9]) via Cython. The experiments were conducted on a Intel Xeon E5-v3 CPU with 32 GB RAM running Linux. The parameters of the proposed model (*cf.* Sect. 3.3) were empirically determined as follows: $\alpha, \sigma = 1$; $\gamma = 0.5$; $C_1, C_2 = 6$.

4.2　Results and Discussion

Table 1 shows the results obtained for both trackers. At the *derf* dataset, our method performs slightly worse than ST-MRF [14] by 3.6% on average in terms of F-Measure. However, we believe that the high tracking performance over this

---

[1] Available online at https://github.com/bombardellif/hhi-stmrftracking.

(a) Frames 2, 6, 12 and 455 of *graduate*.   (b) Frames 2, 10, 17 and 70 of *gymnastics4*.

Fig. 2. Tracking results for videos with tracking objects with low motion. True positives, false positives and false negatives are denoted in green, blue and red, respectively. The proposed method can track objects with little movement more accurately and for a longer time compared to the ST-MRF method [14]. (Color figure online)

dataset should be interpreted cautiously because the experiments were performed on a short portion of the videos (on average 73 frames) due to the limited availability of ground truth annotations (*cf.* Sect. 4.1). This implies that the tracker is less likely to lose the tracking object and also less likely to encounter significant scene changes. Another factor for the high performance over *derf* dataset can be attributed to the relative simplicity of the object motion patterns and relatively large object/picture size ratio which provides more MVs initially associated with the object, thus more reliable input data.

For the VOT2016 dataset, we only show the results for those video sequences in which at least one of the methods obtained an F-measure above 20%. From the table, we observe that the performance of both methods depends highly on the individual sequence and varies strongly within the dataset. In some sequences such as *birds2, sheep, graduate* and *gymnastics4*, we observed that the tracking object has (or appears to have) low motion for some seconds causing most MVs to become zero. Figure 2 shows example frames from two such sequences: *graduate* and *gymnastics4*. In *graduate*, a person runs towards the camera and he appears to be motionless for multiple seconds (except for small arm movements) due to the scene perspective until he finally draws near to the camera and makes a right turn. In the shown portion of *gymnastics4*, the gymnast retains her pose for about two seconds as the (possibly hand-held) camera wiggles briefly. We observe that while ST-MRF loses the tracking object for these cases, our method is able to track them successfully (albeit with some false negatives). The reason why the proposed method handles such cases better than ST-MRF can be attributed to the arc weights of the graph, in which a minimum s-t cut is determined (*cf.* Sect. 3.2). This behavior can be explained by inspecting the individual terms of Eq. (5): if the probabilities $P(\mathbf{x}_n | \omega_n^t = 0)$ and $P(\mathbf{x}_n | \omega_n^t = 1)$ are nearly equal for some block n (*e.g.* background and object have very similar MVs), then the second term $\Psi_n^1(\omega_n^t, \omega_n^{t-1})$, which measures the temporal continuity, becomes more decisive in the objective function (5). This mechanism ensures that the resulting segmentation mask is similar to the one in the previous frame if the object is (or appears to be) motionless.

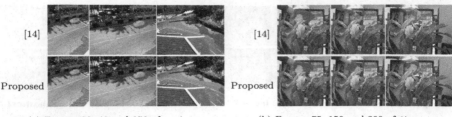

(a) Frames 30, 40 and 150 of *racing*.   (b) Frames 75, 150 and 300 of *tiger*.

Fig. 3. Tracking results for videos with fast motion. True positives, false positives and false negatives are denoted in green, blue and red, respectively. The proposed method yields more precise segmentation masks for fast moving targets than ST-MRF [14]. (Color figure online)

Similarly, our method also performs better in sequences with fast object motion, maintaining higher precision throughout the sequences. Figure 3 shows example frames from two such sequences: *racing* and *tiger*. In *racing*, a car moves on a race track followed by the camera as it makes a turn. In *tiger*, we see a person's arm holding a toy tiger as the person moves the toy with quick, jerky movements behind a flowerpot placed closer to the camera. We observe for both cases that our method manages to track the fast moving object more successfully than ST-MRF. Specifically, our method produces much less false positives in *racing* and does not lose the target object in *tiger* unlike ST-MRF. The success of our method for sequences with fast motion can be explained again by inspecting Eq. (5): if the MVs of the tracking object are very different from the background MVs, then the probability $P(\mathbf{x}_n | \omega_n^t)$ in Eq. (5) becomes more decisive for the optimization. Thus, the importance of the previous mask is suppressed.

Nevertheless, our approach tends to fail in more challenging instances, such as *marching* and *traffic*. The former is a case of complete occlusion, where the marching band member being tracked is rapidly occluded by a person which passes running in front of the camera. The latter is an example of complex camera motion, where the tracking object is followed by a moving camera installed on the helmet of a motorcyclist. One reason for the failure of our method in such cases is that most MVs in the region occupied by the object either do not correspond to the tracking object (as in *marching*) or become hard to distinguish from the background (as in *traffic*), which impairs the segmentation by graph cuts.

In general, both methods have difficulties in performing reliable tracking especially for some of the more challenging sequences in the dataset VOT2016. For those, it is important to notice that compressed-domain approaches have fundamental limitations. One such case is when the object of interest does not occupy a sufficient amount of blocks in the frame, leading to a reduced number of vectors describing its motion. Another issue is the accumulation of the tracking error along the sequence. That is, since the outcome in a given frame depends on the outcome of the previous one, incorrect classifications are propagated and tend to grow with the length of the video. A possible solution to this problem—as proposed by Gül *et al.* [10]—is to periodically regularize the objective function using the color information sampled from the I frames of the video bitstream.

5 Conclusion

In this paper, we present a technique for tracking moving objects in H.264/AVC compressed videos. The proposed approach relies only on motion vectors and block coding modes readily available in the compressed video bitstream. Thus, it requires low processing and storage compared to pixel-domain tracking algorithms. We compared the performance of our method with a state-of-the-art compressed-domain tracking algorithm. We observed that average tracking accuracy significantly depends on the complexity of the scene and motion of the tracking object. In videos with relatively simple motion, both approaches have relatively high tracking accuracy and their performances are comparable. In more challenging sequences, our algorithm achieves a higher average tracking performance for most sequences. Specifically, we observed that our algorithm performs better in sequences containing low motion and fast moving targets, respectively.

Acknowledgments. The research leading to these results has received funding from the German Federal Ministry for Economic Affairs and Energy under the VIRTUOSE-DE project.

References

1. Aimar, L., et al.: x264, the best H.264/AVC encoder - VideoLAN, August 2017. https://www.videolan.org/developers/x264.html
2. Arvanitidou, M.G., Glantz, A., Krutz, A., Sikora, T., Mrak, M., Kondoz, A.: Global motion estimation using variable block sizes and its application to object segmentation. In: 10th Workshop on Image Analysis for Multimedia Interactive Services, pp. 173–176. IEEE (2009)
3. Babu, R.V., Tom, M., Wadekar, P.: A survey on compressed domain video analysis techniques. Multimedia Tools Appl. **75**(2), 1043–1078 (2016)
4. Becker, D., et al.: Visual object tracking in a parking garage using compressed domain analysis. In: Proceedings of the 9th ACM Multimedia System Conference (2018)
5. Besag, J.: Spatial interaction and the statistical analysis of lattice systems. J. Roy. Stat. Soc. Ser. B (Methodol.) **36**, 192–236 (1974)
6. Boykov, Y., Kolmogorov, V.: An experimental comparison of min-cut/max-flow algorithms for energy minimization in vision. IEEE Trans. Pattern Anal. Mach. Intell. **26**(9), 1124–1137 (2004)
7. Galoogahi, H.K., Fagg, A., Huang, C., Ramanan, D., Lucey, S.: Need for speed: a benchmark for higher frame rate object tracking. In: 2017 IEEE International Conference on Computer Vision (ICCV), pp. 1134–1143. IEEE (2017)
8. Goldberg, A.V., Hed, S., Kaplan, H., Tarjan, R.E., Werneck, R.F.: Maximum flows by incremental breadth-first search. In: Demetrescu, C., Halldórsson, M.M. (eds.) ESA 2011. LNCS, vol. 6942, pp. 457–468. Springer, Heidelberg (2011). https://doi.org/10.1007/978-3-642-23719-5_39

9. Goldberg, A.V., Hed, S., Kaplan, H., Kohli, P., Tarjan, R.E., Werneck, R.F.: Faster and more dynamic maximum flow by incremental breadth-first search. In: Bansal, N., Finocchi, I. (eds.) ESA 2015. LNCS, vol. 9294, pp. 619–630. Springer, Heidelberg (2015). https://doi.org/10.1007/978-3-662-48350-3_52

10. Gül, S., Meyer, J.T., Hellge, C., Schierl, T., Samek, W.: Hybrid video object tracking in H.265/HEVC video streams. In: 2016 IEEE 18th Int. Workshop on Multimedia Signal Process, pp. 1–5 (2016)

11. Held, D., Thrun, S., Savarese, S.: Learning to track at 100 FPS with deep regression networks. In: Leibe, B., Matas, J., Sebe, N., Welling, M. (eds.) ECCV 2016. LNCS, vol. 9905, pp. 749–765. Springer, Cham (2016). https://doi.org/10.1007/978-3-319-46448-0_45

12. Kantorov, V., Laptev, I.: Efficient feature extraction, encoding and classification for action recognition. In: CVPR, pp. 2593–2600 (2014)

13. Käs, C., Nicolas, H.: An Approach to trajectory estimation of moving objects in the H.264 compressed domain. In: Wada, T., Huang, F., Lin, S. (eds.) PSIVT 2009. LNCS, vol. 5414, pp. 318–329. Springer, Heidelberg (2009). https://doi.org/10.1007/978-3-540-92957-4_28

14. Khatoonabadi, S.H., Bajić, I.V.: Video object tracking in the compressed domain using spatio-temporal Markov random fields. IEEE Trans. Image Process. **22**(1), 300–313 (2013)

15. Kristan, M., et al.: The visual object tracking VOT2016 challenge results. In: Hua, G., Jégou, H. (eds.) ECCV 2016. LNCS, vol. 9914, pp. 777–823. Springer, Cham (2016). https://doi.org/10.1007/978-3-319-48881-3_54. http://www.springer.com/gp/book/9783319488806

16. Laumer, M., Amon, P., Hutter, A., Kaup, A.: Compressed domain moving object detection based on H.264/AVC macroblock types. In: VISAPP, vol. 1, pp. 219–228 (2013)

17. Laumer, M., Amon, P., Hutter, A., Kaup, A.: Moving object detection in the H.264/AVC compressed domain. APSIPA Trans. Signal Inf. Process. **5**, e18 (2016)

18. Poppe, C., De Bruyne, S., Paridaens, T., Lambert, P., Van de Walle, R.: Moving object detection in the H.264/AVC compressed domain for video surveillance applications. J. Vis. Commun. Image Represent. **20**(6), 428–437 (2009)

19. Prince, S.J.: Computer Vision: Models, Learning, and Inference. Cambridge University Press, Cambridge (2012)

20. Richardson, I.E.: The H.264 Advanced Video Compression Standard. Wiley, Hoboken (2011)

21. Smolić, A., Hoeynck, M., Ohm, J.R.: Low-complexity global motion estimation from P-frame motion vectors for MPEG-7 applications. In: International Conference on Image Processing, vol. 2, pp. 271–274. IEEE (2000)

22. Sühring, K.: H.264/AVC JM reference software, August 2017. http://iphome.hhi.de/suehring/tml/

23. Wiegand, T., Sullivan, G.J., Bjøntegaard, G., Luthra, A.: Overview of the H.264/AVC video coding standard. IEEE Trans. Circuits Syst. Video Technol. **13**(7), 560–576 (2003)

24. Wojaczek, P., Laumer, M., Amon, P., Hutter, A., Kaup, A.: Hybrid person detection and tracking in H.264/AVC video streams. In: VISAPP, vol. 1, pp. 478–485 (2015)

25. Yilmaz, A., Javed, O., Shah, M.: Object tracking: a survey. ACM Comput. Surv. (CSUR) **38**(4), 13 (2006)

26. You, W., Sabirin, M., Kim, M.: Real-time detection and tracking of multiple objects with partial decoding in H.264/AVC bitstream domain. In: Proceedings of SPIE, the International Society for Optical Engineering (2009)
27. Zeng, W., Du, J., Gao, W., Huang, Q.: Robust moving object segmentation on H.264/AVC compressed video using the block-based MRF model. Real-Time Imaging 11(4), 290–299 (2005)

Metric-Driven Learning of Correspondence Weighting for 2-D/3-D Image Registration

Roman Schaffert[1]([⊠])(iD), Jian Wang[2](iD), Peter Fischer[2](iD), Anja Borsdorf[2], and Andreas Maier[1,3](iD)

[1] Pattern Recognition Lab, Friedrich-Alexander Universität Erlangen-Nürnberg, Erlangen, Germany
roman.schrom.schaffert@fau.de
[2] Siemens Healthineers AG, Forchheim, Germany
[3] Graduate School in Advanced Optical Technologies (SAOT), Erlangen, Germany

Abstract. Registration of pre-operative 3-D volumes to intra-operative 2-D X-ray images is important in minimally invasive medical procedures. Rigid registration can be performed by estimating a global rigid motion that optimizes the alignment of local correspondences. However, inaccurate correspondences challenge the registration performance. To minimize their influence, we estimate optimal weights for correspondences using PointNet. We train the network directly with the criterion to minimize the registration error. We propose an objective function which includes point-to-plane correspondence-based motion estimation and projection error computation, thereby enabling the learning of a weighting strategy that optimally fits the underlying formulation of the registration task in an end-to-end fashion. For single-vertebra registration, we achieve an accuracy of 0.74 ± 0.26 mm and highly improved robustness. The success rate is increased from 79.3% to 94.3% and the capture range from 3 mm to 13 mm.

Keywords: Medical image registration · 2-D/3-D registration · Deep learning · Point-to-plane correspondence model

1 Introduction

Image fusion is frequently involved in modern image-guided medical interventions, typically augmenting intra-operatively acquired 2-D X-ray images with pre-operative 3-D CT or MRI images. Accurate alignment between the fused images is essential for clinical applications and can be achieved using 2-D/3-D rigid registration, which aims at finding the pose of a 3-D volume in order to

Electronic supplementary material The online version of this chapter (https://doi.org/10.1007/978-3-030-12939-2_11) contains supplementary material, which is available to authorized users.

© Springer Nature Switzerland AG 2019
T. Brox et al. (Eds.): GCPR 2018, LNCS 11269, pp. 140–152, 2019.
https://doi.org/10.1007/978-3-030-12939-2_11

align its projections to 2-D X-ray images. Most commonly, intensity-based methods are employed [8], where a similarity measure between the 2-D image and the projection of the 3-D image is defined and optimized as e.g. described by Kubias et al. [6]. Despite decades of investigations, 2-D/3-D registration remains challenging. The difference in dimensionality of the input images results in an ill-posed problem. In addition, content mismatch between the pre-operative and intra-operative images, poor image quality and a limited field of view challenge the robustness and accuracy of registration algorithms. Miao et al. [9] propose a learning-based registration method that is build upon the intensity-based approach. While they achieve a high robustness, registration accuracy remains challenging.

The intuition of 2-D/3-D rigid registration is to globally minimize the visual misalignment between 2-D images and the projections of the 3-D image. Based on this intuition, Schmid and Chênes [13] decompose the target structure to local shape patches and model image forces using Hooke's law of a spring from image block matching. Wang et al. [15] propose a point-to-plane correspondence (PPC) model for 2-D/3-D registration, which linearly constrains the global differential motion update using local correspondences. Registration is performed by iteratively establishing correspondences and performing the motion estimation. During the intervention, devices and implants, as well as locally similar anatomies, can introduce outliers for local correspondence search (see Fig. 3a and b). Weighting of local correspondences, in order to emphasize the correct correspondences, directly influences the accuracy and robustness of the registration. An iterative reweighted scheme is suggested by Wang et al. [15] to enhance the robustness against outliers. However, this scheme only works when outliers are a minority of the measurements.

Recently, Qi et al. [11] proposed the PointNet, a type of neural network directly processing point clouds. PointNet is capable of internally extracting global features of the cloud and relating them to local features of individual points. Thus, it is well suited for correspondence weighting in 2-D/3-D registration. Yi et al. [16] propose to learn the selection of correct correspondences for wide-baseline stereo images. As a basis, candidates are established, e.g. using SIFT features. Ground truth labels are generated by exploiting the epipolar constraint. This way, an outlier label is generated. Additionally, a regression loss is introduced, which is based on the error in the estimation of a known essential matrix between two images. Both losses are combined during training. While including the regression loss improves the results, the classification loss is shown to be important to find highly accurate correspondences. The performance of iterative correspondence-based registration algorithms (e.g. [13,15]) can be improved by learning a weighting strategy for the correspondences. However, automatic labeling of the correspondences is not practical for iterative methods as even correct correspondences may have large errors in the first few iterations. This means that labeling cannot be performed by applying a simple rule such as a threshold based on the ground truth position of a point.

In this paper, we propose a method to learn an optimal weighting strategy for the local correspondences for rigid 2-D/3-D registration directly with the criterion to minimize the registration error, without the need of per-correspondence ground truth annotations. We treat the correspondences as a point cloud with extended per-point features and use a modified PointNet architecture to learn global interdependencies of local correspondences according to the PPC registration metric. We choose to use the PPC model as it was shown to enable a high registration accuracy as well as robustness [15]. Furthermore, it is differentiable and therefore lends itself to the use in our training objective function. To train the network, we propose a novel training objective function, which is composed of the motion estimation according to the PPC model and the registration error computation steps. It allows us to learn a correspondence weighting strategy by minimizing the registration error. We demonstrate the effectiveness of the learned weighting strategy by evaluating our method on single-vertebra registration, where we show a highly improved robustness compared to the original PPC registration.

2   Registration and Learned Correspondence Weighting

In the following section, we begin with an overview of the registration method using the PPC model. Then, further details on motion estimation (see Sect. 2.2) and registration error computation (see Sect. 2.3) are given, as these two steps play a crucial role in our objective function. The architecture of our network is discussed in Sect. 2.4, followed by the introduction of our objective function in Sect. 2.5. At last, important details regarding the training procedure are given in Sect. 2.6.

2.1   Registration Using Point-to-Plane Correspondences

Wang et al. [15] measure the local misalignment between the projection of a 3-D volume V and the 2-D fluoroscopic (live X-ray) image I^{FL} and compute a motion which compensates for this misalignment. Surface points are extracted from V using the 3-D Canny detector [1]. A set of contour generator points [4] $\{\mathbf{w}_i\}$, i.e. surface points $\mathbf{w}_i \in \mathbb{R}^3$ which correspond to contours in the projection of V, are projected onto the image as $\{\mathbf{p}_i\}$, i.e. a set of points $\mathbf{p}_i \in \mathbb{R}^3$ on the image plane. Additionally, gradient projection images of V are generated and used to perform local patch matching to find correspondences for $\mathbf{p}_i$ in I^{FL}. Assuming that the motion along contours is not detectable, the patch matching is only performed in the orthogonal direction to the contour. Therefore, the displacement of $\mathbf{w}_i$ along the contour is not known, as well as the displacement along the viewing direction. These unknown directions span the plane Π_i with the normal $\mathbf{n}_i \in \mathbb{R}^3$. After the registration, a point $\mathbf{w}_i$ should be located on the plane Π_i. To minimize the point-to-plane distances $d(\mathbf{w}_i, \Pi_i)$, a linear equation is defined for each correspondence under the small angle assumption. The resulting system of equations is solved for the differential motion $\delta\mathbf{v} \in \mathbb{R}^6$, which contains both rotational components in the axis-angle representation $\delta\boldsymbol{\omega} \in \mathbb{R}^3$ and translational components $\delta \nu \in \mathbb{R}^3$, i.e. $\delta \mathbf{v} = (\delta \boldsymbol{\omega}^\mathsf{T}, \delta \boldsymbol{\nu}^\mathsf{T})^\mathsf{T}$. The correspondence search and motion estimation steps are applied iteratively over multiple resolution levels. To increase the robustness of the motion estimation, the maximum correntropy criterion for regression (MCCR) [3] is used to solve the system of linear equations [15]. The motion estimation is extended to coordinate systems related to the camera coordinates by a rigid transformation by Schaffert et al. [12].

The PPC model sets up a linear relationship between the local point-to-plane correspondences and the differential transformation, i.e. a linear misalignment metric based on the found correspondences. In this paper, we introduce a learning method for correspondence weighting, where the PPC metric is used during training to optimize the weighting strategy for the used correspondences with respect to the registration error.

2.2 Weighted Motion Estimation

Motion estimation according to the PPC model is performed by solving a linear system of equations defined by $\mathbf{A} \in \mathbb{R}^{N \times 6}$ and $\mathbf{b} \in \mathbb{R}^N$, where each equation corresponds to one point-to-plane correspondence and N is the number of used correspondences. We perform the motion estimation in the camera coordinate system with the origin shifted to the centroid of $\{\mathbf{w}_i\}$. This allows us to use the regularized least-squares estimation

$$\delta \mathbf{v} = \arg \min_{\delta \mathbf{v}'} \left(\frac{1}{N} \|\mathbf{A}_s \delta \mathbf{v}' - \mathbf{b}_s\|_2^2 + \lambda \|\delta \mathbf{v}'\|_2^2 \right) \tag{1}$$

in order to improve the robustness of the estimation. Here, $\mathbf{A}_s = \mathbf{S} \cdot \mathbf{A}$, $\mathbf{b}_s = \mathbf{S} \cdot \mathbf{b}$ and λ is the regularizer weight. The diagonal matrix $\mathbf{S} = \mathrm{diag}(\mathbf{s})$ contains weights $\mathbf{s} \in \mathbb{R}^N$ for all correspondences. As Eq. (1) is differentiable w.r.t. $\delta \mathbf{v}'$, we obtain

$$\delta \mathbf{v} = \mathrm{RegPPC}(\mathbf{A}, \mathbf{b}, \mathbf{s}) = (\mathbf{A}_s^\mathsf{T} \mathbf{A}_s + N \cdot \lambda \mathbf{I})^{-1} \mathbf{A}_s^\mathsf{T} \mathbf{b}_s, \tag{2}$$

where $\mathbf{I} \in \mathbb{R}^{6 \times 6}$ is the identity matrix. After each iteration, the registration $\mathbf{T} \in \mathbb{R}^{4 \times 4}$ is updated as

$$\mathbf{T} = \begin{pmatrix} \cos(\alpha)\mathbf{I} + (1 - \cos(\alpha)\mathbf{r}\mathbf{r}^\mathsf{T}) + \sin(\alpha)[\mathbf{r}]_\times & \delta \boldsymbol{\nu} \\ 0 & 1 \end{pmatrix} \cdot \hat{\mathbf{T}} , \tag{3}$$

where $\alpha = \|\delta \boldsymbol{\omega}\|$, $\mathbf{r} = \delta \boldsymbol{\omega}/\|\delta \boldsymbol{\omega}\|$, $[\mathbf{r}]_\times \in \mathbb{R}^{3 \times 3}$ is a skew matrix which expresses the cross product with $\mathbf{r}$ as a matrix multiplication and $\hat{\mathbf{T}} \in \mathbb{R}^{4 \times 4}$ is the registration after the previous iteration [15].

2.3 Registration Error Computation

In the training phase, the registration error is measured and minimized via our training objective function. Different error metrics, such as the mean target registration error (mTRE) or the mean re-projection distance (mRPD) can be used.

For more details on these metrics, see Sect. 3.3. In this work, we choose the projection error (PE) [14], as it directly corresponds to the visible misalignment in the images and therefore roughly correlates to the difficulty to find correspondences by patch matching for the next iteration of the registration method. The PE is computed as

$$e = \text{PE}(\mathbf{T}, \mathbf{T}^{\text{GT}}) = \frac{1}{M} \sum_{j=1}^{M} \| P_{\mathbf{T}}(\mathbf{q}_j) - P_{\mathbf{T}^{\text{GT}}}(\mathbf{q}_j) \|, \qquad (4)$$

where a set of M target points $\{\mathbf{q}_j\}$ is used and j is the point index. $P_{\mathbf{T}}(\cdot)$ is the projection onto the image plane under the currently estimated registration and $P_{\mathbf{T}^{\text{GT}}}(\cdot)$ the projection under the ground-truth registration matrix $\mathbf{T}^{\text{GT}} \in \mathbb{R}^{4 \times 4}$. Corners of the bounding box of the point set $\{\mathbf{w}_i\}$ are used as $\{\mathbf{q}_j\}$.

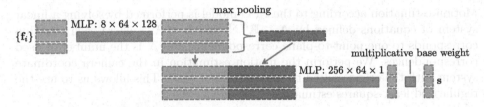

Fig. 1. Modified PointNet [11] architecture used for correspondence weighting. Rectangles with dashed outlines indicate feature vectors (orange for local features, i.e. containing information from single correspondences, and red for global features, i.e. containing information from the entire set of correspondences). Sets of feature vectors (one feature vector per correspondence) are depicted as a column of feature vectors (three correspondences shown here). MLP denotes a multi-layer perceptron, which is applied to each feature vector individually. (Color figure online)

2.4   Network Architecture

We want to weight individual correspondences based on their geometrical properties as well as the image similarity, taking into account the global properties of the correspondence set. For every correspondence, we define the features

$$\mathbf{f}_i = \left(\mathbf{w}_i^{\mathsf{T}} \ \mathbf{n}_i^{\mathsf{T}} \ \text{d}(\mathbf{w}_i, \Pi_i) \ \text{NGC}_i \right)^{\mathsf{T}}, \qquad (5)$$

where NGC_i denotes the normalized gradient correlation for the correspondences, which is obtained in the patch matching step.

The goal is to learn the mapping from a set of feature vectors $\{\mathbf{f}_i\}$ representing all correspondences to the weight vector $\mathbf{s}$ containing weights for all correspondences, i.e. the mapping

$$M_\theta : \{\mathbf{f}_i\} \mapsto \mathbf{s}, \qquad (6)$$

where M_θ is our network, and θ the network parameters.

To learn directly on correspondence sets, we use the PointNet [11] architecture and modify it to fit our task (see Fig. 1). The basic idea behind PointNet is to process points individually and obtain global information by combining the points in a symmetric way, i.e. independent of order in which the points appear in the input [11]. In the simplest variant, the PointNet consists of a multi-layer perceptron (MLP) which is applied for each point, transforming the respective f_i into a higher-dimensional feature space and thereby obtaining a local point descriptor. To describe the global properties of the point set, the resulting local descriptors are combined by max pooling over all points, i.e. for each feature, the maximum activation over all points in the set is retained. To obtain per-point outputs, the resulting global descriptor is concatenated to the local descriptors of each point. The resulting descriptors, containing global as well as local information, are further processed for each point independently by a second MLP. For our network, we choose MLPs with the size of $8 \times 64 \times 128$ and $256 \times 64 \times 1$, which are smaller than in the original network [11]. We enforce the output to be in the range of $[0; 1]$ by using a softsign activation function [2] in the last layer of the second MLP and modify it to re-scale the output range from $(-1; 1)$ to $(0; 1)$. Our modified softsign activation function $f(\cdot)$ is defined as

$$f(x) = \left(\frac{x}{1 + |x|} + 1 \right) \cdot 0.5, \tag{7}$$

where x is the state of the neuron. Additionally, we introduce a global trainable weighting factor which is applied to all correspondences. This allows for an automatic adjustment of the strength of the regularization in the motion estimation step. Note that the network is able to process correspondence sets of variable size so that no fixed amount of correspondences is needed and all extracted correspondences can be utilized.

2.5 Training Objective

We now combine the motion estimation, PE computation and the modified PointNet to obtain the training objective function as

$$\theta = \arg\min_{\theta'} \frac{1}{K} \sum_{k=1}^{K} \text{PE}(\text{RegPPC}(\mathbf{A}_k, \mathbf{b}_k, M_{\theta'}(\{\mathbf{f}_i\}_k)), \mathbf{T}_k^{\text{GT}}), \tag{8}$$

where k is the training sample index and K the overall number of samples. Equation (2) is differentiable with respect to $\mathbf{s}$, Eq. (3) with respect to $\delta\mathbf{v}$ and Eq. (4) with respect to $\mathbf{T}$. Therefore, gradient-based optimization can be performed on Eq. (8).

Note that using Eq. (8), we learn directly with the objective to minimize the registration error and no per-correspondence ground-truth weights are needed. Instead, the PPC metric is used to implicitly assess the quality of the correspondences during the back-propagation step of the training and the weights are adjusted accordingly. In other words, the optimization of the weights is driven by the PPC metric.

2.6 Training Procedure

To obtain training data, a set of volumes $\{V\}$ is used, each with one or more 2-D images $\{I^{\mathrm{FL}}\}$ and a known $\mathbf{T}^{\mathrm{GT}}$ (see Sect. 3.1). For each pair of images, 60 random initial transformations with an uniformly distributed mTRE are generated [5]. For details on the computation of the mTRE and start positions, see Sect. 3.3.

Estimation of correspondences at training time is computationally expensive. Instead, the correspondence search is performed once and the precomputed correspondences are used during training. Training is performed for one iteration of the registration method and start positions with a small initial error are assumed to be representative for subsequent registration iterations at test time. For training, the number of correspondences is fixed to 1024 to enable efficient batch-wise computations. The subset of used correspondences is selected randomly for every training step. Data augmentation is performed on the correspondence sets by applying translations, in-plane rotations and horizontal flipping, i.e. reflection over the plane spanned by the vertical axis of the 2-D image and the principal direction. For each resolution level, a separate model is trained.

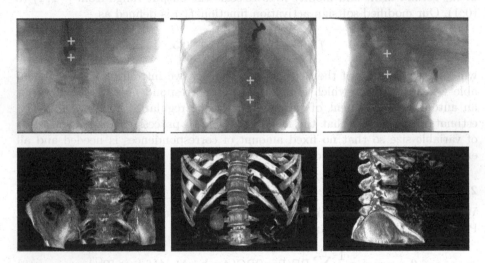

Fig. 2. Examples of 2-D images used as I^{FL} (top row) and the corresponding 3-D images used as V (bottom row) in the registration evaluation. Evaluated vertebrae are marked by a yellow cross in the top row. (Color figure online)

3 Experiments and Results

3.1 Data

We perform experiments for single-view registration of individual vertebrae. Note that single-vertebra registration is challenging due to the small size of the target structure and the presence of neighbor vertebrae. Therefore, achieving a high robustness is challenging. We use clinical C-arm CT acquisitions from the thoracic and pelvic regions of the spine for training and evaluation. Each acquisition consists of a sequence of 2-D images acquired with a rotating C-arm. These images are used to reconstruct the 3-D volume. To enable reconstruction, the C-arm geometry has to be calibrated with a high accuracy (the accuracy is ≤ 0.16 mm for the projection error at the iso-center in our case). We register the acquired 2-D images to the respective reconstructed volume and therefore the ground truth registration is known within the accuracy of the calibration. Vertebra are defined by an axis-aligned volume of interest (VOI) containing the whole vertebra. Only surface points inside the VOI are used for registration. We register the projection images (resolution of 616×480 pixels, pixel size of 0.62 mm) to the reconstructed volumes (containing around 390 slices with slice resolution of 512×512 voxels and voxel size of 0.49 mm). To simulate realistic conditions, we add Poisson noise to all 2-D images and rescale the intensities to better match fluoroscopic images.

The training set consists of 19 acquisitions with a total of 77 vertebrae. For each vertebra, 8 different 2-D images are used. An additional validation set of 23 vertebrae from 6 acquisitions is used to monitor the training process. The registration is performed on a test set of 6 acquisitions. For each acquisition, 2 vertebrae are evaluated and registration is performed independently for both the anterior-posterior and the lateral views. Each set contains data from different patients, i.e. no patient appears in two different sets. The sets were defined so that all sets are representative to the overall quality of the available images, i.e. contain both pelvic and thoracic vertebrae, as well as images with more or less clearly visible vertebrae. Examples of images used in the test set are shown in Fig. 2.

3.2   Compared Methods

We evaluate the performance of the registration using the PPC model in combination with the learned correspondence weighting strategy (PPC-L), which was trained using our proposed metric-driven learning method. To show the effectiveness of the correspondence weighting, we compare PPC-L to the original PPC method. The compared methods differ in the computation of the correspondence weights $\mathbf{s}$ and the regularizer weight λ. For PPC-L, the correspondence weights $\mathbf{s}^L = M_\theta(\{\mathbf{f}\})$ and $\lambda = 0.01$ are used. For PPC, we set $\lambda = 0$ and the used correspondence weights $\mathbf{s}^{PPC}$ are the NGC_i values of the found correspondences, where any value below 0.1 is set to 0, i.e. the correspondence is rejected. Additionally, the MCCR is used in the PPC method only. The minimum resolution level has a scaling of 0.25 and the highest a scaling of 1.0. For the PPC method, registration is performed on the lowest resolution level without allowing motion in depth first, as this showed to increases the robustness of the method. To differentiate between the effect of the correspondence weighting and the regularized motion estimation, we also consider registration using regularized motion estimation. We use a variant where the global weighting factor, which is applied to all points, is matched to the regularizer weight automatically by using our objective function (PPC-R). For the different resolution levels, we obtained a data weight in the range of $[2.0; 2.1]$. Therefore, we use $\lambda = 0.01$ and $s^R = 2.0 \cdot s^{PPC}$. Additionally, we empirically set the correspondence weight to $s^{RM} = 0.25 \cdot s^{PPC}$, which increases the robustness of the registration while still allowing for a reasonable amount of motion (PPC-RM).

3.3 Evaluation Metrics

To evaluate the registration, we follow the standardized evaluation methodology [5,10]. The following metrics are defined by van de Kraats et al. [5]:

- *Mean Target Registration Error:* The mTRE is defined as the mean distance of target points under $\mathbf{T}^{GT}$ and the estimated registration $\mathbf{T}^{est} \in \mathbb{R}^{4 \times 4}$.
- *Mean Re-Projection Distance (mRPD):* The mRPD is defined as the mean distance of target points under $\mathbf{T}^{GT}$ and the re-projection rays of the points as projected under $\mathbf{T}^{est}$.
- *Success Rate (SR):* The SR is the number of registrations with a registration error below a given threshold. As we are concerned with single-view registration, we define the success criterion as a mRPD $\leq 2\,$mm.
- *Capture Range (CR):* The CR is defined as the maximum initial mTRE for which at least 95% of registrations are successful.

Additionally, we compute the gross success rate (GSR) [9] as well as a gross capture range (GCR) with a success criterion of a mRPD $\leq 10\,$mm in order to further assess the robustness of the methods in case of a low accuracy. We define target points as uniformly distributed points inside the VOI of the registered vertebra. For the evaluation, we generate 600 random start transformations for each vertebra in a range of $0\,$mm–$30\,$mm initial mTRE using the methodology described by van de Kraats et al. [5]. We evaluate the accuracy using the mRPD and the robustness using the SR, CR GSR and GCR.

3.4 Results and Discussion

Accuracy and Robustness. The evaluation results for the compared methods are summarized in Table 1. We observe that PPC-L achieves the best SR of 94.3% and CR of 13 mm. Compared to PPC (SR of 79.3% and CR of 3 mm), PPC-R also achieves a higher SR of 88.1% and CR of 6 mm. For the regularized motion estimation, the accuracy decreases for increasing regularizer influence ($0.79 \pm 0.22\,$mm for PPC-R and $1.18 \pm 0.42\,$mm for PPC-RM), compared to PPC ($0.75 \pm 0.21\,$mm) and PPC-L ($0.74 \pm 0.26\,$mm). A sample registration result using PPC-L is shown in Fig. 3d.

For strongly regularized motion estimation, we observe a large difference between the GSR and the SR. While for PPC-R, the difference is relatively small (88.1% vs. 90.7%), it is very high for PPC-RM. Here a GSR of 95.1% is achieved, while the SR is 59.6%. This indicates that while the method is robust, the accuracy is low. Compared to the CR, the GCR is increased for PPC-L

Table 1. Evaluation results for the compared methods. The mRPD is computed for the 2 mm success criterion and is shown as mean ± standard deviation.

Method	mRPD [mm]	SR [%]	CR [mm]	GSR [%]	GCR [mm]
PPC	0.75 ± 0.21	79.3	3	81.8	3
PPC-R	0.79 ± 0.22	88.1	6	90.7	6
PPC-RM	1.18 ± 0.42	59.6	4	95.1	20
PPC-L	0.74 ± 0.26	94.3	13	96.3	22

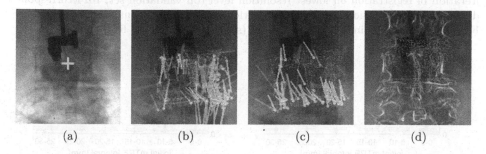

(a)   (b)   (c)   (d)

Fig. 3. Registration example: (a) shows I^{FL} with one marked vertebra to register. Red dots depict initially extracted (b, c) and final aligned (d) contour points. Green lines depict the same randomly selected subset of correspondences, whose intensities are determined by NGC_i (b) and learned weights (c). Final PPC-L registration result overlaid in yellow (d). Also see video in the supplementary material. (Color figure online)

(22 mm vs. 13 mm) and especially for PPC-RM (20 mm vs. 4 mm). Overall, this shows that while some inaccurate registrations are present in PPC-L, they are very common for PPC-RM.

Single Iteration Evaluation. To better understand the effect of the correspondence weighting and regularization, we investigate the registration results after one iteration on the lowest resolution level. In Fig. 4, the PE in pixels (computed using $\{\mathbf{q}_j\}$ as target points) is shown for all cases in the validation set. As in training, 1024 correspondences are used per case for all methods. We observe that for PPC, the error has a high spread, where for some cases, it is decreased considerably, while for other cases, it is increased. For PPC-R, most cases are below the initial error. However, the error is decreased only marginally, as the regularization prevents large motions. For PPC-L, we observe that the error is drastically decreased for most cases. This shows that PPC-L is able to estimate motion efficiently. An example for correspondence weighting in PPC-L is shown in Fig. 3c, where we observe a set of consistent correspondences with high weights, while the remaining correspondences have low weights.

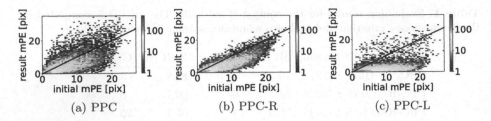

(a) PPC   (b) PPC-R   (c) PPC-L

Fig. 4. Histograms showing initial and result projection error (PE) in pixels for a single iteration of registration on lowest resolution level (on validation set, 1024 correspondences per case). Motion estimation was performed using least squares for all methods. For PPC, no motion in depth is estimated (see Sect. 3.2). (Color figure online)

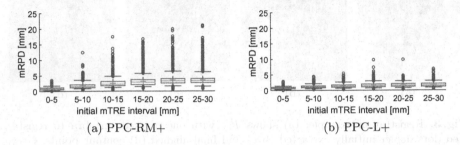

(a) PPC-RM+   (b) PPC-L+

Fig. 5. Box plots for distribution of resulting mRPD on the lowest resolution level for successful registrations for different initial mTRE intervals.

Method Combinations. We observed that while the PPC-RM method has a high robustness (GCR and GSR), it leads to low accuracy. For PPC-L, we observed an increased GCR compared to the CR. In both cases, this demonstrates that registrations are present with a mRPD between 2 mm and 10 mm. As the PPC works reliably for small initial errors, we combine these methods with PPC by performing PPC on the highest resolution level instead of the respective method. We denote the resulting methods as PPC-RM+ and PPC-L+. We observe that PPC-RM+ achieves an accuracy of 0.74 ± 0.18 mm, an SR of 94.6% and a CR of 18 mm, while PPC-L+ achieves an accuracy of 0.74 ± 0.19 mm, an SR of 96.1% and a CR of 19 mm. While the results are similar, we note that for PPC-RM+ a manual weight selection is necessary. Further investigations are needed to clarify the better performance of PPC compared to PPC-L on the highest resolution level. However, this result may also demonstrate the strength of MCCR for cases where the majority of correspondences are correct. We evaluate the convergence behavior of PPC-L+ and PPC-RM+ by only considering cases which were successful. For these cases, we investigate the error distribution after the first resolution level. The results are shown in Fig. 5. We observe that for PPC-L+, a mRPD of below 10 mm is achieved for all cases, while for PPC-RM+, higher misalignment of around 20 mm mRPD is present. The result for PPC-L+ is achieved after an average of 7.6 iterations, while 11.8 iterations were performed on average for PPC-RM+ using the stop criterion defined in [15].

In combination, this further substantiates our findings from the single iteration evaluation and shows the efficiency of PPC-L and its potential for reducing the computational cost.

4   Conclusion

For 2-D/3-D registration, we propose a method to learn the weighting of the local correspondences directly from the global criterion to minimize the registration error. We achieve this by incorporating the motion estimation and error computation steps into our training objective function. A modified PointNet network is trained to weight correspondences based on their geometrical properties and image similarity. A large improvement in the registration robustness is demonstrated when using the learning-based correspondence weighting, while maintaining the high accuracy. Although a high robustness can also be achieved by regularized motion estimation, registration using learned correspondence weighting has the following advantages: it is more efficient, does not need manual parameter tuning and achieves a high accuracy. One direction of future work is to further improve the weighting strategy, e.g. by including more information into the decision process and optimizing the objective function for robustness and/or accuracy depending on the stage of the registration, such as the current resolution level. By regarding the motion estimation as part of the network and not the objective function, our model can also be understood in the framework of precision learning [7] as a regression model for the motion, where we learn only the unknown component (weighting of correspondences), while employing prior knowledge to the known component (motion estimation). Following the framework of precision learning, replacing further steps of the registration framework with learned counterparts can be investigated. One candidate is the correspondence estimation, as it is challenging to design an optimal correspondence estimation method by hand.

Disclaimer: The concept and software presented in this paper are based on research and are not commercially available. Due to regulatory reasons its future availability cannot be guaranteed.

References

1. Canny, J.: A computational approach to edge detection. IEEE Trans. Pattern Anal. Mach. Intell. **6**, 679–698 (1986)
2. Elliott, D.L.: A better activation function for artificial neural networks. Technical report (1993)
3. Feng, Y., Huang, X., Shi, L., Yang, Y., Suykens, J.A.: Learning with the maximum correntropy criterion induced losses for regression. J. Mach. Learn. Res. **16**, 993–1034 (2015)
4. Hartley, R., Zisserman, A.: Multiple View Geometry in Computer Vision, 2nd edn, p. 200. Cambridge University Press, Cambridge (2003)

5. van de Kraats, E.B., Penney, G.P., Tomaževič, D., van Walsum, T., Niessen, W.J.: Standardized evaluation methodology for 2-D-3-D registration. IEEE Trans. Med. imaging **24**(9), 1177–1189 (2005)
6. Kubias, A., Deinzer, F., Feldmann, T., Paulus, D., Schreiber, B., Brunner, T.: 2D/3D image registration on the GPU. Pattern Recogn. Image Anal. **18**(3), 381–389 (2008)
7. Maier, A., et al.: Precision learning: towards use of known operators in neural networks. arXiv preprint arXiv:1712.00374v3 (2017)
8. Markelj, P., Tomaževič, D., Likar, B., Pernuš, F.: A review of 3D/2D registration methods for image-guided interventions. Med. Image Anal. **16**(3), 642–661 (2012)
9. Miao, S., et al.: Dilated FCN for multi-agent 2D/3D medical image registration. In: AAAI Conference on Artificial Intelligence (AAAI), pp. 4694–4701 (2018)
10. Mitrović, U., Špiclin, Ž., Likar, B., Pernuš, F.: 3D–2D registration of cerebral angiograms: a method and evaluation on clinical images. IEEE Trans. Med. Imaging **32**(8), 1550–1563 (2013)
11. Qi, C.R., Su, H., Mo, K., Guibas, L.J.: PointNet: deep learning on point sets for 3D classification and segmentation. In: IEEE Conference on Computer Vision and Pattern Recognition (CVPR), pp. 77–85 (2017)
12. Schaffert, R., Wang, J., Fischer, P., Borsdorf, A., Maier, A.: Multi-view depth-aware rigid 2-D/3-D registration. In: IEEE Nuclear Science Symposium and Medical Imaging Conference (NSS/MIC) (2017)
13. Schmid, J., Chênes, C.: Segmentation of X-ray images by 3D-2D registration based on multibody physics. In: Cremers, D., Reid, I., Saito, H., Yang, M.-H. (eds.) ACCV 2014. LNCS, vol. 9004, pp. 674–687. Springer, Cham (2015). https://doi.org/10.1007/978-3-319-16808-1_45
14. Wang, J., Borsdorf, A., Heigl, B., Köhler, T., Hornegger, J.: Gradient-based differential approach for 3-D motion compensation in interventional 2-D/3-D image fusion. In: International Conference on 3D Vision (3DV), pp. 293–300 (2014)
15. Wang, J., et al.: Dynamic 2-D/3-D rigid registration framework using point-to-plane correspondence model. IEEE Trans. Med. Imaging **36**(9), 1939–1954 (2017)
16. Yi, K.M., Trulls, E., Ono, Y., Lepetit, V., Salzmann, M., Fua, P.: Learning to find good correspondences. In: IEEE Conference on Computer Vision and Pattern Recognition (CVPR), pp. 2666–2674 (2018)

Multi-view X-Ray R-CNN

Jan-Martin O. Steitz[ID], Faraz Saeedan[✉][ID], and Stefan Roth[ID]

Department of Computer Science, TU Darmstadt, Darmstadt, Germany
`faraz.saeedan@visinf.tu-darmstadt.de`

Abstract. Motivated by the detection of prohibited objects in carry-on luggage as a part of avionic security screening, we develop a CNN-based object detection approach for multi-view X-ray image data. Our contributions are two-fold. First, we introduce a novel multi-view pooling layer to perform a 3D aggregation of 2D CNN-features extracted from each view. To that end, our pooling layer exploits the known geometry of the imaging system to ensure geometric consistency of the feature aggregation. Second, we introduce an end-to-end trainable multi-view detection pipeline based on Faster R-CNN, which derives the region proposals and performs the final classification in 3D using these aggregated multi-view features. Our approach shows significant accuracy gains compared to single-view detection while even being more efficient than performing single-view detection in each view.

1   Introduction

Baggage inspection using multi-view X-ray imaging machines is at the heart of most aviation security screening programs. Due to inherent shortcomings in human inspection arising from gradual fatigue, occasional erroneous judgments, and privacy concerns, computer-aided automatic detection of dangerous goods in baggage has long been a sought-after goal [19]. However, earlier approaches, mostly based on hand-engineered features and support vector machines, fell far short of providing detection accuracy comparable to human operators, which is critical due to the sensitive nature of the task [3,8]. Thanks to recent advances in object detection using deep convolutional neural networks [10,11,22,23] with stunning success in photographic images, the accuracy of single-view object detection in X-ray images has improved significantly [16]. Yet, most X-ray machines for baggage inspection provide multiple views (two or four views) of the screening tunnel. An example of this multi-view data is shown in Fig. 1. Multi-view approaches for these applications have been only used in the context of classical methods, but whether CNN-based detectors can benefit is unclear. In fact, [16] found that a naive approach feeding features extracted from multiple views simultaneously to a fully-connected layer for detection leads to a performance drop over the single-view case.

Fueled by applications such as autonomous driving, 3D object detection has lately gained momentum [9]. These 3D detection algorithms, unlike their 2D counterparts, are not general purpose and rely on certain sensor combinations or

© Springer Nature Switzerland AG 2019
T. Brox et al. (Eds.): GCPR 2018, LNCS 11269, pp. 153–168, 2019.
https://doi.org/10.1007/978-3-030-12939-2_12

employ heavy prior assumptions that make them not directly applicable to multi-view object detection in X-ray images. Some of these 3D detection algorithms assume that the shape of the desired object is known in the form of a 3D model [2,24]. Yet, 3D models of objects are more difficult to acquire compared to simple bounding box annotations and a detector that relies on them for training may not generalize well on objects with highly variable shape such as handguns. Other methods use point clouds from laser range finders alone or in conjunction with RGB data from a camera [5,21]. Our setup, in contrast, provides multi-view images of objects in a two channel (dual-energy) format, which is rather different from stereo or point cloud representations. Using 3D convolutions and directly extending existing 2D methods is one possibility, but the computational cost and memory requirements can be prohibitive when relying on very deep CNN backbone architectures such as ResNet [14].

Fig. 1. An example of multi-view X-ray images of hand luggage containing a glass bottle.

In this work, we extend the well-known Faster R-CNN [23] to multi-view X-ray images by employing the idea of late fusion, which enables our use of very deep CNNs to extract powerful features from each individual view, while deriving region proposals and performing the classification in 3D. We introduce a novel *multi-view pooling layer* to enable this fusion of features from single views using the geometry of the imaging setup. This geometry is assumed fixed all through training and testing and needs to be calculated once. We do not assume further knowledge of the detected objects as long as we have sufficient bounding box annotations in 2D. We show that our method, termed *MX-RCNN*, is not only highly flexible in detecting various hazardous object categories with very little extra knowledge required, but is also considerably more accurate while even being more efficient than performing single-view detection in the four views.

2   Related Work

Inspired by the impressive results in 2D object detection, several recent works [20,30,32,33] build upon a 2D detection in an image and then attempt to estimate the 3D object pose. These methods, however, rely predominantly on a set of prior constraints such as objects being located on the ground for estimating the 3D position of the object. These prior constraints do not appear easily extensible to our problem case, since objects inside bags can take an arbitrary orientation and position.

Other approaches have tried to work directly with depth data [18,27,28], where most methods voxelize the space into a regular grid and apply 3D convolutions to the input. While this yields the most straightforward extension of well-proven 2D detectors, which are based on 2D convolution layers, increasing the dimensionality of convolution layers can only be done at very low resolution as denser voxelizations of the space result in unacceptably large memory consumption and processing time. Our method also uses the idea of 3D convolutions but defers them to very late stages in which we switch from 2D to 3D. In doing so, we enable the detector to leverage high image resolution in the input while extracting powerful features that leverage view-consistency.

A number of methods use the geometry of the objects as prior knowledge to infer a 6-DoF object pose. These methods mainly rely on CAD models or ground truth 3D object models and match either keypoints between these models and 2D images [2,24,34] or entire reconstructed objects [25]. Borrowing ideas from robotics mapping, the estimated pose of an object produced by a CNN can also be aligned to an existing 3D model using the iterative closest points (ICP) algorithm [13].

Su et al. [29] proposed a method most closely related to ours, which aggregates features extracted from multiple views of a scene using an elementwise max operation among all views. Yet, unlike our multi-view pooling layer this aggregation is not geometry-aware.

Despite the recent focus on the problem of visual object detection, its application to X-ray images has not received as much attention. Some older methods [3,8] exist for this application, but they perform considerably weaker than deep learning-based methods [1]. However, the use of CNNs on X-ray images for baggage inspection has been limited to the direct application of basic 2D detection algorithms, either with pretraining on photographic images or training from scratch. Jaccard et al. [16] propose a black-box approach to multi-view detection by extracting CNN features from all views, concatenating them, and feeding them to fully-connected layers. Yet, the accuracy fell short of that of the original single-view detection. To the best of our knowledge, there exists no previous end-to-end learning approach that successfully uses the geometry of the X-ray machine to perform a fusion of features from various views.

3 Multi-view X-Ray R-CNN

We build on the standard Faster R-CNN object detection method [23], which works on single-view 2D images and is composed of two stages. They share a common feature extractor, which outputs a feature map. The first stage consists of a Region Proposal Network (RPN) that proposes regions of interest to the second stage. Those regions are then cut from the feature map and individually classified. The RPN uses a fixed set of 9 standard axis-aligned bounding boxes in 3 different aspect ratios and 3 scales, so-called anchor boxes. Those anchor boxes are defined at every location of the feature map. The RPN then alters their position and shape by learning regression parameters in training. Additionally, a score to distinguish between objects and background is learned in a class-agnostic way, which is used for non-maximum suppression and to pass only a subset of top-scoring region proposals to the second stage. The second stage classifies the proposals and outputs additional regression values to fine-tune the bounding boxes at the end of the detection process.

MX-RCNN. The basic concept of our Multi-view X-ray R-CNN (MX-RCNN) approach is to perform feature extraction on 2D images to be able to utilize standard CNN backbones including ImageNet [26] pretraining. This addresses the fact that the amount of annotated X-ray data is significantly lower than that of photographic images. We then combine the extracted feature maps of different projections, or views, into a common 3D feature space in which object detection takes place, identifying 3D locations of the detected objects.

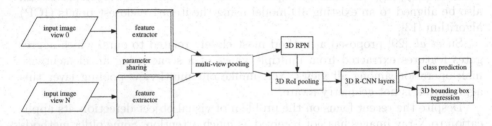

Fig. 2. *Schema of the hybrid 2D-3D MX-RCNN architecture.* The features of each view are extracted independently in 2D and combined in the multi-view pooling layer (*marked in red*). The resulting common 3D feature volume is passed to the RPN and to the RoI pooling layer where regions are extracted for evaluation in the 3D R-CNN layers. (Color figure online)

Our MX-RCNN uses a ResNet-50 [15] architecture, where the first 4 out of its 5 stages are used for feature extraction on the 2D images. Then a novel multi-view pooling layer, provided with the fixed geometry of the imaging setup, combines the feature maps into a common 3D feature volume.

The combined feature space is passed to a RPN, which has a structure similar to the RPN in Faster R-CNN [23], but with 3D convolutional layers instead of 2D ones. Further, it has $6 \times A$ regression parameter outputs per feature volume position, where A is the number of anchor boxes, because for 3D bounding boxes 6 regression parameters are needed. Following Faster R-CNN, we define those regression parameters as

$$t_x = (x - x_a)/w_a \qquad t_y = (y - y_a)/h_a \qquad t_z = (z - z_a)/d_a$$

$$t_w = \log(w/w_a) \qquad t_h = \log(h/h_a) \qquad t_d = \log(d/d_a) \,, \tag{1}$$

where the index a denotes the parameters of the anchor box and with bounding box center (x, y, z), width w, height h, and depth d.

The RPN proposes volumes to be extracted by a Region-of-Interest pooling layer with an output of size $7 \times 7 \times 7$ to cover a part of the feature volume similar in relative size to the 2D case. The 3D regions are then fed into a network similar to the last stage of ResNet-50 in which all convolutional and pooling layers are converted from 2D to 3D and the size of the last pooling kernel is adjusted to fit the feature volume size. In contrast to the 2D stages, these 3D convolutions are trained from scratch since ImageNet pretraining is not possible. Afterwards, the regions are classified and 3D bounding box regression parameters are determined. A schema of our MX-RCNN is depicted in Fig. 2.

3.1 K-means Clustering of Anchor Boxes

When we expand the hand-selected aspect ratios of the Faster R-CNN anchor boxes of 1:1, 1:2, and 2:1 at 3 different scales to 3D, we arrive at a total of 21 anchor boxes. Since this number is large and limits the computational efficiency, we aim to improve over these standard anchor boxes. To that end, we assess the quality of the anchor boxes as priors for the RPN. Specifically, we use their intersection over union (IoU) [17] with the ground-truth annotations of the training set. We instantiate anchor boxes at each position of the feature map used by the RPN and for each ground-truth annotation we find its highest IoU with an anchor box. For the standard anchor boxes expanded to 3D, this yields an average IoU of 0.5.

To improve upon this while optimizing the computational efficiency, we follow the approach of the YOLO9000 object detector [22] and use k-means clustering on the bounding box dimensions (width, height, depth) in the training set to find priors with a better average overlap with the ground-truth annotations. We employ the Jaccard distance [17]

$$d_{\mathrm{J}}(a, b) = 1 - \mathrm{IoU}(a, b) \tag{2}$$

between boxes a and b as a distance metric. We run k-means clustering for various values of k. Figure 3 shows the average IoU between ground-truth bounding boxes and the closest cluster (*blue, circles*). To convert clusters into anchor boxes, they have to be aligned to the resolution of a feature grid. To account for this, we also plot the IoU between the ground-truth bounding boxes and the closest cluster once it has been shifted to the nearest feature grid position (*red, diamonds*). We choose $k = 10$, which achieves an average IoU of 0.56 for the resulting anchor boxes distributed in a grid. This is clearly higher than using the standard 21 hand-selected anchor boxes, while maintaining the training and inference speed of a network with only 10 anchor boxes.

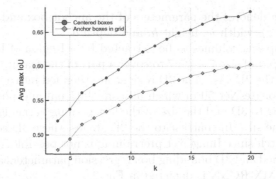

Fig. 3. *Average IoU between ground-truth boxes and the closest cluster from k-means clustering as a function of k.* The IoU is calculated for anchor boxes centered on the ground-truth boxes (*blue, circles*) and for anchor boxes distributed in the grid of the feature map (*red, diamonds*). Even a low number of clusters already outperforms the standard hand-selected anchor boxes (IoU of 0.5). (Color figure online)

3.2   Multi-view Pooling

Our proposed multi-view pooling layer maps the related feature maps of the 2D views of an X-ray recording into a common 3D feature volume by providing it with the known geometry of the X-ray image formation process in the form of a weight matrix. To determine the weights, we connect each group of detector locations related to one pixel in the 2D feature map to their X-ray source to form beams across the 3D space. For each of the output cells of the 3D feature volume, we use the volume of their intersection with the beams normalized by the cell volume as relative weight factors. The multi-view pooling layer then computes the weighted average of the feature vectors of all beams for each output cell, normalized by the number of views in each X-ray recording; we call this variant MX-RCNN$_{avg}$. Additionally, we implemented a version of the multi-view pooling layer that takes the maximum across the weighted feature vectors of all beams for each output cell; we call this variant MX-RCNN$_{max}$. An example of a mapping, specific to our geometry, is shown in Fig. 4.

3.3   Conversion of IoU Thresholds

Since the IoU in 3D (volume) behaves differently than in 2D (area), we aim to equalize for this. Specifically, we aim to apply the same strictness for spatial shifts that are allowed per bounding box dimension such that a proposed object is still considered a valid detection. We assume that the prediction errors of the bounding box regression values are equally distributed across all dimensions. For simplicity, we further assume that errors are only made up of shifts compared to the ground-truth bounding boxes. In 2D, the allowed relative shift s per dimension of a bounding box of arbitrary dimensions for an IoU threshold of t_2 is given by

$$s(t_2) = 1 - \sqrt{2t_2/(t_2 + 1)} \, . \tag{3}$$

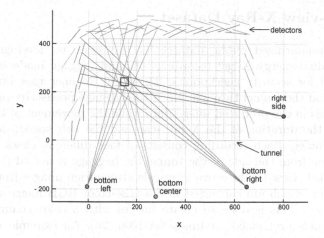

Fig. 4. Example plot illustrating the relevant beams (*color-coded per view*) in the multi-view pooling of a specific output cell (*marked in red*). The actual geometry differs slightly. (Color figure online)

The same relative shift applied to an arbitrarily sized 3D bounding box would require the threshold

$$t_3(s) = (1-s)^3/(2-(1-s)^3) \, . \tag{4}$$

An IoU threshold t_2 applied to the 2D case therefore becomes

$$t_3(t_2) = \frac{\sqrt{2t_2/(1+t_2)}^3}{2 - \sqrt{2t_2/(1+t_2)}^3} \tag{5}$$

for use with 3D bounding boxes if the same strictness per dimension is to be maintained. The evaluation of the PASCAL VOC challenge [7] for detection in 2D images uses a standard threshold of 0.5, which yields a threshold of 0.374 in the 3D detection case.

3.4   Computational Cost

Our single-view Faster R-CNN implementation reaches a frame rate of 3.9 fps for training and 6.1 fps for inference on a NVIDIA GeForce GTX Titan X GPU. 4 frames or images need to be processed for one complete X-ray recording. Our MX-RCNN achieves frame rates of 4.6 fps for training and 7.6 fps for inference; note that it can share work across the 4 frames as they are processed simultaneously. Thus, our method is 18% faster in training and 25% faster in inference. We attribute this to the lower number of regions extracted per recording, because of the common classification stage in the multi-view detector, despite the higher computational costs for its 3D convolutional layers.

4   Multi-view X-Ray Dataset

Lacking a standardized public dataset for this task, we leverage a custom dataset[1] of dual-energy X-ray recordings of hand luggage made by an X-ray scanner used for security checkpoints. The X-ray scanner uses line detectors located around the tunnel through which the baggage passes. Its pixels constitute the x-axis in the produced image data while the movement of the baggage, respectively the duration of the X-ray scan and the belt speed, define the y-axis of the image. Each recording consists of four different views, three from below and one from the side of the tunnel the baggage is moved through. The scans from each view produce two grayscale attenuation images from the dual-energy system, which are converted into a false-color RGB image that is used for the dataset. This is done to create images with 3 color channels that fit available models pretrained on ImageNet-1000 [26]. An example recording is shown in Fig. 5.

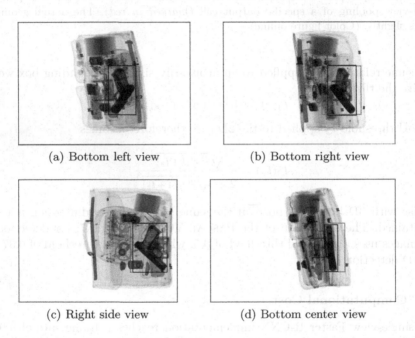

(a) Bottom left view   (b) Bottom right view

(c) Right side view   (d) Bottom center view

Fig. 5. *False-color images of all views of an example X-ray recording of baggage containing a handgun.* The handgun is easier to spot in certain images depending on their angle of projection. Bounding boxes show the original 2D annotations (*black*) and the reprojected 3D annotations (*red*). (Color figure online)

---

[1] Unfortunately, we are not able to release the dataset to the public. Researchers wishing to evaluate on our dataset for comparison purposes are invited to contact the corresponding author.

The following types of recordings are available in the dataset:

Glass Bottle. Recordings of baggage containing glass bottles of different shapes and sizes.

TIP Weapon. Synthetic recordings of baggage where a pre-recorded scan of a handgun is randomly projected onto a baggage recording by a method called Threat Image Projection (TIP) [4]. A limited set of handguns is repeatedly used to generate all recordings.

Real Weapon. Recordings that contain a handgun of various types and are obtained using a conventional scan without the use of TIP.

Negative. Recordings containing neither handguns nor glass bottles.

The synthetic TIP images are only used for training and validation; the complete scans with real weapons are used for testing to evaluate if the trained network generalizes. A detailed overview of the different subsets of the data is given in Table 1. The dataset is split into its subsets such that views belonging to one and the same recording are not distributed over different subsets. PASCAL VOC-style annotations [7] with axis-aligned 2D bounding boxes per view are available for two different classes of hazardous objects, *weapon* and *glassbottle*.

Table 1. Number of recordings (images) in the different subsets of the dataset.

Type / Subset	Train	Validation	Test	Total
Glass Bottle	358 (1432)	40 (160)	209 (836)	607 (2428)
TIP Weapon	1944 (7776)	216 (864)	0 (0)	2160 (8640)
Real Weapon	0 (0)	0 (0)	464 (1856)	464 (1856)
Negative	0 (0)	0 (0)	950 (3800)	950 (3800)
Total	2302 (9208)	256 (1024)	1623 (6492)	4181 (16724)

4.1 3D Bounding Box Annotations

To be able to train and evaluate our multi-view object detection with 3D annotations, we generate those out of more commonly available 2D bounding box annotations. Specifically, we generate axis-aligned 3D bounding boxes from several axis-aligned 2D bounding boxes. Because all our X-ray recordings have at most one annotated object,[2] there is no need to match multiple annotations across the different views. In case of multiple annotated objects per image, a geometrically consistent matching could be used.

Recall the specific imaging setup from above. If we now align the 2D y-axis (belt direction) to the 3D z-axis, the problem of identifying a suitable 3D bounding box reduces to a mapping from the 2D x-axis to a xy-plane in 3D. The

---

[2] The number of annotated objects is a restriction of the dataset only; our detector is able to handle multiple objects per image.

lines of projection between the X-ray sources and the detectors corresponding to the x-axis limits of the 2D bounding boxes define the areas where the object could be located in the xy-plane per view. We intersect those triangular areas using the Vatti polygon clipping algorithm [31] and choose the minimum axis-aligned bounding box containing the resulting polygon as an estimation of the object's position in 3D space. For the z-axis limits of the 3D bounding box, we take the mean of the y-limits of the 2D bounding boxes. An example of the generation process is shown in Fig. 6. Note that while our process of deriving 3D bounding boxes is customized to the baggage screening scenario, analogous procedures can be defined for more general imaging setups.

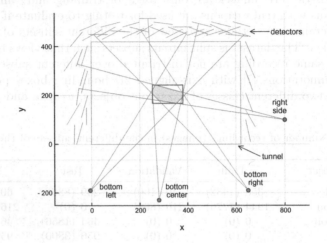

Fig. 6. *Example of the 3D bounding box generation.* The lines of projection (*color-coded per view*) for the 2D bounding box positions overlap in the xy-plane of the 3D volume. The resulting polygon of their intersection (*pink*) is enclosed by the 3D bounding box (*red*). The actual geometry differs slightly. (Color figure online)

Note that in the ideal case, all projection lines would intersect in the 4 corners of the bounding box. However, due to variances in the annotations made independently for each view, this does not hold in practice. As a result, the bounding box enclosing the intersection polygon is an upper bound of the estimated position of the object in 3D space. We thus additionally project the 3D bounding boxes back to the 2D views to yield 2D bounding boxes that include the geometry approximation made in the generation of the 3D bounding box. The difference between an original 2D annotation and a reprojected 3D bounding box can be seen in Fig. 5. We use these 2D annotations to train a single-view Faster R-CNN as a baseline that assumes the same object localization as the multi-view networks trained on the 3D annotations. If more precise 3D bounding boxes are desired, they could be obtained from joint CT and X-ray recordings, which are becoming more common in modern screening machines.

5   Experiments

5.1   Training

We scale all images used for training and evaluation by a factor of 0.5 so they have widths of 384, 384, 352, and 416 px for the views 0 through 3 of each X-ray recording. For all experiments we use a ResNet-50 [14] with parameters pretrained on ImageNet-1000 [26]. The first two stages of the ResNet-50 are fixed and we fine-tune the rest of the parameters. If not mentioned otherwise, hyper-parameters remain unchanged against the standard implementation of Faster R-CNN. All networks are trained by backpropagation using stochastic gradient descent (SGD).

As a baseline we train a standard implementation of single-view Faster R-CNN on the training set without data augmentation. Single-view Faster R-CNN detects objects on all views independently. We start with a learning rate of 0.001 for the first 12 epochs and continue with a rate of 0.0001 for another 3 epochs.

For training and evaluation of our MX-RCNN, we use a mini-batch size of 4 with all related views inside one mini-batch. We reduce the number of randomly sampled anchors in each 3D feature volume from 256 to 128 to better match the desired ratio of up to 1:1 between sampled positive and negative anchors. Additionally, we reduce the number of sampled RoIs to 64 to better match the desired fraction of 25% foreground regions that have an IoU of at least 0.5 with a 3D ground-truth bounding box. We accordingly reduce the learning rate by the same factor [12]. In the multi-task loss of the RPN, we change the balancing factor λ for the regression loss and the normalization by the number of anchor boxes to an empirically determined factor of $\lambda = 0.05$ without additional normalization. In practice, this ensures good convergence of the regression loss. We initialize all 3D convolutional layers as in the standard Faster R-CNN implementation. We then train MX-RCNN$_{avg}$ on the training set for 28 epochs with a learning rate of 0.0005. A cut of the learning rate did not show any benefit when evaluating with the validation set. Additionally, we train MX-RCNN$_{max}$ for 17 epochs with the same learning rate. Again, a learning rate cut did not show any further improvement on the validation set.

5.2   Evaluation Criteria

Since there is no established evaluation criterion for our experimental setting, we are using the average precision (AP), which is the de-facto standard for the evaluation of object detection tasks. Specifically, we compare the trained networks with the evaluation procedure for object detection of the PASCAL VOC challenge that is in use since 2010 [6]. To be considered a valid detection, a proposed bounding box must exceed a certain threshold with a ground-truth bounding box. If multiple proposed bounding boxes match the same ground-truth bounding box, only the one with the highest confidence is counted as a valid detection. The PASCAL VOC challenge uses an IoU of 0.5 as threshold for the case of object detection in 2D images. As discussed in Sect. 3.3, to apply the same strictness for relative shifts that are allowed per dimension, we set this threshold to 0.374 for the evaluation of 3D bounding boxes per recording. Nevertheless, the corresponding IoU threshold we derived for 3D is an estimate. Hence, we additionally project the proposed 3D bounding boxes onto the 2D views and evaluate them per image with a threshold of 0.5 to directly compare to standard 2D detection.

Table 2. *Experimental results of the different networks evaluated on the test set.* For the multi-view networks the evaluation was done with the proposed 3D bounding boxes and their projections onto the 2D views.

Method	Single-view	MX-RCNN$_{avg}$		MX-RCNN$_{max}$	
Evaluation	2D	3D	2D	3D	2D
Weapon AP	85.56 %	**92.28 %**	90.32 %	89.01 %	87.73 %
Glassbottle AP	96.90 %	**98.84 %**	95.37 %	98.74 %	95.62 %
Mean AP	91.23 %	**95.56 %**	92.84 %	93.88 %	91.68 %

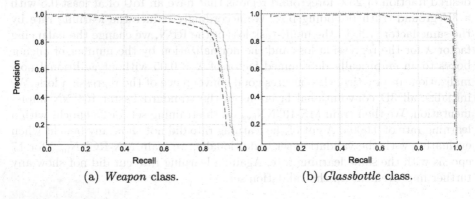

(a) *Weapon* class.   (b) *Glassbottle* class.

Fig. 7. *Precision-recall curves of the different networks evaluated on the test set.* The plots show the precision-recall curves of the single-view (*orange, dashed*), MX-RCNN$_{avg}$ (*turquoise, solid*) and MX-RCNN$_{max}$ (*pink, dotted*) networks. For the multi-view networks the precision-recall curves are shown for the evaluation in 3D.

5.3   Experimental Results

The standard single-view Faster R-CNN [23] used as a baseline reaches 91.2% mean average precision (mAP) per image on the test set (average over classes). With 93.9% mAP per recording, our MX-RCNN$_{max}$ is 2.7% points better than the baseline when evaluating in 3D and 0.5% points better when projected to 2D (91.7% mAP per image). Using a weighted average in the multi-view pooling layer of MX-RCNN (MX-RCNN$_{avg}$) shows consistently better detection accuracy than MX-RCNN$_{max}$ except for the AP of the *glassbottle* class projected to 2D. With an mAP per recording for 3D evaluation of 95.6%, our MX-RCNN$_{avg}$ is 4.4% points better than the baseline when evaluating in 3D and 1.7% better when projected to 2D (mAP of 92.9%). Detailed numbers of the evaluation can be found in Table 2. Additionally, precision-recall curves are provided in Fig. 7 to allow studying the accuracy at different operating points. We observe that the ranking of the curves of the different networks within each object class is consistent with their AP values. Moreover, it becomes apparent that the benefit of the proposed multi-view approach is particularly pronounced in the important high-recall regime.

Table 3. *Tolerance of MX-RCNN for disabling individual views when evaluating on the test set.* The proposed 3D bounding boxes were directly evaluated without reprojection to 2D.

(a) MX-RCNNavg

Views	all	w/o bottom left	w/o bottom right	w/o right side
Weapon AP	92.28 %	82.34 %	85.57 %	53.19 %
Glassbottle AP	98.84 %	91.58 %	98.59 %	92.42 %
Mean AP	95.56 %	86.96 %	92.08 %	72.80 %

(b) MX-RCNNmax

Views	all	w/o bottom left	w/o bottom right	w/o right side
Weapon AP	89.01 %	74.40 %	83.69 %	58.86 %
Glassbottle AP	98.74 %	89.89 %	97.93 %	77.26 %
Mean AP	93.88 %	82.14 %	90.81 %	68.06 %

5.4 Ablation Study

To test the importance of the different views in our multi-view setup on the final detection result, we disabled individual views while evaluating and in the mapping provided to the multi-view pooling layer, respectively. The evaluation was done for both variants of the multi-view pooling layer on the test set and we directly compared the proposed 3D bounding boxes to 3D ground-truth annotations with 0.374 as IoU threshold without reprojecting them to 2D. The detailed results can be found in Table 3. We notice that the tolerance for missing views from below the tunnel is higher than for a missing side view. Also, the impact is more pronounced on weapons whose appearance is more affected by out-of-plane rotations. In general, the use of weighted averaging when combining features in the multi-view pooling seems to be more fault tolerant than the use of a weighted maximum, with the exception of weapons in combination with a missing side view. The results show that the network indeed relies on all views to construct the feature volume and to propose and validate detections.

6   Conclusion

In this paper we have introduced MX-RCNN, a multi-view end-to-end trainable object detection pipeline for X-ray images. MX-RCNN is a two stage detector similar to Faster R-CNN [23] that extracts features from all views separately using a standard CNN backbone and then fuses these features together to shape a 3D representation of the object in space. This fusion happens in a novel multi-view pooling layer, which combines all individual features leveraging the geometry of the X-ray imaging setup. An experimental analysis on a dataset of carry-on luggage containing glass bottles and hand guns showed that when trained with the same annotations, MX-RCNN outperforms Faster R-CNN applied to each view separately and is computationally cheaper than separate processing of all views. We also showed in an ablation study that the method works by far better when the view angles do not all fall in one line (degenerate 3D case), showing that the pipeline is indeed leveraging its 3D feature representation.

Acknowledgements. The authors gratefully acknowledge support by Smiths Heimann GmbH.

References

1. Akçay, S., Kundegorski, M.E., Devereux, M., Breckon, T.P.: Transfer learning using convolutional neural networks for object classification within X-ray baggage security imagery. In: ICIP, pp. 1057–1061 (2016). https://doi.org/10.1109/ICIP.2016.7532519
2. Aubry, M., Maturana, D., Efros, A.A., Russell, B., Sivic, J.: Seeing 3D chairs: exemplar part-based 2D-3D alignment using a large dataset of CAD models. In: CVPR, pp. 3762–3769 (2014). https://doi.org/10.1109/CVPR.2014.487
3. Baştan, M.: Multi-view object detection in dual-energy X-ray images. Mach. Vis. Appl. **26**(7–8), 1045–1060 (2015). https://doi.org/10.1007/s00138-015-0706-x
4. Brudy, T., Schilhab, S.: Projection of hazardous items into X-ray images of inspection objects. Patent WO 2016/001282 AI, January 2016
5. Chen, X., Ma, H., Wan, J., Li, B., Xia, T.: Multi-view 3D object detection network for autonomous driving. In: CVPR, pp. 1907–1915 (2017). https://doi.org/10.1109/CVPR.2017.691
6. Everingham, M., Eslami, S.M.A., Van Gool, L., Williams, C.K.I., Winn, J., Zisserman, A.: The PASCAL visual object classes challenge: a retrospective. Int. J. Comput. Vis. **111**(1), 98–136 (2014). https://doi.org/10.1007/s11263-014-0733-5
7. Everingham, M., Van Gool, L., Williams, C.K.I., Winn, J., Zisserman, A.: The PASCAL visual object classes (VOC) challenge. Int. J. Comput. Vis. **88**(2), 303–338 (2010). https://doi.org/10.1007/s11263-009-0275-4
8. Franzel, T., Schmidt, U., Roth, S.: Object detection in multi-view X-Ray images. In: Pinz, A., Pock, T., Bischof, H., Leberl, F. (eds.) DAGM/OAGM 2012. LNCS, vol. 7476, pp. 144–154. Springer, Heidelberg (2012). https://doi.org/10.1007/978-3-642-32717-9_15
9. Geiger, A., Lenz, P., Urtasun, R.: Are we ready for autonomous driving? The KITTI vision benchmark suite. In: CVPR, pp. 3354–3361 (2012). https://doi.org/10.1109/CVPR.2012.6248074

10. Girshick, R.: Fast R-CNN. In: ICCV, pp. 1440–1448. IEEE (2015). https://doi.org/10.1109/ICCV.2015.169
11. Girshick, R., Donahue, J., Darrell, T., Malik, J.: Region-based convolutional networks for accurate object detection and segmentation. IEEE Trans. Pattern Anal. Mach. Intell. **38**(1), 142–158 (2016). https://doi.org/10.1109/TPAMI.2015.2437384
12. Goyal, P., et al.: Accurate, large minibatch SGD: training ImageNet in 1 hour. arXiv:1706.02677 (2017)
13. Gupta, S., Arbeláez, P., Girshick, R., Malik, J.: Aligning 3D models to RGB-D images of cluttered scenes. In: CVPR, pp. 4731–4740 (2015). https://doi.org/10.1109/CVPR.2015.7299105
14. He, K., Zhang, X., Ren, S., Sun, J.: Deep residual learning for image recognition. In: CVPR, pp. 770–778 (2016). https://doi.org/10.1109/CVPR.2016.90
15. He, K., Zhang, X., Ren, S., Sun, J.: Identity mappings in deep residual networks. In: Leibe, B., Matas, J., Sebe, N., Welling, M. (eds.) ECCV 2016. LNCS, vol. 9908, pp. 630–645. Springer, Cham (2016). https://doi.org/10.1007/978-3-319-46493-0_38
16. Jaccard, N., Rogers, T.W., Morton, E.J., Griffin, L.D.: Automated detection of smuggled high-risk security threats using deep learning. In: ICDP 2016, pp. 1–6 (2016). https://doi.org/10.1049/ic.2016.0079
17. Jaccard, P.: The distribution of the Flora in the Alpine Zone. New Phytol. **11**(2), 37–50 (1912). https://doi.org/10.1111/j.1469-8137.1912.tb05611.x
18. Li, B.: 3D fully convolutional network for vehicle detection in point cloud. In: IROS, pp. 1513–1518 (2016). https://doi.org/10.1109/IROS.2017.8205955
19. Mery, D., Svec, E., Arias, M., Riffo, V., Saavedra, J.M., Banerjee, S.: Modern computer vision techniques for X-ray testing in baggage inspection. IEEE Trans. Syst. Man Cybern. Syst. **15**(2), 682–692 (2016). https://doi.org/10.1109/TSMC.2016.2628381
20. Mousavian, A., Anguelov, D., Flynn, J., Košecká, J.: 3D bounding box estimation using deep learning and geometry. In: CVPR, pp. 5632–5640 (2017). https://doi.org/10.1109/CVPR.2017.597
21. Qi, C.R., Liu, W., Wu, C., Su, H., Guibas, L.J.: Frustum pointnets for 3D object detection from RGB-D data. In: CVPR, pp. 918–927 (2018)
22. Redmon, J., Farhadi, A.: YOLO9000: better, faster, stronger. CVPR (2017). https://doi.org/10.1109/CVPR.2017.690
23. Ren, S., He, K., Girshick, R., Sun, J.: Faster R-CNN: towards real-time object detection with region proposal networks. IEEE Trans. Pattern Anal. Mach. Intell. **39**(6), 1137–1149 (2017). https://doi.org/10.1109/TPAMI.2016.2577031
24. Romea, A.C., Torres, M.M., Srinivasa, S.: The MOPED framework: object recognition and pose estimation for manipulation. Int. J. Robot. Res. **30**(10), 1284–1306 (2011). https://doi.org/10.1177/0278364911401765
25. Rothganger, F., Lazebnik, S., Schmid, C., Ponce, J.: 3D object modeling and recognition using local affine-invariant image descriptors and multi-view spatial constraints. Int. J. Comput. Vis. **66**(3), 231–259 (2006). https://doi.org/10.1007/s11263-005-3674-1
26. Russakovsky, O., et al.: ImageNet large scale visual recognition challenge. Int. J. Comput. Vis. **115**(3), 211–252 (2015). https://doi.org/10.1007/s11263-015-0816-y
27. Song, S., Xiao, J.: Sliding shapes for 3D object detection in depth images. In: Fleet, D., Pajdla, T., Schiele, B., Tuytelaars, T. (eds.) ECCV 2014. LNCS, vol. 8694, pp. 634–651. Springer, Cham (2014). https://doi.org/10.1007/978-3-319-10599-4_41
28. Song, S., Xiao, J.: Deep sliding shapes for amodal 3D object detection in RGB-D images. In: CVPR, pp. 808–816 (2016). https://doi.org/10.1109/CVPR.2016.94

29. Su, H., Maji, S., Kalogerakis, E., Learned-Miller, E.G.: Multi-view convolutional neural networks for 3D shape recognition. In: ICCV, pp. 945–953 (2015). https://doi.org/10.1109/ICCV.2015.114
30. Tulsiani, S., Malik, J.: Viewpoints and keypoints. In: CVPR, pp. 1510–1519 (2015)
31. Vatti, B.R.: A generic solution to polygon clipping. Commun. ACM **35**(7), 56–63 (1992). https://doi.org/10.1145/129902.129906
32. Xiang, Y., Choi, W., Lin, Y., Savarese, S.: Data-driven 3D voxel patterns for object category recognition. In: CVPR, pp. 1903–1911 (2015). https://doi.org/10.1109/CVPR.2015.7298800
33. Xiang, Y., Choi, W., Lin, Y., Savarese, S.: Subcategory-aware convolutional neural networks for object proposals and detection. In: WACV, pp. 924–933 (2017). https://doi.org/10.1109/WACV.2017.108
34. Zhu, M., et al.: Single image 3D object detection and pose estimation for grasping. In: ICRA, pp. 3936–3943 (2014). https://doi.org/10.1109/ICRA.2014.6907430

Ex Paucis Plura: Learning Affordance Segmentation from Very Few Examples

Johann Sawatzky[✉], Martin Garbade, and Juergen Gall

University of Bonn, Bonn, Germany
{sawatzky,garbade,gall}@iai.uni-bonn.de

Abstract. While annotating objects in images is already time-consuming, annotating finer details like object parts or affordances of objects is even more tedious. Given the fact that large datasets with object annotations already exist, we address the question whether we can leverage such information to train a convolutional neural network for segmenting affordances or object parts from very few examples with finer annotations. To achieve this, we use a semantic alignment network to transfer the annotations from the small set of annotated examples to a large set of images with only coarse annotations at object level. We then train a convolutional neural network weakly supervised on the small annotated training set and the additional images with transferred labels. We evaluate our approach on the IIT-AFF and Pascal Parts dataset where our approach outperforms other weakly supervised approaches.

1 Introduction

In order to use an object, an autonomous system has to precisely localize the parts of the object which are responsible for a certain type of interaction between this object and another object or the actor and the object. In comparison to object parts, affordances, which can be considered as functional attributes of objects, are more abstract since they generalize across object classes. Object parts from different object categories can share the same affordance class, if they share some similarity with respect to geometrical, categorical and physical properties, which in turn determines their functionality and usability. An example would be the shaft of a hammer and that of a tennis racket which would be both summarized under the class 'graspable'.

Recently several approaches have been proposed that use CNNs for detecting or segmenting affordances in images [18,19,25,26,34,36]. However, the cost of data annotation constitutes a bottleneck for semantic segmentation in general and that of functional object parts in particular. While generating pixel-wise annotations of objects is already very time-consuming compared to bounding-box annotations, annotating even finer details like parts or affordances at large quantities as it is required for CNNs becomes infeasible.

In this work we show how to extend a tiny training set containing images with affordance annotations to make the training of a semantic segmentation CNN

© Springer Nature Switzerland AG 2019
T. Brox et al. (Eds.): GCPR 2018, LNCS 11269, pp. 169–184, 2019.
https://doi.org/10.1007/978-3-030-12939-2_13

feasible. We assume that for the training set, we have only a handful of images per object category (6 images per tool class in our experiments). For each image, the bounding box of the object and the bounding boxes for all affordances of the object parts are given. Since training a CNN on such a small training set will be prone to overfitting, we make use of additional data where objects are already annotated by bounding boxes, but annotations of affordances or object parts are missing. We term the additional dataset as unlabeled since the images are not labeled in terms of affordances. Such data is already available, for instance, in form of object detection datasets.

In order to train the CNN on both datasets, *i.e.*, the small dataset with affordance annotations and the large dataset with only object annotations, we transfer the affordance annotations from the small dataset to the unlabeled images of the large dataset. For the label transfer, we use a semantic alignment network, which is trained without supervision, to find for each unlabeled image the most similar labeled image. Despite of having only bounding box annotations of affordances, we then train a CNN for pixel-wise affordance segmentation weakly supervised on both datasets. We evaluate our approach on the IIT-AFF dataset [26] and the Pascal Parts dataset [6] where our approach outperforms other segmentation approaches that are also trained weakly supervised.

2   Related Work

Most related to our work are approaches for weakly supervised semantic segmentation and approaches for affordance detection or segmentation.

The task of weakly supervised semantic segmentation is to learn pixel-wise classification from a more coarse level of supervision. The different approaches vary in the type of supervision cues: [29,30,32] use image level labels as supervision to train semantic segmentation models while casting weakly supervised learning as a constrained optimization or a multiple instance learning problem, respectively. [2,20] leverage user annotated scribbles and individual key points to provide either sparse object labels or object location priors. [12,28] apply expectation maximization for weakly supervised training. While both approaches use image level labels, [7,13,28] additionally use annotated object bounding boxes while [12,27] uses saliency masks for supervision. Another paradigm, called simple-to-complex [38,41], consists of first training a model using simple images, *i.e.*, images containing a single object category followed by the training on complex images, *i.e.*, images with multiple objects. [41] combine an object proposal generator [1] with a proposal selection module thereby linking semantic segmentation and object localization. [16] improves the training procedure by using multiple loss functions. [3] combines saliency and attention maps to approximate the ground truth annotation. Some approaches explore the concept of region based mining, *i.e.*, an initial localization seed is expanded to the size of objects [14,40]. While these works address object segmentation, a few works focus on weakly supervised semantic part detection [17] or segmentation [23].

Various image domains have been explored for affordance detection or segmentation. The context of affordances also strongly differs depending on the task such as understanding human body parts [21], classifying environment affordances [31,34], or detecting affordances of real world objects that robots interact with [24]. [37] use predefined primary tools to infer object functionalities from 3D point clouds. [39] detect grasp affordances by combining the global object poses with its local appearance. [15] detect object affordances by observing object-action interactions performed by humans. Recently there have been several works that rely on deep convolutional neural networks for affordance detection [18,19,25,26,34,36]. [11] propose a region alignment layer to align the input image space with the feature map space. [8] detect multiple affordance classes in the object, instead of binary classes as in [11].

3   Label Transfer for Affordance Segmentation

Since annotating affordances or parts of objects is time-consuming, our goal is to train a convolutional network that segments affordances in images on a very small set of annotated images and additional unlabeled images. An overview of the approach is given in Fig. 1.

Our training set consists of a few example images for each object category where the affordances are annotated by bounding boxes. Since large datasets for object detection exist, we make use of them to extend the training set. These datasets, however, do not provide any annotations of affordances or parts but only bounding boxes for the objects. We therefore transfer the affordance labels from our training set to the objects from an object detection dataset. To this end, we first use a semantic alignment network to retrieve for each unlabeled image the most similar annotated training image to transfer the annotations (Sect. 3.1). We then train a fully convolutional network on the original training set and the extended set with transferred labels and use this model for inference (Sect. 3.2).

3.1   Semantic Alignment Network for Similarity Estimation

For similarity matching between annotated example objects and unannotated query objects, we use the semantic alignment network proposed in [33]. It takes two images I_s and I_t and predicts an affine transformation T_{aff} and a thin plate spline transformation T_{tps} whose concatenation semanticly aligns I_s to I_t. The transformations are subsequently predicted by two networks only differing in the final layer.

First the feature maps of both images $f_{ij:}^s$ and $f_{kl:}^t$, where i and j are the spatial coordinates in the source image I_s and k and l are the spatial coordinates in the target image I_t, are extracted in two Siamese branches. Then, a 4D-tensor S of space match scores is obtained via

$$s_{ijkl} = \frac{\langle f_{ij:}^s, f_{kl:}^t \rangle}{\sqrt{\sum_{a,b}\langle f_{ab:}^s, f_{kl:}^t \rangle^2}}. \tag{1}$$

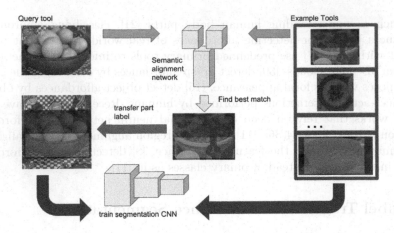

Fig. 1. In order to train a network to segment affordances from a very small set of examples, we transfer labels to unlabeled images. The training data consists of a set of objects where affordances are annotated by bounding boxes (right). This training set is very small and comprises only a few examples per object category. We then collect more examples of objects from an object detection dataset, i.e., the bounding box and the name of the object are given but not the affordances (left). To transfer the annotation labels of the training set to the new images, we use a semantic alignment network to find for each new image the most similar image in the training set. The bounding box annotations of the affordances are then transferred to the matched images and a CNN is then trained on all images. Best viewed in color.

Next, the parameters G of the geometrical transformation T_G are calculated from the space match score tensor S. This yields then the 4D inlier mask tensor M:

$$m_{ijkl} = \begin{cases} 1 & \text{if } d(T_G(i,j),(k,l)) < \tau \\ 0 & \text{otherwise.} \end{cases} \tag{2}$$

where d is the Euclidean distance. For τ, we use the same value as in [33]. Combining M and S provides the soft inlier count, a measure for the quality of the alignment:

$$c = \sum_{i,j,k,l} s_{ijkl} m_{ijkl}. \tag{3}$$

Intuitively, the feature vectors of pixels in the target and the warped image should be similar if the points are spatially close ($m_{ijkl} = 1$). Therefore, $-c$ serves as a training loss.

We use the pre-trained model [33], which has been first trained on synthetic data obtained from the Pascal dataset [9] and then finetuned with image pairs from the PF-PASCAL dataset [10]. Since the loss does not require human supervision and the network does not explicitly take any note of the object class, the model generalizes to unseen object classes. We therefore can use the model trained on Pascal classes on the IIT-AFF dataset.

The approach, however, fails for large transformations. Already 2D rotations by more than 30° lead to poor semantic alignments. We therefore augment each of the annotated examples by rotating it by 90°, 180° and 270° and flipping it. To find the best match in our annotated training set $\{I_i\}_{i\in\{1,...n\}}$ for a query image J, we compute (3) for J and each image I_i, which contains the same object class as J. The best match for J is then given by the image I_k with the highest soft inlier count c.

Figure 2 shows some examples for the top 3 matches.

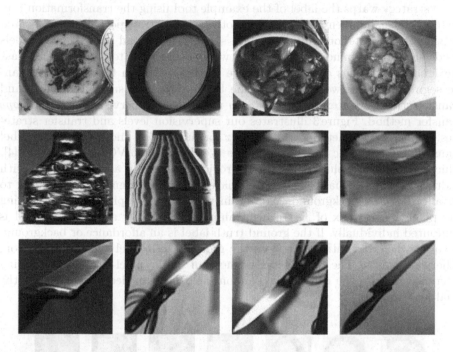

Fig. 2. Some query tools (left column) and the top 3 matching example tools with decreasing proximity from left to right. Except for the second match for the knife, the matching procedure retrieves tools seen from a similar viewpoint and having same orientation. Best viewed in color.

In order to transfer the affordance labels from I_k to J, the estimated warping transformation could be used. However, our experiments reveal that the estimated transformations are not accurate enough for transferring the labels. Instead, we scale I_k to match the size of J and copy the annotations from I_k to J.

3.2   Semantic Segmentation

In our experiments, we will investigate two supervision levels and two transfer strategies. In the first supervision setting, the affordances of example tools are pixel-wise annotated. In the second setting, the affordances of example tools are annotated by bounding boxes. In the latter case, we obtain a rough pixelwise annotation by setting all pixel labels inside an annotated bounding box to its affordance class. If a pixel is located inside multiple affordance bounding boxes, it receives the affordance label of the smallest bounding box. We refer to these supervision levels by *bbox* and *pixelwise*. The *copy* strategy simple resizes and copies the labels of the example tool onto the query tool. The *warp* strategy warps the label of the example tool using the transformation predicted by the alignment network. For both transfer strategies, all pixels located outside the object bounding boxes are set to background and all pixel labels inside the object bounding boxes which were not assigned to an affordance class are ignored and thus do not contribute to the loss when training the semantic segmentation network. We combine the notations of supervision level and transfer strategy, for example *bbox-copy* means *bbox* supervision level and *copy* transfer method. Figure 3 illustrates our supervision levels and transfer strategies. The proposed method assumes *bbox* for supervision and uses *copy* for label transfer. For semantic segmentation, we use the deeplab VGG architecture [4], which is a fully convolutional network providing as output a feature map f with width and height equal to the input image and each channel corresponding to an affordance or background. We obtain the affordance probability by taking the pixelwise softmax of f. During training, the loss for a particular pixel is computed individually. If the ground truth label is an affordance or background it equals the cross entropy between the ground truth label and the prediction, otherwise it is 0. The overall loss is the sum of the pixel-wise losses. During inference, we use the conditional random field layer of deeplab on top of the final feature map.

Fig. 3. Illustration of our supervision levels and transfer strategies. From left to right: query tool, matched example tool, aligned example tool, *bbox-copy* labels, *pixelwise-copy* labels, *bbox-warp* labels, *pixelwise-warp* labels. Best viewed in color.

4   Experiments

We conduct our experiments on the IIT-AFF dataset introduced by [26]. It consists of images showing 10 classes of tools in context. There are 6184 images in the trainval set and 2651 images in the test set. The images were collected in a robotics lab or come from the Imagenet dataset [35]. Each tool is annotated with a bounding box. Additionally, each tool class has a predefined set of possible affordances. Tool parts serving an affordance are pixel-wise annotated with it. The tool classes with their affordances are: bowl (wrap, contain), tv (display), pan (contain, grasp), hammer (grasp, pound), knife (cut, grasp), cup (contain, wrap), drill (grasp, engine), racket (grasp, hit), spatula (support, grasp) and bottle (grasp, contain).

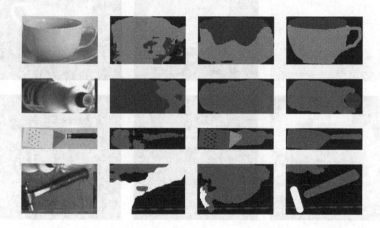

Fig. 4. Qualitative results on bounding boxes: RGB input (first column), DCSP [3] results (second column), our results (third column), ground truth (last column). In contrast to DCSP, our method correctly associates the affordances with the respective object parts. Best viewed in color.

Unless stated otherwise, in all our experiments our unlabeled set comprises the images from the IIT trainval set with 6 example tools per tool class randomly drawn from them to constitute the training set. We use the semantic alignment model trained on PF-PASCAL [10] by [33]. For training and inference with deeplab [4], we use the same setup as in the original paper in the fully supervised setup on Pascal.

4.1   Comparison to State of the Art

To our knowledge there is no work on weakly supervised semantic segmentation which uses the same amount of supervision: A vast object dataset annotated on bounding box level but unlabeled in terms of object part affordances and a tiny dataset with bounding boxes provided for affordances. DCSP [3], which is

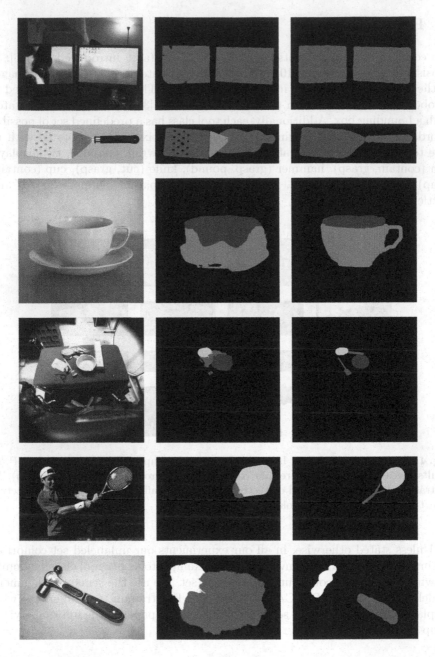

Fig. 5. Qualitative results on IIT-AFF [26]: RGB input (left), our results (middle), ground truth (right). Best viewed in color.

Table 1. Comparison to DCSP [3], a method showing state of the art results on Pascal VOC 2012. We report IoU on the IIT-AFF dataset [26]. For a fair comparison, we train and evaluate DCSP on bounding box crops of tools and the affordance segments of example tools and evaluate ours on the bounding box crops only.

Method	Contain	Cut	Display	Engine	Grasp	Hit	Pound	Support	Wrap grasp	Mean
DCSP [3]	0.340	0.179	0.602	0.214	0.259	0.548	0.242	0.085	0.205	0.297
Proposed	0.616	0.209	0.811	0.364	0.328	0.633	0.345	0.335	0.510	0.461

Table 2. Evaluation of our method on the IIT-AFF dataset [26] for different number of example tools per tool class. We evaluate on full images and report IoU.

# Examples	Contain	Cut	Display	Engine	Grasp	Hit	Pound	Support	Wrap-gr.	Mean
1	0.480	0.152	0.760	0.305	0.293	0.575	0.101	0.134	0.387	0.354
2	0.518	0.191	0.744	0.336	0.267	0.590	0.248	0.096	0.426	0.380
3	0.522	0.182	0.716	0.331	0.269	0.645	0.245	0.136	0.417	0.385
6 (default)	0.564	0.180	0.723	0.329	0.288	0.596	0.295	0.323	0.469	0.419

the current state of the art method for weakly supervised image segmentation on Pascal VOC 2012, uses a list of present classes in an image for supervision. We therefore train DCSP on the bounding boxes of tools from the unlabeled set as well as on the annotated bounding boxes of affordances from the training set. On the unlabeled set, the affordances are inferred from the tool class and used as image labels for supervision. We keep the original training parameters of DCSP, but reduce the learning rate by a factor of 3 since it improved the results of DCSP.

For comparison, we evaluate both methods not on the entire images, but only within the annotated bounding boxes surrounding the objects, since we are interested in how well both methods segment the affordances within a bounding box. The results are reported in Table 1: DCSP achieves a mean IoU of 29.7% while our approach yields 46.1%, thus outperforming DCSP by more then 16%. To analyze if the difficulty for DCSP stems from the localization of affordances on the tool or from the pixel-wise segmentation of the tool itself, we performed an additional experiment. Instead of training DCSP for segmenting affordances, we trained DCSP for segmenting objects. For object segmentation, DCSP performs very well and achieves 53.4% mean IoU for the object categories. Therefore localizing the affordance on the tool constitutes the main challenge. This is also evident from the qualitative comparison shown in Fig. 4. Qualitative results for complete images are shown in Fig. 5.

4.2   Number of Examples

Our proposed evaluation setup uses 6 random examples per tool class, but we also investigated the performance with an even smaller amount of examples, namely 1, 2 and 3 examples per tool class, and report the results in Table 2. Unlike in the previous section, we evaluate on complete test images, but still

Table 3. Comparison of training on the example images only vs. our approach, which uses additional training data by label transfer. We evaluate on full images from the IIT-AFF dataset [26] and report IoU.

Method	Contain	Cut	Display	Engine	Grasp	Hit	Pound	Support	Wrap-gr.	Mean
ex. tools only	0.563	0.000	0.501	0.206	0.226	0.553	0.005	0.016	0.388	0.273
Proposed	0.564	0.180	0.723	0.329	0.288	0.596	0.295	0.323	0.469	0.419

achieve a mean IoU of 41.9%. When using only one example tool per tool class, the performance drops to 35.4%.

4.3   Impact of Additional Training Data

To see if additional training data and transferring the labels from the examples to the additional training data is required at all, we trained our semantic segmentation network only on the images containing at least one of the 60 example tools. Pixels located inside the affordance bounding box of the example tools were set to this affordance class, pixels belonging to any tool bounding box which does not belong to an example tool were ignored during training, and the rest was set to background. Since the number of training images is tiny in this setting, we reduced the number of iterations from 6000 to 300 and the step length during training accordingly to avoid overfitting. As can be seen in Table 3, the performance drops to 27.3% and for the affordances cut, pound, support to almost 0. Our approach is especially beneficial for challenging small affordances.

4.4   Warping vs No Warping

While we simply resize and copy the affordance localization cues from the most similar example tool to the tool of interest, one could also warp the localization cues of the example tool onto the target tool using the transformation provided by the semantic alignment network. On the one hand, this approach has the advantage of potentially better aligning the shape of the tools and therefore better aligning the functional parts. On the other hand, the warping might be reasonable for only some parts of the object but fail for other, in particular small parts. Therefore, the benefit of using the warping transformation or not depends on the affordance classes. The results reported in Table 4 show that warping improves the accuracy for the classes display, engine, and hit, but it decreases the accuracy for the other affordance classes. In average, using the estimated warping transformation for label transfer reduces the accuracy from 41.9% to 39.1%.

4.5   Bounding Box vs. Pixel-Wise Annotation

Obtaining affordance region bounding boxes for example tools is far cheaper than annotating the functional regions pixel-wise. To investigate the potential

Table 4. Comparison of warping the affordance labels from the example tool vs copying them. We evaluate on full images from the IIT-AFF dataset [26] and report IoU.

Method	Contain	Cut	Display	Engine	Grasp	Hit	Pound	Support	Wrap-gr.	Mean
bbox-warped	0.550	0.156	0.730	0.313	0.278	0.640	0.188	0.218	0.443	0.391
Proposed	0.564	0.180	0.723	0.329	0.288	0.596	0.295	0.323	0.469	0.419

Table 5. Comparison of using accurate pixel-wise affordance annotations of the example tools vs. bounding boxes around affordances. We report the results with and without using the estimated warping transformation for label transfer. We evaluate on full images from the IIT-AFF dataset [26] and report IoU.

Method	Contain	Cut	Display	Engine	Grasp	Hit	Pound	Support	Wrap-gr.	Mean
pxlwise copy	0.601	0.245	0.745	0.368	0.388	0.589	0.260	0.333	0.502	0.448
pxlwise warp	0.592	0.190	0.748	0.363	0.354	0.616	0.0	0.278	0.466	0.401
Proposed	0.564	0.180	0.723	0.329	0.288	0.596	0.295	0.323	0.469	0.419

gain from a pixel-wise annotation, we conducted two ablation experiments. In the first, we transfer the pixel-wise affordance annotations from example tools to unlabeled tools without using the estimated warping transformation and in the second we use the estimated warping transformation for label transfer. We report the results in Table 5: Providing pixel-wise affordance annotations for example tools increases the accuracy with and without warping. In case of warping the accuracy increases from 39.1% to 40.1% and without warping the accuracy increases from 41.9% to 44.8%.

4.6 ResNet Features vs. Alignment

To investigate the benefit of the unsupervisedly trained semantic alignment network, we train a semantic segmentation model using an approach identical to the proposed method except for the matching criterion between query tools and example tools. Since the alignment network was trained on Pascal VOC2012, we take the Pascal VOC2012 semantic segmentation Resnet-101 model from [5], and generate the features of the res5c layer for each query tool and each example tool. Note that we use the same CNN backbone as for the semantic alignment network and require the same amount of cross dataset generalisation. After that, we retrieve for each query tool the example tool with the most similar feature map and transfer the labels. Specifically, the cosine distance serves as a measure for the similarity of the vectorized feature maps of two images v, w:

$$d = 1 - \frac{\langle v, w \rangle}{\|v\| \|w\|} \tag{4}$$

As can be seen from Table 6, the ResNet-101 features perform slightly worse than the weak alignment network.

Table 6. Comparison of two matching strategies between query tools and example tools: The proposed strategy uses the loss of a semantic alignment network trained in an unsupervised manner, the ablation uses the features of ResNet-101 pretrained on Pascal VOC2012. We evaluate on full images from the IIT-AFF dataset [26] and report IoU.

	Contain	Cut	Display	Engine	Grasp	Hit	Pound	Support	Wrap grasp	Mean
Features	0.573	0.206	0.705	0.348	0.287	0.608	0.262	0.322	0.423	0.415
Proposed	0.564	0.180	0.723	0.329	0.288	0.596	0.295	0.323	0.469	0.419

4.7 Oracle Experiment: Ground Truth Bounding Box for Each Affordance of Each Query Tool

In this ablation experiment we investigate what is achievable if the bounding boxes around affordances are not only given for the example tools but also for all query tools. All pixels inside an affordance bounding box are set to this affordance. In case of a pixel belonging to multiple affordance bounding box, it is assigned to the affordance with the smallest bounding box. All other pixels are set to background. After that, the semantic segmentation network is trained and used for inference as in our proposed method. We report the results in Table 7. This additional supervision improves the results to 52.6%, however, at the cost of additional annotations of query tools, while our method does not require any additional annotation once object bounding boxes are given. For example, it could be applied to the affordances of objects in the COCO dataset [22]. Even if the bounding boxes are not given for a custom data set, they can be generated using a weakly supervised object detection system, e.g. [42].

Table 7. Results if ground truth bounding boxes would be given for each affordance of each query tool vs. our method. We evaluate on full images from the IIT-AFF dataset [26] and report IoU.

	Contain	Cut	Display	Engine	Grasp	Hit	Pound	Support	Wrap grasp	Mean
gt-bbox	0.686	0.217	0.747	0.521	0.389	0.722	0.382	0.466	0.606	0.526
Proposed	0.564	0.180	0.723	0.329	0.288	0.596	0.295	0.323	0.469	0.419

4.8 Evaluation on the Pascal Parts Dataset

We finally evaluate our approach on the Pascal Parts dataset [6]. It contains images from the Pascal VOC dataset, which belong to the categories bird, cat, cow, dog, horse, person, and sheep. For each category, 4 to 5 semantic body parts are annotated. The task of part segmentation differs from affordance segmentation since different object classes do not share the same part category, *e.g.*, leg of horse and leg of sheep are considered as two different part classes in Pascal Parts. This is in contrast to affordances, which are shared among different tool classes. Since our method can be applied to both tasks, we also evaluate our approach on this dataset by randomly sampling 6 example objects per object class. Our approach outperforms the current state of the art by +3.5% as can be seen in Table 8.

Table 8. Evaluation on the Pascal Parts [6]. Our method outperforms state of the art methods for weakly supervised semantic parts segmentation. As on IIT-AFF dataset [26], we use 6 example objects per object class.

Method	Bird	Cat	Cow	Dog	Horse	Person	Sheep	Mean
[17]	0.099	0.135	0.115	0.141	0.067	0.106	0.105	0.110
[23]	0.111	0.113	0.124	0.142	0.075	0.128	0.106	0.114
Proposed	0.148	0.174	0.115	0.180	0.120	0.108	0.201	0.149

5 Conclusion

In this work, we have shown that a CNN, which is weakly supervised trained for affordance or object part segmentation, can be trained from very few annotated examples. This has been achieved by exploiting a semantic alignment network to transfer annotations from a small set of annotated examples to images that are only annotated by the object class. In our experiments, we have shown that our approach achieves state of the art accuracy on the IIT-AFF dataset [26] and the Pascal Parts dataset [6].

Acknowledgement. The work has been financially supported by the DFG projects GA 1927/5-1 (DFG Research Unit FOR 2535 Anticipating Human Behavior).

References

1. Arbeláez, P.A., Pont-Tuset, J., Barron, J.T., Marqués, F., Malik, J.: Multiscale combinatorial grouping. In: 2014 IEEE Conference on Computer Vision and Pattern Recognition, CVPR 2014, Columbus, OH, USA, 23–28 June 2014, pp. 328–335. IEEE Computer Society (2014)
2. Bearman, A., Russakovsky, O., Ferrari, V., Fei-Fei, L.: What's the point: semantic segmentation with point supervision. In: Leibe, B., Matas, J., Sebe, N., Welling, M. (eds.) ECCV 2016. LNCS, vol. 9911, pp. 549–565. Springer, Cham (2016). https://doi.org/10.1007/978-3-319-46478-7_34
3. Chaudhry, A., Dokania, P.K., Torr, P.H.S.: Discovering class-specific pixels for weakly-supervised semantic segmentation. In: British Machine Vision Conference 2017, BMVC 2017, London, UK, 4–7 September 2017. BMVA Press (2017)
4. Chen, L.C., Papandreou, G., Kokkinos, I., Murphy, K., Yuille, A.L.: Semantic image segmentation with deep convolutional nets and fully connected CRFs. In: International Conference on Learning Representations (2015)

5. Chen, L., Papandreou, G., Kokkinos, I., Murphy, K., Yuille, A.L.: Deeplab: semantic image segmentation with deep convolutional nets, atrous convolution, and fully
   connected CRFs. CoRR abs/1606.00915 (2016)
6. Chen, X., Mottaghi, R., Liu, X., Fidler, S., Urtasun, R., Yuille, A.L.: Detect what
   you can: detecting and representing objects using holistic models and body parts.
   In: 2014 IEEE Conference on Computer Vision and Pattern Recognition, CVPR
   2014, Columbus, OH, USA, 23–28 June 2014, pp. 1979–1986. IEEE Computer
   Society (2014)
7. Dai, J., He, K., Sun, J.: BoxSup: exploiting bounding boxes to supervise convolutional networks for semantic segmentation. In: 2015 IEEE International Conference
   on Computer Vision, ICCV 2015, Santiago, Chile, 7–13 December 2015, pp. 1635–
   1643. IEEE Computer Society (2015)
8. Do, T., Nguyen, A., Reid, I.D., Caldwell, D.G., Tsagarakis, N.G.: Affordancenet:
   an end-to-end deep learning approach for object affordance detection. CoRR
   abs/1709.07326 (2017)
9. Everingham, M., Eslami, S.M.A., Van Gool, L.J., Williams, C.K.I., Winn, J.M.,
   Zisserman, A.: The PASCAL visual object classes challenge: a retrospective. Int.
   J. Comput. Vis. **111**(1), 98–136 (2015)
10. Ham, B., Cho, M., Schmid, C., Ponce, J.: Proposal flow: semantic correspondences
    from object proposals. IEEE Trans. Pattern Anal. Mach. Intell. **40**(7), 1711–1725
    (2018)
11. He, K., Gkioxari, G., Dollár, P., Girshick, R.B.: Mask R-CNN. In: IEEE Interna-
    tional Conference on Computer Vision, ICCV 2017, Venice, Italy, 22–29 October
    2017, pp. 2980–2988. IEEE Computer Society (2017)
12. Hou, Q., Dokania, P.K., Massiceti, D., Wei, Y., Cheng, M., Torr, P.H.S.: Min-
    ing pixels: weakly supervised semantic segmentation using image labels. CoRR
    abs/1612.02101 (2016)
13. Khoreva, A., Benenson, R., Hosang, J.H., Hein, M., Schiele, B.: Simple does it:
    weakly supervised instance and semantic segmentation. In: 2017 IEEE Conference
    on Computer Vision and Pattern Recognition, CVPR 2017, Honolulu, HI, USA,
    21–26 July 2017, pp. 1665–1674. IEEE Computer Society (2017)
14. Kim, D., Cho, D., Yoo, D.: Two-phase learning for weakly supervised object
    localization. In: IEEE International Conference on Computer Vision, ICCV 2017,
    Venice, Italy, 22–29 October 2017, pp. 3554–3563. IEEE Computer Society (2017)
15. Kjellström, H., Romero, J., Kragic, D.: Visual object-action recognition: infer-
    ring object affordances from human demonstration. Comput. Vis. Image Underst.
    115(1), 81–90 (2011)
16. Kolesnikov, A., Lampert, C.H.: Seed, expand and constrain: three principles for
    weakly-supervised image segmentation. In: Leibe, B., Matas, J., Sebe, N., Welling,
    M. (eds.) ECCV 2016. LNCS, vol. 9908, pp. 695–711. Springer, Cham (2016).
    https://doi.org/10.1007/978-3-319-46493-0_42
17. Krause, J., Jin, H., Yang, J., Li, F.: Fine-grained recognition without part annota-
    tions. In: IEEE Conference on Computer Vision and Pattern Recognition, CVPR
    2015, Boston, MA, USA, 7–12 June 2015, pp. 5546–5555. IEEE Computer Society
    (2015)
18. Lenz, I., Lee, H., Saxena, A.: Deep learning for detecting robotic grasps. Inter. J.
    Robot. Res. **34**(4–5), 705–724 (2015)
19. Li, Y., Qi, H., Dai, J., Ji, X., Wei, Y.: Fully convolutional instance-aware semantic
    segmentation. In: 2017 IEEE Conference on Computer Vision and Pattern Recog-
    nition, CVPR 2017, Honolulu, HI, USA, 21–26 July 2017, pp. 4438–4446. IEEE
    Computer Society (2017)

20. Lin, D., Dai, J., Jia, J., He, K., Sun, J.: Scribblesup: scribble-supervised convolutional networks for semantic segmentation. In: 2016 IEEE Conference on Computer Vision and Pattern Recognition, CVPR 2016, Las Vegas, NV, USA, 27–30 June 2016, pp. 3159–3167. IEEE Computer Society (2016)
21. Lin, G., Milan, A., Shen, C., Reid, I.D.: Refinenet: multi-path refinement networks for high-resolution semantic segmentation. In: 2017 IEEE Conference on Computer Vision and Pattern Recognition, CVPR 2017, Honolulu, HI, USA, 21–26 July 2017, pp. 5168–5177. IEEE Computer Society (2017)
22. Lin, T.-Y., et al.: Microsoft COCO: common objects in context. In: Fleet, D., Pajdla, T., Schiele, B., Tuytelaars, T. (eds.) ECCV 2014. LNCS, vol. 8693, pp. 740–755. Springer, Cham (2014). https://doi.org/10.1007/978-3-319-10602-1_48
23. Meng, F., Li, H., Wu, Q., Luo, B., Ngan, K.N.: Weakly supervised part proposal segmentation from multiple images. IEEE Trans. Image Process. **26**(8), 4019–4031 (2017)
24. Myers, A., Teo, C.L., Fermüller, C., Aloimonos, Y.: Affordance detection of tool parts from geometric features. In: IEEE International Conference on Robotics and Automation, ICRA 2015, Seattle, WA, USA, 26–30 May 2015, pp. 1374–1381. IEEE (2015)
25. Nguyen, A., Kanoulas, D., Caldwell, D.G., Tsagarakis, N.G.: Detecting object affordances with convolutional neural networks. In: 2016 IEEE/RSJ International Conference on Intelligent Robots and Systems, IROS 2016, Daejeon, South Korea, 9–14 October 2016, pp. 2765–2770. IEEE (2016)
26. Nguyen, A., Kanoulas, D., Caldwell, D.G., Tsagarakis, N.G.: Object-based affordances detection with convolutional neural networks and dense conditional random fields. In: 2017 IEEE/RSJ International Conference on Intelligent Robots and Systems, IROS 2017, Vancouver, BC, Canada, 24–28 September 2017, pp. 5908–5915. IEEE (2017)
27. Oh, S.J., Benenson, R., Khoreva, A., Akata, Z., Fritz, M., Schiele, B.: Exploiting saliency for object segmentation from image level labels. In: 2017 IEEE Conference on Computer Vision and Pattern Recognition, CVPR 2017, Honolulu, HI, USA, 21–26 July 2017, pp. 5038–5047. IEEE Computer Society (2017)
28. Papandreou, G., Chen, L., Murphy, K.P., Yuille, A.L.: Weakly-and semi-supervised learning of a deep convolutional network for semantic image segmentation. In: 2015 IEEE International Conference on Computer Vision, ICCV 2015, Santiago, Chile, 7–13 December 2015, pp. 1742–1750. IEEE Computer Society (2015)
29. Pathak, D., Krähenbühl, P., Darrell, T.: Constrained convolutional neural networks for weakly supervised segmentation. In: 2015 IEEE International Conference on Computer Vision, ICCV 2015, Santiago, Chile, 7–13 December 2015, pp. 1796–1804. IEEE Computer Society (2015)
30. Pathak, D., Shelhamer, E., Long, J., Darrell, T.: Fully convolutional multi-class multiple instance learning. In: International Conference on Learning Representations Workshop (2015)
31. Pham, T., Do, T.T., Sünderhauf, N., Reid, I.: SceneCut: joint geometric and object segmentation for indoor scenes (2018)
32. Pinheiro, P.H.O., Collobert, R.: From image-level to pixel-level labeling with convolutional networks. In: IEEE Conference on Computer Vision and Pattern Recognition, CVPR 2015, Boston, MA, USA, 7–12 June 2015, pp. 1713–1721. IEEE Computer Society (2015)
33. Rocco, I., Arandjelović, R., Sivic, J.: End-to-end weakly-supervised semantic alignment. In: 2018 IEEE Conference on Computer Vision and Pattern Recognition, CVPR 2018, Salt Lake City, USA, 19–21 June 2018 (2018)

34. Roy, A., Todorovic, S.: A multi-scale CNN for affordance segmentation in RGB images. In: Leibe, B., Matas, J., Sebe, N., Welling, M. (eds.) ECCV 2016. LNCS, vol. 9908, pp. 186–201. Springer, Cham (2016). https://doi.org/10.1007/978-3-319-46493-0_12

35. Russakovsky, O., et al.: Imagenet large scale visual recognition challenge. Int. J. Comput. Vis. **115**(3), 211–252 (2015)

36. Sawatzky, J., Srikantha, A., Gall, J.: Weakly supervised affordance detection. In: 2017 IEEE Conference on Computer Vision and Pattern Recognition, CVPR 2017, Honolulu, HI, USA, 21–26 July 2017, pp. 5197–5206. IEEE Computer Society (2017)

37. Schoeler, M., Wörgötter, F.: Bootstrapping the semantics of tools: affordance analysis of real world objects on a per-part basis. IEEE Trans. Cogn. Dev. Syst. **8**(2), 84–98 (2016)

38. Shen, T., Lin, G., Liu, L., Shen, C., Reid, I.D.: Weakly supervised semantic segmentation based on co-segmentation. In: British Machine Vision Conference 2017, BMVC 2017, London, UK, 4–7 September 2017, BMVA Press (2017)

39. Song, H.O., Fritz, M., Göhring, D., Darrell, T.: Learning to detect visual grasp affordance. IEEE Trans. Autom. Sci. Eng. **13**(2), 798–809 (2016)

40. Wei, Y., Feng, J., Liang, X., Cheng, M., Zhao, Y., Yan, S.: Object region mining with adversarial erasing: a simple classification to semantic segmentation approach. In: 2017 IEEE Conference on Computer Vision and Pattern Recognition, CVPR 2017, Honolulu, HI, USA, 21–26 July 2017, pp. 6488–6496. IEEE Computer Society (2017)

41. Wei, Y., et al.: STC: a simple to complex framework for weakly-supervised semantic segmentation. IEEE Trans. Pattern Anal. Mach. Intell. **39**, 2314–2320 (2017)

42. Zhang, Y., Bai, Y., Ding, M., Li, Y., Ghanem, B.: W2F: a weakly-supervised to fully-supervised framework for object detection. In: 2018 IEEE Conference on Computer Vision and Pattern Recognition, CVPR 2018, Salt Lake City, USA, 19–21 June 2018. IEEE Computer Society (2018)

Oral Session 1: Learning I

Domain Generalization
with Domain-Specific Aggregation
Modules

Antonio D'Innocente[1,2]([⊠]) and Barbara Caputo[2]

[1] Sapienza University of Rome, Rome, Italy
dinnocente@diag.unroma1.it
[2] Italian Institute of Technology, Milan, Italy
{antonio.dinnocente,barbara.caputo}@iit.it

Abstract. Visual recognition systems are meant to work in the real world. For this to happen, they must work robustly in any visual domain, and not only on the data used during training. Within this context, a very realistic scenario deals with *domain generalization*, i.e. the ability to build visual recognition algorithms able to work robustly in several visual domains, without having access to any information about target data statistic. This paper contributes to this research thread, proposing a deep architecture that maintains separated the information about the available source domains data while at the same time leveraging over generic perceptual information. We achieve this by introducing *domain-specific aggregation modules* that through an aggregation layer strategy are able to merge generic and specific information in an effective manner. Experiments on two different benchmark databases show the power of our approach, reaching the new state of the art in domain generalization.

1   Introduction

As artificial intelligence, fueled by machine and deep learning, is entering more and more into our everyday lives, there is a growing need for visual recognition algorithms able to leave the controlled lab settings and work robustly in the wild. This problem has long been investigated in the community under the name of Domain Adaptation (DA): considering the underlying statistics generating the data used during training (source domain), and those expected at test time (target domain), DA assumes that the robustness issues are due to a covariate shift among the source and target distributions, and it attempts to align such distributions so to increase the recognition performances on the target domain. Since its definition [19], the vast majority of works has focused on the scenario where one single source is available at training time, and one specific target source is taken into consideration at test time, with or without any labeled data (for an overview of previous work we refer to Sect. 2). Although useful, this setup is somewhat limited: given the large abundance of visual data produced daily worldwide and uploaded on the Web, it is very reasonable to assume that several

T. Brox et al. (Eds.): GCPR 2018, LNCS 11269, pp. 187–198, 2019.
https://doi.org/10.1007/978-3-030-12939-2_14

source domains might be available at training time. Moreover, the assumption to have access to data representative of the underlying statistic of the target domain, regardless of annotation, is not always realistic. Rather than equipping a seeing machine with a DA algorithm able to solve the domain gap for a specific single target, one would hope to have methods able to solve the problem for *any* target domain. This last scenario, much closer to realistic settings, goes under the name of Domain Generalization (DG, [10]), and is the focus of our work.

Current approaches to DG tend to follow two alternative routes: the first tries to use all source data together in order to learn a joint, general representation for the categories of interest strong enough to work on any target domain [11]. The second instead opts for keeping separated the information coming from each source domain, trying to estimate at test time the similarity between the target domain represented by the incoming data and the known sources, and use only the classifier branch trained on that specific source for classification [14]. Our approach sits across these two philosophies, attempting to get the best of both worlds. Starting from a generic convnet, pre-trained on a general knowledge database like ImageNet [17], we build a new multi-branch architecture with as many branches as the source domains available at training time. Each branch leverages over the general knowledge contained into the pre-trained convnet through a deep layer aggregation strategy inspired by [27], that we call Domain-Specific Aggregation Modules (D-SAM). The resulting architecture is trained so that all three branches contribute to the classification stage through an aggregation strategy. The resulting convnet can be used in an end-to-end fashion, or its learned representations can be used as features in a linear SVM. We tested both options on two different architectures and two different domain generalization databases, benchmarking against all recent approaches to the problem. Results show that our D-SAM architecture, in all cases, consistently achieve the state of the art.

2   Related Works

Most of work in DA has focused on single source scenarios, with two main research threads. The first deals with features, aiming to learn deep domain representations that are invariant to the domain shift, although discriminative enough to perform well on the target [3,4,13,22]. Other methods rely on adversarial loss functions [5,20,23]. Also two-step networks have been shown to have practical advantages [1,24]. The second thread focuses on images. The adversarial approach used successfully for feature-based methods, has also been applied directly to the reduction of the visual domain gap. Various GAN-based strategies [6] have been proposed for generating new images and/or perturb existing ones to mimic the visual style of a domain and reducing the discrepancy at the pixel level [2,18,21]. Recently, some authors addressed the multi-source domain adaptation problem with deep networks. The approach proposed in [26] builds over [5] by replicating the adversarial domain discriminator branch for each available source. Moreover these discriminators are also used to get a perplexity score that indicates how the multiple sources should be combined at test time as in [16]. A similar multi-way adversarial strategy is used also in [28], but this work comes with a theoretical support that frees it from the need of respecting a specific optimal source combination and thus from the need of learning the source weights.

In the DG setting, access to the target data is not allowed, thus the main objective is to look across multiple sources for shared factors in the hypothesis that they will hold also for any new target domain. Deep DG methods are presented in [14,15] and [10]. The first works propose a weighting procedure on the source models, while the second aims at separating the source knowledge into domain-specific and domain-agnostic sub-models. A meta-learning approach was recently presented in [11]: it starts by creating virtual testing domains within each source mini-batch and then it trains a network to minimize the classification loss, while also ensuring that the taken direction leads to an improvement on the virtual testing loss.

Over the last years, it has emerged a growing interest on studying modules and connectivity patterns, and on how to assemble them systematically. Some studies showed how skipping connections can be beneficial for classification and regression. In particular, [8] showed how skipping connections concatenating all the layers in stages is effective for semantic fusion, while [12] exploited conceptually similar ideas for spatial fusion. An unifying framework for these approaches, on which to some extent we build, has been recently proposed in [27]. There the authors proposed two general structures for deep layer aggregation, one iterative and one hierarchical, that capture the nuances of previous works while being applicable in principle to any convnet.

We leverage on this work, proposing a variant of iterative deep aggregation leading to a multi branch architecture, able to conjugate the need for general representations while retaining the strength of keeping information from different sources separated in the domain generalization setting.

3 Domain Specific Aggregation Modules

In this section we describe our aggregation strategy for DG. We will assume to have S source domains and T target domains, denoting with N_i the cardinality of the i_{th} source domain, for which we have $\{x_j^i, y_j^i\}_{j=1}^{N_i}$ labeled samples. Source and target domains share the same classification task; however, unlike DA, the target distribution is unknown and the algorithm is expected to generalize to new domains without ever having access to target data, and hence without any possibility to estimate the underlying statistic for the target domain.

The most basic approach, *Deep All*, consists of ignoring the domain membership of the images available from all training sources, and training a generic algorithm on the combined source samples. Despite its simplicity, *Deep All* outperforms many engineered methods in domain generalization, as shown in [10]. The domain specific aggregation modules we propose can be seen as a way to augment the generalization abilities of given CNN architectures by maintaining a generic core, while at the same time explicitly modeling the single domain specific features separately, in a whole coherent structure.

Our architecture consists of a main branch Θ and a collection of domain specific aggregation modules $\Lambda = \{\lambda_1...\lambda_n\}$, each specialized on a single source domain. The main branch Θ is the backbone of our model, and it can be in principle any pre-trained off-the shelf convnet. Aggregation modules, which we design inspired by an iterative aggregation protocol described in [27], receive inputs from Θ and learn to combine features at different levels to produce classification outputs. At training time, each domain-specific aggregation module learns to specialize on a single source domain. In the validation phase, we use a variation of a leave-one-domain-out strategy: we average predictions of each module but, for each i_{th} source domain, we exclude the corresponding domain-specific module λ_i from the evaluation. We test the model in both an end-to-end fashion and by running a linear classifier on the extracted features. In the rest of the section we describe into detail the various components of our approach (Sects. 3.1 and 3.2) and the training protocol (Sect. 3.3).

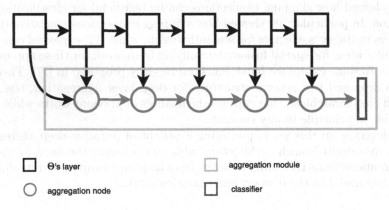

□ Θ's layer   □ aggregation module

○ aggregation node   □ classifier

Fig. 1. Architecture of an aggregation module (purple) augmenting a CNN model. Aggregation nodes (yellow) iteratively process input from Θ's layers and propagate them to the classifier. (Color figure online)

3.1   Aggregation Module

Deep Layer Aggregation [27] is a feature fusion strategy designed to augment a fully convolutional architecture with a parallel, layered structure whose task is to better process and propagate features from the original network to the classifier. Aggregation nodes, the main building block of the augmenting structure, learn to combine convolutional outputs from multiple layers with a compression technique, which in [27] is implemented with 1×1 convolutions followed by batch normalization and nonlinearity. The arrangement of connections between aggregation nodes and the augmented network's original layers yields an architecture more capable of extracting the full spectrum of spatial and semantical informations from the original model [27].

Inspired by the aggregations of [27], we implement aggregation modules as parallel feature processing branches pluggable in any CNN architecture. Our aggregation consists of a stacked sequence of aggregation nodes N, with each node iteratively combining outputs from Θ and from the previous node, as shown in Fig. 1. The nodes we use are implemented as 1×1 convolutions followed by nonlinearity. Our aggregation module visually resembles the Iterative Deep Aggregation (IDA) strategy described in [27], but the two are different. IDA is an aggregation pattern for merging different scales, and is implemented on top of a hierarchical structure. Our aggregation module is a pluggable augmentation which merges features from various layers sequentially. Compared to [27], our structure can be merged with any existing pre-trained model without disrupting the original features' propagation. We also extend its usage to non-fully convolutional models by viewing 2-dimensional outputs of fully connected nodes as 4-dimensional ($N \times C \times H \times W$) tensors whose H and W dimension are collapsed. As we designed these modules having in mind the DG problem and their usage for domain specific learning, we call them Domain-Specific Aggregation Modules (D-SAM).

3.2   D-SAM Architecture for Domain Generalization

The modular nature of our D-SAMs allows the stacking of multiple augmentations on the same backbone network. Given a DG setting in which we have S source domains, we choose a pre-trained model Θ and augment it with S aggregation modules, each of which implements its own classifier while learning to specialize on an individual domain. The overall architecture is shown in Fig. 2.

Our intention is to model the domain specific part and the domain generic part within the architecture. While aggregation modules are domain specific, we may see Θ as the domain generic part that, via backpropagation, learns to yield general features which aggregation modules specialize upon. Although not explicitly trained to do so, our feature evaluations suggest that thanks to our training procedure, the backbone Θ implicitly learns more domain generic representations compared to the corresponding backbone model trained without aggregations.

3.3   Training and Testing

We train our model so that the backbone Θ processes all the input images, while each aggregation module learns to specialize on a single domain. To accomplish this, at each iteration we feed to the network S equal sized mini-batches grouped by domain. Given an input mini-batch x_i from the i_{th} source domain, the corresponding output of our function, as also shown graphically in Fig. 2, is:

$$f(x_i) = \lambda_i(\Theta(x_i)). \tag{1}$$

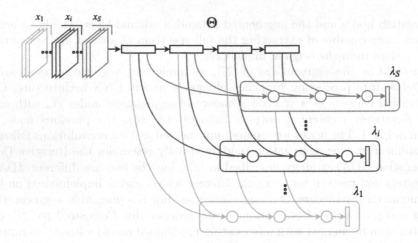

Fig. 2. Simplified architecture with 3 aggregation nodes per aggregation module. The main branch Θ shares features with S specialized modules. At training time, the i_{th} aggregation module only processes outputs relative to the i_{th} domain.

We optimize our model by minimizing the cross entropy loss function $L_C = \sum_c y_{x_j^i,c} \log(p_{x_j^i,c})$, which for a training iteration we formalize as:

$$L(\Theta, \Lambda) = \sum_{i=1}^{S} L_C((\lambda_i \circ \Theta)(x_i)). \qquad (2)$$

We validate our model by combining probabilities of the outputs of aggregation modules. One problem of the DG setting is that performance on the validation set is not very informative, since accuracy on source domains doesn't give much indication of the generalization ability. We partially mitigate this problem in our algorithm by calculating probabilities for validation as:

$$p_{x_j^v} = \sigma\Big(\sum_{i=1, i \neq v}^{S} \lambda_i(\Theta(x_j^v))\Big), \qquad (3)$$

where σ is the softmax function. Given an input image belonging to the k source domain, all aggregation modules besides λ_k participate in the evaluation. With our validation we keep the model whose aggregation modules are general enough to distinguish between unseen distributions, while still training the main branch on all input data.

We test our model both in an end to end fashion and as a feature extractor. For end-to-end classification we calculate probabilities for the label as:

$$p_{x_j^t} = \sigma\Big(\sum_{i=1}^{S} \lambda_i(\Theta(x_j^t))\Big), \qquad (4)$$

When testing our algorithm as a feature extractor, we evaluate Θ's and Λ's features by running an SVM Linear Classifier on the DG task.

4   Experiments

In this section we report experiments assessing the effectiveness of our DSAM-based architecture in the DG scenario, using two different backbone architectures (a ResNet-18 [7] and an AlexNet [9]), on two different databases. We first describe the datasets used (Sect. 4.1), and then we proceed to report the model setup (Sect. 4.2) and the training protocol adopted (Sect. 4.3). Section 4.4 reports and comments upon the experimental results obtained.

4.1   Datasets

We performed experiments on two different databases. The **PACS** database [10] has been recently introduced to support research on DG, and it is quickly becoming the standard reference benchmark for this research thread. It consists of 9.991 images, of resolution 227×227, taken from four different visual domains (Photo, Art paintings, Cartoon and Sketches), depicting seven categories. We followed the experimental protocol of [10] and trained our models considering three domains as source datasets and the remaining one as target.

The **Office-Home** dataset [25] was introduced to support research on DA for object recognition. It provides images from four different domains: Artistic images, Clip art, Product images and Real-world images. Each domain depicts 65 object categories that can be found typically in office and home settings. We are not aware of previous work using the Office-Home dataset in DG scenarios, hence we decided to follow also here the experimental setup introduced in [10] and described above for PACS.

4.2   Model Setup

Aggregation Nodes. We implemented the aggregation nodes as 1×1 convolutional filters followed by nonlinearity. Compared to [27], we did not use batch normalization in the aggregations, since we empirically found it detrimental for our difficult DG targets. Whenever the inputs of a node have different scales, we downsampled with the same strategy used in the backbone model. For ResNet-18 experiments, we further regularized the convolutional inputs of our aggregations with dropout.

Aggregation of Fully Connected Layers. We observe that a fully connected layer's output can be seen as a 4-dimensional (N, C, H, W) tensor with collapsed height and width dimensions, as each unit's output is a function of the entire input image. A 1×1 convolutional layer whose input is such a tensor coincides with a fully connected layer whose input is a 2-dimensional (N, C) tensor, so for simplicity we implemented those aggregations with fully connected layers instead of convolutions (Fig. 3).

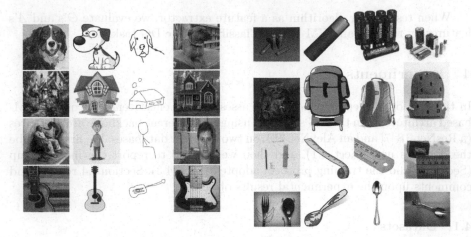

Fig. 3. Exemplar images for the PACS (left) and Office-Home (right) databases, on selected categories. We see that for both databases, the variations among domains for the same category can vary a lot.

Model Initialization. We experimented with two different backbone models: AlexNet and ResNet-18, both of which are pre-trained on the ImageNet 1000 object categories [17]. We initialized our aggregation modules Λ with random uniform initialization. We connected the aggregation nodes with the output of the AlexNet's layers when using AlexNet as backbone, or with the exit of each residual block when using ResNet-18.

4.3 Training Setup

We finetuned our models on $S = 3$ source domains and tested on the remaining target. We splitted our training sets in 90% train and 10% validation, and used the best performing model on the validation set for the final test, following the validation strategy described in Sect. 3. For preprocessing, we used random zooming with rescaling, horizontal flipping, brightness/contrast/saturation/hue perturbations and normalization using ImageNet's statistics. We used a batch size of 96 (32 images per source domain) and trained using SGD with momentum set at 0.9 and initial learning rate at 0.01 and 0.007 for ResNet's and AlexNet's experiments respectively. We considered an epoch as the minimum number of steps necessary to iterate over the largest source domain and we trained our models for 30 epochs, scaling the learning rate by a factor of 0.2 every 10 epochs. We used the same setup to train our ResNet-18 Deep All baselines. We repeated each experiment 5 times, averaging the results.

4.4 Results

We run a first set of experiments with the D-SAMs using an AlexNet as backbone, to compare our results with those reported in the literature by previous works, as AlexNet has been so far the convnet of choice in DG. Results are reported in Table 1. We see that our approach outperforms previous work by a sizable margin, showing the value of our architecture. Particularly, we underline that D-SAMs obtain remarkable performances on the challenging setting where the 'Sketch' domain acts as target.

We then run a second set of experiments, using both the PACS and Office-Home dataset, using as backbone architecture a ResNet-18. The goal of this set of experiments is on one side to showcase how our approach can be easily used with different Θ networks, on the other side to perform an ablation study with respect to the possibility to use D-SAMs not only in an end-to-end classification framework, but also to learn feature representations, suitable for domain generalization. To this end, we report results on both databases using the end-to-end approach tested in the AlexNet experiments, plus results obtained using the feature representations learned by Θ, Λ and the combination of the two. Specifically, we extract and l_2 normalize features from the last pooling layer of each component. We integrate features of Λ's modules with concatenation, and train the SVM classifier leaving the hyperparameter C at the default value. Our results in Tables 2 and 3 show that the SVM classifier trained on the l_2 normalized features always outperforms the corresponding end- to-end models, and that Θ's and Λ's features have similar performance, with Θ's features outperforming the corresponding Deep All features while requiring no computational overhead for inference.

Table 1. PACS end-to-end results using D-SAMs coupled with the AlexNet architecture.

	Deep All [10]	TF [10]	MLDG [11]	SSN [14]	D-SAMs
Art painting	64.91	62.86	**66.23**	64.10	63.87
Cartoon	64.28	66.97	66.88	66.80	**70.70**
Photo	86.67	89.50	88.00	**90.20**	85.55
Sketch	53.08	57.51	58.96	60.10	**64.66**
Avg	67.24	69.21	70.01	70.30	**71.20**

Table 2. PACS results with ResNet-18 using features (top-rows) and end-to-end accuracy (bottom rows).

	Art painting	Cartoon	Sketch	Photo	Avg
Deep All (feat.)	77.06	**77.81**	74.09	93.28	80.56
Θ (feat.)	**79.57**	76.94	75.47	94.16	81.54
Λ (feat.)	79.48	77.13	75.30	94.30	**81.55**
$\Theta + \Lambda$ (feat.)	79.44	77.22	75.33	94.19	81.54
Deep All	77.84	75.89	69.27	95.19	79.55
D-SAMs	77.33	72.43	**77.83**	**95.30**	80.72

Table 3. OfficeHome results with ResNet-18 using features (top rows) and end-to-end accuracy (bottom rows).

	Art	Clipart	Product	Real-World	Avg
Deep All (feat.)	52.66	48.35	71.37	71.47	60.96
Θ (feat.)	54.55	**49.37**	71.38	**72.17**	**61.87**
Λ (feat.)	54.53	49.04	71.57	71.90	61.76
$\Theta + \Lambda$ (feat.)	54.54	49.05	**71.58**	72.03	61.80
Deep All	55.59	42.42	70.34	70.86	59.81
D-SAMs	**58.03**	44.37	69.22	71.45	60.77

5   Conclusions

This paper presented a Domain Generalization architecture inspired by recent work on deep layer aggregation. We developed a convnet that, starting from a pre-trained model carrying generic perceptual knowledge, aggregates layers iteratively for as many branches as the available source domains data at training time. The model can be used in an end-to-end fashion, or its convolutional layers can be used as features in a linear SVM. Both approaches, tested with two popular pre-trained architectures on two benchmark databases, achieve the new state of the art. Future work will further study deep layer aggregation strategies within the context of domain generalization, as well as scalability with respect to the number of sources.

References

1. Angeletti, G., Caputo, B., Tommasi, T.: Adaptive deep learning through visual domain localization. In: International Conference on Robotic Automation (ICRA) (2018)
2. Bousmalis, K., Silberman, N., Dohan, D., Erhan, D., Krishnan, D.: Unsupervised pixel-level domain adaptation with GANs. In: Computer Vision and Pattern Recognition (CVPR) (2017)
3. Carlucci, F.M., Porzi, L., Caputo, B., Ricci, E., Rota Bulò, S.: Autodial: automatic domain alignment layers. In: International Conference on Computer Vision (ICCV) (2017)
4. Carlucci, F.M., Porzi, L., Caputo, B., Ricci, E., Rota Bulò, S.: Just dial: domain alignment layers for unsupervised domain adaptation. In: International Conference on Image Analysis and Processing (2017)
5. Ganin, Y., et al.: Domain-adversarial training of neural networks. J. Mach. Learn. Res. **17**(1), 2030–2096 (2016)
6. Goodfellow, I., et al.: Generative adversarial nets. In: Neural Information Processing Systems (NIPS) (2014)
7. He, K., Zhang, X., Ren, S., Sun, J.: Deep residual learning for image recognition. In: Proceedings of the IEEE Conference on Computer Vision and Pattern Recognition, pp. 770–778 (2016)

8. Huang, G., Liu, Z., Weinberger, K.Q., van der Maaten, L.: Densely connected convolutional networks. In: Proceedings of CVPR (2017)
9. Krizhevsky, A., Sutskever, I., Hinton, G.E.: ImageNet classification with deep convolutional neural networks. In: Advances in Neural Information Processing Systems, pp. 1097–1105 (2012)
10. Li, D., Yang, Y., Song, Y.Z., Hospedales, T.M.: Deeper, broader and artier domain generalization. In: 2017 IEEE International Conference on Computer Vision (ICCV), pp. 5543–5551. IEEE (2017)
11. Li, D., Yang, Y., Song, Y., Hospedales, T.M.: Learning to generalize: meta-learning for domain generalization. In: Conference of the Association for the Advancement of Artificial Intelligence (AAAI) (2018)
12. Lin, T.Y., Dollar, P., Girshick, R., He, K., Hariharan, B., Belongie, S.: Feature pyramid networks for object detection. In: Proceedings of CVPR (2017)
13. Long, M., Zhu, H., Wang, J., Jordan, M.I.: Deep transfer learning with joint adaptation networks. In: International Conference on Machine Learning (ICML) (2017)
14. Mancini, M., Bulò, S.R., Caputo, B., Ricci, E.: Best sources forward: domain generalization through source-specific nets. arXiv preprint arXiv:1806.05810 (2018)
15. Mancini, M., Bulo, S.R., Caputo, B., Ricci, E.: Robust place categorization with deep domain generalization. IEEE Robot. Autom. Lett. (2018)
16. Mansour, Y., Mohri, M., Rostamizadeh, A.: Domain adaptation with multiple sources. In: Neural Information Processing Systems (NIPS) (2009)
17. Russakovsky, O., et al.: ImageNet large scale visual recognition challenge. Int. J. Comput. Vis. (IJCV) **115**(3), 211–252 (2015). https://doi.org/10.1007/s11263-015-0816-y
18. Russo, P., Carlucci, F.M., Tommasi, T., Caputo, B.: From source to target and back: symmetric bi-directional adaptive GAN. In: Computer Vision and Pattern Recognition (CVPR) (2018)
19. Saenko, K., Kulis, B., Fritz, M., Darrell, T.: Adapting visual category models to new domains. In: Daniilidis, K., Maragos, P., Paragios, N. (eds.) ECCV 2010. LNCS, vol. 6314, pp. 213–226. Springer, Heidelberg (2010). https://doi.org/10.1007/978-3-642-15561-1_16
20. Sankaranarayanan, S., Balaji, Y., Castillo, C.D., Chellappa, R.: Generate to adapt: aligning domains using generative adversarial networks. In: Computer Vision and Pattern Recognition (CVPR) (2018)
21. Shrivastava, A., Pfister, T., Tuzel, O., Susskind, J., Wang, W., Webb, R.: Learning from simulated and unsupervised images through adversarial training. In: Computer Vision and Pattern Recognition (CVPR) (2017)
22. Sun, B., Feng, J., Saenko, K.: Return of frustratingly easy domain adaptation. In: Conference of the Association for the Advancement of Artificial Intelligence (AAAI) (2016)
23. Tzeng, E., Hoffman, J., Darrell, T., Saenko, K.: Simultaneous deep transfer across domains and tasks. In: International Conference in Computer Vision (ICCV) (2015)
24. Tzeng, E., Hoffman, J., Darrell, T., Saenko, K.: Adversarial discriminative domain adaptation. In: Computer Vision and Pattern Recognition (CVPR) (2017)
25. Venkateswara, H., Eusebio, J., Chakraborty, S., Panchanathan, S.: Deep hashing network for unsupervised domain adaptation. In: IEEE Conference on Computer Vision and Pattern Recognition (CVPR) (2017)

26. Xu, R., Chen, Z., Zuo, W., Yan, J., Lin, L.: Deep cocktail network: multi-source unsupervised domain adaptation with category shift. In: Computer Vision and Pattern Recognition (CVPR) (2018)
27. Yu, F., Wang, D., Darrell, T.: Deep layer aggregation. arXiv preprint arXiv:1707.06484 (2017)
28. Zhao, H., Zhang, S., Wu, G., Costeira, J.P., Moura, J.M.F., Gordon, G.J.: Multiple source domain adaptation with adversarial learning. In: Workshop of the International Conference on Learning Representations (ICLR-W) (2018)

X-GAN: Improving Generative Adversarial Networks with ConveX Combinations

Oliver Blum[✉], Biagio Brattoli, and Björn Ommer

Heidelberg University, HCI/IWR, Heidelberg, Germany
o.blum90@gmail.com, biagio.brattoli@iwr.uni-heidelberg.de,
ommer@uni-heidelberg.de

Abstract. Recent neural architectures for image generation are capable of producing photo-realistic results but the distributions of real and faked images still differ. While the lack of a structured latent representation for GANs results in mode collapse, VAEs enforce a prior to the latent space that leads to an unnatural representation of the underlying real distribution. We introduce a method that preserves the natural structure of the latent manifold. By utilizing neighboring relations within the set of discrete real samples, we reproduce the full continuous latent manifold. We propose a novel image generation network X-GAN that creates latent input vectors from random convex combinations of adjacent real samples. This way we ensure a structured and natural latent space by not requiring prior assumptions. In our experiments, we show that our model outperforms recent approaches in terms of the missing mode problem while maintaining a high image quality.

1 Introduction

One big challenge in computer vision is the understanding of images and their manifold. Other than discriminative tasks like image/action classification [6,30] and pose estimation [2,5], generative approaches provide a much deeper understanding of the nature of the given data. Therefore, the generation of synthetic data which resembles the real data distribution is major in modern research.

The recent trend of deep generative networks in computer vision led to several models capable to produce photo-realistic images [1,8,12,23,25]. These approaches are mostly based on Generative Adversarial Networks (GAN) [13] and Variational Auto Encoders [27] (VAE). GANs are based on an adversarial game between generator and discriminator, which has been proven successful in generating realistic images. However, GANs are known to suffer from the missing mode problem [13,28]: If the generator becomes strong in producing images of

Electronic supplementary material The online version of this chapter (https://doi.org/10.1007/978-3-030-12939-2_15) contains supplementary material, which is available to authorized users.

T. Brox et al. (Eds.): GCPR 2018, LNCS 11269, pp. 199–214, 2019.
https://doi.org/10.1007/978-3-030-12939-2_15

certain modes the adversarial loss suppresses the generation of more challenging samples. In contrast to the real distribution, for GANs dense areas in the fake data distribution can be observed where images are easily generated, while areas with more difficult samples are not well represented. VAEs are trained to encode and decode images. They are often applied to tackle mode collapse. To fill the space in between the encoded real data representations, VAEs sample from a prior. A Kullback-Leibler-divergence loss [15] (KL-divergence loss) pushes the latent vectors to this prior, that is assumed to match the underlying real distribution. However, this is not necessarily the case: The impact of the overpowering effect of the regularization term (the prior) on VAE training is often referenced in the VAE literature [4,9,10,16,18]. To address the issues of mode collapse and overpowering effect a combination of VAE and GANs is proposed in several publications [1,7,20]. However, all of the proposed methods either still involve a KL-divergence regularization [1,20] or perform the latent vector generation for the GAN training independent of the AE training such that missing modes cannot be fully solved [7]. Other methods rely on the strategy of better representing the latent space [3,10]. However, they still rely on the idea of fitting prior distributions. Currently, the challenge of representing the complex manifold of real images has not yet been addressed satisfactorily (Fig. 1).

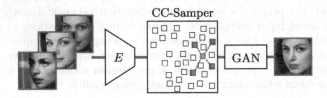

Fig. 1. The principle X-GAN setup. For the creation of latent variables that are used as input of the GAN module, the X-GAN utilities convex combinations of adjacent discrete samples to create new samples from the continuous manifold. This ensures a natural representation of the latent space without enforcing a prior to the distribution.

In this paper, we approach the problem from a different perspective by avoiding any assumption about the probability distribution function but sampling from the entire continuous latent manifold of the given dataset such that no modes are missed. In our model, samples are drawn from the full continuous latent distribution using a non-parametric approach based on a convex combination of adjacent points in the encoding space, without requiring an explicit definition of the latent density function. As this novel approach of drawing latent samples with conveX combinations is our main contribution, we call our model X-GAN.

The dense representation of the latent manifold, provided by means of the convex combinations, makes it possible to condition the generator directly using the position in the latent vectors. Based on this we propose a new method for conditioning our network.

In our experiments, we show that our model outperforms recent methods in terms of missing mode and image realism. In the ablation studies, we substantiate the benefits of the convex combination and the conditioning strategy by illustrating the drawbacks of replacing them with alternative approaches.

2   Related Work

In this section, we introduce several deep generative architectures that attempt to tackle the known issues of mode collapse and overpowering effect. We show that solving both issues with one model is still an unsolved problem.

Variational Auto-Encoder. VAEs rely on the idea of compressing their input with an encoder-network and decoding this latent representation with a generator-network. The network then is trained with an image reconstruction loss. An additional KL-divergence loss pushes the latent representation to resemble a prior distribution, from which samples can be drawn to generate new images. This approach makes the VAE robust against mode collapse. However, the underlying true distribution often is poorly represented by the chosen prior [4,9,10,16,18]. Moreover, VAEs include a distance metric describing the difference between original and generated image. An imperfect choice of this distance metric entails unnatural artifacts in the faked images [11].

Generative Adversarial Network. GANs come with a convenient solution for these problems by learning the loss by an adversarial game between generator and discriminator, without the requirement of enforcing a prior. However, a missing control over the latent space easily results in mode collapse [13,28] as described in Sect. 1.

GAN+VAE. Several recent approaches intend to tackle the previously mentioned issues by combining VAEs and GANs [1,7,20]. The VAE/GAN trains a discriminator along with a VAE. As distance metric, for the autoencoder loss they utilize features provided by the discriminator instead of the pixel-wise distance metrics. This provides a way to learn a distance metric without the drawbacks of the GAN training. The cVAE uses a similar approach which also includes class conditioning. While the VAE/GAN and the cVAE-GAN utilize a prior to draw latent vectors from the continuous distribution, in our model, we use convex combinations. This comes with the advantage of avoiding the overpowering effect.

The Mode-Regularized-GAN [7] (MD-GAN) suggest training a GAN along with an autoencoder without using the KL-divergence loss. In the training procedure, the GAN and the autoencoder are trained alternately with a shared generator network. The MD-GAN attempts to structure the latent space with the autoencoder such that all modes are represented in the latent space. The

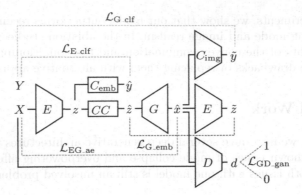

Fig. 2. This figure visualizes the X-GAN architecture. During testing, the X-GAN encodes images $x \in X$ using the encoder E into the latent space $z \in Z$. For the creation of latent variables $\hat{z}$, the X-GAN utilities convex combinations of adjacent real samples. This task is performed by the convex combination sampler CC. The created latent variables are passed on to the generator G that generates synthetic images $\hat{x}$. During the training phase, the images are passed further to a discriminator D, the previously mentioned encoder E and the classification network C_{img}. The network C_{emb} enforces class information into the sample by predicting the label $\hat{y}$ of the latent vectors z. The colored dashed lines that connect two parameters stand for the loss functions with which the X-GAN is trained. (Color figure online)

latent vectors of the GAN module are sampled from a distribution that is independent of the encoded image distribution of the autoencoder. Other than the MD-GAN the encoder of the X-GAN is responsible to define the embedding manifold within the latent space. The latent vectors that are passed to the generator are sampled from this manifold by applying the convex combination strategy. As the autoencoder and the GAN sample from the same shared distribution, the autoencoder also prevents mode collapse for the GAN training.

Latent Space Based Approaches. Apart from combining VAE and GAN, many recent papers focus on optimizing the latent representation.

To better model the single modes of real data distributions, Dilokthanakul et al. [10] utilize a Gaussian mixture model instead of a single Gaussian for the KL-divergence loss. This approach mitigates the issue of overpowering.

The Generative Latent Optimization framework [3] (GLO) represents a slim generative solution that only relies on one generative network. The latent variables themselves are optimized along with the generator by an image-reconstruction-loss. This ensures a solid structured latent space.

The Plug & Play Generative Network (PPGN) [25] involves a network to sample class conditioned latent variables. This ensures that the network generates samples of all classes. This strategy reduces the severity of the missing mode problem as it ensures that all classes are represented in the faked images.

Similarly to the above introduced models, the X-GAN also aims at improving the latent representation. As we focus on side-stepping the overpowering effect, other than the Dilokthanakul et al. [10] and Bojanowski et al. [3] we do not utilize any prior for the latent distribution. Like Nguyen et al. [25] we intend to support the latent structuring by inducing labels without the requirement of the concatenation of sparse label vectors to the dense layer information. In contrast to the PPGN we do not train a conditioning network, but directly encode the conditioning information in the position of the latent vector in the embedding manifold. This supports the encoder finding a solid structure for the latent space which forms the basis for our convex combination approach (Fig. 3).

3   Method

In our model, we use the convex combination strategy to ensure that samples from the entire manifold are created. This approach has no requirement of assuming a prior distribution for the latent space. Thus, our model does not suffer from the overpowering effect. In this section, we will first describe our novel approach to directly sample from the data distribution. Afterwards, we illustrate the model architecture and the training procedure by explaining the utilized loss functions. Finally, we explain our conditioning strategy in the resulting smooth latent distribution.

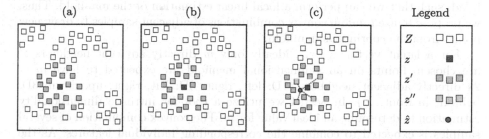

Fig. 3. The three steps for the convex combination strategy. (a) Chose one latent vector $z \in Z$ (dark blue) from the full latent distribution Z and get z', the m nearest neighbors of z in the latent space. (b) Randomly select k samples $z'' \subset z'$. (c) Get $\hat{z}$ as a randomly weighted mean of z'' (see Eq. 1). (Color figure online)

3.1   Convex Combination Strategy

The objective of the convex combination strategy is to provide the generator with samples from the underlying continuous manifold. As the representation of photo-realistic images is a high dimensional, complex manifold, a powerful strategy of drawing samples is required. However, common methods like Kernel-Density-Estimation or Gaussian-Mixture-Models fail due to the curse of dimensionality: Stone [31] proved that the complexity of any estimator grows exponentially with the dimensionality of the density function. However, drawing samples

---

Algorithm 1. Training algorithm for X-GAN

Require: $\{X, Y\}$: training set (images, labels). $\{\theta_E, \theta_G, \theta_D, \theta_{C_{emb}}, \theta_{C_{img}}\}$: initial parameters for $E, G, D, C_{emb}, C_{img}$ (C_{img} pre-trained on $\{X, Y\}$ and fixed during the training). λ: parameter balancing GAN loss compared to the other loss functions. $f(\cdot)$: image feature extracting function.

1: **while** θ_G has not converged **do**
2:      $Z \leftarrow E(X)$
3:      Sample $\{x, y, z\} \sim \{X, Y, Z\}$;
4:      $\hat{z} \leftarrow CC_{k,m}^Z(z)$ (see equation 1) with $\hat{z} \sim P_{\hat{z}}$
5:      $\mathcal{L}_{E\_clf} \qquad \leftarrow -\mathbb{E}_{x \sim P_r}[y \log C_{emb}(E(x))]$
6:      $\mathcal{L}_{EG\_ae} \qquad \leftarrow |f(x_i) - f(G(E(x)))|$
7:      $\mathcal{L}_{GD\_gan} \qquad \leftarrow -(\mathbb{E}_{x \sim p_r}[log(D(x))] + \mathbb{E}_{\hat{z} \sim p_{\hat{z}}}[log(1 - D(G(\hat{z})))])$
8:      $\mathcal{L}_{G\_emb} \qquad \leftarrow |\hat{z} - E(G(\hat{z}))|^2$
9:      $\mathcal{L}_{G\_clf} \qquad \leftarrow -\mathbb{E}_{\hat{z} \sim P_{\hat{z}}}[y \, log(C_{img}(G(\hat{z})))]$
10:     $\theta_E \xleftarrow{\text{adam}} -\nabla_{\theta_E}(\mathcal{L}_{E\_clf} + \mathcal{L}_{EG\_ae})$
11:     $\theta_G \xleftarrow{\text{adam}} -\nabla_{\theta_G}(\mathcal{L}_{EG\_ae} - \lambda\mathcal{L}_{GD\_gan} + \mathcal{L}_{G\_emb} + \mathcal{L}_{G\_clf})$
12:     $\theta_D \xleftarrow{\text{adam}} -\nabla_{\theta_D}(\lambda\mathcal{L}_{GD\_gan})$
13:     $\theta_{C_{emb}} \xleftarrow{\text{adam}} -\nabla_{\theta_{C_{emb}}}(\mathcal{L}_{E\_clf})$

---

from a distribution does not necessarily require the explicit definition of such a function. A natural approach, in this case, is utilizing neighborhood relations: We assume that, the space can be approximated as convex for a small neighborhood, such that we can perform a local linear estimation of the manifold. Thus, we propose to use random convex combinations of adjacent samples to draw new points from the continuous manifold.

For a latent vector $z \in Z$, ideally only m directly adjacent neighbors z' are chosen. Points on an s-dimensional manifold are expected to have $m = 2s$ directly adjacent neighbors (1D: left, right; 2D: left, right, up, down; 3D: behind, in front, ...). In Sect. 4 we utilize a tool for intrinsic dimensionality estimation to determine an ideal value for m. The convex combination of several samples is expected to combine the corresponding individual features. As the latent manifolds from which we sample are high dimensional ($s \sim 50$) we cannot utilize all directly adjacent neighbors: If too many nearest neighbors are chosen, they only share the high-level features as the set is too big to produce an image that exhibits distinct unique features of all individuals. We thus randomly pick k samples $z'' \subset z'$. We then create a set of weights $w_i = \frac{|\hat{w}_i|}{\sum_i |\hat{w}_i|}$, with $i \in \{1, .., k\}$, where $\hat{w}_i \sim \mathcal{N}$ are drawn from a uniform distribution. Given the simplex of weights w_i we create a sample $\hat{z}$ by a convex combination of z''

$$\hat{z} = \sum_{i=0}^k w_i \, z_i'' : CC_{m,k}^Z(z) \text{ , with } \hat{z} \sim P_{\hat{z}}. \tag{1}$$

With the created latent vectors $\hat{z}$ we fill the space between the discrete latent representations z and this way reconstruct the full continuous manifold.

3.2 Image Generation Procedure

This section explains how new images are generated with X-GAN. Thereby, we explain the central role of the convex combination (CC) strategy for guaranteeing the generation of various and realistic images. The utilized network architecture is shown in Fig. 2.

Given a set of images X we use the encoder E to produce an embedding $Z = E(X)$. To create new latent vectors $\hat{z}$ we utilize our novel CC-sampler module. It draws samples from the continuous latent manifold which is defined by the discrete set of image representations Z and thus ensures that no mode representations are missed. Our convex combination strategy samples directly from the real manifold without assuming any prior. On the contrary, VAE enforce a prior on the manifold which may not match the real data distribution, hence it suffers from the overpowering effect. Finally an image $\hat{x} = G(\hat{z})$ can be produced using the generator G. Notice that we only need the networks E and G for the generation of new images.

3.3 Training Procedure

In the following, the training procedure of our proposed method is explained step-by-step. The summarized procedure is shown in Algorithm 1 and a visualization of the network architecture can be found in Fig. 2. The notation of the utilized losses follows the structure $\mathcal{L}_{N\_T}$, with N as the network which is optimized using $\mathcal{L}_{N\_T}$ and the T as the loss type.

The parameter λ balances the GAN loss against to the remaining loss functions. We empirically found that further weighting factors do not improve the results.

Encoder Training. Along with the generator, the encoder is updated with an L1 autoencoder loss on features of the real and the fake images $\mathcal{L}_{EG\_ae}$ (see Algorithm 1 l.7). Therefore, we utilize an image feature extraction function $f(\cdot)$. For the autoencoder loss, no convex combinations are used in the training. The reason for this is that the autoencoder is responsible to shape the basic structure of the latent space. This is done by assigning real images to their corresponding latent representation. VAE would fill the continuous space in between real image embeddings with faked samples that minimize the reconstruction error of all surrounding images. This way of combining features does not necessarily result in realistic images [11]. Thus, we train the autoencoder with discrete latent vectors and utilize a learned GAN loss to train the generator to reconstruct the full continuous distribution defined by convex combinations. Apart from the autoencoder loss, the encoder is trained to minimize a classification loss $\mathcal{L}_{E\_clf}$ (see Algorithm 1 l.6) to cluster the embedding vectors according to their label y in the embedding space. This strategy of inducing conditioning helps to structure the latent space.

GAN Training. So far we have a basic encoding space and we trained E and G to reconstruct the discrete images of the training set. However, we did not train the generator to produce images from latent vectors which are positioned in between the discrete image representations. We propose an adversarial loss $\mathcal{L}_{\text{GD\_gan}}$ (see Algorithm 1 1.8) to fill the space in between samples. To generate input latent variables for the GAN we apply our novel convex combination module to sample from the continuous manifold.

Stabilizing Loss Functions. We propose to additionally train G with an L2 loss $\mathcal{L}_{\text{G\_emb}}$ (see Algorithm 1 1.9) between the input latent vector $\hat{z}$ and the encoded fake image latent vector $E(G(\hat{z}))$. This loss can only be minimized if the generator creates images, that can be mapped back precisely to the latent space. Thus, sudden jumps from one to the other image in the image space are suppressed by this loss. This way, a smooth image transition (such as in Fig. 5) is encouraged.

An additional classification loss $\mathcal{L}_{\text{G\_clf}}$ (see Algorithm 1 1.10) is applied on the synthetic images to reward the generation of recognizable objects. Therefore, it must be ensured that the $\hat{z}$ (Eq. 1) is uniquely assignable to one label by selecting z_i'' from the same class.

3.4   Conditioning

An important feature of generative models is the ability to produce samples that are conditioned on certain characteristic classes. The common procedure of passing a label vector to the generator is to concatenate it to one or several layers of the network. Although this forms a joint representation, neural architectures have problems to capture the complex associations between the two different modalities of sparse and dense information [19]. This is especially the case for fine-grained datasets where the number of classes becomes very large. A more natural way of conditioning, that does not require sparse information, would be to directly encode the class label in the position of a latent vector within the manifold. However, commonly, the full continuous manifold in latent space is not well defined, but a prior distribution is assumed from which samples are drawn. Our model, thanks to the convex-combination strategy, produces a latent space that allows a more natural conditioning of the latent vectors by their position in latent space: The embedding classifier of our model clusters the latent representation according to their class label by means of a classification loss. This supports the encoder in creating a well structured latent space.

In practice, given a set of images x from a common class y we can assume that their embedding vectors $z = E(x)$, can be found in the same cluster in the latent space. Thus, a new sample $\hat{z}$ produced by Eq. 1 will also be placed in this cluster and is naturally conditioned by its position in latent space. This way not only class conditioning but also fine-grained mode conditioning is possible through the encoding in the latent vector.

In Table 3 and Fig. 6(e) we show that our conditioning method produces images that are more realistic than those gained with models utilizing the approach of label concatenation.

4 Experiments

In this section, we describe the experimental setup, the datasets and the model parameters used. Moreover, we explain our evaluation procedures and present their results. In several ablation experiments, we illustrate the advantages of convex combination based sampling.

4.1 Implementation Details

The encoder, generator, and discriminator are all implemented as 6-Layer-CNNs. They utilize batch-normalization [14] and leaky-ReLU as activation function. C_{emb} is a fully connected network with two layers. C_{img} is a VGG-19 network [30], pre-trained on the given dataset and fixed during training. This ensures useful gradients from the beginning of training and avoids overfitting in a later stage. As a feature descriptor f we choose features from intermediate layers of the VGG network as proposed by Chen et al. [8]. Additionally, we add the features of a second VGG-19 network that is trained as a discriminator along with the rest of the model. We set the latent variable size to 512 and the batch size to 80. We choose $\lambda = 2$. That means that we weight the GAN loss twice as high as the remaining loss functions. We train the network with the Adam optimizer [17] with a learning rate of 10^{-4}. For training we only need 16 epochs, what is far less then what is required to train the cVAE-GAN ($\sim$50 epochs) or the MD-GAN ($\sim$100 epochs). For the convex combination sampling, we set the parameters m (total number of nearest neighbors) by estimating the intrinsic dimensionality s of the embedding manifold with a Maximum Likelihood Estimation [21]. For our latent embedding we find a mean (over the classes) of $s = 48$ resulting in $m \approx 100$ (see Sect. 3.1). To maintain individual features for each sample we draw $\hat{z}$ as randomly weighted convex combinations of $k = 5$ adjacent samples. In the evaluation we compare our model with cVAE-GAN [1][1] and MD-GAN [7][2].

Our model is applied to two different datasets: The FaceScrub dataset [26] with images of 530 different individuals and the 102 Category Flower dataset [24]. For the FaceScrub dataset, we followed the alignment procedure suggested by [1]. We want to show that we can maintain a high image quality even for non-aligned image data. Thus, other than Bao et al. [1] we do not perform any preprocessing on the 102 Category flower dataset.

---

[1] cVAE-GAN implementation: https://github.com/tatsy/keras-generative.
[2] MD-GAN implementation: https://github.com/wiseodd/generative-models.

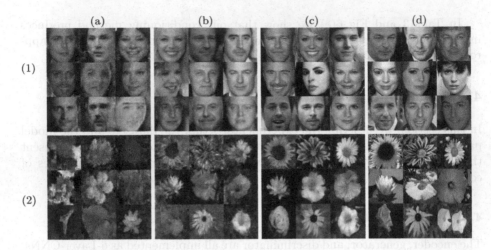

Fig. 4. Comparison of generated samples from different methods on the (1) Face-Scrub dataset [24] and (2) 102 Category Flower dataset [26] (bottom row). The images are generated by (a) MD-GAN [7], (b) cVAE-GAN [1], (c) X-GAN (this work) (d) real. Using the MD-GAN artifacts are clearly visible, the cVAE-GAN and the X-GAN produce photo-realistic images for the aligned faces. For the more challenging flower dataset, which has not been preprocessed, the image quality for the X-GAN is better than for the cVAE-GAN

4.2   Visual Image Quality Comparison

In Fig. 4 we compare our results with MD-GAN and cVAE-GAN. For the Face-Scrub dataset, the MD-GAN generations exhibit noise and artifacts while the cVAE-GAN and the X-GAN produce photo-realistic images. While the cVAE-GAN performs well on the FaceScrub dataset the generated flowers look worse. In the cVAE-GAN paper [1] the authors also evaluate their model with these two datasets and present appealing results. However, other than we do they align the images of both datasets. The fact that still photo-realistic images are generated with X-GAN for the unaligned flower dataset shows, that our model is robust against the missing alignment.

4.3   Discriminator Score for Missing Mode Evaluation

Che et al. [7] propose to utilize a third party discriminator D^* to quantify the robustness of a model towards the missing mode problem. After training D^* on a set of real and fake images the discriminator is applied to a set of test images. The mode of the images that are clearly recognized as real ($D^* \approx 1$) is obviously not represented in the fake image distribution. Thus, the number of test images for which $D^* \approx 1$ serves as a proxy for the degree of mode collapse. As this approach requires a strong discriminator D^* we use the FaceNet [29]³ which is trained on

---

³ Weights/code for FaceNet: https://github.com/davidsandberg/facenet.

Table 1. This table shows the D^*-score for the MD-GAN [7], cVAE-GAN [1] and X-GAN (our model). To obtain this score a third-party-discriminator is trained on a set of real and a set of fake images. Afterwards, it is evaluated on a set of test images. Test samples for which $D^* \approx 1$ are assumed not to be represented by the faked images. Thus, a high D^*-score is a proxy for mode collapse.

Model	$t = 0.90$ [# samples]	$t = 0.95$ [# samples]	$t = 0.97$ [# samples]
MD-GAN	2737 ± 34	2299 ± 62	1952 ± 64
CVAEGAN	325 ± 47	87 ± 22	28 ± 14
X-GAN	$\mathbf{134 \pm 32}$	$\mathbf{15 \pm 10}$	$\mathbf{2 \pm 2}$

the CASIA dataset [22] to produce a face embedding. On top of the FaceNet, we stack a two-layer neural network (D^*). For our experiments, we used three different thresholds $t \in \{0.9, 0.95, 0.97\}$ that determine for which D^* score an image is assumed to be not represented in the fake data. The mean over five runs of this experiment is documented in Table 1. In total 4412 test images are used for the experiment. For a strict threshold of $t = 0.97$, our model exhibits almost no missing representations anymore (2 ± 2), while underrepresented modes for cVAE-GAN are found for 28 ± 14 images. The MD-GAN, even for $t = 0.97$, collapses to almost 50% of the existing modes.

4.4   Image Morphing

The embedding loss (Algorithm 1 l.9) ensures that a smooth transition in the latent space corresponds to a smooth transition in the image space. To visually underpin this, in Fig. 5 we show the results of an image morphing experiment. The corners of the shown image array are real images while the space in between is filled with fake samples. The fact that this is only noticeable in a detailed investigation shows that our synthesized images smoothly supplement the underlying real distribution.

Table 2. This table shows the inception score computed on FaceScrub dataset [24] as a mean of 5×100 K generated images.

Model	Inception score
Real data	2.372 ± 0.003
cVAE-GAN [1]	1.757 ± 0.002
X-GAN	$\mathbf{1.831 \pm 0.003}$

4.5   Inception Score

The realism of generated images is characterized by a high diversity in the distribution and easily recognizable objects. Salimans et al. [28] propose the Inception

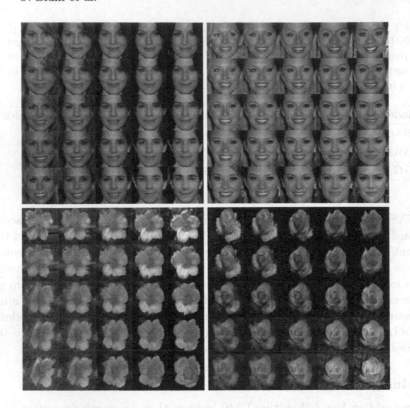

Fig. 5. This figure shows morphing experiments. For each of the shown image-arrays, the four corner images are real and the space in between is filled with fake images gained from weighted convex combinations. The corner images of the upper right image originate from unseen test data. Especially for the illustrated faces, the jump from real to fake data is hardly visible. On a closer inspection of the flower image-arrays, one can recognize the smoother background. The fine features of the flower itself are preserved. This shows that the generated images complement the underlying real distribution well.

Score which relies on the output score of a pre-trained InceptionNet [32]. A high diversity is characterized by a high entropy of the overall score distribution, while a recognizable object corresponds to a low entropy for a single image. In Table 2 we compare the inception score of generated images of our model with cVAE-GAN for the faces dataset. Images generated with our model achieve higher scores.

4.6   Ablation Study

In this section, we quantitatively (see Table 3) and qualitatively (see Fig. 6) evaluate the impacts of removing or replacing parts of X-GAN. Here, we not only illustrate the benefits of the proposed convex combination strategy compared to conventional methods but also present an unsupervised version of the X-GAN.

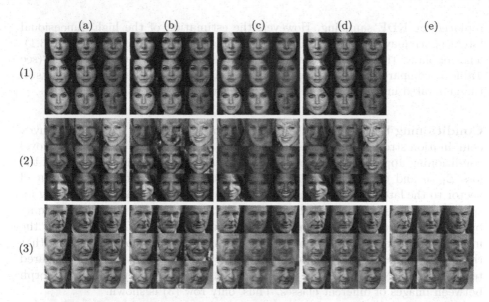

Fig. 6. This figure shows image morphing experiments for each of the performed ablation studies. The images in the corners of the image array are real, while the space in between is filled with faked images. (a) X-GAN, (b) unsupervised X-GAN, (c) KL-Loss, (d) KDE-sampling, (e) concatenate label vector. For each of the image arrays, the four corner images are real, while the space in between is filled with faked images. (1), (2) different individuals in the corner images, (3) different images of the same individual in the corner images.

Unsupervised X-GAN. An unsupervised version of the proposed X-GAN can be obtained by removing the losses $\mathcal{L}_{E\_clf}$ and $\mathcal{L}_{G\_clf}$. Table 3 shows that our model still performs better then the supervised cVAE-GAN. Even though the discriminator score deteriorates, it is still on the same scale as the cVAE-GAN. In the visual evaluation (Fig. 6(b)) it can be seen that the generated images are still sharp and detailed. However, some exhibit artifacts that are not observed for the original X-GAN.

KL-Loss. In this experiment, the convex combination strategy is replaced by the KL-loss based approach proposed by Rosca et al. [27]. This approach enforces a prior to the latent distribution. This results in a deterioration of the inception score and the discriminator score (see Table 3). In the visual analysis in Fig. 6(c) it can be seen that no distinct facial details can be found in the generated bury samples anymore. Unlike the X-GAN generations, there is a clear jump between from the real to the fake images visible.

KDE Sampling. The kernel density estimation (KDE) is a non-parametric approach to estimate the continuous distribution from a set of discrete samples. In this experiment, the creation of latent vectors with convex combinations is replaced by KDE sampling. However, the estimation of the high dimensional latent space may not sufficiently represent the complex manifold (see Sect. 3.1). This explains the deterioration of the inception and discriminator score (see Table 3) compared to the convex combination sampling. The visual artifacts in the generated images underpin the quantitative observations (see Fig. 6(d)).

Conditioning by the Concatenation of Label Vectors. Beside the convex combination strategy, another special feature of the X-GAN model is the novel conditioning approach (see Sect. 3.4). In this ablation experiment, we omit the loss $\mathcal{L}_{E\_clf}$ and condition the latent variables by the concatenation of a label vector to the latent vector. Neural architectures face difficulties when mixing up sparse and dense information. Thus, as it can be seen in Table 3 the conditioning by concatenation performs significantly worse than the X-GAN regarding the inception score and the discriminator score. In Fig. 6(e) a close look shows that the faked images in this ablation study exhibit less distinct features compared to the original X-GAN. As the label vector is discrete, it is pointless to morph between images of different classes. Thus, only row (3) is shown.

Table 3. This table shows the quantitative results of the ablation study. The evaluation metrics are the inception score (see Sect. 4.5) and the discriminator score (see Sect. 4.3). The evaluation approves that the convex combination strategy outperforms conventional approaches (KL-loss and KDE-sampling). Moreover, the superiority of the novel conditioning approach compared to the conventional concatenation of label and latent vectors is approved. Finally, we show that also an unsupervised version of the X-GAN achieves decent inception and discriminator scores.

Model	Inception score	D^* score [# samples]
X-GAN	1.831 ± 0.003	15 ± 10
Unsupervised	1.795 ± 0.003	153 ± 28
KL-loss	1.612 ± 0.002	497 ± 43
KDE-sampling	1.711 ± 0.003	203 ± 34
Concat. label	1.727 ± 0.003	76 ± 21

5   Conclusion

In this paper, we propose a novel strategy of generating a latent vector representation by convex combinations. This enables us to reconstruct the full continuous distribution of the manifold defined by the given dataset. We evaluate our method on two datasets. With various qualitative and quantitative evaluation approaches, we show the X-GAN architecture represents a major step forward in terms of tackling the issue of mode collapse and the overpowering effect.

References

1. Bao, J., Chen, D., Wen, F., Li, H., Hua, G.: CVAE-GAN: fine-grained image generation through asymmetric training. arXiv preprint arXiv:1703.10155 (2017)
2. Bautista, M.A., Sanakoyeu, A., Tikhoncheva, E., Ommer, B.: CliqueCNN: deep unsupervised exemplar learning. In: Advances in Neural Information Processing Systems, pp. 3846–3854 (2016)
3. Bojanowski, P., Joulin, A., Lopez-Paz, D., Szlam, A.: Optimizing the latent space of generative networks. arXiv preprint arXiv:1707.05776 (2017)
4. Bowman, S.R., Vilnis, L., Vinyals, O., Dai, A.M., Jozefowicz, R., Bengio, S.: Generating sentences from a continuous space. arXiv preprint arXiv:1511.06349 (2015)
5. Brattoli, B., Büchler, U., Wahl, A.S., Schwab, M.E., Ommer, B.: LSTM self-supervision for detailed behavior analysis. In: IEEE Conference on Computer Vision and Pattern Recognition (CVPR) (2017)
6. Büchler, U., Brattoli, B., Ommer, B.: Improving spatiotemporal self-supervision by deep reinforcement learning. In: IEEE Conference on Computer Vision and Pattern Recognition (CVPR) (2017)
7. Che, T., Li, Y., Jacob, A.P., Bengio, Y., Li, W.: Mode regularized generative adversarial networks. arXiv preprint arXiv:1612.02136 (2016)
8. Chen, Q., Koltun, V.: Photographic image synthesis with cascaded refinement networks. arXiv preprint arXiv:1707.09405 (2017)
9. Chen, X., Duan, Y., Houthooft, R., Schulman, J., Sutskever, I., Abbeel, P.: Info-GAN: interpretable representation learning by information maximizing generative adversarial nets. In: Advances in Neural Information Processing Systems, pp. 2172–2180 (2016)
10. Dilokthanakul, N., et al.: Deep unsupervised clustering with Gaussian mixture variational autoencoders. arXiv preprint arXiv:1611.02648 (2016)
11. Dosovitskiy, A., Brox, T.: Generating images with perceptual similarity metrics based on deep networks. In: Advances in Neural Information Processing Systems, pp. 658–666 (2016)
12. Esser, P., Sutter, E., Ommer, B.: A variational U-Net for conditional appearance and shape generation. In: Proceedings of the IEEE Conference on Computer Vision and Pattern Recognition, pp. 8857–8866 (2018)
13. Goodfellow, I., et al.: Generative adversarial nets. In: Advances in Neural Information Processing Systems, pp. 2672–2680 (2014)
14. Ioffe, S., Szegedy, C.: Batch normalization: accelerating deep network training by reducing internal covariate shift. In: International Conference on Machine Learning, pp. 448–456 (2015)
15. Joyce, J.M.: Kullback-leibler divergence. In: Lovric, M. (ed.) International Encyclopedia of Statistical Science, pp. 720–722. Springer, Berlin (2011). https://doi.org/10.1007/978-3-642-04898-2
16. Kaae Sønderby, C., Raiko, T., Maaløe, L., Kaae Sønderby, S., Winther, O.: How to train deep variational autoencoders and probabilistic ladder networks. arxiv preprint. arXiv preprint arXiv:1602.02282 (2016)
17. Kingma, D., Ba, J.: Adam: a method for stochastic optimization. arXiv preprint arXiv:1412.6980 (2014)
18. Kingma, D.P., Salimans, T., Welling, M.: Improving variational inference with inverse autoregressive flow. arXiv preprint arXiv:1606.04934 (2016)
19. Kwak, H., Zhang, B.T.: Ways of conditioning generative adversarial networks. arXiv preprint arXiv:1611.01455 (2016)

20. Larsen, A.B.L., Sønderby, S.K., Larochelle, H., Winther, O.: Autoencoding beyond pixels using a learned similarity metric. arXiv preprint arXiv:1512.09300 (2015)
21. Levina, E., Bickel, P.J.: Maximum likelihood estimation of intrinsic dimension. In: Advances in Neural Information Processing Systems, pp. 777–784 (2005)
22. Li, S., Yi, D., Lei, Z., Liao, S.: The CASIA NIR-VIS 2.0 face database. In: Proceedings of the IEEE Conference on Computer Vision and Pattern Recognition Workshops, pp. 348–353 (2013)
23. Milbich, T., Bautista, M., Sutter, E., Ommer, B.: Unsupervised video understanding by reconciliation of posture similarities. In: Proceedings of the IEEE International Conference on Computer Vision (2017)
24. Ng, H.W., Winkler, S.: A data-driven approach to cleaning large face datasets. In: 2014 IEEE International Conference on Image Processing (ICIP), pp. 343–347. IEEE (2014)
25. Nguyen, A., Yosinski, J., Bengio, Y., Dosovitskiy, A., Clune, J.: Plug & play generative networks: conditional iterative generation of images in latent space. arXiv preprint arXiv:1612.00005 (2016)
26. Nilsback, M.E., Zisserman, A.: Automated flower classification over a large number of classes. In: 2008 Sixth Indian Conference on Computer Vision, Graphics & Image Processing, ICVGIP 2008, pp. 722–729. IEEE (2008)
27. Rosca, M., Lakshminarayanan, B., Warde-Farley, D., Mohamed, S.: Variational approaches for auto-encoding generative adversarial networks. arXiv preprint arXiv:1706.04987 (2017)
28. Salimans, T., Goodfellow, I., Zaremba, W., Cheung, V., Radford, A., Chen, X.: Improved techniques for training GANs. In: Advances in Neural Information Processing Systems, pp. 2234–2242 (2016)
29. Schroff, F., Kalenichenko, D., Philbin, J.: FaceNet: a unified embedding for face recognition and clustering. In: Proceedings of the IEEE Conference on Computer Vision and Pattern Recognition, pp. 815–823 (2015)
30. Simonyan, K., Zisserman, A.: Very deep convolutional networks for large-scale image recognition. arXiv preprint arXiv:1409.1556 (2014)
31. Stone, C.J.: Optimal global rates of convergence for nonparametric regression. Ann. Stat., 1040–1053 (1982)
32. Szegedy, C., et al.: Going deeper with convolutions. In: Computer Vision and Pattern Recognition (CVPR) (2015). http://arxiv.org/abs/1409.4842

A Randomized Gradient-Free Attack on ReLU Networks

Francesco Croce[1](✉) and Matthias Hein[2]

[1] Department of Mathematics and Computer Science, Saarland University,
Saarbrücken, Germany
francesco91.croce@gmail.com
[2] Department of Computer Science, University of Tübingen, Tübingen, Germany

Abstract. It has recently been shown that neural networks but also other classifiers are vulnerable to so called adversarial attacks e.g. in object recognition an almost non-perceivable change of the image changes the decision of the classifier. Relatively fast heuristics have been proposed to produce these adversarial inputs but the problem of finding the optimal adversarial input, that is with the minimal change of the input, is NP-hard. While methods based on mixed-integer optimization which find the optimal adversarial input have been developed, they do not scale to large networks. Currently, the attack scheme proposed by Carlini and Wagner is considered to produce the best adversarial inputs. In this paper we propose a new attack scheme for the class of ReLU networks based on a direct optimization on the resulting linear regions. In our experimental validation we improve in all except one experiment out of 18 over the Carlini-Wagner attack with a relative improvement of up to 9%. As our approach is based on the geometrical structure of ReLU networks, it is less susceptible to defences targeting their functional properties.

Keywords: Adversarial manipulation · Robustness of classifiers

1 Introduction

In recent years it has been highlighted that state-of-the-art neural networks are highly non-robust: small changes to an input image, which are basically non-perceivable for humans, change the classifier decision and the wrong decision has even high confidence [6,23]. This calls into question the usage of neural networks in safety-critical systems e.g. medical diagnosis systems or self-driving cars and opens up possibilities to actively attack an ML system in an adversarial way [12,13,18]. Moreover, this non-robustness has also implications on follow-up processes like interpretability. How should we be able to interpret classifier decisions if very small changes of the input lead to different decisions?

This started an arms race looking for both effective defences against adversarial manipulations and new, sophisticated attacking methods to generate adversarial inputs [26]. In the end it turned out that most proposed defences were

© Springer Nature Switzerland AG 2019
T. Brox et al. (Eds.): GCPR 2018, LNCS 11269, pp. 215–227, 2019.
https://doi.org/10.1007/978-3-030-12939-2_16

proven to be ineffective against attacks of type other than that considered by the defence itself [2,4]. Regarding adversarial attacks one can distinguish between exact methods which find the optimal adversarial input with respect to different l_p-norms e.g. wrt to l_1-norm [3], l_∞-norm [10] and recently l_p for $p = 1, 2, \infty$ in [24]. The problem is in general NP-hard [10] and can be formulated as a mixed-integer optimization problem [24] which does not scale to large networks. Therefore early on fast heuristics were proposed to produce adversarial attacks [6,9,14,21] as this is important when one wants to use them in *adversarial training* to robustify the networks. More recently, there has been a focus on methods in the middle range which are close the optimal adversarial input but are still scalable to larger networks, where currently the attack of Carlini and Wagner (CW-attack) [5] is considered to be state-of-the-art.

Another line of research provides robustness guarantees by giving lower bounds on the norm of the minimal perturbation necessary to change the class [8,19,25] but these methods are restricted to one hidden layer [8,19] or rather shallow networks [25] and do not provide adversarial examples.

In this paper we propose a new method for the generation of adversarial inputs for ReLU feedforward neural networks which exploits only the underlying geometric structure of the classifier which are well known to result in continuous piecewise affine functions [1]. We show that on each region where the classifier is affine (linear region) the problem of finding adversarial inputs is thus a quadratic program for $p = 2$. However, as the number of linear regions grows exponentially with depth it is typically impossible to check all of them and thus we propose an efficient exploration strategy. Finally, because of its geometric nature and our random exploration scheme our attack is more resistant to defences which are based on functional properties of the model like gradient based ones. It produces adversarial inputs of high quality outperforming the current state-of-the-art CW-attack [5] on almost all architectures and three data sets which we tested with a relative improvement of up to 9%.

2   Local Linear Representation of ReLU Networks

In the following we consider multi-class classifiers $f : \mathbb{R}^d \to \mathbb{R}^K$ where d is the input dimension and K the number of classes. It is well known that feedforward neural networks which use ReLU activation functions and are linear in the output layer yield continuous piecewise affine functions for each output component, see e.g. [1]. Also residual and convolutional networks with ReLU (as well as leaky ReLU) activation function or max/sum/avg pooling layers lead to continuous piecewise affine classifier functions. However, as these architectures require special care, for simplicity we restrict ourselves to fully connected neural networks.

Definition 1. *A function $h : \mathbb{R}^d \to \mathbb{R}$ is called piecewise affine if there exists a finite set of polytopes $\{Q_r\}_{r=1}^M$ (linear regions of h) such that $\cup_{r=1}^M Q_r = \mathbb{R}^d$ and h is an affine function when restricted to every Q_r.*

We derive now, given an input point x, the explicit formulation of the linear counterpart of f for x and the polytope $Q(x)$ to which x belongs (and on which the f is an affine function). Note that this description need not be unique when x lies on the boundary between two or more linear regions. But as this is a set of measure zero it does not play any role in practice.

Let $L+1$ be the total number of layers and denote the weights and biases by $W^{(l)} \in \mathbb{R}^{n_l \times n_{l-1}}$ and $b^{(l)} \in \mathbb{R}^{n_l}$ for $l = 1, \ldots, L+1$ where $n_0 = d$ and $n_{L+1} = K$. We define the feedforward network in the usual recursive way, where for $x \in \mathbb{R}^d$ we define $g^{(0)}(x) = x$ and the output of the k-th layer before and after applying componentwise the ReLU activation function $\sigma : \mathbb{R} \to \mathbb{R}$, $\sigma(t) = \max\{0, t\}$ as

$$f^{(k)}(x) = W^{(k)} g^{(k-1)}(x) + b^k, \quad \text{and} \quad g^{(k)}(x) = \sigma(f^{(k)}(x)), \quad k = 1, \ldots, L.$$

The final classifier function is given as $f^{(L+1)}(x) = W^{(L+1)} g^{(L)}(x) + b^{(L+1)}$ and decisions are made using $\arg\max_{r=1,\ldots,K} f_r^{(L+1)}(x)$. We define the diagonal matrices $\Delta^{(l)}, \Sigma^{(l)} \in \mathbb{R}^{n_l \times n_l}$ for $l = 1, \ldots, L$ with entries defined as

$$\Delta^{(l)}(x)_{ij} = \begin{cases} \text{sign}(f_i^{(l)}(x)) & \text{if } i = j, \\ 0 & \text{else.} \end{cases}, \quad \Sigma^{(l)}(x)_{ij} = \begin{cases} 1 & \text{if } i = j, f_i^{(l)}(x) > 0, \\ 0 & \text{else.} \end{cases}$$

The matrices $\Delta^{(l)}$ are used later to derive the boundaries of the polytope, while the matrices $\Sigma^{(l)}$ are the linear equivalent to ReLU functions at a specific point. This allows us to write $f^{(k)}(x)$ in terms of matrix and vector products as

$$f^{(k)}(x) = W^{(k)} \Sigma^{(k-1)} \left(W^{(k-1)} \Sigma^{(k-2)} \left(\ldots \left(W^{(1)} x + b^{(1)} \right) \ldots \right) + b^{(k-1)} \right) + b^{(k)}.$$

This can be further rewritten as $f^{(k)}(x) = V^{(k)} x + a^{(k)}$, with $V^{(k)} \in \mathbb{R}^{n_k \times d}$ and $a^{(k)} \in \mathbb{R}^{n_k}$, where

$$V^{(k)} = W^{(k)} \prod_{l=1}^{k-1} \Sigma^{(k-l)} W^{(k-l)}, \quad a^{(k)} = b^{(k)} + \sum_{l=1}^{k-1} \left(\prod_{m=1}^{k-l} W^{(k+1-m)} \Sigma^{(k-m)} \right) b^{(l)}.$$

Note that $V^{(k)}$ and $a^{(k)}$ are accessible via a forward-pass through the network with only slightly increased overhead compared to the normal effort required for computing the output for a given input x. The polytope $Q(x)$ can now be described by the inequalities

$$Q(x) = \left\{ z \in \mathbb{R}^d \mid \Delta^{(l)}(x)(V^{(l)} z + a^{(l)}) \geq 0, \quad l = 1, \ldots, L \right\},$$

where the diagonal matrix $\Delta^{(l)}(x)$ contains the information on which part of the hyperplane x lies. In total one gets $N = \sum_{l=1}^{L} n_l$ inequality constraints describing the polytope and N represents also the total number of hidden neurons of the network. We denote the set of the inequalities defining $Q(x)$ as $\mathcal{S}(Q(x))$.

Finally, the multi-class classifier is described on $Q(x)$ by the affine function

$$f^{(L+1)} = V^{(L+1)} x + a^{(L+1)}.$$

Then the decision region for a class c on $Q(x)$ is the polytope P_c described by $K - 1$ inequalities

$$P_c = \left\{ z \in \mathbb{R}^d \mid \left\langle V_c^{(L+1)} - V_s^{(L+1)}, z \right\rangle + a_c^{(L+1)} - a_s^{(L+1)} \geq 0 \quad \forall s \neq c \right\} \cap Q(x),$$

where $V_r^{(L+1)}$ is the r-th row of $V^{(L+1)}$. The set P_c is again a polytope since obtained as intersection of two polytopes. Note that the intersection with $Q(x)$ is necessary as the linear description for the classifier obtained for x is only valid on $Q(x)$.

In dependency of the application domain of the classifier there might be also other constraints which the input has to fulfill such as box constraints in the case of images. In this case, in all the definitions one has to take the intersection with this constraint set. Without much loss of generality we assume that such a set M is also given as a polytope so that the intersections $Q(x) \cap M$ and $P_c \cap M$ are polytopes as well.

3   Generation of Adversarial Inputs on the Linear Regions

We first define the optimization problem for generating adversarial inputs, that is given a multi-class classifier $f : \mathbb{R}^d \to \mathbb{R}^K$ and an input x we want to find the smallest perturbation $x + \delta$ such that the decision of f for $x + \delta$ is different from that of x. Typical l_p metrics with $p \in \{1, 2, \infty\}$ are used to measure the "size" of the perturbation. In the experiments we choose $p = 2$, but the framework below can be easily extended to $p \in \{1, \infty\}$.

Formally, the problem can be described as the following optimization problem [23]. Suppose that the classifier outputs class c for input x, that is $f_c(x) = \arg\max_{j=1,\dots,K} f_j(x)$ (we assume the decision is unique). The problem of generating the minimal perturbation $x + \delta$ such that the classifier decision changes is equivalent to finding the solution of

$$\min_{\delta \in \mathbb{R}^d} \|\delta\|_p, \qquad \text{s.th.} \quad \max_{l \neq c} f_l(x + \delta) \geq f_c(x + \delta) \quad \text{and} \quad x + \delta \in C, \qquad (1)$$

where C is a constraint set which the generated point $x + \delta$ has to satisfy, e.g., an image has to be in $[0, 1]^d$ but more generally we assume C to be a polytope. The complexity of the optimization problem (1) depends on the classifier f, but it is typically non-convex (see [10] for a hardness result for ReLU networks). Many relaxations and approximate solutions of problem (1) have been proposed in the literature in order to make it computationally tractable, see e.g. [5,16], and for ReLU networks a few formulations have been proposed for the exact solution [3,10,24], most notably [24] which uses mixed-integer programming to achieve this.

However, as we show in the following, the optimization problem (1) can be solved efficiently on any linear region of f. In fact, given a point y in the input space we recall from Sect. 2 that in the polytope $Q(y)$, or equivalently inside the linear region containing y and where the classifier is affine, it holds $f(z) = Vz + a$ for some V, a. Thus the optimization problem

$$\delta = \arg\min_{l \neq c} \|\delta_l\|_p, \tag{2}$$

with δ_l being the solution of

$$\min_{\delta \in \mathbb{R}^d} \|\delta\|_p, \quad \text{s.th.} \quad \langle V_l - V_c, x + \delta \rangle + a_l - a_c \geq 0, \quad x + \delta \in C \cap Q(y), \tag{3}$$

where V_i and a_i are respectively the i-th row and component of V and a, is equivalent to (1) on $Q(y)$. First of all we note that when the class l is fixed and $p = 2$ the resulting optimization problem on $Q(y)$ is a convex quadratic program, whereas for $p \in \{1, \infty\}$ it is a linear program. Further constraints in form of a polytope e.g. box constraints on the input space do not change the type of the optimization problem. Note that it can in principle happen that there exists no feasible point if the decision boundary of f does not intersect the linear region $Q(y)$. Nonetheless, typically one gets at least for one class an adversarial input in this way.

Although the number of linear regions grows exponentially with the size of the networks [1,15], it is finite. Thus one can in principle solve (1) by checking all the linear regions. However, this is clearly infeasible for all possible regions. Thus we develop in the following a mixed randomized strategy of exploration and local search which solves (2) just on a small number of linear regions but nevertheless achieves good quality.

4 A Linear Regions Based Method to Generate Adversarial Examples

As pointed out in the previous section, solving a finite number of problems like (3) suffices to solve problem (1), but enumerating and checking all the linear regions of a generic classifier is not feasible. In the following we motivate our randomized strategy together with several ways to speed-up the computations by either avoiding to solve the QPs by simple checks or how to speed up the QP computation itself.

It is clear that the solution of the QP (3) is typically attained at a face of $Q(y)$ and the solution lies on the decision boundary. At first sight it looks as the optimal next step, after finding a first adversarial input, is to just visit the neighboring polytope to track the decision boundary. Unfortunately, this approach does not work in practice as the solution is attained typically at a face of dimension $m < d - 1$ (more than one linear constraint of the polytope is active). Thus the neighboring region is not uniquely defined and the number of neighboring regions grows roughly exponentially in $d - 1 - m$. Then, one would have to check all of them and this is again infeasible. But even if this was tractable, nevertheless one would still need a strategy in case all of these neighboring regions just lead to worse adversarial inputs.

Algorithm 1. rLR-QP

Input : x original image, δ_{WS} starting perturbation, L set of target classes,
            $n_1, n_2, n_3, n_4, \alpha$ hyperparameters
Output: δ adversarial perturbation

1 $\delta_0 \leftarrow$ solution of problem (2) on $Q(x)$ and $l \in L$
2 **if** $\|\delta_0\|_2 < \|\delta_{WS}\|_2$ **then** $\delta \leftarrow \delta_0$, $u \leftarrow \|\delta_0\|_2$ **else** $\delta \leftarrow \delta_{WS}$, $u \leftarrow \|\delta_{WS}\|_2$;
3 Initialize the set S of n_1 copies of δ
4 **for** $a_1 = 1, ..., n_4$ **do**
5   **Exploration Step:**
6   **foreach** $a_2 = 1, ..., n_3$ **do**
7        $R = \emptyset$
8   **for** $i = 1, ..., n_1$ **do**
9   **foreach** $j = 1, ..., n_2$ **do**
10             $\epsilon \leftarrow$ random point in $B(0, u/a_1)$
11             $R \leftarrow R \cup \{x + S_i + \epsilon\}$
12   **end**
13   **end**
14   **foreach** $y \in R$ **do**
15          $\delta_{temp} \leftarrow$ solution of problem (2) on $Q(y)$ and $l \in L$
16   **if** $\|\delta_{temp}\|_2 < u$ **then** $\delta \leftarrow \delta_0$, $u \leftarrow \|\delta\|_2$;
17          $m = \underset{i=1,...,n_1}{\arg\max} \|S_i\|_2$
18   **if** $\|\delta_{temp}\|_2 < \alpha u$ and $\|\delta_{temp}\|_2 < \|S_m\|_2$ **then** Replace S_m with δ_{temp};
19   **end**
20   **end**
21   **Local Search Step:**
22   **foreach** $j = 1, ..., n_2$ **do**
23       $\epsilon \leftarrow$ random point in $B(0, u/a_1)$
24       $y \leftarrow x + \delta + \epsilon$
25       $\delta_{temp} \leftarrow$ solution of problem (2) on $Q(y)$ and $l \in L$
26   **if** $\|\delta_{temp}\|_2 < u$ **then** $\delta \leftarrow \delta_0$, $u \leftarrow \|\delta\|_2$;
27       $m = \underset{i=1,...,n_1}{\arg\max} \|S_i\|_2$
28   **if** $\|\delta_{temp}\|_2 < \alpha u$ and $\|\delta_{temp}\|_2 < \|S_m\|_2$ **then** Replace S_m with δ_{temp};
29   **end**
30 **end**

This motivates our randomized strategy to select linear regions which is based on an exploration step, in order to get out of a potential suboptimal valley, and a local search strategy, where we just check linear regions in the close vicinity of the current best adversarial input. Please note that we select linear regions by generating randomly points y and then check the corresponding linear region $Q(y)$. Note also that in this way we will be biased to visiting linear regions of high volume, which makes sense as in such way the portion of the input space checked with a limited number of regions tends to be maximized.

The final scheme is summarized in Algorithm 1, which we refer to as *rLR-QP*. Please note that δ is the best adversarial input found so far and $u = \|\delta\|_2$. Another norm than $p = 2$ can be simply optimized by changing the corresponding convex optimization problem in (3). We have the possibility to use adversarial inputs from another method as initialization. Later on we initialize our method with *DeepFool* [16] to speed up the procedure. As a first step the algorithm checks the linear region $Q(x)$ which contains the original input x. This region contains in some cases already the optimal adversarial input. After this initialization phase the algorithm alternates between the exploration step and the local search step. In the exploration step we keep a set of adversarial inputs which are up to α times suboptimal, where $\alpha = 1.5$ in all experiments, and search in their neighborhood. This exploration phase prevents the method to be too much focused on only one region and explores a larger neighborhood of x. The second phase is the local search step where we search in a smaller neighborhood around the best adversarial input found so far. Note that our random sampling on $B(0, u)$ is uniform in the direction and uniform in the radius (this means we are *not* sampling from the uniform distribution on $B(0, u)$). The reason is that we want to have a higher probability for checking also smaller radii, whereas for uniform sampling in high dimensions the samples would be very close to the surface of the sphere.

The parameters n_1, n_2, n_3, n_4 can be used to tune the total number of linear regions that are explored and consequently the runtime of the algorithm. In fact, we have that overall $M = 1 + (n_1 \cdot n_3 + 1) \cdot n_2 \cdot n_4$ points are picked during the process, so that M is an upper bound on how many linear regions are checked (we make sure not to check the same region twice). For the experiments we fix $n_1, n_2 = 10$, $n_3 = 5$, $n_4 = 3$.

After acceptance of the paper we will make code and scripts available.

5   Experiments

In the experiments we compare the performances of our method *rLR-QP* with different state-of-the-art methods. First, we compare our algorithm with an exact method for a small networks guaranteed to find the optimal adversarial input. Second, we apply our method on larger networks, trained both on the original training set and with adversarial training as described in [14]. Finally, we test how the number of points checked by *rLR-QP* improves the quality of the outcome. In all cases, we analyse our results in relation to those obtained by the Carlini-Wagner l_2-attack [5] (*CW*), as it is considered to be state-of-the-art method to produce high quality adversarial examples, and *DeepFool* [16], as it is a very fast method providing already good to high quality adversarial examples which we use as initialization.

Comparison with Provably Optimal Solutions. In [24] problem (1) is solved using a mixed integer programming reformulation. Since we want to evaluate the quality of adversarial examples found by our method (*rLR-QP*), we

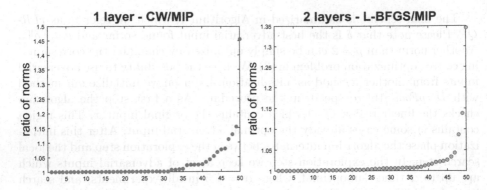

Fig. 1. Effectiveness of attacks. Sorted ratios of the norm of the perturbation found by the attacking methods over the norm of the optimal solution provided by *MIP* (computed on the first 50 images of MNIST test set). Left: performance of *CW* l_2-attack on network N_1. Right: performance of *L-BFGS* on network N_2. In both cases one observes that on about 70% of the points the attacks find solutions close to the optimal ones, while there are approximately 30% of examples where the difference becomes significant and for a few of them even large.

compare them to the minimal solutions obtained as in [24] (*MIP*). Moreover, we also report the performances of other three attacks: *DeepFool*, *L-BFGS* [23] and the *CW* l_2-attack. We train two small neural networks on MNIST dataset: N_1 with 1 hidden layer of 50 units and N_2 with 2 hidden layers of 50 and 15 units. For our method we use the outcome of *DeepFool* as starting point and perform the search over all the 9 target classes. We consider the first 50 images of the test set for the evaluation of adversarial inputs.

We report both the average and the maximum of the ratios $\|\delta\|_2/\|\delta_{MIP}\|_2$, where δ is the perturbation provided by a certain attack while δ_{MIP} is the provably optimal solution of (1) given by *MIP*. As Table 1 shows, *rLR-QP* finds

Table 1. Relative quality of generated adversarial examples. We report the average and the maximum value of the ratios between the 2-norms of the adversarial inputs found by the indicated method and the optimal adversarial inputs generated by the *MIP* method [24] (smaller is better). Two neural networks N_1 (one hidden layer), N_2 (two hidden layers) have been trained on MNIST. The statistics have been computed with the first 50 images of the test set of MNIST. Please notice that our method finds the optimal solution for all 50 test images. All other methods are, sometimes quite significantly, worse.

	rLR-QP (ours)		*DeepFool*		*L-BFGS*		*CW*	
	mean	max	mean	max	mean	max	mean	max
N_1	**1.0000**	**1.0000**	1.1226	1.6059	1.2749	2.2936	1.0269	1.4546
N_2	**1.0000**	**1.0000**	1.1426	1.5953	1.0180	1.3457	1.0686	1.4517

the optimal solution for all 50 test inputs. The other methods instead perform worse and even when the mean is not far from 1 the maximum reaches high values. This behavior is illustrated in Fig. 1 where all the 50 ratios are reported for both CW on N_1 and L-$BFGS$ on N_2 in increasing order. These are the two settings with the *best* mean performance (N_1/CW: 1.027, N_2/L-$BFGS$: 1.018). We see in Fig. 1 that in both cases there are a few outliers on which the performance of the attacks is significantly worse compared to the optimum.

Since it is difficult to provide a fair, complete comparison of the runtime of different methods, we highlight that rLR-QP takes on average around 2 s on N_1 and less than 0.5 s on N_2 to perform on a single image, without any sort of parallelization (see below for further details). We have a shorter time on a more complex network for different reasons. First, the time needed to solve the QPs depends significantly to the size of the optimal solutions themselves (smaller perturbations are usually faster to be computed). Moreover, we did not conduct a wide search in order to tune the hyperparameters $n_1, ..., n_4$ described in Sect. 4, so one might get the same results with smaller computational effort. On the other side, although we reimplemented the MIP algorithm and our implementation might be suboptimal, MIP requires more than 1000 s to complete a run on one image.

Main Experiments. In order to evaluate our method in the task of finding adversarial examples in different settings, we choose three fully connected neural networks with increasing size and depth: 1×1024 with one hidden layer of 1024 units, 5×1024 having 5 hidden layers containing 1024 units each (thus, 5120 hidden units overall) and 10×1024 consisting of 10 hidden layers with 1024 units each (10240 units). Every architecture is trained on three data sets: MNIST, German Traffic Sign (GTS) [22] and CIFAR 10 [11]. Moreover, for each of the previous combinations we train a model on the plain set and another integrating adversarial training (at), using the PGD attack of [14]. However, since we focus on the l_2-norm, we adapted the implementation from [17] to perform the plain gradient update instead of the gradient sign (which corresponds to l_∞-norm and thus is irrelevant for the l_2-norm case) on every iteration. We perform 100 iterations of the PGD attack for every batch. During the training, every batch contains 50% of adversarial and 50% of clean examples.

We apply both *DeepFool*, in the implementation of [20], and CW l_2-attack. For the latter we use its untargeted formulation provided by [17], keeping the settings of the original paper [5] and their code, including 20 restarts, 10000 iterations, learning rate 0.01 and initial constant of 0.001.

We use *DeepFool* as initialization. As we noted that the solution given by *DeepFool* is usually not on the surface representing the boundary between different classes, we conduct a fast binary search over the segment joining the original point x and the adversarial example of *DeepFool* $x + \delta_{DF}$ in order to find the decision boundary. In fact, thanks to the continuity of the classifier f, there exists at least one point on that segment which is still an adversarial example but closer to the clean image. Explicitly we have that

Table 2. Main experiments. We present the statistics of a range of different neural networks trained on different data sets. In particular, we compare the results obtained for networks trained on the *plain training set* and with adversarial training (*at*). Mean, minimum and maximum refer to the values of $\|\delta_{CW}\|_2/\|\delta_{rLR-QP}\|_2$ for CW and $\|\delta_{DF}\|_2/\|\delta_{rLR-QP}\|_2$ for *DeepFool* computed on respectively the first 1000, 700 and 500 images of the test set for 1, 5 and 10 hidden layers models. The improvement rate IR represents the percentage of points on which the norm of perturbation provided by our method is smaller compared to that of the other attack. The number of points where the attack, either CW or *DeepFool*, does not provide an adversarial example is indicated in brackets after the IR. The statistics do not include these points which is an advantage for our competitors.

Data set	Model	CW				DeepFool			
		mean	min	max	IR %	mean	min	max	IR %
MNIST	1 × 1024 plain	1.029	0.827	1.474	94.4	1.157	1.000	13.861	99.9(1)
	1 × 1024 at	1.066	0.454	2.434	83.3	2.107	1.000	26.179	100(49)
	5 × 1024 plain	1.021	0.496	1.471	89.3	1.120	1.001	6.060	100(8)
	5 × 1024 at	1.013	0.585	1.880	75.1	1.404	1.000	11.009	100(4)
	10 × 1024 plain	0.989	0.704	1.535	47.8	1.188	1.000	1.768	100(5)
	10 × 1024 at	0.997	0.270	1.507	67.7(61)	2.084	1.000	5.518	100(4)
GTS	1 × 1024 plain	1.064	0.936	2.065	91.0	1.087	1.000	15.770	96.6
	1 × 1024 at	1.065	0.931	1.944	94.5	1.094	1.000	2.935	99.0
	5 × 1024 plain	1.034	0.509	2.213	79.7	1.222	1.001	2.116	100
	5 × 1024 at	1.036	0.314	3.160	80.1	1.308	1.000	3.248	100
	10 × 1024 plain	1.023	0.563	5.067	76.6(1)	1.346	1.000	4.254	99.8
	10 × 1024 at	1.016	0.533	2.082	68.4	1.583	1.003	3.889	100
CIFAR	1 × 1024 plain	1.090	0.926	1.802	98.3	1.056	1.000	1.966	99.8
	1 × 1024 at	1.080	0.998	1.585	99.9	1.049	1.000	2.747	99.9
	5 × 1024 plain	1.082	0.825	1.783	96.0	1.096	1.001	4.166	100
	5 × 1024 at	1.065	0.769	1.627	94.4	1.090	1.001	1.843	100
	10 × 1024 plain	1.073	0.721	2.225	86.4	1.212	1.002	2.143	100
	10 × 1024 at	1.079	0.644	1.650	86.4	1.160	1.000	1.700	99.8

$$\exists l \quad \text{s.th.} \quad f_c(x) - f_l(x) > 0 \quad \text{and} \quad f_c(x + \delta_{DF}) < f_l(x + \delta_{DF})$$

which implies

$$\exists \delta^* \in \text{conv}(0, \delta_{DF}) \quad \text{s.th.} \quad f_c(x + \delta^*) = f_l(x + \delta^*).$$

Then, we use the approximated $x + \delta^*$ as warm start for our method. If *DeepFool* cannot provide an adversarial example, we perform the linear search between the original point and the origin of $\mathbb{R}^d$ to get the starting point. Moreover, for the 1 hidden layer networks we perform the search of adversarial examples over all the possible target classes, while in the case of 5 and 10 hidden layers we consider only the class the warm start belongs to.

In Table 2 we report, for each setting, mean, minimum and maximum of the ratios $\|\delta_{CW}\|_2/\|\delta_{rLR-QP}\|_2$ and $\|\delta_{DF}\|_2/\|\delta_{rLR-QP}\|_2$, where δ_{CW}, δ_{DF}, δ_{rLR-QP} are the perturbations provided respectively by CW l_2-attack, *DeepFool* and our method, and the percentage of test cases for which $\|\delta_{rLR-QP}\|_2$ is smaller than the other attack. We consider the first 1000 images of the test sets for 1×1024 models, 700 for 5×1024 and 500 for 10×1024. If an attack does not find an adversarial example for a certain image we do not include it in the computations for the statistics. Notice that, unlike the other methods, $rLR\text{-}QP$ always provides a valid adversarial input for all test instances.

Compared to CW attack, on 16 of the 18 models we get an average improvement between 1.3% and 9.0%, while for 10×1024 *at* on MNIST the mean is slightly below 1 but CW attack fails to provide an adversarial example on the 12.2% of cases. Thus it is fair to say that in only one of the 18 experiments, our method is outperformed by the CW attack. The gap is even larger for *DeepFool*, where the average gain with our method is up 110%. Note that the benefit given by the initial binary search is not crucial to achieve this improvement, as can be seen in Table 3 where the statistics both before and after the linear search are shown.

More Iterations of $rLR\text{-}QP$. A natural question is whether allowing our method to check more linear regions can improve significantly the results or does our $rLR\text{-}QP$ algorithm get stuck in some suboptimal area of the input space. We consider the neural network 1×1024 *at* on MNIST, as it has many points where our results are worse than those of CW attack. We want to check if for the images with $\|\delta_{CW}\|_2/\|\delta_{rLR-QP}\|_2 < 0.95$ an improvement is possible. Then, we rerun our method, with the same hyperparameters, using the adversarial example $x + \delta_{rLR-QP}$ produced by $rLR\text{-}QP$ the first time as warm start for the new run. Unlike the first application, we restrict the target class to that of the starting point. Then, we iterate the same procedure a few times, always using the newest perturbation as starting point.

Table 3 shows the evolution of the statistics and the gradual gain in terms of quality. It is interesting that, even if the average improvement between the first and second iterations is the largest, the maximum gain is high also in the successive steps (it is of 45.7% at the fifth application). Furthermore, the progressive increase of the mean appears almost constant and this indicates that further applications of the algorithm will lead to further improvement (for example the second largest increase of the mean of the ratios, 1.0%, is attained the sixth time we run the algorithm). Overall, this means that running our method for a longer time (increasing n_4) can yield better solutions.

Implementation Details. Our algorithm is coded in MATLAB, relies on Gurobi solver [7] for the optimization processes and runs at the moment on CPUs. As it is stated in [5] a direct comparison of the runtime of different methods might be misleading as both implementation and hardware used are hardly similar. We would like to point out that our technique does not benefit at the moment of any kind of parallelization. It is however likely that major improvements in computational speed can be obtained by an adaptation that allows to exploit completely the hardware potential, including GPUs.

Table 3. Evolution of quality over time. We here consider the network 1×1024 *at* trained on MNIST and the 79 images which after the first application of our method have $\|\delta_{CW}\|_2 / \|\delta_{rLR-QP}\|_2 < 0.95$. We show the statistics (mean, minimum, maximum) of the ratios $\|\delta_{CW}\|_2 / \|\delta_{rLR-QP}\|_2$ and the number N of points for which $\|\delta_{rLR-QP}\|_2 < \|\delta_{CW}\|_2$ before performing our method (that is considering the outcome of *DeepFool*, without and with the binary search) and after multiple iterations of it. Moreover, we present the progressive improvement at each step compared to the previous one. It is clear that there are improvements across all the categories and in particular for 24 of 79 points we have that the perturbation of our method at the end is smaller than the one provided by CW.

Step	CW			N	progr. improv.	
	mean	min	max		mean	max
DeepFool	0.500	0.236*	0.893	0	–	–
DeepFool + binary search	0.511	0.235	0.893	0	–	–
I application of rLR-QP	0.865	0.454	0.949	0	–	–
II application of rLR-QP	0.905	0.454	1.292	15	4.9%	44.5%
III application of rLR-QP	0.908	0.550	1.292	16	0.5%	21.2%
IV application of rLR-QP	0.912	0.550	1.292	18	0.4%	12.9%
V application of rLR-QP	0.918	0.550	1.292	20	0.8%	45.7%
VI application of rLR-QP	0.927	0.550	1.292	23	1.0%	30.1%
VII application of rLR-QP	0.930	0.550	1.292	24	0.4%	31.4%

* for one point *DeepFool* does not produce an adversarial input, hence we perform the binary search on the segment joining the original image and the origin of $\mathbb{R}^d$. We do not include this point in the statistics for *DeepFool* and this is why the minimum after "*DeepFool* + binary search" is worse than after only *DeepFool*.

6   Outlook

From the implementation side we will implement the current method using GPUs or if a full GPU implementation is unreasonable do a mixed CPU-GPU implementation. The use of GPUs will then allow also to extend the method easily to convolutional neural networks and related variants which also yield continuous piecewise affine functions if only max- and avg-pooling are used for the convolutional layers and ReLU is used for the fully connected layers.

References

1. Arora, R., Basuy, A., Mianjyz, P., Mukherjee, A.: Understanding deep neural networks with rectified linear unit. In: ICLR (2018)
2. Athalye, A., Carlini, N., Wagner, D.A.: Obfuscated gradients give a false sense of security: circumventing defenses to adversarial examples. arXiv:1802.00420 (2018)
3. Carlini, N., Katz, G., Barrett, C., Dill, D.L.: Provably minimally-distorted adversarial examples. arXiv:1709.10207v2 (2017)

4. Carlini, N., Wagner, D.: Adversarial examples are not easily detected: bypassing ten detection methods. In: ACM Workshop on Artificial Intelligence and Security (2017)
5. Carlini, N., Wagner, D.A.: Towards evaluating the robustness of neural networks. In: IEEE Symposium on Security and Privacy, pp. 39–57 (2017)
6. Goodfellow, I.J., Shlens, J., Szegedy, C.: Explaining and harnessing adversarial examples. In: ICLR (2015)
7. Gurobi Optimization, Inc.: Gurobi optimizer reference manual (2016). http://www.gurobi.com
8. Hein, M., Andriushchenko, M.: Formal guarantees on the robustness of a classifier against adversarial manipulation. In: NIPS (2017)
9. Huang, R., Xu, B., Schuurmans, D., Szepesvari, C.: Learning with a strong adversary. In: ICLR (2016)
10. Katz, G., Barrett, C., Dill, D., Julian, K., Kochenderfer, M.: Reluplex: an efficient SMT solver for verifying deep neural networks. In: CAV (2017)
11. Krizhevsky, A., Nair, V., Hinton, G.: CIFAR-10 (Canadian Institute for Advanced Research). http://www.cs.toronto.edu/~kriz/cifar.html
12. Kurakin, A., Goodfellow, I.J., Bengio, S.: Adversarial examples in the physical world. In: ICLR Workshop (2017)
13. Liu, Y., Chen, X., Liu, C., Song, D.: Delving into transferable adversarial examples and black-box attacks. In: ICLR (2017)
14. Madry, A., Makelov, A., Schmidt, L., Tsipras, D., Valdu, A.: Towards deep learning models resistant to adversarial attacks. In: ICLR (2018)
15. Montufar, G., Pascanu, R., Cho, K., Bengio, Y.: On the number of linear regions of deep neural networks. In: NIPS (2014)
16. Moosavi-Dezfooli, S., Fawzi, A., Fawzi, O., Frossard, P.: Universal adversarial perturbations. In: CVPR (2017)
17. Papernot, N., et al.: CleverHans v2.0.0: an adversarial machine learning library. arXiv:1610.00768 (2017)
18. Papernot, N., McDonald, P., Wu, X., Jha, S., Swami, A.: Distillation as a defense to adversarial perturbations against deep networks. In: IEEE Symposium on Security & Privacy (2016)
19. Raghunathan, A., Steinhardt, J., Liang, P.: Certified defenses against adversarial examples. In: ICLR (2018)
20. Rauber, J., Brendel, W., Bethge, M.: Foolbox: a python toolbox to benchmark the robustness of machine learning models
21. Moosavi-Dezfooli, S.-M., Fawzi, A., Frossard, P.: DeepFool: a simple and accurate method to fool deep neural networks. In: CVPR, pp. 2574–2582 (2016)
22. Stallkamp, J., Schlipsing, M., Salmen, J., Igel, C.: Man vs. computer: benchmarking machine learning algorithms for traffic sign recognition. Neural Netw. 32, 323–332 (2012)
23. Szegedy, C., et al.: Intriguing properties of neural networks. In: ICLR, pp. 2503–2511 (2014)
24. Tjeng, V., Tedrake, R.: Verifying neural networks with mixed integer programming. arXiv:1711.07356v1 (2017)
25. Wong, E., Kolter, J.Z.: Provable defenses against adversarial examples via the convex outer adversarial polytope. arXiv:1711.00851v2 (2018)
26. Yuan, X., He, P., Zhu, Q., Bhat, R.R., Li, X.: Adversarial examples: attacks and defenses for deep learning. arXiv:1712.07107 (2017)

Cross and Learn: Cross-Modal
Self-supervision

Nawid Sayed[✉], Biagio Brattoli[✉], and Björn Ommer[✉]

Heidelberg University, HCI/IWR, Heidelberg, Germany
n.sayed@stud.uni-heidelberg.de,
{biagio.brattoli,bjorn.ommer}@iwr.uni-heidelberg.de

Abstract. In this paper we present a self-supervised method for representation learning utilizing two different modalities. Based on the observation that cross-modal information has a high semantic meaning we propose a method to effectively exploit this signal. For our approach we utilize video data since it is available on a large scale and provides easily accessible modalities given by RGB and optical flow. We demonstrate state-of-the-art performance on highly contested action recognition datasets in the context of self-supervised learning. We show that our feature representation also transfers to other tasks and conduct extensive ablation studies to validate our core contributions.

1 Introduction

In the last decade, Convolutional Neural Networks (CNNs) have shown state of the art accuracy on a variety of visual recognition tasks such as image classification [18], object detection [10] and action recognition [33]. The success of CNNs is based on *supervised learning* which heavily relies on large manually annotated datasets. These are costly to obtain, however unannotated data in form of images and videos have become easily available on a very large scale. Recently this encouraged the investigation of *self-supervised learning* approaches which do not require semantic annotations for the data. Here the general procedure involves pretraining a network on a surrogate task which requires semantic understanding in order to be solved. Although the gap is closing, self-supervised approaches usually cannot compete with feature representations obtained by supervised pretraining on large scale datasets such as ImageNet [31] or Kinetics [15].

In this paper, we use cross-modal information as an alternative source of supervision and propose a new method to effectively exploit mutual information in order to train powerful feature representations for both modalities. The main motivation of our approach is derived from the following observation: Information shared across modalities has a much higher semantic meaning compared to information which is modality specific. We showcase this point in Fig. 1 where we present a tuple of pairs obtained from an action recognition video dataset. We can see that cross-modal information such as the barbell or the baseball bat

© Springer Nature Switzerland AG 2019
T. Brox et al. (Eds.): GCPR 2018, LNCS 11269, pp. 228–243, 2019.
https://doi.org/10.1007/978-3-030-12939-2_17

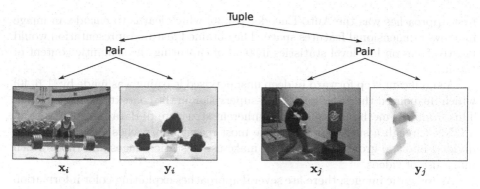

Fig. 1. A tuple of pairs obtained from UCF-101 using RGB and optical flow as modalities. The cross-modal information (barbell, bat, person) has a much higher semantic meaning than the modality specific information (background, camera movement, noise)

provide good clues to identify the action. On the other hand modality specific information such as the background or camera motion do not help to identify the action.

Feature representations which are sensitive to cross-modal information and invariant to modality specific content are therefore desirable. The latter condition is fulfilled if the feature representations of a pair are similar to each other. The former condition is fulfilled if the feature representations are also dissimilar across different pairs. To achieve that we utilize a trainable two stream architecture with one network per modality similar to [33] and propose two different loss contributions which guide the networks to learn the desired feature representations.

For our method we require paired data from different modalities on a large scale. We therefore apply our method to video data which provide very easily accessible modalities RGB and optical flow in practically unlimited quantity. Our choice for the modalities is also motivated by past work where it has been shown that RGB and optical flow complement each other in the context of action recognition [33].

In order to demonstrate the effectiveness of our cross-modal pretraining, we conduct extensive experimental validation and a complete ablation study on our design choices. Our method significantly outperforms state-of-the-art unsupervised approaches on the two highly contested action recognition datasets UCF-101 [34] and HMDB-51 [19] while pretraining for only *6h GPU time* on a single NVIDIA Titan X (Pascal). We also show the transferability of our feature representation to object classification and detection by achieving competitive results on the PASCAL VOC 2007 benchmark.

2   Related Work

In recent years, unsupervised deep learning has been an hot topic for the research community due to the abundance of unannotated data. One of the first approaches was the Auto-Encoder [16, 36] which learns to encode an image in a lower dimensional features space. The obtained feature representation would mostly focus on low level statistics instead of capturing the semantic content of the input.

A significant step forward in deep unsupervised learning was made by [1, 6, 40] which introduced the paradigm of self-supervision in the context of deep learning. This family of methods exploits the inherent structure of data in order to train a CNN through a surrogate task. The most recent approaches can generally be divided into two groups, those which make use of static images and those which make use of videos.

As for static images, there are several approaches exploiting color information [20, 42] and spatial context [6, 26, 28]. For the latter an image is tiled into patches and their relative position is exploited as a supervisory signal in order to obtain a good feature representation. These approaches have shown reliable results on the task of object detection and surface normal estimation. There is also a variety of works which specifically aim to learn reliable posture representations without supervision [3, 4, 23, 30, 32].

Approaches which use video data mainly exploit temporal context as source of supervision [2, 4, 5, 24, 40]. A common idea is to shuffle frames of a video clip and use a network to reconstruct or verify the correct chronological order [9, 21, 24]. The obtained feature representations generalize well to action recognition. Closely related to our approach is the work of Purushwalkam and Gupta [30]. They use RGB and optical flow data obtained from videos and learn a feature representation which transfers to the task of pose estimation. Although they achieve good results for action recognition, our method exploits cross-modal information in RGB and optical flow data much more effectively.

There is a large body of work which demonstrates the effectiveness of utilizing multimodal data in order to solve a variety of tasks. For example [8, 33] show that RGB and optical flow are complementary modalities in the context of action recognition.

Gupta et al. [11] train a feature representation for depth data by distilling the knowledge from a teacher network pretrained on ImageNet [31]. The work of [38] proposes cross-modal ranking in conjunction with structure preserving constrains in order to learn a joint feature representation between image and text data. Both works show successful cross-modal supervision but rely on annotated data, which is not required for our approach.

The work of [25] utilizes a bimodal deep autoencoder in order to learn a shared feature representation for the audio and visual stream of video data. Similarly [41] extends this work to temporal feature representations.

3   Approach

In this section we present an efficient method for representation learning utilizing two different modalities. Our goal is to obtain feature representations which are sensitive to cross-modal information while being invariant to modality specific content. As already explained in the introduction, these conditions are fulfilled by feature representations which are similar for a pair and dissimilar across different pairs. To achieve the former we propose a cross-modal loss L_{cross} and to achieve the latter we utilize a diversity loss L_{div}, both of which act directly in feature space thus promising better training signals.

Our method requires paired data from two different modalities $\mathbf{x} \in X$ and $\mathbf{y} \in Y$, which is available in most use cases i.e. RGB and optical flow. We utilize a two-stream architecture with trainable CNNs in order to obtain our feature representations $f(\mathbf{x})$ and $g(\mathbf{y})$. With exception of the first layer, the networks share the same architecture but do not share weights. To calculate both loss contributions we need a tuple of pairs $\mathbf{x}_i, \mathbf{y}_i$ and $\mathbf{x}_j, \mathbf{y}_j$ from our dataset. A visualization of our method is provided in Fig. 2.

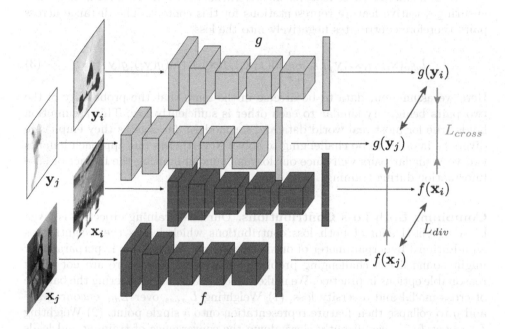

Fig. 2. Visualization of our model. Networks of same color share weights and are denoted by f (red, dark) and g (blue, bright) respectively. f and g are trained so that the cross-modal distance (vertical) decreases while the distance between different pairs (horizontal) increases (Color figure online)

Cross-Modal Loss. In order to enforce cross-modal similarity between f and g we enforce the feature representations of a pair to be close in feature space via some distance d. Solving this task requires the networks to ignore information which is only present in either $\mathbf{x}$ or $\mathbf{y}$

$$L_{cross}(\mathbf{x}_i, \mathbf{y}_i, \mathbf{x}_j, \mathbf{y}_j) = \frac{1}{2} \left[\mathrm{d}(f(\mathbf{x}_i), g(\mathbf{y}_i)) + \mathrm{d}(f(\mathbf{x}_j), g(\mathbf{y}_j)) \right]. \qquad (1)$$

We utilize the bounded cosine distance for d, which is given by

$$d(\mathbf{a}, \mathbf{b}) = 1 - \frac{\mathbf{a} \cdot \mathbf{b}}{|\mathbf{a}| \cdot |\mathbf{b}|} \leq 2. \tag{2}$$

We prevent singularities during training by adding a small ϵ into the square-root of the euclidean norm. We also experimented with the unbounded euclidean distance for d, as done in [11] but found that it leads to an unstable training.

Diversity Loss. We obtain diversity by enforcing the feature representation for both modalities to be distant across pairs with respect to the same distance d as before. This spreads the features of different pairs apart in feature space. Due to the cross-modal loss these features mostly encode cross-modal information, thus ensuring sensitive feature representations for this content. The distance across pairs therefore contributes negatively into the loss

$$L_{div}(\mathbf{x}_i, \mathbf{y}_i, \mathbf{x}_j, \mathbf{y}_j) = -\frac{1}{2} \left[d(f(\mathbf{x}_i), f(\mathbf{x}_j)) + d(g(\mathbf{y}_i), g(\mathbf{y}_j)) \right]. \tag{3}$$

Here we assume our data to be diverse in the sense that the probability of the two pairs being very similar to each other is sufficiently low. This assumption holds true for most real world data and for modern datasets as they emphasize diversity in order to be challenging to solve. Nevertheless our approach handles two very similar pairs well since our loss is bounded limiting the impact of false information during training.

Combining Both Loss Contributions. Our final training objective is given by a weighted sum of both loss contributions which leaves the weighting as an additional hyperparameter of our method. Determining this hyperparameter might sound like a challenging problem but we find that there are not many reasonable options in practice. We make two observations considering the balance of cross-modal and diversity loss. (1) Weighting L_{cross} over L_{div} encourages f and g to collapse their feature representation onto a single point. (2) Weighting L_{div} over L_{cross} significantly slows down the convergence of training and leads to a worse feature representation. It is important to note that these observations only hold true if the distance distributions in both loss contributions can quickly be equalized by the network during training. This is usually the case for modern deep CNN architectures with multiple normalization layers.

Given our observations, we weight both loss contributions equally which yields our final loss

$$L(\mathbf{x}_i, \mathbf{y}_i, \mathbf{x}_j, \mathbf{y}_j) = L_{cross}(\mathbf{x}_i, \mathbf{y}_i, \mathbf{x}_j, \mathbf{y}_j) + L_{div}(\mathbf{x}_i, \mathbf{y}_i, \mathbf{x}_j, \mathbf{y}_j). \tag{4}$$

We obtain our training signal by randomly sampling B tuples ($2B$ pairs) from our dataset and averaging the loss in Eq. 4 across the tuples. In Sect. 4.5 we further validate our design choices.

4 Experiments

In this section we quantitatively and qualitatively evaluate our self-supervised cross-modal pretraining mainly using RGB and optical flow as our modalities of choice. We will therefore refer to f and g as *RGB-network* and *OF-network* respectively. First, we present the implementation details for the self-supervised training. Afterwards, we quantitatively evaluate our feature representation by fine-tuning onto highly contested benchmarks and show a qualitative evaluation of the learned feature representation. Finally, we close with an extensive ablation study where we validate our design choices.

4.1 Implementation Details

We use the CaffeNet [14,18] architecture as this is well established for representation learning and extract our feature representation from fc6 after the ReLU activation. We use dropout with $p = 0.5$. If not stated otherwise, we use batch normalization [12] on all convolutional layers in order to be comparable with [21]. We conduct our experiments using pytorch [29].

We use the trainset of UCF-101 for our pretraining in order to be consistent with previous work, the (TV-L_1) optical flow data is pre-computed using the OpenCV [13] implementation with default parameters. Due to having temporally ordered data we use a stack of 10 consecutive optical flow frames and its temporally centered RGB frame for each pair. This is motivated by past work [30,33] which show that additional optical flow frames are beneficial for motion understanding. The input of the OF-network therefore has 20 channels.

During training we randomly sample 60 videos ($B = 30$ tuples) and from each video we randomly sample a pair. Similarly to [21,24] the latter sampling is weighted by the average flow magnitudes in a pair which reduces the number of training samples without meaningful information.

The following augmentation scheme is applied independently to both pairs. Given the optical flow stack and the RGB frame we first rescale them to a height of 256 conserving the aspect ratio. We then randomly crop a 224×224 patch and apply random horizontal flips, both of which are done identically across the 10 flow frames and the RGB frame. We further augment the flow stack by applying random temporal flips (augmentation from [30]) and subtract the mean [33]. Additionally we apply channel splitting [21] which yields a color-agnostic input forcing the network to learn a less appearance based representation.

We find that a proper choice for ϵ is crucial for the stability of our training and recommend using $\epsilon = 1e-5$ or bigger. We use SGD with momentum of 0.9 and weight decay of $5e-4$ with an initial learning rate of 0.01 which is reduced to 0.001 after 50 K iterations. Training is stopped after 65 K iterations and requires only *6h GPU time* on a NVIDIA Titan X (Pascal).

4.2 Action Recognition

We evaluate our approach on the action recognition datasets UCF-101 and HMDB-51 which emerged as highly contested benchmarks for unsupervised representation learning on videos. To show the versatility of our approach we also utilize the considerably deeper VGG16 architecture, using its fc6 layer as our feature representation. We train on a single GPU using $B = 12$ and a learning rate of 0.005 for a total of 160K iterations, leaving all other hyperparameters unchanged. Pretraining on a single GPU completes in less than two days.

Datasets. The action recognition datasets are typically divided in three splits. UCF-101 is composed of 13K video clips per split, 9.5K for training and 3.5 K for testing, divided in 101 action categories. HMDB-51 consists of 51 classes with 3.5K videos for training and 1.4K for testing per split. Although both datasets are created in a similar manner, HMDB-51 is more challenging as there can be multiple samples from the same video with different semantic labels (draw sword, sword exercise, sword fight). Samples from different classes can therefore have very similar appearance or posture information and require an understanding of motion to be distinguished properly [19].

Finetuning Protocol. We start with a randomly initialized CaffeNet and use the parameters of our pretrained RGB-network to initialize the convolutional and batch normalization layers (FC-layers start from scratch). For training and testing we follow the common finetuning protocol of [33] in order to be comparable with previous work [21,24]. We provide test classification accuracies over 3 splits for both datasets. In order to ensure that the test set of UCF-101 does not contain images which have been previously seen during pretraining we conduct pretraining and finetuning on the same split.

Table 1. Test classification accuracies over 3 splits for different pretraining schemes. If not stated otherwise the referenced methods use the CaffeNet architecture. +: indicates only Split 1. Our RGB-network outperforms previous state-of-the-art self-supervised methods especially on HMDB-51, while also being very efficient

	Dataset	Traintime	UCF-101	HMDB-51
Random	None	None	48.2	19.5
ImageNet [21]	ImageNet	3 days	67.7	28.0
Shuffle and Learn [24]	UCF-101	–	50.2	18.1
VGAN [37] (C3D)	flickr (2M videos)	>2 days	52.1	–
LT-Motion [22] (RNN)	NTU (57K videos)	–	53.0	–
Pose f. Action [30] (VGG)	UCF, HMDB, ACT	–	55.0	23.6
OPN [21]	UCF-101	40 h	56.3	22.1
Our	UCF-101	6 h	**58.7**	**27.2**
Random (VGG16)+	None	None	59.6	24.3
Our (VGG16)+	UCF-101	1.5 days	70.5	33.0

Results. As shown in Table 1, our approach outperforms the previous state-of-the-art method [21] by over 2% and 5% on UCF-101 and HMDB-51 respectively. For the latter dataset our network almost closed the gap to its ImageNet pretrained counterpart. As mentioned before HMDB-51 requires a better understanding of motion and is not easily solved by appearance information. This favors our method because solving our pretraining task requires a good understanding of motion. Compared to past approaches which make use of optical flow [22,30] our method exploits motion information much more effectively. We further expand this point in our qualitative evaluation and ablation studies.

4.3   Transfer Learning

In this section, we evaluate the transferability of our learned feature representation to object classification and detection. To this end we use the Pascal VOC 2007 benchmark and compare to other recent unsupervised learning methods.

Datasets. The Pascal VOC 2007 dataset [7] provides annotation for 20 classes on 10K images, containing in total 25K annotated objects. The images are split equally between training/validation and testing set. The annotations provide class label and bounding box location for every object.

The ACT [39] dataset is composed of 11K video clips of people performing various actions. The dataset contains 43 different action categories which can be summarized to 16 super-classes. For our pretraining we use the trainset containing 7K videos and do not make use of the semantic labels.

Pretraining and Finetuning Protocol. We apply our model onto the training videos from UCF-101, HMDB-51 and ACT [39] which yield about 20K videos during pretraining. We double the number of iterations to 130K (dropping learning rate at 100K) and leave all other hyperparameters unchanged. Similar to Sect. 4.2 we use the Convolutional layers of our RGB-network to initialize a new CaffeNet for finetuning but we do not transfer the batch normalization layers, as suggested by [21]. In order to be comparable to [21] we finetune our RGB-network on Pascal VOC for the multi-class classification task following Krähenbühl et al. [17] protocol and use Fast-RCNN [10] framework when fine-tuning for object detection.

Results. Table 2 shows a comparison of our approach to other unsupervised learning methods. Among the methods which do not make use of ImageNet data we improve upon state-of-the-art in both categories. We also show competitive accuracy in object classification among methods which do use ImageNet data. This result is remarkable as the datasets we used for pretraining are very dissimilar to the ImageNet or Pascal VOC dataset. This demonstrates the transferability of the feature representation obtained by our method.

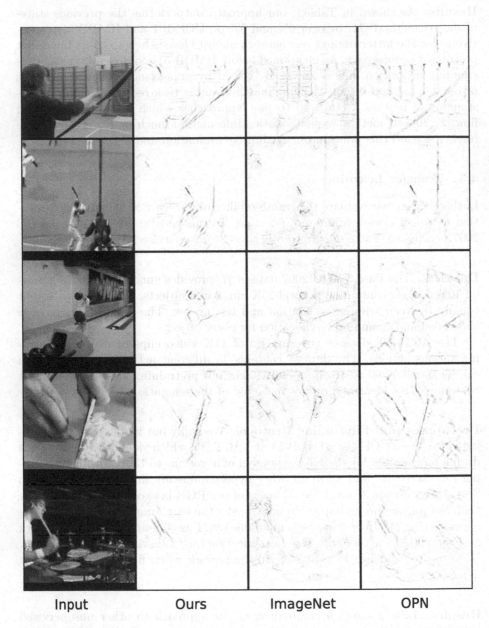

| Input | Ours | ImageNet | OPN |

Fig. 3. Comparison of the input activations for different models. The first column represents the input sample, second is our RGB-network, third is an ImageNet pretrained network and lastly OPN [21]. The activation are computed using guided backpropagation [35]. In contrast to the other approaches our network is able to identify meaningful objects (Bow, bowling ball, drumstick ...) while also ignoring irrelevant background content

| Input | Ours | ImageNet | OPN |

Fig. 4. Additional input activations for our RGB-network, ImageNet pretraining and OPN [21]. Our network is also capable of identifying small moving objects (table tennis ball, pen), and ignore most of the background

Table 2. Results for Pascal VOC 2007 classification and detection. First segment shows baseline performance for supervised training. Methods in the second segment used large scale image data to pretrain their models whereas methods in the last segment used video data during pretraining

	Dataset	Traintime	Classification	Detection
ImageNet [21]	ImageNet	3 days	78.2	56.8
Context [6]	ImageNet	4 weeks	55.3	46.6
Counting [27]	ImageNet	–	67.7	51.4
Jigsaw [26]	ImageNet	2.5 days	67.6	53.2
Jigsaw++ [28]	ImageNet	–	72.5	56.5
Shuffle and Learn	UCF-101	–	54.3	39.9
OPN [21]	UCF, HMDB, ACT	>2 days	63.8	46.9
Our	UCF, HMDB, ACT	12 h	**70.7**	**48.1**

4.4 Qualitative Evaluation

In this section we present a qualitative evaluation of our learned feature representations by showing input gradients obtained from high-level layers. We calculate the input layer activations for our pretrained RGB-network and compare to other approaches on the UCF-101 testset. To obtain the results in Figs. 3 and 4 we use guided backpropagation [35] on the 100 strongest activations in pool5 of the networks. We can see that our training leads the network to focus on key moving objects involved in an action (bowling ball, drumstick, pen...) while ignoring irrelevant background information. Contrary, the ImageNet and OPN pretrained networks take the entire appearance of the scene into account indicating a more appearance based feature representation.

4.5 Ablation Study

In this section we give a complete ablation study on all of our design choices. We start by investigating the effectiveness of our model without using optical flow as second modality. Afterwards we reveal that our method is mutually beneficial for the used modalities. We close by demonstrating the importance of our cross-modal loss and show that a more mainstream model design yields inferior results. We conduct our evaluation with CaffeNet on split 1 of UCF-101 and HMDB-51 only using UCF-101 for pretraining.

Using Stack of Frame Differences as Second Modality. In the works of [9] and [21] reliable results were achieved using stack of frame differences (SOD) for action recognition. Inspired by their findings we train our model using RGB and SOD as modalities (we use the term SOD-network for g in this context). We apply the same data sampling procedure as described in Sect. 4.1 with slight

Table 3. Comparing different choices of modalities. The left segment shows test accuracies obtained by using RGB and optical flow as modalities whereas the right segment reports test accuracies using RGB and SoD. We observe that all modalities benefit significantly from our pretraining

Dataset	Pretraining	RGB	OF	RGB	SOD
UCF-101	Random weights	49.1	76.4	49.1	64.5
UCF-101	Our	**59.3**	**79.2**	**55.4**	**66.3**
HMDB-51	Random weights	19.2	47.1	19.2	30.8
HMDB-51	Our	**27.7**	**51.7**	**23.5**	**33.3**

modifications. To obtain a SOD we sample 5 RGB frames and calculate the difference between successive frames yielding us a SOD with 4 frame differences. The RGB input is then just the temporally centered RGB frame. We only apply random crops and random horizontal flips to SOD but keep the same augmentation as Sect. 4.1 for RGB. All other hyperparameters are kept the same for pretraining and finetuning.

Test classification results on split 1 of UCF-101 and HMDB-51 are reported in the right segment of Table 3. The RGB-network achieves 55.4% and 23.5% test classification accuracy respectively which is still competitive to previous state of the art methods.

Mutual Benefit Between the Modalities. In order to demonstrate the mutual benefit of our method we finetune our obtained OF and SOD-network onto split 1 of UCF-101 and HMDB-51. We apply the same scheme already used for RGB to finetune both networks. We compare to randomly initialized networks and report results in Table 3.

We observe that our pretraining increases the classification accuracy on all used modalities. The OF-network acts supervisory on the RGB-network and also vice versa. This result is quite remarkable given the huge performance gap on the classification task and also holds true for RGB and SOD. Although the weaker modality benefits more from the pretraining it does not drag down the results of the stronger modality but instead gives a considerable boost especially for HMDB-51.

Alternative Design Choices. As already indicated in Sect. 3 we obtain trivial feature representations if we do not utilize the diversity loss. In the following we also demonstrate the importance of our cross-modal loss. To this end we pretrain our model the same way as before but set the cross-modal loss contribution to zero. We then finetune its RGB-network on UCF-101 and HMDB-51 and present our findings in Table 4. Without the cross-modal loss we perform on par with a randomly initialized network which indicates a failed pretraining and highlights the importance of the cross-modal loss.

Table 4. Ablation study for alternative design choices conducted on split 1 of UCF-101 and HMDB-51. Models were pretrained onto UCF-101. Utilizing L_{div} only performs on par with random weights. A more mainstream model design leads to a worse performance

Dataset	Pretraining	RGB	OF
UCF-101	Random weights	49.1	76.4
UCF-101	Only L_{div}	49.0	75.3
UCF-101	Concat	57.6	77.8
UCF-101	Our	**59.3**	**79.2**
HMDB-51	Random weights	19.2	47.1
HMDB-51	Only L_{div}	18.0	47.2
HMDB-51	Concat	24.5	49.9
HMDB-51	Our	**27.7**	**51.7**

To validate our design choices further we now compare to a more mainstream approach of exploiting cross-modal information which is inspired by the work of [30]. We concatenate the fc6 layers of our RGB and OF-network (8192 channels) and put a modified CaffeNet binary classifier (fc7, fc8) on top of it. We preserve our sampling and augmentation protocol described in Sect. 4.1 in order to be as comparable to our approach as possible. Given two pairs x_i, y_i and x_j, y_j we now exploit the mutual information by posing a binary classification surrogate task. We assign the combinations x_i, y_i and x_j, y_j positive labels whereas x_i, y_j and x_j, y_i obtain negative labels. Essentially the network has to figure out if a presented RGB frame and flow stack belong to the same pair or not. We pretrain this model using the Cross-Entropy loss and use the same hyperparameters as our original model. Finetuning is then performed for both modalities in the same way as before. We reference this alternative model as Concat.

Results for our Concat model can be found in Table 4. We observe that the RGB-network of the Concat model is outperforming its randomly initialized counterpart but achieves significantly worse results than our pretraining.

5   Conclusion

Recently self-supervised learning emerged as an attractive research area since unannotated data is available on a large scale whereas annotations are expensive to obtain. In our work we reveal cross-modal information as an alternative source of supervision and present an efficient method to exploit this signal in order to obtain powerful feature representations for both modalities. We evaluate our method in the context of action recognition where we significantly outperform previous state-of-the-art results on the two highly contested action recognition datasets UCF-101 and HMDB-51. We also show the transferability of our feature representations by achieving competitive results in object classification and detection. We close out by conducting an extensive ablation study in which we validate all our design choices.

Acknowledgments. We are grateful to the NVIDIA corporation for supporting our research, the experiments in this paper were performed on a donated Titan X (Pascal) GPU.

References

1. Agrawal, P., Carreira, J., Malik, J.: Learning to see by moving. In: Proceedings of the IEEE International Conference on Computer Vision (2015)
2. Bautista, M., Fuchs, P., Ommer, B.: Learning where to drive by watching others. In: Proceedings of the German Conference Pattern Recognition (2017)
3. Bautista, M., Sanakoyeu, A., Sutter, E., Ommer, B.: CliqueCNN: deep unsupervised exemplar learning. In: Proceedings of the Conference on Advances in Neural Information Processing Systems (NIPS) (2016)
4. Brattoli, B., Büchler, U., Wahl, A.S., Schwab, M.E., Ommer, B.: LSTM self-supervision for detailed behavior analysis. In: IEEE Conference on Computer Vision and Pattern Recognition (CVPR) (2017)
5. Büchler, U., Brattoli, B., Ommer, B.: Improving spatiotemporal self-supervision by deep reinforcement learning. In: Ferrari, V., Hebert, M., Sminchisescu, C., Weiss, Y. (eds.) ECCV 2018. LNCS, vol. 11219, pp. 797–814. Springer, Cham (2018). https://doi.org/10.1007/978-3-030-01267-0_47
6. Doersch, C., Gupta, A., Efros, A.A.: Unsupervised visual representation learning by context prediction. In: Proceedings of the IEEE International Conference on Computer Vision (2015)
7. Everingham, M., Van Gool, L., Williams, C.K.I., Winn, J., Zisserman, A.: The PASCAL Visual Object Classes Challenge 2007 (VOC2007) Results. http://www.pascal-network.org/challenges/VOC/voc2007/workshop/index.html
8. Feichtenhofer, C., Pinz, A., Zisserman, A.: Convolutional two-stream network fusion for video action recognition. In: IEEE Conference on Computer Vision and Pattern Recognition (CVPR) (2016)
9. Fernando, B., Bilen, H., Gavves, E., Gould, S.: Self-supervised video representation learning with odd-one-out networks. In: IEEE Conference on Computer Vision and Pattern Recognition (CVPR) (2017)
10. Girshick, R.B.: Fast R-CNN. CoRR (2015)
11. Gupta, S., Hoffman, J., Malik, J.: Cross modal distillation for supervision transfer. In: Proceedings of the IEEE Conference on Computer Vision and Pattern Recognition (2016)
12. Ioffe, S., Szegedy, C.: Batch normalization: accelerating deep network training by reducing internal covariate shift. arXiv preprint arXiv:1502.03167 (2015)
13. Itseez: Open source computer vision library (2015). https://github.com/itseez/opencv
14. Jia, Y., et al.: Caffe: Convolutional architecture for fast feature embedding. arXiv preprint arXiv:1408.5093 (2014)
15. Kay, W., et al.: The kinetics human action video dataset. CoRR (2017)
16. Kingma, D.P., Welling, M.: Auto-encoding variational bayes. arXiv preprint arXiv:1312.6114 (2013)

17. Krähenbühl, P., Doersch, C., Donahue, J., Darrell, T.: Data-dependent initializations of convolutional neural networks. arXiv preprint arXiv:1511.06856 (2015)
18. Krizhevsky, A., Sutskever, I., Hinton, G.E.: ImageNet classification with deep convolutional neural networks. In: Advances in Neural Information Processing Systems (2012)
19. Kuehne, H., Jhuang, H., Garrote, E., Poggio, T., Serre, T.: HMDB: a large video database for human motion recognition. In: Proceedings of the International Conference on Computer Vision (ICCV) (2011)
20. Larsson, G., Maire, M., Shakhnarovich, G.: Colorization as a proxy task for visual understanding. arXiv preprint arXiv:1703.04044 (2017)
21. Lee, H.Y., Huang, J.B., Singh, M.K., Yang, M.H.: Unsupervised representation learning by sorting sequences. In: IEEE International Conference on Computer Vision (ICCV) (2017)
22. Luo, Z., Peng, B., Huang, D.A., Alahi, A., Fei-Fei, L.: Unsupervised learning of long-term motion dynamics for videos. In: IEEE Conference on Computer Vision and Pattern Recognition (CVPR) (2017)
23. Milbich, T., Bautista, M., Sutter, E., Ommer, B.: Unsupervised video understanding by reconciliation of posture similarities. In: Proceedings of the IEEE International Conference on Computer Vision (ICCV) (2017)
24. Misra, I., Zitnick, C.L., Hebert, M.: Unsupervised learning using sequential verification for action recognition (2016)
25. Ngiam, J., Khosla, A., Kim, M., Nam, J., Lee, H., Ng, A.Y.: Multimodal deep learning. In: ICML (2011)
26. Noroozi, M., Favaro, P.: Unsupervised learning of visual representations by solving jigsaw puzzles. In: Leibe, B., Matas, J., Sebe, N., Welling, M. (eds.) ECCV 2016. LNCS, vol. 9910, pp. 69–84. Springer, Cham (2016). https://doi.org/10.1007/978-3-319-46466-4_5
27. Noroozi, M., Pirsiavash, H., Favaro, P.: Representation learning by learning to count. arXiv preprint arXiv:1708.06734 (2017)
28. Noroozi, M., Vinjimoor, A., Favaro, P., Pirsiavash, H.: Boosting self-supervised learning via knowledge transfer. arXiv preprint arXiv:1805.00385 (2018)
29. Paszke, A., Gross, S., Chintala, S., Chanan, G.: PyTorch (2017)
30. Purushwalkam, S., Gupta, A.: Pose from action: unsupervised learning of pose features based on motion. arXiv preprint arXiv:1609.05420 (2016)
31. Russakovsky, O., et al.: ImageNet large scale visual recognition challenge. Int. J. Comput. Vis. (IJCV) **115**, 211–252 (2015)
32. Sanakoyeu, A., Bautista, M., Ommer, B.: Deep unsupervised learning of visual similarities. Pattern Recogn. **78**, 331–343 (2018)
33. Simonyan, K., Zisserman, A.: Two-stream convolutional networks for action recognition in videos. In: Conference on Neural Information Processing Systems (NIPS) (2014)
34. Soomro, K., Zamir, A.R., Shah, M.: UCF101: a dataset of 101 human actions classes from videos in the wild. arXiv preprint arXiv:1212.0402 (2012)
35. Springenberg, J.T., Dosovitskiy, A., Brox, T., Riedmiller, M.: Striving for simplicity: the all convolutional net. arXiv preprint arXiv:1412.6806 (2014)
36. Vincent, P., Larochelle, H., Lajoie, I., Bengio, Y., Manzagol, P.A.: Stacked denoising autoencoders: learning useful representations in a deep network with a local denoising criterion. J. Mach. Learn. Res. **11**, 3371–3408 (2010)
37. Vondrick, C., Pirsiavash, H., Torralba, A.: Generating videos with scene dynamics. In: Conference on Neural Information Processing Systems (NIPS) (2016)

38. Wang, L., Li, Y., Lazebnik, S.: Learning deep structure-preserving image-text embeddings. CoRR (2015)

39. Wang, X., Farhadi, A., Gupta, A.: Actions ∼ transformations. In: CVPR (2016)

40. Wang, X., Gupta, A.: Unsupervised learning of visual representations using videos. In: Proceedings of the IEEE International Conference on Computer Vision (2015)

41. Yang, X., Ramesh, P., Chitta, R., Madhvanath, S., Bernal, E.A., Luo, J.: Deep multimodal representation learning from temporal data. CoRR (2017)

42. Zhang, R., Isola, P., Efros, A.A.: Colorful image colorization. In: Leibe, B., Matas, J., Sebe, N., Welling, M. (eds.) ECCV 2016. LNCS, vol. 9907, pp. 649–666. Springer, Cham (2016). https://doi.org/10.1007/978-3-319-46487-9_40

KS(conf): A Light-Weight Test if a ConvNet Operates Outside of Its Specifications

Rémy Sun[1] and Christoph H. Lampert[2(✉)]

[1] École Normale Supérieure de Rennes (ENS Rennes), Bruz, France
[2] Institute of Science and Technology Austria (IST Austria), Klosterneuburg, Austria
chl@ist.ac.at

Abstract. Computer vision systems for automatic image categorization have become accurate and reliable enough that they can run continuously for days or even years as components of real-world commercial applications. A major open problem in this context, however, is quality control. Good classification performance can only be expected if systems run under the specific conditions, in particular data distributions, that they were trained for. Surprisingly, none of the currently used deep network architectures have a built-in functionality that could detect if a network operates on data from a distribution it was not trained for, such that potentially a warning to the human users could be triggered.

In this work, we describe KS(conf), a procedure for detecting such *outside of specifications (out-of-specs)* operation, based on statistical testing of the network outputs. We show by extensive experiments using the ImageNet, AwA2 and DAVIS datasets on a variety of ConvNets architectures that KS(conf) reliably detects out-of-specs situations. It furthermore has a number of properties that make it a promising candidate for practical deployment: it is easy to implement, adds almost no overhead to the system, works with all networks, including pretrained ones, and requires no a priori knowledge of how the data distribution could change.

1 Introduction

With the renaissance of deep convolutional networks (ConvNets), computer vision systems have become accurate and reliable enough to perform tasks of practical relevance autonomously over long periods of time. This has opened opportunities for the deployment of automated image recognition systems in many commercial settings, such as in video surveillance, self-driving vehicles, and social media. A major concern our society has about automatic decision systems is their reliability: if decisions are made by a trained classifier instead of a person, how can we be sure that the system works reliably now, and that it will continue to do so in the future?

Quality control for trained systems typically relies on extensive testing, making use of data that (a) was not used during training, and (b) reflects the conditions at prediction time. If a system works well on a sufficiently large amount of

© Springer Nature Switzerland AG 2019
T. Brox et al. (Eds.): GCPR 2018, LNCS 11269, pp. 244–259, 2019.
https://doi.org/10.1007/978-3-030-12939-2_18

data fulfilling both conditions, practical experience as well as machine learning theory tell us that it will also work well in the future. We call this *operating within the specifications (within-specs)*.

In practice, problems emerge when the possibility exists that the data distribution at prediction time differs from our expectations at training time, i.e. when condition (b) is violated. Such *operating outside of the specifications (out-of-specs)* can happen for a variety of reasons, ranging from user errors, over lens errors or sensor fatigue, to unexpected objects occurring in the images, and even deliberate sabotage. Standard performance guarantees do not hold anymore in the out-of-specs situations, and the prediction quality often drops substantially. This is irrespective of how well and on how much data a network was originally trained: even a network that works with 100% accuracy under within-specs conditions can produce predictions at chance level when operating out-of-specs.

This phenomenon is in principle well known, but it has largely been ignored by academics, who control the experimental setting and can thereby avoid out-of-specs conditions. For practitioners, however, the out-of-specs problem has emerged as one of the major obstacles for deplaying deep learning solutions for real-world applications. Consequently, today's most successful classification architectures, multi-class ConvNets, are completely unable to tell if they operate inside or outside their specifications. For example, for any input, even random noise, they will always predict one of the class labels from the training set.

One can imagine many ways to mitigate this problem, for example, changing the network's architecture and/or its training objective. However, any method that requires changes to the training procedure strongly reduces the real-world applicability of such approaches. The reason is that training ConvNets requires expert knowledge and large computational resources. In practice, most end users rely on pretrained networks, which they use as black boxes. This means they can only influence the inputs and observe the network outputs. Sometimes, even influencing the inputs might not be possible, e.g. in embedded devices, such as smart cameras, or in security related appliances that prevent such manipulations.

Consequently, it is highly desirable to have an automatic test that can reliably tell when a ConvNet operates out-of-specs, e.g. to send a warning to a human operator, but that does not require modifications to any ConvNet internals. Our main contribution in this work is such a test, KS(conf), which is light-weight and theoretically well-founded. In the subsequent sections, we introduce the test, discuss its properties and experimentally validate its performance.

2   Testing for Out-of-Specs Operation

The task of a test for out-of-specs operation is to determine whether the conditions under which a classifier currently operates differs from the conditions for which it was created. Assuming a fully automatic classification system, the only difference that can occur is a change in the input data distribution between training/validation and prediction time. This reasoning leads to a canonical blueprint for identifying out-of-specs behavior: perform a statistical test if any batch of data observed at prediction time originates from the same underlying data distribution as data for which we know it reflects within-specs operation. Working with batches has the advantage that it will be possible to tune the sensitivity of the method, because statistical tests become more and more reliable the more samples they operate on. In contrast, any method that, e.g., tries to classify individual test-time images into outliers and regular samples is inherently less powerful, as it cannot judge all properties of the observed distribution. For example, it might be completely acceptable for a network to occasionally encounter a very dark image, but if at some time all input images become underexposed that suggests a problem in the image acquisition pipeline.

While statistical tests are powerful, they tend to suffer heavily from the *curse of dimensionality*. In practice, reliable tests between sets of inputs (i.e. high-dimensional images) are intractable. Therefore, and because ultimately we are interested in the network predictions anyway, we propose to work with the distribution of network outputs. For a multi-class classifier with many classes, the outputs are multi-dimensional, though, and their distribution might still be intractable. Therefore, we suggest to use only the real-valued confidence scores of the predicted labels. These values are one-dimensional, available in most practical applications, and, as our experiments will show, they provide a strong proxy for detecting changes in the distribution of inputs. Because evaluating the network is a deterministic function, the output-based test does not add additional false positives to the test: if reference and test-time distribution of the inputs are identical, then the distribution of outputs will be identical as well. It would in principle be possible that an output-based test overlooks relevant differences between the input distributions. Our experiments will show, however, that for a well-designed test this seems to be at best a minor issue.

In addition to the probabilistic aspects, a test that aims at practical application should have additional features, which we formulate as further conditions:

- **universal.** The same test procedure should be applicable to different network architectures.
- **pretrained-ready.** The test should be applicable to pretrained and fine-tuned networks and not require any specific steps during network training.
- **black-box ready.** The test should not require knowledge of any ConvNet internals, such as the depth, activation functions, or weight matrices.
- **non-parametric.** The test should not require a priori knowledge on *how* the data distribution could change.

2.1   Notation

We assume an arbitrary fixed ConvNet, f, with K outputs, i.e. for an input image X we obtain an output vector $Y := f(X)$ with $Y \in \mathbb{R}^K$. Assuming a standard multi-class setting with a softmax activation function at the output layer, we have $0 \leq Y[k] \leq 1$ for $k = 1, \ldots, K$ and $\sum_{k=1}^{K} Y[k] = 1$. For any output Y, the predicted class label is $C := \arg\max_{k=1}^{K} Y[k]$, with ties broken arbitrarily. The confidence of this prediction is $Z := Y[C]$, i.e. the Cth entry of the output Y, or equivalently $Z := \max_{k=1}^{K} Y[k]$, the largest entry of Y.

We treat X as a random variable with (unknown) underlying probability distribution P_X. Consequently, Z becomes a random variable as well, and we call its induced probability distribution P_Z. We can now formally state the problem that we try to solve.

Definition 1. *A classifier is said to* operate out-of-specs, *if the input data distribution, P_X, at prediction time differs from the one at training time. It is said to* predict out-of-specs, *if the output score distribution, P_Z, at prediction time differs from the one at training time.*

In the rest of the paper, we demonstrate that testing for *out-of-specs prediction* can serve as an easy to implement and computationally light-weight proxy of testing for *out-of-specs operations*.

2.2   KS(conf): Kolmogorov-Smirnov Test of Confidences

We suggest a procedure for out-of-specs testing called KS(conf), which stands for *Kolmogorov-Smirnov test of confidences*. Its main component is the application of a Kolmogorov-Smirnov (KS) test [16] to the distribution of confidence values. KS(conf) consists of three main routines: *calibration, batch testing* and (optionally) *filtering*.

Calibration. In the calibration step, we establish a reference distribution for within-specs conditions. It is meant to be run when the classifier system is installed at its destination, but a human expert is still present to ensure that the environment is indeed within-specs for the duration of the calibration phase.

To characterize the within-specs regime, we use a set of validation images, $X_1^{\text{val}}, \dots, X_n^{\text{val}}$ and their corresponding confidence scores, $Z_1^{\text{val}}, \dots, Z_n^{\text{val}}$. For simplicity we assume all confidence values to be distinct. In practice, this can be enforced by perturbing the values by a small amount of random noise.

The random variable Z is one-dimensional with known range. Therefore, one can, in principle, estimate its probability density function (pdf) from a reasonably sized set of samples, e.g. by dividing the support $[0, 1]$ into regular bins and counting the fraction of samples falling into each of them. For our purposes, uniform bins would be inefficient, though, because ConvNet confidence scores are typically far from uniformly distributed. To avoid a need for data-dependent binning, KS(conf) starts with a processing step. First, we estimate the *inverse cumulative distribution function (inv-cdf)*, F^{-1}, which is possible without binning. First, we sort the confidence values such that we can assume the values $Z_1^{\text{val}}, \dots, Z_n^{\text{val}}$ in monotonically increasing order. Then, for any $p \in [0, 1]$, the estimated *inv-cdf* value at p is obtained by linear interpolation:

$$F^{-1}(p) = \frac{k}{n} + \frac{p - Z_k^{\text{val}}}{n(Z_{k+1}^{\text{val}} - Z_k^{\text{val}})} \quad \text{for } k \in \{0, \dots, n\} \text{ with } p \in [Z_k^{\text{val}}, Z_{k+1}^{\text{val}}], \quad (1)$$

with the convention $Z_0^{\text{val}} = 0$ and $Z_{n+1}^{\text{val}} = 1$.

For KS(conf), the quantities we ultimately work with are $Z' := F^{-1}(Z)$, where F^{-1} remains fixed after calibration. By definition of F^{-1}, the random variable Z' is distributed approximately uniformly in $[0, 1]$, when Z's distribution matches the distribution at calibration time. If the distribution of Z changes at a later time, this will be reflected by the distribution of Z' differing from uniformity. The above transformation is useful for two reasons: in the *batch testing* phase, we will not have to compare two arbitrary distributions to each other, but only the currently observed distribution with the uniform one. In the *filtering* stage we will be able to rely on easy-to-use and efficient uniform bins.

Batch Testing. The main step of KS(conf) is *batch testing*, which determines at any time of the classifier's runtime if the system predicts within-specs or out-of-specs. This step happens at prediction time after the system has been deployed to perform its actual task.

Testing is performed on batches of images, $X'_1, \ldots, X'_m$, that can, but do not have to, coincide with the image batches that are often used for efficient Conv-Nets evaluation on parallel architectures such as GPUs. We apply the inv-cdf that was learned during calibration to the corresponding network confidences, resulting in values, $Z'_1, \ldots, Z'_m$, which, as above, we consider sorted. We then compute the Kolmogorov-Smirnov test statistics:

$$\text{KS} := \max \left(\max_{k=1,\ldots,m} \left\{ Z'_k - \frac{k-1}{m} \right\}, \quad \max_{k=1,\ldots,m} \left\{ \frac{k}{m} - Z'_k \right\} \right). \quad (2)$$

KS reflects the biggest absolute difference between the (empirical) cdf of the observed batch and a linear increasing reference cdf. For a system that operates within-specs (and therefore predicts within-specs), Z' will be close to uniformly distributed, and KS can be expected to be small. It will not be exactly 0, though, because of random fluctuations and finite-sample effects. A particularly appealing property of the KS is that its distribution can be determined and used to derive confidence thresholds [16]. This results in the Kolmogorov-Smirnov (KS) test: for any $\alpha \in [0, 1]$ there is a threshold θ_α, such that when we consider the test outcome *positive* for KS $> \theta_\alpha$, then the expected probability of a false positive test result is α. The values θ_α can be computed numerically [15] or approximated well (in the regime $n \gg m$ that we are mainly interested in) by $\theta_\alpha \approx \left(\frac{-0.5 \log(\frac{\alpha}{2})}{m} \right)^{\frac{1}{2}}$.

The KS-test has several advantages over other tests. In particular, it is *distribution-free*, i.e. the thresholds θ_α are the same regardless of what the distribution $P_{Z'}$ was. Also, it is invariant under reparameterization of the sample space, which in particular means that the KS statistics and the test outcome we compute in comparing Z' to the uniform distribution is in fact identical to the one for comparing original Z to the within-specs distribution. Also, it means that KS(conf) is not negatively affected from networks that produce overly confident outputs, and the KS score itself is compatible with and not affected by potential network score calibration techniques.

Filtering. A particularly challenging case of out-of-specs operation is when the distribution at prediction time is almost the reference one, but a certain fraction of the data is unexpected, e.g. images of object classes that were not present at training time. In such cases, only sending a warning to a human operator might not be a satisfactory solution: the difference in distribution is subtle and might not become apparent from just looking at the input data. We suggest to help the operator by highlighting *which* of the images in the batch are suspicious and the likely cause of the alarm. Unfortunately, on the level of individual samples it is not possible to identify suspicious examples with certainty, except when the reference distribution and the unexpected data are so different that they have disjoint support. Instead, we suggest a *filtering* approach: if a batch of images triggers the out-of-specs test, we accompany the warning with a small number of example images from the batch. The example images should contain as high a fraction of unexpected samples as possible.

In KS(conf), we propose to use a density ratio criterion: if the desired number of example images is w and the batch size is m, we split the interval $[0, 1]$ uniformly into $\lceil \frac{n}{w} \rceil$ bins. We count how many of the values $Z'_1, \ldots, Z'_m$ fall into each bin, and identify the bin with the highest count. The expected number of samples per bin is w (up to rounding), and the selected bin contains at least that many samples. To reduce that number to exactly w, we take a random subset.

The filtering procedure can be expected to produce a subset with a ratio of suspicious to expected images as high as the highest ratio of density between them. This is, because the reference distribution is uniform, so samples from the reference distribution contribute equally to each bin. A bin that contains many more samples than the expected value is therefore likely the result of the uneven distribution of unexpected images.

Resource Requirements. As the above description shows, the KS(conf) test can be implemented in a straight-forward way and requires only standard components, such as sorting and binning. The largest resource requirements occur during *calibration*, where the network has to be evaluated for n inputs and the resulting confidence values have to be sorted. The *calibration* step is performed only once and offline though, before actually running the classification system in production mode, so a $O(n \log n)$ runtime is not a major problem, and even very large n remain practical. A potential issue is the $O(n)$ storage requirements, if calibration is meant to run on very small devices or very large validation sets. Luckily, there exist specific data structures that allow constructing approximate (inv-)cdfs of arbitrary precision in an incremental way from streaming data. For example, *t-digests* [6] use adaptive bins to build an empirical cdf in a streaming fashion. The memory requirements can be made $O(1)$ this way, with well-understood trade-offs between the memory footprint and the quality of the cdf approximation.

The *batch testing* step runs during the standard operation of the classification system and therefore needs to be as efficient as possible. Implemented as described above, it requires applying the inv-cdf function, which typically requires a binary search, sorting the list of m confidence values and identifying the maximum out of $2m$ values. Consequently, the runtime complexity is $O(m \log n)$ and the memory requirement is $O(m)$. With only logarithmic overhead, the added computational cost is typically negligible compared to evaluating the ConvNet itself. For even more restricted settings, incremental variants of the Kolmogorov-Smirnov test have been developed, see e.g. [20].

The *filtering* step also adds very little overhead. The transformed confidence values are already available and the bins are regularly spaced, so creating the bin counts and finding the bin with the largest number of entries requires only $O(m)$ operations and $O(m)$ memory.

2.3   Related Work

The problem of differences between data distributions at training and prediction time are well known, see e.g. [2]. Nevertheless, none of the existing ConvNet architectures for image classification have the built-in functionality to identify when they operate outside of their specifications. Instead, one typically tries to ensure that at least out-of-specs prediction will not occur, e.g. by training invariant representations [7]. Most such *domain adaptation* methods, however, require samples from the data distribution at prediction time and specific modifications of the network training, so they are not applicable for end users, who rely on pretrained classifiers. An exception is [21], which acts at prediction time, but only addresses changes in class priors. A specific out-of-specs situation is when new classes occur in the input data. Specific systems to handle these have been suggested for *incremental* [19] or *open set learning* [3,13]. These methods also work at training time, though, and only for specific classifier architectures.

In [4], the authors describe a method for recognizing atypical individual samples that might stem from any data distribution. The method is not precise enough for real-world applications, but we compare to it in our experimental section. A similar route is followed by recent efforts on failure prediction, i.e. when the output of a classifier is incorrect [1,5,29]. This task is orthogonal to ours, as it applies to the situation where the network operates on data from the within-specs distribution, but nevertheless some outputs should not be trusted. These methods classify individual samples and are therefore not able to tell differences on the distributional level. Similarly, score calibrating [8,18] fulfills a different purpose, as it only influences how confident the network is about individual examples. Combining score calibration with KS(conf) poses no problem, though, as the KS-statistics is left invariant by monotonic per-output operations.

On the mathematical level, our work shares some characteristics with *concept drift detection* in time series. Most such methods are not directly applicable, because they require label annotations (e.g. [9,27]) or low-dimensional data (e.g. [14,23]). An exception is [30], which even discusses the use of a Kolmogorov-Smirnov test. That is in the context of binary classifiers, though, without a clear way to generalize the results to multi-class classification with large label sets.

3 Experiments

In this section, we report on an experimental evaluation of KS(conf) and other baselines for detecting out-of-specs operation. As most detection tasks, out-of-specs detection can be analyzed in terms of two core quantities: the *false positive rate (FPR)* which should be as low as possible, and the *true positive rate (TPR)* which should be as high as possible. While both quantities are important in practice, they play different roles. The TPR should be high, because it measures the ability of the test to perform the task it was designed for: detecting out-of-specs behavior. The FPR should be low, because otherwise the test will annoy the users with false alarms, which typically has the consequence that the test is switched off or its alarms ignored. A practical test should therefore allow its FPR to be controlled and ideally adjusted on-the-fly to a user-specific preference level. Our experimental protocol reflects this setting: for different expected FPRs we will report the TPR in a variety of settings explained below.

For KS(conf), adjusting the FPR is straightforward, as it directly corresponds to the α parameter. When relying on the closed-form expression or tabulated values for the threshold, α can be changed at any time without overhead. Otherwise, adjusting α requires calling a numeric subroutine, but the expensive calibration step never has to be re-run, and no validation data is required. Many other tests, in particular the *mean* baseline we describe later, do not have this property. To adjust their FPR, one has to repeat a calibration step, which in particular requires access to new or previously stored validation data.

3.1 Experimental Protocol

We analyze the behavior of KS(conf) and other tests in different scenarios by performing a large-scale study using five popular ConvNet architectures: ResNet50 [10] and VGG19 [24] are standards in the computer vision community; SqueezeNet [12] and MobileNet25 [11] have smaller computational and memory requirements, making them suitable, e.g., for mobile and embedded applications; NASNetAlarge [31] achieves state-of-the-art performance in the ImageNet challenges, but is quite large and slow. Details of the networks are given in Table 1.

As main data source, we use the ImageNet ILSVRC 2012 dataset [22] that consists of natural images of 1000 object categories. All ConvNets are trained on the 1.2 million training images[1]. We use the 50.000 validation images to characterize the within-specs behavior in the calibration phase and the 100.000 test images to simulate the situation at prediction time. We do not make use of ground truth labels of the validation and test part at any time, as those would not be available for an actually deployed system either.

Our experimental evaluation has two parts. First, we establish how well KS(conf) and the baselines respect the chosen false positive rates, and how well they are able to detect changes of the input image distribution. We also benchmark KS(conf)'s ability to identify a set of suspicious images out of a stream of

---

[1] We use the pretrained models from https://github.com/taehoonlee/tensornets.

Table 1. Details of the ConvNets used for the experimental evaluation. Evaluation time (excluding image preprocessing and network initialization) for different batch sizes (bs) on powerful GPU hardware (NVIDIA Tesla P100) or weak CPU hardware (Raspberry Pi Zero). Missing entries are due to memory limitations.

Network name	ILSVRC2012 error (top-5)	Number of parameters	speed: GPU			CPU
			$bs = 1$	$bs = 10$	$bs = 100$	$bs = 1$
MobileNet25 [11]	24.2%	0.48 M	3.3 ms	5.2 ms	34 ms	682 ms
SqueezeNet [12]	21.4%	1.2 M	5.7 ms	10.1 ms	113 ms	2288 ms
ResNet50 [10]	7.9%	26 M	12.2 ms	34.1 ms	293 ms	—
VGG19 [24]	10.2%	144 M	9.9 ms	53.5 ms	385 ms	—
NASNetAlarge [31]	3.9%	94 M	45.8 ms	227.9 ms	2107 ms	—

images that contains ordinary as well as unexpected images. Second, we provide further insights by analyzing how different network architectures react to a variety of changes in the input distribution, e.g. due to sensor modifications, based on how easy or hard it is for KS(conf) to detect those.

3.2 Baselines

There is no established standard for testing if the distribution of network outputs coincides between training and prediction time. However, one can imagine a variety of ad-hoc ways, and we include some of them as experimental baselines.

Mean-Based Tests. It is a generally accepted fact in the community that ConvNets are very confident (often too confident) in their decisions for data of the type they were trained on, but less confident on other data. This suggests a straight-forward test for out-of-specs behavior: for a batch of images, compute the average confidence and report a positive test if that value lies below a threshold.

We include several baselines based on this reasoning that differ in how they set the threshold. The main two constructions are:

- *z*-test. We compute the mean, μ, and variance, σ^2, of the confidence values on the validation set. Under an assumption of Gaussianity, the distribution of the average confidence over a within-specs batch of size m will have variance σ^2/m. We set the threshold to identify the lower α-quantile of that Gaussian.
- (non-parametric) mean test. To avoid the assumption of Gaussianity, we use a bootstrap-like strategy: we sample many batches from the validation set and compute the mean confidence for each of them. The threshold is set such that at most a fraction α of the batches is flagged as positive.

Furthermore, we include a log-*z* and log-*mean* test. These do the same as the *z*-test and the *mean*-tests, respectively, but work with the logarithms of confidence values instead of the actual values.

The above tests are asymmetric: they will detect if the mean confidence becomes too low, but not if it becomes too high. To be safe, we also include symmetric versions of the above tests, for which we determine two thresholds, an upper and a lower one, allowing for $\alpha/2$ false positives on each side.

Label-Based Test. Instead of using the confidence values, it would also be possible to detect out-of-specs behavior from the distribution of actually predicted labels.

- χ^2 **test.** During calibration, we compute the relative frequency of labels on the validation set. For any batch, we perform a χ^2 goodness-of-fit test, whether the empirical distribution is likely to originate from the stored one and report a positive test if the p-value lies below the desired FPR.

Single-Sample Test. Previous work on *open world* classification has suggested to predict for each sample if it comes from a known or unknown class. While this task is not the same as identifying when a network operates in out-of-specs condition, we nevertheless compare to the state-of-the-art method [4] as a reference baseline from the literature.

3.3   Results: False Positive Rates

As discussed above, it is a crucial property of a test to have a controllable (and ideally arbitrarily low) false positive rate. We check this for KS(conf) and the batch-based baselines by running all tests on batches sampled randomly from the ILSVRC test set, i.e. fully in within-specs conditions. Therefore, all positive tests are false positives, and the fraction of tests that are positive is the FPR.

The results are depicted in Fig. 1, where we report the average FPR over 10.000 random batches. One can see that KS(conf), *mean* and *log-mean* tests, as well as their symmetric counterparts, respect the FPR well. For KS(conf), this is expected, as the underlying Kolmogorov-Smirnov test has well understood

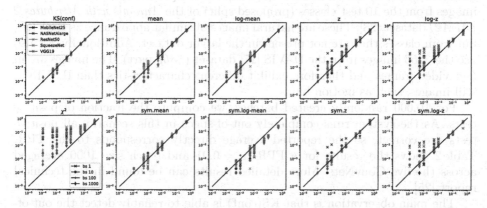

Fig. 1. False positive rates of KS(conf) and baselines for different ConvNets and different batch sizes (*bs*). *x*-axis: target FPR, *y*-axis: observed FPR.

statistics and universal thresholds are available. For the other four tests, the thresholds are obtained from simulating the procedure of testing on within-specs data many timés. This ensures that the FPR is respected, but it requires access to the validation data any time the FPR is meant to be adapted, and it can be very time consuming, especially if small FPRs are desired.

In contrast, z-test and log-z test and their symmetric variants often produce more false positives than intended, especially for small batch sizes. This is because their thresholds are computed based on an assumption of Gaussianity, which is a good approximation only for reasonably large batch sizes. Finally, the label-based χ^2-test produces far too many false positives. The likely reason for this is the high dimensionality of the data: a rule of thumb says that the χ^2-test is reliable when each bin of the distribution has at least 5 expected entries. This criterion is clearly violated in our situation, where the number of samples in a batch is often even smaller than the number of bins.

We also applied the *single-sample test* [4] to all ILSVRC samples, which resulted in (not tunable) FPRs of 0.13 (MobileNet25), 0.16 (VGG19), 0.08 (ResNet50), 0.07 (SqueezeNet) and 0.07 (NASNetAlarge), which is clearly too high for usage in a real-world system. Consequently, we exclude the *label-based test* and the *single-sample test* from further experiments. We keep the z and log-z tests, but with the caveat that they should only be used with large batches.

In summary, of all methods, only KS(conf) achieves the two desirable properties that the FPR is respected for all batch sizes, and that adjusting the thresholds is possible efficiently and without access to validation data.

3.4   Results: Detection Rate

The ultimate quality measure for any test is whether, at a fixed FPR, it can reliably detect changes in the input distribution. To measure this, we operate the ConvNets under out-of-specs conditions by evaluating them on image data that has different characteristics than ILSVRC. Specifically, we use the 7913 images from the 10 test classes (proposed split) of the *Animals with Attributes 2 (AwA2)* dataset [28]. These are natural images of similar appearance as ILSVRC, but from classes that are not present in the larger dataset. Additionally, we also use the 3456 images from the DAVIS [17] dataset (*480p* part). The images are in fact video frames and therefore exhibit different characteristics than ILSVRC's still images, such as motion blur.

For 10.000 randomly created batches, we compute the fraction of positive tests. As the system runs completely out-of-specs in this scenario, all positive tests are correct, so the reported average directly corresponds to the TPR. Table 2 shows the results for a FPR $\alpha = 0.01$ and batch size 1000 averaged across the five ConvNets. More detailed results can be found in the technical report [25].

The main observation is that KS(conf) is able to reliably detect the out-of-specs behavior for all data sources, but none of the other tests are. All mean-based tests fail in at least some cases. To shed more light on this effect, we

Table 2. True positive rates of KS(conf) and baselines, averaged across 5 ConvNets, under different out-of-specs conditions. Failing test (TPR < 1) are marked in bold.

	KS(conf)	mean	logmean	z	log-z	sym. mean	sym. log-mean	sym. z	sym. log-z
AwA2-bat	1.00	1.00	1.00	1.00	1.00	1.00	1.00	1.00	1.00
AwA2-blue whale	1.00	**0.20**	**0.00**	**0.20**	0.00	**0.80**	0.00	**0.80**	**0.62**
AwA2-bobcat	1.00	**0.00**	**0.00**	**0.00**	**0.00**	1.00	**0.00**	1.00	1.00
AwA2-dolphin	1.00	1.00	**0.79**	1.00	**0.79**	1.00	**0.66**	1.00	**0.70**
AwA2-giraffe	1.00	1.00	1.00	1.00	1.00	1.00	1.00	1.00	1.00
AwA2-horse	1.00	1.00	1.00	1.00	1.00	1.00	1.00	1.00	1.00
AwA2-rat	1.00	1.00	1.00	1.00	1.00	1.00	1.00	1.00	1.00
AwA2-seal	1.00	**0.20**	**0.20**	**0.20**	**0.20**	1.00	**0.20**	1.00	1.00
AwA2-sheep	1.00	**0.01**	**0.00**	**0.00**	**0.00**	**0.65**	**0.00**	**0.63**	**0.82**
AwA2-walrus	1.00	1.00	1.00	1.00	1.00	1.00	1.00	1.00	1.00
DAVIS	1.00	1.00	1.00	1.00	1.00	1.00	1.00	1.00	1.00

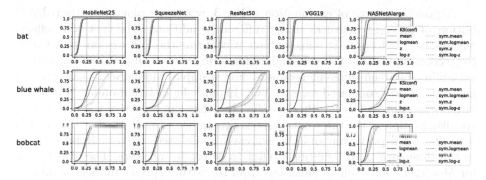

Fig. 2. Selected results for detecting out-of-specs behavior of different tests for different ConvNets and data sources. x-axis: proportions between unexpected (AwA2) and expected (ILSVRC) data in batch. y-axis: detection rate (TPR).

performed more fine-grained experiments, where we create batches as mixtures of *ILSVRC2012-test* and *AwA2* images with different mixture proportions. Figure 2 shows exemplary results as a curve of mixture proportion versus TPR, see [25] for the complete figure. The results fall into three characteristic classes: (1) some sources, here *bat*, are identified reliably by all tests for all ConvNets. (2) other sources, here *bobcat*, are identified reliably by some tests, but not at all by others. (3) for some sources, here *blue whale*, tests show different sensitivities, i.e. some tests work only for high mixture proportions. Interestingly, the results differ substantially between networks. For example, for ResNet50, perfect detection occurs at lower mixture proportions than for MobileNet25. For NASNetAlarge on *blue whale* data, the *sym.mean* and *log-mean* tests work as least as well as KS(conf), but the same tests on the same images fail completely for VGG19.

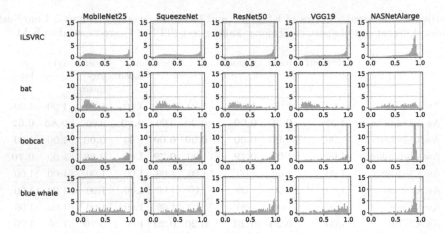

Fig. 3. Distribution of confidence scores for different ConvNets and data sources. x-axis: confidence score, y-axis: normalized probability.

A possible source of explanation is Fig. 3, where we plot the output distribution of different networks under different conditions. The first row reflects within-specs behavior. To some extent, it confirms the folk wisdom that Conv-Net scores are biased towards high values. However, it also shows remarkable variability between different networks. For example, MobileNet25 has a rather flat distribution compared to, e.g., VGG19, and the distribution for NASNetA-large peaks not at 1 but rather at 0.9. The other three rows of the figure show the distribution in the three out-of-specs situations of Fig. 2. For *bat*, the pattern is as one can expect from an unknown class: confidences are overall much lower, so the difference in distribution is easy to detect for all tests. The distribution for *blue whale* data differs much less from the within-specs situation, making it harder to detect. Finally, *bobcat* shows truly unexpected behavior: the networks are overall more confident in their predictions than for within-specs data. This explains in particular why the single-sided mean-based tests fail in this case.

Overall, our experiments show that KS(conf) works reliably in all experimental conditions we tested. This is in agreement with the expectations from theory, as the underlying Kolmogorov-Smirnov test is known to have asymptotic power 1, meaning that if given enough data, it will detect any possible difference between distributions. In contrast to this, the mean-based tests show highly volatile behavior, making them unsuitable as a reliable out-of-specs test.

3.5   Results: Filtering

To benchmark the ability of KS(conf) to filter out images of an unexpected distribution, we run the filtering routine in the setting of the previous section, i.e. when the data at prediction time is a mixture of ILSVRC and AwA2 images. Each time KS(conf) reports a positive test, we identify a subset of 10 images and measure how many of them were indeed samples from the AwA2 classes. There is no established baseline for this task, so we compare against the intuitive baseline of reporting the subset consisting of the 10 images with lowest confidence.

A figure of results can be found in the extended technical report [25]. It shows that KS(conf) consistently creates better subsets than random selection would. Selecting the images of lowest confidence instead sometimes works well, but it also badly fails in some cases, where it performs worse than even random sampling. The reason lies in the fact that out-of-specs operation does not always cause lower ConvNet confidences, as we had already observed in Fig. 3.

3.6   Results: Camera System Changes

Another important reason for an automatic imaging systems to operate out-of-specs is changes to the camera system. We benchmark the performance of KS(conf) to detect such, sometimes subtle, changes by running it on images that we obtain from the ILSVRC test set by applying characteristic manipulations. Because of the results of the previous section and space limitations, we only report on the results of KS(conf) here, not the baselines. Our main goal is to gain insight into how different ConvNets react if their inputs change due to external effects, such as incorrect camera installation, incorrect image exposure, or broken sensor pixels. Specifically, we perform the following manipulations.

- **loss-of-focus.** We blur the image by filtering with a Gaussian kernel.
- **sensor noise.** We add Gaussian random noise to each pixel.
- **dead pixels.** We set a random subset of pixels to pure black or white.
- **wrong geometry.** We flip the image horizontally or vertically or rotate it by 90, 180 or 270°,
- **incorrect RGB/BGR color handling.** We swap R and B color channels.
- **over-/under-exposure.** We scale all image intensities towards 0 or 255.

Details of their implementation and plots of the results can be found in [25]. In the following, we summarize the main results. With a sensitive statistical test, such as KS(conf), it is possible to detect even subtle changes to the input images from the distribution of output scores. This includes cases that are hardly visible to the human eye, such as weak Gaussian smoothing, a small number of dead pixels, or a small amount of additive noise. All networks are affected by such manipulations, with VGG19 reacting more robustly than the others. Contrary to classic computer vision, ConvNets are generally not invariant to changes in the exposure level. For most networks, already a scale factor of 1/2 can be detected reliably. An exception is NASNetAlarge, that seems more invariant to (small amounts of) scaling and exposure changes. All networks are invariant to horizontal flips of the image, presumably because this is explicitly enforced during training. Vertical flips, rotations and incorrect color channels, however, are easily detectable. This is useful, as it allows, e.g., an automatic detection if a camera system has been wrongly installed or runs with wrong preprocessing.

4   Conclusions

In this work, we discussed the importance of being able to identify when a classifier operates outside of its specifications, i.e. when the data distribution it operates on differs from the distribution of data it was trained for. We described a procedure, KS(conf), based on the classical statistical Kolmogorov-Smirnov test, applied to the distribution of the confidence values of the predicted labels. By extensive experiments we showed that KS(conf) reliably identifies out-of-specs behavior in a variety of settings, including images of unexpected classes in the data, as well as effects of incorrect camera settings or sensor fatigue. We hope that our work leads to more research on making ConvNet classifiers trustworthy. Our code and data are available from https://cvml.ist.ac.at/publications.html.

Acknowledgments. This work was funded in parts by the European Research Council under the European Union's Seventh Framework Programme (FP7/2007-2013)/ERC grant agreement no. 308036.

References

1. Bansal, A., Farhadi, A., Parikh, D.: Towards transparent systems: semantic characterization of failure modes. In: Fleet, D., Pajdla, T., Schiele, B., Tuytelaars, T. (eds.) ECCV 2014. LNCS, vol. 8694, pp. 366–381. Springer, Cham (2014). https://doi.org/10.1007/978-3-319-10599-4_24

2. Ben-David, S., Blitzer, J., Crammer, K., Kulesza, A., Pereira, F., Vaughan, J.W.: A theory of learning from different domains. Mach. Learn. **79**(1–2), 151–175 (2010)

3. Bendale, A., Boult, T.: Towards open world recognition. In: Conference on Computer Vision and Pattern Recognition (CVPR) (2015)

4. Bendale, A., Boult, T.: Towards open set deep networks. In: Conference on Computer Vision and Pattern Recognition (CVPR) (2016)

5. Daftry, S., Zeng, S., Bagnell, J.A., Hebert, M.: Introspective perception: learning to predict failures in vision systems. In: International Conference on Intelligent Robots (IROS) (2016)

6. Dunning, T., Ertl, O.: Computing extremely accurate quantiles using t-digests (2014). github.com

7. Ganin, Y., Lempitsky, V.: Unsupervised domain adaptation by backpropagation. In: International Conference on Machine Learing (ICML) (2015)

8. Guo, C., Pleiss, G., Sun, Y., Weinberger, K.Q.: On calibration of modern neural networks. In: International Conference on Machine Learing (ICML) (2017)

9. Harel, M., Mannor, S., El-Yaniv, R., Crammer, K.: Concept drift detection through resampling. In: International Conference on Machine Learning (ICML) (2014)

10. He, K., Zhang, X., Ren, S., Sun, J.: Deep residual learning for image recognition. In: Conference on Computer Vision and Pattern Recognition (CVPR) (2016)

11. Howard, A.G., et al.: Mobilenets: efficient convolutional neural networks for mobile vision applications. arXiv:1704.04861 (2017)

12. Iandola, F.N., Han, S., Moskewicz, M.W., Ashraf, K., Dally, W.J., Keutzer, K.: SqueezeNet: AlexNet-level accuracy with 50x fewer parameters and <0.5 MB model size. arXiv:1602.07360 (2016)

13. Jain, L.P., Scheirer, W.J., Boult, T.E.: Multi-class open set recognition using probability of inclusion. In: Fleet, D., Pajdla, T., Schiele, B., Tuytelaars, T. (eds.) ECCV 2014. LNCS, vol. 8691, pp. 393–409. Springer, Cham (2014). https://doi.org/10.1007/978-3-319-10578-9_26

14. Kuncheva, L.I., Faithfull, W.J.: PCA feature extraction for change detection in multidimensional unlabeled data. IEEE Trans. Neural Netw. (T-NN) **25**(1), 69–80 (2014)

15. Marsaglia, G., Tsang, W.W., Wang, J.: Evaluating Kolmogorov's distribution. J. Stat. Softw. Articles **8**(18), 1–4 (2003)

16. Massey Jr., F.J.: The Kolmogorov-Smirnov test for goodness of fit. J. Am. Stat. Assoc. **46**(253), 68–78 (1951)

17. Perazzi, F., Pont-Tuset, J., McWilliams, B., Van Gool, L., Gross, M., Sorkine-Hornung, A.: A benchmark dataset and evaluation methodology for video object segmentation. In: Conference on Computer Vision and Pattern Recognition (CVPR) (2016)

18. Platt, J.: Probabilistic outputs for support vector machines and comparisons to regularized likelihood methods. In: Advances in Large Margin Classifiers. Cambridge University Press (1999)

19. Rebuffi, S.A., Kolesnikov, A., Sperl, G., Lampert, C.H.: iCaRL: incremental classifier and representation learning. In: Conference on Computer Vision and Pattern Recognition (CVPR) (2016)

20. dos Reis, D.M., Flach, P., Matwin, S., Batista, G.: Fast unsupervised online drift detection using incremental Kolmogorov-Smirnov test. In: SIGKDD (2016)

21. Royer, A., Lampert, C.H.: Classifier adaptation at prediction time. In: Conference on Computer Vision and Pattern Recognition (CVPR) (2015)

22. Russakovsky, O., et al.: ImageNet large scale visual recognition challenge. Int. J. Comput. Vis. (IJCV) **115**(3), 211–252 (2015)

23. Sethi, T.S., Kantardzic, M., Hu, H.: A grid density based framework for classifying streaming data in the presence of concept drift. J. Intell. Inf. Syst. **46**(1), 179–211 (2016)

24. Simonyan, K., Zisserman, A.: Very deep convolutional networks for large-scale image recognition. arXiv:1409.1556 (2014)

25. Sun, R., Lampert, C.H.: KS(conf): A light-weight test if a ConvNet operates outside of its specifications. arXiv:1804.04171 (2018)

26. Tange, O.: Gnu parallel - the command-line power tool. USENIX Mag. **36**(1), 42–47 (2011). http://www.gnu.org/s/parallel

27. Wang, H., Abraham, Z.: Concept drift detection for streaming data. In: International Joint Conference on Neural Networks (IJCNN) (2015)

28. Xian, Y., Lampert, C.H., Schiele, B., Akata, Z.: Zero-shot learning - a comprehensive evaluation of the good, the bad and the ugly. IEEE Trans. Pattern Anal. Mach. Intell. (T-PAMI) (2018)

29. Zhang, P., Wang, J., Farhadi, A., Hebert, M., Parikh, D.: Predicting failures of vision systems. In: Conference on Computer Vision and Pattern Recognition (CVPR) (2014)

30. Zliobaite, I.: Change with delayed labeling: when is it detectable? In: International Conference on Data Mining Workshops (2010)

31. Zoph, B., Vasudevan, V., Shlens, J., Le, Q.V.: Learning transferable architectures for scalable image recognition. arXiv:1707.07012 (2017)

Joint Oral Session 1

Sublabel-Accurate Convex Relaxation with Total Generalized Variation Regularization

Michael Strecke$^{(\boxtimes)}$ and Bastian Goldluecke

University of Konstanz, Konstanz, Germany
{michael.strecke,bastian.goldluecke}@uni-konstanz.de

Abstract. We propose a novel idea to introduce regularization based on second order total generalized variation (TGV) into optimization frameworks based on functional lifting. The proposed formulation extends a recent sublabel-accurate relaxation for multi-label problems and thus allows for accurate solutions using only a small number of labels, significantly improving over previous approaches towards lifting the total generalized variation. Moreover, even recent sublabel accurate methods exhibit staircasing artifacts when used in conjunction with common first order regularizers such as the total variation (TV). This becomes very obvious for example when computing derivatives of disparity maps computed with these methods to obtain normals, which immediately reveals their local flatness and yields inaccurate normal maps. We show that our approach is effective in reducing these artifacts, obtaining disparity maps with a smooth normal field in a single optimization pass.

1 Introduction

Many computer vision tasks can be formulated as continuous optimization problems over a label assignment $u : \Omega \to \Gamma$, where $\Omega \subset \mathbb{R}^d$ denotes the image domain and $\Gamma \subset \mathbb{R}^n$ the label domain. Correct solutions are characterized as the minimizers of an energy functional $E(u)$, which is designed in such a way that low-energy configurations correspond to some desired property, such as u being a smooth disparity map consistent with a given stereo pair. Thus, the energy E typically consists of a (non-convex) point-wise label cost which optimizes the fit to the observed data, and a regularization term which models interactions between neighbouring points. In order to find the optimal solutions u, approaches based on Markov random fields (MRFs) [4,9] discretize Ω as a set of nodes (e.g., pixels or superpixels) and Γ as a set of labels $\{1, \ldots, \ell\}$, with the graph cut class of methods as a popular way to obtain minimizers [13]. Notably, the construction by Ishikawa [12] allows to obtain globally optimal solutions for convex interactions despite the data term being non-convex. A spatially continuous reformulation of this approach [18], based on the idea of functional lifting or the calibration method [1], reduces grid bias and memory requirements. Other

T. Brox et al. (Eds.): GCPR 2018, LNCS 11269, pp. 263–277, 2019.
https://doi.org/10.1007/978-3-030-12939-2_19

related work in this context studies more general regularizers based on embeddings of the labels [14], structured label spaces [7,10] or the relationship between discrete and continuous approaches [23].

However, using a *discrete* label space does not allow for a faithful approximation of the underlying *continuous* model in practical problems such as image denoising or stereo matching. The above approaches [12,18] often yield results which exhibit a strong label bias degrading the result for a coarse sampling, or the discretization leads to unreasonably high demands in memory when using a finer sampling. In [15,16], Moellenhoff et al. thus substantially generalize the idea of functional lifting and derive formulations based on a fully continuous model. While their work allows for a sublabel-accurate approximation of the original (possibly nonconvex) energy, the results still exhibit some fine scale staircasing artifacts as can be seen in Fig. 1. This is particularly bad if derivatives of the result are required, such as in the above example, where normal maps are computed directly from the disparity maps [22], as this strongly emphasizes the artifacts. In practice, the normal maps become useless for subsequent tasks such as intrinsic image decomposition. Thus, [22] propose a two-pass framework, with a separate optimization pass for surface normal maps. While this achieves very good results, it is conceptually not as elegant as solving a single problem.

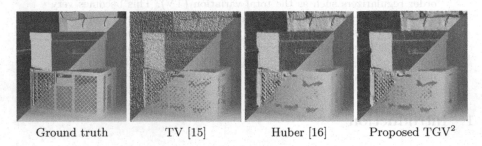

Ground truth   TV [15]   Huber [16]   Proposed TGV^2

Fig. 1. Recent sublabel-accurate optimization algorithms [15,16] yield accurate and at first glance smooth disparity maps (bottom right corners). However, the surface normal maps (top left corners) obtained from the disparity maps by computing derivatives [22] are often still very noisy due to staircasing artifacts. The proposed approach penalizes second order derivatives based on the TGV^2-prior and yields smooth disparity and normal maps in a single optimization pass.

1.1   Contribution

In this work, we propose an empirical extension to the framework by Moellenhoff et al. [15,16], which is based on the total generalized variation (TGV) [5]. Although a mathematical validation of our approximation remains open, we demonstrate in quantitative experiments that our method obtains reasonable solutions to the optimization problem. In particular, we clearly improve over a previous approach to approximately lifting the total generalized variation [20], arriving closer to the optimal solution with less label bias due to sublabel accuracy. Furthermore, we show that our regularization effectively manages to remove staircasing artifacts produced e.g. by total variation (TV) regularization as in [15], and provides similarly accurate normals when applied to a disparity estimation task as the approach [22], which explicitly smoothes normals in a post-processing step.

2   Background and Related Work

2.1   Preliminaries

Our formulation is an empirical extension to the one proposed by Moellenhoff et al. [16], who propose a fully continuous model inspired by the celebrated Mumford-Shah functional [2,17],

$$E(u) = \int_{\Omega \setminus J_u} f(x, u(x), \nabla u(x)) \, dx$$
$$+ \int_{J_u} d\left(x, u^-(x), u^+(x), \nu_u(x)\right) \, d\mathcal{H}^{n-1}(x). \tag{1}$$

The model is composed of two different integrands for the region $\Omega \setminus J_u$, where u is continuous, and the $(n-1)$-dimensional discontinuity set $J_u \subset \Omega$. The integrand $f : \Omega \times \Gamma \times \mathbb{R}^n \to [0, \infty]$ for the continuous part is a combined dataterm and regularizer, where the regularizer penalizes variations in terms of the gradient ∇u. On the discontinuity set J_u, the function $d : \Omega \times \Gamma \times \Gamma \times \mathcal{S}^{n-1} \to [0, \infty]$ penalizes jumps from u^- to u^+ in unit direction ν_u.

The energy (1) is defined for u in the space of *special functions of bounded variation* ($\mathcal{SBV}$). This is a subset of the space of functions $\mathcal{BV}(\Omega)$ of bounded variation, which are those functions $u \in L^1(\Omega; \mathbb{R})$ such that the total variation

$$\text{TV}(u) = \sup \left\{ \int_\Omega u \text{Div} \varphi \, dx : \varphi \in C_c^1(\Omega; \mathbb{R}^n) \right\} \tag{2}$$

is finite. Functions in $\mathcal{SBV}(\Omega)$ are now exactly those $u \in \mathcal{BV}(\Omega)$ whose distributional derivative Du can be decomposed into a continuous and a jump part as required for (1),

$$Du = \nabla u \cdot \mathcal{L}^n + (u^+ - u^-)\nu_u \cdot \mathcal{H}^{n-1} \lfloor J_u, \tag{3}$$

with $\mathcal{L}^n$ denoting the n-dimensional Lebesgue measure and $\mathcal{H}^{n-1} \lfloor J_u$ the $(n-1)$-dimensional Hausdorff measure restricted to the jump set J_u.

In the above formulation, f can be nonconvex in the first two variables, and thus allows a surprisingly large class of vision problems to be represented by (1). Although this makes (1) a difficult nonconvex optimization problem, Moellenhoff et al. [16] found a sublabel-accurate formulation which employs a piecewise convex relaxation of the energy between labels. As we build upon their framework, we follow [16] and make the following simplifying assumptions on the components of the energy (1):

– The Lagrangian f in (1) is seperable into a possibly nonconvex dataterm $\rho : \Omega \times \Gamma \to \mathbb{R}$ and convex regularizer $\eta : \Omega \times \mathbb{R}^n$,

$$f(x, t, g) = \rho(x, t) + \eta(x, g). \tag{4}$$

– The isotropic jump regularizer d in (1) is induced by a concave function $\kappa : \mathbb{R}_{\geq 0} \to \mathbb{R}$:

$$d(x, u^-, u^+, \nu_u) = \kappa(|u^- - u^+|) \|\nu_u\|_2 \tag{5}$$

– The range $\Gamma = [\gamma_1, \gamma_\ell] \subset \mathbb{R}$ is a compact interval divided into $k = \ell - 1$ intervals at the boundaries $\gamma_i, i \in \{1, \dots, \ell\}$. Although most formulations work for arbitrary label intervals, we assume equidistant labels for simplicity of notation and denote the label distance by h.

2.2 Functional Lifting

The basic idea for the convex relaxation used in [16] makes use of the fact that for binary segmentation problems, the total variation (2) penalizes the length of the boundary. This was first used in [1,3,6] to derive convex relaxation of nonconvex optimization problems and applied to imaging problems by Pock et al. [18]. An illustration of this idea of reformulating the energy as the flux through the complete graph G_u of the objective u for the 1D case is shown in Fig. 2.

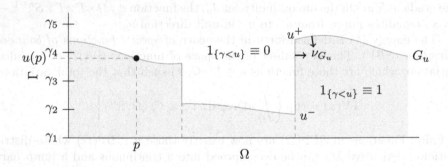

Fig. 2. The central idea behind the convex relaxation of (1) is to reformulate the problem in terms of the complete graph $G_u \subset \Omega \times \Gamma$ of $u : \Omega \to \Gamma$. Since the dimensionality of this reformulation is higher than the dimensionality of the original problem, this is often referred to as *lifting* the problem.

The reformulation in terms of the characteristic function $1_{\{\gamma < u\}}$ of the subgraph $\{\gamma < u\} := \{(x, \gamma) \in \Omega \times \Gamma : \gamma < u(x)\}$ is given by

$$E(u) = F(1_{\{\gamma < u\}}) = \sup_{\varphi \in \mathcal{K}} \int_{G_u} \langle \nu_{G_u}, \varphi \rangle \, \mathrm{d}\mathcal{H}^d, \tag{6}$$

where

$$\mathcal{K} = \left\{ (\varphi_x, \varphi_t) \in \mathcal{C}_c^1(\Omega \times \mathbb{R}; \mathbb{R}^d \times \mathbb{R}) \mid \forall x \in \Omega : \forall t, t' \in \mathbb{R} : \right.$$

$$\varphi_t(x,t) + \rho(x,t) \geq \eta^*(x, \varphi_x(x,t)), \quad (7)$$

$$\left\| \int_t^{t'} \varphi_x(x,\tau) \, d\tau \right\|_2 \leq \kappa(|t - t'|) \right\}, \quad (8)$$

and η^* denotes the *convex conjugate* of the regularizer η. The normal ν_{G_u} in (6) is given by the distributional derivative of the characteristic function of the subgraph $D1_{\{\gamma < u\}}$, allowing for the reformulation

$$F(1_{\{\gamma < u\}}) = \sup_{\varphi \in \mathcal{K}} \int_{\Omega \times \Gamma} \langle D1_{\{\gamma < u\}}, \varphi \rangle \, d(x, \gamma), \quad (9)$$

which is then relaxed to

$$\inf_{v \in \mathcal{C}} \sup_{\varphi \in \mathcal{K}} \int_{\Omega \times \mathbb{R}} \langle Dv, \varphi \rangle \, d(x, \gamma), \quad (10)$$

where

$$\mathcal{C} = \{ v \in \mathcal{BV}_{\mathrm{loc}}(\Omega \times \mathbb{R}; [0,1]) \mid \forall t \leq \gamma_1 : v(x,t) = 1,$$
$$\forall t > \gamma_\ell : v(x,t) = 0, v(x, \cdot) \text{ non-increasing}\}. \quad (11)$$

The key contribution of [16] is an elegant discretization of the variables v and φ, allowing for a sublabel-accurate approximation of the original energy. Their representation of the primal variable v uses coefficients for each label interval $\Gamma_i = [\gamma_i, \gamma_{i+1}]$, denoted by $\hat{v}(x,i) \in [0,1]$ to allow for continuous values in between the labels even after discretization. Writing the lifted primal variable coefficients as a vector allows for computation of the final result by just summing over the entries of that vector.

For an illustration see the point p in Fig. 2, where the discretization of the lifted variable yields:

$$\hat{v}(p, \cdot) = \sum_{i=1}^k e_i \hat{v}(p, i) = h \cdot [1, 1, 0.8, 0]^T. \quad (12)$$

An intuitive derivation for this representation is also given in [15], where the vector in (12) is interpreted as a linear interpolation between labels γ_3 and γ_4, which are represented by $[1, 1, 0, 0]^T$ and $[1, 1, 1, 0]^T$, respectively.

Using a piecewise linear approximation for the dual variable φ_t, the authors of [16] arrive at a sublabel-accurate approximation of the original energy, enabling an implementation of the constraints (7) and (8) individually on each label interval Γ_i as orthogonal projections onto the epigraphs of η^* and ρ_i^*. Here $\rho_i = \rho + \delta_{\Gamma_i}$, which shows that this implementation computes the convex envelope of the original dataterm on each interval Γ_i. In particular, they show that for regularizers η that are support functionals of convex sets, yielding η^* as an indicator function only attaining the values 0 and ∞, the constraint (7) allows for a separation of dataterm and regularizer as implemented for the total variation in [15].

2.3   The Total Generalized Variation

The *total generalized variation* (TGV) of order k was defined in [5] and has subsequently successfully been used for example to reconstruct smooth 3D surfaces [8,19]. Generalizing from the definition (2) of the total variation, it is defined as

$$\mathrm{TGV}_\alpha^k(u) := \sup\left\{ \int_\Omega u \mathrm{Div}^k \psi \, dx \,\middle|\, \psi \in \mathcal{C}_c^k(\Omega; \mathrm{Sym}^k(\mathbb{R}^d)), \right. \tag{13}$$
$$\left. \left\|\mathrm{Div}^l \psi\right\|_{2,\infty} \leq \alpha_l, l = 0, \dots, k-1\right\},$$

with weights $\alpha = [\alpha_0, \dots, \alpha_{k-1}]$. The space $\mathrm{Sym}^k(\mathbb{R}^d)$ denotes the symmetric k-tensors on $\mathbb{R}^d$, e.g., the space $S^{d \times d}$ of symmetric $d \times d$ matrices for $k = 2$.

We will focus on the case $k = 2$, where one can get an intuition of how TGV penalizes variations by deriving the "primal" formulation [5]

$$\mathrm{TGV}_\alpha^2(u) = \inf_{w \in \mathcal{C}^1(\Omega; \mathbb{R}^d)} \alpha_1 \|\nabla u - w\|_{2,1} + \alpha_0 \|\mathcal{E}(w)\|_{2,1}. \tag{14}$$

From (14), the TGV_α^2 penalty can be interpreted as an optimal balancing of first and second order derivative norms. Ranftl et al. [20] use this formulation to develop an approximation of the total generalized variation for nonconvex dataterms using the lifting approach [18]. They specialize the first integral in (1) to obtain

$$\min_{u,w} \alpha \overbrace{\int_\Omega \|Dw\|_2 \, \mathrm{d}x}^{E_1(w|u)} + \underbrace{\int_\Omega \|Du - w\|_2 \, \mathrm{d}x + \lambda \int_\Omega \rho(x, u) \, \mathrm{d}x}_{E_2(u|w)}, \tag{15}$$

which separates the problem into a convex subproblem E_1, optimized over w for a fixed u using standard techniques, and a nonconvex subproblem E_2, where w is assumed to be fixed and the lifted optimization [18] is applied to solve for u. In the implementation of [20], u is allowed to deviate up to half the label distance in each direction to allow for smooth surfaces.

3   Lifting the Total Generalized Variation

In our approach to lifting the total generalized variation, we make use of the fact that the framework of [16] allows for a *label-wise* optimization of the problem.

Since at discontinuities, TGV approximates the total variation (cf. [5]), we set $\kappa(a) = a$ in (1) and focus on the formulation for η as TGV_α^2 in the following. The main idea of our approach is motivated by the fact that the only difference between the definitions of TV (2) and TGV (13) is a more constrained set of dual variables in TGV. Based on this observation, we set η^* in the constraint set (7) to the indicator function

$$\eta^*(\varphi_x) = \delta_{\{-\mathrm{Div}_x\psi\|\|\psi\|\leq\alpha_0,\|\mathrm{Div}_x\psi\|\leq\alpha_1\}}(\varphi_x). \tag{16}$$

This way, we perform TGV regularization on each label interval individually, just as it has been done for TV in [15]. The constraints can be implemented in the publicly available framework prost[1] presented in [15] by using Lagrange multipliers w to enforce equality of φ_x to the negative divergence of some vector field ψ. One can see this by rewriting

$$\begin{aligned}
\mathrm{TGV}_\alpha^2 &= \sup_{\|\varphi_x\|\leq\alpha_1,\|\psi\|\leq\alpha_0} \inf_w \{\langle\nabla u - w, \varphi_x\rangle + \langle\mathcal{E}w, \psi\rangle\} \\
&= \sup_{\|\varphi_x\|\leq\alpha_1,\|\psi\|\leq\alpha_0} \inf_w \{\langle\nabla u, \varphi_x\rangle + \langle w, -\varphi_x - \mathrm{Div}\psi\rangle\}.
\end{aligned} \tag{17}$$

The lifted implementation uses the same piecewise constant discretization of the spatial variables as explained in [16], while for the dual variable φ_t (which has not changed in our formulation) a piecewise linear discretization is chosen to allow for piecewise convex sublabel-accurate approximation of the original energy.

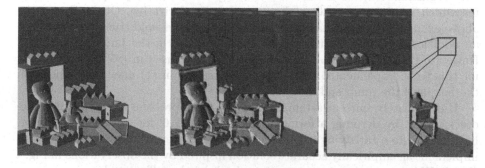

Fig. 3. A naive application of label-wise TGV leads to artifacts in the normal field at disparity label transitions. **Left:** Ground truth normal map, **Center:** One can see label artifacts ("kinks" in the wall on the left) for $\ell = 4$ labels, **Right:** With $\ell = 8$ labels, there are more artifacts at different locations for the $k = 7$ label boundaries.

However, if we just penalize label-wise with TGV, the solution exhibits artifacts which indicate that our formulation is not yet entirely correct. This can be observed in Fig. 3, where we display the resulting normal maps from this naive implementation for light field depth estimation task (cf. Sect. 4 for more details).

---

[1] https://github.com/tum-vision/prost.

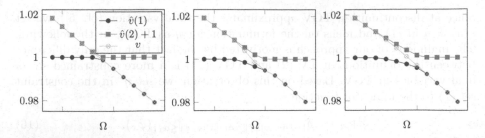

Fig. 4. Left: Synthetic 1D example for two label indicator functions (red and blue), where the exact result is a line with constant slope (green). **Center:** Label-wise TGV tends to oversmooth the coefficients $\hat{v}$ according to the second order component at the transition to constant maximal or minimal value of the respective label, leading to artifacts when computing the result v as the sum of the coefficients. **Right:** Our additional prior penalizing differences in the second order gradients of neighboring labels yields a consistent result. (Color figure online)

One can obtain an intuition for why these artifacts appear when observing a 1D closeup of the artifacts as shown in Fig. 4 (Center). One can see that especially the lower label is oversmoothed by the TGV prior towards the label boundary (constant 1.0) on the left. This leads to an irregularity in the final result retrieved as the sum over the labels. The desired result is shown in Fig. 4 (Left) and illustrates that the plane with constant slope would be best approximated by both labels allowing a sharp transition to the label boundary at a single pixel.

The theoretical reason behind this failure is that when we just perform label-wise regularization, we assume every change of label is a jump discontinuity, for which we do not penalize the second order derivative. Obviously, as the above example shows, this assumption does not always hold true. Thus, we need an additional penalty for the second order gradient in the jump penalization. However, the basic framework developed in [1,3,6] used in [16] does not allow for this to be implemented, since the jump penalty in (1) may only depend on the height of the jump and its direction.

Unfortunately, current attempts at solving this problem in a principled theoretical way, by deriving a formulation based on [1,6] for a TGV-based prior, have not led to a satisfying implementation so far. Nevertheless, we managed to implement an empirically accurate solution inspired by the observations in Fig. 4 (Left). We observe that in most points, both label coefficients have a constant slope (either zero, or the slope of the resulting plane), yielding zero second order derivatives. Nonzero second order derivatives only appear at a single point for both coefficients, where $\hat{v}(1)$ changes from the slope of the result to constant 1.0 and $\hat{v}(2)$ changes from constant 0.0 to the slope of the result. Thus, we need to penalize different second order derivatives across neighboring labels. Since enforcing this relation using a hard constraint would make the lifting obsolete as the dual variables would be the same across all labels, we enforce a soft constraint $\|\hat{\psi}(x, i+1) - \hat{\psi}(x, i)\| \leq \alpha_0$, effectively penalizing $\alpha_0 \|\mathcal{E}\hat{w}(x, i+1) - \mathcal{E}\hat{w}(x, i)\|$. Thus, we impose the same penalty on these differences as on the second order part itself. Figure 4 (Right) shows how this approach successfully removes the artifacts in the 1D closeup. Due to the additional penalty, both labels receive a similar amount of second order smoothing, which cancel each other out, yielding a consistent surface structure after retrieving the final result. Figure 5 shows the results for the normal maps, which are now almost free of discretization artifacts.

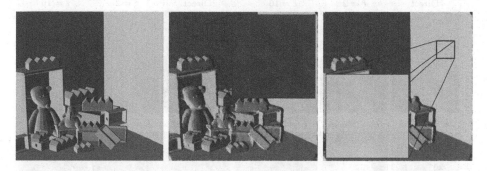

Fig. 5. Our proposed method correctly penalizes different second order derivatives across different labels and thus can remove the label wise artifacts from the naive approach in Fig. 3. **Left:** Ground truth normal map, **Center and Right:** Results of the proposed lifted implementation with $\ell = 4$ and $\ell = 8$ labels, respectively.

4   Experiments

4.1   ROF Denoising

In order to verify the quality of our lifted approximation to the total generalized variation experimentally, we first apply our formulation to the convex ROF denoising problem [21] where the dataterm is designed for Gaussian noise,

$$\rho(x,t) = (t - f(x))^2 \tag{18}$$

for a grayscale input image $f : \Omega \to \mathbb{R}$. For this convex energy, the convex envelope of the energy used for direct optimization as well as for the case $\ell = 2$ is the same as for lifted versions with higher numbers of labels. In Fig. 6, we compare our method to quadratic and Huber regularization as enabled by [16] (see [18] for derivations of the epigraphical projections required), and to our implementation of the baseline TGV^2 lifting approach [20]. The energies for Huber and quadratic regularization are computed in a straightforward way from their definitions using the resulting u. For the TGV energies, we first solve subproblem $E_2(w|u)$ in (15) for w as an instance of ROF given u, and then compute the final energy using the resulting pair u and w. One can see that even for small numbers of labels, our approach manages to achieve similar energies as the direct optimization, the differences to the direct energy only being slightly larger than for Huber and quadratic regularization demonstrated in [16]. The baseline approach [20], however, despite allowing values in between the labels, still has a strong label bias. Since the parameters in (15) are different from the original TGV parameters in (14), we compute them as $\lambda = \frac{1}{\alpha_1}$ and $\alpha = \frac{\alpha_0}{\alpha_1}$ to have a fair comparison.

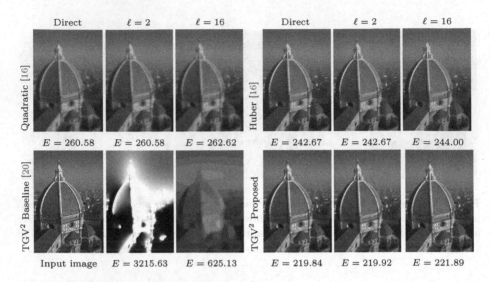

Fig. 6. Results of different regularizers for convex ROF-denoising with different numbers of labels. The proposed method recovers the original energy with only slightly larger margins than for Huber and Quadratic regularization which have been demonstrated in [16], while the baseline method [20] shows strong label artifacts. Note: the direct TGV^2 optimization result displayed for TGV^2 proposed is the same as for the baseline approach [20], where we show the input image instead.

4.2   Robust Truncated Quadratic Denoising

In practice, the simple ROF denoising term [21] is only of limited use because the model does not account for possible outliers which are often present in a captured image (i.e., salt-and-pepper noise). For this kind of noise, a truncated version of the dataterm can achieve better results, penalizing outliers with a constant value,

$$\rho(x,t) = \frac{\alpha}{2} \min\{(t - f(x))^2, \nu\}. \tag{19}$$

Figure 7 shows that our TGV-based lifted regularization achieves good results already for $\ell = 10$ labels, similarly as quadratic and Huber regularization with the approach in [16]. In contrast, the baseline TGV approach [20] exhibits a strong label bias for $\ell = 10$ and severe oversmoothing for $\ell = 20$. The energies displayed in Fig. 7 show a corresponding substantial improvement of our approach compared to the baseline TGV relaxation [20].

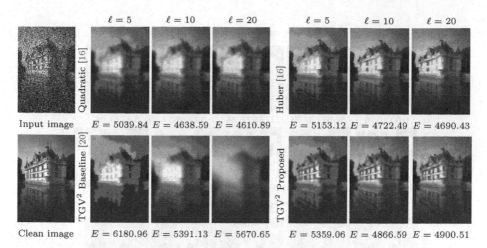

Fig. 7. Results of different regularizers for nonconvex truncated ROF denoising with different numbers of labels. The quadratic regularizer oversmooths details and Huber exhibits similar piecewise constant artifacts at the total variation. The proposed method retains details and results in smooth transitions, while the baseline method [20] does exhibit label artifacts and severe oversmoothing for the same parameter setting.

4.3 Light Field Disparity Estimation

We evaluate our formulation on the light field disparity estimation task with a special focus on the quality of surface normals. Since the behaviour of our algorithm across different numbers of labels was already evaluated in the previous experiments, we focus on a comparison of TV, Huber, and the proposed TGV^2 regularization with $\ell = 8$ labels and compare it to the approach by Strecke et al. [22], which explicitly smoothes the normal map derived from sublabel-accurate TV-based optimization of disparity using [15] in a post-processing step. This method is still among the top-ranked algorithms for surface normal quality on the benchmark [11]. To have a fair comparison of how the regularization influences the result, we use the same dataterm used in [22] and refer to their work for details on how it is constructed and implemented. Figures 8 and 9 demonstrate that we manage to achieve similar results as [22], denoted as OFSY 330DNR in the figures, without the need of computing the surface normals explicitly for optimization or running two optimization passes. One can further see that our approach yields significantly better results in this respect than TV or Huber regularization.

Besides the *Median Angular Error (MAE)* for planar and non-planar surfaces in Figs. 8 and 9 shows that the quality of our obtained disparity maps, measured by the percentage of pixels deviating more than 0.07 from the ground truth. This so-called *BadPix(0.07)* measure is similar to the approach [22].

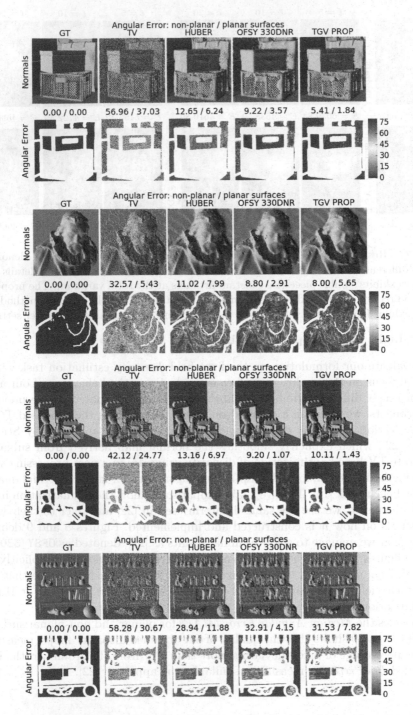

Fig. 8. Normal maps and *Median Angular Errors* obtained on the benchmark training dataset [11] for different regularizers and the method in [22].

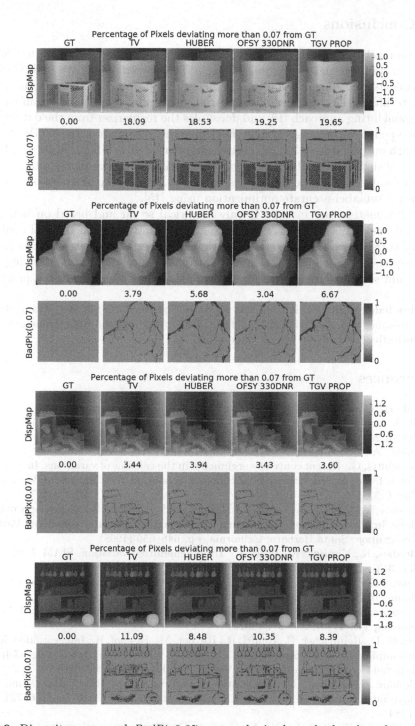

Fig. 9. Disparity maps and *BadPix0.07* errors obtained on the benchmark training dataset [11] for different regularizers and the method [22].

5 Conclusions

Our approach extends the recent functional lifting approaches [15,16] to obtain experimentally accurate solutions using a TGV-based prior. We show in our experiments that our formulation significantly improves over the previous approach to lifting the total generalized variation [20], which is based on an earlier functional lifting approach [18] and decouples the regularizer from the data term. When applied to the task of light field disparity estimation, our TGV^2-based approach outperforms other regularizers implemented in [15,16] in terms of the quality of surface normals. In a single pass optimization, we manage to achieve similar results as [22], who explicitly smooth the normal map in a post-processing step after sublabel-accurate optimization using [15].

Unfortunately, our method is only empirical so far and based on heuristic observations - while results are convincing, it currently lacks theoretical verification of correctness. However, we hope that the insights presented in this paper can inspire future studies on a more principled approach towards deriving our constraint sets, as our experiments indicate that they seem to work in practice.

Acknowledgements. This work was supported by the ERC Starting Grant "Light Field Imaging and Analysis" (LIA 336978, FP7-2014) and the SFB Transregio 161 "Quantitative Methods for Visual Computing".

References

1. Alberti, G., Bouchitté, G., Dal Maso, G.: The calibration method for the Mumford-Shah functional and free-discontinuity problems. Calc. Var. Partial Differ. Equ. **16**(3), 299–333 (2003)
2. Blake, A., Zisserman, A.: Visual Reconstruction. MIT Press, Cambridge (1987)
3. Bouchitté, G.: Recent convexity arguments in the calculus of variations. In: Lecture Notes from the 3rd International Summer School on the Calculus of Variations, Pisa (1998)
4. Boykov, Y., Veksler, O., Zabih, R.: Markov random fields with efficient approximations. In: Proceedings of International Conference on Computer Vision and Pattern Recognition, Santa Barbara, California, pp. 648–655 (1998)
5. Bredies, K., Kunisch, K., Pock, T.: Total generalized variation. SIAM J. Imaging Sci. **3**(3), 492–526 (2010)
6. Chambolle, A.: Convex representation for lower semicontinuous envelopes of functionals in L^1. J. Convex Anal. **8**(1), 149–170 (2001)
7. Cremers, D., Strekalovskiy, E.: Total cyclic variation and generalizations. J. Math. Imaging Vis. **47**(3), 258–277 (2012)
8. Ferstl, D., Reinbacher, C., Ranftl, R., Rüther, M., Bischof, H.: Image guided depth upsampling using anisotropic total generalized variation. In: Proceedings of International Conference on Computer Vision, pp. 993–1000. IEEE (2013)
9. Geman, S., Geman, D.: Stochastic relaxation, Gibbs distributions, and the Bayesian restoration of images. IEEE Trans. Pattern Anal. Mach. Intell. **6**, 721–741 (1984)
10. Goldluecke, B., Strekalovskiy, E., Cremers, D.: Tight convex relaxations for vector-valued labeling. SIAM J. Imaging Sci. **6**(3), 1626–1664 (2013)

11. Honauer, K., Johannsen, O., Kondermann, D., Goldluecke, B.: A dataset and evaluation methodology for depth estimation on 4D light fields. In: Lai, S.-H., Lepetit, V., Nishino, K., Sato, Y. (eds.) ACCV 2016. LNCS, vol. 10113, pp. 19–34. Springer, Cham (2017). https://doi.org/10.1007/978-3-319-54187-7_2
12. Ishikawa, H.: Exact optimization for Markov random fields with convex priors. IEEE Trans. Pattern Anal. Mach. Intell. **25**(10), 1333–1336 (2003)
13. Kolmogorov, V., Zabih, R.: What energy functions can be minimized via graph cuts. IEEE Trans. Pattern Anal. Mach. Intell. **26**(2), 147–159 (2004)
14. Lellmann, J., Becker, F., Schnörr, C.: Convex optimization for multi-class image labeling with a novel family of total variation based regularizers. In: IEEE International Conference on Computer Vision (ICCV) (2009)
15. Moellenhoff, T., Laude, E., Moeller, M., Lellmann, J., Cremers, D.: Sublabel-accurate relaxation of nonconvex energies. In: Proceedings of International Conference on Computer Vision and Pattern Recognition (2016)
16. Möllenhoff, T., Cremers, D.: Sublabel-accurate discretization of nonconvex free-discontinuity problems. In: International Conference on Computer Vision (ICCV), Venice, Italy, October 2017
17. Mumford, D., Shah, J.: Optimal approximations by piecewise smooth functions and associated variational problems. Commun. Pure Appl. Math. **42**, 577–685 (1989)
18. Pock, T., Cremers, D., Bischof, H., Chambolle, A.: Global solutions of variational models with convex regularization. SIAM J. Imaging Sci. **3**, 1122–1145 (2010)
19. Ranftl, R., Gehrig, S., Pock, T., Bischof, H.: Pushing the limits of stereo using variational stereo estimation. In: IEEE Intelligent Vehicles Symposium (2012)
20. Ranftl, R., Pock, T., Bischof, H.: Minimizing TGV-based variational models with non-convex data terms. In: Kuijper, A., Bredies, K., Pock, T., Bischof, H. (eds.) SSVM 2013. LNCS, vol. 7893, pp. 282–293. Springer, Heidelberg (2013). https://doi.org/10.1007/978-3-642-38267-3_24
21. Rudin, L.I., Osher, S., Fatemi, E.: Nonlinear total variation based noise removal algorithms. Phys. D **60**, 259–268 (1992)
22. Strecke, M., Alperovich, A., Goldluecke, B.: Accurate depth and normal maps from occlusion-aware focal stack symmetry. In: Proceedings of International Conference on Computer Vision and Pattern Recognition (2017)
23. Zach, C., Häne, C., Pollefeys, M.: What is optimized in convex relaxations for multilabel problems: connecting discrete and continuously inspired map inference. IEEE Trans. Pattern Anal. Mach. Intell. **36**(1), 157–170 (2014)

Oral Session 2: Motion and Video I

On the Integration of Optical Flow and Action Recognition

Laura Sevilla-Lara[1,2]([⊠]), Yiyi Liao[2,3]([⊠]), Fatma Güney[4]([⊠]),
Varun Jampani[5]([⊠]), Andreas Geiger[2,6]([⊠]), and Michael J. Black[2]([⊠])

[1] Facebook, Menlo Park, USA
laurasevilla@fb.com
[2] Max Planck Institute for Intelligent Systems, Tübingen, Germany
{yiyi.liao,andreas.geiger,black}@tuebingen.mpg.de
[3] Zhejiang University, Hangzhou, China
[4] Oxford University, Oxford, UK
fatma.guney@tuebingen.mpg.de
[5] NVIDIA, Santa Clara, USA
varunjampani@gmail.com
[6] University of Tuebingen, Tübingen, Germany

Abstract. Most of the top performing action recognition methods use optical flow as a "black box" input. Here we take a deeper look at the combination of flow and action recognition, and investigate why optical flow is helpful, what makes a flow method good for action recognition, and how we can make it better. In particular, we investigate the impact of different flow algorithms and input transformations to better understand how these affect a state-of-the-art action recognition method. Furthermore, we fine tune two neural-network flow methods end-to-end on the most widely used action recognition dataset (UCF101). Based on these experiments, we make the following five observations: (1) optical flow is useful for action recognition because it is invariant to appearance, (2) optical flow methods are optimized to minimize end-point-error (EPE), but the EPE of current methods is not well correlated with action recognition performance, (3) for the flow methods tested, accuracy at boundaries and at small displacements is most correlated with action recognition performance, (4) training optical flow to minimize classification error instead of minimizing EPE improves recognition performance, and (5) optical flow learned for the task of action recognition differs from traditional optical flow especially inside the human body and at the boundary of the body. These observations may encourage optical flow researchers to look beyond EPE as a goal and guide action recognition researchers to seek better motion cues, leading to a tighter integration of the optical flow and action recognition communities.

Keywords: Optical flow · Action recognition · Video understanding

© Springer Nature Switzerland AG 2019
T. Brox et al. (Eds.): GCPR 2018, LNCS 11269, pp. 281–297, 2019.
https://doi.org/10.1007/978-3-030-12939-2_20

1   Introduction

Traditionally, the computer vision problem has been divided into sub-problems or modules that are easier to solve, with the goal of putting them together later to solve the larger problem. Some examples include motion, depth, and edge estimation at the lower level, attribute extraction at the middle level, and object or action recognition at the higher level. This had yielded rapid progress in separate communities focused on specific sub-problems.

Fig. 1. Frames from the UCF101 dataset [30], sampled from the categories *ApplyEye-Makeup, Fencing, Knitting, PlayingGuitar, HorseRiding*. A single frame often contains enough information to correctly guess the category.

In the video domain, two common sub-problems are motion estimation and action recognition, which are most commonly combined in a straightforward way. Motion is estimated as the optical flow of the scene, typically by minimizing brightness constancy error, with the goal of achieving accurate flow in terms of end-point-error (EPE), which is the average Euclidean distance between the ground truth and the estimated flow. The optical flow and the raw images are the input to the next module, which computes the video label [28,34]. This approach, although widely used, is based on a few untested hypotheses that we examine in this paper.

Hypothesis 1: *The optical flow between two frames is a good feature for video classification.* While it may seem intuitive to include image motion in a task related to video, often video categories in current datasets can be identified from a single image as illustrated in Fig. 1. Many actions are uniquely defined by human-object interactions, which can be recognized in a single frame [36]. Thus one may ask whether motion, in the form of optical flow, is necessary for action recognition. There is the observation in the literature [33], however, that classification accuracy using exclusively optical flow as input, can be even higher than classification accuracy using exclusively the raw images in some standard datasets [20,30]. This is surprising since current datasets show a large correlation between scenes/objects and categories (i.e.: water and the category "Kayaking", or guitars and "PlayingGuitar" appear together often), and flow seems to lack much of this explicit object information.

Consequently, we ask: *What makes motion such a useful feature for video classification?* Intuitively it would seem that motion trajectories contain information useful for recognition. We test this hypothesis by randomly shuffling the flow fields in time. We observe that the accuracy decreases only a small amount, suggesting that trajectories are not the main source of information in optical flow. Since the flow has been computed between adjacent frames, there is still temporal information in the input. Consequently, we remove the temporal information completely by shuffling the frames *before* computing the flow. We observe that the accuracy decreases further but is still 60 times higher than chance. Thus we argue that most of the value of optical flow in current architectures is that it is a representation of the scene invariant to appearance. This may be related to recent findings [7] that show that at very large scale, networks using only optical flow have lower accuracy than networks using only images. The intuition is that as the training set becomes larger, more examples of different illuminations, clothing or backgrounds are seen, making generalization easier and invariance to appearance less crucial.

We test the hypothesis that much of the value of optical flow is that it is a representation invariant to appearance. For this we alter the appearance of the input and observe that accuracy from optical flow goes down marginally by 1%, while accuracy from raw images goes down by 50%. This suggests that the motion trajectories are not the root of the success of optical flow, and that establishing useful motion representations remains an open problem that optical flow on its own does not address.

Hypothesis 2: More accurate flow methods will yield better action recognition methods, or in other words, *the accuracy of optical flow is correlated with accuracy of action recognition.* Here we test this hypothesis by using several optical flow methods as input to a baseline action recognition system and recording their classification accuracy. We also measure their accuracy on standard optical flow benchmarks [6,15] and compute the correlation between these two measurements. Surprisingly, we observe that the EPE of a flow method is poorly correlated with the classification accuracy of a system that uses it as input. We further observe that certain properties of the estimated flow field are more correlated with classification accuracy than others. In particular, the accuracy at motion boundaries and the correct estimation of small displacements are correlated with performance. Overall, this suggests that the prevailing approach of combining optical flow, optimized for EPE, with classification systems may not be optimal.

Hypothesis 3: *Optical flow is the best motion representation for action recognition.* Optical flow is often formulated as the problem of estimating the 2D projection of the true 3D motion of the world. In the light of the findings above one may wonder if there exists a criterion by which to choose a particular optical flow method for an action recognition system? To answer this question, we combine the two modules, optical flow estimation and action recognition, in an end-to-end trainable network. We fine-tune the optical flow network by optimizing the final classification accuracy of the full model rather than using the traditional EPE loss, which encourages good performance in classical optical flow benchmarks. In our experiments, we consider two different deep learning-based flow models (FlowNet [8] and SpyNet [24]). After end-to-end training, the networks still compute a representation that looks like optical flow but that improves action recognition performance compared to the original flow. In the case of FlowNet, performance on classical flow benchmarks decreases while, for SpyNet, there is no significant change. Finally, we compare the original optical flow to the new motion representation qualitatively and quantitatively, and observe that the new motion fields are most different on the human body and near the boundary of the body; that is the networks appear to focus on the human and their motion.

The conclusions drawn by this paper shed new light on the way optical flow and video recognition modules are used today. In summary, our conclusions are:

- Optical flow is useful for action recognition as it is invariant to appearance, even when temporal coherence is not maintained.
- EPE of current methods is not well correlated with action recognition accuracy, and thus improving EPE may not improve action recognition.
- Flow accuracy at boundaries and for small displacements matters most for action recognition.
- Training optical flow to minimize classification error instead of EPE improves action recognition results.
- Optical flow that is learned to minimize classification differs on the human body and near the boundary of the body.

These experiments suggest that classical optical flow, developed in isolation, may not be the best representation for video and action classification. This argues against the modular approach to vision and in favor of a more integrated approach.

2   Related Work

Optical Flow Estimation. The field of optical flow has made significant progress by focusing on improving numerical accuracy on standard benchmarks. Flow is seen as a source of input for tracking, video segmentation, depth estimation, frame interpolation, and many other problems. It is assumed that optimizing for low EPE will produce flow that is widely useful for many tasks. EPE, however, is just one possible measure of accuracy and others have been used in the literature, such as angular error [3] or frame interpolation error [2].

While there is extensive research on optical flow, here we focus on methods that use deep learning because these can be trained end-to-end on different tasks with different loss functions. Applying learning to the optical flow problem has been hard because there is limited training data with ground truth flow. Early approaches used synthetic data and broke the problem into pieces to make learning possible with limited data [26,31].

The first end-to-end trainable deep convolutional network is FlowNet [8], which is trained on synthetic data to minimize EPE. The results, however, are not on par with top methods, mostly due to inaccuracies for very large or very small displacements. To address this issue, Ranjan and Black [24] propose SpyNet, a combination of the traditional pyramid approach and convolutional networks. This reduces the size of the network, and improves numerical results. The top performing learning-based flow method is FlowNet2 [13]. Here the authors stack multiple FlowNet modules [8] together, train a separate network to focus on small displacements, and experiment carefully with training schedules. The network is complex but produces competitive, though not top, results on the Sintel benchmark [6] while being near the best monocular methods for KITTI 2015 [21]. The complexity makes it difficult to train as part of a system because each component is trained separately and accuracy is sensitive to different training schedules.

Here we retrain both FlowNet and SpyNet on the action recognition problem and find consistent results. In both cases, training on the recognition loss results in a motion representation that is better for action recognition.

Motion and Action Recognition. For human action recognition, there is significant evidence to suggest the importance of motion as a cue. Johansson [17] argues for separating form from motion and demonstrates that 10–12 dots located at the joints of a moving person are sufficient for human observers to recognize a range of human actions. Bobick and Davis [4] show that humans and algorithms can recognize actions in very low resolution video sequences where, in any given frame, the action is unrecognizable. These results would suggest that optical flow can and does play an important role in action recognition. As a counterpoint, however, Koenderink et al. [19] show that movies can undergo significant spatial and temporal distortions yet human observers can still recognize the actions in them. Even with frames that are scrambled in space and time, people can robustly recognize human actions.

More computationally, Jhuang et al. [16] ask what it is about the flow field that is important for human action recognition. They note that "the motion boundaries around a person's body contour seem to contain information for action recognition that is as important as the optical flow within the region of the body." This hints at the idea that flow may be useful for not only extracting *motion*, as suggested by Johansson, but also *form*, that is the shape of the objects performing the action.

Learning Action Recognition. Top performing deep learning methods for action recognition use one or more architecture styles in order to capture temporal structure: two-streams, 3D convolutions or recurrent neural networks (RNNs). Two-stream architectures [10,28,33,34] typically contain two parallel networks adapted from the image recognition literature, such as VGG [29] or Inception [14]. One network, often referred to as the spatial stream, takes as input one or more images. The other network referred to as the temporal stream takes as input one or more flow fields. At test time, the predictions of each of these networks are combined to output the final label. Many different variants of this architecture have been explored and improved upon the basic structure [9,11,27]. Another common style is the use of 3D convolutions [18,32]. These architectures operate on the video as a volume, and thus they may not use optical flow, as the temporal structure is expected to be captured implicitly by the convolution in the third dimension. Carreira and Zisserman [7] propose I3D, which combines elements of these two styles. Finally, RNNs architectures like long short-term memory networks (LSTMs) [23], have also shown successful results.

The action recognition literature is very broad and a thorough review is beyond our scope. Here we focus on two-stream networks because they tend to have top performance and because they use optical flow as input, which makes them most relevant to us. Since flow is computed from the image sequence, one could argue that a network trained to do action recognition could learn to compute flow if it is useful, making the explicit computation of optical flow unnecessary. Of course, whether this works on not may depend on the network architecture. In fact, ablative studies confirm [33,34] that the use of computed optical flow (i.e.: using the temporal stream) improves classification over using only the images (i.e.: using only the spatial stream). This indicates the difficulty of learning the task end-to-end. As noted for FlowNet2, even supervised training of a flow network can be tricky.

One of the most widely used two-stream networks is Temporal Segment Networks (TSN) [34]. Each of the streams is composed by an "inception with batch normalization" network [14]. Small snippets of are sampled throughout the video and predictions on each of these subsets are aggregated in the end. Here we work with this model as our baseline.

The most related work to ours is the unpublished (arXiv) ActionFlowNet [22]. Here the authors also explore the idea of using action classification accuracy as a loss to fine-tune an optical flow network, obtaining similar numerical improvements. However, that work does not study in detail the interaction of the two modules (flow and action recognition) but focuses more on the general numerical improvement of the action recognition task, adding, for example, a multi-task loss that combines EPE and action recognition. Instead, here we focus on understanding why flow is useful for action recognition, what makes a flow method better or worse for action recognition and how flow changes after fine-tuning on action recognition. In particular, we show experiments varying the temporal structure of the flow and the appearance of the input image (Sect. 3), provide a comprehensive study of the correlation of EPE and action recognition accuracy with 6 different flow methods (Sect. 4) and analyze how flow fields change after fine-tuning on the action recognition task (Sect. 5).

3   Why Use Optical Flow as Input for Video Classification?

Although it may seem intuitive to use explicit motion estimation as input for a task involving video, one could argue that using motion is not essential. Some possible arguments are that categories in current datasets can be identified from a single frame, and more broadly many objects and actions in the visual world can be identified from a single frame. On the other hand, there is evidence that motion contains useful information for recognition of humans, as shown in Johansson's work [17]. One could also argue that the raw video stream implicitly

Fig. 2. Samples of modified input videos. Left: original image. Middle: modified image, by sampling a different colormap, referred as "altered colormap". Right: modified image by scaling channel values, referred as "shift color". (Color figure online)

contains the information present in optical flow and, if a network needs this, it can compute it.

Despite these arguments, it has been shown in the action recognition literature that using optical flow as input in addition to the raw images improves classification performance [33]. Thus why is optical flow useful for action recognition?

The intuitive answer is that, as in the case of Johansson's work [17], motion trajectories contain enough information to recognize actions. We test this hypothesis by removing temporal coherence in the input video and measuring how this affects recognition accuracy. We remove temporal coherence by shuffling the flow fields randomly in the temporal dimension.

We choose the state-of-the-art Temporal Segment Network (TSN) [34] for our experiments as it is widely used and exploits a two-stream network, which lets us experiment with the two input modalities separately (images used for the spatial stream and flow used for the temporal stream). We evaluate this network on the UCF101 dataset [30]. The temporal stream of the TSN processes the optical flow in blocks of 5 flow fields, corresponding to 6 image frames. We perform the temporal shuffling at test time in the input videos, within each block[1]. The ordering of the temporal shuffle is random within each block. This breaks temporal coherence.

The results are shown in Table 1. While the recognition accuracy decreases when the trajectories are disrupted, the overall accuracy is still surprisingly high (78.64%, table entry "Flow (shuffled flow fields)"), which suggests that coherent temporal trajectories are not the most important feature for recognition, at least in this particular set up and considering this particular architecture.

There is still, however, some temporal information encoded in the shuffled flow fields since each of these is computed from two temporally adjacent frames. We remove this temporal information completely by applying the same shuffling scheme to the original input RGB frames before computing the optical flow. At this point, the flow does not correspond to the physical motion in general,

---

[1] We do not experiment shuffling the frames and using them as input to the spatial stream because it takes a single frame at a time, thus the temporal ordering is already discarded.

but it still captures the shapes of moving objects. The results are also shown in Table 1. This time the recognition accuracy decreases to 59.5% (table entry "Flow (shuffled images)"). While this is a substantial drop, it is still well above chance-level accuracy which is ∼1%, suggesting that much of the value of the optical flow is not even in the motion per se.

Table 1. Action recognition accuracy with modified inputs. Removing temporal structure by shuffling ("shuffled flow fields" and "shuffled images") affects the performance of the network, but it is still far from chance, suggesting that the benefit of the flow is not just that it represents motion. Modifying the appearance of the input images ("altered colormap" and "shift color") hurts the performance when using only the images but leaves the performance unchanged when using flow.

Input	Accuracy
Flow	86.85%
RGB	85.43%
Flow (shuffled flow fields)	78.64%
Flow (shuffled images)	59.55%
Flow (altered colormap)	84.30%
RGB (altered colormap)	34.23%
Flow (shift color)	85.71%
RGB (shift color)	62.65%

We argue that instead much of the value of optical flow is that it is invariant to the appearance of the input images, resulting in a simpler learning problem as less variance needs to be captured by the action recognition network. To illustrate this, let us consider two videos (one in the training set and one in the test set) that are identical except that the actor is wearing differently colored clothing. If we use the raw images as input to the recognition method, the representation of these two videos will be different and therefore it will be more difficult to learn from one and generalize to the other. However, if we first input such videos to a flow method, the flow of both videos will be very similar, making it easier for the recognition system to learn from one and generalize to the other.

We test this intuition by altering the colormap of the UCF101 and observing the change in accuracy. We do this by converting the RGB images to grayscale and then converting them back to color with a randomly sampled colormap (e.g.: jet, brg, hsv). An example of this mapping in shown in Fig. 2. Results are shown in Table 1. We observe that using the modified images as input the accuracy drops by 50% (from the original result in entry "RGB" to "RGB (altered colormap)"), while using only the flow (computed from the modified images) the accuracy decreases only marginally (table entry "Flow (altered colormap)"). While this alteration of the appearance could resemble the case of two videos where the person is wearing different color clothing, it may result in a very large change over the entire frame. To explore what happens with a smaller change of appearance, we also alter the input frames by scaling the value of each channel by a random coefficient between 0.3 and 1. The result of this change is much less noticeable in the image, but it still impacts the performance of the network using only images by 20%, while it leaves the accuracy of the network using optical flow almost the same. While these results are not surprising, they confirm with numerical evidence the intuition that the temporal structure is not responsible for the success of optical flow in many action recognition applications. Instead, the invariance to appearance of the representation is key (Fig. 3).

4   Is Optical Flow Accuracy Correlated with Action Recognition Accuracy?

Progress in the optical flow and the action recognition communities has been mostly independent. However, it remains unclear if these separate advances lead to a common goal. In other words, does a better optical flow method (as judged by the optical flow community) improve action recognition accuracy? In this section we test whether EPE, which is the standard metric for optical flow, is correlated with classification accuracy.

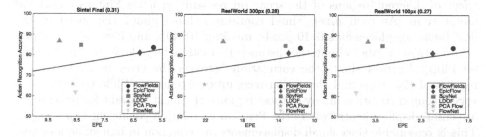

Fig. 3. Action recognition accuracy vs. EPE. We observe that action recognition accuracy is not very highly correlated in general with EPE on Sintel and Real-World Scenes.

We use the temporal stream of the TSN network [34], and create different versions, fine-tuning each of them with a different optical flow method. These optical flow methods are chosen to cover a wide range of accuracies and styles (deep learning based, variational, etc.). We choose FlowFields [1], EpicFlow [25], LDOF [5], PCAFlow [35], FlowNet [8] and Spynet [24]. We take the TSN [34] pre-trained using DenseFlow as initialization and fine-tune it with each flow method separately. To validate the fairness of the initialization scheme, we also conducted experiments with the initial model trained on ImageNet. Both initialization schemes lead to the same ranking of flow methods on action recognition. The results are displayed in Fig. 4.

Since there is no ground truth flow on UCF101, we measure the flow methods according to their performance on standard benchmarks. For a fair evaluation, we consider both the synthetic MPI Sintel dataset [6] and the recently introduced, more realistic Real-World Scenes dataset of Janai et al. [15]. Figure 4 shows the end-point-error (EPE) of each flow method in terms of action recognition accuracy on the UCF101 dataset, along with the correlation score. Note that the EPE along the horizontal axis is in decreasing order as smaller EPE indicates better flow in general. Since the FlowNet model fine-tuned on MPI Sintel is not released, we evaluate FlowNet ourselves by submitting it to the Sintel server. For the Real-World Scenes, we present the EPE value on a clean version with 100px flow magnitude without motion, and also a hard version with 300px flow magnitude in addition to motion blur.

Figure 4 shows that smaller EPE does not correlate strongly with better action recognition. For example, LDOF has relatively large EPE on both Sintel and Real-World Scenes, but it produces the best performance when used as input for action recognition. Although the EPE rankings of these flow methods vary between different datasets, the correlation between flow error and action recognition accuracy is relatively weak.

This finding may be attributed to the fact that EPE is computed and averaged over the entire image. However, not all flow vectors contain the same amount of information for action recognition. For example boundaries contain information about shape, which is useful for recognition but large camera motions in the background may not be very informative. We analyze the effect of different regions of the scene on recognition using Sintel's additional annotations. At each pixel, Sintel contains a label about the speed of the flow (small displacements 0–10 pixels, medium 10–40p, and large 40+p). Sintel also contains a label about the distance to motion boundary (0–10p, 10–60p, 60–140p). Figure 4 shows the correlation between the error in each of these regions of the scene and the action recognition accuracy. While there is not a very strong correlation in any of these regions, the most relevant for recognition are small displacements (where the Pearson correlation coefficient is $\rho = 0.89$). This is reasonable since small displacements are common in human actions (eg. knitting, applying eye make up, etc.) such as those present in UCF101. The second most important regions are boundaries ($\rho = 0.72$), which inform about shape. These two correlations are statistically significant at the 0.05 level, using a one-tailed test since we only expect positive correlations.

This analysis is useful in order to select an optical flow method from an existing repertoire for action recognition. However, it also leads to the question – while improving EPE may lead to progress on action recognition, could there be a better and more direct metric for the task?

5   Are There Better Motion Representations for Action Recognition than Optical Flow?

Current approaches that use motion cues for action recognition follow a sequential procedure: first they compute flow and then use it as input to a classification network (for example, TSN uses DenseFlow). The assumption of this approach

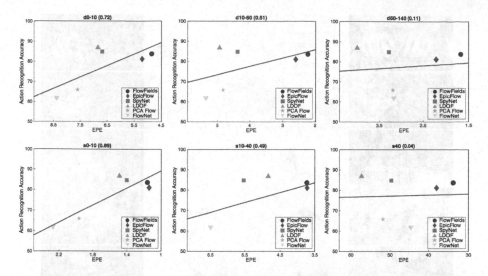

Fig. 4. Action recognition accuracy vs. EPE in specific regions of the scene. The regions are categorized according to distance to the boundary ("d0–10", "d10–60", and "d60–140" are pixels less than 10p away from a motion boundary, 10–60p and 60–140p, respectively), and according to speed ("s0–10", "s10–40" and "s40+" are pixels that move less than 10p, between 10 and 40, and more than 40, respectively). We observe that error at small displacements and close to the boundary the correlation with recognition accuracy is higher.

is that accurate flow (measured by EPE) is useful for action recognition. However, our experiment of Sect. 4 shows that this correlation is weak. Thus can we instead use action recognition accuracy as an optimization criterion? In this section we train the optical flow network to learn a better motion representation directly from the high level task of action recognition.

We use TSN as the recognition network, and experiment with both SpyNet and FlowNet as optical flow modules. We start from the generic flow models and fine-tune them using the action recognition loss back-propagated through the TSN. We use the TSN models fined-tuned to each of the flow methods in the experiment of the previous section, and keep them fixed to observe how the optical flow changes[2]. We follow the training scheme of TSN with 3 blocks of 6 consecutive frames (5 flow fields) randomly sampled. We use a small learning rate of $1e-7$, as in the original FlowNet.

Experiments on Action Recognition and Optical Flow. We find that learning to compute flow to recognize actions improves the motion features and thus the action recognition accuracy. Results are shown in Table 2. In this table we present different evaluation schemes. Using the evaluation scheme of TSN (named "25 Sn. + Data Aug." in the table) we observe that FlowNet improves

---

[2] The SpyNet model is slightly different in this section than the previous one, since we used the end-to-end trainable version.

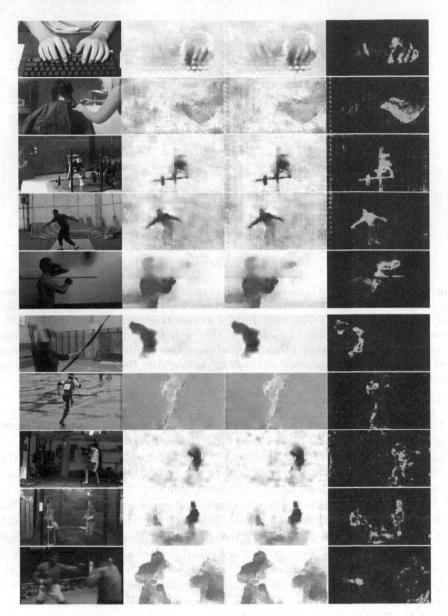

Fig. 5. Comparison of estimated flow fields from a network trained to minimize EPE and the same trained to minimize classification error. Top: Results from FlowNet. Bottom: Results from SpyNet. Each series of 4 images represent the first of the input images, the two flow fields, and the Euclidean distance between the two flow vectors at each pixel (red means higher distance, and blue means lower distance). Flow vectors noticeably change more around motion boundaries and where humans are located. In the case of FlowNet we observe the appearance of a checker-board pattern attributed to the upconvolution (https://distill.pub/2016/deconv-checkerboard/), but we observe that it does not affect the improvement of performance for action recognition. SpyNet does not exhibit the artefact since it does not contain upconvolution. (Color figure online)

Table 2. Action recognition accuracy using optical flow trained on EPE vs. trained on action recognition accuracy. We test using multiple evaluation schemes. In "3 Sn." we take 3 snippets of 5 flow frames, and average the predictions; in "25 Sn." the same with 25 snippets; and in "25 Sn. + Data Aug." the same with the overcropping data augmentation process of TSN. Learning to compute flow for action recognition improves recognition accuracy, across all evaluation schemes and for both flow networks.

Model	EPE loss	Action loss
FlowNet (3 Sn.)	45.97%	**50.51%**
FlowNet (25 Sn.)	45.96%	**50.98%**
FlowNet (25 Sn. + Data Aug.)	56.86%	**59.41%**
SpyNet (3 Sn.)	68.75%	**70.45%**
SpyNet (25 Sn.)	70.26%	**71.50%**
SpyNet (25 Sn. + Data Aug.)	80.91%	**81.47%**

by almost 3% and SpyNet by 0.5%. In this evaluation scheme, 25 snippets (each snippet being a 5 flow field window) are sampled and evaluated and their predictions averaged. In addition, there is data augmentation at test time, where each snippet is "overcropped"[3] 10 times. While this evaluation scheme produces higher accuracy values, it is expensive at test time. Therefore we also show the results of evaluating without data augmentation (named "25 Sn." in the table), where absolute accuracy decreases but we observe the same pattern, of both FlowNet and SpyNet improving their accuracy after learning using the action recognition loss. Finally, we use a light evaluation scheme with only 3 snippets ("3 Sn."). We observe that both flow methods improve their accuracy even more (4% in the case of FlowNet and 2% in the case of SpyNet) in this evaluation scheme that takes in less image evidence, and therefore the quality of the features becomes more apparent. These improvements across all models and evaluation schemes suggest that task-specific flow estimation may be beneficial for solving higher level tasks. We also evaluate the task-specific models on Sintel and observe a similar or slight increase in EPE (Table 3). This is consistent with the results of the previous section where EPE does not correlate strongly with recognition accuracy.

Experiments on the Statistics of the New Motion Representation. What do the learned task-specific optical flow fields represent? We compare the flow fields estimated by the model trained on EPE and the model trained on action recognition. The comparisons are shown in Fig. 5. For each pair of flow fields, the figure shows the first image, the two optical flow fields (using an EPE loss and an action recognition loss), and the Euclidean distance between the two. We observe that most changes occur in two very specific regions of the scene: at motion boundaries and where humans are located. This behavior is consistent

---

[3] This overcropping process consists of cropping the top-left corner, top-right corner, center, bottom-left corner and bottom-right corner, and their flipped counterparts.

Table 3. Evaluation in Sintel of FlowNet and SpyNet, trained on EPE and trained on action recognition accuracy. EPE slightly increases after the networks are fine-tuned for action recognition.

Method	EPE all	EPE matched	EPE unmatched
FlowNet (EPE loss)	8.552	5.053	37.051
FlowNet (Action loss)	8.654	5.149	37.185
SpyNet (EPE loss)	10.715	6.377	46.046
SpyNet (Action loss)	10.719	6.400	45.906

both in SpyNet and FlowNet. Some examples of this effect are the fingers on the typing right hand, the boundary of the person doing push-ups or the arm of the person doing archery. To help us quantify this change we use the Mask-RCNN method [12], to estimate the regions where humans are. We compare the average change of flow at each pixel inside versus outside the human mask. The results are shown in Table 4. In both networks pixel values change one order of magnitude more in regions where humans are located than outside. We quantify the change at boundaries by computing the edge of the mask and dilating it to obtain a thickness of 20 pixels, which captures pixels 10p away from the boundary. In Table 4 we observe that pixels at the boundary change an order of magnitude more than pixels elsewhere. This suggests that flow at boundaries and at objects of interest (in this case humans), is most important for recognition.

Table 4. Statistics of the new motion representation. Regions of the scene where the optical flow changes most during training. We observe that in both methods flow changes most at boundaries and on the human regions.

Method	Human pixels	Non-human pixels	Boundary pixels	Non-bound. pixels
SpyNet	0.1181	0.0169	0.1054	0.0185
FlowNet	0.5046	0.0721	0.4683	0.0821

6   Conclusion

We presented an analysis of two computer vision building blocks (optical flow and action recognition). These two modules are often used together but their interaction has hardly been analyzed. Through thorough experimentation with one of the state-of-the-art action recognition methods and a wide range of optical flow methods we make a number of observations. Optical flow is useful because it is invariant to appearance, even when the flow vectors are inaccurate. We also observe that the traditional EPE metric is weakly correlated with action recognition accuracy but EPE at boundaries and on small displacements is more relevant for recognition. To compute flow that is better for the task we also learned optical flow to directly minimize action recognition error. This leads to numerical improvements on action recognition accuracy. We observed that these improvements arise from changes in the flow on the human body and near the boundary of the body. We believe that our observations will help optical flow researchers who are interested in applications of optical flow for recognition tasks, as well as action recognition researchers who wish to make better decisions about their motion representations.

Disclosure: MJB has received research funding from Intel, Nvidia, Adobe, Facebook, and Amazon. While MJB is a part-time employee of Amazon, this research was performed solely at, and funded solely by, MPI.

References

1. Bailer, C., Taetz, B., Stricker, D.: Flow fields: dense correspondence fields for highly accurate large displacement optical flow estimation. In: International Conference on Computer Vision (ICCV) (2015)
2. Baker, S., Scharstein, D., Lewis, J.P., Roth, S., Black, M.J., Szeliski, R.: A database and evaluation methodology for optical flow. Int. J. Comput. Vis. **92**(1), 1–31 (2011)
3. Barron, J.L., Fleet, D.J., Beauchemin, S.S.: Performance of optical flow techniques. Int. J. Comput. Vis. **12**(1), 43–77 (1994). https://doi.org/10.1007/BF01420984
4. Bobick, A., Davis, J.: An appearance-based representation of action. In: International Pattern Recognition (ICPR) (1996)
5. Brox, T., Malik, J.: Large displacement optical flow: descriptor matching in variational motion estimation. Pattern Anal. Mach. Intell. (PAMI) 500–513 (2011). https://doi.org/10.1109/TPAMI.2010.143
6. Butler, D.J., Wulff, J., Stanley, G.B., Black, M.J.: A naturalistic open source movie for optical flow evaluation. In: Fitzgibbon, A., Lazebnik, S., Perona, P., Sato, Y., Schmid, C. (eds.) ECCV 2012. LNCS, vol. 7577, pp. 611–625. Springer, Heidelberg (2012). https://doi.org/10.1007/978-3-642-33783-3_44
7. Carreira, J., Zisserman, A.: Quo vadis, action recognition? A new model and the kinetics dataset. CoRR abs/1705.07750 (2017). http://arxiv.org/abs/1705.07750
8. Dosovitskiy, A., et al.: FlowNet: learning optical flow with convolutional networks. In: International Conference on Computer Vision (ICCV) (2015)
9. Feichtenhofer, C., Pinz, A., Wildes, R.P.: Spatiotemporal residual networks for video action recognition. CoRR abs/1611.02155 (2016)
10. Feichtenhofer, C., Pinz, A., Zisserman, A.: Convolutional two-stream network fusion for video action recognition. In: Computer Vision and Pattern Recognition (CVPR) (2016)
11. Girdhar, R., Ramanan, D., Gupta, A., Sivic, J., Russell, B.C.: ActionVLAD: learning spatio-temporal aggregation for action classification. CoRR abs/1704.02895 (2017)
12. He, K., Gkioxari, G., Dollár, P., Girshick, R.: Mask R-CNN. arXiv preprint arXiv:1703.06870 (2017)
13. Ilg, E., Mayer, N., Saikia, T., Keuper, M., Dosovitskiy, A., Brox, T.: FlowNet 2.0: evolution of optical flow estimation with deep networks. In: Computer Vision and Pattern Recognition (CVPR) (2017)

14. Ioffe, S., Szegedy, C.: Batch normalization: accelerating deep network training by reducing internal covariate shift. In: International Conference in Machine Learning (ICML), pp. 448–456 (2015). http://jmlr.org/proceedings/papers/v37/ioffe15.pdf
15. Janai, J., Güney, F., Wulff, J., Black, M., Geiger, A.: Slow flow: exploiting high-speed cameras for accurate and diverse optical flow reference data. In: Computer Vision and Pattern Recognition (CVPR) (2017)
16. Jhuang, H., Gall, J., Zuffi, S., Schmid, C., Black, M.J.: Towards understanding action recognition. In: International Conference on Computer Vision (ICCV), pp. 3192–3199 (2013)
17. Johansson, G.: Visual perception of biological motion and a model for its analysis. Percept. Psychophys. **14**(2), 201–211 (1973). https://doi.org/10.3758/BF03212378
18. Karpathy, A., Toderici, G., Shetty, S., Leung, T., Sukthankar, R., Fei-Fei, L.: Large-scale video classification with convolutional neural networks. In: Computer Vision and Pattern Recognition (CVPR) (2014)
19. Koenderink, J., Richards, W., van Doorn, A.J.: Space-time disarray and visual awareness. i-Perception **3**, 159–165 (2012)
20. Kuehne, H., Jhuang, H., Garrote, E., Poggio, T., Serre, T.: HMDB: a large video database for human motion recognition. In: International Conference on Computer Vision (ICCV) (2011)
21. Menze, M., Geiger, A.: Object scene flow for autonomous vehicles. In: Computer Vision and Pattern Recognition (CVPR) (2015)
22. Ng, J.Y., Choi, J., Neumann, J., Davis, L.S.: ActionFlowNet: learning motion representation for action recognition. CoRR abs/1612.03052 (2016). http://arxiv.org/abs/1612.03052
23. Ng, J.Y., Hausknecht, M.J., Vijayanarasimhan, S., Vinyals, O., Monga, R., Toderici, G.: Beyond short snippets: deep networks for video classification. CoRR abs/1503.08909 (2015). http://arxiv.org/abs/1503.08909
24. Ranjan, A., Black, M.J.: Optical flow estimation using a spatial pyramid network. In: Computer Vision and Pattern Recognition (CVPR) (2017)
25. Revaud, J., Weinzaepfel, P., Harchaoui, Z., Schmid, C.: EpicFlow: edge-preserving interpolation of correspondences for optical flow. In: Computer Vision and Pattern Recognition (CVPR) (2015)
26. Roth, S., Black, M.J.: On the spatial statistics of optical flow. Int. J. Comput. Vis. **74**(1), 33–50 (2007)
27. Sigurdsson, G.A., Divvala, S.K., Farhadi, A., Gupta, A.: Asynchronous temporal fields for action recognition. CoRR abs/1612.06371 (2016)
28. Simonyan, K., Zisserman, A.: Two-stream convolutional networks for action recognition in videos. In: Advances in Neural Information Processing Systems (NIPS), pp. 568–576 (2014)
29. Simonyan, K., Zisserman, A.: Very deep convolutional networks for large-scale image recognition. CoRR abs/1409.1556 (2014)
30. Soomro, K., Roshan Zamir, A., Shah, M.: UCF101: a dataset of 101 human actions classes from videos in the wild. In: CRCV-TR-12-01 (2012)
31. Sun, D., Roth, S., Lewis, J.P., Black, M.J.: Learning optical flow. In: Forsyth, D., Torr, P., Zisserman, A. (eds.) ECCV 2008. LNCS, vol. 5304, pp. 83–97. Springer, Heidelberg (2008). https://doi.org/10.1007/978-3-540-88690-7_7
32. Tran, D., Bourdev, L., Fergus, R., Torresani, L., Paluri, M.: Learning spatiotemporal features with 3D convolutional networks. In: International Conference on Computer Vision (ICCV), pp. 4489–4497 (2015)
33. Varol, G., Laptev, I., Schmid, C.: Long-term temporal convolutions for action recognition. Pattern Anal. Mach. Intell. (PAMI) **40**, 1510–1517 (2017)

34. Wang, L., et al.: Temporal segment networks: towards good practices for deep action recognition. In: Leibe, B., Matas, J., Sebe, N., Welling, M. (eds.) ECCV 2016. LNCS, vol. 9912, pp. 20–36. Springer, Cham (2016). https://doi.org/10.1007/978-3-319-46484-8_2

35. Wulff, J., Black, M.J.: Efficient sparse-to-dense optical flow estimation using a learned basis and layers. In: Computer Vision and Pattern Recognition (CVPR), pp. 120–130 (2015)

36. Yao, B., Fei-Fei, L.: Grouplet: a structured image representation for recognizing human and object interactions. In: Computer Vision and Pattern Recognition (CVPR) (2010)

Context-driven Multi-stream LSTM (M-LSTM) for Recognizing Fine-Grained Activity of Drivers

Ardhendu Behera[✉][iD], Alexander Keidel[iD], and Bappaditya Debnath[iD]

Department of Computer Science, Edge Hill University, Ormskirk L39 4QP, UK
{beheraa,keidela,debnathb}@edgehill.ac.uk
https://www.edgehill.ac.uk/computerscience/

Abstract. Automatic recognition of in-vehicle activities has significant impact on the next generation intelligent vehicles. In this paper, we present a novel Multi-stream Long Short-Term Memory (M-LSTM) network for recognizing driver activities. We bring together ideas from recent works on LSTMs, transfer learning for object detection and body pose by exploring the use of deep convolutional neural networks (CNN). Recent work has also shown that representations such as hand-object interactions are important cues in characterizing human activities. The proposed M-LSTM integrates these ideas under one framework, where two streams focus on appearance information with two different levels of abstractions. The other two streams analyze the contextual information involving configuration of body parts and body-object interactions. The proposed contextual descriptor is built to be semantically rich and meaningful, and even when coupled with appearance features it is turned out to be highly discriminating. We validate this on two challenging datasets consisting driver activities.

1 Introduction

Recognition and description of human action/activities in videos and images is a fundamental challenge in computer vision. Over the last two decades, it has been extensively studied and has generated a rich volume of literature [2,15]. It has received increasing attention due to far-reaching applications such as intelligent video surveillance, robotics and AI, human computer interactions, sports analysis, autonomous and intelligent vehicles. Recognising videos requires analysing spatio-temporal data, as well as effective processing and representation of visual and temporal information. Over the years, this representation is dominated by hand-crafted features such as space-time interest points [22,23], joint shape and motion descriptors [4,24,39], feature-level relationships [21,32] and object-hand interactions [3,9,13], due to their superior performance. This has

Electronic supplementary material The online version of this chapter (https://doi.org/10.1007/978-3-030-12939-2_21) contains supplementary material, which is available to authorized users.

© Springer Nature Switzerland AG 2019
T. Brox et al. (Eds.): GCPR 2018, LNCS 11269, pp. 298–314, 2019.
https://doi.org/10.1007/978-3-030-12939-2_21

been challenged by the recent advances in Deep Convolutional Neural Network (DCNN) [11,12,26]. However, extending these networks on video analysis (i.e. temporal data) introduce many new challenges, which are often addressed using temporal modeling. Recently, Long Short-Term Memory (LSTM), a specialized form of Recurrent Neural Network (RNN) is often used to handle temporal data [18]. This is mainly due to the fact that it can encode state, capture temporal ordering and long range dependencies. LSTMs combined with CNNs have shown great performance in video classification tasks [8,27], learning long-term motion dependencies and spatial-temporal relations [25] and precipitation nowcasting [42]. However, it increases network complexity that requires training of a very large number of parameters and tuning many different hyper-parameters. This could be challenging, especially in real-world applications (e.g. robotics and autonomous vehicles) in which there are constraints on power, processing time, size, area and weight.

Recently, there is a growing interest to address the above-mentioned problem via *transfer learning* (TL), aiming to reduce training time and improve performance [29,43]. The initial convolutional layers in deep CNNs produce features with a surprising level of generality (i.e. useful for most images) [29,43]. This generality is a key characteristic of TL that influences the initialization of a target network with layers and trained weights from a base network and is very effective. However, for video-based human activity recognition, most works focus on image-based TL but less work has been done on video-based TL and the best way to do this is still an open question.

In the context of intelligent and (semi-)autonomous vehicles, there is a prominent role of understanding and predicting in-vehicle activities. This would also allow monitoring driver activity (e.g. use of phone, eating and drinking, etc.) and readiness for a takeover request (TOR) [20] in AVs, defined by the National Highway Traffic Safety Administration (NHTSA). This is also a step toward the eventual implementation of the "cognitive car" [14] and self-learning autonomous vehicles (AVs) [6] concepts, which are aimed to learn from the in-vehicle activities to provide a better experience for its occupants and optimize their performance. In this work, we focus on fine-grained in-vehicle (e.g. driver) activity recognition. The term *fine-grained* is similar to the one in [30], aims to distinguish between activities involving little differences. The drivers' activity can be seen as a fine-grained recognition problem (e.g. texting vs talking over phone).

In this paper, we propose a novel deep neural network called Multi-stream LSTM (M-LSTM) for recognising fine-grained activities. The proposed network benefits from the TL by using per-frame CNN features from different layers of available pre-trained CNN models (e.g. VGG16 [34]) as appearance features. We evaluate our M-LSTM network from one stream upto four streams. Our network is flexible and if required, it can accommodate more input streams depending on the target application. The goal is to maximize the use of TL in order to minimize the training complexity and resources while still achieving competitive performance on this fine-grained activity recognition task. This work includes the following novel contributions:

- We demonstrate the effectiveness of our novel Multi-stream LSTM (M-LSTM) for fine-grained activity recognition task. The network is light-weight and can be trained using CPU. It is flexible to accommodate more streams.
- We explore the benefit of TL and validate the significance of context represented by high-level knowledge involving our novel body pose and body-object interactions descriptor. The inclusion of context leads to significant improvements in results. Although LSTMs have been used for action recognition, but in this work we analyze the importance of contextual information influences the way LSTMs are used.
- We are the first to report the video-based activity recognition using the State Farm dataset [7] and the "Distracted Driver" dataset [1], which are aimed to recognise driver's state/activity. All the existing approaches [1,16,36] are based on the single image classification.

2   Related Works

Video-based human activity recognition has made considerable progress. Traditional approaches described in [2,15] are based on hand-crafted features. Recently, these hand-crafted features are replaced with the deep features due to their superior performance. Wang *et al.* [40] replaced the hand-crafted features with CNN features and stacked optical flow, resulting in improved performance. Simonyan and Zisserman [34] have used a two-streams network for action recogniton in which video frames and stacked optical flow are fed as two separate streams. In [33], Ryoo *et al.* used pooled feature representation, which gave superior performance using CNN features.

Long Short-Term Memory (LSTM) models have shown great performance in activity recognition and often used to combine multiple streams of information [8,35,44]. Singh *et al.* [35] have shown that combining full image features with bounding box features improves performance in video classification for fine-grained actions. Wu *et al.* [41] combine several streams: a spatial CNN fed into an LSTM, an optical flow CNN fed into a second LSTM, and an audio spectrogram CNN for video classification. LSTMs have also shown improved performance over two-streams CNNs in recognising activities [8,44].

The traditional vision-based in-vehicle activity monitoring approaches are mostly focused on cues involving driver's upper-body parts (e.g. face, eye, hand and head) and their movements [19,28,38]. These approaches are often targeted at automatic detection of safe/unsafe driving behaviors (e.g. drowsiness, fatigue, distractions, emotions, etc.) using hand-crafted features (e.g. LBP, HOG, Haar-like) combined with classical machine learning algorithms such as SVM and AdaBoost. Understanding driver's activities (e.g. using phone, eating, drinking, etc.) is vital not only for safe driving but also for the autopilot hand-over process for the next generation self-learning AVs. Recently, there has been some progress in using CNN models in monitoring [1,16,36]. However, the adaptation of the state-of-art CNN models driven by the contextual information is yet to be explored. In this paper, we aim to address this.

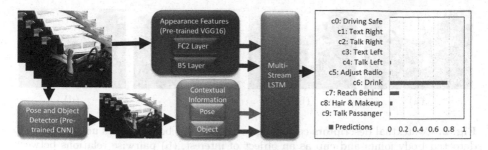

Fig. 1. Overview of the proposed Multi-stream LSTM (M-LSTM) for driver's activity recognition

A good progress has been made in recognising activity using latest approaches such as LSTMs and CNNs. Most of these models are trained on very large datasets and often requires multiple days, even when GPUs are used. It has also been shown that the action recognition performance in still images has significantly improved by incorporating person-objects interactions [11,26] and contextual cues such as body pose [12]. These cues are also vital for video-based activity recognition. Such cues are affiliated to pixel-level and therefore, incorporating these cues in existing LSTMs and CNNs would result in further increase in complexity of these models for video-based activity recognition. As a result, it would be difficult to adapt these models in applications targeted to robotics and autonomous systems. In this work, we revise these contextual cues and represent it as a high-level contextual knowledge that encodes body-pose and hand-object interactions by considering pairwise relationships. These relationships are extrated by exploring the per-frame configuration of the body parts and objects. This is feasible due to the recent development of the state-of-the-art objects [17] and body-parts [5] detector to operate in real-time. We also explore the suggestion in [29] to extract static appearance feature using TL via deep image classification network such as VGG16 [34]. Here we make the observation that use of different level of abstractions (i.e. from different layers) is very useful. We propose a novel Multi-stream LSTM (M-LSTM) which is relatively shallow (upto 8 layers) to integrate contextual cues, long-term sequence information and different levels appearance feature to recognize fine-grained activity of a driver.

3   Proposed Activity Recognition Approach

The overview of the proposed framework is shown in Fig. 1. The architecture has three main components: (1) Transferable deep CNN features, (2) contextual cues involving body pose and body-object interaction and (3) the proposed Multi-stream LSTM (M-LSTM) for sequence modeling and activity recognition.

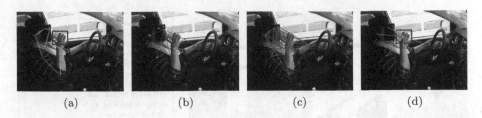

(a)   (b)   (c)   (d)

Fig. 2. Contextual descriptors capturing body pose and body-objects interactions: (a) detected body joints and cup as an object of interest, (b) pairwise relations between nose and the rest of the body joints, (c) all possible pairwise relations between detected body joints, and (d) pairwise relations between detected cup and various body joints.

3.1 Transferable Deep CNN Features

Most of the state-of-the-art deep CNN pre-trained models are publicly available. These models are trained on a large dataset such as ImageNet [31]. Such models learn from very general (e.g. Gabor filters, edges, color blobs) to task-specific features as we move from first-layer to the last-layer [43] and thus, often applied to new dataset with no/minimal fine-tuning. Therefore, it allows us to leverage their power for video analysis when using them as feature extractors. We use VGG16 [34] to extract features at two different extraction points: (1) Block5 (B5) pooling and (2) FC2 (Fully connected). The aim is to extract appearance features denoting various level of abstraction to compare their suitability for a given task.

3.2 Contextual Descriptors

In this work, context refers to the representation of high-level knowledge involving human pose and human-object interactions. Our contextual descriptors are aimed to represent this knowledge effectively. Human action is often perceived from the body pose i.e. configuration of body parts in images. This configuration often provides discriminative appearance cues in differentiating various actions (e.g. standing vs sitting vs bending). However, many fine-grained non-driving activities (e.g. texting, talking over phone, eating, drinking, etc.) exhibit similar body parts configuration. Thus, it is difficult to distinguish them using only body parts. In such cases, involved objects (e.g. cup, bottle, phone, etc.) and its interaction with the body parts play a key role in differentiating these activities. Therefore, we use contextual descriptors to represent relationships between body parts and objects, as well as between various body parts (Fig. 2).

Body Pose Descriptor. The proposed body pose descriptor translates the body parts configuration to a feature vector by encoding relationships between various body parts (Fig. 2c). We use the state-of-the-art Part Affinity Fields (PAFs) [5], which can detect the body parts of multiple person in real-time. It gives output as location (i.e. x, y position in image plane) of 18 body joints:

(1) nose, (2) neck, (3) right shoulder, (4) right elbow, (5) right wrist, (6) left shoulder, (7) left elbow, (8) left wrist, (9) right hip, (10) right knee, (11) right ankle, (12) left hip, (13) left knee, (14) left ankle, (15) right eye, (16) left eye, (17) right ear and (18) left ear. We use the upper-body (knee and above) and there-fore, 16 joints (except both ankles) are considered. There are inevitable noises (missing joints and false detection) and is mainly due to occlusions and contents resulting from driving circumstances and environmental situations. Therefore, detecting all joints accurately would be difficult even if one fine-tuned/re-trained the model on the target dataset. Our goal is to minimize this noise while creat-ing the descriptor and thus, we consider pairwise relations between all possible detected joints. For example, if an elbow is noisy (false detection or undetected) then the relationships between other detected joints (e.g. neck, shoulder, wrist, etc.) would be able to capture the body pose.

There are 16 joints, resulting 120 ($\frac{16 \times 15}{2}$) possible unique pairs. For each pair, we compute a relational feature f. Let's consider a pair of joints j_1 and j_2, located at (x_1, y_1) and (x_2, y_2), respectively. Their relationship is represented using distance $r = \sqrt{(x_2 - x_1)^2 + (y_2 - y_1)^2}$ and orientation $\theta = \arctan(\frac{y_2 - y_1}{x_2 - x_1})$. The angle θ is binned into h number of bins and the magnitude r contributes to the respective bin(s) where the θ falls into. As a result, f is sparse and its dimension is the number of bins h. We apply the L_2 normalisation to f. The process continues for all 120 pairs and concatenate them to represent our pose descriptor $D_p = [f_1, f_2, \cdots, f_{120}]$ of length $120 \times h$.

Body-Object Descriptor. Similar to the pose descriptor, our body-object descriptor captures the pairwise relationship between the body joints and involved objects. This relationship encodes the relative position of an object with respect to a given joint in a scene. Thus, we need to detect the commonly used objects (e.g. mobile phone, water bottle, cup, etc.). Similar to the body joints, we use the TL approach for objects detection i.e. using a pre-trained detector on the target dataset. We benefit from the state-of-the-art deep CNN models, which have achieved remarkable results. One such model is the combi-nation of Faster R-CNN with Inception ResNet-V2 [17]. This model is trained on COCO dataset consisting 330K images, 1.5 million objects instances and 80 object categories.

Our focus is on the *object of interest* (e.g. phone, bottle, cup, etc.). A common observation is that the size of these objects is small with respect to the size of the driver (Fig. 2d) and appears in the vicinity of the driver's bounding box. Thus, we use the bounding box information (size and aspect ratio) to select the objects of interest. We could have selected these based on their types. However, we noticed that there are noises (e.g. wrongly labeled) in detection and is mainly due to occlusion by the driver's hand, as well as the use of TL since the detector is trained on a different dataset. It is observed that often mobile phones and coffee mugs are detected as a remote, cup as a wine glass. Our aim is to model contextual cues (configuration of objects with respect to joints) to discriminate the fine-grained activities. Thus, we argue that if an object is wrongly labeled,

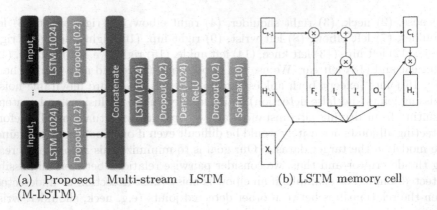

(a) Proposed Multi-stream LSTM
(M-LSTM)

(b) LSTM memory cell

Fig. 3. (a) Proposed relatively shallow (up to 8 layers) Multi-stream LSTM (M-LSTM) and (b) an LSTM memory cell used in this work from [18].

the combined configuration of body joints and object would provide enough cues for discriminating various activities. For example, if a phone is labeled as a mug then based on the arm configuration, its position with respect to other body parts (e.g. torso, head, etc.) and the object's position with respect to body parts, would provide cue in discriminating *texting* vs *talking* vs *drinking*.

A total of 25 objects of interest are selected on the target datasets [1,7] by considering their relative size (area $< 1/4$th of the driver's bounding box) and position (bounding box overlap $> 80\%$) with respect to the driver's bounding box. The proposed body-object descriptor (D_o) captures the pairwise relationship between 16 body joints and the detected objects. D_o encodes this relationship as a histogram of oriented relation $\hat{f}$ (Fig. 2d), which is computed similar to the body joints relational feature f (Fig. 2b) in the pose descriptor D_p. A total of 400 (25×16) pairwise relations ($\hat{f_1}...\hat{f_{400}}$) are stacked to represent our body-object descriptor $D_o = [\hat{f_1}, \hat{f_2}, ..., \hat{f_{400}}]$ of length $400 \times h$ (h angle bins).

3.3 Multi-stream Long Short-Term Memory (M-LSTM) Network

The proposed Multi-stream LSTM (M-LSTM) network for fine-grained activity recognition is shown in Fig. 3a. The aim is to combine multiple feature types in order to take the best advantage of data representation with multiple levels of abstractions and allow the model to learn activities from these representations. The proposed M-LSTM is inspired by [10]. It is light-weight and consists of LSTM, Dropout, FC and Softmax layers. The architecture is flexible so that more input streams could easily be added and takes advantage of off-the-shelf CNN features, which have shown impressive performance in visual recognition tasks [29,43]. The inputs consist of per-frame appearance and contextual features. The sequential information in the M-LSTM is captured by the two LSTM layers - one is in individual stream and the other is after the fusion (Fig. 3a). It should be noted that all our input features are based on transfer learning i.e.

CNN features, object and body parts detectors are not trained/fune-tuned on the target dataset.

LSTM is a special type of Recurrent Neural Network (RNN). It is capable of learning long-term dependencies by incorporating memory units that allow the network to learn, forget previous hidden states and update hidden states, when required [8]. The M-LSTM network uses the LSTM architecture described in [18] (Fig. 3b). At a given timestep t, the M-LSTM takes input $x_t = [D_p^t, D_o^t, F_1^t, F_2^t]$, consisting body pose D_p^t, body-object interactions D_o^t, and CNN feature F_1^t and F_2^t extracted from the respective FC2 and Block5 layer of the VGG16 [34]. The model updates at time t given the memory cells for long-term c_{t-1} and short-term h_{t-1} recall from the previous timestep $t-1$ and is by:

$$
\begin{aligned}
i_t &= tanh(W_{xi}x_t + W_{hi}h_{t-1} + b_i) \\
j_t &= sigm(W_{xj}x_t + W_{hj}h_{t-1} + b_j) \\
f_t &= sigm(W_{xf}x_t + W_{hf}h_{t-1} + b_f) \\
o_t &= tanh(W_{xo}x_t + W_{ho}h_{t-1} + b_o) \\
c_t &= c_{t-1} \odot f_t + i_t \odot j_t \\
h_t &= tanh(c_t) \odot o_t
\end{aligned}
\tag{1}
$$

Where W_* denotes weight matrices, b_* biases, $\odot$ element-wise vector product, respectively. The LSTM has two kinds of hidden states: c_t and h_t which allow it to make complex decisions over a short period of time. It also includes an input gate i_t, input modulation gate j_t contributing to memory, forget gate f_t, output gate o_t as a multiplier between the memory gates (Fig. 3b). The gates i_t and f_t can be seen as knobs allowing the LSTM to selectively consider its current input or forgets its previous memory. Similarly, the output gate o_t learns how much memory cell c_t need to be transferred to the hidden state h_t. These additional memory cells give the ability to learn extremely complex and long-term temporal dynamics in comparison to the RNN. Moreover, LSTM provides the ability to remember information and recall it at a later point in time when needed and is suitable for solving video recognition problems.

4   Experiments, Results and Discussion

We use the State Farm [7] and "Distracted Driver" [1] dataset, comprised of inwards facing dashboard camera images depicting ten fine-grained activities: (c0) safe driving, (c1) texting - right, (c2) talking on the phone - right, (c3) texting - left, (c4) talking on the phone - left, (c5) operating the radio, (c6) drinking, (c7) reaching behind, (c8) hair and makeup, and (c9) talking to passenger.

In the State Farm [7] dataset, there are 260 clips (22,424 images) from 26 drivers (mixture of male and female from different ethnicity). There are 10 clips (one for each activity) per driver. Similarly, in the "Distracted Driver" dataset [1], there are 310 clips (17,308 images) from 31 drivers. This dataset has also 10 classes and 10 clips per driver. In our experiment, we uniformly sampled 30 frames per clip. Let's say there are m number of frames in a given clip and we wish to sample the desired $n = 30$ frames by selecting a frame at position

$j = 0 \ldots m - 1$ in the original clip, where $j = \| \frac{i \times m}{n} \|$ for $i = 0 \ldots n - 1$. For our experiment, 70% (180 videos from 18 drivers in [7] and 220 videos from 22 drivers in [1]) of the dataset is used for training and the rest 30% (80 and 90 clips form the rest of the 8 and 9 drivers in [7] and [1], respectively) for validation. We select this split so that the validation set consists of entirely unseen drivers.

We explore all possible permutations using 4 different features. Our experiments provide multiple outcomes: (1) performance of transferable features from different layers (B5 pooling and FC2) of VGG16 [34], (2) performance of contextual descriptors like body pose and body-object interaction in comparison to CNN features, (3) the impact on performance using various combinations of features, and (4) the influence of temporal information (number of frames) on performance for live monitoring.

We use default image size (224 × 224) for CNN features (B5 and FC2) using pre-trained VGG16 [34], resulting feature length of 4096 (FC2) and 25088 (B5). For our contextual descriptors, we have experimented with different number of bins ($h = 6, 9, 12$ and 18) and found better performance for $h = 12$, resulting the size 1440 (120 × 12) and 4800 (400 × 12) for the pose and body-object interaction descriptor, respectively.

In the proposed M-LSTM, the number of layers, their orders and parameters are selected based on the performance. The final M-LSTM is shown in Fig. 3a. Each clip in the dataset consists of a single activity and therefore, we are interested in the class probability distribution once M-LSTM has observed the entire sequence. To achieve this, many approaches exist [44]: (1) using the prediction at the last frame of a given clip; (2) max pooling the predictions over the entire clip; (3) summing all of the frames predictions over time and returning the most frequent. We have experimented our model by using approaches (1) and (2). Using approach (1) i.e. without temporal pooling layer, we have observed the per-frame accuracy, its effect on the number of input frames and the minimum number of frames required for a good early prediction. The models are trained using the RMSprop [37] optimizer to minimize the categorical cross entropy $L_v = - \sum_c y_{v,c} log(p_{v,c})$, where p are the predictions, y are the targets, v denotes the training video and c denotes the class. One-stream model is trained using a learning rate (lr) of 2×10^{-5}; two-, three- and four-streams of 5×10^{-5}, with all other parameters are assigned with default values. A Linux PC (Intel i7-5930K, 12 cores, 3.5 GHZ) with NVIDIA Quadro P6000 24GB GPU is used for our experiments. The models are trained for 50 epochs with a batch size of 32. Training time of each model is just under 20 min. The same training takes around 2:37h using CPU, which is still a viable option.

For evaluation, we use accuracy (ACC) and average precision (AP). ACC assigns equal cost to false positives and false negatives. Whereas, AP summarizes precision-recall curve. We also compute multi-class log loss $logLoss = -\frac{1}{V} \sum_v \sum_c y_{v,c} log(p_{v,c})$, where v represents test videos, c denotes activity labels, p implies predictions and y denotes targets. It quantifies the accuracy of a classifier by penalizing confident false classifications. For example, if a classifier assigns a very small probability to a correct class then the corresponding contribution to the log loss will be very large. An ideal classifier will have zero log loss. The performance of the M-LSTM is shown in Table 1. There are four sets of rows representing the performance of one-stream to the four-streams. The left column is for the State Farm dataset [7] and the right column is for the "Distracted Driver" [1] dataset. The given performance is based on our proposed M-LSTM without temporal pooling in Fig. 3a. The performance is measured as the *argmax* of the final softmax layer. The best performance is shown as bold within a given set. It is clear that as we add more streams the performance improves in both the datasets.

Table 1. Performance of the proposed M-LSTM: from one-stream to four-streams using State Farm [7] (left column) and "Distracted Driver" [1]. The performance is the *argmax* of the output from the softmax layer. All values are in percentages except for the log loss. Lower value of the log loss is better. The best performance is shown in bold for a given dataset with one or more input streams

	ACC	AP	Log loss	ACC	AP	Log loss
	State Farm [7] dataset			Distracted Driver [1] dataset		
One-stream						
Pose	48.75	60.00	5.61	12.22	12.20	2.25
FC2	52.50	72.50	2.70	30.00	34.18	2.44
Object	61.25	75.25	3.06	**42.22**	44.23	2.40
B5	**77.50**	**85.00**	**1.32**	38.89	**47.46**	**1.94**
Two-streams						
FC2+Pose	60.00	77.50	2.23	34.44	38.49	2.38
Pose+Object	61.25	73.75	5.01	**44.44**	48.64	4.00
B5+Pose	81.25	**91.25**	1.05	34.44	43.51	2.02
FC2+B5	81.25	88.75	0.99	36.67	49.23	1.88
FC2+Object	77.50	81.25	1.10	41.11	**54.69**	**1.87**
B5+Object	**85.00**	90.00	**0.69**	43.33	53.16	1.97
Three-streams						
FC2+Pose+Object	76.25	88.75	1.68	47.78	57.68	2.08
FC2+B5+Pose	78.75	87.50	1.16	34.44	40.22	2.28
FC2+B5+Object	86.25	**96.25**	0.51	46.67	52.83	1.75
B5+Pose+Object	**87.50**	**96.25**	0.62	**52.22**	**59.66**	**1.66**
Four-streams						
FC2+B5+Pose+Object	91.25	95.00	0.45	37.78	53.11	1.72

Performance on State Farm Dataset. [7] For CNN features (FC2 and B5), the ACC of B5 is 25% better than the FC2 (Table 1, left column). In [29], CNN feature from FC layer is used for the visual recognition task. This shows the CNN features are dependent on the target dataset type and more than one extraction point should be considered while using transfer learning. Moreover, when we combine features from multiple extraction points (FC2+B5), the performance is better than the single ones. When our contextual information (body pose and body-object interactions) is added, the ACC increase by 10% (B5+Pose+Object) in comparison to the B5 alone. Similarly, adding this information to FC2, the performance increased by 33.75% and this explains the significance of our high-level contextual descriptors. Our model gives the best performance (ACC: 91.25%), when all four-streams are used. The confusion matrix for one-stream to four-streams using the B5, is shown in Fig. 4. If we compare the one-stream (Fig. 4a) with four-streams (Fig. 4d), the performance of most of the activities is improved or same except the activity c0 - *safe driving* and c1 - *texting right*. The c0 is confused with c1. This could be due to both c0 (both hand on steering) and c1 exhibit similar body pose and the cell phone is often occluded because of the dashboard camera position. The four-streams performance of activity c3 - *texting - left* drops by 12% in comparison to the three-streams model (Fig. 4d vs 4c). This 12% is confused with the c4 - *talking on the phone - left*. This is mainly due to one of the subject's left hand is close to the head while texting and based on the subject's pose and phone position with respect to the body, the model recognized as talking left and could be the influence of contextual information. Whereas, using B5, the model recognises this one correctly (Fig. 4a).

Performance on Distracted Driver Dataset. [1] The performance of the proposed approach using the "Distracted Driver" dataset [1] is presented in Table 1 (right column). Similar to the State Farm [7], the performance increases as we add more streams. However, the overall performance is quite low in comparison to the State Farm [7]. This could be due to the fact that the data in [1] was being collected from seven different countries in four different cars with several variations in driving conditions. Whereas, State Farm [7] data was collected using one car in a controlled environment i.e. a truck dragging the car around on the streets - so the drivers weren't really driving.

In one-stream, the standout performance (ACC: 42.22%) is our contextual descriptor using body-object interactions (Table 1, right column). When this descriptor is combined with others, the overall performance is improved (B5+Object: 43.33%, Pose+Object: 44.44% and FC2+object: 41.11%). This demonstrates the significance of our proposed context-driven model. The best performance on this dataset is the combination of three streams i.e. B5+Pose+Object (ACC: 52.22%). When the fourth stream FC2 is integrated to it, the performance dropped to 37.78%. Therefore, the FC2 feature is not as good as the B5. A similar trend was observed in the State Farm [7] dataset as well.

Performance Using Temporal Pooling Layer. We have experimented with the use of temporal pooling (max pooling) layer. This temporal pooling layer

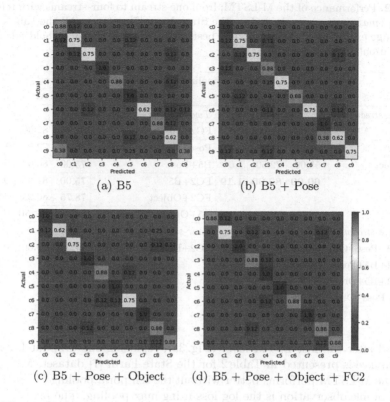

Fig. 4. Confusion matrices for one-stream to four-streams based on B5.

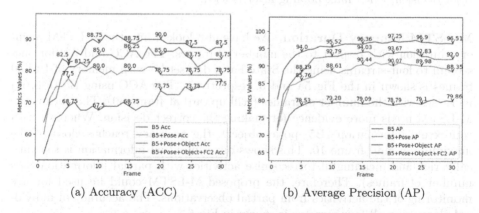

(a) Accuracy (ACC)   (b) Average Precision (AP)

Fig. 5. Activity recognition performance (average over 8 drivers and each with 10 activity classes) for one-stream to four-streams based on B5. The proposed M-LSTM model's ACC (a) and AP (b) over the model's memory duration in frames using the State Farm dataset [7].

Table 2. Performance of the M-LSTM: from one-stream to four-streams with temporal pooling (*max pooling*), evaluated on the State Farm [7] dataset. All the values are in percentage except for the log loss. The best performance is shown in bold for a given combination(s) of input stream(s)

	M-LSTM with max pooling using State Farm [7] dataset						
	ACC	AP	Loss		ACC	AP	Loss
One-stream				*Two-streams*			
Pose	35.00	55.00	2.23	FC2+Pose	62.50	82.50	1.31
FC2	51.25	71.25	1.96	Pose+Object	56.25	72.50	1.72
Object	55.00	72.50	1.64	B5+Pose	75.00	80.00	0.85
B5	**60.00**	**80.00**	**1.19**	FC2+B5	75.00	87.50	0.88
				FC2+Object	78.75	86.25	0.92
				B5+Object	**81.25**	**92.50**	**0.53**
Three-streams				*Four-streams*			
FC2+Pose+Obj	76.25	88.75	0.91	FC2+B5+Pose+Object	87.50	95.00	0.50
FC2+B5+Pose	75.00	87.50	0.76				
FC2+B5+Obj	83.75	**95.00**	**0.49**				
B5+Pose+Obj	**86.25**	91.25	0.52				

is added after the last LSTM layer (Fig. 3a), replacing the dropout layer. The performance is presented in Table 2 for the State Farm [7] dataset. Most of the time, the M-LSTM performs better without the temporal pooling (Table 1). The other notable observation is the log loss using max pooling. The performance is better (lower is better) than without the max pooling, except in the four-streams model. This implies the M-LSTM is more confident (high probability) in making right decision, when max pooling layer is used.

M-LSTM Memory Duration. We have also looked into the M-LSTM memory duration with respect to the number of frames. The ACC and AP for one-stream to four-streams using the State Farm dataset [7] with memory of 1 to 30 frames is shown in the Fig. 5a and b, respectively. The ACC using B5 (Fig. 5a) increases with the number of frames (still upward at frame 30). This means the M-LSTM needs more evidence for making the correct decision. Whereas, with contextual information (B5+pose+object), the accuracy reaches close to the maximum around frame 10. This shows our contextual information is semantically rich and meaningful to recognise activities with partial information (less number of frames). Therefore, the proposed M-LSTM could be used for live monitoring of the activities from partial observations. The accuracy of individual class using all four streams is shown in Fig. 6.

Performance Comparison with State-of-the-Art. As mentioned earlier, we are the first to report video-based activity recognition on these datasets [1,7]. The existing approaches [1,16,36] were evaluated using still images. For still

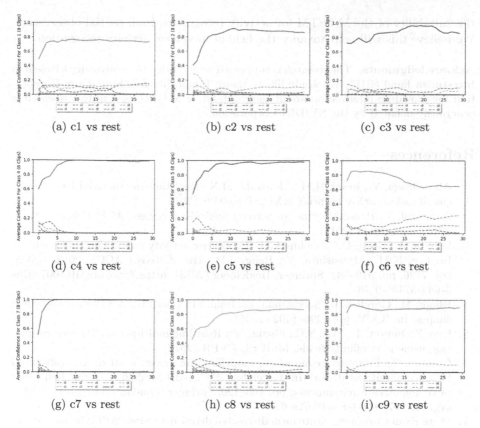

(a) c1 vs rest   (b) c2 vs rest   (c) c3 vs rest

(d) c4 vs rest   (e) c5 vs rest   (f) c6 vs rest

(g) c7 vs rest   (h) c8 vs rest   (i) c9 vs rest

Fig. 6. Individual activity performance (average accuracy over 8 drivers) of our M-LSTM over the model's memory duration in frames. The accuracy using four-streams (B5+Pose+Object+FC2): the solid line is the predicted activity and the dotted lines are the rest of the activities using the State Farm dataset [7].

images, Hssayeni et al. [16] reported the accuracy of 85% using State Farm [7] and Abouelnaga et al. [1] has achieved accuracy of 95.17% using their "Distracted Driver" dataset. However, [1] has used the validation images from the seen drivers i.e. for a given driver and activity, part of the video frames used in training and the rest for testing. In our experiments, we use entirely unseen drivers for testing.

5 Conclusion

We have developed a Multi-stream LSTM (M-LSTM) network for recognizing fine-grained activities of drivers. The network is light-weight and flexible to accommodate one or more input streams. We demonstrated how our proposed network learns to recognize fine-grained activities by exploring transfer learning and combining features with different levels of abstractions, as well as contextual features involving body pose and body-objects interactions. We further analyzes the suitability of the M-LSTM for activity recognition from partial observation. We believe this will help advance the field of in-vehicle activity recognition.

Acknowledgments. The research is supported by the Edge Hill University's Research Investment Fund (RIF). We would like to thank Taylor Smith in State Farm Corporation for providing information about their dataset. The GPU used in this research is generously donated by the NVIDIA Corporation.

References

1. Abouelnaga, Y., Eraqi, H.M., Moustafa, M.N.: Real-time distracted driver posture classification. arXiv preprint arXiv:1706.09498 (2017)
2. Aggarwal, J., Ryoo, M.: Human activity analysis: a review. ACM Comput. Surv. **43**(3), 16:1–16:43 (2011)
3. Behera, A., Hogg, D.C., Cohn, A.G.: Egocentric activity monitoring and recovery. In: Lee, K.M., Matsushita, Y., Rehg, J.M., Hu, Z. (eds.) ACCV 2012. LNCS, vol. 7726, pp. 519–532. Springer, Heidelberg (2013). https://doi.org/10.1007/978-3-642-37431-9_40
4. Blank, M., Gorelick, L., Shechtman, E., Irani, M., Basri, R.: Actions as space-time shapes. In: ICCV, pp. 1395–1402 (2005)
5. Cao, Z., Simon, T., Wei, S.E., Sheikh, Y.: Realtime multi-person 2D pose estimation using part affinity fields. In: IEEE CVPR (2017)
6. Carsten, O.: From driver models to modelling the driver: what do we really need to know about the driver? In: Cacciabue, P.C. (ed.) Modelling Driver Behaviour in Automotive Environments, pp. 105–120. Springer, London (2007). https://doi.org/10.1007/978-1-84628-618-6_6
7. State Farm Corporate: State farm distracted driver detection (2016). https://www.kaggle.com/c/state-farm-distracted-driver-detection
8. Donahue, J., et al.: Long-term recurrent convolutional networks for visual recognition and description. IEEE Trans. PAMI **39**(4), 677–691 (2017)
9. Fathi, A., Farhadi, A., Rehg, J.M.: Understanding egocentric activities. In: ICCV (2011)
10. Feichtenhofer, C., Pinz, A., Zisserman, A.: Convolutional two-stream network fusion for video action recognition. In: IEEE CVPR, pp. 1933–1941 (2016)
11. Girdhar, R., Ramanan, D.: Attentional pooling for action recognition. In: Advances in NIPS, pp. 33–44 (2017)
12. Gkioxari, G., Girshick, R., Malik, J.: Contextual action recognition with R*CNN. In: ICCV, pp. 1080–1088 (2015)
13. Gupta, A., Davis, L.S.: Objects in action: an approach for combining action understanding and object perception. In: CVPR (2007)
14. Heide, A., Henning, K.: The "cognitive car": a roadmap for research issues in the automotive sector. Ann. Rev. Control **30**(2), 197–203 (2006)
15. Herath, S., Harandi, M., Porikli, F.: Going deeper into action recognition: a survey. Image Vis. Comput. **60**, 4–21 (2017)
16. Hssayeni, M., Saxena, S., Ptucha, R., Savakis, A.: Distracted driver detection: deep learning vs handcrafted features. Electron. Imaging **10**, 20–26 (2017)
17. Huang, J., et al.: Speed/accuracy trade-offs for modern convolutional object detectors. In: IEEE CVPR, pp. 3296–3297 (2017)

18. Jozefowicz, R., Zaremba, W., Sutskever, I.: An empirical exploration of recurrent network architectures. In: ICML, pp. 2342–2350 (2015)
19. Kaplan, S., Guvensan, M.A., Yavuz, A.G., Karalurt, Y.: Driver behavior analysis for safe driving: a survey. IEEE Trans. Int. Transp. Syst. **16**(6), 3017–3032 (2015). https://doi.org/10.1109/TITS.2015.2462084
20. Kim, H.J., Yang, J.H.: Takeover requests in simulated partially autonomous vehicles considering human factors. IEEE Trans. Hum.-Mach. Syst. **47**(5), 735–740 (2017). https://doi.org/10.1109/THMS.2017.2674998
21. Kovashka, A., Grauman, K.: Learning a hierarchy of discriminative space-time neighborhood features for human action recognition. In: IEEE CVPR (2010)
22. Laptev, I., Lindeberg, T.: Space-time interest points. In: ICCV, pp. 432–439 (2003)
23. Laptev, I., Marszalek, M., Schmid, C., Rozenfeld, B.: Learning realistic human actions from movies. In: CVPR (2008)
24. Liu, J., Luo, J., Shah, M.: Recognizing realistic actions from videos "in the wild". In: IEEE CVPR, pp. 1996–2003 (2009)
25. Luo, Z., Peng, B., Huang, D.A., Alahi, A., Fei-Fei, L.: Unsupervised learning of long-term motion dynamics for videos. arXiv preprint arXiv:1701.01821, vol. 2 (2017)
26. Mallya, A., Lazebnik, S.: Learning models for actions and person-object interactions with transfer to question answering. In: Leibe, B., Matas, J., Sebe, N., Welling, M. (eds.) ECCV 2016. LNCS, vol. 9905, pp. 414–428. Springer, Cham (2016). https://doi.org/10.1007/978-3-319-46448-0_25
27. Ng, J.Y.H., Hausknecht, M., Vijayanarasimhan, S., Vinyals, O., Monga, R., Toderici, G.: Beyond short snippets: deep networks for video classification. In: CVPR (2015)
28. Ranft, B., Stiller, C.: The role of machine vision for intelligent vehicles. IEEE Trans. Int. Veh. **1**(1), 8–19 (2016). https://doi.org/10.1109/TIV.2016.2551553
29. Razavian, A.S., Azizpour, H., Sullivan, J., Carlsson, S.: CNN features off-the-shelf: an astounding baseline for recognition. In: IEEE CVPRW, pp. 512–519 (2014)
30. Rohrbach, M., Amin, S., Andriluka, M., Schiele, B.: A database for fine grained activity detection of cooking activities. In: IEEE CVPR, pp. 1194–1201, June 2012
31. Russakovsky, O., et al.: ImageNet large scale visual recognition challenge. IJCV **115**(3), 211–252 (2015)
32. Ryoo, M.S., Aggarwal, J.K.: Spatio-temporal relationship match: video structure comparison for recognition of complex human activities. In: ICCV (2009)
33. Ryoo, M.S., Rothrock, B., Matthies, L.H.: Pooled motion features for first-person videos. In: IEEE CVPR (2014)
34. Simonyan, K., Zisserman, A.: Very deep convolutional networks for large-scale image recognition. arXiv preprint arXiv:1409.1556 (2014)
35. Singh, B., Marks, T.K., Jones, M., Tuzel, O., Shao, M.: A multi-stream bi-directional recurrent neural network for fine-grained action detection. In: IEEE CVPR, pp. 1961–1970 (2016)
36. Singh, D.: Using convolutional neural networks to perform classification on state farm insurance driver images. Technical report. Stanford University, Stanford, CA (2016)
37. Tieleman, T., Hinton, G.: Lecture 65-rmsprop: divide the gradient by a running average of its recent magnitude. COURSERA: Neural Networks for Mach. Learn. **4**(2), 26–31 (2012)
38. Trivedi, M.M., Gandhi, T., McCall, J.: Looking-in and looking-out of a vehicle: computer-vision-based enhanced vehicle safety. IEEE Trans. Int. Transp. Syst. **8**(1), 108–120 (2007). https://doi.org/10.1109/TITS.2006.889442

39. Wang, H., Kläser, A., Schmid, C., Liu, C.L.: Dense trajectories and motion boundary descriptors for action recognition. IJCV **103**(1), 60–79 (2013)
40. Wang, L., Qiao, Y., Tang, X.: Action recognition with trajectory-pooled deep-convolutional descriptors. In: IEEE CVPR (2015)
41. Wu, Z., Jiang, Y.G., Wang, X., Ye, H., Xue, X., Wang, J.: Fusing multi-stream deep networks for video classification. arXiv preprint arXiv:1509.06086 (2015)
42. Xingjian, S., Chen, Z., Wang, H., Yeung, D.Y., Wong, W.K., Woo, W.C.: Convolutional LSTM network: a machine learning approach for precipitation nowcasting. In: Advances in NIPS, pp. 802–810 (2015)
43. Yosinski, J., Clune, J., Bengio, Y., Lipson, H.: How transferable are features in deep neural networks? In: NIPS, pp. 3320–3328 (2014)
44. Yue-Hei Ng, J., Hausknecht, M., Vijayanarasimhan, S., Vinyals, O., Monga, R., Toderici, G.: Beyond short snippets: deep networks for video classification. In: IEEE CVPR, pp. 4694–4702 (2015)

3D Fluid Flow Estimation with Integrated Particle Reconstruction

Katrin Lasinger[1]([✉])[iD], Christoph Vogel[2], Thomas Pock[2,3][iD],
and Konrad Schindler[1][iD]

[1] Photogrammetry and Remote Sensing, ETH Zurich, Zürich, Switzerland
`katrin.lasinger@geod.baug.ethz.ch`
[2] Institute of Computer Graphics and Vision,
Graz University of Technology, Graz, Austria
[3] AIT Austrian Institute of Technology, Vienna, Austria

Abstract. The standard approach to densely reconstruct the motion in a volume of fluid is to inject high-contrast tracer particles and record their motion with multiple high-speed cameras. Almost all existing work processes the acquired multi-view video in two separate steps: first, a per-frame reconstruction of the particles, usually in the form of soft occupancy likelihoods in a voxel representation; followed by 3D motion estimation, with some form of dense matching between the precomputed voxel grids from different time steps. In this sequential procedure, the first step cannot use temporal consistency considerations to support the reconstruction, while the second step has no access to the original, high-resolution image data. We show, for the first time, how to *jointly* reconstruct both the individual tracer particles and a dense 3D fluid motion field from the image data, using an integrated energy minimization. Our hybrid Lagrangian/Eulerian model explicitly reconstructs individual particles, and at the same time recovers a dense 3D motion field in the entire domain. Making particles explicit greatly reduces the memory consumption and allows one to use the high-resolution input images for matching. Whereas the dense motion field makes it possible to include physical a-priori constraints and account for the incompressibility and viscosity of the fluid. The method exhibits greatly ($\approx70\%$) improved results over a recent baseline with two separate steps for 3D reconstruction and motion estimation. Our results with only two time steps are comparable to those of state-of-the-art tracking-based methods that require much longer sequences.

1 Introduction

The capture and recovery of 3D motion in a transparent medium is a complex and challenging task, with important applications in different fields of science

Electronic supplementary material The online version of this chapter (https://doi.org/10.1007/978-3-030-12939-2_22) contains supplementary material, which is available to authorized users.

© Springer Nature Switzerland AG 2019
T. Brox et al. (Eds.): GCPR 2018, LNCS 11269, pp. 315–332, 2019.
https://doi.org/10.1007/978-3-030-12939-2_22

Fig. 1. From 2D images of a fluid injected with tracer particles, recorded at two consecutive time steps, we jointly reconstruct the particles Q and a dense 3D motion field $\mathcal{U}$. The example shows the experimental setup of [24].

and technology: Observations of fluid motion and fluid-structure interaction form the basis of experimental fluid dynamics. Measuring and understanding flow and turbulence patterns is important for aero- and hydrodynamics in the automotive, aeronautic and ship-building industries, e.g. to design efficient shapes and to test the elasticity of components. Biological sciences are another application field, e.g., behavioral studies about aquatic organisms that live in flowing water [25].

A state-of-the-art technology to capture fluid motion in the laboratory is *particle image velocimetry* (PIV) [2,32]. The underlying idea is to inject tracer particles into the fluid, which densely cover the illuminated volume of interest, and to record them with high-speed cameras from multiple viewpoints. Figure 1 shows the basic setup: 3D particle positions and a dense motion field are recovered from a set of input images from two consecutive time steps.

Due to computational limitations, early variants were restricted to 2D, by illuminating only a thin slice of the volume, thus neglecting interactions between different slices. More recent methods operate on the full 3D volume, but divide the problem in two independent steps. First, they recover the 3D particle distribution in the volume using all views at a single time step, by means of *tomographic PIV* (TomoPIV) [14], or sparse representations [29]. Second, they employ dense correspondence estimation between consecutive particle volumes to obtain the 3D motion of the fluid. The latter step is often simply an exhaustive matching of large enough local 3D windows [10,11,13] or, more recently, a variational flow estimation [20], with suitable priors on the motion field to limit the size of the matching window. We argue that any such two-step approach is sub-optimal, for several reasons. At each time step, the same particles are reconstructed without looking at the images at the other time step, effectively halving the available data. E.g., ignoring that a particle strongly supported by the later frame "must have come from somewhere". Similarly, valuable information is lost when discarding the input images after the first step. E.g., one cannot check whether a weak particle that unnaturally distorts the motion field "should be there at all"; particularly since physical limitations in practice restrict camera placement to narrow baselines, such that the initial reconstruction is ambiguous. Moreover, to achieve a resolution similar to the original images the volume must be discretized at high resolution, making the computation memory-hungry and expensive. Also, it is well documented that large 3D matching windows are needed for good performance, which undermines the benefits of high resolution.

In this work we propose a *joint energy model* for the reconstruction of the particles and the 3D motion field, so as to capture the inherent mutual dependencies. The model uses the full information – all available images from both time steps at full resolution – to solve the problem. We opt for a hybrid *Lagrangian/Eulerian* approach: particles are modeled individually, while the motion field is represented on a dense grid. Recovering explicit particle locations and intensities avoids the need for a costly 3D parameterization of voxel occupancy, as well as the use of a large matching window. Instead, it directly compares evidence for single particles in the images, yielding significantly higher accuracy.

To represent the motion field, we opt for a trilinear finite element basis. Modeling the 3D motion densely allows us to incorporate physical priors that account for incompressibility and viscosity of the observed fluid [20]. This can be done efficiently, at a much lower voxel resolution than would be required for particle reconstruction, due to the smoothness of the 3D motion field [11, 20].

We model our problem in a variational setting. To better resolve particle ambiguities, we add a prior to our energy that encourages sparsity. In order to overcome weak minima of the non-convex energy, we include a proposal generation step that detects putative particles in the residual images, and alternates with the energy minimization. For the optimization itself, we can rely on the very efficient *inertial Proximal Alternating Linearized Minimization* (iPALM) [9, 30]. It is guaranteed to converge to a stationary point of the energy and has a low memory footprint, so that we can reconstruct large volumes.

Compared to our baselines [14] and [20], which both address the problem sequentially with two independent steps, we achieve particle reconstructions with higher precision and recall, at all tested particle densities; and greatly improved motion estimates. The estimated fluid flow visually appears on par with state-of-the-art techniques like [36], which use tracking over multiple time steps and highly engineered post-processing [15, 38].

2   Related Work

In experimental fluid mechanics, two strategies have evolved for flow estimation from tracer particles: PIV and *particle tracking velocimetry* (PTV) [2, 32]. PIV outputs a dense velocity field (Eulerian view), while PTV computes a flow vector at each particle location (Lagrangian view). The first method to operate in 3D was 3D-PTV [22], where individual particles are detected in different views, triangulated and tracked over time. Yet, as the particle density increases the particles quickly start to overlap in the images, leading to ambiguities. Therefore, 3D-PTV is only recommended for densities <0.005 ppp (particles per pixel). To handle higher densities, [14] introduced Tomo-PIV. They first employ a tomographic reconstruction (e.g. MART) [3] per time step, to obtain a 3D voxel space of occupancy probabilities. Cross-correlation with large local 3D windows ($\geq 35^3$) [10, 11, 13] then yields the flow. Effectively, this amounts to matching particle constellations, assuming constant flow in large windows, which smoothes the output to low effective resolution. Recently, a new particle tracking method

Shake-the-Box (StB) was introduced [36]. It builds on the idea of *iterative parti-cle reconstruction* (IPR) [46], where triangulation is performed iteratively, with a local position and intensity refinement after every triangulation step.

None of the above methods accounts for the physics of (incompressible) fluids during reconstruction. In StB [36], a post-process interpolates sparse tracks to a regular grid, at that step (but not during reconstruction), physical constraints can be included. Variational approaches that impose physical consistent regu-larization were first proposed for the 2D PIV setup, e.g. [34,35]. [20] combine TomoPIV with variational 3D flow estimation and account for physical con-straints, with a regularizer derived from the stationary Stokes equations, similar to [34]. However, their data term requires a huge, high-resolution intensity vol-ume, and a local window of 11^3 voxels for matching, which lowers spatial resolu-tion, albeit less than earlier local matching. [16] proposed a similar approach for dye-injected two-media fluids. Their aim are visually pleasing, rather than phys-ically correct results, computed for relatively small volumes ($\approx 100^3$ voxels). We note that dye leads to data that is very different from tracer particles, e.g., it pro-duces structures that can be matched more easily, but does not evenly cover the volume. [12] use compressive sensing to jointly recover the location and motion of a sparse, time-varying signal with a mathematical recovery guarantee. Results are only shown for small grids (256^3), and the physics of fluids is not consid-ered. [4] introduce a joint approach for 3D reconstruction and flow estimation, however, without considering physical properties of the problem. Their purely Eulerian, voxel-based setup limits the method to small volume sizes, i.e., the method is only evaluated on a $61 \times 61 \times 31$ grid and a rather low seeding density of 0.02 ppp. [47] propose a joint formulation for their single-camera PIV setup. The volume is illuminated by rainbow-colored light planes that encode depth information. This permits the use of only a single camera with the drawback of lower depth accuracy and limited particle density. Voxel occupancy probabilities are recovered on a 3D grid. To handle the ill-conditioned problem from a single camera, constraints on particle sparsity and motion consistency (including phys-ical constraints) are incorporated in the optimization. The method operates on a "thin" maximum volume of $512 \times 270 \times 20$. The single-camera setup does not allow a direct comparison with standard 3D PIV/PTV, but can certainly not compete in terms of depth resolution. In contrast, by separating the representation of particles and motion field, our hybrid Lagrangian/Eulerian approach allows for sub-pixel accurate particle reconstruction and large fluid volumes. Finally, [33] propose a hybrid discrete particle and continuous variational motion estimation approach. However, particle reconstruction and motion estimation are performed sequentially and without a physically motivated regularization of the flow.

Volumetric fluid flow is also related to variational scene-flow estimation, espe-cially methods that parameterize the scene in 3D space [5,42]. Like those, we search for the geometry and motion of a dynamic scene and exploit multiple views, yet our goal is a dense reconstruction in a given volume, rather than a pixel-wise motion field. Scene flow has undergone an evolution similar to the one for 3D fluid flow. Early methods started with a fixed, precomputed geometry estimate [31,44], with a notable exception [17]. Later work moved to a joint reconstruction of geometry and motion [5,40,42]. Likewise, [14,20] precompute the 3D tracer particles [14] before estimating their motion. The present paper is, to our knowledge, the first in multi-camera PIV to jointly determine the explicit particle geometry and (physically-constrained) motion of the fluid. Hence, our model can be seen either as an extension of the flow algorithm [20] to simultaneously reconstruct the particles, or an extension of TomoPIV with sparse representations [28,29], to simultaneously reconstruct the particles at both time steps, and the associated motion field.

Several scene flow methods [23,41,43] overcome the large state space by sampling geometry and motion proposals, and perform discrete optimization over those samples. In a similar spirit, we employ IPR to generate discrete particle proposals, but then combine them with a continuous, variational optimization scheme. We note that discrete labeling does not suit our task: The volumetric setting would require a large number of labels (3D vectors), and enormous amounts of memory. And it does not lend itself to sub-voxel accurate inference.

3   Method

To set the scene, we restate the goal of our method: densely predict the 3D flow field in a fluid seeded with tracer particles, from multiple 2D views acquired at two adjacent time steps.

We aim to do this in a direct, integrated fashion. The joint particle reconstruction and motion estimation is formulated as a hybrid Lagrangian/Eulerian model, where we recover individual particles and keep track of their position and appearance, but reconstruct a continuous 3D motion field in the entire domain. A dense sampling of the motion field makes it technically and numerically easier to adhere to physical constraints like incompressibility. In contrast, modeling particles explicitly takes advantage of the low particle density in PIV data. Practical densities are around 0.1 particles per pixel (ppp) in the images. Depending on the desired voxel resolution, this corresponds to $10-1000\times$ lower volumetric density. Our complete pipeline is depicted in Fig. 2. It alternates between generating particle proposals (Sect. 3.2) based on the current residual images (starting from the raw input images), and energy minimization to update all particles and motion vectors (Sect. 3.3). The correspondent energy model is described in Sect. 3.1. In the process, particle locations and flow estimates are progressively refined and provide a better initialization for further particle proposals.

Particle triangulation is highly ambiguous, so the proposal generator will inevitably introduce many spurious "ghost" particles (Fig. 3). A sparsity term in the energy reduces the influence of low intensity particles that usually correspond to such ghosts, while true particles, given the preliminary flow estimate, receive additional support from the data of the second time step. In later iterations, already reconstructed particles vanish in the residual images. This allows for a refined localization of remaining particles, as particle overlaps are resolved.

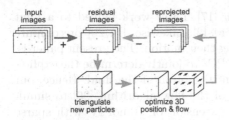

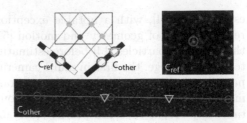

Fig. 2. Particle position and flow estimation pipeline. We alternate between joint optimization of 3D particle positions and dense flow vectors, and adding new candidate particles by triangulation from the residual images.

Fig. 3. A particle in the reference camera (circle) can lead to multiple epipolar-consistent putative matches (circles). However, only a subset of them represents true 3D particles (triangles). *Left*: 1D-illustration. *Right*: peak in reference camera (0.1ppp). *Bottom:* other camera view with 5 putative matches that are consistent over all 4 cameras. (Color figure online)

Notation and Preliminaries. The scene is observed by K calibrated cameras $\mathcal{K}_k, k = 1, \ldots, K$, recording the images $\mathcal{I}_k^t$ at time t. Parameterizing the scene with 3D entities obviates the need for image rectification. In our formulation we do not commit to a particular camera model and instead define a generic projection operator Π_k per camera. We note that fluid experiments typically need sophisticated models to deal with refraction (air-glass and glass-water), or an optical transfer function derived from volume self-calibration. Both are not the focus of this work and can be found in the respective literature, e.g. [37,45].

The dependency on time is denoted via superscript t_0, t_1, and omitted when possible. We denote the set of particles $\mathcal{Q} := \{(p_i, c_i)\}_{i=1}^Q$, composed of a set of intensities $\mathcal{C} := \{c_i\}_{i=1}^Q, c_i \in \mathbb{R}_0^+$ and positions $\mathcal{P} := \{p_i\}_{i=1}^Q$, where each $p_i \in \mathbb{R}^3$ is located in the rectangular domain $\Omega \subset \mathbb{R}^3$. The 3D motion field at position $x \in \Omega$, between times t_0 and t_1, is $u(x, \mathcal{U})$. The set $\mathcal{U}$ contains motion vectors $u \in \mathbb{R}^3$ located at a finite set of positions $y \in \mathcal{Y} \subset \Omega$. If we let these locations coincide with the particle positions, we would arrive at a fully Lagrangian design, also referred to as *smoothed particle hydrodynamics* [1,26]. In this work, we prefer a fixed set $\mathcal{Y}$ and represent the functional $u(x, \mathcal{U})$ by trilinear interpolation, i.e. we opt for an Eulerian description of the motion. Our model is, thus, similar to the so-called *particle in cell design* [48]. W.l.o.g. we assume $\mathcal{Y} \subset \Omega \cap \mathbb{Z}^3$, i.e., we set up a regular grid of vertices $\mathbf{i} \in \mathcal{Y}$ of size $N \times M \times L$, which induce a voxel covering $V(\Omega)$ of size $N - 1 \times M - 1 \times L - 1$ of the whole domain. Each grid vertex $\mathbf{i} = (\mathbf{i}_1, \mathbf{i}_2, \mathbf{i}_3)^\mathsf{T}$ is associated with a trilinear basis function: $\mathbf{b_i}(x) := \prod_{l=1}^3 \max(0, 1 - |x_l - \mathbf{i}_l|)$, for $x = (x_1, x_2, x_3)^\mathsf{T}$. The elements $u_\mathbf{i} \in \mathcal{U}$ now represent the coefficients of our motion field function $u(x, \mathcal{U}), x \in \Omega$ that is given by:

$$u(x, \mathcal{U}) = \big(u_1(x, \mathcal{U}), u_2(x, \mathcal{U}), u_3(x, \mathcal{U})\big)^\mathsf{T}, \quad u_l(x, \mathcal{U}) = \sum_{\mathbf{i} \in \mathcal{Y}} \mathbf{b_i}(x) u_{\mathbf{i},l}, l = 1, 2, 3. \quad (1)$$

3.1   Energy Model

With the definitions above, we can write the energy

$$E(\mathcal{P},\mathcal{C},\mathcal{U}) := \frac{1}{2}E_{\mathrm{D}}(\mathcal{P},\mathcal{C},\mathcal{U}) + \frac{\lambda}{2}E_{\mathrm{S}}(\mathcal{U}) + \mu E_{\mathrm{Sp}}(\mathcal{C}), \tag{2}$$

with a data term E_{D}, a smoothness term E_{S} operating on the motion field, and a sparsity prior E_{Sp} operating on the intensities of the particles.

Data Term. To compute the data term, the images of all cameras at both time steps are predicted from the particles' positions and intensities, and the 3D motion field. E_{D} penalizes deviations between predicted and observed images:

$$E_D(\mathcal{P},\mathcal{C},\mathcal{U}) := \sum_{t\in\{t_0,t_1\}}\sum_{k=1}^{K} \int_{\Gamma_k} \left| \mathcal{I}_k^t(x) - \sum_{i=1}^{Q} \Pi_k(c_i \cdot \mathcal{N}(p_i + [t=t_1]\cdot u(p_i,\mathcal{U}),\sigma)(x)) \right|_2^2 \mathrm{d}x.$$
$$\tag{3}$$

Following an additive (in terms of particles) image formation model, we integrate over the image plane Γ_k of camera k; $[\cdot]$ denotes the Iverson bracket. We model individual particles $(p,c) \in \mathcal{Q}$ as Gaussian blobs with variance σ^2. Particles do not exhibit strong shape or material variations. Their distance to the light source does influence the observed intensity. But since it changes smoothly and the cameras record with high frame-rate, assuming constant intensity is a valid approximation for our two-frame model.

In practice, the projection in (3) can be assumed to be almost orthographic, with little perspective distortion of the particles. The depth range of the volume Ω is small compared to the distance from the camera. Hence, we assume that particles remain Gaussian after a projection into the image. In that regime, and omitting constant terms, the expression for a projected particle simplifies to

$$\Pi\big(\mathcal{N}(\cdot,\sigma)(x)\big) \approx \mathcal{N}\big(\Pi(\cdot),\sigma\big)(x) \propto \sigma^{-1}\exp\big(-|\Pi(\cdot)-x|^2\sigma^{-2}\big). \tag{4}$$

When computing the derivatives of (3) w.r.t. the set of parameters, we do not integrate the particle blobs over the whole image, but restrict the area of influence of (4) to a radius of 3σ, covering 99.7% of its total intensity.

Sparsity Term. The majority of the generated candidate particles do not correspond to *true* particles. To remove the influence of the huge set of low-intensity ghost particles one can exploit the expected sparsity of the solution, e.g. [29]. In other words, we aim to reconstruct the observed scenes with *few, bright* particle, by introducing the following energy term:

$$E_{\mathrm{Sp}}(\mathcal{C}) := \sum_{i=1}^{Q} |c_i|_\diamond + \delta_{\{\geq 0\}}(c_i). \tag{5}$$

Here, $\delta_\Delta(\cdot)$ denotes the indicator function of the set Δ. This term additionally excludes negative intensities. Although not directly related to sparsity, we identified (5) a convenient spot to include this constraint. Popular sparsity-inducing norms $|\cdot|_\diamond$ are either the 1- or 0-norm $(|\cdot|_\diamond = |\cdot|_1$, respectively $|\cdot|_\diamond = |\cdot|_0)$. We have investigated both choices and prefer the stricter 0-norm for the final model. The 0-norm counts the number of non-zero intensities and rapidly discards particles that fall below a certain intensity threshold (modulated by μ in (2)). While the 1-norm only gradually reduces the intensities of weakly supported particles.

Smoothness Term. To define a suitable smoothness prior we follow [20] and employ a quadratic regularizer per component of the flow gradient, plus a term that enforces a divergence-free motion field:

$$E_S(\mathcal{U}) := \int_\Omega \sum_{l=1}^3 |\nabla u_l(x, \mathcal{U})|_2^2 + \delta_{\{0\}}(\nabla \cdot u(x, \mathcal{U})) \mathrm{d}x. \tag{6}$$

It has been shown in [20] that (6) has a physical interpretation, in that the stationary Stokes equations emerge as the Euler-Lagrange equations of the energy (6), including an additional force field. Thus, (6) models the incompressibility of the fluid, while λ represents its viscosity. [20] also suggest a variant in which the hard divergence constraint is replaced with a soft penalty:

$$E_{S,\alpha}(\mathcal{U}) := \int_\Omega \sum_{l=1}^3 |\nabla u_l(x, \mathcal{U})|_2^2 + \alpha |\nabla \cdot u(x, \mathcal{U})|^2 \mathrm{d}x. \tag{7}$$

This version simplifies the numerical optimization, trading off speed for accuracy. For adequate (large) α, the results are similar to the hard constraint in (6). Equation (6) requires the computation of the divergence $\nabla\cdot$ and gradients ∇ of the 3D motion field. Following the definition (1) of the flow field, both entities are linear in the coefficients $\mathcal{U}$ and constant per voxel $v \in V(\Omega)$. A valid discretization of the divergence operator can be achieved via the divergence theorem:

$$\int_v \nabla u(x) \mathrm{d}x = \int_{\partial v} \langle \nu(x), u(x, \mathcal{U}) \rangle \mathrm{d}x = \sum_i \int_{\partial v} b_i(x) \langle \nu(x), u_i \rangle \mathrm{d}x = \frac{1}{4} \sum_{l,(i,j) \in \mathcal{Y} \cap v : i-j=e_l} u_{i,l} - u_{j,l}, \tag{8}$$

where we let $\nu(x)$ denote the outward-pointing normal of voxel v at position $x \in v$ and e_l the unit vector in direction l. The final sum considers pairs of corner vertices $(\mathbf{i}, \mathbf{j}) \in \mathcal{Y} \cap v$ of voxel v, adjacent in direction l. The definition of the per-voxel gradient follows from (1) in a similar manner.

3.2 Particle Initialization

To obtain an initial set of 3D particle locations we employ a direct detect-and-triangulate strategy like IPR [46] and iteratively triangulate putative particles, in alternation with the minimization of energy (2). Particle triangulation is extremely ambiguous and not decidable with local cues (Fig. 3). Instead, *all* plausible correspondences are instantiated. One can interpret the process as a proposal generator for the set of particles, which interacts with the sparsity constraint (5). This proposal generator creates new candidate particles where image evidence remains unexplained. The sparsity prior ensures that only "good" particles survive and contribute to the data costs, whereas those of low intensity that are inconsistent with our model become "zero-intensity" particles. Particles of low intensity are uncommon in reality. In each iteration the set of zero-intensity particles are actively discarded from Q to reduce the workload. Note that this does not change the energy of the current solution. After the first particles and a coarse motion field have been reconstructed, a better initialization is available to spawn further particles, in locations suggested by the residual maps between predicted and observed images. Particles that contribute to the data are retained in the subsequent optimization and help to refine the motion field, etc. The procedure is inspired by the heuristic, yet highly efficient, iterative approach of [46]. They also refine particle candidates triangulated from residual images. Other than theirs, our updated particle locations follow from a joint spatio-temporal objective, and thus also integrate information from the second time step. In more detail, each round of triangulation proceeds as follows: first, detect peaks in 2D image space for all cameras at time step t_0. In the first iteration this is done in the raw inputs, then in the residual images $\mathcal{I}_{k,\text{res}}^{t_0} := \int_{\Gamma_k} \mathcal{I}_k^{t_0}(x) - \sum_{i=1}^{Q} \Pi_k(c_i \cdot \mathcal{N}(p_i, \sigma)(x)) dx$. Peaks are found by non-maximum suppression with a 3×3 kernel, followed by sub-pixel refinement of all peaks with intensity above a threshold I_{min}. We treat one of the cameras, $k = 1$, as reference and compute the entry and exit points to Ω for a ray passing through each peak. Reprojecting the entry and exit into other views yields epipolar line segments, along which we scan for (putatively) matching peaks (Fig. 3). Whenever we find peaks in all views that can be triangulated with a reprojection error below a tolerance ϵ, we generate a new candidate particle. Its initial intensity is set as a function of the intensity in the reference view and the number of candidates: if m proposals p_i are generated at a peak in the reference image, we set $c_i := \mathcal{I}_1(\Pi_1(p_i)) K/(K - 1 + m)$ for each of them.

3.3   Energy Minimization

Our optimization is embedded in a two-fold coarse-to-fine scheme. On the one hand, we start with a larger value for σ, so as to increase the particles' basins of attraction and improve convergence. During optimization, we progressively reduce σ until we reach $\sigma = 1$, meaning that a particle blob covers approximately the same area as in the input images. On the other hand, we also start at a coarser grid $\mathcal{Y}$ and refine the grid resolution along with σ.

To minimize the non-convex and non-smooth energy (2) for a given σ, we employ PALM [9], in its inertial variant [30]. Because our energy function is semi-algebraic [9], it satisfies the Kurdyka-Lojasiewicz property [8], therefore the sequence generated by PALM globally converges to a critical point of the energy. The key idea of PALM is to split the variables into blocks, such that the problem is decomposed into one smooth function on the entire variable set, and a sum of non-smooth functions in which each block is treated separately. We start by arranging the locations and intensities of the particles Q into two separate vectors $\mathbf{p} := (p_1^\mathsf{T}, \ldots, p_Q^\mathsf{T})^\mathsf{T} \in \mathbb{R}^{3Q}$ and $\mathbf{c} := (c_1, \ldots, c_Q)^\mathsf{T} \in \mathbb{R}^Q$. Similarly, we stack the coefficients of the trilinear basis $\mathbf{u} := (u_{i,1}^\mathsf{T}, u_{i,2}^\mathsf{T}, u_{i,3}^\mathsf{T})_{i \in \mathcal{Y}}^\mathsf{T} \in \mathbb{R}^{3NML}$. With these groups, we split the energy functional into a smooth part H and two non-smooth functions, $F_\mathbf{c}$ for the intensities $\mathbf{c}$ and $F_\mathbf{u}$ for the motion vectors $\mathbf{u}$:

$$E(\mathbf{p}, \mathbf{c}, \mathbf{u}) := H(\mathbf{p}, \mathbf{c}, \mathbf{u}) + F_\mathbf{c}(\mathbf{c}) + F_\mathbf{u}(\mathbf{u}) + F_\mathbf{p}(\mathbf{p}), \text{ with}$$

$$H(\mathbf{p}, \mathbf{c}, \mathbf{u}) := E_D(\mathbf{p}, \mathbf{c}, \mathbf{u}) + \lambda \sum_{l=1}^3 \|\nabla \mathbf{u}_l\|^2, \tag{9}$$

$$F_\mathbf{c}(\mathbf{c}) := \mu E_{Sp}(\mathbf{c}), \ F_\mathbf{u}(\mathbf{u}) := \delta_{\{0\}}(\nabla \cdot \mathbf{u}) \text{ and } F_\mathbf{p}(\mathbf{p}) := 0.$$

For notation convenience, we define $F_\mathbf{p}(\mathbf{p}) := 0$. The algorithm then alternates the steps of a proximal forward-backward scheme: take an explicit step w.r.t. one block of variables $z \in \{\mathbf{p}, \mathbf{c}, \mathbf{u}\}$ on the smooth part H of the energy function, then take a backward (proximal) step on the non-smooth part F_z w.r.t. the same variables. That is, we alternate steps of the form

$$z^{n+1} = \operatorname{prox}_t^{F_z}(z) := \arg\min_y F_z(y) + \frac{t}{2}\|y - z\|^2, \text{ with } z = z^n - \frac{1}{t}\nabla_z H(\cdot, z^n, \cdot),$$
$$\tag{10}$$

with a suitable step size $1/t$ for each block of variables. Here and in the following, the placeholder variable z can stand for $\mathbf{c}$, $\mathbf{p}$ or $\mathbf{u}$, as required.

A key property is that, throughout the iterations, the partial gradient of function H w.r.t. a variable block $z \in \{\mathbf{p}, \mathbf{c}, \mathbf{u}\}$ must be globally Lipschitz-continuous with some modulus L_z at the current solution:

$$\|\nabla_z H(\cdot, z_1, \cdot) - \nabla_z H(\cdot, z_2, \cdot)\| \le L_z(\cdot, \cdot)\|z_1 - z_2\| \ \forall z_1, z_2. \tag{11}$$

In other words, before we accept an update z^{n+1} computed with (10), we need to verify that the step size t in (10) fulfills the descent lemma [7]:

$$E(\cdot, z^{n+1}, \cdot) \le E(\cdot, z^n, \cdot) + \langle \nabla_z H(\cdot, z^n, \cdot), z^{n+1} - z^n \rangle + \frac{t}{2}\|z^{n+1} - z^n\|^2. \tag{12}$$

Note that Lipschitz continuity of the gradient of H has to be verified only locally, at the current solution. This property allows for a back-tracking approach to determine the Lipschitz constant, e.g. [6]. Algorithm 1 provides pseudo-code for our scheme to minimize the energy (9). To accelerate convergence we apply extrapolation (lines 4/8/12). These inertial steps, c.f. [6,30], significantly reduce the number of iterations in the algorithm, while leaving the computational cost per step practically untouched. It is further convenient to not only reduce the step sizes (lines 7/11/15 in Algorithm 1), but also to increase them, as long as (12) is fulfilled, to make the steps per iteration as large as possible.

One last thing needs to be explained, namely how we find the solution of the proximal steps on the intensities $\mathbf{c}$ and flow vectors $\mathbf{u}$. The former can be solved point-wise, leading to the following 1D-problem:

$$\operatorname{prox}_t^{F_c}(\bar{c}) := \arg\min_c \mu|c|_\diamond + \delta_{\{\ge 0\}}(c) + \frac{t}{2}|c - \bar{c}|^2, \tag{13}$$

Algorithm 1. iPalm implementation for energy (9)

1: **procedure** IPALM($\mathbf{p}^0, \mathbf{c}^0, \mathbf{u}^0$)
2:     $\mathbf{p}^{-1} \leftarrow \mathbf{p}^0; \mathbf{c}^{-1} \leftarrow \mathbf{c}^0; \mathbf{u}^{-1} \leftarrow \mathbf{u}^0; \tau \leftarrow \frac{1}{\sqrt{2}}; L_\mathbf{p} \leftarrow 1; L_\mathbf{c} \leftarrow 1; L_\mathbf{u} \leftarrow 1;$
3:     **for** n:=0 to n_{steps} and while not converged **do**
4:         $\hat{\mathbf{p}} \leftarrow \mathbf{p}^n + \tau(\mathbf{p}^n - \mathbf{p}^{n-1});$ // inertial step
5:         **while** true **do**
6:             $\mathbf{p}^{n+1} := \hat{\mathbf{p}} - 1/L_\mathbf{p} \nabla_\mathbf{p} H(\hat{\mathbf{p}}, \mathbf{c}^n, \mathbf{u}^n);$
7:             **if** $\mathbf{p}^{n+1}, L_\mathbf{p}$ fulfill (12) **then break**; **else** $L_\mathbf{p} = 2L_\mathbf{p};$
8:         $\hat{\mathbf{c}} \leftarrow \mathbf{c}^n + \tau(\mathbf{c}^n - \mathbf{c}^{n-1});$ // inertial step
9:         **while** true **do**
10:             $\mathbf{c} := \hat{\mathbf{c}} - 1/L_\mathbf{c} \nabla_\mathbf{c} H(\mathbf{p}^{n+1}, \hat{\mathbf{c}}, \mathbf{u}^n); \mathbf{c}^{n+1} := \text{prox}_{L_\mathbf{c}}^{F_\mathbf{c}}(\mathbf{c});$ // Eq. (10)
11:             **if** $\mathbf{c}^{n+1}, L_\mathbf{c}$ fulfill (10) **then break**; **else** $L_\mathbf{c} = 2L_\mathbf{c};$
12:         $\hat{\mathbf{u}} \leftarrow \mathbf{u}^n + \tau(\mathbf{u}^n - \mathbf{u}^{n-1});$ // inertial step
13:         **while** true **do**
14:             $\mathbf{u} := \hat{\mathbf{u}} - 1/L_\mathbf{u} \nabla_\mathbf{u} H(\mathbf{p}^{n+1}, \mathbf{c}^{n+1}, \hat{\mathbf{u}}); \mathbf{u}^{n+1} := \text{prox}_{L_\mathbf{u}}^{F_\mathbf{u}}(\mathbf{u});$ // Eq. (10)
15:             **if** $\mathbf{u}^{n+1}, L_\mathbf{u}$ fulfill (12) **then break**; **else** $L_\mathbf{u} = 2L_\mathbf{u};$

which admits for a closed-form solution for both norms ($\diamond \in \{0, 1\}$):

$$\text{prox}_t^{|\cdot|_0}(\bar{c}) := \begin{cases} 0 & \text{if } t\bar{c}^2 < 2\mu \text{ or } \bar{c} < 0 \\ \bar{c} & \text{else,} \end{cases}, \qquad \text{prox}_t^{|\cdot|_1}(\bar{c}) := \max(0, \bar{c} - \mu/t). \quad (14)$$

The proximal step for the flow vector $\mathbf{u}$, $\text{prox}_t^{F_\mathbf{u}}(\bar{\mathbf{u}}) := \arg\min_{\mathbf{u}} \delta_{\{0\}}(\nabla \cdot \mathbf{u}) + \frac{t}{2}\|\mathbf{u} - \bar{\mathbf{u}}\|^2$, requires the projection of $\bar{\mathbf{u}}$ onto the space of divergence-free 3D vector fields. Given $\bar{\mathbf{u}}$, the solution is independent of the step size $1/t$, which we omit in the following. We construct the Lagrangian by introducing the multiplier ϕ, a scalar vector field whose physical meaning is the pressure in the fluid [20]:

$$\min_{\mathbf{u}} \max_{\phi} \frac{1}{2}\|\mathbf{u} - \bar{\mathbf{u}}\|^2 + \phi^\mathsf{T} \nabla \cdot \mathbf{u}. \quad (15)$$

To prevent confusion, we introduce $D\mathbf{u}$ as matrix notation for the linear divergence operator ($\nabla \cdot \mathbf{u}$) in (8). The KKT conditions of the Lagrangian yield a linear equation system. Simplification with the Schur complement leads to a Poisson system, which we solve for the pressure ϕ to get the divergence-free solution:

$$\text{prox}_t^{F_\mathbf{u}}(\bar{\mathbf{u}}) := \bar{\mathbf{u}} - D^\mathsf{T}\phi \quad \text{with } D^\mathsf{T}D\phi = D^\mathsf{T}\bar{\mathbf{u}}. \quad (16)$$

Again interpreted physically, the divergence of the motion field is removed by subtracting the gradient of the resulting pressure field. For our problem of fluid flow estimation, it is not necessary to exactly solve the Poisson system in every iteration. Instead, we keep track of the pressure field ϕ during optimization, and warm-start the proximal step. In this way, a few (10–20) iterations of preconditioned conjugate gradient descent suffice to update ϕ.

If we replace the hard divergence constraint with the soft penalty $E_{S,\alpha}$ from (7), we add $E_{S,\alpha}$ to the smooth function H in (9). Then only the proximal step on the intensities $\mathbf{c}$ is needed in Algorithm 1. We conclude by noting that accelerating the projection step is in itself an active research area in fluid simulation [19,39].

4 Evaluation

There is no other measurement technique that could deliver ground truth for fluid flow. We follow the standard practice and generate datasets for quantitative evaluation via *direct numerical simulations* (DNS) of turbulent flow, using the *Johns Hopkins Turbulence Database* (JHTDB) [21,27]. This allows us to render realistic input images with varying particle densities and flow magnitudes, together with ground truth vectors on a regular grid. We evaluate how our approach performs with different smoothness terms, particle densities, initialization methods, particle sizes and temporal sampling rates. Additionally, we show results on "test case D" of the 4th International PIV Challenge [18]. We quantitatively compare to the best performing method [36] and refer to the supplementary material for further comparisons as well as additional visualizations, also with the experimental setup of Fig. 1.

Simulated Dataset. We follow the guidelines of the 4th International PIV Challenge [18] for the setup of our own dataset: Randomly sampled particles are rendered to four symmetric cameras of resolution 1500×800 pixels, with viewing angles of $\pm 35°$ w.r.t. the yz-plane of the volume, respectively $\pm 18°$ w.r.t. the xz-plane. If not specified otherwise, particles are rendered as Gaussian blobs with $\sigma = 1$ and varying intensity. We sample 12 datasets from 6 non-overlapping spatial and 2 temporal locations of the forced isotropic turbulence simulation of the JHTDB. Discretizing each DNS grid point with 4 voxels, identical to [18], each dataset corresponds to a volume size of $1024 \times 512 \times 352$. For our flow fields with flow magnitudes up to 8.8 voxels, we use 10 pyramid levels with downsampling factor 0.94. At every level we alternate between triangulation of candidate particles and minimization of the energy function (at most 40 iteration per level).

The effective resolution of the reconstructed flow field is determined by the particle density. At a standard density of ≈ 0.1 ppp and a depth range of 352 voxels, we get a density of ≈ 0.0003 particles per voxel. This suggests to estimate the flow on a coarser grid. We empirically found a particle density of 0.3 per voxel to still deliver good results. Hence, we operate on a subsampled voxel grid of 10-times lower resolution per dimension in all our experiments, to achieve a notable speed-up and memory saving. The computed flow is then upsampled to the target resolution, with barely any loss of accuracy.

We always require a 2D intensity peak in all four cameras to instantiate a candidate particle. We start with a strict threshold of $\epsilon = 0.8$ for the triangulation error, as suggested in [46], which is relaxed to $\epsilon = 2.0$ in later iterations. The idea is to first recover particles with strong support, and gradually add more ambiguous ones, as the residual images become less cluttered. We set $\lambda = 0.01$

Table 1. Endpoint error (AEE), angular error (AAE) and absolute divergence (AAD) for different regularizers (0.1 ppp).

	E_S	$E_{S,64}$	$E_{S,0}$	[20]
AEE	0.136	0.135	0.157	0.406
AAE	2.486	2.463	2.870	6.742
AAD	0.001	0.008	0.100	0.001

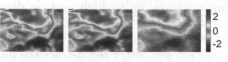

Fig. 4. Detail from an xy-slice of the flow in X-direction. *Left to right:* Ground truth, our method and result of [20].

for our dataset. Since λ corresponds to the viscosity it should be adapted for other fluids. We empirically set the sparsity weight $\mu = 0.0001$.

Regularization. Our framework allows us to plug in different smoothness terms. Following [20], we show results for hard (E_S) and soft divergence regularization ($E_{S,\alpha}$). *Average endpoint error* (AEE), *average angular error* (AAE), and *average absolute divergence* (AAD) are displayed in Table 1. Compared to our default regularizer E_S, removing the divergence constraint ($\alpha = 0$), increases the error by $\approx 15\%$. With the soft constraint at high $\alpha = 64$, the results are equal to those of E_S. We also compare to the method [20]. Our joint model improves the performance by $\approx 70\%$ over that recent baseline, on both error metrics. In Fig. 4 we visually compare our results (with hard divergence constraint) to those of [20]. The figure shows the flow in X-direction in one particular xy-slice of the volume. Our method recovers a lot finer details, and is clearly closer to the ground truth.

Particle Density and Initialization Method. There is a trade-off for choosing the seeding density: A higher density raises the observable spatial resolution, but at the same time makes matching more ambiguous. This causes false positives, commonly called "ghost particles". Very high densities are challenging for all known reconstruction techniques. The additive image formation model of Eq. (3) also suggests an upper bound on the maximal allowed particle density. Table 2 reports results for varying particle densities. We measure recall (fraction of reconstructed ground truth particles) and precision (fraction of reconstructed particles that coincide with true particles to <1 pixel).

To provide an upper bound, we initialize our method with ground truth particle locations at time step 0 and optimize only for the flow estimation. We also evaluate a sequential version of our method, in which we separate energy (2) into particle reconstruction and subsequent motion field estimation. In addition to our proposed IPR-like triangulation, we initialize particles with a popular volumetric tomography method (*MART*) [14]. *MART* creates a full, high-resolution voxel grid of intensities (with, hopefully, lower intensities for ghost particles and very low ones in empty space). To extract a set of sub-voxel accurate 3D particle locations we perform peak detection, similar to the 2D case for triangulation. Since *MART* always returns the same particle set we run it only once, but increase the number of iterations for the minimizer from 40 to 160.

Starting from a perfect particle reconstruction (*true particles*) the flow estimate improves with increasing particle density. Remarkably, our proposed iterative triangulation approach achieves results comparable to the ground truth initialization, up to high particle densities and is able to resolve most particle ambiguities. In contrast, *MART* and the sequential baseline struggle with increasing particle density, which supports our claim that joint energy minimization can better reconstruct the particles.

Table 2. Influence of particle density on our joint approach, as well as several baselines.

ppp	IPR joint			IPR sequential			MART			true particles		
	AEE	*prec.*	*recall*	AEE	*prec.*	*recall*	AEE	*prec.*	*recall*	AEE	*prec.*	*recall*
0.1	0.136	99.98	99.95	0.136	99.97	99.96	0.232	70.39	83.93	0.136	100	100
0.125	0.124	91.00	99.95	0.157	61.55	97.55	0.270	48.51	73.83	0.125	100	100
0.15	0.115	82.82	99.95	0.310	33.46	85.09	0.323	44.61	70.17	0.118	100	100
0.175	0.111	71.37	99.93	0.332	26.63	71.07	0.385	40.89	65.29	0.110	100	100
0.2	0.108	55.43	99.86	0.407	19.42	64.26	0.506	36.88	58.13	0.106	100	100

Particle Size. For the above experiments, we have rendered the particles into the images as Gaussian blobs with fixed $\sigma = 1$, and the same is done when re-rendering for the data term, respectively, proposal generator. We now test the influence of particle size on the reconstruction, by varying σ. Table 3 shows results with hard divergence constraint and fixed particle density 0.1, for varying $\sigma \in [0.6 \ldots 1.6]$. For small enough particles, size does not matter, very large particles lead to more occlusions and degrade the flow. Furthermore, we verify the sensitivity of the method to unequal particle size. To that end, we draw an individual σ for each particle from the normal distribution $\mathcal{N}(1, 0.1^2)$, while still using a fixed $\sigma = 1$ during inference. As expected, the mismatch between actual and rendered particles causes slightly larger errors.

Temporal Sampling. To quantify the stability of our method to different flow magnitudes we modify the time interval between the two discrete time steps and summarize the results in Table 4, together with the respective maximum flow magnitude $|u|_2$. For lower frame rate (1.25x and 1.5x), and thus larger magnitudes, we set our pyramid downsampling factor to 0.93.

PIV Challenge. Unfortunately, no ground truth is provided for the data of the 4th PIV Challenge [18], such that we cannot run a quantitative evaluation on that dataset. However, Schanz et al. [36] kindly provided us results for their method, StB, for snapshot 10. StB was the best-performing method in the challenge with an endpoint error of $\approx$0.24 voxels (compared to errors >0.3 for all competitors). The average endpoint difference between our approach and StB is <0.14 voxels. In Fig. 5 both results appear to be visually comparable, yet, note that StB includes a tracking procedure that requires data of multiple time steps (15 for the given particle density 0.1). We show additional visualizations and a qualitative comparison with the ground truth in the supplementary material.

Table 3. Influence of particle size on reconstruction quality (0.1 ppp).

σ	0.6	0.8	1	1.2	1.4	1.6	$\mathcal{N}_{1,0.1^2}$
AEE	0.194	0.135	0.136	0.140	0.217	0.235	0.155
AAE	3.388	2.465	2.486	2.561	4.002	4.575	2.879

Table 4. Varying the sampling distance between frames (0.1 ppp).

Temp. dist	0.75x	1.0x	1.25x	1.5x
AEE	0.102	0.136	0.170	0.283
Max. $|u|_2$	6.596	8.795	10.993	13.192

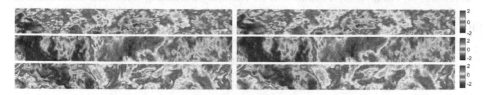

Fig. 5. xy-slice of the flow field for snapshot 10 of the 4th PIV Challenge. *Top to bottom: X, Y, Z* flow components. *Left:* multi-frame StB [36]. *Right:* our 2-frame method.

5 Conclusion

We have presented the first variational model that *jointly* solves sparse particle reconstruction and dense 3D fluid motion estimation in PIV data for the common multi-camera setup. The sparse particle representation allows us to utilize the high-resolution image data for matching, while keeping memory consumption low enough to process large volumes. Densely modeling the fluid motion in 3D enables the direct use of physically motivated regularizers, in our case viscosity and incompressibility. The proposed joint optimization captures the mutual dependencies of particle reconstruction and flow estimation. This yields results that are clearly superior to traditional, sequential methods [14,20]; and, using only 2 frames, competes with the best available multi-frame methods, which require sequences of 15–30 timesteps.

Acknowledgements. This work was supported by ETH grant 29 14-1. Christoph Vogel acknowledges support from the ERC starting grant 640156, 'HOMOVIS'.

References

1. Adams, B., Pauly, M., Keiser, R., Guibas, L.J.: Adaptively sampled particle fluids. In: ACM SIGGRAPH (2007)
2. Adrian, R., Westerweel, J.: Particle Image Velocimetry. Cambridge University Press, Cambridge (2011)
3. Atkinson, C., Soria, J.: An efficient simultaneous reconstruction technique for tomographic particle image velocimetry. Exp. Fluids **47**(4), 553 (2009)
4. Barbu, I., Herzet, C., Mémin, E.: Joint estimation of volume and velocity in TomoPIV. In: 10th International Symposium on Particle Image Velocimetry - PIV13 (2013)
5. Basha, T., Moses, Y., Kiryati, N.: Multi-view scene flow estimation: a view centered variational approach. In: CVPR (2010)

6. Beck, A., Teboulle, M.: A fast iterative shrinkage-thresholding algorithm for linear inverse problems. SIAM J. Imaging Sci. **2**(1), 183–202 (2009)
7. Bertsekas, D.P., Tsitsiklis, J.N.: Parallel and Distributed Computation: Numerical Methods. Prentice-Hall, Upper Saddle River (1989)
8. Bolte, J., Daniilidis, A., Lewis, A.: The Lojasiewicz inequality for nonsmooth subanalytic functions with applications to subgradient dynamical systems. SIAM J. Optim. **17**(4), 1205–1223 (2007)
9. Bolte, J., Sabach, S., Teboulle, M.: Proximal alternating linearized minimization for nonconvex and nonsmooth problems. Math Program. **146**(1), 459–494 (2014)
10. Champagnat, F., Plyer, A., Le Besnerais, G., Leclaire, B., Davoust, S., Le Sant, Y.: Fast and accurate PIV computation using highly parallel iterative correlation maximization. Exp. Fluids **50**(4), 1169 (2011)
11. Cheminet, A., Leclaire, B., Champagnat, F., Plyer, A., Yegavian, R., Le Besnerais, G.: Accuracy assessment of a Lucas-Kanade based correlation method for 3D PIV. In: International Symposium Applications of Laser Techniques to Fluid Mechanics (2014)
12. Dalitz, R., Petra, S., Schnörr, C.: Compressed motion sensing. In: Lauze, F., Dong, Y., Dahl, A.B. (eds.) SSVM 2017. LNCS, vol. 10302, pp. 602–613. Springer, Cham (2017). https://doi.org/10.1007/978-3-319-58771-4_48
13. Discetti, S., Astarita, T.: Fast 3D PIV with direct sparse cross-correlations. Exp. Fluids **53**(5), 1437–1451 (2012)
14. Elsinga, G.E., Scarano, F., Wieneke, B., Oudheusden, B.W.: Tomographic particle image velocimetry. Exp. Fluids **41**(6), 933–947 (2006)
15. Gesemann, S., Huhn, F., Schanz, D., Schröder, A.: From noisy particle tracks to velocity, acceleration and pressure fields using B-splines and penalties. In: International Symposium on Applications of Laser Techniques to Fluid Mechanics (2016)
16. Gregson, J., Ihrke, I., Thuerey, N., Heidrich, W.: From capture to simulation: connecting forward and inverse problems in fluids. ACM ToG **33**(4), 139 (2014)
17. Huguet, F., Devernay, F.: A variational method for scene flow estimation from stereo sequences. In: ICCV (2007)
18. Kähler, C.J., et al.: Main results of the 4th international PIV challenge. Exp. Fluids **57**(6), 97 (2016)
19. Ladický, L., Jeong, S., Solenthaler, B., Pollefeys, M., Gross, M.: Data-driven fluid simulations using regression forests. ACM ToG **34**(6), 199 (2015)
20. Lasinger, K., Vogel, C., Schindler, K.: Volumetric flow estimation for incompressible fluids using the stationary stokes equations. In: ICCV (2017)
21. Li, Y., et al.: A public turbulence database cluster and applications to study Lagrangian evolution of velocity increments in turbulence. J. Turbul. **9**, N31 (2008). https://doi.org/10.1080/14685240802376389
22. Maas, H.G., Gruen, A., Papantoniou, D.: Particle tracking velocimetry in three-dimensional flows. Exp. Fluids **15**(2), 133–146 (1993)
23. Menze, M., Geiger, A.: Object scene flow for autonomous vehicles. In: CVPR (2015)
24. Michaelis, D., Poelma, C., Scarano, F., Westerweel, J., Wieneke, B.: A 3D time-resolved cylinder wake survey by tomographic PIV. In: ISFV12 (2006)
25. Michalec, F.G., Schmitt, F., Souissi, S., Holzner, M.: Characterization of intermittency in zooplankton behaviour in turbulence. Eur. Phys. J. **38**(10), 108 (2015)
26. Monaghan, J.J.: Smoothed particle hydrodynamics. Rep. Progress Phys. **68**(8), 1703 (2005)
27. Perlman, E., Burns, R., Li, Y., Meneveau, C.: Data exploration of turbulence simulations using a database cluster. In: Conference on Supercomputing (2007)

28. Petra, S., Schröder, A., Wieneke, B., Schnörr, C.: On sparsity maximization in tomographic particle image reconstruction. In: Rigoll, G. (ed.) DAGM 2008. LNCS, vol. 5096, pp. 294–303. Springer, Heidelberg (2008). https://doi.org/10.1007/978-3-540-69321-5_30

29. Petra, S., Schröder, A., Schnörr, C.: 3D tomography from few projections in experimental fluid dynamics. In: Nitsche, W., Dobriloff, C. (eds.) Imaging Measurement Methods for Flow Analysis. NNFM, vol. 106, pp. 63–72. Springer, Heidelberg (2009). https://doi.org/10.1007/978-3-642-01106-1_7

30. Pock, T., Sabach, S.: Inertial proximal alternating linearized minimization (iPALM) for nonconvex and nonsmooth problems. SIAM J. Imaging Sci. 9(4), 1756–1787 (2016)

31. Rabe, C., Müller, T., Wedel, A., Franke, U.: Dense, robust, and accurate motion field estimation from stereo image sequences in real-time. In: Daniilidis, K., Maragos, P., Paragios, N. (eds.) ECCV 2010. LNCS, vol. 6314, pp. 582–595. Springer, Heidelberg (2010). https://doi.org/10.1007/978-3-642-15561-1_42

32. Raffel, M., Willert, C.E., Wereley, S., Kompenhans, J.: Particle Image Velocimetry: A Practical Guide. Springer, Heidelberg (2013). https://doi.org/10.1007/978-3-540-72308-0

33. Ruhnau, P., Guetter, C., Putze, T., Schnörr, C.: A variational approach for particle tracking velocimetry. Meas. Sci. Technol. 16(7), 1449 (2005)

34. Ruhnau, P., Schnörr, C.: Optical stokes flow estimation: an imaging-based control approach. Exp. Fluids 42(1), 61–78 (2007)

35. Ruhnau, P., Stahl, A., Schnörr, C.: On-line variational estimation of dynamical fluid flows with physics-based spatio-temporal regularization. In: Franke, K., Müller, K.-R., Nickolay, B., Schäfer, R. (eds.) DAGM 2006. LNCS, vol. 4174, pp. 444–454. Springer, Heidelberg (2006). https://doi.org/10.1007/11861898_45

36. Schanz, D., Gesemann, S., Schröder, A.: Shake-the-box: Lagrangian particle tracking at high particle image densities. Exp. Fluids 57(5), 70 (2016)

37. Schanz, D., Gesemann, S., Schröder, A., Wieneke, B., Novara, M.: Non-uniform optical transfer functions in particle imaging: calibration and application to tomographic reconstruction. Meas. Sci. Technol. 24(2), 024009 (2012). https://doi.org/10.1088/0957-0233/24/2/024009

38. Schneiders, J.F., Scarano, F.: Dense velocity reconstruction from tomographic PTV with material derivatives. Exp. Fluids 57(9), 139 (2016)

39. Tompson, J., Schlachter, K., Sprechmann, P., Perlin, K.: Accelerating eulerian fluid simulation with convolutional networks. CoRR abs/1607.03597 (2016)

40. Valgaerts, L., Bruhn, A., Zimmer, H., Weickert, J., Stoll, C., Theobalt, C.: Joint estimation of motion, structure and geometry from stereo sequences. In: Daniilidis, K., Maragos, P., Paragios, N. (eds.) ECCV 2010. LNCS, vol. 6314, pp. 568–581. Springer, Heidelberg (2010). https://doi.org/10.1007/978-3-642-15561-1_41

41. Vogel, C., Schindler, K., Roth, S.: Piecewise rigid scene flow. In: ICCV (2013)

42. Vogel, C., Schindler, K., Roth, S.: 3D scene flow estimation with a rigid motion prior. In: ICCV (2011)

43. Vogel, C., Schindler, K., Roth, S.: 3D scene flow estimation with a piecewise rigid scene model. IJCV 115(1), 1–28 (2015)

44. Wedel, A., Brox, T., Vaudrey, T., Rabe, C., Franke, U., Cremers, D.: Stereoscopic scene flow computation for 3D motion understanding. IJCV 95(1), 29–51 (2011)

45. Wieneke, B.: Volume self-calibration for 3D particle image velocimetry. Exp. Fluids 45(4), 549–556 (2008)

46. Wieneke, B.: Iterative reconstruction of volumetric particle distribution. Meas. Sci. Technol. **24**(2), 024008 (2012). https://doi.org/10.1088/0957-0233/24/2/024008
47. Xiong, J., et al.: Rainbow particle imaging velocimetry for dense 3D fluid velocity imaging. ACM Trans. Graph. **36**(4), 36:1–36:14 (2017)
48. Zhu, Y., Bridson, R.: Animating sand as a fluid. ACM ToG **24**(3), 965–972 (2005)

Joint Oral Session 2

NRST: Non-rigid Surface Tracking
from Monocular Video

Marc Habermann[1]([✉])(iD), Weipeng Xu[1]([✉])(iD), Helge Rhodin[2]([✉])(iD),
Michael Zollhöfer[3]([✉])(iD), Gerard Pons-Moll[1]([✉])(iD),
and Christian Theobalt[1]([✉])(iD)

[1] Max Planck Institute for Informatics, 66123 Saarbrücken, Germany
{mhaberma,wxu,gpons,theobalt}@mpi-inf.mpg.de
[2] EPFL, 1015 Lausanne, Switzerland
helge.rhodin@epfl.ch
[3] Stanford University, Stanford, CA 94305, USA
zollhoefer@cs.stanford.edu
https://www.mpi-inf.mpg.de/home/, https://www.epfl.ch/,
https://www.stanford.edu/

Abstract. We propose an efficient method for non-rigid surface tracking from monocular RGB videos. Given a video and a template mesh, our algorithm sequentially registers the template non-rigidly to each frame. We formulate the per-frame registration as an optimization problem that includes a novel texture term specifically tailored towards tracking objects with uniform texture but fine-scale structure, such as the regular micro-structural patterns of fabric. Our texture term exploits the orientation information in the micro-structures of the objects, e.g., the yarn patterns of fabrics. This enables us to accurately track uniformly colored materials that have these high frequency micro-structures, for which traditional photometric terms are usually less effective. The results demonstrate the effectiveness of our method on both general textured non-rigid objects and monochromatic fabrics.

1 Introduction

In this paper, we propose NRST, an efficient method for non-rigid surface tracking from monocular RGB videos. Capturing the non-rigid deformation of a dynamic surface is an important and long-standing problem in computer vision. It has a wide range of real world applications in fields such as virtual/augmented reality, medicine and visual effects. Most of the existing methods are based on multi-view imagery, where expensive and complicated system setups are required [3,23,25]. There also exist methods that rely on only a single depth or RGB-D camera [18,19,42,44]. However, these sensors are not as ubiquitous as RGB cameras, and these methods cannot be applied on plenty of existing video

Electronic supplementary material The online version of this chapter (https://doi.org/10.1007/978-3-030-12939-2_23) contains supplementary material, which is available to authorized users.

footage which is found on social media like YouTube. There are also monocular RGB methods [30,43], of course with their own limitations; e.g., they rely on highly textured surfaces and they are often times slow.

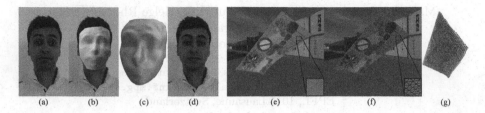

Fig. 1. We propose an efficient method for interactive non-rigid surface tracking from monocular RGB videos for general objects such as faces ((a)–(d)). Given the input image (a) our reconstruction nicely overlays with the input (b) and looks also plausible from another view point (c). The textured overlay looks realistic as well (d). Furthermore, our novel texture term leads to improved reconstruction quality for fabrics given a single video (e). Again the overlayed reconstruction (f) aligns well, and also in 3D (g) our result (red) matches the ground truth (blue). (Color figure online)

In this work, we present a method which is able to densely track the non-rigid deformations of general objects such as faces and fabrics from a single RGB video (Fig. 1). To solve this challenging problem, our method relies on a textured mesh template of the deforming object's surface. Given the input video, our algorithm sequentially registers the template to each frame. More specifically, our method automatically reproduces a deformation sequence of the template model that coincides with the non-rigid surface motion in the video. To this end, we formulate the per-frame registration as a non-linear least squares optimization problem – with an objective function consisting of a photometric alignment and several regularization terms. The optimization is computationally intensive due to the large number of residuals in our alignment objective. To address this, we adapt the efficient GPU-based Gauss-Newton solver of Zollhoefer et al. [44] to our problem that allows for deformable object tracking at interactive frame rates.

Besides the efficiency of the algorithm, the core contribution of our approach is a novel texture term that exploits the orientation information in the micro-structures of the tracked objects, such as the yarn patterns of fabrics. This enables us to track uniformly colored materials which have high frequency patterns, for which the classical color-based term is usually less effective.

In our experimental results, we evaluate our method qualitatively and quantitatively on several challenging sequences of deforming surfaces. We use well established benchmarks, such as pieces of cloth [31,40] and human faces [39,43]. The results demonstrate that our method can accurately track general non-rigid objects. Furthermore, for materials with regular micro-structural patterns, such as fabrics, the tracking accuracy is further improved with our texture term.

2   Related Work

There is a variety of approaches that reconstruct geometry from multiple images, e.g., template-free methods [3], variational ones [25] or object specific approaches [23]. Although multi-view methods can produce accurate tracking results, their setup is expensive and hard to operate. Some approaches use a single RGB-D sensor instead [9,10,18,19,36,42,44]. They manage to capture deformable surfaces nicely and at high efficiency, some even build up a template model alongside per-frame reconstruction. The main limitations of these methods are that the sensors have a high power consumption, they do not work outdoors, the object has to be close to the camera and they cannot use the large amount of RGB-only video footage provided by social media. On these grounds, we aim for a method that uses just a single RGB video as input. In the following, we focus on related monocular reconstruction and tracking approaches.

Monocular Methods. Non-rigid structure from motion methods, which do not rely on any template, try to infer the 3D geometry from a single video by using a prior-free formulation [4], global models [37], local ones [27] or solving a variational formulation [6]. But they often either capture the deformations only coarsely, are not able to model strong deformations, typically require strongly textured objects or rely on dense 2D correspondences. By constraining the setting to specific types of objects such as faces [7], very accurate reconstructions can be obtained, but at the expense of generality. Since in recent years, several approaches [11,22] build a 3D model given a set of images, and even commercial software[1] is available for this task, template acquisition has become easier. Templates are an effective prior for the challenging task of estimating non-rigid deformations from single images as demonstrated by previous work [1,2,14–17,21,24,28–33,40,43]. But even if a template is used, ambiguities [30] remain and additional constraints have to be imposed. Theoretical results [1] show that only allowing isometric deformations [24] results in a uniquely defined solution. Therefore, approaches constrain the deformation space in several ways, e.g., by a Laplacian regularization [21] or by non-linear [32] or linear local surface models [29]. Salzmann et al. [28] argued that relaxing the isometric constraint is beneficial since it allows to model sharp folds. Moreno-Noguer et al. [17] and Malti et al. [16] even go beyond this and show results for elastic surfaces; Tsoli and Argyros [38] demonstrated tracking surfaces that undergo topological changes but require a depth camera. Other approaches investigate how to make reconstruction more robust under faster motions [33] and occlusions [20], or try to replace the feature-based data term by a dense pixel-based one [15] and to find better texture descriptors [8,12,26]. Brunet et al. [2] and Yu et al. [43] formulate the problem of estimating non-rigid deformations as minimizing an objective function which brings them closest to our formulation. In particular, we adopt the photometric, spatial and temporal terms of Yu et al. [43] and combine them with an isometric and acceleration constraint as well as our novel texture term.

---

[1] http://www.agisoft.com/.

Along the line of monocular methods, we propose NRST, a template-based reconstruction framework that estimates the non-rigidly deforming geometry of general objects from just monocular video. In contrast to previous work, our approach does not rely on 3D to 2D correspondences and due to the GPU-based solver architecture it is also much faster than previous approaches. Furthermore, our novel texture term enables tracking of regions with little texture.

3   Method

The goal is to estimate the non-rigid deformation of an object from T frames $I^t(x, y)$ with $t \in \{1, ..., T\}$. We assume a static camera and known camera intrinsics. Since this problem is in general severely under-constrained, it is assumed that a template triangle mesh of the object to be tracked is given as the matrix $\hat{\mathbf{V}} \in \mathbb{R}^{N \times 3}$ where each row contains the coordinates of one of the N vertices. According to that, $\hat{\mathbf{V}}_i$ is defined as the ith vertex of the template in vector form. This notation is also used for the following matrices. The edges of the template are given as the mapping $\mathcal{N}(i)$. Given a vertex index $i \in \{1, 2, ..., N\}$, it returns the set of indices sharing an edge with $\hat{\mathbf{V}}_i$. The F faces of the mesh are represented as the matrix $\mathbf{F} \in \{1, ..., N\}^{F \times 3}$. Each row contains the vertex indices of one triangle. The UV map is given as the matrix $\mathbf{U} \in \mathbb{N}^{N \times 2}$. Each row contains the UV coordinates for the corresponding vertex. The color $\mathbf{C}_i \in \{0, ..., 255\}^3$ of vertex i can be computed by a simple lookup in the texture map I_{TM} at the position $\mathbf{U}_i$. The color of all vertices is stored in the matrix $\mathbf{C} \in \{0, ..., 255\}^{N \times 3}$. Furthermore, it is assumed that the geometry at time $t = 1$ roughly agrees with the true shape shown in the video so that the gradients of the photometric term can guide the optimization to the correct solution without being trapped into local minima. The non-rigidly deformed mesh at time $t + 1$ is represented as the matrix $\mathbf{V}^{t+1} \in \mathbb{R}^{N \times 3}$ and contains the updated vertex positions according to the 3D displacement from t to $t + 1$.

3.1   Non-rigid Tracking as Energy Minimization

Given the template $\hat{\mathbf{V}}$ and our estimate of the previous frame $\mathbf{V}^t$, our method sequentially estimates the geometry $\mathbf{V}^{t+1}$ of the current frame $t + 1$. We jointly optimize per-vertex local rotations denoted by $\mathbf{\Phi}^{t+1}$ and vertex locations $\mathbf{V}^{t+1}$. Specifically, for each time step the deformation estimation is formulated as the non-linear optimization problem

$$(\mathbf{V}^{t+1}, \mathbf{\Phi}^{t+1}) = \underset{\mathbf{V}, \mathbf{\Phi} \in \mathbb{R}^{N \times 3}}{\arg \min} \; E(\mathbf{V}, \mathbf{\Phi}), \tag{1}$$

with

$$\begin{aligned}
E(\mathbf{V}, \mathbf{\Phi}) = {} & \lambda_{\text{Photo}} E_{\text{Photo}}(\mathbf{V}) + \lambda_{\text{Smooth}} E_{\text{Smooth}}(\mathbf{V}) + \lambda_{\text{Edge}} E_{\text{Edge}}(\mathbf{V}) \\
& + \lambda_{\text{Arap}} E_{\text{Arap}}(\mathbf{V}, \mathbf{\Phi}) + \lambda_{\text{Vel}} E_{\text{Vel}}(\mathbf{V}) + \lambda_{\text{Acc}} E_{\text{Acc}}(\mathbf{V}).
\end{aligned} \tag{2}$$

λ_{Photo}, λ_{Smooth}, λ_{Edge}, λ_{Vel}, λ_{Acc}, λ_{Arap} are hyperparameters set before the optimization starts and afterwards they are kept constant. $E\,(\mathbf{V}, \boldsymbol{\Phi})$ combines different cost terms ensuring that the mesh deformations agree with the motion in the video. The resulting non-linear least squares optimization problem is solved with the GPU-based Gauss-Newton solver based on the work of Zollhoefer et al. [44] where we adapted the Jacobian and residual implementation to our energy formulation. The high efficiency is obtained by exploiting the sparse structure of the system of normal equations. For more details we refer the reader to the approach of Zollhoefer et al. [44]. Now, we will explain the terms in more detail.

Photometric Alignment. The photometric term

$$E_{\text{Photo}}(\mathbf{V}) = \sum_{i=1}^{N} \left\| \sigma \left(I^{t+1} * \mathbf{G}_w \left(\Pi\left(\mathbf{V}_i\right) \right) - \mathbf{C}_i \right) \right\|^2 \tag{3}$$

densely measures the re-projection error. $\|\cdot\|$ is the Euclidean norm, $*$ is the convolution operator and $\mathbf{G}_w$ is a Gaussian kernel with standard deviation w. We use Gaussian smoothing on the input frame for more stable and longer range gradients. $\Pi(\mathbf{V}_i) = (\frac{u}{w}, \frac{v}{w})^\top$ with $(u, v, w)^\top = \mathbf{I}\mathbf{V}_i$ projects the vertex $\mathbf{V}_i$ on the image plane and $I^{t+1} * \mathbf{G}_w$ returns the RGB color vector of the smoothed frame at position $\Pi\,(\mathbf{V}_i)$ which is compared against the pre-computed and constant vertex color $\mathbf{C}_i$. Here, $\mathbf{I} \in \mathbb{R}^{3\times3}$ is the intrinsic camera matrix. σ is a robust pruning function for wrong correspondences with respect to color similarity. More specifically, we discard errors above a certain threshold because in most cases they are due to occlusions.

Spatial Smoothness. Without regularization, estimating 3D geometry from a single image is an ill-posed problem. Therefore, we introduce several spatial and temporal regularizers to make the problem well-posed and to propagate 3D deformations into areas where information for data terms is missing, e.g., poorly textured or occluded regions. The first prior

$$E_{\text{Smooth}}\,(\mathbf{V}) = \sum_{i=1}^{N} \sum_{j \in \mathcal{N}(i)} \left\| (\mathbf{V}_i - \mathbf{V}_j) - (\hat{\mathbf{V}}_i - \hat{\mathbf{V}}_j) \right\|^2 \tag{4}$$

ensures that if a vertex $\mathbf{V}_i$ changes its position, its neighbors $\mathbf{V}_j$ with $j \in \mathcal{N}(i)$ are deformed such that the overall shape is still spatially smooth compared to the template mesh $\hat{\mathbf{V}}$. In addition, the prior

$$E_{\text{Edge}}\,(\mathbf{V}) = \sum_{i=1}^{N} \sum_{j \in \mathcal{N}(i)} \left(\|\mathbf{V}_i - \mathbf{V}_j\| - \|\hat{\mathbf{V}}_i - \hat{\mathbf{V}}_j\| \right)^2 \tag{5}$$

ensures isometric deformations which means that the edge length with respect to the template is preserved. In contrast to E_{Smooth}, this prior is rotation invariant.

Finally, the as-rigid-as-possible (ARAP) prior [34]

$$E_{\text{Arap}}(\mathbf{V}, \mathbf{\Phi}) = \sum_{i=1}^{N} \sum_{j \in \mathcal{N}(i)} \left\| (\mathbf{V}_i - \mathbf{V}_j) - \mathcal{R}(\mathbf{\Phi}_i)(\hat{\mathbf{V}}_i - \hat{\mathbf{V}}_j) \right\|^2, \tag{6}$$

allows local rotations for each of the mesh vertices as long as the relative position with respect to their neighborhood remains the same. Each row of the matrix $\mathbf{\Phi} \in \mathbb{R}^{N \times 3}$ contains the per-vertex Euler angles which encode a local rotation around $\mathbf{V}_i$. $\mathcal{R}(\mathbf{\Phi}_i)$ converts them into a rotation matrix.

We choose a combination of spatial regularizers to ensure that our method can track different types of non-rigid deformations equally well. For example, E_{Smooth} is usually sufficient to track facial expressions without large head rotations. But tracking rotating objects can only be achieved with rotational invariant regularizers (E_{Edge}, E_{Arap}). In contrast to Yu et al. [43], we adopt the Euclidean norm in Eqs. 4 and 6 instead of the Huber loss because it led to visually better results.

Temporal Smoothness. To enforce temporally smooth reconstructions, we propose two additional priors. The first one is defined as

$$E_{\text{Velocity}}(\mathbf{V}) = \sum_{i=1}^{N} \left\| \mathbf{V}_i - \mathbf{V}_i^t \right\|^2 \tag{7}$$

and ensures that the displacement of vertices between t and $t+1$ is small. Second, the prior

$$E_{\text{Acc}}(\mathbf{V}) = \sum_{i=1}^{N} \left\| (\mathbf{V}_i - \mathbf{V}_i^t) - (\mathbf{V}_i^t - \mathbf{V}_i^{t-1}) \right\|^2 \tag{8}$$

penalizes large deviations of the current velocity direction from the previous one.

3.2   Non-rigid Tracking of Woven Fabrics

Tracking of uniformly colored fabrics is usually challenging for classical color-based terms due to the lack of color features. To overcome this limitation, we inspected the structure of different garments and found that most of them show line-like micro-structures due to the manufacturing process of the woven threads, see Fig. 2 left. Those can be recorded with recent high resolution cameras such that reconstruction algorithms can make use of those patterns. To this end, we propose a novel texture term to refine the estimation of non-rigid motions for the case of woven fabrics. It can be combined with the terms in Eq. 2. Now, we will explain our novel data term in more detail.

Histogram of Oriented Gradient (HOG). Based on HOG [5] we compute for each pixel (i, j) of an image the corresponding histogram $\mathbf{h}_{i,j} \in \mathbb{R}^b$ where b is the number of bins that count the total number of gradient angles present in the neighborhood of pixel (i, j). To be more robust with respect to outliers

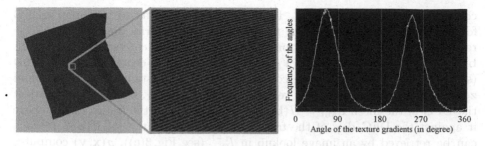

Fig. 2. Histogram of oriented gradients of woven fabrics. Left. The neighborhood region with the center pixel in the middle. Right. The corresponding histogram.

and noise we count the number of gradients per angular bin irrespective of the gradient magnitude and only if the magnitude is higher than a certain threshold. Compared to pure image gradients, HOG is less sensitive to noise. Especially for woven fabrics, image gradients are very localized since changing the position in the image can lead to large differences in the gradient directions due to the high frequency of the image content. HOG instead averages over a certain window so that outliers are discarded.

Directions of a Texture. Applying HOG to pictures of fabrics reveals their special characteristics caused by the line like patterns (see Fig. 2). There are two dominant texture gradient angles α and $\beta = ((\alpha + 180) \mod 360)$ perpendicular to the lines. So α provides the most characteristic information of the pattern in the image at (i, j) and can be computed as the angle whose bin has the highest frequency in $\mathbf{h}_{i,j}$. α is then converted to its normalized 2D direction, also called *dominant frame gradient* (DFG), which is stored in the two-valued image $I_{\mathrm{Dir}}(i, j)$. To detect image regions that do not contain line patterns, we set $I_{\mathrm{Dir}}(i, j) = (0, 0)^\top$ if the highest frequency is below a certain threshold.

Texture-based Constraint. Our novel texture term

$$E_{\mathrm{Tex}}(\mathbf{V}) = \sum_{i=1}^{F} \| \rho (\mathbf{d}_{\mathrm{M},i}, \mathbf{d}_{\mathrm{F},i}) \|^2 \tag{9}$$

ensures now that for all triangles the projected DFG $\mathbf{d}_{\mathrm{M},i}$ parametrized on the object surface agrees with the frame's DFG $\mathbf{d}_{\mathrm{F},i}$ at the location of the projected triangle center. An overview is shown in Fig. 3. More precisely, by averaging $\mathbf{U}_k, \mathbf{U}_m, \mathbf{U}_l$ one can compute the pixel position $\mathbf{z}_{\mathrm{TM},i} \in \mathbb{R}^2$ of the center point of the triangle $\mathbf{F}_i = (k, m, l)$ in the texture map. Now, the neighborhood region for HOG around $\mathbf{z}_{\mathrm{TM},i}$ is defined as the 2D bounding box of the triangle. The HOG descriptor for $\mathbf{z}_{\mathrm{TM},i}$ can be computed and by applying the concept explained in the previous paragraph one obtains the DFG $\mathbf{d}_{\mathrm{TM},i}$ (see Fig. 3(a)). Next, we define $\mathbf{b}_{\mathrm{TM},i} = \mathbf{z}_{\mathrm{TM},i} + \mathbf{d}_{\mathrm{TM},i}$ and express it as a linear combination of the triangles' UV coordinates leading to the *barycentric coordinates* $\mathbf{B}_{i,1}, \mathbf{B}_{i,2}, \mathbf{B}_{i,3}$ of the face $\mathbf{F}_i$. They form together with the other triangles the barycentric coordinates matrix $\mathbf{B} \in \mathbb{R}^{F \times 3}$. Each row represents the texture map's DFG for the respective triangle of the mesh in an implicit form. Since $\mathbf{b}_{\mathrm{TM},i}$ can be represented as a linear combination, one can compute the corresponding 3D point $\mathbf{b}_{3\mathrm{D},i} = \mathbf{B}_{i,1}\mathbf{V}_k + \mathbf{B}_{i,2}\mathbf{V}_m + \mathbf{B}_{i,3}\mathbf{V}_l$ as well as the triangle center $\mathbf{z}_{3\mathrm{D},i} \in \mathbb{R}^3$ in 3D (see Fig. 3(b)). The barycentric coordinates remain constant, so that $\mathbf{b}_{3\mathrm{D},i}$ and $\mathbf{z}_{3\mathrm{D},i}$ only depend on the mesh vertices $\mathbf{V}_k$, $\mathbf{V}_m$ and $\mathbf{V}_l$. One can then project the DFG of the mesh $\mathbf{d}_{\mathrm{M},i} = \Pi(\mathbf{b}_{3\mathrm{D},i}) - \Pi(\mathbf{z}_{3\mathrm{D},i})$ into the frame and compare it against the DFG $\mathbf{d}_{\mathrm{F},i}$ of the frame $t+1$ at the location of $\Pi(\mathbf{z}_{3\mathrm{D},i})$ which can be retrieved by an image lookup in I_{Dir}^{t+1} (see Fig. 3(c)). $\rho(\mathbf{x}, \mathbf{y})$ computes the minimum of the differences between $\mathbf{x}, \mathbf{y}$ and $\mathbf{x}, -\mathbf{y}$ iff both $\mathbf{x}$ and $\mathbf{y}$ are non-zero vectors (otherwise we are not in an area with line patterns) and the directions are similar up to a certain threshold to be more robust with respect to occlusions and noise. As mentioned above, there are two DFGs in the frame for the case of line patterns. We assume the initialization is close to the ground truth and choose the minimum of the two possible directions.

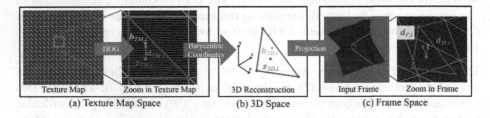

(a) Texture Map Space   (b) 3D Space   (c) Frame Space

Fig. 3. Overview of the proposed texture term.

4   Results

All experiments were performed on a PC with an NVIDIA GeForce GTX 1080Ti and an Intel Core i7. In contrast to related methods [43], we achieve interactive frame rates using the energy proposed in Eq. 2.

4.1   Qualitative and Quantitative Results

Now, we evaluate NRST on datasets for general objects like faces where we disable E_{Tex}. After that, we compare our approach against another monocular method. Finally, we evaluate our proposed texture term on two new scenes showing line-like fabric structures, perform an ablation study and demonstrate interesting applications. More results can be found in the supplemental video.

Qualitative Evaluation for General Objects. In Fig. 4 we show frames from our monocular reconstruction results. We tested our approach on two face sequences [39,43] where templates are provided. Note that NRST precisely reconstructs facial expressions. The 2D overlay (second column) matches the input

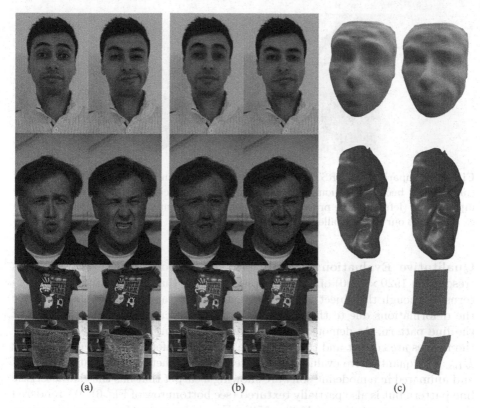

(a)   (b)   (c)

Fig. 4. Reconstructions of existing datasets [31,39,40,43]. Input frames (a). Textured reconstructions overlayed on the input (b). Deformed geometries obtained by our method (rendered from a different view point) (c).

and also in 3D (third column) our results look realistic. Furthermore, we evaluated on the datasets of Varol et al. [40] and Salzmann et al. [31] showing fast movements of a T-shirt and a waving towel. Again for most parts of the surface the reconstructions look accurate in 2D since they overlap well with the input and they are also plausible in 3D. This validates that our approach can deal with the challenging problem of estimating 3D deformations from a monocular video for general kinds of objects.

Comparison to Yu et al. [43]. Figure 5 shows a qualitative comparison between our method and the one of Yu et al. [43]. It becomes obvious that both capture the facial expression, but the proposed approach is faster than the one of Yu et al. due to our data-parallel GPU implementation. In particular, on their sequence our method runs at 15 fps whereas their approach takes several seconds per frame. More sidy-by-side comparisons on this sequence can be found in the supplemental video.

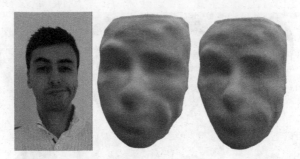

Fig. 5. Comparison of NRST's reconstruction (right) and the one of Yu et al. [43] (middle). It becomes obvious that both capture the facial expression shown in the input frame (left), but the proposed approach is significantly faster than the one of Yu et al. due to our data-parallel GPU implementation.

Qualitative Evaluation for Fabrics. The top row of Fig. 6 shows frames (resolution 1920 × 1080) of a moving piece of cloth that has the typical line patterns. Although the object is sparsely textured, our approach is able to recover the deformations due to the texture term, which accurately tracks the DFG of the line pattern. As demonstrated in the last column, the estimated angles for the frames are correct and therefore give a reliable information cue exploited by E_{Tex}. For quantitative evaluation, we created a synthetic scene that is modeled and animated in a modeling software showing a carpet that has the characteristic line pattern but is also partially textured (see bottom row of Fig. 6). We rendered the scene at a resolution of 1500 × 1500. E_{Tex} helps in the less textured regions where E_{Photo} would fail. The last column shows how close our reconstruction (red) is with respect to ground truth (blue).

Ablation Analysis. Apart from the proposed texture term, our energy formulation is similar to the one of Yu et al. [43]. To validate that E_{Tex} improves the reconstruction over a photometric-only formulation, we perform an ablation study. We measured the averaged per-vertex Euclidean distance between the ground truth mesh and our reconstructions. For the waving towel shown in Fig. 6 bottom, we obtained an error of 26.8 mm without E_{Tex} and 25.5 mm if we also use our proposed texture term leading to an improvement of 4.8%. The diagonal of the 3D bounding box of the towel is 3162 mm. For the rotation sequence (resolution 800 × 800) shown in Fig. 7 the color variation is very limited since background and object have the same color. In contrast to E_{Photo} alone, E_{Tex} can rotate the object leading to an error of 4.1 mm for the texture-only case and 6.7 mm for the photometric-only setting. So E_{Tex} improves over E_{Photo} by 38.8%.

4.2 Applications

Our method enables several applications such as free view point rendering or re-texturing on general deformable objects or for virtual face make-up (see Fig. 8).

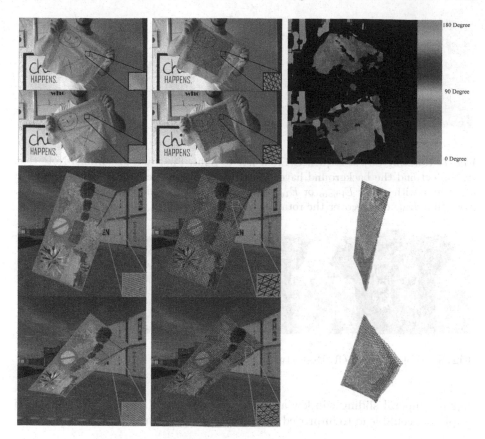

Fig. 6. Reconstruction of line patterns. Top from left to right. Input frames. Textured reconstructions overlayed on the frames. Color coded visualization of the estimated dominant frame angles. Regions where no line pattern was detected are visualized in black. Bottom from left to right. Input frames. Textured reconstructions overlayed on the frames. Ground truth geometries (blue) and our reconstructions (red). (Color figure online)

Since our approach estimates the deforming geometry, one can even change the scene lighting for the foreground such that the shading remains realistic.

4.3   Limitations

By the nature of the challenging task of monocular tracking of non-rigid deformations, our method has some limitations which open up directions for future work. Although, our proposed texture term uses more of the information contained in the video than a photometric-only formulation, there are still image cues that can improve the reconstruction like shading and the object contour as demonstrated by previous work [13, 41]. So, one could combine them in a unified framework. To increase robustness, the deformations could be jointly estimated

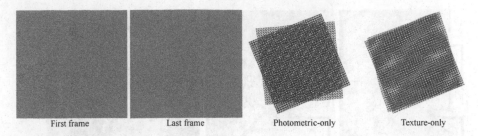

Fig. 7. Rotating object sequence. From left to right. First and last frame. Note that the object and the background have the same color. The reconstructions (red) of the last frame with either E_{Photo} or E_{Tex} overlayed on the ground truth geometry (blue). Note that E_{Tex} can recover the rotation in contrast to E_{Photo}. (Color figure online)

Fig. 8. Applications. Left. Re-textured shirt. Right. Re-textured and re-lighted face.

over a temporal sliding window as proposed by Xu et al. [41] and an embedded graph [35] could lead to improved stability by reducing the number of unknowns.

5   Conclusion

We presented an optimization-based analysis-by-synthesis method that solves the challenging task of estimating non-rigid motion, given a single RGB video and a template. Our method tracks non-trivial deformations of a broad class of shapes, ranging from faces to deforming fabric. Further, we introduce specific solutions tailored to capture woven fabrics, even if they lack clear color variations. Our method runs at interactive frame rates due to the GPU-based solver that can efficiently solve the non-linear least squares optimization problem. Our evaluation shows that the reconstructions are accurate in 2D and 3D which enables several applications such as re-texturing.

References

1. Bartoli, A., Gérard, Y., Chadebecq, F., Collins, T.: On template-based reconstruction from a single view: analytical solutions and proofs of well-posedness for developable, isometric and conformal surfaces. In: CVPR (2012)

2. Brunet, F., Hartley, R., Bartoli, A., Navab, N., Malgouyres, R.: Monocular template-based reconstruction of smooth and inextensible surfaces. In: Kimmel, R., Klette, R., Sugimoto, A. (eds.) ACCV 2010. LNCS, vol. 6494, pp. 52–66. Springer, Heidelberg (2011). https://doi.org/10.1007/978-3-642-19318-7_5
3. Carceroni, R.L., Kutulakos, K.N.: Multi-view scene capture by surfel sampling: from video streams to non-rigid 3D motion, shape & reflectance. In: ICCV (2001)
4. Dai, Y., Li, H., He, M.: A simple prior-free method for non-rigid structure-from-motion factorization. IJCV **107**, 101–122 (2014)
5. Dalal, N., Triggs, B.: Histograms of oriented gradients for human detection. In: CVPR (2005)
6. Garg, R., Roussos, A., Agapito, L.: Dense variational reconstruction of non-rigid surfaces from monocular video. In: CVPR (2013)
7. Garrido, P., Valgaerts, L., Wu, C., Theobalt, C.: Reconstructing detailed dynamic face geometry from monocular video. TOG **32**, 158 (2013)
8. Gårding, J.: Shape from texture for smooth curved surfaces in perspective projection. J. Math. Imaging Vis. **2**, 327–350 (1992)
9. Jordt, A., Koch, R.: Fast tracking of deformable objects in depth and colour video. In: BMVC, pp. 1–11 (2011)
10. Jordt, A., Koch, R.: Direct model-based tracking of 3D object deformations in depth and color video. IJCV **102**(1–3), 239–255 (2013)
11. Labatut, P., Pons, J.P., Keriven, R.: Efficient multi-view reconstruction of large-scale scenes using interest points, delaunay triangulation and graph cuts. In: ICCV (2007)
12. Liang, J., DeMenthon, D., Doermann, D.: Flattening curved documents in images. In: CVPR (2005)
13. Liu-Yin, Q., Yu, R., Agapito, L., Fitzgibbon, A., Russell, C.: Better together: joint reasoning for non-rigid 3D reconstruction with specularities and shading. In: BMVC (2016)
14. Ma, W.J.: Nonrigid 3D reconstruction from a single image. In: ISAI (2016)
15. Malti, A., Bartoli, A., Collins, T.: A pixel-based approach to template-based monocular 3D reconstruction of deformable surfaces. In: ICCV Workshops (2011)
16. Malti, A., Hartley, R., Bartoli, A., Kim, J.H.: Monocular template-based 3D reconstruction of extensible surfaces with local linear elasticity. In: CVPR (2013)
17. Moreno-Noguer, F., Salzmann, M., Lepetit, V., Fua, P.: Capturing 3D stretchable surfaces from single images in closed form. In: CVPR (2009)
18. Newcombe, R.A., Fox, D., Seitz, S.M.: DynamicFusion: reconstruction and tracking of non-rigid scenes in real-time. In: CVPR (2015)
19. Newcombe, R.A., et al.: KinectFusion: real-time dense surface mapping and tracking. In: International Symposium on Mixed and Augmented Reality (2011)
20. Ngo, D.T., Park, S., Jorstad, A., Crivellaro, A., Yoo, C.D., Fua, P.: Dense image registration and deformable surface reconstruction in presence of occlusions and minimal texture. In: ICCV (2015)
21. Östlund, J., Varol, A., Ngo, D.T., Fua, P.: Laplacian meshes for monocular 3D shape recovery. In: Fitzgibbon, A., Lazebnik, S., Perona, P., Sato, Y., Schmid, C. (eds.) ECCV 2012. LNCS, vol. 7574, pp. 412–425. Springer, Heidelberg (2012). https://doi.org/10.1007/978-3-642-33712-3_30
22. Pan, Q., Reitmayr, G., Drummond, T.: ProFORMA: probabilistic feature-based on-line rapid model acquisition. In: BMVC (2009)
23. Perriollat, M., Bartoli, A.: A quasi-minimal model for paper-like surfaces. In: CVPR (2007)

24. Perriollat, M., Hartley, R., Bartoli, A.: Monocular template-based reconstruction of inextensible surfaces. IJCV **95**, 124–137 (2011)
25. Pons, J.P., Keriven, R., Faugeras, O.: Modelling dynamic scenes by registering multi-view image sequence. In: CVPR (2005)
26. Rao, A.R.: Computing oriented texture fields. Comput. Vis. Graph. Image Process.: Graph. Models Image Process. **53**, 157–185 (1991)
27. Russell, C., Fayad, J., Agapito, L.: Energy based multiple model fitting for non-rigid structure from motion. In: CVPR (2011)
28. Salzmann, M., Fua, P.: Reconstructing sharply folding surfaces: a convex formulation. In: CVPR (2009)
29. Salzmann, M., Fua, P.: Linear local models for monocular reconstruction of deformable surface. Trans. Pattern Anal. Mach. Intell. **33**, 931–944 (2011)
30. Salzmann, M., Lepetit, V., Fua, P.: Deformable surface tracking ambiguities. In: CVPR (2007)
31. Salzmann, M., Moreno-Noguer, F., Lepetit, V., Fua, P.: Closed-form solution to non-rigid 3D surface registration. In: Forsyth, D., Torr, P., Zisserman, A. (eds.) ECCV 2008. LNCS, vol. 5305, pp. 581–594. Springer, Heidelberg (2008). https://doi.org/10.1007/978-3-540-88693-8_43
32. Salzmann, M., Urtasun, R., Fua, P.: Local deformation models for monocular 3D shape recovery. In: CVPR (2008)
33. Shen, S., Shi, W., Liu, Y.: Monocular template-based tracking of inextensible deformable surfaces under L_2-norm. In: Zha, H., Taniguchi, R., Maybank, S. (eds.) ACCV 2009. LNCS, vol. 5995, pp. 214–223. Springer, Heidelberg (2010). https://doi.org/10.1007/978-3-642-12304-7_21
34. Sorkine, O., Alexa, M.: As-rigid-as-possible surface modeling. In: SGP (2007)
35. Sumner, R.W., Schmid, J., Pauly, M.: Embedded deformation for shape manipulation. ACM Trans. Graph. **26**(3) (2007). Article no. 80. https://doi.org/10.1145/1276377.1276478. ISSN: 0730-0301
36. Tao, Y., et al.: DoubleFusion: real-time capture of human performance with inner body shape from a depth sensor. In: IEEE Conference on Computer Vision and Pattern Recognition (2018)
37. Torresani, L., Hertzmann, A., Bregler, C.: Non-rigid structure-from-motion: estimating shape and motion with hierarchical priors. Trans. Pattern Anal. Mach. Intell. **30**, 878–892 (2008)
38. Tsoli, A., Argyros, A.: Tracking deformable surfaces that undergo topological changes using an RGB-D camera. In: 3DV, October 2016
39. Valgaerts, L., Wu, C., Bruhn, A., Seidel, H.P., Theobalt, C.: Lightweight binocular facial performance capture under uncontrolled lighting. SIGGRAPH Asia (2012)
40. Varol, A., Salzmann, M., Fua, P., Urtasun, R.: A constrained latent variable model. In: CVPR (2012)
41. Xu, W., et al.: MonoPerfCap: human performance capture from monocular video. TOG **37**, 27 (2018)
42. Xu, W., Salzmann, M., Wang, Y., Liu, Y.: Nonrigid surface registration and completion from RGBD images. In: Fleet, D., Pajdla, T., Schiele, B., Tuytelaars, T. (eds.) ECCV 2014. LNCS, vol. 8690, pp. 64–79. Springer, Cham (2014). https://doi.org/10.1007/978-3-319-10605-2_5
43. Yu, R., Russell, C., Campbell, N.D.F., Agapito, L.: Direct, dense, and deformable: template-based non-rigid 3D reconstruction from RGB video. In: ICCV (2015)
44. Zollhoefer, M., et al.: Real-time non-rigid reconstruction using an RGB-D camera. TOG **33**, 156 (2014)

Oral Session 3: Applications

Counting the Uncountable: Deep Semantic Density Estimation from Space

Andres C. Rodriguez[(✉)] and Jan D. Wegner

ETH Zurich, Stefano-franscini-platz 5, 8093 Zurich, Switzerland
{andres.rodriguez,jan.wegner}@geod.baug.ethz.ch

Abstract. We propose a new method to count objects of specific categories that are significantly smaller than the ground sampling distance of a satellite image. This task is hard due to the cluttered nature of scenes where different object categories occur. Target objects can be partially occluded, vary in appearance within the same class and look alike to different categories. Since traditional object detection is infeasible due to the small size of objects with respect to the pixel size, we cast object counting as a density estimation problem. To distinguish objects of different classes, our approach combines density estimation with semantic segmentation in an end-to-end learnable convolutional neural network (CNN). Experiments show that deep semantic density estimation can robustly count objects of various classes in cluttered scenes. Experiments also suggest that we need specific CNN architectures in remote sensing instead of blindly applying existing ones from computer vision.

Keywords: Remote sensing · Computer vision · Density estimation · Deep learning

1 Introduction

We propose deep semantic density estimation for objects of sub-pixel size in satellite images. Satellite image interpretation is a challenging but very relevant research topic in remote sensing, ecology, agriculture, economics, and cartographic mapping. Since the launch of the Sentinel-2 satellite configuration of the European Space Agency (ESA) in 2015, anyone can download multi-spectral images of up to 10 m ground sampling distance (GSD) for free. At the same time, Sentinel-2 offers high revisit frequency delivering an image of the same spot on earth roughly every 5 days. However, for applications that need more high-resolution evidence like detecting and counting objects (e.g., supply chain management, financial industry), spatial resolution is too poor to apply traditional object detectors. In this work, we thus propose to circumnavigate explicit object detection by turning the counting problem into a density estimation task. Furthermore, we add semantic segmentation to be able to count objects of very specific object categories embedded in cluttered background. We integrate semantic segmentation and density estimation into one concise, end-to-end

© Springer Nature Switzerland AG 2019
T. Brox et al. (Eds.): GCPR 2018, LNCS 11269, pp. 351–362, 2019.
https://doi.org/10.1007/978-3-030-12939-2_24

learnable deep convolutional neural network (CNN) to count objects of 1/3 the size of the GSD. Semantic Segmentation is a standard task in computer vision and has seen significant performance gains since the comeback of deep learning. The major goal is predicting a class label per pixel over an entire image. A rich set of benchmark challenges and datasets like Cityscapes [6] and Pascal VOC 2012 [8] help making rapid progress in this field while continuously reporting current state-of-the-art in online rankings. Typical objects classes of interest are buildings, persons and vehicles that are (i) clearly visible in the image, (ii) large in size (usually several hundreds of pixels) (iii) and can be distinguished from background and further classes primarily relying on shape and RGB texture. Much of this can be transferred with minor adaptions to overhead imagery of <2 m GSD acquired by drones, aerial sensors, and very high-resolution space-borne platforms [12,20,21,25][1]. In contrast, objects like cars, trees, and buildings constitute a single pixel or less in remote sensing imagery of Sentinel-2 (10m GSD) and Landsat (40m GSD). While this resolution is sufficient for semantic segmentation of large, homogeneous regions like crops [26,30], counting individual object instances in cluttered background becomes hard. Here, high spectral resolution comes to the rescue. Deep learning techniques can greatly benefit from high spectral resolution that conveys object information invisible to human sight. It can learn complex relations between spectral bands to identify object-specific spectral signatures that support pixel-accurate semantic segmentation.

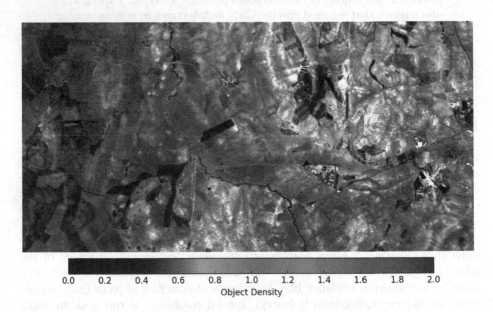

Fig. 1. Density of Olive oil trees in Jaén, Spain, overlaid to a greyscale version of the aerial image. Densities below 0.5 were trimmed for visualization.

[1] See the ISPRS semantic labeling benchmark for an overview http://www2.isprs.org/commissions/comm3/wg4/results.html.

Our workflow goes as follows: We manually annotate a small sample of the object class of interest in Google Earth aerial images. Large-scale groundtruth is obtained by training Faster R-CNN [27] and then predicting for thousands of object instances. Object detections are manually cleansed and turned into smooth density estimates by filtering with a smoothing kernel. An example for groundtruth of olive tree density is given in Fig. 1, where we plot the density obtained from high-resolution aerial images. This reference is used to train, validate, and test our deep semantic density estimation model using Sentinel-2 images. It turns out that deep semantic density estimation can robustly count specific object instances of size well below the GSD by making use of both, spatial texture and spectral signature. We demonstrate that our method robustly scales to $>200\,km^2$ counting >1.6 Mio. object instances.

Our main contributions are: (1) We introduce end-to-end learnable deep semantic density estimation for objects of sub-pixel size, (2) we provide a simplified network architecture that takes advantage of low spatial but high spectral image resolution, (3) we show that standard network architectures from computer vision are inappropriate for this task, and (4) we provide a new, large-scale dataset for object counting in satellite images of moderate resolution.

2 Related Work

There is ample literature for semantic segmentation and object detection in both, computer vision and remote sensing. A full review is beyond the scope of this paper and the reader is referred to top-scoring submissions of benchmarks like Cityscapes [6], MSCOCO [14], and the ISPRS semantic labeling challenge.

Semantic Segmentation has seen significant progress since the invention of fully convolutional neural networks (FCN) [18]. Various improvements to the original architecture have been proposed. For example, more complex Encoder-Decoder models learn features in a lower-dimensional representation and then upscale to the original resolution using deconvolutional layers, making use of middle layer representations or bilinear interpolation [2,13,24,29]. Further ideas include atrous convolutions to prevent lowering the resolution of the learned features and keeping a large receptive field [3–5]. Other approaches are based on pyramid pooling where features are learned in different resolutions and then merged in different ways to deal with objects of different sizes and scales [4,5,16].

Object Detection is related to semantic segmentation. Instead of assigning one class label per pixel, its objective is detecting all instances of a specified object class in an image. This translates to automatically drawing bounding boxes around objects but leaving background unlabeled. One of the most widely used deep learning detectors is Faster R-CNN [27], which extracts scale-invariant features for object proposals. Other approaches compute features for different scales and extract the most relevant scale-features [15]. A more sophisticated variant of object detection is instance segmentation, which adds detailed per-pixel boundaries per object. Today's quasi gold standard is Mask R-CNN [9] that builds on Faster R-CNN and adds a dense feature map to predict instance boundaries.

Density Estimation is about predicting the local distribution of objects without explicitly detecting them. It is a good option in cases where actual objects cannot be clearly identified due to low spatial image resolution, occlusions etc. One application scenario in computer vision is crowd analysis, where ground level images or image sequences from surveillance cameras are used to estimate the number of people [22,31]. An interesting strategy to ease the learning procedure are ranking operations [17] for density estimation. See [1] for a complete review of crowd counting and density estimation. In remote sensing, density estimation has been used for a variety of applications. [7,28] use deep learning to estimate population density using satellite imagery across large regions. Similarly, [32] estimate densities of buildings in cities with support vector regression and a rich set of texture features. More closely related to our work, [11] estimate forest canopy density from Landsat images, whereas [23] estimate biomass density in wetlands from Worldview-2 imagery. These methods inspire our research because they demonstrate that satellite imagery can be used for density estimates of objects with sizes significantly below the GSD. However, all methods have in common that they compute densities of objects that are densely populating the respective image without (much) clutter. In contrast, we propose fine-grained, species-specific density estimates in scenes where the target class could be one out of many. To the best of our knowledge, we are the first to couple fine-grained semantic segmentation with density estimation for cluttered scenes in satellite images. Moreover, we formulate our method as an end-to-end learnable CNN that learns all features for semantics and density estimation simultaneously from the data.

3   Methods

In this section we describe the technical approach. One problem with basically unrecognizable objects in satellite images is manual annotation of reference data. It is impossible to manually segment individual trees or cars in the Sentinel-2 images of 10 meters GSD. We thus resort to Google Maps overhead images of much higher resolution for groundtruth labeling.

Ground Truth. We apply the Faster R-CNN Object detector [27] to very high-resolution ($1m$ GSD) Google Maps images to identify and count reference objects. The detector is tuned to achieve high recall to then manually remove false positive predictions. This allows us to obtain a highly detailed count per area that is used as ground truth to test our model on lower resolution satellite imagery. To down-sample our ground truth to a $10m$ resolution image, we apply a Gaussian kernel with a $\sigma = K/\pi$, where K is the down-scale ratio between the high resolution Google Maps images and the lower resolution satellite image (we chose $K = 10$). We compute the mean over a window of $K \times K$ pixels to obtain the sub-sampled ground truth. The semantic segmentation label is obtained by thresholding densities with a score above 0.5 as object class, and as background otherwise. Note that we use only cloud-free Sentinel-2 images that are closest to the sensing date of the high resolution imagery in Google Maps. Most Sentinel-2 bands have larger GSD than 10 m and we thus need to resample them. We upscale the 20m GSD bands (B5, B6, B7, B8, B10, B11) to 10 m using bilinear interpolation. 60 m bands were not used in our experiments due to their low resolution and the low information they convey for vegetation datasets.

Semantic Segmentation and Density Estimation. Although semantic segmentation and density estimation are different tasks, they are related and can benefit each other. For mutual, fruitful cooperation of both tasks, we set up a joint training procedure such that most features can be used for either of the goals. Adding the semantic segmentation to density estimation also allows to compute classification metrics from standard semantic segmentation literature. Our approach consists of using ResNet blocks, which contain mainly convolutional layers, to obtain features from the input image. Then, for each task, we add an independent convolutional layer at the end of each architecture. For all training experiments, our Loss is defined as:

$$Loss = \underbrace{CrossEntropy(y_{label}, \hat{y}_{label})}_{L_{semantic}} + \underbrace{(y_{density} - \hat{y}_{density})^2}_{L_{density}} \tag{1}$$

where $\hat{y}$ is the predicted estimate for each task. We test four different network architectures in our experiments to verify which provides the best basis for our approach. We begin with the DeepLab V2 (*DL2*) architecture [3], which uses atrous convolutions to obtain filters that have a larger receptive field. These convolutions, inspired from signal processing "à-trous algorithm" [19], have filters that are dilated with zeros to increase the spatial view of a filter without increasing the number of parameters. Moreover, we experiment with the updated version DeepLab V3 (*DL3*) [4], where pyramid pooling with several atrous convolution filters is implemented. Note that this method is a top performing architecture for semantic segmentation on Cityscapes and PASCAL VOC 2012 datasets, and can therefore be viewed as state-of-the-art in semantic image segmentation. Our third architecture (*Ours*) consists of a simplified 6 Layers ResNet [10] where our fourth variant (*Ours Atrous*) adds a last layer of atrous convolutions.

For both simplified ResNet architectures (*Ours* and *Ours Atrous*) we change all striding operations to 1 and use 6 consecutive ResNet Blocks (Fig. 2). Our method moves away from lower dimensional representations but instead keeps details. 6 layers showed a good performance where deeper networks only had marginal to insignificant improvements at a much higher computational cost. The original architecture was designed for typical computer vision images with few, relatively large objects (>100 pixels per object) per image. In our case, thousands of object instances of sub-pixel size are present in the image. We want to retain as many details as possible and therefore set stride to 1. We compensate the potential increase in parameters by reducing the size of the receptive field. In fact, we can tolerate learning contextual knowledge within smaller neighborhoods because it is less important in our case.

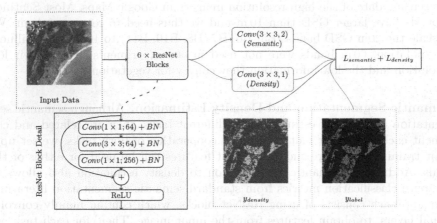

Fig. 2. *Ours* architecture: $Conv(n \times n, M)$ convolution with M filters of size $n \times n$. BN: batch normalization. Input data is first passed through a $Conv(3 \times 3, 256) + BN$ layer before being fed to the first ResNetBlock. Blue and green colors indicate semantic and density connections, respectively. For *Ours Atrous*, all convolutions of the last block before the loss are changed to atrous convolutions. (Color figure online)

4   Experiments

In order to test how robust deep semantic density estimation is to changes in texture, object density and size, we create four different datasets. Three datasets contain trees (olive, coconut, oil palm) with different planting patterns and one dataset contains cars[2]. A summary of all datasets is given in Table 1. Note that object sizes range between $1/3$ and $1/4$ of a Sentinel-2 pixel (Ratio Areas). Object densities of the tree datasets are around 1, whereas the car dataset has highest object density (>5 cars per pixel on average) and smallest object size. Our semi-automated groundtruth annotation procedure involving Faster R-CNN allows us to massively extend our label set across large regions to >200 km^2 with >1.6 Mio. object instances in total (Table 1). We validate outcomes of Faster R-CNN predictions on small, manually labeled hold out regions. Intersection over Union (IoU) ranges between 0.82 and 0.97 for Coconut and Olives, respectively. We achieve highest recall for cars (0.92) and lowest for coconut (0.77).

---

[2] Cars are reacquired VW Diesels sitting in a desert graveyard at the Southern California Logistics Airport in Victorville, USA.

Table 1. Datasets: [a]Mean object density per pixel excluding object free pixels. [b]Ratio areas $= Area_{Object}/Area_{Pixel}$

Dataset	Area (km^2)	Object count	Object density[a]	Ratio areas[b]
Coconuts	77.9	258.7×10^3	0.97	0.36
Palm	104.6	537.5×10^3	1.16	0.36
Olives	129.0	853.7×10^3	0.90	0.39
Cars	0.8	18.3×10^3	5.36	0.26

Semantic Segmentation and Density Estimation. Results of deep semantic density estimation for all architectures are presented in Table 2 and absolute numbers of object counts are shown in Table 3. A visual comparison of ground truth and predictions in Figs. 3 and 4 and the respective χ^2 distance between ground truth distribution $y_{density}$ and predicted distribution $\hat{y}_{density}$ (Table 2, right column) show good performance. *Ours* and *Ours atrous* architectures outperform standard computer vision architectures that build in many downsampling (and upsampling) steps in their network. Results for cars show that there is a natural limitation of our method in terms of minimum object size and maximum object density. While cars can be identified very well (high IoU), there exact number is much harder to estimate (higher MSE, MAE compared to the tree datasets). Moreover, MSE is significantly higher than the MAE, which is caused by outliers in high density areas where lower densities are erroneously predicted (Fig. 4). Our method seems to have a slight tendency to underestimate high density areas that are surrounded by regions of much lower density. This shortcoming of our method can be observed if comparing ground truth high density areas of olives (red) with the respective, underestimated predictions in the middle row of Fig. 3. This effect translates to slightly underestimating the number of instances globally by <5% for all datasets (cf. Table 3).

Comparison of Architectures. Our simple architectures *Ours* and *Ours Atrous* consistently outperform *DL2* and *DL3*. *DL2* and *DL3* use strided convolutions to learn lower dimensional representations of the image, which generates higher level features over large areas to learn context. This seems less important in cases where the extent of individual objects in the image is small compared to the pixel size. In fact, strided convolutions and forcing the network to learn lower dimensional representations risks loosing high frequency information in the satellite images. We compare activation maps of architectures *DL2* and *Ours* on the coconut dataset in Fig. 5 to visualize this argument. One can observe that filters learned by *DL2* loose details (Fig. 5(a)) required for a fine-grained density prediction in contrast to *Ours* (Fig. 5(b)). Recall that both, *DL2* and *DL3*, use bicubic upsampling at different rates to obtain predictions at the original scale. By removing strided convolutions in our architectures, we avoid the need for upscaling predictions already from the start.

358   A. C. Rodriguez and J. D. Wegner

Table 2. Semantic Segmentation and Density Estimation over test areas. In **bold** the best performing metric per object class. χ^2 Distance is the histogram distance between ground truth $y_{density}$ and predicted $\hat{y}_{density}$

Object	Architecture	Semantic segmentation			Density		
		IoU	Precision	Recall	MSE	MAE	χ^2 distance
Coconut	DL2	0.459	0.673	0.591	0.191	0.355	69.7×10^3
	DL3	0.528	0.645	0.744	0.168	0.341	62.5×10^3
	Ours	0.625	**0.775**	0.763	0.126	**0.265**	**50.6×10^3**
	Ours Atrous	**0.649**	0.756	**0.821**	**0.122**	0.273	81.6×10^3
Palm	DL2	0.565	0.710	0.734	0.307	0.421	93.8×10^3
	DL3	0.580	0.694	0.779	0.276	0.415	88.6×10^3
	Ours	0.660	**0.795**	0.796	**0.192**	**0.314**	**75.8×10^3**
	Ours Atrous	0.542	0.544	**0.993**	0.672	0.668	97.1×10^3
Olives	DL2	0.777	**0.921**	0.833	0.235	0.363	**30.9×10^3**
	DL3	0.811	0.883	0.909	0.175	0.331	35.6×10^3
	Ours	**0.861**	0.901	0.952	**0.135**	**0.270**	34.5×10^3
	Ours Atrous	0.858	0.893	**0.957**	0.162	0.302	46.5×10^3
Cars	DL2	0.789	0.928	0.841	8.743	2.235	21.3×10^1
	DL3	0.753	0.892	0.829	8.454	2.319	25.1×10^1
	Ours	0.931	0.936	0.994	2.319	1.077	**1.6×10^1**
	Ours Atrous	**0.941**	**0.944**	**0.996**	**1.940**	**0.991**	3.8×10^1

Table 3. Object counting performance with lowest MSE and MAE error. *Ours* for tree objects and *Ours Atrous* for Cars.

Object	Object count		
	Ground truth	Prediction	Diff %
Coconut	88.49×10^3	84.65×10^3	−4.34
Palm	143.14×10^3	137.13×10^3	−4.20
Olives	64.05×10^3	62.34×10^3	−2.68
Cars	4.33×10^3	4.13×10^3	−4.58

Band Importance. Sentinel-2 satellites are multi-spectral sensors designed for vegetation monitoring. Spectral signatures of different vegetation types and plant species can help distinguishing objects, in contrast to mostly texture-based features in RGB images. In order to verify the contribution of this additional spectral evidence, we train and test *Ours Atrous* with different band settings. Each run leaves away bands to test their importance. We contrast results on vegetation with results for cars. We show results of this analysis in Table 4, where high *IoU* values of column *Semantic* indicate good identification of objects while low *MSE* and *MAE* values of *Density* mean correct object counting. It turns

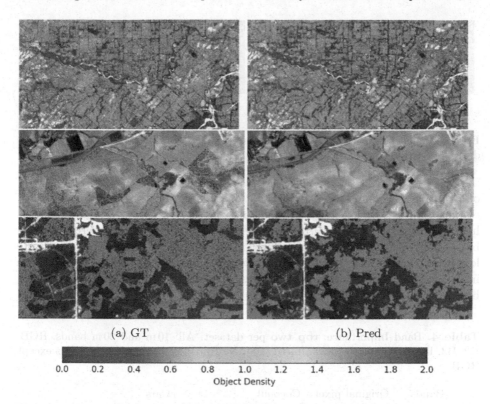

(a) GT   (b) Pred

0.0   0.2   0.4   0.6   0.8   1.0   1.2   1.4   1.6   1.8   2.0
Object Density

Fig. 3. Density estimation results. Top: Coconut; Middle: Olives; Bottom: Palm. Densities below 0.5 were trimmed for visualization. (Color figure online)

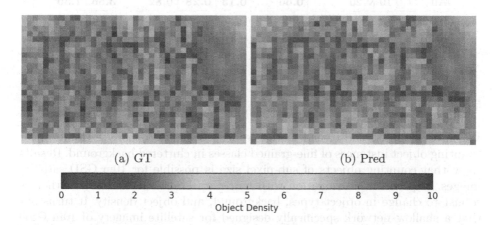

(a) GT   (b) Pred

0   1   2   3   4   5   6   7   8   9   10
Object Density

Fig. 4. Car density, densities below 0.5 were trimmed for visualization.

| (a) DL2 | (b) Ours |

Fig. 5. Final activation maps of (a) *DL2* and (b) *Ours* for a test region of the coconut dataset. *Ours* better retains details than *DL2*.

out that deep semantic density estimation requires both, spectral and spatial evidence for vegetation whereas this is not the case for cars. 10 m RGB bands help counting trees (low *MSE* and *MAE* with RGB bands) whereas infared bands help identifying them (high *IoU* for *All* and *No RGB*). Infrared bands are less important for cars because, unlike plants, they do not reflect characteristic infrared signatures. Prediction is based mostly on texture in the image provided by the 10 m RGB bands.

Table 4. Band Importance: **top two** per dataset. All: 10 m and 20 m bands. RGB: B2, B3, B4. RGBI: RGB plus infrared (B8). No RGB: all 10 m and 20 m bands except RGB.

Bands	Original pixel resolution [m]	Coconut			Cars		
		Semantic	Density		Semantic	Density	
		IoU	MSE	MAE	IoU	MSE	MAE
All	10 & 20	**0.66**	**0.13**	**0.28**	0.82	**3.56**	**1.39**
RGB	10	0.49	0.26	0.41	**0.83**	3.53	1.40
RGB I	10	0.55	**0.16**	**0.33**	0.77	3.68	1.42
No RGB	10 & 20	**0.63**	0.19	0.35	0.81	4.45	1.57

5   Conclusion

We have proposed end-to-end learnable deep semantic density estimation for counting object instances of fine-grained classes in cluttered background. Results show that counting objects of sub-pixel size is possible for 10m GSD satellite images. Experimental evaluation with four datasets shows that our method is robust to change in object types, background, and object density. It turns out that a shallow network specifically designed for satellite imagery of 10m GSD and sub-pixel objects outperforms more sophisticated, state-of-the-art architectures from computer vision. This signifies that direct application of networks tailored for vision to remote sensing images should be done with care. In our experiments, we find that any down-sampling operation inside the network risks loosing precious details. We should thus always keep in mind the particularities of remote sensing imagery in terms of object scale, GSD, (nadir) perspective and (high) spectral resolution. If carefully considered during the network design process, these specific properties offer new possibilities in network design.

Acknowledments. This project is funded by Barry Callebaut Sourcing AG as a part of a Research Project Agreement with ETH Zurich.

References

1. A survey of recent advances in CNN-based single image crowd counting and density estimation. Pattern Recogn. Lett. **107**, 3–16 (2018). Video Surveillance-oriented Biometrics
2. Badrinarayanan, V., Kendall, A., Cipolla, R.: SegNet: a deep convolutional encoder-decoder architecture for image segmentation. IEEE Trans. Pattern Anal. Mach. Intell. **39**(12), 2481–2495 (2017)
3. Chen, L., Papandreou, G., Kokkinos, I., Murphy, K., Yuille, A.L.: DeepLab: semantic image segmentation with deep convolutional nets, atrous convolution, and fully connected CRFs. IEEE Trans. Pattern Anal. Mach. Intell. **40**(4), 834–848 (2018)
4. Chen, L., Papandreou, G., Schroff, F., Adam, H.: Rethinking atrous convolution for semantic image segmentation. CoRR
5. Chen, L., Zhu, Y., Papandreou, G., Schroff, F., Adam, H.: Encoder-decoder with atrous separable convolution for semantic image segmentation. CoRR
6. Cordts, M., et al.: The cityscapes dataset for semantic urban scene understanding. In: Proceedings of the IEEE Conference on Computer Vision and Pattern Recognition (CVPR) (2016)
7. Doupe, P., Bruzelius, E., Faghmous, J., Ruchman, S.G.: Equitable development through deep learning: the case of sub-national population density estimation. In: Proceedings of the 7th Annual Symposium on Computing for Development, p. 6. ACM (2016)
8. Everingham, M., Van Gool, L., Williams, C.K.I., Winn, J., Zisserman, A.: The PASCAL Visual Object Classes Challenge 2012 (VOC2012) Results. http://www.pascal-network.org/challenges/VOC/voc2012/workshop/index.html
9. He, K., Gkioxari, G., Dollár, P., Girshick, R.: Mask R-CNN. In: 2017 IEEE International Conference on Computer Vision (ICCV), pp. 2980–2988 (2017)
10. He, K., Zhang, X., Ren, S., Sun, J.: Deep residual learning for image recognition. In: Proceedings of the IEEE Conference on Computer Vision and Pattern Recognition, pp. 770–778 (2016)
11. Joshi, C., De Leeuw, J., Skidmore, A., van Duren, I., van Osten, H.: Remotely sensed estimation of forest canopy density: a comparison of the performance of four methods. Int. J. Appl. Earth Obs. Geoinf. **8**(2), 84–95 (2006)
12. Kuo, T.S., Tseng, K.S., Yan, J.W., Liu, Y.C., Frank Wang, Y.C.: Deep aggregation net for land cover classification. In: The IEEE Conference on Computer Vision and Pattern Recognition (CVPR) Workshops, June 2018
13. Lin, G., Milan, A., Shen, C., Reid, I.: RefineNet: multi-path refinement networks for high-resolution semantic segmentation. In: 2017 IEEE Conference on Computer Vision and Pattern Recognition (CVPR), pp. 5168–5177 (2017)
14. Lin, T.Y., et al.: Microsoft COCO: common objects in context. In: Fleet, D., Pajdla, T., Schiele, B., Tuytelaars, T. (eds.) ECCV 2014. LNCS, vol. 8693, pp. 740–755. Springer, Cham (2014). https://doi.org/10.1007/978-3-319-10602-1_48

15. Liu, W., et al.: SSD: single shot multibox detector. In: Leibe, B., Matas, J., Sebe, N., Welling, M. (eds.) ECCV 2016. LNCS, vol. 9905, pp. 21–37. Springer, Cham (2016). https://doi.org/10.1007/978-3-319-46448-0_2
16. Liu, W., Rabinovich, A., Berg, A.C.: ParseNet: looking wider to see better. CoRR
17. Liu, X., van de Weijer, J., Bagdanov, A.D.: Leveraging unlabeled data for crowd counting by learning to rank. In: The IEEE Conference on Computer Vision and Pattern Recognition (CVPR), June 2018
18. Long, J., Shelhamer, E., Darrell, T.: Fully convolutional networks for semantic segmentation. In: Proceedings of the IEEE Conference on Computer Vision and Pattern Recognition, pp. 3431–3440 (2015)
19. Mallat, S.: A Wavelet Tour of Signal Processing: The Sparse Way, 3rd edn. Academic Press Inc., Orlando (2008)
20. Marmanis, D., Wegner, J.D., Galliani, S., Schindler, K., Datcu, M., Stilla, U.: Semantic segmentation of aerial images with an ensemble of CNNs. ISPRS Ann. Photogramm. Remote Sens. Spat. Inf. Sci. **3**, 473 (2016)
21. Máttyus, G., Luo, W., Urtasun, R.: DeepRoadMapper: extracting road topology from aerial images. In: International Conference on Computer Vision, vol. 2 (2017)
22. Meynberg, O., Cui, S., Reinartz, P.: Detection of high-density crowds in aerial images using texture classification. Remote Sens. **8**(6), 470 (2016)
23. Mutanga, O., Adam, E., Cho, M.: High density biomass estimation for wetland vegetation using Wordlview-2 imagery and random forest regression algorithm. Int. J. Appl. Earth Obs. Geoinf. **18**, 399–406 (2012)
24. Pohlen, T., Hermans, A., Mathias, M., Leibe, B.: Full-resolution residual networks for semantic segmentation in street scenes. In: The IEEE Conference on Computer Vision and Pattern Recognition (CVPR), July 2017
25. Postadjian, T., Le Bris, A., Sahbi, H., Mallet, C.: Investigating the potential of deep neural networks for large-scale classification of very high resolution satellite images. ISPRS Ann. Photogramm. Remote Sens. Spat. Inf. Sci. **4**, 183 (2017)
26. Pryzant, R., Ermon, S., Lobell, D.: Monitoring ethiopian wheat fungus with satellite imagery and deep feature learning. In: The IEEE Conference on Computer Vision and Pattern Recognition (CVPR) Workshops, July 2017
27. Ren, S., He, K., Girshick, R., Sun, J.: Faster R-CNN: towards real-time object detection with region proposal networks. IEEE Trans. Pattern Anal. Mach. Intell. **39**(6), 1137–1149 (2017)
28. Robinson, C., Hohman, F., Dilkina, B.: A deep learning approach for population estimation from satellite imagery. In: Proceedings of the 1st ACM SIGSPATIAL Workshop on Geospatial Humanities, pp. 47–54. ACM (2017)
29. Ronneberger, O., Fischer, P., Brox, T.: U-Net: convolutional networks for biomedical image segmentation. In: Navab, N., Hornegger, J., Wells, W.M., Frangi, A.F. (eds.) MICCAI 2015. LNCS, vol. 9351, pp. 234–241. Springer, Cham (2015). https://doi.org/10.1007/978-3-319-24574-4_28
30. Russwurm, M., Korner, M.: Temporal vegetation modelling using long short-term memory networks for crop identification from medium-resolution multi-spectral satellite images. In: The IEEE Conference on Computer Vision and Pattern Recognition (CVPR) Workshops, July 2017
31. Shang, C., Ai, H., Bai, B.: End-to-end crowd counting via joint learning local and global count. In: 2016 IEEE International Conference on Image Processing (ICIP), pp. 1215–1219 (2016)
32. Zhang, T., Huang, X., Wen, D., Li, J.: Urban building density estimation from high-resolution imagery using multiple features and support vector regression. IEEE J. Sel. Top. Appl. Earth Obs. Remote Sens. **10**(7), 3265–3280 (2017)

Acquire, Augment, Segment and Enjoy: Weakly Supervised Instance Segmentation of Supermarket Products

Patrick Follmann[1,2]([✉]) [iD], Bertram Drost[1] [iD], and Tobias Böttger[1,2] [iD]

[1] MVTec Software GmbH, Arnulfstr. 205, 80634 Munich, Germany
{follmann,drost,boettger}@mvtec.com
[2] Technical University of Munich, 80333 Munich, Germany
https://www.mvtec.com/research

Abstract. Grocery stores have thousands of products that are usually identified using barcodes with a human in the loop. For automated checkout systems, it is necessary to count and classify the groceries efficiently and robustly. One possibility is to use a deep learning algorithm for instance-aware semantic segmentation. Such methods achieve high accuracies but require a large amount of annotated training data.

We propose a system to generate the training annotations in a weakly supervised manner, drastically reducing the labeling effort. We assume that for each training image, only the object class is known. The system automatically segments the corresponding object from the background. The obtained training data is augmented to simulate variations similar to those seen in real-world setups.

Our experiments show that with appropriate data augmentation, our approach obtains competitive results compared to a fully-supervised baseline, while drastically reducing the amount of manual labeling.

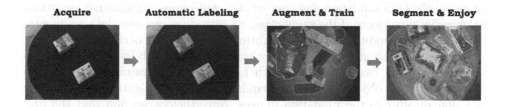

Acquire   Automatic Labeling   Augment & Train   Segment & Enjoy

1 Introduction

The classification and localization of objects are important subtasks in many computer vision applications, such as autonomous driving, grasping objects with a robot, or quality control in a production process. Recently, end-to-end trainable convolutional neural networks (CNNs) for instance segmentation have been successfully applied in the settings of everyday photography or urban street scenes. This is possible due to the advances in CNN architectures [8] and due to the availability of large-scale datasets, such as ImageNet [20], COCO [15] or

Cityscapes [2]. For many industrial challenges, the object categories are very specific and the intra- and inter-class variability is rather small. For example, existing automatic checkout systems in supermarkets identify isolated products that are conveyed on a belt through a scanning tunnel [4,10]. Even though such systems often provide a semi-controlled environment and know which products may appear, external influences and intra-class variations cannot be completely avoided. Furthermore, the system's efficiency is higher if non-isolated products can be identified as well. To fine-tune a network for such an application, it is crucial to have a large amount of annotated training data. However, the manual annotation of such a dataset is time-consuming and expensive. Hence, it is of great interest to be able to train instance segmentation models with as little labeling effort as possible.

A recent dataset for this challenge is D2S [5], which contains 21000 images of 60 common supermarket products. The overall objective of that dataset is to realistically model real-world applications such as an automatic checkout, inventory, or warehouse system. It contains very few training images, which are additionally significantly less complex and crowded than the validation and test images. However, the training images are not simple enough to efficiently use weak supervision to generate labels.

In this work, we present a system that allows to train an instance segmentation model in an industrial setting like D2S with weak supervision. To facilitate this, each of the D2S object categories is captured individually on a turntable. The object regions are labeled automatically using basic image processing techniques. The only manual input is the class of the object on the turntable. This allows to create annotations for instance-aware semantic segmentation of reasonable quality with minimal effort, essentially by only taking a few images of each object category.

In a second step, we assemble complex training scenes using various kinds of data augmentation like the ones proposed in [5]. Moreover, to address the challenges in the D2S validation and test set, i.e., reflections, background variations or neighboring objects of the same class, we introduce two new data augmentation stages that additionally model lighting variations and occlusion.

In our experiments, we thoroughly evaluate the weakly generated annotations against the baseline trained with fully-supervised training data. Due to partially different objects, a different acquisition setup and lighting changes there is a domain-shift to the validation images. Nevertheless, we find that the proposed method allows for an overall detection performance of 68.9% compared to 80.1% of a fully-supervised baseline without domain-shift. Hence, it is possible to produce competitive segmentation results with a very simple acquisition setup, virtually no label effort, and suitable data augmentation.

2   Related Work

Weakly Supervised Instance Segmentation. Solving computer vision tasks with weakly annotated data has become a major topic in recent years. It can significantly reduce the amount of manual labeling effort and thus make solving new tasks feasible. For example, Deselaers *et al.* [3] learn *generic knowledge* about object bounding boxes from a subset of object classes. This is used to support learning new classes without any location annotation. This allows them to train a functional object detector from weakly supervised images only. Similarly, Vezhnevets *et al.* [22] attempt to learn a supervised semantic segmentation method from weak labels that can compete with a fully supervised one. Recently, there has been work that attempts to train instance segmentation models from bounding box labels or by assuming only parts of the data is labeled with pixel-precise annotations. For example, the work by Hu *et al.* [9] attempts to train instance segmentation models over a large set of categories, where most instances only have box annotations. They merely assume a small fraction of the instances have mask annotations that have been manually acquired. Khoreva *et al.* [11] train an instance segmentation model by using GrabCut [19] foreground segmentation on bounding box ground truth labels.

In contrast to the above works, our weak supervision only assumes the object class of each training image and does not require bounding boxes of the single objects or their pixel-precise annotations. We use basic image processing techniques and a simple acquisition setup to learn competitive instance segmentation models from weak image annotations.

Data Augmentation. Since we restrict the training images to objects of a single class on a homogeneous background, it is essential to augment the training data with more complex, artificial, images. Otherwise, state-of-the-art instance segmentation methods fail to generalize to more complex scenes, different backgrounds or varying lighting conditions. This is often the case for industrial applications, where a huge effort is necessary to obtain a large amount of annotated data. Hence, extending the training dataset by data augmentation is common practice [21]. Augmentation is often restricted to global image transformations such as random crops, translations, rotations, horizontal reflections, or color augmentations [12]. However, for instance-level segmentations, it is possible to extend these techniques to generate completely new images. For example, in [6,14,23], new artificial training data is generated by randomly sampling objects from the training split of COCO [15] and pasting them into new training images. However, since the COCO segmentations are coarse and the intraclass variation is extremely high, the augmentation brings limited gain. On the other hand, in the D2S dataset [5], it is difficult to obtain reasonable segmentation results without any data augmentation. The training set is designed to mimic the restrictions of industrial applications, which include little training data and potentially much more complex test images than training images.

Analogously to the above works, we perform various types of data augmentation to increase complexity and the amount of the training data. However, we go a step further and address specific weaknesses of the state of the art on D2S by explicitly generating artificial scenes with neighboring and touching objects. To furthermore gain robustness to changing illumination, we also render the artificial scenes under different lighting conditions by exploiting the depth information.

3 Weak Annotations

The goal is to generate annotations for the Densely Segmented Supermarket dataset (D2S) [5] with as little effort as possible. For this, we built an image acquisition setup similar to the one described in [5] and attempt to automatically generate the pixel-wise object annotations. A handful of training images is acquired for each object in D2S such that each view of the object is captured. The training images are kept very simple. Each contains only instances of a single class and the instances do not touch each other. During the acquisition process, only the category of the object on the turntable has to be set manually. This does not result in additional work, as one has to collect the classes that have already been captured, anyway. Together with the simple acquisition setup, these restrictions allow to generate the pixel-precise annotations of the objects automatically. We present different approaches, one with background subtraction and the other based on salient object detection.

3.1 Acquisition

To be able to reduce the label and acquisition effort to a bare minimum, the image acquisition setup is constructed in a very basic manner. A high-resolution industrial RGB camera with 1920×1440 pixels is mounted above a turntable. The turntable allows to acquire multiple views of each scene without any manual interaction. To increase the perspective variation, the camera is mounted off-center with respect to the rotation center of the turntable. Additionally, a stereo camera that works with projected texture is fixed centrally above the turntable. In Sect. 4, we show how the depth images may be used to extend the capabilities of data augmentation. The setup used for the image acquisition and its dimensions are depicted in Fig. 1.

To make the automatic label generation as simple and robust as possible, the background of the turntable is set to a plain colored brown surface. In an initial step, we keep the background color fixed for every training image. In a next step, we further use a lighter brown background to improve the automatic segmentation of dark or transparent objects such as avocados or bottles. The datasets are denoted with the prefix weakly and weakly cleaned, respectively. A few example classes where the lighter background significantly improved the automatic labels are displayed in Fig. 2.

Note that, although the acquisition setup is very similar to that of the original D2S setup, there is a domain shift between the new training images and original D2S images. In particular, the camera pose relative to the turntable is not the same and the background and the lighting slightly differs. Maybe the most significant differences is, however, that some of the captured objects are different from those in original D2S. For example the vegetables and fruit categories have a slightly different appearance and some packaging, e.g., for the classes clementine or apple_braeburn_bundle are not the same as in D2S.

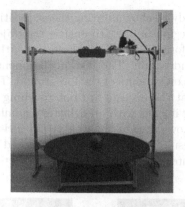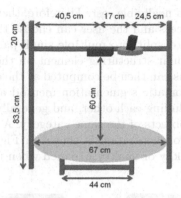

Fig. 1. The *D2S* image acquisition setup. Each scene was rotated ten times using a turntable. For each rotation, three images are acquired with different illuminations.

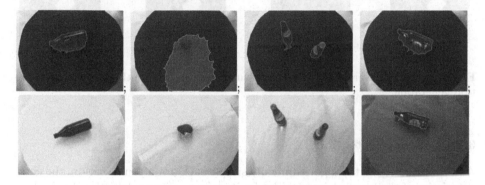

Fig. 2. Examples where the light background used for `weakly_cleaned` significantly improves the automatic segmentations over those from the dark background used for `weakly`.

The two classes `oranges` and `pasta_reggia_fusilli` were not available for purchase anymore and therefore, the respective D2S training scenes (without labels) were used.

3.2 Background Subtraction

We utilize the simple setting of the training images and automatically generate the segmentations by background subtraction. To account for changing illumination of the surrounding environment, an individual background image was acquired for each training scene. By subtracting the background image from each image, a foreground region can be generated automatically with an adaptive binary threshold [17]. Depending on the object and its attributes, we either use the V channel from the HSV color space, or the summed absolute difference of each of the RGB channels. The results for both color-spaces can be computed with negligible cost. Therefore, they can already be shown during the acquisition process and the user can choose the better region online. To ensure the object is not split into multiple small parts, we perform morphological closing with a circular structuring element on the foreground region. The instance segmentations can then be computed as the connected components of the foreground. The automatic segmentation method assumes that the objects are not touching or occluding each other, and generally works for images with an arbitrary number of objects of the same category. A schematic overview of the weakly supervised region generation is shown in Fig. 3. The resulting training set is denoted as `weakly` or `weakly_cleaned` when using a lighter background for dark objects.

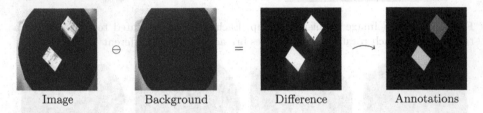

| Image | Background | Difference | Annotations |

Fig. 3. Schematic overview of the weakly supervised ground truth instance segmentation generation.

3.3   Saliency Detection

As an alternative to the algorithmically simple background subtraction, the characteristics of the training images also invite to use saliency detection methods to identify the instances. Currently, the best methods are based on deep learning and require fine-tuning to the target domain [1,13]. Hence, they require manually labeling at least for a subset of the data. A more generic approach is that of the *Saliency Tree* [16]. It is constructed in a multi-step process. In a first step, the image is simplified into a set of primitive regions. The partitions are merged into a saliency tree based on their saliency measure. The tree is then traversed and the salient regions are identified. The salient region generation requires no fine-tuning to the target domain and achieves top ranks in recent benchmarks [1,13].

We use the Saliency Tree to generate saliency images for each of the (cleaned) training images. The foreground region is then generated from the saliency image by a simple thresholding and an intersection with the region of the turntable. Also here, morphological closing and opening with a small circular structuring element is used to close small holes and smooth the boundary. Analogously to the background subtraction, the single instances are computed as the connected components of the foreground region. Qualitatively, we found that a threshold of 40 was a good compromise between too large and too small generated regions. For some rather small objects, using this threshold results in regions that almost fill the whole turntable. To prevent those artifacts, we iteratively increase the threshold by ten until the obtained total area of the regions is smaller than 30% of the turntable area. However, even with this precaution, in some cases the obtained instances may be degenerated. A few examples and failure cases or both the background subtraction and the saliency detection are displayed in Fig. 4. We denote the annotations obtained with the saliency detection method by `saliency cleaned`.

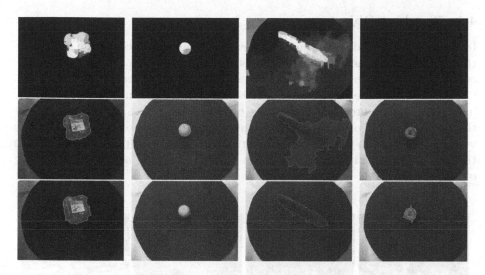

Fig. 4. The automatic labels for saliency detection (second row) and background subtraction (third row) are displayed. In general, the saliency detection and the background subtraction return similar results (first column). In rare cases, the saliency detection outperforms the background subtraction and returns more complete regions. In the third and fourth column some typical failure cases of the saliency detection scheme are displayed. Either it fails completely (fourth column), or it is hard to find a reasonable threshold (third column).

4 Data Augmentation

One of the challenges of applying deep-learning based CNNs is the large amount of training data that is required to obtain competitive results. In the real-world applications discussed in this work, the acquisition and labeling of training data can be expensive as it requires many manual tasks. To mitigate this issue, we use data augmentation, where additional training data is created automatically based on a few manually acquired simple images. The images generated by the data augmentation model and simulate the variations and complexity that commonly occur when applying the trained network.

To augment the training data, we randomly select between 3 and 15 objects from the training set, crop them out of the training image utilizing the generated annotation and paste them onto a background image similar to the one from D2S training images. The objects are placed at a random location with a random rotation. This generates complex scenes, where multiple objects of different instances may be overlapping each other. However, since this does not address all the difficulties within the D2S validation and test set, we also introduce two new augmentation techniques to specifically address these difficulties, namely *touching objects* and *reflections*.

4.1   Touching Objects

In the validation and test set of D2S there are many instances of the same class that touch each other. The existing instance segmentation schemes have difficulties to find the instance boundaries and often return unsatisfactory results. Often, if objects are close, the methods only predict a single instance or the instances extend into the neighboring object. Hence, we specifically augment the training set by generating new images where instances of the same class are very close to or even touching each other. We denote the respective dataset with the suffix `neighboring`. Figure 5 shows some examples of augmented touching objects.

Fig. 5. Examples for augmented reflections using a simulation of a spotlight.

4.2   Reflections

To create even more training data, we augment the original data by rendering artificial scenes under different lighting conditions. For this, we use the registered 3D sensor and RGB camera to build textured 3D models of the different object instances. Random subsets of those instances are then placed at random locations to create new, artificial scenes. Since we do not know the surface characteristics of the individual objects, we use a generic Phong shader [18] with varying spotlight location and spotlight and ambient light intensity to simulate real-world lighting. We use this approach also because in real-world scenarios, lighting can vary drastically compared to the training setup. For example, different checkout counters can have different light placements, while others might be close to a window such that the time of day and the weather influence the local lighting conditions. We denote the respective dataset with the suffix `reflections`. Example images of the `reflections` set are shown in Fig. 6.

Fig. 6. Examples for augmented reflections using a simulation of a spotlight.

5   Experiments

All of the experiments are carried out on D2S [5], as the datasets splits are explicitly designed for the use of data augmentation. In comparison to the validation and test sets, the complexity of the scenes in the training set are a lot lower in terms of object count, occlusions, and background variations. Moreover, the data augmentation techniques introduced in Sect. 4 are well-suited for industrial setting, where the intra-class variations are mainly restricted to rigid and deformable transformations and background or lighting changes. D2S contains 60 object categories in 21.000 pixel-wise labeled images.

We do not want to carry out a review of instance segmentation methods, but focus on the analysis of the weakly supervised setting and the different augmentations. Therefore, we use the competitive instance segmentation method Mask R-CNN [8] for our experiments. We choose the original Detectron [7] implementation in order to make the results easy to reproduce.

Setup. To speed up the training and evaluation process, we downsized D2S by a factor of 4, which results in an image resolution of 480×360 px. Note that we also adapted the image size parameters of Mask R-CNN accordingly, such that no scaling has to be carried out during training or evaluation.

All models were trained using two NVIDIA GTX1080Ti GPUs. We used the original hyperparameters from Detectron except for the following: a batch size of 5 images per GPU (resulting in 10 images per iteration) and a base learning rate of 0.02 (reduced to 0.002 after 12k iterations). We trained for 15000 iterations and initialized with weights pretrained on COCO.

For the evaluation of our results, we used the *D2S* validation set. As is common in instance segmentation, the mean average precision [%] averaged over IoU-thresholds from 0.5 to 0.95 in steps of 0.05 is used as performance measure.

Baseline. As a baseline for the weakly supervised setting, we used the high quality, manually generated annotations from the D2S training set using the original split as provided in [5]. To better compare and separate the effect of the data augmentation from the effect of having better training data, we also augmented this high quality training set. Except for reflections (which requires depth information), the augmentation can be done analogously to the weakly supervised setting. Because the annotations fit almost perfectly, the object crops contain only a very small amount of background surroundings compared to the

Table 1. Results. Ablation study for different ways of generating the annotations and different augmentations. The performance is given in terms of mAP percentage values. * indicates the set that gave the best results in combination with specific augmentations. Abbreviations for augmentation types are as follows: `neighboring` (NB), `random background` (RB), `reflections` (RE).

Training set	Baseline	Weakly	Weakly cleaned	Saliency cleaned
train	48.3	8.5	15.9	16.5
train + augm 2500	77.0	62.8	64.8	55.7
train + augm 5000*	77.8	62.2	61.9	55.4
train + augm 10000	78.4	65.0	63.0	55.8
train + augm 20000	78.4	65.0	62.7	59.7
* + NB	78.5	63.7	62.5	59.2
* + RB	78.5	64.9	68.0	58.7
* + RE	-	-	66.9	59.7
* + NB + RB	**80.1**	**66.8**	**68.9**	60.2
* + NB + RB + RE	-	-	68.5	**61.9**

crops from the weak annotations. Therefore, one can expect the best results for the baseline.

Results. For all types of underlying annotations, `baseline`, `weakly`, `weakly cleaned` and `saliency cleaned`, we made similar experiments. First, we trained the model only on the training images, denoted as `train`. Second, we augmented 2500, 5000, 10000, or 20000 images as described at the beginning of Sect. 4 and added them to `train`, respectively (`augm`). Third, we augmented 2000 images both with touching objects (`neighboring`) or on a random background (`random background`). Additionally, for `weakly cleaned` and `saliency cleaned`, we generated 2000 images with `reflections` (on random background). The corresponding mAP values on the D2S validation set (in quartersize) are shown in Table 1.

The images obtained for our weakly supervised training are significantly less complex than the D2S validation images; there are no touching or occluding objects and always only one category per image. This large domain shift results in a very poor performance of the models trained only on `train` compared to the `baseline` (*c.f.* row 1 of Table 1). Normal augmentation strongly improves the results, e.g., from 8.5% to 65.0% for `weakly`. Note that for the normal augmentation, the annotation quality seems to be less important, as `weakly cleaned` is on the same mAP-level as `weakly`. Only `saliency cleaned` performs significantly worse, probably due to some corrupt automatically generated annotations. The specific augmentation types `neighboring` (NB), `random background` (RB) and `reflections` (RE) further help to improve the result to 68.9% for `weakly cleaned`, which is more than four times better than the `train`-result. NB, RB and RE are indeed complementary augmentation types as each of them

consistently helps to improve upon `train + augm 5000`. In Fig. 7 some qualitative results are displayed. They show that using the specific augmentations
indeed helps to improve on the typical failures cases that they address. Also
note that the relative improvement using specific augmentations is higher in the
weakly setting than for the `baseline` (*e.g.* 7% for `weakly cleaned` *vs.* 2.3% for
`baseline`).

Usually with a higher number of training data the results of models with
a high number of parameters are improved. However, we found that the best
results are obtained if the specific augmentation sets of step three and four are
added to `train + augm 5000`. A reason could be the domain-shift between D2S
validation and the augmented images. For completeness, we show results for
`augm 2500` and `augm 10000` in the supplementary material.

ground truth   train   + augm 5000   + specific

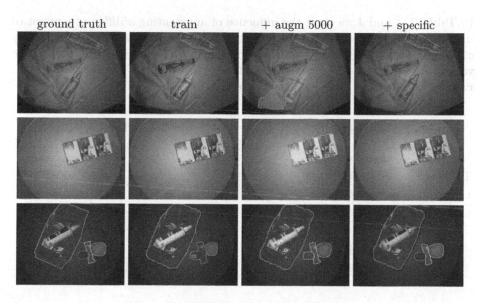

Fig. 7. Qualitative Results. Improvements for `weakly_cleaned` using specific augmentations: (*top*) random `backgrounds`, (*middle*) `neighboring` objects, (*bottom*)
`reflections`.

6   Conclusion

We have presented a system that allows to train competitive instance segmentation methods with virtually no label effort. By acquiring very simple training
images, we were able to automatically generate reasonable object annotations for
the D2S dataset. To tackle the complex validation and test scenes, we propose to
use different types of data augmentation to generate artificial scenes that mimic
the expected validation and test sequences. We present new data augmentation
ideas to help improve scenes where touching objects and changing illumination

is a problem. The results indicate that the weakly supervised models yield a very good trade-off between annotation effort and performance. This paves the way for cost-effective implementations of semantic segmentation approaches by lifting the requirement of acquiring large amounts of training images.

Using imperfect annotations, we also found that increasing the number of augmented images does not always improve the result. We believe that reducing the domain-shift to the test set by generating more realistic augmentations is an open topic that could resolve this problem. Additionally, we found that data augmentation can be beneficial even if the number of labeled training images is already large.

Appendix

In Tables 2, 3 and 4 we show the influence of augmenting a different amount of images and adding specific augmentations for `baseline`, `weakly`, and `weakly cleaned`, respectively. The performance is given in terms of mAP percentage values. Abbreviations for augmentation types are as follows: `neighboring` (NB), `random background` (RB), `reflections` (RE).

Table 2. Baseline results

Training set	augm 2500	augm 5000	augm 10000
train	48.3	48.3	48.3
train + augm	77.0	77.8	78.4
+ NB	77.3	78.5	78.3
+ RB	78.2	78.5	79.1
+ NB + RB	79.3	**80.1**	79.9

Table 3. Weakly results

Training set	augm 2500	augm 5000	augm 10000
train	8.5	8.5	8.5
train + augm	62.8	62.2	65.0
+ NB	64.0	63.7	65.8
+ RB	64.0	64.9	63.5
+ NB + RB	64.0	**66.8**	65.3

Table 4. Weakly cleaned results

Training set	augm 2500	augm 5000	augm 10000
train	15.9	15.9	15.9
train + augm	64.8	61.9	63.0
+ NB	65.0	62.5	64.7
+ RB	65.9	68.0	65.8
+ RE	68.1	66.9	65.3
+ NB + RB	65.9	**68.9**	66.9
+ NB + RB + RE	68.4	68.5	66.9

References

1. Borji, A., Cheng, M.M., Jiang, H., Li, J.: Salient object detection: a benchmark. IEEE Trans. Image Process. **24**(12), 5706–5722 (2015)
2. Cordts, M., et al.: The cityscapes dataset for semantic urban scene understanding. In: Proceedings of the IEEE Conference on Computer Vision and Pattern Recognition (CVPR), pp. 3213–3223 (2016)
3. Deselaers, T., Alexe, B., Ferrari, V.: Weakly supervised localization and learning with generic knowledge. Int. J. Comput. Vis. **100**(3), 275–293 (2012)
4. ECRS: RAPTOR. https://www.ecrs.com/products/point-of-sale-pos/accelerated-checkout/. Accessed 20 June 2018
5. Follmann, P., Böttger, T., Härtinger, P., König, R., Ulrich, M.: MVTec D2S: densely segmented supermarket dataset. In: Ferrari, V., Hebert, M., Sminchisescu, C., Weiss, Y. (eds.) ECCV 2018. LNCS, vol. 11214, pp. 581–597. Springer, Cham (2018). https://doi.org/10.1007/978-3-030-01249-6_35
6. Follmann, P., König, R., Härtinger, P., Klostermann, M.: Learning to see the invisible: end-to-end trainable amodal instance segmentation. CoRR abs/1804.08864 (2018). http://arxiv.org/abs/1804.08864
7. Girshick, R., Radosavovic, I., Gkioxari, G., Dollár, P., He, K.: Detectron (2018). https://github.com/facebookresearch/detectron
8. He, K., Gkioxari, G., Dollar, P., Girshick, R.: Mask R-CNN. In: Proceedings of the IEEE International Conference on Computer Vision (ICCV), pp. 1059–1067 (2017)
9. Hu, R., Dollár, P., He, K., Darrell, T., Girshick, R.: Learning to segment every thing. In: Proceedings of the IEEE Conference on Computer Vision and Pattern Recognition (CVPR) (2018)
10. ITAB: HyperFLOW. https://itab.com/en/itab/checkout/self-checkouts/. Accessed 20 June 2018
11. Khoreva, A., Benenson, R., Hosang, J., Hein, M., Schiele, B.: Simple does it: weakly supervised instance and semantic segmentation. In: Proceedings of the IEEE Conference on Computer Vision and Pattern Recognition (CVPR), pp. 876–885 (2017)
12. Krizhevsky, A., Sutskever, I., Hinton, G.E.: Imagenet classification with deep convolutional neural networks. In: Advances in Neural Information Processing Systems, pp. 1097–1105 (2012)
13. Li, H., Lu, H., Lin, Z., Shen, X., Price, B.: Inner and inter label propagation: salient object detection in the wild. IEEE Trans. Image Process. **24**(10), 3176–3186 (2015)
14. Li, K., Malik, J.: Amodal instance segmentation. In: Leibe, B., Matas, J., Sebe, N., Welling, M. (eds.) ECCV 2016. LNCS, vol. 9906, pp. 677–693. Springer, Cham (2016). https://doi.org/10.1007/978-3-319-46475-6_42
15. Lin, T.-Y., et al.: Microsoft COCO: common objects in context. In: Fleet, D., Pajdla, T., Schiele, B., Tuytelaars, T. (eds.) ECCV 2014. LNCS, vol. 8693, pp. 740–755. Springer, Cham (2014). https://doi.org/10.1007/978-3-319-10602-1_48
16. Liu, Z., Zou, W., Le Meur, O.: Saliency tree: a novel saliency detection framework. IEEE Trans. Image Process. **23**(5), 1937–1952 (2014)
17. Otsu, N.: A threshold selection method from gray-level histograms. IEEE Trans. Syst. Man Cybern. **9**(1), 62–66 (1979)
18. Phong, B.T.: Illumination for computer generated pictures. Commun. ACM **18**(6), 311–317 (1975)
19. Rother, C., Kolmogorov, V., Blake, A.: Grabcut: interactive foreground extraction using iterated graph cuts. In: ACM Transactions on Graphics (TOG), vol. 23, pp. 309–314. ACM (2004)

20. Russakovsky, O., et al.: ImageNet large scale visual recognition challenge. Int. J. Comput. Vis. **115**(3), 211–252 (2015)
21. Simard, P.Y., Steinkraus, D., Platt, J.C., et al.: Best practices for convolutional neural networks applied to visual document analysis. In: Proceedings of the International Conference on Document Analysis and Recognition (ICDAR), vol. 3, pp. 958–962 (2003)
22. Vezhnevets, A., Ferrari, V., Buhmann, J.M.: Weakly supervised semantic segmentation with a multi-image model. In: Proceedings of the IEEE International Conference on Computer Vision (ICCV), pp. 643–650 (2011)
23. Zhu, Y., Tian, Y., Metaxas, D., Dollar, P.: Semantic amodal segmentation. In: Proceedings of the IEEE Conference on Computer Vision and Pattern Recognition (CVPR), pp. 1464–1472 (2017)

Vehicle Re-identification in Context

Aytaç Kanacı[1(✉)], Xiatian Zhu[2], and Shaogang Gong[1]

[1] Queen Mary University of London, London E1 4NS, UK
{a.kanaci,s.gong}@qmul.ac.uk
[2] Vision Semantics Limited, London E1 4NS, UK
eddy@visionsemantics.com

Abstract. Existing vehicle re-identification (re-id) evaluation benchmarks consider strongly artificial test scenarios by assuming the availability of high quality images and fine-grained appearance at an almost constant image scale, reminiscent to images required for Automatic Number Plate Recognition, e.g. VeRi-776. Such assumptions are often invalid in realistic vehicle re-id scenarios where arbitrarily changing image resolutions (scales) are the norm. This makes the existing vehicle re-id benchmarks limited for testing the true performance of a re-id method. In this work, we introduce a more realistic and challenging vehicle re-id benchmark, called Vehicle Re-Identification in Context (VRIC). In contrast to existing vehicle re-id datasets, VRIC is uniquely characterised by vehicle images subject to more realistic and unconstrained variations in resolution (scale), motion blur, illumination, occlusion, and viewpoint. It contains 60,430 images of 5,622 vehicle identities captured by 60 different cameras at heterogeneous road traffic scenes in both day-time and night-time. Given the nature of this new benchmark, we further investigate a multi-scale matching approach to vehicle re-id by learning more discriminative feature representations from multi-resolution images. Extensive evaluations show that the proposed multi-scale method outperforms the state-of-the-art vehicle re-id methods on three benchmark datasets: VehicleID, VeRi-776, and VRIC (Available at http://qmul-vric.github.io).

1 Introduction

Vehicle re-identification (re-id) aims at searching vehicle instances across non-overlapping camera views by image matching [17]. Influenced by the recent extensive studies on person re-id [7,12,13,24,26,28,31,36,37], vehicle re-id has started to gain increasing attention in the past two years, which promises the potential for more flexible means for vehicle recognition and search than Automatic Number Plate Recognition (ANPR). However, vehicle re-id by visual appearance is a challenging task due to the very similar appearance of different vehicle instances of the same model type and colour, and a significant visual appearance variation of the same vehicle instance in different camera views.

Current vehicle re-id studies are mainly driven by two benchmark datasets, VehicleID [17] and VeRi-776 [19]. While having achieved significant performance improvement (e.g. from 61.44% by [19] to 92.35% Rank-1 by [29] on VeRi-776),

© Springer Nature Switzerland AG 2019
T. Brox et al. (Eds.): GCPR 2018, LNCS 11269, pp. 377–390, 2019.
https://doi.org/10.1007/978-3-030-12939-2_26

the scalability of existing re-id algorithms to real-world vehicle re-id applications remains unclear. This is because existing benchmarks represent somewhat rather artificial tests using high-quality images of high resolution, no motion blur, limited weather conditions and occlusion (Table 1 and Fig. 1). This is more reminiscent to imaging conditions for ANPR than what is typical for vehicle re-id in wide-view traffic scenes "in-the-wild".

In this work, we introduce a new benchmark dataset called **Vehicle Re-Identification in Context** (VRIC) for more realistic and challenging vehicle re-identification. VRIC consists of 60,430 images of 5,656 vehicle IDs collected from 60 different cameras in traffic scenes. VRIC differs significantly from existing datasets in that *unconstrained* vehicle appearances were captured with variations in imaging resolution, motion blur, weather condition, and occlusion. This VRIC dataset aims to provide a more realistic vehicle re-id evaluation benchmark.

We make two contributions: (1) We create and introduce a more realistic vehicle re-id benchmark VRIC that contains vehicle images of *unconstrained* visual appearances with variations in resolution, motion blur, weather setting, and occlusion. This dataset is created from the UA-DETRAC benchmark [30] originally designed for object detection and multi-object tracking in traffic scenes, therefore reflecting appropriately and providing the necessary vehicle re-id environmental context and viewing conditions. This new benchmark will be publicly released. (2) We further investigate a Multi-Scale (resolution) Vehicle Feature (MSVF) learning model to address the inherent and significant multi-scale resolution in vehicle visual appearances from typical wide-view traffic scenes, currently an unaddressed problem in vehicle re-id due to the lack of a suitable benchmark dataset. Extensive comparative evaluations demonstrate the effectiveness of the proposed MSVF method in comparison to the state-of-the-art vehicle re-id techniques on the two existing benchmarks (VehicleID [17] and VeRi-776 [19]) and the newly introduced VRIC benchmark.

Table 1. Characteristics of vehicle re-id datasets.

Dataset	Images	IDs	Cameras	Resolutions Width × Height (Mean)	Motion Blur	Illumination	Occlusion
VehicleID [17]	113,123	15,524	-	345.4 × 376.1	No	Limited	No
VeRi-776 [19]	51,034	776	20	376.1 × 345.4	No	Limited	No
VD1 [32]	846,358	141,756	-	424.8 × 411.0	No	Limited	No
VD2 [32]	690,518	79,763	-	401.3 × 376.4	No	Limited	No
VRIC (Ours)	60,430	5,622	120	65.9 × 103.0	Unconstrained	Unconstrained	Unconstrained

2   Related Work

Vehicle Re-identification. Whist vehicle re-id is less studied than person re-id [2–4, 7, 13–15, 24, 27, 31, 36], there are a handful of existing methods. Notably,

VehicleID   VeRi-776   VRIC

Fig. 1. Example images of VehicleID, VeRi-776 and VRIC. Images in each row depict the same vehicle instance. VRIC images exhibit significantly more unconstrained variations in resolution, motion blur, occlusion/truncation and illumination within each vehicle bounding-box images.

Feris *et al.* [6] proposed an attribute-based re-id method. The vehicles are firstly classified by different attributes like car model types and colours. The re-id matching is then conducted in the attribute space. Dominik *et al.* [34] used 3D bounding boxes for rectifying car images and then concatenate colour histogram features of vehicle image pairs. A binary linear SVM model is then trained to verify whether a pair of images have the same identity. Both methods rely heavily on weak hand-crafted visual features in a complex multi-step based approach, suffering from weak discriminative model generalisation.

More recently, deep learning techniques have been exploited to vehicle re-id. Liu *et al.* [19] explored a deep neural network to estimate the visual similarities between vehicle images. Liu *et al.* [17] designed a Coupled Clusters Loss (CCL) to boost a multi-branch CNN model for vehicle re-id. Kanaci [9] explored the appearance difference at the coarse-grained vehicle model level. All these methods utilise the global appearance features of vehicle images and ignore local discriminative regions. To explore local information and motivated by the idea of landmark alignment [35] in both face recognition [25] and human body pose estimation [21], Wang *et al.* [29] considered 20 vehicle keypoints for learning and aligning local regions of a vehicle for re-id. Clearly, this approach comes with extra cost of exhaustively labelling these keypoints in a large number of vehicle images, and the implicit assumption of having sufficient image resolution/details for computing these keypoints.

Additionally, space-time contextual knowledge has also been exploited for vehicle re-id subject to structured scenes [19,22]. Liu *et al.* [19] proposed a spatio-temporal affinity approach for quantifying every pair of images. Shen *et al.* [22] further incorporated spatio-temporal path information of vehicles. Whilst this method improves the re-id performance on the VeRi-776 dataset, it may not generalise to complex scene structures when the number of visual spatio-temporal path proposals is very large with only weak contextual knowledge available to facilitate model decision.

In contrast to all existing methods as above, we address a different problem of learning multi-scale feature representation for vehicle re-id.

Vehicle Re-identification Benchmarks. There are in total four vehicle re-id benchmarks reported in the literature. Liu *et al.* [17] introduced the "VehicleID" benchmark with a total of 221,763 images from 26,267 IDs. In parallel, Liu *et al.* [18] created "VeRi-776", a smaller scale re-id dataset (51,035 images of 776 IDs) but with space-time annotations among 20 cameras in a road network. Recently, Yan *et al.* [32] presented two larger datasets (846,358 images of 141,756 IDs in "VD1", 690,518 images of 79,763 IDs in "VD2") with similar visual characteristics as VehicleID.

Whilst these existing benchmarks have contributed significantly to the development of vehicle re-id methods, they only represent *constrained* test scenarios due to the rather artificial assumption of having high quality images of constant resolution (Table 1). This makes them limited for testing the true robustness of re-id matching algorithms in typically *unconstrained* wide-view traffic scene imaging conditions. The VRIC benchmark introduced in this work addresses this limitation by providing a vehicle re-id dataset conditions giving rise to changes in resolution, motion blur, weather, illumination, and occlusion (Fig. 2).

3   The Vehicle Re-identification in Context Benchmark

3.1   Dataset Construction

We want to establish a realistic vehicle re-id evaluation benchmark with natural visual appearance characteristics and matching challenges (Sect. 1). To this end, it is necessary to collect a large number of vehicle images/videos from wide-view traffic scenes. In the following, we describe the process of constructing the Vehicle Re-Identification in Context (VRIC) benchmark.

Source Video Data. Given highly restricted access permission of typical surveillance video data, we propose to reuse existing vehicle related datasets publicly available in the research community.

In particular, we selected the UA-DETRAC object detection and tracking benchmark [30] as the source data of our VRIC benchmark, based on following considerations:

1. All videos were captured from the real-world traffic scenes (e.g. roads), reflecting realistic context for vehicle re-id.
2. It covers 24 different surveillance locations with diverse environmental conditions therefore offering a rich spectrum of test scenarios without bias towards particular viewing conditions.
3. It contains rich object and attribute annotations that can facilitate vehicle re-id labelling.

The UA-DETRAC videos were recorded at 25 frames per second (fps) with a frame resolution of 960 × 540 pixels (Fig. 3). Samples of the whole scene images are shown in Fig. 2(b, c).

Fig. 2. Example vehicle bounding-box and whole scene images of the VRIC benchmark. (a) Samples of vehicle bounding-box images. (b) The *near* and *far* views in a wide-view traffic scene. (c) UA-DETRAC video scenes with different illumination due to changing weather conditions (sunny, cloudy and rainy) and time (day and night). (d) Vehicle matching pairs (each column) from some example test vehicle instances.

Vehicle Image Filtering and Annotation. To construct a vehicle re-id dataset, we used 60 UA-DETRAC training videos with object bounding box annotations. For vehicle identity (ID) annotation, we started with assigning a unique label to each vehicle trajectory per UA-DETRAC video and then manually verified the ID duplication cases. Since all these raw videos were collected from different scenes and time durations, we found little duplicated trajectories in terms of identity. To ensure sufficient vehicle appearance variation, we throw away short trajectories with less than 20 frames and bounding boxes smaller than 24×24. By doing so, we obtained 5,622 vehicle IDs across all 60 videos.

In terms of vehicle instance resolution, the average image resolution of all 60,430 vehicle bounding-boxes is 69.8×107.5 pixels in width × height, with a variance of 32 to 280 pixels due to the unconstrained distances between vehicles and cameras. This presents inherently a multi-scale re-id matching challenge.

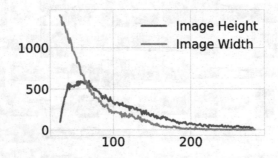

Fig. 3. Vehicle instance scale distributions in VRIC.

3.2   Evaluation Protocol

Data Split. For model training and testing using the VRIC dataset as a benchmark, we randomly split all 5,622 vehicle IDs into two non-overlapping halves: 2,811 for training, and 2,811 for testing. To remove data redundancy, we performed random frame-wise sub-sampling of the training trajectories. Since there is no cross-camera pairwise ID matches (UA-DETRAC is about single-camera object detection/tracking), we simulated cross-view variation by distant sampling between probe and gallery images.

In particular, we defined two pseudo views, *near* or *far*, for each video/camera and then built the probe/gallery sets from the test trajectories by randomly sampling each in two pseudo views. It is shown in Fig. 2(b) that the *near* and *far* views present very different viewing conditions and hence allowing for a good simulation of two non-overlapping camera views. In this sense, VRIC contains a total 120 pseudo camera views from the 60 original camera views with unconstrained condition diversity.

We adopted the standard single-shot evaluation setting, i.e. one image per vehicle per view. From the above, we obtained 54,808/5,622 training/testing images for the VRIC benchmark. The data partition and statistics are summarised in Table 2.

Table 2. Data statistics and partition in VRIC.

Partition	All	Training set	Test set	
			Probe	Gallery
IDs	5,622	2,811	2,811	2,811
Images	60,430	54,808	2,811	2,811

Performance Metrics. For re-id performance measure, we used the *Cumulative Matching Characteristic* (CMC) rates [10]. The CMC is computed for each individual rank k as the cumulative percentage of the truth matches for probes returned at ranks $\leq k$. In practice, the Rank-1 rate is often used as a strong indicator of an algorithm's efficacy.

4   Deep Learning Multi-scale Vehicle Representation

We aim to learn a deep representation model from a set of n vehicle images $\mathcal{I} = \{I_i\}_{i=1}^n$ with the corresponding vehicle ID labels as $\mathcal{Y} = \{y_i\}_{i=1}^n$. These training images capture the visual appearance variations of n_{id} different IDs under multiple camera views, with $y_i \in [1, \cdots, n_{id}]$. In typical surveillance scenes, vehicles are often captured at varying scales (resolutions), which causes significant interview feature representation discrepancy in re-id matching. In this work, we investigate this problem in vehicle re-id by exploring image pyramid representation [1,11].

Specifically, we exploit the potential of learning ID discriminative pyramidal representations originally designed for person re-id [4]. Our objective is to extract and represent complementary appearance information of vehicle ID from multiple resolution scales concurrently in order to optimise re-id matching under significant view changes. We call this model **Multi-Scale Vehicle Representation** (MSVR). Our approach differs notably from existing vehicle re-id models typically assuming single-scale representation learning.

MSVR Overview. The overall MSVR network design is depicted in Fig. 4. Specifically, MSVR consists of $(m + 1)$ sub-networks: (1) m branches of sub-networks each for learning discriminative scale-specific visual features. Each branch has an identical structure. (2) One fusion branch for learning the discriminative integration of m scale-specific representations of the same vehicle image. To maximise the complementary advantage between different scales of

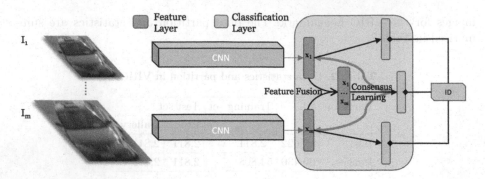

Fig. 4. Overview of Multi-Scale Vehicle Representation (MSVR) learning for discriminative vehicle re-id at varying spatial resolutions. MSVR learns vehicle re-id sensitive feature representations from image pyramid by an network architecture of multiple branches all of which are optimised concurrently (consensus feedback shown in red, see Eq. (4)) subject to the same ID label constraints. Importantly, an inter-scale interaction mechanism is enforced to further enhance the scale-generic feature learning. (Color figure online)

feature representation in learning, we concurrently optimise per-scale discriminative representations with scale-specific and scale-generic (combined) learning subject to the same ID label supervision. Critically, we further propagate multi-scale consensus as feedback to regulate the learning of per-scale branches. Next, we detail three MSVR components: (1) Single-Scale Representation; (2) Multi-Scale Consensus; (3) Feature Regularisation.

(1) Single-Scale Representation. We exploit the MobileNet [8] to design single-scale branches due to its favourable trade-off between model complexity and learning capability. To train a single-scale branch, we use the softmax cross-entropy loss function to optimise vehicle re-id sensitive information from ID labels. Formally, we first compute the class posterior probability $\tilde{y}$ of a training image I:

$$p(\tilde{y} = y | I) = \frac{\exp(\boldsymbol{w}_y^\top \boldsymbol{x})}{\sum_{k=1}^{n_{\mathrm{id}}} \exp(\boldsymbol{w}_k^\top \boldsymbol{x})} \tag{1}$$

where $\boldsymbol{x}$ and y refer to the feature vector and ground-truth label of I, n_{id} the number of training IDs, and $\boldsymbol{w}_k$ the classifier parameters of class k. The training loss is then defined as:

$$\mathcal{L}_{\mathrm{ce}} = -\log\left(p(\tilde{y} = y | I)\right) \tag{2}$$

(2) Multi-Scale Consensus. We learn multi-scale consensus on vehicle ID classes between m scale-specific branches. We achieve this using joint-feature based classification. First, we obtain joint feature of different scales by vector fusion. In MobileNets, feature vectors are computed by global average pooling of the last CNN feature maps with dimension of 1024. Hence, this fusion produces a $1024 \times m$-D feature vectors. We then use this combined features to perform classification for providing multi-scale consensus on the ID labels. We again adopt the cross-entropy loss (Eq. (2)) as in single-scale representation learning.

(3) Feature Regularisation. We regularise the single-scale branches by multi-scale consensus for imposing interaction between different scale representations in model learning. Specifically, we propagate the consensus as an auxiliary *feedback* to regularise the learning of each single-scale branch concurrently. We first compute for each training sample a soft probability prediction (i.e. a consensus representation) $\tilde{P} = [\tilde{p}_1, \cdots, \tilde{p}_i, \cdots, \tilde{p}_{n_{\mathrm{id}}}]$ as:

$$\tilde{p}_i = \tilde{p}(\tilde{y} = i | \boldsymbol{I}) = \frac{\exp(\frac{z_i}{T})}{\sum_k \exp(\frac{z_k}{T})}, \quad i \in [1, \cdots, n_{\mathrm{id}}] \tag{3}$$

where z is the logit and T the temperature parameter (higher values leading to softer probability distribution). We empirically set $T = 1$ in our experiments. Then, we use the consensus probability $\tilde{P}$ as the *teacher* signal to guide the learning process of each single-scale branch (*student*). To quantify the alignment between these predictions, we use the cross-entropy measurement which is defined as:

$$\mathcal{H}(\tilde{P}, P) = -\frac{1}{n_{\mathrm{id}}} \sum_{i=1}^{n_{\mathrm{id}}} \left(\tilde{p}_i \ln(p_i) + (1 - \tilde{p}_i) \ln(1 - p_i) \right) \tag{4}$$

The objective loss function for each single-scale branch is then:

$$\mathcal{L}_{\mathrm{scale}} = \mathcal{L}_{\mathrm{ce}} + \lambda \mathcal{H}(\tilde{P}, P) \tag{5}$$

where the hyper-parameter λ ($\lambda = 1$ in our experiments) is the weighting between two loss terms. $P = [p_1, \cdots, p_{n_{\mathrm{id}}}]$ defines the probability prediction over all n_{id} identity classes by the corresponding single-scale branch (Eq. (1)). As such, each single-scale branch learns to correctly predict the true ID label of training sample ($\mathcal{L}_{\mathrm{ce}}$) by the corresponding scale-specific representation and to match the consensus probability estimated based on the scale-generic representation ($\mathcal{H}$).

MSVR Deployment. In model test, we deploy the fusion branch's representation for multi-scale aware vehicle re-id matching. We use only a generic distance metric without camera-pair specific distance metric learning, e.g. the L2 distance. Based on the pairwise distance, we then return a ranking of gallery images as the re-id results. For successful tasks, the true matches for a given probe image are should be placed among top ranks.

5   Experiments

Datasets. For evaluation, in addition to the newly introduced VRIC dataset, we also utilised two most popular vehicle re-id benchmarks. The **VehicleID** [17] dataset provides a training set with 113,346 from 13,164 IDs and a test set with 19,777 images from 2,400 identities. It adopts the single-shot re-id setting, with only one true matching for each probe. Following the standard setting, we repeated 10 times of randomly selected probe and gallery sets in our experiments. The **VeRi-776** dataset [19] has 37,778 images of 576 IDs in training set and 200 IDs in test set. The standard probe and gallery sets consist of 1,678 and 11,579 images, respectively. The data split statistics are summarised in Table 3.

Table 3. Data split of vehicle re-id datasets evaluated in our experiments.

Dataset	Training IDs/images	Probe IDs/images	Gallery IDs/images
VehicleID [17]	13,164/113,346	2,400/17,377	2,400/2,400
VeRi-776 [19]	576/37,778	200/1,678	200/11,579
VRIC (**Ours**)	2,811/54,808	2,811/2,811	2,811/2,811

Performance Metrics. For VehicleID and VRIC, we used the CMC measurement to evaluate re-id performance. For VeRi-776, we additionally adopted the *mean Average Precision* (mAP) due to its multi-shot nature in the gallery of the test data. Specifically, for each probe, we compute the area under its Precision-Recall curve, i.e. Average Precision (AP). The mAP is then computed as the mean value of APs for all probes. This metric considers both precision and recall performance, and hence providing a more comprehensive evaluation.

Implementation Details. In the MSVR model, we used 2 resolution scales, 224×224 and 160×160. We adopted the ADAM optimizer and set the initial learning rate to 0.0002, the weight decay to 0.0002, the β_1 to 0.5, the mini-batch size to 8, the max-iteration to 100,000. Model initialization was done with ImageNet [5] pretrained weights. The data augmentation includes random cropping and horizontal flipping.

Evaluation. Table 4 compares MSVR with state-of-the-art methods on three benchmarks. We make these main observations as follows:
(1) Under the standard visual appearance based evaluation setting (the top part), MSVR outperforms all other competitors with large margins – MSVR surpasses the best competitor in Rank-1 rate by 24.38% (88.56–64.18) on VeRi-776, 24.82% (62.02–38.20) on VehicleID, and 16.73% (46.61–30.55) on VRIC. This demonstrates the consistent superiority of MSVR over alternative methods

in vehicle re-id, showing the importance in modelling multi-scale representation for vehicle re-id.

(2) Benefited from more training data plus space-time contextual knowledge and fine-grained local key-point supervision, the OIFE model achieves the best performance on VeRi-776. However, such advantages from additional data and knowledge representation is generically beneficial to all models including the MSVR when applied.

(3) We carefully reproduced two very recent methods, OIFE(Single-Branch) [29] and Siamese-Visual [22], and obtained inconsistent results compared to the reported performances of these two models. In particular, the performance of OIFE(Single-Branch) decreases on VeRi-776 and VehicleID. This is mainly due to that the original results are based on a larger multi-source training set with 225,268 training images of 36,108 IDs (from VehicleID [17], VeRi-776 [19], BoxCars [23] and CompCars [33]), *versus* the standard 100,182 training images of 13,164 IDs on VehicleID, *i.e.* 2.2 times more training images and 2.7 times more training ID labels, and the standard 37,778 training images of 576 IDs on VeRi-776, *i.e.* 6.0 times more training images and 62.7 times more training ID labels, respectively. In contrast, the result of Siamese-Visual (ResNet50 based) increases on VeRi-776. It is worth pointing out that we trained this model using the cross-entropy classification loss and cannot make it converge with pairwise inner-product loss.

Table 4. Comparative vehicle re-id results on three benchmarking datasets. Upper part of table lists methods trained with only the images available from the respective datasets for fair comparison of the methods; lower part lists methods trained with additional datasets and/or labels. *: By our reimplementation. E: Extra information and annotation, e.g. number plates, local key-points, space-time prior knowledge. M: Multiple vehicle re-id and classification datasets are combined for training. †: Result from [29].

Method	Notes	VeRi-776 [19]		VehicleID [17]		VRIC		Publication
		Rank-1	mAP	Rank-1	Rank-5	Rank-1	Rank-5	
LOMO [16]		25.33	9.64	-	-	-	-	CVPR'15
FACT [18]		50.95	18.49	-	-	-	-	ICME'16
Mixed Diff + CCL [17]		-	-	38.20	50.30	-	-	CVPR'16
Siamese-Visual [22]		41.12	29.40	-	-	-	-	ICCV'17
Siamese-Visual [22]	*	64.18	31.54	36.83	57.97	30.55	57.30	ICCV'17
OIFE(Single Branch) [29]	*	60.13	31.81	32.86	52.75	24.62	50.98	ICCV'17
MSVF		**88.56**	**49.30**	**63.02**	**73.05**	**46.61**	**65.58**	**Ours**
KEPLER [20] †	M	68.70	33.53	45.40	68.90	-	-	TIP'15
FACT + Plate + Space-Time [19]	E	61.44	27.77	-	-	-	-	ECCV'16
Siamese-CNN + Path-LSTM [22]	E	83.49	**58.27**	-	-	-	-	ICCV'17
OIFE(Single Branch) [29]	M	88.66	45.50	63.20	80.60	-	-	ICCV'17
OIFE(4Views) [29]	ME	89.43	48.00	**67.00**	**82.90**	-	-	ICCV'17
OIFE(4Views + Space-Time) [29]	ME	**92.35**	51.42	-	-	-	-	ICCV'17

Further Analysis. Table 5 compares the performances of a single-scale and a multi-scale feature representations of the MSVR model. It is evident that the multi-scale representation learning with MSVR has performance benefit across all three datasets with varying resolution scale changes. This shows that the overall effectiveness of MSVR in boosting vehicle re-id matching performance. Moreover, the model performance gain on VRIC is the largest, which is consistent with the more significant scale variations exhibited in the VRIC vehicle images (Fig. 1 and Table 1).

Table 5. Comparing single-scale and multi-scale representations of MSVR. Gain is measured as the performance difference of MSVR over the *mean* of single-scale variants.

Dataset	VeRi-776 [19]		VehicleID [17]		VRIC	
Metrics (%)	Rank-1	mAP	Rank-1	Rank-5	Rank-1	Rank-5
Scale-224	88.37	47.37	62.80	72.54	43.55	61.88
Scale-160	87.43	46.81	60.29	71.15	43.62	62.77
MSVR	**88.56**	**49.30**	**63.02**	**73.05**	**46.61**	**65.58**
Gain (%)	+0.76	+2.11	+1.47	+1.20	**+3.02**	**+3.25**

6   Conclusion

In this work we introduced a more realistic and challenging vehicle re-identification benchmark, Vehicle Re-Identification in Context (VRIC), to enable the design and evaluation of vehicle re-id methods to more closely reflect real-world application conditions. VRIC is uniquely characterised by unconstrained vehicle images from large scale, wide scale traffic scene videos inherently exhibiting variations in resolution, illumination, motion blur, and occlusion. This dataset provides a more realistic and truthful test and evaluation of algorithms for vehicle re-id "in-the-wild". We further investigated a multi-scale learning representation by exploiting a pyramid based deep learning method. Experimental evaluations demonstrate the effectiveness and performance advantages of our multi-scale learning method over the state-of-the-art vehicle re-id methods on three benchmarks VeRi-776, VehicleID, and VRIC.

References

1. Adelson, E.H., Anderson, C.H., Bergen, J.R., Burt, P.J., Ogden, J.M.: Pyramid methods in image processing. RCA Eng. **29**(6), 33–41 (1984)
2. Ahmed, E., Jones, M., Marks, T.K.: An improved deep learning architecture for person re-identification. In: IEEE Conference on Computer Vision and Pattern Recognition (2015)
3. Chen, Y., Zhu, X., Gong, S.: Deep association learning for unsupervised video person re-identification. In: British Machine Vision Conference (2018)

4. Chen, Y.C., Zhu, X., Zheng, W.S., Lai, J.H.: Person re-identification by camera correlation aware feature augmentation. IEEE Trans. Pattern Anal. Mach. Intell. **40**(2), 392–408 (2018)
5. Deng, J., Dong, W., Socher, R., Li, L.J., Li, K., Fei-Fei, L.: Imagenet: a large-scale hierarchical image database. In: IEEE Conference on Computer Vision and Pattern Recognition (2009)
6. Feris, R.S., et al.: Large-scale vehicle detection, indexing, and search in urban surveillance videos. IEEE Trans. Multimedia **14**(1), 28–42 (2012)
7. Gong, S., Cristani, M., Yan, S., Loy, C.C.: Person Re-identification. Springer, Heidelberg (2014). https://doi.org/10.1007/978-1-4471-6296-4
8. Howard, A.G., et al.: Mobilenets: efficient convolutional neural networks for mobile vision applications. arXiv preprint arXiv:1704.04861 (2017)
9. Kanacı, A., Zhu, X., Gong, S.: Vehicle reidentification by fine-grained cross-level deep learning. In: BMVC AMMDS Workshop, vol. 2 (2017)
10. Klare, B.F., et al.: Pushing the frontiers of unconstrained face detection and recognition: Iarpa janus benchmark A. In: IEEE Conference on Computer Vision and Pattern Recognition (2015)
11. Lazebnik, S., Schmid, C., Ponce, J.: Beyond bags of features: spatial pyramid matching for recognizing natural scene categories. In: IEEE Conference on Computer Vision and Pattern Recognition (2006)
12. Li, M., Zhu, X., Gong, S.: Unsupervised person re-identification by deep learning tracklet association. In: Ferrari, V., Hebert, M., Sminchisescu, C., Weiss, Y. (eds.) ECCV 2018. LNCS, vol. 11208, pp. 772–788. Springer, Cham (2018). https://doi.org/10.1007/978-3-030-01225-0_45
13. Li, W., Zhao, R., Xiao, T., Wang, X.: DeepReID: deep filter pairing neural network for person re-identification. In: IEEE Conference on Computer Vision and Pattern Recognition (2014)
14. Li, W., Zhu, X., Gong, S.: Person re-identification by deep joint learning of multiloss classification. In: International Joint Conference of Artificial Intelligence (2017)
15. Li, W., Zhu, X., Gong, S.: Harmonious attention network for person re-identification. In: IEEE Conference on Computer Vision and Pattern Recognition (2018)
16. Liao, S., Hu, Y., Zhu, X., Li, S.Z.: Person re-identification by local maximal occurrence representation and metric learning. In: IEEE Conference on Computer Vision and Pattern Recognition (2015)
17. Liu, H., Tian, Y., Wang, Y., Pang, L., Huang, T.: Deep relative distance learning: tell the difference between similar vehicles. In: IEEE Conference on Computer Vision and Pattern Recognition (2016)
18. Liu, X., Liu, W., Ma, H., Fu, H.: Large-scale vehicle re-identification in urban surveillance videos. In: IEEE International Conference on Multimedia and Expo (2016)
19. Liu, X., Liu, W., Mei, T., Ma, H.: A deep learning-based approach to progressive vehicle re-identification for urban surveillance. In: Leibe, B., Matas, J., Sebe, N., Welling, M. (eds.) ECCV 2016. LNCS, vol. 9906, pp. 869–884. Springer, Cham (2016). https://doi.org/10.1007/978-3-319-46475-6_53
20. Martinel, N., Micheloni, C., Foresti, G.L.: Kernelized saliency-based person re-identification through multiple metric learning. IEEE Trans. Image Process. **24**(12), 5645–5658 (2015)
21. Newell, A., Yang, K., Deng, J.: Stacked hourglass networks for human pose estimation. In: Leibe, B., Matas, J., Sebe, N., Welling, M. (eds.) ECCV 2016. LNCS,

vol. 9912, pp. 483–499. Springer, Cham (2016). https://doi.org/10.1007/978-3-319-46484-8_29

22. Shen, Y., Xiao, T., Li, H., Yi, S., Wang, X.: Learning deep neural networks for vehicle re-id with visual-spatio-temporal path proposals. In: IEEE International Conference on Computer Vision (2017)

23. Sochor, J., Herout, A., Havel, J.: Boxcars: 3D boxes as CNN input for improved fine-grained vehicle recognition. In: IEEE Conference on Computer Vision and Pattern Recognition, pp. 3006–3015 (2016)

24. Sun, Y., Zheng, L., Deng, W., Wang, S.: SVDNet for pedestrian retrieval. In: IEEE International Conference on Computer Vision (2017)

25. Taigman, Y., Yang, M., Ranzato, M., Wolf, L.: Deepface: closing the gap to human-level performance in face verification. In: IEEE Conference on Computer Vision and Pattern Recognition, pp. 1701–1708 (2014)

26. Wang, H., Zhu, X., Gong, S., Xiang, T.: Person re-identification in identity regression space. Int. J. Comput. Vis. **126**, 1288–1310 (2018)

27. Wang, J., Zhu, X., Gong, S., Li, W.: Transferable joint attribute-identity deep learning for unsupervised person re-identification. In: IEEE Conference on Computer Vision and Pattern Recognition (2018)

28. Wang, T., Gong, S., Zhu, X., Wang, S.: Person re-identification by video ranking. In: Fleet, D., Pajdla, T., Schiele, B., Tuytelaars, T. (eds.) ECCV 2014. LNCS, vol. 8692, pp. 688–703. Springer, Cham (2014). https://doi.org/10.1007/978-3-319-10593-2_45

29. Wang, Z., et al.: Orientation invariant feature embedding and spatial temporal regularization for vehicle re-identification. In: IEEE International Conference on Computer Vision (2017)

30. Wen, L., et al.: UA-DETRAC: a new benchmark and protocol for multi-object detection and tracking. arXiv abs/1511.04136 (2015)

31. Xiao, T., Li, H., Ouyang, W., Wang, X.: Learning deep feature representations with domain guided dropout for person re-identification. In: IEEE Conference on Computer Vision and Pattern Recognition. IEEE (2016)

32. Yan, K., Tian, Y., Wang, Y., Zeng, W., Huang, T.: Exploiting multi-grain ranking constraints for precisely searching visually-similar vehicles. In: IEEE International Conference on Computer Vision, pp. 562–570 (2017)

33. Yang, L., Luo, P., Change Loy, C., Tang, X.: A large-scale car dataset for fine-grained categorization and verification. In: IEEE Conference on Computer Vision and Pattern Recognition (2015)

34. Zapletal, D., Herout, A.: Vehicle re-identification for automatic video traffic surveillance. In: IEEE Conference on Computer Vision and Pattern Recognition Workshops, pp. 1568–1574 (2016)

35. Zhang, Z., Luo, P., Loy, C.C., Tang, X.: Facial landmark detection by deep multi-task learning. In: Fleet, D., Pajdla, T., Schiele, B., Tuytelaars, T. (eds.) ECCV 2014. LNCS, vol. 8694, pp. 94–108. Springer, Cham (2014). https://doi.org/10.1007/978-3-319-10599-4_7

36. Zhong, Z., Zheng, L., Zheng, Z., Li, S., Yang, Y.: Camera style adaptation for person re-identification. In: IEEE Conference on Computer Vision and Pattern Recognition (2018)

37. Zhu, X., Wu, B., Huang, D., Zheng, W.S.: Fast open-world person re-identification. IEEE Trans. Image Process. **27**(5), 2286–2300 (2018)

Low-Shot Learning of Plankton Categories

Simon-Martin Schröder[1]( ), Rainer Kiko[2], Jean-Olivier Irisson[3],
and Reinhard Koch[1]

[1] Department of Computer Science, Kiel University, Kiel, Germany
{sms,rk}@informatik.uni-kiel.de
[2] GEOMAR Helmholtz-Centre for Ocean Research, Kiel, Germany
rkiko@geomar.de
[3] Sorbonne Université, CNRS, Laboratoire d'Océanographie de Villefanche, LOV,
Villefranche-sur-mer, France
irisson@obs-vlfr.fr

Abstract. The size of current plankton image datasets renders manual classification virtually infeasible. The training of models for machine classification is complicated by the fact that a large number of classes consist of only a few examples. We employ the recently introduced weight imprinting technique in order to use the available training data to train accurate classifiers in absence of enough examples for some classes.

The model architecture used in this work succeeds in the identification of plankton using machine learning with its unique challenges, i.e. a limited number of training examples and a severely skewed class size distribution. Weight imprinting enables a neural network to recognize small classes immediately without re-training. This permits the mining of examples for novel classes.

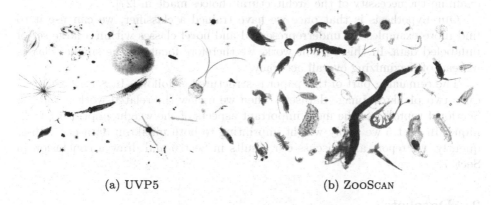

(a) UVP5   (b) ZooScan

Fig. 1. Example images from both datasets.

T. Brox et al. (Eds.): GCPR 2018, LNCS 11269, pp. 391–404, 2019.
https://doi.org/10.1007/978-3-030-12939-2_27

1   Introduction

Planktonic organisms – drifters in the ocean – cover a large size range from nanometer-sized bacteria to meter-sized jellyfishes. While some of these organisms such as the planktonic copepods can be observed nearly everywhere, others occupy only small niches. Past observations allow an overview of the most abundant groups but we can expect that the number of classes will keep increasing with increasing sampling effort.

Current imaging systems (e.g. UVP5, ZooScan, ISIIS, FlowCytoBot [6,13,21, 25]) that target the micro to macroplankton size range (approx. $10\,\mu m$ to $10\,cm$) yield large amounts of image data every day. The size of the resulting datasets renders manual classification virtually infeasible. Therefore, accurate machine classification is a critical step in the processing of these data. Usually, the result is later verified by human experts. Even the annotation of pre-classified data is still labor-intensive [7,12], which is why maximally accurate models are crucial.

This work is part of a larger undertaking with the aim of continually monitoring newly acquired data for classes that have been overlooked so far. The observation of new kinds of objects means that the machine classification models need to be updated to incorporate these novel classes. In addition, plankton image datasets typically consist of few classes with many examples and many classes with only a few examples. A major problem is therefore the scarcity of training data for a large number of classes.

Here we tackle the question of how available labeled data can be used to train accurate machine classifiers when some class sizes in the training data set are very small, which is known as *low-shot learning*. We employ a recently presented method for low-shot learning called *weight imprinting* [27] that is able to incorporate new classes into a model without re-training it from scratch.

The contribution of this present paper is a rigorous evaluation of whether weight imprinting works satisfactorily for two plankton image datasets. We also examine the necessity of the architectural choices made in [27].

Our hypothesis is that once we have trained a classifier, we can use it to find more examples for underrepresented and novel classes within a large set of unlabeled data. In this current work, we therefore focus on the smaller classes instead of maximizing overall accuracy.

The remaining part of this paper is structured as follows. In Sect. 2 we introduce two plankton image datasets. Then we review the related work in Sect. 3. Section 4 reproduces the most important aspects of the weight imprinting technique. In Sect. 5 we apply weight imprinting to both plankton datasets. Subsequently, we report and discuss our results in Sect. 6 and draw a conclusion in Sect. 7.

2   Datasets

We evaluate the approach on two datasets extracted from the plankton image database EcoTaxa [24]. The objects were sampled on numerous cruises in many parts of the world's oceans. The first dataset (UVP5) consists of 588,121 pelagic underwater images acquired with the UVP5 [25]. The images were sorted by experts into 65 classes. The dataset is available from the authors upon reasonable request. The second dataset (ZooScan) [10] consists of 1,433,282 wet net samples digitized with the ZooScan system [13] and sorted into 93 classes. We use a subset of 1,146,684 images for training and validation.

Both datasets are severely imbalanced, as shown in Fig. 2 for the UVP5 dataset. The 10% most populated classes contain more than 77% of all objects and the class sizes span multiple orders of magnitude. Figure 1 shows some exemplary objects from both datasets.

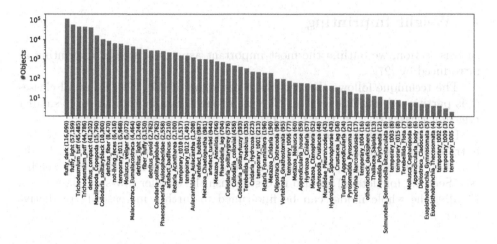

Fig. 2. UVP5 dataset: classes ordered by their size in the training set. The class sizes span five orders of magnitude.

3   Related Work

One-Shot and Low-Shot Learning. One-shot and low-shot learning is concerned with training a model with only one or a few training examples for each class.

Low-shot learning using neural networks usually incorporates two phases [15]. In the *representation learning* phase, the learner finds a suitable feature space, usually guided by a set of base classes with abundant examples. In the *low-shot learning* phase, a classifier is trained that incorporates both base and low-shot classes. Different approaches emphasize different aspects of the process [3]: the discriminative approach is concerned with learning powerful features, the generative approach enlarges the training set by augmentation or generation and the network structural approach utilizes new types of classifiers.

Weight imprinting [27], label diffusion [9], and metric learning [20] belong to the third category. They provide low-shot learning without having to retrain the whole model from scratch.

Classification of Plankton Images. Classification of plankton images is traditionally performed using shallow models, like Support Vector Machines or Random Forests, trained with handcrafted local features measured on the image (e.g. size, grey level distribution, etc.) [1,8,11,13,28].

Since Kaggle's National Data Science Bowl competition to sort data from ISIIS [6], there has been a slow transition towards deep models [4,14,18,22,26].

In the representation learning phase, we rely on the observations of [22] regarding the classification of plankton images with deep learning models, i.e. that the initialization with pre-trained weights outperforms random initialization.

4   Weight Imprinting

In this section, we outline the most important aspects of weight imprinting as introduced by [27].

The technique follows the two-phase paradigm of [15]: The set of all classes C is partitioned into *base classes* C_0 with enough training data and the smaller *low-shot classes* C_+, i.e. $C = C_0 \cup C_+$.

In the representation learning phase, a convolutional neural network (CNN) is trained to distinguish the base classes with enough training data C_0. In the low-shot learning phase, the classifier is then updated with calculated weights (see Sect. 4.2 for details) to also to distinguish the smaller low-shot classes C_+. Finally, the whole model can be fine-tuned to further increase its predictive power.

4.1   Neural Network Model

The model consists of two stages: A feature extractor network $f : I \rightarrow \mathbb{R}^d$ maps an input image $x \in I$ to an L_2-normalized d-dimensional feature vector $\hat{y}$. The second stage is a modified softmax classifier $g : \mathbb{R}^d \rightarrow [0,1]^{|C|}$ that maps the feature activations to a discrete probability distribution of $|C|$ classes.

$$g_i(y) = \frac{\exp(s \cdot \hat{w}_i^{\mathsf{T}} \hat{y})}{\sum\limits_{j \in C} \exp(s \cdot \hat{w}_j^{\mathsf{T}} \hat{y})} \tag{1}$$

$\hat{w}_i$ is the weight vector corresponding to class i and is normalized to unit length as well. The scalar product $\hat{w}_i^{\mathsf{T}} \hat{y}$ is the angle or cosine similarity [19] between the feature vector and the weight vector. A weight vector $\hat{w}_i$ therefore acts as a template for class i. s is a learnable scale factor that allows the probabilities to match the one-hot encoding of classes [29].

4.2 Low-Shot Learning

To learn a new class $c_+ \in C_+$, the weight matrix is extended by a column w_+. It follows from the above characterization of weight vectors $\hat{w}_i$ and image feature vectors $\hat{y}$ that they are interchangeable. Therefore, w_+ can be calculated directly from the feature vectors of the examples of class c_+. In the simplest case, if only one single training example x_+ belongs to c_+, the weight vector is equal to its feature vector, i.e. $w_+ = f(x_+)$. In the general case, if c_+ consists of multiple examples ($|c_+| \geq 1$), the weight vector is calculated as the arithmetic average of the image features, i.e. $w_+ = \frac{1}{|c_+|} \sum_{x_+ \in c_+} f(x_+)$, and renormalized. The scalar product $\hat{w}_+^T \hat{y}$ then acts as a nearest mean classifier [20] using the cosine similarity. The underlying assumption is that the distribution of the examples is unimodal for each new class c_+.

5 Experiments

This section describes the experiments to evaluate the ability of weight imprinting to incorporate new classes into a plankton classification model without completely re-training from scratch.

5.1 Network Architecture

The model architecture is summarized in Table 1. The feature extractor network is based on the ResNet18 architecture, as it has a favorable accuracy-speed trade-off [2]. It is initialized with weights pre-trained on the ImageNet dataset [16]. The grayscale plankton images are converted to color images to fit the pre-trained model. We use 512-dimensional embeddings as we observed that the 64-dimensional embeddings from the original paper delayed the convergence of the training and did not bring an advantage. The last three layers implement the operations required for the weight imprinting as described in Sect. 4.1 and are initialized randomly.

Table 1. Network architecture.

Layer	#Parameters	Output shape
Input		$128 \times 128 \times 3$
ResNet18	11 M	$4 \times 4 \times 512$
Global Average Pooling		512
Linear Layer (Embedding)	262 k	512
Normalization		512
Linear Layer $(\hat{w}_i)_{i \in C}$	$512 \cdot |C|$	$|C|$
Scale	1	$|C|$

The whole model is fine-tuned to the task at hand, following the common practice [5]. Each experiment is carried out with three-fold cross-validation. To counter the class imbalance in the dataset we randomly subsample 1000 samples from the larger classes for each training epoch independently. Early stopping is used to avoid overfitting to the training split. To treat all classes equally, we weight the validation loss by the inverse class size. The initial learning rate is set to 1×10^{-4} and decreased whenever the validation loss plateaus until it reaches 1×10^{-8}. The Adam algorithm [17], an extension to stochastic gradient descent, is used for parameter optimization. The batch size is set to 128 images. The images are cropped to their tight bounding box and padded to a square with a minimum edge length of 128 px. Images larger than 128 px are shrunken to this size. The grey values are scaled to the $[0, 1]$ range. We perform training-time augmentation using random rotations in $90°$ steps, random horizontal and vertical flips and Gaussian noise with $\sigma = 0.001$. The models are trained using the PyTorch deep learning library [23] on an NVIDIA GeForce GTX 1070 GPU.

5.2   Baselines

As a baseline (BL), we train the whole network on all classes $C = C_0 \cup C_+$ jointly and without altering the weights in a separate step. Larger classes are subsampled, smaller classes oversampled. We also conduct an ablation experiment to examine the necessity of the architectural choices made in [27] by comparing the original architecture to two modified versions where we removed the weight normalization (BL-W) and subsequently the feature normalization as well (BL-WF).

5.3   Representation Learning

In the first phase of model training, the model learns the base classes C_0. For the UVP5 dataset, we selected the classes with more than 1000 members in the training split (22 classes out of 65) as base classes. For the ZooScan dataset, the classes with more than 1500 members in the training split (44 classes out of 93) were selected as base classes.

The network is trained until the validation loss does not decrease for 25 epochs. No oversampling is performed because the minimum class size (1000 or 1500) is equal to or larger than the number of images needed per epoch (1000).

5.4   Low-Shot Learning

Now, the low-shot weights of the base network are set to their calculated values. For this purpose, we apply the feature extractor part of the network to every image. For each low-shot class $c_i \in C_+$, we calculate the mean feature vector, re-normalize it, and write it into the entry $\hat{w}_i$ of the weight matrix in the classifier part of the network corresponding to the respective class. We compare the described mean imprinting (MI) to random imprinting (RI), where $\hat{w}_i$ is initialized randomly.

5.5 Fine-Tuning

Finally, the imprinted networks are fine-tuned (MI+FT, RI+FT). Classes with less than 1000 examples are oversampled to counteract the class imbalance.

6 Results and Discussion

Tables 2 and 3 list the evaluation results for the UVP5 and ZOOSCAN datasets, respectively. Both datasets behave comparably regarding the success of weight imprinting. We show the arithmetic average and standard deviation of three validation splits. Macro precision and macro recall are reported for base and low-shot classes separately. We do not report accuracy as it is mainly influenced by the base classes that contain most of the examples. Bold entries are global maxima, italic entries are maximal among their respective group.

Figures 3 and 4 show how precision and recall of individual classes depend on the size of the respective class. The vertical line divides low-shot classes (left) and base classes (right). To show the general tendency, the graphs contain a LOWESS fit for each set of classes. The figures compare MI, MI+FT, and BL. They are best viewed in color.

Table 4 lists the amount of time required to train a model to convergence in each condition, respectively.

Table 2. Macro precision and recall (UVP5).

	Base classes		Low-shot classes	
	Macro precision	Macro recall	Macro precision	Macro recall
MI	0.569 ± 0.019	0.466 ± 0.051	0.030 ± 0.001	0.149 ± 0.023
MI+FT	*0.581 ± 0.001*	*0.644 ± 0.002*	*0.121 ± 0.035*	*0.296 ± 0.035*
RI	0.538 ± 0.024	*0.675 ± 0.015*		0
RI+FT	**0.593 ± 0.008**	0.642 ± 0.005	*0.163 ± 0.026*	*0.299 ± 0.022*
BL	*0.539 ± 0.004*	**0.689 ± 0.003**	**0.366 ± 0.049**	0.265 ± 0.022
BL-W	0.489 ± 0.006	0.634 ± 0.015	0.212 ± 0.033	0.289 ± 0.014
BL-WF	0.487 ± 0.017	0.555 ± 0.087	0.157 ± 0.010	**0.302 ± 0.006**

6.1 Low-Shot Learning

For both datasets, mean imprinting (MI) leads to a better precision for the base classes than random imprinting (RI) and to a nonzero recall and precision of the low-shot classes. However, recall for the base classes is impaired. This was expected because as the low-shot classes are initialized with plausible locations in the feature space, they will draw off objects from the base classes.

Table 3. Macro precision and recall with standard deviation (ZOOSCAN).

	Base classes		Low-shot classes	
	Macro precision	Macro recall	Macro precision	Macro recall
MI	0.701 ± 0.001	0.716 ± 0.006	0.066 ± 0.008	0.205 ± 0.010
MI+FT	*0.724 ± 0.005*	*0.771 ± 0.002*	*0.174 ± 0.010*	*0.650 ± 0.010*
RI	0.663 ± 0.006	**0.823 ± 0.003**		0
RI+FT	**0.731 ± 0.005**	0.775 ± 0.003	*0.187 ± 0.003*	*0.664 ± 0.003*
BL	*0.627 ± 0.008*	*0.812 ± 0.005*	**0.459 ± 0.019**	0.614 ± 0.002
BL-W	0.544 ± 0.010	0.793 ± 0.007	0.350 ± 0.025	0.675 ± 0.021
BL-WF	0.502 ± 0.019	0.747 ± 0.028	0.242 ± 0.013	**0.709 ± 0.012**

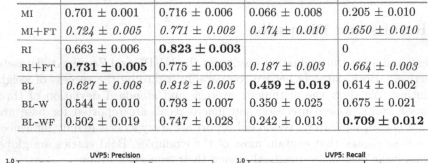

Fig. 3. UVP5: Comparison of per-class precision and recall for mean imprinting (MI), fine-tuning (MI+FT), and training from scratch (BL). (Color figure online)

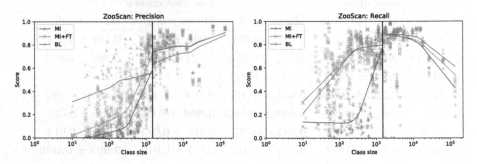

Fig. 4. ZOOSCAN: Comparison of per-class precision and recall for mean imprinting (MI), fine-tuning (MI+FT), and training from scratch (BL). (Color figure online)

Table 4. Training times (s).

	UVP5	ZOOSCAN
MI	0.476 ± 0.026	2.120 ± 0.500
MI+FT	6588.105 ± 989.882	10 550.683 ± 961.637
BL	10 261.286 ± 425.061	22 182.181 ± 665.596

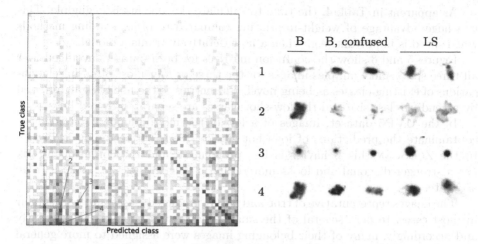

Fig. 5. Mean imprinting: confusion matrix and failure cases (UVP5, validation set). Four of the entries with the most objects from a base class falsely predicted as a low-shot class are numbered. Representative images of the true base class (B) and the predicted low-shot class (LS), as well as two confused images (B falsely predicted as LS) are shown for each entry. 1: Copepoda vs. Cladocera, 2: fluffy dark vs. t003, 3: Collodaria solitary black vs. other dark sphere, 4: fluffy dark vs. t015. *See the electronical version for a magnified view.* (Color figure online)

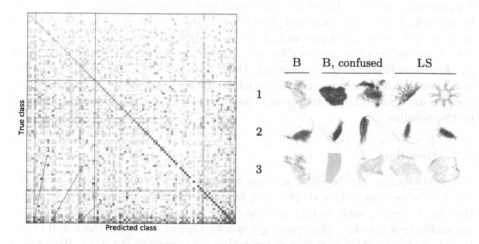

Fig. 6. Mean imprinting: confusion matrix and failure cases (ZooScan, validation set). Three of the entries with the most objects from a base class falsely predicted as a low-shot class are numbered. Representative images of the true base class (B) and the predicted low-shot class (LS), as well as two confused images (B falsely predicted as LS) are shown for each entry. 1: Detritus vs. Ephyra, 2: Calanoida vs. Calocalanus pavo, 3: Detritus vs. scale. *See the electronical version for a magnified view.* (Color figure online)

As apparent in Table 4, the time to calculate the weights is negligible. This is a huge advantage of weight-imprinting compared to other training methods when speed is important, e.g. when a user iteratively trains a model.

Figures 5 and 6 show the confusion matrices for both datasets averaged over all three splits and examples images for the three or four most often misclassifications of existing classes as being novel. The entries of the matrices are ordered by ascending class size and the low-shot classes are separated by red lines.

In the UVP5 dataset, images of a few of the more abundant base classes contaminate the predictions of low-shot classes (lower left rectangle in Fig. 5). In the ZooScan this behavior is less pronounced and the confusion matrix has a stronger diagonal and looks more uniform (Fig. 6), i.e. the model is more accurate.

The images representative of true and falsely predicted classes are very similar in most cases. In fact, several of the smaller classes were defined only recently and accordingly, many of their belonging images were assigned to more general classes in earlier days. We therefore suspect that some of the "errors" made by the models originate from an incoherent labeling of the data. Another type of error is the confusion of classes that differ only by a minuscule feature, for example the missing tail of the Cladocera in Fig. 5 or the regular shape of the Ephyra in Fig. 6.

6.2   Fine-Tuning

Fine-tuning (MI+FT) always improves over mean imprinting alone (MI). This is in agreement with [27]. However, fine-tuning a mean imprinted model does not yield better results than fine-tuning a randomly initialized model (RI+FT). In fact, both perform in a very similar way, while most scores are slightly higher for random initialization. Here, our results differ from [27]. The reason is presumably overfitting of the weight imprinted models to too few samples in the training split. Finetuning a mean imprinted model roughly halves the training time compared to the baseline.

6.3   Baselines

When comparing the baseline models amongst each other, it is apparent that the best scores are achieved with weight normalization and feature normalization (BL). Taking away weight normalization (BL-W) and subsequently feature normalization (BL-WF), the scores get worse. One exception is the recall of the low-shot classes which is maximal for minimal restrictions (BL-WF). We assume that feature and weight normalization have a regularizing effect that leads to a better generalization of the model.

Regarding the low-shot classes, a model trained from scratch (BL) leads to a significantly higher precision and recall than an imprinted model (MI) and to a better or equal recall than a fine-tuned model (MI+FT).

For the base classes, all three conditions behave roughly similarly, although the precision of BL is slightly worse than of MI and MI+FT. This can be explained by the fact that during the representation learning phase of MI and MI+FT, the models learn features that are explicitly adapted to the base classes. Fine-tuning does not seem to destroy this advantage. Conversely, when training on all classes jointly (BL), the features are adapted to all classes equally (and not primarily to the base classes). This also explains the better scores of BL concerning the low-shot classes.

The negative slope of the recall of the base classes in the ZOOSCAN dataset can be explained by the decreasing sampling rate of the base classes, where down to 1% (for the largest classes) of the available examples are used in each training epoch. Therefore, the model may not be able to capture the full variability of the data.

Training a model from scratch takes roughly twice as long as finetuning a mean imprinted model.

6.4   Dataset Maintenance

When collecting plankton images, it is important to constantly monitor the newly acquired data for previously overlooked classes and to update the models accordingly. When a dataset is extended by a novel class, more examples of this novel class have to be found among a large number of images. These examples can be found in new unlabeled data and may also hide in existing labeled data, as in some cases they might have been assigned to a more general class before the introduction of the novel class.

Figures 3 and 4 show how precision and recall are linked to the class size for all models (BL, MI, and MI+FT). Although the imprinting of weights (MI) does not achieve the best scores, its huge advantage is the instant integration of novel data.

Correspondingly, the model may serve as a tool to quickly build up a collection of images in order to train a more powerful classifier later. As weight imprinting allows instant (i.e. in less than one second) re-training for every additional training example without much overhead (see Sect. 4.2), it can be used during a process of iterative example mining: The model is initialized using one or few examples of a class. It is then used to classify unlabeled data and a human operator validates these classifications. The positive examples are used to improve the classifier. In this way, the suggestions will get increasingly better in every iteration.

For the suggestions to be useful, they have to contain positive examples at all, which manifests in a non-zero recall. In the ZOOSCAN dataset, the recall is stable at an average of approx. 0.2 for even the smallest classes. In the UVP5 dataset, the recall is low for most classes. However, there are notable outliers with a recall of up to 1.0. Further research is needed to figure out what makes these outliers special.

As a result, weight imprinting is useful in the mining of additional examples for small and novel classes in both plankton image datasets. The actual implementation of the described procedure will be a task for the future.

The incoherent labeling of novel low-shot classes and existing base classes apparent in the evaluation underlines the usefulness of weight imprinting to keep a dataset consistently labeled when the set of classes evolves.

7 Conclusion

Deep learning models often fail when it comes to training classifiers with very little training data. This is the case for a considerable number of classes in both plankton image datasets. We therefore employed *weight imprinting* [27], a low-shot learning method. When applying this method to plankton image datasets, it allows a model to incorporate underrepresented classes without overly impairing the performance on the base classes.

Weight imprinting resulted in an acceptable recall for the low-shot classes immediately without re-training the neural network. This permits the extension of a training set by examples of a novel class as soon as a single example of this class is observed.

Even when training from scratch, the underlying network architecture performs better than a model without normalization of features and weights in most cases. Apart from a reduced training time, we observed no significant advantage of an imprinted and fine-tuned model over a model trained from scratch.

In summary, the techniques in question, i.e. normalization of features and weights and weight imprinting, are able to advance the identification of plankton using machine learning with its unique challenges, i.e. a limited number of training examples, a severely skewed class size distribution and ever-emerging novel classes.

Acknowledgements. Rainer Kiko was supported by the Deutsche Forschungsgemeinschaft (DFG) as part of the Collaborative Research Centre (SFB) 754 "Climate-Biogeochemistry Interactions in the Tropical Ocean." Rainer Kiko, Reinhard Koch and Simon-Martin Schröder were furthermore supported by grants CP1650 and CP1733 of the Cluster of Excellence 80 "The Future Ocean." "The Future Ocean" is funded within the framework of the Excellence Initiative by the Deutsche Forschungsgemeinschaft (DFG) on behalf of the German federal and state governments. Jean-Olivier Irisson was supported by CNRS LEFE-MANU through project DL-PIC.

References

1. Blaschko, M.B., et al.: Automatic in situ identification of plankton. In: 2005 Seventh IEEE Workshops on Applications of Computer Vision (WACV/MOTION 2005), vol. 1, pp. 79–86. IEEE (2005)
2. Canziani, A., Paszke, A., Culurciello, E.: An Analysis of Deep Neural Network Models for Practical Applications (2016). http://arxiv.org/abs/1605.07678
3. Choe, J., Park, S., Kim, K., Park, J.H., Kim, D., Shim, H.: Face generation for low-shot learning using generative adversarial networks. In: ICCVW 2017, pp. 1940–1948 (2017)

4. Christiansen, S., et al.: Particulate matter flux interception in oceanic mesoscale eddies by the polychaete Poeobius sp. Limnol. Oceanogr. **63**, 2093–2109 (2018)
5. Chu, B., Madhavan, V., Beijbom, O., Hoffman, J., Darrell, T.: Best practices for fine-tuning visual classifiers to new domains. In: Hua, G., Jégou, H. (eds.) ECCV 2016. LNCS, vol. 9915, pp. 435–442. Springer, Cham (2016). https://doi.org/10.1007/978-3-319-49409-8_34
6. Cowen, R.K., Guigand, C.M.: In situ ichthyoplankton imaging system (ISIIS): system design and preliminary results. Limnol. Oceanogr.: Methods **6**, 126–132 (2008)
7. Culverhouse, P.F., Macleod, N., Williams, R., Benfield, M.C., Lopes, R.M., Picheral, M.: An empirical assessment of the consistency of taxonomic identifications. Marine Biol. Res. **10**, 73–84 (2014)
8. Culverhouse, P.F., et al.: Automatic classification of field-collected dinoflagellates by artificial neural network. Marine Ecol. Progress Ser. **139**(1/3), 281–287 (1996)
9. Douze, M., Szlam, A., Hariharan, B., Jégou, H.: Low-shot learning with large-scale diffusion (2017). https://arxiv.org/pdf/1706.02332.pdf
10. Elineau, A., et al.: ZooScanNet: plankton images captured with the ZooScan (2018). http://doi.org/10.17882/55741
11. Ellen, J., Li, H., Ohman, M.D.: Quantifying California current plankton samples with efficient machine learning techniques. In: OCEANS 2015 - MTS/IEEE Washington, pp. 1–9. IEEE (2015)
12. Faillettaz, R., Picheral, M., Luo, J.Y., Guigand, C., Cowen, R.K., Irisson, J.O.: Imperfect automatic image classification successfully describes plankton distribution patterns. Methods Oceanogr. **15–16**, 60–77 (2016)
13. Gorsky, G.: Digital zooplankton image analysis using the ZooScan integrated system. J. Plankton Res. **32**(3), 285–303 (2010)
14. Graham, B., van der Maaten, L.: Submanifold Sparse Convolutional Networks (2017). http://arxiv.org/abs/1706.01307
15. Hariharan, B., Girshick, R.: Low-shot visual recognition by shrinking and hallucinating features. In: 2017 IEEE International Conference on Computer Vision (ICCV), pp. 3037–3046. IEEE (2017)
16. Deng, J., Dong, W., Socher, R., Li, L.-J., Li, K., Fei-Fei, L.: ImageNet: a large-scale hierarchical image database. In: 2009 IEEE Conference on Computer Vision and Pattern Recognition, pp. 248–255. IEEE (2009)
17. Kingma, D.P., Ba, J.: Adam: A Method for Stochastic Optimization (2014). http://arxiv.org/abs/1412.6980
18. Lee, H., Park, M., Kim, J.: Plankton classification on imbalanced large scale database via convolutional neural networks with transfer learning. In: 2016 IEEE International Conference on Image Processing (ICIP), pp. 3713–3717. IEEE (2016)
19. Luo, C., Zhan, J., Wang, L., Yang, Q.: Cosine Normalization: Using Cosine Similarity Instead of Dot Product in Neural Networks (2017). http://arxiv.org/abs/1702.05870
20. Mensink, T., Verbeek, J., Perronnin, F., Csurka, G.: Distance-based image classification: generalizing to new classes at near-zero cost. IEEE Trans. Pattern Anal. Mach. Intell. **35**(11), 2624–2637 (2013)
21. Olson, R.J., Sosik, H.M.: A submersible imaging-in-flow instrument to analyze nano-and microplankton: Imaging FlowCytobot. Limnol. Oceanogr.: Methods **5**(6), 195–203 (2007)
22. Orenstein, E.C., Beijbom, O.: Transfer learning and deep feature extraction for planktonic image data sets. In: 2017 IEEE Winter Conference on Applications of Computer Vision (WACV), pp. 1082–1088. IEEE (2017)

23. Paszke, A., et al.: Automatic differentiation in PyTorch. In: Advances in Neural Information Processing Systems (NIPS), vol. 30, pp. 1–4 (2017)
24. Picheral, M., Colin, S., Irisson, J.O.: EcoTaxa (2017). http://ecotaxa.obs-vlfr.fr/
25. Picheral, M., Guidi, L., Stemmann, L., Karl, D.M., Iddaoud, G., Gorsky, G.: The Underwater Vision Profiler 5: an advanced instrument for high spatial resolution studies of particle size spectra and zooplankton. Limnol. Oceanogr.: Methods 8(1), 462–473 (2010)
26. Py, O., Hong, H., Zhongzhi, S.: Plankton classification with deep convolutional neural networks. In: 2016 IEEE Information Technology, Networking, Electronic and Automation Control Conference, pp. 132–136 (2016)
27. Qi, H., Brown, M., Lowe, D.G.: Low-shot learning with imprinted weights. In: Proceedings of the IEEE Conference on Computer Vision and Pattern Recognition, pp. 5822–5830 (2018)
28. Sosik, H.M., Olson, R.J.: Automated taxonomic classification of phytoplankton sampled with imaging-in-flow cytometry. Limnol. Oceanogr.: Methods 5(6), 204–216 (2007)
29. Wang, F., Xiang, X., Cheng, J., Yuille, A.L.: NormFace: L_2 hypersphere embedding for face verification. In: Proceedings of the 2017 ACM on Multimedia Conference, MM 2017, pp. 1041–1049. ACM Press, New York (2017)

Poster Session 2

Poster Session 2

Multimodal Dense Stereo Matching

Max Mehltretter[1]($\boxtimes$), Sebastian P. Kleinschmidt[2], Bernardo Wagner[2], and Christian Heipke[1]

[1] Institute of Photogrammetry and GeoInformation,
Leibniz Universität Hannover, Hannover, Germany
{mehltretter,heipke}@ipi.uni-hannover.de
[2] Institute of Systems Engineering - Real Time Systems Group,
Leibniz Universität Hannover, Hannover, Germany
{kleinschmidt,wagner}@rts.uni-hannover.de

Abstract. In this paper, we propose a new approach for dense depth estimation based on multimodal stereo images. Our approach employs a combined cost function utilizing robust metrics and a transformation to an illumination independent representation. Additionally, we present a confidence based weighting scheme which allows a pixel-wise weight adjustment within the cost function. We demonstrate the capabilities of our approach using RGB- and thermal images. The resulting depth maps are evaluated by comparing them to depth measurements of a Velodyne HDL-64E LiDAR sensor. We show that our method outperforms current state of the art dense matching methods regarding depth estimation based on multimodal input images.

1 Introduction

The reconstruction of depth information from a set of images is a well-known problem in the fields of photogrammetry and computer vision. For this task, the identification of image correspondences is an essential prerequisite. However, in the presence of difficult environmental conditions such as lighting or weather changes, the performance of state of the art correspondence identification techniques is limited. This task becomes even more challenging if cameras of different imaging modalities are used, which are operating in different parts of the electromagnetic spectrum. In this case, correspondences of image features of one modality may be represented differently or may be absent altogether in images of other modalities. However, multimodal imaging may help to make current computer vision algorithms more robust due to additional spectral information: Thermal imaging is insensitive to lighting variations and therefore still works when RGB-cameras fail. Consequently, establishing spatial relations between images of different modalities is relevant for a variety of applications. In medical diagnosis for example, multimodal image fusion algorithms have shown notable achievements in improving the clinical accuracy of decisions based on medical images [13]. Whereas most multimodal approaches for medical applications are

© Springer Nature Switzerland AG 2019
T. Brox et al. (Eds.): GCPR 2018, LNCS 11269, pp. 407–421, 2019.
https://doi.org/10.1007/978-3-030-12939-2_28

only confronted with objects of a limited and known anatomic atlas, more general computer vision applications have to deal with a larger variety of objects and environments. Therefore, they have a different focus and varying requirements. The presented work uses the advantages of multimodal imaging for dense depth estimation using a multimodal stereo setup.

The overall aim of the current work is to investigate the feasibility of dense depth estimation from multimodal stereo images. For this purpose, we examine the performance of a dense image matching approach using one thermal- and one RGB image as input data. We demonstrate the possibility to reconstruct an environment densely even if its representation in the images differs greatly. Our main contributions on this topic are:

- A combined cost function utilizing robust metrics and a transformation to an illumination independent representation.
- A confidence based weighting scheme which allows adjusting the weights within the cost function pixel-wise.

2   Related Work

2.1   Multimodal Image Fusion

The combination of RGB and thermal imaging is useful for a series of applications as pedestrian detection and tracking as well as silhouette extraction (e.g. [2,4,7,20,33]), agricultural applications (e.g. [21,26]), maintenance (e.g. [28]) and traffic monitoring (e.g. [1]). Multimodal image registration has been realized using contours [8], Harris Corners [10], Hough lines [12], wavelet transformations [27] or the intrinsic and extrinsic camera calibration [15]. Beside merging image features of different modalities only using two-dimensional information, depth information of a depth sensor [16] or structure from motion techniques [17] can be used for feature association. Based on spatially aligned multimodal images, the authors of [15] perform an analysis of the statistical and spatial distribution of sparse image features for RGB, IR and thermal imaging and conclude, that only a relatively small quantity of sparse image features has corresponding image features across modalities for the evaluated scenario. The results indicate a potential limit for the number of transferable image features across imaging modalities.

For multimodal dense matching, the performance of current state of the art techniques is limited as well: Because area-based cross-correlation only works insufficiently for a thermal stereo setup, [6] obtains phase congruency maps for two thermal images before correlation is performed. The authors conclude, that their method is more robust than matching the greyscale images directly. The work presented in [25] investigates the feasibility of matching multimodal features in a stereo setup consisting of an RGB and a thermal camera. The authors introduce a novel feature descriptor based on the combination of the phase congruency and the spatial distribution of the contours in a window around the extracted point.

2.2   Dense Image Matching

Finding correspondences between images of different modalities (e.g. RGB and thermal) and between those taken under different lighting conditions leads to a similar problem: In general, the grey- or RGB-values of such an image pair cannot be transformed to each other in a global linear manner. Rather, the transformations depend on the different depicted objects and therefore vary locally. However, most of the published approaches focus on image pairs which were taken under similar conditions and with the same type of sensor (e.g. [9,31]). Hence, they assume the scene to appear similarly in all images. Consequently, these methods are not robust against influences which have an impact on the imaging process, as changing illumination or contrast. Only a few methods like [14,23,24] address this problem. Nevertheless, most of them rely on strong assumptions and therefore have a quite limited range of application: The assumptions made in [23] for example, are only valid if the sun is the only significant light source. Besides, [14] can only handle specific changes in illumination. Consequently, common dense matching approaches are neither sufficient for solving multimodal fusion nor for matching under varying illumination conditions, because they are based on assumptions which do not hold under these conditions.

3   Method

3.1   Imaging Process

Infrared (IR) thermal imaging, captures radiation in the electromagnetic spectrum from approximately 0.9 to 14 µm. All objects with a temperature above 0 K emit thermal radiation. Because most thermal cameras operate surrounded by atmospheric gases, only radiation can be reasonably used for thermal imaging, which line up with the atmospheric window, i.e. is not absorbed by the atmosphere. As a result, there are only two ranges of IR wavelength which are typically used for thermal imaging: The short or medium wavelength band (SW/MW) and the long wavelength band (LW). The general setup of a thermal camera is very similar to the one of a typical RGB camera which also consists of a lens focussing radiation on a detector arranged as a focal plane array. Consequently, also similar mathematical models are used to describe the imaging process of a thermal camera with respect to reflection, refraction, and transmission. As summarized in [22], there are multiple reasons why many state of the art computer vision algorithms have a worse performance on thermal images than on RGB images. One major problem is more significant Gaussian image noise: In RGB imaging most objects only reflect light, and the resulting brightness level can typically be covered by a common exposure/gain level for the dynamic range of the camera. In contrast, in thermal imaging all objects with a temperature above 0 K emit thermal radiation, and thermal imaging typically has to deal with a much higher dynamic range. Additionally, the emission of an object in the thermal spectrum depends on the object's temperature. Finally, the appearance of an object changes over time due to thermal balancing effects causing significant changes in the appearance of the object in the thermal image.

As described in this section, RGB and thermal imaging capture different wavelengths of the electromagnetic spectrum and therefore represent different aspects of their environment. Moreover, material transitions often provide different appearances in the visual spectrum as well as in the thermal image due to different thermal capacity and emissivity. Even though, because of the similar properties of visual and thermal radiation regarding reflection, refraction, and transmission, visual and thermal images not only depend on the reflected or emitted radiation in the specific ranges only, but also on the scene geometry from which light is reflected or emitted. These common factors are used in our method to establish multimodal image correspondences.

3.2   Multimodal Dense Matching

In general, it is advantageous for dense image matching if the images are stereo-rectified beforehand, as then the task of correspondence determination is reduced from a two-dimensional problem to one where homologous features lie in horizontal lines. To perform this kind of rectification, the cameras' intrinsic parameters as well as their relative orientation are assumed to be known. Subsequently, an approach based on Semi-Global Matching [9] and a combined cost function [24] is applied to estimate disparity maps for the thermal as well as the RGB image.

Combined Cost Function. In order to densely reconstruct an environment from images that depict it in greatly different manners, a robust matching approach is crucial. For RGB and thermal images, it will typically not be possible to linearly transform the grey values from one domain to the other. Consequently, either a metric is needed which is robust against these kinds of differences or a transformation has to be used which brings both images into a common representation. In this work, a cost function is introduced which considers both approaches. For this purpose, various metrics are combined:

$$C(x, d) = \sum_n \lambda_n \cdot C_n(x, d) . \tag{1}$$

The combined cost function is computed for each pixel x and disparity d and is defined as the weighted sum of the individual functions. The weights λ_n represent the confidence of the corresponding cost functions in the current pixel. All weights add up to one. More information on the weights is provided later in this section.

In order to combine the response of the individual metrics to a consistent cost function, the value range of the responses has to be considered. In this context, not only the size of the support region for cost aggregation is relevant, but also the type of similarity measure used. For example, when comparing a Census filter plus Hamming distance with a SAD metric, the responses are not only within various intervals but also show different distributions over these intervals. Consequently, a sum of these responses, weighted or not, can lead to a situation in which the influence of one metric is canceled out by the dominating one. Hence, the metric responses are normalized within $[0; 1]$ and spread over the whole interval.

Metrics. The combined cost function consists of four elements: a modified Census transformation (MC), Zero-mean Normalized Cross-Correlation (ZNCC), Normalized Sum of Squared Differences (NSSD) and a triangle-based depth prediction approach. All of them are applied to the images transformed by phase congruency [18] instead of the original images. This procedure is described in detail in the subsequent section.

Proposed in [34], the modified Census transformation extends the original concept [30] by intensifying the use of cross-correlation information. For this purpose, the pixels within the support region are not only compared to the center pixel, but to the mean value of the region as well. Keeping in mind that the image pair consists of a thermal and a RGB image, the grey value distribution in both images may differ greatly. Consequently, the corresponding maps obtained by phase congruency may vary also. Therefore, this modified version of the Census transformation better suits our application.

With respect to these properties, the sum of squared differences has to be modified as well, in order to be able to apply this metric to these kind of image pairs effectively. For this purpose, the results of the metric are assumed to be normally distributed and the standard score is utilized for normalization:

$$NSSD(x,d) = \frac{1}{\gamma \cdot |X_L|} \sum_{\tilde{x} \in X_L} \left(\frac{I_L(\tilde{x}) - \mu_L}{\sigma_L} - \frac{I_R(\tilde{x} - d) - \mu_L}{\sigma_R} \right)^2, \qquad (2)$$

$$C_{NSSD}(x,d) = min\left(NSSD(x,d), 1\right), \qquad (3)$$

where $|X_L|$ is the number of pixels within the support region of x in the left image and $\tilde{x}$ are the single elements. The mean and standard deviation of the support region in the corresponding image are denoted as μ and σ, respectively. Finally, the parameter γ is used to normalize the resulting value before truncation in Eq. 3.

The last element of the combined cost function is a triangle-based depth prediction which is based on the approach originally proposed in [3]. In order to adjust this process to the specified data, the images are transformed via phase congruency prior to feature detection. Consequently, the moments of this transformation are used for the detection step [19]. Afterwards, the feature points are matched using the edge histogram descriptor proposed in [25] and the matching strategy suggested in [24]. Subsequently, a Delaunay triangulation is applied to the features for both images individually. In a final step, a disparity is predicted for every pixel within the triangles by interpolating the disparity values of the corresponding vertices. Thus, the corresponding cost function is defined as:

$$C_T(x,d) = min\left(\frac{|d - d_{T,x}|}{d_0}, 1\right), \qquad (4)$$

where $d_{T,x}$ is the interpolated disparity at pixel x within triangle T and d_0 is the threshold for the maximum distance to the prediction. To avoid wrong predictions, triangles that are not surface consistent must be filtered out. Here, this is done via three criteria: The number of pixels within a triangle, the maximum edge length and the inclination of the triangle relative to the image plane.

Phase Congruency. Originally proposed in [18], phase congruency is an image transformation which allows a representation which is invariant to differences in illumination and contrast. The image is then analyzed in the frequency domain within a local context and is based on the concept of the local energy model. In contrast to many other approaches that operate in the frequency domain, phase congruency utilizes phase information, not amplitudes. While [25] has already shown its capability to operate on thermal RGB image pairs in order to find sparse correspondences, within this work the transformation is used to convert the images into a representation that allows the use of common dense matching approaches.

Due to the Time-Frequency Uncertainty Principle it is not possible to accurately determine the spatial position and frequency simultaneously. Thus, the conventional approach is applied, utilizing a bank of Log-Gabor filters to approximate the phase congruency. The bank contains filters for various scales n and orientations Θ which are applied on an image $I(x)$ with:

$$PC(x) = \frac{\sum_\Theta \sqrt{(\sum_n (I(x) * M_{n\Theta}^e))^2 + (\sum_n (I(x) * M_{n\Theta}^o))^2}}{\sum_\Theta \sum_n (A_{n\Theta}(x)) + \epsilon}, \qquad (5)$$

$$A_{n\Theta}(x) = \sqrt{(I(x) * M_{n\Theta}^e)^2 + (I(x) * M_{n\Theta}^\Theta)^2}, \qquad (6)$$

where $PC(x)$ is the phase congruency value and $A_{n\Theta}(x)$ the amplitude of the response in pixel x. The even and odd symmetric components of the Log-Gabor filters are denoted as $M_{n\Theta}^e$ and $M_{n\Theta}^o$, respectively. In order to prevent a division by zero, ϵ is added to the denominator in Eq. 5.

Fig. 1. RGB and thermal images with their corresponding phase congruency.

After phase congruency was applied on two images, a matching metric $F(*, *)$ is used to compute the similarity of the transformation results I_{PC}^L and I_{PC}^R. The cost function is then constructed as follows:

$$C_{PC}(x, d) = F(I_{PC}^L(x), I_{PC}^R(x - d)). \qquad (7)$$

Besides, the result of the phase congruency itself, the maximum and minimum moment of the transformation can be utilized as well. By filtering these values with certain thresholds, edges and corners can be extracted [19]. As it is directly based on the transformation, the invariance against changes in illumination and contrast also applies here.

$$M = \frac{1}{2}\left(c + a + \sqrt{b^2 + (a - c)^2}\right), \tag{8}$$

$$m = \frac{1}{2}\left(c + a - \sqrt{b^2 + (a - c)^2}\right). \tag{9}$$

In order to determine edges and corners, the values of the moments are compared to two thresholds ϵ_E and ϵ_C: If the maximum moment $M > \epsilon_E$ in a certain point, this point is labeled as 'edge' and if $M > \epsilon_E$ and the minimum moment $m > \epsilon_C$ the point is labeled as 'corner'. The corresponding coefficients are defined as:

$$a = \sum_{\Theta}(PC(\Theta)cos(\Theta))^2, \tag{10}$$

$$b = 2\sum_{\Theta}(PC(\Theta)cos(\Theta) \cdot PC(\Theta)sin(\Theta)), \tag{11}$$

$$c = \sum_{\Theta}(PC(\Theta)sin(\Theta))^2, \tag{12}$$

where $PC(\Theta)$ represents the phase congruency value regarding only orientation Θ, but all scales. The sum is then calculated for all the orientations used.

Confidence Based Weighting. The influence of the different metrics utilized within the combined cost function is controlled by their weights. Thus, the selection of suitable weights is a crucial task to obtain accurate results. While the approach proposed in [24] uses constant weights, the significance of the individual metrics can vary greatly, when operating on different parts of an image. Consequently, constant weights can only be a compromise over all pixels and in general, they will not be optimal.

To overcome this problem, a dynamic weighting scheme is proposed in this work. For this purpose, the weights of the single metrics are adjusted pixelwise based on their confidence for the current pixel. To do so, in [11] different approaches were evaluated: Some are based on local attributes of the curve corresponding to the cost function, others analyze the entire curve and a third group utilizes the left-right consistency assumption. However, most of these concepts are not suitable to compare different kinds of metrics. Furthermore, in general, a more complex analysis leads to more reliable results. Thus, we propose to not only consider characteristics of the resulting cost curve but to introduce expectations on an 'ideal' cost curve, as well. For this purpose, the confidence measure is based on the difference between the curve of the cost function and a predefined reference curve:

$$\rho(x) = \begin{cases} \sqrt{\dfrac{1}{n} \sum_{d}^{n} (R(d) - C(x,d))^2}, & \text{if } |c_0 - c_1| > \epsilon \\ 0, & \text{otherwise} \end{cases} \tag{13}$$

$$R(d) = 1 - \exp(-\omega \cdot (d - c_0)^2). \tag{14}$$

To ensures the uniqueness of the solution, the confidence ρ of a metric is only computed if the difference between the smallest (c_0) and the second smallest (c_1) value of the cost function is bigger than a predefined threshold ϵ. Otherwise, it is set to zero. The confidence itself is defined as the RMS-Error between the cost function C and the reference function R, for which R is specified by its extension ω and minimum, which is placed at c_0. The proposed confidence measure is used for all matching metrics except for the triangle-based depth prediction. Based on the definition of the prediction approach, the corresponding cost curve always has the same shape. Consequently, the comparison to a reference curve would result in a constant value. Instead, the distance $g(x,T)$ between the current pixel and the closest vertex of triangle T is used to measure the confidence as proposed in [3]:

$$\rho_T(x) = \exp\left(-\frac{g(x,T)}{\sigma}\right), \tag{15}$$

where σ is a non-negative constant that controls the degree to which the confidence value descends. Finally, the weights λ are the confidence values normalized over the sum of all confidences:

$$\lambda_n = \frac{\rho_n}{\sum \rho}. \tag{16}$$

Optimization and Post-processing. In the final step, the optimal disparity value for every pixel is determined by optimizing the cost volume produced by the combined cost function. For this purpose, Semi-Global Matching [9] is used. As suggested in the original work, gradient information is introduced to adjust the penalties. For this purpose, the edge map extracted from the maximum moment of the phase congruency is utilized. The resulting disparity maps are post-processed by filtering for speckles first and applying a left-right consistency check afterwards. To be able to demonstrate the capability of the proposed approach only, no interpolation is applied subsequently.

4   Evaluation

4.1   Experimental Setup

To evaluate our approach, we use a *FLIR A655sc* thermal camera, a *FLIR Grasshopper3 GS3-U3-23S6C* RGB-camera, and a *Velodyne HDL64E S2* LiDAR

Fig. 2. Setup to evaluate our multimodal dense matching approach: FLIR A655sc *(left)*, Velodyne HDL64E S2 *(center)*, FLIR Grasshopper3 GS3-U3-23S6C *(right)*.

sensor. All sensors are rigidly connected. The baseline between the camera centers of the RGB and the thermal camera has a length of 0.393 m. The resulting setup is shown in Fig. 2. The RGB camera works at a framerate of 7 Hz whereas the thermal camera captures images at 50 Hz. Because both cameras are working untriggered at different measurement rates, time synchronization is performed according to [16] using global timestamps. The resulting maximum time difference between the images can be computed to be less than 10 ms. The extrinsic calibration between the cameras and the laser scanner was performed according to [32]. To determine the extrinsic calibration between the cameras, we used a multimodal chessboard with patterns with specific color and thermal emissivity properties, which can be clearly recognized in both imaging modalities as described in [16]. Furthermore, to better distinguish the patterns of the chessboard in the thermal image, the chessboard is actively heated using heat pads applied on the backside of the patterns. Additionally, the patterns are coated by materials with varying emissivity.

The presented approach is evaluated using a dataset consisting of 15 multimodal stereo images taken outside. The dataset covers artificial structures as buildings and cars as well as natural vegetation. Besides minor variations in the scene caused by environmental influences as wind, the scenes are assumed to be static. Furthermore, the distance to the objects in the scene varies between 2 m and 50 m, with a median of 5 m.

4.2 Error Metric

In order to evaluate the depth estimation error of our approach, lidar data is utilized as ground truth. For this purpose, the acquired 3D point clouds are projected into image space using the results of the intrinsic and extrinsic calibration:

$$_{(RGB)}\mathbf{x} = _{(RGB)}\mathbf{M} \cdot {}^{(RGB)}\mathbf{T}_{(L)} \cdot {}_{(L)}\mathbf{X}, \tag{17}$$

where $\mathbf{X}$ is a 3D point and $\mathbf{x}$ its 2D correspondence. ${}^{(RGB)}\mathbf{T}_{(L)}$ is the transformations from the lidar to the RGB camera coordinate system. Finally, $_{(RGB)}\mathbf{M}$

is the projection matrix of the camera. To compute the 2D image coordinates, Euclidean normalization is applied. The error is then estimated for every pixel that is set in the ground truth image obtained by the laser scanner. Furthermore, a pixel is considered as correct if the distance between the dense image matching result and the ground truth is lower than a specified error bound. Lastly, the overall error is defined as the percentage of pixels which are considered as incorrect.

In general, an error bound of 20% of the depth was used. This value was chosen due to the challenging setup and associated lower expected accuracy compared to traditional dense image matching applications. It is mainly used to compare our approach against others (see Table 1) and to demonstrate the contribution of the different components (see Fig. 4 on the right). Additionally, a more differentiated evaluation of the error is given in Fig. 4 on the left, providing results with varying error bounds in the range of 5%–25%.

4.3   Results

Based on the error metric described above, the results were evaluated in a qualitative as well as a quantitative manner. On average 63.4% of the estimated disparity values are classified as correct. As can be seen in Fig. 3, especially for structured areas and borders between different materials depth can be reconstructed accurately. This is based on the fact, that both are clearly visible in thermal as well as in RGB images. Conversely, textured but flat surfaces like facades and asphalt are challenging for this kind of application. Because of their varying appearance, they are not or only insufficiently visible in the spectrum covered by thermal imaging. This can also be observed when comparing the phase congruency maps obtained from both modalities shown in Fig. 1: The structure of the wall, as well as the ground is only visible in the transformed RGB image. Moreover, Fig. 3 and Table 1 show that the estimated disparity maps do not cover the complete image and consequently, not all ground truth points. This is based on the fact that no interpolation is performed at the end. Consequently, depth cannot be reconstructed in occluded areas as well as for pixels at edges which are only visible in one image.

Based on the error metric described in the previous section, we have also evaluated our approach with different error bounds for the depth. As can be seen in Fig. 4 on the left side, utilizing an error bound of 20%, 63.4% of the available ground truth points can be reconstructed correctly, and more than 40% of the points have a difference between estimation and ground truth which is smaller than 10% of their distance to the camera. Furthermore, the right side of Fig. 4 shows the importance of every single metric for the overall approach: Using Zero-mean Normalized Cross-Correlation (ZNCC) exclusively, only 51.5% of the depth estimations are correct. Compared to this baseline, the combined cost function approach increases the performance by more than 10% to 63.4%.

To demonstrate the advantages of our approach regarding multimodal images, we compared our method against conventional dense matching approaches based on the error bound of 20%. As shown in Table 1, conventional

Fig. 3. Qualitative results of the proposed approach. From top to bottom: RGB image, thermal image, disparity map (from large values in red to small values in blue) and error map (from a small error in green to a large one in red - white points are not covered by the estimation). The disparity and error maps are related to the RGB image. (color figure online)

Table 1. Comparison against conventional dense matching approaches

Method	Correctly reconstructed pixels in %	Coverage of ground truth points in %
Elas Matcher [5]	15.1	0.3
SPS Stereo [29]	15.4	94.8
Illum. invariant matching [24]	54.5	23.2
Ours	63.4	60.5

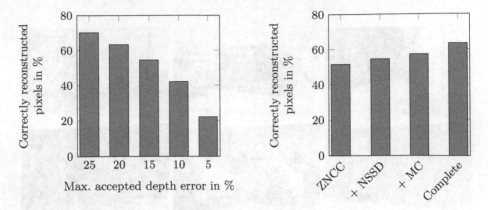

Fig. 4. Left: Percentage of pixels with a correct depth estimation according to varying thresholds which are based on the ground truth data. Right: Comparison of the performance of our approach using subsets of the proposed metrics.

methods are not suitable for this kind of data in general. With a coverage of ground truth points of less than 1%, the Elas Matcher [5] even failed completely. This clarifies once again the challenge that the combination of RGB and thermal images presents to dense image matching.

5   Conclusion

In this paper, we have presented a new approach for multimodal dense depth estimation based on stereo images of an RGB- and a thermal camera. To solve this task we developed a cost function combining different robust metrics which are applied to an illumination independent image representation. Furthermore, we introduced a new confidence based weighting scheme which allows a pixel-wise weight adjustment within a cost function. We evaluated our approach based on 15 multimodal image pairs including ground truth data of a 64 channel lidar sensor and demonstrated, that our approach correctly estimates disparity values for on average 63.4% of the estimated disparity values.

To further examine the performance of the presented approach, a more diverse dataset including additional lighting and temperature variations would be beneficial. Additionally, a common public multimodal dataset including ground truth data would allow a more competitive comparison.

As far as the authors know, we presented the first dense matching approach designed for the special requirements resulting from multimodal stereo setups. As shown in our experiments, the presented approach outperforms current state of the art dense matching methods regarding depth estimation based on multimodal images.

Acknowledgements. This work was supported by the German Research Foundation (DFG) as a part of the Research Training Group i.c.sens [GRK2159] and the MOBILISE initiative of the Leibniz Universität Hannover and TU Braunschweig.

References

1. Alldieck, T., Bahnsen, C.H., Moeslund, T.B.: Context-aware fusion of RGB and thermal imagery for traffic monitoring. Sensors **16**(11) (2016). https://doi.org/10.3390/s16111947

2. Bhanu, B., Han, J.: Kinematic-based human motion analysis in infrared sequences. In: Proceedings of the Sixth IEEE Workshop on Applications of Computer Vision (2002)

3. Bulatov, D., Wernerus, P., Heipke, C.: Multi-view dense matching supported by triangular meshes. ISPRS J. Photogramm. Remote Sens. **66**(6), 907–918 (2011)

4. Conaire, C., Cooke, E., O'Connor, N., Murphy, N., Smearson, A.: Background modelling in infrared and visible spectrum video for people tracking. In: IEEE Computer Society Conference on Computer Vision and Pattern Recognition - Workshops (2005)

5. Geiger, A., Roser, M., Urtasun, R.: Efficient large-scale stereo matching. In: Kimmel, R., Klette, R., Sugimoto, A. (eds.) ACCV 2010. LNCS, vol. 6492, pp. 25–38. Springer, Heidelberg (2011). https://doi.org/10.1007/978-3-642-19315-6_3

6. Guo, L., Zhang, G., Wu, J.: Infrared image area correlation matching method based on phase congruency. In: International Conference on Artificial Intelligence and Computational Intelligence (2010)

7. Han, J., Bhanu, B.: Fusion of color and infrared video for moving human detection. Pattern Recognit. **40**(6), 1771–1784 (2007). https://doi.org/10.1016/j.patcog.2006.11.010

8. Heather, J.P., Smith, M.I.: Multimodal image registration with applications to image fusion. In: 7th International Conference on Information Fusion, vol. 1, p. 8 (2005). https://doi.org/10.1109/ICIF.2005.1591879

9. Hirschmuller, H.: Stereo processing by semiglobal matching and mutual information. IEEE Trans. Pattern Anal. Mach. Intell. **30**(2), 328–341 (2008)

10. Hrkać, T., Kalafatić, Z., Krapac, J.: Infrared-visual image registration based on corners and hausdorff distance. In: Ersbøll, B.K., Pedersen, K.S. (eds.) SCIA 2007. LNCS, vol. 4522, pp. 383–392. Springer, Heidelberg (2007). https://doi.org/10.1007/978-3-540-73040-8_39

11. Hu, X., Mordohai, P.: A quantitative evaluation of confidence measures for stereo vision. IEEE Trans. Pattern Anal. Mach. Intell. **34**(11), 2121–2133 (2012)

12. Istenic, R., Heric, D., Ribaric, S., Zazula, D.: Thermal and visual image registration in hough parameter space. In: 14th International Workshop on Systems, Signals and Image Processing and 6th EURASIP Conference focused on Speech and Image Processing, Multimedia Communications and Services, pp. 106–109 (2007). https://doi.org/10.1109/IWSSIP.2007.4381164

13. James, A.P., Dasarathy, B.V.: Medical image fusion: a survey of the state of the art. CoRR abs/1401.0166 (2014)

14. Kim, S., Ham, B., Kim, B., Sohn, K.: Mahalanobis distance cross-correlation for illumination-invariant stereo matching. IEEE Trans. Circuits Syst. Video Technol. **24**(11), 1844–1859 (2014)

15. Kleinschmidt, S.P., Wagner, B.: Probabilistic fusion and analysis of multimodal image features. In: 18th International Conference on Advanced Robotics, pp. 498–504 (2017)
16. Kleinschmidt, S.P., Wagner, B.: Spatial fusion of different imaging technologies using a virtual multimodal camera. In: Madani, K., Peaucelle, D., Gusikhin, O. (eds.) Informatics in Control, Automation and Robotics. LNEE, vol. 430, pp. 153–174. Springer, Cham (2018). https://doi.org/10.1007/978-3-319-55011-4_8
17. Kleinschmidt, S.P., Wagner, B.: Visual multimodal odometry: robust visual odometry in harsh environments. In: IEEE International Symposium on Safety, Security and Rescue Robotics (2018)
18. Kovesi, P.: Image Features from Phase Congruency. Videre: J. Comput. Vis. Res. 1(3), 1–26 (1999)
19. Kovesi, P.: Phase congruency detects corners and edges. In: The Australian Pattern Recognition Society Conference: DICTA, pp. 309–318 (2003)
20. Krotosky, S.J., Trivedi, M.M.: Mutual information based registration of multimodal stereo videos for person tracking. Comput. Vis. Image Underst. 106(2–3), 270–287 (2007). https://doi.org/10.1016/j.cviu.2006.10.008
21. Leinonen, I., Jones, H.G.: Combining thermal and visible imagery for estimating canopy temperature and identifying plant stress. J. Exp. Bot. 55(401), 1423–1431 (2004)
22. Lin, S.S.: Review: extending visible band computer vision techniques to infrared band images. Technical report, MS-CIS-01-04, GRASP Laboratory, Computer Vision and Information Science Department, University of Pennsylvania (2001)
23. Maddern, W., Stewart, A., McManus, C., Upcroft, B., Churchill, W., Newman, P.: Illumination invariant imaging: applications in robust vision-based localisation, mapping and classification for autonomous vehicles. In: Proceedings of the IEEE International Conference on Robotics and Automation - Workshop, vol. 2, p. 3 (2014)
24. Mehltretter, M., Heipke, C.: Illumination invariant dense image matching based on sparse features. In: 38. Wissenschaftlich-Technische Jahrestagung der DGPF und PFGK18 Tagung in München, vol. 27, pp. 584–596 (2018)
25. Mouats, T., Aouf, N.: Multimodal stereo correspondence based on phase congruency and edge histogram descriptor. In: Proceedings of the 16th International Conference on Information Fusion, pp. 1981–1987. IEEE (2013)
26. Raza, S., Sanchez, V., Prince, G., Clarkson, J., Rajpoot, N.M.: Registration of thermal and visible light images of diseased plants using silhouette extraction in the wavelet domain. Pattern Recognit. 7(48), 2119–2128 (2015)
27. Shah, P., Merchant, S.N., Desai, U.B.: Fusion of surveillance images in infrared and visible band using curvelet, wavelet and wavelet packet transform. Int. J. Wavelets, Multiresolution Inf. Process. 8(2), 271–292 (2010)
28. Vidas, S., Moghadam, P.: HeatWave: a handheld 3D thermography system for energy auditing. Energy Build. 66, 445–460 (2013)
29. Yamaguchi, K., McAllester, D., Urtasun, R.: Efficient joint segmentation, occlusion labeling, stereo and flow estimation. In: Fleet, D., Pajdla, T., Schiele, B., Tuytelaars, T. (eds.) ECCV 2014. LNCS, vol. 8693, pp. 756–771. Springer, Cham (2014). https://doi.org/10.1007/978-3-319-10602-1_49
30. Zabih, R., Woodfill, J.: Non-parametric local transforms for computing visual correspondence. In: Eklundh, J.-O. (ed.) ECCV 1994. LNCS, vol. 801, pp. 151–158. Springer, Heidelberg (1994). https://doi.org/10.1007/BFb0028345
31. Zbontar, J., LeCun, Y.: Stereo matching by training a convolutional neural network to compare image patches. J. Mach. Learn. Res. 17(1–32), 2 (2016)

32. Zhang, Q., Pless, R.: Extrinsic calibration of a camera and laser range finder. In: International Conference on Intelligent Robots and Systems, pp. 2301–2306 (2004)
33. Zhao, J., Cheung, S.S.: Human segmentation by geometrically fusing visible-light and thermal imageries. Multimedia Tools Appl. **73**(1), 61–89 (2014). https://doi.org/10.1007/s11042-012-1299-2
34. Zhu, S., Yan, L.: Local stereo matching algorithm with efficient matching cost and adaptive guided image filter. Vis. Comput. **33**(9), 1087–1102 (2017)

Deep Distance Transform to Segment Visually Indistinguishable Merged Objects

Sören Klemm, Xiaoyi Jiang(✉), and Benjamin Risse

Faculty of Mathematics and Computer Science, Univeristy of Münster,
Münster, Germany
{klemms,xjiang,b.risse}@uni-muenster.de

Abstract. We design a two stage image segmentation method, comprising a distance transform estimating neural network and watershed segmentation. It allows segmentation and tracking of colliding objects without any assumptions on object behavior or global object appearance as the proposed machine learning step is trained on contour information only. Our method is also capable of segmenting partially vanishing contact surfaces of visually merged objects. The evaluation is performed on a dataset of collisions of *Drosophila melanogaster* larvae manually labeled with pixel accuracy. The proposed pipeline needs no manual parameter tuning and operates at high frame rates. We provide a detailed evaluation of the neural network design including 1200 trained networks.

1 Introduction

Estimating individual shapes from visually indistinguishable and merged objects is a challenging task in Computer Vision [16]. Particularly biomedical data often comprises multiple nearby objects such as touching cells, tissues or animals. A reliable pixel-wise segmentation of such entities would enable precise shape and motion quantifications but is still an unsolved problem for most circumstances. For example, behavioral studies are limited by our ability to disambiguate the posture of identically looking individuals during collisions preventing quantitative studies of collective behavior and interactions [2].

1.1 Related Work

Segmenting indistinguishable objects over time has gained an increasing attention due to the need to track popular model organisms such as worms and larvae [3,10–12,16]. In general, work on resolving collisions can be divided into two groups: (1) Identity assignments after separation and (2) intra collision segmentation.

The first group of approaches aims on assigning the same identities (IDs) to well separated individuals before and after a collision. The *idTracker* extracts

© Springer Nature Switzerland AG 2019
T. Brox et al. (Eds.): GCPR 2018, LNCS 11269, pp. 422–433, 2019.
https://doi.org/10.1007/978-3-030-12939-2_29

fingerprints of separated objects before a collision and tries to match the fingerprints after the collision using correlograms of color and/or brightness [11]. Recently this approach has been extended using two independent neural networks (NNs) to detect collisions and to identify individuals using convolutional neural networks [13]. Fiaschi *et al.* model collisions as a mass flow of multiple, potentially overlapping, intensities and use weakly supervised structured learning to assign IDs [3].

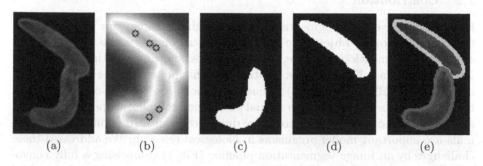

(a)   (b)   (c)   (d)   (e)

Fig. 1. Outline of our proposed method: From a gray level image (a) a neural network estimates a signed distance transform. (b) Local minima in this distance map (blue circles) are used as seeds for a watershed segmentation separating visually merged objects (c)+(d). An overlay of the resultant individual contours on the input image is given in (e). (Color figure online)

Intra collision segmentation algorithms aim to disambiguate the precise posture and motion before, during and after the collision on a frame-by-frame basis. Risse *et al.* have developed FIM^{2c}, an imaging setup utilizing fluorescent labeling to allow decomposition of 2-larvae collisions [12]. Since only situations involving a labeled and an unlabeled animal can be resolved approximately 50% of all collisions can be disambiguated. Michels *et al.* use Reversible Jump Morkov Chain Monte Carlo (RJMCMC) methods to tackle collisions as a filtering problem [10]. Larvae are explicitly modeled based on discrete spine points. While this approach works for collisions of multiple larvae, it is computationally expensive and needs prior information on larval behavior an motion patterns. Yurchenko and Lempitsky propose deep singling out networks (SON), an NN based approach, that generates a fingerprint for the central object in a cluster. This fingerprint is than matched to descriptors of single objects in a database using nearest neighbor search [16]. The basic assumption of this approach is that the objects' behavior and appearance do not change during the collision, which does not hold in many situations. A NN approach for segmenting larvae in real time on low-cost hardware has been proposed by Scherzinger *et al.* [15]. However, their network does not allow labeling individual objects. Bai and Urtasun proposed an NN-based method to segment visually overlapping man-made objects [1]. Despite the different context this approach shares some similarity to our approach: The authors combine an NN which predicts a vector field pointing away from object contours with a second network, producing a quantized 16-level watershed transform. The output of the second network is then segmented using thresholding. This approach needs a previous semantic segmentation and works best for large object while strongly relying on a set of manually tuned parameters. In addition, appearance features such as color are available rendering their approach infeasible for merged indistinguishable objects.

1.2   Contribution

In order to develop a segmentation and tracking strategy for visually indistinguishable moving objects we built our system on the same publicly available datasets mentioned above, namely videos showing multiple interacting Drosophila larvae. These datasets feature four distinct challenges: (1) individual larvae are visually identical; (2) frequent collisions are recognised during high-throughput recordings; (3) these animal go through complex shape deformations; and (4) larval boundaries tend to merge during collisions. In addition, these animals are important model organisms in biological research. We addressed these challenges by an image segmentation pipeline (Fig. 1) comprising a fully convolutional neural network (FCN) based preprocessing stage to estimate a signed distance transform with respect to individual contours. Since the NN is trained on a single image basis there are no assumptions on particular shape deformations of the tracked objects. More importantly, distance maps are independent of the object appearance such as color or texture. Since the size of the training samples is chosen such that the object outline is never completely covered we also achieve invariance with respect to the overall object shape. Furthermore, the distance transform estimation is not limited to the number of objects involved in a collision. Apart from the hyper parameters of the NN, the segmentation pipeline is parameter free. Resultant distance transformations are used in a seed based watershed segmentation to allow collision decomposition with pixel accuracy. We provide an in-depth evaluation of 48 NN topologies trained in a 5-fold double cross validation setting, hence drawing results from over 1200 trained networks. This evaluation includes effects of the recently proposed self normalizing scaled exponential linear units (SELUs) [7].

2   Learn to Predict a Distance Transform

Training an NN on detecting indistinguishable merged objects (e.g. colliding larval contours) directly is a poorly conditioned problem due to highly imbalanced classes and weak gradients. Instead, our training goal is a signed distance transform of the larval contours. Given an intensity image $I(x, y); x, y \in \mathbb{N}; 0 \le x < c; 0 \le y < r$, where r and c is the number of rows and columns respectively let $L = \{l_1, \ldots, l_N\}$ be a set of larvae ($N \ge 2$). Each larva l_i is defined by a set of pixels belonging to the i-th animal. The binary contour image as $C(x, y)$ is then defined by

$$C(x,y) = \begin{cases} 1, & \text{if } \exists i \in 1 \ldots N : (x,y) \in l_i, \text{ and} \\ & \exists (x^*, y^*) \in \mathcal{N}_4((x,y)) : (x^*, y^*) \notin l_i \\ 0, & \text{otherwise} \end{cases} \quad (1)$$

with $\mathcal{N}_4((x,y))$ being the 4-neighborhood of (x,y). The signed distance transform can then be defined as:

$$D(x,y) = \text{sign}(x,y) \cdot \min |(\hat{x}, \hat{y}) - (x,y)|_2 : \quad \forall C(\hat{x}, \hat{y}) = 1 \quad (2)$$

with

$$\text{sign}(x,y) = \begin{cases} -1, & \text{if } \exists i \in 1 \ldots N : (x,y) \in l_i \\ 1, & \text{otherwise} \end{cases} \quad (3)$$

We set a clipping value of ± 25 pixels for the distance transform to reduce negative effects of uncertainties in areas far away from the contours. The value was chosen to be slightly larger than the width of typical larvae to prevent clipping on the inside. To avoid the vanishing gradient problem caused by tanh activations, we limit the normalized distances to values between -0.9 and 0.9 by scaling [9]. Taken together our training goal is defined as:

$$D(x,y) = 0.9 \cdot \max(-1, \min(1, D(x,y)/25)) \quad (4)$$

All NNs are trained to learn a transformation $F(I(x,y)) = \tilde{D}(x,y) \approx D(x,y)$. Although learning the distance transform is much better conditioned than the original contour segmentation task, it is still necessary to improve training convergence by using a weighted Euclidean loss L:

$$L(F) = \sum_{(x,y)} (\tilde{D}(x,y) - D(x,y))^2 \cdot (1 + W(x,y)) \quad (5)$$

Here, the weight function is defined as:

$$\tilde{W}(x,y) = g_3 * C(x,y)$$
$$W(x,y) = \min(1, \tilde{W}(x,y)/P_{99}) \quad (6)$$

where g_σ is a Gaussian kernel with standard deviation σ and size $3\sigma \times 3\sigma$[1] and P_{99} being the 99-th percentile of all values of $\tilde{W}$ for a given sample. In general W assigns additional weights on all contour areas, while clipping to P_{99} reduces the influence of Y-junctions of contours between two colliding larvae.

We train NN topologies, derived from the well-known U-Net architecture [14]. Padding is used in all convolutional layers to keep the size of the feature maps constant. The network topology is parameterized by the number of filter kernels in the first convolutional layers c and the number of pooling layers, which we call depth d. Furthermore, we evaluate if SELU [7] or ReLU activation leads to performance changes during training or inference. Additionally, the influence of

---

[1] Please note that reasonable small values ($1 < \sigma \leq 7$) lead to comparable results.

the activation between the two convolutions at the beginning of each stage is evaluated: The original approach is using an activation between both convolutional layers (called 'double' in the remainder of this document), whereas we also train topologies without these intermediate activation functions. Table 1 shows two detailed examples of the tested topologies and an overview of the number of trainable parameters for each topology.

Table 1. Examples of evaluated network topologies and their trainable parameters. 'c' refers to convolutional, 'd' refers to deconvolutional and 'con' to concatenation layers. The notation $k \times k$ refers to a receptive field size. Values in square brackets show the number of output channels of the respective layer. The table on the right shows an overview of the number of trainable parameters.

parameters: 320 / 9248 / 18496 / 36928 / 73856 / 147584 / 328832 / 8256 / 8224 / 2080 / 33 / 337857

d=2; c=32; relu; single:
c 3x3 [32], c 3x3 [32], relu, pool 2x2, c 3x3 [64], c 3x3 [64], relu, pool 2x2, c 3x3 [128], c 3x3 [128], relu, d 2x2 [64], con [128], c 1x1 [64], relu, d 2x2 [32], con [64], c 1x1 [32], relu, c 1x1 [1], tanh, ∑

d=1; c=16; selu; double:
c 3x3 [16], selu, c 3x3 [16], selu, pool 2x2, c 3x3 [32], selu, c 3x3 [32], selu, ... , d 2x2 [16], con [32], c 1x1 [16], relu, c 1x1 [1], tanh, ∑

parameters: 160 / 2320 / 4640 / 9248 / 2064 / 528 / 17 / 18977

d	c	params
1	8	4817
1	16	18977
1	32	75329
2	8	21297
2	16	84705
2	32	337857
3	8	87025
3	16	347233
3	32	1387201
4	8	349553
4	16	1396577
4	32	5583041

3   Segmenting Objects

A seed based watershed is used for the final segmentation step. From the estimated distance transform $\tilde{D}$, we find a set $\mathcal{S}_{min}$ of local minima, filtered using non-maximum suppression in an area of 5×5 pixels. We also store local maxima of the background in $\mathcal{S}_{max}$ (Fig. 2a). Algorithm 1 shows how masks are created from this seeds.

Assuming that n and k seeds are found within two objects l_a and l_b respectively, there are $n \cdot k$ correct and hence identical masks for l_a, while there are at most $(n-1)$ incorrect (i.e. partial) masks. Figure 2b shows examples of unique masks containing correct (Mask1 and Mask2) and partial masks.

Once we know the correct masks, an ID is assigned to every mask, by choosing the ID with maximum overlap from the previous frame. If that ID is already taken, for example because of over segmentation or crossovers, a new ID is assigned. If and only if no previous frame is available (i.e. the first frame of a sequence) the IDs are taken from the ground truth segmentation.

For evaluation of the segmentation quality two common scores Dice and intersection over union (IoU) ranging from 0 (worst) to 1 (best) are used. Given a ground truth larvae mask m and a segmentation $\tilde{m}$, they are calculated as:

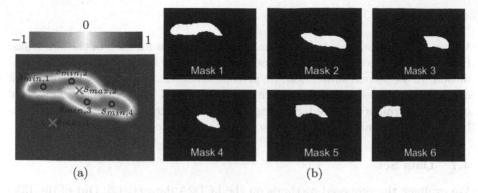

Fig. 2. Example of segmentation results for an exemplary input $\tilde{D}$ containing 2 local minima for each object and 2 background components shown in (a). (b) 12 mask proposals generated from 4 foreground seeds can be aggregated into 6 unique masks. The number of supporting proposals per mask is from top left to bottom right: 4, 4, 1, 1, 1, 1.

```
Data: D̃                                        // distance transform estimate
Sₘᵢₙ                                           // list of filtered local minima
Sₘₐₓ                                           // list of background seeds
Result: list_of_masks
foreach s1 in Sₘᵢₙ do
    foreach s2 in Sₘᵢₙ \ {s1} do
        _, mask1, mask2 = watershed(-abs(D̃), Sₘₐₓ, s1, s2)
        if mask1 in candidates then
            inc_mask_count(mask1)
        else
            candidates.append(mask1)
        // repeat for mask 2
    end
end
sortCandidatesByCount(masks)                    // highest count first
foreach mask in candidates do
    if (!any(mask \ candidates == 0)) then
        list_of_masks.append(mask)
    end
end
```

Algorithm 1. Generation of object masks from seeds in the distance transform estimate. Mask candidates are added only if they contain pixels not covered by any other accepted mask.

$$Dice = \frac{2 \cdot |\tilde{m} \cap m|}{|\tilde{m}| + |m|} \qquad\qquad IoU = \frac{|\tilde{m} \cap m|}{|\tilde{m} \cup m|} \qquad (7)$$

Both scores are calculated for individual masks. Each frame is assigned the average score of all segments found. Each sequence is assigned the average score of all frames. All calculations are done on the test sets, not previously seen by any network. Due to the double cross validation we can provide results averaged over all 60 sequences.

4   Results

Within this section we provide quantitative evaluation for each of the two tasks. First, we describe the preparation of the datasets for training, testing and validation. In the second subsection, we present results on the machine learning task of estimating the distance transform from gray level images. Finally, we show overall performance on the larvae segmentation task by applying the watershed-based segmentation approach to the predicted distance transforms.

4.1   Data Set

We evaluate the proposed methods on the LCD2A dataset [12]. Out of the 1352 sequences, we took 60 sequences (1989 frames), showing collisions between two larvae, and performed manual pixel-wise labeling of the colliding larvae. Each sequence was reduced to consecutive frames in which larvae collide (i.e. contours intersect). To force unique and robust ID assignments after the collision one leading and one trailing frame was added, showing both larvae separated. Hence, the number of frames per sequence varies from 3 to 116.

The available sequences were split into 5 sets, which were chosen such that they contain approximately the same amount of frames, while sequences were never split across sets. The first set was put aside as test set, while the remaining 4 sets were joined and split into 5 sets again, using the same approach. Out of these 5 sets, one set was chosen as validation set and the 4 remaining sets were used to train a network with the given hyperparameters. This facilitates a double 5-fold cross validation.

The statistics presented in the following sections are calculated across the 5-fold double cross validation. Every sequence in the data set can be assigned to one test set. From the 5 networks trained with this sequence in the test set the one with the lowest validation error is chosen as the classifier for calculation of the test loss. Due to the different complexities of collisions and larvae behavior and the small number of collision sequences per validation split (9 to 11), the losses in different validation folds deviate significantly. Table 2 shows those average losses for all test (columns) and validation (rows) folds before normalization to give an idea of the differences in complexity. Hence, for plotting in Fig. 3 all losses are normalized using the mean loss value across all tested networks in this test and validation fold.

Table 2. Average loss values across all tested networks for each cross validation fold.

Validation	Test				
	0	1	2	3	4
0	13.65	6.57	5.79	6.74	7.83
1	14.18	6.09	6.96	6.07	13.79
2	12.16	7.21	13.04	6.69	5.95
3	7.37	47.19	6.95	4.86	5.97
4	48.62	6.11	12.12	6.14	10.21

4.2   Distance Transform

All NN training runs were performed using the same hyper parameters for mini-batch stochastic gradient descent. The Adam optimizer [6] was used with parameters set to default values $\beta_1 = 0.1$, $\beta_2 = 0.999$ and $\epsilon = 10^{-8}$, the minibatch size was set to 25 samples and L_2 weight regularization, a weight decay of $2 \cdot 10^{-4}$ was set. All NNs were trained for 10 epochs. All weights were initialized using the initialization method from [4], biases were initialized to 0. Training was performed on different machines equipped with NVIDIA GTX1080 GPUs using Caffe [5] and Barista [8].

The training data comprised 64×64 pixel windows randomly sampled from each frame. 50 samples per frame were cropped, while ensuring that at least 25% of the window area was covered by larvae. For training, each sample and its mirrored version were rotated by 90, 180, 270° to increase the available training data. No data augmentation was performed for the validation and testing data.

Figure 3 shows the results of the hyper parameter grid search. Subfigure 3a shows that the shallowest networks of depth 1 are not competitive. Networks starting with 32 channels in the first stage are significantly slower to train. The performance gain achieved with this increased model capacity differs across network depth. An increase in model size is best achieved by increasing model depth, as can be seen in Subfig. 3b. Data points also suggest, that deeper networks do no longer profit from a higher number of channels. Subfigure 3c shows a more detailed view of the more powerful topologies. It is evident, that 3 and 4 layer topologies achieve the best performance for a given training speed. Stepping from 16 to 32 channels leads to a slight performance increase for the depth 3 and depth 4 networks, while training time increases significantly. Only the shallow network shows a significant increase in performance for this step. Subfigure 3d shows a detailed evaluation of the tested activation functions. Training speed slows down as expected for double activations, when compared to their single counterparts. This comes at no performance increase for ReLU or SELU and depth 3 or 4 networks. Furthermore, SELU activated networks are always outperformed by their ReLU counterparts.

In the following subsection we investigate whether the average loss functions have an impact on the final segmentation performance. We will focus the evaluation on those designs having a good performance to speed ratio.

4.3   Segmentation

For the evaluation of segmentation performance we focus on those network topologies already identified as best performers in Subsect. 4.2. Hence, we investigate networks of depths 3 and 4 starting with 16 channels. In order to get an idea of the influence of a quality drop in the distance estimation caused by smaller networks, potentially usable in low-cost hardware, we also present results on a smaller network starting with 8 channels and a depth of 3. Finally, we also evaluate the quality and processing time of the pipeline containing largest network. The segmentation is based on the estimated distance transform created by

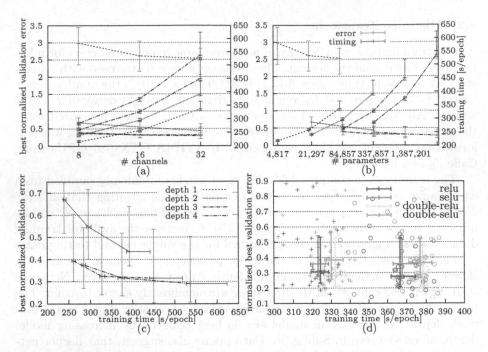

Fig. 3. Results of performance comparison of all tested network topologies as presented in Sect. 2. Error bars show the 0.2, 0.5 and 0.8 percentiles. (a) Best normalized validation error for the trained topologies (red, left axis) and time in seconds needed to train for one epoch (blue, right axis) depending on number of channels in the first layer. (b) Error and timings w.r.t. number of trainable parameters (cf. Table 1). (c) Relation of validation error and training time for networks of depths 2, 3 and 4. This also provides a more detailed view on the performance of the best networks. (d) Comparison of speed and performance for the best performing networks of depth 3 (left cluster, crosses) and 4 (right cluster, circles) and 16 channels in the first layer depending on the kind of activation. (Color figure online)

the best performing net across all validation runs. Performance is measured on testing data using an Intel Core i5-4590 CPU @ 3.30 GHz equipped with 16 GB RAM and a GeForce GTX 1050Ti GPU running Cuda 9.2 and CuDNN.

Our findings are presented in Table 3. Best results in the intersection over union and Dice scores is achieved by networks of depth 4. The differences are, however, only marginal and show that the overall performance does not rely heavily on choosing the correct network. Although there were no notable quality differences on the validation losses, the 'double' activations seem to improve the quality of the distance transform estimate. Overall speed of our method is currently governed by the time needed to calculate the watershed for all possible pairs of seed points. Larger networks, although consuming more time for processing the input, produce smoother results, hence generating less seed points which speeds up the generation of the proposed masks. Compared to the results

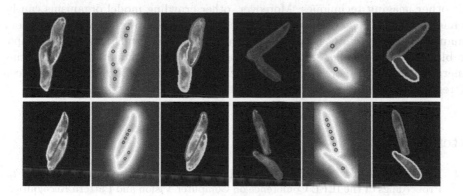

Table 3. Segmentation results on the LCD2A dataset. Average values across all sequences are reported for the intersection over union (IoU) and Dice score. We also report the number of IDs labeled wrong after the collision and the computation time per frame averaged over all sequences. The table on the right shows results on the LCD2A data set as reported in [10].

	IoU	Dice	ID [%]	ms	IoU	Dice	ID [%]	ms
	depth 3; 16 channels				depth 4; 16 channels			
relu	0.89	0.94	**0.0**	87.9	0.88	0.93	3.3	82.5
selu	0.85	0.90	2.3	93.9	0.89	0.94	1.7	93.0
double-relu	0.88	0.93	1.7	82.4	**0.90**	**0.95**	**0.0**	**78.9**
double-selu	0.86	0.91	**0.0**	91.0	0.89	0.94	**0.0**	94.0
c=8	depth 3; 8 channels				depth 4; 32 channels			
relu	0.84	0.89	6.7	93.2	0.89	0.94	1.7	89.0
selu	0.83	0.89	1.7	102.6	0.89	0.94	**0.0**	99.4
double-relu	0.84	0.89	5.0	90.5	0.87	0.92	**0.0**	88.0
double-selu	0.82	0.87	11.7	97.1	0.87	0.92	1.7	101.1

RJMCMC results

samples	ID [%]	ms
300	2.3	24
1000	1.6	87
1500	1.2	142

Fig. 4. Example distance transform estimates and segmentations

presented in [10], our method achieves better ID preservation at comparable or even faster speed.

5   Conclusion

We have presented and evaluated a two stage method, combining a neural network for estimation of a signed distance transform and classical seed-based watershed segmentation to faithfully segment merged objects. By learning the distance transformation rather than visually discriminative features such as color we achieve an appearance invariant pixel classification which can separate visually indistinguishable objects. Besides the parameters explained in Sect. 2, which can be derived from object properties and are robust to reasonable changes, the proposed pipeline has no manually tuned parameters. We furthermore evaluated the properties of the recently proposed self normalizing scaled exponential linear units based on training more than 1200 networks to identify the optimal neural network topology for this task. We could show that for none of the tested topologies SELU activated networks outperformed ReLU activation. Furthermore, the ID preservation properties of our method are robust with respect to the chosen topology as soon as the model reaches a certain threshold of complexity (350k trainable parameters). The usability was demonstrated on segmenting interacting Drosophila larvae which is a popular model organisms in Biology. Our results outperform the state-of-the-art approaches in both accuracy and computational time. Additionally, the proposed method provides pixel-wise segmentation for every frame in a collision sequence without the need for an object model. Figure 4 shows examples of the resulting segmentation for qualitative evaluation.

In the future we will extract the training data for the deep distance transform automatically by using the FIM^{2c} technique which can be used to generate segmentations of labeled and unlabeled animals [12]. The resultant network can then be used to resolve the remaining ambiguous collisions and will generalize to other imaging techniques. Moreover, other crawling model organisms can be imaged via FIM^{2c} so that our pipeline can be applied to other animals without manual labeling effort. Based on the results of [15], which builds on comparable but much smaller network topologies, we are confident that segmenting merged objects in more demanding environments with lower contrast between foreground and background and lower resolution is also possible.

References

1. Bai, M., Urtasun, R.: Deep watershed transform for instance segmentation. In: Proceedings of the IEEE Conference on Computer Vision and Pattern Recognition, pp. 2858–2866 (2017). https://doi.org/10.1109/CVPR.2017.305
2. Dell, A.I., et al.: Automated image-based tracking and its application in ecology. Trends Ecol. Evol. **29**(7), 417–428 (2014). https://doi.org/10.1016/j.tree.2014.05.004
3. Fiaschi, L., et al.: Tracking indistinguishable translucent objects over time using weakly supervised structured learning. In: Proceedings of the IEEE Conference on Computer Vision and Pattern Recognition, pp. 2736–2743 (2014). https://doi.org/10.1109/CVPR.2014.356
4. Glorot, X., Bengio, Y.: Understanding the difficulty of training deep feedforward neural networks. In: Proceedings of the 13th International Conference on Artificial Intelligence and Statistics, pp. 249–256 (2010)
5. Jia, Y., et al.: Caffe: Convolutional architecture for fast feature embedding. CoRR abs/1408.5093 (2014)
6. Kingma, D.P., Ba, J.: Adam: a method for stochastic optimization. CoRR abs/1412.6980 (2014)
7. Klambauer, G., Unterthiner, T., Mayr, A., Hochreiter, S.: Self-normalizing neural networks. In: Proceedings of the 30th Annual Conference on Neural Information Processing Systems, pp. 972–981 (2017)
8. Klemm, S., Scherzinger, A., Drees, D., Jiang, X.: Barista - a graphical tool for designing and training deep neural networks. CoRR abs/1802.04626 (2018)

9. LeCun, Y., Bottou, L., Orr, G.B., Müller, K.: Efficient backprop. In: Montavon, G., Orr, G.B., Müller, K. (eds.) Neural Networks: Tricks of the Trade. Lecture Notes in Computer Science, vol. 7700, 2nd edn, pp. 9–48. Springer, Heidelberg (2012). https://doi.org/10.1007/978-3-642-35289-8_3

10. Michels, T., Berh, D., Jiang, X.: An RJMCMC-based method for tracking and resolving collisions of drosophila larvae. IEEE/ACM Trans. Comput. Biol. Bioinform. (2017). https://doi.org/10.1109/TCBB.2017.2779141

11. Pérez-Escudero, A., Vicente-Page, J., Hinz, R.C., Arganda, S., de Polavieja, G.G.: idTracker: tracking individuals in a group by automatic identification of unmarked animals. Nat. Methods 11, (2014). https://doi.org/10.1038/nmeth.2994

12. Risse, B., Otto, N., Berh, D., Jiang, X., Kiel, M., Klämbt, C.: FIM^{2c}: multicolor, multipurpose imaging system to manipulate and analyze animal behavior. IEEE Trans. Biomed. Eng. 64(3), 610–620 (2017). https://doi.org/10.1109/TBME.2016.2570598

13. Romero-Ferrero, F., Bergomi, M.G., Hinz, R., Heras, F.J.H., de Polavieja, G.G.: idtracker.ai: tracking all individuals in large collectives of unmarked animals. CoRR abs/1803.04351 (2018)

14. Ronneberger, O., Fischer, P., Brox, T.: U-Net: convolutional networks for biomedical image segmentation. In: Proceedings of the 18th International Conference on Medical Image Computing and Computer-Assisted Intervention, pp. 234–241 (2015). https://doi.org/10.1007/978-3-319-24574-4_28

15. Scherzinger, A., Klemm, S., Berh, D., Jiang, X.: CNN-based background subtraction for long-term in-vial FIM imaging. In: Proceedings of the 17th International Conference on Computer Analysis of Images and Patterns, pp. 359–371 (2017). https://doi.org/10.1007/978-3-319-64689-3_29

16. Yurchenko, V., Lempitsky, V.S.: Parsing images of overlapping organisms with deep singling-out networks. In: Proceedings of the IEEE Conference on Computer Vision and Pattern Recognition, pp. 4752–4760 (2017). https://doi.org/10.1109/CVPR.2017.505

Multi-class Cell Segmentation Using CNNs with F_1-measure Loss Function

Aaron Scherzinger[1], Philipp Hugenroth[1], Marike Rüder[2], Sven Bogdan[2], and Xiaoyi Jiang[1(✉)]

[1] Faculty of Mathematics and Computer Science, University of Münster, Münster, Germany
xjiang@uni-muenster.de
[2] Institute for Physiology and Pathophysiology, Department of Molecular Cell Physiology, Philipps-University Marburg, Marburg, Germany

Abstract. Cell segmentation is one of the fundamental problems in biomedical image processing as it is often mandatory for the quantitative analysis of biological processes. Sometimes, a binary segmentation of the cells is not sufficient, for instance if biologists are interested in the appearance of specific cell parts. Such a setting requires multiple foreground classes, which can significantly increase the complexity of the segmentation task. This is especially the case if very fine structures need to be detected. Here, we propose a method for multi-class segmentation of Drosophila macrophages in in-vivo fluorescence microscopy images to segment complex cell structures such as the lamellipodium and filopodia. Our approach is based on a convolutional neural network, more specifically the U-net architecture. The network is trained using a loss function based on the F_1-measure which we have extended for multi-class scenarios to account for class imbalances in the image data. We compare the F_1-measure loss function to a weighted cross entropy loss and show that the CNN outperforms other segmentation approaches.

Keywords: CNN · F_1-measure · Loss function · Cell segmentation

1 Introduction

In neurobiology, it is often of interest to study specific cells and their behavior *in-vivo*, i.e., in the living organism, and compare different genotypes of a model organism in this regard. Usually, such an analysis requires the detection and segmentation of individual cells as a pre-processing step to allow for quantification, tracking, or a more in-depth inspection of the cells' properties. Due to the increasing amount of acquired image data and the complexity of this task, it is not feasible to perform the segmentation procedure manually. Automated cell segmentation is thus one of the fundamental tasks in biomedical image processing. Here, we consider the analysis of Drosophila macrophages [26] which are recorded in-vivo using *Spinning Disk Confocal Microscopy* (SDCM).

© Springer Nature Switzerland AG 2019
T. Brox et al. (Eds.): GCPR 2018, LNCS 11269, pp. 434–446, 2019.
https://doi.org/10.1007/978-3-030-12939-2_30

In order to allow in-vivo imaging of the structures of interest, cells are genetically marked using GFP (*green fluorescent protein*). A 2D image is obtained from the microscopy stack using maximum intensity projection (MIP). An example of such an image is shown in Fig. 1a.

Biologists are interested in the migration behavior of the cells as well as their morphology, i.e., shape, as both are closely related [16, 24]. In this specific case, it is desirable not only to compute a foreground segmentation, i.e., distinguish cells from the background, but also differentiate between different parts of each individual cell. In order to do so, it is necessary to perform a multi-class segmentation. More specifically, the goal is to segment four classes: background as well as *cell body, lamellipodium* (leaf-like structures), and *filopodia* (finger-like structures) of the cells (see Fig. 1b). Such a multi-class segmentation task is particularly challenging, since fluorescence intensity can greatly vary among objects, i.e., different cells, but also within a single cell or part of a cell, especially when considering the lamellipodium (see Fig. 1). Moreover, distinguishing between the filopodia and lamellipodium pixel-wise is often difficult, even for domain experts.

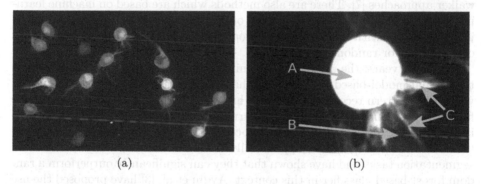

(a)   (b)

Fig. 1. Examples of the input images. (a) SDCM image of *in-vivo* wildtype Drosophila macrophages which have been marked using GFP. (b) Magnified illustration of a single cell. Brightness and contrast have been enhanced for better clarity. Arrows exemplarily mark the three foreground classes relevant for the segmentation: (A) Cell body, (B) Lamellipodium, and (C) Filopodia. (Color figure online)

In recent years, deep learning with neural networks has been shown to be a powerful tool in many different vision applications, often surpassing traditional model-based approaches by a large margin. Consequently, deep learning has also become popular for biomedical image processing, especially when considering cell segmentation tasks (see Sect. 2). Here, we apply a well-established architecture for biomedical segmentation, the U-net [23], as a basis for our segmentation. In order to efficiently train the network with our images, where the class occurences are largely imbalanced, we apply a multi-class version of the F_1-measure loss function that has previously been shown to work well for unbalanced binary classification tasks in the context of biomedical image segmentation [19, 27].

The remainder of this paper is structured as follows. Section 2 will provide a brief overview of related work regarding cell segmentation and the use of deep learning with neural networks in this context. Section 3 will describe the methodology used for the segmentation and will introduce a multi-class version of the F_1-measure loss function. Section 4 will then present the results of a quantitative evaluation using the described methods. Moreover, the network architecture and loss function will be compared against traditional unsupervised segmentation approaches as well as a semi-automated random walker segmentation. Finally, Sect. 5 concludes the paper and gives an outlook on potential future work.

2   Related Work

The diversity of imaging modalities, tissues, and cell types has led to a vast amount of proposed methods for cell segmentation tasks. Traditional image processing approaches that have been applied to cell segmentation range from thresholding [11], watershed [21], level set active contours [5,8], region growing [4], and extremal regions [13] to semi-automated methods such as random walker approaches [7]. There are also methods which are based on machine learning by performing pixel (or, in the case of 3D images, voxel) classification, often in combination with model-based approaches. Such techniques include the use of SVMs [18] or random forests [12].

In recent years, the use of deep learning with neural networks has surpassed traditional model-based methods and handcrafted features in many computer vision and pattern recognition tasks. A historical review of deep learning can be found in [28]. Unsurprisingly, deep learning techniques have also been applied in the context of biomedical image processing and, in particular, cell segmentation. Valen et al. [29] have applied fully convolutional neural networks to cell segmentation tasks and have shown that they can significantly outperform a random forest-based classifier in this context. Aydin et al. [3] have proposed the use of convolutional networks for yeast cell segmentation in fluorescence microscopy images. Ronneberger et al. [23] have proposed the U-net, a fully convolutional neural networks architecture which is specifically tailored towards segmentation tasks in biomedical images. Their network won the cell tracking challenge at ISBI 2015. Sadanandan et al. [25] have also applied a U-net architecture to segment cells in different microscopy imaging modalities. Akram et al. [1] have used neural networks for region proposals of cells and later extended their approach by using an additional fully convolutional network for a pixel-wise segmentation based on the proposed bounding boxes [2]. Raza et al. [22] proposed another neural network architecture, the MIMO-net, for cell segmentation. The U-net architecture was also extended to the case of 3D image segmentation by Milletari et al. [19] and Cicek et al. [10]. The latter architecture was applied to 3D cell segmentation in fluorescence microscopy images similar to our images by Castilla et al. [9]. However, all of the above cases do not distinguish between different parts of the individual cells, i.e., only provide a foreground segmentation of the cells (although some networks provide different foreground classes in the segmentation map for a classification into different cell classes).

3 Methods

3.1 Data

As mentioned before, from an image processing point of view, the data presents several challenges. Fluorescence intensity distributions vary between different regions of an image, but also between individual cells, even when they are neighboring objects in the image. Some cells are relatively bright while others are difficult to distinguish from the background signal. Moreover, this is not only a problem regarding the separation of foreground and background, but translates to the individual foreground classes as well. In some cells the cell body class is brighter than the lamellipodium in others, but when comparing it to different cells, it might have lower intensity. This is also problematic as there are no clear boundaries between the different foreground classes in a single cell, especially between filopodia and lamellipodium. The latter one is particularly difficult to segment as it often has very low fluorescence intensity. All of these problems illustrate that a segmentation solely based on intensity values without any (at least local) context, e.g., a simple thresholding method, will not perform well (see Sect. 4). Furthermore, some of the structures of interest are blurry, which might be partially due to the used imaging technique with a fluorescence signal, and partially due to the cells not being in the focal plane of the microscope. This is especially problematic for the very fine structures of the filopodia.

Another problem is the fact that the lamellipodium and filopodia are difficult (and sometimes impossible) to clearly distinguish, even for domain experts (see Fig. 1b and Fig. 2) and that fine structures like filopodia are often even challenging to visualize [6]. This makes it difficult to provide a ground truth labeling and can potentially also hamper the evaluation of the achieved segmentation results if the ground truth labeling is not reliable. However, it is relatively easy to distinguish the cell body from the two other foreground classes. In discussions with domain experts, it was thus decided to optionally merge the filopodia and lamellipodium classes to a single *protrusion* class, i.e., try to solve a three-class problem instead of a four-class problem. Training of the classifier and evaluation was then performed for the three-class as well as the four-class problem setting.

For training and validation, 90 images with a resolution of 960×608 pixels were manually labeled to obtain pixel-wise ground truth information for all four classes. For the three-class version, the labels of lamellipodium and filopodia were merged afterwards to obtain a labeling of the same images. Figure 2 depicts an example of an original image along with its manual ground truth labeling.

In a pre-processing step, the fluorescence intensities of each individual image were normalized to mean 0 and standard deviation 1. To increase the amount of available training data, data augmentation was applied in multiple ways. First, all images were flipped vertically and both the original image as well as the flipped image were rotated by $90°$, $180°$, and $270°$. This provided 8 times the training data. Moreover, we performed elastic deformation on the images for further increasing the amount of available training images. Afterwards, the images were decomposed into tiles of 428×428. It should be noted that the

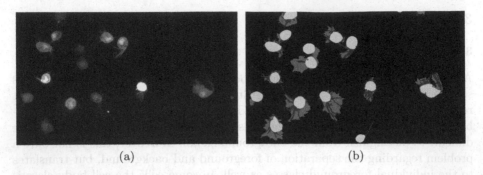

(a)   (b)

Fig. 2. Example of the labeling for the four classes. (a) Original image (brightness and contrast have been enhanced for clarity). (b) Manual ground truth labeling for background (black), cell body (green), lamellipodium (red), and filopodia (blue). Note that some regions, in particular the lamellipodium, are relatively dark in the original image. (Color figure online)

border of the input images is lost in the output segmentation maps due to the receptive field of the network, where each 3×3 convolutional layer reduces the size of the map by one border pixel on each side of the image. When using an input size of 428×428 pixels, the output segmentation maps thus comprise the inner area of 244×244 pixels. Prior to computing the tiles of each image, it is thus padded by mirroring the border so that the entire area of the original image can be used as ground truth information for training. After tiling, all tiles are removed that contain only pixels of one class (e.g., only background pixels). The available data was randomly split into training and validation data in a ratio of 4:1 and that data augmentation was only applied to the training data. In total, this procedure resulted in a training set of 12,497 image tiles (including the data augmentation) and a validation set of 199 tiles.

3.2   Net Architecture and Loss Function

It has already been mentioned that the U-net architecture proposed by Ronneberger et al. [23] performs well on biomedical images, especially in the context of cell segmentation. We therefore utilize this architecture for the multi-class segmentation. In general, the U-net is a convolutional neural net, more specifically a fully convolutional net (FCN), architecture which is designed to perform a pixel-wise classification and is thus suitable for image segmentation tasks. For the most part, the U-net is structured like a standard FCN. It contains a contracting path which consists of convolutional layers in combination with max pooling operations. After the contracting part, i.e., reaching the bottleneck which is given by the lowest resolution created by the pooling operations, the expansion path of the network starts, which uses de-convolution operations to upsample the data until reaching the original image resolution. The novelty that was introduced by the U-net is the use of shortcuts from the pre-bottleneck layers to the post-bottleneck layers that merge detailed local information (from the contraction part) with large-scale global information (from the expansion part). This is done by using concatenation operations at each resolution level that append the activation maps of the high-resolution contraction path to the upsampled maps present in the expansion path. By performing an additional convolution after the concatenation, the high-resolution (but more low-level) features which are the results of the first convolutional operations are combined with the upsampled output. This improves the localization of the features and thus the segmentation quality. For more details on the U-net, please refer to [23].

When examining Fig. 2 it becomes apparent that the classes in the image data are highly imbalanced. This refers to the background-to-foreground ratio when considering a binary segmentation task, but even more so when differentiating between the three foreground classes. In particular, pixels that belong to the filopodia and lamellipodium classes occur significantly less often than the cell body or the background class. For (imbalanced) binary classification problems with a positive (less common) and a negative (more common) class, the F_1-measure is a well-established quality measure to avoid the bias that is present in the accuracy. This can be utilized by applying the F_1-measure as the loss function of a neural network, directly optimizing the quality measure used in the evaluation. It has previously been shown that using the F_1-measure as a loss function shows good results for training neural networks on binary image segmentation tasks with unbalanced class occurrences in a biomedical context [19,27]. Given a binary segmentation S and a ground truth labeling G with n pixels, the number of *true positives* (TP) is given by the number of foreground pixels $s_i \in S, 0 \leq i < n$, which are also labeled as foreground in G, i.e., for which holds that $s_i = 1 = g_i$, where $g_i \in G$ is the corresponding pixel in G. Consequently, the number of *false positives* (FP) corresponds to the number of pixels $s_i \in S$ for which $s_i = 1 \wedge g_i = 0$, and the number of *false negatives* (FN) is given by the number of pixels $s_i \in S$ for which $s_i = 0 \wedge g_i = 1$. The two metrics *Precision* (PR), sometimes also called *Confidence*, and *Recall* (RC), sometimes also referred to as *Sensitivity*, can be defined on the basis of TP, FP, and FN:

$$PR = \frac{TP}{TP + FP} \qquad RC = \frac{TP}{TP + FN} \tag{1}$$

The F_1-measure is then given by the harmonic mean between PR and RC:

$$F_1 = 2 \cdot \frac{PR \cdot RC}{PR + RC} \tag{2}$$

When using a network with a softmax activation function in the output layer, the output map consists of a probability for each pixel, i.e., a value in the range $[0, 1]$, instead of a binary output. To apply the F_1-measure in such a scenario with continous probability outputs, the aforementioned definitions have to be extended. For a probability map O with $o_i \in O$, $0 \leq i < n$, $0 \leq o_i \leq 1$ instead of a binary segmentation S the TP, FP, and FN can be computed as follows:

$$TP = \sum_{i=0}^{n-1} o_i \cdot g_i \qquad FP = \sum_{i=0}^{n-1} o_i \cdot (1 - g_i) \qquad FN = \sum_{i=0}^{n-1} (1 - o_i) \cdot g_i \tag{3}$$

The F_1-measure in Eq. 2 can then also be expressed in terms of the output probabilities o_i and ground truth information g_i for all of the pixels:

$$F_1 = 2 \cdot \frac{PR \cdot RC}{PR + RC} = 2 \cdot \frac{\sum_{i=0}^{n-1} (o_i \cdot g_i)}{\sum_{i=0}^{n-1} (o_i + g_i)} \tag{4}$$

It should be noted that in its more general form (which is called F_β-measure), the equation contains an additional parameter β which can be understood as a weighting factor for Precision and Recall within the score [20]. Here, we set $\beta = 1$ which yields the most commonly applied F_1-measure.

In order to apply the F_1-measure as the loss function for the backpropagation algorithm, it is necessary to compute the gradient given by the partial derivatives with respect to o_j, $0 \leq j < n$, as follows:

$$\frac{\partial F_1}{\partial o_j} = 2 \cdot \frac{g_j \cdot \sum_{i=0}^{n-1} (o_i + g_i) - \sum_{i=0}^{n-1} (o_i \cdot g_i)}{\left[\sum_{i=0}^{n-1} (o_i + g_i)\right]^2} \tag{5}$$

The definition of the F_1-measure loss function given above is applicable in binary classification situations, as the outputs o_i of the network are real-valued probabilities in the range $[0, 1]$ and the ground truth values g_i are either 0 or 1. However, in our scenario the loss needs to take into account more than two classes. For a classification problem with k classes, the output o_i of the network obtained from the softmax activation function is thus a k-dimensional vector, containing a class probability $o_{i,c}$ for each class $c, 0 \leq c < k$. The labels g_i are then given as integer labels for the corresponding class of a pixel, i.e., $g_i \in \mathbb{N}_0, 0 \leq g_i < k$. To extend the loss function to the case of multi-class segmentation, we compute the F_1-measure in a one-vs-all fashion for each individual class (i.e., background, cell body, lamellipodium, and filopodia). We convert the integer class label $g_i, 0 \leq g_i < k$ of pixel i in the ground truth to a one-hot encoding in the form of a k-dimensional vector $\tilde{g}_i$ where all entries are 0 except for the entry that corresponds to the class index of g_i, i.e., $\tilde{g}_{i,j} = 1$ and $\tilde{g}_{i,l,l \neq j} = 0$ for $j = g_i$. We then use output c of the softmax activation function, i.e., the value $o_{i,c}$, to obtain the class probability for class c and compare it to entry c in the ground truth vector $\tilde{g}$, i.e., we compare $o_{i,c}$ to $\tilde{g}_{i,c}$ using Eq. 4. In this way, we compute the F_1-measure loss for each class c separately. The gradient for this class can be calculated accordingly using Eq. 5. The gradients are then averaged over the classes for the backpropagation step.

As an alternative to the multi-class version of the F_1-measure loss function, we have also used the same network architecture and training data with a weighted cross entropy loss function as proposed by Ronneberger et al. [23]. Here, a weight map is utilized for weighting the loss of the individual pixels in order to balance the frequency of the classes in the training data. For details on computing the weight maps and individual class weights, please refer to the description provided in [23].

For training and evaluating the nets, we used the Caffe library [14] in combination with the graphical deep learning tool Barista [15]. The Caffe library was modified to contain the weighted cross entropy loss layer proposed by Ronneberger et al. [23]. The multi-class F_1-measure loss layer was implemented as a custom Python layer. All nets were trained on a machine with an Intel Xeon E5-2695 CPU with 18 physical cores (36 logical cores) at 2.1 GHz (up to 3.3 GHz), 128 GB of main memory, and two NVIDIA Titan X Pascal graphics cards with 12 GB of graphics memory each. Batch size was set to 5 tiles per mini-batch for all training procedures. The networks were trained for 32 epochs.

4   Evaluation and Results

This section presents the results that have been achieved on both the three-class and the four-class version of the segmentation. We have evaluated both the F_1-measure and the weighted cross entropy loss function on both datasets. Moreover, we have applied several baseline methods: Otsu's thresholding, K-means clustering, and Gaussian mixture models (GMM). All of these algorithms are based on the image intensities of individual pixels and are unsupervised, i.e., they do not depend on the ground truth data and were computed on a per-image basis. For GMM, the Gaussian distributions were fitted to the distribution of intensities in the image using Expectation Maximization. In the evaluation, the detected classes in each image are assigned to the ground truth classes in the way that maximizes the overall result for this method, i.e., we assign the classes detected by the segmentation to the classes in the ground truth in an optimal way by testing all possible combinations. Additionally, a semi-automated random walker with a seed generation extension [7] has been applied to the three-class version data. The initial seeds for the random walker were obtained by a sparse labeling performed by a domain expert, i.e., a few user scribbles for each of the classes (for details see [7]). Results for the three-class dataset are listed in Table 1 and results for the four-class dataset are listed in Table 2.

The quantitative results show that, unsurprisingly, the U-net is superior to all baseline methods as well as the semi-automated random walker method (despite its use of manual annotations as initial seeds). While Otsu's thresholding method performs considerably well regarding the background and cell body classes, it is not able to perform a satisfying segmentation of the protrusion class in the three-class data, and even more so the two separate classes in the four-class version of the image data. While K-means clustering of intensity values and GMM share this problem with the finer structures, both methods additionally have more problems to recognize the cell body class. In the three-class data, the semi-automated random walker segmentation provides better results than the baseline methods, but is still significantly outperformed by the neural networks when considering the protrusion class.

Table 1. Results for the three-class dataset. The U-net has been used with the weighted cross entropy (listed as WC) as well as the F_1-measure (listed as F_1) loss function. Listed results are the F_1-measures for each individual class (in a one-vs.-all fashion) as well as the overall result over all classes.

Method	Background	Cell body	Protrusion	Overall
Otsu	0.948	0.826	0.293	0.894
K-means	0.912	0.559	0.204	0.827
GMM	0.919	0.592	0.454	0.840
Random walker	0.975	0.848	0.438	0.943
U-net WC	**0.980**	0.934	**0.852**	**0.961**
U-net F_1	0.974	**0.935**	0.810	0.950

Table 2. Results for the four-class dataset. The U-net has been used with the weighted cross entropy (listed as WC) as well as the F_1-measure (listed as F_1) loss function. Listed results are the F_1-measures for each individual class (in a one-vs.-all fashion) as well as the overall result over all classes.

Method	Backgr.	Cell body	Lamellip.	Filop.	Overall
Otsu	0.952	0.826	0.211	0.291	0.889
K-means	0.903	0.507	0.144	0.265	0.799
GMM	0.907	0.573	0.354	0.268	0.802
U-net WC	0.978	0.923	**0.664**	0.634	0.935
U-net F_1	**0.979**	**0.929**	0.648	**0.641**	**0.936**

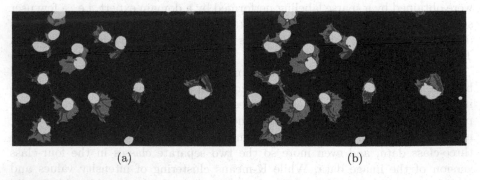

(a)   (b)

Fig. 3. Example illustrating the segmentation quality of the U-net trained with the F_1-measure loss function on the four-class version of the original image depicted in Fig. 2. (a) Ground truth labeling. (b) Segmentation results obtained from the classifier (without applying any post-processing).

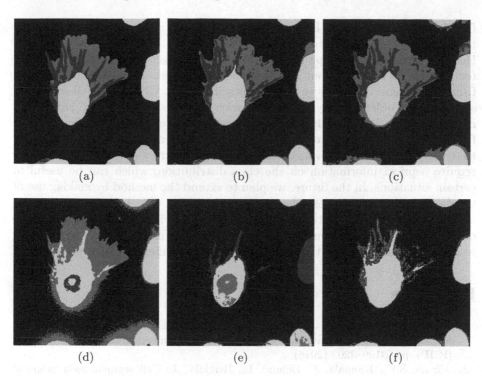

Fig. 4. Exemplary results for a single image tile from the validation set. (a) Ground truth labeling. (b) U-net with F_1-measure loss function. (c) U-net with weighted cross entropy. (d) GMM. (e) K-means. (f) Otsu.

Regarding the two different loss functions used with the U-net, results are relatively similar. The weighted cross entropy seems to perform slightly better on the three-class dataset, while the F_1-measure loss function yields slightly better results for the four-class dataset. The segmentation result for the image depicted in Fig. 2 using the U-net with the F_1-measure loss function is shown in Fig. 3. Exemplary results of all methods tested on the four-class dataset are shown for a single image tile in Fig. 4.

Overall, the results suggest that both loss functions perform similar to each other. The advantage of the F_1-measure is that it uses the class occurrences within a single mini-batch instead of requiring the *a priori* information about the class frequencies in the training set that are necessary for the weighted cross entropy. Since the F_1-measure still performs on par with the weighted cross entropy, it might be preferable in situations where information about the entire training set is not yet available, e.g., when using techniques such as pseudo-labeling [17] with large amounts of unlabeled data for which the class frequencies cannot necessarily be estimated from the training samples, or when more balanced data is used in the labeled training data, but a more unbalanced situation is given in the unlabeled data.

5   Conclusion and Future Work

Here, we have shown the applicability of a well-established neural network architecture, the U-net, to a multi-class segmentation task of cell images obtained from fluorescence microscopy. The results show that CNNs are well-suited for solving this problem as they outperform other methods such as a semi-automated random walker. We have also used the U-net with a multi-class F_1-measure loss function which we compared to a weighted cross entropy loss. Results show that the F_1-measure performs on par the weighted cross entropy, but does not require a priori information on the class distribution, which can be useful in certain situations. In the future, we plan to extend the method by making use of unlabeled images to increase the amount of training data by applying pseudo-labeling [17]. Moreover, tracking the cells and providing a meaningful shape quantification could offer new challenging tasks for machine learning, e.g., by using the extracted shape to automatically classify different genotypes.

References

1. Akram, S.U., Kannala, J., Eklund, L., Heikkilä, J.: Cell proposal network for microscopy image analysis. In: IEEE International Conference on Image Processing (ICIP), pp. 3199–3203 (2016)
2. Akram, S.U., Kannala, J., Eklund, L., Heikkilä, J.: Cell segmentation proposal network for microscopy image analysis. In: Proceedings of Deep Learning and Data Labeling for Medical Applications, pp. 21–29 (2016)
3. Aydin, A.S., Dubey, A., Dovrat, D., Aharoni, A., Shilkrot, R.: CNN based yeast cell segmentation in multi-modal fluorescent microscopy data. In: IEEE Conference on Computer Vision and Pattern Recognition (CVPR) Workshops, pp. 753–759 (2017)
4. Barry, D.J., Durkin, C.H., Abella, J.V., Way, M.: Open source software for quantification of cell migration, protrusions, and fluorescence intensities. J. Cell Biol. **209**(1), 163–180 (2015)
5. Bergeest, J., Rohr, K.: Efficient globally optimal segmentation of cells in fluorescence microscopy images using level sets and convex energy functionals. Med. Image Anal. **16**(7), 1436–1444 (2012)
6. Bernier-Latmani, J., Petrova, T.V.: High-resolution 3D analysis of mouse small-intestinal stroma. Nat. Protoc. **119**(9), 1617–1629 (2016)
7. Bian, A., Scherzinger, A., Jiang, X.: An enhanced multi-label random walk for biomedical image segmentation using statistical seed generation. In: Proceedings of International Conference on Advanced Concepts for Intelligent Vision Systems (ACIVS), pp. 748–760 (2017)
8. Bredies, K., Wolinski, H.: An active-contour based algorithm for the automated segmentation of dense yeast populations on transmission microscopy images. Comput. Vis. Sci. **14**(7), 341–352 (2011)
9. Castilla, C., Maska, M., Sorokin, D.V., Meijering, E., de Solorzano, C.O.: Segmentation of actin-stained 3D fluorescent cells with filopodial protrusions using convolutional neural networks. In: International Symposium on Biomedical Imaging (ISBI), pp. 413–417 (2018)

10. Çiçek, Ö., Abdulkadir, A., Lienkamp, S.S., Brox, T., Ronneberger, O.: 3D U-Net: learning dense volumetric segmentation from sparse annotation. In: Proceedings of Medical Image Computing and Computer-Assisted Intervention (MICCAI), Part II, pp. 424–432 (2016)
11. Espinoza, E., Martinez, G., Frerichs, J., Scheper, T.: Cell cluster segmentation based on global and local thresholding for in-situ microscopy. In: Proceedings of IEEE International Symposium on Biomedical Imaging: From Nano to Macro, pp. 542–545 (2006)
12. Essa, E., Xie, X., Errington, R.J., White, N.S.: A multi-stage random forest classifier for phase contrast cell segmentation. In: Proceedings of International Conference of the IEEE Engineering in Medicine and Biology Society (EMBC), pp. 3865–3868 (2015)
13. Hilsenbeck, O., et al.: FastER: a user-friendly tool for ultrafast and robust cell segmentation in large-scale microscopy. Bioinformatics **33**(13), 2020–2028 (2017)
14. Jia, Y., et al.: Caffe: convolutional architecture for fast feature embedding. In: Proceedings of ACM International Conference on Multimedia (MM), pp. 675–678 (2014)
15. Klemm, S., Scherzinger, A., Drees, D., Jiang, X.: Barista - a graphical tool for designing and training deep neural networks. CoRR abs/1802.04626 (2018). http://arxiv.org/abs/1802.04626
16. Lammel, U., et al.: The drosophila FHOD1-like formin Knittrig acts through Rok to promote stress fiber formation and directed macrophage migration during the cellular immune response. Development **14**(1), 1366–1380 (2014)
17. Lee, D.H.: Pseudo-label: The simple and efficient semi-supervised learning method for deep neural networks. In: ICML Workshop: Challenges in Representation Learning (WREPL) (2013)
18. Marcuzzo, M., Quelhas, P., Campilho, A., Mendonça, A.M., Campilho, A.: Automated arabidopsis plant root cell segmentation based on SVM classification and region merging. Comput. Biol. Med. **39**(9), 785–793 (2009)
19. Milletari, F., Navab, N., Ahmadi, S.: V-Net: fully convolutional neural networks for volumetric medical image segmentation. In: International Conference on 3D Vision (3DV), pp. 565–571 (2016)
20. Pastor-Pellicer, J., Zamora-Martínez, F., Boquera, S.E., Bleda, M.J.C.: F-measure as the error function to train neural networks. In: Proceedings of International Work-Conference on Artificial Neural Networks (IWANN), Part I, pp. 376–384 (2013)
21. Pinidiyaarachchi, A., Wählby, C.: Seeded watersheds for combined segmentation and tracking of cells. In: Roli, F., Vitulano, S. (eds.) Proceedings of Image Analysis and Processing (ICIAP), pp. 336–343 (2005)
22. Raza, S., Cheung, L., Epstein, D.B.A., Pelengaris, S., Khan, M., Rajpoot, N.M.: Mimo-net: a multi-input multi-output convolutional neural network for cell segmentation in fluorescence microscopy images. In: Proceedings of IEEE International Symposium on Biomedical Imaging (ISBI), pp. 337–340 (2017)
23. Ronneberger, O., Fischer, P., Brox, T.: U-Net: convolutional networks for biomedical image segmentation. In: Proceedings of Medical Image Computing and Computer-Assisted Intervention (MICCAI), Part III, pp. 234–241 (2015)
24. Rüder, M., Nagel, B.M., Bogdan, S.: Analysis of cell shape and cell migration of *Drosophila* macrophages in vivo. In: Gautreau, A. (ed.) Cell Migration. MMB, vol. 1749, pp. 227–238. Springer, New York (2018). https://doi.org/10.1007/978-1-4939-7701-7_17

25. Sadanandan, S.K., Ranefall, P., Wählby, C.: Feature augmented deep neural networks for segmentation of cells. In: Proceedings of European Conference on Computer Vision (ECCV) Workshops, Part I, pp. 231–243 (2016)
26. Sander, M., Squarr, A.J., Risse, B., Jiang, X., Bogdan, S.: Drosophila pupal macrophages - a versatile tool for combined ex vivo and in vivo imaging of actin dynamics at high resolution. Eur. J. Cell Biol. **92**(10–11), 349–354 (2013)
27. Scherzinger, A., Klemm, S., Berh, D., Jiang, X.: CNN-based background subtraction for long-term in-vial FIM imaging. In: Proceedings of International Conference on Computer Analysis of Images and Patterns (CAIP), Part I, pp. 359–371 (2017)
28. Schmidhuber, J.: Deep learning in neural networks: an overview. Neural Netw. **61**, 85–117 (2015)
29. Valen, D.A.V., et al.: Deep learning automates the quantitative analysis of individual cells in live-cell imaging experiments. PLoS Comput. Biol. **12**(11), e1005177 (2016)

Improved Semantic Stixels via Multimodal Sensor Fusion

Florian Piewak[1,2](✉)(iD), Peter Pinggera[1](iD), Markus Enzweiler[1](iD),
David Pfeiffer[1](iD), and Marius Zöllner[2,3](iD)

[1] Daimler AG, R&D, Stuttgart, Germany
florian.piewak@daimler.com
[2] Karlsruhe Institute of Technology (KIT), Karlsruhe, Germany
[3] Forschungszentrum Informatik (FZI), Karlsruhe, Germany

Abstract. This paper presents a compact and accurate representation
of 3D scenes that are observed by a LiDAR sensor and a monocular
camera. The proposed method is based on the well-established Stixel
model originally developed for stereo vision applications. We extend this
Stixel concept to incorporate data from multiple sensor modalities. The
resulting mid-level fusion scheme takes full advantage of the geometric
accuracy of LiDAR measurements as well as the high resolution and
semantic detail of RGB images. The obtained environment model provides a geometrically and semantically consistent representation of the
3D scene at a significantly reduced amount of data while minimizing
information loss at the same time. Since the different sensor modalities
are considered as input to a joint optimization problem, the solution is
obtained with only minor computational overhead. We demonstrate the
effectiveness of the proposed multimodal Stixel algorithm on a manually
annotated ground truth dataset. Our results indicate that the proposed
mid-level fusion of LiDAR and camera data improves both the geometric
and semantic accuracy of the Stixel model significantly while reducing
the computational overhead as well as the amount of generated data in
comparison to using a single modality on its own.

1 Introduction

Research on autonomous vehicles has attracted a large amount of attention
in recent years, mainly sparked by the complexity of the problem and the
drive to transform the mobility space. One key to success are powerful environment perception systems that allow autonomous systems to understand and act
within a human-designed environment. Stringent requirements regarding accuracy, availability, and safety have led to the use of sensor suites that incorporate
complimentary sensor types such as camera, LiDAR, and RADAR. Each sensor modality needs to leverage its specific strengths to contribute to a holistic
picture of the environment.

D. Pfeiffer—Contributed while with Daimler AG.

© Springer Nature Switzerland AG 2019
T. Brox et al. (Eds.): GCPR 2018, LNCS 11269, pp. 447–458, 2019.
https://doi.org/10.1007/978-3-030-12939-2_31

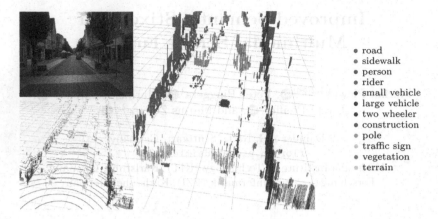

- road
- sidewalk
- person
- rider
- small vehicle
- large vehicle
- two wheeler
- construction
- pole
- traffic sign
- vegetation
- terrain

Fig. 1. Example of a multimodal Stixel scene (right) generated based on a camera image (top left) and a semantic point cloud (bottom left). Note that only *object* Stixels are visualised. The colors correspond to the Cityscapes semantic class color coding [6]. (Color figure online)

The sensor output usually involves quantities that are derived from raw measurements, such as detailed semantics [5,22] or object instance knowledge [29,30]. The different representations provided by the various sensor types are typically fused into an integrated environment model, for example an occupancy grid map [20], to successfully tackle high-level tasks such as object tracking [27] and path planning [3].

Fusing the massive amounts of data provided by multiple different sensors represents a significant challenge in a real-time application. As a way out, mid-level data representations have been proposed that reduce the amount of sensor data but retain the underlying information at the same time. A prime example of such a mid-level representation is the so-called Stixel-World [2,7,13,21,26] that provides a compact, yet geometrically and semantically consistent model of the observed environment. Thereby a 3D scene is represented by a set of narrow vertical segments, the Stixels, which are described individually by their vertical extent, geometric surface, and semantic label. The Stixel concept was originally applied to stereo camera data, where the segmentation is primarily based on dense disparity data as well as pixel-level semantics obtained from a deep neural network [7,13,26].

In this paper, we propose to transfer the Stixel concept into the LiDAR domain to develop a compact and robust mid-level representation for 3D point clouds. Moreover, we extend the Stixel-World to a multimodal representation by incorporating both camera and LiDAR sensor data into the model. The specific combination of the high resolution and semantic detail of RGB imagery with the supreme distance accuracy of LiDAR data in the multimodal Stixel-World results in a very powerful environment representation that outperforms the state-of-the-art (see Fig. 1). Our main contributions can be summarized as follows:

- A compact and robust mid-level representation for semantic LiDAR point clouds based on the Stixel-World.
- A multimodal fusion approach integrated into the proposed mid-level representation.
- A detailed performance analysis and quantitative evaluation of the proposed methods.

Fig. 2. Example of a multimodal Stixel scene (right, colors = Cityscapes semantic class [6], each image column is separated into multiple semantic Stixels) and the corresponding LiDAR distance image (center, blue = close, red = far) projected to a cylindrical view. The corresponding camera image is shown on the left. (Color figure online)

2 Related Work

The multimodal Stixel approach presented in this paper combines LiDAR distance measurements with the point-wise semantic labeling information obtained from both LiDAR and a monocular camera. We relate our approach to three different categories of existing work: semantic labeling, sensor fusion, and compact mid-level data representations.

First, semantic labeling describes a range of techniques for the measurement-wise (e.g. pixel-wise) assignment of object class or object type. The topic has been well explored within the camera domain [5,10,17,25]. In contrast, semantic labeling for 3D point clouds is a relatively recent topic [23,24], which has mainly been studied on indoor [1,8] or stationary outdoor datasets [12]. Within road scenarios, Wu et al. [28] introduced a Fully Convolutional Neural Network (FCN) approach based on the SqueezeNet architecture [14] for semantic labeling of vehicles, pedestrian and cyclists within 3D LiDAR point cloud data. A 2D cylindrical projection of the point cloud (see Fig. 2) is applied, enabling the application of efficient image-based filter kernels. Piewak et al. [22] extend this concept and propose an improved network architecture which is able to perform high-quality semantic labeling of a 3D point cloud based on 13 classes similar to the Cityscapes Benchmark suite [6]. As the multimodal Stixel approach proposed in this paper utilizes semantics from both LiDAR and camera data, we apply the approach of [22] to directly extract the detailed point-wise semantics from LiDAR data. This results in a class representation similar to the camera domain, where we make use of the efficient FCN architecture described by Cordts et al. [5].

Second, different fusion strategies can be applied to the multimodal data of various sensors. Several approaches perform so-called low-level fusion by directly combining the raw data to obtain a joint sensor representation, which is then used for object detection [11] or semantic labeling [19]. A different method commonly used within the autonomous driving context is high-level fusion [20], where the sensor data is processed independently and the results are later combined on a more abstract level. In this paper, we present a novel fusion concept which integrates the sensor data on mid-level, reducing the data volume while minimizing information loss. This representation can further be integrated into a more abstract environment model such as an occupancy grid [20].

Third, the presented multimodal Stixel approach is closely related to other compact mid-level representations in terms of the output data format. In particular, we refer to the Stixel-World obtained from camera imagery, which has successfully been applied with [4,16,21] and without [4,15] the use of stereoscopic depth information. The integration of camera-based semantic labeling information into the Stixel generation process was presented in [5,13,26], thereby further improving robustness and promoting the semantic consistency of the result. The Stixel concept has also been adapted to other image-based sensor techniques, for example to a camera-based infrared depth sensor as shown in [18]. Forsberg [9] makes use of a LiDAR scanner to obtain depth information for the Stixel generation process. Similarly to an early idea in [21], the LiDAR point cloud is simply projected into the camera image to replace the original dense disparity information with the sparse LiDAR-based depth measurements. In contrast, we employ a LiDAR-specific sensor model that is particularly tailored to exploit the superior geometric accuracy of the LiDAR sensor over a stereo camera. Finally, we integrate semantics from both LiDAR and camera data into the Stixel generation process to obtain a high-quality, comprehensive mid-level 3D representation of the environment.

3 Method

The proposed Stixel model is inspired by the stereoscopic camera approaches of [7,21,26]. After a general definition of the Stixel representation, we describe the transfer of the Stixel model to the LiDAR domain as well as the adapted Stixel generation process.

3.1 Stixel Definition

Stixels are segments which represent sensor data in a compact fashion while retaining the underlying semantic and geometric properties. Generally, the segmentation of an image represents a 2D optimization problem which is challenging to solve in a real-time environment. Instead, Stixels are optimized column-wise, which reduces the optimization task to a 1D problem that can be efficiently solved via dynamic programming [21]. As a result, each column is separated into rectangular stick-like segments S called Stixels. Within the LiDAR domain, we represent the input data as an ordered set of columns of the LiDAR scan, obtained from a cylindrical projection of the 3D measurements onto a 2D grid, as shown in Fig. 2. Each Stixel $s_i = (b, t, r, l, c)$ is represented by the bottom row index b and the top row index t, describing its vertical extent with regard to the vertically ordered measurements $M = (m_1, \ldots, m_h)$. Additionally, each Stixel has a semantic label l, a structural class c, and a distance r to the sensor or the ideal ground plane (depending on the structural class c). There are three different Stixel structural classes, i.e. *support* ($\mathcal{G}$) for flat regions such as road surface or sidewalk, *object* ($\mathcal{O}$) for obstacles such as people or vehicles, and *sky* ($\mathcal{S}$) for areas without LiDAR measurements, as indicated in Fig. 3.

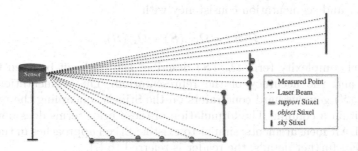

Fig. 3. Exemplary Stixel extraction based on a vertical LiDAR scan column.

3.2   Stixel Model

The vertically ordered (bottom to top) set of measurements $M = (m_1, \ldots, m_h)$ is processed column-wise (see Fig. 2) and contains LiDAR depth measurements $D = (d_1, \ldots, d_h)$ as well as semantics from the camera $L_{cam} = (l_{cam_1}, \ldots, l_{cam_h})$ and the LiDAR $L_{lidar} = (l_{lidar_1}, \ldots, l_{lidar_h})$, respectively. The extraction of semantics from the LiDAR is done using the LiLaNet architecture of [22]. The semantic information of the camera is associated to the 3D LiDAR points based on the so-called Autolabeling technique [22], which projects the LiDAR points into the image plane in order to associate the semantics provided by a state-of-the-art image-based FCN to each point.

Based on this definition the posterior distribution $P(S|M)$ of the Stixels S given the measurements M of a column is defined using the likelihood $P(M|S)$ as well as the prior $P(S)$ as

$$P(S|M) = \frac{P(M|S) \cdot P(S)}{P(M)}. \qquad (1)$$

Here, the Stixels $S = (s_1, \ldots, s_n)$ are vertically ordered in accordance with the measurement vector M. Formulating the posterior distribution in the log-domain yields

$$P(S|M) = e^{-E(S,M)}, \qquad (2)$$

where $E(\boldsymbol{S}, \boldsymbol{M})$ represents an energy function similar to [7], defined as

$$E(\boldsymbol{S}, \boldsymbol{M}) = \Theta(\boldsymbol{S}, \boldsymbol{M}) + \Omega(\boldsymbol{S}) - \log(P(\boldsymbol{M})). \tag{3}$$

Note that $\Theta(\boldsymbol{S}, \boldsymbol{M})$ represents the data likelihood, $\Omega(\boldsymbol{S})$ the segmentation prior, and $P(\boldsymbol{M})$ a normalizing constant. In contrast to camera-based Stixel applications, as discussed in Sect. 2, the proposed approach puts forward a LiDAR-specific sensor model to better integrate the accurate LiDAR geometry into the Stixel-World. This will be discussed within the next subsections.

Prior. The prior $\Omega(\boldsymbol{S})$ puts constraints on the Stixel model in terms of model complexity and segmentation consistency with

$$\Omega(\boldsymbol{S}) = \Omega_{mc}(\boldsymbol{S}) + \Omega_{sc}(\boldsymbol{S}). \tag{4}$$

The model complexity term $\Omega_{mc}(\boldsymbol{S})$ describes the trade-off between the compactness and the accuracy of the representation. The segmentation consistency $\Omega_{sc}(\boldsymbol{S})$ governs hard constraints on the Stixels concerning the relation of Stixels within a column. The formulation of these prior terms does not depend on the LiDAR measurements, similar to existing Stixel approaches in the camera domain. For further details, the reader is referred to [7].

Data Likelihood. The data likelihood represents the matching quality of the measurements $\boldsymbol{M}$ to a given set of Stixels $\boldsymbol{S}$, considering three different data modalities: LiDAR geometry, LiDAR semantics, and camera semantics:

$$
\begin{aligned}
\Theta(\boldsymbol{S}, \boldsymbol{M}) = \sum_{s_i \in S} \sum_{m_j \in M_i^*} & \beta_{geo_{lidar}} \Theta_{geo}(\boldsymbol{s}_i, \boldsymbol{d}_j, \boldsymbol{d}_{j-1}) \\
& + \beta_{sem_{lidar}} \Theta_{sem_{lidar}}(\boldsymbol{s}_i, \boldsymbol{l}_{lidar_j}) \\
& + \beta_{sem_{cam}} \Theta_{sem_{cam}}(\boldsymbol{s}_i, \boldsymbol{l}_{cam_j}).
\end{aligned}
\tag{5}
$$

Here $\boldsymbol{M}_i^*$ represents a subset of the measurements $\boldsymbol{M}$ associated to a specific Stixel $\boldsymbol{s}_i$. The parameters $\beta_{geo_{lidar}}$, $\beta_{sem_{lidar}}$, and $\beta_{sem_{cam}}$ represent weighting parameters of each modality, which are described within this subsection.

LiDAR Geometry. The LiDAR geometry data likelihood consists of three elements defined as follows:

$$
\begin{aligned}
\Theta_{geo}(\boldsymbol{s}_i, \boldsymbol{d}_j, \boldsymbol{d}_{j-1}) = \Theta_{dist}(\boldsymbol{s}_i, \boldsymbol{d}_j) &+ \Theta_{gr}(\boldsymbol{s}_i, \boldsymbol{d}_j, \boldsymbol{d}_{j-1}) \\
&+ \Theta_{sens}(\boldsymbol{s}_i, \boldsymbol{d}_j).
\end{aligned}
\tag{6}
$$

First of all, the relation of a LiDAR depth measurement $\boldsymbol{d}_j$ and the Stixel $\boldsymbol{s}_i$ is given by the term $\Theta_{dist}(\boldsymbol{s}_i, \boldsymbol{d}_j)$. We represent this data likelihood as a mixture of a normal distribution, encoding the sensor noise based on the variance σ, and an uniform distribution representing outlier measurements with an outlier rate of p_{out} similar to [7].

In addition to the common depth likelihood definition $\Theta_{dist}(s_i, d_j)$, two additional likelihood terms are defined to take advantage of LiDAR-specific measurement properties: a ground term $\Theta_{gr}(s_i, d_j, d_{j-1})$ and a sensor term $\Theta_{sens}(s_i, d_j)$. The ground term assesses the consistency of the data with an assumed ground model, based on the gradient between two measurements

$$\phi(d_j, d_k) = \arctan\left(\frac{\Delta z_{jk}}{d_{ground_{jk}}}\right) = \arctan\left(\frac{z_k - z_j}{\sqrt{x_k^2 + y_k^2} - \sqrt{x_j^2 + y_j^2}}\right). \quad (7)$$

Note that a geometric LiDAR measurement $d_j = (r_j, \alpha_{h_j}, \alpha_{v_j})$ is represented using polar coordinates and consists of a measured distance r_j, a horizontal angle α_{h_j}, and a vertical angle α_{v_j}. Based on these polar coordinates, the Cartesian coordinates (x_j, y_j, z_j) are extracted.

The gradient ϕ obtained from the high-quality LiDAR measurements provides structural information of the environment to distinguish between flat surfaces such as ground (low gradient) and obstacles (high gradient). This information is encoded into an object existence probability using a parametrized hyperbolic tangent as

$$P_{ob}(d_j, d_{j-1}) = \frac{1 + \tanh(\beta_{gr,steep}(\phi(d_j, d_{j-1}) - \beta_{gr,shift}))}{2}. \quad (8)$$

Note that the parameters $\beta_{gr,steep}$ and $\beta_{gr,shift}$ adapt the sensitivity of the gradient model. Subsequently, the data likelihood based on the ground model is defined as

$$\Theta_{gr}(s_i, d_j, d_{j-1}) = \begin{cases} -\log(1 - P_{ob}(d_j, d_{j-1})) & \text{if } \phi \text{ is def. and } c_i = \mathcal{G} \\ -\log(P_{ob}(d_j, d_{j-1})) & \text{if } \phi \text{ is def. and } c_i = \mathcal{O} \\ 0 & \text{if } \phi \text{ is undef. or } c_i = \mathcal{S} \end{cases}. \quad (9)$$

Note that the data likelihood based on the ground model is set to zero when the gradient is undefined, which can be caused by missing reflections of the LiDAR laser light (e.g. if the laser beam is pointing to the sky). However, both the vertical and horizontal angles of the polar coordinate of the so-called invalid measurement are still available.

In case of an invalid measurement, the data likelihood based on both the ground model and the depth matching cannot be processed. For this reason we introduce the sensor term $\Theta_{sens}(s_i, d_j)$ to the likelihood formulation, which is based on the vertical distribution of measurement angles of the LiDAR sensor. We assume that a *sky* Stixel is more likely to occur at larger vertical angles, which is encoded into a parametrized hyperbolic tangent similar to Eq. (8) as

$$P_S(\alpha_{v_j}) = \frac{1 + \tanh(\beta_{sens,scale}(\alpha_{v_j} - \beta_{sens,shift}))}{2}. \quad (10)$$

A similar definition is used with regard to small vertical angles and *support* Stixels by inverting the vertical angle $P_{\mathcal{G}}(\alpha_{v_j}) = P_{\mathcal{S}}(-\alpha_{v_j})$. Consequently, the sensor term contribution for invalid points is defined by

$$\Theta_{sens}(\boldsymbol{s}_i, \boldsymbol{d}_j) = \begin{cases} -\log(P_{\mathcal{S}}(\alpha_{v_j})) & \text{if } \boldsymbol{d}_j \text{ is invalid and } c_i = \mathcal{S} \\ -\log(P_{\mathcal{G}}(\alpha_{v_j})) & \text{if } \boldsymbol{d}_j \text{ is invalid and } c_i = \mathcal{G} \\ -\log(1 - P_B(\alpha_{v_j})) & \text{if } \boldsymbol{d}_j \text{ is invalid and } c_i = \mathcal{O} \\ \infty & \text{if } \boldsymbol{d}_j \text{ is valid and } c_i = \mathcal{S} \\ 0 & \text{if } \boldsymbol{d}_j \text{ is valid and } c_i \in \{\mathcal{G}, \mathcal{O}\} \end{cases} , \qquad (11)$$

with $P_B(\alpha_{v_j}) = P_{\mathcal{S}}(\alpha_{v_j}) + P_{\mathcal{G}}(\alpha_{v_j})$. Note that a hard constraint is inserted to prohibit *sky* Stixels resulting from valid measurements.

Semantic Information. The semantic information obtained from the LiDAR data is utilized in a similar way as in the Stixel-World of the camera domain. Each semantic measurement l_{lidar_j} holds a probability estimate $P_{l_{lidar_j}}(l)$ of each class l conditioned on the input data, which can be obtained from the underlying semantic labeling method. We make use of the LiLaNet architecture of [22] to compute the point-wise LiDAR-based semantic information. The definition of the semantic data likelihood is adapted from [26] and [7] as

$$\Theta_{sem_{lidar}}(\boldsymbol{s}_i, l_{lidar_j}) = -\log(P_{l_{lidar_j}}(l_i)). \qquad (12)$$

To obtain high resolution semantic information from the camera image, we make use of the efficient FCN architecture described by Cordts et al. [5]. Fusing this information into the proposed multimodal Stixel approach enables the combination of high resolution camera semantics with geometrically accurate information of the LiDAR. For this purpose we apply the projection technique of [22] to extract the semantic information of the camera by projecting the LiDAR measurements into the semantically labeled image. Each LiDAR measurement then holds additional semantic information from the camera domain l_{cam_j} which is processed similar to Eq. (12) based on the probability $P_{l_{cam_j}}(l)$ for each semantic class l with

$$\Theta_{sem_{cam}}(\boldsymbol{s}_i, l_{cam_j}) = -\log(P_{l_{cam_j}}(l_i)). \qquad (13)$$

Note that this definition is independent of the LiDAR-based semantics which enables the extraction of different domain specific semantic classes l from camera and LiDAR. Especially the camera-based FCN [5] extracts more semantic classes based on the higher resolution as well as the larger receptive field as the LiDAR-based FCN [22]. Hence, the domain specific strengths of each sensor modality and the differing object appearance within the LiDAR and the camera are combined to increase the semantic consistency of the multimodal Stixel result.

3.3   Stixel Generation

Based on the proposed Stixel model, Stixels are generated by finding the maximum-a-posteriori solution of Eq. (1). This is equal to the minimization of the energy function given in Eq. (3). Note, that the probability of the measurement $P(M)$ represents a scaling factor which is ignored within the optimization process. To solve this 1D column-wise optimization process, a dynamic programming approach is used similar to the original Stixel formulation (c.f. [21] and [7]).

4 Experiments

To evaluate our proposed multimodal Stixel model, we use the manually annotated dataset of Piewak et al. [22]. The dataset consists of manually annotated semantic LiDAR point clouds recorded from a vehicle in various traffic scenarios, and further includes corresponding image data captured by a front-facing monocular camera. This enables both a semantic evaluation of our proposed method based on the manually annotated semantic LiDAR data and a geometric evaluation based on the LiDAR depth data. Due to the sensor configuration within the dataset, the evaluation is restricted to the area inside the field of view of the camera. We evaluate various performance metrics on a point-wise basis to measure the geometric and semantic consistency as well as the compactness of the model:

1. Outlier Rate
   A relative distance deviation of the original LiDAR depth measurement from the associated Stixel of more than 5% is declared as an outlier. Based on this formulation the outlier rate is defined as the ratio of the number of outliers to the number of total LiDAR points.
2. Intersection over Union (IoU)
   Based on the manually annotated semantic ground truth, an IoU of the Stixels to the ground truth LiDAR points can be calculated similar to [6].
3. Compression Rate
   The data compression rate θ defines the ratio between the number of stixels $n_{stixels}$ and number of original LiDAR points n_{points} via

$$\theta = 1 - \frac{n_{stixels}}{n_{points}}. \tag{14}$$

The quantitative results are illustrated in Fig. 4. First, the impact of the LiDAR semantic weight $\beta_{sem_{lidar}}$ is evaluated while the LiDAR geometry weight is set to $\beta_{geo_{lidar}} = 1$ and the camera semantics is deactivated ($\beta_{sem_{cam}} = 0$). We observe that the semantic consistency is constantly increasing with an increase of the LiDAR semantic weight. At the same time, the compression rate increases as well as the outlier rate. Putting too much focus on the semantic input thus reduces the number of individual Stixels and yields a model purely tuned to the LiDAR semantics. In turn, consistency with the underlying geometry decreases.

Considering the multimodality in our model by activating the camera semantics, the compression rate as well as the outlier rate slightly decreases. The semantic consistency further improves until the weighting of the camera semantics $\beta_{sem_{cam}}$ reaches the weighting of the LiDAR semantics $\beta_{sem_{lidar}}$. However,

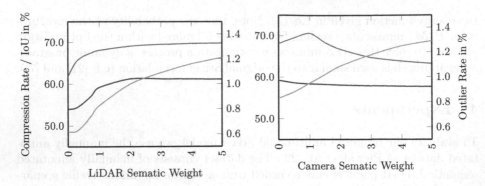

Fig. 4. Impact of considering the semantic information within the multimodal Stixel model with a constant LiDAR geometry weight ($\beta_{geo_{lidar}} = 1$). Left: adaption of the LiDAR semantic weight $\beta_{sem_{lidar}}$ based on a deactivated camera semantics ($\beta_{sem_{cam}} = 0$). Right: adaption of the camera semantic weight $\beta_{sem_{cam}}$ based on a LiDAR semantic weight $\beta_{sem_{lidar}} = 1$

the camera semantics on its own reaches a lower IoU after the transfer to the LiDAR domain (see Table 1). This demonstrates the potential of our novel multimodal Stixel approach, which creates a compact, geometrically and semantically consistent mid-level representation by combining the advantages of different sensor domains to reach a higher accuracy than each modality on its own. Our proposed method of equally weighting the different modalities represents the best combination with regard to the semantic consistency as well as a good compromise concerning the outlier rate and the compression rate. This setup outperforms the original Stixel-World based on a stereoscopic camera regarding the geometric and the semantic consistency of the data representation (see Table 1).

Table 1. Comparison of the original Stixel World (based on a stereoscopic camera), the different independent Stixel optimization modalities, and the combined multimodal representation.

	Stereo camera [7][a]	LiDAR depth only	LiDAR semantic only	Camera semantic only	Multi-modality
Outlier rate in %	6.7	**0.62**	28.8	35.3	0.95
IoU in %	66.5	61.8	70.0	60.8	**70.6**
Compression rate in %	_	54.0	81.2	**85.3**	58.3

[a]Results of the original Stixel-World (stereo camera) are added for comparison based on [7]. No evaluation is done on our dataset.

5   Conclusion

In this paper, we presented the multimodal Stixel-World, a Stixel-based environment representation to directly leverage both camera and LiDAR sensor data. Our design goal is to jointly represent accurate geometric and semantic information based on a multi-sensor system within a compact and efficient environment model. To this end we introduce a LiDAR-specific sensor model that exploits the geometric accuracy of LiDAR sensors as well as a mid-level fusion technique to combine valuable semantic information from both camera and LiDAR. In our experiments we demonstrated the benefits of our multimodal Stixel-World over unimodal representations in terms of representation and compression quality by outperforming the original Stixel-World based on a stereoscopic camera. Moreover, our presented multimodal Stixel approach can easily be extended to other sensor modalities as long as they can be projected into a common structured data format.

References

1. Armeni, I., Sax, S., Zamir, A.R., et al.: Joint 2D-3D-semantic data for indoor scene understanding. arXiv preprint arXiv:1702.01105 (2017)
2. Badino, H., Franke, U., Pfeiffer, D.: The Stixel World - a compact medium level representation of the 3D-world. In: Denzler, J., Notni, G., Süße, H. (eds.) DAGM 2009. LNCS, vol. 5748, pp. 51–60. Springer, Heidelberg (2009). https://doi.org/10.1007/978-3-642-03798-6_6
3. Bai, H., Cai, S., Ye, N., et al.: Intention-aware online POMDP planning for autonomous driving in a crowd. In: International Conference on Robotics and Automation, ICRA (2015)
4. Benenson, R., Mathias, M., Timofte, R., Van Gool, L.: Fast Stixel computation for fast pedestrian detection. In: Fusiello, A., Murino, V., Cucchiara, R. (eds.) ECCV 2012. LNCS, vol. 7585, pp. 11–20. Springer, Heidelberg (2012). https://doi.org/10.1007/978-3-642-33885-4_2
5. Cordts, M.: Understanding Cityscapes: efficient urban semantic scene understanding. Ph.D. thesis. Technische Universität Darmstadt (2017)
6. Cordts, M., Omran, M., Ramos, S., et al.: The Cityscapes dataset for semantic urban scene understanding. In: Conference on Computer Vision and Pattern Recognition, CVPR (2016)
7. Cordts, M., Rehfeld, T., Schneider, L., et al.: The Stixel World: a medium-level representation of traffic scenes. Image Vis. Comput. **68**, 40–52 (2017)
8. Dai, A., Chang, A.X., Savva, M., et al.: ScanNet: richly-annotated 3D reconstructions of indoor scenes. In: Conference on Computer Vision and Pattern Recognition, CVPR (2017)
9. Forsberg, O.: Semantic Stixels fusing LIDAR for scene perception (2018)
10. Garcia-Garcia, A., Orts-Escolano, S., Oprea, S., et al.: A review on deep learning techniques applied to semantic segmentation. arXiv preprint arXiv:1704.06857 (2017)
11. Gupta, S., Girshick, R., Arbeláez, P., Malik, J.: Learning rich features from RGB-D images for object detection and segmentation. In: Fleet, D., Pajdla, T., Schiele, B., Tuytelaars, T. (eds.) ECCV 2014. LNCS, vol. 8695, pp. 345–360. Springer, Cham (2014). https://doi.org/10.1007/978-3-319-10584-0_23

12. Hackel, T., Savinov, N., Ladicky, L., et al.: Semantic3D.net: a new large-scale point cloud classification benchmark. Ann. Photogram. Remote Sens. Spat. Inf. Sci. (ISPRS) **IV-1/W1**, 91–98 (2017)
13. Hernandez-Juarez, D., Schneider, L., Espinosa, A., et al.: Slanted Stixels: representing San Francisco's Steepest streets. In: British Machine Vision Conference, BMVC (2017)
14. Iandola, F.N., Han, S., Moskewicz, M.W., et al.: SqueezeNet: AlexNet-level accuracy with 50x fewer parameters and <0.5MB model size. arXiv preprint arXiv:1602.07360 (2016)
15. Levi, D., Garnett, N., Fetaya, E.: StixelNet: a deep convolutional network for obstacle detection and road segmentation. In: British Machine Vision Conference, BMVC (2015)
16. Liu, M.Y., Lin, S., Ramalingam, S., et al.: Layered interpretation of street view images. In: Robotics: Science and Systems. Robotics: Science and Systems Foundation (2015)
17. Long, J., Shelhamer, E., Darrell, T.: Fully convolutional networks for semantic segmentation. In: Conference on Computer Vision and Pattern Recognition, CVPR (2015)
18. Martinez, M., Roitberg, A., Koester, D., et al.: Using technology developed for autonomous cars to help navigate blind people. In: Conference on Computer Vision Workshops, ICCVW (2017)
19. Muller, A.C., Behnke, S.: Learning depth-sensitive conditional random fields for semantic segmentation of RGB-D images. In: Conference on Robotics and Automation, ICRA (2014)
20. Nuss, D., Reuter, S., Thom, M., et al.: A random finite set approach for dynamic occupancy grid maps with real-time application. arXiv preprint arXiv:1605.02406 (2016)
21. Pfeiffer, D.: The Stixel World - a compact medium-level representation for efficiently modeling dynamic three-dimensional environments. Ph.D. thesis. Humboldt-Universität Berlin (2012)
22. Piewak, F., Pinggera, P., Schäfer, M., et al.: Boosting LiDAR-based semantic labeling by cross-modal training data generation. arXiv preprint arXiv:1804.09915 (2018)
23. Qi, C.R., Yi, L., Su, H., et al.: PointNet++: deep hierarchical feature learning on point sets in a metric space. In: Advances in Neural Information Processing Systems, NIPS (2017)
24. Riegler, G., Ulusoy, A.O., Geiger, A.: OctNet: learning deep 3D representations at high resolutions. In: Computer Vision and Pattern Recognition, CVPR (2017)
25. Sankaranarayanan, S., Balaji, Y., Jain, A., et al.: Learning from synthetic data: addressing domain shift for semantic segmentation. arXiv preprint arXiv:1711.06969 (2017)
26. Schneider, L., Cordts, M., Rehfeld, T., et al.: Semantic Stixels: depth is not enough. In: Intelligent Vehicles Symposium, IV (2016)
27. Vu, T.D., Burlet, J., Aycard, O., et al.: Grid-based localization and local mapping with moving object detection and tracking. J. Inf. Fusion **12**(1), 58–69 (2011)
28. Wu, B., Wan, A., Yue, X., et al.: SqueezeSeg: convolutional neural nets with recurrent CRF for real-time road-object segmentation from 3D LiDAR point cloud. arXiv preprint arXiv:1710.07368 (2017)
29. Yang, F., Choi, W., Lin, Y.: Exploit all the layers: fast and accurate CNN object detector with scale dependent pooling and cascaded rejection classifiers. In: Conference on Computer Vision and Pattern Recognition, CVPR (2016)
30. Zhou, Y., Tuzel, O.: VoxelNet: end-to-end learning for point cloud based 3D object detection. arXiv preprint arXiv:1711.06396 (2017)

Convolve, Attend and Spell:
An Attention-based
Sequence-to-Sequence Model for
Handwritten Word Recognition

Lei Kang[1,2]($\boxtimes$), J. Ignacio Toledo[1]($\boxtimes$), Pau Riba[1]($\boxtimes$), Mauricio Villegas[2]($\boxtimes$),
Alicia Fornés[1]($\boxtimes$), and Marçal Rusiñol[1]($\boxtimes$)

[1] Computer Vision Center, Universitat Autónoma de Barcelona, Barcelona, Spain
{lkang,jitoledo,priba,afornes,marcal}@cvc.uab.es
[2] omni:us, Berlin, Germany
{lei,mauricio}@omnius.com

Abstract. This paper proposes Convolve, Attend and Spell, an attention-based sequence-to-sequence model for handwritten word recognition. The proposed architecture has three main parts: an encoder, consisting of a CNN and a bi-directional GRU, an attention mechanism devoted to focus on the pertinent features and a decoder formed by a one-directional GRU, able to spell the corresponding word, character by character. Compared with the recent state-of-the-art, our model achieves competitive results on the IAM dataset without needing any pre-processing step, predefined lexicon nor language model. Code and additional results are available in https://github.com/omni-us/research-seq2seq-HTR.

1 Introduction

Handwriting Text Recognition (HTR) has interested the Pattern Recognition community for many years. Transforming images of handwritten text into machine readable format has an important amount of application scenarios, such as historical documents, mail-room processing, administrative documents, etc. But the inherent high variability of handwritten text, the myriad of different writing styles and the amount of different languages and scripts, make HTR an open research problem that is still challenging. With the rise of neural networks and deep learning architectures, HTR has reached, as many other applications, an important performance boost. The recognition of handwritten text was, in fact, one of the first application scenarios of convolutional neural networks, when LeCun *et al.* proposed in the late nineties such architectures [16] for recognizing handwritten digits from the MNIST dataset. In the literature, several other

Electronic supplementary material The online version of this chapter (https://doi.org/10.1007/978-3-030-12939-2_32) contains supplementary material, which is available to authorized users.

methods have been proposed for tackling the HTR task such as Hidden Markov Models (HMM) [4,6,11], Recurrent Neural Networks (RNN) and Connectionist Temporal Classification (CTC) [15,18,20,23,27], or nearest neighbor search methods in embedding spaces [1,14,21].

Inspired in the latest advances in machine translation [2,25], image captioning [28] or speech recognition [3,8], we believe that sequence-to-sequence models backed with attention mechanisms [5,24] have a significant potential to become the new state-of-the-art for HTR tasks. Recurrent architectures suit the temporal nature of text, written usually from left to right, and attention mechanisms have proven to be quite performant when paired with such recurrent architectures to focus on the right features at each time step. Sequence-to-sequence (seq2seq) models follow an encoder-decoder paradigm. In our case, the encoder part consists of a Convolutional Neural Network (CNN) that extracts low-level features from the written glyphs, that are then sequentially encoded by an Recurrent Neural Network (RNN). The decoder is another RNN that will decode one character at each time step, thus spelling the whole word. An attention mechanism is introduced as a bridge between the encoder and the decoder, in order to provide a high-correlated context vector that focuses on each character's features at each decoding time step.

The contributions of this work are twofold. On the one hand, we present a novel attention-based seq2seq model, whose performance is comparable to that of other state-of-the-art approaches. Our architecture does not need any pre-processing step of the handwritten text such as de-slanting, baseline normalization, etc. The proposed approach is able to recognize the handwritten texts without the need of any predefined lexicon nor a language model. On the other hand, we also provide a deep investigation for content- and location-based attention formulations, and other strategies such as attention smoothing, multinomial sampling and label smoothing. In this paper we focus on the specific task of isolated word recognition, and we present our results in the widely known offline IAM dataset, comparing our performance with a collection of different approaches from the literature.

The rest of the paper is organized as follows. Section 2 reviews the relevant works for handwritten text recognition. Afterwards, Sect. 3 introduces the proposed architecture. Section 4 presents our experimental results and performs a comparison of the proposed method against the state-of-the-art. Finally, Sect. 5 draws the conclusions and future work.

2   Related Work

Handwritten text recognition approaches can be grouped into four different categories: HMM-based approaches, RNN-based approaches, nearest neighbor-based approaches and attention-based approaches. We will discuss methods from each of these big groups below.

HMM-based approaches were the first ones to reach a reasonable performance level [9]. Bianne-Bernard *et al.* [4] built a handwriting recognizer based on HMM, decision tree and a set of expert-based questions. Bluche et al. [6] proposed a method of the combination of hidden Markov models (HMM) and convolutional neural networks (CNN) for handwritten word recognition. Giménez et al. [11] provided a method using windowed Bernoulli mixture HMMs. However, with the rise of deep learning, such HMM proposals have been outperformed.

The second group of methods corresponds to RNN-based approaches. Graves et al. [12] first proposed to use Long Short-Term Memory (LSTM) cells together with the Connectionist Temporal Classification (CTC) loss to train a multi-time step output recurrent neural network. Later on, in [13] he first provided the Bidirectional Long Short-Term Memory (BLSTM) and CTC model for HTR which outperformed the state-of-the-art HMM-based models. For many years, the use of LSTM with CTC was the state of the art in handwriting recognition and many different variants were proposed. Krishnan et al. [15] perform word spotting and recognition by employing a Spatial Transformer Network (STN), BLSTM and CTC networks. Stuner et al. [23] provide a BLSTM cascade model using a lexicon verification operator and a CTC loss. Wigington et al. [27] perform word and line-level recognition by applying their normalization and augmentation to both training and test images using a CNN-LSTM-CTC network. However, CTC implies that the output cannot have more time steps than the input, this is usually not a problem for HTR tasks, but it is a barrier to further development towards generality and robustness. In addition, CTC only allows monotonic alignments, it may be a valid assumption for word-level or line-level HTR tasks, but it lacks the possibility for further research on paragraph or even more complex article styles.

As an alternative to RNN architectures, some authors proposed to learn embeddings that will map handwritten words to an n-dimensional space in which a nearest neighbor strategy can be applied to find the most likely transcription of a word. Almazán et al. [1] created a fixed length and low dimensional attribute representation known as PHOC. Krishnan et al. [14] proposed to learn such embeddings using a deep convolutional representation. Poznanski et al. [21] provided a CNN-N-Gram based method as word embedding. All the above methods have proven to correctly address the problem of multiple writers, but, as far as we know, they need a predefined lexicon, so they can not recognize out of vocabulary words, which is an important drawback.

Finally, attention-based approaches have been widely used for machine translation, speech recognition and image captioning. Recently, the interest in these approaches for HTR has arisen. Bluche et al. [5] propose an attention-based model for end-to-end handwriting recognition, but the features from the encoding step still needed to be pre-trained using CTC loss in order to be meaningful. This work might be the first successful trial using an attention-based model. Sueiras et al. [24] recently proposed a seq2seq model with attention for handwritten recognition, but they impose a sliding-window approach whose window size needs to be manually tuned which limits the representative power of the CNN features by arbitrarily limiting its field of view. In addition, in the paper they introduced some changes to the widely used Bahdanau [2] content-based attention that are not properly justified. Our seq2seq model outperforms all of those previous proposals.

3   Seq2seq Model with Attention Mechanism

Our attention-based seq2seq model consists of three main parts: an encoder, an attention mechanism and a decoder. Figure 1 shows the whole architecture proposed in this work. Let us detail each of the different parts.

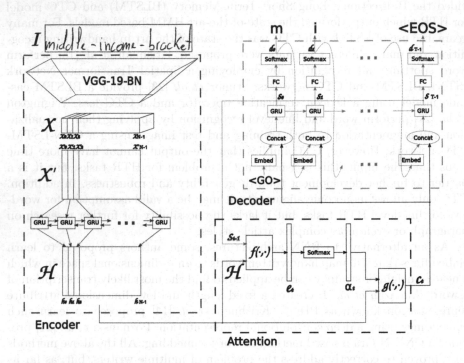

Fig. 1. Architecture of the seq2seq model with attention mechanism.

3.1   Encoder

We start with a CNN to extract visual features. Since we believe that handwritten text images are not visually as complex as real world images, we choose a reasonable CNN architecture such as the VGG-19-BN [22] and initialize it with the pre-trained weights from ImageNet. Then we introduce a multi-layered Bi-directional Gated Recurrent Unit (BGRU) which will involve mutual information and extra positional information for each column, and will encode the sequential nature of handwritten text. For VGG-19-BN network, we removed the last Max pooling layer to be able to tackle short feature sequences. So we use VGG+BGRU as an encoder to transfer the image $\mathcal{I}$ into an intermediate-level feature $\mathcal{X}$, which then is reshaped into a two-dimensional feature map $\mathcal{X}'$. The feature map $\mathcal{X}'$ can be referred as a sequence of column feature vectors $(x'_0, x'_1, \ldots, x'_{N-1})$, where N is the width of the feature map. $\mathcal{H}$ is the output of encoder which shares the same width of $\mathcal{X}'$. Each element $h_i \in \mathcal{H}$ is the output of BGRU at each time step, which will be further used to calculate attention.

3.2   Attention Mechanism

In this section we will discuss two main attention mechanisms, content-based attention and location-based attention.

Content-based Attention. The basic attention mechanism is content-based attention [2]. The intuition is to find the similarity between the current hidden state of the decoder and the word image representation feature map, thus we can find the most correlated feature vectors in the feature map of the encoder, which can be used to predict the current character at the current time step. Let us define α_t as the attention mask vector at time step t, h_i as the hidden state of the encoder at the current time step $i \in \{0, 1, \ldots, N-1\}$, s_t as the hidden state of decoder at current time step $t \in \{0, 1, \ldots, T-1\}$, where T is the maximum length of decoding characters. Then,

$$\alpha_t = \text{Softmax}(e_t) \tag{1}$$

where

$$e_{t,i} = f(h_i, s_{t-1}) = w^T \tanh(W h_i + V s_{t-1} + b) \tag{2}$$

where w, W, V and b are trainable parameters. After obtaining the attention mask vector, the most relevant context vector can be calculated as:

$$c_t = g(\alpha_t, H) = \sum_{i=0}^{N-1} \alpha_{ti} h_i \tag{3}$$

Location-based Attention. The main disadvantage of content-based attention is that it expects positional information to be encoded in the extracted features. Hence, the encoder is forced to add this information, otherwise, content-based attention will never detect the difference between multiple feature representations of same character in different positions. To overcome it, we use an attention mechanism that takes into account the location information explicitly, $i.e.$ location-based attention [8]. Thus, the content-based has been extended to be location-aware by making it take into account the alignment produced at the previous step. First we extract k vectors $l_{t,i} \in \mathbb{R}^k$ for every position i of the previous alignment α_{t-1} by convolving it with a matrix $F \in \mathbb{R}^{k \times r}$:

$$l_t = F * \alpha_{t-1} \tag{4}$$

And then, we replace Eq. 2 by:

$$e_{t,i} = f'(h_i, s_{t-1}, l_t) = w^T \tanh(W h_i + V s_{t-1} + U l_{t,i} + b) \tag{5}$$

where w, W, V, U and b are trainable parameters.

Attention Smoothing. In practice, the attended area is a little narrower than the target character area of the word image. Consequently, we can infer that the model can already get the correct prediction only focusing at the narrow area. However, from the viewpoint of humans, a little wider covering area of the target character would be beneficial. For this reason, we propose to replace the Softmax Eq. 1 with the logistic sigmoid σ proposed by [8]:

$$\alpha_{t,i} = \frac{\sigma(e_{t,i})}{\sum_{i=0}^{N} \sigma(e_{t,i})} \tag{6}$$

3.3   Decoder

The decoder is a one-directional multi-layered GRUs. During each time step t, the concatenation of the embedding vector of the previous time step $\tilde{y}_{t-1}$ and the context vector c_t will be fed into the current GRU unit. The embedding vector for each character in the dataset's vocabulary comes from a look-up table matrix, which is randomly initialized and updated during the training process. The prediction of each time step t is:

$$y_t = \arg\max(\omega(s_t)) \tag{7}$$

where $\omega(\cdot)$ is a linear layer. Then we use the index to fetch the corresponding embedding vector $\tilde{y}_t$ from the look-up table matrix:

$$\tilde{y}_t = \text{Embedding}(y_t) \tag{8}$$

The decoder always starts with the start signal $\langle GO \rangle$ as first input character and ends the decoding process when the end signal $\langle EOS \rangle$ occurs or until the maximum time step T.

The previous embedding vector and current context vector are concatenated to obtain s_t, the hidden state of decoder at current time step. Thus, at each time step of the decoding, the decoder GRU can take advantage of both the information of the previous character and the potentially most relevant visual features, which will benefit the model to make correct predictions. So,

$$s_t = \text{Decoder}([\tilde{y}_{t-1}, c_t], s_{t-1}) \tag{9}$$

where $[\cdot, \cdot]$ is the concatenation of two vectors. There are two techniques that we can adopt to improve the decoding process: multi-nomial decoding and label smoothing.

Multi-nomial Decoding. Inspired by [7], during the training process, instead of choosing the character that has the highest probability from the Softmax output d_t at time step t, multiple indices can be sampled from the multi-nomial probability distribution located in the Softmax output d_t. But to keep the model simple, here we sample only one index but in a random way based on the multi-nomial probability distribution, and this index corresponds to a specific character. Although only one index has been sampled, it allows the decoder to explore other alternative decoding paths towards the final word prediction, which could make the decoder more robust and lead to better performance, although it will absolutely take longer epochs to train.

Label Smoothing. Label smoothing [26] is a regularization mechanism to prevent the model from making over-confident predictions. It encourages the model to have higher entropy at its prediction, and therefore it makes the model more adaptable and improve generalization. We regularize the groundtruth by replacing the hard 0 and 1 classification targets with targets of $\frac{\varepsilon}{k}$ and $1 - \frac{k-1}{k}\varepsilon$. In this paper, we choose the $\varepsilon = 0.4$.

4   Experiments

In this section, we report the experiments performed to evaluate our attention-based seq2seq model and discuss the techniques that could be potentially helpful for HTR tasks. We finally make a comparison among the state-of-the-art works.

4.1   Dataset

As the IAM Handwriting dataset [17] is the most popular one for handwritten text recognition tasks, we carried out our experiments based on it. The IAM dataset consists of 115320 isolated and labeled words written by 657 writers. For the partition, we chose the most widely used one: the RWTH Aachen partition, which consists of 55081, 8895 and 25920 words in training, validation and test sets, respectively. All of these sets are disjoint, and no writer has contributed to more than one set. We selected all the words whose segmentation are marked "OK" (even when there are some errors among the "OK" words, we still keep them), so we obtain 47981, 7554 and 20305 words in each partition. Examples of the training and test images are shown in Fig. 2.

4.2   Implementation Details

All experiments were run using the PyTorch system [19] on an NVIDIA GTX 1080 Ti. Training was done using Adam optimizer with an initial learning rate of $2 \cdot 10^{-4}$ and a batch size of 32. We set the dropout probability to be 50% for all the GRU layers except the last layer of both encoder and decoder. We have run

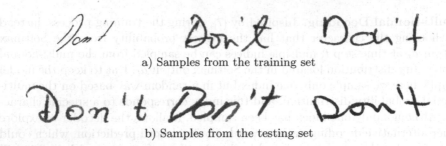

a) Samples from the training set

b) Samples from the testing set

Fig. 2. Samples from the IAM dataset of the word "Don't".

some experiments based on different number of layers and size of hidden state, and the final decision of these hyper-parameters will be discussed in Sect. 4.3.

All the images have been resized to a fixed height of 64 pixels while keeping the original ratio of the length/height. With the fixed height size of 64 pixels, the longest word has the length of 1011 pixels, so we padded zeros to the right of every word image so as to share the same shape of 64×1011.

4.3   Results

All results presented use the standard performance measures: character error rate (CER) and word error rate (WER) [10]. The CER is computed as the Levenshtein distance which is the sum of the character substitutions (S), insertions (I) and deletions (D) that are needed to transform one string into the other, divided by the total number of characters in the groundtruth word (N). Formally,

$$CER = \frac{S + I + D}{N} \tag{10}$$

Similarly, the WER is computed as the sum of the word substitutions (S_w), insertions (I_w) and deletions (D_w) that are required to transform one string into the other, divided by the total number of words in the groundtruth (N_w). Formally,

$$WER = \frac{S_w + I_w + D_w}{N_w} \tag{11}$$

Since our experiments are at word level, WER becomes the percentage of incorrectly recognized words.

At first, we need to find out relatively perfect parameters for sizes of hidden state and hidden layers of both encoder and decoder. As the hidden state of the decoder should be initialized by the encoder, we always keep the size of the hidden state and the number of hidden layers the same for both the encoder and decoder. We tried 1, 2 and 3 layers, 128, 256, 512 and 1024 sizes, being a total of 12 experiments. From the results shown in Table 1, we can observe that the relatively best parameters are 2 layers and 512 size for both the encoder and decoder.

Table 1. Validation CER comparison changing the size of the hidden state and number of layers.

Size	Number of layers		
	1	2	3
128	5.57	6.07	6.09
256	5.13	5.33	5.69
512	5.05	**5.01**	5.34
1024	5.19	5.03	5.10

Table 2. Ablation study for the proposed model tested on the IAM dataset, character error rates are computed from validation set.

Attention	AttnSmooth	Multinomial	LabelSmooth	Valid-CER	Valid-WER
Content	–	–	–	5.79	15.91
	–	–	✓	5.08	13.88
Location	–	–	–	5.49	14.74
	–	–	✓	**5.01**	**13.61**
	–	✓	–	5.53	14.53
	–	✓	✓	5.03	13.66
	✓	–	–	5.72	15.92
	✓	–	✓	5.34	14.62
	✓	✓	–	5.84	15.85
	✓	✓	✓	5.56	14.85

As detailed in Sect. 3, we explored some techniques for potential improvements. Table 2, shows that the best performance was achieved using location-based attention and label smoothing. Studying the table, we can see that the label smoothing is really helpful. The location-based attention is just slightly better than the content-based one. The reason behind this little improvement is that the use of the BGRU in the encoder can already encode some positional information to the feature map. Contrary, once we encode the positional information explicitly, the result improves. In conclusion, the location-based attention still meets our expectation.

Concerning attention smoothing and multi-nomial decoding, they seem not helping our model. On the one hand, the original Softmax attention is already good (attention visualization can be found in Figs. 3 and 4), therefore smoothing the attention may introduce noise, which could harm the model. On the other hand, multi-nomial decoding enables the proposed approach to explore new decoding paths. This exploration was expected to make our model more robust, however, it has showed that this technique is still not able to outperform our best result in the table. This probably means that the multi-nomial decoding really makes our model harder to train.

Table 3. Comparison with the state-of-the-art methods.

Idea	Method	Lexicon[a]	LM	Pre-processing	Pre-train	CER	WER
HMMs	Giménez et al. [11]	tr+va+te	✓	✓	–	–	25.80
	Bluche et al. [6]	te	✓	✓	–	–	23.70
	Bianne et al. [4]	tr+va+te	–	–	–	–	21.90
RNN + CTC	Mor et al. [18]	–	–	–	–	–	20.49
	Pham et al. [20]	–	–	–	–	13.92	31.48
	Krishnan et al. [15]	–	✓	–	Synthetic	6.34	16.19
	Wiginton et al. [27]	–	–	✓	–	6.07	19.07
	Stunner et al. [23]	2.4M	✓	–	–	**4.77**	**13.30**
Nearest Neighbor Search	Almazán et al. [1]	te	–	–	–	11.27	20.01
	Krishnan et al. [14]	te+90K	–	–	Synthetic	6.33	14.07
	Poznanski et al. [21]	tr+te	✓	✓	Synthetic	**3.44**	**6.45**
Attention	Bluche et al. [5]	–	–	–	CTC	12.60	–
	Sueiras et al. [24]	–	–	✓	–	8.80	23.80
	Ours	–	–	–	–	**6.88**	**17.45**

[a]Vocabulary of all words occurring in training (tr), validation (va) and test set (te). 2.4 million (2.4M) and 90 thousand (90K) words lexicon.

Table 3 shows the most popular approaches on the IAM word-level dataset, however, most of them have applied different pre-processings on the original dataset. For HMM-based approaches, Giménez et al. [11] corrected the slant in the image and made the gray level normalization. Bluche et al. [6] also corrected the slant in the image, enhanced the image contrast and added 20 white pixels on left and right to model the empty context. Bianne et al. [4] trained the model using all training and validation sets. These approaches have already been outperformed, since the RNN- and nearest neighbor-based approaches perform pretty well. In the case of RNN-based approaches, Mor et al. [18] filtered out punctuation and short words, and trained the model using training and validation sets. Krishnan et al. [15] has been pre-trained using synthetic data. Wiginton et al. [27] cleaned the punctuation and upper-cases, used the profile normalization and applied test augmentation.

Since the nearest neighbor-based approaches cannot work without lexicons, they cannot be widely used in daily or industrial use cases. In addition, Krishnan et al. [14] has also pre-trained using synthetic data, cleaned punctuation and upper-cases and applied test augmentation. Poznanski et al. [21] used a pre-trained model from synthetic data and applied test augmentation.

The bottom rows of Table 3 correspond to attention-based approaches, which are relatively new for handwriting recognition and have a significant potential for development. But Bluche et al. [5] has been pre-trained using CTC loss in order to get meaningful feature representation. Sueiras et al. [24] corrected the line skew and the slant in the images, normalized the height of the characters based on baseline and corpus line.

Among all those approaches, some of them have utilized language model (LM) explicitly. Even though no language model is used in our system, the RNN of the decoder might learn the relations between characters in the training vocabulary.

In summary, we can observe that our results are the best among the attention-based approaches and comparable to other state-of-the-art approaches especially with neither dataset pre-processing, model pre-training on synthetic dataset nor using CTC loss.

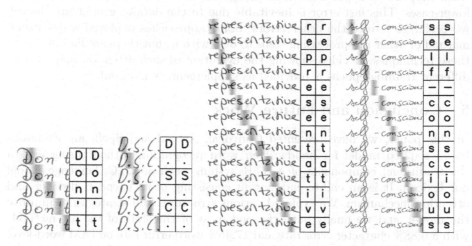

Fig. 3. Examples where the attention mechanisms correctly focuses on the right characters and we obtain a good transcription (Left: Prediction, Right: Groundtruth).

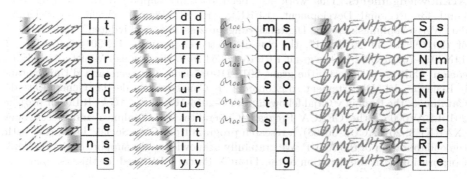

Fig. 4. Examples where we obtain an incorrect transcription (Left: Prediction, Right: Groundtruth).

4.4   Error Analysis

Some attention examples are visualized in Figs. 3 and 4. In Fig. 3, the predictions are correct and the attentions are perfectly aligned to each character as we expected. However, in Fig. 4, the errors in the first two images are due to the slant of the words and very different writing styles in comparison to the training set. Concerning the third image, if we only look at the isolated word image, actually it is hard to tell the transcription even as a human. According to this error, a language model could be used to improve the prediction. The error in the fourth image is due to the mismatch of the image and groundtruth label, while they are all upper-cases in the image but in the label all the characters are lower-cases. This last error is inevitable due to the dataset grountruth, hence, we prefer to reduce the other errors. Some approaches deployed a deslanting method or other pre-processing steps to deal with it, but there are limitations to these techniques. A video showing the evolution of such attention maps across different training epochs is provided as supplementary material.

5   Conclusion and Future Work

In this paper, we have presented Convolve, Attend and Spell, an attention-based seq2seq model for handwritten word recognition without using any of the traditional components of a HTR system, such as CTC, language model nor lexicon. It is an end-to-end system consisting of an encoder, decoder and attention mechanism. We explored various structures and strategies to improve the model, and we finally outperformed most of the state of the art methods with a 6.88% character error rate and 17.45% word error rate on IAM word-level dataset. Our future work will be focused on the application of this model to the recognition of text-lines on the IAM dataset, and to explore the incorporation of language models into the seq2seq models.

Acknowledgements. This work has been partially supported by the European Fund for Regional Development (EFRE), Pro FIT-Project "Vollautomatisierung der Wertschöpfungskette im Digitalisierungsprozess von Archivdaten" with support of IBB/EFRE in 2016/2017, the Spanish research projects TIN2014-52072-P and TIN2015-70924-C2-2-R, the grant FPU15/06264 from the Spanish Ministerio de Educación, Cultura y Deporte, the grant 2016-DI-087 from the Secretaria d'Universitats i Recerca del Departament d'Economia i Coneixement de la Generalitat de Catalunya, the Ramón y Cajal fellowship RYC-2014-16831, the AGAUR Llavor project 2016LLAV00057, the CERCA Program/Generalitat de Catalunya and RecerCaixa (XARXES, 2016ACUP-00008), a research program from Obra Social "La Caixa" with the collaboration of the ACUP. We gratefully acknowledge the support of the NVIDIA Corporation with the donation of the Titan X Pascal GPU used for this research.

References

1. Almazán, J., Gordo, A., Fornés, A., Valveny, E.: Word spotting and recognition with embedded attributes. IEEE Trans. Pattern Anal. Mach. Intell. **36**(12), 2552–2566 (2014)
2. Bahdanau, D., Cho, K., Bengio, Y.: Neural machine translation by jointly learning to align and translate. arXiv preprint arXiv:1409.0473 (2014)
3. Bahdanau, D., Chorowski, J., Serdyuk, D., Brakel, P., Bengio, Y.: End-to-end attention-based large vocabulary speech recognition. In: Proceedings of the IEEE International Conference on Acoustics, Speech and Signal Processing, pp. 4945–4949 (2016)

4. Bianne-Bernard, A.L., Menasri, F., Mohamad, R.A.H., Mokbel, C., Kermorvant, C., Likforman-Sulem, L.: Dynamic and contextual information in HMM modeling for handwritten word recognition. IEEE Trans. Pattern Anal. Mach. Intell. **33**(10), 2066–2080 (2011)
5. Bluche, T., Louradour, J., Messina, R.: Scan, attend and read: end-to-end handwritten paragraph recognition with MDLSTM attention. In: Proceedings of the IAPR International Conference on Document Analysis and Recognition, pp. 1050–1055 (2017)
6. Bluche, T., Ney, H., Kermorvant, C.: Tandem HMM with convolutional neural network for handwritten word recognition. In: Proceedings of the IEEE International Conference on Acoustics, Speech and Signal Processing, pp. 2390–2394 (2013)
7. Cho, K., et al.: Learning phrase representations using RNN encoder-decoder for statistical machine translation. arXiv preprint arXiv:1406.1078 (2014)
8. Chorowski, J.K., Bahdanau, D., Serdyuk, D., Cho, K., Bengio, Y.: Attention-based models for speech recognition. In: Proceedings of the International Conference on Neural Information Processing Systems, pp. 577–585 (2015)
9. España-Boquera, S., Castro-Bleda, M.J., Gorbe-Moya, J., Zamora-Martinez, F.: Improving offline handwritten text recognition with hybrid HMM/ANN models. IEEE Trans. Pattern Anal. Mach. Intell. **33**(4), 767–779 (2011)
10. Frinken, V., Bunke, H.: Continuous handwritten script recognition. In: Doermann, D., Tombre, K. (eds.) Handbook of Document Image Processing and Recognition, pp. 391–425. Springer, London (2014). https://doi.org/10.1007/978-0-85729-859-1_12
11. Giménez, A., Khoury, I., Andrés-Ferrer, J., Juan, A.: Handwriting word recognition using windowed Bernoulli HMMs. Pattern Recogn. Lett. **35**, 149–156 (2014)
12. Graves, A., Fernández, S., Gomez, F., Schmidhuber, J.: Connectionist temporal classification: labelling unsegmented sequence data with recurrent neural networks. In: Proceedings of the International Conference on Machine Learning, pp. 369–376 (2006)
13. Graves, A., Liwicki, M., Fernández, S., Bertolami, R., Bunke, H., Schmidhuber, J.: A novel connectionist system for unconstrained handwriting recognition. IEEE Trans. Pattern Anal. Mach. Intell. **31**(5), 855–868 (2009)
14. Krishnan, P., Dutta, K., Jawahar, C.: Deep feature embedding for accurate recognition and retrieval of handwritten text. In: Proceedings of the International Conference on Frontiers in Handwriting Recognition, pp. 289–294 (2016)
15. Krishnan, P., Dutta, K., Jawahar, C.: Word spotting and recognition using deep embedding. In: Proceedings of the IAPR International Workshop on Document Analysis (2018)
16. LeCun, Y., Bottou, L., Bengio, Y., Haffner, P.: Gradient-based learning applied to document recognition. Proc. IEEE **86**(11), 2278–2324 (1998)
17. Marti, U.V., Bunke, H.: The IAM-database: an English sentence database for offline handwriting recognition. Int. J. Doc. Anal. Recogn. **5**(1), 39–46 (2002)
18. Mor, N., Wolf, L.: Confidence prediction for lexicon-free OCR. In: Proceedings of the IEEE Winter Conference on Applications of Computer Vision, pp. 218–225 (2018)
19. Paszke, A., et al.: Automatic differentiation in PyTorch (2017)
20. Pham, V., Bluche, T., Kermorvant, C., Louradour, J.: Dropout improves recurrent neural networks for handwriting recognition. In: Proceedings of the International Conference on Frontiers in Handwriting Recognition, pp. 285–290 (2014)

21. Poznanski, A., Wolf, L.: CNN-N-gram for handwriting word recognition. In: Proceedings of the IEEE Conference on Computer Vision and Pattern Recognition, pp. 2305–2314 (2016)
22. Simonyan, K., Zisserman, A.: Very deep convolutional networks for large-scale image recognition. arXiv preprint arXiv:1409.1556 (2014)
23. Stuner, B., Chatelain, C., Paquet, T.: Handwriting recognition using cohort of LSTM and lexicon verification with extremely large lexicon. CoRR, vol. abs/1612.07528 (2016)
24. Sueiras, J., Ruiz, V., Sanchez, A., Velez, J.F.: Offline continuous handwriting recognition using sequence to sequence neural networks. Neurocomputing **289**, 119–128 (2018)
25. Sutskever, I., Vinyals, O., Le, Q.V.: Sequence to sequence learning with neural networks. In: Proceedings of the International Conference on Neural Information Processing Systems, pp. 3104–3112 (2014)
26. Szegedy, C., Vanhoucke, V., Ioffe, S., Shlens, J., Wojna, Z.: Rethinking the inception architecture for computer vision. In: Proceedings of the IEEE Conference on Computer Vision and Pattern Recognition, pp. 2818–2826 (2016)
27. Wigington, C., Stewart, S., Davis, B., Barrett, B., Price, B., Cohen, S.: Data augmentation for recognition of handwritten words and lines using a CNN-LSTM network. In: Proceedings of the IAPR International Conference on Document Analysis and Recognition, pp. 639–645 (2017)
28. Xu, K., et al.: Show, attend and tell: Neural image caption generation with visual attention. In: Proceedings of the International Conference on Machine Learning, pp. 2048–2057 (2015)

Illumination Estimation Is Sufficient for Indoor-Outdoor Image Classification

Nikola Banić[(✉)] and Sven Lončarić

Image Processing Group,
Department of Electronic Systems and Information Processing,
Faculty of Electrical Engineering and Computing, University of Zagreb,
10000 Zagreb, Croatia
{nikola.banic,sven.loncaric}@fer.hr

Abstract. Indoor-outdoor image classification is a well-known problem for which multiple solutions have been proposed, many of which use both low-level and high-level features put into various models. Despite varying complexity, the accuracy of most of these models is reported to be around 90%. In this paper it is shown that the same accuracy can be obtained by simple manipulation of only low-level features extracted from the image in the early phase of image formation and based on the simplest forms of illumination estimation, namely methods such as Gray-World. Additionally, it is shown how using the built-in camera auto white balance is also enough to effectively achieve state-of-the-art indoor-outdoor classification accuracy. The results are presented and discussed.

1 Introduction

Indoor-outdoor image classification is a well-known problem for which multiple solutions have been proposed in the literature. Some of them are based on using histograms in the Ohta color space, multiresolution simultaneous autoregressive model parameters, and coefficients of a shift-invariant DCT as features [33], using low-level and semantic features [26], capturing high-level concepts from low-level image features [35], using color and texture features [10, 30], integrating low-level features and spatial properties in Bayesian framework [20], using global features that describe color and illumination properties [4], analysing edge straightness [29], using edge and color orientation histogram [23], calculating color correlated temperature and using it for k-NN classification [16], using expert decision functions [7], feeding holistic image features like GIST to different classifiers [31, 34], fusing collaborative representation of local and global spatial features [37]. In addition to relying on low-level features, most of these solutions also include calculation of higher level features as well as using various models for the final classification. While in many cases such approaches increase the complexity of the whole system, the gain in the accuracy of the indoor-outdoor classification does not significantly change and is mostly around 90%. One notable exception can be found in [36] where indoor-outdoor classification accuracy was reported to be over 97%, but no details on the used classifier were given.

© Springer Nature Switzerland AG 2019
T. Brox et al. (Eds.): GCPR 2018, LNCS 11269, pp. 473–486, 2019.
https://doi.org/10.1007/978-3-030-12939-2_33

With the accuracy being very similar across all mentioned approaches, the decisive criteria when choosing a method for indoor-outdoor classification could be the speed and simplicity of the feature extraction and the classification process. Fast and simple methods have the additional benefit of commonly being hardware-friendly and as such they are a natural choice for implementation in embedded systems. In this paper a method based on results of simple low-level statistics-based illumination estimation methods and an additional assumption is proposed. For best accuracy it operates on linear raw images in the early stage of the image formation process, but it can also operate on common sRGB images. The method is shown to achieve state-of-the-art results with practically no significant additional computational cost and it effectively demonstrates that using illumination estimation is sufficient to have indoor-outdoor classification of accuracy that is comparable to that of other state-of-the-art methods.

The paper is structured as follows: Sect. 2 gives the motivation for the new indoor-outdoor classification method, in Sect. 3 this new method is described, experimental results are presented and discussed in Sect. 4, and, finally, Sect. 5 concludes the paper.

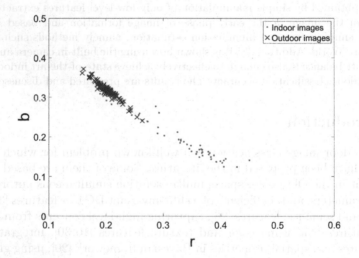

Fig. 1. The rb-chromaticities of the ground-truth illuminations for images of the Panasonic linear benchmark dataset [9].

2   Motivation

One of the image properties that has been linked to the image being an indoor or an outdoor one is scene illumination [5,8]. Namely, indoor illumination tends to be more reddish because of the artificial illumination sources that are usually subjectively warmer than the daylight, e.g. incandescent light bulb, while on the other hand outdoor illumination tends to be more blueish, especially in

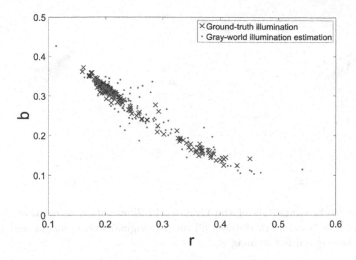

Fig. 2. The rb-chromaticities of the ground-truth illuminations and Gray-world illumination estimations for images of the Panasonic benchmark dataset [9].

the shadows where a significant amount of illumination is affected by the light reflected from the sky. This can easily be demonstrated by observing the illumination color on various indoor and outdoor images. Image datasets that come with such information for each image are computational color constancy [11] benchmark datasets. In these datasets the illumination color in each image was extracted by putting a calibration object in the scene of each image and later reading the value of its achromatic surfaces, which effectively represents the illumination color that influences the image. In the best case this reading is performed on minimally processed raw images that are linear with respect to scene radiance since this also alters the real illumination color minimally. The chromaticities, i.e. colors normalized so that their RGB components sum up to 1, of ground-truth illumination from one of the linear NUS datasets [9] are given in Fig. 1, which shows that there is a more or less clear distinction between the two illumination types in the rb-chromaticity plane. Based on Fig. 1 it is evident that illumination may be a useful feature for indoor-outdoor classification.

However, the main problem here is that in most cases scene illumination is unknown. This problem can be solved by applying illumination estimation, the main step of computational color constancy and also an ill-posed problem that has led to numerous proposals of illumination estimation methods [17]. Illumination estimation is usually performed on linear raw images at the beginning of a camera's image processing pipeline [22] because such images are in accordance with the image formation model most commonly used by illumination estimation methods [17]. While no illumination estimation method gives satisfactory accuracy in all conditions, even illumination estimations of the simplest statistics-based methods still appear "to correlate *roughly* with the actual illuminant" [12] as shown in Fig. 2 for the case of Gray-world method [6]. Although there are

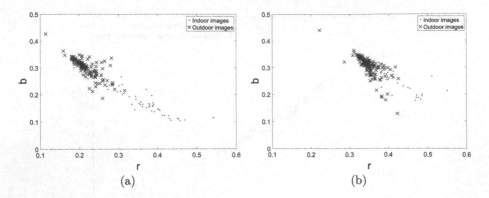

Fig. 3. The rb-chromaticities of the Gray-world illumination estimations for images of the Panasonic benchmark dataset [9] on (a) original linear images and (b) sRGB version of the original linear images.

visible differences between the ground-truth illuminations and the Gray-world illumination estimations, for the purpose of indoor-outdoor classification it is more important that the latter's clustering is similar to the one shown in Fig. 1. As shown in Fig. 3(a), this appears to be the case. It must be stressed again here that this is the case only for linear raw images, while for the more commonly used sRGB images the Gray-world illumination estimations would be arranged as shown in Fig. 3(b). Therefore, if illumination estimation results are to be used for indoor-outdoor image classification, it is better if they are calculated on linear images since sRGB images are highly non-linear because of the numerous post-processing techniques applied to them [22].

3   The Proposed Method

3.1   Formal Statement

Based on the previous section, a new method for indoor-outdoor classification can be proposed. Its main step is to apply an illumination estimation method to the linear version of a given image and then, depending on the illumination estimation color's position in the chromaticity space, to decide whether the image scene was taken indoor or outdoor. All of this is under the assumption that an image taken outdoor will mostly have a typically colder outdoor illumination and an image taken indoor will mostly have a typically warmer indoor illumination. This means that the method boils down to a binary illumination classification.

As mentioned earlier, the chosen illumination estimation method does not need to be highly accurate to guarantee accurate classification. With that in mind, it seems reasonable to choose some of the simplest and fastest methods with an accuracy high enough to produce satisfactory classification results. One of the best candidates for such a methods is the already mentioned Gray-world method, which is centered around the Gray-world assumption that states that the average scene reflectance is achromatic. This means that any deviation from the gray mean is directly attributed to illumination $\mathbf{e}$, which is then given as

$$\mathbf{e} = \frac{\int \mathbf{f}(x)dx}{\int dx} \tag{1}$$

where x is a given image pixel and $\mathbf{f}$ is the image.

Another advantage of the Gray-world method is that it has no parameters that would have to be tuned, which additionally adds to its simplicity of use. A similar method that also has no parameters is the White-patch method [14,25]. Nevertheless, because of its sensitivity to noise, its accuracy is usually among the poorest ones [9,17] and therefore it is not used here.

The final step is to decide the criteria when a given illumination estimation is going to be treated as one of an indoor or one of an outdoor image. Since for illumination chromaticities there is a strong linear connection between the red and blue chromaticities [1,2,21], comparing only red ones should also give satisfactory results and additionally reduce the computation. Therefore, on a given training dataset it is enough to find the red chromaticity threshold that separates the illumination estimations of indoor and outdoor images with the greatest accuracy and use it later on the test set. The pseudocodes for training and applying the proposed method are given in Algorithms 1 and 2, respectively.

Algorithm 1. Training

Input: image set $\mathbb{I}$, image labels $\mathbb{L}$, illumination estimation function m
Output: red chromaticity threshold t

1: $\mathbb{E} \leftarrow \{\}$ ▷ Illumination estimations
2: **for** $\mathbf{I}_i \in \mathbb{I}$ **do**
3:      $\mathbf{e}^{(i)} = m\left(\mathbf{I}_i\right)$ ▷ $\mathbf{e}^{(i)} = \left(e_R^{(i)}, e_G^{(i)}, e_B^{(i)}\right)$
4:      $\mathbb{E} \leftarrow \mathbb{E} \cup \left\{\mathbf{e}^{(i)}\right\}$ ▷ Storing illumination estimations for all images
5: **end for**
6: $n = |\mathbb{I}|$ ▷ number of images
7: $t = \underset{r \in [0,1]}{\arg\max} \sum_{i=1} \begin{cases} 1, & \text{if } L_i = 0 \text{ and } e_R^{(i)} \leq r \\ 1, & \text{if } L_i = 1 \text{ and } e_R^{(i)} > r \\ 0, & \text{if } L_i = 0 \text{ and } e_R^{(i)} > r \\ 0, & \text{if } L_i = 1 \text{ and } e_R^{(i)} \leq r \end{cases}$ ▷ $L_i \in \mathbb{L}$ is 0 for outdoor and 1 for an indoor images

---

3.2 Overcoming Limitations

The main disadvantage of the proposed method is that to achieve best accuracy, it has to operate on linear raw images, which are impractical for direct usage due to their increased storage size and high dynamic range. However, as shown

Algorithm 2. Application

Input: image $\mathbf{I}$, illumination estimation function m, red chromaticity threshold t

Output: image label L

1: $\mathbf{e} = m\,(\mathbf{I})$ $\triangleright \mathbf{e} = (e_R, e_G, e_B)$

2: $L = \begin{cases} 0, & \text{if } e_R \leq t \\ 1, & \text{if } e_R > t \end{cases}$

in Sect. 4, operating on sRGB images results in a much lower accuracy, which means that to keep high accuracy, operating on linear raw images should be kept as well. There are several possible solutions for this.

The most direct way to overcome the described limitation of directly storing raw images is to store enough information to restore the original raw image from a given sRGB image. Namely, there are solutions that require "no calibration of the camera and can reconstruct the original RAW to within 0.3% error with only a 64 KB overhead for the additional data" [27,28]. In this case the required additional data is stored in the exchangeable image file format (Exif) metadata. While this helps to restore enough information for a successful illumination estimation, it unfortunately disables other useful metadata from being stored and used later.

A better solution that additionally removes the need for performing separate illumination estimation is to simply use the information obtained from the camera's built-in illumination estimation system. These information can be taken from the Exif metadata by reading the values of fields *Red Balance* and *Blue Balance*, which represent the channel gains by which the red and blue channels have to be multiplied in order remove the illumination influence. By simply inverting these values, using 1 as the green multiplier, and then normalizing them all so that they all sum up to 1, the chromaticity of the camera's illumination estimation is obtained. It can now be used instead of the one given by Gray-world or some other method. As a matter of fact, these values are often stored in metadata of JPEG files written by many contemporary camera models, which means that they can be easily extracted and used by the proposed method.

4   Experimental Results

4.1   Tested Methods

Three variants of the proposed method were tested using the results of applying Gray-world to linear images, the results of applying Gray-world to sRGB images, and the results of the camera's built-in illumination estimation. As for other methods, the papers in which they are described often lack important implementation details and therefore a simple high-level feature method was created for the purpose of comparison instead. This method will be denoted as **high-level features** and it is trained by first extracting the values of the penultimate layer of the ResNet-50 network [19] after applying it to training images. These values are then used as features for a linear SVM [32], which is then trained for given indoor-outdoor labels. When this method is applied to a new image, its ResNet-50 features are calculated and used as the input for the trained SVM for the final classification result. Three-fold cross-validation was used to obtain the accuracy results for both the proposed method and high-level features method.

4.2 Datasets

In order to be able to simultaneously test the proposed method on both linear and sRGB images, the eight NUS datasets [9] were used. They were chosen because they provide the linear images, their sRGB versions, and the original raw file for each image from which the Exif metadata i.e. camera's built-in auto white balance multipliers can be read. The indoor-outdoor labels for their combined 1736 images were obtained through manual annotation. The three-fold cross-validation was performed individually for each of the eight datasets with each of them being created by another camera model. Since all eight NUS datasets contain images of practically the same scenes, it is possible to see the influence of various sensors on the classification accuracy of the proposed method.

Additional experiments were carried out for the Dresden dataset [18] on a subset of images whose files contained white balance metadata. The goal of the experiment was to see the influence of sensors of some older camera models, not all of which are professional, on the accuracy of the proposed method. Since the scenes in this dataset are massively repeated, the high-level features method results should be disregarded since they have an unfair advantage. Finally, the subset of the reprocessed version [24] of the ColorChecker dataset [15] taken with Canon EOS 5D camera model was used. The Canon EOS-1DS camera model subset was not used since its image files do not contain the required metadata.

      (a)   (b)

Fig. 4. Failure cases of the proposed method when the Gray-world method is used for illumination estimation: (a) a falsely predicted indoor scene and (b) a falsely predicted outdoor scene.

Table 1. Combined results of several methods on the images of all NUS datasets [9]; O stands for outdoor, I for indoor, camera for built-in illumination estimation, and GW for Gray-world.

Method		GW on linear		GW on sRGB		Built-in		High-level features	
Actual label		O	I	O	I	O	I	O	I
Predicted label	O	1245	112	1214	247	1269	89	1200	89
	I	44	335	75	200	20	358	152	295
Accuracy		0.9101		0.8145		0.9372		0.8611	

Table 2. Results of several methods on the images of the all NUS datasets [9] for individual cameras; O stands for outdoor, I for indoor, built-in for camera's illumination estimation, and GW for Gray-world.

Camera	Method			
	GW on linear	GW on sRGB	Built-in	High-level features
Canon EOS-1Ds Mark III	0.9112	0.8649	0.9344	0.8649
Canon EOS 600D	0.9050	0.8250	0.9450	0.8700
Fujifilm X-M1	0.9031	0.7551	0.9235	0.8571
Nikon D5200	0.9200	0.8600	0.9300	0.8600
Olympus E-PL6	0.9183	0.8365	0.9519	0.8750
Panasonic Lumix DMC-GX1	0.9212	0.7635	0.9360	0.8473
Samsung NX2000	0.9208	0.7673	0.9455	0.8366
Sony SLT-A57	0.8881	0.8246	0.9328	0.8731

4.3   Accuracy

Table 1 shows the obtained accuracies for the proposed method using Gray-world on linear images, Gray-world on sRGB images, and camera built-in illumination estimation, as well as the results of the SVM classification by using high-level features on the NUS datasets. It can be seen that the proposed method obtained the best accuracy when it used camera's built-in illumination estimation, but that simultaneously the version that used Gray-world illumination estimation on linear images is not far behind. As for using Gray-world illumination estimation obtained on sRGB images, the obtained accuracy is significantly lower, which clearly demonstrates the superiority of using linear images. Finally, when the results of the high-level features are observed, the obtained accuracy is relatively high when it is considered that the size of the training set was not particularly great and that the setup was simple. Table 2 shows the accuracies obtained on individual cameras i.e. NUS datasets. It can be seen that for some of the present camera models the accuracy of the proposed method can go as high as 95%.

Except for Canon EOS-1Ds Mark III, all other models were produced in years 2011, 2012, or 2013. The images from the Dresden dataset give the possibility to see the accuracy of the proposed method on images obtained by older camera models produced from 2004 to 2008, which is up to 9 years difference when

Table 3. Combined results of several methods on the images of the subset of the Dresden dataset [18]; O stands for outdoor, I for indoor, camera for built-in illumination estimation, and GW for Gray-world.

Method		GW on sRGB		Built-in		High-level features	
Actual label		O	I	O	I	O	I
Predicted label	O	2300	599	2387	627	2509	107
	I	316	1074	229	1046	104	1569
Accuracy		0.7867		0.8004		0.9508	

Table 4. Results of several methods on the images of the subset of the Dresden dataset [18] for individual cameras; O stands for outdoor, I for indoor, built-in for camera's illumination estimation, and GW for Gray-world.

Camera	Method		
	GW on sRGB	Built-in	High-level features
Nikon D200	0.8391	0.8923	1.0000
Nikon D70	0.8699	0.8293	0.7236
Nikon D70s	0.7711	0.7793	0.8011
Olympus mju 1050 SW	0.7962	0.7173	0.9885
Panasonic DMC-FZ50	0.6917	0.7358	0.9989
Pentax OptioA40	0.8229	0.9091	0.9859
Pentax OptioW60	0.7396	0.8281	0.9271

compared to models used for the NUS dataset. The results are shown in Tables 3 and 4. While for some models the accuracy of the proposed method also goes up to 90%, the overall accuracy for all models combined is significantly lower when compared to the one obtained on the NUS datasets despite the fact that all camera models were used to take very similar images of the same scenes.

Finally, Table 5 shows the result for the subset of the reprocessed ColorChecker dataset taken by the Canon EOS 5D camera model, which was announced back in year 2005. Unlike with NUS datasets, here using Gray-world results obtained on sRGB images makes the proposed method to have a higher accuracy then when Gray-world results obtained on linear images are used. Additionally, the accuracy of the proposed method with the camera's built-in illumination estimation is only slightly worse then the high-level features method.

Examples of failure cases of the proposed method when using Gray-world for illumination estimation are shown in Fig. 4. The main reason for the falsely predicted outdoor image is its reddish content, which by definition of Gray-world as the mean value of the image resulted in a warmer illumination estimation, which in turn resulted in the false prediction that the scene is an outdoor one. As for the falsely predicted indoor scene, it can be argued that the scene was taken next to a window and was thus under the direct influence of the outdoor

Table 5. Results of several methods on the Canon EOS 5D images of the reprocessed version [24] of the ColorChecker dataset [15]; O stands for outdoor, I for indoor, camera for built-in illumination estimation, and GW for Gray-world.

Method		GW on linear		GW on sRGB		Built-in		High-level features	
Actual label		O	I	O	I	O	I	O	I
Predicted label	O	275	120	287	79	300	48	289	23
	I	37	50	25	91	12	122	34	136
Accuracy		0.6743		0.7842		0.8755		0.8817	

illumination, which in turn again resulted in a false prediction. It is thus visible that the accuracy and the very nature of the used illumination estimation method also plays an important role in shaping the accuracy of the proposed method.

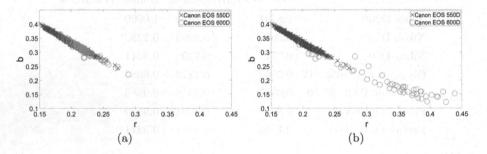

(a)   (b)

Fig. 5. The rb-chromaticities of the ground-truth illumination of the outdoor images of the Cube dataset [3] taken with a Canon EOS 550D illumination estimations compared to rb-chromaticities of ground-truth illumination of image subset of the Canon 600D dataset [9] taken (a) outdoor and (b) indoor.

4.4   Discussion

The presented results demonstrate that the proposed method obtains around 90% accuracy for classifying images as being indoor or outdoor. Since this is on the level of similar state-of-the-art methods, it can be said that using information obtained from illumination estimation on linear images is sufficient for indoor-outdoor image classification. As a matter of fact, the proposed method obtains the best results when the already present camera's auto white balance illumination estimation is used, which means that the added computation cost is minimal, unlike with other proposed solutions. This means that the proposed method is hardware-friendly in addition to being accurate, which lowers the cost.

The best results were observed for the newer camera models, which may be a sign that the characteristics and quality of camera's sensor also play an important role in the overall methods accuracy. Nevertheless, since all of the used cameras did not take images of the same scenes, it is hard to draw a definite conclusion and more experiments are required to answer this question properly.

Beside the sensor, another important factor is the used illumination estimation method. The mentioned Gray-world method is one of the simplest methods. Substituting it with a slightly advanced method, e.g. Shades-of-Gray [13] that uses a predefined Minkowski mean, can already bring significant accuracy gains. In the case of linear ColorChecker by using Shades-of-Gray instead of Gray-world on linear images the accuracy rises from 67.43% to 78.01%.

When analyzing the accuracy results, it can be seen that the proposed method has a significantly higher sensitivity for outdoor images than for indoor images. The explanation for this is that very often indoor images have outdoor illumination coming in through the window, while illumination typical for indoor scenes will influence outdoor scenes only in extreme cases of sunrise or sunset. To better illustrate this high outdoor sensitivity, it is useful to take a look at the rb-chromaticities of ground-truth illumination of the Cube dataset [3] that contains only outdoor images with known illumination. When these chromaticities are compared to indoor illumination chromaticities, it can be seen that only few of Cube's 1365 outdoor illuminations get mixed with indoor illuminations, while it is much often the case that one of the indoor illumination finds itself being inside of the outdoor illumination cluster. This can be seen in Fig. 5 where Cube's ground-truth illumination is compared to the one of the Canon 600D dataset [9]. This dataset was chosen because it was taken with the Canon EOS 600D camera, the successor of the Canon EOS 550D camera that was used to create the Cube dataset, so it was assumed that the sensor differences are small enough not to significantly affect the position of illumination chromaticities.

Finally, it must be stated that with contemporary state-of-the-art deep learning methods it is definitely possible to achieve much higher accuracies than reported in this paper, especially with large amounts of given data. However, the main advantage of the proposed method with respect to that lays in the fact that the reported accuracies were obtained by using only simple statistics with sound theoretical backing, which in turn means that only a relatively small of training images is required. Additionally, when compared to deep learning networks, the proposed method comes with practically no computational cost.

5   Conclusions

A new indoor-outdoor classification method has been proposed. It is based on comparing the results of illumination estimation obtained on linear images and despite being simpler than state-of-the-art methods, it achieves accuracy of same level. The method was shown to work especially accurately if a given camera's built-in auto white balance system was used to provide illumination estimations. When using illumination estimations calculated on sRGB images, the accuracy becomes significantly lower. Future research will include combining illumination estimation with other simple features in order to increase the overall accuracy.

Acknowledgment. We thank the anonymous reviewers for their kind suggestions. This work has been supported by the Croatian Science Foundation under Project IP-06-2016-2092.

References

1. Banić, N., Lončarić, S.: Color Cat: remembering colors for illumination estimation. IEEE Sig. Process. Lett. **22**(6), 651–655 (2015)
2. Banić, N., Lončarić, S.: Using the red chromaticity for illumination estimation. In: 2015 9th International Symposium on Image and Signal Processing and Analysis (ISPA), pp. 131–136. IEEE (2015)
3. Banić, N., Lončarić, S.: Unsupervised learning for color constancy. arXiv preprint arXiv:1712.00436 (2017)
4. Barla, A., Odone, F., Verri, A.: Histogram intersection kernel for image classification. In: 2003 Proceedings of the International Conference on Image Processing, ICIP 2003, vol. 3, p. III-513. IEEE (2003)
5. Bianco, S., Ciocca, G., Cusano, C., Schettini, R.: Improving color constancy using indoor-outdoor image classification. IEEE Trans. Image Process. **17**(12), 2381–2392 (2008)
6. Buchsbaum, G.: A spatial processor model for object colour perception. J. Franklin Inst. **310**(1), 1–26 (1980)
7. Chen, C., Ren, Y., Kuo, C.-C.J.: Large-scale indoor/outdoor image classification via expert decision fusion (EDF). In: Jawahar, C.V., Shan, S. (eds.) ACCV 2014. LNCS, vol. 9008, pp. 426–442. Springer, Cham (2015). https://doi.org/10.1007/978-3-319-16628-5_31
8. Cheng, D., Abdelhamed, A., Price, B., Cohen, S., Brown, M.S.: Two illuminant estimation and user correction preference. In: Proceedings of the IEEE Conference on Computer Vision and Pattern Recognition, pp. 469–477 (2016)
9. Cheng, D., Prasad, D.K., Brown, M.S.: Illuminant estimation for color constancy: why spatial-domain methods work and the role of the color distribution. JOSA A **31**(5), 1049–1058 (2014)
10. Cvetković, S.S., Nikolić, S.V., Ilić, S.: Effective combining of color and texture descriptors for indoor-outdoor image classification. Facta Universitatis Ser. Electron. Energ. **27**(3), 399–410 (2014)
11. Ebner, M.: Color Constancy. The Wiley-IS&T Series in Imaging Science and Technology. Wiley, Chichester (2007)
12. Finlayson, G.D.: Corrected-moment illuminant estimation. In: Proceedings of the IEEE International Conference on Computer Vision, pp. 1904–1911 (2013)
13. Finlayson, G.D., Trezzi, E.: Shades of gray and colour constancy. In: Color and Imaging Conference, vol. 2004, pp. 37–41. Society for Imaging Science and Technology (2004)
14. Funt, B., Shi, L.: The rehabilitation of MaxRGB. In: Color and Imaging Conference, vol. 2010, pp. 256–259. Society for Imaging Science and Technology (2010)
15. Gehler, P.V., Rother, C., Blake, A., Minka, T., Sharp, T.: Bayesian color constancy revisited. In: 2008 IEEE Conference on Computer Vision and Pattern Recognition, CVPR 2008, pp. 1–8. IEEE (2008)
16. Ghomsheh, A.N., Talebpour, A.: A new method for indoor-outdoor image classification using color correlated temperature. Int. J. Image Process **6**(3), 167–181 (2012)

17. Gijsenij, A., Gevers, T., Van De Weijer, J.: Computational color constancy: survey and experiments. IEEE Trans. Image Process. **20**(9), 2475–2489 (2011)
18. Gloe, T., Böhme, R.: The 'Dresden Image Database' for benchmarking digital image forensics. In: Proceedings of the 2010 ACM Symposium on Applied Computing, pp. 1584–1590. ACM (2010)
19. He, K., Zhang, X., Ren, S., Sun, J.: Deep residual learning for image recognition. In: Proceedings of the IEEE Conference on Computer Vision and Pattern Recognition, pp. 770–778 (2016)
20. Hu, G.H., Bu, J.J., Chen, C.: A novel Bayesian framework for indoor-outdoor image classification. In: 2003 International Conference on Machine Learning and Cybernetics, vol. 5, pp. 3028–3032. IEEE (2003)
21. Joze, V., Reza, H.: Estimating the colour of the illuminant using specular reflection and exemplar-based method. Ph.D. thesis, Applied Sciences: School of Computing Science (2013)
22. Kim, S.J., Lin, H.T., Lu, Z., Süsstrunk, S., Lin, S., Brown, M.S.: A new in-camera imaging model for color computer vision and its application. IEEE Trans. Pattern Anal. Mach. Intell. **34**(12), 2289–2302 (2012)
23. Kim, W., Park, J., Kim, C.: A novel method for efficient indoor-outdoor image classification. J. Sig. Process. Syst. **61**(3), 251–258 (2010)
24. Shi, L., Funt, B.: Re-processed version of the gehler color constancy dataset of 568 images (2018). http://www.cs.sfu.ca/~colour/data/
25. Land, E.H.: The retinex theory of color vision. Sci. Am. **237**(6), 108–128 (1977)
26. Luo, J., Savakis, A.: Indoor vs outdoor classification of consumer photographs using low-level and semantic features. In: 2001 Proceedings of the International Conference on Image Processing, vol. 2, pp. 745–748. IEEE (2001)
27. Nguyen, R.M., Brown, M.S.: RAW image reconstruction using a self-contained sRGB-JPEG image with only 64 KB overhead. In: Proceedings of the IEEE Conference on Computer Vision and Pattern Recognition, pp. 1655–1663 (2016)
28. Nguyen, R.M., Brown, M.S.: RAW image reconstruction using a self-contained sRGB-JPEG image with small memory overhead. Int. J. Comput. Vis. **126**(6), 637–650 (2018)
29. Payne, A., Singh, S.: Indoor vs. outdoor scene classification in digital photographs. Pattern Recogn. **38**(10), 1533–1545 (2005)
30. Serrano, N., Savakis, A., Luo, A.: A computationally efficient approach to indoor/outdoor scene classification. In: 2002 Proceedings of the 16th International Conference on Pattern Recognition, vol. 4, pp. 146–149. IEEE (2002)
31. Shwetha, T., Shaila, H.: Indoor outdoor scene classification in digital images. Int. J. Electr. Electron. Comput. Syst. **2**(11–12), 34–38 (2014)
32. Steinwart, I., Christmann, A.: Support Vector Machines. ISS. Springer Science & Business Media, New York (2008). https://doi.org/10.1007/978-0-387-77242-4
33. Szummer, M., Picard, R.W.: Indoor-outdoor image classification. In: 1998 Proceedings of the IEEE International Workshop on Content-Based Access of Image and Video Database, pp. 42–51. IEEE (1998)
34. Tahir, W., Majeed, A., Rehman, T.: Indoor/outdoor image classification using gist image features and neural network classifiers. In: 2015 12th International Conference on High-Capacity Optical Networks and Enabling/Emerging Technologies (HONET), pp. 1–5. IEEE (2015)
35. Vailaya, A., Figueiredo, M.A., Jain, A.K., Zhang, H.J.: Image classification for content-based indexing. IEEE Trans. Image Process. **10**(1), 117–130 (2001)

36. Zhu, Y., Newsam, S.: Land use classification using convolutional neural networks applied to ground-level images. In: Proceedings of the 23rd SIGSPATIAL International Conference on Advances in Geographic Information Systems, p. 61. ACM (2015)

37. Zou, J., Li, W., Chen, C., Du, Q.: Scene classification using local and global features with collaborative representation fusion. Inf. Sci. **348**, 209–226 (2016)

DeepKey: Towards End-to-End Physical Key Replication from a Single Photograph

Rory Smith[✉] and Tilo Burghardt

Department of Computer Science, SCEEM, University of Bristol, Bristol, UK
rs14369@bristol.ac.uk, tilo@cs.bris.ac.uk

Abstract. This paper describes DeepKey, an end-to-end deep neural architecture capable of taking a digital RGB image of an 'everyday' scene containing a pin tumbler key (e.g. lying on a table or carpet) and fully automatically inferring a printable 3D key model. We report on the key detection performance and describe how candidates can be transformed into physical prints. We show an example opening a real-world lock. Our system is described in detail, providing a breakdown of all components including key detection, pose normalisation, bitting segmentation and 3D model inference. We provide an in-depth evaluation and conclude by reflecting on limitations, applications, potential security risks and societal impact. We contribute the DeepKey Datasets of 5,300+ images covering a few test keys with bounding boxes, pose and unaligned mask data.

1 Introduction and Overview

Imaging the detailed structural properties of physical keys is easily possible using modern high-resolution cameras or smartphones. Such photography may be undertaken by the rightful owner of a key to produce a visual backup or by an untrusted third party. The latter could potentially image keys unnoticed, particularly when considering scenarios that expose key rings in plain sight in public (e.g. on a table at a cafe) or even private environments (e.g. on a kitchen counter visible through a window).

In this paper we show that fully automated physical key generation from photographic snapshots is a technical reality. Despite a low physical duplication accuracy experienced with the described system, this raises wider questions and highlights the need for adequate countermeasures. In particular, we will explain here how a visual end-to-end convolutional neural network (CNN) architecture can be used to generate 3D-printable pin tumbler key models from single RGB images without user input. To the best of our knowledge the proposed system is the first one that automates the task – that is compared to published semi-manual approaches of potentially much higher replication quality [12].

As depicted in Fig. 1, the deep neural network (DNN) pipeline put forward here takes an 'everyday' scene containing a Yale pin tumbler key as input. It

© Springer Nature Switzerland AG 2019
T. Brox et al. (Eds.): GCPR 2018, LNCS 11269, pp. 487–502, 2019.
https://doi.org/10.1007/978-3-030-12939-2_34

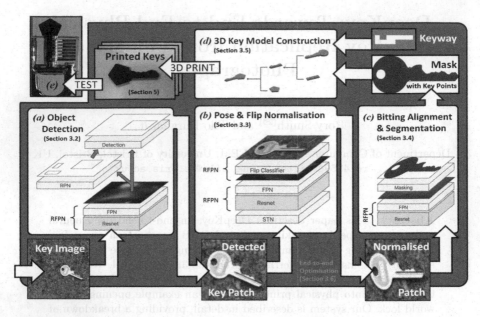

Fig. 1. DeepKey architecture. Overview of pipeline to generate a physical pin tumbler key from an RGB photograph. *(a) Key detection:* images are fed to a Resnet-101-v2 [9] backbone followed by a feature pyramid network (FPN) [13], together referred to as an RFPN component. This RFPN, a region proposal network (RPN), and a detection network combinedly perform proposal filtering, bounding box regression and content classification [17]. *(b) Pose normalisation:* translation, scale, rotation and warp normalisation of detected key patches is then implemented via a spatial transformer network (STN) [10], whilst a specialised RFPN controls flipping. *(c) Bitting extraction:* segmentation of normalised patches is based on Mask R-CNN [7] inferring binary bitting masks via an extended RFPN. *(d) Key inference:* masks are finally converted to 3D-printable models to yield plastic prints of Yale keys. *(e) Physical tests:* given models of sufficient quality, these key prints may open real-world locks, although many distinct models may be required.

then breaks vision-based key reconstruction down into a sequence of distinct inference tasks: first, keys are detected in the scene via a pose-invariantly trained Faster R-CNN [17] component, whose outputs are transformed into a unified pose domain by a customised spatial transformer network (STN) [10]. These pose-normalised patches containing aligned instances are used to infer the bitting pattern, exploiting the concepts of Mask R-CNN [7].

Finally, alignment and projection of the bitting mask onto a known 'keyway' yields a CAD entity, which may be 3D-printed into a physical object. Using portions of the DeepKey Datasets as training information, our network pipeline is first optimised at the component level before final steps proceed in a forward-feeding end-to-end manner allowing for optimisation by the discovery of weight correlations.

Before describing our architecture, training and recorded performance in detail, we briefly review methodologies and prior work relevant to the application.

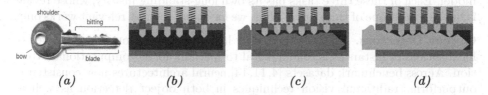

Fig. 2. Pin tumbler keys and locks. *(a) Pin tumbler keys:* for a given manufacturer type the non-public key information is encoded in the bitting, which is the target of the visual reconstruction. A key's keyway is a secondary level of security, but is publicly available, given the key type is known. Allowed cuts adhere to a maximum adjacent cut specification (MACS) to ensure insertion and extraction of the key is always possible. *(b–d) Pin tumbler locks:* unlocking requires raising a set of stacked pins to particular, key-specific heights such that the entire cylinder can rotate cleanly.

2 Related Work and Context

2.1 Vision-based Key Replication

For this proof of concept we focus on the vision-based replication of Yale pin tumbler keys only, a widely used key class and lock arrangement. As shown in Fig. 2, pin tumbler locks require the key to raise a set of stacked pins at different heights such that the entire plug may rotate cleanly. This is achieved by cuts made into one edge of the key, known as the 'bitting'. For a given pin tumbler lock type, such as Yale, it is the bitting alone that encodes the information unique to an individual key. A key type's remaining geometric information including its 'keyway' frontal profile is publicly available via manufacturer type patents that legally prevent the reproduction of uncut keys without a license. Even without accurate schematics, a key's frontal profile can be determined from a single photo of the key's lock visible from the outside of the door [2].

Existing Vision-based Key Replication. Computational teleduplication of physical keys via optical decoding was first published by Laxton et al. [12] who designed a semi-automated system named 'Sneakey'. Their software requires the user to crop the key from an image and annotate manually two separate point sets: a key-type-dependent one enabling planar homographic normalisation to a rectified pose, and a lock-dependent one for decoding the individual bitting code.

2.2 Deep Learning Concepts

In this paper, we assume the key type to be fixed and the keyway to be known. Automating vision-based key replication based on this, then evolves around solving three 'classic' vision tasks: that is object(-class) detection and localisation [11] of keys, rigid key pose estimation and normalisation [10], as well as image segmentation [7] to extract the bitting pattern. A projection of the bitting onto the known keyway will then generate a scale-accurate description as a CAD model. Each of these three tasks has its own long-standing history, whose review is beyond the scope of this paper. Thus, we focus on the most relevant works only.

Object Detectors. For the pipeline at hand, mapping from input images to localisations of instances is fundamental to spatially focus computational attention. Across benchmark datasets [4,11,14] neural architectures now consistently outperform traditional vision techniques in both object detection as well as image classification [3,11,16,21]. Region-based convolutional neural networks (R-CNNs) [6] combine these tasks by unifying candidate localisation and classification – however, in its original form, R-CNNs are computationally expensive [5]. By sharing operations across proposals as in Fast R-CNN or SPPnet [5,8] efficiency can be gained, although proposal estimation persists to be a bottleneck. To address this, Ren et al. introduced region proposal networks (RPNs) [17], which again share features during detection, resulting in the Faster R-CNN [17]. We use this approach here for initial candidate key detection, noting that various alternative architectures such as YOLO [16] and Overfeat [20] are also viable.

Network Substructure. The base component in Faster R-CNNs, also referred to as its 'backbone', can be altered or exchanged without breaking the approach's conceptual layout. Practically, deeper backbone networks often lead to improved detection performance [21]. In response to this observation and as suggested by He et al. [7], we utilise the well-tested 101-layer Resnet-101-v2 [9] backbone in our work with final weight sharing (see Sect. 3.6). As shown in Fig. 5, its output feeds into a feature pyramid network (FPN) [13] similar in spatial layout to traditional scale-space feature maps [1]. When considering the detection application at hand where key height and width can vary vastly, the explicit use of an FPN helps to detect keys at these various scales *fast*. Moreover, together with the backbone, it forms a versatile RFPN network pair.

Normalisation and Segmentation. Fundamentally, RFPN components learn scale-space features and, thus, have been shown to support a versatile array of mapping tasks [7,17] – including segmentation. Mask R-CNNs [7] exemplify this practically by adding further convolutional and then de-convolutional layers to an RFPN in order to map to a binary mask (see Fig. 7). We base our segmentation architecture off this concept, but apply modifications to increase the final mask resolution (see Sect. 3.4). Additionally, spatial transforms arising from variance in viewpoint are rectified. Spatial transformer networks (STNs) [10] are designed to deal with this task, although traditionally in an implicit way, where the parameters of the transformation matrix that affects the image are not known. Our STN estimates transformation matrix parameters directly after object detection, unifying the representation and production of orthonormal key views for segmentation (see Fig. 6).

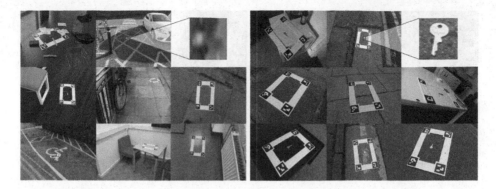

Fig. 3. DeepKey datasets. *(left) Lower resolution dataset A:* examples from 2, 653 'everyday' scenes resolved at 5184×3456 pixels containing both rectification patterns for training and an ordinary pin tumbler key at resolutions ranging from 78×21 to 746×439 primarily used to train key detection components; *(right) Higher resolution dataset B:* examples from 2, 696 scenes of seven different pin tumbler keys and rectification patterns resolved at 5184 × 3456 pixels with key resolutions from 171 × 211 to 689 × 487 pixels primarily used to train bitting segmentation networks. Lowest resolution key patches from both datasets are visualised in the upper-right-most images.

3 DeepKey Implementation

3.1 Generation of Training Information

We collected 5, 349 images of a few keys provided in two separate DeepKey Datasets[1] A and B, detailed in Fig. 3, plus a tiny extra Test C (see Sect. 5) featuring a key not contained in either set. Set A contains distant shots of common environments that may contain keys – such as tables, carpets, road surfaces, and wooden boards. Set B contains shots with keys at higher resolution, but less environmental context. We divide the datasets into a traditional split of approx. 70% for system training and a withheld portion of remaining images for validation. To allow for automatic data annotation, we developed a physical marker frame which is placed around keys in the real world (see Figs. 3 and 4), with placement aided by a custom-developed mobile app using an iPhone 7 smartphone. The marker board essentially provides four points, which can be used during a post-processing step to calculate a projective transform per image. This automatic meta-annotation allows us to reduce labelling and produce larger training sets with exact parameterisation for backpropagation during learning.

3.2 Pose-Invariant Key Detection

Our detailed detection architecture is depicted in Fig. 5. Woven around a Faster R-CNN layout with a training RPN proposal limit of 200 we utilise a Resnet-101-v2 as the network backbone. An empirical study of similar alternatives as shown

---

[1] DeepKey Datasets can be requested via https://data.bris.ac.uk.

Fig. 4. Perspective ground truth and augmentation. *(left) Marker frame:* Annotation of training images via 4 ArUco markers, pasted on a rigid card base. Automatic labelling locates each marker and generates a bounding box and transformation matrix per image. *(right) Synthetic data augmentation:* The application of pseudo-random crop, scale, flip and shift augmentations to the data yields further synthetic data. Shown are an original example image (top left) and three derived augmentations next to it. In addition, the two right-most images illustrate the marker frame exclusion augmentation used as an alternative evaluation strategy (see Sect. 4).

in Fig. 5 (right) confirms its efficacy. Inspired by Mask R-CNN [7], the FPN fed by this backbone provides improved scale-dependent detection performance. It takes Resnet blocks $C2, C3, C4, C5$ and adds lateral connections as shown in Fig. 5. We feed in resized images at 224×224 pixels and used a pooling size of 8×8 when resizing cropped feature-map regions. With training images augmented from DeepKey Datasets A and B, we first froze our backbone to fine-tune remaining layers via SGD with momentum ($\lambda = 0.9$) with batch size 16 and learning rate (LR) of 0.001 for 400 epochs – before unfreezing the backbone and lowering the LR by factor 10 and optimizing for 400 epochs further. We use log losses for RPN and detection head classification as detailed in [17], and a smooth L1 loss as defined in [5] for bounding box regression. We evaluate the detection component in detail in Sect. 4 where Fig. 9 visualises results. Note that we carry out a comparative study confirming that the potential presence of marker frame pixels in the receptive fields of network layers has no application-preventing impact on key detection performance.

3.3   Pose Normalisation

In order to map key detections into unified pose we opt to use traditional geometric transform operations fuelled by deep network predictions of eight perspective transform parameters as well as flips. Figure 6 (left) shows the used architecture in detail. Following [24], an STN first predicts eight parameters forming a transformation matrix, which are applied to the input via a projective transform. Rather than applying STNs in a traditional unsupervised manner, we train against our labelled dataset of transform parameters, using an averaged

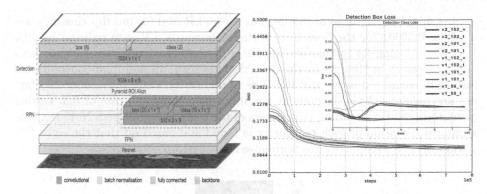

Fig. 5. Detection network architecture. *(left) Component details:* in-depth description of the layout of our detection component, where Resnet-101-v2 is used as the backbone. *(right) Backbone performance study:* results depict the performance impact of using different networks as backbone. Note the performance/size trade-of struck by Resnet-101-v2 compared to the various alternatives investigated.

L2 norm loss (MSE) detailed in [18]. Note that we do not use the features from our Resnet-101 backbone, but instead opt to take a shallower number of convolutions from the raw image. A subsequent flip classification network determines whether the key requires flipping such that its bitting faces up, readily aligned for bitting segmentation. Using SGD with momentum ($\lambda = 0.9$) and batch size 32, pose normalisation and flip classification are repeatedly trained on DeepKey Dataset B key patches, with random augmentations resolved at 128×128 pixels, against pre-computed marker frame ground truths as detailed in Fig. 4.

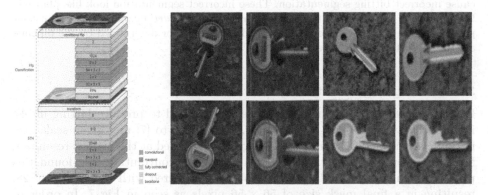

Fig. 6. Pose normalisation architecture. *(left) Component details:* in order to normalise pose, an STN predicts 8 mapping parameters on whose basis a perspective transform is applied (white). Subsequently, a classification network determines whether or not an image flip should be performed. *(right) Examples of normalised keys:* representative sample patches before and after pose normalisation and flip correction.

Inspired by [10], pose normalisation uses a LR of 0.01 and flip classification a LR of 0.00001 for the first 400 epochs. Afterwards, LRs are reduced by 10× before continuing for further 400 epochs. Flip classification uses a softmax cross entropy loss as in [18]. As in the detection network, all non-final convolutional and fully connected layers use ReLU as non-linearity. Only fully-connected layers are regularised via dropout at an empirically optimised rate of 0.3. During pose normalisation training parameters of the loss are normalised. Note that the standard deviation of each parameter is found and based on that the eight free parameters $\theta_0, \theta_1, \theta_2 \ldots \theta_7$ are normalised to speed up convergence.

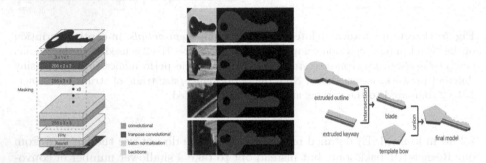

Fig. 7. Segmentation architecture, mask examples and key modelling. *(left) Component overview:* normalised key crops are fed through our modified Mask-RCNN head, where the additional deconvolutions and larger pool size provides us greater output resolution. *(middle) Segmentation examples after end-to-end optimisation:* final pose normalisations and bitting segmentations after running test samples through the full end-to-end system. Masks are resized from 56 × 56 pixel output. Top 2 examples show valid bitting segmentation whereas others highlight cases where normalisation errors cause incorrect bitting segmentation. These incorrect segmentation look like plausible key masks but do not match the ground truth. *(right) Modelling process:* separate components of the key that are either provided by the user or determined by the pipeline are fused together to create a printable STL file.

3.4   Bitting Segmentation

Figure 7 depicts how normalised patches are utilised to produce bitting masks inspired by Mask R-CNN [7]. However, in contrast to [7] and given scale pre-normalisation, we only compute FPN layer $P2$ encoded at the highest resolution and use 8 convolutions (rather than 4) before de-convolution. We found this provides higher precision in mask outputs when paired with a pool size of 28, resulting in a final mask size of 56 × 56 pixels as seen in Fig. 7. In order to accurately align the output mask with the keyway, we define ground truth masks with small activation areas of two key points as further pixel classes to train on – following [7]. We use DeepKey Dataset B at a LR of 0.001 and SGD with momentum ($\lambda = 0.9$) for training. LR was reduced by a factor 10 after 400 epochs before running further 400 epochs. As given in [7], our masking loss was average binary cross entropy loss with a per-pixel sigmoid on final layer logits.

3.5   3D Model Generation and Printing

The estimated key mask, key points, keyway profile and real-world keyway height are used for 3D key model generation. Binarisations of the bitting mask are transformed into a series of key boundary points. Using this description, this bitting and the known keyway can be extruded along orthogonal axes and key point locations are aligned (scaled + translated) with the keyway via scripts [15], where the final key blade is constructed by union and attachment of a standard key bow before outputting an STL file printable using [22].

3.6   Final Optimisation via an End-to-End Pipeline

After training all subcomponents as described, we then progress to the end-to-end training of components by forwarding data generated by each subcomponent as training data to subsequent components in order to optimise the overall system. This two-step process of bootstrapping each subcomponent's weights from separately provided ground truth mitigated the effect of early stage errors.

During end-to-end training, we only generate training data from the DeepKey Dataset B adjusting the detection component to take input sizes of 1024×1024 (up from the 224×224 standard of [11]) due to resolution requirements of the later stages. Additionally, we use input batches of 2 and a detection proposal limit of 32 so that later stages experience an effective batch size of 64 because of GPU size limitations – all other training parameters are inherited from the definitions provided in each subcomponent's section. Inputs are processed end-to-end for 200 epochs to train with frozen backbones, followed by a further 800 epochs at 1/10 LR, and a final 800 epochs with unfrozen backbones and a batch size of only 2 at a LR of 10^{-7}.

In order to fit the end-to-end pipeline onto Blue Crystal 4 [23] Nvidia P100 GPU nodes used for all optimisations of this paper, we opted to share the learned weights between the three backbone instances across the architecture. Despite weight sharing, performance improvements can still be recorded under our forwarding end-to-end paradigm.

4   Results

This section discusses and evaluates in detail metrics that quantify the performance of each subcomponent and the overall DeepKey system. For detection evaluation, six different types of test data arrangements will be used, all derived from withheld testset portions of the DeepKey Datasets: (1) first, 875 withheld original low-resolution images from Dataset A; (2) 875 images derived from the former via augmentation (reminder of Fig. 4); (3) 889 withheld original high-resolution images from Dataset B; (4) 889 images derived from the former via augmentation; (5) 889 withheld original high resolution images from Dataset B with marker frame removal; and (6) 889 images derived from the former via augmentation. All subsequent component evaluations utilise Dataset variation 3.

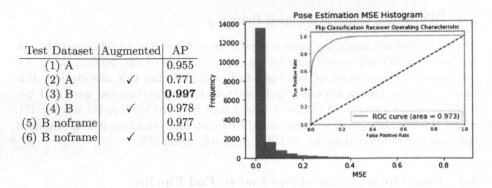

Test Dataset	Augmented	AP
(1) A		0.955
(2) A	✓	0.771
(3) B		**0.997**
(4) B	✓	0.978
(5) B noframe		0.977
(6) B noframe	✓	0.911

Fig. 8. Detection and normalisation visualisations and metrics. *(left) Detection AP metrics:* results are shown for all six test cases covering original test data, geometric augmentations, as well as 'noframe' tests with augmentation of colours of all marker pixels and those outside the marker black. *(right) Pose normalisation metrics:* pose normalisation results in low parameter value MSE achieved on the DeepKey TestSet B, where flip classification achieves an AUC of 0.973.

Marker frame removal is applied to guarantee full independence from marker-board presence during tests. Whilst augmentations (see Sect. 3) allow for validation using a larger number of geometric transforms than found in the data gathered, in order to ensure we are not applying augmentations to manipulate object detection results in our favour, we also compare to non-augmented data. Figure 8 (left) shows an overview of key detection performance results for all six test data arrangements. Figure 9 then exemplifies detection and quantifies localisation regression. It provides a precision-recall analysis of improvements provided by localisation regression.

It can be seen that key-class object detection produces the highest AP of 0.997 upon the original DeepKey Testset B. The system achieves a lower AP when full augmentation is applied. Our results show only a negligible decrease in AP when removing marker information. Thus, the bias towards images containing markers as introduced in training is small – key detection AP on the original DeepKey Testset B reduces by 2.00% from $AP = 0.997$ to $AP = 0.977$ upon marker frame removal from test instances. Figure 8 (right) shows an overview of pose normalisation performance results, where the process can be seen depicted in Figure 6 (right) key samples are successfully normalised and flipped. We record the MSE across all values of the transformation matrices generated by pose normalisation inference to produce a histogram showing the error distribution. In addition, we produce a receiver operating characteristic (ROC) plot for flip classification. Our flip classification network operates with an AUC of 0.973. Via the application of Gradcam [19], it can be seen that, as depicted in Fig. 10, the network activations of this component focus indeed on key bitting and shoulder during flip classification, as required to determine orientation. Transformation estimation performs as described in Fig. 8 (right), however, a small absolute error

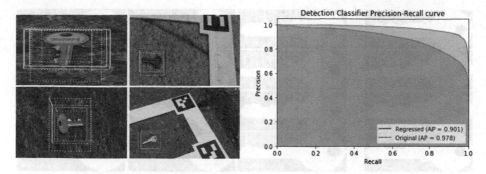

Fig. 9. Detection head performance. *(left) Correct proposal samples:* four input images and their detection head bounding box regressions. Dotted boxes indicate original proposals from the RPN and are depicted with their regressed solid box counterparts by similarly coloured lines. In the featured samples, the firstly somewhat misaligned RPN proposals are regressed to common bounding boxes that correctly bound their target keys. *(right) Precision-recall metric:* precision-recall curve for the first ($AP = 0.901$) and then the regressed final detection head proposals ($AP = 0.978$ as reported in Fig. 8) when run on augmented images derived from DeepKey Testset B. (Color figure online)

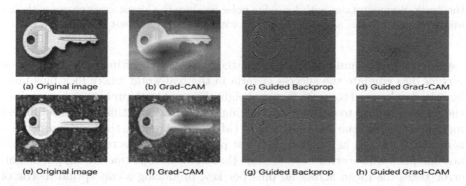

Fig. 10. Flip classification visualisation. *(a, e) Original input patches:* RGB normalised key crops of the flipped and unflipped classes. *(b, f) Grad-CAM heatmaps:* overlayed on top of original images showing areas of interest to the final convolutional layer before fully connected layers and predictions. Note how on the flipped key the shoulder of the key is seen as interesting to the final layer whereas on the unflipped key, the key bitting is used. *(c, g) Guided back-propagation:* visualisation of features important to the prediction. *(d, h) Guided grad-CAM:* combining Grad-CAM with guided back-prop to highlight potentially class-discriminative features.

can of course still result in a clearly visible transformation error, as depicted by non-horizontal keys in Figs. 6 (right).

When evaluating the bitting segmentation, we take an approach contrary to the standard in image segmentation: rather than only calculating the pixel mask IoU as in [7], we also focus our evaluation on the bitting of the keys by casting

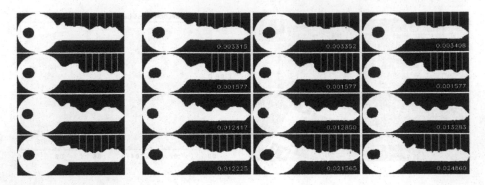

Fig. 11. Bitting segmentation error visualisation. Ground truth masks in left column, segmentation examples of this key on the right. Per-mask errors are given on each mask. *(top to bottom) MPE:* error is calculated as max difference between ground truth cut height and measured segmentation cut height at virtual pin locations. This metric favours keys with shallow bittings as segmentations tend to smooth. *Mean:* error is calculated as mean difference between ground truth cut height and measured cut height at virtual pin locations. We find this metric scores best on validation keys of a similar type to those in the training set, which exhibit little variation. *IoU:* error is the pixelwise intersection between mask and ground truth, divided by the area of the mask. Segmentations with low edge noise produce the lowest error scores with this metric. *Unseen MPE:* same as *MPE*, but with an unseen key, not in dataset A or B.

rays at manually annotated locations required for pin lifting in a lock. These *virtual pins* emulate the success criteria in the real-world where lock pins must be raised or lowered to a satisfactory height. Figure 11 comprehensively visualises the metrics we use to evaluate the bitting segmentation, utilising three different metrics: (top row) the 'max pin height' (MPE) error reflects the largest difference across all cuts on a key, and is the most practical metric as reality requires that not one pin produce error beyond some threshold; (second row) 'mean pin height' error takes the mean across all pins per key, producing a conceptual metric of how far the bitting of a key is from ground truth; (third row) 'pixel IoU' is included for the sake of comparison.

The practically most relevant metric is that of MPE: Fig. 11 (bottom) includes a mask never seen in training data (outside DeepKey Datasets A and B) with an MPE of 0.0122 – we use example output to print a physical sample and successfully open its target lock as shown in Fig. 12. For this test, we estimate physical operation capable of unlocking the target when used with a key showing a segmentation error of $MPE <= 0.012$, however, we note that higher quality locks will feature lower bitting error tolerances. Across our validation set, mean MPE is 0.039, far higher than the quality example given in Fig. 11 (top).

5   Physical Proof-of-Concept

Consequently, according to the result statistics, only a small proportion of physical replicas generated are expected to work in opening the target lock. To provide

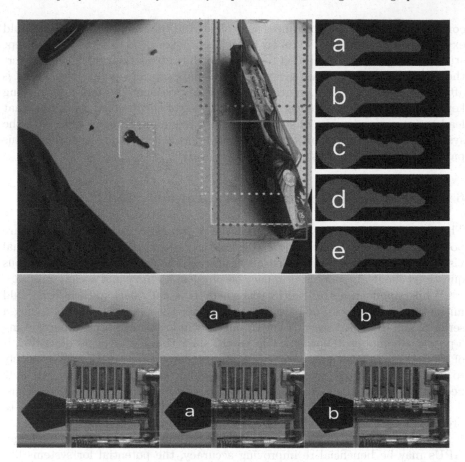

Fig. 12. Physical key prediction example. *(top-left) Example of unseen image:* sample image from the unseen DeepKey dataset C, without the inclusion of any marker frames. The selected key detection undergoes normalisation and is rectified, which in turn allows segmentation to successfully take place. *(top-right) Sampled segmentations:* 5 manually selected samples from the end-to-end segmentation output used to print physical keys for tests. *(bottom) 3D printed key opens lock:* red ground truth key raises all lock pins to their valid positions. Print (a) resulting from the above end-to-end system output also raises all lock pins to sufficient levels, although they are visibly slightly different from those of the ground truth key. A secondary print (b) exhibits too large deviance in bitting to open the lock. (Color figure online)

a proof of concept that real-world locks can indeed be opened using the system, we evaluate the full pipeline empirically using a tiny, new set of test images (withheld DeepKey Dataset C) of a hitherto, unseen key exemplified in the top left image of Fig. 12. We manually select the top 5 end-to-end masks – three of these masks can be seen in Fig. 11 (bottom). From this test set of 5, we find that only 1 is capable of unlocking the target lock as shown in Fig. 12. Although the heights of the pins differ from the ground truth key, the lock still operates correctly due to in-built tolerances as explained in the results section. We would expect truly high-quality locks to reject such a key. For this proof-of-concept study many prints were needed to yield one that opens the target lock. Nevertheless, the study shows that given an image of appropriate quality, the system *is* after possibly many trials eventually capable of producing a valid, lock-opening key from a single visual image. Further analyses of the detailed conditions that lead to images and prints of sufficient quality to successful open locks with the system would be an important step, however, this is outside the scope of this paper and would require significant further work.

6   Reflection, Potential Societal Impact, and Conclusion

The usability of basic key imagery for the production of key models that are potentially capable of unlocking a physical target lock, be that via a traditional vision system [12] or via a deep learning approach such as DeepKey, raises various questions about any potential impact on physical security and society overall.

Whilst applications for legitimate owners to visually backup their keys could mitigate accidental loss, one also has to consider the case of assailants taking a series of still RGB pictures of a key through a window and printing replicas using a potentially mobile 3D printer. Our results show that DeepKey, as described, is of limited use in such a scenario since multiple key models and prints are likely to be required, as not every model will be valid, and the number of attempts needed will rise as the lock quality increases due to lower error tolerances. Thus, it is probable that many prints, possibly 10s or even 100s may be needed to produce a working key using DeepKey depending on the scenario.

Whilst we believe that increased final prediction resolution trained via larger GPUs may be beneficial re improving accuracy, the potential for systems like DeepKey to cause a general threat to public lock-users is also hamstrung by the large variety of lock types available today. We assessed only the application of automated key model prediction to one type of Yale pin tumbler keys.

Most importantly, however, everyone should consider that basic countermeasures such as avoidance of visual exposure or bitting-covering key rings are simple and effective ways to deny unwanted key imaging. New architectures and approaches to lock-based security such as those featuring multi-sided 3D bittings may also be effective in minimising the risk of unwanted photographic capture. Magnetic locks in particular provide security properties outside the visual domain since the key's secret is encoded in the orientation of embedded magnets. Due to the lack in visual variance of such keys, any visual system would be entirely ineffective in capturing the key's secret information.

We hope that the publication of DeepKey can inspire research into countermeasures and legitimate security applications, whilst also acting as an early warning: academia, lock producers, authorities and the general public must be alerted to the growing potential of deep learning driven visual attacks in an unprepared physical security world.

References

1. Adelson, E.H., Bergen, J.R., Burt, P.J., Ogden, J.M.: Pyramid methods in image processing. RCA Eng. **29**(4), 33–41 (1984)
2. Burgess, B., Wustrow, E., Halderman, J.A.: Replication prohibited: attacking restricted keyways with 3D-printing. In: WOOT (2015)
3. Dai, J., et al.: Deformable convolutional networks. CoRR abs/1703.06211 (2017). https://doi.org/10.1109/ICCV.2017.89, http://arxiv.org/abs/1703.06211
4. Everingham, M., Van Gool, L., Williams, C.K.I., Winn, J., Zisserman, A.: The PASCAL Visual Object Classes Challenge 2012 (VOC 2012) Results. http://www.pascal-network.org/challenges/VOC/voc2012/workshop/index.html
5. Girshick, R.B.: Fast R-CNN. In: 2015 IEEE International Conference on Computer Vision (ICCV), pp. 1440–1448 (2015). https://doi.org/10.1109/ICCV.2015.169
6. Girshick, R.B., Donahue, J., Darrell, T., Malik, J.: Rich feature hierarchies for accurate object detection and semantic segmentation. CoRR abs/1311.2524 (2013). https://doi.org/10.1109/CVPR.2014.81, http://arxiv.org/abs/1311.2524
7. He, K., Gkioxari, G., Dollár, P., Girshick, R.B.: Mask R-CNN. In: 2017 IEEE International Conference on Computer Vision (ICCV), pp. 2980–2988 (2017). https://doi.org/10.1109/ICCV.2017.322
8. He, K., Zhang, X., Ren, S., Sun, J.: Spatial pyramid pooling in deep convolutional networks for visual recognition. CoRR abs/1406.4729 (2014). https://doi.org/10.1109/TPAMI.2015.2389824, http://arxiv.org/abs/1406.4729
9. He, K., Zhang, X., Ren, S., Sun, J.: Deep residual learning for image recognition. In: 2016 IEEE Conference on Computer Vision and Pattern Recognition (CVPR), pp. 770–778 (2016). https://doi.org/10.1109/CVPR.2016.90
10. Jaderberg, M., Simonyan, K., Zisserman, A., Kavukcuoglu, K.: Spatial transformer networks. In: NIPS (2015)
11. Krizhevsky, A., Sutskever, I., Hinton, G.E.: Imagenet classification with deep convolutional neural networks. In: NIPS (2012). https://doi.org/10.1145/3065386
12. Laxton, B., Wang, K., Savage, S.: Reconsidering physical key secrecy: teleduplication via optical decoding. In: ACM Conference on Computer and Communications Security (2008). https://doi.org/10.1145/1455770.1455830
13. Lin, T.Y., Dollár, P., Girshick, R.B., He, K., Hariharan, B., Belongie, S.J.: Feature pyramid networks for object detection. In: 2017 IEEE Conference on Computer Vision and Pattern Recognition (CVPR), pp. 936–944 (2017). https://doi.org/10.1109/CVPR.2017.106
14. Lin, T., et al.: Microsoft COCO: common objects in context. CoRR abs/1405.0312 (2014). http://arxiv.org/abs/1405.0312
15. Marius Kintel, C.W.: Openscad. http://www.blender.org/
16. Redmon, J., Farhadi, A.: YOLO9000: better, faster, stronger. CoRR abs/1612.08242 (2016). http://arxiv.org/abs/1612.08242
17. Ren, S., He, K., Girshick, R.B., Sun, J.: Faster R-CNN: towards real-time object detection with region proposal networks. IEEE Trans. Pattern Anal. Mach. Intell. **39**, 1137–1149 (2015). https://doi.org/10.1109/TPAMI.2016.2577031
18. Schmidhuber, J.: Deep learning in neural networks: an overview. CoRR abs/1404.7828 (2014). https://doi.org/10.1016/j.neunet.2014.09.003, http://arxiv.org/abs/1404.7828
19. Selvaraju, R.R., Cogswell, M., Das, A., Vedantam, R., Parikh, D., Batra, D.: Grad-CAM: visual explanations from deep networks via gradient-based localization. In: 2017 IEEE International Conference on Computer Vision (ICCV), pp. 618–626 (2017). https://doi.org/10.1109/ICCV.2017.74

20. Sermanet, P., Eigen, D., Zhang, X., Mathieu, M., Fergus, R., LeCun, Y.: OverFeat: integrated recognition, localization and detection using convolutional networks. CoRR abs/1312.6229 (2013)
21. Simonyan, K., Zisserman, A.: Very deep convolutional networks for large-scale image recognition. CoRR abs/1409.1556 (2014)
22. Ultimaker BV: Ultimaker 2 plus technical specifications (2016). https://ultimaker.com/en/products/ultimaker-2-plus/specifications
23. Univeristy of Bristol Advanced Computing Research Centre: Blue crystal phase 4 (2017). https://www.acrc.bris.ac.uk/acrc/phase4.htm
24. Zakka, K.: Spatial transformer network implementation, January 2017. https://github.com/kevinzakka/spatial-transformer-network

Deriving Neural Network Architectures Using Precision Learning: Parallel-to-Fan Beam Conversion

Christopher Syben[1,2]([✉]), Bernhard Stimpel[1,2], Jonathan Lommen[1,2], Tobias Würfl[1], Arnd Dörfler[2], and Andreas Maier[1]

[1] Pattern Recognition Lab, Department of Computer Science,
Friedrich-Alexander-Universität Erlangen-Nürnberg, Erlangen, Germany
christopher.syben@fau.de
[2] Department of Neuroradiology, Universitätsklinikum Erlangen,
Friedrich-Alexander-Universität Erlangen-Nürnberg, Erlangen, Germany

Abstract. In this paper, we derive a neural network architecture based on an analytical formulation of the parallel-to-fan beam conversion problem following the concept of precision learning. The network allows to learn the unknown operators in this conversion in a data-driven manner avoiding interpolation and potential loss of resolution. Integration of known operators results in a small number of trainable parameters that can be estimated from synthetic data only. The concept is evaluated in the context of Hybrid MRI/X-ray imaging where transformation of the parallel-beam MRI projections to fan-beam X-ray projections is required. The proposed method is compared to a traditional rebinning method. The results demonstrate that the proposed method is superior to ray-by-ray interpolation and is able to deliver sharper images using the same amount of parallel-beam input projections which is crucial for interventional applications. We believe that this approach forms a basis for further work uniting deep learning, signal processing, physics, and traditional pattern recognition.

Keywords: Machine learning · Precision learning · Hybrid MRI/X-ray imaging

1 Introduction

Deep learning is a game-changer in many perceptual tasks ranging from image classification over segmentation to localization [2]. A major disadvantage of perceptual problems is that no prior knowledge on how the classes and labels are obtained is available. As such a large body of literature exists that investigates different network topologies for different applications. As result, we managed to replace *hand-crafted features* with *hand-crafted networks*.

Recently, these techniques also emerge to other fields in signal processing. One of them is medical image reconstruction in which surprising results have

© Springer Nature Switzerland AG 2019
T. Brox et al. (Eds.): GCPR 2018, LNCS 11269, pp. 503–517, 2019.
https://doi.org/10.1007/978-3-030-12939-2_35

been obtained [4, 16]. For signal processing, however, we do have prior knowledge available that can be reused in the network design. The use of these prior operators reduces the number of unknowns of the network, therewith the amount of required training samples, and the maximal training error bounds [6]. Up to now, this *precision learning* approach was only used to augment networks with prior knowledge and or to add more flexibility into existing algorithms [3, 10, 14, 15]. In this paper, we want to extend this approach even further: we demonstrate that we can derive a mathematical model to tackle a problem under consideration and use deep learning to formulate different hypothesis on efficient solution schemes that are then found as the point of optimality of a deep learning training process.

In particular, we aim in this paper at an efficient convolution-based solution for parallel-to-fan-beam conversion. Up to now, such an efficient algorithm was unknown and the state-of-the-art to address this problem is rebinning of rays that is inherently connected to interpolation and a loss of resolution.

The problem at hand is not only interesting in terms of algorithmic development, it also has an immediate application. Novel hybrid medical scanners will be able to combine Computed Tomography (CT) and Magnetic Resonance Imaging (MRI) in a single device for interventional applications [8, 13]. While CT offers high spatial and temporal resolution, MRI allows for the visualization of soft-tissue contrast, vessels without the use of contrast agent, and there is no need for harmful ionizing radiation.

However, acquisition on MR devices is slow compared to CT. Flat-panel detectors allow image-guided interventions using fluoroscopic projection images that can be acquired at high frame-rates with up to 30 frames per second. This is a challenging time constraint for MRI. Recent developments indicate that MRI is also able to perform projection imaging at acceptable frame rates [5]. Yet the two modalities are inherently incompatible, as MRI typically operates in a parallel projection geometry and X-rays emerge from a source point that restricts them to fan- and cone-beam geometries.

Recent publications elaborate on the idea of MR/X-ray projection fusion and extend the MR acquisition such that the final MR-projection image shows the same perspective distortion as the X-ray projection [5, 11, 12]. Current approaches, however, rely on rebinning that requires interpolation which inherently reduces the resolution of the generated images. In this paper, we propose to derive an image rebinning method from the classical theory. However, as this would require an expensive inverse of a large matrix, we propose to replace the operation with a highly efficient convolution that is inspired by the classical filtered back-projection solution in CT. Here, we examine two cases for this convolution: a projection-independent and a projection-dependent one.

2   Methods

In the first section we shortly describe the link between X-ray and MRI projections using rebinning [11], afterwards we revisit the discrete form of the reconstruction problem, which is then followed by our proposed problem description.

Subsequently the network topology will be derived following the precision learning paradigm. This section is concluded by a description of the training process and the used training data.

2.1   Linking MRI and X-ray Acqusition

The link between the X-ray and MRI acquisition is given by the central slice theorem. This has first been demonstrated by Syben et al. [11] for simulation data and was later applied for the construction of X-ray projections from MRI measurement data [5]. Their approach is inspired by the geometric rebinning method which allows the reconstruction of fan-beam data by resampling the fan-beam acquisition to a parallel-beam acquisition.

They follow the central slice theorem which states that the Fourier transform of a 1D projection of a 2D object can be found in the 2D Fourier transform of the object along a radial line with the same orientation as the detector. Because the MRI can sample the Fourier transform of the object, parallel projections can be acquired. This relationship combined with the geometric rebinning method can be used to convert a set of parallel projections to one fan-beam projection as shown in Fig. 1.

In their publication they analyze the sub-sampling capability of this method. In this context, full sampling means that the MR device acquires one parallel projection for each fan-beam detector pixel. Thus sub-sampling is related to the case where less parallel projections are acquired with respect to the number of fan-beam detector pixels. They show that only few projections are necessary to create the target fan-beam projection with a small error [11]. Following their geometric rebinning method two steps of interpolation in spatial domain are required: first an interpolation between two projections with different projection angles is carried out followed by an interpolation between the pixels of the parallel-beam projection.

2.2   The Tomographic Reconstruction Problem

The CT imaging procedure from acquiring X-ray projections to the reconstructed object information can be described in discrete linear algebra. The acquisition of the projection images of the object can be described with

$$Ax = p, \tag{1}$$

where A is the system matrix describing the geometry of the imaging system. x is the object itself and p are the projections of x under the described geometry A. Correspondingly the reconstruction can be obtained with

$$x = A^{-1}p, \tag{2}$$

where A^{-1} is the inverse of the system matrix, which can not be inverted since it is a tall matrix. Thus, the reconstruction is conducted using the left-side pseudo

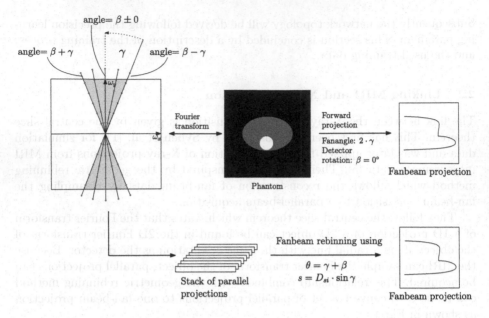

Fig. 1. MRI to X-ray link and geometric rebinning method proposed by Syben et al. [11].

inverse which gives the approximation with minimal distance to the inverse in a $\ell 2$-norm sense.

$$x = A^\top(AA^\top)^{-1}p \tag{3}$$

where $A^\top$ is the transposed system matrix, which can be algorithmically described as the back-projection operator. For a full scan with 180° of rotation in parallel geometry, the inverse bracket is a filtering step in the Fourier domain and can be described as

$$x = A^\top F^H K F p \tag{4}$$

where F, F^H is the Fourier and inverse Fourier transform, respectively. K is the so called Ramp filter represented in a diagonal matrix. Together the pseudo inverse this describes the filtered back-projection algorithm in a discrete fashion.

2.3   Rebinning Using Tomographic Reconstruction

As shown in [10], the discrete description of the reconstruction problem can be used to derive a network topology and to learn the reconstruction filter. In the following, we use this idea to derive an optimization problem to find a filter which can be used to transform several parallel projections to one fan-beam projection. A fan-beam projection can be created by

$$A_f x = p_f, \tag{5}$$

where A_f describes the system matrix for a fan-beam projection and p_f is the respective projection. The necessary parallel projections which contain the information for the fan-beam projection can be found in the Fourier domain (or K-space of the MRI system) in a wedge region [11] which is defined by the fan angle of the fan-beam geometry. These parallel projections can be described with

$$A_p x = p_p, \tag{6}$$

where A_p is the system matrix generating the projections p_p from object x under the parallel-beam geometry. The object x in Eq. 5 can be substituted by the reconstruction using the inverse of the system matrix and the projections from Eq. 3 in Sect. 2.2:

$$A_f \underbrace{A_p^\top (A_p A_p^\top)^{-1} p_p}_{\text{Parallel reconstruction } x} = p_f. \tag{7}$$

In principle, the above equation is hard to solve, as the reconstruction task from this very small set of projections is ill-posed and there is no analytical closed-from solution known. However, we now simply postulate that there exists a projection-independent filter which is a close approximation the above inverse bracket. As in Sect. 2.2, this allows us to express the solution as a multiplication with an diagonal filter matrix K in Fourier domain:

$$A_f A_p^\top F^H K F p_p = \hat{p}_f, \tag{8}$$

where $\hat{p}_f$ is the approximated fan-beam projection under the above stated assumption. Now the only unknown operation in above equation is K that can be determined using an objective function:

$$f(K) = \frac{1}{2} \| A_f A_p^\top F^H K F p_p - p_f \|_2^2. \tag{9}$$

The gradient of function f is with respect to K is

$$\frac{\partial f(K)}{\partial K} = F A_p A_f^\top (A_f A_p^\top F^H K F p_p - p_f)(F p_p)^\top. \tag{10}$$

Note that this gradient is determined automatically by back-propagation to update the weights of layer K, if Eq. 8 is implemented by means of a neural network as already observed for a different application in [10]. Thus, the network topology for a network which learns the transformation from several parallel projections to one fan-beam projection could be derived by the presented approach.

2.4   Network

The network topology can be directly derived from the description of the objective function in Eq. 9 and is shown in Fig. 2. Projectors and back-projectors are

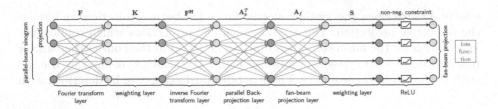

Fig. 2. Network based on objective function (Eq. 9).

scaled to each other in terms of sampling density and number of projections. Since we mix a parallel back-projector with a fan-beam forward projector and aim at different sampling densities we added an additional scaling layer S to the network to compensate accordingly.

Implementation Details

We have implemented the network using Tensorflow [1]. Thus, the Fourier and inverse Fourier transform are layers provided by the Tensorflow framework. The parallel projector and back-projector as well as the fan-beam projector and back-projector are unmatched pairs and are implemented as custom ops in Tensorflow using Cuda kernels. For the back-propagation the respective operation is assigned to the layers for the gradient calculation.

2.5 Training Process

Training Data

For the training we use numerical phantoms which bring their different characteristics into the training process (Fig. 3). The first type of phantoms are homogeneous objects that fill the field of view like ellipses and circles. The second type contain a homogeneous field of view filling ellipse with contains varying number of elongated ellipses (in the following called bars). The third type of phantoms uses only bars without the surrounding ellipsoid. As a last type we use phantoms which contain normal distributed noise.

In the following list, the number test phantoms are listed:

- 1 Ellipse phantom
- 1 Circle phantom
- 8 Ellipse-bar phantoms (with increasing number of bars from 1 up to 8)
- 5 Bar phantoms (with increasing number of bars from 1 to 5
- 50 Noise phantoms (Normal distributed noise)

The parallel projections and respective label projections (fan-beam) are based on the following geometry:

- Trajectory: [0°, 25°, 45°, 65°, 90°]
- Source detector distance (SDD): 1200 mm

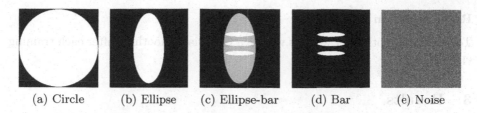

(a) Circle   (b) Ellipse   (c) Ellipse-bar   (d) Bar   (e) Noise

Fig. 3. Phantom types in training set.

- Source isocenter distance (SID): 900 mm
- Parallel and fan-beam detector size: 512 pixel
- Reconstruction size: 256 × 256

Thus, the training data set consists of partial parallel projections according to the method described in [10] using the given angles in the trajectory for β. The respective label fan-beam projection is generated for each angle of the trajectory for each phantom. All projections are generated using the implemented projection layers. The performance of the network is validated using the Shepp-Logan phantom [9].

Training Setup

The training process is divided into two steps. In the first step, the scaling layer S is trained while K remains fixed. After the training of the scaling layer S converges, the scaling factor is fixed and the training of the filter K is started. This separation is based on two thoughts. First, the scaling layer fixes an occurring problem due to the mix up of the different forward- and backprojection geometries and is not part of the unknown operator. The second point is that by dividing the learning process into two parts the learning rate for the scaling layer can be much higher and therefore speed up the whole training process. Furthermore the separation ensures that the calculated loss w.r.t. the label projection can express the deviation from the real fan-beam projection and is not distracted by a scaling factor due to the mixed forward- and backprojection. The filter K is initialized with the Ram-Lak filter [7], which is an optimal discrete reconstruction filter for a complete data acquisition and therefore can be interpret as a strong pre-training of the network. We train on different sub-sampling factors, starting with full sampling and continuing by successively sub-sampling to 15, 7, 5 and 3 projections. This allows us to compare with the geometrical rebinning approach [11].

Projection-dependent vs. Projection-independent

To determine which type of filter performs the best, we performed all experiments on the different sub-sampling levels using both a projection-dependent and a projection-independent of version of K.

Regularization

To achieve smooth filter weights we use a Gaussian smoothing after each training epoch.

3   Results

The performance of the network is evaluated in three steps. First we analyze the performance for the different sub-sampling stages using the Shepp-Logan phantom and the fan-beam forward projection of the phantom as ground truth (GT). Afterwards, the results are compared with the geometrical approach with certain sub-sampling factors. To provide a better qualitative impression of the performance we subsequently present a comparison based on a 3D phantom using a stacked fan-beam approach. The network performance analysis is followed by a presentation of the learned filter types.

Network Performance

In Fig. 4 the rebinning performance of the learned network for the projection-dependent filter using the Shepp-Logan phantom with different sub-sampling factors is shown. All results show a similar shape as the line profile of the GT projection. The full sampling as well as the sub-sampling case using 15 projections show a noisy behavior. The noise is less for the sub-sampling cases using 7, 5 and 3 projections, respectively. For all versions, except for the case with 7 projections, the rebinned signal overshoots the GT signal at the edges of the object.   For the projection-independent version of the filter (Fig. 5) similar but strengthened behavior can be observed. For all four rebinning types the projection-independent counterpart is more noisy and overshoots or undershoots more extensively, especially for the rebinning with 5 projections.

However, the noisiness of the 1D plots is misleading as the visual impression of the rebinned MR-projections from the head phantom show in Fig. 6. Even though the noisy behavior of the previous evaluation can be observed in the line profiles of the different sub-sampling methods, the noise level is not the main factor of the observed image impression. The experiment with 15 projections gives a sharp

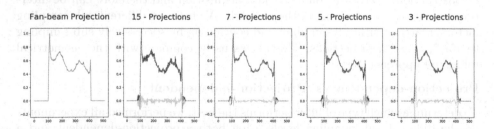

Fig. 4. Sub-sampling comparison of the projection-dependent filter with the GT projection of the Shepp-Logan phantom. The plot colors are red for the reference, blue for the respective line profile and green for the difference. (Color figure online)

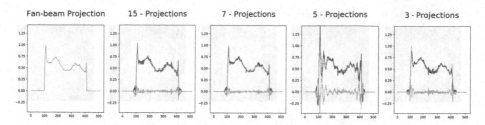

Fig. 5. Sub-sampling comparison of the projection-independent filter applied on the Shepp-Logan phantom. The plot colors are red for the reference, blue for the respective line profile and green for the difference. (Color figure online)

visual impression of the object, although it suffers from the strongest noise. The line profiles of the network trained with 5 and 3 projections show a reduced noise level compared to the network using 15 projections, but high-frequency artifacts and blurriness towards the edges of the image can be observed in the image.

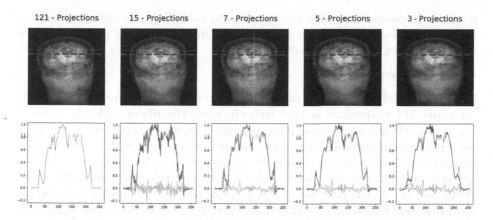

Fig. 6. Sub-sampling comparison of the projection-dependent filter applied on the MR head phantom. The plot colors are red for the reference, blue for the respective line profile and green for the difference. (Color figure online)

For the projection-independent filter results, a similar but strengthened behavior can be observed in Fig. 7. The filter for 15 projections provides a similar visual impression as the projection-dependent counterpart. The strength of the noise is stronger for the filter with 7, 5, and 3 projections than their respective projection-dependent counterpart. The high frequency artifacts are much stronger for the case with 5 and 3 projections.

In Fig. 8 both filter types, projection-independent and projection-dependent are compared to the performance of the geometrical rebinning [11]. For the experiment 15 out of the acquired 121 projections of the head phantom are used. Both filters provide a sharper image impression compared to the reference

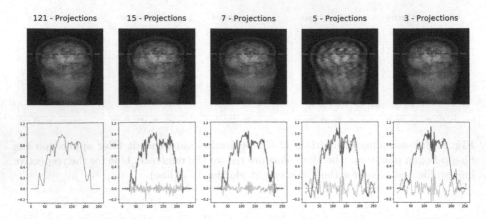

Fig. 7. Sub-sampling comparison projection-independent filter, real data. The plot colors are red for the reference, blue for the respective line profile and green for the difference. (Color figure online)

method. In comparison with the geometrical rebinning method the results of both filters show high frequency artifacts at the edges of the phantom, which can be also seen in the line profiles.

Filter Appearance

In Fig. 9 the different learned projection-independent filters are shown. The filter using 512 projections is very smooth, while the filters with 15, 7, and 5 projections show high frequency components with a large amplitude. The filter for 3 projections has a high frequency component too, but with a much smaller amplitude. Furthermore, the amplitude of the filter is decreased compared to the initialization and the other filters. The learned projection-dependent filters are shown in Fig. 10. The filter for 512 projections shows in the middle a shape like the projection-independent counterpart, but drops off at the edges. While this is also true for the filter for 15 projections, the filter for 7, 5 and 3 projections are converging towards a U-shape.

4   Discussion

The results of the 1D fan-beam projections prove that our proposed analytical description of the rebinning process can be carried out learning the unknown operators in the problem description. The results of the MR head phantom provide a sharper visual impression than the rebinning method proposed Syben et al., although the noise level in the line profiles is much higher. The blurry visual impression of their approach is linked to the necessary interpolation in their method. Especially for image-guided interventions the sharpness is important to provide a clear impression of the vessels and interventional devices. Although the line profile for geometric rebinning overlaps very well with the projection

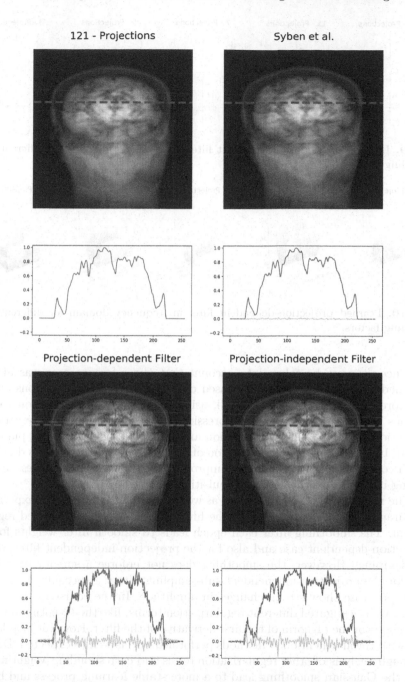

Fig. 8. Comparison of the geometrical rebinning methods and filter type using 15 projections out of the acquired 121 MR. The reference image with 121 projections is created by the geometrical rebinning method. The plot colors are red for the reference, blue for the respective line profile and green for the difference. (Color figure online)

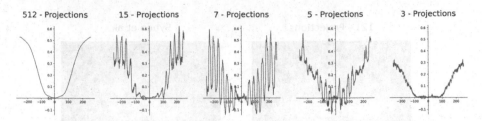

Fig. 9. Learned projection-independent filter in frequency domain for different sub-sampling factors.

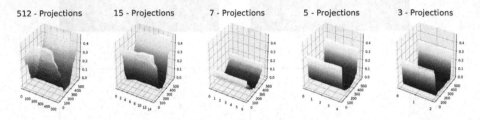

Fig. 10. Learned projection-dependent filter in frequency domain for different sub-sampling factors.

reference, it must be taken into account that the reference case was already rebinned with this method itself based on all existing MR projections and is, therefore, already smoothed. Overall, using the learned filter based on 15 projections provides the best visual impression, while the amount of necessary MR projections is small. These observation are confirmed by the analysis published in [11]. In general, additional reduction of the number of projections is desirable, which could be achieved by further improving the filter learning process, e.g. by linking it directly to the k-space acquisition scheme.

The results of the 1D projections as well as the stacked fan-beam experiment encourage a detailed discussion of the filter, its shape and the applied regularization. The smoothing after each epoch leads to smooth filter weights for the projection-dependent case and also for the projection-independent filter for the full sampling. However, the smoothing does not enforce a smooth filter function for the projection-independent sub-sampling filters. Especially the 7 and 5 projection case show strong changes in amplitude. In the course of the experiments, we investigated different regularization terms, like the $\ell2$-norm on the filter weights or the $\ell1$-norm of the first derivative of the filter. However, regularization with the aforementioned methods performed not as well as expected. Despite thorough analysis of other regularization terms and corresponding weighting factors, the Gaussian smoothing lead to a more stable learning process and better results. However, a more profound method to achieve smooth filter weights is desirable. For this we started to look closer into regularizing the filter using the Lipschitz continuity. Certainly a more consistent regularization especially for the projection-independent filter has to be found. Such a regularization could open the opportunity to reduce the number of used projections in the rebinning process while preserving the sharp visual impression. Furthermore, introducing a symmetry constraint for the filter could improve the learning behavior and the outcome filter shape, while at the same time the number of parameters which have to be learned are reduced by a factor of 2.

The results lead to several interesting questions which should be considered in further research. The impact of the number of used projections on the rebinning process as well as the covered frequency spectrum of the used phantoms on the filter shape are a promising line for subsequent work. The observed artifacts and the high frequency component in the projection-independent filter could be caused by insufficient coverage of the frequency space in the training process. Also the selection of the projections means a certain coverage of the wedge in the Fourier space as proposed by Syben et al. Furthermore the shape of the projection-dependent filter compared the 512 projection with the 3 projection filter version invites for further experiments. The U-like shape of the projection-dependent filter in the 5 and 3 projection cases removes large amounts of low frequencies. With regard to MR acquisition, this could lead to a higher acquisition speed, as fewer frequencies have to be acquired in the K-space. Similar thoughts can be made with respect to the projection-independent filter with 7 projections. While it is more likely that the high change in amplitude is linked to the above discussion of the frequency spectrum and selected projections the question arises if a introduction of sparsity could lead to a sparse selection of frequencies.

Note that this is not the only approach for fan-beam MR imaging. Wachowicz et al. [12] propose a method using additional non-linear gradient coils to directly acquire distorted images. Their approach is based on additional hardware, while we are demonstrate an acquisition approach which can be achieved without additional hardware.

An overall interesting observation is the performance of the derived network topology. The results show that we can substitute the inversed bracket of right inverse of the system matrix by a filter in the frequency domain. The network topology to learn such a filter could be derived used the precision learning approach introduced in [6].

5   Conclusion

We presented an alternative description of the rebinning process in terms of a projection-dependent or -independent filter. Based on the reconstruction problem and the problem description, we derived a network topology which allows to learn the unknown operators. Our proposed method provides a sharper image impression than the state-of-the-art method, since the necessary interpolation and thus smoothing steps can be avoided. Furthermore, the filter design is done entirely data-driven. The presented results encourage further investigation of the method. With deeper insight in the learning process, we assume that a further reduction of the necessary number of projections without losing the sharp image impression is possible. Additionally, as a next step the filter learning process may be extended to cone-beam projections. We hope that a better understanding of the filter will enable us to further reduce the number of data points to be recorded in k-space and, in the best case, to reduce them to points analytically determined by the filter. In the future, we want to combine our approach with MR acquisition trajectories specially adapted to our case.

Overall the results encourage to apply the proposed concept of learning unknown operators in other domains. In future we want to explore the applicability to other domains especially to the field of signal theory.

Acknowledgement. This work has been supported by the project P3-Stroke, an EIT Health innovation project. EIT Health is supported by EIT, a body of the European Union.

References

1. Abadi, M., et al.: TensorFlow: a system for large-scale machine learning. In: OSDI, vol. 16, pp. 265–283 (2016)
2. Christlein, V., et al.: Tutorial: deep learning advancing the state-of-the-art in medical image analysis. In: Maier-Hein, K.H., et al. (eds.) Bildverarbeitung für die Medizin 2017. I, pp. 6–7. Springer, Heidelberg (2017). https://doi.org/10.1007/978-3-662-54345-0_6
3. Fu, W., et al.: Frangi-Net: a neural network approach to vessel segmentation. In: Maier, A., Deserno, T., Handels, H., Maier-Hein, K., Palm, C., Tolxdorff, T. (eds.) Bildverarbeitung für die Medizin 2018, pp. 341–346 (2018)
4. Huang, Y., Würfl, T., Breininger, K., Liu, L., Lauritsch, G., Maier, A.: Some investigations on robustness of deep learning in limited angle tomography. In: Frangi, A.F., Schnabel, J.A., Davatzikos, C., Alberola-López, C., Fichtinger, G. (eds.) MICCAI 2018. LNCS, vol. 11070, pp. 145–153. Springer, Cham (2018). https://doi.org/10.1007/978-3-030-00928-1_17
5. Lommen, J., et al.: MR-projection imaging for interventional X/MR-hybrid applications. In: Proceedings of the 49th Annual Meeting of the German Society for Medical Physics (2018)
6. Maier, A.K., et al.: Precision learning: towards use of known operators in neural networks. CoRR abs/1712.00374 (2017). http://arxiv.org/abs/1712.00374
7. Ramachandran, G., Lakshminarayanan, A.: Three-dimensional reconstruction from radiographs and electron micrographs: application of convolutions instead of fourier transforms. Proc. Nat. Acad. Sci. **68**(9), 2236–2240 (1971)
8. Fahrig, R., et al.: A truly hybrid interventional MR/X-ray system: feasibility demonstration. J. Magn. Reson. Imaging **13**(2), 294–300 (2001). https://doi.org/10.1002/1522-2586(200102)13:2<294::AID-JMRI1042>3.0.CO;2-X
9. Shepp, L.A., Logan, B.F.: The fourier reconstruction of a head section. IEEE Trans. Nucl. Sci. **21**(3), 21–43 (1974)
10. Syben, C., et al.: Precision learning: reconstruction filter kernel discretization. In: Noo, F. (ed.) Proceedings of the Fifth International Conference on Image Formation in X-Ray Computed Tomography, pp. 386–390 (2018)

11. Syben, C., Stimpel, B., Leghissa, M., Dörfler, A., Maier, A.: Fan-beam projection image acquisition using MRI. In: Skalej, M., Hoeschen, C. (eds.) 3rd Conference on Image-Guided Interventions & Fokus Neuroradiologie, pp. 14–15 (2017)

12. Wachowicz, K., Murray, B., Fallone, B.: On the direct acquisition of beam's-eye-view images in MRI for integration with external beam radiotherapy. Phys. Med. Biol. **63**(12), 125002 (2018)

13. Wang, G., et al.: Vision 20/20: simultaneous CT-MRI - next chapter of multi-modality imaging. Med. Phys. **42**, 5879–5889 (2015). https://doi.org/10.1118/1.4929559

14. Würfl, T., Ghesu, F.C., Christlein, V., Maier, A.: Deep learning computed tomography. In: Ourselin, S., Joskowicz, L., Sabuncu, M.R., Unal, G., Wells, W. (eds.) MICCAI 2016. LNCS, vol. 9902, pp. 432–440. Springer, Cham (2016). https://doi.org/10.1007/978-3-319-46726-9_50

15. Würfl, T., et al.: Deep learning computed tomography: learning projection-domain weights from image domain in limited angle problems. IEEE Trans. Med. Imaging **37**(6), 1454–1463 (2018). https://doi.org/10.1109/TMI.2018.2833499

16. Zhu, B., Liu, J.Z., Cauley, S.F., Rosen, B.R., Rosen, M.S.: Image reconstruction by domain-transform manifold learning. Nature **555**(7697), 487 (2018)

Detecting Face Morphing Attacks
by Analyzing the Directed Distances
of Facial Landmarks Shifts

Naser Damer[1(✉)] 📵, Viola Boller[1], Yaza Wainakh[1], Fadi Boutros[1],
Philipp Terhörst[1], Andreas Braun[1], and Arjan Kuijper[1,2]

[1] Fraunhofer Institute for Computer Graphics Research IGD, Darmstadt, Germany
naser.damer@igd.fraunhofer.de
[2] Mathematical and Applied Visual Computing, TU Darmstadt,
Darmstadt, Germany

Abstract. Face morphing attacks create face images that are verifiable
to multiple identities. Associating such images to identity documents
lead to building faulty identity links, causing attacks on operations like
border crossing. Most of previously proposed morphing attack detection approaches directly classified features extracted from the investigated image. We discuss the operational opportunity of having a live
face probe to support the morphing detection decision and propose a
detection approach that take advantage of that. Our proposed solution
considers the facial landmarks shifting patterns between reference and
probe images. This is represented by the directed distances to avoid confusion with shifts caused by other variations. We validated our approach
using a publicly available database, built on 549 identities. Our proposed
detection concept is tested with three landmark detectors and proved to
outperform the baseline concept based on handcrafted and transferable
CNN features.

1 Introduction

Face recognition technology is gaining deployment ground in different application
fields [23]. This is mainly driven by the recent performance spikes achieved by
the deep learning based solutions [37] and the high social acceptance of faces
compared to other biometric modalities [5]. This enabled a variety of applications
including enhanced surveillance, border control, user convenience in consumer
devices, and different identity management processes.

Presentation attacks on face recognition

Just as face recognition systems deployment is on the rise, the attacks on such
systems are becoming more innovative. Some of the conventional attacks are the
presentation attacks (spoofing) that aim at impersonating a different identity

T. Brox et al. (Eds.): GCPR 2018, LNCS 11269, pp. 518–534, 2019.
https://doi.org/10.1007/978-3-030-12939-2_36

by presenting a copy of their characteristics [9,20], disguised face attacks that aim at disabling face detection or recognition using some physical objects [12], and moving the face in an intention to avoid identification [8]. More recently, Ferrara et al. [14] presented a new form of attack in their paper titled "The magic passport". This attack aims at presenting one face reference image that is, automatically and by human experts, successfully matched to more than one person. This is referred to as the face morphing attack and it can cause a crucial security gap when such morphed images are used in travel or identity documents, which would allow multiple subjects to verify their identity to the one associated with the document. This faulty subject link to the document identity can lead to a wide range of illegal activities, including financial transactions, illegal immigration, human trafficking, and circumventing legal black identity lists.

Morphing two faces together would act as a smoothing operator for some parts of the image, because of the pixel interpolation involved. Morphing detection solutions based on the direct classification of features extracted on the pixel level, e.g. by a convolutional neural network (CNN) [28], can depend in their training on detecting these smoothing (or other) artifacts caused by the morphing method. Previous works have only considered direct classification of features extracted from the investigated reference face images.

The Availability of Live Probes

In operation, there are two main processes where a morphed image are in direct interaction with the official authorities, and therefore the attack detection is feasible. These operations are:

1. The issuing of the identity (or travel) document: when applying for an identity or travel document, many countries (e.g. Germany) require the applicants to provide a printed face picture. This process is the main point of attacks for morphed images, as an applicant can provide a morphed image. The process of depending on a printed image is still the case because of different image quality restrictions [18], as well as, traditional, societal, legal, financial reasons. This make the document issuing process vulnerable to morphing attacks. However, the issuing process usually require the presence of the related person, and therefore a live probe of their faces is possible, even if it did not meet the identity required image quality restrictions and was not used in the document itself.

2. Verifying the identity of a subject with identity (or travel) document: the document issuing process might not be protected against morphing attacks, and it cannot be controlled in different countries. However, foreign travel and identity documents are still accepted as an identity verification tool in security critical processes like border control and financial transactions. Therefore, the authorities in the non-issuing country only interact with these documents when they verify the identity of their holders. In this scenario as well, the subject holding the document is present for a possible live face probe.

Both of the listed operations require the presence of the associated subject (the owner of the document), or in a morphing attack case, one of the subjects who were morphed into the attack image (an attacker). Therefore, live probe images can be captured when presenting the reference morphed image, whether at the passport/ID-card issuing office or at the verification site (e.g. border check) [35]. These live probes can be used as additional information to check if the referenced image is morphed or not.

This Work

In this work, we benefit from these live probes by presenting a novel approach utilizing them to enhance the performance of the attack detection. The proposed approach is based on our assumption, that facial landmark shifts between an investigated reference image and a live probe caused by the morphing process have a detectable pattern, compared to the shifts caused by normal capture variabilities (noise, pose, illumination variations, etc.). To materialize a solution based on this assumption, we detected facial landmarks on the reference and probe images and calculated a landmarks shifts vector to represent their shift patterns. Three state-of-the art landmarks detectors were investigated to analyze their effect on the attack detection performance. To create the landmarks shift vector, we started by using a straight forward solution that consider the absolute distance between corresponding landmarks. To gain more insight on the relative shift relations, we proposed a second solution that calculate this vector by considering directed distances (in two axes) between the corresponding landmarks.

Unlike previous works, we evaluate our proposed approaches, along with the conventional baseline approach, on a publicly available morphed face database. To enable a wider range of evaluation with the baseline detection concept, we considered image feature extraction methods of two different natures, handcrafted classical image descriptors and transferable CNN-based representations. The used database is significantly larger and has higher diversity of subjects, as it is based on 549 different identities, while previous works considered databases based on up to 163 identities.

As will be demonstrated later, our proposed detection concept proved to enhance the morphing detection accuracy in comparison to that of the traditional work-flow used in the state-of-the-art works, as well as to solutions based on absolute landmark shifts. Detection performance was significantly improved when using the directed distances to represent landmark shifts. We found a variation in the performance between different landmark detectors, emphasizing the importance of their accuracy. However, they all performed better than the baseline at most operation points within our proposed detection concept.

2   Related Works

The possibility of creating a morphed face image, out of two images of two subjects, was introduced by Ferrara et al. [14]. They compared a small number of morphed images with images of the original subjects using two face recognition solutions, and concluded with the high vulnerability of face recognition to such attacks. This has driven the work on similar attacks on different modalities such as fingerprints [13] and irises [30]. Further studies considered the human expert vulnerability to morphed face images when comparing faces [15,32]. These works concluded that human experts, to a large extend, can fail in detecting morphed face images.

Ramachandra et al. [29] were first to propose the automatic detection of morphed face images, by extracting local image descriptors as the Binarised Statistical Image Features (BSIF) that tries to capture textural properties of the image. These features were then used within a Support Vector Machine (SVM) to classify images into morphed or bona fide (not morphed) ones. Scherhag et al. [36] considered a scenario in which a morphed image is printed and scanned (re-digitized) before morphing detection. They presented a re-digitized database and uncovered the vulnerability of a commercial-off-the-shelf and open-source (CNN-based) face recognition solutions to both the digital and re-digitized morphed face images. Baseline detection methods built on micro-texture based features showed higher vulnerability to the re-digitized images, which can be explained by the changes on the pixel level information. Ramachandra et al., in further works, improved the morphed face detection accuracy by considering features extracted from a pre-trained Convolutional Neural Network (CNN) [28], and compared between the possibilities of detecting morphed images versus averaged images [27]. Although some of these works tried to address the issue of depending on the vulnerable pixel-level information by evaluating on re-digitized images, the methods themselves were not changed and are inherently dependent on such information. Neubert [24] considered the detection problem from another perspective, by analyzing continuous image degradation based on JPEG compression. From a similar perspective, Hildebrandt et al. proposed a detection solution based on Benford's law characteristics on quantized Discrete Cosine Transformation (DCT) coefficients of JPEG-compressed images [17]. These approaches are inherently sensitive to noise because they depend on creating multiple artificial self-references and measures the distance from these references to the input. Agarwal et al. [1] addressed a similar problem under a different scenario by evaluating the possibility of attacking a face recognition system by a video created by the Snapchat swapping function and proposed a detection approach based on weighted local magnitude pattern, in a scenario that considers the attacks as probes rather than references.

A standardized manner to evaluate the vulnerability of biometric systems to morphing attacks was recently proposed by Scherhag et al. [35]. Their work mentioned the operational validity of having a live probe capture in the attack detection process, but did not provide any experimental implementation or evaluation of the mentioned possibility. A recent work by Ferrara et al. [16] viewed the morphing attack problem from a different perspective by proposing an approach to revert the morphed face image (demorph) enough to reveal the identity of the legitimate document owner, given a bona fide capture. All the discussed previous works developed and evaluated their approaches based on databases prepared at their labs and that are not publicly, which limits the possibility of cross-lab incremental research. These database were also of relatively limited size, including between 104 [28] and 163 [27] different subjects. The so far discussed morphed face detection solutions built their classification decisions directly based on features extracted from images, which raises the concerns on pixel-level and micro-texture feature dependency. Recently, a solution have been proposed to utilize the landmark shifts to build an attack detection decision [34]. However, this solution [34] considered absolute distance and angles rather than the shift directional patterns, which resulted in a high confusion between attacks and face variations (e.g. pose, expression) and therefore a poor attack detection performance.

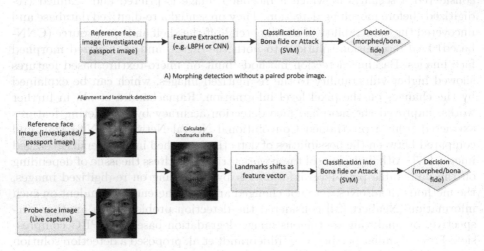

Fig. 1. Work-flows of different approaches for morphed face image detection: (A) the conventional work-flow based on features extracted only from the investigated reference image, and (B) the proposed method based on facial landmarks shifts between a probe image and the investigated reference image.

3   Methodology

This section starts by presenting the baseline morphing attack detection concept used in state-of-the-art works, and in this work as a baseline solution. Our proposed landmarks-based concept and solution details are later presented in this section.

3.1 Baseline Solutions

The baseline approach is based on the decision work-flow utilized in the previous works, mentioned in the related work section, is shown in Fig. 1-A. In this work-flow, features are extracted from the investigated reference image. These features are used as an input to a classifier that will build a decision labeling the investigated image as a morphed or a bona fide one.

We considered image feature extraction methods of two different natures to enable a wider range of conceptual evaluation and more diverse comparison to the state-of-the-art detection concept (looking only at the reference attack). The first is the hand crafted classical image descriptors, the Local Binary Pattern Histogram (LBPH) [2]. The second is based on transferable deep-CNN features. Both types of features were previously utilized for the detection of face morphing under the traditional work-flow, without a paired probe image [28,29].

The LBPH features were extracted from the cropped face image. A histogram was calculated for each block of an 8×8 grid of blocks in the face image. These histograms were concatenated to produce the final feature vector describing the image. Each LBP was extracted within a radius of 1 pixel and 8 neighbor pixels. The transferable deep-CNN features were extracted using the well performing, and relatively small OpenFace NN4.SMALL2 model [3]. OpenFace [3] is a general-purpose face recognition library based on the deep neural network (DNN) FaceNet architecture suggested in [37]. Given an aligned and cropped face image, this pre-trained network produces a highly discriminant representation (feature vector) of 128 elements. The extracted feature vector from an image, whether from CNN or LBPH, is classified by a support vector machine (SVM) classifier, to be originated from a morphed or a bona fide image. The SVM utilized a Radial Basis Function (RBF) kernel to map the variables into a high dimensional space and allows a better class separation. The SVM hyperparameters were found using Bayesian optimization. The SVM classifier produces a decision score that represent the probability of the input image being a morphed one rather than a bona fide one. This classical baseline approach will be referred to as feature vector classification (FVC). When it utilize LBPH features it will be called FVC-LBPH and when it uses transferable CNN features it will be called FVC-CNN.

3.2 Proposed Landmarks-based Solution

Concept Overview: The proposed concept in this work is based on utilizing the practical opportunity of having a live probe of the possible attacker face, and use this additional information source to make more accurate attack detections. To integrate this additional information, our proposed solution considers the facial landmarks in both the investigated reference and the live probe images. We build our solution on the assumption that the shifts of these landmarks (between reference and probe images) follows identifiable patterns when a morphed reference is considered, in comparison to shifts cause by conventional bona fide capture variations.

The proposed detection work-flow is visualized in Fig. 1-B. Here, the landmarks in both, the reference and probe, images are detected. Based on these landmarks, a feature vector is created to represent the corresponding shifts in the landmarks locations. This landmarks shifts vector is then used to classify the reference image into a morphing attack or a bona fide image. Examples visualizing the mentioned shifts in the landmarks locations are shown in Fig. 2. The images on the left (a, b) represent the landmarks detected on a morphed attack image (red) and a bona fide probe (blue), while the images on the right (c, d) are of a bona fide reference (green) and probe (blue) of the same subject. One can notice a less symmetrical (around the vertical axis) location shifts in the bona fide image pairs, in comparison to the pairs including an attack image.

In the rest of this section, we present the three different methods used to detect the facial landmarks. We also discuss the creation of the landmarks shifts representing vector, with two levels of retained information. As well as the classifier used to make the detection decision.

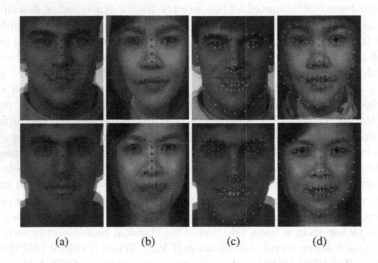

(a)   (b)   (c)   (d)

Fig. 2. Examples of facial landmarks detected in (a) & (b) morphed attack reference images (landmarks in red) vs. bona fide probes (landmarks in blue) of subject 1 (top) and subject 2 (bottom), whom reference images created the attack image. In (c) & (d) these landmarks are shown for bona fide references (landmarks in green) of subject 1 (top) and 2 (bottom) with their corresponding probe images (landmarks in blue). Each image presents a pair of reference-probe overlapping face images. The images are of the same person and captured in a different session for (c) & (d), and of the a person involved in creating the morphed image (with an image from a different session) and his resulting morphed attack image. (Color figure online)

Landmark Detection: To present a wider range of evaluation of the proposed detection concept, three state-of-the-art facial landmarks detectors are used.

The detectors are used to detect 68 facial landmarks as defined in [33]. These detectors are:

1. Ensemble of regression trees (ERT) [21]: this detector was proposed by Kazemi et al. who used a cascade of regressors to efficiently estimate the face's landmark positions directly from a sparse subset of pixel intensities. They presented a general framework based on gradient boosting to learn an ensemble of regression trees that optimizes the sum of square error loss and naturally handles partially labeled data [21].
2. Explicit shape regression (ESR) [6]: here, Cao et al. presented a method that directly learn a vectorial regression function to infer the whole facial shape from the image and explicitly minimize the alignment errors over the training data [6].
3. Regressing local binary features (LBF) [31]: this detector was proposed by Ren et al. where they used a set of local binary features, and a locality principle for learning these features. They proposed to learn a set of highly discriminative local binary features for each facial landmark independently, then use these to jointly learn a linear regression for the final landmark detection output [31].

Shift Representation: The shifts between the corresponding landmarks detected in the reference and probe facial images should be represented in a feature vector form to enable a standard classification process. This feature vector will be referred to here as a landmark shift vector (LS). Using one of the landmark detectors presented in the last section, each face image (probe or reference) will be defined by the locations of $N = 68$ landmarks. These landmarks will be defined by their relative location (pixel wise) to the upper left corner of the detected face area (origin). This set of landmark representation of the reference and probe images consequently will be defined as:

$$ref = \{(x_n, y_n)\}_{n=1,...,N} \tag{1}$$
$$probe = \{(x_n, y_n)\}_{n=1,...,N}, \tag{2}$$

where the values $x_{ref,n}, x_{probe,n}, y_{ref,n}$, and $y_{probe,n}$ describe the x and y axes pixel-displacement of the landmark n from the origin point, for the reference and probe images.

The direct approach to create LS is to consider the absolute distance between the corresponding landmarks in the probe and reference images, as proposed very recently in [34]. This is implemented by calculating the Euclidean (L2) distance between these corresponding points, resulting in an N dimensional LS vector where a given n^{th} entry is defined by

$$[LS_{D2}(ref, probe)]_{n=1,...,N} = \sqrt{(x_{ref,n} - x_{probe,n})^2 + (y_{ref,n} - y_{probe,n})^2}. \tag{3}$$

The defined LS_{D2} vector represents the absolute landmark shifts, and thus have no shift direction information. One can imagine that different kind of shifts can appear in the same form in this representation. These shifts can occur either from a morphing attack origin, or from capture variations, like slight pose changes. This will inherently make the morphing attack detector unstable under less-than-perfect capture scenarios.

To avoid the apparent shortcomings of the LS_{D2} representation, we propose to use the directed distances between the corresponding landmarks, rather than the absolute ones. This will give the classification process a more in-depth view on the relative movements of the landmarks between the reference and morphed image. Such a representation, based on the directed shift distances in the horizontal and vertical axes will be referred to as LS_{DD}. This representation will be $2N$-dimensional, and its mth entry is defined as:

$$[LS_{DD}(ref, probe)]_{m=1,...,2N} = \begin{cases} x_{ref,k} - x_{probe,k} & \text{for } k = \frac{m}{2} & \text{if } m \text{ is even} \\ y_{ref,k} - y_{probe,k} & \text{for } k = \frac{m+1}{2} & \text{if } m \text{ is odd} \end{cases}.$$

(4)

Classification: The vector representations, LS_{2D} or LS_{DD}, are used within a classifier to detect if they originate from an attack or a bona fide reference. To eliminate the effect of the classification approach in the comparison, the same classification setup used for the baseline solution is used for our proposed solution. Namely, an SVM using an RBF kernel, with the hyperparameters found using Bayesian optimization.

Our proposed approach will be refered to based on the used landmarks detector (ERT, ESR, or LBF) and landmarks shifts representation (LS_{2D} or LS_{DD}). Resulting in six possible combinations (2D-ERT, 2D-ESR, 2D-LBF, DD-ERT, DD-ESR, DD-LBF).

4   Experimental Setup

This section presents the database used in this work. It also discusses the experimental setup in preparation of the results in the next section.

4.1   Data

This work is developed and evaluated using the recently released, public, and freely available Biometix face morphing dataset (for vulnerability research) [4]. It must be mentioned that all previous works reported results on privately created databases.

The database was created by Biometix Pty Ltd based on the FERET face database [25,26]. From the FERET database, 549 frontal face images, each of a different subject, were selected to create the morphed images database. This resulted in 1082 morphed images, of identity pairs selected by the database creators to be visually similar. The morphing was performed by detecting 68 landmarks on the face. The mean face points for each image are calculated and each image is then warped to sit on these coordinates. Only the facial area is morphed and stitched into one of the original morphed images [22]. The original 549 frontal face images were considered as the bona fide face images in our experiments. Examples of the Biometix face morphing dataset (for vulnerability research) [4] are shown in Fig. 3.

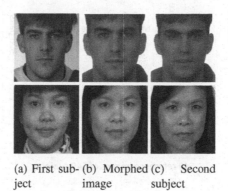

(a) First sub- (b) Morphed (c)   Second
ject   image   subject

Fig. 3. Two morphed face image examples of the Biometix face morphing dataset [4] (in the middle). The two face images [25, 26] of both identities used to create the morphed images are shown on the right and left sides.

To investigate morphing detection that involve a bona fide probe image, we built a database of paired images between the investigated reference (whether morphed or bona fide) images and the probe (assumed to be live captures) images. Each reference image is paired with images of the same user (one pair for each of the two users in case of morphed references). However, the probe images are the frontal face images of the same users captured in different sessions than the reference images. This results in a total of 920 images used as probes, which are all the frontal images of the reference identities, of the original database, captured in sessions other than the references capture sessions. These probe images are paired (genuine pairs) with the investigated morphed reference (1082 images), so that there are pairs between each of the original identities (making the morph) and the morphed image. This resulted in 3583 reference-probe pairs, where the reference is a morphed image. These probe images are also paired with the bona fide references resulting in 920 reference-probe pairs, where the reference is a bona fide image. Given the possible reference morphing attack detection scenarios discussed in Sect. 1, i.e. during document issue and identity verification, only the genuine pairs of references and probes are relevant, as an imposter pair defies the attack goal by principle. The database structure is presented in Fig. 4.

The data is split in 5 parts to enable cross validation, i.e. evaluating over the complete data. The splits were performed so that there is minimum identity overlap between them and all splits have almost the same number of samples/pairs

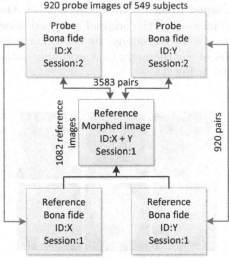

Fig. 4. The database structure including the pairing between the references (bona fide and morphed) and the probe images. Morphed references and pairs containing morphed references are in red. Probes, bona fide reference, and pairs containing bona fide reference are in green. (Color figure online)

($\pm$1). The multiple possibilities of pairing the images in the detection approaches that consider a paired probe, results in a higher number of evaluation samples. To enable a direct performance comparison with the traditional morphing detection (without paired probe, Fig. 1-A), the investigated reference image was also tested individually in the traditional manner for each evaluated paired images. This resulted in multiple evaluations of some of the reference samples.

To prove the vulnerability of face recognition to this morphing database, the vulnerability of the open-source CNN-based OpenFace as described in [3] is demonstrated in Fig. 5. As expected, the CNN-based face recognition performs well when it comes to face verification. This can be seen by the small overlap area between the imposter and genuine scores distribution. A successful morphing attack will produce comparison scores (with any of the two original identities) that lies in the same range of the bona fide genuine scores. Knowing that, the vulnerability of the OpenFace solution to morphing attacks is very significant, as the attack scores distribution covers a very similar area to that of the bona fide genuine scores.

4.2   Image Pre-processing

The face regions of all the images were detected using a multi-scale sliding detection window based on histograms of oriented gradients (HOG) features [7]. The faces were then aligned by utilizing the transformation approach proposed by

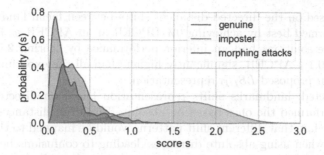

Fig. 5. The comparison score (here the score is a measure of dissimilarity/distance) distributions of bona fide genuine and imposter comparisons scores compared to the distribution of the morphed face attacks comparisons scores distribution from the Open-Face CNN-based face recognition algorithm. The vulnerability of the face recognition algorithm to the morphing attacks is clear, as the attacks comparison scores are in a very close range to the bona fide genuine scores.

Kazemi and Sullivan [21]. The aligned and detected faces are then cropped and downsized to a 246 × 246 pixels image.

4.3   Experiments

The experiments performed included measuring the morphing attack detection performance for the two baseline solutions (FVC-LBPH & FVC-CNN), our intermediate solution based on absolute distances (2D-ERT, 2D-ESR, 2D-LBF), and our proposed solution based on directed distances (DD-ERT, DD-ESR, DD-LBF).

The performance of the morphed face detection is presented as a trade-off between two error rates, the Attack Presentation Classification Error Rate (APCER) and Bona Fide Presentation Classification Error Rate (BPCER) as defined by the ISO/IEC 30107-3 [19] and advised by recent works [35]. Here, the APCER is the proportion of morphed face presentations incorrectly classified as bona fide presentations. The BPCER is the proportion of bona fide presentations incorrectly classified as morphed face attacks. BPCER values achieved at fixed APCER rates are reported to enable direct comparison between different solutions at certain operation points. Lower values of BPCER and APCER indicates higher detection performance. A detection error tradeoff (DET) curve plotting APCER vs. BPCER is also presented to provide a comparative view of this trade-off on a continuous range of operation points.

5   Results

The morphed face detection performance achieved by the baseline concept and the proposed concept are presented in Table 1. It is noticed that our proposed solution, based on the directed distances shifts between facial landmarks (DD-LBF), performed best by achieving 0% BPCER at an APCER as low as 0.1%. The baseline solutions had an inferior performance by scoring 2.50 to 5.11% BPCER at 0.1% APCER, significantly higher than all the experimental setups including our proposed LS_{DD} representation.

As expected, landmarks shifts representation based on directed distances (DD) outperformed the ones based on absolute Euclidean distances (D2). This is due to the fact that different shift patterns would be mapped to the same representation when using absolute distances, leading to confusions between shifts induced by morphing and naturally occurring shifts induced by the capture quality variations.

Table 1. The morphed face detection performance of the different concepts and experiment settings given as BPCER values achieved at fixed APCER. Our proposed detection approach, based on directed distances, consistently outperforms the baseline (FVC) approach. The two lowest BPCER values achieved at each fixed APCER are in bold.

APCER		BPCER at fixed APCER							
		0.10%	0.30%	0.50%	1.00%	2.00%	3.00%	5.00%	10.00%
Base-line FVC	FVC-CNN	5.11%	5.11%	3.70%	3.26%	0.22%	0.21%	**0.11%**	0.00%
	FVC-LBPH	2.50%	1.63%	0.33%	0.21%	**0.00%**	**0.00%**	**0.00%**	0.00%
Landmark shifts distance (L2)	D2-ERT	74.86%	64.04%	54.20%	40.76%	27.00%	1803%	10.16%	4.26%
	D2-ESR	86.44%	69.62%	55.52%	36.61%	25.57%	21.63%	14.75%	7.43%
	D2-LBF	81.74%	60.22%	46.33%	36.39%	26.22%	22.40%	16.61%	8.41%
Landmark shifts directed distance	DD-ERT	**1.53%**	**0.11%**	**0.00%**	**0.00%**	**0.00%**	**0.00%**	**0.00%**	0.00%
	DD-ESR	1.74%	0.76%	**0.32%**	0.11%	0.11%	0.11%	0.11%	0.00%
	DD-LBF	**0.00%**	**0.00%**	**0.00%**	**0.00%**	**0.00%**	**0.00%**	**0.00%**	0.00%

Different landmarks detectors led to varying performances, although all out-performing the baseline solutions at most operation points. The LBF detector resulted in the lowest error rates, producing 0% BPCER all over the investigated APCER range. This performance was followed closely by the ERT detector at lower, and thus more relevant, APCER range. While the ESR detector performed relatively poorly at the low APCER range and improved at higher ranges. This can be reasoned by the more accurate landmark detection of the LBF and ERT solutions compared to the ESR, as demonstrated in [21] and [31].

The DET curves achieved by the different experimental settings of the proposed solution (based on the LS_{DD} representation), along with the baseline solutions, are presented in Fig. 6. Here, on a more detailed APCER range, one can notice the high accuracy of the proposed solution based on the LS_{DD} representation in comparison to the baseline solutions. Best detections results were achieved by the highly accurate ERT and LBF landmark detectors, followed by the ESR detector, all within our proposed concept.

The overall results prove the significance of including the operationally-feasible probe image in the detection process. The high detection performance of

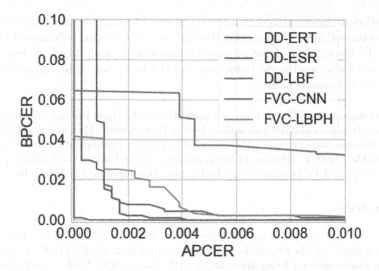

Fig. 6. DET curves achieved by the two baseline solutions and the different experimental settings of the proposed solution based on the landmarks shifts measure by directed distances. The superiority of the proposed DD-LPF solution is clear by achieving 0% BPCER on a very low APCER range. This is followed by solutions of the same proposed concept, using different landmark detectors. The performance of the solutions based on the LS_{D2} representations is not shown here as they lay on a higher error range.

our proposed solution also points out the importance of deploying an accurate landmarks detector and including the direction information of landmarks shifts. Further evaluations need to be made on the effect of perspective distortion [11], relevant in such use scenarios, on landmarks-based attack detection performance. Furthermore, novel techniques of morphing attacks that rendered the classical attack detection solutions vulnerable, such as ones based on generative adversarial networks [10], are yet to be evaluated on our proposed solution.

6   Conclusion

In this work, we proposed a novel approach of integrating information from a live probe face image to classify an investigate reference image into a morphing attack or a bona fide one. Previous morphing detection works built their classification decision based only on features extracted from the investigated images. Our proposed solution is based on the assumption that the facial landmarks shifts between reference and probe images follows identifiable patterns when a morphed attack reference is considered, in comparison to shifts cause by conventional capture variations in bona fide references. In contrast to previous works, our solution, along with two baseline solutions, were evaluated on a publicly available morphed faces database built on a relatively large number of different identities. Our proposed concept was tested in combination with three state-of-the-art landmarks detectors and proved to significantly outperform the baseline concept utilized in state-of-the-art attack detection solutions. Our analysis proved the validity of the proposed solution and emphasized the importance of accurate facial landmarks detection and the inclusion of directional information of the landmarks shifts.

Acknowledgment. This work was supported by the German Federal Ministry of Education and Research (BMBF) as well as by the Hessen State Ministry for Higher Education, Research and the Arts (HMWK) within CRISP. Portions of the research in this paper use the FERET database of facial images collected under the FERET program, sponsored by the DOD Counterdrug Technology Development Program Office [25,26].

References

1. Agarwal, A., Singh, R., Vatsa, M., Noore, A.: SWAPPED! Digital face presentation attack detection via weighted local magnitude pattern. In: 2017 IEEE International Joint Conference on Biometrics, IJCB 2017, Denver, CO, USA, 1–4 October 2017, pp. 659–665. IEEE (2017)
2. Ahonen, T., Hadid, A., Pietikäinen, M.: Face recognition with local binary patterns. In: Pajdla, T., Matas, J. (eds.) ECCV 2004. LNCS, vol. 3021, pp. 469–481. Springer, Heidelberg (2004). https://doi.org/10.1007/978-3-540-24670-1_36
3. Amos, B., Ludwiczuk, B., Satyanarayanan, M.: OpenFace: a general-purpose face recognition library with mobile applications. Technical report, CMU-CS-16-118, CMU School of Computer Science (2016)
4. Biometix Pty Ltd.: Face morphing dataset (for vulnerability research) (2017). http://www.biometix.com/2017/09/18/new-face-morphing-dataset-for-vulnerability-research/
5. Bolle, R., Pankanti, S.: Biometrics, Personal Identification in Networked Society: Personal Identification in Networked Society. Kluwer Academic Publishers, Norwell (1998)
6. Cao, X., Wei, Y., Wen, F., Sun, J.: Face alignment by explicit shape regression. In: 2012 IEEE Conference on Computer Vision and Pattern Recognition, Providence, RI, USA, 16–21 June 2012, pp. 2887–2894. IEEE Computer Society (2012)
7. Dalal, N., Triggs, B.: Histograms of oriented gradients for human detection. In: 2005 IEEE Computer Society Conference on Computer Vision and Pattern Recognition (CVPR 2005), San Diego, CA, USA, 20–26 June 2005, pp. 886–893. IEEE Computer Society (2005)
8. Damer, N., et al.: CrazyFaces: unassisted circumvention of watchlist face identification. In: 9th IEEE International Conference on Biometrics Theory, Applications and Systems, BTAS 2018, Los Angeles, California, USA, 22–25 October 2018. IEEE (2018)
9. Damer, N., Dimitrov, K.: Practical view on face presentation attack detection. In: Wilson, R.C., Hancock, E.R., Smith, W.A.P. (eds.) Proceedings of the British Machine Vision Conference 2016, BMVC 2016, York, UK, 19–22 September 2016. BMVA Press (2016)
10. Damer, N., Saladié, A.M., Braun, A., Kuijper, A.: MorGAN: recognition vulnerability and attack detectability of face morphing attacks created by generative adversarial network. In: 9th IEEE International Conference on Biometrics Theory, Applications and Systems, BTAS 2018, Los Angeles, California, USA, 22–25 October 2018. IEEE (2018)

11. Damer, N., et al.: Deep learning-based face recognition and the robustness to perspective distortion. In: 24th International Conference on Pattern Recognition, ICPR 2018, Beijing, China, August 2018. IEEE (2018)

12. Dhamecha, T.I., Nigam, A., Singh, R., Vatsa, M.: Disguise detection and face recognition in visible and thermal spectrums. In: Fiérrez, J., Kumar, A., Vatsa, M., Veldhuis, R.N.J., Ortega-Garcia, J. (eds.) International Conference on Biometrics, ICB 2013, Madrid, Spain, 4–7 June 2013, pp. 1–8. IEEE (2013)

13. Ferrara, M., Cappelli, R., Maltoni, D.: On the feasibility of creating double-identity fingerprints. IEEE Trans. Inf. Forensics Secur. **12**(4), 892–900 (2017)

14. Ferrara, M., Franco, A., Maltoni, D.: The magic passport. In: IEEE International Joint Conference on Biometrics, Clearwater, IJCB 2014, FL, USA, 29 September–2 October 2014, pp. 1–7. IEEE (2014)

15. Ferrara, M., Franco, A., Maltoni, D.: On the effects of image alterations on face recognition accuracy. In: Bourlai, T. (ed.) Face Recognition Across the Imaging Spectrum, pp. 195–222. Springer, Cham (2016). https://doi.org/10.1007/978-3-319-28501-6_9

16. Ferrara, M., Franco, A., Maltoni, D.: Face demorphing. IEEE Trans. Inf. Forensics Secur. **13**(4), 1008–1017 (2018)

17. Hildebrandt, M., Neubert, T., Makrushin, A., Dittmann, J.: Benchmarking face morphing forgery detection: application of stirtrace for impact simulation of different processing steps. In: 5th International Workshop on Biometrics and Forensics, IWBF 2017, Coventry, United Kingdom, 4–5 April 2017, pp. 1–6. IEEE (2017)

18. International Civil Aviation Organisation (ICAO): ICAO draft technical report: portrait quality (reference facial images for MRTD). Technical report (version), September 2017

19. International Organization for Standardization: ISO/IEC DIS 30107-3:2016: information technology - biometric presentation attack detection - part 3: testing and reporting. Standard (2017)

20. Kähm, O., Damer, N.: 2D face liveness detection: an overview. In: Brömme, A., Busch, C. (eds.) Proceedings of the International Conference of Biometrics Special Interest Group, 2012 BIOSIG, Darmstadt, Germany, 6–7 September 2012. LNI, vol. 197, pp. 1–12. IEEE/GI (2012)

21. Kazemi, V., Sullivan, J.: One millisecond face alignment with an ensemble of regression trees. In: 2014 IEEE Conference on Computer Vision and Pattern Recognition, CVPR 2014, Columbus, OH, USA, 23–28 June 2014, pp. 1867–1874. IEEE Computer Society (2014)

22. Mallick, S.: Face morph using opencv - c++/python (2016). https://www.learnopencv.com/face-morph-using-opencv-cpp-python/

23. Markets and Markets: Facial recognition market by component (software tools and services), technology, use case (emotion recognition, attendance tracking and monitoring, access control, law enforcement), end-user, and region - global forecast to 2022. Report, November 2017

24. Neubert, T.: Face morphing detection: an approach based on image degradation analysis. In: Kraetzer, C., Shi, Y.-Q., Dittmann, J., Kim, H.J. (eds.) IWDW 2017. LNCS, vol. 10431, pp. 93–106. Springer, Cham (2017). https://doi.org/10.1007/978-3-319-64185-0_8

25. Phillips, P.J., Moon, H., Rizvi, S.A., Rauss, P.J.: The FERET evaluation methodology for face-recognition algorithms. IEEE Trans. Pattern Anal. Mach. Intell. **22**(10), 1090–1104 (2000)

26. Phillips, P.J., Wechsler, H., Huang, J., Rauss, P.J.: The FERET database and evaluation procedure for face-recognition algorithms. Image Vis. Comput. **16**(5), 295–306 (1998)

27. Ramachandra, R., Raja, K.B., Venkatesh, S., Busch, C.: Face morphing versus face averaging: vulnerability and detection. In: 2017 IEEE International Joint Conference on Biometrics, IJCB 2017, Denver, CO, USA, 1–4 October 2017, pp. 555–563. IEEE (2017)

28. Ramachandra, R., Raja, K.B., Venkatesh, S., Busch, C.: Transferable deep-CNN features for detecting digital and print-scanned morphed face images. In: 2017 IEEE Conference on Computer Vision and Pattern Recognition Workshops, CVPR Workshops, Honolulu, HI, USA, 21–26 July 2017, pp. 1822–1830. IEEE Computer Society (2017)

29. Ramachandra, R., Raja, K.B., Busch, C.: Detecting morphed face images. In: 8th IEEE International Conference on Biometrics Theory, Applications and Systems, BTAS 2016, Niagara Falls, NY, USA, 6–9 September 2016, pp. 1–7. IEEE (2016)

30. Rathgeb, C., Busch, C.: On the feasibility of creating morphed iris-codes. In: 2017 IEEE International Joint Conference on Biometrics, IJCB 2017, Denver, CO, USA, 1–4 October 2017, pp. 152–157. IEEE (2017)

31. Ren, S., Cao, X., Wei, Y., Sun, J.: Face alignment at 3000 FPS via regressing local binary features. In: 2014 IEEE Conference on Computer Vision and Pattern Recognition, CVPR 2014, Columbus, OH, USA, 23–28 June 2014, pp. 1685–1692. IEEE Computer Society (2014)

32. Robertson, D.J., Kramer, R.S.S., Burton, A.M.: Fraudulent ID using face morphs: experiments on human and automatic recognition. PLoS One **12**(3), 1–12 (2017)

33. Sagonas, C., Antonakos, E., Tzimiropoulos, G., Zafeiriou, S., Pantic, M.: 300 faces in-the-wild challenge: database and results. Image Vis. Comput. **47**, 3–18 (2016)

34. Scherhag, U., Budhrani, D., Gomez-Barrero, M., Busch, C.: Detecting morphed face images using facial landmarks. In: Mansouri, A., El Moataz, A., Nouboud, F., Mammass, D. (eds.) ICISP 2018. LNCS, vol. 10884, pp. 444–452. Springer, Cham (2018). https://doi.org/10.1007/978-3-319-94211-7_48

35. Scherhag, U., et al.: Biometric systems under morphing attacks: assessment of morphing techniques and vulnerability reporting. In: Brömme, A., Busch, C., Dantcheva, A., Rathgeb, C., Uhl, A. (eds.) International Conference of the Biometrics Special Interest Group, BIOSIG 2017, Darmstadt, Germany, 20–22 September 2017. LNI, vol. P-270, pp. 149–159. GI/IEEE (2017)

36. Scherhag, U., Ramachandra, R., Raja, K.B., Gomez-Barrero, M., Rathgeb, C., Busch, C.: On the vulnerability of face recognition systems towards morphed face attacks. In: 5th International Workshop on Biometrics and Forensics, IWBF 2017, Coventry, United Kingdom, 4–5 April 2017, pp. 1–6. IEEE (2017)

37. Schroff, F., Kalenichenko, D., Philbin, J.: FaceNet: a unified embedding for face recognition and clustering. In: IEEE Conference on Computer Vision and Pattern Recognition, CVPR 2015, Boston, MA, USA, 7–12 June 2015, pp. 815–823. IEEE Computer Society (2015)

KloudNet: Deep Learning for Sky Image Analysis and Irradiance Forecasting

Dinesh Pothineni[1], Martin R. Oswald[1(✉)], Jan Poland[2], and Marc Pollefeys[1]

[1] ETH Zürich, Zürich, Switzerland
martin.oswald@inf.ethz.ch
[2] ABB Corporate Research, Baden, Switzerland

Abstract. We present a novel image-based approach for estimating irradiance fluctuations from sky images. Our goal is a very short-term prediction of the irradiance state around a photovoltaic power plant 5–10 min ahead of time, in order to adjust alternative energy sources and ensure a stable energy network. To this end, we propose a convolutional neural network with residual building blocks that learns to predict the future irradiance state from a small set of sky images. Our experiments on two large datasets demonstrate that the network abstracts upon local site-specific properties such as day- and month-dependent sun positions, as well as generic properties about moving, creating, dissolving clouds, or seasonal changes. Moreover, our approach significantly outperforms the established baseline and state-of-the-art methods.

1 Introduction

Large scale integration of photovoltaic (PV) energy into power grids has become reality. While this environmentally friendly energy source has undoubtedly many advantages, it is well known that its strong fluctuations may seriously affect the stability of the power grids. Most prominently, rapid changes in the cloud conditions cause rapid changes in local solar irradiance which have a direct impact on the power generated by PV power plants [24]. As a measure of mitigating the stability risks, grid operators have started to introduce requirements such as ramp rate limitations on renewable power sources to be integrated. One of the first places where a 10% per minute ramp rate had been introduced is Puerto Rico [12].

In this paper we investigate the image-based prediction of irradiance levels for PV sites. We use a single fisheye camera observing the sky and especially the clouds around a PV site to predict irradiance levels 5–10 min ahead of time. Within this time frame, it is possible to adjust alternative power sources (e.g. Diesel generators, batteries, etc.) or otherwise compensate the expected power loss or surplus. Also, for possible curtailment within a typical ramp rate limitation framework [12], this is the proper time period to consider. Forecasting in the minute ranges is often referred to as *very short term forecasting* or *nowcasting*, in contrast to short term forecasting which typically ranges over several hours ahead and is rather used to support allocation of energy production.

© Springer Nature Switzerland AG 2019
T. Brox et al. (Eds.): GCPR 2018, LNCS 11269, pp. 535–551, 2019.
https://doi.org/10.1007/978-3-030-12939-2_37

Besides PV power forecasting, our approach can be useful in numerous further applications. Learned relationships between sky images and PV plant behavior may enable more accurate condition monitoring for the PV plant. Other applications that depend on local weather and cloud conditions, not necessarily with a focus on forecasting, and hence may benefit from our methods include building automation (automatic control of roof windows or window blinds; Heating, Ventilation and Air Conditioning management, etc.), aviation (hot-air ballooning, gliding, paragliding, parachuting, kite flying or model aircraft flying), marine applications (sailing, vessel routing, etc.), wind power, and more.

Contributions. Our contributions can be summarized as follows.

- We present a novel end-to-end deep learning framework using residual neural networks for short-term irradiance forecasting from sky images. To the best of our knowledge this is the first work to approach this problem with recent machine learning techniques.
- We present a detailed ablation study comparing various network architectures and different training modes and parameter settings with respect to their test accuracy to select the best model.
- Our approach does not require any location specific modeling or expert intervention, leading to robust forecasting framework which outperforms classical approaches [28] on two large datasets.

2 Related Work

For very short term PV forecasting, a number of methods are commonly used (compare also [26]):

1. **Persistence** refers to the concept of always predicting that the present situation (i.e. irradiance level) will persist. Persistence is a very good model on average: Statistically, the present condition will persist in a large fraction of the time. Hence, in benchmarks that evaluate very short term forecasting methods with common statistical criteria, persistence is often a hard to beat baseline. However, persistence fails to predict fluctuations.
2. **Statistical models** [10,22,38–40] use local information (e.g. past irradiance) to derive predictions in a data driven way. They capture patterns in the training data in order to identify a predictive model. Simple statistical models are based on few simple input quantities, like past power production, irradiance, temperature, etc. None of the candidate simple quantities is appropriate to reliably predict power fluctuation. E.g. a dip in power production on a partly cloudy day comes from a cloud that covers the sun. Even though a slight increase in power production may precede the dip since the cloud reflects more light before it covers the sun, no reliable prediction can be derived from this situation. The cloud could as well pass by the sun.
3. **Sensor based methods** use additional sensors, mostly local cameras or satellite images. For very short term forecasting however, satellite images are usually not sufficiently high resolution both in space and time [26]. Camera based methods are discussed in detail below.

4. **Numerical weather predictions** (NWP) are typically too coarse in spatial and time resolution to give a useful answer to the problem of local very short term PV power prediction. They are rather used for short to mid term forecasting. Moreover, they are computationally very expensive.

Camera-based Very Short Term Forecasting. Early applications of whole-sky camera systems to determining the degree of solar occlusion and cloud coverage are reported in [6,31]. The applications of sky cameras for very short term forecasting is much more recent, one of the first such systems has been presented in [9]. It reports a binary classification accuracy around 70% for a 5 min ahead prediction. Since then, the number of publications on this topic has rapidly increased, e.g. [4,7,20,21,32–35]. The general approach in these works is based on conventional image processing and follows very similar lines:

1. Images are periodically captured, e.g. every 5–10 s, often with HDR fusion of different exposures.
2. An image at one time step is transformed to a binary cloud map by a *cloud segmentation* step which in most cases uses some (adaptive) thresholding of the red to blue ratio of the individual pixels.
3. Cloud motion is determined via *optical flow* methods to subsequent images.
4. The cloud motion is extrapolated into the future for a prediction.

The clear usefulness of such very short term forecast systems has attracted a number of commercial players. Since 2015, there exist commercial offerings, e.g. from SteadySun [2] and Reuniwatt [1]. IBM used a similar approach inside an ensemble method and reported significant accuracy improvements [19].

The baseline and benchmark for the present work is given by long term experiments with the conventional image processing approach. It is implemented in a similar manner as described in [28] and evaluated for one year in two different PV plant sites in Europe. In addition, a commercial product was acquired and tested in yet another location in Australia. In all three installations, the long term average classification accuracy of predicting clear vs. occluded irradiance conditions 5 min ahead has been around 80%. Moreover, it can be observed that predicting persisting conditions is significantly easier than predicting changing conditions: The average long term classification accuracy in the presence of a change drops to around 50% for all three installations.

The conventional image processing approach works well in favorable situations, when the clouds are clearly distinguishable from the clear sky, their motion pattern is predictable, and the sun is not too close to the horizon of the fisheye camera (in which case clouds coming from the border of the horizon cannot be seen in advance). In the absence of favorable conditions, prediction accuracy drops significantly. While the case where the sun is close to the horizon will remain challenging (and can be mitigated with the installation of several cameras), the other two challenges can be potentially addressed with the deep CNN approach we propose here, except for extreme situations such as shown in Fig. 8. It is often in hazy or foggy conditions or with dark clouds as in storms, that it is hard to distinguish if a single pixel in the image is clear or occluded. Here, a feature that is constructed based on a wider region of the image is typically superior. And in cases of unclear motions, optical flow may be too inflexible to reasonably predict into the future, while these motion patterns may still be learnable from data.

Neural Networks for Irradiance Forcasting. There are few applications of deep convolutional neural networks in meteorology yet. Some initial work reports their use for weather forecast [16] and classification [11]. Analysis of the cloud coverage (however based on snapshot images) has been discussed in [25].

By now, there is a large number of established deep neural network architectures that have been shown to perform well on many segmentation and classification tasks, for instance, AlexNet [18], VGG-net [36], ZFNet [41], GoogleNet [37] and many more. Most of them have improved over Alexnet with increasingly deeper architectures. Due to the problem of vanishing gradients [5], deeper architectures do not necessarily perform better and a common remedy to the vanishing gradient problem are batch normalization layers [17]. A very successful approach which does not suffer from the vanishing gradient problem are residual networks (ResNet) [13] which are currently among the best performing network architectures for segmentation and classification tasks.

To our knowledge, no prior work has yet attempted to tackle the problem of irradiance forecasting directly with deep neural networks in an end-to-end fashion. We present a machine learning framework based on ResNet that pushes the accuracy rates of irradiance forecasting by a significant margin.

3 Method

Our main objective is to build a local short term forecasting model to predict the state of cloud cover over the surface area of a PV plant. Convolutional neural networks are known to be very good at extracting global features and learning image classification problems usually better than regression problems. Therefore, we modeled the forecasting problem as a classification problem. The most important events for PV power compensation management are clouds moving in front of the sun, with a significant drop in irradiance values. Therefore, for our application we can sufficiently well approximate the irradiance level with a two state classification problem (cloudy, clear sky) which results in a much easier learning problem.

Power vs. Irradiance Forecasting. In this paper, we focus on learning irradiance forecasts. We point out that learning power forecasts for a given PV plant that is co-located with the camera can be expected to work equally well. Our experience with this application indicates that, despite the fact that the power is collected over a larger area compared to the point nature of the irradiance sensor, their predictions behave very similarly. In fact, the power signal is usually a slightly smoothed version of the irradiance signal (except for plant failures, which are out of scope for this work).

fisheye camera   irradiance sensor   masks   example sky images

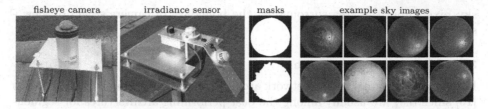

Fig. 1. Overview of our data acquisition setup and input data. From left to right: input fisheye camera, irradiance sensor for ground truth measurements, clear sky masks and example sky images from our dataset originating from 2 different sites showing variances regarding sky, clouds, rain, fog, snow, noise etc. (top images: *SiteIT*, bottom images: *SiteCH*).

Datasets. Since our method is tightly related to image data, we describe our dataset here before the method description. We have access to two datasets that have been acquired in two regions: one test site in Italy (denoted by *SiteIT*) and one in the swiss mountains (denoted by *SiteCH*).

The hardware setup for both sites was identical. For capturing high quality sky images, four images of 1600×1600 pixels resolution were acquired with different exposure times ($\{200, 400, 700, 1100\}$ ms) and then combined into a single HDR image. For both sites data measurements were captured with a fisheye camera and the irradiance sensor every 8 s over time period of 11 months, resulting in about 4.2 million HDR images and corresponding irradiance values for each site. See Fig. 1 for an overview.

Clear Sky Model. The clear sky model describes the ideal irradiance for an entirely cloud-free day and for a particular geographic location (latitude, longitude and elevation). We used the Perez-Ineichen clear sky model [27] to simulate global horizontal irradiance (GHI), direct normal irradiance (DNI) and diffuse horizontal irradiance (DHI) under clear sky conditions.

Classification Model. In order to create a classification task, we transform the measured irradiance values into binary values by comparing the sensor data to the clear sky model and threshold them at 80%. This gives us the ground truth data for the learning task to classify whether a particular image contains an occluded or a clear sky.

To help the neural network recognize the temporal connection between current and future states, we also considered an augmented state set Σ, which contains pairs of the current and the future state. In sum, we investigate and compare the following two state sets:

- **4 labels** - pair of present & future state (**PFS**):
  $\Sigma = \{(occluded, occluded), (occluded, clear), (clear, occluded), (clear, clear)\}$
- **2 labels** - future state only (**FS**): $\Sigma = \{occluded, clear\}$

Data Preprocessing. Our image preprocessing involves downsampling ($1600 \times 1600 \rightarrow 224 \times 224$), masking and normalization. With the masking we filter non-sky pixels from the area surrounding the boundary of camera's field of view - see Fig. 1 middle.

3.1 Network Architecture

For our convolutional neural network architecture we use residual building blocks [13] since they are usually among the best performing architectures for segmentation and classification tasks.

The inputs to all models are initialized with an initial convolution layer of kernel size 7×7, stride of 2×2 and 64 filter maps. This is followed by a max pooling layer of pool size 3×3, and stride of 2×2. These are connected to subsequent residual blocks in the second, third level, each with different number of filter maps and output dimensions. Each level consists of n residual blocks that are connected with skip connections, which forwards the residual mapping to the next block. Shortcut connections are used directly when input and output dimensions match with each other. Details of convolution and activation layers at various depths are specified in Table 1 and it closely follows the architecture introduced in [13]. However when the dimensions increase as the blocks move to higher level of feature maps, we use the projection shortcut suggested in [14] i.e., 1×1 convolution layer with appropriate stride length as part of the shortcut connection. This transforms the input dimensions to match the output dimensionality of the next block. These type of connections are indicated in Fig. 2. The merged output from the final residual block is subjected to a batch normalization and activation layer. The batch normalization layer solves the internal covariate shift problem, which refers to slower training caused by the adaptation of weights that occurs between intermediate layers. Batch normalization causes a regularizing effect for the data flow between intermediate layers and allows for higher learning rates and to remove dropout layers from the architecture which can slow down learning.

We used rectified linear units (ReLu: $f(x) = max(0, x)$) as the activation function in our models. After the convolutions, an average pooling layer is used to sum up the spatial information to generate a feature map for each corresponding class category. This is followed by a fully connected layer and ends up with a softmax layer for final classification outputs.

Residual Block Units. We consider two variants of residual blocks in this work: (a) A basic residual block with two convolutional layers, a pre-normalization layer added before the shortcut connections followed by an activation after the addition of outputs. (b) A pre-activated block in which the batch normalization and activation layers are before the weight layers. This has for instance shown improvements on the CIFAR-10 dataset [14].

A graphical illustration of both residual blocks is shown in Fig. 2(a), (b).

4 Experiments and Results

Setup. All experiments were conducted on a shared GPU cluster managed by a slurm workload scheduler, with either Nvidia Titan X 12 GB or Nvidia GTX 1080

8 GB card. The network model pipeline was written in Python using Keras [8] deep learning framework and Tensorflow [3] as the computational backend.

Training Details. We split our dataset into strictly disjunct sets for training, validation and testing. We test two options for the split (1) by month: we took the first 6 months for training and validation (70/30%) and the remaining months for testing; or (2) interleaved: The training data has been sampled from the dataset, and validation was split from training in an interleaving way i.e., every 5th day of the week and additional 10% of the sequences randomly sampled from rest of the week.

Further, we always ensured proper balancing of all classes during training. If not otherwise noted all experiments predict the irradiance class 5 min ahead of time. We used categorical cross entropy loss function and trained the network with the Adam optimizer using an adaptive learning rate scheduler.

4.1 Ablation Study

In this section we investigate various network architectures and parameter settings and measure their performance in order to explore which changes have positive performance impact.

Table 1. Layered architecture specifications of our residual network for 3 different network sizes. The last row shows the computational complexity of the network in floating point operations per second (FLOPs).

Layer name	Output size	18-layer	34-layer	50-layer
conv1	112×112	7×7, 64, stride 2		
		3×3 max pool, stride 2		
conv2_x	56×56	$\begin{bmatrix} 3 \times 3, 64 \\ 3 \times 3, 64 \end{bmatrix} \times 3$	$\begin{bmatrix} 3 \times 3, 64 \\ 3 \times 3, 64 \end{bmatrix} \times 3$	$\begin{bmatrix} 1 \times 1, 64 \\ 3 \times 3, 64 \\ 1 \times 1, 256 \end{bmatrix} \times 3$
conv3_x	28×28	$\begin{bmatrix} 3 \times 3, 128 \\ 3 \times 3, 128 \end{bmatrix} \times 3$	$\begin{bmatrix} 3 \times 3, 128 \\ 3 \times 3, 128 \end{bmatrix} \times 3$	$\begin{bmatrix} 1 \times 1, 128 \\ 3 \times 3, 128 \\ 1 \times 1, 512 \end{bmatrix} \times 3$
conv4_x	14×14	$\begin{bmatrix} 3 \times 3, 256 \\ 3 \times 3, 256 \end{bmatrix} \times 3$	$\begin{bmatrix} 3 \times 3, 256 \\ 3 \times 3, 256 \end{bmatrix} \times 3$	$\begin{bmatrix} 1 \times 1, 256 \\ 3 \times 3, 256 \\ 1 \times 1, 1024 \end{bmatrix} \times 3$
conv5_x	7×7	$\begin{bmatrix} 3 \times 3, 512 \\ 3 \times 3, 512 \end{bmatrix} \times 3$	$\begin{bmatrix} 3 \times 3, 512 \\ 3 \times 3, 512 \end{bmatrix} \times 3$	$\begin{bmatrix} 1 \times 1, 512 \\ 3 \times 3, 512 \\ 1 \times 1, 2048 \end{bmatrix} \times 3$
	1×1	Average pool, 100-d, fc, softmax		
FLOPs		1.8×10^9	3.6×10^9	3.8×10^9

Single Frame Input. An initial series of experiments were conducted using a single camera frame input. The setup was initially tested with a CNN similar to Alexnet [18] with some modifications. The input layer is initialized with 11×11 size convolution filters. Further, we added a batch normalization layer [17] for the lower level 3×3 convolution filters and a dropout layer was added before the fully connected layer. Rmsprop was used as the optimizer for the model, categorical cross entropy as a loss function. The network was trained end-end without any pre-trained weights. After training for 83 epochs the network attained 83% accuracy on training data with 0.614 loss on validation.

Table 2. Comparison of model performance for different network architectures using single frame input.

Model	Epochs	Train-loss	Train-accuracy	Val-loss	Val-accuracy
Alexnet	83	0.0492	0.831	0.6141	0.8102
VGG-16	72	0.0904	0.87	0.6258	0.8287
ResNet18-BA	**57**	**0.0847**	**0.99**	**0.4973**	**0.8801**

The same setup was trained with the VGG-16 architecture [36], with pre-trained weights from the Imagenet challenge as initialization. The pre-trained weights did not have any noticeable effect on our dataset compared to random initialization, as our training dataset is quite large and has no related images from Imagenet. Stochastic gradient descent was used as the optimizer function and cross-entropy as a loss function with a learning rate of 0.1. A mini batch size of 32 was used with $3 \times 224 \times 224$ input dimensions. As shown in Table 2, the VGG model has improved training performance over the previous model with 87% on training data after 72 epochs of training, with slightly better performance over validation data. For comparison, we applied the same experiment to the ResNet18-BA with basic residual blocks as described before which shows superior performance.

Sequential Frame Input. In order to let the network also learn about temporal relationships like cloud movements, we changed the network to allow an input of N sequential images by horizontally concatenating the images. For the experiment we used a mini batch size of 16 and sequence length of 9 (SQ9) and compared it to the single frame version as well as a deeper ResNet with 50 layers. The results listed in Table 3 indicate that the sequential input leads to better estimates especially on the validation set and the deeper single input ResNet50 overfits on the training data. Later, in Table 5 we also show that a network input with only 2 sequential images (SQ2) is sufficient to yield a similar 1–2% acurracy increase. Instead of horizontally concatenating the sequential images, we also tried feeding the sequential images as additional parallel color channels. That is, instead of increasing the images size, we increase the number of color channels, for instance, for two sequential RGB images, we get 6 channels (6CH). As also shown in Table 5, this input encoding performs better (4–6% accuracy increase compared to single frame input), probably because local correspondences and movements can then be better captured by this network architecture.

Basic vs. Pre-activated Residual Blocks. As described in Sect. 3.1 we considered two types of residual blocks: basic and pre-activated residual blocks, which are depicted in Fig. 2(a), (b). Figure 2(c) shows a performance comparison of networks with these residual blocks. Table 4 shows the corresponding quantitative results. The evaluation results indicate that the pre-activated units yield better accuracy which is why we selected them for all remaining experiments.

Table 3. Comparison of ResNet with sequential input and varying depth. *BA - basic residual block, SQ9 - sequential input (9 images)*

Model	Input	Train-loss	Train-accuracy	Val-loss	Val-accuracy
ResNet18-BA	224 × 224 × 3	0.0966	**0.99**	0.6357	0.9103
ResNet18-BA-SQ9	2016 × 224 × 3	0.0904	**0.99**	**0.3883**	**0.9225**
ResNet50-BA	224 × 224 × 3	**0.0847**	**0.99**	0.5053	0.9139

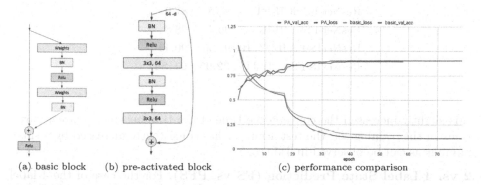

(a) basic block   (b) pre-activated block   (c) performance comparison

Fig. 2. Architecture of different residual block structures. Representation of (a) basic and (b) fully pre-activated network blocks *(BN = batch normalization; ReLu = rectified linear unit)*. (c) shows accuracy and loss during the training epochs for both residual blocks in comparison.

Training with Interleaving Data. In the previous experiments the disjunct split between training and test data was done by months. Since we do not have data for a full year, but only for 11 months (July 2015 till May 2016), we were training the network on data from mostly fall and winter and testing the network on data from spring and summer. In order to let the network better learn about seasonal changes, we re-organize training and test images in an interleaved manner such that both sets cover all available months and are still disjunct. Although

Table 4. Network performance with basic and preactivated residual blocks.
BA - basic residual block, PA - pre-activated residual block

Model	Input	Train-loss	Train-acc	Val-loss	Val-acc
ResNet18-BA	224 × 224	0.1415	0.992	0.4973	0.8944
ResNet18-PA	224 × 224	**0.1086**	**0.999**	**0.4764**	**0.9037**

Table 5. Comparison of results from all models tested on both test sites.
PFS = present-future state, FS = future state, SIN = single frame, SQ2 = sequential input (2 images), 6CH = 6 channel sequential input, AG = augmentation, IL = interleaving, JT = joint training, SiteIT = site in Italy, SiteCH = site in Switzerland

Model	Test accuracy [%] on	
	SiteIT	*SiteCH*
ResNet-PFS-SIN	74.8	70.2
ResNet-PFS-SQ2	75.7	71.6
ResNet-PFS-6CH-AG	78.9	74.1
ResNet-PFS-IL-JT	85.1	80.2
ResNet-FS-6CH	88.77	84.75
ResNet-FS-6CH-PT	N/A	87.9
ResNet-FS-6CH-IL	90.7	88.8
ResNet18-FS-IL-JT-10	92.36	90.45
ResNet18-FS-6CH-JT	**92.93**	**91.34**

this slightly increased the convergence time of the training due to larger variations in the training set, the test accuracy has consistently increased by a small number as can be observed in Table 5.

2 vs. 4 Label State Prediction (FS vs. PFS). For the case of the 4 label state, the amount of training data per class becomes more unbalanced. We therefore also experimented with data augmentation (AG) and added horizontally flipped images for the rare classes. In the Fig. 3 we present a detailed distribution of our model performance for the 4 label case (PFS) on various cloud state transitions in the 5 min horizon. The plots show that the model has good accuracy for recognizing the change classes i.e., where the present and future state differs. For example, clear to occluded state is hard to recognize in the short term period and this is very essential in the business of power production and consumption for planning. Our model tested on *SiteIT* shows, that 52% of the days have more than 70% of accuracy, similarly 70.9% of the days have more than 60% accuracy in correctly forecasting the clear sky transition to occluded.

Joint Training and Cross Site Testing. In order to study how well networks generalize, we compare the testing performance of a network on a test site when

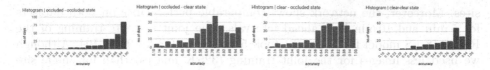

Fig. 3. Histogram of class-wise accuracy per day, with ResNet18-JT trained on both sites, tested on *SiteIT* for the 4 label case (i.e. classes represent state transitions).

Table 6. Test accuracy comparison with cross site testing or joint training. The comparison shows that joint training on both datasets gives superior network results. Further, a 10 min ahead prediction yields comparable accuracies to the 5 min prediction results on both sides. *FS = future state, IL = interleaving, 10 = 10 min prediction, JT = joint training, SiteIT = site in Italy, SiteCH = site in Switzerland. Here, we simplified the model naming: all models used the 6 channel approach (6CH) and pre-activated residual units (PU).*

Model	Trained on	Test accuracy [%] on	
		SiteIT	*SiteCH*
ResNet18-FS	*SiteIT*	88.7	71.4
ResNet18-FS-IL	*SiteIT*	90.7	72.8
ResNet18-FS	*SiteCH*	65.1	87.9
ResNet18-FS-IL	*SiteCH*	65.4	88.4
ResNet18-PFS-IL-JT	*SiteIT+SiteCH*	85.1	80.2
ResNet18-FS-IL-JT	*SiteIT+SiteCH*	**92.93**	**91.34**
ResNet18-FS-IL-JT-10	*SiteIT+SiteCH*	92.36	90.45

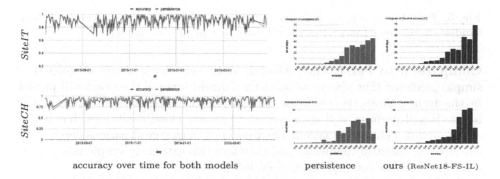

accuracy over time for both models   persistence   ours (ResNet18-FS-IL)

Fig. 4. Performance comparison to persistence model. The persistence model always predicts the same state as the current input state. The histograms show the number of days reaching a particular accuracy value (top: *SiteIT*, bottom: *SiteCH*).

it was only trained on another test side. Further, we investigate the network performance if it was trained jointly on both test sites. Table 6 clearly shows that joint training significantly improves the network performance on both test sites. Moreover, the network shows comparable performance on both datasets for 5 min and 10 min look ahead intervals. The joint test site training of the Resnet18-FS model for 65 epochs took 5 days on a GTX 1080 GPU. Although we used less images for the joint training (325 K images) than for single site training (1.2 M images), the network shows superior performance on both test sites due to an increased data variety and possibly better generalization.

4.2 Comparison to Baselines

For reference, we compare our approach qualitatively and quantitatively to natural baselines which we describe in the following.

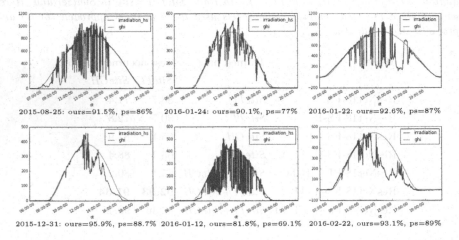

2015-08-25: ours=91.5%, ps=86%   2016-01-24: ours=90.1%, ps=77%   2016-01-22: ours=92.6%, ps=87%

2015-12-31: ours=95.9%, ps=88.7% 2016-01-12, ours=81.8%, ps=69.1% 2016-02-22: ours=93.1%, ps=89%

Fig. 5. Full-day samples and prediction accuracy results on days with high irradiation volatility (ours = ResNet18-FS-IL; ps = persistence model).

Comparison to Persistance Model. With *persistence model* we refer to a simple predictor that always assumes the current state of the cloud will persist in the future. Since the predictor will always forecasts the same state as the input, it will perform well with respect to steady cloud conditions, but it can never predict a change situation. The frequency of change situations depends on the site and seasonal conditions and therefore this extremely simple predictor is a natural baseline for experimental evaluations.

In Fig. 4 we show a comparison between the persistence model and our ResNet18-FS-IL model. In 61% of the days our model achieves more than 90% of accuracy in *SiteIT*, and 89% of the days has more than 80% accuracy. Similarly, 56% of the days in *SiteCH* has more than 90% accuracy and 86% of the days has more than 80% overall accuracy. Further, Fig. 5 illustrates various samples for full-day high volatile irradiance curves and corresponding accuracies for our model in comparison to the persistence model.

Comparison to Classical Pipeline. The second baseline method resembles a classical sequential image processing pipeline with edge detection, optical flow-based cloud tracking and subsequent irradiance forcasting. Our implementation follows similar processing steps of cloud tracking approach by Richardson *et al.* [28]. Figure 6 shows the results of this approach in comparison to our best performing network ResNet18-FS-IL. With an overall accuracy of 92.9%, our ResNet approach outperforms the classical method significantly which reaches only 83% accuracy, on a reference data set for *SiteIT*. (This dataset was constructed to evaluate the classical image processing approach and contains the most interesting out of all days wrt. irradiance fluctuation, it ranges over the whole year.)

Performance by Transition Type. As seen above, the classical approach predicts exhibits less accuracy for changing conditions (roughly 50%) than overall (roughly 80%). A similar observation is mostly true for KloudNet, but less pronounced, as shown in Fig. 7 for ResNet18-PFS-JT. The classification accuracy for changing conditions drops by about 15% wrt. the total classification accuracy.

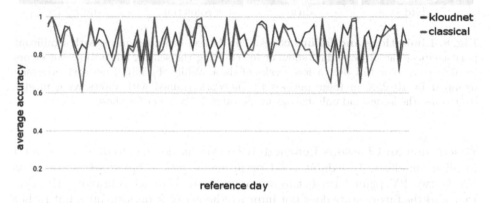

Fig. 6. Comparison of our ResNet18-FS-IL model to a classical cloud-tracking pipeline [28] on a reference dataset for *SiteIT*. Our overall accuracy of 92.9% significantly outperforms the classical pipeline which has an accuracy of 83%.

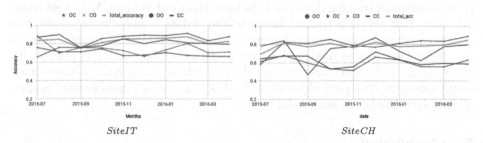

Fig. 7. Monthly performance of ResNet18-PFS-JT model over various cloud state transitions for both sites. The results are slightly better for *SiteIT*, but generally very similar.

Limitations and Failure Cases. For such a large dataset, not all captured images are always perfect. The camera sensor has sometimes been covered by animals, dirt, snow or ice. Moreover, several weeks of images have a color tint due to a sensor error. Some examples are depicted in Fig. 8. In practice, a prediction system should be robust to a certain degree of interferences. In our experiments several network architecture had significant performance drops (20–25%) in these situations. Since a reasonable amount of such cases is part of the training set, especially the networks with interleaved training was able to tackle these disturbances with only small performance reductions (3–5%).

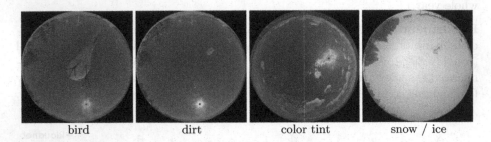

bird   dirt   color tint   snow / ice

Fig. 8. Limitations and failure cases. The dataset contains images with significant perturbances like objects, dirt, snow or ice covering the sensor, but also sensor errors leading to a color tint over a few weeks of data. While the initial network accuracy dropped by 20–25% in these periods the network trained with interleaving mostly overcomes the issues and only has accuracy rates 3–5% lower for those cases.

Discussion and Lessons Learned. KloudNet has learned to overcome several localization effects to exhibit good performance over a broad set of scenarios across two PV plants. Predicting an augmented state set containing the current and the future state does not improve the network performance, but rather complicates training due to additional unbalancing of training examples among classes. Merged input channel layers and pre-activated units improve model performance. The network with shared input layers has outperformed all. This shows that variation in training data can help more than just volume. Year-wise training shows that networks trained on one season of data can predict instances from another part of the year reasonably well. Transfer learning experiments indicate that KloudNet can be used to improve performance on other PV plants with noisy datasets. In summary, our novel approach achieved reliable very short-term forecasts with pure sky image models that do not involve any explicit geographic, weather or seasonal data.

5   Conclusion

We presented a novel CNN-based approach for short-term irradiance class forecasting based on fisheye sky images. In contrast to classical approaches that explicitly model seasonal cloud and sun movement, our model learns all these sophisticated relations purely from training data without the need to provide specific geographic or weather data. Moreover, if sufficiently represented in the training set, the trained network also becomes reasonably robust to sensor failures (color tint) and partial sensor occlusions (birds, dirt, snow, ice). In several experiments on two large datasets we showed how changes of parameters and architecture impact the model performance. Moreover, our approach achieves very low error rates on challenging datasets with a high diversity of cloud- and atmospheric conditions, as well as, it compares favorably to established baselines and state-of-the-art pipelines. Future work will investigate other successful network architectures like U-Net [29] or LSTMs [15]. Another promising direction for future research is the direct end-to-end learning of controllers for grid-friendly PV plants, e.g. by reinforcement learning [23] or imitation learning [30].

Acknowledgements. This work received funding from the Horizon 2020 research and innovation programme under grant No. 637221 (Built2Spec).

References

1. Reuniwatt. http://reuniwatt.com. Accessed 03 July 2018
2. SteadySun. http://steady-sun.com. Accessed 03 July 2018
3. Abadi, M., et al.: TensorFlow: large-scale machine learning on heterogeneous distributed systems. arXiv preprint arXiv:1603.04467 (2016)
4. Ai, Y., Peng, Y., Wei, W.: A model of very short-term solar irradiance forecasting based on low-cost sky images. In: American Institute of Physics Conference Proceedings (2017)
5. Bengio, Y., Simard, P., Frasconi, P.: Learning long-term dependencies with gradient descent is difficult. IEEE Trans. Neural Netw. 5(2), 157–166 (1994)
6. Borkowski, J., Chai, A.T., Mo, T., Green, A.E.O.: Cloud effects on middle ultraviolet global radiation. Acta Geophysica Polonica 25(4), 287–301 (1977)
7. Chauvin, R., Nou, J., Thil, S., Traoré, A., Grieu, S.: Cloud detection methodology based on a sky-imaging system. Energy Procedia 69, 1970–1980 (2015). International Conference on Concentrating Solar Power and Chemical Energy Systems, SolarPACES, p. 2014
8. Chollet, F., et al.: Keras (2015). https://keras.io
9. Chow, C., et al.: Intra-hour forecasting with a total sky imager at the UC San Diego solar energy testbed. Solar Energy 85, 2881–2893 (2011)
10. Diagne, H.M., David, M., Lauret, P., Boland, J., Schmutz, N.: Review of solar irradiance forecasting methods and a proposition for small-scale insular grids. Renew. Sustain. Energy Rev. 27, 65–76 (2013)
11. Elhoseiny, M., Huang, S., Elgammal, A.: Weather classification with deep convolutional neural networks. In: International Conference on Image Processing (2015)
12. Gevorgian, V., Booth, S.: Review of PREPA technical requirements for interconnecting wind and solar generation. Technical Report NREL/TP-5D00-57089, National Renewable Energy Laboratory (2013)
13. He, K., Zhang, X., Ren, S., Sun, J.: Deep residual learning for image recognition. In: CVPR, pp. 770–778 (2016). https://doi.org/10.1109/CVPR.2016.90

14. He, K., Zhang, X., Ren, S., Sun, J.: Identity mappings in deep residual networks. In: Leibe, B., Matas, J., Sebe, N., Welling, M. (eds.) ECCV 2016. LNCS, vol. 9908, pp. 630–645. Springer, Cham (2016). https://doi.org/10.1007/978-3-319-46493-0_38
15. Hochreiter, S., Schmidhuber, J.: Long short-term memory. Neural Comput. 9(8), 1735–1780 (1997). https://doi.org/10.1162/neco.1997.9.8.1735
16. Larraondo, P.R., Inza, I., Lozano, J.A.: Automating weather forecasts based on convolutional networks. In: ICML 17 Workshop on Deep Structured Prediction (2017)
17. Ioffe, S., Szegedy, C.: Batch normalization: accelerating deep network training by reducing internal covariate shift. In: ICML, pp. 448–456 (2015)
18. Krizhevsky, A., Sutskever, I., Hinton, G.E.: ImageNet classification with deep convolutional neural networks. In: NIPS, pp. 1106–1114 (2012)
19. Lu, S., et al.: Machine learning based multi-physical-model blending for enhancing renewable energy forecast - improvement via situation dependent error correction. In: Proceedings of the European Conference on Computer Vision (ECCV), pp. 31–45 (2015)
20. Magnone, L., Sossan, F., Scolari, E., Paolone, M.: Cloud motion identification algorithms based on all-sky images to support solar irradiance forecast. In: Photovoltaic Specialists Conference (2017)
21. Marquez, R., Coimbra, C.F.: Intra-hour DNI forecasting based on cloud tracking image analysis. Solar Energy 91, 327–336 (2013)
22. Mellit, A.: Artificial intelligence technique for modelling and forecasting of solar radiation data - a review. Int. J. Artif. Intell. Soft Comput. 1, 52–76 (2008)
23. Mnih, V., et al.: Human-level control through deep reinforcement learning. Nature 518(7540), 529–533 (2015)
24. Nguyen, H.T., Pearce, J.M.: Estimating potential photovoltaic yield with r.sun and the open source geographical resources analysis support system. Solar energy 84(5), 831–843 (2010)
25. Onishi, R., Sugiyama, D.: Deep convolutional neural network for cloud coverage estimation from snapshot camera images. SOL Atmos. 13, 235–239 (2017)
26. Pelland, S., et al.: Photovoltaic and solar forecasting: state of the art. Technical report IEA PVPS T14–01:2013, International Energy Agency, October 2013
27. Perez, R., et al.: A new operational model for satellite-derived irradiances: description and validation. Solar Energy 73(5), 307–317 (2002)
28. Richardson, W., Krishnaswami, H., Vega, R., Cervantes, M.: A low cost, edge computing, all-sky imager for cloud tracking and intra-hour irradiance forecasting. Sustainability 9, 1–17 (2017)
29. Ronneberger, O., Fischer, P., Brox, T.: U-Net: convolutional networks for biomedical image segmentation. In: Navab, N., Hornegger, J., Wells, W.M., Frangi, A.F. (eds.) MICCAI 2015. LNCS, vol. 9351, pp. 234–241. Springer, Cham (2015). https://doi.org/10.1007/978-3-319-24574-4_28
30. Ross, S., Gordon, G., Bagnell, D.: A reduction of imitation learning and structured prediction to no-regret online learning. In: Gordon, G., Dunson, D., Dudík, M. (eds.) International Conference on Artificial Intelligence and Statistics, vol. 15, pp. 627–635 (2011)
31. Sabburg, J., Wong, J.: Evaluation of a ground-based sky camera system for use in surface irradiance measurement. J. Atmos. Oceanic Technol. 16, 752–759 (1998)
32. Schmidt, T., et al.: Short-term solar forecasting based on sky images to enable higher PV generation in remote electricity networks. Renew. Energy Environ. Sustain. 2, 23 (2017)

33. Schmidt, T., Kalisch, J., Lorenz, E., Heinemann, D.: Evaluating the spatio-temporal performance of sky-imager-based solar irradiance analysis and forecasts. Atmos. Chem. Phys. **16**, 3399–3412 (2016)
34. Scolari, E., Sossan, F., Paolone, M.: Irradiance prediction intervals for PV stochastic generation in microgrid applications. Solar Energy **139**, 116–129 (2016)
35. Scolari, E., Sossan, F., Paolone, M.: Photovoltaic-model-based solar irradiance estimators: performance comparison and application to maximum power forecasting. IEEE Trans. Sustain. Energy **9**, 35–44 (2018)
36. Simonyan, K., Zisserman, A.: Very deep convolutional networks for large-scale image recognition. CoRR abs/1409.1556 (2014). http://arxiv.org/abs/1409.1556
37. Szegedy, C., et al.: Going deeper with convolutions. In: CVPR (2015)
38. Wolff, B., Kramer, O., Heinemann, D.: Selection of numerical weather forecast features for PV power predictions with random forests. In: Data Analytics for Renewable Energy Integration - 4th ECML PKDD Workshop, pp. 78–91 (2016)
39. Wolff, B., Lorenz, E., Kramer, O.: Statistical learning for short-term photovoltaic power predictions. In: Lässig, J., Kersting, K., Morik, K. (eds.) Computational Sustainability. SCI, vol. 645, pp. 31–45. Springer, Cham (2016). https://doi.org/10.1007/978-3-319-31858-5_3
40. Yadav, A.K., Chandel, S.: Solar radiation prediction using artificial neural network techniques: a review. Renew. Sustain. Energy Rev. **33**, 772–781 (2014)
41. Zeiler, M.D., Fergus, R.: Visualizing and understanding convolutional networks. In: Fleet, D., Pajdla, T., Schiele, B., Tuytelaars, T. (eds.) ECCV 2014. LNCS, vol. 8689, pp. 818–833. Springer, Cham (2014). https://doi.org/10.1007/978-3-319-10590-1_53

Learning Style Compatibility
for Furniture

Divyansh Aggarwal[1], Elchin Valiyev[2], Fadime Sener[2(✉)], and Angela Yao[2]

[1] IIT Jodhpur, Jodhpur, India
aggarwal.1@iitj.ac.in
[2] University of Bonn, Bonn, Germany
s6elvali@uni-bonn.de, {sener,yao}@cs.uni-bonn.de

Abstract. When judging style, a key question that often arises is whether or not a pair of objects are compatible with each other. In this paper we investigate how Siamese networks can be used efficiently for assessing the style compatibility between images of furniture items. We show that the middle layers of pretrained CNNs can capture essential information about furniture style, which allows for efficient applications of such networks for this task. We also use a joint image-text embedding method that allows for the querying of stylistically compatible furniture items, along with additional attribute constraints based on text. To evaluate our methods, we collect and present a large scale dataset of images of furniture of different style categories accompanied by text attributes.

1 Introduction

Understanding visual styles is important for application domains such as art, cinematography, advertising, and so on. Previous research in this domain focused primarily on recognition, *e.g.* of photo æsthetic quality [3], building styles [9], illustration and painting styles [7,16,26], city architectures [5], clothing styles [18]. Beyond recognition, however, style becomes a difficult concept to quantify, since it is a subjective and fine-grained problem. In this paper, we address the problem of style compatibility. We ask whether two objects – furniture specifically, are stylistically congruent, *e.g. "How well does this chair match that table?"*. Answering such a question would be greatly useful for supporting interior design, but is highly challenging, as it requires the ability to recognize features and attributes characteristic of specific styles across multiple object categories.

Recently, a few works have addressed style compatibility, though their focus is on clothing [10,23,31]. Our work is inspired by [31], which uses a Siamese network to measure compatibility between different types of clothing. Siamese networks have shown great success in measuring fine-grained visual similarities [1,21,32].

Electronic supplementary material The online version of this chapter (https://doi.org/10.1007/978-3-030-12939-2_38) contains supplementary material, which is available to authorized users.

© Springer Nature Switzerland AG 2019
T. Brox et al. (Eds.): GCPR 2018, LNCS 11269, pp. 552–566, 2019.
https://doi.org/10.1007/978-3-030-12939-2_38

In this work, we investigate the use of different Siamese architectures in assessing furniture style compatibility.

Style, as a high-level semantic concept, can be conveyed not only through the visual appearance, but also through text descriptions. As style data is often compiled from retail resources on the web [1, 10], the text tags and meta-data that often accompany images can also serve as an additional source of information. As such, we also use a joint visual-text embedding for learning stylistic compatibility. Such a model can make stylistically compatible recommendations in the presence of constraints such as the type of furniture, material and color.

To evaluate our methods, we collect and present the Bonn Furniture Styles Dataset. This is a large-scale dataset of approximately 90,000 images of furniture, drawn from six types and 17 different styles. To the best of our knowledge, the only dataset of furniture to date is the Singapore Furniture Dataset from Hu *et al.* [12] and is too small (~3000 images) to effectively learn deep models. Our dataset is more challenging and in addition, each image is accompanied by text descriptions of the furniture, with key attributes such as material, color, and so on.

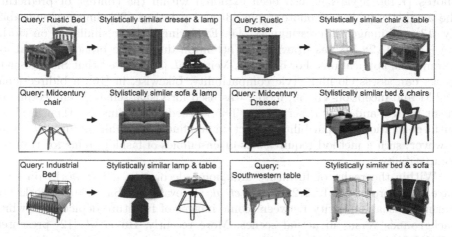

Fig. 1. Applying our categorical Siamese model (see Sect. 3.3), we show the two most stylistically compatible furniture items with respect to the query item. Note that our model is specifically trained across different types of furniture. (Color figure online)

We experiment using the Singapore Furniture Dataset [12] as well as our own large-scale dataset. Our findings show that Siamese networks are not only very successful at evaluating furniture style compatibility but also that compatibility can be assessed with only mid-level features. This opens up the possibility of deploying such a network efficiently on resource-constrained platforms and allows individuals to assess furniture compatibility in their own home with mobile devices. Our main contributions can be summarized as follows:

- We explore Siamese networks for learning the style compatibility of furniture and show that style, as a high-level semantic concept, is sufficiently encoded by the middle layers of convolutional networks. As such, style compatibility can already be assessed using relatively short CNNs without much loss in performance in comparison to full-depth CNNs.
- We use a joint visual-text embedding which can make style-aware furniture recommendations with additional text-based constraints.
- We collected a new large-scale dataset of furniture of different styles, along with associated text descriptions such as category, color, material etc. The dataset will be made publicly available and will be of interest for those working not only on style understanding but also on image attributes and fine-grained image understanding.

2   Related Work

Recognizing visual styles in computer vision has been addressed for classifying classic painting styles [16,26], building architectures [9] and illustrations and photos [7,15]. Style has also been explored within the context of predicting the aesthetic quality of photographs [3] and paintings [20], image memorability [13] and image "interestingness" [4]. Exploring stylistic similarity on clothing [17,18,27,28,31] has drawn a lot attention due to the broad potential for commercial applications. For example, Veit *et al.* [31] showed that Siamese networks can assess clothing style compatibility. Likewise, in [10], a bidirectional LSTM and Inception-V3 [30] model was used for visual-semantic embedding of outfit images and their descriptions. The learned embedding are then used for outfit generation, compatibility prediction and finding matching item tasks. Note however, such a method requires sets or ensembles of fashion items for training compatibility.

Within the realm of furniture and home decoration a few works on style have been proposed [1,12,22]. Bell *et al.* [1] evaluated Siamese networks for learning visual similarity between iconic images of furniture depicted on white backgrounds versus in actual scenes. More recently, Hu *et al.* [12] presented a CNN for furniture style classification, testing on their own collected dataset with style labels from industry professionals. A work similar to ours in spirit [22], tries to assess compatibility of furniture, but is based on learning a compatibility function for 3D models and requires computing geometric features for each 3D model. Additionally it doesn't account for material and texture which can carry important information about the style.

3   Style Compatibility Models

Our interest in learning about style compatibility of furniture is manifested in two tasks. First and foremost, we would like to be able to assess the style compatibility of two furniture items. We refer to this as the compatibility task. Secondly, given an image of an item of furniture, we would like to be able to retrieve, without knowing its style, other items which are stylistically compatible. Furthermore, we would like to place constraints on the retrieval, *e.g.* the type of item, or its color, material *etc.* We refer to the second task as the retrieval task.

To tackle these two tasks, we learn Siamese architectures (Sects. 3.1 to 3.3) to serve as a stylistic similarity metric between pairs of furniture images. These architectures can directly address the compatibility task. They can also naturally be extended to the retrieval task by making pairwise computations of a query image with respect to a collection of images and returning those which have the highest compatibility score. To apply a constrained query, we use using joint visual-text embeddings (Sect. 3.4) for representing both text and images in the same semantic space.

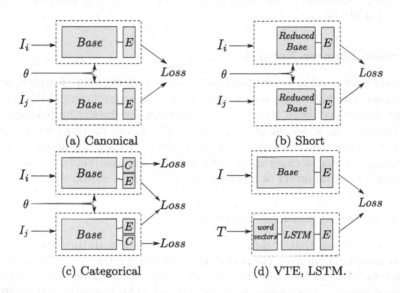

Fig. 2. Structure of our models. *Base* - base model, *E* - embedding layer, *C* - dense layer for classification, *T* - text as concatenated meta-data, *VTE* - visual-text embeddings.

3.1   Canonical Siamese Networks

The Siamese architecture joins two sub-networks at their output [2] to make some inference about a pair of input data and are commonly used for comparison. Typically, the base of the sub-networks have the same configuration and parameter set. For our *Canonical* Siamese configuration (see Fig. 2a), we use a pre-trained CNN as the base and add a fully connected layer E with D-dimensional output on top, and apply a contrastive loss to learn an embedding that maps similarly styled furniture items close to each other and different styles further apart:

$$L_{\text{can}}(I_i, I_j, Y, \theta) = Y \cdot \frac{1}{2} D_\theta(I_i, I_j)^2 + (1 - Y) \cdot \frac{1}{2} \max[0, m - D_\theta(I_i, I_j)]^2 \quad (1)$$

where (I_i, I_j, Y) is a sample pair of images I_i and I_j with compatibility label $Y \in \{0, 1\}$ ($Y = 1$ for a positive, compatible pair and $Y = 0$ for a negative non-compatible pair). $D_\theta(I_i, I_j)$ is a distance measure between I_i and I_j. The first term of the loss minimizes the distance between positive image pairs, while the second term of the loss encourages the distance between negative pairs to be as large as possible, up to some margin $m > 0$. Such a margin m is necessary, since it is possible to push negative pairs arbitrarily far from each other and thereby dominate the loss function. Siamese networks maps an image I_i into a D-dimensional embedding location x_i. In our experiments, we use the Euclidean distance on these output locations of images I_i and I_j as the distance, i.e. $D_\theta(I_i, I_j) = \|x_i - x_j\|^2$. The margin m is determined via cross-validation. Note that the canonical model does not directly receive any style labels during training; styles are defined implicitly from positive compatible and negative non-compatible pairs.

3.2   Short Siamese Network

Convolutional neural networks learn feature hierarchies, where features increase in semantic complexity as one progresses through the layers [33]. The mid-network layers have been shown to be important for preserving painting styles when transferring styles for photographs [8,14]. Based on this observation, we hypothesize that the later layers of a pretrained CNN are not necessary for differentiating style and experiment with a *Short* Siamese network (see Fig. 2b) with only the initial layers of a pre-trained CNN as an alternative base.

3.3   Categorical Siamese Network

It has been shown that including a classification loss during the training of Siamese model can improve the performance of image retrieval [1,25]. To leverage style labels, we combine similarity learning and classification into a multi-task setup and define a *Categorical* Siamese network. This network adds a soft-max layer to the base network so that it produces both an embedding and classification output C (See Fig. 2c). The loss for the Categorical Siamese is defined as:

$$L_{\text{cat}}(I_i, C_i, I_j, C_j, Y, \theta) = L_{\text{can}}(I_i, I_j, Y, \theta) + L_C(I_i, C_i, \theta) + L_C(I_j, C_j, \theta), \quad (2)$$

where L_{can} is the contrastive loss of the canonical network (see Eq. 1), C_i and C_j are the style annotations, and L_C is a categorical cross-entropy:

$$L_C = -\frac{1}{N} \sum_{n=1}^{N} \sum_i y_i \log \hat{y}_i, \quad (3)$$

where y is the output of the soft-max layer and $\hat{y}$ is the ground truth.

3.4 Joint Visual-Text Embeddings

We can further enhance our understanding of style and style compatibility by leveraging the text information from the meta-data of the product images. In particular, we extract meta-data for a product's coloring, material, and furniture type, in addition to its style. It is highly challenging to work with such meta-data because such information is not consistently available for all the images; furthermore it can be of variable length *e.g.* *"cream, wood, dresser"* or *"ruby english tea, hardwood fabric, sofa"*.

Our objective is to learn a joint embedding space to which both images and text meta-data can be projected (see Fig. 2d). Images and correctly associated meta-data should be kept close together and vice versa for non-matching images and meta-data. We do this in a similar way as DeViSE [6], by projecting both image and text features into a common D-dimensional embedding space, E, while minimizing a hinge rank loss:

$$L_{\text{joint}}(I_i, T_i, \theta) = \sum_{j \neq i} \max[0, m - S_\theta(I_i, T_i) + S_\theta(I_i, T_j)] \tag{4}$$

where (I_i, T_i) is a sample pair of image I_i and sequence of text T_i. Image and text features can be projected into the embedding positions x_I and x_T in the D-dimensional embedding space, E. Then, $S_\theta(I_i, T_i)$ is the dot product similarity between the vectors x_I and x_T of image I_i and text T_i. T_i represents the correct text for image I_i, while T_j is the text for images other than I_i. This loss encourages correct image and text pairs (I_i, T_i) to have a higher similarity score than the wrong pairs (I_i, T_j) by a margin m.

To represent the meta-data for each product as a fixed-length feature vector (300 in our case), we convert each word in the meta-data to its word2vec [24] representation and apply it as input to a 1-layer Long Short Term Memory network [11] (LSTM) with 300 hidden nodes. The corresponding images are passed through a base network and projected into the joint embedding space.

4   Bonn Furniture Styles Dataset

We collect a dataset of 90,298 furniture images with corresponding text meta-data from Houzz.com, a website specialized in architecture, decoration and interior design. We focus only on iconic images, depicting the furniture on a white background, so as to minimize crosstalk from distractors that may be present in images of the item within a scene. Text meta-data contain information as manufacturer, size, weight, materials, subcategories (e.g. folding chair, dining chair, armchair) and, most importantly, the style.

Our dataset has the six most popular categories of furniture on Houzz.com: beds (6594), chairs (22247), dressers (16885), lamps (32403), sofas (4080) and tables (8183). The distribution of styles per category are shown in Fig. 4. Figure 3 provides examples of the styles for the "bed" and "chair" categories.

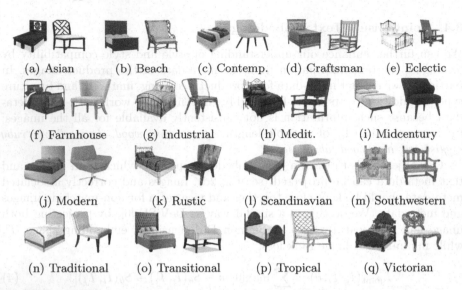

(a) Asian   (b) Beach   (c) Contemp.   (d) Craftsman   (e) Eclectic

(f) Farmhouse   (g) Industrial   (h) Medit.   (i) Midcentury

(j) Modern   (k) Rustic   (l) Scandinavian   (m) Southwestern

(n) Traditional   (o) Transitional   (p) Tropical   (q) Victorian

Fig. 3. *"Beds"* and *"chairs"* from the 17 styles. Style similarity may be encoded in material (3k), geometric curvatures (3q) or colour (3e). (Color figure online)

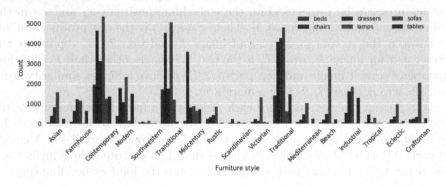

Fig. 4. Style distribution across categories in the Bonn Furniture Styles Dataset

Because our dataset and corresponding labels are extracted from the web, it tends to be noisy with mis-labelled data and duplicates. We first remove outliers by fine-tuning GoogLeNet [29] for the six categories of furniture based on a dataset of 25k images retrieved from the web. Samples with the lowest soft-max scores are considered to be irrelevant and removed. We find duplicates by thresholding on the Hamming distance between computed Perceptual Hash [19] values. When detecting duplicates, we remove one of the two duplicates if the style annotations are the same; if they are annotated with different styles, we remove both. This step also removes different colored versions of the same product.

5 Experiments

5.1 Setup, Training Details and Evaluation

As a base model, we use a pre-trained GoogLeNet [29] with the last layer removed. The embedding layer linearly transforms the 1024 dimensional feature vector output from GoogLeNet [29] into a 256-dimensional embedding feature. For the short Siamese, we first consider the GoogLeNet [29] layers up to Inception 4c and apply an average pooling that produces a 512-dimensional vector, to which we then append the embedding layer. For further comparisons, we also experimented with short networks with layers up to Inception 4b, 3b, and 3a.

To generate training pairs, we use a *strategic sampling* [31] that creates positive pairs only from different categories, *i.e.* same style, different types of furniture. This pushes the embedding to focus solely on the style compatibility and not on the similarities between items from the same furniture types. Negative pairs, on the other hand, are pairs of different styles drawn randomly from all types of furniture, both same and different.

We split the dataset into train, validation and test sets according to a 68:12:20 ratio. Our final training set of pairs has 2.2M pairs, while the validation and test sets have 200k pairs; similar to [31], we keep a 1:16 ratio of positive and negative pairs. We also test on the Singapore Furniture Dataset [12], using provided splits. Due to the smaller size of this dataset, we are able to generate 2.2M pairs for training but only 11K pairs for validation and 65K pairs for testing.

All networks are trained in two stages; first we back-propagate only over the embedding/classification layer (with learning rate $\epsilon = 0.01$, weight decay $\rho = 0.9$) for 50 iterations and then do a fine-tuning over the entire network with a lower learning rate ($\epsilon = 0.0001$). Overall training takes eight epochs. Embedding/classification soft-max layer weights are randomly initialized.

For training the visual-text embeddings, we create batches of a reference image and 16 other randomly sampled images from different styles than the reference. These sets of 17 images, along with their concatenated textual data are then considered as one batch for training the embeddings. The optimizer used for training is RMSProp with a learning rate $\epsilon = 0.001$. The base model for extracting the features from the image is kept fixed, so that only the visual embedding weights is learned. However, for the text part of the model, the entire LSTM as well as the textual embedding weights are learned from scratch.

To determine the margin parameter m in Eq. 1, we cross-validate to set a value of $m = 50$ for the canonical and short Siamese networks and $m = 1000$ for the categorical network.

We evaluate the compatibility task performance with area under the ROC curve (AUC). The Siamese networks, when presented with a pair of images, return a compatibility score between 0 (not compatible at all) and 1 (fully compatible). An AUC value of 0.5 is equal to taking a random guess, while 1.0 indicates perfect discrimination. For the retrieval task, we report recall@K which measures the fraction of times the correct item was found among top K results.

5.2 Comparison of Siamese Network Architectures

First, we compare the performance of three different Siamese network architectures presented in Sects. 3.1 to 3.3. As a baseline, we fine-tuned the base network GoogLeNet [29] model to explicitly classify furniture styles, and extracted the CNN features before the classification layer. Later on we compute the Euclidean distance between the CNN features of pairs of images as a measure of similarity. The ROC curves are shown in Fig. 5. We find that the canonical and categorical Siamese networks perform very similarly on the compatibility task, with AUCs of 0.7501 and 0.7546 respectively. While the categorical Siamese has only a marginally higher AUC than the canonical, the real impact of the additional categorical cross-entropy loss terms is in the fact that it helps training to converge much faster. After one epoch, the AUC of the categorical Siamese is already 0.732, as opposed to 0.710 for the canonical Siamese.

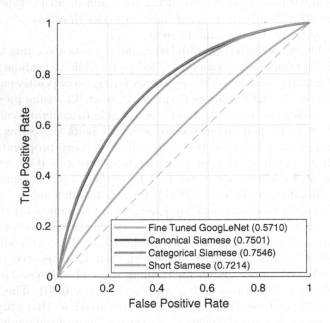

Fig. 5. Evaluation of models over test pairs generated from our Houzz.com dataset. The plot illustrates ROC curves and corresponding AUC (indicated as "area"). The dashed line represents random performance (AUC = 0.5).

More interesting, however, is the performance of the short Siamese network. With an AUC of 0.7214, it performs only a little bit worse than the much deeper canonical version. Such a small gap in performance can be explained by the nature of the stylistic features. Most of the stylistic cues can be visually recognized on a local level, rather than the overall view. For example, the *"Tropic"* style is characterized by woven fabric, whereas *"Victorian"* stands out from specific ornaments and curves. As such, the majority of the relevant features can

Table 1. Evaluation of short Siamese models along with the total number of network parameters. For the short Siamese networks, we consider GoogLeNet [29] layers up to Inception 3a, 3b, 4b and 4c.

	Inception 3a	Inception 3b	Inception 4b	Inception 4c	Canonical Siamese
AUC	0.6419	0.6938	0.7201	0.7214	0.7501
Params	$\approx 0.3M$	$\approx 0.7M$	$\approx 1.5M$	$\approx 1.9M$	$\approx 6M$

be captured by the mid-network convolutional layers of a deep network. Given that the short Siamese has much less parameters ($\approx 1.9M$ versus $\approx 6M$ for the canonical Siamese), it would be more advantageous for resource-limited scenarios such as deployments on a mobile device. In Table 1, we present comparisons for different short Siamese networks along with the number of parameters required.

Style-Based Comparison of All Models: Figure 6 depicts the AUC scores of the categorical Siamese on the compatibility task over the 17 style classes. Among others, *"Victorian"* and *"Midcentury"* styles have the highest AUCs. We attribute this to *"Victorian"* furniture usually having dark wood color with distinct ornaments and sometimes a golden coating. Similarly, *"Midcentury"* furniture can easily be distinguished by inclined legs. In contrast, *"Eclectic"* and *"Southwestern"* styles have the lowest AUCs; the poor performance can be attributed to both a lower number of images in the dataset (see Fig. 4) and large visual variance across furniture types.

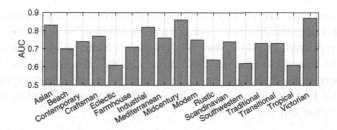

Fig. 6. AUC scores of the categorical Siamese network on the compatibility task over 17 style classes in the Bonn Furniture Styles Dataset.

5.3   Style Transferability

From Compatibility to Classification and Vice Versa: We want to test how well our Siamese networks, trained for style compatibility are able to perform on classifying styles. To do so, we train a linear SVM on the features extracted from the embedding layer of the categorical Siamese model and report our classification results in Table 2. We compare this with a fine-tuned version of the base network, *i.e.* GoogLeNet. We find that our proposed dataset is very difficult; the fine-tuned baseline has a classification accuracy of only 0.41, in comparison to the Singapore dataset [12], which has a classification of 0.66. Using the features learned from the embedding of the categorical Siamese, we get better classification performance on our large-scale dataset (0.49), but slightly worse on the smaller Singapore dataset (0.64). In comparison, the best reported classification results on this dataset is 0.70, achieved through an SVM classification of a combination of fine-tuned CNN features and hand-crafted features [12]. Given that the differences to our categorical Siamese is only marginal, we conclude that the features learned by the Siamese network are good representations of the style class.

Table 2. First two columns: comparison of style classification accuracy for a fine-tuned GoogLeNet versus a linear SVM trained on embedding vectors produced by categorical Siamese network. Second two columns: comparison of AUC scores for compatibility assessment between a fine-tuned GoogLeNet versus the categorical Siamese network.

	Classification		Compatibility	
Model	Bonn styles	Singapore [12]	Bonn styles	Singapore [12]
Fine-tuned GoogLeNet	0.4141	**0.6580**	0.5710	0.6184
Categorical Siamese	**0.4920**	0.6362	**0.7546**	**0.8289**

The reverse case, however, of using features learned for classification for determining style compatibility (see Sect. 5.2), does not hold as well (see Table 2). As previously reported, the AUC for the categorical Siamese is significantly higher than the fine-tuned GoogLeNet (0.7546 vs 0.5710). We find a similar trend for the Singapore dataset (0.8289 vs 0.6184). Based on these two experiments, we conclude that features learned for style compatibility are well-suited for performing classification but not vice versa.

Cross-Dataset Testing: We investigated the transferability of features learned on one dataset to another by training on our proposed dataset and testing on the Singapore Furniture Dataset [12]. This dataset has similar types of furniture distributed over 16 styles, 14 of which do not appear in our dataset (only Mediterranean and modern are common to both datasets). We find that the categorical Siamese model trained on our proposed dataset is able to achieve an AUC score of 0.7129 on the Singapore Furniture Dataset [12]. This suggests that our network is able to generalize to the notion of style similarity, even when encountering never-seen-before styles. When we try the reverse, however, *i.e.* training on the Singapore dataset and testing on ours, the AUC is a much lower 0.5534. We attribute the difference in the performance to the size difference of the two datasets (90K vs. 3K). Although both datasets have almost equal number of style classes, our dataset has more data for each class which allows the deep model to learn finer grained similarities from higher amount of variations within each style across furniture types.

5.4   Stylistic Image Retrieval

We evaluate the Siamese model's ability to correctly retrieve stylistically similar images in Table 3. To evaluate the ranking we report recall@K, $K \in 1, 5, 10$. The performance of the different models in the retrieval task mirror that of the compatibility task. The canonical and categorical models perform similarly, with the categorical being slightly better, while the canonical is a little bit lower. In Fig. 1, we show example retrieval results for the categorical Siamese network.

Table 3. Stylistic-based retrieval results using Siamese networks. We report recall@K (high is good).

	R@1	R@5	R@10
Canonical	33.7	64.1	75.6
Categorical	34.5	64.8	74.9
Short	29.8	63.2	76.7

5.5   Retrieval with Text Constraints

To retrieve stylistically compatible images with additional text constraints, we use the joint visual-text embeddings from Sect. 3.4. We project the query image features extracted from the GoogLeNet to the joint embedding space position x_I. Similarly, for the text, which is used as a constraint, we first extract the LSTM [11] features and then project them to the joint embedding space position x_T. The sum of these two vectors, $x_{sum} = x_I + x_T$, is another position in this space and we return the results based on a nearest-neighbour search in the joint embedding space using x_{sum} as our query vector.

As a baseline, we use the style text of the query image along with text constraints. We measure the recall of the style and furniture type for such queries and report recall@K, $K \in 1, 3, 5, 10$ in Table 4 and example retrievals in Fig. 7. Admittedly, our recall performance is not so impressive; however there is only a small drop from querying with images versus text and even the image query is still several times better than chance. One should consider the difficulty of this task, which is expressed qualitatively in Fig. 7: It can be seen that retrieving exact matches is quite difficult, given the available text attributes. Nonetheless, we can still maintain style and category similar to the query image constrained with text.

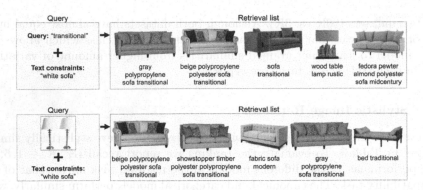

Fig. 7. Applying our visual text embedding model for queries constrained with text (see Sect. 3.4). In the second row, the style of lamps is "transitional".

Table 4. Retrieval with text constraints. We report recall@K (high is good)

	Style+category				Exact match			
	R@1	R@3	R@5	R@10	R@1	R@3	R@5	R@10
Text query	0.8	1.9	4.9	6.9	0.3	0.3	0.6	0.8
Image query	0.1	1.2	3.0	5.9	0	0	0.2	0.7

6   Conclusion

In this work we tackle the problem of learning style compatibility for furniture and addressed two different style tasks – one assessing compatibility between pairs of images, and one querying for stylistically compatible images. To accomplish this, we propose and test several Siamese architectures. Our evaluations show that Siamese networks excel at capturing the stylistic compatibility; in addition, these networks can be reduced to only low- and mid-level layers of pre-trained CNNs and still perform comparably with full CNNs, thereby enabling efficient deployments. In addition, we use a joint visual-text embedding model for making stylistically compatible recommendations, while constraining the queries by attributes like furniture type, color and material. For evaluation, we collected an extensive dataset of furniture images of different style categories, along with textual annotations which we will release publicly. We report comprehensive evaluations on our dataset and show that it is very beneficial for style understanding with and without text.

References

1. Bell, S., Bala, K.: Learning visual similarity for product design with convolutional neural networks. ACM Trans. Graph. **34**, 98 (2015)
2. Bromley, J., Guyon, I., LeCun, Y., Säckinger, E., Shah, R.: Signature verification using a "siamese" time delay neural network. In: Cowan, J.D., Tesauro, G., Alspector, J. (eds.) Advances in Neural Information Processing Systems 6, pp. 737–744. Morgan-Kaufmann (1994). http://papers.nips.cc/paper/769-signature-verification-using-a-siamese-time-delay-neural-network.pdf
3. Datta, R., Joshi, D., Li, J., Wang, J.Z.: Studying aesthetics in photographic images using a computational approach. In: Leonardis, A., Bischof, H., Pinz, A. (eds.) ECCV 2006. LNCS, vol. 3953, pp. 288–301. Springer, Heidelberg (2006). https://doi.org/10.1007/11744078_23
4. Dhar, S., Ordonez, V., Berg, T.L.: High level describable attributes for predicting aesthetics and interestingness. In: Proceedings of the 2011 IEEE Conference on Computer Vision and Pattern Recognition, CVPR 2011 (2011)
5. Doersch, C., Singh, S., Gupta, A., Sivic, J., Efros, A.: What makes paris look like paris? ACM Trans. Graph. **31**(4) (2012)
6. Frome, A., et al.: DeViSE: a deep visual-semantic embedding model. In: Advances in Neural Information Processing Systems 26 (2013)
7. Garces, E., Agarwala, A., Gutierrez, D., Hertzmann, A.: A similarity measure for illustration style. ACM Trans. Graph. **33**, 93 (2014)
8. Gatys, L.A., Ecker, A.S., Bethge, M.: A neural algorithm of artistic style. arXiv preprint arXiv:1508.06576 (2015)
9. Goel, A., Juneja, M., Jawahar, C.V.: Are buildings only instances?: exploration in architectural style categories. In: Proceedings of the Eighth Indian Conference on Computer Vision, Graphics and Image Processing, ICVGIP 2012 (2012)
10. Han, X., Wu, Z., Jiang, Y., Davis, L.S.: Learning fashion compatibility with bidirectional LSTMs. CoRR (2017)
11. Hochreiter, S., Schmidhuber, J.: Long short-term memory. Neural Comput. **9**(8), 1735–1780 (1997)
12. Hu, Z., et al.: Visual classification of furniture styles. ACM Trans. Intell. Syst. Technol. (2017)
13. Isola, P., Xiao, J., Parikh, D., Torralba, A., Oliva, A.: What makes a photograph memorable? IEEE Trans. Pattern Anal. Mach. Intell. **36**, 1469–1482 (2014)
14. Johnson, J., Alahi, A., Fei-Fei, L.: Perceptual losses for real-time style transfer and super-resolution. In: Leibe, B., Matas, J., Sebe, N., Welling, M. (eds.) ECCV 2016. LNCS, vol. 9906, pp. 694–711. Springer, Cham (2016). https://doi.org/10.1007/978-3-319-46475-6_43
15. Karayev, S., et al.: Recognizing image style. arXiv preprint arXiv:1311.3715 (2013)
16. Keren, D.: Painter identification using local features and naive Bayes. In: Proceedings of Pattern Recognition Conference. IEEE (2002)
17. Kiapour, M.H., Han, X., Lazebnik, S., Berg, A.C., Berg, T.L.: Where to buy it: matching street clothing photos in online shops. In: Proceedings of the 2015 International Conference on Computer Vision. IEEE Press (2015)
18. Kiapour, M.H., Yamaguchi, K., Berg, A.C., Berg, T.L.: Hipster wars: discovering elements of fashion styles. In: Fleet, D., Pajdla, T., Schiele, B., Tuytelaars, T. (eds.) ECCV 2014. LNCS, vol. 8689, pp. 472–488. Springer, Cham (2014). https://doi.org/10.1007/978-3-319-10590-1_31

19. Krawetz, N.: Looks like it (2011). http://www.hackerfactor.com/blog/index.php?/archives/432-Looks-Like-It.html
20. Li, C., Chen, T.: Aesthetic visual quality assessment of paintings. IEEE J. Sel. Top. Sign. Proces. **3**, 236–252 (2009)
21. Lin, T.Y., Cui, Y., Belongie, S., Hays, J.: Learning deep representations for ground-to-aerial geolocalization. In: Proceedings of the IEEE Conference on Computer Vision and Pattern Recognition (2015)
22. Liu, T., Hertzmann, A., Li, W., Funkhouser, T.: Style compatibility for 3D furniture models. ACM Trans. Graph. **34**, 85 (2015)
23. McAuley, J., Targett, C., Shi, Q., Van Den Hengel, A.: Image-based recommendations on styles and substitutes. In: Proceedings of the 38th International ACM SIGIR Conference on Research and Development in Information Retrieval. ACM (2015)
24. Řehůřek, R., Sojka, P.: Software framework for topic modelling with large corpora. In: Proceedings of the LREC 2010 Workshop on New Challenges for NLP Frameworks. ELRA (2010)
25. Sangkloy, P., Burnell, N., Ham, C., Hays, J.: The sketchy database: learning to retrieve badly drawn bunnies. ACM Trans. Graph. **35**, 119 (2016). Proceedings of SIGGRAPH
26. Shamir, L., Macura, T., Orlov, N., Eckley, D.M., Goldberg, I.G.: Impressionism, expressionism, surrealism: automated recognition of painters and schools of art. ACM Trans. Appl. Percept. **7**, 8 (2010)
27. Simo-Serra, E., Fidler, S., Moreno-Noguer, F., Urtasun, R.: Neuroaesthetics in fashion: modeling the perception of fashionability. In: Proceedings of the Computer Vision and Pattern Recognition Conference (CVPR 2015). IEEE Press (2015)
28. Simo-Serra, E., Ishikawa, H.: Fashion style in 128 floats: joint ranking and classification using weak data for feature extraction. In: Proceedings of the Conference on Computer Vision and Pattern Recognition (CVPR) (2016)
29. Szegedy, C., et al.: Going deeper with convolutions. In: Computer Vision and Pattern Recognition (CVPR) (2015)
30. Szegedy, C., Vanhoucke, V., Ioffe, S., Shlens, J., Wojna, Z.: Rethinking the inception architecture for computer vision. In: Proceedings of the IEEE Conference on Computer Vision and Pattern Recognition (2016)
31. Veit, A., Kovacs, B., Bell, S., McAuley, J., Bala, K., Belongie, S.: Learning visual clothing style with heterogeneous dyadic co-occurrences. In: Proceedings of the IEEE International Conference on Computer Vision (2015)
32. Wang, J., et al.: Learning fine-grained image similarity with deep ranking. In: Proceedings of the IEEE Conference on Computer Vision and Pattern Recognition (2014)
33. Zeiler, M.D., Fergus, R.: Visualizing and understanding convolutional networks. In: Fleet, D., Pajdla, T., Schiele, B., Tuytelaars, T. (eds.) ECCV 2014. LNCS, vol. 8689, pp. 818–833. Springer, Cham (2014). https://doi.org/10.1007/978-3-319-10590-1_53

Temporal Interpolation as an Unsupervised Pretraining Task for Optical Flow Estimation

Jonas Wulff[1,2]([⊠]) and Michael J. Black[1]

[1] Max-Planck Institute for Intelligent Systems, Tübingen, Germany
wulff@mit.edu, black@tuebingen.mpg.de
[2] MIT CSAIL, Cambridge, MA, USA

Abstract. The difficulty of annotating training data is a major obstacle to using CNNs for low-level tasks in video. Synthetic data often does not generalize to real videos, while unsupervised methods require heuristic losses. Proxy tasks can overcome these issues, and start by training a network for a task for which annotation is easier or which can be trained unsupervised. The trained network is then fine-tuned for the original task using small amounts of ground truth data. Here, we investigate frame interpolation as a proxy task for optical flow. Using real movies, we train a CNN unsupervised for temporal interpolation. Such a network implicitly estimates motion, but cannot handle untextured regions. By fine-tuning on small amounts of ground truth flow, the network can learn to fill in homogeneous regions and compute full optical flow fields. Using this unsupervised pre-training, our network outperforms similar architectures that were trained supervised using synthetic optical flow.

1 Introduction

In recent years, the successes of deep convolutional neural networks (CNNs) have led to a large number of breakthroughs in most fields of computer vision. The two factors that made this possible are a widespread adoption of massively parallel processors in the form of GPUs and large amounts of available annotated training data. To learn good and sufficiently general representations of visual features, CNNs require tens of thousands to several hundred million [28] examples of the visual content they are supposed to process, annotated with labels teaching the CNNs the desired output for a given visual stimulus.

For some tasks such as image classification or object detection it is possible to generate massive amounts of data by paying human workers to manually annotate images. For example, writing a description of an image into a textbox or dragging a rectangle around an object are tasks that are easy to understand and relatively quick to perform. For other tasks, especially those related to video, obtaining ground truth is not as easy. For example, manual annotation of dense optical flow, motion segmentation, or tracking of objects requires not just the annotation of a huge number of instances (in the first two cases one would ideally

© Springer Nature Switzerland AG 2019
T. Brox et al. (Eds.): GCPR 2018, LNCS 11269, pp. 567–582, 2019.
https://doi.org/10.1007/978-3-030-12939-2_39

want one annotation per pixel), but an annotator would also have to step back and forth in time to ensure temporal consistency [17]. Since this makes the task both tedious and error-prone, manually annotated data is rarely used for low-level video analysis.

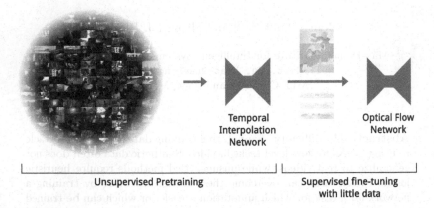

Fig. 1. Overview of our method. Using large amounts of unlabelled data we train a temporal interpolation network without explicit supervision. We then fine-tune the network for the task of optical flow using small amounts of ground truth data, outperforming similar architectures that were trained supervised.

An alternative is to use synthetic data, for example from animated movies [4], videogames [26], or generated procedurally [19]. The problem here is that synthetic data always lives in a world different from our own. Even if the low-level image statistics are a good match to those of the real world, it is an open question whether realistic effects such as physics or human behavior can be learned from synthetic data.

A different approach to address the issue of small data is to use *proxy tasks*. The idea is to train a network using data for which labels are easy to acquire, or for which unsupervised or self-supervised learning is possible. Training on such data forces the network to learn a latent representation, and if the proxy task is appropriately chosen, this representation transfers to the actual task at hand. The trained network, or parts thereof, can then be fine-tuned to the final task using limited amounts of annotated data, making use of the structure learned from the proxy task. An example proxy task for visual reasoning about images is colorization, since solving the colorization problem requires the network to learn about the semantics of the world [16]. Another example is context prediction [5], in which the proxy task is to predict the spatial arrangement of sub-patches of objects, which helps in the final task of object detection.

What, then, would be a good proxy task for video analysis? One core problem in the analysis of video is to compute temporal correspondences between frames. Once correspondences are established, it is possible to reason about the temporal evolution of the scene, track objects, classify actions, and reconstruct the geometry of the world. Recent work by Long *et al.* [18] proposed a way to learn about correspondences without supervision. They first train a network to interpolate between two frames. For each point in the interpolated frame, they then backpropagate the derivatives through the network, computing which pixels in the input images most strongly influence this point. This, in turn, establishes correspondences between the two maxima of these derivatives in the input images. Their work, however, had two main shortcomings. First, using a complete backpropagation pass to compute each correspondence is computationally expensive. Second, especially in unstructured or blurry regions of the frame, the derivatives are not necessarily well located, since a good (in the photometric sense) output pixel can be sampled from a number of wrongly corresponding sites in the input images; frame interpolation does not need to get the flow right to produce a result with low photometric error. This corresponds to the classical aperture problem in optical flow, in which the flow is not locally constrained, but context is needed to resolve ambiguities. Consequently, so far, the interpolation task has not served as an effective proxy for learning flow.

In this work, we address these shortcomings and show that, treated properly, the interpolation task can, indeed, support the learning of optical flow. To this end, we treat training for optical flow as a two-stage problem (Fig. 1). In the first stage, we train a network to estimate the center frame from four adjacent, equally spaced frames. This forces the network to learn to establish correspondences in visually distinct areas. Unlike previous work, which used only limited datasets of a few tens of thousands frames such as KITTI-RAW [8], we use a little under one million samples from a diverse set of datasets incorporating both driving scenarios and several movies and TV series. This trains the network to better cope with effects like large displacements and motion and focus blur. Thanks to this varied and large body of training data, our network outperforms specialized frame interpolation methods despite not being tailored to this task.

In a second stage, we fine-tune the network using a small amount of ground-truth optical flow data from the training sets of KITTI [8] and Sintel [4]. This has three advantages. First, after fine-tuning, the network outputs optical flow directly, which makes it much more efficient than [18]. Second, this fine-tuning forces the network to group untextured regions and to consider the context when estimating the motion; as mentioned above, this can usually not be learned from photometric errors alone. Third, compared to fully unsupervised optical flow algorithms [1,21], during training our method does not employ prior assumptions such as spatial smoothness, but is purely data-driven.

Our resulting network is fast and yields optical flow results with superior accuracy to the comparable networks of FlowNetS [6] and SpyNet [24] which were trained using large amounts of labeled, synthetic optical flow data [24]. This demonstrates that (a) when computing optical flow, it is important to use real data for training, and (b) that temporal interpolation is a suitable proxy task to learn from to make learning from such data feasible.

2   Previous Work

CNNs for Optical Flow. In the past years, end-to-end training has had considerable success in many tasks of computer vision, including optical flow. The first paper demonstrating end-to-end optical flow was FlowNet [6], which used an architecture similar to ours, but trained on large amounts of synthetic ground truth optical flow. In follow-up work [12], the authors propose a cascade of hourglass networks, each warping the images closer towards each other. Furthermore, they significantly extend their training dataset (which is still synthetic). This leads to high performance at the cost of a complicated training procedure.

Taking a different direction, SpyNet [24] combines deep learning with a spatial pyramid. Similar to classical optical flow methods, each pyramid level computes the flow residual for the flow on the next coarser scale, and successively warps the input frame using the new, refined flow. This allows the authors to use a very simple network architecture, which in turns leads to high computational efficiency. The training, however, is still done using the same annotated training set as [6]. The recently proposed PWC-Net [31] uses ideas of both, and computes the flow in a multiscale fashion using a cost volume on each scale, followed by a trained flow refinement step.

A different approach is to not train a network for full end-to-end optical flow estimation, but to use trained networks inside a larger pipeline. Most commonly, these approaches use a network to estimate the similarity between two patches [11,34], effectively replacing the data cost in a variational flow method by a CNN. The resulting data costs can be combined with spatial inference, for example belief-propagation [11], or a cost volume optimization [34]. A network trained to denoise data can also be used as the proximal operator in a variational framework [20]. In the classical optical flow formulation, this would correspond to a network that learns to regularize.

All these approaches, however, require large amounts of annotated data. For real sequences, such training data is either hard to obtain for general scenes [14], or limited to specific domains such as driving scenarios [8]. Synthetic benchmarks [4,19,26], on the other hand, often lack realism, and it is unclear how well their training data generalizes to the real world.

Hence, several works have investigated unsupervised training for optical flow estimation. A common approach is to let the network estimate a flow field, warp the input images towards each other using this flow field, and measure the similarity of the images under a photometric loss. Since warping can be formulated as a differentiable function [13], the photometric loss can be back-propagated, forcing the network to learn better optical flow. In [35], the authors combine the photometric loss with a robust spatial loss on the estimated flow, similar to robust regularization in variational optical flow methods [29]. However, while their training is unsupervised, they do not demonstrate cross-dataset generalization, but train for Flying Chairs [6] and KITTI [8] using matching training sets and separately tuned hyper-parameters. In [25], the authors use the same approach, but show that a network that is pre-trained using the same dataset as in [6] can be fine-tuned to different output scenarios. Similarly, USCNN [1] uses only a single training set. Here, the authors do not use end-to-end training, but instead use a photometric loss to train a network to estimate the residual flow on different pyramid layers, similar to [24]. The recently proposed UnFlow [21] uses a loss based on the CENSUS transform and computes the flow in both forward and backward direction. This allows the authors to integrate occlusion reasoning into the loss; using an architecture based on FlowNet2, they achieve state-of-the-art results on driving scenarios. All these methods require manually chosen heuristics as part of the loss, such as spatial smoothness or forward-backward consistency-based occlusion reasoning. Therefore, they do not fully exploit the fact that CNNs allow us to overcome such heuristics and to purely "let the data speak". In contrast, our method does not use any explicitly defined heuristics, but uses an unsupervised interpolation task and a small number of ground truth flow fields to learn about motion.

Several approaches use geometrical reasoning to self-supervise the training process. In TransFlow [2], the authors train two networks, a first, shallow one estimating a global homography between two input frames, and a second, deep network estimating the residual flow after warping with this homography. Since they use the homography to model the ego-motion, they focus on driving scenarios, and do not test on more generic optical flow sequences. In [9], a network is trained to estimate depth from a single image, and the photometric error according to the warping in a known stereo setup induced by the depth is penalized. Similarly [36] trains a network to estimate depth from a single image by learning to warp, but use videos instead of stereo. SfM-Net [7] learns to reduce a photometric loss by estimating the 3D structure of the world, the motion of the observer, and the segmentation into moving and static regions, which is enough to explain most of the motion of the world. However, as most other methods, it is only tested on the restricted automotive scenario.

Simliar to self-supervision using geometric losses, Generative Adversarial Networks [10] have been used to learn the structure of optical flow fields. In [15], the GAN is trained to distinguish between the warping errors caused by ground truth and wrongly estimated optical flow. Only the discriminator uses annotated data; once trained, it provides a loss for unsupervised training of the flow itself.

Frame Interpolation. Instead of warping one input frame to another, it is also possible to train networks to interpolate and extrapolate images by showing them unlabeled videos at training time. A hybrid network is used in [27], where a shared contractive network is combined with two expanding networks to estimate optical flow and to predict the next frame, respectively. Similar to us, they hypothesize that temporal frame generation and optical flow share some internal representations; however, unlike us they train the optical flow network completely with labeled data, and do not test on the challenging Sintel test set. Similarly, [32] trains a network to anticipate the values of intermediate feature maps in the future. However, they are not interested in the motion itself, but in the future higher-level scene properties such as objects and actions. Niklaus *et al.* [23] propose a video interpolation network, where the motion is encoded in an estimated convolutional kernel; however, the quality of this implicit motion is never tested. As mentioned above, the work most similar to ours is [18], where a CNN is trained to interpolate between frames and subsequently used to compute correspondences between images. Unlike our work, however, they require expensive backpropagation steps to establish the correspondences; we show that using a small amount of training data can teach the network to translate between its internal motion representation and optical flow, resulting in significantly improved performance.

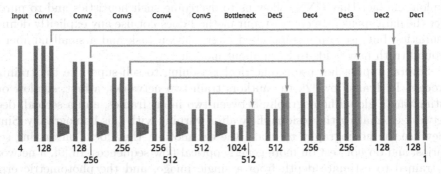

Fig. 2. Architecture of our network. The outputs of 3×3 convolutional layers are shown in blue, the output of 2×2 max-pooling operations in red, $2\times$ transposed convolutions in green, and side-channel concatenation in orange. Not shown are leaky ReLUs after each layer except the last and batch normalization layers. The numbers indicate the number of channels of each feature map.

3 A Frame Interpolation Network

The core hypothesis of our work is that in order to properly perform temporal interpolation, it is necessary to learn about the motion of the world. Temporal interpolation, however, is a task that does not require explicit supervision; with proper selection of input and output frames, every video sequence can serve as a supervisory signal. Therefore, we start by training a network for the task of interpolation in an unsupervised manner. Given four frames (as shown in Fig. 3 in red), the task of our network is to interpolate the center frame, shown in green in Fig. 3. Empirically, we found that using four input frames resulted in approximately 13% lower errors (2.04 px EPE) on the optical flow estimation task than using two frames (2.31 px EPE). We believe that the reasons for this are that with more than two frames (a) it is easier to reason about higher order temporal effects (*ie.* non-zero acceleration), and (b) it enables the network to reason about occlusions, which requires at least three frames [30]. We hence use four input frames for both the interpolation and the optical flow estimation task. We use grayscale images as input and output, since we found the final optical flow to have lower errors with grayscale than with color images.

Fig. 3. Our network predicts the center frame (green) from four neighboring, equally spaced frames (red). To ensure equal spacing of the input frames, the unmarked frames (second from the left and right) are not taken into account. (Color figure online)

Network Architecture. Similar to [18], we use a standard hourglass architecture with side-channels, as shown in Fig. 2. This simple architecture is nevertheless surprisingly effective in many different applications, such as optical flow computation [6] and unsupervised depth estimation [36]. Our network consists of five convolutional blocks (`Conv1` to `Conv5` in Fig. 2), each of which contains three 3×3 convolutional layers followed by batch normalization layers and leaky ReLUs. Between the blocks, we use max-pooling to reduce the resolution by a factor of two. Within each block, all layers except the last output the same number of feature maps. `Conv5` is followed by a bottleneck block consisting of two convolutional layers and a transposed convolution. The output is then successively upscaled using a series of decoder blocks (`Dec5` to `Dec1`). Each consists of two convolutional layers and (except for `Dec1`) a transposed convolution which doubles the resolution, again interleaved with leaky ReLUs and batch normalization layers.

To preserve high frequency information, we use side channels as in [6], shown in orange in Fig. 2. The output of the transposed convolutions are concatenated with the appropriate outputs from the convolutional layers. The last convolutional layer of `Dec1` directly outputs the monochrome output image and is not followed by a nonlinearity. Table 1 summarizes the number of inputs and outputs of each convolutional block.

Table 1. Number of input and output channels per layer block.

	Conv1	Conv2	Conv3	Conv4	Conv5	Bottleneck	Dec5	Dec4	Dec3	Dec2	Dec1
Input	4	128	128	256	256	512	1024	1024	512	512	256
Output	128	128	256	256	512	1024	1024	512	512	256	1

Training Data. Unsupervised training would in theory allow us to train a network with infinite amounts of data. Yet, most previous works only use restricted datasets, such as KITTI-RAW. Instead, in this work we aim to compile a large, varied dataset, containing both cinematic sequences from several movies of different genres as well as more restricted but very common sequences from driving scenarios. As movies, we use *Victoria* and *Birdman*. The former was filmed in a true single take, and the later was filmed and edited in such a way that cuts are imperceptible. In addition, we use long takes from the movies *Atonement*, *Children of Men*, *Baby Driver*, and the TV series *True Detective*. Shot boundaries would destroy the temporal consistency that we want our network to learn and hence would have to be explicitly detected and removed; using single-take shots eliminates this problem.

For the driving scenarios, we use KITTI-RAW [22] and Malaga [3], the first of which contains several sequences and the second of which contains one long shot of camera footage recorded from a driving car. For each sequence, we use around 1% of frames as validation, sampled from the beginning, center, and end of the sequence and sampled such that they do not overlap the actual training data. The only difference is KITTI-RAW, which is already broken up into sequences. Here, we sample full sequences to go either to the training or validation set, and use 10% for the validation set. This ensures that the validation set contains approximately the same amount of frames from driving and movie-like scenarios. Table 2 summarizes the datasets used and the amount of frames from each.

In total, we thus have approximately 464K training frames. However, in movie sequences, the camera and object motions are often small. Therefore, during both training and validation, we predict each frame twice, once from the adjacent frames as shown in Fig. 3, and once with doubled spacing between the frames. Therefore, a target frame at time t provides two training samples, one where it is predicted from the frames at $t - 3, t - 1, t + 1$, and $t + 3$, and one where it is predicted from $t - 6, t - 2, t + 2$, and $t + 6$. This ensures that we have a sufficient amount of large motions in our frame interpolation training set. In total, our training and validation sets contain 928,410 and 16,966 samples, respectively.

Training Details. As shown in Fig. 3, each training sample of our network consists of the four input frames and the center frame which the network should predict. During training, each quadruple of frames is separately normalized by subtracting the mean of the four input frames and dividing by their standard deviation. We found this to work better than normalization across the full dataset. We believe the reason for this is that in correspondence estimation, it is more important to consider the structure *within* a sample than the structure across samples, the later of which is important for classification tasks. To put it differently, whether a light bar or a dark bar moves to the right does not matter for optical flow and should produce the same output.

As data augmentation, we randomly crop the input images to rectangles with the aspect ratio 2:1, and resize the cropped images to a resolution of 384×192 pixel, resulting in randomization of both scale and translation. For all input frames belonging to a training sample, we use the same crop. Furthermore, we randomly flip the images in horizontal and vertical direction, and randomly switch between forward and backward temporal ordering of the input images. We use a batch size of 8, train our network using ADAM and use a loss consisting of a structural similarity loss (SSIM) [33] and an L_1 loss, weighted equally. The initial learning rate is set to $1e - 4$, and halved after 3, 6, 8, and 10 epochs. We train our network for 12 epochs; after this point, we did not notice any further decrease in our loss on the validation set.

Table 2. Training data for interpolation.

Source	Type	Training frames	Validation frames
Birdman	Full movie	155,403	1,543
Victoria	Full movie	188,700	1,878
KITTI-RAW	Driving	39,032	3,960
Malaga	Driving	51,285	460
Atonement	Movie clip	7,062	44
Children of Men	Movie clip	9,165	65
Baby Driver	Movie clip	3,888	14
True Detective	Movie clip	8,388	57
Total		464,205	8,483

4   From Interpolation to Optical Flow

Given a frame interpolation network, it has been shown before [18] that motion is learned by the network and can be extracted. However, this only works for regions with sufficient texture. In unstructured areas of the image, the photometric error that is used to train the frame interpolation is not informative, and even a wrong motion estimation can result in virtually perfect frame reconstruction.

What is missing for good optical flow estimation, then, is the capability to group the scene and to fill in the motion in unstructured regions, *ie.* to address the aperture problem. Furthermore, the mechanism used to extract the motion in [18] is slow, since it requires a complete backpropagation pass for each correspondence. To effectively use frame interpolation for optical flow computation, two steps are thus missing: (a) to add knowledge about grouping and region fill-in to a network that can compute correspondences, and (b) to modify the network to directly yield an optical flow field, making expensive backpropagation steps unnecessary at test time. Luckily, both objectives can be achieved by fine-tuning the network to directly estimate optical flow, using only a very limited amount of annotated ground truth data.

For this, we replace the last layer of the `Dec1` block with a vanilla 3×3 convolutional layer with two output channels instead of one, and train this network using available ground truth training data, consisting of the training sets of KITTI-2012 [8], KITTI-2015 [22] and the clean and final passes of MPI-Sintel [4], for a total of about 2500 frames. We use 10% of the data as validation.

We again use ADAM with an initial learning rate of 10^{-4}, halve the learning rate if the error on the validation set has not decreased for 20 epochs, and train for a total of 200 epochs using the endpoint error as the loss. Except for the temporal reversal, we use the same augmentations as described above.

As we will see in the next section, this simple fine-tuning procedure results in a network that computes good optical flow, and even outperforms networks with comparable architecture that were trained using large amounts of synthetically generated optical flow.

5   Experiments

In this section, we demonstrate the effectiveness of our method for interpolation and optical flow estimation, and provide further experiments showing the importance of pre-training and the effects of reduced ground truth data for fine-tuning.

5.1   Temporal Interpolation

To evaluate the interpolation performance of our network, we compare with [23], a state-of-the-art method for frame interpolation. Unlike ours, [23] is specifically designed for this task; in contrast, we use a standard hourglass network. We compute temporal interpolations for 2800 frames from natural movies, a synthetic movie (Sintel), and driving scenarios. All frames were not previously seen in training. To compute interpolated color frames, we simply run our network once for each input color channel. Table 3 shows results on both PSNR and SSIM. For [23], we report both the $\mathcal{L}_1$ and $\mathcal{L}_F$ results; according to [23], the former is better suited for numerical evaluation, while the later produces better visual results. We outperform both variants in both metrics.

Fig. 4. Visual interpolation results (unseen data). From top to bottom: linear blending; interpolation using [23], $\mathcal{L}_F$ variant; interpolation using our method; ground truth. While the results from [23] are sharper, they produce significant artifacts, for example the tree in the right example. Our method tends to be blurrier, but captures the gist of the scene better; this is reflected in the superior quantitative results.

Table 3. Interpolation performance in PSNR (SSIM).

	Real movie	Synthetic movie	Driving	All
[23], $\mathcal{L}_1$	33.15 (0.915)	25.73 (0.841)	18.26 (0.664)	28.80 (0.854)
[23], $\mathcal{L}_F$	32.98 (0.911)	25.44 (0.825)	18.04 (0.631)	28.59 (0.843)
Ours	**34.68 (0.928)**	**26.46 (0.859)**	**19.76 (0.710)**	**30.13 (0.8741)**

Figure 4 shows quantitative results of the interpolation for all three scenarios. Visually, the interpolation results are good. In particular, our method can handle large displacements, as can be seen in the helmet strap in Fig. 4, first column, and the tree in Fig. 4, third column. The results of [23] tend to be sharper; however, this comes with strong artifacts visible in the second row of Fig. 4. Both the helmet strap and the tree are not reconstructed significantly better than when using simple linear blending (first row); our method, while slightly blurry, localizes the objects much better.

5.2 Optical Flow

Results on Benchmarks. To demonstrate the effectiveness of our method, dubbed *IPFlow* for Interpolation Pretrained Flow, we test the optical flow performance on the two main benchmarks, KITTI [8,22] and MPI-Sintel [4]. Since our method uses four input frames, we double the first and last frames to compute the first and last flow field within a sequence, respectively, thereby obtaining flow corresponding to all input frames. Furthermore, like FlowNet [6], we perform a variational post-processing step to remove noise from our flow field. Computing the flow on a NVIDIA M6000 GPU takes 60 ms for the CNN; the variational refinement takes 1.2 s.

Fig. 5. Visual results. From top to bottom: Input image; Ground truth flow; Result of IPFlow; Training from scratch. The flow computed using pure training from scratch is reasonable, but using pre-training yields significantly better optical flow maps.

Table 4. Quantitative evaluation of our method.

	Sintel		Kitti-2012	Kitti-2015
	Clean	Final		
Supervised methods				
FlowNet2-ft [12]	**4.16**	**5.74**	**1.8**	**11.48%**
FlowNetS+ft+v [6]	6.16	7.22	9.1	
SpyNet+ft [24]	6.64	8.36	4.1	35.07%
Un- and semisupervised methods				
DSTFlow [25]	10.41	11.28	12.4	39%
USCNN [1]		8.88		
Semi-GAN [15]	6.27	7.31	6.8	31.01%
UnFlow-CSS [21]	9.38	10.22	**1.7**	**11.11%**
IPFlow (ours)	**5.95**	**6.59**	3.5	29.54%
IPFlow-Scratch	8.35	8.87		

Table 4 shows the errors on the unseen test sets (average endpoint error for Sintel and KITTI-2012, F1-All for KITTI-2015); Fig. 5 shows qualitative results. While we do not quite reach the same performance as more complicated architectures such as FlowNet2 [12] or UnFlow-CSS [21][1], on all datasets we outperform methods which are based on simple architectures comparable to ours, including those that were trained with large amounts of annotated ground truth data (FlowNetS+ft+v [6] and SpyNet [24]). For these simple architectures, pre-training using a slow-motion task is hence superior to pre-training using synthetic, annotated optical flow data. UnFlow-CSS is the only method outperforming ours on KITTI that does not require large amounts of annotated frames; yet, they use a considerably more complicated architecture and only achieve state-of-the-art results in driving scenarios and not on Sintel.

Performance Without Pretraining. To evaluate whether the Sintel training data might be enough to learn optical flow by itself, we also tried training our network from scratch. We test two training schedules, first using the same learning parameters as for the fine-tuning, and second the well-established *s_short* schedule from [12]. As shown in Fig. 6, the network is able to learn to compute optical flow even without pre-training, and benefits from using the *s_short* schedule[2]. However, at convergence the error of the network without pre-training on unseen validation data is around 50% higher. This is also visible in Table 4, where *IPFlow-Scratch* denotes the training from scratch using *s_short*; again,

---

[1] For UnFlow, test set results are only available for the -CSS variant, which is based on a FlowNet2 architecture. The simpler UnFlow-C is not evaluated on the test sets.

[2] For fine-tuning after pretraining, *s_short* gives higher errors than our schedule.

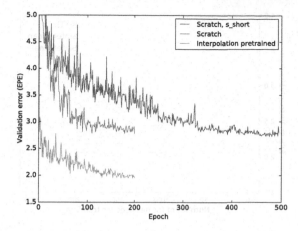

Fig. 6. Using interpolation as pre-training, the network learns to adapt to optical flow. Flow can also be learned without pre-training, but in this case the error is 50% higher.

the errors are considerably higher. Thus, important properties of motion must have been learned during the unsupervised pretraining phase.

Using a Low Number of Fine-Tuning Frames. As we just showed, using only the training set and no fine-tuning results in significantly worse performance; pre-training from interpolation is clearly beneficial. However, this now points to another, related question: Once we have a pre-trained network, how much annotated training data is actually required to achieve good performance? In other words, does pre-training free us from having to annotate or generate thousands of ground truth optical flow frames, and if so, how large is this effect?

We tested this question by repeating the finetuning procedure using only a small amount (25–200) of randomly chosen frames from the respective training sets. Since the scenario for using very few annotated frames points to application-specific optical flow (for example, flow specifically for driving), we perform this experiment separately for different datasets, KITTI (containing both KITTI-2015 [22] and KITTI-2012 [8]), Sintel (clean) and Sintel (final). All trained networks are tested on the same validation set for the respective dataset, and we repeated the experiment three times and averaged the results.

Figure 7 shows the results. While using only 25 frames is generally not enough to estimate good optical flow, the performance quickly improves with the number of available training frames. After seeing only 100 training frames, for all datasets the performance is within 0.5 px EPE of the optimal performance achievable when using the full training sets for the respective dataset. This shows that a interpolation-pretrained network such as the one presented here can be quickly and easily tuned for computing flow for a specific application, and does not require a large amount of annotated ground truth flow fields.

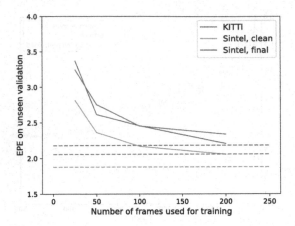

Fig. 7. Fine-tuning with a small amount of frames. With only 100 frames, the performance on all validation sets gets within $0.5px$ EPE of the optimal performance. The dashed lines show the performance when using the full training set for each dataset.

6   Conclusion

In this work, we have demonstrated that a network trained for the task of interpolation does learn about motion in the world. However, this is only true for image regions containing sufficient texture for the photometric error to be meaningful. We have shown that, using a simple fine-tuning procedure, the network can be taught to (a) fill in untextured regions and (b) to output optical flow directly, making it more efficient than comparable, previous work [18]. In particular, we have shown that only a small number of annotated ground truth optical flow frames is sufficient to reach comparable performance to large datasets; this provides the user of our algorithm with the choice of either increasing the accuracy of the optical flow estimation, or to require only a low number of annotated ground truth frames. Demonstrating the importance of pre-training, we have shown that the same network without the interpolation pre-training performs significantly worse; our network also outperforms all other methods with comparable architectures, regardless whether they were trained using full supervision or not. As a side effect, we have demonstrated that, given enough and sufficiently varied training data, even a simple generic network architecture outperforms a specialized architecture for frame interpolation.

Our work suggests several directions for future work. First, it shows the usefulness of this simple proxy task for correspondence estimation. In the analysis of still images, however, we often use a proxy task that requires some *semantic* understanding of the scene, in the hope of arriving at internal representations of the image that mirror the semantic content. As video analysis moves away from the pixels and more towards higher-level understanding, finding such proxy tasks for video remains an open problem. Second, even when staying with the problem of optical flow estimation, we saw that optimized pipelines together with synthetic training data still outperform our method. We believe, however, that even those algorithms could benefit from using a pre-training such as the one described here; utilizing it to achieve true state-of-the-art performance on optical flow remains for future work.

Lastly, the promise of unsupervised methods is that they scale with the amount of data, and that showing more video to a method like ours would lead to better results. Testing how good an interpolation (and the subsequent flow estimation) method can get by simply watching more and more video remains to be seen.

Acknowledgements and Disclosure. JW was supported by the Max Planck ETH Center for Learning Systems. MJB has received research funding from Intel, Nvidia, Adobe, Facebook, and Amazon. While MJB is a part-time employee of Amazon, this research was performed solely at, and funded solely by, MPI.

References

1. Ahmadi, A., Patras, I.: Unsupervised convolutional neural networks for motion estimation. In: 2016 IEEE International Conference on Image Processing (ICIP), pp. 1629–1633, September 2016. DOI: https://doi.org/10.1109/ICIP.2016.7532634
2. Alletto, S., Abati, D., Calderara, S., Cucchiara, R., Rigazio, L.: TransFlow: unsupervised motion flow by joint geometric and pixel-level estimation. Technical report, arXiv preprint arXiv:1706.00322 (2017)
3. Blanco, J.L., Moreno, F.A., Gonzalez-Jimenez, J.: The malaga urban dataset: high-rate stereo and LiDARs in a realistic urban scenario. Int. J. Robot. Res. **33**(2), 207–214 (2014). https://doi.org/10.1177/0278364913507326
4. Butler, D.J., Wulff, J., Stanley, G.B., Black, M.J.: A naturalistic open source movie for optical flow evaluation. In: Fitzgibbon, A., Lazebnik, S., Perona, P., Sato, Y., Schmid, C. (eds.) ECCV 2012. LNCS, vol. 7577, pp. 611–625. Springer, Heidelberg (2012). https://doi.org/10.1007/978-3-642-33783-3_44
5. Doersch, C., Gupta, A., Efros, A.A.: Unsupervised visual representation learning by context prediction. In: ICCV (2015)
6. Dosovitskiy, A., et al.: FlowNet: learning optical flow with convolutional networks. In: International Conference on Computer Vision (ICCV) (2015)
7. Fragkiadaki, A., Seybold, B., Sukthankar, R., Vijayanarasimhan, S., Ricco, S.: Self-supervised learning of structure and motion from video. arxiv 2017 (2017)
8. Geiger, A., Lenz, P., Stiller, C., Urtasun, R.: Vision meets robotics: the KITTI dataset. Int. J. Robot. Res. **32**(11), 1231–1237 (2013). https://doi.org/10.1177/0278364913491297
9. Godard, C., Mac Aodha, O., Brostow, G.J.: Unsupervised monocular depth estimation with left-right consistency. In: CVPR, July 2017
10. Goodfellow, I., et al.: Generative adversarial nets. In: NIPS (2014)
11. Güney, F., Geiger, A.: Deep discrete flow. In: ACCV (2016)
12. Ilg, E., Mayer, N., Saikia, T., Keuper, M., Dosovitskiy, A., Brox, T.: FlowNet 2.0: evolution of optical flow estimation with deep networks. In: CVPR (2017)
13. Jaderberg, M., Simonyan, K., Zisserman, A., Kavukcuoglu, k.: Spatial transformer networks. In: NIPS (2015)
14. Janai, J., Güney, F., Wulff, J., Black, M., Geiger, A.: Slow Flow: exploiting high-speed cameras for accurate and diverse optical flow reference data. In: CVPR (2017)

15. Lai, W.S., Huang, J.B., Yang, M.H.: Semi-supervised learning for optical flow with generative adversarial networks. In: NIPS (2017)
16. Larsson, G., Maire, M., Shakhnarovich, G.: Colorization as a proxy task for visual understanding. In: CVPR (2017)
17. Liu, C., Freeman, W.T., Adelson, E.H., Weiss, Y.: Human-assisted motion annotation. In: CVPR (2008)
18. Long, G., Kneip, L., Alvarez, J.M., Li, H., Zhang, X., Yu, Q.: Learning image matching by simply watching video. In: Leibe, B., Matas, J., Sebe, N., Welling, M. (eds.) ECCV 2016. LNCS, vol. 9910, pp. 434–450. Springer, Cham (2016). https://doi.org/10.1007/978-3-319-46466-4_26
19. Mayer, N., et al.: A large dataset to train convolutional networks for disparity, optical flow, and scene flow estimation. In: CVPR (2016)
20. Meinhardt, T., Moller, M., Hazirbas, C., Cremers, D.: Learning proximal operators: using denoising networks for regularizing inverse imaging problems. In: ICCV (2017)
21. Meister, S., Hur, J., Roth, S.: UnFlow: unsupervised learning of optical flow with a bidirectional census loss. arXiv preprint arXiv:1711.07837 (2017)
22. Menze, M., Heipke, C., Geiger, A.: Discrete optimization for optical flow. In: Gall, J., Gehler, P., Leibe, B. (eds.) GCPR 2015. LNCS, vol. 9358, pp. 16–28. Springer, Cham (2015). https://doi.org/10.1007/978-3-319-24947-6_2
23. Niklaus, S., Mai, L., Liu, F.: Video frame interpolation via adaptive separable convolution. In: ICCV (2017)
24. Ranjan, A., Black, M.J.: Optical flow estimation using a spatial pyramid network. Technical report, arXiv (2016)
25. Ren, Z., Yan, J., Ni, B., Liu, B., Yang, X., Zha, H.: Unsupervised deep learning for optical flow estimation. In: AAAI Conference on Artificial Intelligence (2017)
26. Richter, S.R., Hayder, Z., Koltun, V.: Playing for Benchmarks. In: ICCV (2017)
27. Sedaghat, N., Zolfaghari, M., Brox, T.: Hybrid learning of optical flow and next frame prediction to boost optical flow in the wild. Technical report, arXiv:1612.03777 (2017)
28. Sun, C., Shrivastava, A., Singh, S., Gupta, A.: Revisiting unreasonable effectiveness of data in deep learning era. In: ICCV (2017)
29. Sun, D., Roth, S., Black, M.: A quantitative analysis of current practices in optical flow estimation and the principles behind them. Int. J. Comput. Vis. **106**(2), 115–137 (2014). https://doi.org/10.1007/s11263-013-0644-x
30. Sun, D., Sudderth, E., Black, M.J.: Layered segmentation and optical flow estimation over time. In: CVPR (2012)
31. Sun, D., Yang, X., Liu, M.Y., Kautz, J.: PWC-Net: CNNs for optical flow using pyramid, warping, and cost volume. arXiv preprint arXiv:1709.02371 (2017)
32. Vondrick, C., Pirsiavash, H., Torralba, A.: Anticipating visual representations from unlabeled video. In: CVPR (2016)
33. Wang, Z., Bovik, A.C., Sheikh, H.R., Simoncelli, E.P.: Image quality assessment: from error visibility to structural similarity. IEEE Trans. Image Process. **13**(4), 600–612 (2004). https://doi.org/10.1109/TIP.2003.819861
34. Xu, J., Ranftl, R., Koltun, V.: Accurate optical flow via direct cost volume processing. In: CVPR (2017)
35. Yu, J.J., Harley, A.W., Derpanis, K.G.: Back to basics: unsupervised learning of optical flow via brightness constancy and motion smoothness. In: Hua, G., Jégou, H. (eds.) ECCV 2016. LNCS, vol. 9915, pp. 3–10. Springer, Cham (2016). https://doi.org/10.1007/978-3-319-49409-8_1
36. Zhou, T., Brown, M., Snavely, N., Lowe, D.G.: Unsupervised learning of depth and ego-motion from video. In: CVPR (2017)

Decoupling Respiratory and Angular Variation in Rotational X-ray Scans Using a Prior Bilinear Model

Tobias Geimer[1,2,3]([✉]), Paul Keall[4][iD], Katharina Breininger[1], Vincent Caillet[4], Michelle Dunbar[4], Christoph Bert[2,3][iD], and Andreas Maier[1,2][iD]

[1] Pattern Recognition Lab, Department of Computer Science,
Friedrich-Alexander-Universität Erlangen-Nürnberg, Erlangen, Germany
`tobias.geimer@fau.de`
[2] Erlangen Graduate School in Advanced Optical Technologies (SAOT),
Friedrich-Alexander-Universität Erlangen-Nürnberg, Erlangen, Germany
[3] Department of Radiation Oncology, Universitätsklinikum Erlangen,
Friedrich-Alexander-Universität Erlangen-Nürnberg, Erlangen, Germany
[4] ACRF Image X Institute, The University of Sydney, Sydney, Australia

Abstract. Data-driven respiratory signal extraction from rotational X-ray scans is a challenge as angular effects overlap with respiration-induced change in the scene. In this paper, we use the linearity of the X-ray transform to propose a bilinear model based on a prior 4D scan to separate angular and respiratory variation. The bilinear estimation process is supported by a B-spline interpolation using prior knowledge about the trajectory angle. Consequently, extraction of respiratory features simplifies to a linear problem. Though the need for a prior 4D CT seems steep, our proposed use-case of driving a respiratory motion model in radiation therapy usually meets this requirement. We evaluate on DRRs of 5 patient 4D CTs in a leave-one-phase-out manner and achieve a mean estimation error of 3.01% in the gray values for unseen viewing angles. We further demonstrate suitability of the extracted weights to drive a motion model for treatments with a continuously rotating gantry.

Keywords: Bilinear model · Motion model · Respiratory signal · X-ray projection · Feature extraction

1 Introduction

Extracting information about a patient's breathing state from X-ray projections is important for many time-resolved application, such as CT reconstruction or motion compensation in image-guided radiation therapy (IGRT) [8]. In the context of CT imaging, respiratory motion during the scan time introduces data inconsistencies that, ultimately, manifest in reconstruction artifacts. These effects can be mitigated by incorporating non-linear motion models into state-of-the-art algorithms for motion-compensated reconstruction [11]. In IGRT, the

© Springer Nature Switzerland AG 2019
T. Brox et al. (Eds.): GCPR 2018, LNCS 11269, pp. 583–594, 2019.
https://doi.org/10.1007/978-3-030-12939-2_40

consequences of respiratory motion may be particularly harmful if not addressed properly. Here, malignant tumor cells are irradiated following an optimized dose distribution that is the result of treatment planning based on CT imaging. However, respiratory motion may lead to a displacement of the target volume during irradiation, resulting in underdosage of the tumor and, ultimately, the potential survival of malignant cells [8]. Motion tracking represents the state-of-the-art procedure, where the treatment beam is continuously following the tumor motion. However, this process requires sophisticated motion monitoring, often incorporating motion models to estimate internal deformation from the available imaging modalities such as on-board X-ray imagers.

Many data-driven approaches have been proposed to extract respiratory information from X-ray projections, ranging from the established Amsterdam Shroud [15] to more sophisticated approaches based on epipolar consistency [1]. In the context of respiratory motion models [11] used to estimate internal deformation fields in IGRT [7], their main drawback is the fact that most of these methods only extract a 1D signal, that, at best, can be decomposed into amplitude and phase [5]. When the motion representation is covered by a statistical shape model (SSM) [3,11], it is highly desirable to extract more features to allow for a lower reconstruction error. While approaches exist that extract multiple respiratory features from X-ray projections [6], they are restricted to static acquisition angles. As training a separate model for every possible static angle is infeasible, these methods are typically not suited for applications with a continuously rotating gantry, such as cone-beam CT or volumetric arc therapy.

With both angular and respiratory variation present in the X-ray images of a rotational scan, we aim to separate these effects by expressing them as the two domains of a bilinear model with corresponding rotational and respiratory feature space. A mathematical foundation to decompose multiple sources of variation was given by De Lathauwer et al. [4] who formulated Higher-order Singular Value Decomposition (HOSVD) on a tensor of arbitrary dimensionality. Meanwhile, bilinear models have seen use in many fields including medical applications. Among others, Tenenbaum et al. [13] used a bilinear model to separate pose and identity from face images, while Çimen et al. [2] constructed a spatio-temporal model of coronary artery centerlines.

In this work, we show that due to the linearity of the X-ray transform, a bilinear decomposition of respiratory and angular variation exists (Sect. 2.1). Subsequently, Sects. 2.2 and 2.3 will cover both model training and its application in feature estimation. With the simultaneous estimation of both bilinear weights being an ill-posed problem, we propose a B-spline interpolation of rotational weights based on prior knowledge about the trajectory angle. With known rotational weights, the task of estimating respiratory weights reduces to a linear one. We validate our model in a leave-one-phase-out manner using digitally reconstructed radiographs (DRRs) of five patient 4D CTs consisting of eight respiratory phases each. The main purpose of our evaluation is to give a proof-of-concept of the proposed decoupling process. In addition, we provide first indication that the extracted respiratory features contain volumetric information suitable for driving a motion model.

2   Material and Methods

2.1   X-ray Transform Under Respiratory and Angular Variation

An X-ray projection $p_{i,j} \in \mathbb{R}^{N^2 \times 1}$ at rotation angle $\phi_i \in [0, 2\pi)$ and respiratory phase $t_j \in [0, 1)$ is given by the X-ray transform $R_i \in \mathbb{R}^{N^2 \times N^3}$ applied to the volume $v_j \in \mathbb{R}^{N^3 \times 1}$

$$p_{i,j} = R_i \, v_j, \tag{1}$$

where N indicates the arbitrary dimension of the volume and projection image. It has been shown that the respiratory-induced changes in the anatomy can be described by an active shape model of the internal anatomy [11]:

$$v_j = M \, a_j + \bar{v}, \tag{2}$$

where $\bar{v}$ is the data mean of the mode, $M \in \mathbb{R}^{N^3 \times f}$ contains the eigenvectors corresponding to the first f principal components, and $a_j \in \mathbb{R}^{f \times 1}$ are the model weights corresponding to phase t_j. Thus, Eq. 1 can be further processed to

$$p_{i,j} = R_i \, (M \, a_j + \bar{v})$$
$$= M_i^R \, a_j + \bar{p}_i. \tag{3}$$

Now, $M_i^R \in \mathbb{R}^{N^2 \times f}$ represents a model (with mean $\bar{p}_i = R_i \, \bar{v}$) for describing the projection image $p_{i,j}$ under the fixed angle ϕ_i given the respiratory weights a_j. The inversion of the X-ray transform R itself is ill-posed for a single projection. However, M_i^R can be inverted more easily with a_j encoding mostly variation in superior-inferior direction observable in the projection. As a result, respiratory model weights can be estimated from a single projection image if the angle-dependent model matrix is known [6].

Furthermore, we propose a X-ray transform R_i to be approximated by a linear combination using a new basis of X-ray transforms, such that

$$R_i = \sum_k b_{k,i} R_k. \tag{4}$$

This essentially mimics Eq. 2 with R_k describing variation in the projection images solely caused by the rotation of the gantry. The resulting scalar factors $b_{k,i}$ form the weight vector $b_i = [\ldots, b_{k,i}, \ldots]$. Note that in this formulation, we implicitly assume a continuous trajectory and that the breathing motion is observable from each view. This gives rise to a bilinear formulation for any given projection image $p_{i,j}$. However, bilinear models typically do not operate on mean-normalized data. Therefore, we use the decomposition described in Eq. 2 without mean subtraction:

$$
\begin{aligned}
\boldsymbol{p}_{i,j} &= \boldsymbol{R}_i \left(\boldsymbol{M} \, \boldsymbol{a}_j \right) \\
&= \sum_k b_{k,i} \, \boldsymbol{R}_k \left(\boldsymbol{M} \, \boldsymbol{a}_j \right) \\
&= \sum_k b_{k,i} \, \boldsymbol{M}_k^R \, \boldsymbol{a}_j \\
&= \mathcal{M} \times_1 \boldsymbol{a}_j \times_2 \boldsymbol{b}_i,
\end{aligned} \tag{5}
$$

where $\mathcal{M} \in \mathbb{R}^{N^2 \times f \times g}$ is a model tensor with respiratory and rotational feature dimensionality f and g. Here, $\times_*$ denotes the mode product along the given mode $*$. For more details on tensor notation please refer to [9].

2.2   Model Training

For model training, a prior 4D CT scan is required yielding F phase-binned volumes $\boldsymbol{v}_j$, $j \in \{1, \ldots, F\}$. Using the CONRAD software framework [10], DRRs are computed at G angles ϕ_i, $i \in \{1, \ldots, G\}$ along a circular trajectory. The resulting $F \cdot G$ projection images $\boldsymbol{p}_{i,j}$ form the data tensor $\mathcal{D} \in \mathbb{R}^{N^2 \times F \times G}$. Using HOSVD [4] we perform dimensionality reduction on the data tensor. First, $\mathcal{D}$ is unfolded along mode k:

$$
\mathcal{D}_{(k)} \in \mathbb{R}^{d_k \times \left(\prod_{l \neq k} d_l \right)}.
$$

Fig. 1-left illustrates the unfolding process. Second, SVD is performed on each unfolded matrix

$$
\mathcal{D}_{(k)} = \boldsymbol{U}_k \boldsymbol{S}_k \boldsymbol{V}_k^\top, \tag{6}
$$

which yields the tensor basis $\{\boldsymbol{U}_k\}_{k=1}^K$ to project $\mathcal{D}$ onto (see Fig. 1-right):

$$
\mathcal{D} = \mathcal{M} \times_{k=1}^K \boldsymbol{U}_k. \tag{7}
$$

Finally, $\mathcal{D}$ can be described by a model tensor $\mathcal{M}$:

$$
\underbrace{\mathcal{D}}_{N^2 \times F \times G} = \underbrace{\mathcal{M}}_{N^2 \times f \times g} \times_1 \underbrace{\boldsymbol{A}}_{F \times f} \times_2 \underbrace{\boldsymbol{B}}_{G \times g}, \tag{8}
$$

where $\boldsymbol{A}$ and $\boldsymbol{B}$ carry the low-dimensional ($f \ll F$, $g \ll G$) model weights for respiratory and angular variation, respectively.

2.3   Weight Estimation

Given an observed projection image $\boldsymbol{p}_{x,y}$ at unknown respiratory phase t_y and angle ϕ_x, our objective is to find coefficients $\boldsymbol{a}_y$, $\boldsymbol{b}_x$ for respiration and rotation to best represent the observation in terms of the model:

$$
\boldsymbol{p}_{x,y} = \mathcal{M} \times_1 \boldsymbol{a}_y \times_2 \boldsymbol{b}_x. \tag{9}
$$

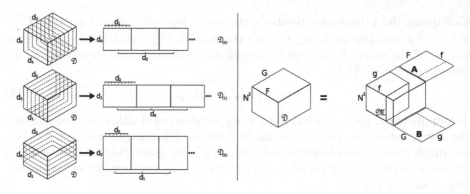

Fig. 1. Left: Tensor unfolding concatenates the slices of a tensor along a selected mode. Right: Dimensionality reduction (HOSVD) of the rotational and respiratory domain.

However, as a_y and b_x need to be optimized simultaneously, this task is highly ill-posed. Tenenbaum *et al.* [13] used an Expectation-Maximization algorithm to cope with this problem in their separation of identity and pose in face images. However, they benefit from the fact that only the pose is a continuous variable whereas identity is a discrete state, drastically simplifying their EM-approach. In our case, both respiratory and angular variation have to be considered continuous. Fortunately, we can incorporate prior knowledge about the trajectory into the estimation process. From the trajectory, the angle of each projection image is known even though the corresponding weights b_x are only given for particular angles within the training samples. Consequently, interpolating the desired rotational weights using those within the training set seems feasible under the assumption of a continuous non-sparse trajectory.

Rotational B-spline Interpolation. Using the rotation angle as prior knowledge, we propose extending the bilinear model with a B-spline curve fitted to the rotational weights b_i from training:

$$b(u) = \sum_{i=1}^{G} b_i \mathcal{N}_i(u), \tag{10}$$

with $\mathcal{N}_i$ being the B-spline basis functions. Using a uniform parametrization with respect to the training angles, $u(\phi)$ of new angle ϕ is given as

$$u(\phi) = \frac{\phi - \phi_{\min}}{\phi_{\max} - \phi_{\min}}. \tag{11}$$

Respiratory Weight Computation. With the rotational weight interpolated, multiplying $\mathcal{M}$ and $b\left(u\left(\phi_x\right)\right)$, first removes the angular variation:

$$\mathcal{M}_x^R = \mathcal{M} \times_2 b\left(u\left(\phi_x\right)\right) \in \mathbb{R}^{N^2 \times f \times 1}. \tag{12}$$

Collapsing the 1-dimension results in the angle-dependent model matrix $\boldsymbol{M}_x^R \in \mathbb{R}^{N^2 \times f}$ for the new angle ϕ_x. Closing the loop to Eq. 3 without mean, computation of the respiratory weights simplifies to a linear problem solved via the pseudo-inverse of $\boldsymbol{M}_x^R$:

$$a_y = \left(\boldsymbol{M}_x^R\right)^{-1} \boldsymbol{p}_{x,y}. \tag{13}$$

For application, the extracted respiratory weights could either be used as input for a respiratory model [7] to estimate internal deformation fields, or for data augmentation in the context of cone-beam CT by generating additional gated projections for different rotational weights $\boldsymbol{b}_i$ at the constant phase corresponding to a_x (see Eq. 5).

2.4   Data and Experiments

Evaluation was performed on 4D CTs of five patients, consisting of eight phase-binned volumes each at respiratory states 0%, 15%, 50%, 85%, 100% inhale, and 85%, 50%, 15% exhale. Using CONRAD [10], DRRs of size 512×512 with an 0.8 mm isotropic pixel spacing were created by forward projecting each of the $F = 8$ volumes at $G = 60$ angles over a circular trajectory of 360° (in 6° steps). Consequently, the full data tensor $\mathcal{D}$ featured a dimensionality of $512^2 \times 8 \times 60$ for each patient. With the model being patient-specific, the following experiments were conducted individually for each patient and results were averaged where indicated.

Experiment 1. Our goal is to provide a proof-of-concept of the bilinear decoupling and to investigate how accurately respiratory weights can be extracted using the proposed method. For each patient, a dense bilinear model was trained on the entire data tensor to assess the variance explained by the respiratory domain. For comparison, a SSM (linear PCA with mean normalization) of the 4D CT volumes was trained to assess weights and variance prior to the influence of the X-ray transform.

Experiment 2. To investigate how well a previously unseen projection image for unknown angles and breathing phase can be decomposed into rotational and respiratory weights, every 6th angle (10 in total) was removed from training. Further, leave-one-out evaluation was performed, were each phase was subsequently removed prior to training, resulting in a sparser data tensor of size $512^2 \times 7 \times 50$. In this scenario, the dense bilinear model provided a reference for the features to be expected. In the evaluation step, the corresponding projection image and its respective trajectory angle were fed to the model and the rotational and respiratory weights were estimated as described in Sect. 2.3. From these weights, the projection image was rebuilt and model accuracy was assessed with respect to the mean gray-value error between the reconstructed image and the original.

Experiment 3. To assess their use for predicting 3D information, the bilinear respiratory weights were used as a driving surrogate for a motion model [11], which, apart from the surrogate, usually consists of an internal motion representation

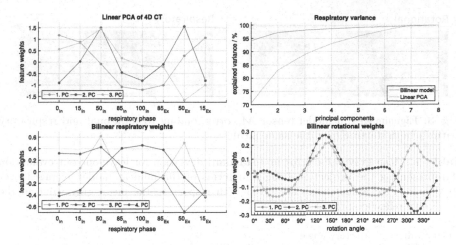

Fig. 2. Feature weights for the first few principal components for linear PCA on the 4D CT (t. l.), bilinear respiratory (b. l.) and rotational weights (b. r.) as well as the explained variance caused by respiration in the linear and bilinear case (t. r.).

and a internal-external correlation model. For motion representation, a SSM was trained for each test phase on the remaining seven 4D CT volumes (Eq. 2). With the 4D SSM weights and bilinear respiratory weights showing similar behavior but differing in scale (Fig. 2), multi-linear regression [14] was chosen to correlate the bilinear weights to the 4D SSM weights. True to the leave-one-out nature, the regression matrix $W \in \mathbb{R}^{e \times f}$ was trained between the weights of the seven remaining phases relating bilinear respiratory weights of feature dimension $f = 6$ to 4D SSM weights of dimension $e = 5$ (see also results of experiment 1). The rebuilt 3D volume was then compared to the ground truth volume in the 4D CT in terms of HU difference.

3   Results and Discussion

Experiment 1. Figure 2 shows the weights of the first few principal components for the linear PCA of the volumes as well as each phase and angle in the projection images. Notably, both first bilinear components are near constant. Unlike linear PCA (Eq. 2), data in the bilinear model does not have zero-mean (Eq. 5). Consequently, the first component points to the data mean while variation in the respective domain is encoded starting from the second component [13]. Appropriately, the $(n + 1)$-th bilinear respiratory component corresponds to the n-th linear component of the 4D CT indicating that separation of respiratory and angular variance in the projections is in fact achieved. Additionally, the respiratory variance explained by the principal components is plotted (top right). Most of the variance in the bilinear case is already explained by movement towards the mean. Thus, the linear components better reflect that four components accurately describe over 90% of the data variance. As a consequence

Rotational ————————→   Respiratory ————————→

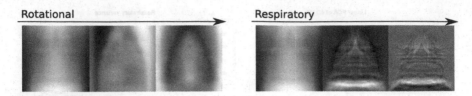

Fig. 3. Eigenimages in model tensor $\mathcal{M}$ corresponding to rotational and respiratory features both starting from the same mean.

Table 1. Mean gray value error and standard deviation for leave-one-out evaluation of representing the projection images in terms of the bilinear model averaged over all phases. Percentage values are given with respect to the mean gray value in the respective reference projection image

Gray value error [%]	Trajectory angle									
	18°	54°	90°	126°	162°	198°	234°	270°	306°	342°
Pat 1	3.20 ± 3.41	2.68 ± 2.40	3.74 ± 4.02	3.88 ± 4.00	4.82 ± 4.72	3.17 ± 2.97	2.79 ± 2.53	3.95 ± 3.89	5.43 ± 6.33	4.66 ± 4.78
Pat 2	2.63 ± 2.41	2.54 ± 2.27	2.84 ± 2.75	3.03 ± 2.80	3.37 ± 3.01	2.88 ± 2.62	2.67 ± 2.38	3.06 ± 2.85	3.20 ± 2.70	4.07 ± 3.54
Pat 3	2.78 ± 2.64	2.56 ± 2.37	3.05 ± 3.35	3.58 ± 3.87	3.64 ± 3.16	2.86 ± 2.65	2.62 ± 2.39	3.08 ± 2.91	4.71 ± 5.03	4.28 ± 3.83
Pat 4	1.72 ± 1.58	1.67 ± 1.51	1.81 ± 1.65	2.12 ± 2.39	1.94 ± 1.72	1.78 ± 1.57	1.78 ± 1.56	1.98 ± 1.77	2.26 ± 2.15	2.43 ± 2.19
Pat 5	2.68 ± 2.69	2.47 ± 2.35	2.76 ± 2.49	2.98 ± 2.90	2.96 ± 2.61	2.95 ± 3.07	2.56 ± 2.41	2.96 ± 2.69	3.36 ± 3.02	3.57 ± 3.19

of the two last mentioned results, one more feature should be extracted than expected by the volumetric 4D SSM, when using the bilinear weights as the driving surrogate. This is also the motivation for the 5×6 regression matrix chosen in experiment 3. Figure 3 shows the eigenimages corresponding to angular and respiratory variation, respectively. Noticeably, the rotational eigenimages contain mostly low-frequent variation inherent to the moving gantry whereas the respiratory direction encodes comparably high-frequent changes.

Experiment 2. Regarding the bilinear decomposition, Table 1 lists the percentage mean gray value error in the reconstructed projection images for each test-angle averaged over all estimated phases. The average error was 1.28 ± 1.27 compared to a reference mean gray value of 44.14 ± 12.39. Exemplarily for one phase-angle combination of patient 1, Fig. 4 shows the leave-one-out estimation result for $85\%_{\mathrm{Ex}}$ and 234°. The proposed B-spline interpolation yields rotational weights close to the dense bilinear model up to the 10th component. Since both sets of weights correspond to slightly different eigenvectors, due to one model being trained on less data, deviation especially in the lower components is to be expected. Still, four to five respiratory weights are estimated accurately which,

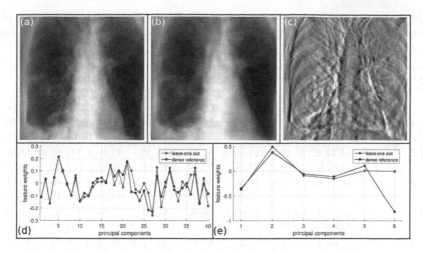

Fig. 4. Example reconstruction for 85% exhale phase at 234° angle. (a) Original DRR sample. (b) Leave-one-out bilinear reconstruction. (c) Difference image with level/window −0.15/3.75. (d) Rotational weights from dense bilinear model and interpolated weights for the loo estimation. (e) Respiratory weight estimate.

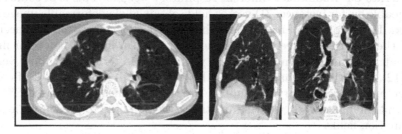

Fig. 5. Estimation visualization for patient 1 at 85% exhale phase estimated from projections at 234° angle. The overlay displays the original CT in cyan and the estimated volume in red, adding up to gray for equal HU. (Color figure online)

as shown previously, is sufficient to recover over 90% respiratory variance. As such, we believe they contain much more information than just the respiratory phase.

Experiment 3. To substantiate this assumption, Table 2 provides the mean HU-errors in the estimated CT volumes using projections at the ten test angles for each patient. Errors showed very small deviation w.r.t. the acquisition angle, indicating that the respiratory domain is extracted sufficiently regardless of the view. Given an HU range from −1000 to 3000, a mean error of 25 to 100 indicates reasonable performance. For visualization, Fig. 5 shows the estimated CT for patient 1 at 85% exhale phase, that was estimated using a projection at a trajectory angle of 234°. Deviation is most prominent at vessel structures within the lung as well as at the left side of the diaphragm.

Table 2. Mean voxel error and standard deviation in HU for each patient and phase averaged over all voxels and angles. The average standard deviation between angles was only 1.87 HU within the same patient

Mean voxel error [HU]	Respiratory phase							
	0_{In}	15_{In}	50_{In}	85_{In}	100_{In}	85_{Ex}	50_{Ex}	15_{Ex}
Pat 1	21.64 ± 51.42	17.26 ± 42.38	22.48 ± 51.42	15.13 ± 33.69	16.68 ± 38.87	16.53 ± 38.19	23.82 ± 55.06	21.59 ± 51.87
Pat 2	84.24 ± 149.73	59.15 ± 94.72	51.50 ± 74.01	42.42 ± 54.16	48.06 ± 65.61	42.39 ± 56.18	47.66 ± 65.68	58.86 ± 86.28
Pat 3	46.47 ± 64.85	58.57 ± 86.78	46.56 ± 67.06	50.69 ± 74.59	45.38 ± 63.01	48.80 ± 72.00	47.60 ± 68.27	42.25 ± 55.54
Pat 4	82.01 ± 114.07	60.47 ± 69.10	53.99 ± 58.59	50.00 ± 50.49	51.09 ± 52.06	53.65 ± 56.30	86.92 ± 123.08	67.74 ± 77.82
Pat 5	87.08 ± 133.69	64.21 ± 82.35	56.32 ± 67.89	50.17 ± 57.58	52.17 ± 59.19	50.91 ± 60.12	56.74 ± 68.84	117.47± 159.99

In this scenario, the motion representation is covered by a HU-based SSM to generate CT volumes for different respiratory weights. This is of course interchangeable by, for instance, 3D vector fields obtained via deformable image registration. In the context of motion tracking in IGRT, the estimated displacements could then be used to steer the treatment beam according to the tumor motion while at the same time enabling quality assurance in terms of 4D dose verification [12]. However, the main focus of this work was to provide proof-of-concept for the angular-respiratory decoupling process for which a HU-based SSM was sufficient. In future work, we will investigate the potential to predict entire dense deformation fields.

Our current leave-one-out evaluation assumed two simplifications, that will pose additional challenges. First, a perfect baseline registration of the training CT to the projection images may not be the case in every scenario. However, for the case of radiation therapy accurate alignment of patient and system is a prerequisite for optimal treatment. Second, no anatomical changes between the 4D CT and the rotational scan are taken into account. Further investigation on how these effects interfere with the decomposition are subject to future work.

4   Conclusion

In this paper, we demonstrate that the X-ray transform under respiratory and angular variation can be expressed in terms of a bilinear model given a continuous trajectory and that motion is observable in every projection. Using a prior 4D CT, we show that projection images on the trajectory can be bilinearly decomposed into rotational and respiratory components. Prior knowledge about the gantry angle is used to solve this ill-posed out-of-sample problem. Results for both 2D DRRs and estimated 3D volumes demonstrate that up to five components of the respiratory variance are recovered independent of the view-angle.

These explain more than 90% of the volumetric variation. As such, recovery of 3D motion seems possible. Currently our study is limited by two simplifications, namely perfect alignment and no inter-acquisition changes. Their investigation is subject to future work.

Acknowledgement. This work was partially conducted at the ACRF Image X Institute as part of a visiting research scholar program. The authors gratefully acknowledge funding of this research stay by the Erlangen Graduate School in Advanced Optical Technologies (SAOT).

References

1. Aichert, A., et al.: Epipolar consistency in transmission imaging. IEEE Trans. Med. Imaging **34**(11), 2205–2219 (2015). https://doi.org/10.1109/TMI.2015.2426417
2. Çimen, S., Hoogendoorn, C., Morris, P.D., Gunn, J., Frangi, A.F.: Reconstruction of coronary trees from 3DRA using a 3D+t statistical cardiac prior. In: Golland, P., Hata, N., Barillot, C., Hornegger, J., Howe, R. (eds.) MICCAI 2014. LNCS, vol. 8674, pp. 619–626. Springer, Cham (2014). https://doi.org/10.1007/978-3-319-10470-6_77
3. Cootes, T.F., Taylor, C.J., Cooper, D.H., Graham, J.: Active shape models - their training and application. Comput. Vis. Image Underst. **61**(1), 38–59 (1995)
4. De Lathauwer, L., De Moor, B., Vandewalle, J.: A multilinear singular value decomposition. SIAM J. Matrix Anal. Appl. **21**(4), 1253–1278 (2000)
5. Fassi, A., et al.: Surrogate-driven deformable motion model for organ motion tracking in particle radiation therapy. Phys. Med. Biol. **60**(4), 1565–1582 (2015). https://doi.org/10.1088/0031-9155/60/4/1565
6. Fischer, P., Pohl, T., Faranesh, A., Maier, A., Hornegger, J.: Unsupervised learning for robust respiratory signal estimation from x-ray fluoroscopy. IEEE Trans. Med. Imaging **36**(4), 865–877 (2017). https://doi.org/10.1109/TMI.2016.2609888
7. Geimer, T., Unberath, M., Birlutiu, A., Wölfelschneider, J., Bert, C., Maier, A.: A kernel-based framework for intra-fractional respiratory motion estimation in radiation therapy. In: Proceedings of IEEE International Symposium on Biomed Imaging, pp. 1036–1039 (2017)
8. Keall, P.J., et al.: The management of respiratory motion in radiation oncology report of AAPM Task Group 76. Med. Phys. **33**(10), 3874–3900 (2006). https://doi.org/10.1118/1.2349696
9. Kolda, T.G., Bader, B.W.: Tensor decompositions and applications. SIAM Rev. **51**(3), 455–500 (2009). https://doi.org/10.1137/07070111X
10. Maier, A., et al.: CONRAD-a software framework for cone-beam imaging in radiology. Med. Phys. **40**(11), 111914 (2013). https://doi.org/10.1118/1.4824926
11. McClelland, J.R., Hawkes, D.J., Schaeffter, T., King, A.P.: Respiratory motion models: a review. Med. Image Anal. **17**(1), 19–42 (2013). https://doi.org/10.1016/j.media.2012.09.005
12. Prasetio, H., Wölfelschneider, J., Ziegler, M., Serpa, M., Witulla, B., Bert, C.: Dose calculation and verification of the vero gimbal tracking treatment delivery. Phys. Med. Biol. **63**(3), 035043 (2018). https://doi.org/10.1088/1361-6560/aaa617
13. Tenenbaum, J.B., Freeman, W.T.: Separating style and content with bilinear models. Neural Comput. **12**(6), 1247–1283 (2000)

14. Wilms, M., Werner, R., Ehrhardt, J., Schmidt-Richberg, A., Schlemmer, H.P., Handels, H.: Multivariate regression approaches for surrogate-based diffeomorphic estimation of respiratory motion in radiation therapy. Phys. Med. Biol. **59**(5), 1147–1164 (2014). https://doi.org/10.1088/0031-9155/59/5/1147
15. Yan, H., et al.: Extracting respiratory signals from thoracic cone beam CT projections. Phys. Med. Biol. **58**(5), 1447–64 (2013). https://doi.org/10.1088/0031-9155/58/5/1447

Oral Session 4: Learning II

Inference, Learning and Attention Mechanisms that Exploit and Preserve Sparsity in CNNs

Timo Hackel, Mikhail Usvyatsov, Silvano Galliani, Jan Dirk Wegner, and Konrad Schindler[✉]

Photogrammetry and Remote Sensing, ETH Zürich, Zürich, Switzerland
schindler@ethz.ch

Abstract. While CNNs naturally lend themselves to densely sampled data, and sophisticated implementations are available, they lack the ability to efficiently process sparse data. In this work we introduce a suite of tools that exploit sparsity in both the feature maps and the filter weights, and thereby allow for significantly lower memory footprints and computation times than the conventional dense framework, when processing data with a high degree of sparsity. Our scheme provides *(i)* an efficient GPU implementation of a convolution layer based on direct, sparse convolution; *(ii)* a filter step within the convolution layer, which we call *attention*, that prevents fill-in, i.e., the tendency of convolution to rapidly decrease sparsity, and guarantees an upper bound on the computational resources; and *(iii)* an adaptation of back-propagation that makes it possible to combine our approach with standard learning frameworks, while still exploiting sparsity in the data and the model.

1 Introduction

Deep neural networks are nowadays the most successful tool for a wide spectrum of computer vision task [18,23,31]. A main reason for their spectacular comeback, perhaps even the single most important factor, is the enormous gain in computational efficiency brought about by massively parallel computing on GPUs. Both the response maps (feature maps) within the neural network and the parameters (filter weights) of the network form regular grids that are conveniently stored and processed as tensors. However, while naturally suited for image processing, regular grids are a suboptimal representation for data such as line drawings or irregular 3D point clouds (Fig. 1). E.g., the latter are typically acquired with line-of-sight instruments, thus the large majority of points lies on a small number of 2D surfaces. When represented as 3D voxel grid they therefore exhibit a high degree of sparsity, as most voxels are empty; while at the same time 3D data processing with CNNs is challenged by high memory demands [3,14,24,38].

A counter-measure is to make explicit the sparsity of the feature maps and store them in a sparse data representation, see Fig. 2. Moreover, it can also be

T. Brox et al. (Eds.): GCPR 2018, LNCS 11269, pp. 597–611, 2019.
https://doi.org/10.1007/978-3-030-12939-2_41

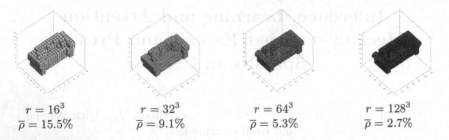

$r = 16^3$ $r = 32^3$ $r = 64^3$ $r = 128^3$
$\bar{p} = 15.5\%$ $\bar{p} = 9.1\%$ $\bar{p} = 5.3\%$ $\bar{p} = 2.7\%$

Fig. 1. Sparsity in 3D data analysis. The density $\bar{p}$ of occupied voxels is low in 3D data from Modelnet40, and decreases with increasing voxel resolution.

Fig. 2. With suitable computational mechanisms, sparsity in the input can be preserved throughout the CNN. Shown are the activations for one channel of the 1st, 2nd and 3rd convolution layers on MNIST for a dense network (left) and for a sparse network with upper bound $\rho_{up} = 15\%$ (right).

beneficial to represent the CNN parameters in a sparse fashion to improve runtime and – perhaps more important for modern, deep architectures – memory footprint; especially if the sparsity is promoted already during training through appropriate regularisation. It is obvious that, in a sufficiently sparse setting, a significant speed-up can be achieved by performing convolutions *directly*, incrementally updating a layer's output map only where there are non-zero entries in the input map as well as non-zero filter weights. This has recently been confirmed independently by two concurrent works [8,27]. Direct convolution guarantees that only the minimum number of necessary operations is carried out. However, the selective updating only at indexed locations makes parallelisation harder. This may be the reason why, to our knowledge, no practical implementations with sparse feature maps exist. In this work we develop a framework to exploit both sparse feature maps and sparse filter parameters in CNNs. To that end *(i)* we provide a sparse *Direct Convolution Layer*, as well as sparse versions of the *ReLU* and *max-pooling* layers; *(ii)* we extend the backpropagation algorithm to preserve sparsity and make our sparse layers usable with existing optimisation routines that are available in modern deep learning frameworks, which have been designed for dense data; *(iii)* we propose to add a density-dependent regulariser that encourages sparsity of the feature maps, and a pruning step that suppresses small filter weights. This regularisation in fact guarantees that the network gets progressively faster at its task, as it receives more training. All these steps have been implemented on GPU as extensions of *Tensorflow*, for generic n-dimensional tensors. The source code is available at https://github.com/TimoHackel/ILA-SCNN. In a series of experiments, we show that it outperforms its dense counterpart in terms of both runtime and memory footprint when processing sufficiently sparse data.

2 Related Work

Dense CNN for Sparse Data

Neural networks, usually of the deep, convolutional network flavour, offer the possibility to completely avoid heuristic feature design and feature selection. They are at present immensely popular in 2D image interpretation. Recently, deep learning pipelines have been adapted to voxel grids [19,24,28,38], RGB-D images [34] and video [17], too. Being completely data-driven, these techniques have the ability to capture appearance as well as geometric object properties. Moreover, their multi-layered, hierarchical architecture is able to encode a large amount of contextual information. A general drawback when directly applying 3D-CNNs to (dense) voxel grids derived from (originally sparse) point clouds is the huge memory overhead for encoding empty space. Computational complexity grows cubically with voxel grid resolution, but in fact high resolution would only be needed at object surfaces.

Data Sparsity

Therefore, more recent 3D-CNNs exploit the *sparsity of occupied voxels* prevalent in practical voxel grids. In [9] a sparse CNN is introduced, which is however limited to small resolutions (in the paper, up to 80^3) due to decreasing sparsity in convolutional layers. Another strategy is to resort to an octree representation [32, 35]. Since the octree partitioning depends on the object at hand, an important question is how to automatically adapt to previously unseen objects. While [32] assume the octree structure to be known at test time, [35] learn to predict it together with the labels. In [13] a coarse-to-fine scheme is used to hierarchically predict the values of small blocks of voxels in an octree. Another strategy is to rely only on a small subset of discriminative points, while neglecting the large majority of less informative ones [21,29,30]. The idea is that the network learns how to select the most informative points and aggregates information into global descriptors of object shape via fully-connected layers. This allows for both shape classification and per-point labeling using only a small subset of points, resulting in significant speed and memory gains. Bilateral convolutional layers [16] map the data into permutohedral space, thus also exploiting sparsity in the data, but do not have a mechanism to exploit parameter sparsity. Recently [10,11] advocate the strategy to perform convolutions only on non-zero elements in the feature map and find correspondences via hash tables. However, limiting activations to non-zero inputs can increase the error and slow down learning.

Parameter Sparsity

Several works address the situation that the model *parameters* are sparse. Denil *et al.* [5] reduce the network parameters by exploiting low rank matrix factorisation. Liu *et al.* [22] exploit the decomposition of matrices to perform efficient convolutions with sparse kernel parameters. Some authors [6, 15] approximate convolutional filters to achieve a faster runtime, moreover it has been proposed to reduce the number of parameters by pruning connections [12] or imposing sparsity in an already trained network [37].

Direct Convolutions
The works [8, 26, 27] are the most related ones to our approach, in that they also perform convolutions in a direct manner to efficiently exploit sparsity in network parameters and feature maps. While [27] use compressed rows as sparse format for the filter parameters, neither [8] nor [27] uses a sparse format for both filter parameters and feature maps. Parashar *et al.* [26] implement sparse convolutions on custom-designed hardware to achieve an energy- and memory-efficient CNN. Even though all three works follow a similar idea, only the latter exploits sparsity in both the parameters and the data, with compressed sparse blocks; but requires dedicated, non-standard hardware.

3   Method

It is a general theme of computing to speed up computations and reduce memory usage by exploiting sparsity in the data. In the following section, we propose a number of ways to do the same for the specific case of neural network layers, always keeping in mind the specific requirements and limitations of modern GPU architectures. Throughout, sparse tensors are represented and manipulated in a format similar to *Coordinate List*[1], which stores indices into the sparsely populated grid and the corresponding data entries in separate tensors, and is available in the "SparseTensor" implementation of *Tensorflow*. To minimise memory overhead, the indices of the form $\{batch, index_x, index_y, ..., channel\}$ are compressed into unique $1D$ keys and only expanded when needed.

To achieve coalesced memory access, which permits efficient caching, the tensors for feature maps are sorted w.r.t. batches and within each batch w.r.t. channels. Likewise, filter weights are sorted w.r.t. the output channels and within each channel w.r.t. the input channels. Compared to dense tensors, the sparse representation naturally adds some overhead. For instance, in our implementation we use 64 bit keys, and 32 bit depth for feature maps. Consequently, storing a dense feature map (100% density) required 3× more memory. For densities <33% the sparse representation is more efficient, and at low densities the savings can be quite dramatic, e.g., at density 1% it uses 97% less memory.

Sparse Convolution
Our convolutional layer is designed to work with sparse tensors for both feature maps and filter weights. Feature maps are updated incrementally with *atomic operations*, c.f. Algorithm 1, where atomic operations are small enough to be thread-safe, even if no locking mechanism is used. In that respect it is similar to

---

[1] We have also experimented with other sparse formats, like compressed sparse blocks; but found none of them to work as well, in part due to limitations and idiosyncrasies of current GPU hardware.

Algorithm 1. Direct Sparse Convolution with Attention

1: decompress filter and data indices from 1D to kD
2: **for** $b \in [0 : batch\_count]$ **do**
3:      **for** $oc \in [0 : out\_channel\_count]$ **do**
4:          initialize dense *buffer* with 0
5:          **for** $ic \in [0 : in\_channel\_count])$ **do**
6:              **for** $\{id, val\} \in$ data(b, ic) **do**
7:                  **for** $\{fid, fval\} \in$ *filter(oc, ic)* **do**
8:                      compute *uid* with get_update_id(id, fid)
9:                      atomically add $val \cdot fval$ to *buffer* at *uid*
10:         get *non-zero* entries from *buffer*
11:         add *bias* to non-zero entries in *buffer*
12:         select k largest responses from *non-zero* entries
13:         compress ids of k largest responses from kD to 1D
14:         write k largest features and ids as sparse output

---

two concurrent works [26,27]. In practice, the incremental update is limited by the current hardware design, since atomic operations are slightly slower than non-atomics: at present, off-the-shelf GPUs do not offer native support for atomic floating point operations in shared memory, although they do for more costly CAS instructions. Yet incremental updating is significantly faster, because it performs only the minimum number of operations necessary to obtain the convolution, while avoiding to multiply or add zeros.

The sparse convolution is computed sequentially per output channel and batch, but in parallel across input channels, features and filter weights. Its result is stored in a temporary, dense buffer with batch size and channel depth 1 This buffer increases quadratically for 2D images, cubically for 3D volumes, *etc.* Still, it is in practice a lot smaller than a typical dense tensor with correct dimensionality for batches and channels, such that volumes up to 512^3 can be processed on a single graphics card (Nvidia Titan Xp, 12 GB).

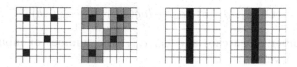

Fig. 3. Fill-in (loss of sparsity) due to convolutions depends on the data distribution. Uniformly distributed data is affected most strongly, e.g., in 3D every $3 \times 3 \times 3$ filter will increase the density by a factor of 27, until data is dense.

Preserving Sparsity with Attention

Convolution with kernels larger than (1×1) generates fill-in, i.e., it reduces the sparsity of a feature map, by construction. See Fig. 3. This "smearing out" of the sparse inputs usually only has a small influence on the output of the network,

---

Algorithm 2. Backpropagation for convolutional layer

```
 1: initialize bp_data with shape(input_values) and 0
 2: initialize bp_filter with shape(filter_weights) and 0
 3: decompress filter and data indices from 1D to kD
 4: for b ∈ [0 : batch_count] do
 5:     for oc ∈ [0 : out_channel_count] do
 6:         initialize dense buffer with gradients(b, oc)
 7:         for ic ∈ [0 : in_channel_count]) do
 8:             for {id, val} ∈ data(b, ic) do
 9:                 for {fid, fval} ∈ filter(oc, ic) do
10:                     compute uid with get_update_id(id, fid)
11:                     get gradient g from buffer at uid
12:                     atomically add g · fval to bp_data at id
13:                     atomically add g · val to bp_filter at fid
```

---

see the experiments. But it considerably increases memory consumption and runtime, especially when occurring repeatedly over multiple layers. In order to guarantee upper bounds on the memory footprint and runtime of the network, we apply a k-selection filter [2] on each output channel, keeping only the k strongest responses. This can be seen as an approximation of the exact convolution where small responses are suppressed, but using an adaptive threshold that suppresses only as many values as necessary to maintain the desired degree of sparsity.

The parameter k controls the sparsity, and thus the memory consumption, of the convolutional layers. Processes that aim to optimally direct and manage the limited resources available for some cognitive task are commonly referred to as *attention*. We have implemented two versions of our simple attention mechanism via k-selection: *(i)* acts on the raw responses, so it prefers large positive responses, making it similar to a rectified linear unit; *(ii)* picks the k values with the largest absolute values, expressing a preference for responses with large magnitude. The time complexity of this layer to convolve data of dimension k, resolution s_d and density ρ_d, with filters of size s_f and density ρ_f, is

$$O\big((\rho_d \cdot \rho_f \cdot s_f^k \cdot c_{in} + log(s_d^k)) \cdot s_d^k \cdot c_{out} \cdot b\big), \tag{1}$$

with b the number of batches and c_{in}, c_{out}, the number of input and output channels, respectively.

Pooling Layer
Our sparse pooling layer has three straight-forward stages. First, assign features to an output (hyper-)voxel, by dividing the data channels of their index by strides. Second, sort the data w.r.t. voxels, so that responses within the same voxel are clustered together. Third, apply the pooling operator separately to each cluster. The time complexity for this is

$$O\big(\rho_d \cdot s_d^k \cdot log(\rho_d \cdot s_d^k) \cdot c_{in} \cdot b\big). \tag{2}$$

Direct Sparse Backpropagation

Our target for back-propagation is again to skip operations that can be avoided due to sparsity. We must propagate error gradients only to all those features which have produced evidence, in the form of non-zero responses during the forward pass. Yet, the performance issues already discussed for the forward pass apply also to the backward pass: back-propagation through a convolution layer is itself a convolution that leads to fill-in, increasing memory use and runtime.

Contrary to the forward pass, it is not advisable to bound the fill-in with the k-selection technique, since this will not prevent the back-propagated error gradients from spreading to zero activations and vanishing, while smaller gradients flowing towards non-zero activations might be missed. It is evident that this effect could seriously slow down the training process. Hence, we propose to use a stricter back-propagation, which only propagates errors L to non-zero features x and model parameters w:

$$\frac{\partial L}{\partial x_i} = \begin{cases} 0 & \text{for } x_i = 0 \\ \frac{\partial L}{\partial y}\frac{\partial y}{\partial x_i}, \text{ else} \end{cases} \quad , \quad \frac{\partial L}{\partial w_i} = \begin{cases} 0 & \text{for } w_i = 0 \\ \frac{\partial L}{\partial y}\frac{\partial y}{\partial w_i}, \text{ else} \end{cases}. \quad (3)$$

Here, weights are considered equal to zero only if they have been explicitly removed by pruning, so as to avoid suppressing the gradients of weights that pass through $w_i = 0$ while changing sign. Note the similarity of our approximated back-propagation to back-propagation through any layer with *ReLU* activation: Conventional back-propagation sets values to zero in function of the layer output y_i, whereas we do so in function of the input x_i.

Neglecting zero-elements slightly reduces the efficiency per learning iteration, since not all error gradients are propagated anymore. However, it has a number of advantages: *(i)* The tensors used for back-propagation have fixed size and shape. Therefore, one can still use optimisation frameworks that have been designed for dense data, and expect fixed and known array dimensions; *(ii)* By considering only gradients on non-zero elements of the forward pass, back-propagation can be implemented in a clean and transparent manner. E.g. for convolutional layers one obtains Algorithm 2, which is very similar to Algorithm 1; *(iii)* Once a filter weight has been set to zero, it will remain zero. Below, we will describe how this property can be used to guarantee that the network gets progressively faster at its task as the learning proceeds and it sees more training data.

Adaptive Density Regularisation

There is a computationally more efficient way to encourage sparsity of the feature maps, such that the sparsity thresholds are rarely exceeded in the first place, and the more costly k-selection step is avoided. The *ReLU* non-linearity used in most modern CCNs, by definition, truncates negative activations to zero while leaving positive ones unchanged. This means that we can include a regularisation that pushes down the values (not magnitudes) of filter weights and biases. By doing so, more weights will be driven into the negative region, where they are extinguished by the subsequent *ReLU*. Moreover, the same idea can be used to reduce sparsity when it is not needed, and optimally use the available resources: when too few activations are >0, one drives the filter weights up, so that fewer of them are suppressed by the $ReLU$. To achieve the desired effect, we simply add a bias b to the L_2-regularisation, so that the regulariser becomes $\sum(w+b)^2$. The scalar b is positive when the density ρ is too large, and negative when it is overly small:

$$b = \begin{cases} o + b_1 \cdot (\rho - \rho_{up}) & \rho > \rho_{up} \quad \text{(exceeds available resources)} \\ -b_2 \cdot (\rho_{up} - \rho) & \rho \leq \rho_{up} \quad \text{(not using available resources)} \end{cases} \quad (4)$$

with ρ_{up} the upper bound implied by the k-selection filter, and o, b_1, $b_2 \geq 0$ control parameters. The offset o adds an additional penalty for exceeding the available resources, since this case requires the use of the k-selection filter and, hence, increases the computational load.

Parameter Pruning

As explained above, our training algorithm has the following useful properties: *(i)* The regulariser encourages small model parameters. *(ii)* The sparse back-propagation ensures that, once set to zero, model parameters do not reappear in later training steps. Together, these two suggest an easily controllable way to progressively favour sparsity during training: At the end of every training epoch we screen the network for weights w that are very small, $|w_i| < \epsilon$. If the magnitude of a weight w_i stays low for two consecutive epochs (meaning that it was already close to zero before, and that did not change during one epoch of training) we conclude that it has little influence on the network output and prune it (one-warning-shot pruning). We note that a small weight should not be pruned when first detected, without warning shot: it could have a large gradient and just happen to be at its zero-crossing from a large positive to a large negative value (or vice versa) at the end of the epoch. On the contrary, it is very unlikely to observe a weight exactly at its zero-crossing twice in a row.

Since a weight, once set to zero, will not reappear with our sparse back-propagation, every pruning can only reduce the number of non-zero weights. It is thus guaranteed that the network become sparser, and therefore also faster at the task it is learning, as it sees more training data. Note, it is well documented that biological systems get faster at a task with longer training [25,33].

4   Evaluation

In this section we evaluate the impact of density upper bounds and regularisation on runtime and classification accuracy. The sparse network structures were implemented into the Tensorflow framework and programmed in C++/CUDA with a python interface. Our experiments were run on PCs with Intel Core i7 7700 K processors, 64 GB RAM and Titan Xp GPUs. Detailed specifications about the different CNN variants used in the experiments (in both sparse and dense versions) are given in the appendix.

To start with, we use a synthetic dataset of sparse random tensors to evaluate the memory footprint and runtime of our convolutional layer and to compare it against the dense layers of Tensorflow version 1.4 (compiled with Cuda 9.0 and

CuDNN 6.0). We conduct different experiments to evaluate the effects of our sparse network on classification accuracy: First, the impact of upper bounds on classification is evaluated by performing a grid search on the upper bound ρ_{up} in the convolutional layers. For this experiment the MNIST data set [20] is used, as it is small enough to perform grid search in a reasonable amount of time and can be interpreted as sparse data (1D lines in 2D images). Second, the effects of pruning on runtime and classification accuracy are shown using the Modelnet data set [38], by varying the strength λ of the regularisation. Modelnet40 provides 3D CAD models of 40 different classes. Furthermore, the classification results of different baseline methods are compared on this data set. Modelnet40 is trained for 90 epochs with learning rate 0.001, using, using *adagrad* [7].

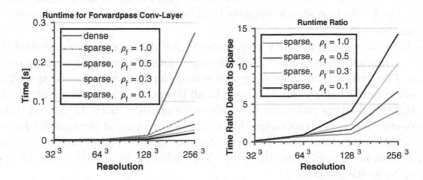

Fig. 4. Runtime [s] of a dense convolution layer in Tensorflow and of our sparse convolution layer, for different resolutions r^3. At high resolutions the sparse version is much more efficient.

Table 1. Memory consumption of a dense conv layer in Tensorflow and of our sparse conv layer, for different resolutions r^3, with $\rho_{up} = 1/r$, minibatch size 32 and output depth 8. At high resolutions the sparse version is much more efficient.

Resolution	32^3	64^3	128^3	256^3	512^3
Dense [GB]	0.04	0.27	2.15	17.18	137.28
Sparse 32 [GB]	$2 \cdot 10^{-3}$	$8 \cdot 10^{-3}$	0.03	—	—
Sparse 64 [GB]	$3 \cdot 10^{-3}$	0.013	0.05	0.2	0.8
Sparse Temp [GB]	$3 \cdot 10^{-4}$	0.002	0.016	0.13	1.07

Runtime and Memory Footprint

For the evaluation of runtime, convolutions are performed on a sparse voxel grid filled with random numbers. The resolution of the voxel grid r^3 is varied between $r = 16$ and $r = 256$. To achieve the expected data density of a 2D surface in a 3D voxel grid, the data density ρ as well as the upper bound on the per-channel density ρ_{up} are set to $\rho = \rho_{up} = \frac{1}{r}$. To run dense convolution at resolution $r = 256$, the mini-batch size and channel depth had to be set to 1 (Protobuf limits each single tensor to 2 GB), while the number of output channels was set to 8. The density ρ_f of the filter weights is varied between 0.1 and 1. As baseline we use the convolutional layer of Tensorflow [1], which performs convolutions via the fast Fourier transform and batched general matrix-matrix multiplication from cuBlas, as front end to cuDNN [4]. We note that processing only a single input channel does not play to the strength of our sparse network. Moreover, Tensorflow is able to use the full capability of the GPU, while our implementation is limited to operating in global memory, due to the weak support for atomic floating point operations in shared memory. The effect of this limitation is particularly pronounced at small resolution and high density, whereas for high resolutions and low densities its influence fades. In particular, at $r = 256$ and $\rho_f = 0.1$, we are 14× faster with strong density regularisation, so that the k-selection step is bypassed; and still 7× faster including k-selection filtering. See Fig. 4.

Table 1 shows the memory requirements for dense and sparse convolution layers at various resolutions r. Dense convolutions require only a single output tensor. The sparse implementation uses tensors for indices and data as well as a temporary buffer, which can be reused in all layers. For the experiment the data type is 32 bit floating point, for the indices we consider both 32 bit and 64 bit.[2] As expected, our sparse representation needs less memory at the sparsity levels of realistic 3D point cloud data. In particular, our sparse version makes it possible to work with large resolutions up to $r = 512^3$, which is impossible with the dense version on existing hardware.

Contribution of Small Feature Responses

In the context of sparsity the question arises, whether zero-valued features contribute valuable information. Two recent works tried to answer this question. On the one hand, Graham et al. [11] found that they reach the same accuracies as dense networks for their application, while completely neglecting zero-valued features. On the other hand, Uhrig [36] concluded that for certain tasks zero-valued features may be beneficial. For our network it is possible to assess the importance of small feature responses (not limited to exact zero-values) by training neural networks with varying upper bounds. For this experiment, CNNs are trained on MNIST for 10 epochs without regularisation, using the *adagrad* optimiser and a learning rate of 0.01.

The pixels in MNIST were set to zero when their value $v \in [0, 255]$ was below a threshold of $v < 50$, to obtain a sparse dataset with average density $\overline{\rho_{in}} = 0.23$, while the upper bound ρ_{up} ranges from $\rho_{up} = 0.035$ to $\rho_{up} = 0.095$. Note that even though letters can be interpreted as 1D lines in 2D images, the MNIST data has a low resolution of only 28×28 pixels. Hence, the data is still not extremely sparse. Lower upper bounds guarantee a small memory footprint, and also yield slightly faster runtime per epoch. The price to pay is slower convergence, because some gradients are lost during backpropagation; and a slight performance penalty for very strict bounds (<1.5% for the strictest setting $\rho_{up} = 0.035$).

---

[2] 32 bit indices can only be used for resolutions $r \leq 128^3$ due to buffer overflows.

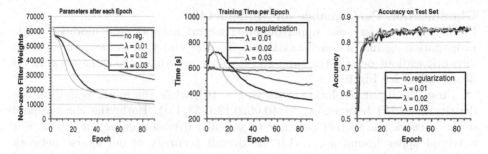

Fig. 5. Influence of adaptive density regularisation and pruning on *(left)* the number of non-zero filter weights, *(middle)* the runtime per training epoch, and *(right)* the accuracy on the Modelnet40 test set. Strong regularisation and pruning save a lot of memory and time without noticeable impact on accuracy.

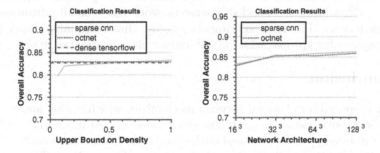

Fig. 6. Performance of sparse network on Modelnet40, compared to the equivalent dense network and Octnet. *(left)* accuracy for different upper density bounds; *(right)* accuracy for different input resolutions.

Regularisation and Pruning

With our sparsity-inducing pruning and regularisation, we expect faster runtime. In order to verify this behaviour, neural networks are trained on Modelnet40 with varying regularisation scales $\lambda \in \{0, 0.1, 0.2, 0.3\}$. The bias for density-based regularisation is computed with $b_1 = b_2 = o = 0.1$. Stronger regularisation decimates the number of (non-zero) filter weights faster, as shown in Fig. 5. It can also be seen that the number of parameters converges when only important weights are left. The drop in non-zero weights also reduces runtime. After 90 epochs, a network regularised with $\lambda = 0.3$ is 51% faster than one trained without regularisation and pruning, even though only the first nine out of twelve convolution layers are set to be sparse. Strong regularisation initially causes an increase in runtime, by driving up the number of non-zero weights to use the available resources via the bias term b_2. The classification accuracy for all tested regularisation scales quickly converges to practically identical values, as shown in Fig. 5. We point out that pruning finds the most suitable sparsity pattern *for a given training set*. When using a pruned model for transfer learning, it may be safer to re-initialize the removed filter weights of the sparse representation with zeros before fine-tuning.

Classification Performance on Modelnet40

Finally, we compare our upper-bounded neural network and modified back-propagation against a conventional net. To that end we run Octnet3, a dense network without octree structure, and a sparse version of the same network on Modelnet40, see Fig. 6.

First, the input resolution is set to $r = 16^3$, while the upper bound on the density is varied between $\rho_{in} \in \{0.06, 0.12, 0.33, 1.0\}$. Both, the conventional dense network and Octnet converge to a similar overall accuracy of ≈ 0.83. For a trivial upper bound $\rho_{in} = 1.0$ the overall accuracy of our sparse network is also practically the same. Very low upper bounds up to $\rho_{in} = 0.12$ yield slightly worse results on the 16^3 inputs, for the lowest bound $\rho_{in} = 0.06$ the drop in performance reaches $\approx 3\%$ points. Second, the resolution of the input is gradually increased: $r \in \{16^3, 32^3, 64^3, 128^3\}$. Both the sparse network and Octnet yield similar results, for all resolutions. Octnet performs slightly better on $r = 32^3$, while our bounded, sparse network has a small advantage at all other resolutions. The two experiments suggest that reasonable upper bounds and our sparse backpropagation do not reduce classification accuracy.

5 Conclusion

We have proposed novel neural network mechanisms which exploit and encourage sparseness in both feature maps and model parameters. At practically useful resolutions, our novel sparse layers and back-propagation rule significantly reduce *(i)* memory footprint and *(ii)* runtime of convolutional layers for sufficiently sparse data. Moreover, our approach guarantees upper bounds on the memory requirements and runtime of the network. For classification tasks the performance of our sparse network is comparable to its dense counterpart as well as Octnet. In future work, it will be interesting to employ sparsity also for other tasks. Our implementation is fully compatible with Tensorflow and has been released as open-source code. We hope, that hardware support for sparse convolutions will improve further on future consumer GPUs, as demonstrated by [26]; thus further boosting the performance of sparse, high-dimensional CNNs.

Appendix: Network Architectures

Table 2 shows the network architectures of our experiments. Depending on the type of data and the goal of the experiment, we used the following network specifications (both for the dense and the sparse version, where applicable):

- For MNIST, we run OctNet3-24^2 with 10 output classes. ρ_{21} is set as specified in the paper text and $\rho_{22} = 2 \cdot \rho_{21}$.
- For Modelnet40 we have $c = 40$ different output classes and employ the following variants:
  1. For the regularisation experiment (Fig. 5) we use OctNet3-64^3 with $\rho_{41} = 0.06$, $\rho_{42} = 0.14$, $\rho_{43} = 0.33$.
  2. Figure 6 *(left)* has been generated with OctNet3-16^3 with varying upper bounds $\rho_{11} = \{0.06, 0.12, 0.33, 1\}$, $\rho_{12} = \{0.12, 0.24, 0.33, 1\}$.

3. For Fig. 6 *(right)* the following networks were used: OctNet3-16^3 with $\rho_{11} = \rho_{12} = 1$; OctNet3-$32^3$ with $\rho_{31} = 0.14$, $\rho_{32} = 0.33$, $\rho_{33} = 0.66$; OctNet3-64^3 with $\rho_{41} = 0.06$, $\rho_{42} = 0.14$, $\rho_{43} = 0.33$; OctNet3-128^3 with $\rho_{51} = 0.02$, $\rho_{52} = 0.06$, $\rho_{53} = 0.14$.

Table 2. In our evaluation, we use different OctNet3 network architectures, similar to those also used by Riegler et al. [32]

OctNet3-16^3	OctNet3-24^2	OctNet3-32^3	OctNet3-64^3	OctNet3-128^3	OctNet3-256^3
conv(1, 8, ρ_{11})	conv(1, 8, ρ_{21})	conv(1, 8, ρ_{31})	conv(1, 8, ρ_{41})	conv(1, 8, ρ_{51})	conv(1, 8, ρ_{61})
conv(8, 8, ρ_{11})	conv(8, 8, ρ_{21})	conv(8, 8, ρ_{31})	conv(8, 8, ρ_{41})	conv(8, 8, ρ_{51})	conv(8, 8, ρ_{61})
conv(8, 8, ρ_{11})	conv(8, 8, ρ_{21})	conv(8, 8, ρ_{31})	conv(8, 8, ρ_{41})	conv(8, 8, ρ_{51})	conv(8, 8, ρ_{61})
maxPooling(2)	maxPooling(2)	maxPooling(2)	maxPooling(2)	maxPooling(2)	maxPooling(2)
conv(8, 16, ρ_{12})	conv(8, 16, ρ_{22})	conv(8, 16, ρ_{32})	conv(8, 16, ρ_{42})	conv(8, 16, ρ_{52})	conv(8, 16, ρ_{62})
conv(16, 16, ρ_{12})	conv(16, 16, ρ_{22})	conv(16, 16, ρ_{32})	conv(16, 16, ρ_{42})	conv(16, 16, ρ_{52})	conv(16, 16, ρ_{62})
conv(16, 16, ρ_{12})	conv(16, 16, ρ_{22})	conv(16, 16, ρ_{32})	conv(16, 16, ρ_{42})	conv(16, 16, ρ_{52})	conv(16, 16, ρ_{62})
sparseToDense()	sparseToDense()	maxPooling(2)	maxPooling(2)	maxPooling(2)	maxPooling(2)
		conv(16, 24, ρ_{33})	conv(16, 24, ρ_{43})	conv(16, 24, ρ_{53})	conv(16, 24, ρ_{63})
		conv(24, 24, ρ_{33})	conv(24, 24, ρ_{43})	conv(24, 24, ρ_{53})	conv(24, 24, ρ_{63})
		conv(24, 24, ρ_{33})	conv(24, 24, ρ_{43})	conv(24, 24, ρ_{53})	conv(24, 24, ρ_{63})
		sparseToDense()	sparseToDense()	sparseToDense()	sparseToDense()
			maxPooling(2)	maxPooling(2)	maxPooling(2)
			conv(24, 32)	conv(24, 32)	conv(24, 32)
			conv(32, 32)	conv(32, 32)	conv(32, 32)
			conv(32, 32)	conv(32, 32)	conv(32, 32)
				maxPooling(2)	maxPooling(2)
				conv(32, 40)	conv(32, 40)
				conv(40, 40)	conv(40, 40)
				conv(40, 40)	conv(40, 40)
					maxPooling(2)
					conv(40, 48)
					conv(48, 48)
					conv(48, 48)
dropout(0.5)					
fully-connected(1024)					
fully-connected(c)					

References

1. Abadi, M., et al.: TensorFlow: a system for large-scale machine learning. In: USENIX OSDI (2016)
2. Alabi, T., Blanchard, J.D., Gordon, B., Steinbach, R.: Fast k-selection algorithms for graphics processing units. J. Exp. Algorithmics **17** (2012)
3. Brock, A., Lim, T., Ritchie, J., Weston, N.: Generative and discriminative voxel modeling with convolutional neural networks. arXiv preprint arXiv:1608.04236 (2017)
4. Chetlur, S., et al.: CUDNN: efficient primitives for deep learning. arXiv preprint arXiv:1410.0759 (2014)
5. Denil, M., Shakibi, B., Dinh, L., de Freitas, N., et al.: Predicting parameters in deep learning. In: NIPS (2013)
6. Denton, E.L., Zaremba, W., Bruna, J., LeCun, Y., Fergus, R.: Exploiting linear structure within convolutional networks for efficient evaluation. In: NIPS (2014)
7. Duchi, J., Hazan, E., Singer, Y.: Adaptive subgradient methods for online learning and stochastic optimization. J. Mach. Learn. Res. **12**, 2121–2159 (2011)
8. Engelcke, M., Rao, D., Wang, D.Z., Tong, C.H., Posner, I.: Vote3Deep: fast object detection in 3D point clouds using efficient convolutional neural networks. arXiv preprint arXiv:1609.06666 (2017)
9. Graham, B.: Spatially-sparse convolutional neural networks. arXiv preprint arXiv:1409.6070 (2014)
10. Graham, B., Engelcke, M., van der Maaten, L.: 3D semantic segmentation with sub-manifold sparse convolutional networks. arXiv preprint arXiv:1711.10275 (2017)
11. Graham, B., van der Maaten, L.: Submanifold sparse convolutional networks. arXiv preprint arXiv:1706.01307 (2017)
12. Han, S., Pool, J., Tran, J., Dally, W.: Learning both weights and connections for efficient neural network. In: NIPS (2015)
13. Häne, C., Tulsiani, S., Malik, J.: Hierarchical surface prediction for 3D object reconstruction. arXiv preprint arXiv:1704.00710 (2017)
14. Huang, J., You, S.: Point cloud labeling using 3D convolutional neural network. In: ICPR (2016)
15. Jaderberg, M., Vedaldi, A., Zisserman, A.: Speeding up convolutional neural networks with low rank expansions. arXiv preprint arXiv:1405.3866 (2014)
16. Jampani, V., Kiefel, M., Gehler, P.V.: Learning sparse high dimensional filters: image filtering, dense CRFs and bilateral neural networks. In: CVPR (2016)
17. Karpathy, A., Toderici, G., Shetty, S., Leung, T., Sukthankar, R., Fei-Fei, L.: Large-scale video classification with convolutional neural networks. In: CVPR (2014)
18. Krizhevsky, A., Sutskever, I., Hinton, G.E.: ImageNet classification with deep convolutional neural networks. In: NIPS (2012)
19. Lai, K., Bo, L., Fox, D.: Unsupervised feature learning for 3D scene labeling. In: ICRA (2014)
20. LeCun, Y., Bottou, L., Bengio, Y., Haffner, P.: Gradient-based learning applied to document recognition. Proc. IEEE **86**(11), 2278–2324 (1998)
21. Li, Y., Pirk, S., Su, H., Qi, C.R., Guibas, L.J.: FPNN: field probing neural networks for 3D data. In: NIPS (2016)
22. Liu, B., Wang, M., Foroosh, H., Tappen, M., Pensky, M.: Sparse convolutional neural networks. In: CVPR (2015)
23. Long, J., Shelhamer, E., Darrell, T.: Fully convolutional networks for semantic segmentation. In: CVPR (2015)

24. Maturana, D., Scherer, S.: VoxNet: a 3D convolutional neural network for real-time object recognition. In: IROS (2015)
25. Nissen, M.J., Bullemer, P.: Attentional requirements of learning: evidence from performance measures. Cogn. Psychol. **19**(1), 1–32 (1987)
26. Parashar, A., et al.: SCNN: an accelerator for compressed-sparse convolutional neural networks. In: International Symposium on Computer Architecture (2017)
27. Park, J., et al.: Faster CNNs with direct sparse convolutions and guided pruning. In: ICLR (2017)
28. Prokhorov, D.: A convolutional learning system for object classification in 3-D lidar data. IEEE Trans. Neural Netw. **21**(5), 858–863 (2010)
29. Qi, C.R., Su, H., Mo, K., Guibas, L.J.: PointNet: deep learning on point sets for 3D classification and segmentation. In: CVPR (2017)
30. Qi, C.R., Yi, L., Su, H., Guibas, L.J.: PointNet++: deep hierarchical feature learning on point sets in a metric space. arXiv preprint arXiv:1706.02413 (2017)
31. Ren, S., He, K., Girshick, R., Sun, J.: Faster R-CNN: towards real-time object detection with region proposal networks. In: NIPS (2015)
32. Riegler, G., Ulusoy, A.O., Geiger, A.: OctNet: learning deep 3D representations at high resolutions. In: CVPR (2017)
33. Robertson, E.M.: The serial reaction time task: implicit motor skill learning? J. Neurosci. **27**(38), 10073–10075 (2007)
34. Song, S., Xiao, J.: Deep sliding shapes for amodal 3D object detection in RGB-D images. In: CVPR (2016)
35. Tatarchenko, M., Dosovitskiy, A., Brox, T.: Octree generating networks: efficient convolutional architectures for high-resolution 3D outputs. arXiv preprint arXiv:1703.09438 (2017)
36. Uhrig, J., Schneider, N., Schneider, L., Franke, U., Brox, T., Geiger, A.: Sparsity invariant CNNs. arXiv preprint arXiv:1708.06500 (2017)
37. Wen, W., Wu, C., Wang, Y., Chen, Y., Li, H.: Learning structured sparsity in deep neural networks. In: NIPS (2016)
38. Wu, Z., et al.: 3D ShapeNets: a deep representation for volumetric shapes. In: CVPR (2015)

End-to-End Learning of Deterministic Decision Trees

Thomas M. Hehn[✉] and Fred A. Hamprecht

Heidelberg Collaboratory for Image Processing Interdisciplinary Center for Scientific Computing, Heidelberg University, 69115 Heidelberg, Germany
t.m.hehn@tudelft.nl

Abstract. Conventional decision trees have a number of favorable properties, including interpretability, a small computational footprint and the ability to learn from little training data. However, they lack a key quality that has helped fuel the deep learning revolution: that of being end-to-end trainable. Kontschieder 2015 has addressed this deficit, but at the cost of losing a main attractive trait of decision trees: the fact that each sample is routed along a small subset of tree nodes only. We here propose a model and Expectation-Maximization training scheme for decision trees that are fully probabilistic at train time, but after an annealing process become deterministic at test time. We analyze the learned oblique split parameters on image datasets and show that Neural Networks can be trained at each split. In summary, we present an end-to-end learning scheme for deterministic decision trees and present results on par or superior to published standard oblique decision tree algorithms.

1 Introduction

When selecting a supervised machine learning technique, we are led by multiple and often conflicting criteria. These include: how accurate is the resulting model? How much training data is needed to achieve a given level of accuracy? How interpretable is the model? How big is the computational effort at train time? And at test time? How well does the implementation map to the available hardware?

These days, neural networks have superseded all other approaches in terms of achievable accuracy of the predictions; but state of the art networks are not easy to interpret, are fairly hungry for training data, often require weeks of GPU training and have a computational and memory footprint that rules out their use on small embedded devices. Decision trees achieve inferior accuracy, but are fundamentally more frugal.

T. M. Hehn—Corresponding author is now at TU Delft.

Electronic supplementary material The online version of this chapter (https://doi.org/10.1007/978-3-030-12939-2_42) contains supplementary material, which is available to authorized users.

© Springer Nature Switzerland AG 2019
T. Brox et al. (Eds.): GCPR 2018, LNCS 11269, pp. 612–627, 2019.
https://doi.org/10.1007/978-3-030-12939-2_42

Both neural networks and decision trees are composed of basic computational units, the perceptrons and nodes, respectively. A crucial difference between the two is that in a standard neural network, all units are being evaluated for every input; while in a decision tree with I inner split nodes, only $\mathcal{O}(\log I)$ split nodes are visited. That is, in a decision tree, a sample is routed along a single path from the root to a leaf, with the path conditioned on the sample's features.

It is this sparsity of the sample-dependent computational graph that piques our interest in decision trees; but we also hope to profit from their ability to learn their comparatively few parameters from a small training set, and their relative interpretability.

One hallmark of neural networks is their ability to learn a complex combination of many elementary decisions jointly, by end-to-end training using backpropagation. This is a feature that has so far been missing in deterministic decision trees, which are usually constructed greedily without subsequent tuning. We here propose a mechanism to remedy this deficit.

1.1 Contributions

- We propose a decision tree whose internal nodes are probabilistic and hence differentiable at train time. As a consequence, we are able to train the internal nodes jointly in an end-to-end fashion. This is true for linear nodes, but the property is maintained for more complex nodes, such as small Convolutional Neural Networks (CNNs) (Sect. 3.4).
- We derive an expectation-maximization style algorithm for finding the optimal parameters in a split node (Sect. 3.3). We develop a probabilistic split criterion that generalizes the long-established information gain [24]. The proposed criterion is asymptotically identical to information gain in the limit of very steep non-linearities, but allows to better model class overlap in the vicinity of a split decision boundary (Sect. 3.2).
- We demonstrate good results by making the nodes deterministic at test time, sending each sample along a unique path of only $\mathcal{O}(\log I)$ out of the I inner nodes in a tree. We evaluate the performance of the proposed method on the same datasets as used in related work [22] (Sect. 4.1) and find steeper learning curves with respect to tree depth, as well as higher overall accuracy. We show the benefit of regularizing the spatial derivatives of learned features when samples are images or image patches (Sect. 4.2). Finally, we report preliminary experiments with minimalistic trees with CNNs as split feature.

2   Related Work

Decision trees and decision tree ensembles, such as random forests [1], are widely used for computer vision [4] and have proven effective on a variety of classification tasks [7]. In order to improve their performance for a specific task, it is common practice to engineer its features to a specific task [8,14,16]. Oblique linear and non-linear classifiers using more than one feature at a time have been benchmarked in [18], but the available algorithms are, in contrast to our approach, limited to binary classification problems.

There have been several attempts to train decision trees using gradient optimization techniques for more complex split functions. Similarly to our approach, [19] have successfully approximated information gain using a sigmoid function and a smoothness hyperparameter. However, that approach does not allow joint optimization of an entire tree.

In [22], the authors also propose an algorithm for optimization of an entire tree with a given structure. They show a connection between optimizing oblique splits and structured prediction with latent variables. As a result, they formulate a convex-concave upper bound on the tree's empirical loss. In order to find an initial tree structure, the work also relies on a greedy algorithm, which is based on the same upper bound approach [21]. Their method is restricted to linear splits and relies on the kernel trick to introduce higher order split features as opposed to our optimization, which allows more complex split features.

Other advances towards gradient-based decision tree optimization rely on either fuzzy or probabilistic split functions [10,13,30]. In contrast to our approach, the assignment of a single sample to the leaves remains fuzzy, respectively probabilistic, during prediction. Consequently, all leaves and paths need to be evaluated for every sample, which annihilates the computational benefits of trees.

We build on reference [13], which is closest to our work. The authors use sigmoid functions to model the probabilistic routes and employ the same log-likelihood objective. In contrast to their work, we derive the alternating optimization using the Expectation-Maximization approach as in [11] and aim for a deterministic decision tree for prediction. Also, they start from a random, but balanced tree, because their algorithm does not learn the structure of the tree. In [28], a greedy strategy is applied to learn neural networks for each split node and hence learn the structure of the tree. However, their approach is lacking end-to-end learning capabilities. In contrast, we have provided a unified framework which enables greedy learning as well as end-to-end learning for deterministic decision trees at test time.

Finally, connections between neural networks and decision tree ensembles have been examined. In [29,31] decision tree ensembles are cast to neural networks, which enables gradient descent training. As long as the structure of the trees is preserved, the optimized parameters of the neural network can also be mapped back to the random forest. Subsequently, [26] cast stacked decision forests to convolutional neural networks and found an approximate mapping back. In [9,17] several models of neural networks with separate, conditional data flows are discussed.

Our work builds on various ideas of previous work, however, none of these algorithms provide a unified framework to learn deterministic decision trees with arbitrary split functions in an end-to-end fashion.

3 Methods

Consider a classification problem with input space $\mathcal{X} \subset \mathbb{R}^p$ and output space $\mathcal{Y} = \{1, ..., K\}$. The training set is defined as $\{x_1, ..., x_N\} = \mathcal{X}_t \subset \mathcal{X}$ with corresponding classes $\{y_1, ..., y_N\} = \mathcal{Y}_t \subset \mathcal{Y}$. We propose training a probabilistic decision tree model, which becomes deterministic at test time.

3.1 Standard Decision Tree and Notation

In binary decision trees (Fig. 1c), split functions $s : \mathbb{R} \to [0, 1]$ determine the routing of a sample through the tree, conditioned on that sample's features. The split function controls whether the splits are deterministic or probabilistic. The prediction is made by the leaf node that is reached by the sample.

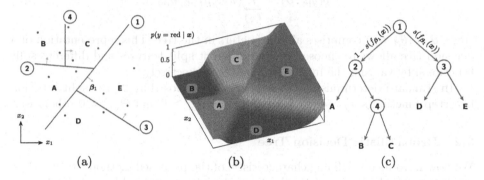

Fig. 1. Probabilistic oblique decision trees. (a) A feature space with a binary classification problem tessellated by an example oblique decision tree. The oblique splits (1-4) partition the feature space into five different leaves (A–E). (b) The predicted $p(y = \text{red} \mid x)$ (Eq. 2) of the oblique decision tree when a probabilistic split (Eq. 3) is used. (c) The corresponding tree diagram. (Color figure online)

Split Nodes. Each split node $i \in \{1, ..., I\}$ computes a split feature from a sample, and sends that feature to into a split function. That function is a map $f_{\beta_i} : \mathbb{R}^p \to \mathbb{R}$ parametrized by β_i. For example, *oblique splits* are a linear combination of the input as in $f_{\beta_i}(x) = (x^T, 1) \cdot \beta_i$ with $\beta_i \in \mathbb{R}^{p+1}$. Similarly, an axis-aligned split perpendicular to axis a is represented by an oblique split whose only non-zero parameters are at index a and $p + 1$. We write $\theta_\beta = (\beta_1, ..., \beta_I)$ to denote the collection of all split parameters in the tree.

Leaf Nodes. Each leaf $\ell \in \{1, ..., L\}$ stores a categorical distribution over classes $k \in \{1, ..., K\}$ in a vector $\pi_\ell \in [0, 1]^K$. These vectors are normalized such that the probability of all classes in a leaf sum to $\sum_{k=1}^{K}(\pi_\ell)_k = 1$. We define $\theta_\pi = (\pi_1, ..., \pi_L)$ to include all leaf parameters in the tree.

Paths. For each leaf node there exists one unique set of split outcomes, called a path. We define the probability that a sample x takes the path to leaf ℓ as

$$\mu_\ell(x; s, \theta_\beta) = \prod_{r \in \mathcal{R}_\ell} s(f_{\beta_r}(x)) \prod_{l \in \mathcal{L}_\ell} \left(1 - s(f_{\beta_l}(x))\right). \tag{1}$$

Here, $\mathcal{R}_\ell \subset \{1, ..., I\}$ denotes the splits on the path which contain ℓ in the right subtree. Analogously, $\mathcal{L}_\ell \subset \{1, ..., I\}$ denotes splits which contain ℓ in the left subtree. In Fig. 1c this means that $\mathcal{R}_B = \{2\}$ and $\mathcal{L}_B = \{1, 4\}$. Also note that in the following, we will omit the s dependency whenever we do not consider a specific function.

The prediction of the entire decision tree is given by multiplying the path probability with the corresponding leaf prediction:

$$p(y|x; \theta) = \sum_{\ell=1}^{L} (\pi_\ell)_y \mu_\ell(x; \theta_\beta). \tag{2}$$

Here, $\theta = (\theta_\beta, \theta_\pi)$ comprises all parameters in the tree. This representation of a decision tree allows to choose between different split features and different split functions, by varying the functions f and s, respectively.

In standard deterministic decision trees as proposed in [2], the split function is a step function $s(x) = \Theta(x)$ with $\Theta(x) = 1$ if $x > 0$ and $\Theta(x) = 0$ otherwise.

3.2   Probabilistic Decision Tree

We now introduce a defining characteristic of the proposed method. Rather than sending a sample deterministically down the left or right subtree, depending on its features x, we send it left or right with a probability

$$s(f(x)) = \sigma(f(x)) = \frac{1}{1 + e^{-f(x)}}. \tag{3}$$

This corresponds to regarding each split in the tree as a Bernoulli decision with mean $\sigma(f(x))$ and as a result Eq. 2 is the expected value over the possible outcomes. Figure 1b shows the prediction from Eq. 2 in the probabilistic case for a class $y = $ "red" on the classification problem illustrated in Fig. 1a.

To train our probabilistic decision trees, we choose as objective the maximization of the empirical log-likelihood of the training data:

$$\max_{\theta} \mathcal{L}(\theta; \mathcal{X}_t, \mathcal{Y}_t) = \max_{\theta} \sum_{n=1}^{N} \log p(y_n|x_n; \theta). \tag{4}$$

Importantly, while we propose to use a probabilistic decision tree for training, we use a deterministic decision tree for prediction. To better match the models used at train and test time, we introduce a hyperparameter γ, which steers the steepness of the split function by scaling the split feature [19]

$$s(f(x)) = \sigma_\gamma(f(x)) = \sigma(\gamma f(x)). \tag{5}$$

Note, for $\gamma \rightarrow \infty$ the model resembles a deterministic decision tree, since $\sigma_\infty(f(x)) = \Theta(f(x))$. During training, we iteratively increase γ, akin a temperature cooling schedule in deterministic annealing [27].

3.3   Expectation-Maximization

For the optimization of the log-likelihood (Eq. 4), we propose a gradient-based, EM-style optimization strategy, which requires f and s to be differentiable with respect to the split parameters β_i. The derivation of the EM-algorithm for this model follows the spirit of [11]. We introduce additional latent random variables $z_{n,\ell}$, which indicate that leaf ℓ generated the class label of a given data point x_n. Including these latent variables, the optimization objective (Eq. 4) becomes the complete-data log-likelihood (including latent variables)

$$\mathcal{L}(\theta; \mathcal{X}_t, \mathcal{Y}_t, \mathcal{Z}_t) = \sum_{n=1}^{N} \sum_{\ell=1}^{L} z_{n,\ell} \log \left((\pi_\ell)_{y_n} \mu_\ell(x_n; \theta_\beta) \right). \tag{6}$$

E-Step. In the Expectation-Step, the expected value of the complete-data log-likelihood over the latent variables given the previous parameters θ' is computed

$$Q(\theta|\theta') = E_{\mathcal{Z}_t|\mathcal{X}_t, \mathcal{Y}_t; \theta'} [\mathcal{L}(\theta; \mathcal{X}_t, \mathcal{Y}_t, \mathcal{Z}_t)]. \tag{7}$$

For this purpose, it is necessary to compute the probability that $z_{n,\ell} = 1$ for each training sample n:

$$h_{n,\ell} := p(z_{n,\ell} = 1 \mid x_n, y_n; \theta') \tag{8}$$

$$= \frac{p(y_n \mid z_{n,\ell} = 1, x_n; \theta') p(z_{n,\ell} = 1 \mid x_n; \theta')}{p(y_n \mid x_n; \theta')} \tag{9}$$

$$= \frac{(\pi'_\ell)_{y_n} \mu_\ell(x_n; \theta'_\beta)}{\sum_{\ell'=1}^{L} (\pi'_{\ell'})_{y_n} \mu_{\ell'}(x_n; \theta'_\beta)}. \tag{10}$$

Thus, the expectation value of the complete-data log-likelihood yields

$$Q(\theta|\theta') = \sum_{n=1}^{N} \sum_{\ell=1}^{L} h_{n,\ell} \log \left((\pi_\ell)_{y_n} \mu_\ell(x_n; \theta_\beta) \right). \tag{11}$$

M-Step. In the Maximization-Step of the EM-Algorithm, the expectation value computed in the E-Step (Eq. 11) is maximized to find updated parameters

$$\max_\theta Q(\theta|\theta'). \tag{12}$$

Due to the latent variables we introduced, it is now possible to separate the parameter dependencies in the logarithm into a sum. As a result, the leaf predictions and split parameters are optimized separately. The optimization of the leaf predictions including the normalization constraint can be computed directly as

$$(\pi_\ell)_k = \frac{\sum_{n=1}^{N} \mathbb{1}(y_n = k)h_{n,\ell}}{\sum_{n=1}^{N} h_{n,\ell}}. \tag{13}$$

Here, the indicator function $\mathbb{1}(y_n = k)$ equals 1 if $y_n = k$ and 0 otherwise. The optimization of the split parameters in the M-Step is performed using gradient based optimization. The separated objective for the split parameters without the leaf predictions is

$$\max_{\theta_\beta} \sum_{n=1}^{N} \sum_{\ell=1}^{L} h_{n,\ell} \log \mu_\ell(x_n; \theta_\beta). \tag{14}$$

We use the first-order gradient-based stochastic optimization Adam [12] for optimization of the split parameters.

In summary, each iteration of the algorithm requires evaluation of Eqs. 10 and 13, as well as at least one update of the split parameters based on Eq. 14. This iterative algorithm can be applied to a binary decision tree of any given structure.

3.4   Complex Splits and Spatial Regularization

The proposed optimization procedure only requires the split features f to be differentiable with respect to the split parameters. As a result, it is possible to implement more complex splits than axis-aligned or oblique splits. For example, it is possible to use a small Convolutional Neural Network (CNN) as split feature extractor for f and learn its parameters (Sect. 4.4).

Furthermore, the optimization objective can also include regularization constraints on the parameters. This is useful to avoid overfitting and learn more robust patterns. When the inputs are from images, spatial regularization also reveals more discernible spatial structures in the learned parameters without sacrificing accuracy (Sect. 4.2). To encourage the learning of coherent spatial patterns at each split, we introduce a spatial regularization term

$$-\lambda \sum_{i=1}^{I} \beta_i^T M \beta_i \tag{15}$$

to the maximization objective of the split features (Eq. 14) [5]. The matrix M denotes the Laplacian matrix when interpreting the image as a grid graph. For a single pixel, corresponding to weight β_i, the diagonal element M_{ii} contains the number of neighboring pixels. If pixels i and j are neighboring pixels, then $M_{ij} = M_{ji} = -1$. All remaining elements in M are 0. This regularization term penalizes spatial finite differences, encouraging similar parameters for neighboring pixels. The hyperparameter λ controls the regularization strength, with higher λ leads to stronger regularization.

3.5 Structure Learning

The foregoing shows how to fit a decision tree to training data, given the tree topology (parameter learning). We now turn to the learning of the tree itself (structure learning). We recommend, and evaluate in Sect. 4.1, a greedy strategy: Starting at the root, each split is considered and trained as a tree stump, consisting of one split and two leaf nodes.

Since there are only two leaves, the log-likelihood objective (Eq. 4) then resembles an approximation of the widely popular information gain criterion [24,25] (Sect. 3.6). The previously found splits, in the more shallow levels of the tree, deterministically route data to the split currently being trained. In particular this means that, at first, the root split is trained on the entire training data. After training of the first split, both leaves are discarded and replaced by new splits. According to the root split, the training data is deterministically divided into two subsets, which are now used to train the corresponding child nodes. This procedure is repeated until, some stopping criterion, e.g. maximum depth, maximum number of leaves or leaf purity, is reached. After this greedy structure learning, the nodes in the entire resulting tree can be finetuned jointly as described in Sect. 3.3, this time with probabilistic routing of all training data.

3.6 Relation to Information Gain and Leaf Entropies

We now show that maximization of the log-likelihood of the probabilistic decision tree model approximately minimizes the weighted entropies in the leaves. The steeper the splits become, the better the approximation.

To establish this connection we use hyperparameter γ to control the steepness of the probabilistic split function (Eq. 5). We introduce the function $\ell(x)$ that returns the index of the leaf sample x reaches when the path is evaluated deterministically

$$\ell(x) = \sum_{\ell=1}^{L} \ell \lim_{\gamma \to \infty} \mu_\ell(x; \sigma_\gamma, \theta_\beta). \tag{16}$$

This simplifies the log-likelihood objective (Eq. 4) to

$$\max_\theta \sum_{n=1}^{N} \log(\pi_{\ell(x_n)})_{y_n} \tag{17}$$

because each sample reaches only one leaf. Let $N_{\ell,k}$ be the number of training samples in leaf ℓ with class k and $N_\ell = \sum_{k=1}^{K} N_{\ell,k}$ denote all training samples in leaf ℓ. Since training samples with the same class and in the same leaf contribute the same term, the equations may be rearranged to

$$\max_\theta \sum_{\ell=1}^{L} \sum_{k=1}^{K} N_{\ell,k} \log(\pi_\ell)_k. \tag{18}$$

With $\gamma \to \infty$, the optimal leaf predictions are the same as in a standard, deterministic decision tree, i.e. $(\boldsymbol{\pi}_\ell)_k = \frac{N_{\ell,k}}{N_\ell}$. Accordingly, the objective can be rewritten as

$$\max_{\theta} \lim_{\gamma \to \infty} \mathcal{L}(\theta; \mathcal{X}_t, \mathcal{Y}_t) = \min_{\theta} \sum_{\ell=1}^{L} \frac{N_\ell}{N} H_\ell. \tag{19}$$

Here, $H_\ell = -\sum_{k=1}^{K} (\boldsymbol{\pi}_\ell)_k \log(\boldsymbol{\pi}_\ell)_k$ denotes the entropy in leaf ℓ.

In conclusion, we have shown that for $\gamma \to \infty$, maximizing the log-likelihood objective minimizes a weighted sum of leaf entropies. For the special case of a single split with two leaves, this is the same as maximizing the information gain. Consequently, the log-likelihood objective (Eq. 4) can be regarded as a generalization of the information gain criterion [24] to an entire tree.

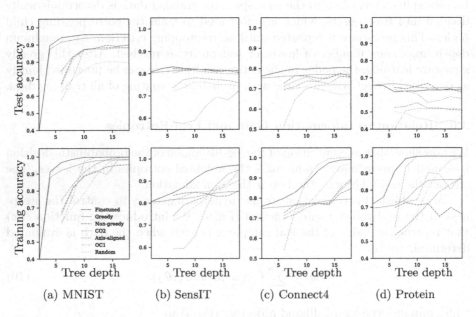

(a) MNIST   (b) SensIT   (c) Connect4   (d) Protein

Fig. 2. Performance of deterministic oblique decision trees. Accuracy of *Greedy* trained (solid, light red line) and *Finetuned* oblique decision trees (solid, dark red line) on test and training sets is compared against other algorithms. The maximum tree depth varies from 2 to 18 with stepsize 2. Dashed lines represent results reported in [22]. (Color figure online)

4 Experiments

We conduct experiments on data from very different domains: first, on the multivariate but unstructured datasets used in [22] (Sect. 4.1). Next, we show that the proposed algorithm can learn meaningful spatial features on *MNIST*, *FashionMNIST* and *ISBI*, as has previously been demonstrated in neural networks but not in decision trees (Sect. 4.2). Then, we demonstrate the same property on a real-world biological image processing task (Sect. 4.3). Finally, we deliver proof of principle that a deterministic decision tree with complex split nodes can be trained end-to-end, by using a small neural network in each split node (Sect. 4.4).

4.1 Performance of Oblique Decision Trees

We compare the performance of our algorithm in terms of accuracy to all results reported in [22]. They only compare single, unpruned trees, since common ensemble methods such as bagging and boosting as well as pruning can be applied to all algorithms. In order to provide a fair comparison, we also refrain from pruning, ensembles and regularization.

Datasets. Reference [22] reports results on the following four datasets. The multi-class classification datasets *SensIT (combined)*, *Connect4*, *Protein* and *MNIST* are obtained from the LIBSVM repository [6]. When a separate test set is not provided, we randomly split the data into a training set with 80% of the data and use 20% for testing. Likewise, when no validation set is provided, we randomly extract 20% of the training set as validation set. In a preprocessing step, we normalize the data to zero mean and unit variance of the training data.

Compared Algorithms. The final model for prediction is always a deterministic decision tree with either oblique or axis-aligned splits. The following algorithms were evaluated in [22]. *Axis-aligned*: conventional axis-aligned splits based on information gain. *OC1*: oblique splits optimized with coordinate descent as proposed in [20]. *Random*: selected the best of randomly generated oblique splits based on information gain. *CO2*: greedy oblique tree algorithm based on structured learning [21]. *Non-greedy*: non-greedy oblique decision tree algorithm based on structured learning [22]. We compare the results of these algorithms with our proposed algorithms. Here, *Greedy* denotes a greedy initialization where each oblique split is computed using the EM optimization. For each depth, we apply the *Finetune* algorithm to the tree obtained from the *Greedy* algorithm at that depth.

Hyperparameters and Initialization. We keep all hyperparameters fixed and conduct a grid search only over the number of training epochs in $\{20, 35, 50, 65\}$, using a train/validation split. The test data is only used to report the final performance.

For gradient-based split parameter optimization, we use the Adam optimizer [12] with default parameters ($\alpha = 0.001, \beta_1 = 0.9, \beta_2 = 0.999, \epsilon = 10^{-8}$) and a batch size of 1000 with shuffled batches. The split steepness hyperparameter is set to $\gamma = 1.0$ initially and increased by 0.1 after each epoch (one epoch consists of the split parameter θ_β updates of all training batches as well as the update of the leaf predictions θ_π).

Initial split directions are sampled from the unit sphere and the categorical leaf predictions are initialized uniformly random.

Results. Figure 2 shows the test and training statistical accuracy of the different decision tree learning algorithms. The accuracy of a classifier is defined as the ratio of correctly classified samples in the respective set. It was evaluated for a single tree at various maximum depths. The red solid lines show the result of our proposed algorithm, the dashed lines represent results from [22].

Our algorithms achieve higher test accuracy than previous work, especially in extremely shallow trees. The highest increase in test accuracy is observed on the *MNIST* data set. Here, we significantly outperform previous approaches for oblique decision trees at all depths. In particular, an oblique decision tree of depth 4 is already sufficient to surpass all competitors.

Likewise, on *Connect4* our approach performs better at all depths. Notably, a decision tree of depth 2 is sufficient to exceed previous approaches.

On *SensIT* and *Protein* we perform better than or on par with the *Non-greedy* approach proposed in [22]. However, experiments with regularization of leaf features have shown that with more hyperparameter tuning overfitting may be reduced, e.g. on the *Protein* dataset and thus the results may be improved. We did not include this here, as we aimed to provide a fair comparison and show the performance given very little fine-tuning.

Generally, our algorithm also trains more accurate oblique decision trees on of the depth complexity on the training data.

In conclusion, our experiments show that our proposed algorithm is able to learn more accurate deterministic oblique decision trees than previous approaches. Furthermore, we refrained from hyperparameter tuning to show that the approach even works well with default parameters.

4.2   Spatially Regularized Parameters

We now investigate the effects of spatial regularization (Sect. 3.4) on the parameters of oblique decision trees learned with our algorithm. For this purpose, we train oblique decision trees on the *MNIST* digit dataset [15], the *FashionM-NIST* fashion product dataset [32] and the *ISBI* image partitioning dataset [3] comprising serial section Transmission Electron Microscopy images. In Fig. 3, we visualized selected parameters of the oblique splits at various depths with and without regularization. In both cases, we selected the parameters that displayed the best visible structures. For *MNIST* and *FashionMNIST*, the parameters were reshaped to 28×28 images, such that each parameter pixel corresponds to the respective pixel in the training images. To solve the segmentation task on *ISBI*, we provide a sliding window of size 31×31 as features for each pixel in the center of the window. Moreover, we linearly normalized the parameters to the full grayscale range.

Results. Regularization penalizes differences in adjacent parameters. The parameters without regularization appear very noisy and it is difficult for the

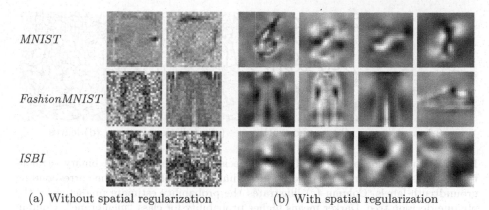

MNIST				
FashionMNIST				
ISBI				
(a) Without spatial regularization		(b) With spatial regularization		

Fig. 3. Visualizations of oblique split parameters learned with and without spatial regularization (Sect. 3.4). The parameters are learned on different datasets, viz. *MNIST* [15] (top row), *FashionMNIST* [32] (center row) and *ISBI* [3] (bottom row). Parameters trained with spatial regularization show visible structures and patterns, whereas parameters learned without regularization appear noisy. In both cases, we selected the parameters that show the best visible structures.

human eye to identify structures. In contrast, in the experiments with regularization the algorithm learns smoother parameter patterns, without decreasing the accuracy of the decision trees. The regularized parameters display structures and recognizable patterns. The patterns learned on the *MNIST* show visible sigmoidal shapes and even recognizable digits. On the *FashionMNIST* dataset, the regularized parameters display the silhouettes of coats, pants and sneakers. Likewise, our algorithm is able to learn the structures of membranes on the real-world biological electron microscopy images from the *ISBI* dataset.

4.3   Image Segmentation

We test the applicability of the proposed decision tree algorithm for image segmentation on the ISBI challenge dataset [3]. This image partitioning benchmark comprises serial section Transmission Electron Microscopy images and binary annotations of neurons and membranes (Fig. 4a).

For every pixel, we provide a sliding window around the current pixel as input features to the oblique decision tree. Consequently, the learned parameters at each split node can be regarded as a spatial kernel. We learn an oblique decision tree of depth 8 with a maximum of 256 leaves with our greedy EM algorithm. We use the default parameters as described in Sect. 4.1 and train each split for 40 epochs.

Results. Figure 4 shows a sample image of the input, the groundtruth labels, the predicted probability of our oblique decision tree and the color-coded leaf affiliation. The visualization of the prediction shows pixels more likely to be of class "membrane" in darker color. In the color-coded leaf affiliation, each

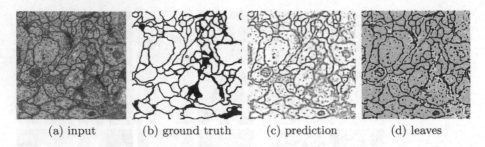

(a) input   (b) ground truth   (c) prediction   (d) leaves

Fig. 4. Visualization of results of oblique decision trees on the ISBI binary segmentation dataset. Column (a) shows the input image and column (b) the corresponding groundtruth labels. Column (c) illustrates the probability estimate predicted by the oblique decision tree. Darker means higher probability for class "membrane". Column (d) shows the leaf affiliation in the oblique decision tree. The leaves from left to right are equidistantly assigned to grayscale values from black to white.

grayscale value represents a leaf in the oblique decision tree. Darker pixels have reached a leaf further on the left side of the decision tree.

In the prediction most of the membranes are correctly identified. However, many mitochondria are falsely classified as membrane. Interestingly, the leaf affiliation is fairly regular, implying that most adjacent pixels are routed to the same leaf, in spite of some variation in appearance. The leaf affiliation could also be provided as additional feature in order to stack classifiers.

4.4   CNN Split Features

In a preliminary experiment, we test the effectiveness of Convolutional Neural Networks as split features on *MNIST*. At each split we trained a very simple CNN of the following architecture: Convolution 5×5 kernel @ 3 output channels $\rightarrow$ Max Pool 2×2 $\rightarrow$ ReLU $\rightarrow$ Convolution 5×5 @ 6 $\rightarrow$ Max Pool 2×2 $\rightarrow$ ReLU $\rightarrow$ Fully connected layer 96×50 $\rightarrow$ ReLU $\rightarrow$ Fully connected layer 50×1. The final scalar output is the split feature, which is the input to the split function. Again, we train greedily to initialize the tree, however we split nodes in a best-first manner, based on highest information gain. As a result, the trees can be fairly unbalanced despite impure leaves. We now choose to stop at a maximum of 10 leaves, as we aim to increase interpretability and efficiency by having one expert leaf per class.

Results. In this setting, we achieve a test accuracy of 0.982 ± 0.003 deterministic evaluation of nodes. This model provides interesting benefits in interpretability and efficiency, which are the main advantages of decision trees. When a sample was misclassified it is straightforward to find the split node that is responsible for the error. This offers interpretability as well as the possibility to improve the overall model. Other methods, such as *OneVsOne* or *OneVsRest* multi-class approaches, provide similar interpretability, however at a much higher cost at test time. This is due to the fact that in a binary decision tree with K leaves, i.e. a leaf for each class, it is sufficient to evaluate $\mathcal{O}(\log K)$ split nodes. In *OneVsOne* and *OneVsAll* it is necessary to evaluate $K(K-1)/2$ and respectively K different classifiers at test time.

5   Conclusion

We have presented a new approach to train deterministic decision trees with gradient-based optimization in an end-to-end manner. We show that this approach outperforms previous algorithms for oblique decision trees. The approach is not restricted in the complexity of the split features and we have provided preliminary evidence of the effectiveness of more complex split features, such as convolutional neural networks. Moreover, our approach allows imposing additional regularization constraints on the learned split features. We have demonstrated these capabilities by visualizing spatially regularized parameters on image processing datasets. The overall approach provides high flexibility and the potential for accurate models that maintain interpretability and efficiency due to the conditional data flow.

Source code of the implementation in PyTorch [23] is available at http://www.github.com/tomsal/endtoenddecisiontrees.

Acknowledgments. The authors gratefully acknowledge financial support by DFG grant HA 4364/10-1.

References

1. Breiman, L.: Random forests. Mach. Learn. **45**(1), 5–32 (2001)
2. Breiman, L., Friedman, J., Olshen, R.A., Stone, C.J.: Classification and Regression Trees. Chapman & Hall/CRC, London (1984)
3. Cardona, A., et al.: An integrated micro- and macroarchitectural analysis of the drosophila brain by computer-assisted serial section electron microscopy. PLOS Biol. **8**(10), 1–17 (2010). https://doi.org/10.1371/journal.pbio.1000502
4. Criminisi, A., Shotton, J.: Decision Forests for Computer Vision and Medical Image Analysis. Springer, Berlin (2013). https://doi.org/10.1007/978-1-4471-4929-3
5. Eilers, P.H.C., Marx, B.D.: Flexible smoothing with B-splines and penalties. Stat. Sci. **11**, 89–121 (1996)
6. Fan, R.E., Lin, C.J.: LIBSVM data: classification, regression and multi-label (2011). http://www.csie.ntu.edu.tw/~cjlin/libsvmtools/datasets/
7. Fernández-Delgado, M., Cernadas, E., Barro, S., Amorim, D.: Do we need hundreds of classifiers to solve real world classification problems? J. Mach. Learn. Res. **15**, 3133–3181 (2014)
8. Gall, J., Lempitsky, V.: Class-specific hough forests for object detection. In: 2009 IEEE Conference on Computer Vision and Pattern Recognition, pp. 1022–1029, June 2009. https://doi.org/10.1109/CVPR.2009.5206740
9. Ioannou, Y., et al.: Decision forests, convolutional networks and the models in-between. arXiv:1603.01250 (March 2016)

10. Jordan, M.I.: A statistical approach to decision tree modeling. In: Proceedings of the Seventh Annual Conference on Computational Learning Theory, COLT 1994, New York, NY, USA, pp. 13–20 (1994)
11. Jordan, M.I., Jacobs, R.A.: Hierarchical mixtures of experts and the em algorithm. Neural Comput. 6(2), 181–214 (1994). https://doi.org/10.1162/neco.1994.6.2.181
12. Kingma, D., Ba, J.: Adam: a method for stochastic optimization. In: ICLR (2015)
13. Kontschieder, P., Fiterau, M., Criminisi, A., Rota Bulò, S.: Deep neural decision forests. In: ICCV (2015)
14. Kontschieder, P., Kohli, P., Shotton, J., Criminisi, A.: GeoF: geodesic forests for learning coupled predictors. In: The IEEE Conference on Computer Vision and Pattern Recognition (CVPR), June 2013
15. LeCun, Y., Bottou, L., Bengio, Y., Haffner, P.: Gradient-based learning applied to document recognition. Proc. IEEE 86(11), 2278–2324 (1998)
16. Lepetit, V., Lagger, P., Fua, P.: Randomized trees for real-time keypoint recognition. In: 2005 IEEE Computer Society Conference on Computer Vision and Pattern Recognition (CVPR 2005), vol. 2, pp. 775–781, June 2005. https://doi.org/10.1109/CVPR.2005.288
17. McGill, M., Perona, P.: Deciding how to decide: dynamic routing in artificial neural networks. In: Precup, D., Teh, Y.W. (eds.) Proceedings of the 34th International Conference on Machine Learning. Proceedings of Machine Learning Research, PMLR, International Convention Centre, Sydney, Australia, 06–11 August 2017, vol. 70, pp. 2363–2372. http://proceedings.mlr.press/v70/mcgill17a.html
18. Menze, B.H., Kelm, B.M., Splitthoff, D.N., Koethe, U., Hamprecht, F.A.: On oblique random forests. In: Gunopulos, D., Hofmann, T., Malerba, D., Vazirgiannis, M. (eds.) ECML PKDD 2011. LNCS (LNAI), vol. 6912, pp. 453–469. Springer, Heidelberg (2011). https://doi.org/10.1007/978-3-642-23783-6_29
19. Montillo, A., et al.: Entanglement and differentiable information gain maximization. In: Criminisi, A., Shotton, J. (eds.) Decision Forests for Computer Vision and Medical Image Analysis. ACVPR, pp. 273–293. Springer, London (2013). https://doi.org/10.1007/978-1-4471-4929-3_19
20. Murthy, K.V.S.: On growing better decision trees from data. Ph.D. thesis, The Johns Hopkins University (1996)
21. Norouzi, M., Collins, M.D., Fleet, D.J., Kohli, P.: Co2 forest: improved random forest by continuous optimization of oblique splits. arXiv:1506.06155 (2015)
22. Norouzi, M., Collins, M.D., Johnson, M., Fleet, D.J., Kohli, P.: Efficient non-greedy optimization of decision trees. In: NIPS, December 2015
23. PyTorch: http://www.pytorch.org/
24. Quinlan, J.R.: Induction of decision trees. In: Shavlik, J.W., Dietterich, T.G. (eds.) Readings in Machine Learning. Morgan Kaufmann, Los Altos (1990). Originally published in Mach. Learn. 1, 81–106 (1986)
25. Quinlan, J.R.: C4.5: Programs for Machine Learning. Morgan Kaufmann Publishers Inc., San Francisco (1993)
26. Richmond, D., Kainmueller, D., Yang, M., Myers, E., Rother, C.: Mapping autocontext decision forests to deep convnets for semantic segmentation. In: Wilson, R.C., Hancock, E.R., Smith, W.A.P. (eds.) Proceedings of the British Machine Vision Conference (BMVC), pp. 144.1–144.12. BMVA Press, September 2016. https://doi.org/10.5244/C.30.144
27. Rose, K., Gurewitz, E., Fox, G.C.: Statistical mechanics and phase transitions in clustering. Phys. Rev. Lett. 65, 945–948 (1990). https://doi.org/10.1103/PhysRevLett.65.945

28. Rota Bulo, S., Kontschieder, P.: Neural decision forests for semantic image labelling. In: The IEEE Conference on Computer Vision and Pattern Recognition (CVPR), June 2014

29. Sethi, I.K.: Entropy nets: from decision trees to neural networks. Proc. IEEE **78**(10), 1605–1613 (1990)

30. Suárez, A., Lutsko, J.F.: Globally optimal fuzzy decision trees for classification and regression. IEEE Trans. Pattern Anal. Mach. Intell. **21**(12), 1297–1311 (1999)

31. Welbl, J.: Casting random forests as artificial neural networks (and profiting from it). In: Jiang, X., Hornegger, J., Koch, R. (eds.) GCPR 2014. LNCS, vol. 8753, pp. 765–771. Springer, Cham (2014). https://doi.org/10.1007/978-3-319-11752-2_66

32. Xiao, H., Rasul, K., Vollgraf, R.: Fashion-MNIST: a novel image dataset for benchmarking machine learning algorithms. arXiv:1708.07747 (2017)

Taming the Cross Entropy Loss

Manuel Martinez[(✉)] and Rainer Stiefelhagen

Karlsruhe Institute of Technology, Karlsruhe, Germany
{manuel.martinez,rainer.stiefelhagen}@kit.edu

Abstract. We present the Tamed Cross Entropy (TCE) loss function, a robust derivative of the standard Cross Entropy (CE) loss used in deep learning for classification tasks. However, unlike other robust losses, the TCE loss is designed to exhibit the same training properties than the CE loss in noiseless scenarios. Therefore, the TCE loss requires no modification on the training regime compared to the CE loss and, in consequence, can be applied in all applications where the CE loss is currently used. We evaluate the TCE loss using the ResNet architecture on four image datasets that we artificially contaminated with various levels of label noise. The TCE loss outperforms the CE loss in every tested scenario.

1 Introduction

The most common way to train Convolutional Neural Networks (CNNs) for classification problems is to use stochastic gradient descent coupled with the Cross Entropy (CE) loss. The CE loss is popular mainly due to its excellent convergence speeds, alongside its excellent performance in terms of Top-1 and Top-5 classification accuracy.

However, the CE loss is not without weaknesses. Theoretically, the CE is proven to be a calibrated loss [20], and thus should provide well-behaved probability estimates, however, in reality a different behavior is observed: the calibration of a classifier using the CE loss worsens as the classification accuracy improves [7]. As a consequence, many techniques have been proposed to improve calibration (*e.g.*, Bayesian Neural Networks [1]).

A related problem of the CE loss is its suboptimal performance when dealing with noisy data [5]. Although complex CNNs architectures have shown considerable robustness to noise in the training dataset [3,17,18], noisy labels and outliers are still a significant problem, particularly when dealing with weak labels. As a consequence, the problem of dealing with label noise when learning has been studied extensively [4].

In particular, there are loss functions for classification tasks that are more robust or have more discriminative power than the CE. For example, the pairwise loss [8] and the triplet loss [19] are effective ways to learn discriminative features between individual classes. Also, the OLE loss [15] explicitly maximizes intra-class similarity and inter-class margin, and thus, improves its discriminative power with respect to the CE. However, such losses are either slower or significantly more complex to apply than the CE.

© Springer Nature Switzerland AG 2019
T. Brox et al. (Eds.): GCPR 2018, LNCS 11269, pp. 628–637, 2019.
https://doi.org/10.1007/978-3-030-12939-2_43

Ghosh *et al.* [5] used a risk minimization framework to analyze the CE loss, the Mean Absolute Error (MAE) loss, and the Mean Squared Error (MSE) loss, for classification tasks under artificially added label noise. Their results show that the MAE is inherently robust to noise, while the CE is particularly vulnerable to label noise, and the MSE should perform better than the CE but worse than the MAE. Sadly, being an ℓ_1 loss, the MAE has abysmal convergence properties and is not well suited for practical use.

We aim to offer a more convenient alternative to the currently available losses for robust classification. We follow the same spirit than Huber *et al.* [10] and Girshick *et al.* [6], who independently hand crafted a robust regression loss by fusing the MSE loss and the MAE loss together, and thus obtained a loss with the convergence properties of the MSE, and the robustness to noise of the MAE.

Our result is the Tamed Cross Entropy (TCE) loss, which is derived from the CE and thus it shares the same convergence properties, while, at the same time, its more robust to noise. Instead of fusing two losses, we started from the CE and designed guidelines on how the gradient of our tentative TCE should behave in order to behave like the CE and be robust to outliers.

Finally, to design the actual TCE, we used a power normalization over the CE gradient to make it compatible with our previously designed guidelines. We choose this kind of regularization because power normalizations have already been used with great success to robustify features [12].

The gradient of the TCE is identical to the gradient of the CE if the predicted confidence with respect to the actual label is high, and tends to zero if the predicted confidence of with respect to the actual label is low. This way, training samples that produce low confidence values (ideally outliers or mislabeled data), generate a reduced feedback response.

To ensure that the TCE can be used as a drop-in replacement for the CE, we used the reference implementation for the ResNet [9] architecture and we replaced the CE with the TCE without altering any configuration parameters. We also tested the performance of the TCE against the CE, the MSE, and the MAE losses in the same scenario, and we also evaluated the robustness of the loss functions against uniformly distributed label noise.

In all tested cases, our TCE outperformed the CE while having almost the same convergence speed. Furthermore, with 80% of random labels, the TCE offers Top-1 accuracy improvements of 9.36%, 9.80%, and 4.94% in CIFAR10+, CIFAR100+, and VSHN respectively.

2   Taming the Negative Log Likelihood Loss

2.1   Background

The cross entropy loss is commonly used after a softmax layer that normalizes the output of the network, and is defined as:

$$\text{Softmax}(\mathbf{o}) = \frac{e^{\mathbf{o}}}{\sum_{j=1}^{N} e^{\mathbf{o}_j}}, \tag{1}$$

whereas the cross entropy between two N sized discrete distributions $\mathbf{p} \in [0,1]^N$ and $\mathbf{q} \in (0,1]^N$ is:

$$H(\mathbf{p}, \mathbf{q}) = -\sum_{i=1}^{N} \mathbf{p}_i \log \mathbf{q}_i, \qquad (2)$$

where $\mathbf{p}$ corresponds to the classification target, and $\mathbf{q}$ the output of the softmax layer, *i.e.*, the likelihood predicted per class.

Is it important to note that the actual value of the loss function does not affect in any way the training procedure, as only its gradient is used during back propagation. We analyze the gradient of the cross entropy loss with respect to the log-likelihood, which is a commonly used trick. Using $\mathbf{p} \in \{0,1\}^N$, the partial derivatives of the CE loss with respect to the predicted log-likelihoods are:

$$\frac{\partial H(\mathbf{p}, \mathbf{q})}{\partial \log \mathbf{q}_i} = \begin{cases} 0 & \text{if } \mathbf{p}_i = 0, \\ -1 & \text{if } \mathbf{p}_i = 1. \end{cases} \qquad (3)$$

2.2   Design Goals

We define the following set of design goals in order to guide us in the design process towards a robust classification goal:

1. We want the gradient of the TCE loss ($\hat{H}$) to be proportional to the gradient of the CE loss. This way we expect that both losses will behave in a similar way. We aim to:

$$\nabla \hat{H}(\mathbf{p}, \mathbf{q}) \propto \nabla H(\mathbf{p}, \mathbf{q}). \qquad (4)$$

2. If the network is confident about the predicted class, *i.e.*, $\mathbf{q}_i \to 1$, we want the TCE to behave exactly like the CE.

$$\nabla \hat{H}(\mathbf{p}, \mathbf{q}) = -1 \quad \text{if } p_i = 1 \text{ and } q_i \to 1. \qquad (5)$$

3. We aim to reduce the impact of outliers by reducing the feedback from the gradient when there is a large discrepancy between a prediction and its associated label:

$$\nabla \hat{H}(\mathbf{p}, \mathbf{q}) = 0 \quad \text{if } p_i = 1 \text{ and } q_i \to 0. \qquad (6)$$

To summarize, we aim to design a function whose gradient behaves in the following way:

$$\frac{\partial \hat{H}(\mathbf{p}, \mathbf{q})}{\partial \log \mathbf{q}_i} \approx \begin{cases} 0 & \text{if } \mathbf{p}_i = 0, \\ -1 & \text{if } \mathbf{p}_i = 1 \text{ and } \mathbf{q}_i \to 1, \\ 0 & \text{if } \mathbf{p}_i = 1 \text{ and } \mathbf{q}_i \to 0. \end{cases} \qquad (7)$$

2.3   The Gradient of the Tamed Cross Entropy Loss

We suggest the following gradient that fulfills the requirements expressed in Eq. 7:

$$\frac{\partial \hat{H}_\alpha(\mathbf{p}, \mathbf{q})}{\partial \log \mathbf{q}_i} = \begin{cases} 0 & \text{if } \mathbf{p}_i = 0, \\ -(1 - \log \mathbf{q}_i)^{-\alpha} & \text{if } \mathbf{p}_i = 1. \end{cases} \tag{8}$$

We based our regularization on the domain $[1, \infty)$ of the power function, which we applied to the $\log \mathbf{p}_i$ term. And we control the regularization factor using the parameter $\alpha \in \mathbb{R}^+$.

The loss function that corresponds with the gradient presented in Eq. 8 is:

$$\hat{H}_\alpha(\mathbf{p}, \mathbf{q}) = \frac{1}{1 - \alpha} \sum_{i=1}^{N} \mathbf{p}_i \left((1 - \log \mathbf{q}_i)^{1-\alpha} - \frac{1}{1 - \alpha} \right). \tag{9}$$

We can observe the behavior of both $\hat{H}_\alpha$ and $\nabla \hat{H}_\alpha$ in Fig. 1. Also, note that $\hat{H}_\alpha$ corresponds to H, when α equals 0.

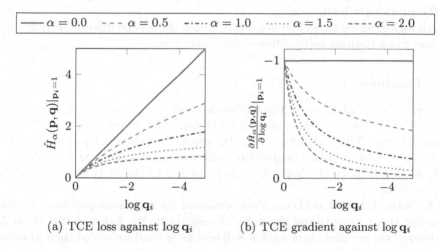

(a) TCE loss against $\log \mathbf{q}_i$ (b) TCE gradient against $\log \mathbf{q}_i$

Fig. 1. The CE (case $\alpha = 0.0$) has a constant gradient when plotted against $\log \mathbf{q}_i$, thus its response is independent of the confidence estimate of the prediction. On the other hand, TCE's gradient gets smaller as the confidence estimate of the prediction decreases.

3   Experiments

3.1   Experimental Setup

We evaluate the TCE against the CE loss and other baselines on four datasets: MNIST [14], CIFAR10 [13], CIFAR100 [13], and VSHN [16]. All datasets are well known, and consist of 32×32 pixel images. MNIST, CIFAR10, and VSHN contain 10 classes each, while CIFAR100 contains 100 different classes.

Our training setup is based on the reference implementation for the ResNet [9], implemented in Torch [2]. We train the same architecture (ResNet-20) for all datasets, and we use the default training strategy, which is optimized for the CE loss we aim to replace. For CIFAR10 and CIFAR100 we apply common data augmentation schemes (shifting and mirroring), thus we decorate both datasets with a "+" mark on the evaluation. On MNIST and VSHN we apply only shifting, as they depict numbers. We normalize the data using the channel means and standard deviation. We use an initial learning rate of 0.1, a Nesterov momentum of 0.9, batch size of 128, and weight decay of $1e-4$. We train for 256 epochs, and we divide the learning rate by 10 at epoch 128, and again at epoch 192.

We hold out 5000 images from the training set of each dataset and we use them as a validation set. Such validation set is used only to determine at which epoch the lowest validation error is obtained. Then, we run 5 times each experiment (using the entire training data) and we report the mean and the standard deviation (when significant) of the test error captured at the epoch determined by the previous validation step.

All losses can be computed efficiently, hence there is no discernible difference in time when training using different loss functions.

3.2   Baselines

We compare our TCE loss to the CE loss we aim to replace, as well as the MSE and the MAE losses, both suggested by Ghosh *et al.* [5] as robust alternatives to the CE loss. The Huber loss [10], also known as SmoothL1 loss [6], is a well known loss used in robust regression, however there is no need to evaluate it as it is equivalent to the MSE loss when applied to the $[0,1]$ domain used for classification.

As both MSE and MAE are losses designed for regression problems, we had to adapt them prior to use them for classification. We followed the Torch [2] guidelines: we prefixed them with a Softmax later, and we scaled their gradient by the number of classes in the output.

3.3   Top-1 Accuracy Under Uniform Label Noise

A common experiment to evaluate robustness in deep learning is to perform an experiment where we apply uniformly distributed random labels to a portion of the training dataset [3,5,11,18]. In this setup, the noise ratio (η) determines the proportion of the training dataset corrupted with random labels, and we evaluated our losses on the four datasets using $\eta \in \{0.0, 0.2, 0.4, 0.6, 0.8\}$.

We group the full results of this experiment on the challenging CIFAR100+ dataset in Table 1. We group the results on the 10-class datasets in the Table 2, where we only show the results for $\eta \in \{0.0, 0.4, 0.8\}$ for space reasons.

Table 1. Evaluation of our TCE loss against alternatives using a ResNet-20 on CIFAR100+. We used the reference ResNet implementation and default parameters except for the loss function. A proportion of the training dataset (η) had its labels replaced randomly. CIFAR100+ is a complex dataset with 100 classes, and thus we can observe how neither MSE nor TCE with $\alpha = 2$ converge when $\eta = 0.8$. Less extreme values of α are able to converge just as well as the CE loss while outperforming it. The MAE loss, as expected, failed to converge under the default training parameters.

Noise (η)	CIFAR100+				
	0.0	0.2	0.4	0.6	0.8
CE	68.18	61.16	54.52	44.08	20.30
MSE	67.78	62.81	55.98	42.48	15.41
MAE	1.00	1.00	1.00	1.00	1.00
TCE $\alpha = 0.5$	68.25	63.58	57.88	48.10	25.13
TCE $\alpha = 1.0$	68.33	64.11	59.90	51.59	29.58
TCE $\alpha = 1.5$	**68.45**	**65.10**	61.07	**53.76**	**30.10**
TCE $\alpha = 2.0$	66.81	64.37	**61.51**	52.09	18.75

Top-1 Accuracy (%)

Table 2. Evaluation of our TCE loss against alternatives using a ResNet-20 on MNIST, CIFAR10+, and VSHN. We used the reference ResNet implementation and default parameters except for the loss function. A proportion of the training dataset (η) had its labels replaced randomly. Our TCE loss offers generally better performance than the CE and the MSE losses, in particular when the training labels are noisy. The MNIST dataset is not challenging anymore, and even when training with 80% of noisy labels the default configuration offers excellent performance.

Noise (η)	MNIST			CIFAR10+			VSHN		
	0.0	0.4	0.8	0.0	0.4	0.8	0.0	0.4	0.8
CE	99.69	99.25	97.77	92.10	83.73	63.59	96.57	93.77	85.50
MSE	99.73	99.22	98.01	**92.15**	84.90	63.30	96.95	94.21	85.31
MAE	-	-	10.28	10.00	10.00	10.00	-	-	-
TCE $\alpha = 0.5$	**99.77**	99.30	98.02	92.13	85.19	63.86	96.76	93.94	85.46
TCE $\alpha = 1.0$	99.74	99.33	98.09	91.99	87.12	63.14	97.06	94.56	86.35
TCE $\alpha = 1.5$	99.72	99.46	98.17	91.79	87.99	65.62	97.04	95.51	87.30
TCE $\alpha = 2.0$	99.74	**99.59**	**98.76**	91.82	**88.40**	**72.95**	**97.09**	**96.15**	**90.44**

Top-1 Accuracy (%)

We observe that, when using default training regimes, the MAE norm fails to converge, something expected from a pure ℓ_1 norm loss. Although in [5] it is argued that the MSE should be more robust to noise than the CE, the improvement is small and only occurs on low noise factors (*i.e.*, $\eta \leq 0.4$). In general terms, both CE and MSE losses obtain similar performance.

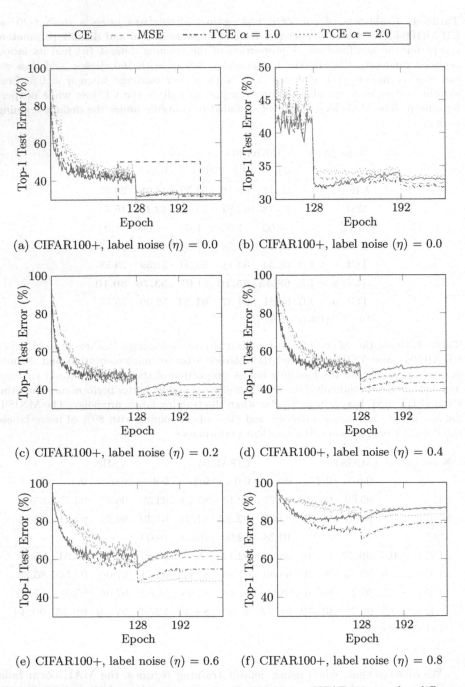

(a) CIFAR100+, label noise $(\eta) = 0.0$ (b) CIFAR100+, label noise $(\eta) = 0.0$

(c) CIFAR100+, label noise $(\eta) = 0.2$ (d) CIFAR100+, label noise $(\eta) = 0.4$

(e) CIFAR100+, label noise $(\eta) = 0.6$ (f) CIFAR100+, label noise $(\eta) = 0.8$

Fig. 2. Test error curves during training ResNet20 on CIFAR100+ under different losses, and different noise ratios. Note that (b) is a detail of (a), where we can observe how the CE loss performance worsens even without label noise. The TCE and MSE losses are more robust to accuracy regressions.

On the other hand, the TCE losses achieve the best Top-1 accuracy in all but one case, where it is second best after MSE. For $\eta = 0.8$, the TCE improves Top-1 accuracy by 9.36% in CIFAR10+, 9.80% in CIFAR100+, and 4.94% in VSHN. Furthermore, the TCE loss shows little sensitivity to its regularization parameter, offering solid performances for $\alpha \in \{0.5, 1.0, 1.5, 2.0\}$.

3.4 Learning Behavior Under Label Noise

In Fig. 2 we show the test set accuracy during training for the CIFAR100+ dataset with different levels of noise.

The first stage of training, with a learning rate of 10^{-1}, correspond to the annealing stage, and it generally shows little overfitting behavior. In this stage, the CE loss converges the fastest, and the TCE with $\alpha = 1$ performs similarly. On the other hand, when using $\alpha = 2$, the convergence ratio of the TCE is similar to that of the MSE loss.

At the epoch 128, we reduce the learning rate to 10^{-2}, and all losses experience a significant drop in the error rate. However, after this drop, the networks start to overfit on the mislabeled images, raising the error rate. Although this effect grows stronger together with the noise (η), it is still present even with $\eta = 0$, as can be seen in Fig. 2b.

3.5 Top-1 Accuracy vs. Convergence Speed

In Fig. 3 we evaluate Top-1 Accuracy against convergence speed. We measure convergence speed by counting how many epochs are necessary for the network

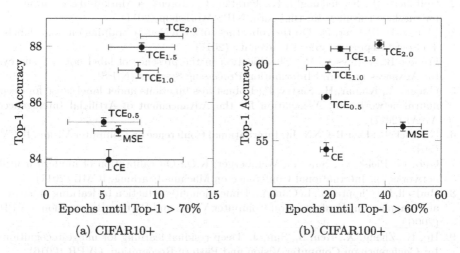

(a) CIFAR10+   (b) CIFAR100+

Fig. 3. We compare accuracy against convergence speed on CIFAR10+ and CIFAR100+ datasets with 40% of random labels. The vertical axis shows the accuracy obtained by each loss. The horizontal axis shows the number of epochs needed to reach the first plateau. Error bars represent standard deviation.

to achieve an accuracy threshold. We observe a large variance when measuring convergence speed in 10-class datasets like CIFAR10+ (see Fig. 3a), thus our analysis will be based only on the CIFAR100+ results (Fig. 3b).

For $\alpha \leq 1$, the TCE loss shows approximately the same convergence speed than the CE loss, but better accuracy. Only for $\alpha > 1$ the TCE keeps growing slower, but never reaches the slow convergence speed of the MSE.

This results seem to indicate that TCE with $\alpha = 1.5$ offers the best trade-off between accuracy and convergence speed.

4   Conclusions

We have proposed a new loss function, named Tamed Cross Entropy (TCE), that behaves like the popular CE loss but is more robust to universal label noise. The TCE loss is friendly to use and can be applied to classification tasks where the CE loss is currently used without altering the training parameters. We found experimentally that the only regularization parameter of the TCE loss has a limited effective range $0 < \alpha < 2$, and changes in α do not have dramatic effects on the performance of the loss. We expect to extend this work in the future by applying the TCE loss to more classification tasks, as well as weakly supervised tasks.

References

1. Cobb, A.D., Roberts, S.J., Gal, Y.: Loss-calibrated approximate inference in Bayesian neural networks. arXiv preprint arXiv:1805.03901 (2018)
2. Collobert, R., Kavukcuoglu, K., Farabet, C.: Torch7: a Matlab-like environment for machine learning. In: BigLearn, NIPS Workshop (2011)
3. Flatow, D., Penner, D.: On the robustness of ConvNets to training on noisy labels. Technical Report. Stanford University (2017)
4. Frénay, B., Verleysen, M.: Classification in the presence of label noise: a survey. In: Advances in Neural Information Processing Systems (NIPS)
5. Ghosh, A., Kumar, H., Sastry, P.: Robust loss functions under label noise for deep neural networks. In: Association for the Advancement of Artificial Intelligence, AAAI (2017)
6. Girshick, R.: Fast R-CNN. In: International Conference on Computer Vision, ICCV (2015)
7. Guo, C., Pleiss, G., Sun, Y., Weinberger, K.Q.: On calibration of modern neural networks. In: International Conference on Machine Learning, ICML (2017)
8. Hadsell, R., Chopra, S., LeCun, Y.: Dimensionality reduction by learning an invariant mapping. In: Conference on Computer Vision and Pattern Recognition, CVPR (2006)
9. He, K., Zhang, X., Ren, S., Sun, J.: Deep residual learning for image recognition. In: Conference on Computer Vision and Pattern Recognition, CVPR (2016)
10. Huber, P.J., et al.: Robust estimation of a location parameter. Ann. Math. Stat. **35**, 73–101 (1964)
11. Jindal, I., Nokleby, M., Chen, X.: Learning deep networks from noisy labels with dropout regularization. In: International Conference Data Mining, ICDM (2016)

12. Koniusz, P., Yan, F., Mikolajczyk, K.: Comparison of mid-level feature coding approaches and pooling strategies in visual concept detection. Comput. Vis. Image Underst. (CVIU) **117**, 479–492 (2013)
13. Krizhevsky, A., Hinton, G.: Learning multiple layers of features from tiny images. Technical report (2009)
14. LeCun, Y., Bottou, L., Bengio, Y., Haffner, P.: Gradient-based learning applied to document recognition. Proc. IEEE **86**(11), 2278–2324 (1998)
15. Lezama, J., Qiu, Q., Musé, P., Sapiro, G.: OLE: orthogonal low-rank embedding, a plug and play geometric loss for deep learning. In: Conference on Computer Vision and Pattern Recognition, CVPR (2018)
16. Netzer, Y., Wang, T., Coates, A., Bissacco, A., Wu, B., Ng, A.Y.: Reading digits in natural images with unsupervised feature learning. In: NIPS Workshop on Deep Learning and Unsupervised Feature Learning (2011)
17. Prakash, A., Moran, N., Garber, S., DiLillo, A., Storer, J.: Protecting JPEG images against adversarial attacks. In: Data Compression Conference, DCC (2018)
18. Rolnick, D., Veit, A., Belongie, S., Shavit, N.: Deep learning is robust to massive label noise. arXiv preprint arXiv:1705.10694 (2017)
19. Schroff, F., Kalenichenko, D., Philbin, J.: FaceNet: a unified embedding for face recognition and clustering. In: Conference on Computer Vision and Pattern Recognition, CVPR (2015)
20. Tewari, A., Bartlett, P.L.: On the consistency of multiclass classification methods. J. Mach. Learn. Res. **8**, 1007–1025 (2007)

Supervised Deep Kriging for Single-Image Super-Resolution

Gianni Franchi[1(✉)], Angela Yao[2], and Andreas Kolb[1]

[1] Institute for Vision and Graphics, University of Siegen, Siegen, Germany
{gianni.franchi,andreas.kolb}@uni-siegen.de
[2] University of Bonn, Bonn, Germany
yao@cs.uni-bonn.de

Abstract. We propose a novel single-image super-resolution approach based on the geostatistical method of kriging. Kriging is a zero-bias minimum-variance estimator that performs spatial interpolation based on a weighted average of known observations. Rather than solving for the kriging weights via the traditional method of inverting covariance matrices, we propose a supervised form in which we learn a deep network to generate said weights. We combine the kriging weight generation and kriging process into a joint network that can be learned end-to-end. Our network achieves competitive super-resolution results as other state-of-the-art methods. In addition, since the super-resolution process follows a known statistical framework, we are able to estimate bias and variance, something which is rarely possible for other deep networks.

1 Introduction

Super-resolution aims to transform low resolution (LR) images into images with high resolution (HR). In computer vision, super-resolution is relevant for applications where high-frequency information and detailing is desirable yet not always captured, *e.g.* medical imaging, satellite imaging, surveillance, etc. Our interest is in single image super-resolution (SISR), a special case where only one LR image is available. SISR is an ill-posed inverse problem with multiple solutions, *i.e.* multiple HR images could lead to the same LR image after applying a low-resolution filter.

SISR been solved with many different approaches. Early approaches relied on spatial relationships present in the image and include nearest neighbours [4], bi-cubic interpolation [13]. Other techniques build upon the assumption that the underlying signal is sparse, *e.g.* compressive sensing [8] and dictionary learning [30]. These early approaches tend to yield HR images which are blurry and or noisy, due mainly to the fact that these methods are crafted heuristically. As a result, they cannot sufficiently recover enough information to yield sharp photo-realistic images.

Electronic supplementary material The online version of this chapter (https://doi.org/10.1007/978-3-030-12939-2_44) contains supplementary material, which is available to authorized users.

ⓒ Springer Nature Switzerland AG 2019
T. Brox et al. (Eds.): GCPR 2018, LNCS 11269, pp. 638–649, 2019.
https://doi.org/10.1007/978-3-030-12939-2_44

Deep learning, and more specifically, convolutional neural networks (CNNs) [16], has afforded significant performance gains in SISR. The newest frameworks [14,15,17,24,25] learn feature representations for super-resolution in a supervised end-to-end manner and are achieving ever-improving performance both in terms of speed and quantitative evaluation. However, despite their impressive results, most deep networks are being used as black boxes to make point estimates. The regressed outputs represent only a mean value and give no indication of model uncertainty. In the case of SISR, this means that we make (possibly very accurate) guesses for the unknown pixels, but we have no idea how good these guesses are. This can be highly problematic for applications such as microscopy or medical imaging, where model confidence is just as important as the actual output.

We would like to leverage the strong learning capabilities of deep networks and embed them within a known statistical framework for which we can derive model uncertainty. As such, we propose *deep kriging* to solve SISR. Kriging [5,20] is a geostatistics method used for spatial interpolation of attributes such as topography and natural resources. It has close relations to Gaussian process (GP) regression, although some sources oversimplify and describe the two as being equivalent. The main difference is that kriging makes stationary and ergodic assumptions on the random field representing the data, while GP regression considers it as a Gaussian process.[1]

Kriging interpolates unknown values by taking a weighted average of known values and results in an unbiased estimator with minimum variance. One can solve for the weights by inverting a covariance matrix computed on the known instances. Kriging makes for a natural extension to the application of SISR, where HR images are interpolated from pixels observed in the LR version of the image. The computational cost of the kriging is cubic with respect to the number of known instances; hence it is preferable to work locally. However, interpolated results are often overly smooth and depend on the choice of the covariance function.

Our contributions can be summarized as follows:

- We propose a novel deep learning-based statistical estimator with SISR results competitive with state-of-the-art.
- We propose a deep kriging approach that solves for kriging weights and performs the kriging in a single network; this allows us to perform a supervised form of spatial interpolation which can be applied not only to SISR, but other geostatistical computations such as field reconstructions.
- Our proposed deep kriging is a hybrid deep learning and statistical framework for which we can derive statistical bias and variance; such measures of model performance and uncertainty are not commonly available for other deep networks, making us the first to model and compute pixel uncertainty in deep SISR approaches.

---

[1] We refer the reader to our supplementary materials for a more detailed comparison of the two.

2   Related Work

Prior to the use of deep learning, SISR approaches applied variants of dictionary learning [7–9,22,30]. Patches were extracted from the low-resolution images and mapped to their corresponding high-resolution version which are then stitched together to increase the image resolution. Other learning-based approaches to increase image resolution include [1,32,33].

State-of-the-art SISR methods are deep-learning-based [14,15,17,24,25]. The VDSR [14] and DRCN [15] approaches showed the benefits of working with image residuals for super-resolution. The DRRN approach [25] generalizes VDSR and concludes that the deeper the network, the better the super-resolved image. We also use a residual network in our approach, but unlike all the other deep SISR methods, we are solving for a set of filter weights to perform the super-resolution with our network rather than directly estimating the HR image itself.

Several unsupervised techniques have also been developed for SISR [18,29], though their performance is usually poorer than supervised approaches. One work of note [10], uses GP regression to perform super-resolution and resembles ours in spirit in that we both model pixel intensities as a random process regressed from neighbouring pixels. However, [10] is unsupervised while our approach learn the weights from supervise examples.

Our proposed approach can be thought of as a form of local filtering [3], and is most similar in spirit to works which combine deep learning and GP regression [6, 28]. However, we differ from these techniques since we do not apply GP regression but a modified version of local kriging. These techniques are similar to us in that they also consider the data to follow a random process. However, we do not explicitly learn the covariance matrix, which offers us more flexibility in the relationships we wish to express. Furthermore, we treat each image as following a random process; the set of training images is then a set of random processes, while the aforementioned works consider all the training data to follow the same process.

3   Deep Kriging

We begin with a short overview on classical kriging in Sect. 3.1 before we introduce our proposed method of supervised kriging in Sect. 3.2 and elaborate on its statistical properties in Sect. 3.3. Finally, we show how the proposed form of deep kriging can be implemented in a deep network in Sect. 3.4.

3.1   Classical Kriging

Consider an image f as a realization of a random field F. This random field is a collection of random variables, *i.e.* $F = \{F_i\}$ where each F_i is a random variable and i is a position index. Unknown values on f at position x^*, $\hat{f}_*{}^2$, can

---

[2] For concise notation, we use $\hat{f}_*$ to denote $\hat{f}(x^*)$, f_i to denote $f(x_i)$ and $w_i^* = w_i(x^*)$.

be interpolated linearly from n known realizations f_i, with normalized weights w_i, i.e.

$$\hat{f}_* = \sum_{i=1}^{n} w_i(x^*)f_i, \quad \text{with} \quad \sum_{i=1}^{n} w_i(x^*) = 1. \tag{1}$$

In classical kriging, all known realizations are used in the interpolation and n is the number of pixels in the image, though local variants have been proposed and studied in [21, 23].

The weights $\{w_i\}$ are found by minimizing the true risk:

$$R(\omega) = \mathbb{E}\left[(F_* - \hat{F}_*)^2\right] = \text{var}\left(F_* - \hat{F}_*\right). \tag{2}$$

We can equate the $\mathbb{E}[\cdot]$ with the $\text{var}(\cdot)$ term in Eq. 2 because the constraint that the weights must sum up to 1 implies that $\mathbb{E}[f_* - \hat{f}_*] = 0$. However, since we do not have access to different realizations of the random field, this variance cannot be solved directly.

To infer the variance from a single event, the theory of geostatistics replaces the classical statistics assumption of having independent and identically distributed (iid) random variables with assumptions of stationarity and ergodicity on the random field. The random field is assumed to be first and second order stationary. This means that $\mathbb{E}_{F^i}(f^i(x))$ does not depend on x and that $\mathbb{E}_{F^i}(f^i(x) \times f^i(x + \tau))$ depends only on τ. In addition, the field is assumed to be second order ergodic, so a covariance or mean estimate in the probability domain is equivalent in the spatial domain. This second assumption implies that an empirical covariance can be estimated and depends only on a distance τ between two realizations, i.e. $\tau = \|x_i - x_j\|$. However, it is difficult to work directly with the empirical covariance, since it can be noisy and also is not guaranteed to form a positive semi-definite matrix. As such, in kriging, we use the true covariance by fitting a parametric model. While different models can be used, the most common one is Gaussian, with covariance C_{ij} between points x_i and x_j defined as $C_{ij} = C_0 \exp\left(-\frac{1}{\sigma^2}\|x_i - x_j\|^2\right)$, where C_0 and σ are parameters of the model.

A Lagrange multiplier (with constant λ) can be used to minimize the risk function with the constraints on the weights w_i, leading to the following cost function:

$$\mathcal{L}(w) = \text{var}\left(F_* - \hat{F}_*\right) + 2\lambda\left(\sum_{i=1}^{n} w_i(x^*) - 1\right), \tag{3}$$

and the associated solution expressed in matrix form as:

$$\begin{pmatrix} C_{11} & \cdots & C_{1n} & 1 \\ \vdots & \ddots & \vdots & \vdots \\ C_{1n} & \cdots & C_{nn} & 1 \\ 1 & \cdots & 1 & 0 \end{pmatrix} \begin{pmatrix} w_1(x^*) \\ \vdots \\ w_n(x^*) \\ -\lambda \end{pmatrix} = \begin{pmatrix} C_{1*} \\ \vdots \\ C_{n*} \\ 1 \end{pmatrix}. \tag{4}$$

The process of kriging then is reduced to solving for the weights w_i. This involves inverting the covariance matrix on the left. Since the matrix is of dimension $(n+1)$, where n is the number of observed pixels in the image (patch), it can be very computationally expensive. Even though one can limit n with local kriging, n needs to be sufficiently large in order to accurately capture and represent the spatial relationships. We aim to bypass the matrix inversion and still maintain sufficient generalization power by using a deep network to directly learn the weights instead.

3.2 Supervised Kriging

Consider E, a subset of the discrete space $\mathbb{Z}^2$, as a representation of the support space of a 2D image. We denote an image as $f \in \mathbb{R}$ and f_i as its value at pixel $x_i \in E$. This assumes we work with greyscale images, which is a standard assumption made in most SISR algorithms [14,15,25].

We assume that we are given a set of n_1 training image pairs $\{(\tilde{f}^i, f^i)\}, i \in [1, n_1]$, where $\tilde{f}^i$ is an up-sampled low resolution version of f^i with the same size. Our objective is to super-resolve the low-resolution images of the test set $\mathcal{N}_{\text{test}} = \{\tilde{f}^i\}_{i=1}^{n_2}$. We further assume that $\tilde{f}^i$ is a realization of a first and second moment stationary random process $\tilde{F}^i$. For convenience we denote $\tilde{F}^i$ the distribution of the random process. In addition f is a realization of a random field F. We denote the training set as $\{\tilde{f}^i, f^i\}_{i=1}^{n_1} \sim \mathcal{M}$, where $\mathcal{M}$ is a joint meta-distribution where each training pair $(\tilde{f}^i, f^i) \sim \tilde{F}^i \times F^i$ follows its own random process.

In classical kriging, the estimated $\hat{f}(x)$ is expressed as a linear combination of all the observed samples $i.e.$ pixels of f. In the case of super-resolution, the observations come from the low-resolution image $\tilde{f}(x)$. Furthermore, we estimate $\hat{f}(x)$ as a linear combination of only local observations of some window radius $\mathcal{K}$, leading to the estimator:

$$\hat{f}_* = \sum_{k \in \{\|x_k - x^*\|_1 \leq \mathcal{K}\}} \omega_k(x^*)\tilde{f}_k \quad \text{with} \quad \sum_{k \in \{\|x_k - x^*\|_1 \leq \mathcal{K}\}} \omega_k(x^*) = 1. \qquad (5)$$

When no confusion is possible we denote $\hat{F}_* = \sum_{k_1=1}^{n} \omega_k(x^*)\tilde{F}_k^i$, with $n = (2\mathcal{K} + 1)^2$. We found that a window of 7×7 provided the best results. To find ω, we want to minimize the true risk as given in Eq. 2, leading to:

$$R(\omega) = \sum_{i=1}^{n_1} \mathbb{E}_{F^i \times \tilde{F}^i} \left[\left(F_*^i - \hat{F}^i \right)^2 \right]. \qquad (6)$$

This risk is a compromise between the geostatistical model and the deep learning model, where the covariance of each field is learned through supervised learning. Furthermore, if we replace the true expectation with the empirical one and the random field with its realization, we arrive at

$$R(\omega) = \sum_{i=1}^{n_1} \sum_{j=1}^{N_i} \left[\left(f_*^i - \sum_{k=1}^{n} \omega_k(x^*)\tilde{f}_k^i \right)^2 \right], \qquad (7)$$

where N_i is the number of pixels in image f^i.

Now, rather than solving for the weights ω by inverting the covariance matrix in Eq. 4, we propose learning this set of weights directly with a CNN. This allow us to capture and model more complex spatial relationships between the data than the classical model with covariances. As such, the estimator becomes $\hat{f}(x, \tilde{f}, g, \theta)$, where $w = g(\tilde{f}, \theta)$, with g and θ representing the CNN network function and its parameters respectively.

3.3 Statistical Properties

We can derive statistical properties for our proposed estimator $\hat{F}$. Given $\{\omega_1, \ldots, \omega_n\}$, the bias can be expressed as

$$\mathrm{bias}(x) = \mathbb{E}_{\tilde{F}|\omega_1,\ldots,\omega_n}\left[\tilde{F}(x) - \hat{F}(x)\right]$$

$$= \mathbb{E}_{\tilde{F}|\omega_1,\ldots,\omega_n}\left[\tilde{F}(x)\right] - \mathbb{E}_{\tilde{F}|\omega_1,\ldots,\omega_n}\left[\hat{F}(x)\right]$$

$$= \mathbb{E}_{\tilde{F}|\omega_1,\ldots,\omega_n}\left[\tilde{F}(x)\right] - \sum_{k_1=1}^{n}\omega_{k_1}(x_j)\mathbb{E}_{\tilde{F}|\omega_1,\ldots,\omega_n}\left[\tilde{F}(x)\right].$$

Since $\sum_{k_1=1}^{n}\omega_{k_1}(x_j) = 1$ and the random field is first-order stationary, we are left with zero bias according to the weights of the neural network, *i.e.* $\mathrm{bias}(x) = 0$. In other words, our network does not add bias to the field $\tilde{F}$. As such, from F to $\tilde{F}$, if the two fields have the same first moment, then no bias added to F^3. This point is critical since in classical statistics a good estimator should have zero bias and minimal variance.

By definition, the variance of our estimator $\hat{F}$ is

$$V_{\tilde{F}}(x) = \mathbb{E}_{\tilde{F}}\left[\hat{F}(x)^2\right] - \left(\mathbb{E}_{\tilde{F}}[\hat{F}(x)]\right)^2. \tag{8}$$

Again, we estimate the covariance given $\{\omega_1, \ldots, \omega_n\}$. Since we assume that $\tilde{F}$ is second-order stationary, the covariance of $\tilde{F}$ depends only on the distance between two points, *i.e.*

$$\mathbb{E}_{\tilde{F}}\left[\tilde{F}(x_k)\tilde{F}(x_{k'})\right] = \tilde{C}(\|x_k - x_{k'}\|_2) - \mu^2. \tag{9}$$

By setting $\mu = \mathbb{E}_{\tilde{F}}[\tilde{F}(x)]$, we arrive at:

$$V_{\tilde{F}|\omega_1,\ldots,\omega_n}(x) = \sum_{(k,k')\in[1,(2\times\mathcal{K}+1)^2]^2}\omega_k(x)\omega_{k'}(x)\tilde{C}(\|x_k - x_{k'}\|_2) \tag{10}$$

where the covariance $\tilde{C}(\cdot)$ is estimated from the low resolution image $\tilde{f}$. The variance depends on the position x. Note, however, since we directly estimate the weights $\omega(x^*)$ without making assumptions on the covariance function, we cannot compute the variance and an approximation is needed to estimate the covariance empirically from $\tilde{f}$. Equation 10 however is particularly interesting since it shows that the estimator variance at x is directly proportional to the variance of $\tilde{f}$ and the different values of ω near x. The bigger these values are, the more uncertain the estimator is.

---

[3] Of course, we cannot account for the low resolution process that produced $\tilde{F}$.

3.4   Network Implementation and Training

So far, the theory which we have presented on supervised kriging is generic and does not indicate how one should minimize the risk in Eq. 7 to solve for the kriging weights. We solve for the weights with a CNN network which we show in Fig. 1. The weight estimation branch is composed of a residual network of 9 residual units; the residual unit itself has 2 convolutional layers, each preceded by a batch normalization [12] and a ReLU.

This branch follows a similar architecture as [14,25], with the difference that they apply this architecture to directly estimate the HR image, while we use it to estimate our kriging weights, *i.e.* as a local dynamic filter [3]. In addition, contrary to [25] our network is not recurrent.

The network learns a total of 20 convolution layers to determine the kriging weights. The first 19 are of depth 128, the last prediction layer has depth $(2 \times \mathcal{K}+1)^2$ and outputs the kriging weight vector $\omega(x) = [\omega_1(x), \ldots, \omega_{(2 \times \mathcal{K}+1)^2}(x)]$. The weights are applied to the repeated input image via a point-wise multiplication and summation along the depth dimension to yield the HR output. Overall, the network with $\mathcal{K} = 3$ is very lightweight, inference on a 320×480 sized image takes only 0.10 s with a titan X.

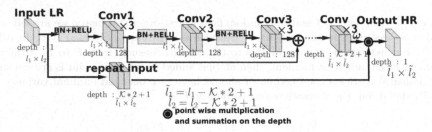

Fig. 1. Overview of the network structure. The input image goes through two branches. The first one calculates the weights ω; the second copies the input image for an efficient application of the weights via point-wise multiplication.

Note our network is actually learning how to estimate the kriging weights ω, *i.e.* as a local dynamic filter. To derive this dynamic filter end-to-end, we adapt the following formulation of the Eq. 5 in convolution terms:

$$\tilde{f}_i(x^*) = \sum_{k \in \{\|x_k - x^*\|_1 \leq \mathcal{K}\}} \omega_k(x^*) \left(\tilde{f}_i * h_k \right)(x_k) \quad \text{with} \quad \sum_{k \in \{\|x_k - x^*\|_1 \leq \mathcal{K}\}} \omega_k(x^*) = 1 \tag{11}$$

with $h_k(x) = \delta(x - x_k)$ or the Dirac function. The h_k filter is denoted by *"repeat input"* in Fig. 1, since applying the Dirac functions in each position x^* is a way to extract the pixel neighbourhood at position x^*. After having determined the weights, we normalize them so that they sum up to 1, as given by the constraint in Eq. 11. We point-wise multiply the normalized weights to the output of the repeat filter; to arrive at the super-resolved image, we simply sum along the depth.

We implement our network in Tensorflow, minimizing the loss in Eq. 7 with the Adam optimizer, a batch size of 8 and a learning rate of 10^{-4}. We apply gradient clipping and dropout between the last ReLU and the convolution layer that predicts

ω, with a dropout rate of 0.3. The effective depth of our network is $d = 2 + 2 \times U$, with U the number of times the residual units are applied. In our case, we use $U = 9$.

4 Experiments

4.1 Datasets, Pre-processing and Evaluation

For training, we follow [14,25] and use the 291 images combined from [31] and the Berkeley Segmentation datasets [19]. We further augment the data by rotating ($90°$, $180°$ and $270°$) and scaling the data ($\times 2$, $\times 3$, $\times 4$). We limit to these fixed grades of rotation and scaling to follow the same protocol as [25]. Like [14,25], we work with patches of size 31×31, sampled from the augmented dataset with a stride of 21. Testing is then performed on the four commonly used benchmarks: *Set 5* [2], *Set 14* [15], *B100* [19] and *Urban 100* [11]. To be consistent with [14,25], we convert the RGB images to YCbCr and only resolved the Y component. This is then combined with an upsampled Cb and Cr component and converted back into RGB. Up-sampling is done via bi-cubic interpolation.

We evaluate the resulting super-resolved images quantitatively with the peak signal-to-noise ratio (PSNR): $\mathrm{PSNR}(\tilde{f}, f_{\mathrm{ref}}) = \log_{10}\left(\frac{255^2}{\sum_{i=1}^{N}(\tilde{f}(x_i) - f_{\mathrm{ref}}(x_i))^2}\right)$, where f_{ref} and $\tilde{f}$ are the ground truth and the super-resolved images respectively and N refers to the number of pixels in the (high-resolution) image. A higher PSNR corresponds to better results. We also evaluate using Structural Similarity (SSIM) [27], which measures the similarity between two images. The closer the SSIM value is to 1, the more similar the super-resolved image to the ground truth high resolution image.

4.2 Comparison to State-of-the-Art

We compare our PSNR and SSIM measures for the different scales against state-of-the-art in Table 1. The first two methods, bi-cubic and local kriging are unsupervised, while all others are supervised approaches. We use the Matlab implementation of bicubic interpolation.

For the local kriging, we use a neighbourhood of 90×90 and a stride of 81. At this sparse setting, unsupervised kriging does very well in comparison to bicubic interpolation. However, it is already extremely slow, since for each patch, we need to compute the empirical covariance, true covariance, and then invert the covariance matrix. In total, it takes approximately 1 min for an image of size 320×480. In comparison, our proposed deep kriging, on the same image, applied densely is one magnitude faster, and takes only 0.25 s with a titan x.

Looking at our approach (reported in the second last column in Table 1) with respect to the supervised methods, our performance is comparable to the DRRN [25] B1U9 setting, DRCN [15] and VSDR [14]; all three have networks with depth similar to ours. The best results are reported by the DRRN B1U25 [25], which has 50 convolution layers and is more than twice as deep as our network.

Given the trend of the community to work on deep learning-based approaches for super-resolution, as well as the fact that no labelled data is required for training, one can work with (infinitely) large datasets [17,26]. For fair comparison with state-of-the-art, however, we omit from this table the techniques which do not use the fixed 291 image training set as per the training protocol set by [14,25].

4.3 Model Uncertainty

One of the key strengths of our technique is the fact that we can estimate model uncertainty. We show in Fig. 2 the estimated variance for each pixel based on Eq. 10. To evaluate this equation, we need to apply covariance models for f and $\tilde{f}$. We do this by first estimating the empirical covariance $c(\tau) = \sum_i f(x_i)f(x_i + \tau) - \mu$ and then solving for C_0 and σ of the Gaussian model in Sect. 3.1 that is the closest to the empirical covariance.

The main advantage of our model of uncertainty is that we can have information on the black box CNN. It gives us feedback about the reliability of results provided by an unknown image. One can see in Fig. 2 our uncertainty estimate. The estimated variance has a higher value than the real PSNR this is due to the fact that we have a noisy estimation of the PSNR from a low resolution image. Holistically, however, the are similar, in that areas with high variance corresponds to high PSNR. Quantitatively, we find for Set 5 that 91.9% of the super-resolved pixel values fall within 3 standard deviations based on the estimated variance. In addition, we evaluate the similarity between the images resulting from the PSNR and the one resulting from the variance in set 5. We use the correlation to measure the similarity and find that these images have high correlation up to 0.8.

Input Image Bicubic local kriging DRRN   ours   variance RMSE real
                                      B1U9   estimate

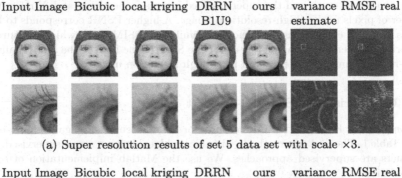

(a) Super resolution results of set 5 data set with scale ×3.

Input Image Bicubic local kriging DRRN   ours   variance RMSE real
                                      B1U9   estimate

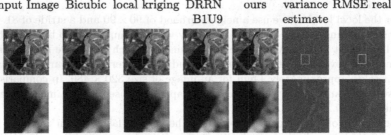

(b) Super resolution results of set 5 data set with scale ×3.

Fig. 2. Super resolution results

Table 1. Results of various super resolution techniques. The column 3rd and 4th are unsupervised. The other columns are trained on the 291 data set [19,31]. The Urban 100 set having no images at scale 3 we did not evaluate it.

Dataset	Scale	Bicubic PSNR/SSIM	local kringing PSNR/SSIM	SRCNN PSNR/SSIM	VDSR PSNR/SSIM	DRCN PSNR/SSIM	DRRN B1U9 PSNR/SSIM	DRRN B1U25 PSNR/SSIM	ours PSNR/SSIM
Set 5	×2	33.66/0.930	35.68/0.923	36.66/0.953	37.53/0.959	37.63/0.959	37.66/0.959	37.74/0.959	37.65/0.960
	×3	30.39/0.868	31.72/0.864	32.75/0.909	33.66/0.921	33.82/0.923	33.93/0.923	34.04/0.924	33.94/0.923
	×4	28.42/0.810	29.83/0.814	30.48/0.862	31.35/0.883	31.53/0.885	31.58/0.886	31.68/0.889	31.56/0.886
Set 14	×2	30.24/0.869	31.26/0.874	32.45/0.907	33.03/0.912	33.04/0.912	33.19/0.913	33.23/0.914	33.10/0.912
	×3	27.55/0.774	27.94/0.781	29.30/0.822	29.77/0.831	29.76/0.831	29.94/0.831	29.96/0.834	29.81/0.831
	×4	26.00/0.703	26.43/0.715	27.50/0.751	28.01/0.767	28.02/0.767	28.02/0.767	28.18/0.770	28.08/0.771
B 100	×2	29.56/0.843	31.06/0.848	31.36/0.888	31.90/0.8960	31.85/0.894	32.01/0.897	32.05/0.897	32.01/0.896
	×3	27.21/0.8431	27.86/0.7357	31.36/0.8879	28.82/0.7976	28.80/0.7963	28.91/0.7992	28.95/0.800	28.82/0.800
	×4	25.96/0.668	26.55/0.665	26.90/0.711	27.29/0.725	27.23/0.723	27.35/0.726	27.38/0.728	27.36/0.727
Urban 100	×2	26.88/0.840	28.32/0.843	29.50/0.895	30.76/0.914	30.75/0.913	31.02/0.916	31.23/0.919	30.95/0.921
	×3	24.46/0.735	25.06/0.715	29.50/0.799	27.14/0.715	27.15/0.828	27.38/0.833	27.53/0.838	
	×4	23.14/0.658	23.70/0.627	24.52/0.722	25.19/0.752	25.14/0.751	25.35/0.757	25.44/0.764	25.10/0.749

5 Conclusions

In this paper, we have proposed a joint deep learning and statistical framework for single image super-resolution based on a form of supervised kriging. We solve for the kriging weights in the manner of a local dynamic filter and apply it directly to the low resolution image, all within a single network that can be learned end-to-end. Since we work within the known statistical framework of kriging, we can estimate model uncertainty, something typically not possible for deep networks. More specifically, we show through derivations that the statistical estimator generated by our network is unbiased and we calculate its variance.

Acknowledgement. This research was funded by the German Research Foundation (DFG) as part of the research training group GRK 1564 Imaging New Modalities.

References

1. Anbarjafari, G., Demirel, H.: Image super resolution based on interpolation of wavelet domain high frequency subbands and the spatial domain input image. ETRI J. **32**(3), 390–394 (2010)
2. Bevilacqua, M., Roumy, A., Guillemot, C., Alberi-Morel, M.: Low-complexity single-image super-resolution based on nonnegative neighbor embedding (2012)
3. De Brabandere, B., Jia, X., Tuytelaars, T., Gool, L.V.: Dynamic filter networks. In: NIPS (2016)
4. Chang, H., Yeung, D., Xiong, Y.: Super-resolution through neighbor embedding. In: CVPR, vol. 1, p. I. IEEE (2004)
5. Cressie, N.: Statistics for Spatial Data. Wiley, Hoboken (2015)
6. Damianou, A., Lawrence, N.: Deep Gaussian processes. In: Artificial Intelligence and Statistics, pp. 207–215 (2013)

7. Dong, W., Zhang, L., Shi, G., Wu, X.: Image deblurring and super-resolution by adaptive sparse domain selection and adaptive regularization. IEEE Trans. Image Process. (TIP) **20**(7), 1838–1857 (2011)
8. Donoho, D.L.: Compressed sensing. IEEE Trans. Inf. Theory **52**(4), 1289–1306 (2006)
9. Freeman, W., Jones, T., Pasztor, E.: Example-based super-resolution. IEEE Comput. Graph. Appl. **22**(2), 56–65 (2002)
10. He, H., Siu, W.C.: Single image super-resolution using Gaussian process regression. In: CVPR (2011)
11. Huang, J., Singh, A., Ahuja, N.: Single image super-resolution from transformed self-exemplars. In: CVPR, pp. 5197–5206 (2015)
12. Ioffe, S., Szegedy, C.: Batch normalization: accelerating deep network training by reducing internal covariate shift. In: International Conference on Machine Learning, pp. 448–456 (2015)
13. Keys, R.: Cubic convolution interpolation for digital image processing. IEEE Trans. Acoust. Speech Signal Process. **29**(6), 1153–1160 (1981)
14. Kim, J., Lee, J.K., Lee, K.M.: Accurate image super-resolution using very deep convolutional networks. In: CVPR (2016)
15. Kim, J., Lee, J.K., Lee, K.M.: Deeply-recursive convolutional network for image super-resolution. In: CVPR (2016)
16. LeCun, Y., Bottou, L., Bengio, Y., Haffner, P.: Gradient-based learning applied to document recognition. Proc. IEEE **86**(11), 2278–2324 (1998)
17. Lim, B., Son, S., Kim, H., Nah, S., Lee, K.M.: Enhanced deep residual networks for single image super-resolution. In: CVPR Workshops (2017)
18. Marquina, A., Osher, S.: Image super-resolution by TV-regularization and Bregman iteration. J. Sci. Comput. **37**(3), 367–382 (2008)
19. Martin, D., Fowlkes, C., Tal, D., Malik, J.: A database of human segmented natural images and its application to evaluating segmentation algorithms and measuring ecological statistics. In: ICCV, vol. 2, pp. 416–423 (2001)
20. Matheron, G.: Random Sets and Integral Geometry. Wiley, Hoboken (1975)
21. Meier, F., Hennig, P., Schaal, S.: Local Gaussian regression. arXiv preprint arXiv:1402.0645 (2014)
22. Peleg, T., Elad, M.: A statistical prediction model based on sparse representations for single image super-resolution. IEEE Trans. Image Process. (TIP) **23**(6), 2569–2582 (2014)
23. Pronzato, L., Rendas, M.J.: Bayesian local kriging. Technometrics **59**, 293–304 (2017)
24. Sajjadi, M.S.M., Scholkopf, B., Hirsch, M.: EnhanceNet: single image super-resolution through automated texture synthesis. In: ICCV, October 2017
25. Tai, Y., Yang, J., Liu, X.: Image super-resolution via deep recursive residual network. In: CVPR, June 2017
26. Tong, T., Li, G., Liu, X., Gao, Q.: Image super-resolution using dense skip connections. In: ICCV, October 2017
27. Wang, Z., Bovik, A., Sheikh, H., Simoncelli, E.: Image quality assessment: from error visibility to structural similarity. IEEE Trans. Image Process. (TIP) **13**(4), 600–612 (2004)
28. Wilson, A.G., Hu, Z., Salakhutdinov, R., Xing, E.P.: Deep kernel learning. In: AISTATS (2016)

29. Xu, L., Jia, J.: Two-phase kernel estimation for robust motion deblurring. In: Daniilidis, K., Maragos, P., Paragios, N. (eds.) ECCV 2010. LNCS, vol. 6311, pp. 157–170. Springer, Heidelberg (2010). https://doi.org/10.1007/978-3-642-15549-9_12

30. Yang, J., Wang, Z., Lin, Z., Cohen, S., Huang, T.: Coupled dictionary training for image super-resolution. IEEE Trans. Image Process. (TIP) **21**(8), 3467–3478 (2012)

31. Yang, J., Wright, J., Huang, T., Ma, Y.: Image super-resolution via sparse representation. IEEE Trans. Image Process. (TIP) **19**(11), 2861–2873 (2010)

32. Zhang, K., Gao, X., Tao, D., Li, X.: Single image super-resolution with non-local means and steering kernel regression. IEEE Trans. Image Process. (TIP) **21**(11), 4544–4556 (2012)

33. Zhao, S., Han, H., Peng, S.: Wavelet-domain HMT-based image super-resolution. In: International Conference on Image Processing (ICIP), vol. 2, pp. II–953. IEEE (2003)

Information-Theoretic Active Learning for Content-Based Image Retrieval

Björn Barz$^{(\boxtimes)}$ (iD), Christoph Käding (iD), and Joachim Denzler (iD)

Friedrich Schiller University Jena, Ernst-Abbe-Platz 2, 07743 Jena, Germany
bjoern.barz@uni-jena.de
http://www.inf-cv.uni-jena.de

Abstract. We propose Information-Theoretic Active Learning (ITAL), a novel batch-mode active learning method for binary classification, and apply it for acquiring meaningful user feedback in the context of content-based image retrieval. Instead of combining different heuristics such as uncertainty, diversity, or density, our method is based on maximizing the mutual information between the predicted relevance of the images and the expected user feedback regarding the selected batch. We propose suitable approximations to this computationally demanding problem and also integrate an explicit model of user behavior that accounts for possible incorrect labels and unnameable instances. Furthermore, our approach does not only take the structure of the data but also the expected model output change caused by the user feedback into account. In contrast to other methods, ITAL turns out to be highly flexible and provides state-of-the-art performance across various datasets, such as MIR-FLICKR and ImageNet.

Keywords: Batch-mode active learning · Image retrieval

1 Introduction

For content-based image retrieval (CBIR) [25,30], just classifying the query image is, in general, not sufficient. Since images encode complex semantic and stylistic information—sometimes more than text can express—a single query is usually insufficient to comprehend the search interest of the user. A common approach to overcome this issue is enabling the user to provide *relevance feedback* by tagging some retrieval results as relevant or irrelevant [4,6,31]. This way, however, the user will only be able to give feedback regarding images about which the retrieval system is already very confident.

The effect of relevance feedback could hence be significantly improved when the user is not asked to provide feedback regarding the currently top-scoring results, but for those instances of the dataset that are most informative for the

Electronic supplementary material The online version of this chapter (https://doi.org/10.1007/978-3-030-12939-2_45) contains supplementary material, which is available to authorized users.

T. Brox et al. (Eds.): GCPR 2018, LNCS 11269, pp. 650–666, 2019.
https://doi.org/10.1007/978-3-030-12939-2_45

Fig. 1. Comparison of candidate batches selected for the second annotation round by ITAL with the selection of TCAL [5] on 4 exemplary queries from the MIRFLICKR [16] dataset. The border colors correspond to different topics that could be associated with the query. Obviously, ITAL explores much more diverse relevant topics than TCAL.

classifier to distinguish between relevant and irrelevant images. Finding such a set of most informative samples is the objective of *batch-mode active learning (BMAL)* [2,12,15,32], which has recently been explored for CBIR [3,5]. However, the performance of existing approaches usually varies substantially between datasets, which is not only observable in our experiments, but also in comparative evaluations in the existing literature (*e.g.*, [15]).

In this work, we propose *Information-Theoretic Active Learning (ITAL)*, a BMAL method for relevance feedback that does not suffer from this instability, but provides state-of-the-art performance across different datasets. This is demonstrated by a comparison of our approach with a variety of competitor methods on 5 image datasets of very different type and structure. Our method for selecting unlabeled samples for annotation by the user (*a*) implicitly maintains both diversity and informativeness of the candidate images, (*b*) employs an explicit model of the user behavior for dealing with the possibility of incorrect annotations and *unnameable instances* [19], *i.e.*, images which the user cannot classify at all, (*c*) takes the model output change caused by the expected user feedback into account, (*d*) can easily be parallelized for processing large datasets, and (*e*) works with as few as a single initial training sample.

The user model allows ITAL to compensate for unreliable users, who are likely to make mistakes or to refuse giving feedback. It acts as an implicit mechanism for controlling the trade-off between redundancy and diversity of the batch of samples selected for annotation. Because care has to be taken not only that all images in the batch of unlabeled samples selected for annotation are *informative* individually, but that they are also *diverse* compared to each other to avoid unnecessary redundant feedback. The majority of existing works on BMAL try to achieve this using a combination of several heuristics to simultaneously maximize the *diversity* within the batch and the *uncertainty* of the selected samples or their *density* in the dataset [2,3,5,12,32,33].

Our proposed ITAL method, in contrast, aims to maximize the mutual information (MI) between the expected user feedback and the relevance model. By taking the joint distribution of the predictive relevance of the samples in the batch into account, the MI criterion implicitly maintains diversity without the need for any heuristics or manually tuned linear combinations of different criteria. Instead, our method does not only take the structure of the data and the current relevance predictions into account, but also considers the expected impact that annotating the selected samples would have on the predicted relevance after updating the model. This integration of the expected model output change (EMOC) has successfully been used for one-sample-at-a-time active learning [9], but, to the best of our knowledge, not been applied to BMAL yet.

However, computing the expected model output change requires relevance models that can be updated efficiently. In addition, both the relevance model and the active learning technique should be capable of working with as few training data as a single positive query example provided by the user. We achieve both by using a Gaussian process (GP) [26] for classification, which can be fitted to a single training sample and can be updated using a closed-form solution without the need for iterative optimization. This is in contrast to many other works on active learning, which are based on logistic regression [14,23] or support vector machines (SVMs) [2,5,12,31] as classification technique. Moreover, SVMs require a fair amount of both positive and negative initial training data for learning a robust hyperplane. Thus, such an approach is not feasible for image retrieval.

Figure 1 illustrates the advantages of our approach: While existing methods often select images similar to the query, but with high uncertainty (*e.g.*, only dogs for a dog query or birds for a bird query), ITAL additionally explores the different meanings of the query image. The query showing a bird in front of the sea could as well refer to images of the sea or to animals at the sea in general. The dog query, on the other hand, could refer to images showing two dogs, images of dogs in general, or images of white animals. Finally, the user providing the beach image as query could be interested in images of the coast, of creatures at the beach, or also just in images of people in action without necessarily being at the beach. All these various options are explored by ITAL, which actively asks the user for the feedback to resolve these ambiguities.

We will briefly review related methods in the following section and explain our ITAL method in detail in Sect. 3. The experiments mentioned above are presented in Sects. 4 and 5 concludes this paper.

2   Related Work

The use of active learning methods is, of course, not limited to information retrieval applications, but also evident in the scenario of manual annotation of large unlabeled datasets: One would prefer spending money and human effort on labeling the most useful samples instead of outliers. Thus, active learning has been extensively studied for several years across various application domains, including binary classification [2,8,9,15,31], multi-class classification [14,17,19, 23,32], and regression [13,20,22].

With regard to batch-mode active learning (BMAL), most existing methods employ some combination of the criteria uncertainty, diversity, and density: Brinker [2] proposes to select samples close to the decision boundary, while enforcing diversity by minimizing the maximum cosine similarity of samples within the batch. Similarly, "Sampling by Uncertainty and Density (SUD)" [33] selects samples maximizing the product of entropy and average cosine similarity to the nearest neighbors and "Ranked Batch-mode Active Learning (RBMAL)" [3] constructs a batch by successively adding samples with high uncertainty and low maximum similarity to any other already selected sample. "Triple Criteria Active Learning (TCAL)" [5], on the other hand, first selects a subset of uncertain samples near the decision boundary, divides them into k clusters, and chooses that sample from each cluster that has the minimum average distance to all other samples in the same cluster. Following a more complex approach, "Uncertainty Sampling with Diversity Maximization (USDM)" [32] finds a trade-off between the individual entropy of the samples in the batch and their diversity by formulating this optimization problem as a quadratic program, whose parameters to be determined are the ranking-scores of the unlabeled samples.

In addition, two works use an information-theoretic approach and are, thus, particularly similar to our method:

Guo and Greiner [14] propose to maximize the mutual information between the selected sample and the remaining unlabeled instances, given the already labeled data. They reduce this objective to the minimization of conditional entropy of the predictive label distribution of the unlabeled samples, given the existing labels and a proxy-label for the selected instance. With regard to the latter, they make an optimistic guess assuming the label which would minimize mutual information. If this guess turns out to be wrong, they fall back to uncertainty sampling for the next iteration.

Though the results obtained by this approach called MCMI[min]+MU are convincing, it is computationally demanding and not scalable to real-world scenarios, even though the authors already employed some assumptions to make it more tractable. In particular, they assume that the conditional entropy of a set of samples can be decomposed as a sum of the entropy of individual samples. However, this assumption ignores relationships between unlabeled samples and is hence not suitable for a batch-mode scenario.

In our work, we employ different approximations and Gaussian processes to enable the use of mutual information for BMAL. Using Gaussian processes instead of logistic regression or SVMs also allows us to take the impact of user feedback on the model output into account, since updating a GP does not involve iterative algorithms.

On the other hand, Li and Guo [23] employ mutual information as a measure for the information density of the unlabeled samples and combine it with the conditional entropy of their individual labels as uncertainty measure. Similar to our approach, they use a GP to estimate the mutual information, but then employ logistic regression for the actual classification. Furthermore, their method cannot be applied to a batch-mode scenario and does not scale to large datasets, so that they need to randomly sub-sample the unlabeled data.

Our ITAL method, in contrast, forms a consistent framework, provides a batch-mode, considers the impact of annotations on the model output, and relies solely on the solid theoretical basis of mutual information to implicitly account for uncertainty, density, and diversity.

3   Information-Theoretic Active Learning

We begin with a very general description of the idea behind our ITAL approach and then describe its individual components in more detail. The implementations of ITAL and the competing methods described in Sect. 4.2 are available as open source at https://github.com/cvjena/ITAL/.

3.1   Idea and Ideal Objective

Let $\mathfrak{U} = \{x_1, \ldots, x_m\}$ be a set of features of unlabeled samples and $\mathfrak{L} = \{(x_{m+1}, y_{m+1}), \ldots, (x_{m+\ell}, y_{m+\ell})\}$ be a set of features of labeled samples $x_i \in \mathbb{R}^d$ and their labels $y_i \in \{-1, 1\}$. The label 1 is assigned to relevant and -1 to irrelevant samples. $\mathfrak{X} = \{x_1, \ldots, x_m, x_{m+1}, \ldots, x_{m+\ell}\}$ denotes the set of all $n = m + \ell$ samples. In the scenario of content-based image retrieval, $\mathfrak{L}$ usually consists initially of the features of a single relevant sample: the query image provided by the user. However, queries consisting of multiple and even negative examples are possible as well.

Intuitively, we want to ask the user for relevance feedback for a batch $u \subseteq \mathfrak{U}$ of $k = |u|$ unlabeled samples, whose feedback we expect to be most helpful for classifying the remaining unlabeled instances, i.e., assessing their relevance to the user. Note that these chosen samples are also often referred to as "queries" in the active learning literature. To avoid confusion caused by this conflicting terminology, we will refer to the query image as "query" and to the unlabeled samples chosen for annotation as "candidates".

Ideally, the most informative batch u of candidates can be found by maximizing the conditional mutual information $\mathfrak{I}(R, F \mid u)$ between the relevance R of both labeled and unlabeled samples, which is a multivariate random variable over the space $\{-1, 1\}^n$ of relevance labels, and the user feedback F, being a multivariate random variable over the space $\{-1, 0, 1\}^n$ of possible feedbacks. A feedback of 0 represents the case that the user has not given any feedback for a certain candidate. This option is a special feature of our approach, which allows the user to omit candidates that cannot be labeled reliably.

Since the size n of the dataset can be huge, this problem is not solvable in practice. We will show later on how it can be approximated to become tractable. But for now, let us consider the ideal optimization objective:

$$u = \operatorname*{argmax}_{\hat{u} \subseteq \mathfrak{U}} \mathfrak{I}(R, F \mid \hat{u}). \tag{1}$$

Writing the mutual information (MI) in terms of entropy reveals the relationship of our approach to uncertainty sampling by maximizing the entropy $H(R \mid u)$ of the candidate batch [23, 32, 33] or minimizing the conditional entropy $H(R \mid F, u)$ [14]:

$$\Im(R, F \mid u) = H(R \mid u) - H(R \mid F, u). \tag{2}$$

In contrast to pure uncertainty maximization, we also take into account how the relevance model is expected to change after having obtained the feedback from the user: To select those samples whose annotation would reduce uncertainty the most, we maximize the difference between the uncertainty $H(R \mid u)$ according to the current relevance model and the uncertainty $H(R \mid F, u)$ after an update of the model with the expected user feedback.

In contrast to existing works [23, 32, 33], we do not assume $H(R \mid u)$ to be equal to the sum of individual entropies of the samples, but use their joint distribution to compute the entropy. Thus, maximizing $H(R \mid u)$ is also a possible novel approach, which will be compared to maximization of MI in the experiments (cf. Sect. 4).

In more detail, the mutual information can be decomposed into the following components (a derivation is provided in the supplemental material):

$$\Im(R, F \mid u) = \sum_{\substack{r \in \{-1,1\}^n \\ f \in \{-1,0,1\}^n}} \left[P(R = r \mid u) \cdot P(F = f \mid R = r, u) \right.$$

$$\left. \cdot \log\left(\frac{P(R = r \mid F = f, u)}{P(R = r \mid u)} \right) \right]. \tag{3}$$

The individual terms can be interpreted as follows:

- $P(R \mid u) = P(R)$ is the probability of a certain relevance configuration according to the current relevance model.
- $P(R \mid F, u)$ is the probability of a certain relevance configuration after updating the relevance model according to the user feedback. Thus, $\frac{P(R \mid F, u)}{P(R \mid u)}$ quantifies the model output change. Compared to other active learning techniques taking model output change into account, e.g., EMOC [9], we do not just consider the change of the predictive mean, but of the joint relevance probability and hence take all parameters of the distributions into account.
- $P(F \mid R, u)$ is the probability of observing a certain feedback, given that the true relevance of the samples is already known. One might assume that the feedback will always be equal to the true relevance. However, users are not perfect and tend to make mistakes or prefer to avoid difficult samples (so-called *unnameable instances* [19]). Thus, this term corresponds to a *user model* predicting the behavior of the user.

In the following Subsects. 3.2 and 3.3, we will first describe our relevance and user model, respectively. Thereafter, we introduce assumptions to approximate Eq. (1) in the Subsects. 3.4 and 3.5, since finding an optimal set of candidates would require exponential computational effort.

3.2 Relevance Model

We fit a probabilistic regression to the training data $\mathcal{L}$, $i.e.$, the query images and the images annotated so far, using a Gaussian process [26, Chap. 2] with an RBF kernel given by the kernel matrix $K \in \mathbb{R}^{n \times n}$ over the entire dataset $\mathfrak{X}$:

$$K_{ij} = \sigma_{\text{var}}^2 \cdot \exp\left(-\frac{\|x_i - x_j\|^2}{2 \cdot \sigma_{\text{ls}}^2} \right) + \sigma_{\text{noise}}^2 \cdot \delta_{ij} , \tag{4}$$

where δ_{ij} is the Kronecker delta function with $\delta_{ij} = 1 \leftrightarrow i = j$ and zero otherwise, and σ_{var}, σ_{ls}, and σ_{noise} are the hyper-parameters of the kernel.

The computation of the kernel matrix can be performed off-line in advance and does hence not contribute to the run-time of our active learning method. However, if time and memory required for computing and storing the kernel are an issue, alternative kernels for efficient large-scale Gaussian process inference [27] can be used.

The prediction of the Gaussian process for any finite set of k samples consists of a multivariate normal distribution $\mathcal{N}(\mu, \Sigma)$ over continuous values $\hat{y} \in \mathbb{R}^k$, where $\mu \in \mathbb{R}^k$ is a vector of predictive means of the samples and $\Sigma \in \mathbb{R}^{k \times k}$ is their predictive joint covariance matrix. Let $p(\hat{y}) = \mathcal{N}(\hat{y} \mid \mu, \Sigma)$ denote the probability density function of such a distribution.

We use this probabilistic label regression for binary classification by considering samples x_i with $\hat{y}_i > 0$ as relevant. The probability of a given relevance configuration $r \in \{-1, 1\}^n$ for the samples in $\mathfrak{X}$ is hence given by

$$P(R = r) = \int_{a_1}^{b_1} \cdots \int_{a_n}^{b_n} p(y_1, \ldots, y_n) \, dy_n \cdots dy_1, \tag{5}$$

with

$$a_i = \begin{cases} 0, & r_i = 1, \\ -\infty, & r_i = -1, \end{cases} \qquad b_i = \begin{cases} \infty, & r_i = 1, \\ 0, & r_i = -1, \end{cases} \tag{6}$$

for $i = 1, \ldots, n$. This is a multivariate normal distribution function, which can be efficiently approximated using numerical methods [11].

The posterior probability $P(R \mid F, u)$ can be obtained in the same way after updating the GP with the expected feedback. For such an update, it is not necessary to re-fit the GP to the extended training data from scratch, which would involve an expensive inversion of the kernel matrix of the training data. Instead, efficient updates of the inverse of the kernel matrix [24] can be performed to obtain updated predictions at a low cost. This is an advantage of our GP-based approach compared with other methods relying on logistic regression ($e.g.$, [14, 23]), which requires expensive iterative optimization for updating the model.

3.3 User Model

We employ a simple, but plausible user model for $P(F \mid R, u)$, which comes along with a slight simplification of the optimization objective in Eq. (1): First of all, we assume that if we already know the true relevance $r = [r_1, \ldots, r_n]^\top$ of all samples, the feedback f_i given by the user for an individual sample x_i is conditionally independent from the feedback provided for the other samples. More formally:

$$P(F = f \mid R = r, u) = \prod_{i=1}^{n} P(F_i = f_i \mid R_i = r_i, u). \qquad (7)$$

Clearly, if a sample x_i has not been included in the candidate batch u, the user cannot give feedback for that sample, i.e., $x_i \notin u \rightarrow f_i = 0$. Furthermore, we assume that the user will, on average, label a fraction p_{label} of the candidate samples. For each labeled sample, the user is assumed to provide an incorrect label with probability p_{mistake}. In summary, this user model can be formalized as follows:

$$P(F_i = f_i \mid R_i = r_i, u) = \begin{cases} 0, & x_i \notin u \wedge f_i \neq 0, \\ 1, & x_i \notin u \wedge f_i = 0, \\ 1 - p_{\text{label}}, & x_i \in u \wedge f_i = 0, \\ p_{\text{label}} \cdot p_{\text{mistake}}, & x_i \in u \wedge f_i \neq r_i, \\ p_{\text{label}} \cdot (1 - p_{\text{mistake}}), & x_i \in u \wedge f_i = r_i. \end{cases} \qquad (8)$$

The fact that $\left(\exists_{i \in \{1,\ldots,n\}} : x_i \notin u \wedge f_i \neq 0 \right) \rightarrow P(F = f \mid R = r, u) = 0$ allows us to adjust the sum in Eq. (3) to run over only 3^k instead of 3^n possible feedback vectors, where $k \ll n$ is the batch size and independent from the size n of the dataset. This is not an approximation, but an advantage of our user model, that decreases the complexity of the problem significantly.

Modeling the user behavior can enable the active learning technique to find a trade-off between learning as fast as possible by asking for feedback for very diverse samples and improving confidence regarding existing knowledge by selecting not extremely diverse, but slightly redundant samples. The latter can be useful for difficult datasets or tasks, where the user is likely to make mistakes or to refuse to give feedback for a significant number of candidates. Nevertheless, the assumption of a perfect user, who labels all samples in the batch and never fails, is an interesting special case since it results in a simplification of the MI term from Eq. (3) and can reduce computation time drastically:

$$(p_{\text{label}} = 1 \wedge p_{\text{mistake}} = 0) \rightarrow$$

$$\mathfrak{I}(R, F \mid u) = \sum_{r \in \{-1,1\}^n} \left[P(R = r \mid u) \cdot \log \left(\frac{P(R = r \mid F = r, u)}{P(R = r \mid u)} \right) \right]. \qquad (9)$$

3.4   Approximation of Mutual Information

Even with the perfect user assumption, evaluating Eq. (9) still involves a summation over 2^n possible relevance configurations, which does not scale to large datasets. To overcome this issue, we employ an approximation based on the assumption, that the probability of observing a certain relevance configuration depends only on the samples in the current candidate batch:

$$P(R = r \mid u = \{x_{i_1}, \dots, x_{i_k}\}) \; = \; P(R_{i_1} = r_{i_1}, \dots, R_{i_k} = r_{i_k}). \qquad (10)$$

This means that we indeed condition $P(R \mid u)$ on the current batch u, though actually $P(R \mid u) = P(R)$ holds for the original problem formulation.

This assumption allows us to restrict the sum in Eq. (3) to 2^k instead of 2^n possible relevance configurations, leading to the approximate mutual information

$$\tilde{\mathfrak{I}}(R, F \mid u) = 2^{n-k} \sum_{\substack{r \in \{-1,1\}^k \\ f \in \{-1,0,1\}^k}} \Bigg[P(R_u = r) \cdot P(F_u = f \mid R_u = r)$$

$$\cdot \log \left(\frac{P(R_u = r \mid F_u = f)}{P(R_u = r)} \right) \Bigg] \qquad (11)$$

with $u = \{x_{i_1}, \dots, x_{i_k}\}$ and, by an abuse of notation, $R_u = [R_{i_1}, \dots, R_{i_k}]^\top$ (analogously for F_u). The number of involved summands now does not depend on the size of the dataset anymore, but only on the number k of candidates chosen at each round for annotation.

On the other hand, this assumption also restricts the estimation of the expected model output change, expressed by the term $P(R_u \mid F_u)/P(R_u)$, to the current batch, which is probably the most severe drawback of this approximation. However, estimating the model output change for the entire dataset would be too expensive and the experiments in Sect. 4.4 show that our approach can still benefit from the expected model output change. Future work might explore the option of taking a tractable subset of context into account additionally.

3.5   Greedy Batch Construction

Although the computational effort required to calculate the approximate MI given in Eq. (11) is independent from the size of the dataset, finding the exact solution to the optimization problem from Eq. (1) would still require computing the MI for all possible 2^m candidate batches $u \subseteq \mathfrak{U}$ of unlabeled samples. Since we do not want to confront the user with an unlimited number of candidates anyway, we set the batch size to a fixed number k, which leaves us with a number of $\binom{m}{k}$ possible candidate batches.

Assessing them all would involve a polynomial number of subsets and is, thus, still too time-consuming in general. On first sight, one might think that this problem can be solved more efficiently using dynamic programming, but this is unfortunately not an option since the MI is not adequately separable.

Thus, we follow a linear-time greedy approach to approximate the optimal batch by successively adding samples to the batch [13], taking their relationship to already selected samples into account: We first select the sample x_{i_1} with maximum $\tilde{\mathfrak{I}}(R, F \mid u = \{x_{i_1}\})$. The second sample x_{i_2} is chosen to maximize MI together with x_{i_1}. This continues until the batch contains k samples.

At each iteration, the unlabeled samples eligible for being added to the current batch can be treated completely independently from each other, allowing for straightforward parallelization.

4 Experiments

We demonstrate the performance of our ITAL approach on five image datasets of varying type and structure, described in Sect. 4.1, and compare it against several existing active learning techniques briefly explained in Sect. 4.2. The quantitative results in Sect. 4.4 show that ITAL is the only method that can provide state-of-the-art performance across all datasets. Qualitative examples are shown in Fig. 1 and failure cases are included in the supplemental material.

4.1 Datasets

All datasets used in our experiments consist of multiple classes and are divided into a training and a test set. We define image retrieval tasks for each dataset as follows: Pick a single random instance from the training set of a certain class as query image and consider all other images belonging to that class as relevant, while instances from other classes are irrelevant. Batch-mode active learning is performed for 10 successive rounds with a batch-size of $k = 4$ candidates per round and retrieval performance is evaluated after each round by means of average precision on the test set. This process is repeated multiple times with different random queries for each class and we report the mean average precision (mAP) over all repetitions.

Note that our goal is not to achieve state-of-the-art performance in terms of classification accuracy, but with respect to the active learning objective, *i.e.*, obtaining better performance after fewer feedback rounds.

The smallest dataset used is the **Butterflies** dataset [18], comprising 1,500 images of 5 different species of butterflies captured over a period of 100 years. We use the CNN features provided by the authors and, following their advice, reduce them to 50 dimensions using PCA. A random stratified subset of 20% of the dataset is used as test set.

Second, we use the **USPS** dataset [10] consisting of 9,300 gray-scale images of handwritten digits, scanned from envelopes by the U.S. Postal Service. The number of images per class is very unevenly distributed. All images have a size of 16×16 pixels and are used without further feature extraction as 256-dimensional feature vectors. We use the canonical training-test split provided with the dataset.

As a more real-word use-case, we perform evaluation on the **13 Natural Scenes** dataset [7] and the **MIRFLICKR-25K** dataset [16]. The former consists of more than 3,400 images from 13 categories of natural scenes such as forests, streets, mountains, coasts, offices, or kitchens. The latter comprises

25,000 images, each assigned to a subset of 14 very general topics such as "clouds", "tree", "people", "portrait" etc. Thus, query images can belong to multiple categories and will be ambiguous. Asking the user the right questions is hence of great importance. There are also "wide-sense annotations" assigning images to categories if they could be related to a small degree. If a candidate image is annotated in this way, we consider it as unnameable during our simulation. For both datasets, we extracted image features from the first fully-connected layer of the VGG-16 convolutional neural network [29], pre-trained for classification on ImageNet, and reduce their dimensionality to 512 using PCA. Experiments in the supplemental material show that the relative performance of the different methods is not very sensitive w.r.t. the dimensionality of the features. 25% of the natural scenes and 20% of the MIRFLICKR dataset are used as test set.

Finally, we derive further challenging image retrieval tasks from the **ImageNet Large Scale Visual Recognition Challenge (ILSVRC)** [28], which comprises more than 1,2 million images from 1,000 classes. Following Freytag et al. [9], we obtain binary classification tasks by randomly choosing a single positive and 19 negative classes. This is repeated 25 times and 10 random queries are chosen for each task, leading to a total of 250 image retrieval scenarios. We use the bag-of-words (BoW) features provided with ImageNet instead of CNN features, mainly for two reasons: First, the BoW features are public and hence facilitate reproduction. Second, most neural networks are pre-trained on ImageNet, which could bias the evaluation.

The number of random repetitions per class for the natural scenes and the MIRFLICKR dataset has been set to 10 as well, while we use 25 queries per class for USPS and 50 for the butterflies dataset.

The features of all datasets were scaled to be in $[0, 1]$.

4.2   Competitor Methods

We compare ITAL with a variety of baselines and competing methods, including **SUD** [33], **TCAL** [5], **RBMAL** [3], and the method of Brinker [2] referred to as "**border_div**" in the following. All these native BMAL methods have been described in Sect. 2.

In addition, we evaluate the following successful one-by-one active learning techniques in the BMAL scenario by selecting the k samples with the highest selection scores: Uncertainty sampling for SVM active learning by choosing samples close to the decision boundary (**border**) [31], uncertainty sampling for Gaussian processes (**unc**) [21], where uncertainty is defined as the ratio between absolute predictive mean and predictive standard deviation, and sample selection by maximizing the expected model output change (**EMOC**) [9].

All methods have to compete against the baselines of **random** selection, selecting the **topscoring** samples with maximum predictive mean, resembling the standard retrieval scenario [1], and variance sampling (**var**) by maximizing the difference of the sum of variances and the sum of covariances in the batch.

Finally, we also investigate maximizing the **joint entropy** $H(R_{i_1}, \ldots, R_{i_k}) = -\sum_{r \in \{-1,1\}^k} P(R_u = r) \cdot \log(P(R_u = r))$ of candidate batch $u = \{x_{i_1}, \ldots, x_{i_k}\}$. Being a component of our ITAL method, this is also a novel approach, but lacks the model output change term and the user model (cf. Eq. (2)).

We also tried applying **USDM** [32], **MCMI[min]** [14] and **AdaptAL** [23], especially since the latter two also maximize a mutual information criterion. However, all these methods scale so badly to datasets of realistic size, that they could not be applied in practice. AdaptAL, for example, would require 14 h for composing a single batch on MIRFLICKR, which is clearly intractable. Our ITAL method, in contrast, can handle this dataset with less than a minute per batch. These three competitors could, thus, only applied to USPS, MIRFLICKR, and ImageNet by randomly sub-sampling 1000 candidates to choose from, as suggested by Li et al. [23]. This usually leads to a degradation of performance, as can be seen from the results reported in the supplemental material.

4.3 Hyper-parameters

The hyper-parameters of the RBF kernel, *i.e.*, σ_{ls}, σ_{var}, and σ_{noise} (cf. Sect. 3.2), potentially have a large impact on the performance of the active learning methods. However, the overall goal is to eventually obtain a classifier that performs as well as possible. Therefore, we determine the optimal kernel hyper-parameters for each dataset using tenfold cross-validation on the training set and alternating optimization to maximize mean average precision. This optimization aims only for good classification performance independent of the active learning method being used and the same hyper-parameters are used for all methods.

With regard to the hyper-parameters of the user model used by ITAL, we employ the perfect user assumption for being comparable to competing methods that do not model the user. An experiment evaluating the effect of different user model parameters is presented in Sect. 4.5.

In case that other methods have further hyper-parameters, we use the default values provided by their authors.

4.4 Results

Figure 2 depicts the average precision obtained on average after 10 feedback rounds using the different BMAL methods. On the Butterflies dataset, ITAL obtains perfect performance after the least number of feedback rounds. TCAL and border_div perform similar to ITAL on USPS, but ITAL learns faster at the beginning, which is important in interactive image retrieval scenarios. While sampling candidates based on batch entropy behaves almost identical to ITAL on Butterflies, USPS, and MIRFLICKR, it is slightly superior on the Natural Scenes dataset, but fails to improve after more than 4 rounds of feedback on the ImageNet benchmark, where ITAL is clearly superior to all competitor methods. This indicates that taking the effect of the expected user feedback on the model output change into account is of great benefit for datasets as diverse as ImageNet.

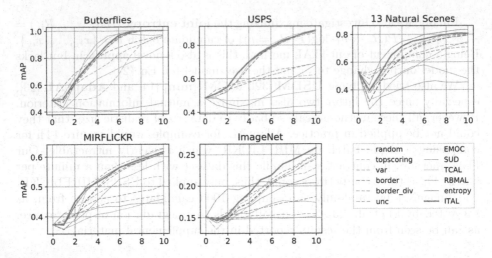

Fig. 2. Comparison of retrieval performance after different numbers of feedback rounds for various active learning methods. The thick, orange line corresponds to our proposed method. Figure is best viewed in color. (Color figure online)

Since it is often desirable to compare different methods by means of a single value, we report the area under the learning curves (AULC) in 1, divided by the number of feedback rounds so that the best possible value is always 1.0. In all cases, our method is among the top performers, achieving the best of all results in 3 out of 5 cases. The improvement over the second-best method on 13 Natural Scenes and ImageNet is significant on a level of <1% and on a level of 7% on USPS, according to Student's paired t-test.

The performance of the competing methods, on the other hand, varies significantly across datasets. ITAL, in contrast, is not affected by this issue and provides state-of-the-art performance independent from the characteristics of the data. To make this more visible, we construct a ranking of the tested methods for each dataset and report the average rank in 1 as well. ITAL achieves the best average rank and can thus be considered most universally applicable.

This is of high importance because, in an active learning scenario, labeled data is usually not available before performing the active learning. Thus, adaptation of the AL method or selection of a suitable one depending on the dataset is difficult. A widely applicable method such as ITAL is hence very desirable.

4.5   Effect of the User Model

To evaluate the effect of the user model integrated into ITAL, we simulated several types of users behaviors on the 13 Natural Scenes dataset: (a) an aggressive user annotating all images but assigning a wrong label in 50% of the cases, (b) a conservative user who always provides correct labels but only annotates 25% of the images on average, and (c) a blend of both, labeling 50% of the candidate images on average and having a 25% chance of making an incorrect annotation.

Table 1. Area under the learning curves from Fig. 2. The numbers in parentheses indicate the position in the ranking of all methods. The best value in each column is set in bold face, while the second-best and third-best values are underlined.

Method	Area under Learning Curve (AULC)					Avg. Rank
	Butterflies	USPS	Nat. Scenes	MIRFLICKR	ImageNet	
random	0.7316 (8)	0.5416 (8)	0.5687 (8)	0.4099 (9)	0.1494 (9)	8.4
topscoring	0.5991 (11)	0.5289 (9)	0.5419 (9)	0.4358 (7)	0.1708 (7)	8.6
var	0.6800 (9)	0.5550 (7)	0.5831 (5)	0.3957 (10)	0.1383 (11)	8.4
border	0.7434 (6)	0.6393 (5)	0.5775 (7)	0.4559 (6)	0.1743 (4)	5.6
border_div	0.7456 (5)	<u>0.6465</u> (3)	<u>0.6031</u> (3)	**0.4795** (1)	<u>0.1791</u> (3)	<u>3.0</u>
unc	0.7373 (7)	0.6391 (6)	0.5793 (6)	0.4585 (5)	0.1725 (5)	5.8
EMOC	<u>0.7561</u> (2)	0.4723 (10)	0.4654 (11)	0.4357 (8)	0.1483 (10)	8.2
SUD	0.3887 (12)	0.3903 (12)	0.3766 (12)	0.3883 (11)	0.1626 (8)	11.0
TCAL	**0.7720** (1)	0.6459 (4)	0.6016 (4)	0.4688 (4)	0.1708 (6)	3.8
RBMAL	0.6023 (10)	0.4457 (11)	0.5046 (10)	0.3732 (12)	0.1356 (12)	11.0
entropy (ours)	<u>0.7512</u> (3)	<u>0.6484</u> (2)	**0.6547** (1)	<u>0.4703</u> (3)	<u>0.1793</u> (2)	<u>2.2</u>
ITAL (ours)	0.7511 (4)	**0.6522** (1)	<u>0.6233</u> (2)	<u>0.4731</u> (2)	**0.1841** (1)	**2.0**

The same active learning methods as in the previous sections are applied and the parameters p_{label} and $p_{mistake}$ of ITAL are set accordingly.

The results presented in the supplemental material show that the user model helps ITAL to make faster improvements than with the perfect user model. A possible reason for this effect is that the parameters of the user model control an implicit trade-off between diversity and redundancy used by ITAL: For an imperfect user, selecting samples for annotation more redundantly can help to reduce the impact of wrong annotations. However, ITAL performs reasonably well even with the perfect user assumption. This could hence be used to speed-up ITAL noticeably with only a minor loss of performance.

5   Conclusions

We have proposed information-theoretic active learning (ITAL), a novel batch-mode active learning technique for binary classification, and applied it successfully to image retrieval with relevance feedback. Based on the idea of finding a subset of unlabeled samples that maximizes the mutual information between the relevance model and the expected user feedback, we propose suitable models and approximations to make this NP-hard problem tractable in practice. ITAL does not need to rely on manually tuned combinations of different heuristics, as many other works on batch-mode active learning do, but implicitly trades off uncertainty against diversity by taking the joint relevance distribution of the instances in the dataset into account.

Our method also features an explicit user model that enables it to deal with unnameable instances and the possibility of incorrect annotations. This has been demonstrated to be beneficial in the case of unreliable users.

We evaluated our method on five image datasets and found that it provides state-of-the-art performance across datasets, while many competitors perform well on certain datasets only. Moreover, ITAL outperforms existing techniques on the ImageNet dataset, which we attribute to its ability of taking the effect of the expected user feedback on the model output change into account.

Acknowledgements. This work was supported by the German Research Foundation as part of the priority programme "Volunteered Geographic Information: Interpretation, Visualisation and Social Computing" (SPP 1894, contract number DE 735/11-1).

References

1. Ayache, S., Quénot, G.: Evaluation of active learning strategies for video indexing. Sig. Process.: Image Commun. **22**(7), 692–704 (2007)
2. Brinker, K.: Incorporating diversity in active learning with support vector machines. In: International Conference on Machine Learning (ICML), pp. 59–66 (2003)
3. Cardoso, T.N., Silva, R.M., Canuto, S., Moro, M.M., Gonçalves, M.A.: Ranked batch-mode active learning. Inf. Sci. **379**, 313–337 (2017)
4. Cox, I.J., Miller, M.L., Minka, T.P., Papathomas, T.V., Yianilos, P.N.: The Bayesian image retrieval system, pichunter: theory, implementation, and psychophysical experiments. IEEE Trans. Image Process. **9**(1), 20–37 (2000)
5. Demir, B., Bruzzone, L.: A novel active learning method in relevance feedback for content-based remote sensing image retrieval. IEEE Trans. Geosci. Remote Sens. **53**(5), 2323–2334 (2015)
6. Deselaers, T., Paredes, R., Vidal, E., Ney, H.: Learning weighted distances for relevance feedback in image retrieval. In: International Conference on Pattern Recognition (ICPR), pp. 1–4. IEEE (2008)
7. Fei-Fei, L., Perona, P.: A Bayesian hierarchical model for learning natural scene categories. In: IEEE Conference on Computer Vision and Pattern Recognition (CVPR), vol. 2, pp. 524–531. IEEE (2005)
8. Freytag, A., Rodner, E., Bodesheim, P., Denzler, J.: Labeling examples that matter: relevance-based active learning with Gaussian processes. In: Weickert, J., Hein, M., Schiele, B. (eds.) GCPR 2013. LNCS, vol. 8142, pp. 282–291. Springer, Heidelberg (2013). https://doi.org/10.1007/978-3-642-40602-7_31
9. Freytag, A., Rodner, E., Denzler, J.: Selecting influential examples: active learning with expected model output changes. In: Fleet, D., Pajdla, T., Schiele, B., Tuytelaars, T. (eds.) ECCV 2014. LNCS, vol. 8692, pp. 562–577. Springer, Cham (2014). https://doi.org/10.1007/978-3-319-10593-2_37
10. Friedman, J., Hastie, T., Tibshirani, R.: Example: ZIP code data (Ch. 11.7). In: The Elements of Statistical Learning. Springer Series in Statistics, New York (2001)
11. Genz, A.: Numerical computation of multivariate normal probabilities. J. Comput. Graph. Stat. **1**(2), 141–149 (1992)
12. Giang, N.T., Tao, N.Q., Dung, N.D., The, N.T.: Batch mode active learning for interactive image retrieval. In: 2014 IEEE International Symposium on Multimedia (ISM), pp. 28–31. IEEE (2014)

13. Guestrin, C., Krause, A., Singh, A.P.: Near-optimal sensor placements in Gaussian processes. In: International Conference on Machine Learning (ICML), pp. 265–272. ACM (2005)
14. Guo, Y., Greiner, R.: Optimistic active-learning using mutual information. In: IJCAI, vol. 7, pp. 823–829 (2007)
15. Guo, Y., Schuurmans, D.: Discriminative batch mode active learning. In: Advances in Neural Information Processing Systems (NIPS), pp. 593–600 (2008)
16. Huiskes, M.J., Lew, M.S.: The MIR flickr retrieval evaluation. In: Proceedings of the 2008 ACM International Conference on Multimedia Information Retrieval, MIR 2008. ACM, New York (2008)
17. Jain, P., Kapoor, A.: Active learning for large multi-class problems. In: IEEE Conference on Computer Vision and Pattern Recognition (CVPR), pp. 762–769. IEEE (2009)
18. Johns, E., Mac Aodha, O., Brostow, G.J.: Becoming the expert - interactive multi-class machine teaching. In: IEEE Conference on Computer Vision and Pattern Recognition (CVPR), pp. 2616–2624. IEEE (2015)
19. Käding, C., Freytag, A., Rodner, E., Bodesheim, P., Denzler, J.: Active learning and discovery of object categories in the presence of unnameable instances. In: IEEE Conference on Computer Vision and Pattern Recognition (CVPR), pp. 4343–4352 (2015)
20. Käding, C., Rodner, E., Freytag, A., Mothes, O., Barz, B., Denzler, J.: Active learning for regression tasks with expected model output changes. In: British Machine Vision Conference (BMVC) (2018)
21. Kapoor, A., Grauman, K., Urtasun, R., Darrell, T.: Active learning with Gaussian processes for object categorization. In: IEEE International Conference on Computer Vision (ICCV), pp. 1–8. IEEE (2007)
22. Krause, A., Guestrin, C.: Nonmyopic active learning of Gaussian processes: an exploration-exploitation approach. In: International Conference on Machine Learning (ICML), pp. 449–456. ACM (2007)
23. Li, X., Guo, Y.: Adaptive active learning for image classification. In: IEEE Conference on Computer Vision and Pattern Recognition (CVPR), pp. 859–866 (2013)
24. Lütz, A., Rodner, E., Denzler, J.: I want to know more—efficient multi-class incremental learning using Gaussian processes. Pattern Recogn. Image Anal. 23(3), 402–407 (2013)
25. Niblack, C.W., et al.: QBIC project: querying images by content, using color, texture, and shape. In: Storage and Retrieval for Image and Video Databases, vol. 1908, pp. 173–188. International Society for Optics and Photonics (1993)
26. Rasmussen, C.E., Williams, C.K.: Gaussian Processes for Machine Learning, vol. 1. MIT Press, Cambridge (2006)
27. Rodner, E., Freytag, A., Bodesheim, P., Fröhlich, B., Denzler, J.: Large-scale Gaussian process inference with generalized histogram intersection kernels for visual recognition tasks. Int. J. Comput. Vis. 121(2), 253–280 (2017)
28. Russakovsky, O., et al.: ImageNet large scale visual recognition challenge. Int. J. Comput. Vis. (IJCV) 115(3), 211–252 (2015)
29. Simonyan, K., Zisserman, A.: Very deep convolutional networks for large-scale image recognition. arXiv preprint arXiv:1409.1556 (2014)
30. Smeulders, A.W., Worring, M., Santini, S., Gupta, A., Jain, R.: Content-based image retrieval at the end of the early years. IEEE Trans. Pattern Anal. Mach. Intell. (TPAMI) 22(12), 1349–1380 (2000)
31. Tong, S., Chang, E.: Support vector machine active learning for image retrieval. In: ACM International Conference on Multimedia, pp. 107–118. ACM (2001)

32. Yang, Y., Ma, Z., Nie, F., Chang, X., Hauptmann, A.G.: Multi-class active learning by uncertainty sampling with diversity maximization. Int. J. Comput. Vis. **113**(2), 113–127 (2015)
33. Zhu, J., Wang, H., Yao, T., Tsou, B.K.: Active learning with sampling by uncertainty and density for word sense disambiguation and text classification. In: International Conference on Computational Linguistics, vol. 1 (2008)

Oral Session 5: Optimization and Clustering

Oral Session 5: Optimization and Clustering

AFSI: Adaptive Restart for Fast Semi-Iterative Schemes for Convex Optimisation

Jón Arnar Tómasson[1(✉)], Peter Ochs[2], and Joachim Weickert[1]

[1] Mathematical Image Analysis Group,
Faculty of Mathematics and Computer Science, Campus E1.7, Saarland University,
66041 Saarbrücken, Germany
{tomasson,weickert}@mia.uni-saarland.de
[2] Mathematical Optimization Group, Faculty of Mathematics and Computer Science,
Campus E1.7, Saarland University, 66041 Saarbrücken, Germany
ochs@math.uni-sb.de

Abstract. Smooth optimisation problems arise in many fields including image processing, and having fast methods for solving them has clear benefits. Widely and successfully used strategies to solve them are accelerated gradient methods. They accelerate standard gradient-based schemes by means of extrapolation. Unfortunately, most acceleration strategies are generic, in the sense, that they ignore specific information about the objective function. In this paper, we implement an adaptive restarting into a recently proposed efficient acceleration strategy that was coined Fast Semi-Iterative (FSI) scheme. Our analysis shows clear advantages of the adaptive restarting in terms of a theoretical convergence rate guarantee and state-of-the-art performance on a challenging image processing task.

1 Introduction

The high dimensionality of many variational problems in image processing or computer vision dictates the usage of first-order optimisation algorithms. These are iterative schemes that combine gradient information to construct a sequence of improving approximations to a solution of the variational problem. The simplest instance is the well-known Steepest Descent Method. While the complexity of each iteration is usually very cheap, their efficiency highly depends on the curvature of the objective function to be minimised. In flat regions, short gradient vectors must be compensated by large step sizes while in steep regions the opposite configuration appears.

Essentially, this information is captured by the second derivative (Hessian) of the objective function, which is not available for first-order methods. A successful

Electronic supplementary material The online version of this chapter (https://doi.org/10.1007/978-3-030-12939-2_46) contains supplementary material, which is available to authorized users.

strategy to deal with this problem is provided by accumulating momentum in steep regions, which is used in flat regions to preserve the speed. This is the underlying idea of *accelerated gradient schemes*, which are widely used to solve the aforementioned problems. The accelerated gradient scheme that we consider is the Fast Semi-Iterative Scheme (FSI) [5]. The efficiency of this method comes from a clever extrapolation step with cyclically varying parameters.

However, this is an idealised picture. Around a steep local minimum or along a long ramp, accumulating too much momentum leads to oscillatory behaviour [14]. These are just two different (simplified) pictures of optimisation scenarios, which indicate that optimisation algorithms should *adapt* to the objective function. Of course, the situation is significantly more complex for high dimensional problems.

In this paper, we introduce an adaptive restart strategy for FSI. Our adaptation rule comes with several significant advantages: (i) The algorithm *automatically selects* the cycle length of FSI, an otherwise problem-sensitive *parameter*; (ii) it efficiently solves a wide variety of problems, and shows state-of-the-art performance on a difficult image processing problem; and (iii) we prove a worst-case convergence rate, which is not available for the FSI method.

Paper Organisation. Section 2 introduces the underlying accelerated gradient method, FSI, which directly leads to the difficult question of selecting its cycle length parameter. After discussing related work in Sect. 3, we introduce our adaptive restarting that automatically selects a good cycle length for FSI in Sect. 4. The convergence of this adaptive FSI (AFSI) scheme is studied in Sects. 5 and 6 demonstrated the high quality of AFSI in image processing. Section 7 concludes the paper and provides a brief outlook.

2   Fast Semi-Iterative Schemes

FSI schemes have been introduced recently by Hafner et al. [5]. They are versatile strategies that accelerate the simplest solvers for four problem classes: the explicit scheme for parabolic partial differential equations, Richardson's iteration for linear systems of equations, the gradient descent method for convex optimisation problems, and the projected gradient descent method for constrained convex optimisation problems. This acceleration is achieved by an extrapolation step in the direction from the previous to the current iterate. While FSI schemes have been introduced in the context of image analysis applications, they have also been used successfully in other fields [1].

In the present paper we are interested in the FSI schemes that solve smooth convex optimisation problems of type

$$\min_{x \in \mathbb{R}^N} F(x) \tag{1}$$

where ∇F is Lipschitz continuous with constant L. The classical gradient descent method for this problem reads

$$x^{k+1} = x^k - \omega \, \nabla F(x^k), \tag{2}$$

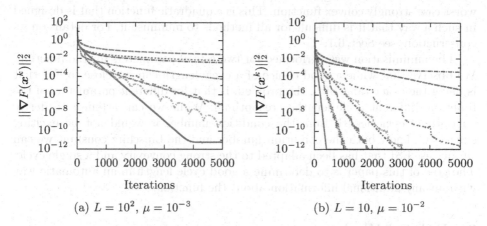

(a) $L = 10^2$, $\mu = 10^{-3}$ (b) $L = 10$, $\mu = 10^{-2}$

Fig. 1. Convergence plots of FSI with different cycle lengths for solving Nesterov's worst case problem. The problem dimension is $N = 10^5$ and we explore two difference parameter choices for L and μ. The convergence is measured in terms of the squared Euclidean norm of the gradient of the objective. FSI that has been optimally adapted to the strong convexity is used as a baseline. The optimal cycle length for FSI can change significantly depending on the problem parameters.

where the upper index denotes the iteration number, and the step size parameter ω must satisfy $\omega \in (0, 2/L)$ for stability reasons.

FSI accelerates gradient descent by considering the cyclic iteration

$$\boldsymbol{x}^{m,\,k+1} = \boldsymbol{x}^{m,\,k} - \alpha_k\,\omega\,\nabla F(\boldsymbol{x}^{m,\,k}) + (\alpha_k - 1)(\boldsymbol{x}^{m,\,k} - \boldsymbol{x}^{m,\,k-1}) \qquad (3)$$

with $\boldsymbol{x}^{m,-1} := \boldsymbol{x}^{m,0}$ and extrapolation parameter $\alpha_k = \frac{4k+2}{2k+3}$. The inner iteration index k ranges from 0 to $K - 1$, where K denotes the cycle length. The outer index m counts the cycles. In [5] it has been argued that the cycle length K is responsible for the efficiency of the method, while the number of cycles influences the accuracy. In practice there is a natural tradeoff between both parameters, and it requires hand tuning to obtain the highest convergence speed for a given number of iterations. This may be burdensome. Therefore, in this paper, we suggest an automatic adaptive selection of this parameter.

For strongly convex problems with convexity parameter μ (i.e. $F(\boldsymbol{x}) - \frac{\mu}{2}||\boldsymbol{x}||^2$ is convex), Hafner et al. [5] suggest to consider only a single cycle with step size $\omega = \frac{2}{L+\mu}$ and modified extrapolation parameters

$$\alpha_0 = \frac{2(L+\mu)}{3L+\mu}, \quad \alpha_k = \frac{1}{1 - \frac{\alpha_{k-1}}{4}\left(\frac{L-\mu}{L+\mu}\right)^2}. \qquad (4)$$

While this removes the need to select the cycle length it requires us to know the strong convexity parameter μ.

Figure 1 demonstrates the difficulty of selecting the cycle length of FSI. It shows the performance of different FSI cycle lengths compared to FSI that has been adapted to the strong convexity. The function being minimised is Nesterov's worst case strongly convex function. This is a quadratic function that is designed in such a way that it is difficult for all methods to minimise it. For details on its construction, see Sect. 6.1.

The minimisation was performed for two sets of parameters for the function. We observe that while a good choice of a cycle length can get close to FSI that is using the exact value of μ, the problem is that for different parameters of the function, different cycle lengths are optimal. While we can attempt to derive an optimal cycle length from the condition number it would not be exciting since if we know both the condition number and the Lipschitz constant we can simply use FSI that has been adapted to the strong convexity and a single cycle. The goal of this paper is to determine a good cycle length in an automatic way without any additional information about the function.

3   Related Work

A classic gradient-based method is Polyak's heavy ball method [12] which has the following updating rule:

$$x^{k+1} = x^k - \alpha \nabla F(x^k) + \beta(x^k - x^{k-1}), \tag{5}$$

where the inertial parameter $\beta \in [0, 1)$ controls the momentum we gain and $\alpha \in (0, \frac{2(1+\beta)}{L})$ is the step size. As shown in [5], FSI schemes for convex optimisation can be viewed as a variant of Polyak's heavy ball method by allowing cyclically varying parameters; see (3).

A closely related method is Nesterov's accelerated gradient descent [7]. The accelerated gradient descent has the following updating rule:

$$y^k = x^k + \beta_k(x^k - x^{k-1}),$$
$$x^{k+1} = y^k - \frac{1}{L} \nabla F(y^k), \tag{6}$$
$$\beta_k = \theta_k(\theta_{k-1}^{-1} - 1),$$

where $\theta_0 := \theta_{-1} := 1$ and $\frac{1-\theta_{k+1}}{\theta_{k+1}^2} \leq \frac{1}{\theta_k^2}$. Here the extrapolated point is also used in the evaluation of the gradient. This allows the accelerated gradient descent to respond to an increase in the function values earlier, reducing its oscillatory behaviour.

A common choice for the inertial parameter is $\beta_k = \frac{k-1}{k+2}$. Comparing it to the inertial parameter of FSI, $(\alpha_k - 1) = (k - \frac{1}{2})/(k + \frac{3}{2})$, we observe that β_k converges to 1 at a slower rate than $(\alpha_k - 1)$. If we fix the cycle length of FSI to some K then $(\alpha_k - 1)$ will be bounded from above by the constant $(\alpha_K - 1) < 1$ and for a large enough k, β_k will overtake it.

Like FSI, the accelerated gradient descent can be adapted to the strong convexity of a function with the parameter choice [8, Sect. 2.2.1]:

$$\beta_k = \frac{\sqrt{L} - \sqrt{\mu}}{\sqrt{L} + \sqrt{\mu}}. \tag{7}$$

A closer relative to FSI is the restarted accelerated gradient descent introduced by O'Donoghue and Candès [11]. Just like FSI the restarted accelerated gradient descent also cyclically varies its parameters and resets its momentum. O'Donoghue and Candès consider both a fixed restart interval, and two different adaptive schemes:

– *Function scheme*: Restart whenever

$$F(x^k) > F(x^{k-1}). \tag{8}$$

– *Gradient scheme*: Restart whenever

$$\langle \nabla F(y^{k-1}), x^k - x^{k-1} \rangle > 0. \tag{9}$$

While the function scheme offers monotonicity it can be numerically unstable. The gradient scheme works better in practice and is often cheaper to compute.

Another restarting scheme for the accelerated gradient descent was recently proposed by Su, Boyd and Candès [14]. The scheme restarts when it detects decreasing speed. This can be detected with the following restart criterion:

– *Speed based scheme*: Restart whenever

$$\|x^k - x^{k-1}\| < \|x^{k-1} - x^{k-2}\|. \tag{10}$$

Although this scheme often performs worse than the gradient scheme it comes with the advantage of a linear worst case convergence rate.

While the heavy ball method, the restarted accelerated gradient descent and obviously FSI are the closest to our work, there exist many extensions of the heavy ball method and the accelerated gradient descent. For example, FISTA [2] extends the accelerated gradient descent to include non-smooth functions, and iPiano [10] extends the heavy ball method to include non-smooth and non-convex functions. These methods are all closely related to the momentum method that is frequently applied in machine learning [13, 15].

FED [4] uses another acceleration strategy instead of accumulating momentum. FED uses step sizes that on their own are unstable but can be combined into a stable cycle. In the linear setting this is equivalent to FSI [5].

4   Adaptive Restarting

In Sect. 2 we saw that in general selecting a good cycle length for the FSI solver is difficult. For specific tasks we might be able to find cycle lengths that work well in practice but this requires some extra work from the user. Instead of the user needing to adapt FSI to the problem, FSI should adapt in an automatic way.

We seek a simple criterion that is both cheap to compute, and yields a performance that is comparable to an expert selecting the cycle length manually for a specific task.

One way to achieve this is using adaptive restarts [11]. The idea comes from the observation that the function values of momentum based methods start to oscillate if the inertia parameter is set higher than the optimal value.

To visualise this we consider the heavy ball method in 2D. The heavy ball method can be thought of as a ball rolling down some landscape. If our landscape is a bowl then it is easy to see that if the friction between the bowl and ball is low the ball will roll past the minimum and up the other side of the bowl. If we want to get to the minimum fast it is a natural idea to simply stop the ball whenever it starts going upwards.

Therefore, the idea of adaptive restarting is to discard the momentum whenever the function values start increasing. Since the gradient is always pointing upwards in the function, we can go into a new cycle when the following condition is met:

$$\langle \nabla F\left(x^k\right), x^k - x^{k-1}\rangle > 0. \tag{11}$$

This leads to *Adaptive FSI (AFSI)* schemes for strongly convex optimisation.

Since we discard the entire momentum once it is pointing towards higher function values, the advantage of the accelerated gradient descent discussed in Sect. 3 becomes less obvious. With the oscillatory behaviour taken care of explicitly, the faster growing inertial parameter and larger step sizes of FSI become more attractive.

Algorithm 1 shows the general idea of AFSI. In each iteration we need to compute one additional inner product. When compared to the rest of the iteration this is not expensive.

Let us compare our restart strategy from (11) to the function scheme from (8) and the gradient scheme from (9). While we designed it to prevent an increase in function values like the function scheme, it shares the structure with the gradient scheme. The difference is where we evaluate the gradient. When deciding whether the momentum at x^k should be reset or used for the extrapolation step from (6), the gradient scheme uses the gradient information from the previous intermediary point y^{k-1}. Our scheme uses the gradient information from the current iterate x^k, this is illustrated in Fig. 2. While our scheme requires an extra gradient evaluation when applied to Nesterov's accelerated gradient descent, FSI requires the gradient at x^k anyway. Therefore no extra gradient evaluations are required when implementing AFSI. In the next section we will see that evaluating the restarting condition at the current iterate gives us monotonicity of the

---

Algorithm 1. AFSI

$\omega \in \left(0, \frac{2}{L}\right)$, $x^{-1} := x^0$, $k := 0$

while stopping criterion is not met **do**

 if $\langle \nabla f(x^k), x^k - x^{k-1} \rangle > 0$ {Check the reset condition} **then**

  $x^{-1}, x^0 \leftarrow x^{k-1}$ { Reset the momentum}

  $k \leftarrow 0$

 end if

 $\alpha_k \leftarrow \frac{4k+2}{2k+3}$

 $x^{k+1} \leftarrow x^k - \alpha_k \omega \nabla f(x^k) + (\alpha_k - 1)(x^k - x^{k-1})$

 $k \leftarrow k + 1$

end while

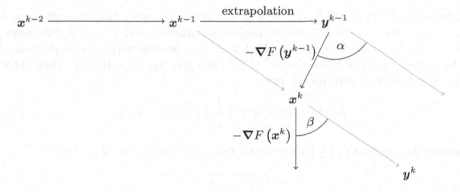

Fig. 2. This figure illustrates the difference between the gradient scheme from (9) and our scheme. When deciding whether the momentum at x^k (in red) should be reset or used to compute y^k, the schemes use gradient information from different locations. The gradient scheme resets when the angle α is obtuse and our scheme resets when β is obtuse. (Color figure online)

function values. This combines the theoretical properties of the function scheme with the numerical stability and cheap computation of the gradient scheme.

5 Theoretical Insights

While resetting the momentum term and going into a new cycle when it is pointing towards higher function values sounds intuitive, it can also be motivated directly by the convergence analysis of FSI. If we know that the algorithm goes into a new cycle whenever the inequality from (11) is satisfied we have the additional information that all previous iterates satisfy

$$\langle \nabla F\left(x^k\right), x^{k-1} - x^k \rangle \geq 0. \tag{12}$$

This term appears in a lot of useful inequalities from convex analysis and knowing its sign proves to be very useful. The fact that it allows us to ignore a lot of terms in the convergence analysis of FSI can be considered a motivation for the restart condition from (11). We can use the subgradient inequality (see for example [8, Sect. 2.1.1])

$$F(y) \geq F(x) + \langle \nabla F(x), y - x \rangle \tag{13}$$

to conclude that

$$F(x^k) \leq F(x^{k-1}). \tag{14}$$

This tells us that AFSI is a descent method. Note that we are not able to conclude this with the gradient scheme from (9).

By applying (12) repeatedly in the convergence analysis we can derive the following linear convergence rate for AFSI. The proof can be found in the supplementary material.

Theorem 1. *Let $F : \mathbb{R}^N \to \mathbb{R}$ be a smooth strongly convex function with convexity parameter μ and a L-Lipschitz continuous gradient with $L > \mu$. Furthermore, let F^* be the unique minimum of F. Let $(x^k)_{k \in \mathbb{N}}$ be generated by a single cycle of Algorithm 1 with initialisation $x^0 \in \mathbb{R}^N$, and step size $\omega \in \left(0, \frac{1}{L}\right)$. Then AFSI has the following convergence rate:*

$$F(x^k) - F^* \leq q^k C\left(\frac{L}{\mu}\right)(F(x^0) - F^*), \tag{15}$$

where the constant $C\left(\frac{L}{\mu}\right)$ depends on the condition number L/μ and

$$q := \sqrt{\frac{\frac{L}{\mu}}{2\mu\omega(1 - L\omega) + \frac{L}{\mu}}}. \tag{16}$$

The convergence rate from Theorem 1 is optimised for $\omega = \frac{1}{2L}$, where we have

$$q = \sqrt{\frac{1}{\frac{1}{2}\left(\frac{\mu}{L}\right)^2 + 1}}. \tag{17}$$

Figure 3 shows how the convergence rate compares to the convergence rate of gradient descent, and the optimal convergence rate in the sense of Nemirovski and Yudin [6,8]. While the convergence rate provided by Theorem 1 is worse than the convergence rate of gradient descent, it is linear. This is an improvement over FSI. Section 6 shows that in practice we observe much faster convergence. The constant C is in general not very large and for $L/\mu \geq 25$ we have $C(L/\mu) = 1$.

6 Experiments

6.1 Nesterov's Worst Case Functions

Nesterov's worst case functions are a family of functions that are designed to be difficult to minimise for all methods. They are defined by [8, Sect. 2.1.4]:

$$F_{\mu,L}(x) = \frac{L - \mu}{8}\left(x_1^2 + \sum_{i=1}^{+\infty}(x_i - x_{i+1})^2 - 2x_1\right) + \frac{\mu}{2}\|x\|_2^2 \tag{18}$$

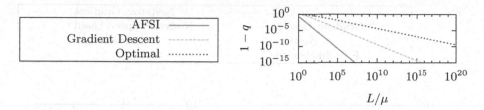

Fig. 3. Plot of 1 minus the convergence rate as a function of the condition number L/μ for AFSI, gradient descent, and the optimal convergence rate for the class of strongly convex smooth functions. While the worst case convergence rate of AFSI is worse than gradient descent, it is linear.

for strongly convex functions, and [8, Sect. 2.1.2]

$$F_{k,L}(\boldsymbol{x}) = \frac{L}{4}\left(\frac{1}{2}\left(x_1^2 + \sum_{i=1}^{2k}(x_i - x_{i+1})^2 + x_{2k+2}^2\right) - x_1\right) \qquad (19)$$

for convex functions. The difficulty arises when we initialise with $\boldsymbol{x}^0 := \boldsymbol{0}$, then at iteration k, $\boldsymbol{x}^k$ will at most have k nonzero entries. The nonzero entries of the minimum $\boldsymbol{x}^*$ then provide a bound on the convergence rate. For the class of strongly convex functions the worst case function is defined for $\mathbb{R}^{+\infty} \to \mathbb{R}$. Therefore, when approximating it the problem dimension should be large compared to the number of iterations taken.

For the convex problem the function has a parameter $k \leq (N-1)/2$. This parameter governs at which iteration the following lower bound holds:

$$F_{k,L}(\boldsymbol{x}^k) - F^* \geq \frac{3L\|\boldsymbol{x}^0 - \boldsymbol{x}^*\|^2}{32(k+1)^2}. \qquad (20)$$

While this proves that for all iterations k there exists a function such that the bound holds, it is important to note that for a specific instance of the function it is only guaranteed to hold at a single iteration k. Since the function is not designed to be difficult to minimise at any other iteration we can argue that the performance after iteration k is not interesting.

Since we are using adaptive restarting the obvious method to compare AFSI to is Nesterov's accelerated gradient descent with adaptive restarting that was introduced by O'Donoghue and Candes [11]. We consider 2 restarting schemes, the gradient scheme from (9), and the speed based scheme of Su et al. from (10).

In Fig. 4 we observe that AFSI can get close to FSI adapted to the strong convexity with the optimal parameters and can even beat the accelerated gradient descent adapted to the convexity. For this problem the gradient scheme for the accelerated gradient descent has not yet reset its momentum. Therefore, it is still identical to the accelerated gradient descent from (6). The speed based scheme performs better but it cannot achieve the performance of AFSI.

While our analysis was only conducted for strongly convex functions we also evaluate the performance on Nesterov's worst case convex function with

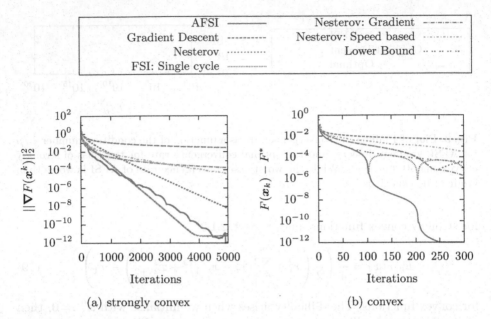

AFSI	———	Nesterov: Gradient	—·—·—·—
Gradient Descent	----------	Nesterov: Speed based	············
Nesterov	············	Lower Bound	·· ··· ··
FSI: Single cycle	··················		

(a) strongly convex   (b) convex

Fig. 4. Convergence plots of AFSI, FSI that has been optimally adapted to the strong convexity, Nesterov's accelerated gradient descent that has been optimally adapted to the strong convexity, and Nesterov's accelerated gradient descent with the gradient based restarting scheme from (9) and the speed based restarting scheme from (10). The methods are solving Nesterov's worst case problem. The strongly convex problem in (a) has the dimension 10^5, and parameters $L = 10^2$ and $\mu = 10^{-3}$. The convergence is measured in terms of the squared Euclidean norm of the gradient. The convex problem in (b) has the dimension 10^3, and parameters $k = 50$ and $L = 1$. The residual of the objective is used to evaluate the convergence. AFSI achieves state-of-the-art performance and even outperforms Nesterov's optimal method for both functions.

$k = 50$. We observe that we keep the state-of-the-art performance of FSI in the interesting part of the function. Once we get past it, AFSI becomes superior. Here the gradient scheme for the accelerated gradient descent works as intended by restarting once the function values start to increase. At this point AFSI is already in its third cycle.

We observe that the speed based scheme performs worse than the gradient scheme due to restarting too early. Since the convergence rate of the speed based scheme is linear it will overtake the accelerated gradient descent without restarting. This happens after around 1000 iterations.

6.2 Non-quadratic Minimisation

For this experiment we consider the following functional:

$$E(u) = \frac{1}{2} \int_\Omega \left(\Psi((u - f)^2) + \alpha\Psi(|\boldsymbol{\nabla} u|^2) \right) dx dy \qquad (21)$$

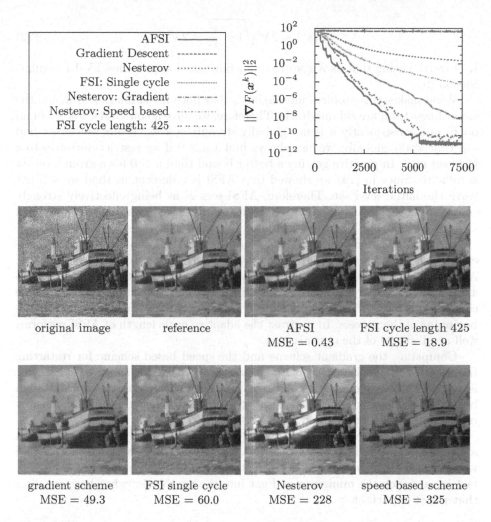

Fig. 5. Denoising with $\alpha = 1$, $\lambda = 0.1$, and a black initialisation. Comparison of AFSI, FSI, and Nesterov's accelerated gradient descent with and without adaptive restarting. The solutions and mean square error (MSE) of the methods after 500 iterations are shown above. The solution of the gradient descent method (not shown) is still the black initialisation after 500 iterations. The reference solution is obtained with 20000 iterations of Nesterov's method restarted with the gradient scheme. The cycle length of 425 was hand-tuned for the best performance. AFSI reaches a low MSE faster than the other methods, and converges faster than FSI for all fixed cycle lengths.

and its discretised counterpart $F : \mathbb{R}^N \to \mathbb{R}$. Here we aim to remove noise from an image $f : \Omega \to \mathbb{R}$ by finding an image $u : \Omega \to \mathbb{R}$ that is both similar to f and is smooth. To achieve this we use the Charbonnier penaliser [3]:

$$\Psi(s^2) = 2\lambda^2 \sqrt{1 + \frac{s^2}{\lambda^2}} - 2\lambda^2. \tag{22}$$

It is worth noting that as λ goes to 0 our functional approaches TV-L1 regularisation [9].

What makes this problem interesting is that both the similarity term and the smoothness term are subquadratic. Therefore, we have no quadratic lower bound on F, and consequently it is not globally strongly convex. While we cannot find a μ that works globally, we can always find a $\mu > 0$ if we restrict ourselves to a level set of F. In practice getting a better bound than $\mu > 0$ for a given level set is difficult. Since in (14) we showed that AFSI is a descent method we will not leave the initial level set. Therefore, AFSI sees F as being effectively strongly convex even if globally it is not. In other words, AFSI can adapt to the local structure of F while FSI uses the global information.

In Fig. 5 we observe that this does indeed give AFSI and the restarted accelerated gradient descent an advantage over their counterparts without restarts. AFSI even performs better than FSI that has the cycle length tuned by hand to 425 for the fastest convergence. While this cycle length results in a comparable convergence rate once we are close to the minimum it is not well suited at the beginning of the process. In contrast the adaptive cycle length of AFSI performs well at all stages of the optimisation.

Comparing the gradient scheme and the speed based scheme for restarting the accelerated gradient descent, we again observe that the speed based scheme is restarting too frequently. While the gradient scheme converges faster than both the speed based scheme and the accelerated gradient descent without any restarting, it converges slower than AFSI.

We observe that while a single FSI cycle converges slowly it achieves a good approximation quickly. This is exactly what allows FSI to perform so well once we apply adaptive restarting. For a restarted method we only care about how fast it can reach the minimum and get into the next cycle, what happens after that is not important.

7   Conclusions and Future Work

We have introduced *Adaptive FSI* (AFSI) schemes for strongly convex optimisation problems. They provide an automatic way of selecting the cycle length for FSI schemes. Since we no longer have an extra parameter, we have a method that is both simple to implement and simple to use. We can show that AFSI offers additional stability guarantees over FSI where the cycle length is a free parameter.

Our experiments demonstrate that when the strong convexity parameter of the function is known we can get close to the performance of the optimal methods. Additionally, when no useful bound on the strong convexity parameter is available AFSI can outperform them.

While we have only considered FSI schemes for unconstrained optimisation, FSI schemes can also be used for solving parabolic and elliptic partial differential equations, and for constrained optimisation [5]. In our ongoing work, we are studying how to extend the results for AFSI to these other types of FSI schemes.

Acknowledgements. Our research has been partially funded by the Cluster of Excellence on Multimodal Computing and Interaction within the Excellence Initiative of the German Research Foundation (DFG) and by the ERC Advanced Grant INCOVID. This is gratefully acknowledged.

References

1. Bähr, M., Dachsel, R., Breuß, M.: Fast solvers for solving shape matching by time integration. In: Annual Workshop of the AAPR, vol. 42, pp. 65–72, May 2018
2. Beck, A., Teboulle, M.: A fast iterative shrinkage-thresholding algorithm for linear inverse problems. SIAM J. Imaging Sci. **2**(1), 183–202 (2009)
3. Charbonnier, P., Blanc-Feraud, L., Aubert, G., Barlaud, M.: Deterministic edge-preserving regularization in computed imaging. IEEE Trans. Image Process. **6**(2), 298–311 (1997)
4. Grewenig, S., Weickert, J., Bruhn, A.: From box filtering to fast explicit diffusion. In: Goesele, M., Roth, S., Kuijper, A., Schiele, B., Schindler, K. (eds.) DAGM 2010. LNCS, vol. 6376, pp. 533–542. Springer, Heidelberg (2010). https://doi.org/10.1007/978-3-642-15986-2_54
5. Hafner, D., Ochs, P., Weickert, J., Reißel, M., Grewenig, S.: FSI schemes: fast semi-iterative solvers for PDEs and optimisation methods. In: Rosenhahn, B., Andres, B. (eds.) GCPR 2016. LNCS, vol. 9796, pp. 91–102. Springer, Cham (2016). https://doi.org/10.1007/978-3-319-45886-1_8
6. Nemirovski, A., Yudin, D.: Problem Complexity and Method Efficiency in Optimization. Wiley-Interscience Series in Discrete Mathematics. Wiley, Hoboken (1983)
7. Nesterov, Y.: A method of solving a convex programming problem with convergence rate $O(1/k^2)$. Soviet Math. Doklady **27**, 372–376 (1983)
8. Nesterov, Y.: Introductory Lectures on Convex Optimization: A Basic Course. Springer, Heidelberg (2004). https://doi.org/10.1007/978-1-4419-8853-9
9. Nikolova, M.: A variational approach to remove outliers and impulse noise. J. Math. Imaging Vis. **20**(1), 99–120 (2004)
10. Ochs, P., Chen, Y., Brox, T., Pock, T.: iPiano: inertial proximal algorithm for non-convex optimization. SIAM J. Imaging Sci. (SIIMS) **7**, 1388–1419 (2014)
11. O'Donoghue, B., Candès, E.: Adaptive restart for accelerated gradient schemes. Found. Comput. Math. **15**(3), 715–732 (2015)
12. Polyak, B.: Some methods of speeding up the convergence of iteration methods. USSR Comput. Math. Math. Phys. **4**, 1–17 (1964)
13. Rumelhart, D., Hinton, G., Williams, R.: Learning internal representations by error propagation. In: Rumelhart, D., McClelland, J. (eds.) Parallel Distributed Processing: Explorations in the Microstructure of Cognition, vol. 1, chap. 8, pp. 318–362. MIT Press, Cambridge (1986)
14. Su, W., Boyd, S., Candès, E.: A differential equation for modeling Nesterov's accelerated gradient method: theory and insights. J. Mach. Learn. Res. **17**, 1–43 (2016)
15. Sutskever, I., Martens, J., Dahl, G., Hinton, G.: On the importance of initialization and momentum in deep learning. In: Dasgupta, S., McAllester, D. (eds.) Proceedings of the 30th International Conference on Machine Learning. Proceedings of Machine Learning Research, vol. 28, pp. 1139–1147. PMLR, Atlanta, 17–19 June 2013

Invexity Preserving Transformations for Projection Free Optimization with Sparsity Inducing Non-convex Constraints

Sebastian Mathias Keller$^{(\boxtimes)}$ (iD), Damian Murezzan (iD), and Volker Roth (iD)

University of Basel, Spiegelgasse 1, Basel, Switzerland
`sebastianmathias.keller@unibas.ch`

Abstract. Forward stagewise and Frank Wolfe are popular gradient based projection free optimization algorithms which both require convex constraints. We propose a method to extend the applicability of these algorithms to problems of the form $\min_x f(x)$ $s.t.$ $g(x) \leq \kappa$ where $f(x)$ is an invex (Invexity is a generalization of convexity and ensures that all local optima are also global optima.) objective function and $g(x)$ is a non-convex constraint. We provide a theorem which defines a class of monotone component-wise transformation functions $x_i = h(z_i)$. These transformations lead to a convex constraint function $G(z) = g(h(z))$. Assuming invexity of the original function $f(x)$ that same transformation $x_i = h(z_i)$ will lead to a transformed objective function $F(z) = f(h(z))$ which is also invex. For algorithms that rely on a non-zero gradient ∇F to produce new update steps invexity ensures that these algorithms will move forward as long as a descent direction exists.

1 Introduction

In this work we consider constrained optimization problems of the form

$$\min_x f(x) \quad s.t. \quad g(x) \leq \kappa, \tag{1}$$

where $x \in \mathbb{R}^p$, f is a differentiable invex function and g is an arbitrary, typically non-convex function. Within this wide class of problems we specifically focus on constraints $g(x)$ which can be made quasi-convex in a new variable $z \in \mathbb{R}^p$ by way of coordinate-wise transformations $x_j = h(z_i)$, $j = 1, \ldots, p$. This subset of problems is still relatively large. For instance, many problems in *sparse regression* with "sub ℓ_1"-penalties, i.e. non-convex penalties that produce sparser solutions than the *lasso*, fall into this class (The topic of non-convex constraint

---

S. M. Keller and D. Murezzan—Equal contribution.

Electronic supplementary material The online version of this chapter (https:// doi.org/10.1007/978-3-030-12939-2_47) contains supplementary material, which is available to authorized users.

T. Brox et al. (Eds.): GCPR 2018, LNCS 11269, pp. 682–697, 2019.
https://doi.org/10.1007/978-3-030-12939-2_47

regression has been discussed in multiple publications, e.g. [4,6,7,10,15,16,23]). The main advantage of having a quasi-convex constraint in the new variables is that certain optimization techniques, which rely on a convex feasible region, can now be applied. In particular, we focus on projection-free algorithms of *forward stagewise* type or on the highly related class of Frank Wolfe algorithms. These algorithms have properties which make them interesting in light of practical applications. For instance, forward stagewise methods are closely related to well-studied boosting algorithms, they are conceptually simple and computationally efficient, and they allow the computation (or dense sampling) of the whole *solution path* – i.e. the set of all solutions for a sequence of increasing constraint values – without any additional computational costs. Frank-Wolfe algorithms, on the other hand, are well studied from a theoretical point of view, and (local) convergence guaranties for problems involving non-convex functions f are available. When one is interested in the whole solution path (and arguably in most practical applications this is the case, e.g. performing model selection for the constraint value κ), the use of variable transformations $t : \mathbb{R}^p \to \mathbb{R}^p$, $x \mapsto z$ might induce local extrema in the minimization problem in Eq. (1). This in turn will pose a problem for gradient-based optimization strategies. We will show that this problem can be circumvented for transformations $h^{-1} : \mathbb{R}^p \to \mathbb{R}^p$, $x \mapsto z$ that fulfil certain criteria – basically invertability and smoothness of both h an h^{-1}. Such transformations keep the function $F(z) = (f \circ h)(z) = f(h(z))$ invex in the new variable z. This means that gradient-based methods evaluating $\nabla_z F(z)$ cannot get stuck in local minima. And assuming a sufficiently relaxed constraint value, the constructed solution path will indeed end at the unconstrained solution $\min_z F(z)$, provided that the minimum exists. Despite the fact that $F(z)$ has this invexity property, we cannot guarantee *joint invexity* of $F(z)$ and $G(z) = g(h(z))$, which would be necessary to prove that the solution path connects pointwise-optimal solutions. Panels (a) and (b) of Fig. 1 show a Gaussian function $f(x)$ (solid lines) where the positions of the respective minima differ only slightly. The problem is minimizing the function $f(x)$ over the depicted non-convex feasible region $g(x)$ (dotted lines). The result of the variable transformation, the functions $F(z)$ and $G(z)$, are shown in panels (c) and (d) where the constraint has now become convex. Minimization is performed in the z-space where one observes that the solution paths have changed considerably for only minor changes in the location of the minimum. In general, it would not be realistic to expect a guarantee of reconstructing the optimal solution path for a non-convex optimization problem. Nevertheless from a practical point of view the correctness of both the starting point[1] and the end point of the solution path is of considerable value as all solution paths will eventually converge towards the same end point as the constraint is relaxed. Furthermore any local extrema or saddlepoints of $F(z)$ introduced at the border of the

---

[1] In the supplementary materials, we provide an analytical proof which shows that for least squares regression problems the first active variable will always be correctly identified by the forward-stagewise method independent of the constraint. For other functions, the correctness of the first active variable can easily be empirically verified.

constraint region can always be escaped as κ is increased and no "re-starts" will ever become necessary. This too is a direct consequence of the invexity of $F(z)$. The solution path in the original variable is obtained by transforming back into x-space. The remainder of this paper is structured as follows. After a discussion of related work in Sect. 2, we briefly review the concept of invexity and prove invexity of $F(z)$ for certain transformations $x_j = h(z_j)$ in Sect. 3 and how to adapt it to different applications. We show how the proposed transformations allow regression problems to be formulated for several non-convex penalties (see Table 1), highlighting the easy applicability of the method to new models. In addition, we present a new algorithm for the sparse information bottleneck [19] which improves upon the previous algorithm by several orders of magnitude. Section 4 then discusses the general form of forward-stagewise and Frank-Wolfe algorithms in the transformed variable $z = h^{-1}(x)$ and finally in Sect. 5 we show several experiments on the proposed applications.

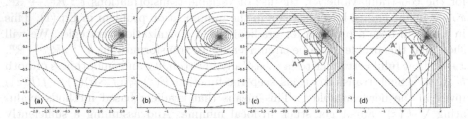

Fig. 1. The minimum of the Gaussian function $f(x)$ in panel (a) is located at $(2.0/1.0)$ and at $(1.8/1.0)$ in panel (b). After transforming $f(x)$ and the feasible region $g(x)$ into the new variable z, $F(z) = (f \circ h)(z) = f(h(z))$ has become invex whereas $G(z) = (g \circ h)(z) = g(h(z))$ is now convex (panels c, d). Using the forward stagewise algorithm which requires a convex feasible region, optimization is performed in z-space. Due to the differently located minima, the solution path for panels (a, c) is constructed by including first the dimension x_1 (A) into the active set followed by x_2 (B) once the correlation of x_1 with the residual has become small enough. In panels (b, d) the reverse sequence is observed: first x_2 (A') is included followed by x_1 (B'). From points C, C' onwards the weights of both dimensions is increased in alternating fashion till the minimum is reached for a sufficiently relaxed constraint value κ. The difference in solution paths reflects the non-convex nature of the optimization problem and illustrates that solution paths in such a setting can in general not be guaranteed to connect pointwise-optimal solutions.

2   Related Work

Projection-free constrained convex optimization such as generalized forward stagewise and Frank-Wolfe are well known optimization algorithms. [11] provides details between the connection of forward stagewise and lasso optimization.

Due to a different objective function, forward stagewise tries to minimize the arc-length of the solution path while lasso optimises the cost function at each point of the solution path. Consequently forward stagewise produces smoother solution paths compared to lasso, while retaining most of its properties (forward stagewise solutions converge to *monotone* lasso solutions as the step size ϵ tends towards zero [11]). A generalized version, which works for generic convex problems, is described in [21]. Frank-Wolfe was introduced in [5]. Recently it has increased in popularity due to its ability to efficiently solve a wide range of problems, as reviewed in [12]. Contrary to forward stagewise, Frank Wolfe is a point-estimator and will *not* construct a solution path. Both forward stagewise and Frank-Wolfe linearise the target function at each step and need a constraint for which the linearised problem is easily solved in order to be efficient. This is usually only the case for convex constraints. The concept of invexity is explained in [1] (a minor correction to this article was added by [8]), and described in detail in [17]. Invexity is a concept not well known to the machine learning community, although there exists work on it, e.g. [3,14].

Table 1. Overview of non-convex constraints, elementwise transformations and convex transformed constraints. It is assumed that $x_j \geq 0 \ \forall j$ and $z_j \geq 0 \ \forall j$ for the log and group log penalties, $\frac{\pi}{3} \geq z_j \geq 0 \ \forall j$ for the inverse tangent penalty and $\frac{2}{\gamma} \geq z_j \geq 0 \ \forall j$ for the rational polynomials penalty.

	Constraint $g(x)$	Transformation $x_j = h(z_j)$	Transformed constraint $g(z)$
Log penalty	$\sum_j \log(\gamma x_j + 1)$	$x_j = \frac{1}{\gamma}(\exp(z_j) - 1)$	$\sum_j z_j$
Log-group lasso	$\sum_i w_i \log(\gamma \|x_{I_i}\|_\infty + 1)$	$x_j = \frac{1}{\gamma}(\exp(z_j) - 1)$	$\sum_i w_i \|z_{I_i}\|_\infty$
Inverse tangent penalty	$\sum_j \text{atan}(\frac{1 + 2\gamma x_j}{\sqrt{3}}) - \frac{\pi}{6}$	$x_j = \frac{\sqrt{3}\,\tan(z_j + \frac{\pi}{6}) - 1}{2\gamma}$	$\sum_j z_j$
Rational polynomials	$\sum_j \frac{x_j}{1 + \gamma x_j/2}$	$x_j = \frac{2z_j}{\gamma z_j - 2}$	$\sum_j z_j$

3   Transformations Ensuring Invexity of the Objective Function

Invexity, as defined below, is an extension of convexity, i.e. every convex function is also an invex function. To recover the usual definition of a differentiable convex function one has to set $\eta(z, z') = z - z'$ in Definition 1.

Definition 1. *Let $Z \subseteq \mathbb{R}^p$ be an open set. The differentiable function $F : Z \to \mathbb{R}$ is invex if there exists a vector function $\eta : Z \times Z \to \mathbb{R}^p$ such that $F(z) - F(z') \geq \eta(z, z')^T \nabla_z F(z'), \ \forall z, z' \in Z$.*

An alternative definition of invexity is given by [1] in the following theorem:

Theorem 1. *F is invex if and only if every stationary point is a global minimum.*

The proof can be found in [1]. We now define a class of transformations $h(\cdot)$ under which the invexity property of function f is preserved.

Theorem 2. *Let $X, Z \subseteq \mathbb{R}^p$ be open sets, and let $f : X \to \mathbb{R}$ be invex and differentiable. Let h be a differentiable bijective function $h : Z \to X, z \mapsto x$ with differentiable inverse h^{-1}. Then $F(z) = (f \circ h)(z) = f(h(z))$ is invex on Z.*

Proof. Invexity of $f = F \circ h^{-1}$ and the chain rule imply

$$(F \circ h^{-1})(x) - (F \circ h^{-1})(y) \geq \eta(x, y)^T \nabla (F \circ h^{-1})(y)$$
$$= \eta(x, y)^T \nabla F(h^{-1}(y)) \nabla h^{-1}(y).$$

If $\nabla_z F(z^\star) = 0$, there exists an $y \in X$ s.t. $h(z^\star) = y$ and $h^{-1}(y) = z^\star$. It follows that $(F \circ h^{-1})(x) \geq F(z^\star) \ \forall x \in X$. Since h is one-to-one, $F(z) \geq F(z^\star) \ \forall z \in Z$. Hence, every stationary point of F yields a global minimum on Z, so F is invex on Z. □

Remark: As the proposed optimization method with non-convex constraints relies on every stationary point of the unconstrained objective function being a guaranteed global minimum, the class of quasiconvex functions is in general not permissible here. Furthermore the class of invex functions and the class of quasiconvex functions have only partial overlap, e.g. $f_1(x) = x^3, x \in \mathbb{R}$, is quasiconvex, but not invex, since $x = 0$ is a stationary point which is not a minimum point whereas $f_2(x, y) = x^3 + x - 10y^3 - y$ is invex as no stationary points exist, but not quasiconvex: following Definition 1 and choosing $z' = (0, 0)$, $x = 2$ and $y = 1$, yields $f(x, y) - f(z') < 0$ but $(x - y)\nabla f(z') > 0$. On the other hand, the class of pseudoconvex functions presents an unnecessary restriction as every pseudoconvex function is invex whereas the reverse is not true. See [9].

A particular sub-class of bijective functions $h(\cdot)$ on $Z \subseteq \mathbb{R}^p$ consists of strictly monotone increasing functions that are defined in a coordinate-wise manner, i.e. $h_j = h(z_j)$, $j = 1, .., p$ and map 0 onto itself[2], i.e. $h(0) = 0$. We will restrict ourselves to this type of coordinate-wise transformations for the remainder of this work.

Application Example I: Logarithmic Constraints for Sparse Regression.
In the context of regression, one possibility to ensure interpretability is to enforce sparsity of the coefficients. We now discuss transformations $h(\cdot)$ for families of constraint functions that are frequently used in the context of sparsity (for a list of example functions, see Table 1). One interesting class of non-convex constraints uses the concavity of the logarithm. These logarithmic constraints arise naturally as a means to interpolate between the ℓ_0-"norm" and the ℓ_1-norm:

$$g(x; \gamma) = \sum_{j=1}^{p} \log(\gamma|x_j| + 1). \tag{2}$$

---

[2] This is a crucial property in the context of sparse regression, as only then the sparsity patterns in x- and z-space are identical.

Used as a regularizer, such a constraint will often increase the sparsity of the solution of a linear regression problem even in comparison to lasso. The major problem for the application of our method to a regression setting is the domain of the x_j. Due to the required monotonicity of the constraint function $g(\cdot)$ (see Theorem 2), it is not possible to use penalties containing the absolute value function $|\cdot|$ on domains other than $\mathbb{R}_{\geq 0}$. This prevents the direct applicability of the method to regression and other settings where negative values are a possibility. For regression, this problem can be circumvented by doubling the number of predictors as described in the *monotone lasso* [11]. There x is replaced by $x_j^+ = \frac{1}{2}(|x_j| + x_j)$ and $x_j^- = \frac{1}{2}(|x_j| - x_j)$ which implies that $x_j^+ \geq 0, x_j^- \geq 0 \ \forall \ j$. The problem is thus redefined as $f(x = x^+ - x^-)$ s.t. $g(|x| = x^+ + x^-)$. This leads to a regression problem which is entirely defined on $\mathbb{R}_{\geq 0}$. Applied to least squares regression with a log-constraint, we obtain

$$\min_x \ \sum_{i=1}^n (b_i - [\sum_{j=1}^p a_{ij} x_j^+ - \sum_{j=1}^p a_{ij} x_j^-])^2 \tag{3}$$

$$\text{s.t.} \ \sum_{j=1}^p \log(\gamma(x_j^+ + x_j^-) + 1) \leq \kappa \text{ and } x_j^+ \geq 0, \ x_j^- \geq 0 \forall j = 1, \ldots, p. \tag{4}$$

If one analyses the KKT conditions of this problem, it can be seen that $x_j^+ > 0$ implies $x_j^- = 0$ (A detailed proof for general $f(x)$ and $g(x)$ can be found in the supplement). This allows us to write $g(x^+ + x^-) = g(\tilde{x})$ with $\tilde{x} = [x^+, x^-]$:

$$\sum_{j=1}^p \log(\gamma(x_j^+ + x_j^-) + 1) = \sum_{j=1}^{2p} \log(\gamma \tilde{x} + 1) \leq \kappa. \tag{5}$$

By substituting $\tilde{x}_j = h(\tilde{z}_j) = \frac{1}{\gamma}[\exp(\tilde{z}_j) - 1]$ in Eq. (5) this expression is transformed to the convex lasso constraint on $\mathbb{R}_{\geq 0}^{2p}$, i.e. $G(\tilde{z}; \gamma) = \sum_{j=1}^{2p} \tilde{z}_j$, while the loss function in Eq. (3) goes from convex to being invex. Theorem 2 requires the existence of the gradient of $F(z)$ at all points, which is not the case for $F(z = 0)$ if we consider only the closed set $\mathbb{R}_{\geq 0}^{2p}$. However, we can always fulfill this requirement by simply enlarging the domain of h^{-1} to include the neighbourhood of 0 (this requires f to be differentiable at 0, but we already stated this condition previously). This is always possible, since $h^{-1}(\tilde{x}) = \log(\gamma \tilde{x} + 1)$ is well-defined and differentiable at $x = 0$. Note that this argument would not be valid for ℓ_p-"norms" with $0 < p < 1$, since these functions are not differentiable at zero.

Application Example II: Sparse Information Bottleneck. The information bottleneck was introduced by [22]. Its goal is to compress a random variable X into a variable T, such that the mutual information $I(X; T)$ is minimized while the mutual information with a target variable Y, i.e. $I(Y; T)$, is maximized. In the *Gaussian IB*, one considers jointly Gaussian random vectors $X \in \mathbb{R}^p$ and $Y \in \mathbb{R}^q$. It follows that the optimal compression T is a noisy projection,

$T = AX + \eta$ with independent standard normal noise $\eta \sim N(0, I)$, [2]. The original formulation only allowed for discrete variables, but [2] extended the method to Gaussian variables and [20] proposed an extension to variables with a joint Gaussian copula. The problem we want to improve upon with our method is the sparse meta-gaussian information bottleneck discussed in [19], which also introduces sparsity to the compressed variable T. In this variant of the Gaussian IB, the actual optimization problem can be formulated as

$$\min_a \log |P_{X|Y} D_a + I| - \log |P_X D_a + I| \quad s.t. \quad \log |P_X D_a + I| \leq \kappa, \quad (6)$$

where P_X is the correlation matrix of X, and $P_{X|Y}$ denotes the conditional correlation of X, given Y. Note that for the case $P_X = I$, the penalty (6) reduces to

$$g_\gamma(x) = \sum_{j=1}^{p} \log(\gamma x_j + 1). \quad (7)$$

on the non-negative reals, which in turn allows for an element-wise transformation $x_j = h(z_j; \gamma) = \frac{1}{\gamma}(\exp(z_j) - 1)$. In general, the transformed constraint has a more complicated form with curved level sets (an image of the level-sets is available in the supplement), for which we have a solution in the next section.

Group-Sparse Constraints. The group lasso method is a generalization of the lasso to allow for sparsity on the level of grouped variables. One frequently used version of the group lasso uses a $\ell_{1,\infty}$ "block norm" $g(x) = \sum_j \|y_j\|_\infty$, where a vector y_j contains a group of variables. The constraint families in Eq. (2) (from the Paper), (11) and (12) (from Appendix Sect. 3) are all of the form $g(x) = \sum_j h^{-1}(x_j)$ and can be extended to group-sparse versions that are "below" the group-lasso block-norm, if we substitute x_j by $\|y_j\|_\infty$. Since the infinity-norm of the group is defined as the maximum within the group, and since we assume that we operate on the non-negative reals, for a group y_j containing l variables we have $\|y_j\|_\infty = \max\{y_{j1}, \ldots, y_{jl}\}$. By using a strictly monotone increasing element-wise transformation $y_{ji} = h(z_{ji})$ we arrive at

$$h^{-1}(\|y_j\|_\infty) = h^{-1}(\max\{h(z_{j1}), \ldots, h(z_{jl})\}) \quad (8)$$

$$= h^{-1}(h(\max\{z_{j1}, \ldots, z_{jl}\})) \quad (9)$$

$$= \max\{z_{j1}, \ldots, z_{jl}\}, \quad (10)$$

which again is simply the non-negative version of the group-lasso constraint.

Other Usable Non-convex Constraints. In applications like image denoising, several authors, e.g [13], have proposed to use sparsity penalties that either involve the inverse tangent function or rational polynomials.

$$g_\gamma(x) = \sum_{j=1}^{p} \text{atan}(\frac{1 + 2\gamma|x|}{\sqrt{3}}). \quad (11)$$

$$g_\gamma(x) = \sum_{j=1}^{p} \frac{|x|}{1 + \gamma|x|/2}. \quad (12)$$

Together with the augmentation trick in Eq. (4), and similar to the log-penalties discussed above, both versions can be transformed to lasso constraints with variable transformations $h(z)$ whose inverses are differentiable at zero.

4 Algorithms

Before discussing the algorithms, we now make two basic remarks.

1. The algorithms we are presenting require a convex constraint G. We consider non-convex constraint functions g which are transformed into convex functions $G = g(h(\cdot))$ by a mapping $h(\cdot)$ that fulfils the requirements of Theorem 2. For an initially invex function f, invexity of the objective function $F = f(h(\cdot))$ is preserved under that same mapping h.
2. The algorithms presented here will perform update steps as long as there is a non-zero gradient. The existence of a continuation criterion for the presented algorithms is guaranteed by the invexity of the objective function: As the algorithms only consider ∇F, update steps are performed as long as the constraint remains active.

4.1 Forward Stagewise

General Forward Stagewise Procedures. For two convex functions $f(x)$ and $g(x)$ the general form of the forward-stagewise method is described in [21]. Here we assume g to be *non-convex*. Applying the doubling of predictors $x \mapsto \tilde{x} = [x^+, x^-]$ described in our "Application Example I" and substituting $\tilde{x}_j = h(z_j)$ in f we obtain the invex function $F(z) = (f \circ h)(z)$ and the convex function $G(z) = g(h(z))$. It is now possible to use projection-free optimization methods like forward stagewise to find the minimum of $F(z)$ constrained by $G(z)$. The general forward stagewise procedure is:
Initialize $z^{(0)} = 0$. Repeat while $G(z) < \kappa$:

$$L^{(j)} = \nabla F(z)\big|_{z=z^{(j)}}, \tag{13}$$

$$\Delta_\beta = \operatorname*{argmin}_\beta \beta^t L^{(j)} \quad s.t. \quad G(\beta) \le \epsilon \text{ and } \beta \ge 0, \tag{14}$$

$$z^{(j+1)} = z^{(j)} + \Delta_\beta. \tag{15}$$

In some cases, the increment Δ_β can be found analytically, see [21] for a general discussion of penalty functions that have this property. For the lasso constraint on the non-negative reals, i.e. $G(z; \gamma) = g(h(z; \gamma)) = \sum_j z_j$, the increment has the form:
Initialize $z^{(0)} = 0$. Repeat while $G(z) < \kappa$ and $L_i^{(j)} < 0$ for any i:

$$L^{(j)} = \nabla F(z)\big|_{z=z^{(j)}}, \tag{16}$$

$$i = \operatorname*{argmin}_i L_i^{(j)}, \tag{17}$$

$$z^{(j+1)} = z^{(j)} + \epsilon \cdot e_i, \tag{18}$$

where e_i is the unit vector for dimension i. Note that log-constraints for sparse "sub-lasso" regression in Eq. (2), as well as inverse tangent penalties and rational polynomials (see Table 1) can be easily transformed to this non-negative lasso setting.

Forward Stagewise with First Order Taylor Approximation. In some cases, however, the transformed constraint $G(z)$ is convex but has a more complicated structure (than the ℓ_1-region). For this case we propose the *Forward stagewise with first order Taylor approximation*. With $\epsilon \ll 0$ we are allowed to replace $G(\beta)$ in Eq. 14 with its Taylor expansion around zero. If the transformation h has succeeded in mapping the non-convex constraint onto a convex constraint *close* to the ℓ_1 shape, truncating the series after the linear term is often sufficient to obtain a good approximation. For instance in case of the "Sparse Information Bottleneck", using only the linear term, the increment Δ_β is approximated as follows $\log|PD + I| \approx trace(PD) = trace(D)$. The latter identity follows from P being a correlation matrix with ones on the diagonal. In practice, this approximation leads to virtually indistinguishable results when compared to the numerically computed "true" solution of Δ_β, but at a considerable computational speed-up. We demonstrate this in the experiment section (see Fig. 6).

4.2   Frank-Wolfe Algorithms

Frank-Wolfe was introduced in [5]. Recently it has increased in popularity due to its ability to efficiently solve a wide range of problems, as reviewed in [12]. Contrary to forward stagewise, Frank Wolfe is a point-estimator and will *not* construct a solution path. Both forward stagewise and Frank-Wolfe linearise the objective function at each step and need a constraint for which the linearised problem is easily solved in order to be efficient. This is usually only the case for convex constraints. Formally, Frank-Wolfe algorithms use simple modifications of the general forward-stagewise update steps. In particular, the computation of the increment in Eq. (14) is modified to include the *whole* constraint region $\{\beta : G(\beta) \leq \kappa\}$:

$$\Delta_\beta = \underset{\beta}{\operatorname{argmin}} \ \beta^t L^{(j)} \quad s.t. \quad G(\beta) \leq \kappa \text{ and } \beta \geq 0 \qquad (19)$$

Further, the update in Eq. (15) has a slightly modified form using convex mixtures of the old value and the new increment Δ_β

$$z^{(j+1)} = (1 - t)z^{(j)} + t\Delta_\beta. \qquad (20)$$

Due to this high formal similarity, the use of variable transformations $h(\cdot)$ has the same implications for Frank-Wolfe algorithms as it has for forward stagewise algorithms. It should be noted, however, that Frank-Wolfe algorithms cannot be directly used to compute a solution path. A potential "path"-variant is discussed in [21], but compared to forward-stagewise algorithms, this variant has dramatically increased computational costs. On the other hand, Frank-Wolfe methods have some local convergence guarantees which are not available in this form for forward-stagewise methods. The choice between the two algorithms therefore depends on the actual requirements. Important to note is that all guarantees (see [12]) provided by forward stagewise and Frank Wolfe apply only to the transformed problem where the constraint is convex. These guarantees have no meaning in the original problem, as neither forward stagewise nor Frank Wolfe are applicable in a non-convex setting. Nevertheless, the progress, i.e. the decrease in the loss function along the solution path, will be identical for the original and the transformed problem as shown in Eq. 21. For an optimization problem of the form of Eq. 1, the minimization is performed in z-space and the following holds:

$$\begin{aligned}
F(z) - F(z') &= (f \circ h)(z) - (f \circ h)(z') \\
&= f(h(z)) - f(h(z')) \\
&= f(x) - f(x').
\end{aligned} \tag{21}$$

This means that for an algorithm constructing a series of intermediate solutions the difference between two such solutions will be the same in both spaces.

5   Experiments

5.1   Topographic Plots of Two Dimensional Solution Paths

Figure 2 shows the optimization path generated by Frank Wolfe for a two dimensional problem and the solution path produced by forward stagewise for that same problem. The penalty used is given in Eq. 2. As one can see, the boundary of the constrained region has a non-convex shape in the original problem, while the transformed problem has a ℓ_1 constraint. For forward stagewise, the sparsity of the path is expressed by its course parallel to the coordinate axis: first, the w_2 dimension is included into the model then followed by the w_1 dimension. All points on the path are intermediate solutions corresponding to different values of κ. Intermediate points of the Frank Wolfe procedure on the other hand do in general not correspond to a specific value of κ.

5.2   Solution Paths in Dependence of γ

In Fig. 3, we compare the solution paths generated by forward stagewise for different values of γ (using the log penalty given in Eq. 2). The dataset used to generate these plots consisting of $n = 100$ samples, $p = 300$ predictors and the coefficients $x = [5, 5, 5, 5, 5, 0, ..., 0, -1, -1, -1, -1, -1]$. Thus, there are 10 non-zero coefficients. The correlation matrix Σ is generated by $\Sigma_{ij} = min(i, j) * \frac{1}{p}$, which means the negative coefficients are highly correlated and the positive ones uncorrelated. We add Gaussian noise with $\sigma^2 = 50$ to the response values. The

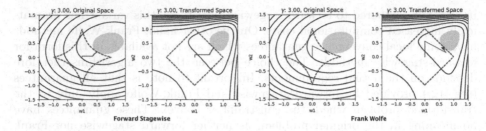

Fig. 2. Plots of two dimensional forward stagewise solution path (left) and Frank Wolfe optimization path (right). Red path corresponds to the solution (or optimization) path, blue dashed line denotes the boundaries of the constrained region and the green surface shows the area for which all values of the loss function are smaller than the solution found by the algorithm. The right plots show the transformed loss over the ℓ_1 norm, on the left side the least squares loss with log-penalty is shown. Plot is for $\gamma = 5.0$ and $\kappa = 1$. (Color figure online)

top panels show the size of the coefficients in dependence of the training loss while the bottom panels show the test loss as a function of the training loss. The red, vertical line depicts the minimum loss on the test set. The two leftmost panels use the log-penalty with a small γ value of 0.001. This corresponds approximately to a ℓ_1 regularization, and the coefficient paths look like a typical lasso path. The right and centre panels also use the log-penalty, but with a γ value of 0.5 respectively 3.0. We see that the coefficient paths with higher γ values are generally sparser. The test error for the best model as well as the number of active coefficients decrease as γ increases. A higher γ value also means that new coefficients will enter the model at later stages and already selected coefficients will end up with higher absolute values.

5.3   Monotone Increasing Solution Paths for Forward Stagewise

In [11], it is shown that the path optimized by forward stagewise differs from a solution path computed by the lasso in case of highly correlated predictors. We reproduce their experiment and show that similar observations can be made for non-convex penalties. As a comparison, we use the sparsenet package by [16] (available in the R-repository). Sparsenet also constructs a path for non-convex penalties, although in their case they use the MC+ penalty from [23]. The experimental setup is as follows: The data consist of 60 samples with 1000 dimension. The dimensions are divided into 20 groups of the same size. Samples are drawn from a multivariate Gaussian, where the correlation between each member of a group is $\rho = 0.95$, members of different groups are uncorrelated. For each group, there is a non-zero coefficient in the solution vector, each drawn from a standard Gaussian. Gaussian noise is added to the output variable with a standard deviation of $\sigma = 6$. We plot the obtained solution paths in Fig. 4. One observes that the effect of the monotonicity of the forward stagewise paths carry over to the sparse version ($\gamma = 5$) while the sparsenet coefficients fluctuate much

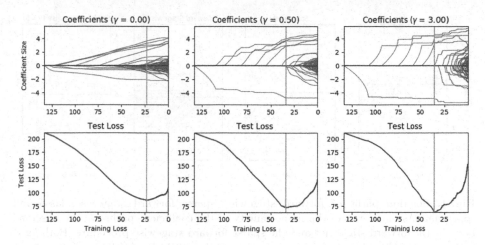

Fig. 3. From left to right: solution paths for log penalty with $\gamma = 0.001$, $\gamma = 1$ and $\gamma = 5$. Top panels depict the size of coefficients, bottom panels the error on the test set. On the y axis, the training loss is given. Each point on the y axis corresponds to a valid model. The panel on the left side approximates the lasso problem. The center and right panels show increased sparsity compared to the lasso solutions.

more. This is explained by the different objectives these algorithms optimize: Forward stagewise optimizes the arc-length of the path, and therefore leads to a far smoother solution path by preventing the path from changing drastically between subsequent solutions. Lasso on the other hand optimizes the cost function at each point of the solution path. In addition, sparse forward stagewise is more efficient in computing the solution path compared to forward stagewise when a similar dense solution path is wanted (15 s for sparse forward stagewise vs 45 s for sparsenet on a 2.9 GHz Intel Core i5).

5.4   Regression on Artificial Data

In this experiment, the goal is to assess if an increase in sparsity can help to find a better model than it is possible with regular lasso regression or forward stagewise. For this, a dataset consisting of 50 features and 40 samples is created. In the underlying model, only four coefficients are related to the target. In Fig. 5, the first and last two coefficients have a coefficient size of $[-20, -10, 10, 20]$. Noise with a standard deviation of 15 is added to the result. All input features are correlated to each other with a correlation coefficient of 0.1. Figure 5 shows the result of this experiment. All models use cross correlation to select the correct sparsity level. The top model on the left corresponds to lasso regression (model taken from the sklearn library [18]), the middle one to forward stagewise and the bottom one to sparse forward stagewise (with $\gamma = 5$). All models are tested on a test set and the scores on training and test set can be seen on the right. Overall, sparse forward stagewise leads to better test performance with a slightly worse training performance. If we look at the coefficients, its apparent that sparse

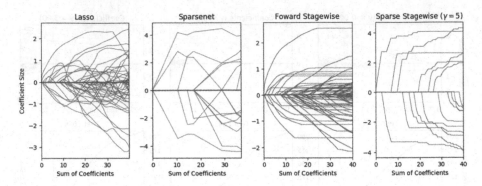

Fig. 4. Solution paths of forward stagewise, sparse forward stagewise, lasso and sparsenet. As one can see, the monotonicity of the coefficient paths can be observed both in the forward stagewise and the sparse forward stagewise procedure. Both lasso and sparsenet show bigger variations in the solution path due to the impact of correlated coefficients. This can be explained by the fact that forward stagewise minimizes the arc-length of the solution path, which adds smoothness to the coefficient paths.

forward stagewise includes less spurious features as the other two and better recovers the true magnitude of the coefficients in the underlying model. This is also expected, as the better a model can approximate ℓ_0, the less shrinkage should occur. This experiments can be considered as a ideal case for our method: There are more features than samples in the dataset and there is only a small amount of correlation between the input variables, which favours a model that can perform feature selection while recovering the magnitude of the coefficients without bias.

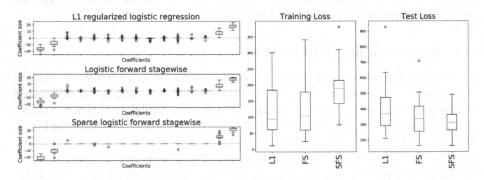

Fig. 5. Coefficient boxplots for ℓ_1 regularized logistic regression (L1), forward stagewise (FS) and sparse forward stagewise with $\gamma = 5$ (SFS). Only 15 coefficients are shown (the first and last two as well as eleven other) to increase the legibility of the figure. Coefficients not shown have also median of zero with some outliers similar to the middle ones visible in the left figure.

5.5   Sparse Gaussian Information Bottleneck

We use the forward-stagewise algorithm with first order Taylor approximation for computing the solution path, i.e. the evolution of the sparse compression coefficients a when the constraint κ is relaxed, of the sparse gaussian information bottleneck. The original algorithm proposed in [19] uses a log-Barrier method and traverses the solution path in the opposite direction: for a very large initial constraint value, this original algorithm starts at a feasible point a with strictly positive coefficients, which are then successively shrinked to zero by tightening the constraint. Typically, however, we are interested in sparse solutions, and this reverse traversal of the solution path is rather inefficient in practice. Our forward-stagewise algorithm, however, starts with the empty vector $a = 0$ and successively includes new positive components when the constraint is relaxed. This conceptual difference leads to a huge difference in computational workloads. On artificial data containing three "informative" features (i.e. dimensions in X which indeed have nonzero mutual information with Y), and many other noisy dimensions, our proposed forward-stagewise algorithm improved the run-time by several orders of magnitude, see the left of Fig. 6. The new algorithm will introduce a error to the solution, as only the first order approximation is used, however, as one can see on the right side of Fig. 6, this error is negligible if one compares the exact and approximate solution.

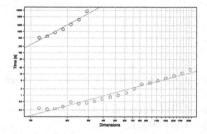 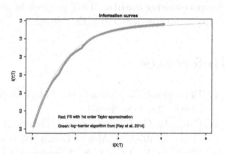

Fig. 6. (Left) Runtime experiments for the sparse meta-Gaussian information bottleneck. The data always contained 2000 samples, the dimensionality of Y was 20. There are three informative dimensions in X, and a varying number of additional noise dimensions (x-axis). Blue points/curve: algorithm proposed in [19], line is linear regression fit. Red: our proposed forward-stagewise algorithm, stopped after 10 variables have been selected. Note that this is a log-log plot. (Right) Comparison of information curves between the log-barrier method and forward stagewise with first order Taylor approximation. As one can see, forward stagewise induces a certain error into the solution, but compared to the exact solution, the error is negligible. (Color figure online)

6   Conclusion

Our contribution is threefold: We first show how popular optimization algorithms of the forward stagewise and Frank Wolfe type can be applied to *non-convex* constraints by means of mapping the non-convex constraints onto a convex ones. Assuming invexity of the initial objective function, the proposed mapping preserves this property such that the transformed objective is again invex. For gradient based optimization algorithms that require convex constraints and rely only on the gradient of the objective function to produce an update step, invexity ensures that there always exists an optimization direction as long as there is a descent direction. In our second contribution we show that several popular non-convex constraints can be mapped onto the ℓ_1 constraint, for which forward stagewise and Frank Wolfe are extremely efficient. Our third contribution deals with situations where non-convex penalties cannot be mapped onto the ℓ_1 region but onto a convex region close to ℓ_1. For this case, we propose a forward stagewise approach with first order Taylor approximation. In the experiment section, we show that in a log-constrained regression setting, we can achieve better generalization performance by trading off less shrinkage for more sparsity compared to lasso. Additionally, we show that a log-constraint optimization problem which arises naturally in the context of the sparse information bottleneck can be solved more efficiently. This is possible by transforming the non-convex constraint in such a way that forward stagewise, a convex optimization algorithm, can be applied. Our approach is able to outperform the previous algorithm by several orders of magnitude.

Acknowledgements. This project is supported by the the Swiss National Science Foundation project CR32I2 159682.

References

1. Ben-Israel, A., Mond, B.: What is invexity? J. Aust. Math. Soc. Ser. B. Appl. Math. **28**, 1–9 (1986)
2. Chechik, G., Globerson, A., Tishby, N., Weiss, Y.: Information bottleneck for Gaussian variables. J. Mach. Learn. Res. **6**(1), 165–188 (2005)
3. Dinuzzo, F., Ong, C.S., Pillonetto, G., Gehler, P.V.: Learning output kernels with block coordinate descent. In: Proceedings of the 28th International Conference on Machine Learning (ICML-2011), pp. 49–56 (2011)
4. Fan, J., Li, R.: Variable selection via nonconcave penalized likelihood and its oracle properties. J. Am. Stat. Assoc. **96**(456), 1348–1360 (2001)
5. Frank, M., Wolfe, P.: An algorithm for quadratic programming. Naval Res. Logistics (NRL) **3**(1–2), 95–110 (1956)
6. Friedman, J.H.: Fast sparse regression and classification. Int. J. Forecast. **28**(3), 722–738 (2012)
7. Gasso, G., Rakotomamonjy, A., Canu, S.: Solving non-convex lasso type problems with dc programming. In: IEEE Workshop on Machine Learning for Signal Processing, MLSP 2008, pp. 450–455. IEEE (2008)
8. Giorgi, G.: On first order sufficient conditions for constrained optima. In: Maruyama, T., Takahashi, W. (eds.) Nonlinear and Convex Analysis in Economic Theory, pp. 53–66. Springer, Heidelberg (1995). https://doi.org/10.1007/978-3-642-48719-4_5
9. Giorgi, G.: On some generalizations of preinvex functions **49** (2008)

10. Gorodnitsky, I.F., Rao, B.D.: Sparse signal reconstruction from limited data using focuss: a re-weighted minimum norm algorithm. IEEE Trans. Signal Process. **45**(3), 600–616 (1997)
11. Hastie, T., Taylor, J., Tibshirani, R., Walther, G.: Forward stagewise regression and the monotone lasso. Electron. J. Stat. **1**, 1–29 (2007). https://doi.org/10.1214/07-EJS004
12. Jaggi, M.: Revisiting Frank-Wolfe: projection-free sparse convex optimization. In: ICML, vol. 1, pp. 427–435 (2013)
13. Lanza, A., Morigi, S., Sgallari, F.: Convex image denoising via non-convex regularization. In: Aujol, J.-F., Nikolova, M., Papadakis, N. (eds.) SSVM 2015. LNCS, vol. 9087, pp. 666–677. Springer, Cham (2015). https://doi.org/10.1007/978-3-319-18461-6_53
14. Li, G., Yan, Z., Wang, J.: A one-layer recurrent neural network for constrained nonsmooth invex optimization. Neural Netw. **50**, 79–89 (2014)
15. Li, X., Zhao, T., Zhang, T., Liu, H.: The picasso package for nonconvex regularized M-estimation in high dimensions in R. Technical report (2015)
16. Mazumder, R., Friedman, J.H., Hastie, T.: SparseNet: coordinate descent with nonconvex penalties. J. Am. Stat. Assoc. **106**(495), 1125–1138 (2011)
17. Mishra, S., Giorgi, G.: Invexity and Optimization. Nonconvex Optimization and Its Applications. Springer, Heidelberg (2008). https://doi.org/10.1007/978-3-540-78562-0
18. Pedregosa, F., et al.: Scikit-learn: machine learning in python. J. Mach. Learn. Res. **12**, 2825–2830 (2011)
19. Rey, M., Fuchs, T., Roth, V.: Sparse meta-Gaussian information bottleneck. In: Proceedings of the 31st International Conference on Machine Learning (ICML-2014), pp. 910–918 (2014)
20. Rey, M., Roth, V.: Meta-Gaussian information bottleneck. In: Advances in Neural Information Processing Systems-NIPS 25 (2012)
21. Tibshirani, R.J.: A general framework for fast stagewise algorithms. J. Mach. Learn. Res. **16**, 2543–2588 (2015)
22. Tishby, N., Pereira, F.C., Bialek, W.: The information bottleneck method. arXiv preprint physics/0004057 (2000)
23. Zhang, C.H.: Nearly unbiased variable selection under minimax concave penalty. Ann. Stat. **38**, 894–942 (2010)

Unsupervised Label Learning on Manifolds by Spatially Regularized Geometric Assignment

Artjom Zern[1]([✉]), Matthias Zisler[1], Freddie Åström[1], Stefania Petra[2], and Christoph Schnörr[1]

[1] Image and Pattern Analysis Group, Heidelberg University, Heidelberg, Germany
artjom.zern@iwr.uni-heidelberg.de
[2] Mathematical Imaging Group, Heidelberg University, Heidelberg, Germany

Abstract. Manifold models of image features abound in computer vision. We present a novel approach that combines unsupervised computation of representative manifold-valued features, called labels, and the spatially regularized assignment of these labels to given manifold-valued data. Both processes evolve dynamically through two Riemannian gradient flows that are coupled. The representation of labels and assignment variables are kept separate, to enable the flexible application to various manifold data models. As a case study, we apply our approach to the unsupervised learning of covariance descriptors on the positive definite matrix manifold, through spatially regularized geometric assignment.

1 Introduction

Manifold-based methods define an active research area in computer vision [19]. Covariance descriptors, in particular, play a prominent role [5]. Covariance descriptors are typically applied to the detection and classification of entire images (e.g. faces, texture) or videos (e.g. action recognition). An important task in this context is to compute a *codebook of covariance descriptors* that can be used solving a task at hand by nearest-neighbor search [6].

The recent work [10] defines a *geometric state-of-the-art method* for computing such codebooks. Embedding descriptors into a Hilbert space (see (4) below) enables to approximate given data by kernel expansion [11] and to determine a sparse subset by ℓ_1-regularization of the expansion coefficients. This method works *entirely in feature space* and ignores the *spatial* structure of codebook assignments to data. Figure 1 illustrates that when covariance descriptors are used as 'labels' for representing *local* image structure, rather than encoding *global* second-order statistics of entire images or videos, then the *spatial structure* of label assignments should also drive the evolution of labels in feature space for unsupervised label learning.

The classical approach for the unsupervised learning of feature prototypes ('labels') is the mean-shift iteration [7,8], which iteratively seeks modes

T. Brox et al. (Eds.): GCPR 2018, LNCS 11269, pp. 698–713, 2019.
https://doi.org/10.1007/978-3-030-12939-2_48

(local peaks) of the feature density distribution through the averaging of features within local neighborhoods. This has been generalized to *manifold-valued* features by [17] by replacing ordinary mean-shifts by Riemannian (Fréchet, Karcher) means [13]. The common way to take into account the *spatial structure* of label assignments is to *augment* the feature space by *spatial coordinates*, e.g. turn a color feature (r, g, b) into the feature vector (x, y, r, g, b). This *merge* of feature space and spatial domain has a conceptual drawback, however: The *same* color vector $(\overline{r}, \overline{g}, \overline{b})$ observed at two *different* locations $(x_1, y_1, \overline{r}, \overline{g}, \overline{b})$, $(x_2, y_2, \overline{r}, \overline{g}, \overline{b})$ defines two *different* feature vectors. Furthermore, clustering spatial coordinates into *centroids* by mean-shifts (together with the features) *differs* from *unbiased spatial regularization* as performed by variational approaches or graphical models, that do *not* depend on the location of centroids and the corresponding shape of local density modes. This work, therefore, studies the problem of representing a given manifold-valued input image with few prototypes, which are learned in an unsupervised way, while performing unbiased spatial regularization in the image domain.

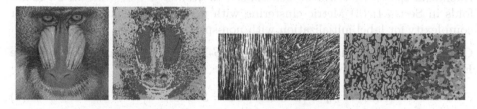

Fig. 1. Local assignments of covariance descriptors $\{G_j\}_{j \in J} \subset \mathcal{P}_d$ from a codebook J to data $\{F_i\}_{i \in I}$ are *noisy*. Different colors represent different codebook entry assignments but do not have any other specific meaning. By definition, *unsupervised* learning rules out the possibility of feature parameters tuning. Rather, covariance descriptors should *evolve* along a flow $G(t)$ driven by *spatially regularized* assignments $W(t)$ that are *not* biased towards spatial centroids and still enable *global* communication on the feature manifold $\mathcal{P}_d$. This is accomplished by our approach (1). (Color figure online)

Contribution. We introduce a novel approach with the following properties:

(i) The approach incorporates and performs *unsupervised learning of manifold-valued features*, henceforth called *labels*. We work with covariance descriptors as a case study. But the approach applies to any feature manifold [17] for which the corresponding Riemannian feature means are well-defined and computationally feasible.

(ii) The evolution of labels (unsupervised learning) is driven by the *spatial regularization of assignments* that is *not* biased towards spatial centroids. This is accomplished by applying the *geometric* approach to image labeling by assignment, recently introduced by [2].

(iii) The smooth settings of both (i), (ii) enables to define a *smooth coupled flow*

$$(\dot{G}, \dot{W}) = \mathcal{V}(G, W) \tag{1}$$

where the evolution of labels G and the evolution of spatially regularized assignments (of labels to data) W *interact*. This interaction keeps both domains (i) and (ii) *separate*, which enables to use alternative feature manifolds with the *same* regularized assignment mechanism.

Organization. Section 2 sketches basic material required to understand the approaches (i) and (ii), which are described in Sect. 3. Our approach is presented in Sect. 4. The concrete iterative scheme corresponding to (1) and geometric numerical integration is given by system of Eq. (30a–30d). We present and discuss experimental results in Sect. 5.

2   Preliminaries

To make this paper self-contained, we briefly sketch three methods that are relevant to our approach: (1) Geometry of the domain of covariance descriptors, S-divergence and Hilbert space embedding; (2) Soft-k-means clustering in Euclidean spaces that will be generalized to *geometric* soft-k-means on manifolds in Sect. 4.1; (3) Metric clustering with performance guarantee and linear complexity for label initialization with non-sparse codebooks.

Geometry of Covariance Descriptors, S-Divergence and Hilbert Space Embedding. The open cone

$$\mathcal{P}_d = \{S \in \mathbb{R}^{d \times d} : S = S^\top, \ S \succ 0\} \tag{2}$$

of symmetric positive definite matrices endowed with the Riemannian *metric* $\langle S_1, S_2 \rangle_S = \langle S^{-1} S_1 S^{-1}, S_2 \rangle = \operatorname{tr}(S^{-1} S_1 S^{-1} S_2)$ forms a Riemannian manifold [3]. Since evaluating the Riemannian *distance* involves a numerically expensive generalized eigenvalue problem, *divergence* functions are used instead as a compromise between respecting the geometry of (2) and computational efficiency (cf. e.g. [6]). We focus on the *symmetric S-(matrix-)divergence* [16]

$$D_S(F, G) = \log \det \left(\frac{F + G}{2} \right) - \frac{1}{2} \log \det(FG), \qquad F, G \in \mathcal{P}_d \tag{3}$$

that emerges as special case of a parametric family of matrix divergence functions [4] and compares favorably to the more common log-Euclidean divergence [1]. Moreover, the S-divergence generates a valid kernel function

$$k_S(F, G) = \exp\left(-\beta D_S(F, G)\right) \quad \text{with} \quad \beta \in \{\tfrac{1}{2}, \tfrac{2}{2}, \dots, \tfrac{d-1}{2}\} \cup [\tfrac{d-1}{2}, \infty) \tag{4}$$

for the embedding $\mathcal{P}_d \to \mathcal{H}$ of covariance descriptors into a reproducing kernel Hilbert space $\mathcal{H}$ [11]. This has been explored recently by [10], see also [5].

Euclidean Soft-k-Means Clustering. The content of this paragraph can be found in numerous papers and textbooks. We merely refer to the survey [18] and to the bibliography therein. It will be generalized to the manifold $\mathcal{P}_d$ (2) of covariance descriptors in Sect. 4.

Given data vectors $x^1, \ldots, x^{|I|}$, we consider the task of determining proto-type vectors $M = \{m^1, \ldots, m^{|J|}\}$ by minimizing the k-means criterion $J(M) = \sum_{i \in I} \min_{j \in J} \|x^i - m^j\|^2$. *Soft-k*-means is based on the *smoothed* objective

$$J_\varepsilon(M) = -\varepsilon \sum_{i \in I} \log \Big(\sum_{j \in J} \exp \big(- \frac{\|x^i - m^j\|^2}{\varepsilon} \big) \Big), \tag{5}$$

which results from approximating the inner minimization problem of $J(M)$ using the log-exponential function [14, p. 27]. Similar to the basic k-means algorithm, *soft-k*-means clustering solves the stationarity condition $\nabla_{m^j} J_\varepsilon(M) = 0$, $j \in J$ by fixed point iteration that iterates the update steps

$$p^i_{\varepsilon, j}(M) = \frac{\exp \big(- d^i_j(M)/\varepsilon \big)}{\sum_{l \in J} \exp \big(- d^i_l(M)/\varepsilon \big)}, \quad d^i_j(M) = \|x^i - m^j\|^2 \tag{6}$$

for every $i \in I, j \in J$ and

$$m^j = \sum_{i \in I} q^j_i(M) x^i, \quad q^j_i(M) = \frac{p^i_{\varepsilon, j}(M)}{\sum_{k \in I} p^k_{\varepsilon, j}(M)}. \tag{7}$$

The distribution $p^i_\varepsilon(M) \in \Delta_k$ represents the *soft-assignment* $p^i_{\varepsilon, j}(M)$ of each data point x^i to each prototype m^j, and the distribution $q^j(M)$ determines the convex combination of data points that determines the prototypes m^j by the *mean-shift* (7).

Greedy Clustering in Metric Spaces. We adopt a simple algorithm from [9] as a preprocessing step for data reduction, due to the following properties: It works in *any metric space* (X, d_X), it has *linear* complexity $\mathcal{O}(kN)$ with respect to the problem size N, and it comes along with a *performance guarantee*.

Given data points $X_N = \{x^1, \ldots, x^N\} \subset X$, the objective is to determine a k-subset $M = \{m^1, \ldots, m^k\}$ that solves the combinatorially hard optimization problem

$$J^*_\infty = \min_{M \subset X_N, |M| = k} \max_{x \in X_N} d_X(x, M). \tag{8}$$

Starting from a first initial point m^1, e.g. chosen randomly, selecting the remaining $k - 1$ points $m^2, \ldots, m^k$ by greedy iteration yields a set M that is a 2-approximation $J_\infty(M) \leq 2J^*_\infty$ of the optimum (8) [9, Theorem 4.3]. As a consequence, the subset of k points of M are uniformly distributed in X_N according to the metric d_X. Figure 2 provides an illustration.

3   Label Learning, Label Assignment

We sketch the recent work of [10] and [2] which motivated our approach, that is presented in Sect. 4.

Fig. 2. Approximation of the metric clustering objective (8). LEFT: 10.000 points on the sphere regarded as manifold equipped with the cosine distance. RIGHT: 200 prototypes determined with linear runtime complexity by metric clustering are *almost uniformly located* in the data set, which qualifies them for unbiased initialization of more complex nonlinear prototype evolutions (Sect. 4). This works in any metric space and is applied in this paper to covariance descriptors on the positive definite matrix manifold (2), to determine non-sparse codebooks as initialization $G(t)|_{t=0}$ of the flow (1).

Sparse Coding of Covariance Descriptors [10]. Given observations $\{F_i\}_{i \in I} \subset \mathcal{P}_d$ and the embedding $\phi \colon \mathcal{P}_d \to \mathcal{H}$ into a Hilbert space induced by the S-divergence (3) and the kernel function (4), the objective function for learning a sparse codebook $G = \{G_j\}_{j \in J} \subset \mathcal{P}_d$ of covariance descriptors reads

$$J(G, y) = \sum_{i \in I} l_\phi(y, F_i, G), \quad l_\phi(y, F_i, G) = \left\| \phi(F_i) - \sum_{j \in J} y_j \phi(G_j) \right\|^2 + \alpha \|y\|_1, \quad (9)$$

where sparsity is enforced through ℓ_1-penalization of the coefficients y. The approach iterates (i) a *sparse coding step* solving $y_i = \operatorname{argmin}_y l_\phi(y, F_i, G)$, $i \in [m]$ while keeping G fixed, and (ii) a *dictionary learning step* evaluating the optimality condition $\nabla_{G_j} J(G) = 0$, $\forall j$. In the particular case of the S-divergence (3), (4), this condition takes the form of an *algebraic Riccati equation* which can be solved numerically with the fixed-point iteration

$$G_j - G_j \mathcal{G}_j(G) G_j = 0, \qquad G_j^{(k+1)} = \left(\mathcal{G}_j(G^{(k)}) \right)^{-1}, \quad j \in J. \quad (10)$$

The map $\mathcal{G}_j(G)$ is given by

$$\mathcal{G}_j(G) = \frac{\sum_i y_{ij} \left(k_S(F_i, G_j) \left(\frac{F_i + G_j}{2} \right)^{-1} - \sum_r y_{ir} k_S(G_j, G_r) \left(\frac{G_j + G_r}{2} \right)^{-1} \right)}{\sum_i y_{ij} \left(k_S(F_i, G_j) - \sum_r y_{ir} k_S(G_j, G_r) \right)}. \quad (11)$$

As discussed in Sect. 1, we point out again that this approach *entirely* works on the feature manifold $\mathcal{P}_d$ with auxiliary variables y, *independent* of the spatial image structure corresponding to the data $\{F_i\}_{i \in I}$.

Regularized Image Labeling on the Assignment Manifold [2]. Given data $\{F_i\}_{i \in I}$ and labels $\{G_j\}_{j \in J}$, assignments $F_i \leftrightarrow G_j$ are represented by the components $W_{i,j}$ of *assignment vectors* $W_i \in \mathcal{S}$, $i \in I$, where $\mathcal{S}$ denotes the open probability simplex equipped with the Fisher-Rao metric. Gathering all vectors into the assignment matrix $W \subset \mathcal{W} \in \mathbb{R}^{|I| \times |J|}$ on the product manifold $\mathcal{W} := \prod_{i \in I} \mathcal{S}$, spatially regularized assignments W are determined as follows.

A distance matrix

$$D \in \mathbb{R}^{|I| \times |J|}, \quad D_i = \big(d(F_i, G_1), \ldots, d(F_i, G_{|J|})\big)^\top, \qquad i \in I \qquad (12)$$

with row vectors D_i, describes the similarity of labels G_j and data F_i based on any distance function $d(\cdot, \cdot)$. Using the mapping (with componentwise multiplication of strictly positive vectors in the numerator)

$$L_p(u) = \frac{p e^u}{\langle p, e^u \rangle}, \qquad p \in \mathcal{S}, \qquad (13)$$

which serves as a first-order approximation of the exponential mapping induced by the Fisher-Rao geometry [2, Proposition 3], the distance matrix D is turned into the likelihood matrix

$$L(W) \in \mathbb{R}^{|I| \times |J|}, \quad L_i(W) = L_{W_i}(-D_i/\rho) = \frac{W_i e^{-D_i/\rho}}{\langle W_i, e^{-D_i/\rho} \rangle}, \quad \rho > 0, \, i \in I. \quad (14)$$

These local assignments are spatially regularized through geometric averaging, resulting in the similarity matrix

$$S(W) \in \mathbb{R}^{|I| \times |J|}, \quad S_i = S_i(W) = \frac{\mathrm{mean}_g\{L_j(W)\}_{j \in \mathcal{N}(i)}}{\langle \mathbb{1}, \mathrm{mean}_g\{L_j(W)\}_{j \in \mathcal{N}(i)} \rangle}, \quad i \in I \quad (15)$$

with $\mathrm{mean}_g\{L_j(W)\}_{j \in \mathcal{N}(i)} = \big(\prod_{j \in \mathcal{N}(i)} L_j(W)\big)^{\frac{1}{|\mathcal{N}(i)|}}$ and spatial neighborhoods $\mathcal{N}(i)$ around each pixel i. Finally, W is determined by maximizing the objective function $J : \mathcal{W} \to \mathbb{R}$, $J(W) := \langle W, S(W) \rangle$. This leads to the Riemannian gradient ascent flow

$$\dot{W}(t) = \nabla_{\mathcal{W}} J(W(t)), \qquad W(0) = \frac{1}{|J|} \mathbb{1}_{|I|} \mathbb{1}_{|J|}^\top := C \qquad (16)$$

initialized at the barycenter C of the assignment manifold corresponding to uniform unbiased assignments. Using the approximation discussed in [2],

$$\nabla J(W(t)) \approx S(W), \qquad (17)$$

where ∇ denotes the Euclidean gradient, the Riemannian gradient flow (16) explicitly reads for each vector

$$\dot{W}_i = W_i\big(S_i(W) - \langle W_i, S_i(W) \rangle \mathbb{1}\big), \qquad i \in I. \qquad (18)$$

Numerical integration of (18) in order to solve for $W(t)$ can be conveniently done on the tangent space $T^I = T \times \cdots \times T := T_C \mathcal{W}$, $T := T_{\frac{1}{|J|} \mathbb{1}} \mathcal{S}$, using the framework suggested by [15]. The pullback of the flow (16) using the map L_C (14) evaluated at the barycenter C takes the form

$$\dot{V}_i(t) = \Pi_T \nabla_i J(W(t)), \qquad V_i(0) = 0, \qquad W_i(t) = L_{C_i}(V_i(t)), \qquad i \in I, \quad (19)$$

where Π_T denotes the orthogonal projection onto the tangent space T. Discretization with the simplest numerical integration method, i.e. explicit Euler-steps with stepsize $h > 0$, and taking into account approximation (17), yields the iterative scheme

$$V_i^{(k+1)} = V_i^{(k)} + h\Pi_T S_i(W^{(k)}), \quad V_i^{(0)} = 0, \quad h > 0, \qquad (20a)$$
$$W_i^{(k+1)} = L_{C_i}(V_i^{(k+1)}), \quad i \in I. \qquad (20b)$$

This update step for supervised smooth geometric image labeling has high potential for parallel implementations and corresponding speed-ups.

Moreover, it has been shown recently [12] how the approach can be used in order to evaluate any given discrete graphical model for image labeling.

4   Label Learning by Assignment

In this section, we detail our approach (1) in two steps concerning the G- and W-component, respectively.

(1) *G-component:* We extend the basic soft-k-means clustering approach (Sect. 2, Eqs. (6), (7)) to an arbitrary feature manifold. In the particular case of the S-divergence, it turns out that the resulting fixed point iteration takes the form of an algebraic Riccati equation, as does the approach [10] – cf. (10), with different mappings $\mathcal{G}_j$, of course.

(2) *W-component:* Since the assignment variables due to (1) turn out to be *probabilities*, we can replace them by the assignment variables of the flow (16) and thus seamlessly enforce *spatial regularization* for manifold-valued soft-k-means clustering of features. Conversely, the resulting evolution of labels $\{G_j\}_{j \in J}$ affects the assignment flow through the distance vectors (12). This defines the W-component of our approach.

We point out once more that covariance descriptors are used here as a case study. They can be replaced or augmented by any other manifold-valued features for which the corresponding operations are mathematically well-defined and computationally feasible.

4.1   Manifold-Valued Soft-k-Means Clustering

Given data and labels $\{F_i\}_{i \in I}, \{G_j\}_{j \in J} \subset \mathcal{P}_d$ as covariance descriptors, we adopt the S-divergence (3) and rewrite the soft-k-means objective (5) in the form

$$J(G) := J(G_1, \ldots, G_{|J|}) = -\varepsilon \sum_{i \in I} \log \Big(\sum_{j \in J} \exp \big(-\frac{D_S(F_i, G_j)}{\varepsilon}\big)\Big), \quad \varepsilon > 0. \quad (21)$$

The Riemannian metric of the positive definite manifold $\mathcal{P}_d$,

$$g_A(U, V) = \mathrm{tr}(A^{-1}U A^{-1}V), \qquad A \in \mathcal{P}_d, \qquad U, V \in S_{\mathrm{sym}}(d, \mathbb{R}) \qquad (22)$$

is also induced by the S-divergence D_S [4, Proposition 3.8]. We regard the argument $G = (G_1, \ldots, G_n)$ of J as points on the product manifold $\prod_{j \in J} \mathcal{P}_d$. The j-th component of the Riemannian gradient of J is a symmetric matrix $(\operatorname{grad} J)_j$ satisfying

$$g_{G_j}\big((\operatorname{grad} J)_j, V\big) = d_j J(V), \qquad \forall V \in S_{\text{sym}}(d, \mathbb{R}), \tag{23}$$

where $d_j J(V)$ denotes the differential of J with respect to G_j applied to a tangent matrix V. Thus, if $d_j J(V) = \operatorname{tr}(UV)$ for some symmetric matrix U, then $(\operatorname{grad} J)_j(G) = G_j U G_j$. We have

$$d_j J(G)(V) = \sum_{i \in I} \underbrace{\frac{\exp\big(-\frac{D_S(F_i, G_j)}{\varepsilon}\big)}{\sum_{l \in J} \exp\big(-\frac{D_S(F_i, G_l)}{\varepsilon}\big)}}_{p_{ij}(G)} d_j D_S(F_i, G_j)(V) \tag{24}$$

where $p_{ij}(G) \in \Delta_n$ are the assignment probabilities of datum F_i to each prototype G_j. Evaluating the differential $d_j D_S(F_i, G_j)$, we have $d_j D_S(F_i, G_j)(V) = \operatorname{tr}\big(((F_i + G_j)^{-1} - \frac{1}{2}G_j^{-1})V\big)$ and thus obtain from (24)

$$(\operatorname{grad} J)_j(G) = \sum_{i \in I} p_{ij}(G) G_j (F_i + G_j)^{-1} G_j - \frac{P_j(G)}{2} G_j, \quad j \in J \tag{25}$$

with $P_j(G) = \sum_{i \in I} p_{ij}(G)$. Setting the gradient to zero and rearranging yields

$$G_j - \sum_{i \in I} q_{ij}(G) G_j \Big(\frac{F_i + G_j}{2}\Big)^{-1} G_j = 0 \quad q_{ij}(G) := \frac{p_{ij}(G)}{P_j}, \quad j \in J \tag{26}$$

where the variable symbols p and q highlight the extension of their counterparts in the Euclidean case (6). Moreover, rewriting the preceding optimality condition in the form

$$G_j - G_j \mathcal{G}_j(G) G_j = 0, \qquad \mathcal{G}_j(G) = \sum_{i \in I} q_{ij}(G) \Big(\frac{F_i + G_j}{2}\Big)^{-1}, \quad j \in J \tag{27}$$

reveals a structure analogous to condition (10) resulting from the approach [10], with different mappings $\mathcal{G}_j$, however. The major difference is that (10) includes the embedding $\mathcal{P}_d \to \mathcal{H}$ of covariance descriptors into the Hilbert space generate by the kernel (4), whereas (27) is directly defined on the feature manifold $\mathcal{P}_d$.

Exploiting this analogy, we adopt the fixed point iteration (10),

$$G_j^{(k+1)} = \big(\mathcal{G}_j(G^{(k)})\big)^{-1}, \quad j \in J \tag{28}$$

with $\mathcal{G}_j$ given by (27). Since $(q_{ij})_{i \in I}$ is a probability vector, it is immediate that $\mathcal{G}_j \colon \mathcal{P}_d \to \mathcal{P}_d$ maps the feature manifold onto itself and that Eq. (28) is well-posed.

4.2   Joint Label Learning and Label Assignment

We modify in this section the schemes (28) and (20a and 20b) so as to obtain an interaction $\{G_j\} \leftrightarrow \{W_i\}$ of label evolution $G(t)$ and label assignments $W(t)$, in both directions. And we explain why these modifications make sense.

$\{G_j\} \rightarrow \{W_i\}$: Changing labels $G(t)$ change the distance matrix (12) to $D(t) = D(G(t))$, which affects the matrices (14) and (15) and in turn the assignment flow (16). Since the distance function $d(\cdot, \cdot)$ defining D by (12) is the S-divergence $D_S(\cdot, \cdot)$ (3) in this paper, and since labels G_j satisfying (27) minimize $D_S(F_i, G_j)$ by minimizing the objective (21), they also maximize the likelihood vectors (14) which are *spatially regularized* to form the similarity matrix (15). The similarity matrix $S(W)$ drives the assignment flow through (20a and 20b) so as to maximize the correlation $\langle W, S(W) \rangle$ between pixelwise label assignments W_i and similarity vectors $S_i(W)$, which represent assignments in the spatial context through the *non-local* geometric diffusion process (15).

$\{W_i\} \rightarrow \{G_j\}$: The *row* vectors W_i can be interpreted as posterior probabilities $W_{ij} = \Pr(G_j | F_i)$ of assigning prototypes $G_j, j \in J$ to data $F_i, i \in I$. Hence these row vectors are of primary importance for the assignment flow, as just discussed. Conversely, the *column* vectors W^j, $j \in J$ with components $(W^j)_i = W_{ij}$ represent *weights* that associate each data point F_i with a label G_j. Normalization $\frac{W_{ij}}{\langle \mathbb{1}, W^j \rangle}$ turns these weights into probability vectors that exactly show up as probabilities $q_{ij}(G)$ in the optimality condition (27), which defines the evolution of labels G_j. Consequently, in order to affect label evolution by *spatially regularized* assignments, we exchange these probabilities so that the mappings $\mathcal{G}_j$, $j \in J$ defining the optimality condition (27) now read

$$\mathcal{G}_j(W) = \sum_{i \in I} q_{ij}(W) \left(\frac{F_i + G_j}{2} \right)^{-1}, \quad q_{ij}(W) = \frac{W_{ij}}{\langle \mathbb{1}, W^j \rangle} \in \mathcal{S}_{|I|}, \; j \in J. \quad (29)$$

4.3   Summary and Discussion

Summing up, the joint flow (1) of labels $\{G_j\}_{j \in J}$ and assignments $\{W_i\}_{i \in I}$ is implemented, with $h > 0$ by the discrete iterative scheme

$$V_i^{(k+1)}(G) = V_i^{(k)}(G) + h \Pi_T S_i(W^{(k)}(G)), \quad G = G^{(k)}, V_i^{(0)} = 0 \quad (30a)$$

$$W_i^{(k+1)}(G) = L_{C_i}(V_i^{(k+1)}(G)), \quad i \in I \quad (30b)$$

$$G_j^{(k+1)}(W) = (\mathcal{G}_j(W))^{-1}, \quad W = W^{(k+1)}, \quad j \in J \quad (30c)$$

$$\mathcal{G}_j(W) = \sum_{i \in I} q_{ij}(W) \left(\frac{F_i + G_j}{2} \right)^{-1}, \quad q_{ij}(W) = \frac{W_{ij}}{\langle \mathbb{1}, W^j \rangle}. \quad (30d)$$

We adopt the **termination criterion** from [2]: The iteration (30a–30d) stops when the average entropy of the assignment variables drops below 10^{-3}, which signals an (almost) unique label assignment and hence also stationarity of the label evolution.

While the dependency $G = G(W)$ is explicit by (30d), the dependency $W = W(G)$ is not: it is given through the distance matrix (12) which defines the vectors S_i of (30a) through (14) and (15). As a consequence, the computation of these matrices, though not expensive, has to be repeated at every step of the iteration (30a–30d).

To conclude this section, we point out and discuss few **further aspects** that characterize our approach **and differences to established work.**

(a) Our approach is affected by *specific* properties of the feature manifold only through the divergence function D_S of (21), and through the structure of the resulting optimality condition (27). The divergence function should induce the Riemannian metric, like (22) in our present case study using covariance descriptors. The optimality condition should admit a numerically convenient iterative scheme, like the fixed point iteration (28). If these properties are satisfied for some feature manifold, our approach can be applied.

(b) The approach [10] works entirely on the feature manifold, as discussed in Sect. 3, whereas our approach additionally takes into account the spatial structure of assignments through regularization. Mean-shift approaches, on the other hand, merge both representations by augmenting feature vectors with spatial coordinates. As a consequence, spatial regularization through averaging is based on the corresponding centroids (spatial coordinates of prototypes). Our approach keeps both representations separate, and spatial regularization through the geometric diffusion process (17) does not involve any centroids.

(c) A natural idea is to replace manifold-valued soft-k-means clustering, i.e. the G-component of our approach, by the approach [10]. This is not directly practicable because the sparse coefficients y of the kernel expansion (9) are *signed,* whereas our approach works with assignment *probabilities.* We leave this problem for future work.

5   Experiments

In this section we show numerical results to illustrate the impact of geometric spatial regularization on unsupervised label evolution on the feature manifold, the empirical convergence rate and the influence of parameter values.

We compare to two state-of-the-art methods: *Assignment Flow* [2] for supervised labeling on the manifold (fixed labels), *Harandi et al.* [10] for unsupervised label learning (no spatial regularization), and the *Local Method,* which is nearest-neighbor labeling based on given initial labels.

Experiment Set-Up. We did not undertake any 'feature-engineering' but constructed only a basic set of covariance feature descriptors consisting of intensities, first and second order partial derivatives: $g = \left(\partial^{0,0}, \partial^{1,0}, \partial^{0,1}, \partial^{2,0}, \partial^{1,1}, \partial^{0,2}\right)$ which, in the case of color images, results in descriptors of size 18×18. For all

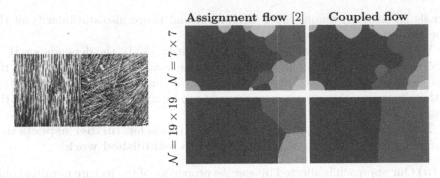

Fig. 3. LEFT: Image combining homogeneous (left) and heterogeneous texture (right). RIGHT: Supervised flow (fixed labels) vs. unsupervised flow (with label evolution) together with weak and strong spatial regularization (bottom vs. top). Our approach (Coupled flow) moves few labels in a proper position on the feature manifold and suppresses redundant ones, through the *sparsifying effect* of spatial regularization and adaptation of labels done *simultaneously*.

methods we used the S-divergence as distance. Initial labels were computed by metric clustering to limit the otherwise infeasible large label space when using the complete data set.

Fixed Labels vs. Evolving Labels, with and Without Spatial Regularization. Figure 3 shows an image with two textures. The texture on the left is more homogeneous than the texture on the right. We compare the *supervised* assignment flow (fixed labels) and our *unsupervised* approach (with label evolution) performing both weak and stronger spatial regularization (top vs. bottom row). Starting from an overcomplete dictionary with 8 initial labels, the supervised approach easily clusters the homogeneous left texture whereas partitions emerge on the right that reflect the heterogeneous texture structure. Our unsupervised approach manages this task with fewer labels. This demonstrates (i) the effect of label evolution and (ii) the sparsifying effect of spatial regularization *done simultaneously*, in order to move few labels in a proper position on the feature manifold and to get rid of the remaining ones.

Figure 4 shows a larger problem instance including the outcome of the Local method and Harandi's unsupervised clustering. We point out that, since label evolutions differ between the approaches, colors merely index label assignments but cannot be compared. Rather, the relative frequencies of label assignments are informative and enable to compare the methods.

We performed two experiments with 8 and 15 initial labels (top vs. bottom row) and fixed strength of spatial regularization. Both the local method and especially Harandi's method are susceptible to small details and noise. The noise suppressing effect of spatial regularization is clearly visible for the supervised assignment flow. Our approach (Coupled flow) additionally combines regularization with label evolution and yields a more coherent result without suppressing details, e.g. at the eyes and the tip of the nose.

Coupled flow   Assignment flow [2]   Local   Harandi [10]

8 labels

15 labels

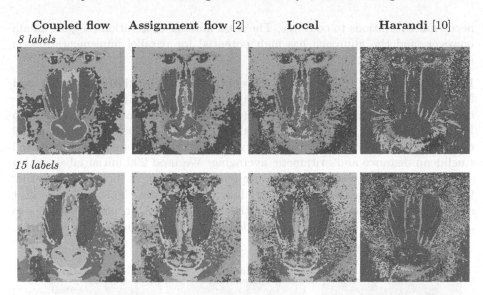

Fig. 4. Impact of spatial regularization (Assignment flow, Coupled flow) and unsupervised label evolution (Harandi, Coupled flow). The Assignment flow consistently suppresses fine details whereas Harandi's approach captures all small variations in the data including noise. The Coupled flow provides a good compromise between suppressing spurious labelings and obtaining a compact, spatially coherent representation through label evolution that preserves visual features (eye region, tip of the nose). (Color figure online)

8 labels   15 labels

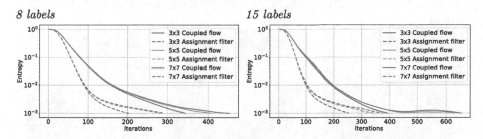

Fig. 5. Entropy of label assignments depending on the iteration number for the Assignment flow and the Coupled flow, for different strengths of spatial regularization. We observe (i) that both labeling processes converge rapidly until the termination criterion (entropy $\leq 10^{-3}$) is met, (ii) stronger spatial regularization requires more iterations to resolve label assignment conflicts, and (iii) the Coupled flow needs more iterations than the supervised Assignment flow, due to the interaction between label evolution and regularized label assignment.

Empirical Convergence Rate. Figure 5 displays the entropy measure of label assignments used as termination criterion for the Assignment flow'and the Coupled flow, for different strengths of spatial regularization. Due to the interaction between label evolution and regularized label assignments, the Coupled flow needs more iterations to converge. The total number of iterations is quite small, however, and the approach has high potential for parallel implementation on modern hardware.

Euclidean Color Clustering (Special Case: Spatially Regularized Mean-Shift; Fig. 6). We demonstrate the flexible applicability of our approach: replacing the positive definite manifold (covariance descriptors) by the Euclidean RGB-space results in spatially regularized mean-shift clustering as a special case. The S-divergence and geometric averaging were replaced by the squared Euclidean distance and arithmetic averaging. We used 200 initial labels which suffice to represent the image structure (compare Input vs. Local). Comparing the Assignment flow and the Coupled flow demonstrates the sparsifying effect of combining label evolution with spatial regularization. In particular, regions around the eyes and the nose are encoded by a smaller number of prototypes.

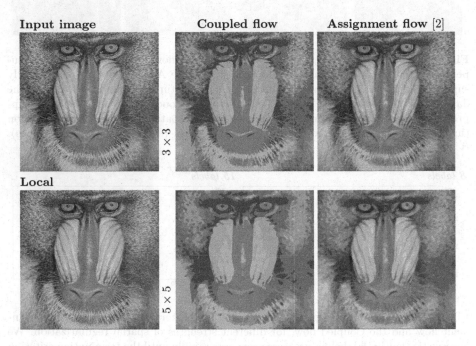

Fig. 6. Replacing the covariance descriptor manifold $\mathcal{P}_d$ by the $\mathbb{R}^3$ color space results in *spatially regularized mean-shift* as a special case. Comparing the Assignment flow (fixed labels) with the Coupled flow (evolving labels), for 200 initial labels and different strengths of spatial regularization (top vs. bottom), demonstrates the sparsifying effect of the *coupled* process, resulting in a more compact representation of the image. In particular, regions around the eyes and the nose are encoded by a smaller number of prototypes. (Color figure online)

Real Images and Texture. We applied the assignment of covariance descriptors to representative urban scenes, that comprise both low-rank image structure (edges of walls, windows, etc.) and texture (trees, roofs, etc.).

Figure 7 shows the results for 15 initial labels whereas Fig. 8 shows the results for 100 initial labels. In both scenarios, the unsupervised method of Harandi consistently returns non-compact oversegmentations, despite performing label evolution. This is significantly different for the Coupled flow, where label evo-

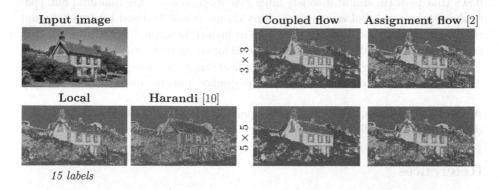

Fig. 7. The Coupled flow yields more homogeneous regions, which can be observed in particular in regions corresponding to the roof, windows and grass. Without prototype adaptation the Assignment flow returns large disconnected regions that are less useful for subsequent image interpretation. The global clustering method of Harandi produces visually pleasing results, but fails to return spatially coherent regions, especially in textured regions of the scene.

Fig. 8. Same set-up as Fig. 7 using 100 initial labels. The observations stated in the caption of Fig. 7 hold here as well. We only point out that with sufficiently strong spatial regularization (bottom row), the Coupled flow managed to adapt labels on the feature manifold, and thus represents more compactly textured regions (tree, roof) in a spatially coherent way.

lution *and* spatial regularization adapt labels on the feature manifold and thus enable more compact representations of textured regions corresponding to the tree and the roof in Fig. 8.

6   Conclusion

We introduced a novel approach in terms of two coupled Riemannian gradient flows that perform simultaneously label evolution on a feature manifold and spatially regularized label assignment. This unsupervised method returns compact representations of local image structure in high-dimensional feature spaces that are statistically significant and hence useful for subsequent image interpretation. The modular design enables flexible applications to various feature manifolds. The algorithm has high potential for fine-grained parallel implementation.

Acknowledgements. This work was supported by the German Research Foundation (DFG), grant GRK 1653.

References

1. Arsigny, V., Fillard, P., Pennec, X., Ayache, N.: Geometric means in a novel vector space structure on symmetric positive-definite matrices. SIAM J. Matrix Anal. Appl. **29**(1), 328–347 (2006)
2. Åström, F., Petra, S., Schmitzer, B., Schnörr, C.: Image labeling by assignment. J. Math. Imaging Vis. **58**(2), 211–238 (2017)
3. Bhatia, R.: Positive Definite Matrices. Princeton University Press, Princeton (2006)
4. Chebbi, Z., Moakher, M.: Means of Hermitian positive-definite matrices based on the log-determinant α-divergence function. Linear Algebra Appl. **436**(7), 1872–1889 (2012)
5. Cherian, A., Sra, S.: Positive definite matrices: data representation and applications to computer vision. In: Minh, H.Q., Murino, V. (eds.) Algorithmic Advances in Riemannian Geometry and Applications. ACVPR, pp. 93–114. Springer, Cham (2016). https://doi.org/10.1007/978-3-319-45026-1_4
6. Cherian, A., Sra, S., Banerjee, A., Papanikolopoulos, N.: Jensen-Bregman LogDet divergence with application to efficient similarity search for covariance matrices. IEEE PAMI **35**(9), 2161–2174 (2013)
7. Comaniciu, D., Meer, P.: Mean shift: a robust approach toward feature space analysis. IEEE Trans. Patt. Anal. Mach. Intell. **24**(5), 603–619 (2002)
8. Fukunaga, K., Hostetler, L.: The estimation of the gradient of a density function, with applications in pattern recognition. IEEE Trans. Inform. Theory **21**(1), 32–40 (1975)
9. Har-Peled, S.: Geometric Approximation Algorithms. AMS, Providence (2011)
10. Harandi, M., Hartley, R., Lovell, B., Sanderson, C.: Sparse coding on symmetric positive definite manifolds using Bregman divergences. IEEE Trans. Neural Netw. Learn. Syst. **27**(6), 1294–1306 (2016)
11. Hofmann, T., Schölkopf, B., Smola, A.J.: Kernel methods in machine learning. Ann. Stat. **36**(3), 1171–1220 (2008)

12. Hühnerbein, R., Savarino, F., Åström, F., Schnörr, C.: Image labeling based on graphical models using Wasserstein messages and geometric assignment. SIAM J. Imaging Sci. **11**(2), 1317–1362 (2018)
13. Karcher, H.: Riemannian center of mass and mollifier smoothing. Commun. Pure Appl. Math. **30**, 509–541 (1977)
14. Rockafellar, R.T., Wets, R.J.B.: Variational Analysis, 3rd edn. Springer, Heidelberg (2009). https://doi.org/10.1007/978-3-642-02431-3
15. Savarino, F., Hühnerbein, R., Åström, F., Recknagel, J., Schnörr, C.: Numerical integration of Riemannian gradient flows for image labeling. In: Lauze, F., Dong, Y., Dahl, A.B. (eds.) SSVM 2017. LNCS, vol. 10302, pp. 361–372. Springer, Cham (2017). https://doi.org/10.1007/978-3-319-58771-4_29
16. Sra, S.: Positive Definite Matrices and the Symmetric Stein Divergence. CoRR abs/1110.1773 (2013)
17. Subbarao, R., Meer, P.: Nonlinear mean shift over Riemannian manifolds. Int. J. Comput. Vis. **84**(1), 1–20 (2009)
18. Teboulle, M.: A unified continuous optimization framework for center-based clustering methods. J. Mach. Learn. Res. **8**, 65–102 (2007)
19. Turaga, P., Srivastava, A. (eds.): Riemannian Computing in Computer Vision. Springer, Cham (2016). https://doi.org/10.1007/978-3-319-22957-7

Author Index

Printed in the United States
By Bookmasters